THE WESTERN EXPERIENCE

Photo: Benozzo Gozzoli, "The Procession of the Magi." Palazzo Medici Riccardi, Florence, Italy. Courtesy of Scala/ Art Resource, NY.

THE WESTERN EXPERIENCE

SIXTH EDITION

MORTIMER CHAMBERS
University of California, Los Angeles

RAYMOND GREW
University of Michigan

DAVID HERLIHY
Late Professor of History
Brown University

THEODORE K. RABB
Princeton University

ISSER WOLOCH
Columbia University

McGRAW-HILL, INC.

New York • St. Louis • San Francisco • Auckland • Bogotá • Caracas • Lisbon • London • Madrid
Mexico City • Milan • Montreal • New Delhi • San Juan • Singapore
Sydney • Tokyo • Toronto

THE WESTERN EXPERIENCE

Photo and Text Credits appear on pages 1063–1069 and on this page by reference.

This book is printed on acid-free paper.

3 4 5 6 7 8 9 0 VNH VNH 9 0 9 8 7 6

ISBN 0-07-011066-2

This book was set in Palatino by CRWaldman Graphic Communications.
The editors were Pamela Gordon and Ira C. Roberts;
the designers were Wanda Lubelska and Wanda Siedlecka;
the production supervisor was Kathryn Porzio.
The photo editor was Deborah Bull/Photosearch.
The cartographer was David Lindroth.
Von Hoffmann Press, Inc., was printer and binder.

Cover art: Benozzo Gozzoli, "The Procession of the Magi" (detail). Palazzo Medici Riccardi, Florence, Italy. Courtesy of Scala/Art Resource, NY.

Library of Congress Cataloging-in-Publication Data

The Western Experience / Mortimer Chambers . . . [et al.].—6th ed.
p. cm.
Includes bibliographical references and index.
ISBN 0-07-011066-2
1. Civilization—History. 2. Civilization, Western—History.
I. Chambers, Mortimer.
CB59.W38 1995
909—dc20 94-17442

About the Authors

Mortimer Chambers is Professor of History at the University of California, Los Angeles. He was a Rhodes scholar from 1949 to 1952 and received an M.A. from Wadham College, Oxford, in 1955 after obtaining his doctorate from Harvard University in 1954. He has taught at Harvard University (1954–1955) and the University of Chicago (1955–1958). He was Visiting Professor at the University of British Columbia in 1958, the State University of New York at Buffalo in 1971, the University of Freiburg (Germany) in 1974, and Vassar College in 1988. A specialist in Greek and Roman history, he is coauthor of *Aristotle's History of Athenian Democracy* (1962), editor of a series of essays entitled *The Fall of Rome* (1963), and author of *Georg Busolt: His Career in His Letters* (1990) and of *Staat der Athener*, a German translation and commentary to Aristotle's *Constitution of the Athenians* (1990). He has edited Greek texts of the latter work (1986) and of the *Hellenica Oxyrhynchia* (1993). He has contributed articles to the *American Historical Review and Classical Philology* as well as other journals, both in America and in Europe.

Raymond Grew is Professor of History at the University of Michigan. He earned both his M.A. (1952) and Ph.D. (1957) from Harvard University in the field of modern European history. He was a Fulbright Fellow to Italy (1954–1955), and Fulbright Travelling Fellow to France (1976, 1990), Guggenheim Fellow (1968–1969), Director of Studies at the Écoles des Hautes Études en Sciences Sociales in Paris (1976, 1987, 1990), and a Fellow of the National Endowment for the Humanities (1979). In 1962 he received the Chester Higby Prize from the American Historical Association, and in 1963 the Italian government awarded him the Unita d'Italia Prize; in 1993 he received the David Pinkney Prize of the Society for French Historical Studies. He is an active member of the A.H.A.; the Society for French Historical Studies; the Society for Italian Historical Studies, of which he has been president; and the Council for European Studies, of which he has twice served as national chair. His books include *Sterner Plan for Italian Unity* (1963), *Crises of Development in Europe and the United States* (1978), and *School, State, and Society: The Growth of Elementary Education in Nineteenth-Century France* (1991). He is the editor of *Comparative Studies in Society and History* and its book series. He has also written on global history and is one of the directors of the Global History Group. His articles and reviews have appeared in a number of European and American journals.

David Herlihy was the Mary Critchfield and Barnaby Keeney Professor of History at Brown University and the author of numerous books and studies on the social history of the Middle Ages. His most recent publications were *Opera Muliebria: Woman and Work in Medieval Europe* (1990); *Medieval Households* (1985); and, in collaboration with Christiane Klapisch-Zuber, *Tuscans and Their Families: A Study of the Florentine Catasto of 1427* (1985). He received his M.A., from the Catholic University of America in 1952, his Ph.D. from Yale University in 1956, and an honorary Doctor of Humanities from the University of San Francisco in 1983. He was a former president of several historical associations, and in 1990 served as president of the American History Association, the largest historical society in America. He was a fellow of the Guggenheim Foundation (1961–1962), the American Council of Learned Societies (1966–1967), the Center for Advanced Study in the Behavioral Sciences (1972–1973), and the National Endowment for the Humanities (1976). He was a fellow of the American Academy of Arts and Sciences and the American Philosophical Society. His articles and reviews have appeared in numerous professional journals, both here and abroad.

Theodore K. Rabb is Professor of History at Princeton University. He received his Ph.D. from Princeton, and subsequently taught at Stanford, Northwestern, Harvard, and Johns Hopkins universities. He is the author of numerous articles and reviews, and has been editor of *The Journal of Interdisciplinary History* since its foundation. Among his books are *The Struggle for Stability in Early Modern Europe* and *Renaissance Lives*. Professor Rabb has held offices in various national organizations, including the American Historical Association and The National Council for Historical Education. He was the principal historian for the PBS series, *Renaissance*.

Isser Woloch is Professor of History at Columbia University. He received his Ph.D. (1965) from Princeton University in the field of eighteenth- and nineteenth-century European history. He has taught at Indiana University and at the University of California at Los Angeles where, in 1967, he received a Distinguished Teaching Citation. He has been a fellow of the A.C.L.S., the National Endowment for the Humanities, the Guggenheim Foundation, and the Institute for Advanced Study at Princeton. His publications include *Jacobin Legacy: The Democratic Movement under the Directory* (1970), *The Peasantry in the Old Regime: Conditions and Protests* (1970), *The French Veteran from the Revolution to the Restoration* (1979), and *Eighteenth-Century Europe: Tradition and Progress, 1715–1789* (1982), and *The New Regime: Transformations of the French Civic Order, 1789–1820s* (1994).

This book is dedicated
to the memory of
David Herlihy
whose erudition and judgment
were central to its creation
and whose friendship and example
continue to inspire
his co-authors

Contents

2

THE FORMING OF GREEK CIVILIZATION 31

3

CLASSICAL AND HELLENISTIC GREECE 63

4

THE ROMAN REPUBLIC 89

5

THE EMPIRE AND CHRISTIANITY 117

6

THE MAKING OF WESTERN EUROPE 151

7

THE EARLY MEDIEVAL EAST 181

8

TWO CENTURIES OF CREATIVITY 211

14

ECONOMIC EXPANSION AND A NEW POLITICS 421

15

WAR AND CRISIS 461

20

THE FRENCH REVOLUTION 637

21

THE AGE OF NAPOLEON 671

22

FOUNDATIONS OF THE NINETEENTH CENTURY: POLITICS AND SOCIAL CHANGE 703

23

LEARNING TO LIVE WITH CHANGE 733

24

NATIONAL STATES AND NATIONAL CULTURES 767

25

EUROPEAN DYNAMISM AND THE NINETEENTH-CENTURY WORLD 803

26

THE AGE OF PROGRESS 839

27

WORLD WAR AND DEMOCRACY 871

28

THE GREAT TWENTIETH-CENTURY CRISIS 907

List of Maps

Introduction

Everyone uses history. We use it to define who we are, to connect our personal experience with the collective memory of the groups to which we belong and to attach ourselves to a particular region, nation, or culture. We invoke the past to explain our hopes and ambitions and to justify our fears and conflicts. The Charter of the United Nations, like the American Declaration of Independence, is based on a view of history. When workers strike or armies march, they cite the lessons of their history. Because history is so important to us psychologically and intellectually, historical understanding is always shifting and often controversial.

Some questions must be asked repeatedly; some issues arise again and again. But historical knowledge is cumulative, for while asking new questions, historians integrate the answers learned from previous studies. History is not merely a subjective exercise in which all opinions are equally valid. No matter what motivated a particular historical question, the answer to it stands until overturned by better evidence. We now know more about the past than ever before and understand it as the people we study could not. Unlike them, we know how their history came out; we can apply methods they did not have, and often we have evidence they never saw. This knowledge and the ways of interpreting it are the collective achievement of thousands of historians.

We also use history for pleasure—as a cultivated entertainment. The biographies of admirable or monstrous men and women, dramatic accounts of important events, and colorful tales of earlier times can be fascinating in themselves. Through these encounters with history, we experience the common human concerns of all people; and through the study of European history, we come to appreciate the ideals and conflicts, the failures and accidents, the social needs and human choices that formed the Western world in which we live. When understood in their historical context, the achievements of European civilization are all the more remarkable, hammered out among competing interests and burning controversies.

The Western Experience was designed to provide a reasonably comprehensive and analytic account of the various circumstances within which, and the processes by which, European society and civilization evolved. This is the book's sixth edition, evidence of a long life sustained with the help of prior revisions. Even so, this edition is more completely rewritten and recast than any of its predecessors—our response to changes in students and in historical study. Each cohort of students carries different experiences, interests, and training into the classroom. These changes are easily exaggerated, but they can be important; and the women and men we teach have taught us enough about what currently engages or confuses them, about the impression of European history they bring to college, and about what they can be expected to take from a survey course to make us want to reconsider the way the book presented its material. This led to a rewriting and reordering that we think has made the book clearer and more accessible without sacrificing our initial goals of writing a sophisticated, interpretive, and analytic history.

Adapting the latest developments in historical understanding to a general work presents a problem of a particular kind. From its first edition, this book incorporated more of the results of quantitative and social history than general European histories usually did, an obvious reflection of the several authors' own research. Each subsequent edition provided an occasion to incorporate current methods and new knowledge, an opportunity to reconsider paragraphs, sections, and whole chapters in the light of new approaches and new research, sometimes literally reconceiving part of the past. Recent work—in demographic, economic, diplomatic, and intellectual history as well as social history, and most of all in gender studies and cultural studies—increases those opportunities, and we have sought to convey something of the excitement of this new understanding. At the same time, we have wanted to preserve a special kind of balance. The professional scholar prefers new perspectives to familiar information, but other readers are less likely to make such distinctions. For them, the latest interpretations need to be integrated with a presentation of standard controversies, of the people and events that are part of our cultural lore, and of the basic information necessary to build a framework for the historical understanding that they are begining to form.

Other kinds of balance are important, too. We believe that this history must be interpretive but also that its readers—instructors, students, and general readers—should be free to use it in many different ways and in conjunction with their own interpretive approaches, their own areas of special knowledge, and their own diverse interests and curiosity. Of course, there is no simple standard by which to judge when such a work is comprehensive enough to offer that freedom yet selective enough to be comprehensible. For this edition, the authors once again jointly planned revision of the entire volume, read and criticized each other's drafts, and benefited from the criticisms and suggestions of more than a score of other scholars and teachers. The book carefully includes evidence from which alternative interpretations can be formulated and a platform that allows classroom teachers of any period to emphasize social, political, cultural, economic, or institutional history in lectures and selected readings.

The use of color throughout the book and a new design obviously make it more attractive, and the maps have been completely redrawn. They convey more information more clearly and allow the basic geography of Europe a visual presence throughout the book. The greater range of illustrations has made it possible for them to be more fully integrated into the text than ever before. We have also adopted the common device of including selections from primary sources, choosing samples that expand points made in the text, provide some flavor of the period under discussion, and grant to the reader some of that independence that comes from personal engagement with historical sources.

Throughout the book, from the earliest civilizations to the present, certain themes are pursued. They appear most distinctly in the early chapters, in discussions of how the land is settled, divided among its inhabitants, and put to use; how production and the division of labor are organized and whether there are slaves, classes that do not work at all, and recognized specialists in fighting or crafts or trade; how the family is structured, the gendered roles within and outside the family, and the relationship of that to the overall social structure; how religion and belief systems are sustained and connected to power; how the political system operates, who participates in it, and how it maintains order and makes war; how the institutions of society and the system of law work to permit or constrain social change; and how the forms of cultural expression relate to the social structure and important issues of an era. Attentive readers will note that these themes, introduced early, are then picked up in subsequent sections of the book as changes in these themes are important for understanding other eras of European history.

We think of that history as the history of Western civilization, but the very concept of a Western civilization is itself the result of history. The Greeks gave the names *east* and *west* to the points on the horizon where the sun rises and sets. Because the impressive Persian Empire and India lay to their east, the Greeks thought of themselves as living in the West, on the edge of the continent they called *Europe*. The distinction between Western civilization and others—ethnocentric, often arbitrary, and frequently exaggerated—continued even as that civilization changed and expanded with the Roman Empire, Christianity, and the European conquest of the New World. The view that this is one civilization, with America tied more closely to ancient Greece than Greece is to Egypt or Spain to Islam, can be easily challenged in every respect save cultural tradition.

The Western Experience gives primary attention to a small part of the world and in doing so honors that cultural tradition. The concentration on Europe includes important examples of city and of rural life; of empires and monarchies and republics; of life before and after industrialization; of societies in which labor was organized through markets, serfdom, and slavery; of cultures little concerned with science and of ones that used changing scientific knowledge; of non-Christian religions and of all the major forms of Christianity in action.

To discuss history in this way is to think comparatively and to employ categories of the social history that has greatly affected historical understanding in the last half of the twentieth century. The desire to broaden the scope of historical writing is not new. As early as the eighteenth century many historians (of whom Voltaire was one) called for a history that was more than chronology, more than an account of kings and battles. In the nineteenth century—even while historical studies paid dominant attention to past politics, diplomacy, and war (taking the evidence primarily from official documents found in state archives)—there were important and systematic efforts to encompass the history of intellectual and cultural trends, of law and constitutions, of religion, and of the economy. Social history, as a field of study, emerged as one of these efforts at broader coverage. For some, it was primarily the history of labor movements. For others, it was the history of daily life—in ancient Rome or Renaissance Florence or old New York as reflected in styles of dress, housing, diet, and so on. This "pots and pans history" was the sort of history featured in historical museums and popular magazines. Appealing in its concreteness, it tended (like the collections of interesting objects that it resembled) to lack a theoretical basis.

Modern social history is more systematic. In the theories and methods it employs, it borrows from the social sciences—especially anthropology, sociology, economics, and political science. It seeks to compensate for the fact that most historical writing has been about the tiny minority of the powerful, rich, and educated (who, after all, left behind the fullest and most accessible records of their activities); and it aims to be mindful of popular culture as well as formal or official culture, as interested in the family and living conditions as in the state and political theory.

The growth of social history facilitated a remarkable expansion in the history of women. Stimulated by contemporary feminism as well as by developments within social history, the history of women has in turn grown into gender studies, a set of approaches that has proved enormously revealing about society as a whole, showing how politics and culture together with leisure and work, are shaped by and reproduce assumptions about gender. This new work has affected the historical understanding of every era and nearly every subfield of history. Gender studies have also tended to draw attention to social symbols and to the values expressed in social behavior, drawing history closer to the literary and philosophical theories underlying what is currently called *cultural studies*. These approaches, as well as the renewed interest in intellectual history, emphasize the role of interpretation over objective science and the relativity of all writing on culture and society.

Such interests, theories, and techniques have greatly expanded the range of useful historical sources and the range of issues historians must consider. They also make those mainstays of historical organization—clear chronology and periodization—more complex. The periodization of history based on the rise and fall of dynasties, on the formation of states, and on the duration of wars and revolutions usually does not fit the periodization most appropriate for highlighting changes in culture and ideas, economic production, or science and technology. Historical surveys have therefore frequently been organized topically as well as chronologically, with special chapters on economic or intellectual developments, which can weaken awareness of interconnection.

In *The Western Experience* an effort has been made to combine the newer approaches with more established perspectives. The tradition of the introductory course in European history (and our cultural tradition as well) is recognized by keeping the book's chapters essentially chronological in sequence, sometimes using groups of chapters to cover a whole period. At the same time each chapter is presented as an interpretative essay, introducing a set of historical problems important to the understanding of the period treated. The information within a chapter serves as evidence to illustrate the interpretive argument, but it is also selected to meet the general requirements of a survey of European history, to provide the basis for constructing a coherent picture of the development of Europe, and to exemplify different kinds of historical interest.

Readers of this book may thus use it as an introduction to historical method, find within it a framework to which they can attach whatever else they know about Western society, and discover here some challenge to their preconceptions—about the past, about how societies are organized, and about how people behave. Historical study is an integrative enterprise in which long-term trends and specific moments, as well as social structure and individual actions, are brought together.

A college course is not the only way to build a personal culture. Nor is history the only path to integrated knowledge. Western history is not the only history one should know, nor is an introductory survey necessarily the best way to learn it. Still, as readers consider and then challenge interpretations offered in this text, they will exercise critical and analytical skills; and they will find that the world beyond (and before) our own lives is relevant to our current concerns. They can acknowledge the greatness of their Western heritage and its distinctiveness, which includes injustice, cruelty, and failure. In doing these things, they will experience the study of history as one of those vital intellectual activities by which we come to know who and where we are.

Acknowledgments

We wish to thank the following reviewers, consultants, and users for their helpful suggestions for *The Western Experience:* Catherine Albanese, Wright State University; Thomas M. Bader, California State University, Northridge; B. D. Bargar, University of South Carolina; Edward E. Barry, Montana State University; S. Scott Bartchy, University of California, Los Angeles; Iris Berger, State University of New York-Albany; Alan E. Bernstein, University of Akron; Charles R. Berry, Wright State University; Thomas Blomquist, Northern Illinois University; Stephen Blum, Montgomery County Community College, PA; Jack Bournazian; Elspeth Brown, Hamilton College, NY; Paul Chardoul, Grand Rapids Junior College; Craig A. Czarnecki, Baltimore, MD; Ronnie M. Day, Eastern Tennessee State University; Michael De Michele, University of Scranton; Bradley H. Dowden, California State University-Sacramento; Veron Egger, Georgia Southern College; Nancy Ellenberger, United States Naval Academy; Elfriede Engel, Lansing Community College, MI; Steven Epstein, University of Colorado at Boulder; R. Finucane, Georgia Southern College; Willard C. Frank, Jr., Old Dominion University, VA; Ellen G. Friedman, Boston College; James Friguglietti, Eastern Michigan College; Laura Gellott, University of Wisconsin at Parkside; Robert Gottfried, Rutgers University; Carl Granquist, Jr., Keene State College; Katherine J. Gribble, Highline Community College, WA; Margot A. Haberhern, Florida Institute of Technology; Barbara Hanawalt, University of Minnesota; Drew Harrington, Western Kentucky University; Patricia Herlihy, Brown University; Neil M. Heyman, San Diego State University; Deborah L. Jones, Lexington, KY; Thomas E. Kaiser, University of Arkansas-Little Rock; Nannerl O. Keohane, Wellesley College; Donald P. King, Whitman College, WA; William J. King, Wright State University; Ellen E. Kittell, University of Oregon; Steven P. Kramer, The University of New Mexico; Lisa Lane, Mira-Costa College; Gordon Lauren, University of Montana; Phoebe Lundy, Boise State University; Gilbert H. McArthur, College of William and Mary; Edward Malefakis, Columbia University; Vesta F. Manning, University of Arizona-Tucson; William Mathews, State University of New York at Potsdam; William Carl Matthews, Ohio State University; Edgar Melton, Wright State University; Carol Menning, University of Toledo; Julius Milmeister, Pittsburgh, PA; Frederick I. Murphy, Western Kentucky University; Sandra Norman, Florida Atlantic University; Peter Pierson, Santa Clara University; Linda J. Piper, The University of Georgia-Athens; Carl Pletsch, Miami University; Philip Racine, Wofford College; Ronald A. Rebholz, Stanford University; John F. Robertson, Central Michigan University; Louisa Sarasohn, Oregon State College; Judy Sealander, Wright State University; Ezel Kural Shaw, California State University, Northridge; Eileen Soldwedel, Edmonds Community College; Alan Spetter, Wright State University; Richard E. Sullivan, Michigan State University; John Sweets, University of Kansas; George Taylor, University of North Carolina at Chapel Hill; Armstrong Starkey, Adelphi University, NY; Richard Wagner, Des Moines Area Community College; Richard Weigel, Western Kentucky University; Robert H. Welborn, Clayton State College; Michael J. Witt, FSC, Christian Brothers College, TN; and Richard M. Wunderli, University of Colorado. We would also like to thank Professor Raymond J. Jirran of Thomas Nelson Community College for his helpful comments and suggestions.

Mortimer Chambers
Raymond Grew
Theodore K. Rabb
Isser Woloch

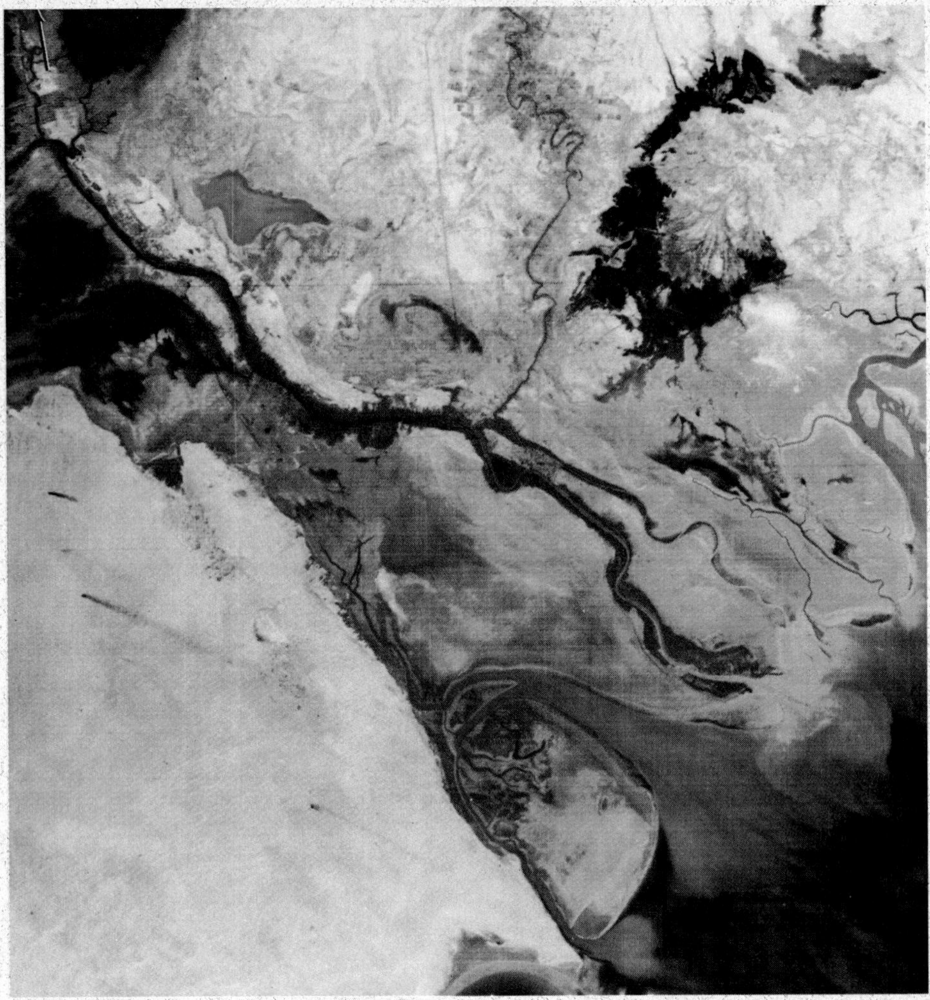

The earth, seen from space, showing the Tigris (east) and Euphrates (west) rivers, which irrigated the cradle of civilization in the Near East.

CHAPTER ONE

The First Civilizations

THE subject of this book is the Western experience—that is, the history of European civilization and its origins in earlier civilizations located in Mesopotamia and around the Mediterranean Sea.

Human beings began to abandon a nomadic existence and live in settled agricultural villages about 8000 B.C. By about 3000 B.C. they had created settlements of some size along the banks of the Tigris, Euphrates, Nile, and Indus rivers. People's efforts to build a better life transformed the agricultural villages into something we can recognize as cities—having a scale and pattern crucial for the development of civilization. In these valleys types of behavior and institutions first appeared that have persisted, in varying forms, throughout all periods of Western civilization.

Powerful kingdoms and great empires, centered on sizable cities, gradually arose in Asia Minor and in Egypt. Their achievement of literacy and their many written records; their long-distance trade; their invention of increasingly ingenious tools, utensils, vehicles, and weapons; their development of monumental architecture and representative art; and their advances in medicine, astronomy, and mathematics marked the change from primitive life and constituted civilization.

I. The Earliest Humans

Our first task as we try to grasp historical chronology is to gain a sense of the overwhelmingly long period that we call "prehistory." The astronomer Carl Sagan has reckoned that, if the entire history of the universe were plotted out over the span of one year, everything that we usually think of as European history—the subject of this book—would have taken place in the last two or three minutes of the year.

Human beings are members of the species Homo sapiens ("thinking human being"), which appeared, according to present evidence, about 350,000 years ago. The immediate predecessor was Homo erectus, which may have emerged as long ago as 1,500,000 years. Back in time beyond Homo erectus is an area of doubt and controversy. There is growing support for the theory that humanity originated in east Africa about 2 million years ago, but this is not yet fully proved.

HUMAN BEINGS AS FOOD GATHERERS

Human beings have always had to try to come to terms with their environment. For the greatest part of their time on earth, they have struggled simply to hunt and gather food. Only relatively recently have people been able to produce food and thus create a stable basis for life. And only within the last few decades have we recognized that we have the power to destroy the environment that nourishes us.

From the beginning of human society, people had to decide how to share labor. Historians have usually guessed that men did most of the hunting and gathering in earliest times, while women nourished the young, but recent research has cast doubt on this pattern. The division of labor was probably flexible, depending on circumstances; even today in some communities women hunt animals and babies are suckled by more than one woman. At times, men may have hunted food while women tended crops as well as bearing the young; in such societies women may have dominated the economic and social organization.

If the men in some community trapped and killed a large animal, this achievement may have enabled them to claim leadership, and physical strength may explain why men have led most societies that have left records. The records themselves have usually been shaped by males, but they still reveal indispensable roles for women as organizers and sustainers of human communities. To the extent that males have taken the lead, it has probably been the result of the need for physical strength to repel aggression. One hunting band, for example, might have had to turn aside the claims of another band to certain territory. In such clashes, we may guess that men assumed leadership through their strength and thus created a division of roles based on sex that gave them dominance of their communities. One result of this social division has been a comparative lack of information about the role of women in history; the reconstruction of this role, the restoring of women to history, has been a leading theme of historical research in the present generation.

The period when people gathered food is often called the Old Stone Age, or Paleolithic Age, and ranges from the beginning of human history to about 10,000 B.C. Even in this early period, some human beings developed a remarkably sophisticated kind of art. The most striking creations we have from food-gathering societies are a series of cave paintings that survive at their finest in Lascaux in France and Altamira in Spain. Most of them show wild animals, enemies of human beings and yet part of their essential support. The paintings may have a quasi-religious meaning as symbolic attempts to gain power over the quarry; scars on the walls suggest that people threw spears at the painted animals, as if to symbolize killing them. If so, the cave paintings provide our earliest evidence for one of the main themes of history: the attempt to communicate with forces outside human control through symbolic action, art, and thought—that is, through religion and ritual acts.

HUMAN BEINGS AS FOOD PRODUCERS

About 10,000 B.C. there occurred the most important event in all human history: People turned from hunting animals and gathering food to producing food from the earth. This event, the rise of agriculture, is called the Neolithic Revolution and introduced the Neolithic, or New Stone, Age.

The word *revolution* usually implies dramatic action over a short time, which was in no way true of this one: Yet revolution it was, for it made possible the feeding of larger populations. The rise of agriculture gave continuity to human existence and demanded long-term planning and the practice of new skills and specialties. Those people not needed in agriculture could engage in hunting (for this skill was still needed), weaving, pottery, metalwork, and trade.

But *why* did this revolution take place? What caused people to turn from the pattern of roaming the countryside that had lasted hundreds of thousands of years? There may be no one simple answer, but it is clear that the earth's glaciers, which had long been advancing from both polar regions toward inhabited areas, began to shrink back toward the poles. This allowed the animals that had been driven by the glaciers into the arms and weapons of human beings to wander away again. To hunt and trap animals now demanded longer journeys in search of less abundant prey: Therefore farming became a necessity.

It has also been suggested that agriculture developed in response to increasing population. Some historians have argued that larger populations in the later (or "upper") Paleolithic Age made it imperative to develop new sources of food. Other historians have denied this, suggesting that a large increase in population became possible only *after* the agricultural revolution had ensured a supply of the necessities that would sustain humanity—domesticated animals (sheep, pigs, cattle), vegetables, and grains. There is probably truth in both views: The need for a new supply of food may have been pressing even as people came to seek more settled homes, rather than face the constant upheavals of a nomadic existence.

Moreover, when people invested much labor in their settlements and knew that their sustenance depended on their land, the issue of protecting and even expanding their claims to territory became of immense importance. Therefore one effect of the agricultural revolution was the impetus to fight over territory—to make war. War is one of the constantly recurring themes of Western civilization. The reasons for making war will vary considerably through the centuries, and the tools of war will become ever more sophisticated; but the willingness to seize a weapon and be willing to shed other people's blood and risk one's own life to protect territory descends from the earliest permanent human settlements.

EARLY NEAR EASTERN VILLAGES

The Neolithic Revolution first occurred among the hills of what is now southern Turkey and northern Iraq, especially in the Zagros hills east of the Tigris River. But, again, why was *this* region the cradle of agriculture? Historians have concluded that only here was there a sufficient supply of animals for domestication along with the needed vegetables and cereals. The earliest known settlements, dating from about 9000 B.C., were unwalled and unfortified, and their people lived in simple huts. About 8000 B.C. the first somewhat larger villages appeared. The oldest seem to have been Jericho and Jarmo, but even

AN OVERVIEW OF EVENTS (ALL DATES B.C.*)

c. 7000	First permanent villages in Near East.
c. 3000	Formation of cities in Sumer; unification of Upper and Lower Egypt.
c. 1900	Hebrews begin immigration into Palestine.
1792–1750	Hammurabi unifies Babylonia and issues his law code.
c. 1595	Sack of Babylon by Hittites.
c. 1570–1085	Egyptian Empire (New Kingdom).
c. 1400–1200	High point of Hittite kingdom.
c. 1230	Exodus of Israelites from Egypt and their invasion of Canaan.
c. 900–612	Assyrian conquests.
559–530	Cyrus founds Persian Empire.
521–486	Rule of Darius in Persia.

*Some historians use an alternate system of dating: B.C.E. (Before the Common Era) and C.E. (Common Era).

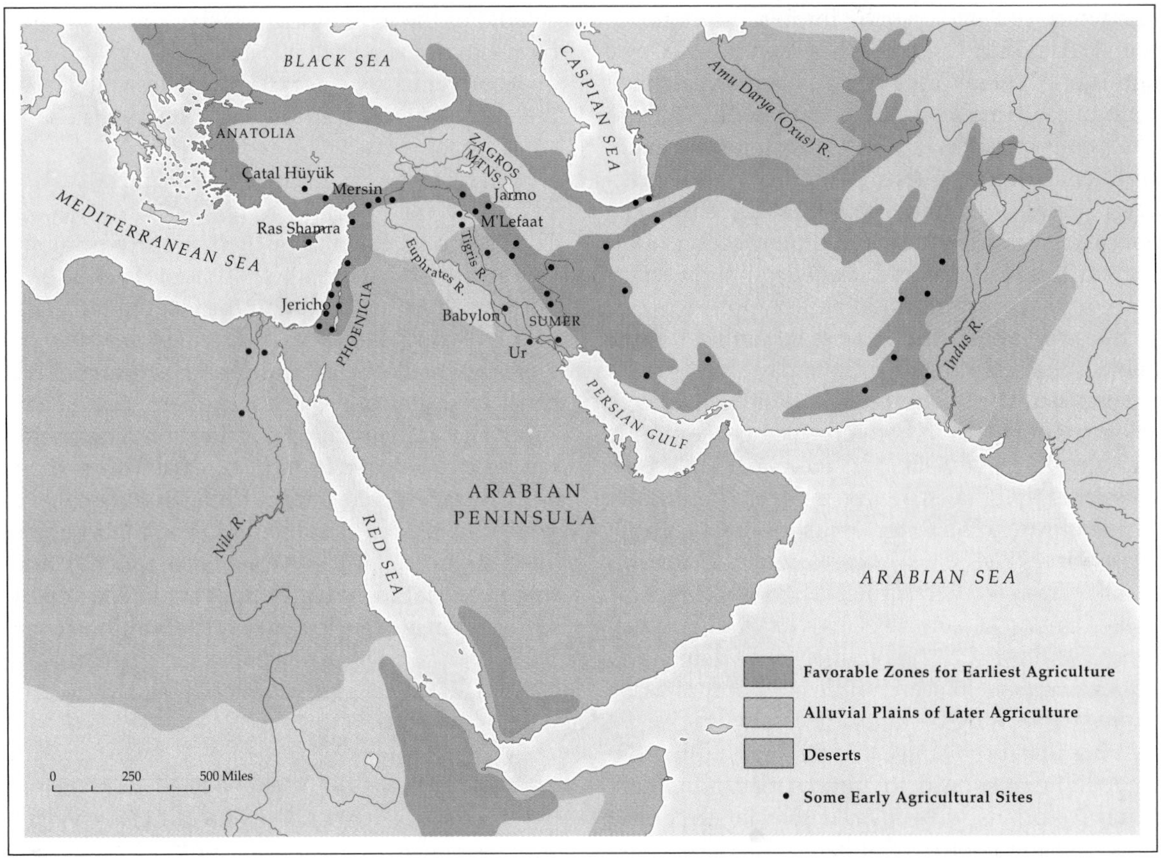

Map 1.1 THE EARLIEST CIVILIZATIONS
Note the famous "fertile crescent," running north from Jericho, then curving southeast toward Sumer; this area supported the first permanent agricultural villages.

these were still small settlements; Jarmo's population is estimated to have been about 150.

As such villages became more permanent, they also became more versatile in their inventions; our first evidence of pottery, for example, comes from what is now Iran and dates from about 6500 B.C. This invention allowed the storage of food and sustained the population in periods when hunting and gathering were more difficult. Another invention, the art of weaving, was practiced in Anatolia, now within modern Turkey, by about 6000 B.C. and provided both new occupations and new resources for a village. About this time, too, people began to travel in crude rafts and in carts with wheels. Potters gradually learned to fashion their wares on the surface of a turning wheel, so that they could make in minutes what had previously taken hours; and the pot, the raft, and the wheel combined to provide the means to transport grain and other goods. Thus arose another institution of all later societies: the mutually profitable exchange of goods in trade, pursued by people skilled enough to make a living at it. Some archaeologists have suggested that a number of towns were formed not for the sake of local agriculture but to serve as trading centers. Trade needs safe routes and a guarantee of safety for traders, which in turn require some kind of political protection and control.

The early agriculturalists were naturally much concerned with breeding and fertility; in their cities we therefore find evidence of attempts at communication with goddesses, in the form of statuettes of unmistakable earth-mothers, with large buttocks and breasts, whose fertile bodies, it was hoped, would make the soil productive. Such figures probably also signify the importance of human mothers, for the villages flourished only if women produced and sustained each new generation. The emphasis on the importance of females and female deities has led some historians (though without clear evidence) to deduce that matriarchy, the political domination of a society by women, existed during the early period of agricultural towns, and that men had to overturn this system in order to gain or regain mastery.

So by stages there arose agrarian communities with communal gods, domesticated animals, simple technologies and economies, and some regulation of social behavior. Yet we must remember how painfully slow was the transition from nomadic hunters to food-producing villagers. And still another 6000 years were to separate such agricultural villages from the first civilizations.

II. The First Civilizations in Mesopotamia

THE EMERGENCE OF CIVILIZATION

From about 3000 B.C., the historian speaks of civilization, a social organization with more complex rules for behavior than those that guided dwellers in caves or the earliest farmers. In a civilization, there are more sophisticated divisions of authority and labor, including duties, powers, and skills that pass down within certain families. Such forms of social life first appear about 3000 B.C., though they were not the result of a sudden explosion but rather of long social development.

The establishment of firm authority requires the acceptance by both governors and the governed of their status; we shall see this balance throughout history, but we shall also observe its collapse when conflict leads to the replacement of one governing group by another. Rulers, however named, arise from among the heads of powerful families. Seeking social order, people give authority to a man or woman who seems to have some special power or ability.

An equally essential part of the social cement, in all periods of civilization, has been law, formally accepted codes of behavior, as distinct from the simple customs of a village. Law may develop slowly, but eventually it is recorded in detailed law codes, which tell us how societies controlled relations among their people. But there is tension, in any civilization, between control and freedom; law codes are thus also a way of restraining encroachment of one citizen on another. The constant discussion and refinement of law is another permanent theme of our history.

Cities are larger and therefore stronger than villages; they have the power to dominate the hinterland and even to enslave its population. Slavery, though deplorable in modern eyes, allowed the enslavers more varied occupations by freeing them from the mundane requirements of existence. As people began to use this new freedom to pursue special skills, some gained a reputation for religious knowledge and became the state's communicators with divine powers; and such is the strength of religious belief that these priests could form a class of advisers whom even kings could not ignore.

Other citizens used their new freedom to develop new arts and crafts. Along with improved techniques of pottery, weaving, and domestication of animals, a major step forward took place when workers discovered how to blend other metals with copper to fashion bronze, especially for weapons. As the first cities reached significant size, humanity thus entered the Bronze Age, which started about 3000 B.C. and ended between 1200 and 1000 B.C.

SUMER

Mesopotamia is a rich alluvial plain created by deposits from the Tigris and Euphrates rivers. At the southern end of this plain arose the first real cities and the first recognizable civilization, in the area known as Sumer. The people of Sumer and their language appear to be unrelated to any other known people or language. By about 3000 B.C. Sumer contained a dozen or more city-states—in other words, cities that were each independent of the others, each ruled by its own king and worshiping its own patron deity, a god that offered protection to the city. The citizens of each city were divided into three classes: nobles and priests, commoners, and slaves. This is the first example of what we shall often meet in history: a recognized, legal division of people into social orders. The king was not considered divine; he held power only so long as he could command support from the powerful priests and nobles.

At the center of a Sumerian city there usually stood a ziggurat, a terraced tower built of baked brick and culminating in a temple, probably for the patron god of the city. A ziggurat might be a stupendous structure: The wall surrounding one of them was some 36 feet thick. The Old Testament contains many echoes from Sumer, and it seems likely that the story in the Bible of the Tower of Babel was ultimately based on the memory of a ziggurat.

In Sumerian culture, the patron god theoretically owned the whole city; but, in fact, much of the land was private property, held mainly by princes and their families but also by private citizens. Most houses were of a single story and were jammed into narrow streets, but some richer houses had two stories and an open court. The people were monogamous, and women held property and took part in business but did not hold political office.

Trade was essential for the growth of Sumerian cities, for, despite the region's astonishing fertility, it lacked good timber and stone. Sumerians pioneered the art of building in baked brick, but to obtain other materials they had to export in exchange such goods as metalwork, in which they became outstanding craftsmen.

Perhaps to bolster their expertise in the essential art of trading, the Sumerians developed a precise system of mathematical notation. Their system was the sexagesimal, in which the number 60 (*sexaginta* in Latin) is one of the main elements; this system has the advantage of including 3, 10, and 12 as factors. One of the longest-lasting legacies of Mesopotamia to our world is this system:

▶ A ziggurat from Ur. The stairway leads up to a room in which a god could rest and take his pleasure. The ziggurat formed the core of a temple compound, while around it were storehouses.

The foot has 12 inches; the day, twice 12 or 24 hours; the minute and hour, 60 units each; and the circle, 360 degrees.

Sumerian Literature The Sumerians' chief contribution to later civilizations was the art of writing. The most important intellectual tool ever discovered, writing enables people to keep records, codify laws, and transmit knowledge. All the record keeping, libraries, and literature of later times are made possible by this invention. We know of some earlier attempts at communication through written symbols, but the Sumerians developed the art in an efficient form. Their script was pictographic: Each sign was originally a simplified picture of the article that the scribe had in mind. In time, scribes reduced the complexity of the system by simplifying pictures and by combining several pictures into one. In this process of abstraction, the meaning of a sign might change. For example, a crude picture of a star was simplified into four wedge-shaped marks and given the meaning of "god" or "heaven."[1] In another kind of refinement, the Sumerian script became at least partly alphabetic and phonetic, rather than remaining purely a system of pictographic writing. Sumerian texts were written on clay tablets by pressing the end of a reed or bone stylus into the wet clay; the resulting wedge-shaped marks are called *cuneiform* (Latin *cuneus*, meaning "wedge"), a name used for all such scripts in whatever language they occur.

The Sumerians had a developed mythology and saw the world as having been created by a god. Moreover, the gods had established the standards by which people had to live. One of their main deities, Enlil, was primarily a storm god who lived in heaven. Normally kind and fatherly, Enlil made the rich soil of Mesopotamia fertile and was credited with designing the plow. At times, however, when Enlil had to carry out the harsh decrees of other gods, he became terrifying. This alternation may reflect the uncertainty bred in the Sumerians by the threat of floods that always hovered over them. When the rivers overflowed and destroyed the crops, the Sumerians thought the gods had withdrawn their

► **A relief showing the Sumerian hero Gilgamesh holding a conquered lion, from the reign of Sargon II of Assyria, eighth century B.C. The relief shows the long continuation of the Sumerian legend.**

[1]The Sumerian method of writing is described by S. N. Kramer in *The Sumerians*, 1963, pp. 302 ff.

favor, and they rationalized such treatment by assuming that they had somehow offended the gods or failed to observe their requirements.

In Sumerian mythology, humanity was almost completely dependent on the gods. Indeed, Sumerian myth taught that the gods had created people merely to provide slaves for themselves. In the Sumerian epic *The Creation of Mankind*, Marduk the creator says, "Let him be burdened with the toil of the gods, that they may freely breathe." Other Sumerian myths foreshadow the biblical accounts of eating from the tree of knowledge in Paradise and of the Flood that covered the earth.

Sargon and the Revival of Ur Wars among the cities of Sumer weakened them and prepared the way for the first great warlord of Western history: Sargon, of the region of Akkad, an area just north of Babylon. He ruled from 2371 to 2316 B.C.[2] and conquered all Mesopotamia; his kingdom even reached the Mediterranean Sea. From Akkad his language is named Akkadian; it is of the Semitic linguistic family. Thus through Sargon we first meet one of the most important of all groups of peoples in Western civilization, the Semites. They spoke a number of related languages including Akkadian, Hebrew, and Canaanite. Akkadian, also written in cuneiform, now replaced Sumerian as a spoken language, although Sumerian continued to be written until about the beginning of the Christian era.

Sargon and his successors ruled from Akkad until about 2230, when invasion, and perhaps internal dissension, dissolved the Akkadian kingdom. The Sumerians then regained control of southern Mesopotamia and established the so-called Third Dynasty of Ur. The chief ruler of this period was Ur-Nammu (2113–2096 B.C.). He created another practice that we will see again and again in history, when he issued the first comprehensive law code and spelled out regulations and penalties for a broad range of offenses. He also established standard weights and measures, a recognition of the importance of trade to the people of his state. His law code is preserved in only fragmentary form, but it is clear that he laid down fines in money rather than calling for physical retribution: "If a man has cut off the foot of another man . . . He shall pay ten shekels . . . If a man has severed with a weapon the bones of another man . . . He shall pay one mina of silver."

THE BABYLONIAN KINGDOM

The cities of southern Mesopotamia succumbed, toward the year 2000 B.C., to the rising power of a Semitic people called Amorites. These invaders destroyed Ur in 2006 and soon established their own capital at Babylon, within the region known as Babylonia. Hammurabi, the sixth king of the dynasty in Babylon itself, finally succeeded in unifying Mesopotamia under his rule.

Hammurabi (1792–1750 B.C.) is a towering figure whose greatest legacy is the most significant of all the documents written down to his time: a cuneiform stone column, now in the Louvre Museum in Paris, recording a long series of legal judgments published under his name. This so-called Code of Hammurabi, like the earlier one of Ur-Nammu, is not a complete constitution or system of law; rather, it is a compilation of those laws and decisions that he thought needed restating. The code includes some 270 sections, much more carefully organized than any earlier one that we know (*see box*, p. 9). Hammurabi has always been considered the primary example of the lawgiver, the man who grasped the organizing power of royal declarations of law; this example was to be followed by many other potentates, whether or not they consciously looked back to the Babylonian model.

We cannot, in a few lines, summarize Hammurabi's fascinating document, which regulates virtually every aspect of relations between citizens. The penalties for crime were severe, to say the least. If a son struck his father, his hand was cut off; if a man broke into a house, he was put to death; anyone who looted a burning home was thrown into the fire. Among the most forward-looking provisions in the code were those regarding the family. Hammurabi evidently recognized the vulnerable position of women and children in his society and took care to protect them. If a man's wife became ill, he could marry

---

[2]Dates in early Near Eastern history are constantly being revised. For dates in this chapter we normally rely on the *Cambridge Ancient History*, 3rd ed., 1970 ff.

Hammurabi's Law Code

Here are some excerpts from the "judgments" laid down by Hammurabi in his famous law code.

"When Marduk [the patron god of Babylon] sent me to rule the people and to bring help to the country, I established law and justice in the language of the land and promoted the welfare of the people. At that time I decreed:

"1. If a man accuses another man of murder but cannot prove it, the accuser shall be put to death.

"2. If a man bears false witness in a case, or cannot prove his testimony, if that case involves life or death, he shall be put to death.

"22. If a man commits robbery and is captured, he shall be put to death.

"23. If the robber is not captured, the man who has been robbed shall, in the presence of the god, make a list of what he has lost, and the city and the governor of the province where the robbery was committed shall compensate him for his loss.

"138. If a man wants to divorce his wife who has not borne him children, he shall give her money equal to her marriage price and shall repay to her the dowry she brought from her father; and then he may divorce her.

"142. If a woman hates her husband and says, "You may not possess me," the city council shall inquire into her case; and if she has been careful and without reproach and her husband has been going about and belittling her, she is not to blame. She may take her dowry and return to her father's house.

"195. If a son strikes his father, they shall cut off his hand.

"196. If a man destroys the eye of another man, they shall destroy his eye.

"197. If he breaks another man's bone, they shall break his bone.

"200. If a man knocks out a tooth of a man of his own rank, they shall knock out his tooth."

The Code of Hammurabi, Robert F. Harper (tr.), 1904, language modified.

another woman but had to continue to support the first wife; and she, if she wished, could move out and keep her dowry. Again, a widower could not seize his dead wife's dowry and spend it but had to save it for her sons; and a widow could keep her dowry, that is, the contribution from her family that she had brought into her marriage. Divorce was also allowed. A wife could divorce her husband for adultery, but only if she had been chaste; if not, she was thrown into the river along with her lover.

MESOPOTAMIAN CULTURE

Hammurabi's subjects used all manner of commercial records (bills, letters of credit, and the like), and their knowledge of mathematics was amazing. They built on foundations laid by the Sumerians, using the sexagesimal system, with 60 as the base. They had multiplication tables, exponents, tables for computing interest, and textbooks with problems for solution.

The Mesopotamians also developed complex systems of astrology and astronomy. It is not certain which science inspired the other, but we have both astrological predictions and astronomic observations from the second millennium. The Babylonian calendar had 12 lunar months and thus had only 354 days, but astronomers learned how to regularize the year by adding a month at certain intervals. When the Hebrews and Greeks wanted to order time through a calendar, they learned the method from the Babylonians. In fact, the calendars of both Jerusalem and Athens were also lunar, with 354 days and a month added from time to time.

III. Egypt

The early cities of Mesopotamia had turbulent histories, falling now to one warlord, now to another. The kingdom of Egypt, by contrast, achieved a nearly incredible permanence; its people and monuments survive even today. The basic element in the long history of Egyptian civilization is the Nile River. The Nile overflows its banks each summer, reviving the land with fresh water and depositing a thick layer of alluvial soil for cultivation. Only this yearly flood protected the Egyptians from starvation.

THE OLD KINGDOM

Early Egypt was divided into two regions, Upper Egypt (the Nile Valley) and Lower Egypt (the river delta). A king, Menes (also known as Narmer), who lived about 3000 B.C., unified Upper and Lower Egypt and established a capital at Memphis. By the beginning of the Old Kingdom, the land had been consolidated under the strong central power of the king, who enjoyed a supremacy that we can hardly imagine today. The king (he was not called *pharaoh* until the New Kingdom) was the owner of all Egypt and considered a god as well. The whole economy was a royal monopoly; and serving the king was a hierarchy of officials, ranging from governors of provinces down through local mayors and tax collectors. Artisans, peasants, and slaves, all working for the king, nourished the whole system.

The supreme monuments of the Old Kingdom are the three immense pyramids, tombs for kings, built at Giza (now within the city of Cairo) between 2600 and 2500 B.C. These staggering feats of engineering dwarf any other monuments from any age. Building such a pyramid may well have been the chief activity of the king during his rule.

▸ Top: The ceremonial palette of King Narmer is a symbolic representation of the unification of Upper and Lower Egypt. This side of the palette shows the king, wearing the white crown of Upper Egypt, smashing the head of an enemy. The god Horus, in the form of a falcon, holds a rope attached to a captive of Lower Egypt, a region symbolized by six papyrus plants.
Bottom: On this side of the palette King Narmer has completed his conquest of Lower Egypt and wears the red crown of that kingdom. He is reviewing the bodies of decapitated victims. The exotic beasts with necks intertwined may symbolize the unity of the two Egypts.

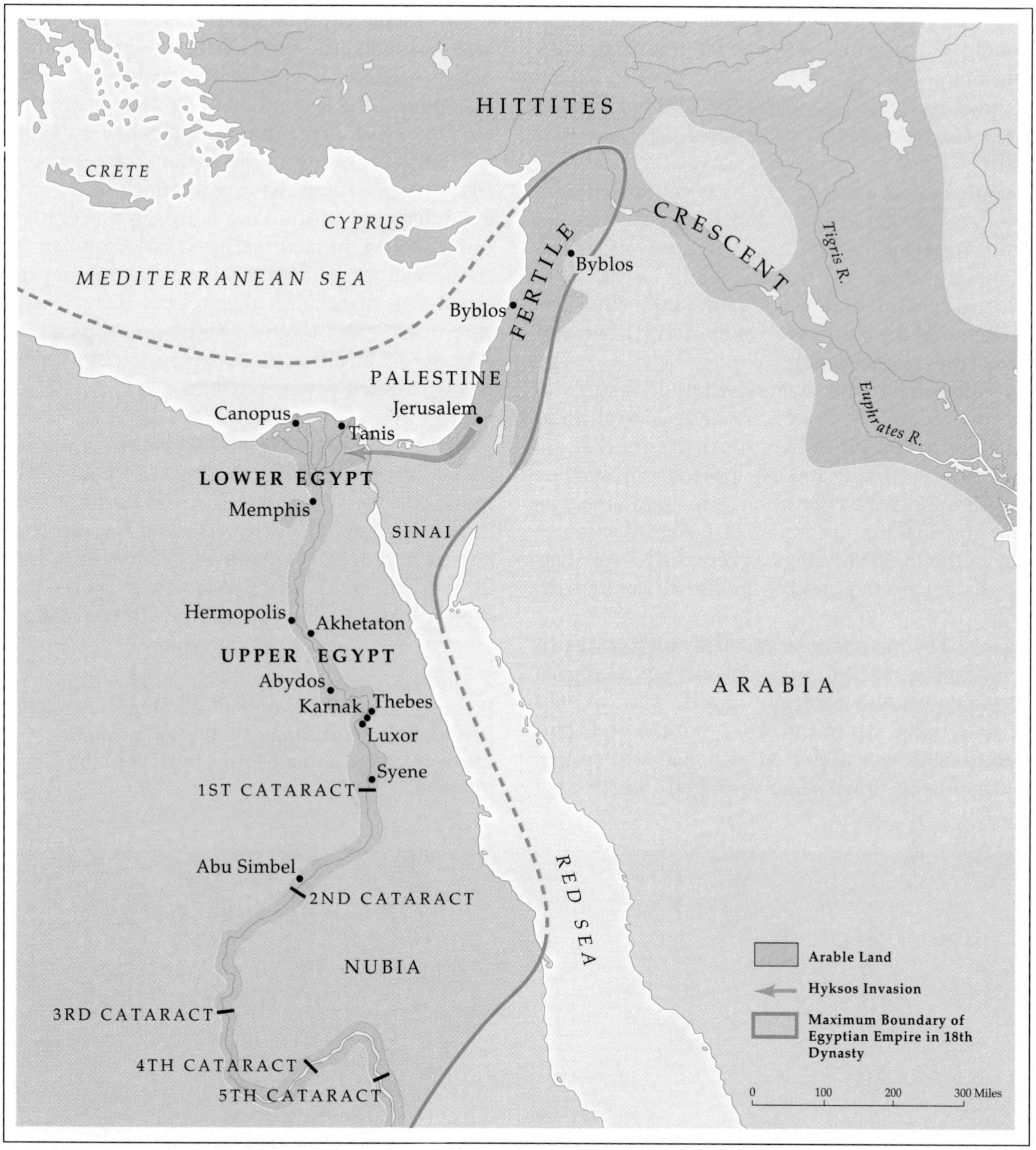

Map 1.2 ANCIENT EGYPT
The kingdom reached from the fourth cataract to the Mediterranean.

Religion The king, together with the gods whom Egyptian belief associated with him, stood at the pinnacle of Egyptian religion. Other gods, who occupied lesser positions in Egyptian theology, appeared in a variety of forms, often as animals, and in origin were probably deities of the villages up and down the Nile. The Egyptians believed in a pleasant life after death, in which people would perform their usual tasks but with more success. The king, already a god, would become a greater god; viziers, priests, and administrators would hold more responsible positions.

For everyone who had lived a good life there would be pleasures such as boating and duck hunting.

In Egyptian mythology, the god who ruled over the dead was Osiris, originally a god of fertility. He had given Egypt its laws and taught the people how to prosper. But he was murdered by his treacherous brother, and his body was cut into fragments, which his loving wife Isis reassembled, thus resurrecting him. Osiris' son, Horus, was identified with the king, who was considered the incarnation of Horus on earth and the center of the world.

In harmony with their expectation of survival beyond death, the Egyptians made careful preparations for the physical needs of the afterlife, especially by placing favored possessions such as jewelry and wine cups into a tomb and embalming and making mummies of the dead. Statues sat in the tombs of kings as receptacles for their spirits in case their bodies should be destroyed.

Maat The Egyptians recognized an abstract ethical quality called *maat,* which Egyptologists translate roughly as "right order." *Maat* existed if everything was in the order that the gods had ordained. It was a kind of primeval and cosmic harmonizing force that arranged all created things in the right relationships. All ancient societies valued order and harmony—most of them had a monarchic system that naturally prized discipline—but the notion of *maat* seems to show a new way of advocating moral behavior. When a society can give a name to the abstract idea of right order without having to attach it to a god, a subtler kind of thinking is taking place. Right order would, indeed, help to hold Egyptian society together. Thus *maat* illustrates another frequent use of religion throughout history: as a carefully crafted tool of politics and a promoter of order, in addition to an expression of people's feeling toward divine powers.

Writing Egyptians developed a form of writing known as *hieroglyphics* ("sacred carvings"). The indispensable key to the Egyptian past has been the Rosetta stone, discovered when Napoleon occupied part of Egypt in A.D. 1798. This stone, now in the British Museum, contains a partly preserved hieroglyphic text along with translations

▶ The step pyramid of Zoser (about 2800 B.C.), the center of a large religious complex, shown with part of the surrounding wall that gave into the courtyard. Note a small shrine in front of the pyramid.

in the cursive Egyptian script that evolved from hieroglyphics and also in Greek, a known language that offered a way of deciphering the other two.

Like the cuneiform script of Mesopotamia, hieroglyphics began as pictorial signs. Experts believe that the Sumerians influenced the Egyptians in the early stages, around 3000 B.C.; but the pictures that the Egyptians developed were mostly original. Hieroglyphics sometimes use merely a picture of the object represented; for example, a small oval represents "mouth." But at some point the scribes decided to use the pictograms as phonetic signs; thus *ra* continued to mean "mouth" but was also used for the sound *r*. Fully developed hieroglyphics, like Sumerian cuneiform, are therefore a combination of pictograms and phonetic signs.

The Egyptians made writing material from the papyrus plants (from which comes our word *paper*) that grew in abundance along the Nile. The reeds of the plant were placed crosswise in layers, then soaked, pressed, and dried to produce sheets and rolls. Because of the dry climate, thousands of papyri have survived in legible condition; most of these come from a later period when the Romans administered Egypt.

▸ The Pyramids of Giza. Left to right, the pyramid of Menkaure, Khefre, and Khufu (the "great" pyramid).

Literature Egyptians developed a rich, lively literature. Their works often dealt, as did their art, with mythology and the afterlife; and their hymns to various deities, poems celebrating the king's victory over death, and stories about the gods reflect the serene Egyptian confidence in the beneficence of the gods. Various texts, collectively known as the Book of the Dead, provide charms and other methods of ensuring a successful transition to the other world.

Success in this world appears as the central concern of another literary genre, appropriately known as "instructions" or "instructions in wisdom." These books, in which a wise man gives advice about how to get ahead in the world, reveal much about Egyptian social attitudes, especially the supreme position of the king. The writers counsel discretion and loyalty: "If you are a man of note sitting in the council of your lord, fix your heart upon what is good. Be silent—this is better than flowers. Speak only if you can unravel the difficulty . . . to speak is harder than any other

An Egyptian papyrus showing an antelope and a lion in a game of chess; a playful scene from daily life.

work. . . . Bend your back to him that is over you, your superior in the king's administration. So will your house endure with its substance, and your pay be duly awarded. To resist him that is set in authority is evil."[3]

We also have scraps of Egyptian love poetry: "It is pleasant to go to the pond in order to bathe in your presence, that I may let you see my beauty in my tunic of finest royal linen, when it is wet." And there are meditations, songs, ghost stories, and fables of all kinds. In fact, not until the Greeks did the ancient world have another literature with the variety and beauty equal to that of Egypt.

Mathematics and Medicine The Egyptians were pioneers in applied science. The need for careful planting in the silt deposits of the Nile forced them to master arithmetic, geometry, and the art of surveying; for an unusually rich overflow might wipe out the boundaries between plots of land, and when this happened the land had to be remeasured.

Medicine in Egypt depended largely on driving out demons from the body. The Egyptians believed that a separate god ruled over each organ and limb, and treatment consisted largely in finding the right chant to appease the appropriate deity and then delivering it in the right tone of voice. Sometimes a sorcerer simply threatened a demon by promising to invoke the aid of the gods if it did not depart at once.

But medicine was not based entirely on magic. One papyrus, a treatise on surgery, displays a more empirical approach to illness. It discusses some 48 medical problems, classified according to the various parts of the body. Whenever possible, the author gives a diagnosis and suggests a treatment. A verdict is often given in one of three forms—"An ailment that I will treat," "An ailment with which I will contend," or "An ailment not to be treated"—probably according to whether the prognosis was favorable, uncertain, or unfavorable. This text is a witness to the birth of a kind of inquiry that transcends haphazard folk medicine. Such maturing and broadening of knowledge independent of magic characterize the civilizing process throughout history.

[3]Adolf Erman, *The Ancient Egyptians: A Sourcebook of Their Writings*, 1966, pp. 61–62 (language modified).

The Invasion of the Hyksos A major disaster befell Egypt about 1720 B.C., the invasion of the Hyksos (the name means roughly "rulers of foreign lands"). Historians are still not certain who these invaders were, but they were probably a group of western Asiatic peoples from Syria and Palestine. They controlled mainly the region of the delta, but by about 1570 B.C. Egyptian warriors from Thebes had counterattacked and had driven the Hyksos from the delta and back into Asia Minor. The period following the expulsion is called the New Kingdom, or the Egyptian Empire.

THE NEW KINGDOM

During the Eighteenth Dynasty the rulers from Thebes, now called *pharaohs,* strengthened the power of the central government over the nobles and organized Egypt into a military state. They enlarged their domain by encroaching on Asia Minor, where they encountered another large kingdom, that of the Hittites. These two kingdoms, the Egyptian and the Hittite, were the most powerful ones down to their time, and also the last great kingdoms of the Bronze Age.

Hatshepsut Within the Eighteenth Dynasty there reigned the first, and greatest, female ruler of ancient times, Hatshepsut. This dynamic woman seized power and in 1503 B.C. had herself crowned king of Egypt, representing this act as the will of the god Amen. It was an act of breathtaking audacity in a social system where men had always held the absolute power of monarch. Perhaps to emphasize her right to rule as king, she had herself portrayed as a sphinx with a beard.

Hatshepsut wanted to be remembered above all as a builder, the restorer of Egypt. "I have repaired," she proclaimed on inscribed walls, "what was destroyed by the Hyksos; I have raised up what was in pieces ever since the Asiatics had been in the Delta, overthrowing what had been made." Her great temple tomb in the Valley of the Kings is the equal in majesty of any other building in Egypt.

Thutmose III, her successor, became Egypt's greatest military statesman. He made 17 expeditions into Asia Minor and expanded the empire as far as the Euphrates River. His successors, exploiting these conquests, grew rich on the tribute paid by subject peoples such as the Israelites, many of whom became slaves in Egypt. With this economic power the Egyptians expanded their trade, honored their gods with more temples, and continued working the rich copper mines in the Sinai peninsula.

Akhnaton's Religious Reform After the conquests of Thutmose III, a dramatic conflict of religions took place in the New Kingdom. This

▶ Queen Hatshepsut of Egypt (1512–1482 B.C.), history's first female ruler, pictured as a sphinx, which was a divine animal. Surrounding her face are a lion's mane and a ceremonial false beard.

struggle arose from a contest between the pharaoh and certain priests and nobles, as each party strove to make its own god the supreme one. Thus the apparent religious battle—not for the last time in history—was, in reality, a political one. Although it was but one event during the centuries of the New Kingdom, the reforming aims of one side in this conflict have fascinated modern observers.

Early in his reign King Amenhotep IV (1379–1362 B.C.) began to oppose the worship of Amen-Re, for centuries the traditional god of the Thebes, and sponsored the worship of the *aton*, the physical disk, or circle, of the sun. Supported by his wife Nefertiti, Amenhotep appears to have been trying to overcome the influence of priests and bureaucrats in Thebes. To advertise the new faith among his people, he changed his own name to Akhnaton, which may be translated as "he who serves Aton." He moved his capital from Thebes to a completely new city called Akhetaton, "the horizon of Aton" (a village called El Amarna today), where he built a temple to Aton. He composed a soaring hymn in praise of Aton, hailing him as the creator of the world—an account of creation comparable to those of the Sumerians and the Israelites.

There is evidence that Akhnaton fought the worship of other gods, and some historians have gone so far as to call him the first monotheist. Such a conception is anachronistic and overlooks how Aton was worshiped: The royal family alone worshiped the god; the Egyptian people were expected to continue to worship the pharaoh himself. Artistic scenes show priests and nobles in attitudes of reverence, but they are addressing their prayers to the pharaoh, not directly to Aton.

The more conservative priests, and probably most Egyptians, continued to worship Amen-Re, and Akhnaton's religious reform ended with his death. The next pharaoh changed his name from Tutankhaton to Tutankhamen, thus indicating

▶ Akhnaton and Nefertiti in a familial scene hold three of their children, while the sun-disk blesses and cherishes them. The style of art (round bellies, slender bodies, elongated jaws) is typical of the Amarna period.

▸ **Syrian subjects presenting tribute to the pharaoh of Egypt on a wall painting at Thebes in the period of the empire.**

that Amen-Re, the older chief deity, was again in favor. The royal court moved back to Thebes, and the city named for Aton, Akhetaton, was abandoned and destroyed. Akhnaton's name was savagely effaced from monuments and king lists, and he was now known as "the criminal of Akhetaton." The young king Tutankhamen reigned for only seven years and was buried with dazzling splendor. His tomb, discovered in A.D. 1922, intact with all its treasures, has remained the most stunning single find in the history of Egyptology.

The New Kingdom now emerged from the period of religious conflict with renewed strength and was led by ambitious pharaohs, the most famous of whom was Ramses II. He fought a major, though inconclusive, battle with the Hittites in 1300 B.C., at Kadesh in Palestine, and carried on the war until the two kingdoms signed a peace treaty in 1284. The temporary peace that Ramses achieved allowed him to spend time and money on remarkable building projects, which became notorious in the Old Testament as the hardest labor of the Israelite slaves. At Karnak, for example, he completed an enormous hall of columns sacred to Amen-Re, who had now fully regained his old position. Ramses' supreme achievement as a builder is the colossal temple that he had carved out of the rocky cliffs along the Nile at Abu Simbel. The building of the Aswan Dam by the modern Egyptians would have drowned the temple and its statues beneath the water of an artificial lake; but an international group of engineers preserved Ramses' desire to be remembered for all time by cutting the outer monuments free and raising them above the level of the water.

A VIEW OF EGYPTIAN SOCIETY

In antiquity, communication by ship was greatly superior to overland transportation in animal-drawn carts. The Nile therefore imposed a natural administrative unity on Egypt. The kings secured their power through the help of ministers and advisers, especially the class of priests, while a complex bureaucracy carried out the routine work of government and saw to the royal monopoly over the economy.

Slaves existed, but the economic difference between free citizens and slaves was not always vast. Both classes worked the fields, labored on

Dates in Egyptian History

The basic source for Egyptian chronology is a list of the rulers compiled about 280 B.C. by Manetho, an Egyptian priest, who wrote in Greek. He grouped the kings into 30 dynasties (later chronicles added a thirty-first). Modern scholars accept Manetho's divisions and have established these approximate dates B.C.:

Archaic Period (Dynasties 1–2)	3100–2700
Old Kingdom (Dynasties 3–6)	2700–2200
First Intermediate Period (Dynasties 7–10)	2200–2050
Middle Kingdom (Dynasties 11–12)	2050–1800
Second Intermediate Period (Dynasties 13–17, invasion of Hyksos)	1800–1570
New Kingdom, or Empire (Dynasties 18–20)	1570–1085
Postempire (Dynasties 21–31)	1085–332
Conquest of Egypt by Persia	525
Conquest of Egypt by Alexander the Great	332

the pyramids, and were indeed the ultimate economic basis for the regime, although their own lives changed little from one generation to another.

It was possible to enter and rise in the Egyptian hierarchy through education. The kings and their gods needed all manner of scribes, treasurers, and functionaries, and Egyptian children might learn the art of writing in a school run by a temple or a palace or even from a private teacher in a village. They studied normally from age 4 to age 16 and could then enter the army or the royal service. Scribes were also needed for the arts of medicine and architecture and for the priesthoods; most priests were men, but some were women.

Egyptian society was liberal in the scope given to women—more so, in fact, than Judaic or Greco-Roman societies. Women could own and pass on property, could appear as witnesses in court, and could initiate action at law if anyone tried to take their land away. Officials were nearly always men, but women sometimes acted as scribes, even treasurers, something unknown in Greece and Rome. Among peasants, women toiled with men in agriculture and did most of the baking and spinning.

We must not overlook the turmoil within Egyptian history: the invasion of the Hyksos, wars in Asia, the collapse of the New Kingdom, and its conquest by Assyria and then by Persia (*see box*). Yet there remains the awesome *permanence* of Egypt: No other state, in the nations we call Western, has ever survived so long. On the whole, over the span of some 30 centuries, life flowed predictably, as did the Nile, making severe demands but bringing the material for a well-earned reward.

IV. The Early Indo-Europeans

Down to this point, our survey has looked at the great kingdoms of the ancient Near East. During the later centuries of these kingdoms, a new family of peoples began to appear, speaking the languages from which the languages of modern Europe were to descend. English, French, Greek, Latin, Russian, Spanish, and the languages of India, Pakistan, and Iran all belong to the family of languages known as Indo-European. These languages descend from a tongue that we call Indo-European, though we have no preserved writings in such a language. Perhaps about 6000 to 5000 B.C. the Indo-European peoples began a slow dispersion across Europe and parts of Asia. Some of them ultimately settled on the Indian subcontinent, while others moved westward into Italy, Greece, central Europe, and Asia Minor.

THE HITTITE KINGDOM

One of the Indo-European peoples was the Hittites. By about 1650 B.C. they established a capital at Hattusha (Boghazköy in modern Turkey). Excavations here have unearthed about 10,000 cuneiform tablets, the decipherment of which has made it possible to recover at least some of Hittite history.

▶ **Soldiers, carved in the living rock, shown guarding a shrine in a cleft at the Hittite site of Yazilikaya near Boghazköy.**

The greatest early warrior of this nation, Murshili I, in the sixteenth century B.C. led armies south as far as Babylon, which he sacked about 1595, thus ending the kingdom once ruled by Hammurabi. Between 1400 and 1200 B.C. the Hittite kingdom reached its zenith. During the reign of Akhnaton in Egypt the Hittites took advantage of the pharaoh's preoccupation with religious reform to tear away from Egypt the region of northern Syria. Under Ramses II, as we have seen, Egypt's attempt to regain this territory led, in 1284 B.C., to a treaty of nonaggression between the two nations. This modern-seeming document shows a growth in the techniques of diplomacy among ancient states.[4]

The Hittites shared various customs with other eastern states. They believed, for example, that the king became a god after death. But they had other features that historians consider characteristic of Indo-European peoples. The whole army formed a kind of assembly, called the *pankus*, which acted as a court of law to punish criminals. Some historians think the *pankus* once chose the kings, but this power had passed away before our records begin, for it seems clear that kings had the right of inheritance. The queen retained her position even after the king's death, perhaps so that her religious duties should not be interrupted. The king was general, chief judge, and high priest, serving the many Hittite gods; the Hittites adopted most of these deities when they entered Asia Minor.

The Hittites had kings, but much of the political power was in the hands of a limited number of families, who received grants of land and were bound to the king by oaths. This system addressed a common problem of all rulers, how to win and maintain loyalty among potentially dangerous rivals.

Like other societies in this era, the Hittites published law codes, which reveal that their society was patriarchal. Fathers gave their daughters in marriage, and a widow was normally married off to her father's next of kin. But women did have some rights of their own; for example, a free woman who married a slave remained free.

[4]Both the Hittite and Egyptian texts of this document are translated in James B. Pritchard (ed.), *Ancient Near Eastern Texts Relating to the Old Testament*, 1969, pp. 199–203.

THE CLOSE OF THE BRONZE AGE

Between 1250 and 1200 B.C. new waves of invaders (probably including mysterious raiders generally called "sea peoples") poured into Asia Minor, breaking up the Hittite kingdom. These peoples had learned the secret of working iron and applied their knowledge to weaponry. As a result, they overcame the older civilizations that still relied on bronze weapons. Between 1200 and 1000 B.C. the Bronze Age disappeared, to be replaced by an Iron Age, in which we still live.

The introduction of iron had profound social and political consequences. Iron, more readily available than bronze, is not only harder but, most important for this discussion, cheaper as well. As a result, more people could own weapons, and states in the Iron Age grew more formidable in war. As more of the population obtained weapons, there followed a partial shrinking of the distance between some socioeconomic groups in the society. Those who now served the state in the army began to claim some role in determining its policies, and the ruling elites had to open their ranks to armed newcomers in order to maintain control over the masses. A noted historian, V. Gordon Childe, hit the mark when he called iron the "democratic metal."

V. Palestine

CANAANITES AND PHOENICIANS

The region of Palestine was originally inhabited by a group of Semitic tribes known as the Canaanites, among whose cities were Jericho and Jerusalem. By about 1200 B.C. the Canaanites had settled mainly in Phoenicia, a narrow region along the Mediterranean Sea. They drew part of their culture from the Mesopotamian and Egyptian states nearby, but they were also innovators. Their outstanding contribution was a simplified alphabet with only about 30 characters that was later adopted by the Greeks and became the ancestor of Western alphabets. It is impossible to overstate the political and social importance of this invention. It ended the long period during which people had to learn thousands of pictorial symbols to be reasonably literate and writing was a mysterious art known to only a few. Especially in the hands of the Greeks, writing brought a knowledge of law codes and historical records within the intellectual reach of ordinary citizens and led to reevaluation of the past and skepticism about mythology.

The Phoenicians lacked the military power to create an empire, but they influenced other cultures, especially through trade on both land and sea. They established trading posts or colonies far from Palestine, the most famous of which was Carthage, a powerful city on the north coast of Africa that controlled parts of North Africa and Spain.

Among the Phoenician articles of trade was a reddish dye that the ancients called *purple*; cloth dyed in this color became a luxury and has remained a mark of royalty or eminence. The Phoenicians were also the first people to treat the art of war as a profession, and because of their sailing ability they provided the navy for the Persian Empire. They and other Canaanite peoples had thus developed a high urban civilization by the time the Israelites began their invasion of the Palestinian coast.

HEBREW SOCIETY

South of Phoenicia is the region of Palestine that today is known as Israel, also settled in antiquity by speakers of the Semitic Hebrew language. The Old Testament of the Bible provides a continuous record of how this people viewed its past, but before historians can use the narratives and chronicles of the Bible as a source, they must take a stand on the credibility of the documents. Scholars in the nineteenth century questioned whether the Old Testament contained unchallengeable, divinely revealed truth. Archaeology in recent years has often confirmed the Bible, at least in questions of geography and topography, but literal accuracy is not, after all, the central issue. Religious traditions of any society, whether or not they are strictly verifiable, can provide historical information, just as do law codes and lists of kings.

The Israelite chroniclers concentrated on a single god and on humanity's relationship to him. This great theme, varied in countless ways, fuses the Old Testament into a story about one god and the history of his chosen people. Unlike Mesopotamian epics, the Bible deals with real people and real times; it combines ethics, poetry, and history into the most influential book in the Western tradition.

The Early Hebrews There is little reason to doubt the biblical tradition that, beginning around 1900 B.C., tribes of nomads began to wander into Palestine from the east. Each one was led by a patriarch, and they did not form a unified society. One such patriarch was Abraham, whose grandson, Jacob, is said to have organized the nomadic people into 12 tribes under the leadership of his 12 sons. Jacob himself also took the name Israel (meaning "God strove" or "God ruled"). The people were therefore a tribal society, unlike the urban society of Sumer or the unified monarchy of Egypt.

Some Israelite tribes settled in Canaan. Others migrated to Egypt, which they abandoned, probably about 1270 B.C., in the "exodus" (*see box*, below). At their head was a man with the Egyptian name of Moses, who led them across the Sinai peninsula during the period of general unrest in the Near East. Moses organized the tribes of Israel and some neighboring Canaanites into a confederation bound by a covenant to the god he named YHWH (by convention, we write this word Yahweh; in English it later became Jehovah) and placed all the people in Yahweh's service. So far as we can tell, this was the first time that any consolidated group in Western civilization accepted one god. This tremendous moment is thus the birth of monotheism.

But *why* did Israel accept one god, in contrast to the rest of the ancient world, where families of deities were the rule? Was Moses perhaps influenced by the monotheism of Akhnaton? We do not know, but we may guess that Moses saw the need to unify his people so that they would be strong enough to regain their home in Palestine; and what could forge a stronger bond than having the whole people swear allegiance to a single god?

Moses proclaimed the new convenant between God and his people on Mount Sinai, in the wastes of the desert. According to the Old Testament Book of Exodus, he received his instructions directly from Yahweh. These instructions, a document of the greatest historical interest, include the Ten Commandments, in which Yahweh issues the terse order "Thou shalt have no other gods before me."

The Salvation of Israel

The Old Testament book of Exodus narrates the escape of the Israelites from Egypt and preserves the hymn of praise sung by Moses and his people after they reached the holy land. The poem celebrates the strength of God and his generosity in saving Israel. It also shows that Israel saw itself as having a special compact with God.

"I will sing to the Lord, for he has triumphed gloriously; the horse and his rider he has thrown into the sea. The Lord is my strength and my song, and he has become my salvation; this is my God, and I will praise him, my father's God, and I will exalt him. The Lord is a man of war; the Lord is his name. Pharaoh's chariots and his host he cast into the sea; and his picked officers are sunk in the Red Sea. The floods cover them; they went down into the depths like a stone. Thy right hand, O Lord, glorious in power, thy right hand, O Lord, shatters the enemy. [. . .] Thou hast led in thy steadfast love the people whom thou has redeemed, thou hast guided them by thy strength to thy holy abode [. . .], the sanctuary, O Lord, which thou hast made for thy abode, the sanctuary, O Lord, which thy hands have established. The Lord will reign for ever and ever."

Exodus 15, *Holy Bible*, Revised Standard Version, 1962.

Early Israelite society was clearly father-dominated through the patriarchs and God, whom they considered their supreme father. This structure shaped the legal status of women. The commandments imply that a woman is the legal possession of her husband: "Thou shalt not covet thy neighbor's house, nor his wife, nor his servant, nor his ox, nor his ass." Marriage occurs through purchase throughout the Old Testament, and a daughter might simply be given as a kind of salary: "Jacob loved Rachel and served seven years to gain her" (Gen. 29:20). The heroism of those women of the Bible who rose above this control—Ruth, Judith, and Deborah, for example—is all the greater.

Moses also laid down a code of laws, which, unlike earlier codes, is a series of laws prescribing ethically right conduct. This appears to be the first intervention of religion into the private behavior of human beings. The historical reality of Moses, the fact that his laws are connected with the experience of a people, and the power of the ethical concerns of that people have given the faith of Israel an immediacy to which Sumerian or Egyptian religion could hardly pretend.

The Israelite Monarchy By a series of attacks on Canaanite cities and by convenants made with other tribes, the Israelites established themselves in Palestine. About 1230 B.C. they invaded Canaanite territory in a campaign aimed at expansion. Biblical stories say that Joshua, the successor of Moses, led the tribes of Israel across the Jordan River and followed God's instructions to take the Canaanite city of Jericho by siege.

During the years of the conquest of Canaan, Israel still lacked a central government. A series of leaders (called "judges"), one of them a woman named Deborah, managed to reunite the people in periods of crisis, but the tribes then habitually drifted apart. According to the Bible, the people finally demanded a king, evidently wanting to imitate the practice of the Canaanites: "We will have a king over us; then we shall be like other nations, with a king to govern us, to lead us out to war and fight our battles" (1 Sam. 8:20). The first king, Saul (1020?–1010?), and his successor, David (1010?–960?), captured Jerusalem and made it Israel's capital. The entire nation now took the name Israel, and during his reign David extended the kingdom to its farthest boundaries.

Solomon, David's son and successor (960?–920?), was famed for his wisdom. Like all great kings of the period, Solomon was a builder. He left behind him the physical memorial that symbolized the faith of Israel through the centuries—the Temple in Jerusalem. But the temple could not compare in size with his magnificent palace and citadel, whose stables, according to tradition, housed 12,000 horses.

Solomon's autocratic rule and extravagance caused resentment among his people, who were heavily taxed to pay for his palace and army. After his death the kingdom split into two parts. The northern half, centered on the ancient town of Shechem, retained the name of Israel; the southern half, ruled from Jerusalem, was now called Judah. Weakened by internal quarrels, the northern kingdom of Israel was conquered in 722 B.C. by the Assyrians to the northeast, who deported much of the population. This scattered people became known in biblical lore as the 10 lost tribes of Israel.

Judah was now the only Israelite kingdom, and from this time on the remaining Israelites are known as Jews. Judah also fell in 586 B.C. to the Chaldean, or Neo-Babylonian, Kingdom. The captives were deported to Babylon, in the so-called Babylonian captivity, but later in the same century they were allowed by the king of Persia to trickle back into Palestine. There were occasional revivals of an independent Jewish kingdom at other times; but in general the Jews became pawns of the various forces that ruled Palestine until 1948, when a revived Jewish state—the republic of Israel—took its place among sovereign nations.

The Faith and the Prophets Judaism was also shaped by a few resolute critics, known as the prophets: men of the people, tradesmen, and preachers, such as Amos, Micah, Hosea, Jeremiah, and Isaiah. They were not kings and had no military power that could make the people listen to their message. The most authoritative prophet had been Moses, and all successors looked back to him for guidance. The later prophets spoke one general message: Israel was becoming corrupt and only a rigid moral reform could

Jeremiah Reproaches Israel

The people of Israel discovered monotheism, but to maintain it was not easy. The prophet Jeremiah warned his people that they were backsliding into worshiping false gods such as Baal, rather than retain allegiance to the one true God.

"The Lord said to me, 'There is revolt among the men of Judah and the inhabitants of Jerusalem. They have turned back to the iniquities of their forefathers, who refused to hear my words; they have gone after other gods to serve them; the house of Israel and the house of Judah have broken my covenant which I made with their fathers. Therefore, thus says the Lord, Behold, I am bringing evil upon them which they cannot escape; though they cry to me, I will not listen to them. [. . .] The Lord once called you, "A green olive tree, fair with goodly fruit"; but with the roar of a great tempest he will set fire to it, and its branches will be consumed. The Lord of hosts, who planted you, has pronounced evil against you, because of the evil which the house of Israel and the house of Judah have done, provoking me to anger by burning incense to Baal.' "

Jeremiah 11, *Holy Bible*, Revised Standard Version, 1962.

save it. Worship of Yahweh had sometimes been blended with that of the gods, or Baalim, of the Canaanites. Luxury, promiscuity, and extravagance were weakening the discipline of Israelite society (*see box*, above).

But even as they denounced the prevalent wickedness, the prophets promised that God would forgive Israel if the people repented, and he would further prove his love to Israel by sending a Messiah. The word *Messiah* (*mashiah* in Hebrew) means a person or even a thing possessing a divine power or purpose; referring to people, it came to mean one "anointed" by God to perform a special mission. From about 200 B.C. onward, Jewish thought held that a king would some day appear, a descendant of David, who would restore the power and glory of Israel on earth. The famous Dead Sea Scrolls (discussed in Chapter 5), ranging in date from the second century B.C. through the first century A.D., often speak of the awaited Messiah. Christians, too, developed their theory of a Messiah, who would return to rule on earth over all humanity: To them, the "anointed one" (*ho christós* in Greek) is Jesus, but to Jews, the hero is still unborn or unknown.

Another event that strengthened Judaism was the organization of the sacred writings. Ezra, who wrote about 445 B.C., is the prototype of a new kind of spiritual leader—the scribe and scholar. He collected and published the first five books of the Old Testament (the Pentateuch); later scholars collected the books of the prophets. The Temple in Jerusalem, destroyed during the Babylonian invasion, was rebuilt during the sixth century B.C. and, in the absence of a free Jewish state, assumed even greater importance as the nucleus of the faith. It fell once more, in A.D. 70, this time to the Romans, who destroyed it. But part of the western wall of the outer court survived, and at this site the Jews were permitted to gather and pray.

THE JEWISH LEGACY

The Jews are the only society originating in the ancient Near East whose traditions have remained vital in modern times. For reasons that no one can fully explain, adversity has never broken the Jewish spirit, and over many centuries the Jews have persisted as a society even without an independent state. Their faith provided the most persuasive answer to the problem that also troubled their neighbors—the nature of the relationship between humanity and God. To Israel, there was only one god; unlike the gods of the pagans, he was an exclusive and intolerant one.

He judged severely, but was also prepared to forgive those who sincerely regretted wrong behavior. He created the world and stood outside the world; he had no association with the world of nature and never appeared as an animal or in any other form. Above all, he was a god for everyone, not just for nobles, priests, and kings. Christianity, the religion of medieval and modern Europe, is a child of Judaism and has drawn upon the morality and ethics of the older faith.

▶ An extreme rarity, the only example of frescoes in a Jewish synagogue showing scenes from the Bible. From Dura Europus, circa A.D. 239; now in a museum at Damascus.

VI. The Near Eastern Empires

A series of general disruptions about 1250 to 1150 B.C. left no state dominant for the next few centuries until the Assyrians began their conquests. They became the first people to accomplish a political unification of large parts of the Near East (see Map 1.3). The Persians, the next great imperialists of this region, built on foundations laid by the Assyrians and ruled with an administrative skill that only the Roman Empire would equal in ancient times. The Persians also developed a widely accepted religion, Zoroastrianism, some of whose doctrines persisted long after the Persian Empire disappeared.

THE ASSYRIAN STATE

The Assyrians were descended from Semitic nomads who had entered northern Mesopotamia about 2500 B.C. and founded the city of Ashur, named after their chief god. From this name comes the designation *Assyrian* for the people. Their language was a Semitic dialect closely resembling that of the Babylonians, and they wrote in the cuneiform script that had originated in Sumer and had remained in general use.

About 900 B.C. the Assyrians began their most important period of conquest and expansion. They became masters of the upper reaches of Mesopotamia, and their territory included Babylonia to the south, the cities of Palestine to

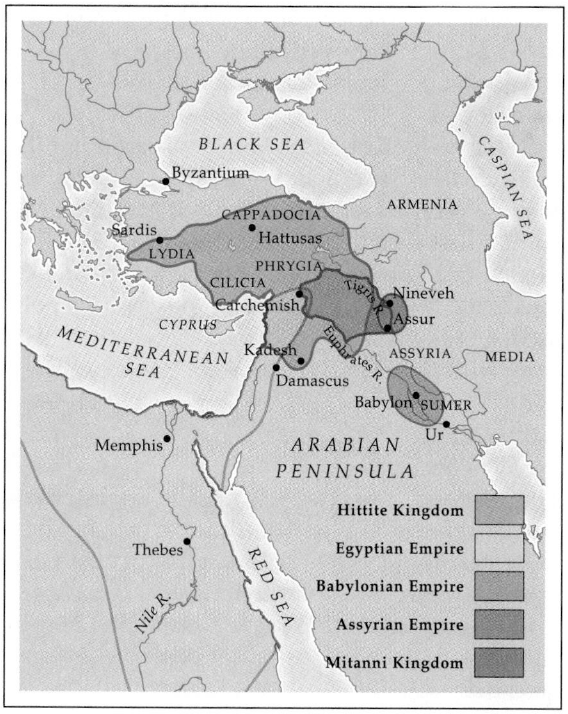

Map 1.3 Three Ancient States
Sumer, Babylonia, and the Hittite kingdom, down to about 1200 B.C.

the west, and Egypt. By the late seventh century their empire embraced most of the Near East.

If any one concept could characterize Assyrian society it would be militarism. The army was especially dominant and efficient, and the Assyrians greatly extended the use of iron weapons. In administering their empire, the Assyrians faced a greater challenge than any earlier state in absorbing large kingdoms such as Egypt and Babylonia. They ruled with a degree of control unknown in any of the earlier conglomerates.

The Assyrian kings exacted heavy payments of tribute as the price of leaving the conquered territories in peace. Some peoples, such as the inhabitants of Judah, escaped further burdens, but other less independent peoples had to accept a vizier, or governor, serving the king. In some cases the imperial government deported subject peoples who might prove troublesome—for example, those inhabitants of Israel who were dispersed within the Assyrian domain. Assyrian armies stationed in the provinces were a further guarantee of stability.

Language became another means of unifying the empire; the Semitic language known as Aramaic was ultimately spoken everywhere in lands dominated by Assyria, and it became the common tongue of the Near East. In Palestine it was spoken by the Jews, including Jesus.

For all their harsh militarism and their brutal rule over their conquered subjects, the Assyrians created magnificent works of art. Much of the wealth extracted from the empire was spent on glorifications of the king and his conquests. Most notable are the reliefs cut on the palace walls at Nineveh, the capital, and elsewhere. The last powerful Assyrian king, Ashurbanipal (668–627), also created a library of cuneiform texts. The largest single group of these texts concerns omens, divination, or observations of the stars, for Assyrian kings relied heavily on omens and their interpretation by priests to guide their policy.

It is hardly surprising that the subjects of the Assyrians watched for any chance to rebel. Finally, in 612 B.C., a combination of forces, led by Babylonians, captured Nineveh, and the Assyrians lost control of their empire.

► **An Assyrian relief showing Ashurbanipal's soldiers attacking a city. Some soldiers swim to the attack; others scale the walls with ladders while defenders fall from the ramparts.**

THE CHALDEANS AND THE MEDES

The Assyrian Empire gave way to two successor states: the Chaldean, or Neo-Babylonian, Kingdom and the Kingdom of the Medes. The Chaldeans, the dominant tribe within a new kingdom based on Babylon, were the most learned astronomers of antiquity. They kept minute records of eclipses, charted a plan of the heavens, and calculated the length of the year mathematically. Their discoveries were passed on to the Greeks and Romans and influenced all medieval and modern astronomy.

Babylon, the capital of the Chaldean Kingdom, was notorious as a center of luxury and wealth. Nebuchadnezzar (604–562 B.C.), the most famous king of the Chaldean dynasty, built lavish temples to the gods and also constructed the terraced roof garden known as the Hanging Gardens, which was considered one of the Seven Wonders of the ancient world.

There now appears a new people, the Iranians, another branch of the Indo-European family of languages. Two Iranian societies especially concern us: the Medes and the Persians. The Medes, living in the area of Media to the east of Mesopotamia, formed a coherent kingdom about 625 B.C., and they took part in the capture of Nineveh in 612 B.C. We know little of their society, because no written documents from Media have yet been found.

Their neighbors, the Persians, lived in the same general area and eventually subdued the Medes. Yet the Medes had enough prestige to be named first in official documents in which both Medes and Persians are mentioned. The Greeks, too, used *Medes* as the term embracing both Medes and Persians, and they called their two wars with the Persian empire the *Medic* wars.

THE PERSIAN EMPIRE

The Persians proceeded to form the largest, most efficient state down to their time. In fact, because of its territorial extent and complexity and the skill with which the Persian kings ruled their domain, many historians would call the Persian state the first "empire," as opposed to a large kingdom.

Map 1.4 FIVE KINGDOMS OF THE NEAR EAST, DOWN TO ABOUT 500 B.C.

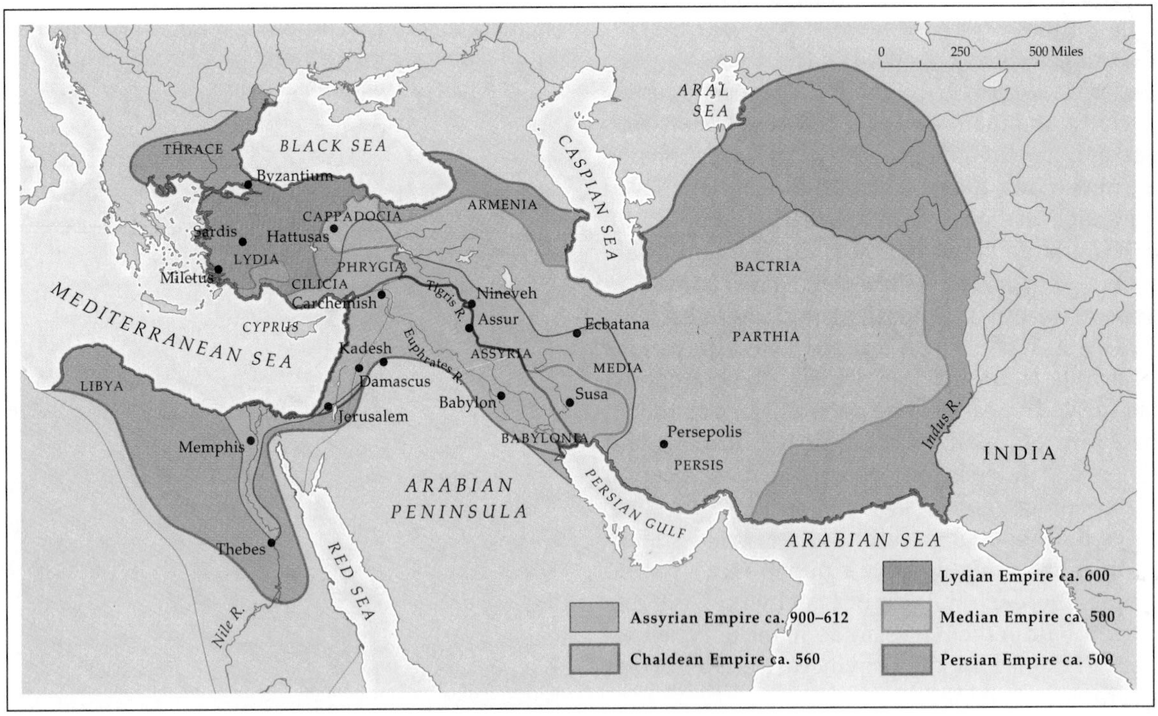

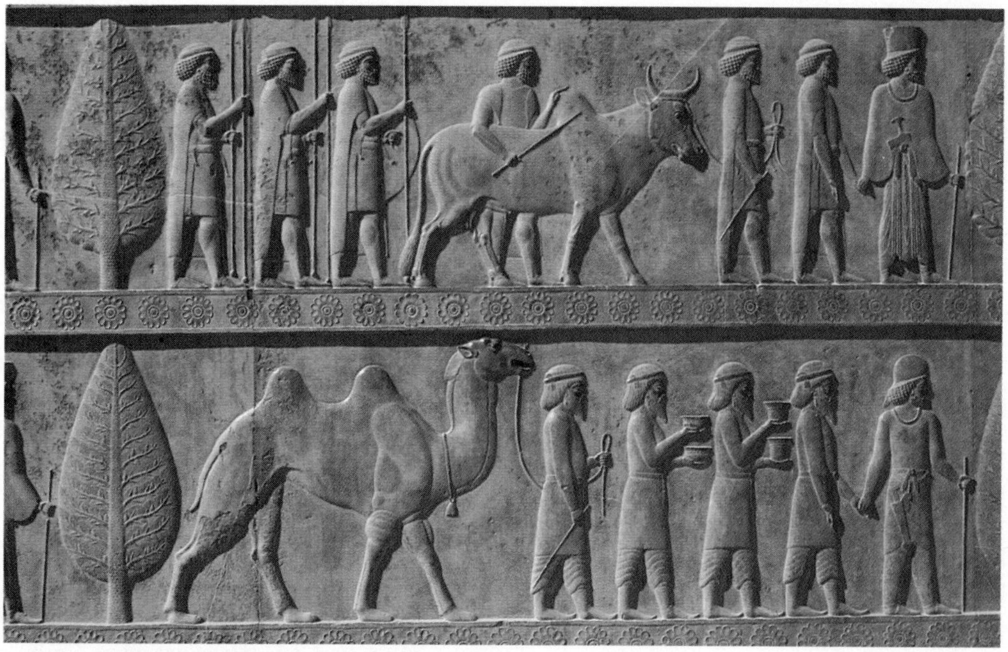

Two panels on a staircase of the great reception hall at the Persian capital, Persepolis. In each panel an official leads a messenger whose followers bear tribute for the king of Persia.

Cyrus The founder of the Persian Empire was King Cyrus (559–530 B.C.). His actions show him as a determined imperialist, and his first conquest was his victory over Media, to the north, in 550. A few years later Cyrus led his forces into western Asia Minor and conquered the kingdom of Lydia. This advance brought the Persian Empire westward as far as the Aegean Sea, which separates Asia Minor from Greece, and set the stage for a direct clash between the vast empire of the Near East and the new culture of the Greeks; but this clash was not to come for another two generations.

To secure the southern flank of his growing empire, Cyrus led his forces against the Chaldeans and captured Babylon. The inhabitants evidently welcomed him, for they offered little resistance. Their judgment was sound; Cyrus treated the city with moderation, not sacking it as an Assyrian conqueror might have done. In fact, his administration was marked by a notable toleration of the customs and religions of the people he brought under his control.

Cyrus' successor, Cambyses (530–522 B.C.), made the third conquest that completed the Persian Empire: He conquered Egypt in 525 B.C., and the rich valley of the Nile remained under Persian rule until Alexander the Great captured it in 332 B.C.

The Persian kings ruled their immense empire from several capital cities, of which Susa and Persepolis were the most famous. The king was the absolute and supreme ruler. His word was law, and he was surrounded with pomp and ceremony; his isolation from his subjects contributed to his reputation for awesome power, which went far to establish the aura of magnificence that has colored monarchy in the Roman Empire and the subsequent kingdoms of Europe.

Darius The most skillful administrator of the Persian Empire was Darius (521–486 B.C.). He left behind a superb monument—a proud summary of his reign written, like the Rosetta Stone from Egypt, in three languages (Old Persian, Akkadian, Elamite). Carved under a relief showing Darius and some of his captives, this text survives high on the face of a rock at Bisitun in Iran. In a series of paragraphs, each beginning "Saith Darius the king," it records his conquests, including that of Babylon, and the defeat and mutilation of his enemies. He also clarifies that he is the only source of law: "As was said by me, thus it was done." The tone and physical setting of this grandiose monument confirm the lofty position of the king. A later inscription on his tomb also proclaimed his devotion to justice: "I am a friend to right, not to wrong. Whoever does harm, I punish him according to the damage he has done." This statement reminds us of the insistence on restitution built into Hammurabi's code and shows how some Near Eastern kings, for all their unchallengeable power, tried to earn a reputation for fairness.

Darius divided his empire into some 20 satrapies, or provinces, each ruled by a satrap ("protector of the realm"). The king, naturally, was the supreme glory of the state, but the satraps had a high degree of independence; they dispensed justice, designed foreign policy, and were in charge of finance. Each satrap, for example, was responsible for collecting an assigned amount of revenue from his province. This system of delegating authority became the model for the Roman Empire when it expanded Rome's domain outside Italy.

▶ Part of the Bisitun inscription in Iran, showing King Darius of Persia (530–486 B.C.) receiving the submission of rebels. Carved in three languages, this inscription provided the key to the decipherment of cuneiform writing.

The Greek historian Herodotus, writing in the fifth century B.C., mentions with admiration the Persian system of roads begun by Cyrus and perfected by Darius. A great highway ran across the empire from the capital at Susa westward to Sardis in Lydia, a distance of more than 1000 miles. The first long highway built anywhere, this road served trade and commerce and also bound the far-flung empire together.

Zoroastrianism The Persian king was never considered divine, but he often served as a priest and claimed to have received his authority from the god of the Persians, Ahura Mazda. The prophet who formed the Persian faith was Zoroaster (also known as Zarathustra). The date of his life and work cannot yet be proved, but a number of historians think he lived about 600 B.C. or soon after. He, too, was not considered divine; rather, he taught that the supreme god, Ahura Mazda, had created the world and directed the heavens and seasons. Around Ahura Mazda gathered good deities such as "Truth," "Righteous Thought," "Devotion," and so on, whose ideals humanity should follow. But Ahura was opposed by Ahriman, a wholly evil spirit—a devil, in fact. Thus Zoroaster taught a dualist religion, although obviously only Ahura is the true god whose message we are to hear. Zoroaster further proclaimed that, after thousands of years, a day of judgment will see the final triumph of good, and those who have followed Ahura will gain paradise and the rest will suffer in the realm of endless night. Thus Zoroaster preached ethical demands on a high level.

Zoroaster also rejected such ancient practices as the sacrifice of animals. The faith he taught demanded recognition of the one good spirit and a life of devotion to Ahura's ideals. His noble thought far outlasted the Persian Empire and resembles doctrines of Christianity, which also has a bad spirit opposed to God, a final judgment, and the possibility of immortality.

The mighty legacy of the ancient Near Eastern societies—including the art of writing, monumental architecture, the development of pottery and weaponry—also influenced the development of their neighbors, the Greeks. They further learned from the older societies the use of coinage, the measurement of time, and forms of diplomacy. The Greeks added to this heritage a radical individualism and a passion for logical argument; their policies and institutions have influenced our own, even more directly and profoundly, as will be apparent when we turn to the Mediterranean and the peoples of Greece.

Recommended Reading

Sources

Lichtheim, Miriam. *Ancient Egyptian Literature: A Book of Readings* (3 vols.). 1973–1980. Excellent gathering of original sources in modern translation.

Pritchard, James B. (ed.). *Ancient Near Eastern Texts Relating to the Old Testament.* 1969. A collection of translations from cuneiform and hieroglyphic texts, with brief commentaries, by eminent scholars.

Studies

Adams, Robert M. *The Evolution of Urban Society,* 1971. Contains chapters on both early Iraq and Mexico.

Albright, William Foxwell. *The Biblical Period from Abraham to Ezra.* 1963. A brief history of Israel by a giant in the field.

The Cambridge Ancient History (3rd ed.) (12 vols.). 1970–in progress. The standard history of the ancient world; chapters by numerous scholars, with wide-ranging bibliographies.

Childe, V. Gordon. *What Happened in History.* 1985. Compact but profound analysis of history by a great anthropologist.

Cook, J. M. *The Persian Empire.* 1983.

Dahlberg, Frances (ed.). *Woman, the Gatherer.* 1981. Studies of the economic and social roles of women in the earliest societies.

Eliade, M. (ed.). *Religions of Antiquity.* 1989. Essays on the various religions of this long epoch.

Emery, Walter B. *Archaic Egypt.* 1961.

Frankfort, Henri. *The Birth of Civilization in the Near East.* 1951. A comparison of early Mesopotamian and Egyptian history.

Frye, Richard N. *The Heritage of Persia.* 1963.

Gardiner, Sir Alan. *Egypt of the Pharaohs.* 1966. A detailed political narrative.

Gurney, O. R. *The Hittites.* 1954. Old but still reliable.

Hallo, William W., and William K. Simpson. *The Ancient Near East: A History.* 1971. American textbook survey of Mesopotamian-Egyptian history.

Kramer, Samuel Noah. *The Sumerians: Their History, Culture, and Character.* 1963. Full portrait of Sumerian society by a leading authority.

Laessøe, Jørgen. *People of Ancient Assyria: Their Inscriptions and Correspondence.* 1963.

Leakey, Richard. *The Making of Mankind.* 1981. By the son of Sir Louis Leakey, presenting a view different from that of the author's father.

Loewe, Raphael. *The Position of Women in Judaism.* 1966. Brief but exact discussion of the role of homemaker in Judaism.

Michalowski, Kazimierz. *Art of Ancient Egypt.* 1969.

Oates, Joan. *Babylon.* 1979. Survey for the nonspecialist.

Olmstead, A. T. *History of the Persian Empire.* 1948.

Price, T. D., and J. A. Brown. *Prehistoric Hunter-Gatherers.* 1985. Earliest techniques of survival and growth of villages.

Roux, Georges. *Ancient Iraq.* 1966. Detailed but readable survey of ancient Mesopotamia.

Saggs, W. F. *The Greatness That Was Babylon.* 1962. Mesopotamian history and society surveyed.

Sahlin, Marshall. *Stone Age Economics.* 1972. The life of earliest humanity.

Skaggs, H. W. F. *Everyday Life in Babylonia and Assyria* (rev. ed.). 1987.

Trigger, B. G. (ed.). *Ancient Egypt: A Social History.* 1983. Chapters by several historians giving modern treatment.

Wilson, John A. *The Culture of Ancient Egypt.* 1956. Subtle treatment of cultural history of Egypt; superb for the history of ideas. A classic.

A magnificent mask of gold foil, found pressed on the face of a ruler of Mycenae, about 1500 B.C. This is one of the first Europeans on whose faces we can look.

CHAPTER TWO

THE FORMING OF GREEK CIVILIZATION

GREEK civilization has been praised by our own more than any other for its creativity, its artistic genius, its intellectual daring. It created forms of thought and expression that have been imitated ever since: philosophy, drama, epic poetry, and history. This civilization honored personal heroism and independence, and its literature is the oldest one with individually known writers.

The Greeks developed a civic culture that broke with the Near Eastern traditions of monarchy. They lived in independent communities, or city-states, in which the most common model seems to have been domination by an upper class of some kind, but even this structure extended power beyond the sole ruler of older civilizations. Citizens of Greek city-states took pride in their temples, their civic traditions, the individual qualities of their own state, their participation in its life. In Athens the government had many features that resembled those of modern democracy. Sparta, Athens' leading rival, chose by contrast a severe, authoritarian form of rule and was the only Greek state to retain a monarchy after it had vanished in all others.

These two states led Greece into its most brilliant victories in war, the defeat of forces twice sent from the vast Persian Empire. They also became the nuclei of alliances that followed this triumph with tragedy, as their rivalry escalated into the long, destructive Peloponnesian War.

I. Crete and Early Greece (Ca. 3000–1100 B.C.)

The first important society in the Greek world developed on the island of Crete, just south of the Aegean Sea. The people of Crete were not Greek: they probably came from western Asia Minor well before 3000 B.C. But their influence on Greek culture was so significant that the history of Greece must begin with Crete.

CRETAN CIVILIZATION

Our major source of knowledge of Cretan civilization is archaeological evidence found in a magnificent villa at Knossos known as the Palace of Minos; the civilization of Crete is thus often called *Minoan*. Greek legend told of the Minotaur (or "Minos-bull"), a monster that lived in a labyrinth (surely a memory of the complex palace) and devoured girls and boys sent to it as tribute. The myth suggests that Greeks had at least a dim recollection of a powerful ruler called Minos, and the historian Thucydides tells of Minos, the powerful king who "cleared the seas of piracy, captured islands, and placed his sons in control over them." Other palaces on Crete exist, but none is so elegant as that at Knossos.

The Palace of Minos was built over a period of about 700 years from 2200 to about 1500 B.C. It was an extensive structure, with a vast eastern courtyard, an impressive grand staircase leading to upper rooms, and many wings and storage chambers. A throne room for the king was added at a late stage of the building, and the throne still survives. The palace even had a plumbing system with water running through fitted clay pipes.

The walls of the palace at Knossos were decorated with frescoes showing the Cretans' delight in nature. Gardens, birds, and animals are vividly portrayed, and one spectacular painting shows young men vaulting over the horns of a bull. The absence of walls around the palace suggests that Minoan civilization was essentially peaceful.

Knossos was clearly the wealthiest of the Cretan cities, and the king was served by an efficient bureaucracy. So far as we can distinguish the roles of the sexes, the rulers were probably men;

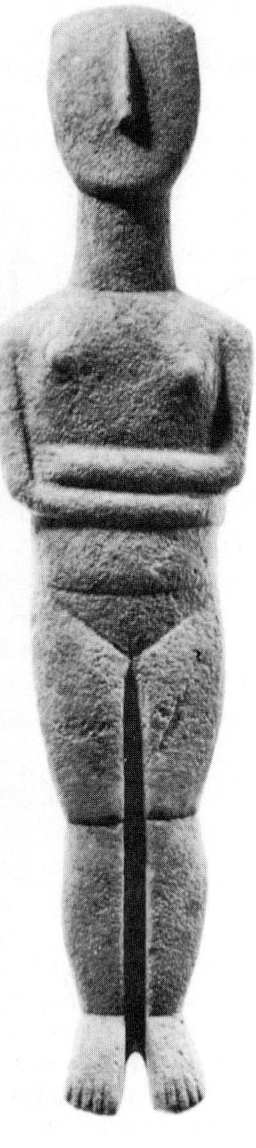

▶ This marble statuette of a goddess is a product of the Cycladic culture (so named from its home in the Cyclades Islands of Greece), which preceded the coming of the Greeks. Carved circa 2800 to 2300 B.C., it represents the early emphasis on female rather than male gods. Neolithic art preferred abstraction to Paleolithic realism and points the way toward later abstract thought. In our own century artists like Brancusi and Mondrian have returned to this type of noble, elegant simplicity.

one wall painting shows a man, often identified as a priest or king, leading an animal to some kind of ceremony. Women had a significant place in this society, for not only were jeweled ladies in elegant gowns portrayed in Minoan wall paintings but they were clearly the object of worship as deities. Statuettes of women have been found, probably goddesses of nature holding snakes in their hands.

Much of the wealth of Crete came from trade, and Cretan pottery has been found far and wide throughout the Mediterranean world. There are about a dozen sites in the Greek world, probably trading posts, called *Minoa*, obviously named after Minos. But we cannot speak of a true Cretan empire with political control of wide areas like the dominions of Assyria or Persia, for Crete lacked the population to conquer and permanently subdue overseas possessions.

CRETE AND THE GREEKS

Yet Minoan civilization influenced the Greek world as it reached its height between 1550 and 1400 B.C. Greek art of this period shows Minoan

Map 2.1 Early Greece during the Bronze Age, ca. 2000–1100 B.C.

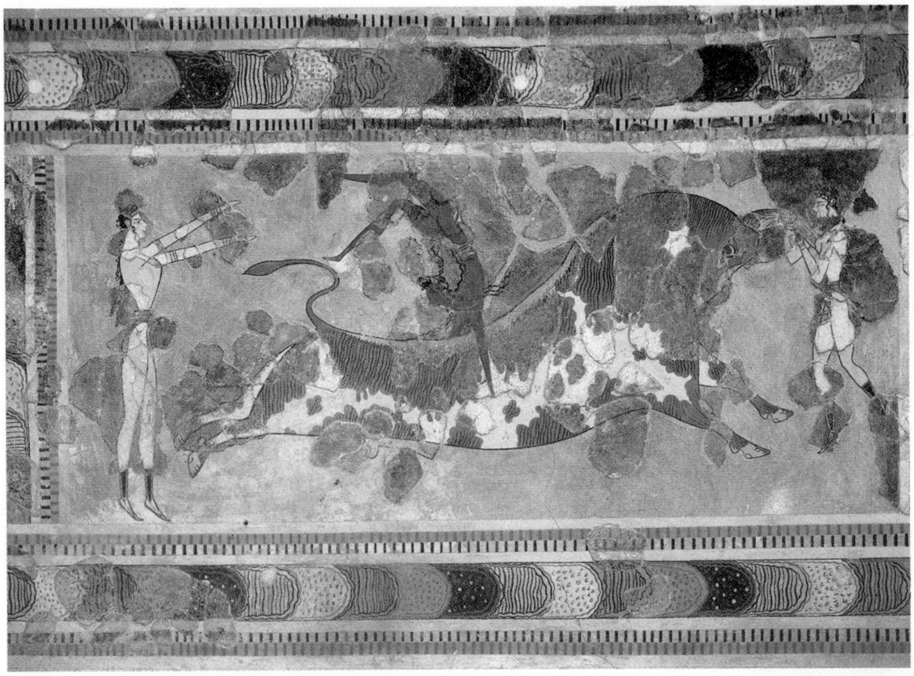

▶ **A wall painting from Knossos, showing athletes vaulting over the horns of a bull. The figure at the right will catch the leaper in the center. The location of this painting in the palace suggests that the sport was a kind of ceremony. The bull may represent raw nature being tamed in this agricultural society.**

influence, and at least two Greek goddesses, Athena and Artemis, were probably adopted from Crete. The Minoans also had interchange with the Greeks through writing. Clay tablets have been found at Knossos in two similar scripts, called Linear A and Linear B. Both scripts are syllabic: Each symbol represents a sound, such as *ko*, rather than a letter of an alphabet. The language written in Linear A, the older script (used circa 1700–1500 B.C.), has not yet been deciphered; but Linear B, the younger of the two scripts (used circa 1450–1400 B.C.), has been deciphered as an early form of Greek. The tablets contain inventories, rosters, and records of all kinds, listing foot stools, helmets, vessels, seeds, and the like.

That these Linear B tablets were written in a form of Greek is a startling discovery, for it shows that the Greeks, who at this time had not developed writing of their own, learned to write their

▶ **A "marine style" vase by a Greek artist, about 1500 B.C., clearly imitating Cretan models. Sea creatures were often used in Minoan pottery in a free, naturalistic style.**

▸ **A large vase from Crete in the Late Minoan II style, circa 1450 to 1400 B.C., when Cretan art came under Greek influence and became more disciplined and geometric. Note the double ax motif, found in the palace at Knossos.**

language in a Cretan script. Their presence on Crete during this period suggests that Greeks had come to dominate Knossos, perhaps through outright military seizure. Probably the only Greek community that could have done this was that of Mycenae.

About 1380 B.C., a catastrophe, whose causes are uncertain, engulfed Knossos and other Cretan cities; several of the stately palaces were burned or destroyed. A massive earthquake shook the island at this time, but the disaster may also have been connected with a quarrel or rebellion against Greek rule.

MYCENAEAN CIVILIZATION (Ca. 1600–1100 B.C.)

The Greeks, the people who spoke and imported the Greek language, began to settle in Greece about 2000 B.C., arriving from the Balkan areas to the north; they were members of the general family of Indo-Europeans who had started to migrate into Europe at an uncertain time, perhaps around 5000 B.C. (see Chapter 1, p. 18). They called themselves Hellenes and their country Hellas; the Greeks still use these names, and only in West European languages are they called *Greeks*, a name given them by the Romans.

The City of Mycenae Geography divides Greece into many small valleys and forced the Greeks to develop independent communities with kings,

Map 2.2 MYCENAE
The most impressive city in Bronze Age Greece, Mycenae, was first settled on its citadel. As the population expanded, a lower town developed, also surrounded by a wall. Outside the walls were terraced agricultural plots.

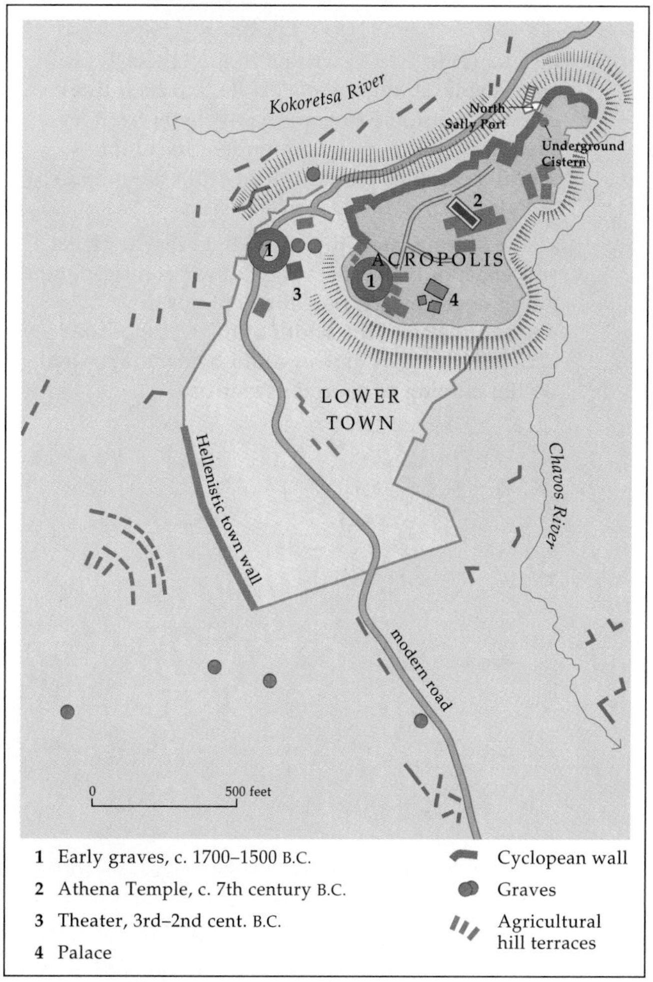

▶ **A tablet in Greek, written in the Linear B script, from Pylos, about 1200 B.C. Note that each line contains a brief listing, probably items from an inventory, followed by a number. Such tablets reveal a complex bureaucracy within the monarchy at Pylos during the Mycenaean Age.**

▶ **The "Lion Gate," the entrance to the citadel at Mycenae, built about 1350 B.C. Two lionesses stand guard over the city; note the depth of the entranceway and the width of the threshold. In early civilizations, power could be demonstrated by the moving of enormous stones.**

but without the direction—or oppression—of a central ruler like a pharaoh. By about 1600 B.C., the Greeks had created wealthy, fortified cities, among which the most prominent was Mycenae, built on a huge citadel in the Peloponnese. The years from 1600 to 1100 B.C. are therefore often called the Mycenaean Age.

Two sets of graves found at Mycenae have given us a glimpse of the wealth and artistic accomplishments of this city. They contained such stunning luxuries as masks of gold foil that were pressed on the faces of the dead and a complete burial suit of gold foil wrapped around a child, as well as swords, knives, and hundreds of gold ornaments. Tablets written in Linear B, attesting a palace bureaucracy, have been found at Mycenae and other sites of the Mycenaean Age.

The Zenith of Mycenaean Power and the Trojan War Between 1400 and 1200 B.C., Mycenae reached the height of its prosperity and created the most imposing monuments in Bronze Age Greece. A mighty decorated gateway with a relief of lions carved over it, known as the Lion Gate, formed the entrance to the walled city. Some rulers were buried in immense vaulted tombs in beehive shape, of which the grandest and best preserved is the so-called Treasury of Atreus, named by modern archaeologists for the legendary father of King Agamemnon; but we do not really know which ruler or rulers were buried here.

Each city of the Mycenaean Age was probably independent under its own king. The only time these cities appear to have united was during the war against Troy, a rich city of obscure ethnic origin in Asia Minor near the Dardanelles. The evident wealth of the city must have offered a tempting prey to pirates and looters. Such was probably the real cause of the war against Troy, but Greek legend explained the war by the romantic story in Homer's *Iliad* about the seduction by a Trojan prince of Helen, the wife of a king of Sparta. Since Homer is the only source recording the Greek attack on Troy, we must proceed with caution if we are to believe that there really was such a war, for Homer was a poet, not a historian. Nevertheless, excavations at Troy have revealed several layers of building, among which one layer, called Troy VII A, was destroyed by some invaders about 1250 B.C., and this may well be the Troy that Homer says the Greeks attacked.

The Decline of Mycenae and the Dorian Invasion
The war against Troy was the last great feat of the Mycenaean Age. Between about 1300 and 1200 B.C., marauders called sea-peoples made trade by sea so dangerous that the export of Mycenaean pottery virtually ended. The identity of these warriors is still uncertain, but their homes

A gold cup from Vaphio, near Mycenae, about 1400 B.C. The man in the center is taming an animal by tying its leg; the animals to the left are already tamed and nestle up against each other.

The most spectacular tomb at Mycenae, the "Treasury of Atreus," built in beehive style about 1300 B.C. The long entrance alley and the tomb itself are almost perfectly preserved.

▸ **The "warrior vase" from Mycenae, showing armed warriors departing for battle; at the left, a woman waves her farewell.**

were probably somewhere in Asia Minor. Even more significant to the collapse of the Mycenaean Age was a series of attacks by land, lasting roughly from 1200 to 1100 B.C.; around 1100 B.C., Mycenae itself was overrun, though not obliterated.

This invasion by land was probably the work of a later wave of Greeks who spoke the Doric dialect of the Greek language. Between about 1200 and 1100 B.C. these Greeks made their way southward from central Greece and settled mainly in the Peloponnese, especially in Corinth and Sparta, which became the most important cities where Doric Greek was spoken.

The period 1100–800 B.C. is called the Dark Age of Greece, because throughout the area there was sharp cultural decline: less elegant pottery, simple burials, no massive buildings. Even the art of writing in Linear B vanished. But the decline was not a total collapse. Farming, weaving, making pottery, the Greek language in spoken form, and other skills survived.

The invasions of the twelfth century B.C., in which the Dorian Greeks played at least a part, ended forever the domination of the palace-centered kings. In a sense, the shattering of the monarchic pattern of the Mycenaean Age can be viewed as liberating. If these monarchies had survived, Greece might have developed as Egypt and Asia Minor did, with centralized rule and priests who interpreted religion in ways that justified kingship. Self-government in Greece might have been delayed for centuries, if it appeared at all.

II. The Greek Renaissance (Ca. 800–600 B.C.)

With the passing of time, Greek culture revived after the Dark Age and entered a period of extraordinary artistic and intellectual vitality. Poetry and art broke new frontiers; the economy expanded, partly through overseas colonization; and the polis, or independent city-state, emerged. Historians borrow a term from a later period and call this movement the Greek Renaissance.

GREEK RELIGION

The Greeks brought with them, during their earliest immigration around 2000 B.C., the worship of some of their gods, above all Zeus, the sky god, whose name is Indo-European; his counterparts are Dyaus in early India, Jupiter in Rome, and Tiu in Norse myths. Other gods were adapted from other regions: Apollo, the sun god, from western Asia Minor; Aphrodite, goddess of love, from Cyprus; Athena, goddess of wisdom, and Artemis, the hunter goddess, from Crete. At a much later stage, Greeks adopted some Egyptian gods (Isis, for example), but there is no solid evidence for the belief, recently put forth, that they received all or even many of their gods from Egypt (*see box*, p. 39).[1]

Greek gods are not the remote, transcendent deities of Mesopotamian peoples. They intervene in human affairs, they assist their favorites, and they are anthropomorphic: That is, they are human-like super-beings, differing from people only in their physical perfection and immortality. Even Mount Olympus, their legendary home, is an actual mountain in northern Greece.

[1]Herodotus, the first historian, writing around 450 B.C., does say this, but he was perhaps so impressed with the antiquity of Egypt, and with the resemblance of gods in the two cultures, that he drew this false conclusion.

The Greeks never developed a code of behavior prescribed by religion, as Israel did. Some acts, such as killing a parent or leaving a relative unburied, were obviously wrong, as were offenses against generally accepted conduct, such as betraying a friend. If people became too arrogant, Nemesis, an avenging force, would sweep down on them and destroy them. But, on the whole, Greek religion had no spirit of evil and scarcely any demanding spirits of good.

The gods were viewed as generally benevolent, but they had to be appeased through offerings and suitable ceremonies. The most remarkable feature of Greek religion—especially in contrast to monarchies of Egypt and Asia Minor—was that the Greeks had priests and priestesses for their temples and smaller shrines, but no priestly class that intervened in politics. To put it simply, the Greeks had no church. Why the Greeks felt they could worship without succumb-

The Debate over Black Athena

Martin Bernal, in **Black Athena**, *has set forth the challenging thesis that Greek civilization, and even much of the Greek language, rest on cultural borrowings from Egypt and the Levant from about 2100 to about 1100 B.C. Bernal also holds that anti-Semitic nineteenth-century scholars deliberately concealed the contribution of Egypt and the Phoenicians. This excerpt, in Bernal's words, summarizes his thesis.*

"The scheme I propose is that while there seems to have been more or less continuous Near Eastern influence on the Aegean over this millennium, its intensity varied considerably at different periods. The first "peak" of which we have any trace was the 21st century. It was then that Egypt recovered from the breakdown of the First Intermediate Period, and the so-called Middle Kingdom was established by the new 11th Dynasty. This not only reunited Egypt but attacked the Levant and is known from archaeological evidence to have had wide-ranging contacts further afield, certainly including Crete and possibly the mainland. [. . .] It is generally agreed that the Greek language was formed during the 17th and 16th centuries B.C. Its Indo-European structure and basic lexicon are combined with a non-Indo-European vocabulary of sophistication. I am convinced that much of the latter can be plausibly derived from Egyptian and West Semitic. This would fit very well with a long period of domination by Egypto-Semitic conquerors. [. . .] [I] discuss some of the equations made between specific Greek and Egyptian divinities and rituals, and the general belief that the Egyptian were the earlier forms and that Egyptian religion was the original one."

Martin Bernal, *Black Athena*, vol. 1, 1987, pp. 17–23 (abridged).

Mary Lefkowitz, a professor of classics at Wellesley College, commented thus on Bernal's work.

"Bernal relies too much on Herodotus's treatment of Egypt. [. . .] [He] cites Herodotus on the Egyptian origin of Greek religion and ritual, discussing the many rough but intriguing parallels that can be drawn between Egyptian and Greek myth and cult. Again, none of these seems in itself conclusive. Nor does Bernal show how the Greeks came to borrow their "philosophy" as well. He does not discuss the implications of Herodotus's very explicit statement that Egyptian habits and customs in his own time were totally different from those of the Greeks. [. . .] [W]ith the data that he has assembled, he may have sharpened the quality of the debate about the origins of Greek culture. But I do not think that he has brought about any dramatic change in the way that the evidence about Greek origins should be interpreted."

The New Republic, Feb. 10, 1992.

ing to the direction of a priestly hierarchy we do not know, but the reason must be connected to the independence of the 600 to 700 individual Greek city-states. There was no king, pharaoh, or emperor who had the power to install such a system. Religion and civic life were intertwined, and the beautiful temples all over Greece were built by decision of the governing power, but not at the orders of priests or viziers.

Most gods were common to all Greeks, and their worship is a sign of a Panhellenic culture that arose during the Greek Renaissance. Each locality, while recognizing the several gods generally, could have its own patron. For example, various gods had temples in Athens, but Athena was accepted as the protecting goddess of the city. Zeus, though worshiped everywhere as the chief god, was the main local deity at Olympia. Apollo was the chief god at Delphi and supposedly inspired the oracle, a woman who gave guidance to inquirers after payment of a fee. The Greek faith in this oracle is another sign of growing common identity among the Greeks. Though never more than a small village, Delphi was adorned with treasure houses built by the various cities to house the gifts they dedicated to Apollo when seeking his guidance.

PUBLIC GAMES

Another sign of a growing community among Greeks is the founding of Panhellenic athletic games in 776 B.C. (This date is commonly agreed to mark the beginning of the "historic" period of Greek civilization: broadly speaking, the period when writing began and we begin to have fairly solid dates for events.)

The first games were held at Olympia, in the Peloponnese, and were dedicated to Zeus; thus from the beginning the games were connected with religion and demonstrate that religious ceremonies in a community could embrace several different practices. But they were also a way of celebrating human perfection and heroism, an aspiration typical of Greek civilization. Originally, the Olympics featured only foot races and wrestling, but gradually they came to include horse and chariot races, boxing, javelin throwing, and other events. Only the winner gained a prize, an olive wreath, but victory also brought rich awards from one's city and lifelong glory. In imitation of the Olympics, other cities founded games, and there was eventually one set of Panhellenic games each year, as well as games in many individual cities.

COLONIZATION (Ca. 750–550 B.C.)

The growth in population during the Dark Age finally forced the Greek cities into foreign colonization: In effect, the mainland Greeks of the eighth and seventh centuries exported their excess population. They colonized vigorously from about 750 to about 550 B.C., and by the end of this period there were Greeks spread throughout the Mediterranean. Wherever they went, they settled on the edge of the sea, never far inland. Colonies, when founded, were wholly independent cities, and among them are some of the great ports of modern Europe: Byzantium (today Istanbul in Turkey), Naples, and Syracuse.

This expansion overseas led to a revival of trade after the stagnation of the Dark Age. The Greeks now had access to a greater food supply, above all grain from southern Italy and the Black Sea. Trade brought prosperity to many Greek cities and, even more important, spread Greek civilization throughout the Mediterranean.

THE ALPHABET

The Greeks apparently lapsed into illiteracy when the Linear B script vanished, soon after 1200 B.C.; but by about 750 B.C. their trade had brought them to Palestine and into contact with the Phoenicians, who used a Semitic script called the alphabet. This alphabet had only some 30 characters, but many different sounds could be represented by these few symbols; and their precision and versatility made this script far easier to master than pictorial cuneiform scripts (see p. 7). Fortunately for the future of European literacy, the Greeks adopted the alphabet, changing some of the characters, which were all consonants, to vowels.

Two versions of the Greek alphabet developed. A Western version made its way to Cumae, a Greek town in Italy, and then to the Etruscans, the people in Italy who then controlled Rome. They passed it on to the Romans, who turned it into the alphabet used throughout the Western world. The Eastern version became the standard alphabet in Greece itself. Much later, many letters of the Greek alphabet were used in the Cyrillic script of Russian and other Slavic languages. Thus large parts of the world today use one or another derivative of the Phoenician alphabet in the form it received from the Greeks.

In Greece, the alphabet was first used in public for the proclamation of laws, which ordinary people could read and grasp; information could circulate more rapidly, with dynamic consequences for political life. Later, from about 500 B.C., especially in Athens, people began to publish every kind of public decision and record on prominently displayed stone inscriptions; these were not simply boastful monuments to a king's victories but were documents enabling citizens to understand and control the activities of the state.

ARCHAIC LITERATURE

The Homeric Epics The greatest literary creations of the Greek Renaissance are the epic poems about the glorious heroes who had supposedly led the war against Troy. The supreme achievements of this tradition are two epics ascribed to Homer, the *Iliad* and the *Odyssey*. The *Iliad* is a portrait—in rolling, majestic verse—of a warrior aristocracy in which greatness in combat is the highest virtue. Heroism is exemplified by the proud warrior Achilles, who withdraws from the siege of Troy when his concubine is taken from him; he then allows his friend Patroclus to wear his armor in combat and, after Patroclus is killed by the Trojan hero Hector, avenges his death by killing Hector in a scene of savage power. The gods take sides with their favorites, but the *Iliad* is essentially a poem about men and women in conflict.

The *Odyssey*, by contrast, celebrates cleverness rather than sheer military prowess. Its hero Odysseus makes his way home after the Trojan War through dozens of adventures that test his skill and tenacity and enable Homer to explore human character and behavior in widely different situations. Eventually Odysseus reaches his home, the island of Ithaca, and drives off a band of suitors who are wooing his noble wife Penelope.

These epics were probably first recited at feasts by traveling bards, but over the years they became known to all through presentation at festivals and finally through study in schools. We have no idea who wrote these great epics. Neither ancient Greeks nor modern scholars have been able to prove whether a person named Homer really lived, whether the epics are the work of one writer or several, and whether they were originally composed orally or in writing. The poems are usually dated to the period around 750 B.C., just when the Greeks were learning to write, and it would be surprising if anyone immediately used this new technique to compose such long sagas; the more probable view is that the poems were composed orally, recited for generations, and written down later. In any case, Homer remained the chief inspiration for Greek literature in all periods.

Hesiod Homer never speaks in the first person (except to invoke the Muses to inspire him), but his successors began to express their own thoughts and feelings and to create a literature of intensely frank self-expression. The first major post-Homeric poet was Hesiod of Boeotia (in central Greece), whose *Works and Days* dates from around 700 B.C. Hesiod was a farmer, and his poem is a farmer's almanac, celebrating agriculture and, in the "days" of the title, telling the reader when to plow and plant. The poem also contains a bitter attack on the injustice of aristocratic landlords ("gift-devouring rulers") toward their peasants.

In his other surviving poem, the *Theogony*, Hesiod recounts the genealogy of the various gods. He narrates frankly the bloody rise of Zeus to supreme divine power. The god Cronus had castrated his own father, Uranus, to gain rule over the world and had killed his own children except Zeus, who escaped. After a long struggle Zeus wins the final battle and becomes supreme. This conflict resembles similar sagas in Hittite literature, in which gods kill and mutilate one another. But the difference in the Greek conception is that the supremacy of Zeus is seen not just as another act of vengeance but as a fulfillment of the proper divine order.

Lyric Poets About 650 B.C. Greek poets began to experiment with a variety of more personal themes. Archilochus of Paros has left us brief poems of brilliant vigor and audacity, written as bursts of self-revelation, a typically Greek kind of literature that has no predecessors in the ancient Eastern cultures. He was a traveler, a man of action, and a mercenary soldier who fell in battle. He criticizes traditional forms of chivalry and can be cynical about supposed aristocratic conduct. He boasts, for example, that he once threw away his shield to save his life and laughs off this unmilitary act: "Never mind, I'll buy another one just as good." His love poetry can be astonishingly frank. In one poem he tenderly yet passionately describes his seduction of a girl, including his own sexual fulfillment.

The most intense and subtle poet of the age was Sappho of the island of Lesbos (about 600 B.C.). We have only one complete poem from her pen and many short quotations (*see box*). She was evidently a widow who maintained a school on Lesbos where young girls learned music, dance, poetry, and elegant dress as preparation for marriage. Sappho sings of the beauty of the girls and the pleasures of love and apparently shared physical love with some of them. In its exact evocation of emotion, its inventive images, its individuality, her poetry reveals a writer of the highest originality and power.

Sappho's Love Poetry

The poetry of Sappho of Lesbos is amazingly sensitive and original. This short excerpt from a poem frankly acknowledges her need for love.

"You have come, and done,
And I was waiting for you
To temper the red desire
That burned my heart."

The following is addressed to a young woman.

"He seems to be a god, that man
Facing you, who leans to be close,
Smiles, and, alert and glad, listens
To your mellow voice.

"And quickens in love at your laughter
That stings my breasts, jolts my heart
If I dare the shock of a glance.
I cannot speak,

"My tongue sticks to my dry mouth,
Thin fire spreads beneath my skin,
My eyes cannot see and my aching ears
Roar in their labyrinths.

"Chill sweat slides down my body,
I shake, I turn greener than grass,
I am neither living nor dead and cry
From the narrow between.

"But endure, even this grief of love."

Translations by Guy Davenport, *Archilochus, Sappho, Alkman*, Berkeley-Los Angeles-London, 1980.

III. The Polis

ORGANIZATION AND GOVERNMENT

For the social and political history of Western civilization, the most important event in the Greek Renaissance was the emergence, soon after 800 B.C., of the independent city-state, the *polis* (plural, *poleis*). Physically, the polis had a central inhabited area (the *astu*), often surrounding a citadel called the *acropolis* ("high city"). Over time, the acropolis came to be reserved for temples, shrines, treasuries, and other official buildings. Within the astu, the nucleus of the city, the people dwelt in closely packed houses, each normally built on more than one level, without internal staircases but with the rooms opening to a courtyard. A wall normally surrounded the astu; outside it, but still part of the polis, were suburbs and fields.

Greek cities usually had a large open space, the *agora*, that served as a main public square and civic center. Although used as a public market, the agora was always a sacred place and, like the acropolis, it housed temples and official buildings. In Athens, the agora was the site of trials, of buildings containing laws and other documents, and of many free-standing inscriptions on marble recording further public business.

The polis was a community of both male and female citizens. Male citizens could vote, pass on their property through wills, and generally participate in civic life; women did not vote but, like men, were protected against seizure and violence. Outside this group, and without civic rights, were slaves and resident aliens. No citizen of a polis had rights in any other polis; thus poleis were both cities and small states. When Greeks referred to the size of the citizen body, they reckoned only adult males, and by this measure the poleis ranged from a few hundred citizens to tens of thousands. Athens, the largest, had from 35,000 to 45,000; if to this we add the estimated number of women, children, resident foreigners, and slaves, the total population of Athens and the outlying villages, which were also part of the polis, was between 200,000 and 300,000 (the whole region is known as Attica). Sparta, by contrast, probably had an adult male population of no more than 12,000.

Despite considerable diversity within the 600 to 700 poleis, one development seems to have been common to all those that we know anything about, namely, the growth of some kind of self-government by the male citizens. The major social problem that Greek poleis solved was how to harness the energies of all the citizens in support of a city, rather than allow the rivalries inherent in such crowded quarters to erupt into civil war. In many poleis (Corinth, for example), oligarchy (a system in which wealthier citizens governed) held sway, while other cities, especially Athens, developed control of affairs by the masses.

Evolution toward self-government is rare in history, and the various forms of self-government that arose in Greece may, like the Greeks' lack of a priestly class, be the result of topography and scale. In a small state, locked within a ring of hills, no monarch could long remain a remote, transcendent figure like those who ruled Eastern kingdoms. Homer attests that the Greeks of the Mycenaean era had kings, but by about 700 B.C. they had vanished—though we can seldom say precisely how—in nearly all poleis. Sparta, the most authoritarian Greek state, was an exception and retained a system with two kings, each descended from a royal family, ruling together. The Spartans apparently felt safer in a system where one king could act as a control over the other.

The wealthier classes—using the term loosely, we may call them aristocrats, but there was no hereditary nobility—must have governed, if Homer is to be believed, through assemblies that originated as the armed forces of the poleis. But as populations increased and armies came to include citizens outside the circle of the elite, the upper classes could no longer ignore the wishes of others. It is significant that the first Greek legal codes defining citizens' rights were published within the seventh century B.C.—evidence that the populace was no longer willing to accept direction from the wealthy.

Also in the seventh century we hear of the first popular leaders who united the masses and overturned the rule of the old aristocracy. These men installed themselves as "tyrants" (the Greek word *tyrannos* meant an autocrat who ruled without strict legal foundation, not necessarily a cruel oppressor). The tyrants, though certainly no sponsors of democracy, did help to undermine rule by the wealthy alone and in a way opened the path to self-government.

THE ECONOMY OF THE POLEIS (Ca. 700–400 B.C.)

The poleis were sufficiently similar to allow a general picture of their economy. The basic activity was agriculture, but in many areas of Greece the soil is thin and rocky, not suited to raising grain or pasturing animals. A shortage of food was therefore a constant threat to economic stability. Some states, as we have seen, drained away part of their excess population through colonization and imported grain from areas on the fringe of the Greek world.

All Greek dwellings were modest, and sanitation was primitive, although the Athenians had a main drain under their central market. Grain, occasionally fish, were staples of the diet; meat was usually reserved for festival days. Breakfast, if taken at all, was a lump of bread dipped in olive oil, which also served as fuel for lamps and even as a kind of soap. Sugar was unknown; the only sweetening agent was honey. With few luxuries available, Greeks could subsist on small incomes. Fishing and farming were suspended in winter, so Greeks had considerable leisure time, which they spent mainly in public places, as is still true today.

The development of an economy based on coinage was slow. Greece did not begin to use coins until about 625 B.C., and even then they played little part in daily trade: The smallest coin was usually a drachma, said to have been at that time the price of a sheep. In the fifth century the use of coinage expanded rapidly. Taxation in poleis paid for the upkeep of walls, drains, roads, harbors, and the like, though Greeks had little grasp of the mechanics of public finance. There were no permanent military treasuries until the 300s B.C., a surprising fact since the cities were so often at war. Infantry soldiers had to arm themselves, but they were paid at the expense of the state. When large projects such as public buildings and maintenance of ships were planned, the expenses were assigned to citizens who were judged capable of bearing the cost.

The Roles of the Sexes In Greek society people found certain roles assigned to them according to their sex. Men were the rulers and leaders, and in no Greek state did women vote or hold offices with the exception of certain priesthoods. They were, however, citizens and could not be violated or sold into slavery.

Thus roughly half the citizens of Greek poleis must have been women, but to reconstruct their place in Greek society is not easy, mainly because nearly all our sources were written by men. Nor is there likely to have been a single view of women in Greek society, as we can see from our oldest source, the Homeric poems. In the *Iliad*, the story opens as Achilles and Agamemnon quarrel over a concubine who is nothing but a sexual slave, while the Trojan hero Hector honors and cherishes his wife Andromache; equally, in Homer's *Odyssey* Penelope, the wife of the absent Odysseus, is a model of wisdom and fidelity.

As we look from the idealized figures of Homer to the women of the polis, we see a much less benign attitude toward women. A woman was always under the control of her *kyrios*, or master—at first her father, then her husband, then her father again if she became divorced or widowed. Her father gave her in marriage with a dowry, normally at about age 15, to a man perhaps 10 to 20 years her senior. Xenophon describes the education of a young wife in obedience and household skills, and the picture is like the training of a young animal. Her main duty, apart from managing the household, was to provide a male heir in order to maintain the family's hold over its property. If the family had no male heir, the property came to a daughter, but she held it only temporarily. She must then be married to the nearest available male relative, thus preventing the property from passing from the family. Yet the duty of women to provide heirs did not cause Greeks to think of a woman as a mere breeding machine. On the contrary, the power, possessed only by women, to bear children seems to have made them objects not only to be cherished but also to be feared.

Since women could be transferred from one husband to another, Greeks were not sure about their fidelity, and adultery was a grave threat because it could bring outsiders into the family and threaten the preservation of property within the correct line. Such suspicions may partly account for some passages by Greek poets and philosophers where women are viewed as undisciplined, emotionally unstable, and sexually inexhaustible. To preserve a woman's fidelity, the door of the home was considered her proper frontier, but such restrictions were not possible for families without servants; yet even when women did go out, they were normally accompanied.

If we have rightly understood the threat that women could present to men, we may be near to understanding why women of Greek drama such as Clytemnestra, Antigone, and Medea are such powerful characters, far stronger and more dangerous than the men in their plays. Again, in myths the furies, who could drive people mad, were female, as was Ate, the spirit that brought punishing destruction; so too the three Fates who spun out the thread of life and cut it off at the end. Yet we must not expect perfect consistency where such emotions are at play. Many of the most revered deities are women: Athena, who was respected for her warlike nature and never had lovers in myth, was also the protecting goddess to the Athenians, who held her in affection.

Aphrodite, who could involve human beings in ruin through sexual passion, was treasured as the model of ideal beauty and was so portrayed in hundreds of statues.

Elegant single women might become paid companions at men's social affairs; the most famous of all, Aspasia, had a long affair with the statesman Pericles and bore him a son. Only these women could participate in the refined intellectual life of the city. Poorer women worked, for example, as seamstresses, nurses, sellers in the market, or prostitutes (these were normally slaves or foreigners).

Modern scholars warn that it is fruitless to wonder whether Greek men and women shared emotional love. The recommendation of Plutarch, that a man should sleep with his wife three times a month, suggests that love played only a modest part in marriage. On the other hand, gravestones from many poleis show the affection in which some women were held; typically, a woman is seated, members of her family stand nearby, and a son or her husband takes her hand in a quiet farewell.

Slavery A great social-economic historian, M. I. Finley, once asked the challenging question: Was Greek civilization based on slave labor? It is undeniable that the presence of slaves gave Greeks freedom to pursue civic affairs. Many Greeks looked down on manual labor as beneath their dignity, and it was usually performed by poor citizens or slaves. The troubling institution of slavery was accepted by all ancient societies and was justified by philosophers like Aristotle, who asserted that nature had divided humanity into natural masters and natural slaves—the latter including all "barbarians," that is, non-Greeks. Nor did anyone in antiquity ever recommend abolishing slavery on the ground that it was morally wrong: The only criticism of it was the occasional warning to manage it efficiently. Greeks commonly obtained slaves through conquest of other territory, though kidnapping and even the sale of children added to recruitment. An ordinary slave might cost about 150 drachmas, roughly four months' pay for a laborer, but a highly skilled one could cost much more.

Industry was rarely more extensive than household craft, and Greece, unlike Rome, did not use gangs of slaves in agriculture; the only industries in which slaves worked in large numbers were mining and stone quarrying, where conditions were atrocious. These and domestic service were the only tasks always assigned to slaves. In a unique exception to this rule, Athens had a police force composed of slaves from Scythia. The Athenian writer Xenophon said, "A man buys a slave to have a companion at work." Potters, shoemakers, and stonecutters might have a slave or two, though a few larger workshops are known: One shield maker, for example, had 120 slaves.

The prejudice against manual labor, and the availability of slaves, may explain why slaves worked on the building of the Parthenon in Athens and were paid the same as free men—one drachma a day, about the same wage paid to soldiers and sailors—and it partly explains the lack of inventions among the Greeks that could have made industry more productive.

SPARTA AND ATHENS (Ca. 700–500 B.C.)

We know little about the internal workings of most poleis, and the two we know best, Sparta and Athens, were not typical; but their importance requires detailed discussion.

Sparta Sparta, the most influential of the Dorian states in the Peloponnese, chose to solve its problem of overpopulation by conquering Messenia, the territory to its west, in a war usually dated 736 to 716 B.C. Only males of demonstrably pure Spartan descent could be full citizens, and they were each given an allotment of land to be worked for them by the Messenians, who were known as helots. They were public slaves, with no rights whatever, but differed from other slaves in Greece in that they could not be bought and sold. Spartan landowners spent their lives in constant military training in order to maintain control over the helots, who outnumbered them by about seven to one.

Around 650 B.C. the Messenians tried to rebel, but the uprising failed, and the Spartans responded by making their army more invincible and their state even more rigid. The new arrangements, attributed to a lawgiver named Lycurgus, date from about 600 B.C. The identity of

Map 2.3 ARCHAIC AND CLASSICAL GREECE, CA. 800–400 B.C.

Lycurgus was obscure even in antiquity, though such a man apparently lived around 800 B.C., and many historians believe that Spartan reformers of around 600 B.C. ascribed their system to him in order to give it the appearance of ancient authority.

In the Spartan regime, oligarchy, or the rule of a small number, was tempered with some measure of democracy. The public assembly included all males over 30, who elected a council of 28 elders over 60 to serve for life and to plan business for the assembly. The assembly also chose five *ephors* ("overseers") each year; they received foreign delegates, summoned the assembly to meet, and in general acted as a check on the power of the kings. When proposals came before the assembly, it was limited to voting yes or no, without debate. As a further safeguard against too much popular control, the ephors and council could simply dismiss the assembly if, in their opinion, it made the wrong choice. Thus the limited democracy of Sparta yielded to its ultimate faith in oligarchy. To Greek political philosophers, Sparta was a superb example of a "mixed" constitution, in which the kings represented the element of monarchy, the council oligarchy, and the citizenry a kind of democracy.

For a time Sparta tried to dominate other Peloponnesian states by outright conquest. But by around 560 B.C. this policy had failed, and about 530 B.C. the Spartans sought strength through alliance rather than warfare by forming the Peloponnesian League with their neighbors. The league is one of the earliest examples of alliance in the Greek world and is a rare instance of the Greeks' transcending the normal exclusiveness of city-state politics. The Spartans led the league but did not wholly control it, and action required approval of the member states.

The Spartan male dedicated most of his life, from age 7 through 60, to soldiering. The warriors lived and trained together, and their discipline could be sadistic. As tests of their courage and resourcefulness, young men were taught to steal if necessary, to go without food and shelter, even at times to kill a helot.

Spartan women also had a life style that other Greeks found extraordinary. Again the military commitments of the state played a role in shaping social practices, for the girls trained in games in order to become physically strong mothers. Spartan men, living with one another, seldom visited their wives, and if a marriage was childless, a woman could bear a child by a man other than her husband. These customs were meant to ensure enough manpower for the army and to focus loyalty on the state, not on the individual family.

Spartans were cut off from the other Greeks by two mountain ranges, and they traded little with other people, even adopting an intrinsically worthless iron currency to maintain their isolation. They rarely traveled and were shielded from new ideas that might have inspired intellectual pursuits such as philosophy or historical writing. Though they did make fine pottery, at least until about 525 B.C., when the art declined, their military regime left little time for or interest in the arts. Thus the isolation of Sparta from other Greeks was both geographic and psychological, but it reflected the deliberate choice of the people.

Athens The city of Athens also had expansionist beginnings, extending its domain by about 700 B.C. to include the whole plain of Attica. It was a large polis with widespread trading interests,

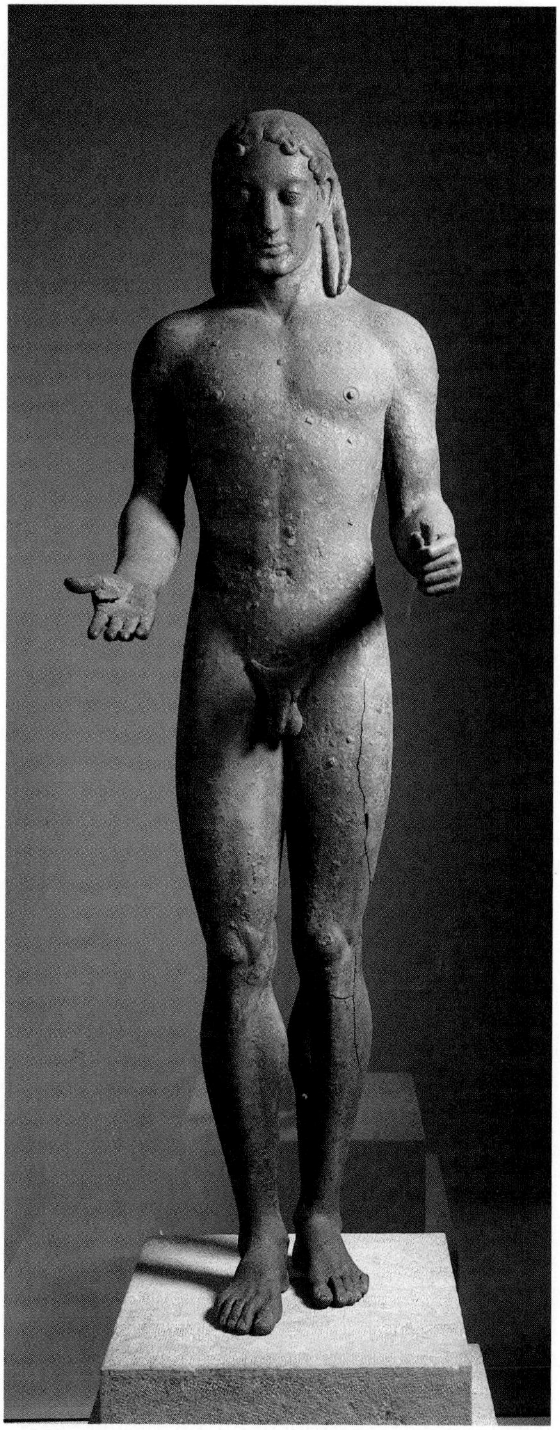

► An Attic kouros, or young man, in the "severe" style, about 510 B.C. The figure is one of ideal physical perfection, typical of the humanity-centered aesthetics of Greece.

and its political currents were strong and turbulent. As the people experimented again and again with their constitution, their political history became the most varied of all the city-states of Greece.

Athens, like other states, once had kings; but the monarchy ended in 683 B.C. (we do not know exactly how), and the city was managed by three (later nine) archons, or administrators, elected annually by an assembly, in which all adult male citizens could vote. After their year in office, the nine archons moved permanently into a council called the Areopagus, which eventually numbered about 300 men. Since it comprised senior men with permanent membership, the Areopagus was probably more influential than the board of archons in setting public policy.

Our first information about a reform in Athens after the monarchy is dated around 621 B.C. when Draco, an otherwise unknown statesman, codified the law on homicide, apparently distinguishing between voluntary and involuntary homicide. This was a large step forward, for early societies often looked on any kind of homicide as defiling the community in the eyes of the gods. This was also another in the series of law codes that established a recognized basis for justice and did away with forcing citizens to rely on the dictates of tribal elders.

Solon and Political Reform In the 500s B.C. Athens went through far-reaching social changes, the likes of which no Greek state had ever seen. As often happens in history, economic conditions demanded a social response. Down to about 600 B.C. the Athenian economy was trying to do the impossible, namely, feed the growing population of Attica from its own limited area; and this strategy caused a nearly desperate social and economic crisis. Some farmers had evidently borrowed food from others who were better off and had gone so deeply into debt in the form of grain that they had lost their own land and had even fallen into slavery by pledging their bodies as security for more food. Their frustration might have exploded into violent revolution had the Athenians not found a rational solution by giving (probably in the 570s) powers of arbitration to Solon, who had been archon in 594 B.C.[2] He was a poet and statesman whose courageous, compassionate work has made him a towering figure in Greek history, indeed in the history of civilization.

Aware that the poor farmers could probably never repay their debts, Solon took the daring step of canceling all agricultural debts and forbade further borrowing against the body. At one stroke the enslaved men were free, but the land they had lost probably remained in the hands of its new owners, who were thus compensated for the cancellation of debt. This legislation left many families without land and made them seek work elsewhere, but the crucial thing was that Solon had prevented civil war. Such arbitration by a private citizen without an army to fight with is heretofore unknown in history.

Since an economic crisis had threatened the community and brought him to power, Solon determined to transform the economy of Athens. He decreed that no product from the soil could be exported except olive oil; by this means he forced the Athenians to cultivate olive trees, which they could grow more successfully than grain. He also changed the commercial weights used by the Athenians, making them the same as those more widely used in Greece, a reform that brought Athens into a wider circle of trade.

He now seized the opportunity to reform the Athenian state, with the aim of breaking the grip of the wealthy and those with eminent family backgrounds on public office. He therefore divided all Athenian citizens into four classes based on their income from farmland and allowed members of the two highest classes to hold office. The significance of this reform is that men could improve their status economically and thus achieve positions of leadership, regardless of their ancestry.

Solon also created a court of appeal, the Heliaea, somehow drawn from the people, but

[2]That Solon was archon in 594 B.C. is fairly certain, and most historians follow ancient sources in dating his reforms to this year as well. But the assumed linkage between his archonship and his reforms was probably only an inference drawn in antiquity, and there is good reason to think that the reforms took place in the 570s; see C. Hignett, *A History of the Athenian Constitution*, 1952, p. 316.

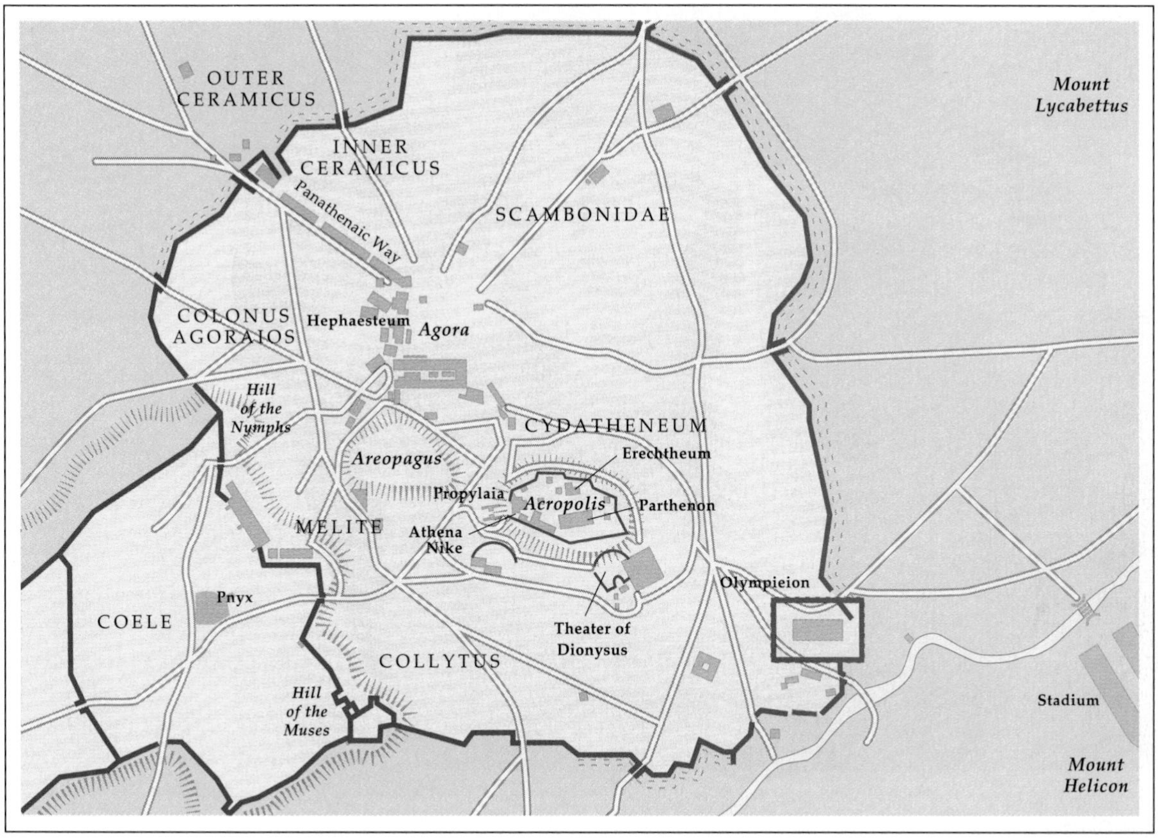

Map 2.4 CLASSICAL ATHENS, ABOUT 400 B.C.

our sources tell us little of how it worked. His chief contribution was to see the common people as a group with grievances and to take bold steps to help them. He thus pointed the state toward eventual democracy, but he did not want to go too far and by no means gave the masses supreme power; in his own poetry he declared, "I gave the people just enough privilege and no more." Nor did his legislation, humane though it was, wholly end the agricultural problem; freeing farmers from servitude was not the same as guaranteeing them enough to eat, and the agony of those peasants who had lost their land continued.

The Tyrant Pisistratus Pisistratus, a popular Athenian military leader supported by poorer farmers from the hill country in eastern Attica, saw his chance in this turmoil. In 561 B.C. he and his followers seized power; though twice driven out, he returned in 546 with a mercenary army to gain permanent control and ruled from that year until his death in 528.

Pisistratus fits well the pattern of the Greek tyrants sketched earlier. He rewarded his supporters with grants of land, surely taken from the estates of landowning aristocrats who had opposed him, thus completing the work of Solon, who lacked the power and probably the will to redistribute land. And like many another "big city boss," he saw to a splendid program of public works. He built temples to Athena and Zeus and established a yearly festival to the god Dionysus. By encouraging dramatic contests at this festival he opened the way for the development of Athenian tragedy in the next century.

He ruled by clothing his despotic power in legal form. The assembly still chose archons, but these were trusted men picked by the tyrant himself. The legal facade was actually one of his chief

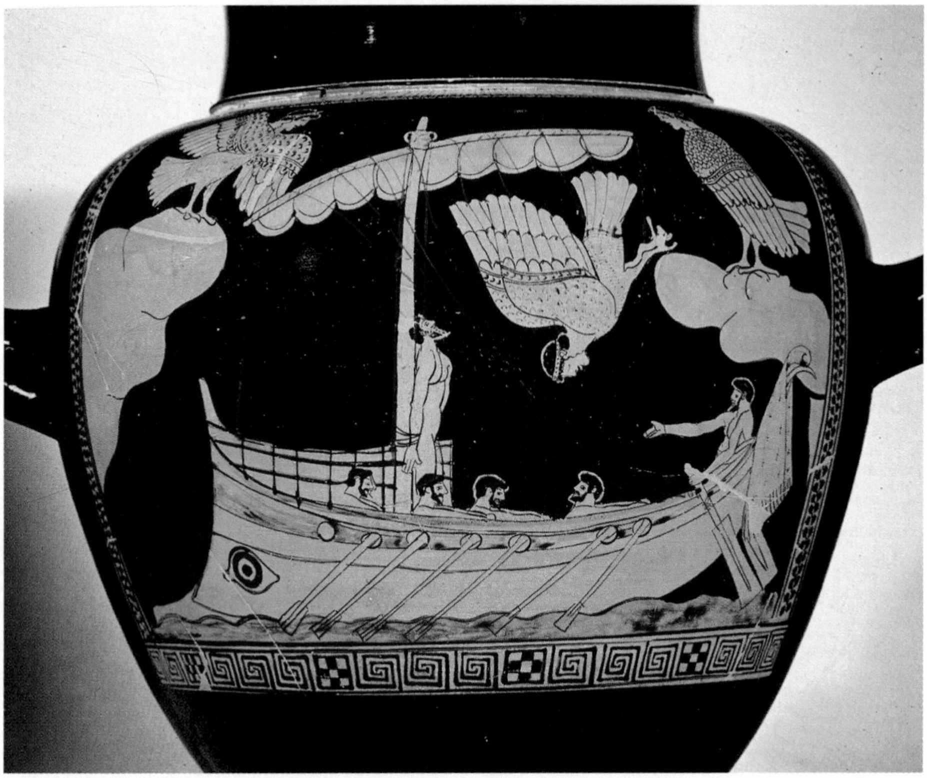

▶ **A superb red-figure vase (the figures are left in the natural red of the clay), illustrating a scene from Homer's *Odyssey*, Book 12. Odysseus, bound to the mast of his ship, listens to the song of the Siren, who guides him into troubled waters; by the Siren Painter, about 490 to 480 B.C.**

contributions, for the Athenians now became familiar with democratic procedures, and this made them receptive to real democracy when it came into existence at the end of the sixth century.

***Cleisthenes and* Demokratia** Pisistratus' son Hippias ruled securely until 514 B.C., when a conspiracy frightened him into using terror as a means to maintain his control. He forced many Athenians into exile, including Cleisthenes, the leader of the Alcmaeonids, a powerful family. While in exile in Delphi, Cleisthenes and his supporters enlisted the help of the Spartans in driving Hippias from Athens in 510. Cleisthenes returned to his native city and in 508—perhaps to secure his own supremacy—carried the social revolution further by proposing a scheme whereby the masses would actually direct the state. The Greek word *demos* means "the people," but in Greek political language it also means "the masses," and the domination of the Athenian state by the whole mass of voters came to be called *demokratia*. Participation extended only to the adult male citizens of Athens, for women, aliens, and slaves did not vote; but this system was by far the closest to a democracy that had ever existed.

Cleisthenes anchored his system in popular support by a stroke of genius: He created a council of 500 members to prepare business for the assembly, allowing all male citizens above 30 to serve in it for a year. In later times (and perhaps from the beginning, though our sources do not say so) councillors were chosen by drawing lots, and no man could serve more than twice. There was a fair chance that every eligible Athenian would be chosen to serve during his lifetime, and this widespread participation in the council ensured that the people would want to maintain the new regime. Within about 50 years this new council came to surpass the old Areopagus council, which continued to exist, in political power.

Cleisthenes also determined to break up the possible influence of regional groups in Attica through a complex system of building blocks. Every man was now enrolled as a citizen within the single village in which he lived, and which kept registers of its citizens. These villages throughout Attica were then grouped into 10 tribes, so composed that each tribe contained citizens from all parts of Attica. The council's 500 men included 50 men from each tribe and were thus automatically a cross section of Athenian citizens. As a result, when the council met to prepare business for the assembly, no single region could dominate the discussion. Each of the 10 tribes fought as a unit in the army, and here, too, men from all over Attica, not from a single region, stood together in each tribal regiment.

The sovereign body was, as before, the assembly, including all adult male citizens, whether landowners or not. The assembly passed laws and resolutions brought before it by the council, elected magistrates, voted for or against war, and accepted alliances with other states.

After passing his reforms in 508 B.C., Cleisthenes vanishes from our sources, but the Athenians continued to refine his system, especially through the use of the lot. In 487 B.C. they began to choose their nine annual archons, the executive committee, by drawing lots from a slate of candidates. Later, in the fifth and fourth centuries, all manner of officials, such as public auditors and managers of public land and mines, were so chosen. The theory behind this practice held that there were many men equally honest and capable of serving in a democracy; and choosing officials by lot reduced corruption and angry competition in the process of selection. Also in 487 B.C., for the first time, a man was expelled from Athens for 10 years by the process of ostracism; Aristotle attributed the practice to Cleisthenes himself, but this remains controversial.

Choosing officials by lot greatly diminished the prestige of such positions and caused the most ambitious men not to bother to seek them. As a result, political power shifted to the 10 generals, who were elected annually and could be reelected. From this point onward we find the great Athenian politicians within the ranks of the generals.

▶ The interesting procedure of ostracism was instituted in Athens about the time of Cleisthenes. Once a year the Athenians could vote for the man they considered most dangerous to the state by inscribing his name on *ostraka*, or scraps of pottery. Six thousand votes in all had to be cast, and the "winner" went at once into exile for 10 years.

IV. The Challenge of Persia

By the beginning of the "classical" period of Greek history, lasting from about 500 to 323 B.C., the Greek states had reached the political form they would retain for more than two centuries. But almost at once they faced their supreme challenge, a clash with the great Persian Empire.

Map 2.5 THE FIRST PERSIAN WAR, 490 B.C.

THE INVASION UNDER DARIUS AND MARATHON (490 B.C.)

King Darius of Persia (521–486 B.C.) had expanded his empire throughout Asia Minor, including the Greek cities on the west coast, the region called Ionia. Some of these Greeks sought their liberty from Persian control in 499 B.C. in the "Ionian revolt," but the revolt collapsed in 493. Darius now proposed to invade Greece itself, largely for the sake of revenge against Athens, which had shown solidarity with the Ionian rebels by sending a force to help them. After a brief campaign in 492, he sent a fleet across the Aegean in 490. The Persians first attacked Eretria, on the island of Euboea, and then landed in Attica on the beach at Marathon, a village north of Athens. The Athenian infantry routed them in a brilliant victory and even marched back to Athens in time to ward off a Persian naval attack. The Athenians never forgot this immortal feat of arms; they lost only 192 men, whose burial mound still stands at Marathon, and the Persians lost about 6400.

THE SECOND PERSIAN WAR (480–479 B.C.)

To avenge this defeat, Darius' son Xerxes (486–465 B.C.) readied a huge force and swore that this time there would be no mistake. Fortunately for Greece and Europe, the Athenians were guided by a shrewd strategist, Themistocles. In 483 B.C., seeing the Persian menace on the horizon, he had persuaded the Athenians to use some newly found veins of silver in their mines to increase greatly the size of their fleet. Early in 480 some 30 Greek states, also fearing annihilation, formed a military alliance and entrusted to the Spartans command on both land and sea.

Map 2.6 THE SECOND PERSIAN WAR, 480–479 B.C. Note the canal cut through Mt. Athos in 492 B.C.

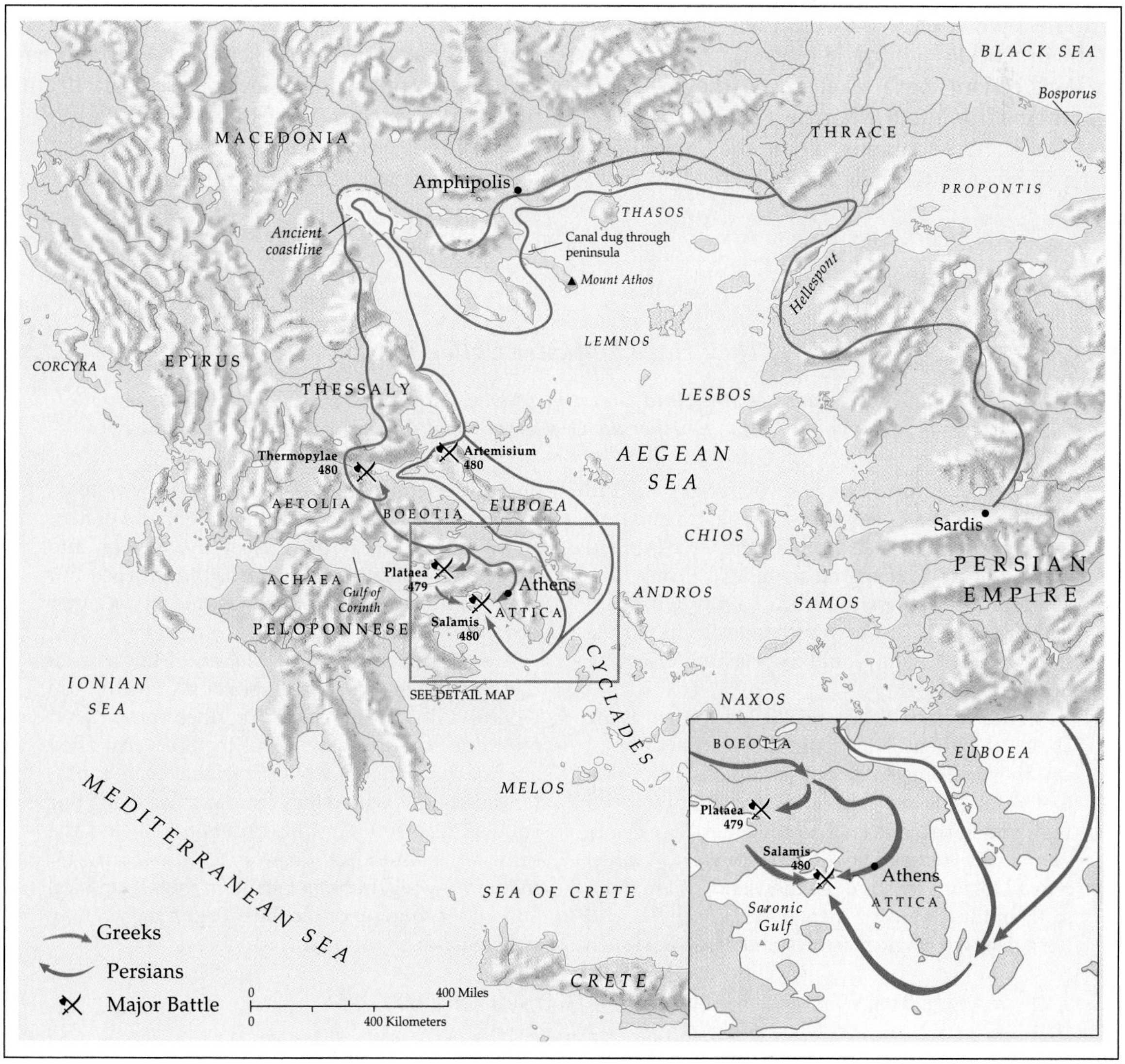

A few months later Xerxes began his march toward Greece with a force of perhaps 60,000 men and 600 ships, in a grandiose amphibious invasion of Europe. The first Greek force sent out in 480 against the Persians was defeated at the pass of Thermopylae in central Greece in a stand always remembered for its heroism. At the same time, a sea battle at nearby Artemisium was inconclusive.

As the Persian forces continued southward, the Athenians abandoned Athens and the Persians burnt the city down. In this nearly desperate situation, Themistocles devised a brilliant trick. He sent a slave to the Persian king with a false message: Themistocles wished him well and advised him that, if he attacked the Greek fleet with his own at once, he would win the decisive battle practically without a blow.

The Persians were taken in by the ruse and sent their ships into the narrows between Athens and the island of Salamis, where the Greek fleet, lying in wait, utterly defeated them. His navy shattered, Xerxes, who had watched the battle from a height, abandoned Greece and marched back toward the Dardanelles (*see box,* below).

Yet the Persians could still have won the war, for a large Persian army remained in central Greece. The reckoning with this force came in a battle in 479 B.C., at the village of Plataea. Once more a Greek army, under the Spartan general Pausanias, crushed the Persians; out of perhaps 50,000 Persians, only a few thousand survived.

The Greeks won a further battle at Mycale on the shore of Asia Minor in 479. The Ionian Greeks now proclaimed their freedom and thus completed the work of throwing off Persian control that they had begun 20 years earlier. The Greek victory over Persia was the most brilliant one in the history of Greek civilization. If the Greeks had lost the war and become another Persian province, it is by no means clear that Greek art, drama, philosophy, historical writing, and above all self-government would have survived—or how different Western civilization might have been.

"They Have a Master Called Law"

As King Xerxes leads his army into Greece in 480 B.C., he asks a former king of Sparta, who is accompanying him, whether the Greeks will really fight against the Persians.

"Now, Demaratus, I will ask you what I want to know. You are a Greek and one from no minor or weak city. So now tell me, will the Greeks stand and fight me?" Demaratus replied, "Your Majesty, shall I tell you the truth, or say what you want to hear?" The king ordered him to tell the truth, saying that he would respect him no less for doing so.

"Your Majesty," he said, "I am not speaking about all of them, only about the Spartans. First, I say they will never accept conditions from you that would enslave Greece; second, that they will fight you in battle even if all the other Greeks join your side." Xerxes said, "Demaratus, let's look at it in all logic: why should a thousand, or ten thousand, or fifty thousand men, if they are all free and not ruled by a single master, stand up against such an army as mine? If they were ruled by one man, like my subjects, I suppose they might, out of fear, show more bravery than usual and, driven into battle by the lash, go up against a bigger force; but if allowed their freedom, they wouldn't do either one."

Demaratus said, "Your Majesty, I knew from the beginning that if I spoke the truth you wouldn't like my message, but, since you ordered me to do so, I told you about the Spartans. They are free men, but not wholly free: they have a master called Law, whom they fear far more than your soldiers fear you. And his orders are always the same—they must not run away from any army no matter how big, but must stand in their formation and either conquer or die. But, Your Majesty, may your wishes be fulfilled."

Herodotus, Book VII, chaps. 101–104 (abridged), M. H. Chambers (tr.).

CHRONOLOGY OF THE PERSIAN WARS

499, autumn	Greek cities of Ionia in Asia Minor revolt from Persian Empire.
498	Athens and Eretria (on island of Euboea) take part in burning of Sardis in Persian Empire.
496	Persians besiege Miletus, leading city in the revolt.
494	Fall of Miletus.
493	End of Ionian revolt.
492, spring	Persian expedition to northern Greece suffers heavy losses in storms.
490, mid-August	Battle of Marathon near Athens; Persians defeated.
486, November	Death of King Darius of Persia; accession of Xerxes.
484, spring–480, spring	Xerxes prepares for new invasion of Greece.
480, spring	Persian army sets out from Sardis.
480, late August	Battles of Thermopylae and Artemisium.
480, late September	Battle of Salamis.
479, early August	Battle of Plataea.
479, mid-August	Battle of Mycale on coast of Asia Minor (according to Herodotus, fought on the same day as Plataea).

V. The Wars of the Fifth Century (479–404 B.C.)

After a brief period of cooperation, the two leading Greek cities, Athens and Sparta, led their allies into the long, tragic war that fatally weakened the Greek poleis.

THE ATHENIAN EMPIRE

The victorious Greeks continued the war against Persia in 479 and 478 B.C., liberating, for example, the Greek city of Byzantium on the Bosporus from Persian control. But in 478 Sparta returned to its perennial isolationism and withdrew from the alliance that had been formed to oppose Persia. In response, many of the newly liberated Greek states met on the island of Delos in 478 and formed an alliance, known as the Delian League, to continue the war and take further vengeance on Persia. Athens was recognized as head of the league and determined which members should supply ships to the common navy and which ones should contribute money. The military campaigns, often fought under the command of the Athenian general Cimon, were successful until the warfare between Greeks and Persians ended about 450. Meanwhile, Athenian control of the league had become stricter through the years. Sometimes Athens forcibly prevented members from withdrawing from the league; sometimes it stationed garrisons or governors in the supposedly independent member states. Athenian domination became unmistakable in 454, when the league transferred its treasury from Delos to

Themistocles, the great Athenian strategist, was ostracized about 472 B.C. This ostrakon, cast against him, says, "Themistocles, son of Neocles, let him depart" (ITO).

Athens. The cash contributions were now nothing but tribute to Athens, and the alliance of equals had become an Athenian empire.

THE AGE OF PERICLES

The leading statesman in the period of the Athenian empire was Pericles (490?–429 B.C.), an aristocrat from a wealthy family who had the support of the common people. Now that the archonship was no longer a position for an ambitious man, Pericles held only the post of general, to which he was reelected from 443 to 429. He was a powerful orator and a highly competent general, and was renowned for his personal honesty; moreover, his policies generally favored the common people. In 447 B.C., for example, he proposed that the Athenians should begin to rebuild the temples on the Acropolis that the Persians had destroyed in their invasion of 480. Between 447 and 432 B.C. they built for their goddess Athena the most nearly perfect of all Greek temples, the Parthenon, and a magnificent gateway to the Acropolis. These public works both beautified the city and provided work for the people.

Moreover, Pericles' lifetime coincided with the zenith of Athenian literature, when Athenian drama, especially, reached its highest development in the plays of Sophocles (a friend of Pericles) and Euripides. So brilliant was this era, and so strongly marked by his leadership, that historians often call the era from 450 to 429 the Age of Pericles. His political dominance drew praise from the historian Thucydides because "he controlled the masses, rather than let them control him. [. . .] Though the state was a democracy in name, in fact it was ruled by the most prominent man."[3]

The expansion of the empire must have been one of the causes for the development of the judicial system. Juries were chosen by lot and comprised 200, 500, or even more citizens drawn from all classes. There was no detailed body of civil or criminal law, and juries had wide powers of interpretation without the possibility of appeal from their decisions. They heard all manner of cases with exception of homicides, which were tried by the Areopagus. Critics of this system saw it as too democratic, but it expressed the spirit of the Greek state: that the average citizen could and should play a part in governing the city.

[3]Thucydides 2.65.

▶ A portion of the frieze from within the Athenian Parthenon, showing officials carrying the robe that will be presented to Athena. On the right, gods sit in conversation, awaiting the procession; note that they are portrayed as larger than the human beings.

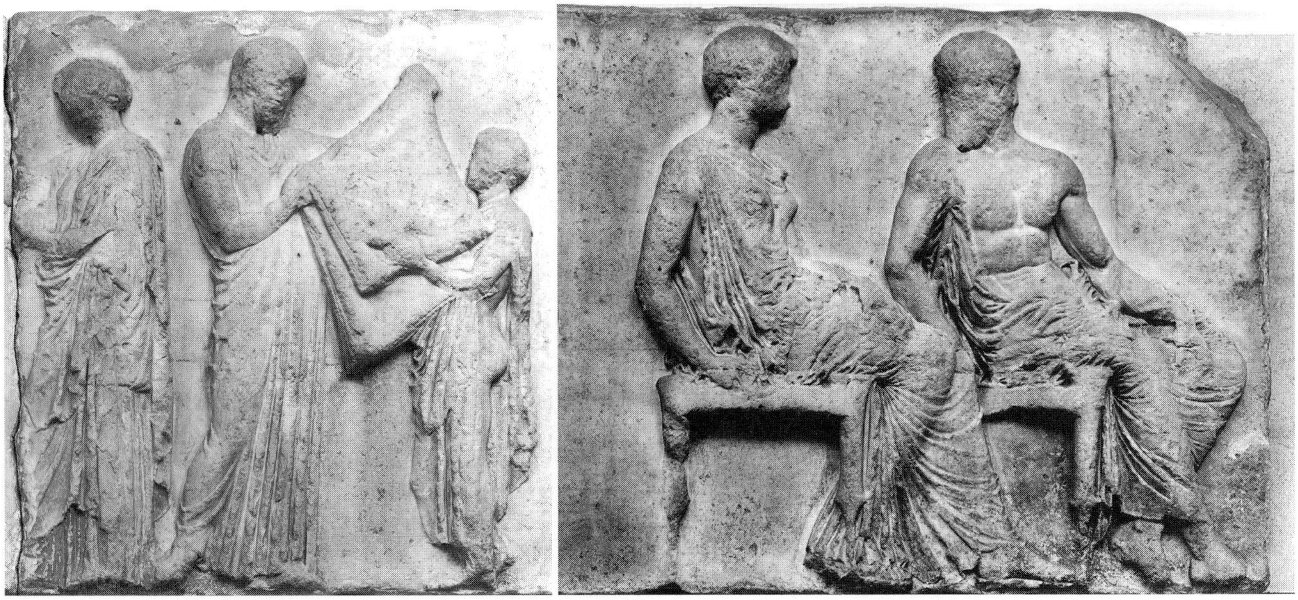

▶ **A Roman copy of an idealized portrait of Pericles, the leading Athenian statesman of his time. The helmet symbolizes his position as commander.**

THE PELOPONNESIAN WAR (431–404 B.C.)

"Historical laws" are difficult to establish and dangerous to use, but the observation of the British historian Lord Acton is hard to resist: "Power tends to corrupt." The Athenian empire, which had emerged out of the heroic victory in the Persian Wars, became more and more dominating over its subject states—its former allies. This movement, and the resentment that it caused, brought about the long war that sealed the doom of the Greek city-states. By far the longest and most dramatic of all collisions in Greek history, it also received an immortal analysis from the greatest of ancient historians, Thucydides of Athens (circa 455–circa 395 B.C.).

The Outbreak of War In the 430s aggressive action by Athens convinced the allies of Sparta that they must declare a preventive war on Athens. First, in 435 Corinth, an ally of Sparta, went to war with one of its colonies, Corcyra (today the main city on the island of Corfu). The quarrel threatened to become a Panhellenic one when Corcyra appealed for help to Athens in 433. Despite the warning of ambassadors from Corinth that any assistance would make war inevitable, the Athenians signed an alliance with Corcyra and actually fought with their new allies in a naval battle against Corinth.

Second, also in 433, the Athenians ordered the town of Potidaea, in northern Greece, to demolish its walls, send hostages to Athens, and banish its magistrates. Though Potidaea was a member of the Athenian empire, these demands infuriated the allies of Sparta, especially Corinth. The allies demanded a meeting of the Peloponnesian League and voted to declare war on the Athenians and their allies. Thucydides gives his opinion that these events were only the immediate, incidental causes of the war: "The truest cause, though the least talked about openly, was that the growth of Athenian power frightened the Spartans and finally compelled them to go to war."[4] This judgment seems accurate, for neither the affair of Corcyra nor that of Potidaea threatened the Spartans directly; more menacing was the general disturbance of the balance of power caused by Athenian boldness.

This war, known as the Peloponnesian War, opposed two kinds of states. Sparta, though the head of the Peloponnesian League, controlled no empire and maintained itself through its own resources. Athens relied on its empire to provide grain for its people and tribute to pay for its navy. Sparta had the strongest army in Greece, and Athens was the chief naval power.

The Archidamian War (431–421 B.C.) The first 10 years of the war are called the Archidamian War, so named for Archidamus, one of the kings of Sparta when the war began. Fighting opened in 431 B.C. but was inconclusive for several years. Sparta sought to break Athenian morale by

[4]Thucydides 1.23.

Map 2.7 GREECE IN 431 B.C., ON THE OUTBREAK OF THE PELOPONNESIAN WAR
Shows the members of the alliances headed by Athens and Sparta.

invading Attica annually, ravaging farms, and then departing for the Peloponnesian harvest. But the Athenians withdrew behind their "long walls" that reached down to their harbor until the enemy left, and Pericles refused to allow the Athenian infantry to challenge Sparta on the field. Instead, the Athenians launched raids by sea against coastal towns in the Peloponnese, but these raids left Sparta untouched. Far more damaging to Athens than the Spartan invasions was a devastating plague (not yet identified with any known disease) that attacked the Athenians, packed inside their walls, in 430 and later years. The plague took thousands of lives within the crowded, unsanitary city; Thucydides survived it and has left us a horrifying description of its effects on the body.

Unfortunately for Athens' effectiveness in the war, Pericles died in 429 B.C. None of his successors could maintain his stable leadership, and some were unscrupulous demagogues playing only for their own temporary power. In the 420s both sides achieved certain successes, but the casualties that all parties suffered in the next few years made them ready to end, or at least suspend, the war. A peace treaty was signed in 421 B.C., called the Peace of Nicias from the Athenian general who led the negotiations.

The "Suspicious Truce" (421–415 B.C.) At this point the Greeks could have turned their backs on war, for both Athens and Sparta had shown courage and neither had gained a decisive advantage. Thucydides called the next few years a time of suspicious truce, but during this period one event demands attention, the brutal subjugation of the small island of Melos by the Athenians in 416.

The Athenians sailed up to this neutral island and commanded the Melians to join the Athenian empire. Thucydides describes the negotiations in a brilliant passage, called the Melian Dialogue, in which envoys on each side argue their cases. It is by no means clear how he could have known what was said by either side, and this dialogue is probably based on his own conjectures. In any case, the Melians protest that they are so few in number that they cannot in any way threaten the Athenians, to which the Athenians reply that it is precisely their weakness that makes them dangerous: If the Athenians allow so small a state to remain neutral, this will show weakness in the Athenians themselves and may tempt their subjects to rebel.

The Athenians brush aside all arguments based on morality and justice and, in the end, seize the island, kill all the adult men (probably 2000 to 3000), and sell the women and children as slaves. Without explicitly stating any moral conclusion, Thucydides shows the Athenians giving way to the corrupting influence of war; as he says in another passage, "War teaches men to be violent."[5]

The Defeat of Athens In 415 B.C. another occasion for war arose. The people of Segesta, a city in Sicily, appealed to Athens for help in a war they were fighting against Syracuse, the leading power on that island. In commenting on the death of Pericles, Thucydides noted that his successors were often lesser men of poor judgment. It was so now, as Alcibiades, a talented young political leader of enormous ambition and—as it later turned out—few scruples, persuaded the Athenian assembly, against the advice of the Athenian general Nicias, to raise a large fleet and attack Syracuse, with himself as one of the generals. This campaign in effect reopened the Peloponnesian War despite the peace treaty of 421 B.C.

Thucydides makes it clear that a quick, resolute attack might well have succeeded, but the Athenians failed to strike when they had a clear advantage. One event that blunted the Athenian attack was the loss of Alcibiades. He was recalled to Athens to stand trial on charges of violating the state's religion, but fearing that his political enemies would be able to secure his conviction, he defected to Sparta and advised them how to fight the Athenians.

In Syracuse, the Athenians finally decided to break off the campaign, but they lost a critical battle in the harbor and could not sail away. Trying to retreat toward the interior of the island, they were cut off and decimated. Those who survived this calamity were imprisoned in terrible conditions in a quarry at Syracuse; as Thucydides grimly says, "Few out of many returned home."

The disaster in Sicily led to many defections among Athens' subjects, but Sparta still could not strike the final blow. The war dragged on for another eight years until, in 405 B.C., the Spartan admiral Lysander captured the Athenian fleet at a spot called Aegospotami, in the Dardanelles. Athens, now deprived of its food supply through the straits, had to surrender in desperate hunger in 404. It abandoned its empire and, as a guarantee for the future and a symbol of humiliation, had to pull down the "long walls" that had protected the population during the war. Sparta proclaimed this event, in language often used by winners of wars, as the "liberation of Greece" and imposed on the Athenians a cruel regime (known as the "30 tyrants"). This hated clique lasted only some eight months, and democracy was restored in 403 B.C.

Athens never regained its former power, although democracy survived for long years after the war. The quality of political leadership had declined after the death of Pericles, as Thucydi-

---

[5]Thucydides 3.82.

des observed. Several times when the war could have ended, ambitious politicians raised support for rash ventures that ended in disaster, of which the Sicilian expedition was only the most notable.

Looking back at the fifth century B.C., we can see that the Greek poleis made little constructive use of their brilliant victory over the invaders from Persia. Freed of a foreign enemy, they divided themselves into two blocs that turned against one another and, like characters in a Greek tragedy, involved themselves in the catastrophe of the Peloponnesian War.

The Athenians lost their empire, which had made them the richest polis in Greek history. Sparta, persuaded by its allies to go to war in 431, had dissolved the Athenian empire, but this empire had been no threat whatever to Sparta's isolated life within the protecting mountains of the Peloponnese. The losses in manpower had been heavy on both sides, but Sparta could less easily sustain these losses because of its smaller population, and in the fourth century it could put fewer and fewer troops in the field.

Besides these losses, there now came a failure of will, a spirit of pessimism and disillusion among Athenian intellectuals. Many thought uncontrolled democracy had led to social decline and military disaster, and they contrasted the discipline of Sparta, the victor, with the frequent chaos of Athenian policy. Thucydides often speaks critically of "the masses" and "the rabble," and similar ideas run through the work of Plato and other philosophers, who asked what had gone wrong with democracy and what system should replace it.

Recommended Reading

Sources

Herodotus. *The Histories.* Aubrey de Sélincourt (tr.). 1954. The only translation to catch the witty personality of the first historian.

Homer. *The Iliad.* Robert Fagles (tr.). 1990. A stirring translation in verse.

———. *The Odyssey.* Richmond Lattimore (tr.). 1968.

Studies

Andrewes, Antony. *The Greeks.* 1973. Chapters on Greek social and political life, not a continuous history.

———. *The Greek Tyrants.* 1963. Brief but highly concentrated book on the tyrants in early Greece.

Boardman, John. *Greek Art.* 1973.

Burkert, Walter. *Greek Religion.* 1987. By the most original and trenchant expert of our times.

Burn, A. R. *The Lyric Age of Greece.* 1960. History and literature in the archaic period.

———. *Persia and the Greeks.* 1962. Accurate narrative of the Persian Wars.

Cartledge, Paul. *Sparta and Lakonia.* 1979. Detailed historical-geographical survey.

Chadwick, John. *The Decipherment of Linear B* (2nd ed.). 1970. A study of the Cretan scripts, with notes on the method of decipherment.

Drews, Robert. *The Coming of the Greeks.* 1988. On the arrival of the Greeks in the general context of migrations.

Ehrenberg, Victor. *From Solon to Socrates.* 1968. A political textbook on the central period of Greek history, with good references to primary sources.

Finley, M. I. *The World of Odysseus.* 1979. The values, customs, and life style of Homeric society, by the leading social-economic historian of his time.

Guthrie, W. K. C. *A History of Greek Philosophy* (6 vols.). 1962–1981. Encyclopedic history, brilliant and sensitive.

Hignett, C. *A History of the Athenian Constitution.* 1952. For advanced students; microscopic study of every problem, often critical of ancient sources.

———. *Xerxes' Invasion of Greece.* 1963. Most detailed narrative; accepts Herodotus over all other evidence.

Hooker, J. T. *The Ancient Spartans.* 1980.

Hopper, R. J. *The Early Greeks.* 1976. Highly readable survey of ancient Greece to the beginning of the Classical period.

Jeffery, L. H. *Archaic Greece: City-States c. 700–500 B.C.* 1976. Mainly a close political narrative.

Kagan, Donald. *The Archidamian War.* 1974. Detailed history of the first part of the Peloponnesian War (followed by two other volumes).

Kitto, H. D. F. *The Greeks.* 1950. Classic appreciation of Greek culture, written with sensitivity and wit.

McGregor, Malcolm F. *The Athenians and Their Empire.* 1987. A narrative, less technical than Meiggs.

Meiggs, Russell. *The Athenian Empire.* 1972. For advanced students; discussion of every historical problem, especially good at interpreting evidence from inscriptions.

Ostwald, Martin. *From Popular Sovereignty to the Sovereignty of Law.* 1986. Detailed study of development of the Athenian state.

Page, Denys L. *History and the Homeric Iliad* (ed. 2). 1966. Especially good on Near Eastern connections with the epic.

Sealey, Raphael. *A History of the Greek City States.* 1976. The best textbook history, concentrating on problems rather than mechanical narrative.

Snodgrass, Anthony. *Archaic Greece: The Age of Experiment.* 1981. Excellent use of archaeological evidence.

de Ste Croix, G. E. M. *The Origins of the Peloponnesian War.* 1972. Really a detailed history of the fifth century; many appendixes on special topics.

Staveley, E. S. *Greek and Roman Voting and Elections.* 1972. Illuminates many practices in the Athenian constitution.

Taylour, Lord William. *The Mycenaeans.* 1983. Solid and learned treatment of earliest Greek civilization.

Vermeule, Emily. *Greece in the Bronze Age.* 1972. Classic work of synthesis by a noted art historian.

Warren, Peter. *The Aegean Civilisations.* 1975. Fully illustrated study of Minoan-Mycenaean period.

Woodhead, A. G. *The Greeks in the West.* 1962. The Greek colonies in Sicily and South Italy.

Zimmern, A. E. *The Greek Commonwealth* (4th ed.). 1924. Despite its age, still a classic portrait of social-political life in Athens.

A superb statue of the god Apollo from the west pediment of the Temple of Zeus at Olympia. In a commanding gesture, the god controls a centaur and symbolically brings Hellenic rationality to bear over an undisciplined universe. The statue combines the power and dignity of a god with the ideal perfection of a human being.

CHAPTER THREE

CLASSICAL AND HELLENISTIC GREECE

THE Peloponnesian War left the two main Greek political alliances, those built around Athens and Sparta, weak and demoralized. The war thus prepared the way for the conquest of Greece in the next century by the Macedonian king Philip II and his son Alexander the Great, who went on to conquer Egypt, Persia, and vast stretches of Asia Minor.

Despite the tumultuous conditions of Greek politics—and perhaps because of the uncertainties and upheavals—the fifth and fourth centuries witnessed an extraordinary flowering of intellectual and artistic achievements. This sudden burst of creative energy was concentrated in time and space to a degree that was unprecedented in history and, some would argue, has never been duplicated. In these years were written the plays of the tragedians Aeschylus, Sophocles, and Euripides, and the comic poet Aristophanes; Herodotus and Thucydides invented the writing of history; and philosophers probed in new ways virtually every phase of human experience.

During the last decades of the fourth century the Greeks, having lost the world of the independent polis, embraced the larger world of Alexander's empire, which brought them into expanded contact with other peoples. There followed a series of intellectual encounters that were to affect dramatically the experience of the West.

I. Classical Greek Culture (Ca. 500–323 B.C.)

In less than two centuries Greek society went through an amazing transformation, nowhere more apparent than in the Greeks' written culture: their drama, their historical writing, and their philosophy. It was an era of Athenian preeminence, and thus the study of Greek civilization in this "golden age" inevitably focuses on Athens.

GREEK TRAGEDY

One of the most lasting achievements of the fifth century B.C. was the creation and perfection of a new literary and theatrical form, tragedy. Greek dramas were written in the most sublime poetry since Homer, and they first appeared in Athens, at religious festivals honoring the god Dionysus. At these celebrations, also marked by dancing and revelry, there were dramatic performances that addressed increasingly serious moral issues. The writers of tragedies derived most of their plots from tales of gods and heroes in Greek mythology, and their central themes are the questions fundamental to all religions: What is humanity's relationship to the gods? What is justice? And if the gods are just, why do they allow people to suffer? That tragic drama arose at this time and in this place may be the result of the new confidence of the Athenians following their victory over Persia and the founding of the Athenian empire. Their inspiration may also have derived from their awareness of how short-lived triumphs can be. Greek tragedy relentlessly pursued its main theme—that worldly success and arrogance can invite destruction.

The surviving plays explore subtle moral problems with shattering power. The stature of the main characters gives the tragedies additional force, for they deal with heroic, strong-willed men and women like Oedipus and Antigone, powerful personalities who are caught in fearful dilemmas. Thus Antigone, in Sophocles' play of that name, defies the ruler of Thebes, who has forbidden her brother a traditional burial because he died in war against the city; she chooses to follow divine, not human, law, and her courageous decision destroys her. Along with these characters there is a chorus of a dozen or so men, who comment on the action and the moral problems in odes set to music.

In the fifth century these dramas were performed before audiences of as many as 15,000 people of all classes; the plays not only moved and inspired but also provided an education in ethics for citizens, who were gripped by the complex debates over which persons were acting justly and which ones should suffer retribution for moral error and crime. Just as philosophy was to explore the subject of ethical responsibility and right conduct, so do the dramas—but with far greater emotional power. Greek tragedies are still performed and filmed, and they continue to inspire operas, plays, and ballets over 2000 years after their creation.

Playwrights presented dramas in sets of three, accompanied by a comic playlet known as a satyr play (probably meant to relieve the heavy emotion of the main drama). Only one such "trilogy" has survived: the *Oresteia*, the tragedy of Orestes, the son of Agamemnon, by Aeschylus, which was produced in 458 B.C. The central theme is the nature of justice, which Aeschylus explores in a tale of multiple murders and vengeance. Agamemnon, the leader of the war against Troy, found his fleet becalmed and had to sacrifice his daughter to revive the winds so that he could fulfill his oath to make war on Troy. On his return, his wife kills him and is in turn killed by her son Orestes, who is finally tried and acquitted in an Athenian court presided over by the goddess Athena. The cycle of retribution runs its course as the themes of fate and revenge focus on the family, all developed through majestic poetry and intense emotion.

In Sophocles, who wrote mainly during the Peloponnesian War, when the very definition of the polis was under challenge, social concerns became central, and the focus shifts to the community. The chorus plays a larger role, and Sophocles adds a third actor (in Aeschylus there are never more than two on the stage at any time) in order to concentrate more on the interplay of characters and the larger issues of society that they explore. He also shows a greater interest in personality than Aeschylus. In *Oedipus the King* he created perhaps the most nearly perfect specimen of surviving Greek tragedy; its central concern is the relationship of the individual and the polis. The play is about Oedipus, king of Thebes, who, through mistaken identity, unknowingly commits the terrible crimes of killing his father and marrying his mother. As the play opens, a religious curse has brought a plague on his people. Oedipus orders a search to discover the offender who has brought this pollution on the city. As the search narrows with terrifying logic to Oedipus himself, he discovers that his crimes of patricide and incest, though unintentional, have disturbed the order of the universe and his polis in particular. The only remedy is for him to serve justice and atone for them. When the truth emerges, Oedipus' wife-mother hangs herself and Oedipus, in a frenzy of remorse and public humiliation, plunges her brooches into his eyes and begins a life of wandering as a blind outcast; once the powerful monarch, he is now a broken, homeless fugitive (*see box*, below).

The Athenian poet Euripides, a contemporary of Sophocles, emphasized above all the psychology of his characters. Reacting to the violence of his times, he throws his characters back on their own searing passions. They forge their own fates, alienated from their societies. As a result, we see in Euripides how the workings of the mind and emotions shape a person's destiny. His intense, even fanatical, characters determine the course of events by their own often savage deeds, though the themes of justice and retribution for crime are still central to the drama.

In Euripides' *Medea*, for example, Jason, Medea's husband, has deserted her for a princess of Corinth. Driven by overwhelming emotion to take revenge, Medea kills the Corinthian girl and then turns on her own children. As love and hatred battle within her, she weeps over her children but, despite a momentary weakening of will, completes her vengeance and kills them. The powerful woman has found her own way of dealing with the terrors of the world.

Oedipus' Self-Mutilation

In Sophocles' tragedy* King Oedipus, *Jocasta, the mother of Oedipus, hangs herself after learning that she has married her own son. An attendant then narrates what follows. (Those he "should never have seen" are the daughters Oedipus fathered by his mother-wife.)

"We saw a knotted pendulum, a noose,
A strangled woman swinging before our eyes.
"The King saw too, and with heart-rending groans
Untied the rope, and laid her on the ground.
But worse was yet to see. Her dress was pinned
With golden brooches, which the King snatched out
And thrust, from full arm's length, into his eyes—
Eyes that should see no longer his shame, his guilt,
No longer see those they should never have seen,
Nor see, unseeing, those he had longed to see,
Henceforth seeing nothing but night . . . To this wild tune
He pierced his eyeballs time and time again,
Till bloody tears ran down his beard—not drops
But in full spate a whole cascade descending
In drenching cataracts of scarlet rain.
"Thus two have sinned; and on two heads, not one—
On man and wife—falls mingled punishment.
Their old long happiness of former times
Was happiness earned with justice; but to-day
Calamity, death, ruin, tears, and shame,
All ills that there are names for—all are here."

Sophocles, *The Theban Plays*, Penguin, 1971, E. F. Watling (tr.), pp. 60–61.

▶ **Roman wall paintings often show scenes from Greek drama and mythology; this painting shows Medea, in Euripides' play, about to kill her children. "My friends, I am resolved to act, to slay my children quickly and depart from this land . . ."**

COMEDY

Comedy abandoned these serious themes and satirized contemporary situations and people in the real world. Almost the only comedies that have come down to us are those written by the Athenian Aristophanes, a younger contemporary of Sophocles and Euripides. Again and again he emphasized the ridiculous in the situation of individuals as well as society at large. Aristophanes used fantasy and burlesque to satirize the Peloponnesian War, political leaders, intellectuals—including Socrates—and the failings of democracy. Whatever his political motives in writing his satires, they sometimes exposed the folly of human behavior more devastatingly than the tragedies. And they were particularly cutting in their depiction of the absurdities of arrogant persons in Athenian society.

The earliest of Aristophanes' 11 surviving plays is the *Acharnians* (425 B.C.), an antiwar comedy from the early years of the Peloponnesian War. He continued his antiwar theme in other plays, notably *Lysistrata,* which he wrote after the disastrous Athenian expedition to Syracuse. In this comedy the women of Athens, despairing of any other means of ending the long war, go on a sex strike that humiliates their blustering menfolk, and they succeed in enlisting the other women of Greece in their cause.

Aristophanes reserved some of his sharpest attacks for the democratic leaders who succeeded Pericles. In *The Knights* (424 B.C.) a general tries to persuade an ignorant sausage-seller to unseat Cleon, one of those leaders:

Sausage-Seller: Tell me this, how can I, a sausage-seller, be a big man like that?

General: The easiest thing in the world. You've got all the qualifications: low birth, marketplace training, insolence.

Sausage-Seller: I don't think I deserve it.

General: Not deserve it? It looks to me as if you've got too good a conscience. Was your father a gentleman?

Sausage-Seller: By the gods, no! My folks were scoundrels.

General: Lucky man! What a good start you've got for public life!

Sausage-Seller: But I can hardly read.

General: The only trouble is that you know anything. To be a leader of the people isn't for learned men, or honest men, but for the ignorant and vile. Don't miss the golden opportunity.[1]

HISTORICAL WRITING

Drama is one way of examining the human condition; writing history is another. The constant wars in the fifth century B.C. prompted some

[1]From L. S. Stavrianos, *Epic of Man to 1500*, 1970.

men to seek to explain why war was their perpetual companion. They looked to the past to understand what causes war and how people behave during conflict. In so doing, they invented a new literary form: history.

Herodotus Herodotus, a Greek from Asia Minor and a contemporary of Sophocles, is rightly called the "Father of History," for he was the first to write a sustained narrative of political events, in his case the Greek victory over Persia. Yet this was no mere chronicle. Herodotus understood that an event like a major war could be seen as a clash between two differing cultures. He therefore began by trying to learn the history of the Persian Empire in order to explain its pressure on Europe.

The most impressive dimension of his work is his demonstration that all the cultures of the ancient world were interconnected. Using travelers' tales, interviews, and oral tradition, much as a modern anthropologist does, he described the character and outlook of the several peoples of the Near East. He also reduced centuries of Near Eastern history into order, chronicling the dynasties and successions from one monarch to another. He did this without the help of any earlier narrative, and the structure he gave to the history of the Persian Empire has not been shaken. He explained the growth of the Persian Empire as the work of powerful, ambitious monarchs, constantly striving for a larger realm. In the end, Herodotus shows his Greek heritage with his verdict that the Greek victory in the Persian Wars was the inevitable triumph of a free society over a despotic one, but he also recognizes the strength and solidity of the Persian Empire and is generally free of racial prejudice. It was his methods for regaining the past, rather than any particular interpretations, that gave him his stature as the pioneer in the writing of history.

Thucydides Greek historians "published" their work by giving readings, perhaps also allowing copies to be made. Thucydides, a younger con-

▶ **An Attic red-figure vase (about 470 B.C.), showing scenes from a school. At left, a master teaches a boy to play the lyre; at right, a boy learns to recite poetry from a scroll held by another master, while another supervises the class.**

temporary of Herodotus, is said to have heard him read, and this may have inspired him when, as a participant in the Peloponnesian War, he decided to write its history. He did not live to finish his work, which breaks off within 411, seven years before the end of the war. Thucydides has a narrower theme than Herodotus, for he concentrates on a limited period and area. Yet he is the more profound inquirer into causation and the motives for the actions of statesmen and warriors. His entire first book, out of the eight that make up his history, explores the causes, both immediate and long-term, for the outbreak of the war. Thucydides brings to bear on events the kind of logical and unemotional analysis that philosophers developed in the late fifth century. Throughout his work he presents a series of speeches and debates about various issues and decisions to lay bare the motives of the participants. The speakers are usually contemptuous of moral principles, and arguments based on justice and mercy, if brought up at all, are ruthlessly swept aside by whichever individual or force has the upper hand. It is by no means clear that Thucydides himself rejected compassion, but he presents the whole war as a cold pursuit of power. It was by such rigorous analysis that he brought order out of the cruelties and disruptions of his age.

In Thucydides' view, the Athenian state was in good order under Pericles because he could control the Athenian people. His political successors, by contrast, allowed the masses to influence decisions, with tragic consequences for Athens, including above all the expedition to Sicily in 415 B.C. Thucydides combines accuracy and concentration on detail with descriptive powers that rival those of the dramatists, particularly when he brings a scene of horror to life. No reader can avoid feeling a chill over the clinical description of the plague that attacked Athens in 430 B.C. or the shattering defeat of the proud armada that

Thucydides: The Melian Dialogue

In 416 B.C., the Athenians mercilessly inform the people of the small island of Melos that they must join the Athenian empire. Thucydides presents the cold logic of their demand.

"***Athenians:*** We will use no fine phrases saying, for example, that we have a right to our empire because we defeated the Persians, or that we have come against you now because of the injuries you have done us. And we ask you not to imagine that you will influence us by saying that you have never done us any harm. You know as well as we do that the strong do what they have the power to do and the weak accept what they have to accept.

"***Melians:*** So you would not agree to our being neutral, friends instead of enemies, but allies of neither side?

"***Athenians:*** No, because it is not so much your hostility that injures us; rather, if we were on friendly terms with you, our subjects would regard that as a sign of weakness in us, whereas your hatred is evidence of our power.

"***Melians:*** We trust that the gods will give us fortune as good as yours, because we are standing for what is right against what is wrong.

"***Athenians:*** Our opinion of the gods and our knowledge of men lead us to conclude that it is a general and necessary law of nature to rule whereever one can. This is not a law that we made ourselves, nor were we the first to act upon it when it was made. We found it already in existence, and we shall leave it to exist forever. We are merely acting in accordance with it, and we know that you or anybody else with the same power as ours would be acting in precisely the same way."

Thucydides, *The Peloponnesian War*, Penguin, 1980, Rex Warner (tr.), Book V, chaps. 89–105 (abridged).

sailed against Syracuse. He is the undisputed master among ancient historians, and for gripping narrative power and philosophical breadth he remains unsurpassed (*see box*, p. 68).

PHILOSOPHY

The supreme intellectual invention of the Greeks is the special search for knowledge called philosophy—the attempt to use reason to discover why things are as they are. Philosophy is born when people are no longer satisfied with supernatural and mythical explanations of the world or of human behavior. It is hard to say just why Greeks gradually became skeptical about the accounts that they inherited in their own mythology, but around 600 B.C. they began to suspect that there was an order in the universe beyond manipulation by the gods—and that human beings could discover it. Life in Greek poleis was conducive to argument and debate, and such conditions encouraged rational inquiry and even dispute. And philosophy, like drama and history, became a means of understanding change and upheaval.

▸ **Roman wall painting, showing Theseus having killed the Minotaur; he is surrounded by grateful Athenian children, whom he has saved from possible death by being devoured by the half-man, half-beast monster.**

The Beginnings of Philosophy The first Greek philosophers lived in the city of Miletus, a prominent trading center on the western shore of Asia Minor in the region of Ionia. Its citizens had direct contact with the ideas and achievements of the Near East, and these intellectual currents must have helped form the city as a center of thought. Soon after 600 B.C., certain Milesians were discovering a world of speculation in an apparently simple yet profoundly radical question: What exists? They sought their answer in some single primal element. One philosopher, Thales, for example, taught that everything in the whole universe was made of water, a notion that echoes Babylonian myths of a primeval flood.

A pupil and follower of Thales, Anaximander of Miletus, held (probably about 560 B.C.) that the origin of everything was an infinite body of matter, which he called "the boundless." A whirling motion within the boundless divided its substance into the hot, which rose to form the heavens, and the cold, which sank and assumed form in the earth and the air surrounding it. A further separation into wet and dry created the oceans and the land. This theory points toward a common later classification of all matter into four elements (earth, air, fire, water). Anaximander also suggested what modern biology has confirmed: that people and other animals developed from fish-like beings.

Among the theories proposed to explain the order or substance of all things were those of Pythagoras of Samos (around 530 B.C.), who developed a strikingly different theory to explain the order of the world. He saw the key to all existence in mathematics and approached the universe through the study of numbers. He discovered the harmonic intervals within the musical scale and stated the Pythagorean theorem about the sum of the sides of a right triangle. Pythagoras went on to say that all objects are similar to numbers, by which he probably meant that within objects there is always a numerically balanced arrangement of parts. He thus anticipated the modern discoveries of mathematical relationships within all things, including even the genetic code in our bodies.

Yet another way of looking at the universe was proposed by one Leucippus and his contemporary, Democritus of Abdera, about 450 B.C. They saw the world as made up of invisibly small particles or atoms (*a-toma* in Greek, meaning "things that cannot be divided"), which simply come together and cohere at random. Death, according to this theory, leads simply to the redistribution of the atoms that make up our body and soul and thus need hold no terror for humanity. The scientific validity of the atomic theory was eventually to be recognized in the modern era; like the Pythagorean and other theories, it attests the ferment of ideas in ancient Greece—ideas that were to influence Western thought for millennia.

The Sophists and Socrates Around 450 B.C. philosophers turned away from speculations about the structure of the universe and toward the study of human beings and the ways they led their lives. The first Greeks to undertake this study were those commonly known as Sophists (*sophistés* in Greek, meaning "expert" or "learned man"). They came from various places to Athens about 450 B.C. and challenged nearly all accepted beliefs. One of the early Sophists, Protagoras, declared that "man is the measure" of everything; that is, human beings and their perceptions are the only measure of whether a thing exists at all. The very existence of the gods, whom people cannot really perceive, is only an undemonstrable assumption. From such a statement it is only a short step to the belief that it is almost impossible to know anything; in the absence of objective knowledge, the only recourse is to make your way through the world by coolly exploiting to your own advantage any situation you encounter.

The Sophists also drew an important distinction between human customs on the one hand and the law of nature on the other. Thus they argued that what was made or designed by people was arbitrary and inferior; what existed naturally was immutable and proper. This argument called into question all accepted canons of good behavior. Freed of moral constraints, the Sophists suggested that intellectual activity was valuable only in helping one succeed in life. They accepted pupils and said they could train them for success in any calling, since in every line of work there are problems to be solved through reasoning. They taught the art of rhetoric, persuasive speech making that could be used to sway an assembly or to defend oneself in court. Their pupils, they implied, could gain power by coolly analyzing the mechanics of politics and by using the skills the Sophists taught them.

The main critic of the Sophists was Socrates (469–399 B.C.), a contemporary of Sophocles and Euripides, who was active during the intellectually dynamic period before and during the Peloponnesian War. He faulted the Sophists for taking pay for teaching, yet failing to teach ethically right behavior. In the course of his critique, Socrates transformed philosophy into an inquiry

▶ The olive was one of the basic crops in Greek agriculture. In this black-figure vase (the figures are painted black, while the background is the natural red of the clay), two men knock olives off a tree at harvest time, while another climbs the branches and a boy gathers the fruit.

Socrates Is Sentenced to Death

Plato's version of Socrates' words to the jury that sentenced him to death:

"You too, gentlemen of the jury, must look forward to death with confidence, and fix your minds on this one belief, which is certain: that nothing can harm a good man either in life or after death, and his fortunes are not a matter of indifference to the gods. This present experience of mine has not come about mechanically; I am quite clear that the time had come when it was better for me to die and to be released from my distractions. [. . .] For my own part I bear no grudge at all against those who condemned me and accused me, although it was not with this kind intention that they did so, but because they thought they were hurting me. [. . .] However, I ask them to grant me one favor. When my sons grow up, gentlemen, if you think that they are putting money or anything else before goodness, take your revenge by plaguing them as I plagued you; and if they fancy themselves for no reason, you must scold them just as I scolded you, for neglecting the important things and thinking that they are good for something when they are good for nothing. If you do this, I shall have had justice at your hands, both I myself and my children.

"Now it is time that we were going, I to die and you to live; but which of us has the happier prospect is unknown to anyone but God."

Plato, *The Last Days of Socrates*, Penguin, 1980, Hugh Tredennick (tr.), p. 76.

about the moral responsibility of people. His basic questions were not, What is the world made of, and How does it operate? but rather, What is right action, and How can I know it is right? His mission was to persuade the young men of Athens to examine their lives in the pursuit of moral truth, for "the unexamined life is not worth living." His technique was to engage his pupils in a dialogue of questions and answers and to refute, correct, and guide them by this "Socratic" method to the right answers. He held that no man is wise who cannot give a logical account of his actions and that knowledge will point to the morally right choices; this belief led to his statement that "knowledge is virtue," one of several Socratic theses that seem paradoxical, for even ignorant men may be virtuous. Yet it was through ironic statements like these that he made people think critically and thus discover moral truths. The Roman orator and essayist Cicero said that Socrates brought philosophy down from the heavens and placed it in the cities of humanity.

Socrates' doctrines and his insistent questioning annoyed many Athenians. He also had political critics, for he was the tutor of several Athenians who had opposed democracy during the last years of the Peloponnesian War (Alcibiades was one of his followers). As a result, he was suspected of sympathy with the enemies of Athenian democracy, and in 399 B.C. he was brought to trial on charges of "worshiping strange gods and corrupting the youth"—a way of implying that Socrates had connections with enemies of the democratic state. One can understand why the Athenian jurors, who had just regained their democratic constitution from a short-lived oligarchy that fell in 403, would have wanted to punish anyone who had collaborated with the oligarchs. Convinced through misguided patriotism, the jury convicted him; when he proposed as his penalty a fine of 100 drachmas, while also ironically requesting an honorary dinner at the town hall, they reacted in anger by voting for the death penalty (*see box*, above). He accepted his fate, declined to seek exile outside his polis—for what would he do elsewhere at age 70?—and drank a cup of poison with simple courage.

Plato Our knowledge of Socrates' thought comes mainly from the writings of his most fa-

▸ **An Etruscan vase (about 520 B.C.) with a scene from Greek literature. Odysseus and his men escape from the Cyclops, Polyphemus, by putting out his only eye (Homer's *Odyssey*, Book 9). This scene is found on several other vases from Greece.**

mous pupil, Plato (428–347 B.C.), for Socrates wrote nothing. Plato continued Socrates' investigation of moral conduct by writing a series of complex and profound philosophical books, mainly in the form of dialogues in which Socrates is the main speaker. In these works, Plato went far beyond the ironic paradoxes proposed by Socrates and sought truth through a subtle process of reasoning and inquiry that modern readers still endlessly discuss and probe.

Plato made his greatest impact on the future of philosophy with his theory of knowledge. Socrates' answer to the question, How can I know what is right? was simply that one must listen to one's conscience. Such reliance on the inner voice within each human being did not satisfy Plato, who believed that we must go beyond the evidence of our senses to find ultimate reality and truth. According to Plato, we see objects as real, but in fact, they are only poor reflections of ideal models, or "forms," which are eternal, perfect originals of any given object or notion.[2] In his *Republic*, Plato illustrates our lack of true perception with a famous metaphor. Imagine men sitting in a cave, facing a wall, with a fire behind them. As others carry objects through the cave, in front of the fire, the men see only vague shadows of the objects and therefore cannot make out the reality. Everything that we see is like these imprecise shadows; so what we see as justice, for example, is nothing but an approximation of the true "form" of justice. Only through long training in philosophy can we learn how to perceive and understand the true ideal forms, which exist outside our world.

Plato presents this thesis in several dialogues, of which the most widely read is *The Republic*. Like some other Athenian intellectuals, Plato opposed democracy as a political system dominated by emotion rather than thought. His repudiation of democracy intensified when a jury was persuaded to condemn Socrates to death, even though he had served the state as a soldier and had committed no crime. Socrates is the main speaker in the *Republic*, and in the work's long debate over the right form of state, he expresses severe criticisms of democracy as a volatile, unpredictable, and ineffective system. Yet it is by no means certain that these opinions were really those of the historical Socrates. It has been argued that Plato was the real antidemocrat and that he put these opinions into the mouth of Socrates. Whatever its source, Plato's denunciation of broad participation by the people in governing has remained a challenge to political theorists ever since.

Looking back at the death of his teacher at the hands of a popular court, Plato sought to dem-

▸ ***Facing page*** **An Attic relief, showing the goddess Athena leaning on her spear and gazing at a tablet, perhaps a list of men fallen in battle. If so, this would justify the name often given to this relief, the "Mourning Athena."**

[2]Plato used the Greek word *idéa*, which means an image that one can see. Thus "form" is a better translation than the English "idea," even though the latter is widely used.

onstrate that people without a philosophical education should never exercise political power. Their chief disqualification was that they had no grasp of reality, since they were unable to perceive the forms. Government should therefore be in the hands of men who had received an education in philosophy. This ruling elite would see to it that "everyone will do his proper task." In Plato's preferred system, a second class, warriors, would defend the state; a third class, workers, would produce the needed material goods. Plato sums up his conception of good government in an epigram: "The state will be ruled well when philosophers become kings and kings become philosophers."[3]

Like other visions of a perfect state, Plato's *Republic* has had little effect on actual constitutions, but its analyses probe nearly every problem of philosophy, from statesmanship to the nature of perception, the power of language, and psychology. Through this rich book run many threads, but one above all: the question, What is justice? As we have seen, the issue of justice was central to Greek drama and also to the debates in the history of Thucydides: Indeed, it recurs throughout the whole fifth century. That the pupil of Socrates, who had seen his teacher condemned in what he considered a brutal distortion of justice, should have been obsessed by this question only emphasizes the degree to which Plato was a product of the Athenian society of his time.

[3]*Republic*, 473 c.

Aristotle Plato had a pupil of equal genius, Aristotle (384–322 B.C.), who was for a time the teacher of Alexander the Great of Macedonia. His investigations, in which he was assisted by his pupils in Athens between 336 and 322 B.C., embraced all fields of learning known to the ancients, including logic, metaphysics, astronomy, biology, physics, politics, and poetry.

Aristotle departed from Plato's theory that there is an ideal reality that cannot be perceived by the senses. For Aristotle each object has a purpose as part of a grand design of the universe. "Nature does nothing by accident," he said. The task of the philosopher is to study these individual objects to discover their purpose; then, from the conclusions he draws, he may ultimately be able to uncover a grand design.

Aristotle made that task his life's work. He and his pupils, meeting in a grove in Athens called the Lyceum, devoted themselves to collecting and systematizing knowledge in all fields. In one of his works, the *Politics*, he classified the types of political constitutions in the Greek world and distinguished three basic forms: monarchy, aristocracy, and moderate democracy. He warned that monarchy can turn into tyranny; aristocracy, into oligarchy; and moderate democracy, into

▶ The so-called Temple of Concord from Agrigento, Sicily. Superb example of a fifth-century Doric temple. The stone was of inferior quality and was originally covered with stucco, still visible on some columns.

radical democracy, or anarchy. Of the three uncorrupted forms, Aristotle expressed a preference for moderate democracy—one in which the masses do not exercise too much power. The chief end of government, in his view, is a good life, for both the individual and the community as a whole. This is an extension of the view expressed in his *Ethics* that happiness is the greatest good of the individual. To achieve this end, people must seek moderation, a mean between extremes of excessive pleasure and ascetic denial—a goal that reflected the Greek principle of harmony and balance in all things.

Aristotle's conception of the universe remained influential in scientific speculation for 2000 years. By about 350 B.C. philosophers generally recognized four elements: earth, air, fire, and water. Aristotle gave them purpose and movement. Air and fire, he said, naturally move upward; and earth and water, downward. Movement he explained by saying that elements seek their natural place. Thus a stone falls because it seems to return to the earth. It also seeks to be at rest; all motion is therefore unnatural and has to be accounted for by an outside force.

To the four elements Aristotle added a fifth, ether, the material of which the stars are made. He explained that the stars move in a natural circular motion, and outside the whole universe there exists an eternal "prime mover," which imparts movement to all the other parts. This prime mover, or God, as Aristotle finally designates him, does not move or change; God is a kind of divine thought or mind which sets the whole universe in motion.

Among the most interesting of all Aristotle's works are his writings on biology, which are based on extensive firsthand observation. In the *Generation of Animals,* he examines the birth and reproduction of animals, birds, fish, insects, and human beings. In the *Parts of Animals,* he discusses the functions of the various parts of the body. Aristotle believed that nature, the creator of living things, designed every part with a specific function. Thus, for example, the lion and wolf were given no vertebrae in the neck, because nature intended that they should have rigid necks for charging their prey. Such explanations are called *teleological* (from the Greek word *telos,* meaning "aim, goal"), and they remained influential for many centuries. Even more influential was Aristotle's effort to classify all that he observed in separate categories. His organizing principles remained the basis for investigations of nature until the scientific revolution of the seventeenth century.

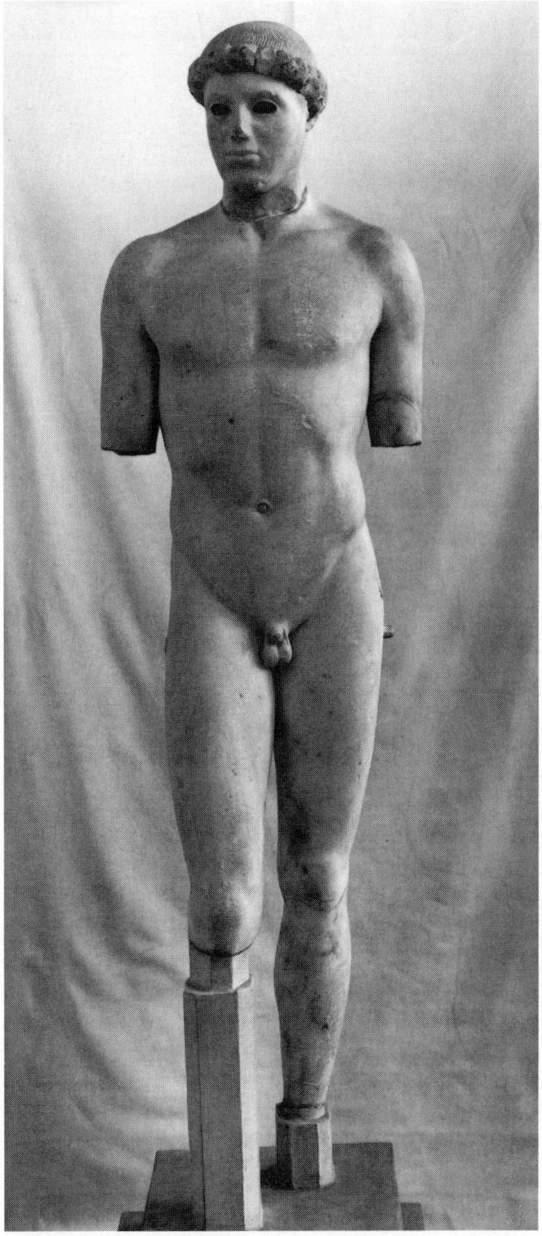

An Attic kouros, or young man, leaning on one foot, showing a movement away from the severe toward a more natural style.

II. The Rise of Macedonia

Plato and Aristotle theorized about the classical polis as it was entering a period of decline. The Peloponnesian War had exacted terrible losses in manpower; and instead of the needed healing period, there followed decades of interstate warfare that left the poleis weaker than ever.

THE WEAKNESSES OF THE POLEIS

Sparta, the victor in the Peloponnesian War, had established a puppet regime of obedient Athenians, known as the Thirty Tyrants, to govern Athens in 404 B.C.; but within a few months popular opposition swept this group away. As the Athenians sought to regain power, they revived their naval league in 394 B.C., though with many fewer members than it had had in the fifth century. But their arrogance had not subsided. Despite their promises to respect the independence of the league's members, the Athenians began to demand tribute from them as they had done under the Delian League. Rebellions followed, and this second league collapsed about 355 B.C.

Map 3.1 MACEDONIA UNDER PHILIP II, 359–336 B.C.

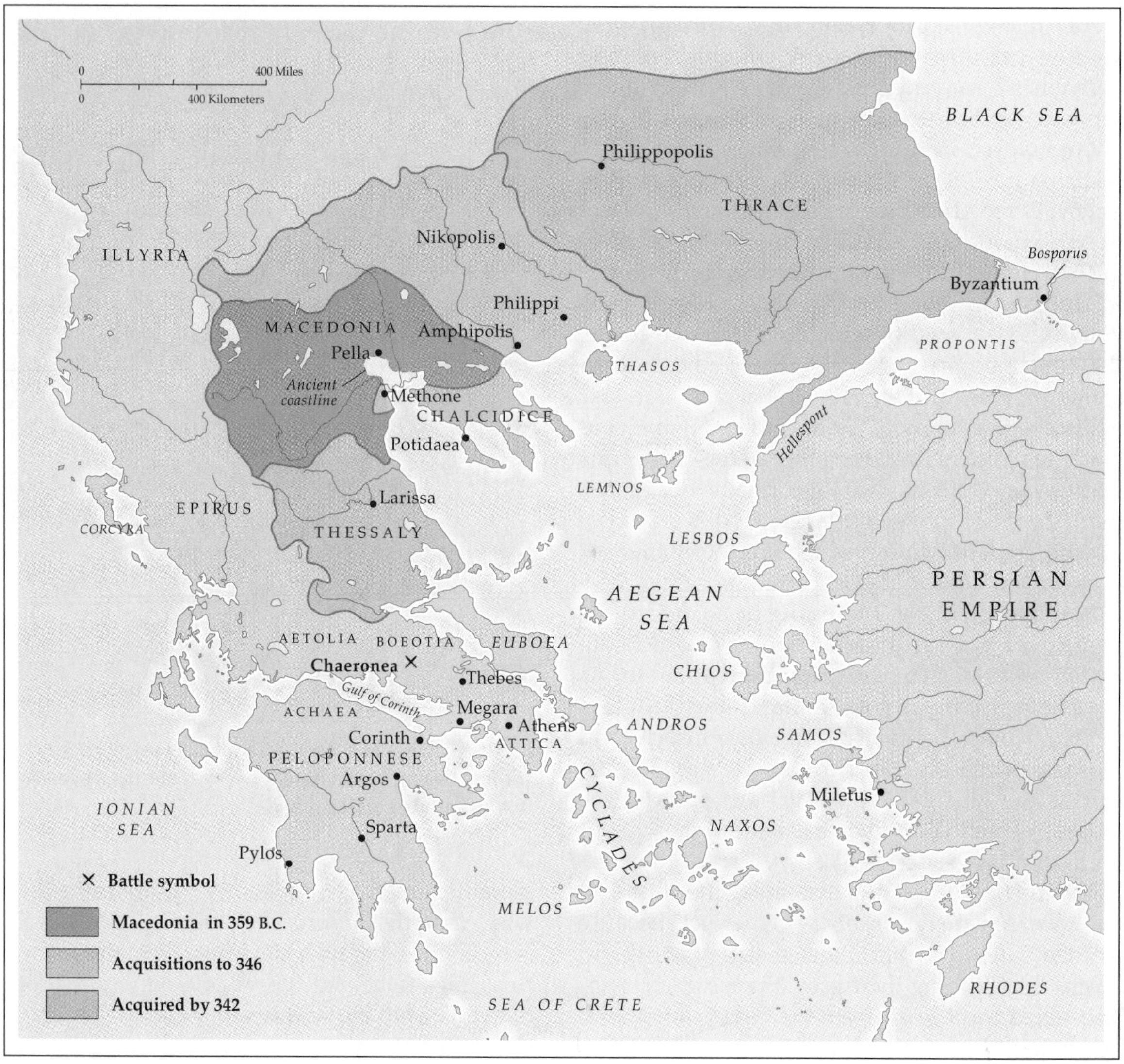

By now there were no longer only two dominant cities in Greece. The polis of Thebes was becoming an important power, siding now with Athens, now with Sparta, in a series of never-ending quarrels. There was no clear trend in these struggles except that the constant intrigue and war, spanning several decades, drained the energies of all the antagonists. In 371 B.C. the brilliant Theban general Epaminondas won a victory over Sparta, which finally exploded the long-held belief in Greece that the Spartan infantry was invincible. The Thebans liberated Sparta's slaves, the helots, and helped them to found their own city, called Megalopolis, in the Peloponnese. The Spartans were thus deprived of much of their territory and of the slaves who had worked their land. A shortage of manpower accelerated the decline in Sparta's strength. Aristotle informs us about 335 B.C. that Spartan armies in the field had fewer than 1000 men, rather than the 4000 or 5000 who had gone into battle during the wars of the fifth century. Epaminondas himself died in another battle near Sparta in 362 B.C., and no comparable leader in any polis took his place. The era of independent city-states was all but over, doomed by the constant wars of the fourth century.

PHILIP II OF MACEDONIA

Macedonia, a kingdom in northern Greece, emerged as a leading power under an ambitious, resourceful king, Philip II, who reigned between 359 and 336 B.C. With shrewd political skill Philip developed his kingdom, built up a powerful army, and planned a program of conquest.

Using both aggression and diplomacy, Philip added poleis and large territories to his kingdom and extended his influence into central Greece. The great Athenian orator Demosthenes (384–322 B.C.), in a series of fiery speeches called "Philippics," beginning in 351, called on his countrymen to recognize the danger from Macedonia and prepare to make war against it. But by the time the Athenians responded, it was too late to halt the Macedonian advance. Philip won a decisive battle against Athens and several other poleis at Chaeronea in 338 B.C. All the city-states of southern Greece, except isolated Sparta, now lay at his mercy. He could have devastated many of them, including Athens, but his sense of tactics warned him not to do so. Instead, he gathered the more important poleis into an obedient alliance called the League of Corinth, which recognized Philip as its leader and agreed to follow him in his next project, an invasion of Persia.

But before Philip could open his Persian war, he was murdered in 336 B.C. by one of his officers who apparently had a personal quarrel with the king. Some historians have wondered whether Philip's wife or his son Alexander may have been involved in a plot to kill Philip and put Alexander on the throne; but tempting as such speculations may be, the sources do not give them clear support.

▶ **The "Getty Bronze," a fourth-century statue in a soft, relaxed style. Surviving bronze statues from Greece are rare.**

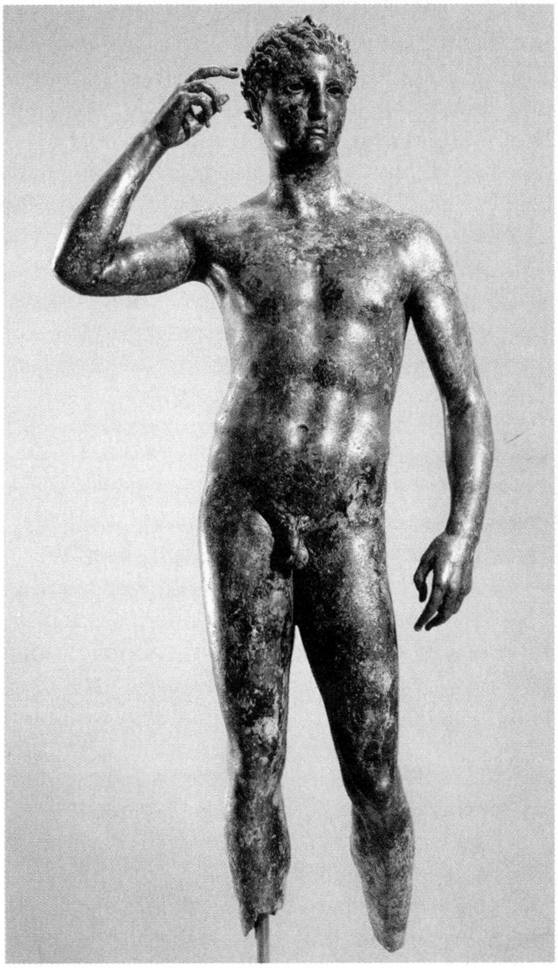

Statue of victorious athlete. Artist unknown. Late 4th century B.C.

ALEXANDER THE GREAT

The empire built by Philip now passed to his son, Alexander III (reigned 336–323 B.C.), known as Alexander the Great, and never has a young warrior prince made more effective use of his opportunities. During his brief reign Alexander created the largest empire the ancient world had known and, more than any other man, became responsible for the eastward expansion of the Greek world.

In the next year, 335, a rumor of Alexander's death caused a democratic revolution in the city of Thebes. Alexander marched on Thebes and sacked it with the utmost brutality, destroying every building except temples and the house of the poet Pindar. Having thus warned the Greek cities against any further rebellions, Alexander began the invasion of the Persian Empire. The Persia that he attacked was a much weaker state than the one that had conquered Babylon or the one that Xerxes had led against the Greeks in 480 B.C. Intrigue and disloyalty had weakened the administration of the empire. Moreover, the king, Darius III, had to rely on Greek mercenary soldiers as the one disciplined element in his infantry, for native troops were mainly untrained. The weakness of Persia helps to explain Alexander's success, but in no way does it diminish his reputation as one of the supreme generals in history. His campaigns were astonishing combinations of physical courage, strategic insight, and superb leadership.

Alexander swept the Persians away from the coast of Asia Minor and in 332 B.C. drove them out of Egypt, a land they had held for two centuries. The Egyptians welcomed him as a liberator and recognized him as their pharaoh. While he was in Egypt (also in 332), Alexander founded the city of Alexandria. He intended this city to serve as a link between Macedonia and the valley of the Nile, and he had it laid out in the grid pattern typical of Greek city planning. Although he did not live to see it, Alexandria remained one of the conqueror's most enduring legacies: a great metropolis thoughout history.

In the next season, 331 B.C., Alexander fought Darius III at Gaugamela, winning a complete victory there that guaranteed he would face little further opposition in Persia. Darius III was murdered by disloyal officers in 330 B.C., and Alexander assumed the title of king of Persia. The expedition had now achieved its professed aim; yet Alexander, for whom conquest was self-expression, continued to make war. During the

▶ The Venus of Cyrene (early third century B.C.), a most elegant, graceful depiction of ideal female beauty.

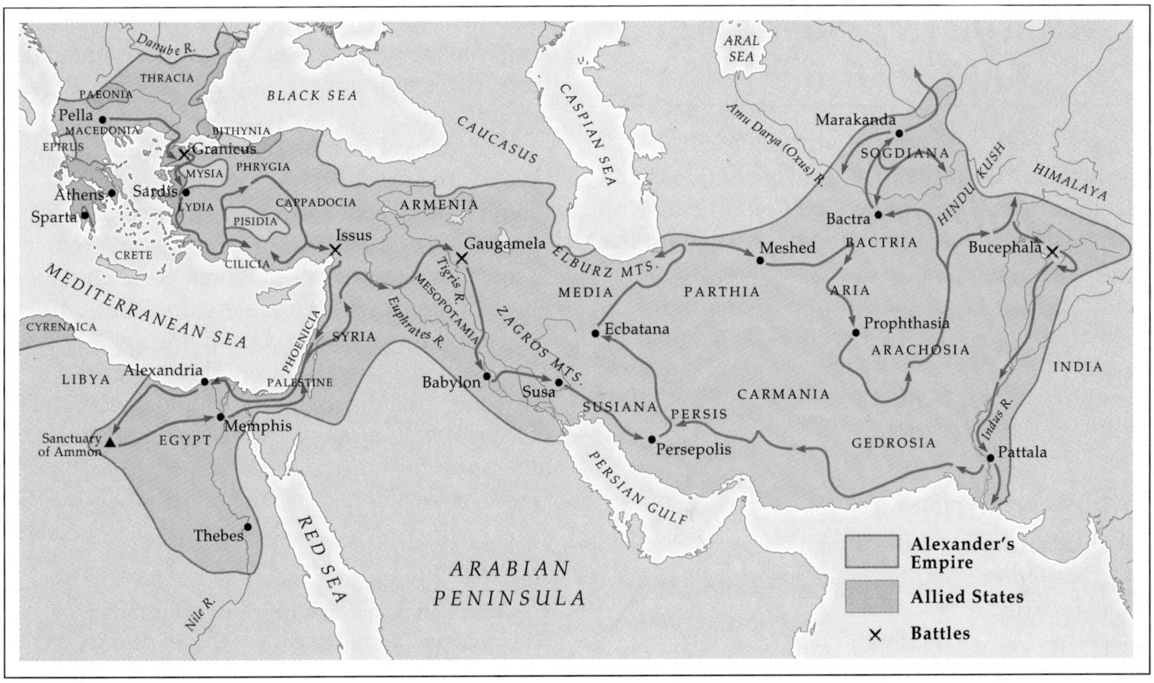

Map 3.2 THE EMPIRE OF ALEXANDER THE GREAT

next few years he campaigned as far east as India, where he crossed the Indus River (see Map 3.3), and finally, in 326 B.C., he began his march back. But at Babylon in 323 B.C., he caught a fever after a bout of heavy drinking, and within a few days he died, not yet 33.

Alexander is a figure of such stature and power that he defies easy interpretation, and even today radically different biographies are written about this most famous man in Greek history. Part of our difficulty is that our best narrative source for his life, the Greek historian Arrian, lived four centuries after Alexander's death; and Arrian, for all his merits, was not the kind of probing historian who might have given us a rounded psychological portrait of the king. Yet it is clear that along with Alexander's courage and drive, perhaps as their necessary accompaniment, came a personality sometimes barely containing a raging animal. He executed a number of his friends for supposedly being aware of conspiracies against him; another one he murdered himself in a sudden fury. On the other hand, Arrian tells the moving story of Alexander's pouring a cup of water, offered him by his parched troops, into the desert because he refused to drink if his men could not.

Nor do we know just what Alexander was trying to accomplish. There is little reason to believe the popular myth that he hoped to conquer the world. His goal may have been a stable empire that would maintain his vast conquests, but if so he failed, for he had designated no successor and the empire disintegrated on his death. Some historians have believed that Alexander had a vision of the unity of the human race and was trying to establish an empire in which different peoples would live in harmony as within one family, but this view is widely, and rightly, rejected as sentimental and too idealistic. Others focus on his acts of cruelty and vindictiveness and see him as a paranoiac tyrant. In any case, no portrait of him should overlook his patronage of scholarship, which extended even to his bringing scientists and geographers with him as he invaded Persia. However we interpret him, he has remained the prototype of a world conqueror. Some of his successors put his portrait on their own coins, and even Roman emperors also issued medallions portraying him, as if to borrow his glory and power for their often threatened reigns.

III. The Hellenistic Age (323–30 B.C.)

We have said that the Classical Age of Greek civilization began about 500 B.C., just after the reform of the Athenian state under Cleisthenes. The next period, the Hellenistic Age, is usually dated from 323 B.C., when Alexander the Great died, to the death of Cleopatra of Egypt in 30 B.C. During this period the Greeks carried their culture throughout the Near East in the movement known as Hellenization.

THE DISSOLUTION OF ALEXANDER'S EMPIRE

Alexander's empire was shattered almost at once after his death, as his generals seized various parts for themselves. By about 275 B.C., after years of warfare and diplomatic intrigue, three large kingdoms emerged. A fourth kingdom was formed about 260 around the city of Pergamum in western Asia Minor. The kings of these states became absolute rulers, with complete authority over their realms. The subsequent history of these kingdoms is one of continual warfare until they were all eventually absorbed by the Roman Republic.

The king of Macedonia controlled northern Greece. The poleis in the south retained their autonomy, and some of them formed defensive leagues to protect their independence from the monarchy. The most influential were the Aetolian League in western Greece and the Achaean League on the northern coast of the Peloponnese. These leagues tried to strengthen themselves by awarding citizenship in the league to all citizens of their member cities; but this principle of confederation for mutual security arrived too late in Greek history to take firm root before Greece fell

▸ A scene from the magnificent "Alexander Sarcophagus" found at Sidon; fourth century B.C. Alexander is shown, left, hunting accompanied by a Persian. Although we have no reason to think Alexander was ever buried in this sarcophagus, the scene symbolizes Alexander's heroism and virility and calls attention to his conquest of the Persian Empire.

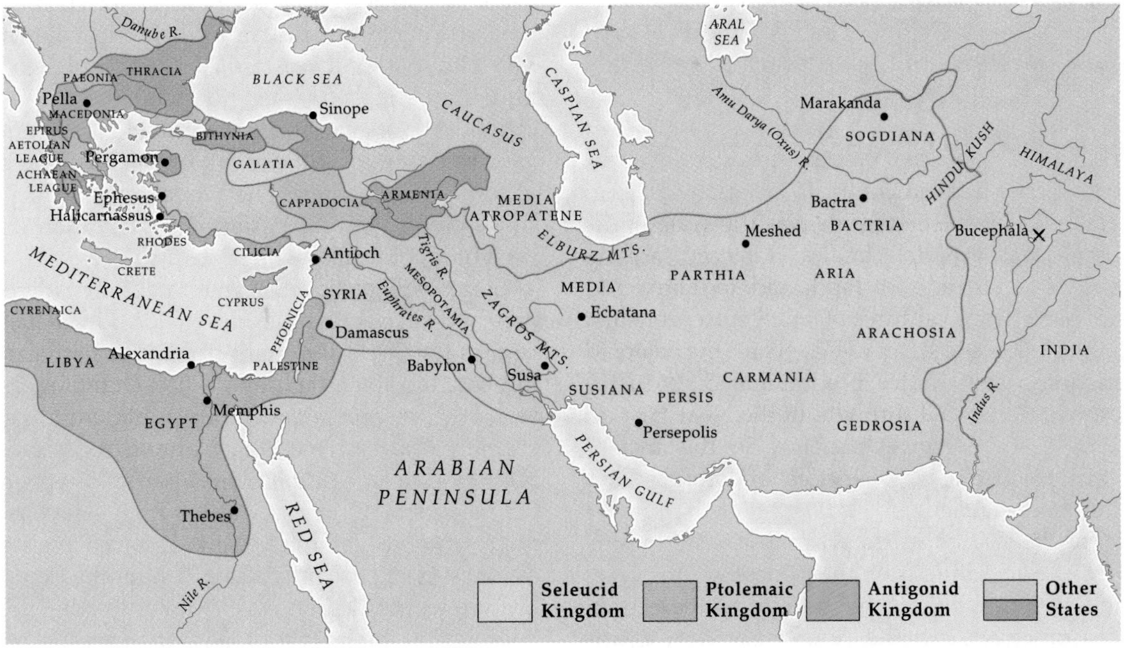

Map 3.3 HELLENISTIC KINGDOMS AFTER ALEXANDER, CA. 240 B.C.

to the expanding Roman Republic. As to the Egyptians and inhabitants of the Near East, they had long seen their rulers as divine or semidivine beings, and the Hellenistic kings in these areas exploited this tendency and established themselves as absolute monarchs who owned the kingdom.

Remarkably, considering the military roots of these kingdoms, the Hellenistic Age witnessed the reemergence of women as rulers. Their power first became evident in Macedonia, where Olympias, the mother of Alexander, was a more important political figure than any other woman in classical Greece. The most famous and skillful of all Hellenistic queens was Cleopatra of Egypt, who manipulated such Roman military leaders as Julius Caesar and Mark Antony to the advantage of her kingdom.

Hellenistic monarchs ruled through strong armies and large bureaucracies, and their systems of taxation were extremely efficient. Certain products, such as oil in Egypt, were royal monopolies and could be traded only at official prices. Greeks usually held the chief public offices in the army and bureaucracy, and rulers did allow some democratic institutions, such as a town council, to function in Near Eastern cities; but the autonomy of these cities was limited to

▶ **The head of Alexander the Great in heroic profile; the obverse of a silver coin issued by Lysimachus, one of Alexander's bodyguards, who after his master's death became king of Thrace.**

local affairs. The king controlled all foreign policy, and he alone granted and could cancel such rights of self-government as the cities enjoyed.

ECONOMIC LIFE

One of the sharpest contrasts between the classical and Hellenistic worlds was the scale of economic activity. In classical Greece, farmers worked small plots of land, and industry and commerce were ventures of small entrepreneurs. In the Hellenistic states of Egypt and the Seleucid kingdom, vast estates predominated. Industry and trade operated throughout the Near East on a larger scale than ever before in the ancient world, requiring the services of bankers and other financial agents.

The Hellenistic world prospered as ambitious Greeks, emigrating from their homeland to make their fortunes, brought new vigor to the economies of Egypt and the Near East. They introduced new crops and new techniques in agriculture to make production more efficient. For example, Greeks had long cultivated vines, and they now enhanced the wines of Egypt. At the same time, they improved and extended the irrigation system and could thus devote more acreage to pasturing animals, which provided leather and cloth for the people and horses for the cavalry.

The growth of long-distance trade was even more remarkable. The Hellenistic rulers encouraged these efforts by establishing a sound money system, building roads and canals, and clearing the seas of pirates. Traders ventured eastward to India and, in the west, beyond the Mediterranean to the Atlantic coasts of Africa and Europe.

The resulting prosperity, however, was unevenly distributed. Rulers and members of the upper classes (usually Greek) amassed great fortunes, but little of this wealth filtered down to the small farmers and laborers. This great disparity between rich and poor led to increasing social conflict.

HELLENISTIC CITIES

The greater part of the vast lands of the new kingdoms was devoted to agricultural pursuits, but it was in the numerous Greek cities founded by Alexander and his successors that the civilization that we call Hellenistic was formed. Most of these new cities were in western Asia, in the Seleucid kingdom. Alexander had founded the brilliant city of Alexandria, in Egypt, but the Ptolemies who ruled Egypt did not follow his example by founding many cities. They considered a docile, rustic civilization far easier to control than citizens of a politically active urban society.

Some Hellenistic cities were magnificently ornate and spectacular. Besides their political institutions the Greeks brought from their homeland many of the amenities of polis life—temples, theaters, gymnasiums, and other public buildings. Pergamum, an outstanding example of city planning, contained a stupendous altar to Zeus, a renowned library, and a theater high above the main city with a superb view. It may have had as many as 100,000 inhabitants (under the Roman Empire its population was about 200,000), while Alexandria, the largest of all, had at least a half million.

Local families in the upper classes copied Greek ways and sent their children to Greek schools. Moreover, a version of Greek, *koiné* ("common") Greek, became an international tongue. Now, for the first time, people could travel to any city in the known civilized world and make themselves understood.

LITERATURE, ART, AND SCIENCE

The most significant literary achievements in the Hellenistic Age were in the field of scholarship. The kings of Egypt took pride in constructing a huge library in Alexandria that probably contained, by about 200 B.C., a half million papyrus rolls. Along with the library they built the Museum, a kind of research institute, where literary, historical, and scientific studies flourished, each employing its own experts. One of the main interests of literary scholars in Alexandria was the literature of the classical period, and among their achievements was the standardization of the Greek text of Homer. By comparing the many versions that had been handed down in manuscripts over the centuries, they were able to establish the text on which modern versions of Homer are based.

The specialization of scholars was characteristic of the growing professionalism of the age. Whereas the citizen of fifth-century Athens could be a farmer, a politician, and a soldier at the same time, now each of these roles was filled by a professional. The army consisted of professional soldiers, while professional bureaucrats ran the government.

▸ Panels from the altar to Zeus at Pergamum, showing gods in combat with giants. Greek art preferred abstraction to reality, and such scenes probably represent the triumph of Greek civilization over non-Greek peoples. The violence and dramatizing are in the "baroque" tradition of Hellenistic art of the second century B.C.

Hellenistic rulers also wanted to glorify their cities and provided generous subsidies for art and architecture. The architecture of the age tends to emphasize size and grandeur, as compared with the simplicity and human scale of classical architecture. Thus the Altar of Zeus from Pergamum, now in Berlin, included a great stairway, flanked by a frieze 400 feet long. The figures on the frieze, typical of Hellenistic sculpture, are carved in high relief, with an almost extravagant emotionalism that makes them seem to burst out of the background. Hellenistic sculpture also differed from that of the classical period through its devotion to realism. Instead of creating figures of ideal perfection, artists now showed individual-

▸ **Bronze statue of a boxer from Rome, second century B.C. Greek sculptors had abandoned statues of ideal beauty and were now experimenting with scenes of frank realism. Note the boxer's battered face and bandaged hands.**

ity in faces and bodies (see picture, above), even depicting physical imperfection or frank ugliness.

Advances in the field of science drew strength from the cross-fertilization of cultures in the Hellenistic Age. The Greeks had long speculated about the nature of the universe, and the Near East had an even longer scientific tradition, particularly in the fields of astronomy and mathematics. After Alexander's conquests joined the two cultures, other conditions favored scientific advance: the increased professionalism of the age, the use of Greek as an international language, and the facilities of the Museum in Alexandria. The result was an age of scientific achievement that was not surpassed until the seventeenth century.

In mathematics, Euclid (about 300 B.C.) compiled a textbook that is still the basis for the study of plane geometry. Some of his theorems were already known, and others (for example, his demonstration that nonparallel lines must meet somewhere) may seem obvious. His remarkable accomplishment was to construct a succession of elegant proofs for these theorems, each based on earlier proofs, starting with the simple proposition that the shortest distance between two points is a straight line. The analytical method of his proofs is a characteristic of Greek thought, for Greek philosophers believed that knowing something entailed being able to prove it.

The greatest mathematician of antiquity—indeed, one of the greatest ever—was Archimedes of Syracuse, who also lived during the Hellenistic era (287?–212 B.C.). He calculated the value of *pi* (the ratio between the circumference and diameter of a circle); he developed a system for expressing immensely large numbers, by using 100,000,000 as the base (as we use 10); and he discovered the ratio between the volumes of a sphere and a cylinder circumscribing it (2:3, a proportion he had engraved on his tombstone). Archimedes was also a pioneer in physics; he demonstrated that a floating body will sink in a liquid only to the point at which it displaces its own weight. He understood the principle of using the lever for lifting massive weights and is said to have proclaimed, "Give me a place where I can stand and I will lift the earth" (that is, outside the earth entirely and with a long enough lever). He also invented the water screw still used for irrigation in Egypt. Tragically, he was murdered by a Roman soldier during the Roman attack on Syracuse in 212 B.C.—as he sat drawing a mathematical figure in the sand.

About 250 B.C., Aristarchus, an astronomer and mathematician, advanced a heliocentric theory of the movement of the planets. The view that the earth revolves around the sun was not new, but Aristarchus refined it by stating that the earth revolves on its own axis while it, together with the other planets, circles the sun. Not until the sixteenth century did astronomers prove the soundness of Aristarchus' system; meanwhile, the Greek astronomic tradition continued to follow an older geocentric theory, which held that the earth was the center of the solar system and that the sun revolved around it. The geocentric theory was the basis for the most important Hellenistic text on astronomy, the *Almagest* of Ptolemy of Alexandria (about A.D. 140). This book systematized Greek study of astronomy and remained the accepted text on the subject for more than 1000 years.

Hellenistic scientists also made important advances in the realm of measurements. Hipparchus calculated the length of the average lunar month to within one second of today's accepted figure. Eratosthenes about 225 B.C. computed the circumference of the earth to be about 28,000 miles, only 3000 miles more than the actual figure. Other scientists worked out the division of time into hours, minutes, and seconds, and of circles into degrees, minutes, and seconds.

PHILOSOPHY AND RELIGION

The change in life style from the relative security of the polis to the increasing uncertainties of a larger world shifted the direction of Greek philosophy. Plato and Aristotle had been philosophers of the polis in the sense that they were concerned with the individual's role in the intimate world of the city-state; the ideal state in their theories would have only a few thousand citizens. But when the city-state came to be governed by a large kingdom headed by a remote ruler, individual men and women could hardly influence its policies even though they were caught up in its wars and its many changes of fortune. Moreover, the large Hellenistic cities lacked the cohesiveness, the sense of belonging among citizens, that had made the classical poleis internally united. In such conditions, philosophers sought means of accommodation with the larger Hellenistic world that was shaping their lives. They tried to provide people with guidance in their personal lives and were less concerned about the nature of the political framework. Thus the two most important schools of Hellenistic philosophy, Epicureanism and Stoicism, were philosophies designed to provide comfort and reassurance for the individual human being.

Epicureans and Stoics Epicurus, who taught in Athens during the generation after Alexander, believed that people should strive above all for tranquillity, which he sought to provide through the atomic theory of Democritus. Our bodies and souls, Epicurus taught, are made up of atoms that cohere only for our lifetimes. When we die, the atoms will be redistributed into the universe again, and nothing of us will remain behind to suffer any desire for the life we have lost. Since death therefore holds no terrors, we should concern ourselves only with leading pleasurable lives, avoiding physical and mental pain. But emotional commitment and passionate love, in Epicurus' view, are equally unrewarding, since they may lead to disappointment and pain. Thus the wise person withdraws from the world to study philosophy and enjoy the companionship of a few friends. Some later Epicureans came close to advocating an almost heedless pursuit of pleasure, but in its early days this philosophy was intended as a powerful antidote to anxiety and suffering.

A different approach to this problem was that of a contemporary of Epicurus—namely, Zeno of Cyprus—who founded a philosophical school known as Stoicism, so named because he taught his pupils in a building in Athens called the Stoa. He believed that a single divine plan governs the universe and that to find happiness one must act in harmony with this plan. One should be patient in adversity, for adversity is a necessary part of the divine plan and one can do nothing to change it. By cultivating a sense of duty and self-discipline, people can learn to accept their fate; they will then become immune to earthly anxieties and will achieve inner freedom and tranquillity. The Stoics did not advocate withdrawal from the world, for they believed that all people, as rational beings, belong to one family. Moreover, to ensure justice for all, the rational person should discover his or her place in the world and consider it a duty to participate in public affairs.

The Stoics advanced ideas that were to have a profound influence on later Western history, especially as they were interpreted in the Roman and Christian visions of civilization: the concept that all humanity is part of a universal family; the virtues of tolerance; and the need for self-discipline, public service, and compassion for the less fortunate members of the human race. Furthermore, while most earlier Greeks had accepted the institution of slavery, the Stoics believed that the practice of exploiting others corrupted the owner (the slave could endure bondage by achieving inner freedom). Stoicism became the most influential philosophy among the educated of the Hellenistic Age and achieved great influence among the Romans, who adopted with conviction the ideals of discipline and fulfillment of public and private duty.

New Religions The search for meaning in life preoccupied all levels of Hellenistic society, but none so painfully as the great masses of the poor. The answers of philosophy were addressed to an intellectual elite: wealthy scholars, as it were, meditating in the study. But the poor—lacking the education, leisure, and detachment for such a pursuit—looked elsewhere for spiritual and emotional sustenance in their daily encounters with the harshness of Hellenistic life. For many, religion answered their need for escape and consolation.

Among the new religious practices were the Near Eastern mystery cults that had some features in common as a result of the frequent intermingling of cultures in the cosmopolitan Near East. They are called mystery cults because they centered on the worship of a savior whose death and resurrection would redeem the sins of humanity; their rituals were secret, known only to the participants, and were elaborate, often wildly emotional; and they nourished hope by promising an afterlife that would compensate for the rigors of life on earth. One of the most popular mystery cults was the worship of the Egyptian deities Isis and Osiris. In this myth, Osiris had been dismembered but was reassembled and saved by Isis, his devoted wife; thus the myth suggested that its followers might also attain salvation and life after death.

All these political, scientific, and intellectual explorations were parts of the legacy of Alexander, the Macedonian who brought Greek civilization and the Greek language into another world. Greek was to be the language in which the New Testament was written, and therefore some historians have also seen his campaigns as preparing the way for Christianity and have even called Christianity his most important legacy. Be this as it may, the Greeks and Macedonians could not maintain permanent control over the remains of Alexander's empire. Not Greece but Rome became the uniting force that passed the legacy of classical civilization to medieval and then to modern Europe.

Recommended Reading

Sources

Aristotle. *The Athenian Constitution.* P. J. Rhodes (tr.). 1984. The great philosopher's brief history and description of the Athenian state, with helpful commentary.

Arrian. *The Campaigns of Alexander the Great.* Aubrey de Sélincourt (tr.). 1958. Our main source for the life of the great conqueror.

Grene, David, and Richmond Lattimore (eds.). *The Complete Greek Tragedies.* 1959. The best collection of modern translations.

Plato. *The Republic.* Desmond Lee (tr.). 1974. The central work of Greek political philosophy.

Studies

Adkins, Arthur W. H. *Merit and Responsibility: A Study in Greek Values.* 1975. A summary of the ethical beliefs of the Greeks.

Cartledge, Paul. *Sparta and Lakonia: A Regional History, 1300–362 B.C.* 1979. Both a physical and a social-political history.

Cawkwell, George. *Philip of Macedon.* 1978. Macedonia before Philip II and the reorganization and expansion of the kingdom.

Dodds, E. R. *The Greeks and the Irrational.* 1951. Brilliant study of the Greek mind.

Dover, K. J. *Greek Homosexuality*. 1978. Dispassionate study of this feature of Greek life.

———. *Greek Popular Morality in the Time of Plato and Aristotle*. 1974. More limited in time than Adkins, by today's leading Hellenist.

Ellis, John R. *Philip II and Macedonian Imperialism*. 1976. Good modern study of the kingdom that was to dominate Greece.

Errington, R. Malcolm. *A History of Macedonia*. Catherine Errington (tr.). 1990. Compact one-volume treatment, carrying the story down through Alexander's successors.

Green, Peter. *Alexander to Actium. The Historical Evolution of the Hellenistic Age*. 1990. Now the most comprehensive historical and cultural survey; a colossal study.

Guthrie, W. K. C. *Socrates*. 1971. Excellent study of the man and his thought.

Hamilton, J. R. *Alexander the Great*. 1973. The best modern portrait of this controversial figure.

Hammond, N. G. L., G. T. Griffith, and F. W. Walbank. *A History of Macedonia* (3 vols.). 1972–1988. Monumental, detailed survey. For advanced students.

Hatzopoulos, Miltiades, and Louisa Lykopoulou. *Philip of Macedon*. 1981. Includes recent archaeological evidence about Macedonia.

Just, Roger. *Women in Athenian Law and Life*. 1988. Solid, often technical.

Kitto, H. D. F. *Greek Tragedy. A Literary Study*. 1969. Probably still the best general book on one of the supreme achievements of the Greeks.

Lacey, W. K. *The Family in Classical Greece*. 1968. Older treatment, still not wholly replaced as introduction.

Long, A. A. *Hellenistic Philosophy: Stoics, Epicureans, Sceptics*. 1974. The best introduction to the philosophies of these schools.

Pomeroy, Sarah B. *Goddesses, Whores, Wives and Slaves*. 1975. A groundbreaking study of the many roles of women in antiquity.

———. *Women in Hellenistic Egypt*. 1989. A study of women in the society offering the most evidence about their status.

Ross. W. D. *Aristotle*. 1956. Comprehensive study by a great master.

Vlastos, Gregory. *Socrates: Ironist and Moral Philosopher*. 1991. Most important recent study of style and significance of Socrates' philosophy.

Walbank, F. W. *The Hellenistic World*. 1982. The best one-volume introduction to the period.

"Noble" Romans, those whose ancestors had been consuls, had the right to have masks representing them carried in funeral processions. This republican noble of about 30 B.C. shows the masks of two of his ancestors.

CHAPTER FOUR

The Roman Republic

THE contrast in the political and social systems of the two great ancient cultures that shaped Western civilization is unmistakable. The Greeks flourished in small, intensely competitive communities, but the Romans established a huge and long-lived empire. The character of the Roman people shines forth throughout their history. They valued discipline, obedience, and social cohesion. When the kings of early Rome disappeared, self-government emerged in a republic, but its practices were never so democratic as those of Athens. And from Rome's earliest days as a republic, the theme of its history was conquest and domination.

The result was the creation of a society that was primarily a military machine. Since an army is not a democracy, but a disciplined body governed by a few experienced men—an oligarchy—the effects were felt in every area of life.

The military machine formed in the Roman Republic united first the Italian peninsula and then the entire Mediterranean basin. In these conquests the state showed political skill, tenacity, and power of calculation easily superior to the volatile policies of Greek city-states. But in the process, a series of military dynasts became so powerful and ambitious that, over the course of a long revolution, they destroyed the republican constitution. This revolution also killed the elements of political freedom that had been put into place under the Republic. The response was the formation of a far more powerful autocracy, from which Europe was to descend—the Roman Empire.

I. The Unification of Italy (to 264 B.C.)

THE GEOGRAPHY OF ITALY

Italy is not, like Greece, divided into many small valleys or islands. The main geographic feature is the Apennine range, which runs diagonally across Italy in the north and then turns southward to bisect the peninsula. North of the Apennines, the Po River flows through a large, fertile valley that was for centuries the home of Celtic peoples known as Gauls. The hills of Italy, unlike those of Greece, are gentle enough for pasturing. The landscape is of unsurpassed beauty; some of the best Roman poetry—by Virgil, Horace, and Catullus—hymns the delights of the land and the pleasure of farming.

EARLY ROME

The legends about the founding of Rome by Aeneas or by Romulus and Remus are myths, so we must depend on archaeology to recover early Roman history. Pottery finds suggest that the site of Rome, along the Tiber River in the plain of Latium, was inhabited as early as 1400 B.C. Ancient scholars relied on myths to date the "founding" of Rome in 753 B.C. This date is not to be taken seriously as the moment when Rome came into existence, but there must have been considerable habitation in the area by that time, especially on the seven hills that surround the city. About 625 B.C. the settlers drained the marshes below the hills and built a central marketplace, the Forum. This was to be forever the center of Roman history.

Etruscans and Greeks Beside the Romans themselves, two other peoples are important in the early history of Rome. The first were the Etruscans, who actually dominated early Rome from about 625 to 509 B.C. The name *Roma* is Etruscan, and at least some of the kings of Rome were Etruscans. The origin of the Etruscans is obscure and has provoked a famous controversy. Some ancient sources say that they were a native European people, while the Greek historian Herodotus asserts that they arrived from Asia Minor. In any case, they appeared in Italy soon after

▶ This sarcophagus is from a late sixth-century Etruscan tomb. The reclining couple on the lid reflects the influence of Greek art on the style of the Etruscans.

The art of Etruscan tombs often showed dancing and banqueting in the afterlife. This fifth-century painting, from the Tomb of the Lionesses at Tarquinia, shows two dancers with jugs of wine.

800 B.C., in the region north of the Tiber River known as Etruria (modern Tuscany). Their language is still undeciphered even though thousands of short Etruscan inscriptions exist.

The Etruscans had an urbane, technologically advanced culture and traded with Greeks and Phoenicians; Greek vases, especially, have been found in Etruscan tombs, and Etruscan art is strongly influenced by that of the Greeks. They also bequeathed to the Romans the technique of building temples, and they introduced the worship of a triad of gods (Juno, Minerva, Jupiter) and the custom of examining the innards of animals to foretell the future.

The second non-Roman people were the Greeks. Beginning about 750, they established about 50 poleis in southern Italy and on the island of Sicily. So numerous were the Greek cities in southern Italy that the Romans called this region *Magna Graecia* ("Great Greece") and thus gave us the name *Greeks* for the people who called themselves Hellenes.[1]

Greek culture from these colonies influenced the Etruscans and, in turn, the Romans. For example, from the village of Cumae, the oldest Greek colony in Italy, the Etruscans learned the Western version of the Greek alphabet and passed it on to Rome; it became the basis for the alphabet used throughout the Western world.

About 500 B.C. (the Romans reckoned the date as 509) Rome somehow freed itself of its last Etruscan king and established a republican form of government. Thereafter, the Etruscans gradually declined as a power until they were finally absorbed by the Romans in the fourth century.

---

[1]The name *Graikoi* (Graeci, or Greeks) probably comes from one or more villages in central Greece called Graia; one such place is mentioned in Homer's *Iliad* (2.498).

The Early Constitution A large part of the history of the Roman Republic concerns the development of its constitution; this was never a written document but rather a set of carefully observed procedures and customs. The Roman system, like that of Sparta, had three major components, which tended to offset and balance one another. The executives were two officers called consuls, who were the supreme civil and military magistrates. On rare occasions the Romans appointed a man as "dictator," whose authority surpassed that of the consuls, but his office was limited to six months. There was also an advisory body of elder statesmen called the Senate. Finally, there were assemblies including all adult male citizens.

The consuls were elected annually by the Assembly of the Centuries, which was made up of the entire army; in this assembly the wealthier citizens voted first and could determine the result if they all voted the same way. This arrangement illustrates the hierarchical and conservative instincts of the Roman mind; so does the law providing that, in cases where the two consuls disagreed, one could block the action of the other, and the consul advocating no action had to prevail. Consuls possessed a right known as *imperium*, which gave them the power to command troops and to execute any other assignments they might receive from the Senate.

There were two other assemblies, the more important being the Assembly of Tribes, which was divided into 35 voting units (or tribes). Membership in a specific tribe was determined by a man's residence. This tribal assembly elected officers who did not command troops and therefore did not have imperium; and these magistrates, known as quaestors and aediles, looked after various financial matters and public works. The other body was the Assembly of Curiae, or wards of the city; this assembly met only to validate decisions taken elsewhere and gradually lost importance. Over the centuries, the Assembly of Tribes became the most active of the three assemblies and passed most of Rome's major laws.

The Senate was the nerve center of the whole state. It did not, in the Republic, pass laws, but it did appoint commanders, assign funds, and generally set the direction of the state. The Roman

▸ This temple in central Rome, from the second century B.C., perhaps dedicated to Portunus, the god of harbors, is a typical Roman temple with a closed room for an image of the god. An altar stood in front. The columns are in the Greek Ionic order, and the temple has a deep basement, common in Etruscan building. Thus the temple unites the three cultures that went into the making of Rome.

▶ **Many inscriptions, written by professional painters, in favor of this or that candidate in elections have been found on the walls of Pompeii, the city buried in the eruption of A.D. 79.**

Senate house, which still stands in the Forum, was thus the cradle of Roman power. The senators (usually about 300) were men who had held elected offices, and membership was for life. Their solid conservatism acted to restrain hotheaded politicians, and more than once they provided the moral leadership that saw the state through a military crisis. Rome had no political parties in the modern sense, but the Senate did have factions that were rivals in the struggle for power.

But the real basis of political power was the family: Indeed, modern historians have learned how to tell the story of the Republic through the study of the family. Alliances, divorces, marriages, and adoptions could all add to the political power of the family. A larger unit, the *gens* (or clan), included a group of related families consisting of, for example, all Romans whose second name was Cornelius or Aemilius. The great clans and their subdivisions contrived to maintain such firm control over high office that by about 100 B.C. it was rare for any man to attain the consulship who lacked ancestors who had already been consuls. Such an outsider (for example, the orator Cicero) was referred to as a "new man."

THE STRUGGLE OF THE ORDERS (494–287 B.C.)

Within the citizen body, the Romans established a distinction that had no parallel in any Greek state. The patricians, a small number of clans (about 5 to 7 percent of the whole people), were recognized as being socially and legally superior to the vast majority, who were called plebeians. Ancient sources do not explain how the distinction arose; it was probably based on wealth gained from owning land and on the less easily defined criterion of social leadership. Membership in the patrician class was based on birth (or, occasionally, adoption), and originally only pa-

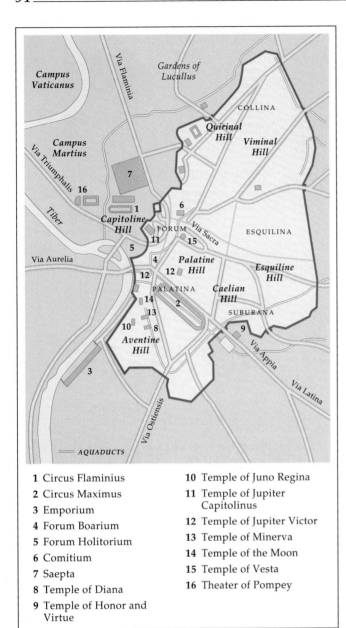

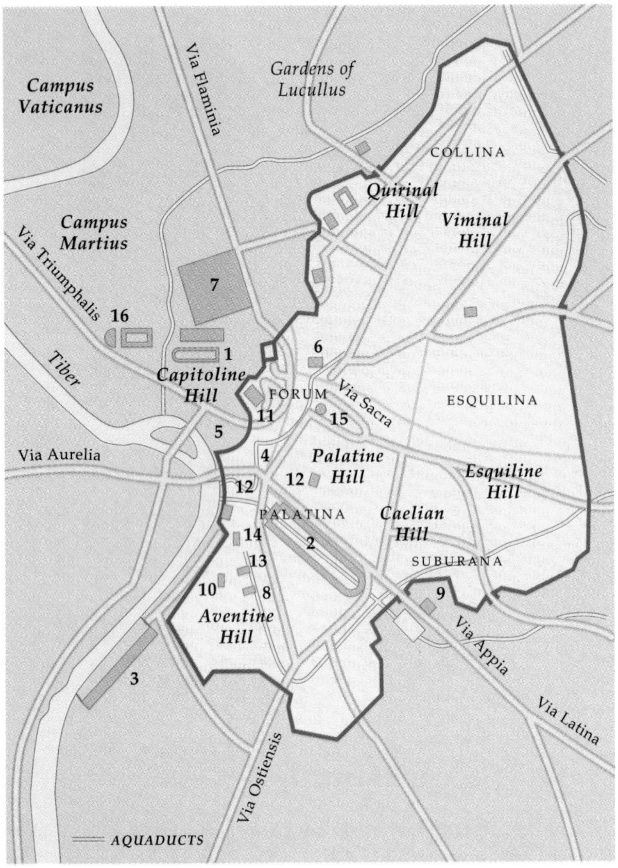

1 Circus Flaminius
2 Circus Maximus
3 Emporium
4 Forum Boarium
5 Forum Holitorium
6 Comitium
7 Saepta
8 Temple of Diana
9 Temple of Honor and Virtue
10 Temple of Juno Regina
11 Temple of Jupiter Capitolinus
12 Temple of Jupiter Victor
13 Temple of Minerva
14 Temple of the Moon
15 Temple of Vesta
16 Theater of Pompey

Map 4.1 THE CITY OF ROME IN REPUBLICAN TIMES

tricians could belong to the Senate and hold office.

The plebeians did gain a number of privileges in a long process called the struggle of the orders (or classes). When the struggle ended, the plebeians could point to significant gains, but the great families were still secure in their domination. Indeed, one effect of the struggle of the orders was to make the state an even more efficient machine for conquest, since the plebeians could now feel that they had a more favorable position within the system and were thus more willing to fight for their country.

Concessions to the Plebeians The plebeians' first victory in the struggle came in 494 B.C., when they evidently threatened to secede from the state.[2] They now obtained the right to elect annually two men, called tribunes, to represent them; the number eventually rose to ten. The powers of the tribunes reveal the Roman genius for political compromise in the interests of a united state. The patricians evidently recognized that spokesmen for the people were a necessary evil, and they took an oath that made it a religious crime to violate or injure the body of a tribune. The "sacrosanctity" of the tribunes allowed them to interfere in any action, since no one could lay hands on them. Out of this protected status arose the famous veto power of the tribunes (sometimes called *intercession*); they could forbid any magistrate from acting and could even arrest consuls. Such power might have threatened to cause anarchy, but in fact, because it reassured the plebeians, it proved to be a stabilizing influence.

Other extensions of privilege to the plebeians included the publication of a code of laws, in 450 B.C. on the so-called 12 wooden tablets, and the right, in 445, to intermarry with patricians. Intermarriage created a patrician-plebeian aristocracy that replaced the original one restricted to patricians alone.

In 367 B.C. it was agreed that one consul each year should be a plebeian. Another office was now created—that of praetor, a kind of assistant consul who also held imperium. Eventually there were eight praetors elected every year, but there were never more than two consuls at a time. Therefore, as the road to the highest office narrowed, a praetor who wanted to become consul was well advised to observe the generally traditional ways of Roman politics.

[2]The sources give contradictory dates for, and accounts of, many events in Roman history down to about 280 B.C.; the order adopted here cannot always be proved right in every detail.

The state also restricted, in 367 B.C., the amount of public land that any citizen could occupy (the precise acreage allowed is disputed). This measure prevented the upper classes from acquiring an overwhelming share of farming land and made possible a dramatic growth of manpower among farmers who could, when necessary, serve in the army. It was, in fact, the huge reserve of fighting men that guaranteed Rome's expansion within Italy and its victories in the long Punic Wars.

The End of the Struggle of the Orders The final concession to the plebeians came in 287 B.C., when a law (the Lex Hortensia)[3] made decisions of the Assembly of Tribes binding on the whole state without further action by any other body. Thus the common people now had the absolute legal right to pass laws; but in practice most legislation had the sponsorship of the Senate before it came before the Assembly of Tribes. The struggle of the orders was a real conflict, and it led to greater power for the plebeians; but the patrician-plebeian upper class managed to control the changes in the constitution before they could lead to the actual direction of affairs by the masses.

THE STRUGGLE OF THE ORDERS

The main stages by which the Roman plebeians attained a measure of equality with the patricians are as follows:

494 B.C.	First "secession" of plebeians; appointment of two tribunes (later rising to ten).
450	The Laws of the Twelve Tables, Rome's first written law code, published.
445	The Lex Canuleia permits marriage between plebeians and patricians.
367	Licinian-Sextian laws limiting amount of public land anyone could hold.
366	First plebeian consul.
287	Laws passed by plebeians are binding on the whole state; final victory of plebeians.

EARLY EXPANSION OF ROME

Rome's First Conquests While the Romans were developing their form of government, they were also expanding their holdings on the Italian peninsula. Sometimes they could use peaceful diplomacy, for example, by making a treaty with other peoples living, like them, in the plain of Latium. More often they turned to outright military conquest in wars that were clearly long and arduous. One important victory was won over the last remaining Etruscan stronghold, the town of Veii, just across the Tiber River, which they took and destroyed in 396 B.C.

The period of conquest was not uniformly successful and was in fact punctuated by one major disaster. About 390 B.C. a large force of Gauls left their stronghold in the Po valley and captured part of Rome. They exacted a ransom as the price of their withdrawal, but Rome then renewed its policy of expansion, showing the resilience that made it, in the words of the historian Edward Gibbon, "sometimes vanquished in battle, always victorious in war."[4] By the 290s Rome dominated the Italian peninsula as far south as the Greek city-states of Magna Graecia.

In the 280s some of the Greek cities summoned Pyrrhus, the king of Epirus (near modern Albania), to direct a campaign against Rome. Pyrrhus fought two successful battles in 280 B.C., but at a heavy cost in casualties to his own men (hence the phrase "a Pyrrhic victory"). The Romans again rebounded from defeat and Pyrrhus abandoned his allies in 275, leaving the Romans free to pursue their conquests. By 265 B.C. Rome controlled the entire Italian peninsula but had not yet mastered the Po valley.

The Roman Federation Rome showed great administrative skill in organizing the conquered

---

[3]All Roman laws were named for their sponsors, in this case one Hortensius; since *lex* is a feminine noun in Latin, the adjective with it must end in *-a*.

[4]*Decline and Fall of the Roman Empire*, chap. 38.

communities by establishing different degrees of privilege and responsibility among them. Residents of a few favored communities were granted the most highly prized status, full Roman citizenship. This meant that they were on the same legal footing as the Romans; they enjoyed the protection of Roman law, they could make legal wills to pass on their property, and they could even hold office in Rome. Members of some other communities became citizens who could not vote but had the right of intermarriage with Romans. At a lower level of privilege were the allied states (*socii*). They received Rome's protection from other peoples and were also liable to provide troops. This carefully designed system of confederation enabled the Romans to solve an administrative problem that had frustrated the Greek poleis: how to control a large territory without having to demolish or transform the conqueror's own institutions. Even more important, the creation of this chain of alliances greatly expanded the manpower available to Rome in its progressive domination of the Mediterranean.

Map 4.2 Italy in 265 B.C., on the Eve of the Punic Wars

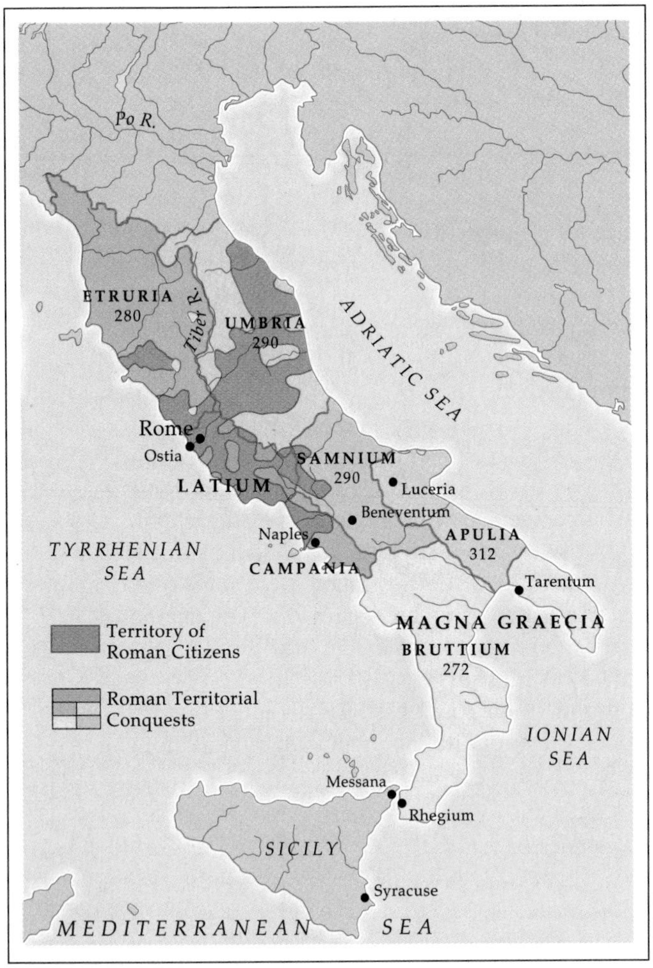

II. The Age of Mediterranean Conquest (264–133 B.C.)

THE PUNIC WARS

Rome—by which we now mean not only the ancient city but also the group of peoples in Italy allied with the city—at last had the strength in population to become a world power. The Romans achieved that goal in three wars with Carthage, a city that had been founded by Phoenicians about 700 B.C. and over the next century had established its own Mediterranean empire. By the time Rome had unified the Italian peninsula, Carthage controlled cities in northern Africa, parts of Spain, the islands of Corsica and Sardinia, and much of Sicily. It was beyond comparison the leading naval power in the western Mediterranean and could live off the tribute paid by its possessions. With good reason a German historian called Carthage "the London of antiquity."

The confrontation with Rome began in 264 B.C. as a minor conflict over the Sicilian city of Messana (modern Messina). The war soon became a contest for control of the island of Sicily itself and was the first of the three Punic Wars, so named from the Latin word *Poeni* for the Phoenicians who had founded Carthage. Roman tenacity finally won this war in 241, but with heavy casualties. Carthage abandoned Sicily entirely, large parts of the island passed to Rome, and it became the first Roman province (a territory outside Italy controlled by Rome). In 238 B.C. the Romans seized the islands of Corsica and Sardinia, formerly held by Carthage, and these islands, administered together, formed the second province.

The second Punic War (219–202 B.C.) was the most critical of the three. A quarrel arose over Saguntum, a town in Spain friendly to Rome. Hannibal, the brilliant Carthaginian general, seized Saguntum, thus in effect opening war with Rome, and determined to carry the war to the enemy. In autumn 218 he led his army from Spain across the Alps and down into Italy. Once there he hoped to arouse the Gallic tribes in the Po valley and break up the alliances of the various peoples with Rome, following which he would conquer Rome itself. In the end, Hannibal's twofold strategy failed. He won a stupendous victory over the Romans at Cannae, in southeastern Italy, in 216 B.C., which has remained a classic study for strategists ever since; but not even then could he arouse the allies to revolt. At least half of them chose to remain loyal to Rome, and without their help Hannibal's manpower was no match for that of the Roman federation.

While Hannibal was in Italy, the Roman commander Publius Cornelius Scipio carried the war into Spain. In 209 B.C. he captured the important city of New Carthage and by 206 he controlled most of Spain. In 204 he landed in Africa, near Carthage itself, where his victories brought about the recall of Hannibal from Italy and set the stage for a final clash between these two great generals and their forces. Scipio won the decisive battle in 202, at Zama in North Africa. In honor of the victory, Scipio received the name *Africanus* and proudly added it to his traditional Roman name. Besides paying Rome a huge indemnity, Carthage had to give up all its territory except its immediate surroundings in Africa and was forbidden to raise an army without Roman permission.

Thus the second war ended in a hard-earned victory for Roman perseverance and skill; but a large bill would later have to be paid. Hannibal had laid waste large tracts of farming land in southern Italy and had driven many farmers off their soil. In casualties, too, the cost to Rome had been severe: It is estimated that Roman military manpower fell from about 285,000 in 218 to about 235,000 in 203.

The third and final Punic War was a squalid affair, lasting from 149 to 146 B.C. There was in Rome a bitterly anti-Carthaginian group, led by a former consul, Marcus Cato, whose name has become symbolic of narrow intolerance. He succeeded in provoking this war and in making it a campaign of punishment against Carthage. Another Scipio, Aemilianus, captured and destroyed Carthage in 146. The city was utterly razed and cursed (the tale that the victors poured salt into the soil is, however, a modern fiction), and the territory became the Roman province called simply Africa. The conquest of the territory formerly held by Carthage in Europe was completed as Rome conquered almost all of Spain by 133 B.C.

EXPANSION IN THE EASTERN MEDITERRANEAN

In the following decades the Romans continued their conquests until they had mastered the whole Mediterranean basin. Historians have long debated whether this policy represented deliberate imperialism or was at least partly accidental. Certainly the first stage was forced on Rome by the king of Macedonia, Philip V (ruled 221–179 B.C.). He drew Rome into war by forming an alliance with Hannibal after the battle of Cannae and thus opened the gate through which, over centuries, Roman troops and administrators

THE ROMAN PROVINCES

The dates when some of the major Roman provinces were formed.

227 B.C.	Sicily and Sardinia.
197	Nearer and Farther Spain.
146	Macedonia; Africa (old territory of Carthage).
129	Asia (old territory of Pergamum).
c. 120	Transalpine Gaul.
62	Syria.
16–13	Three Gauls (northern France, conquered by Caesar).

poured as far east as Armenia and changed the course of European history.

During this era Rome also became involved in war with Antiochus III, the Macedonian ruler of Syria, the kingdom founded by Seleucus after the death of Alexander. Roman forces defeated his army at Magnesia in 190 B.C.—another significant moment in Rome's expansion, as Roman legions left Europe and fought in Asia for the first time.

After further quarrels, the Roman Senate realized that outright annexation of the Greek mainland was the only way to secure its interests. Therefore, in 146 B.C., Macedonia and southern Greece were combined into a province—Rome's first acquisition of territory in the Greek world. Thus the Romans brought to an end the independent political life of mainland Greece, and from this time on their dominance in the Mediterranean could not be denied or reversed.

Some experienced rulers in the region were shrewd enough to perceive what had happened and began a process of accommodation to Rome. For example, in 133 B.C., the last king of Pergamum died without leaving a successor and the Romans found that he had willed his kingdom to Rome—surely because he had seen that the kingdom of Pergamum could not long survive without Roman protection. Four years later Rome created the province of Asia, based on the territory of Pergamum (see Map 4.3). This province possessed great wealth and offered tempting opportunities for a governor of Asia to enrich himself through corruption; the post became highly desirable for ambitious politicians and also brought with it a posting to the pleasant climate of the beautifully built Greek cities.

Map 4.3 THE EXPANSION OF THE ROMAN REPUBLIC, 241—44 B.C.

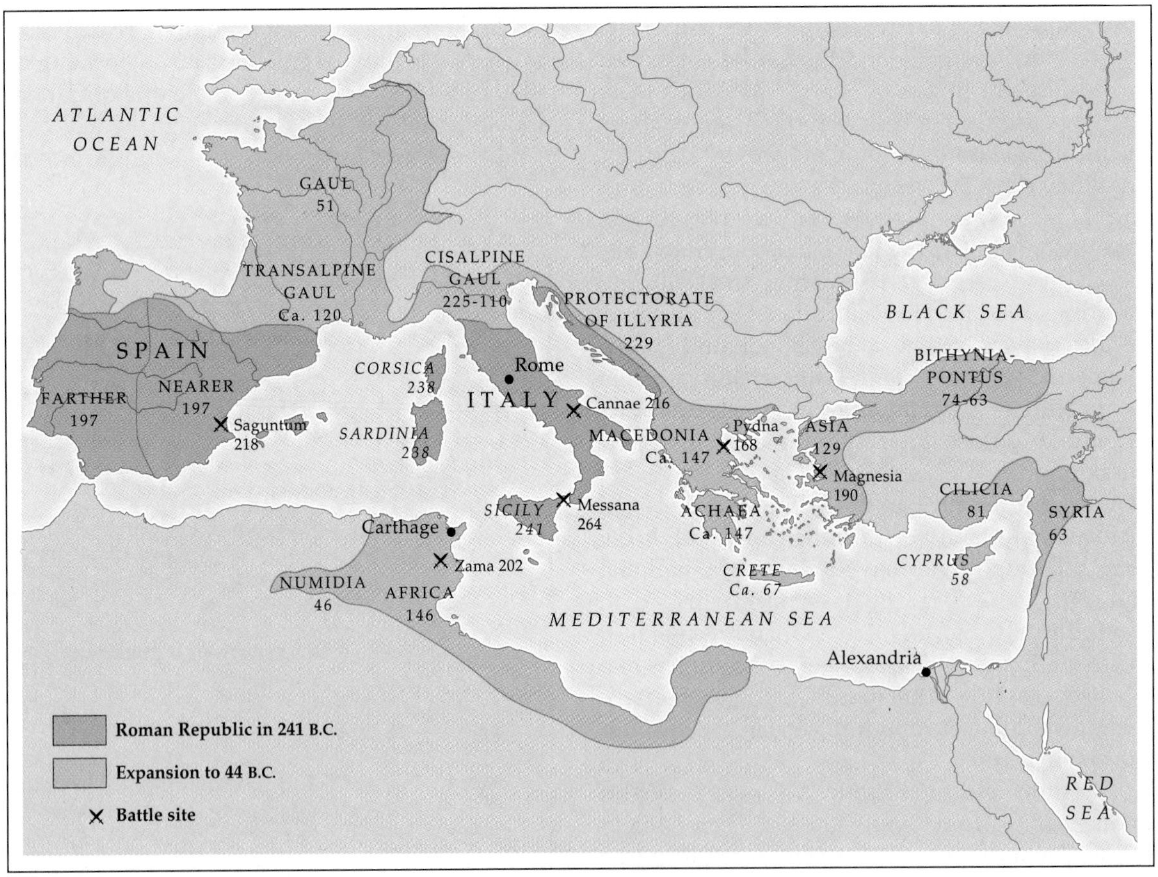

THE NATURE OF ROMAN EXPANSION

Rome's success in its domination of the Mediterranean rested on certain unique historical conditions. Early in its history, events had forced the city to seek defensive alliances. After the expulsion of the Etruscan monarchs, for example, Rome had to unite militarily with its neighbors in the plain of Latium against a possible Etruscan counterattack. Constant wars in the fourth and third centuries, such as the invasion by the Gauls in 390, further emphasized the need for common security. The result was a commitment to, and mastery of, military force that proved to be unsurpassed, and this soon developed into a highly effective and (when necessary) utterly ruthless policy of conquest. Scipio Aemilianus, for example, forced the people of Numantia, in Spain, to surrender in 133 by reducing them to cannibalism and even cut off the hands of 400 young men in a neighboring city who had advocated aiding their Spanish brethren. The Senate at home considered Aemilianus' achievements worthy of a triumphal parade, the highest military honor that Romans could bestow on a successful commander.

Provincial Administration The Latin word *provincia* means "a duty assigned to a magistrate," and the Romans extended the meaning to denote the various regions that they acquired through conquest. The Senate chose the governors for the various provinces, often giving them the title *proconsul* ("in place of a consul"). These governors ruled their provinces with absolute power, though they could not violate Roman law or act illegally against Roman citizens. Some provinces were well ruled, but others were notorious for their corrupt governors. From the Roman view the advantage of the system was its efficiency: Rebellions were not common, and troops stationed in the provinces could maintain control without resorting to massacres.

The provinces furnished financial support for the Roman Republic. Some had to pay tribute in various forms, usually food, while others were assigned a fixed sum of money. In order to obtain these taxes, the state devised a convenient, but corruptible, system of tax collection. Companies of tax collectors bid for the contracts to collect the taxes of certain provinces, especially Asia. They paid the state a fixed sum in advance and then tried to make a profit by collecting taxes in excess of what they had paid. The natives of the provinces were nearly helpless against the raids of the *publicani*, as tax collectors were called. Their only protection was the governor of the province, who was supposed to see that the *publicani* did not collect more than a reasonable amount. Unfortunately, however, the collectors could use their funds as bribes to persuade the governor to overlook their rapacity.[5] These tax collectors came from a nonsenatorial class known as *equestrians* (their name, *equites*, originally meant "cavalry"). Besides collecting taxes, equestrians formed companies to build roads and aqueducts, owned land, and managed businesses of all kinds. Senators were forbidden to be in business, and some equestrians could far outstrip senators in wealth through their multiple enterprises, but they held no political office.

ROMAN SOCIETY IN THE REPUBLIC

The Roman Family The forceful part played by the family in Roman politics was reflected in the organization of the family itself. The Romans accepted direction from the top in most areas of their society, and this kind of structure was built into the family of patricians and plebeians alike. The father of the family, the *paterfamilias*, was the absolute owner of the whole family, which included children, land, other property, animals, and slaves. So long as he lived, his sons, even if married with their own households, remained in his power. On the death of the father, each of his sons became a *paterfamilias* in his own family. Such a severe system differs from anything known in Greece but has parallels in Israelite society.

In early Rome, wives were also legally within the power of their fathers or husbands (again as in ancient Israel), and their chief virtues were considered to be silence and obedience. The sources tell stories about women legally executed by their families for adultery or other offenses. A young woman was normally married at about 14,

[5]Cicero, a firm supporter of the *publicani*, called them "the flower of the Roman equestrians, the ornament of the state, and the foundation of the Republic."

as in Greece, and in early times she was transferred to her new family and lost her right to her native family's property. But this system could not last forever. As Rome became wealthier, the narrow framework of women's lives was loosened. Marriage less often involved the placing of a woman under the absolute power of her husband. The reason for this change was not necessarily a wish to respect women's rights: Rather, it was that wealthy families with well-off daughters did not wish to lose control over their property. Marriages now became less stable, and we find women of prominent families, especially in Rome itself, moving in society, and even from husband to husband, with a freedom impossible in Greece. In apparent alarm at the emancipation of women, the elder Cato supported an existing law forbidding women to possess jewelry and wear colored dresses, which tells us that they were doing so in the second century B.C. Despite Cato's dislike of such women's liberation, we do not find in Rome that undercurrent of fear of the mysterious powers of women that can be seen in Greek myth and literature.

As in Greece, Roman women could not hold office or vote, but they greatly surpassed Greek women as influences behind the scenes. One especially eminent woman was Cornelia, the daughter of Scipio Africanus, the victorious general in the second Punic War. On the death of her husband she refused all offers of marriage, including one from a king of Egypt, and devoted herself to the education of her 12 children, among whom were the tribunes Tiberius and Gaius Gracchus. She was a woman of high education who maintained a salon and whose letters were praised for their elegant style; indeed, she had a position and prominence unparalleled by any woman in classical Greece.

Other women in the Republic also became important as a link between prominent families in marriage alliances, which were arranged by fathers, often for the political advantages they would confer. One notable such marriage made Julius Caesar the father-in-law of Pompey and cemented the alliance of the two men during Caesar's rise to supreme power. Julia, the daughter of the first emperor, Augustus, was also married to men favored by this emperor, in order to continue his family line. The influence of women in politics continued to grow enormously during the Roman Empire, when the long periods of an emperor's reign allowed wives and mothers of rulers to learn and control the levers of power in the imperial court. Yet we must not exaggerate the degree to which Roman women were liberated. In all periods, as in Greece, sarcophagi and tomb reliefs portray men with their wives in conventional poses, and on some inscriptions, the women are praised for modest domestic virtues: "She was chaste, she was thrifty, she remained at home, she spun wool."

Religion Roman religion consisted largely of forms of worship that upheld Roman tradition. Within the household, the father acted as the priest and led the family in its worship of household gods—for example, Janus, the god protecting the doorway; Vesta, the spirit of the hearth; and household spirits known as Lares and Penates.

Public religion, on the other hand, was closely connected with the interest of the state. Priesthoods were mainly political offices, held only by men. Women were, however, responsible for one of the most important religious duties: It fell to six virgins to maintain the sacred fire of Vesta that guarded the hearth of the state. These Vestal Virgins were held in high honor and lived in a spacious, elegant villa in the Forum; by a remarkable exception, these women were freed of the power of their father. Roman rites seem to have been designed mainly to placate the gods—almost to keep them at arm's length through sacrifices. Eventually the rites hardened into patterns whose original meaning had sometimes been forgotten; but so long as the priests did not deviate from routine, the Romans assumed that the gods were satisfied and would not frustrate their enterprises.

As for mythology, nearly all of it was an adaptation of Greek legend, and Roman gods were often Greek deities with Roman names. The Greek father-god Zeus became Iuppiter, or Jupiter; his wife Hera became Juno; Athena became Minerva; Hermes became Mercury; and so on. These gods were officially worshiped in public and also in the home along with the household deities, these latter being minor gods with no connection to the Greek pantheon. Perhaps be-

▶ **A late Republican gravestone showing one Lucius Vibius and his wife and child. Roman realism is evident in the portraiture. The face of the man suggests the determined conservatism that shaped the Roman character during the Republican period.**

cause Greek myths often show gods behaving spitefully or immorally, the Romans also created certain uplifting ideals—such as Virtus (manly conduct), Pax (peace), Fides (loyalty), and Pudor (modesty)—and transformed them into gods.

Early Roman Literature It may seem surprising that it took the Romans centuries to develop a literature. Homeric epic is older than the Greek city-states themselves, but Rome had been independent of the Etruscans for the better part of three centuries before a significant literature emerged. Evidently the Romans needed contact with Greek civilization, which came about during the age of conquest, to stimulate their own literary efforts. After the first Punic War, one Naevius wrote an epic poem (thus imitating Homer), but it has not survived.

The earliest preserved Latin literature is the comedies, influenced by the Greeks, that were written by Plautus (250?–184? B.C.) and Terence (190?–159? B.C.). These playwrights imitated Greek New Comedy, as it is called, in which the plays were entirely fiction. The Romans did not approve of Old Comedy, such as the plays of Aristophanes, which savagely lampooned active politicians. Plautus filled his comedies with stock situations and characters, such as mistaken identities, lecherous old men, and frustrated romances. One of his plays about mistaken identities, the *Menaechmi*, was used by Shakespeare as the model for his *Comedy of Errors*. Terence wrote comedy in a more refined and delicate style than Plautus. His characters are less earthy, and the humor emerges from more subtle situations or such human foibles as greed.

The Greek Polybius (200?–118? B.C.), though not a Latin writer, helped create a Roman literary tradition as a historian of the Roman Republic. He was deported as a hostage to Rome in the 160s, where he met many Roman statesmen and became an expert in Roman history. He wrote a general history of the Greco-Roman world from the first Punic War down to his own times, largely to demonstrate the inevitable domination of the Mediterranean by the Romans.

Polybius believed that much of Rome's success in government was due to its well-designed constitution—a commendable mixed form of state that would probably long maintain Rome's power. He traveled widely and insisted on the need to visit sites in order to grasp the importance of geography to history. His work is analytic and methodical and attempts to revive the high standards of historical writing that Herodotus and Thucydides had established. He is both the most important historian of the Hellenistic Age and the most reliable guide to earlier Roman history.

III. The Roman Revolution (133–27 B.C.)

SOCIAL CHANGE AND THE GRACCHI

The Changing World of Italy The breakdown of the Roman Republic has been called Hannibal's legacy, for the ravages of years of fighting up and down Italy had brought many farmers to the point of ruin. On the other hand, wealthy citizens had enriched themselves with booty and the spoils of war. The less fortunate had often lost their land or were willing to sell it to these newly wealthy men. There had also been a great increase in the slave population on Italian soil from prisoners of war, and these slaves depressed the wages paid to private workers. Often the displaced farmers had little choice but to join the ranks of the permanently unemployed. Their poverty threatened to impede the recruitment of soldiers into the Roman army, for Rome had nothing like a modern war treasury, and only men who had enough money to buy their own armor could be drafted into the legions. Without sufficient recruits, the gains from the conquests might be lost.

Tiberius Gracchus Two ambitious young Roman statesmen, Tiberius and Gaius Gracchus, moved to solve these problems. Their mother, Cornelia, was a well-known daughter of a great family; her father was the Publius Cornelius Scipio Africanus who had won the war against Hannibal. She had married a prominent plebeian politician, Tiberius Gracchus, and thus her sons were plebeian, though descended from the loftiest aristocracy. Tiberius, the older brother (162–133 B.C.), became tribune for 133 and proposed a bill to the Assembly of Tribes that would allow the state to assign parcels of public land, reclaimed from the wealthy, to dispossessed farmers, with the aim of increasing the supply of potential recruits for the army. The bill was opposed by another tribune, who tried to veto it on behalf of vested interests. Tiberius persuaded the people to remove this tribune from office, a dangerous action barely within the constitution. Once such a step had been taken, what tribune would be safe in the future from a similar threat? But the people followed Tiberius, and the bill was passed.

▶ An unknown Roman of the Republic. The realistic portrait shows the dignity and virility of a Roman *paterfamilias*.

The distribution of land was in progress when Tiberius decided to run for reelection. This was a breach of custom, for tribunes held office for only one year. Some of his opponents feared that he might seize permanent leadership of the propertyless and lead them into social revolution. A group of senators, late in 133, took the law into their own hands and provoked a riot in which Tiberius was clubbed to death—an event that gave grim warning of a new intensity in Rome's political struggles. Above all, the taboo against assassination had been violated, and this first step, once taken, became easier to repeat. Despite Tiberius' death, the distribution of land continued, and his enemies even took credit for the success of the project.

Gaius Gracchus Tiberius' younger brother, Gaius, became tribune 10 years later, in 123. He proposed several measures that sought to limit the prerogatives of the Senate. One of the most important concerned the extortion court, which investigated cases of alleged extortion by provincial governors and tax collectors. The jurors, all senators, were usually not severe in judging governors, who were fellow members of the Senate. Gaius had a bill passed that assigned the seats on this jury to members of the equestrian class.

All tax collectors were equestrians, and it was now they who had the potential to favor members of their group who might be accused and brought to trial. Gaius' arrangements were later revised, but he was the first to make the extortion court the subject of a bitter political quarrel.

Gaius weakened his own standing with the people by proposing that Roman citizenship be offered to large numbers of Italians who were not yet Roman citizens. They had been asking for this status to protect themselves against having their land confiscated for distribution to those whom the Romans were resettling. But the voters of Rome, warned by Gaius' opponents that they would now have to share their privileges with outsiders, refused to extend their citizenship.

Like his brother, Gaius Gracchus came to a violent end. After he left office, his enemies asserted that he was planning a revolution. The Senate then instructed one of the consuls for the year 121 to "see to it that the state suffered no harm," thus inviting the consul to use force to suppress the younger Gracchus. When the consul raised a mob to hunt him down, Gaius had one of his own slaves kill him.

The Gracchi had unleashed a whirlwind when they invited the Assembly of Tribes to take a more activist role. It is true that the people had long possessed the right to legislate in this assembly, but they had not always had the will; nor had ambitious tribunes always dared to use such a weapon. But now demagogues began to turn more and more to this assembly to pass bills in favor of their military patrons. From this moment began the slow but sure Roman revolution.

THE ROMAN REVOLUTION

The main landmarks in the Roman revolution were as follows:

133 B.C.	Tiberius Gracchus elected tribune and is killed in riot.
123–2	Gaius Gracchus tribune; equestrians gain control of extortion court; Gaius killed.
107	First consulship of Marius.
91–88	War with Italian allies.
81–79	Sulla's dictatorship.
70	First consulship of Pompey and Crassus.
66	Pompey given command against Mithridates in Asia.
59	Julius Caesar consul, receives command in Gaul.
58–50	Caesar's conquest of Gaul.
49	Caesar invades Italy, opening of civil war.
44	Caesar murdered.
31	Battle of Actium, defeat of Mark Antony.
27	Supremacy of Octavian, later called Augustus; beginning of Roman Empire.

THE YEARS OF THE WARLORDS

The Gracchi could not protect themselves from the violence of the Senate because they had no army. But as Roman conquests brought the state into further wars, powerful generals appeared who did have the support of their armies and used it to seize power. Their struggles against one another undermined the republican constitution and the state finally collapsed into dictatorship.

Marius The first general to play this game was Gaius Marius (157?–86 B.C.), a "new man" from the country near Rome. He is a crucial figure because he changed, radically and forever, the membership of the Roman army and the direction of its loyalty. He gained high prestige by winning a war (111–106 B.C.) against Jugurtha, a king in North Africa. Marius' reputation grew even more after he drove back an attempted invasion (105–101 B.C.) by some Germanic tribes moving toward northern Italy. Such was his stature in this period that he was consul for five consecutive years and dominated politics from 107 to 100 B.C.

In order to raise large numbers of men for the German wars, Marius abolished the old requirement that a soldier had to own at least a modest amount of property, and he also accepted volunteers instead of just drafting men for service. As a result, the army came to be composed largely of poor men who served their commander, received booty from him, relied on him as their main patron, and expected him to obtain for them a grant of land that they could then farm after they were discharged. Thus Marius converted the army into an instrument for ambitious commanders during the remaining years of the Republic and even throughout the Roman Empire.

The War with the Italians The Italian peoples who were Rome's allies had never been granted Roman citizenship, and in 91 B.C. some of them proclaimed themselves independent and opened a war that continued until 88. In the end the Romans negotiated with the Italians and allowed them to acquire citizenship. But the fact that it required a war to obtain this concession shows that both the upper classes—the senators and equestrians—and the common people were still jealous of their privileges.

Senatorial Reaction under Sulla The Italian War made the reputation of another powerful general, Lucius Cornelius Sulla (138?–78 B.C.). In the 80s civil war broke out in Rome among various factions of senators. One group rallied behind Sulla and his legions, seeing in them the best vehicle for their own ambitions. In 88 Sulla invaded the city of Rome itself with his supporters—the first but not the last time that the ancient city was thus seized by Romans themselves. All that Sulla wanted for himself was command of a war against Mithridates, who ruled the kingdom of Pontus (extending along the south coast of the Black Sea) from 120 to 63 B.C. Sulla departed for this campaign in 87 B.C., and during his absence, other politicians, just as unscrupulous as he was, seized Rome in turn. But as soon as Sulla was free of his Eastern war he returned to Italy and once more occupied Rome (November 82). He had hundreds of his opponents executed and had himself named dictator without limit of time, thus breaking the customary six-month limit for holding that office.

Sulla used his supreme power to reshape the state on strictly authoritarian and conservative lines. Two forces, he thought, had menaced the rigid control over Rome that the Senate should enjoy: the tribunes of the people, who had made the Assembly of Tribes more conscious of its power, and the generals who had used the loyalty of their armies to gain political leverage. To deal with the first of these threats, Sulla forced through a law forbidding tribunes to offer legislation without prior approval from the Senate and denying them the right ever to hold any other office—a rule that would make the tribunate unattractive to young men with political ambitions.

Sulla handled the army commanders by restricting their service as governor of a province to a period of one year. This scheme neatly ensured that no commander could remain on the scene long enough to become a familiar hero to his troops and possibly the leader of a new march on Rome. He further established minimum ages

▶ **This idealized statue of the first century B.C. shows the ruthless tyrant Cornelius Sulla in the dignified pose of a classical orator.**

at which a man might hold the various offices in a political career (a consul, for example, had to be 42 or over). He also canceled the work of Gaius Gracchus on the jury system; as one might have expected from this strict traditionalist, he gave all the seats on the juries back to senators.

Sulla resigned the dictatorship in 79 B.C., a rare act in any supreme ruler, but he evidently thought he had put the Senate so firmly in control that he was no longer needed; he died in 78. To his enemies he was pitiless, and his executions of Roman citizens were horrifying, but he was also a clever political strategist. He had done his part for the conservative cause by putting the Senate in charge, but this body proved unable to manage the next generation of warlords.

The Rise of Pompey Sulla had used the tool forged by Marius—an army loyal to a commander—and another warlord soon followed his example, namely Gnaeus Pompeius (106–48 B.C.), usually called Pompey. He first gained a reputation in 77 B.C., when he was sent to Spain to end a revolt there. After completing this task, and while his army was still intact, he helped suppress a rebellion of slaves in Italy led by a Thracian slave named Spartacus. This campaign was already being waged by another ambitious Roman, Marcus Licinius Crassus, the richest man of his time. No sooner was the slave revolt crushed in 71 B.C. than the joint commanders, Pompey and Crassus, marched their armies to the gates of Rome and demanded both consulships for the year 70. Pompey was legally unqualified for this office, for he was only 36 and had held no previous magistracy. The Senate, however, lacked the will to enforce the constitution and resist the two men, and they were elected consuls.

During their consulship Pompey and Crassus canceled several of Sulla's arrangements. They restored to the tribunes their right to propose legislation, and they mixed senators and equestrians in the always controversial juries. At the end of their year in office, both consuls retired without demanding any further appointment—an action that, though at first surprising, was really consistent with Pompey's ambitions. He wanted to be the first man in the state, but he disliked committing himself to open revolution. A modern historian has compared him to Shakespeare's Macbeth: He would not play false and yet would wrongly win.

In 67 B.C. Pompey was next given an extraordinary command to deal with pirates operating in the Mediterranean who were interfering with the grain supply for Rome—a critical matter, since the city had to live on grain shipped to its harbor. Pompey fulfilled his orders and cleared the seas in a swift campaign. Then in 66 B.C. he received through the Tribal Assembly an even more important command in Asia Minor, where Rome was involved in war with Mithridates, Sulla's old enemy, who was still on his throne. Pompey successfully fought the difficult war in Asia Minor and set up a system of client kings, rulers of smaller states whose loyalty to Rome was ensured by the familiar device of "friendship."

Cicero During Pompey's absence overseas, Marcus Tullius Cicero (106–43 B.C.) became the chief nonmilitary statesman in Rome. Like Marius, he was a "new man" from the countryside, but unlike him, he chose a career in law and administration. His administrative skill won for him each successive political office at the earliest possible legal age. He was genuinely dedicated to compromise and political negotiation and thought that such procedures would establish the combined rule of the two upper classes, the senatorial and equestrian.

Cicero was also the most versatile Latin writer of his time, and his polished prose style became the model in Latin for clarity and elegance. His philosophical treatises do not follow the doctrines of any particular school; he was equally interested in Stoicism, the thought of Plato, and several other schools, and he chose whatever seemed persuasive from Greek writings for his own theories. In *On the Republic*, for example, he accepted the Platonic view that wise leaders ought to govern the state, but he disregarded the more technical aspects of Plato's philosophy.

Cicero's political speeches are a continuous record of his career and his frustrated ambitions. He enjoyed his political success as a "new man" and sought a place for himself among the upper classes, believing that they should guide the state along established constitutional lines. Unfortunately, most politicians in the later Republic could be tempted away from any allegiance to the constitution and selfishly followed their own personal advantage. Cicero never became a magnetic leader around whom others gathered. His letters are a frank and often painful record of the compromises that he was forced to make in the treacherous world of Roman politics.

When Pompey returned to Rome in 62 B.C. from his Eastern victories, he had two political aims. He wanted the Senate to ratify the arrangements he had made in Asia Minor; and he requested a grant of land for his men. This latter request, as we have seen, was nothing unusual. It reflected the relationship between a general and his troops, which was that of patron and client—one of the oldest traditions in Rome. But some senators, either jealous or fearful of his prestige, combined to frustrate his wishes. This short-term victory practically doomed the Senate and the Republic, for it drove Pompey into a political alliance with Julius Caesar, who proved to have the revolutionary will that Pompey lacked.

THE FIRST TRIUMVIRATE

Gaius Julius Caesar (100–44 B.C.), a descendant of an old patrician family, returned to Rome in 60 B.C. from his post as governor of Spain. Politically, he is an example of the aristocrat who bases his power on the common people. He, too, had enemies within the Senate, where many looked on him as a brash upstart. They refused his request to be allowed to run for the consulship of 59 in absence and then lead a triumphal parade through the city. Faced with this direct affront to his dignity, Caesar made a political bargain with Pompey and with Crassus, who was also at odds with some powerful senators over a financial matter. The three formed a coalition known to historians as the First Triumvirate, and their united influence at the polls elected Caesar as one of the consuls for 59. To confirm the bargain in a manner customary in Roman politics, Pompey married Caesar's daughter.

Caesar's Consulship and the Gallic War Caesar's influence secured allotments of land for Pompey's army and the approval of his arrangements in the East. Crassus' financial quarrel was also settled to his satisfaction. Caesar then secured for himself the command over Cisalpine Gaul (the Po valley) and the coast of Illyria for a guaranteed period of five years beginning on March 1, 59 B.C. About this time the governor of Transalpine Gaul (Provence, in the south of France) died, and this province was also added to Caesar's command.

Caesar intervened in the politics of the Gallic tribes and opened a series of campaigns that finally brought the whole area of modern France and Belgium under Roman rule. The Romans implanted in Gaul the Latin language, the origin of modern French, Roman technology, and Roman ways in general. Caesar narrated and defended

Map 4.4 GAUL IN THE TIME OF CAESAR

▸ Perhaps the most spectacular classical monument in Europe, the Pont du Gard was built in the first century A.D. to carry water to Nîmes (ancient Nemausus) in France. The water ran through a trough above the top layer of arches. The aqueduct is an example of the Romans' mastery of hydraulic technology and construction in arches.

his actions in his *Commentaries on the Gallic War*, which to this day remains a superb textbook in political-military decision making.

The Gallic War lasted from 58 to 50 B.C. Caesar's two partners in the triumvirate, Pompey and Crassus, were always suspicious of each other, but they maintained fairly good relations and even held a second consulship together in 55. They also had Caesar's command in Gaul renewed for another five years, so that it would not expire until March 1, 49, and they obtained commands for themselves. Crassus lost his life in a war in Syria in 53, while Pompey was given command over the two provinces of Spain, which he governed through assistants, preferring to remain at the center of power near Rome.

THE SUPREMACY OF JULIUS CAESAR

The Break between Caesar and the Senate Caesar's conquest of Gaul greatly enriched the state, but to his enemies it was a cause of dismay. They feared that he might use his victories, and his popularity among the people, to become another, and perhaps a permanent, Sulla. As protection against Caesar, his enemies in the Senate began to draw Pompey into their camp. Some of them had quarreled with him in the past, but they were willing to gamble that they could eliminate him when they no longer needed him.

As 49 B.C. opened, the Senate met in a state near hysteria. A small band of implacable senators forced through a motion ordering Caesar to lay down his command, even though he was then taking no action beyond remaining in his province of Cisalpine Gaul. The Senate passed a decree establishing martial law and ordering Pompey to command the armies of Rome against Caesar. The ill-advised Pompey accepted the command; but in doing so he signed his own death warrant and condemned the Republic to extinction in yet another civil war. Finally, the Senate defied the oldest of Roman traditions by threatening the lives of any tribunes who opposed these extreme measures. They thus handed Caesar a superb theme for his own propaganda: He could proclaim that he was defending the rights of the tribunes, the common people of Rome who had elected them, and the men in his army who had loyally served in the Gallic wars.

Caesar's Invasion of Italy Caesar saw that his enemies were in effect challenging him to war and decided that he had no course but to fight for his dignity and, as he could now assert, for the people and their sacred tribunes. On about January 11, 49 B.C., he crossed the boundary of his province, the small Rubicon River north of Ravenna, thus invading his own country at the head of Roman legions.

Caesar advanced swiftly, and Pompey and his followers had to retreat to Greece; Caesar pursued them and won a decisive battle in 48 B.C. at the town of Pharsalus, in Thessaly. Pompey sought refuge in Egypt, but as he stepped on shore he was murdered by advisers to the pharaoh. After other victories Caesar returned to Rome in 46.

Caesar's Rule to 44 B.C. Caesar now decided to make his rule impregnable and assumed the positions of both dictator and consul. On the model of Sulla he extended his dictatorship beyond the legal six-month limit; then, in 44, he had himself named dictator for life. He swept aside all restraints on his power that Roman tradition might have imposed and took complete authority to pass laws, declare war, and appoint men to office.

As dictator, Caesar saw to a series of rapid reforms in many areas of Roman life. He raised the membership of the Senate to about 900, packing it with many of his veteran officers. From this time onward the Senate lost its former authority as the bulwark of the state. Caesar also divided all Italy into municipal areas, giving each town administrative control over the surrounding countryside. He scaled down his large army by settling many of his soldiers in newly founded colonies and extended Roman citizenship into some of the provinces. His most lasting reform was one by which we still regulate our lives—the establishment of a calendar based on the old Egyptian reckoning of 365 days, with one day added every fourth year. This "Julian" calendar lasted until 1582, when it was revised by Pope Gregory XIII to our present Gregorian calendar.

The Death of Caesar The full effect of Caesar's plans was not to be realized, for on March 15, 44, after four years of supremacy, he fell to the dag-

▸ **An arena in El-Djem, Tunisia, imitating the Colosseum in Rome. Built in the second/third century A.D., this arena could seat 50,000 spectators. Wild animals were housed in the long rectangular pit in the center. Roman buildings were widely copied throughout the Empire as other cities sought to identify themselves with the great capital.**

gers of conspirators led by two of his lieutenants, Marcus Brutus and Gaius Cassius. His autocracy had been a grave affront to the upper class; because their dignity as members of the governing class had been undermined, they united against Caesar and carried out the most famous political murder in all history. It is said that Caesar was warned that morning of an imminent conspiracy and that he brushed the warning aside. As the Senate met near a theater built by Pompey, the killers plunged on him; when he recognized his protégé Marcus Brutus in the group, he said in Greek, "You, too, my boy?" and covered his head with his toga as he fell. His body was carried to the Forum and burned on a rock that still stands in a small temple built to his memory after his death (*see box*, p. 110).

Assessments of Caesar are baffling and controversial, even as they were to his contemporaries. He was pitiless toward Gauls and Germans, and he enriched himself by selling prisoners of war as slaves; but indifference toward captured foreigners was common in the ancient world. In Rome he showed too little respect for republican forms once he became dictator, and for this mistake he paid with his life. On the other hand, in the civil war he was generous enough to dismiss opposing generals whom he had captured, and

The Murder of Julius Caesar

The biographer Plutarch, who wrote about A.D. 120, looked back to describe the scene when Caesar was killed, 44 B.C.

"The place chosen for this murder, where the Senate met on that day, contained a statue of Pompey, one of the adornments for the theater he had built; this made it clear to all that some divine power had guided the deed and summoned it to just that spot. As Caesar entered, the Senate rose as a sign of respect, while those in Brutus' faction came down and stood around his chair. Tillius Cimber seized Caesar's toga with both hands and pulled it down from his neck, which was the signal for the assassination. Casca was the first to strike him in the neck with his sword, but the wound was neither deep nor fatal, and Caesar turned around, grasping and holding the weapon. Those who knew nothing of the plot were terrified and did not dare run away or help Caesar or even utter a sound. But those who came prepared for the murder whipped out their daggers, and Caesar was encircled, so that wherever he turned he met with blows and was surrounded by daggers leveled at his face and eyes and he was grappling with all their hands at once. Everyone was supposed to strike him and have a taste of the murder; even Brutus stabbed him once in the groin. Some say that, as he fought off all the rest, turning his body this way and that and shouting for help, he saw Brutus draw his dagger and pulled his toga down over his head and let himself fall at the base of Pompey's statue, whether by chance or because he was pushed by the assassins. There was blood all around the statue, so that it seemed that Pompey was presiding over the vengeance taken against his enemy, who now lay at his feet and breathed out his life through his wounds. They say he was struck 23 times, and many of the assassins were wounded by one another as they all directed their blows at his body."

Plutarch, *Life of Caesar*, chap. 66 (abridged), M. H. Chambers (tr.).

they lived to fight him another day. Such actions may have rested on cool calculation of their value as propaganda, but they may also show genuine gallantry. No one can question Caesar's fiery leadership. His troops followed him into Italy with enthusiasm and fought with amazing discipline.

Caesar clearly thought that the old institutions of the Senate and the assemblies were obsolete. "The Republic," he is said to have remarked, "is only a name without body or face, and Sulla did not know the ABCs of politics in resigning his dictatorship."[6] The political weakness of the late Republic largely confirms this harsh evaluation. But in the end his authoritarian behavior proved unacceptable to the experienced politicians whom he needed for his administration. Caesar's career thus blends triumph and tragedy. He rose to the absolute summit of Roman politics, but in doing so he destroyed both the Roman Republic and himself.

IV. The End of the Roman Republic

THE SECOND TRIUMVIRATE

Antony and Octavian Brutus, Cassius, and the other assassins imagined that republican government could be restored with Caesar out of the way. Yet partisans of Caesar commanded armies throughout the Roman world, and they were not

[6]Suetonius, *Life of Caesar*, chap. 77.

men who would meekly surrender their powers to the Senate. One survivor was Marcus Antonius, or Mark Antony, a follower of Caesar and consul for the year 44 B.C. Antony tried to seize for himself the provincial command in Cisalpine Gaul, even though the Senate had already assigned it to another governor for the year 43. The Senate turned on him with Cicero, now a senior statesman, leading the attack. The state sent an army out to bring Antony to justice, and it must have seemed to many that the old institutions of the Republic had indeed come back to life.

Among the commanders whom the Senate put in action against Antony was a young man of 19—Caesar's grandnephew and adopted son. His name, originally Gaius Octavius, became Gaius Julius Caesar Octavianus upon his adoption; modern historians call him Octavian, but he called himself Caesar. He used his name skillfully to win a following among Caesar's former soldiers, but he also played the part of a discreet young supporter of the Senate in its battle against Antony. Cicero, the chief supporter of the old constitution, naively wrote of Octavian after their first meeting, "The young man is completely devoted to me."[7]

Octavian and Antony realized that the Senate was committed to the destruction of the Caesarian faction from which they derived their political support. Therefore, in 43, they allied together, and Octavian turned his back on the duty laid on him by the state, to attack Antony. They brought into their partnership a lesser commander, Lepidus; then, following the example of Sulla and others, they invaded Rome and made themselves the military rulers of the ancient capital. Faced with their armies, the Senate had to acknowledge their leadership, and a tribune proposed a law that turned the state over to their control for a period of five years; their official duties were "to provide order for the state"—a charge broad enough to supply a legal basis for nearly any action they might wish to take. Thus was formed the Second Triumvirate. In due course their collective power was renewed for another five years.

[7]*Letters to Atticus,* 14.11 (April 25, 44 B.C.).

Brutus and Cassius, seeing that they did not have popular support, fled to the East and managed to gain control of the provinces of Syria and Macedonia. But in 42 B.C. the triumvirs eliminated these enemies at the Battle of Philippi in northern Greece. To reward their troops with land, the rulers had already marked out the territory of no fewer than 18 prosperous towns in Italy. The rule of the Second Triumvirate (43–33 B.C.) was thus made secure by the seizure and redistribution of property. Further security was provided by a series of "trials" mounted against those who had had the bad luck to be on the losing side. As in the time of Sulla, the autocrats brushed aside the traditional guarantees of Roman law as they coldly purged their enemies. One of those killed without trial was Cicero.

OCTAVIAN TRIUMPHANT

Suspicion now began to grow between the two major partners, Antony and Octavian (Lepidus had been forced into retirement when he tried to take control of Sicily away from Octavian). The basic cause of their enmity was the lust for supreme power, and Antony did his own cause grave harm by remaining in the East for long periods, fighting the Parthian kingdom, which had taken certain Roman territories after the death of Crassus in 53. Octavian stayed in Rome and skillfully exploited the rumors that surrounded Antony's romance with Cleopatra VII of Egypt. In particular, Octavian falsely asserted that Antony was planning to place this Eastern queen in command of the state.

The final break between the two men came in 32 B.C. Octavian raised a large force from Italy and the western provinces; led by his skillful general Marcus Agrippa, this force defeated Antony in 31 B.C. at Actium, a promontory on the western coast of Greece. Antony withdrew to Egypt and took refuge with Cleopatra, and his army surrendered to Octavian.

The next year Octavian unhurriedly advanced on Alexandria for the reckoning with Antony and Cleopatra. Antony took his own life, and Cleopatra soon followed him. With Cleopatra's death ended the last Macedonian kingdom and, therefore, the Hellenistic Age, which had begun with the death of Alexander the Great in 323.

V. The Founding of the Roman Empire

AUGUSTUS AND THE PRINCIPATE

When Octavian returned to Rome in 29 B.C. from his conquest of Egypt, his supremacy was beyond challenge. The issue now was whether he would solve the problem that had defeated Caesar: how to rule without seeming to be an autocrat. He achieved this by restoring the appearance—but no more—of republican government. His designated candidates ran for office, and a willing Senate executed only the policies that he favored. Republican structures remained intact, but they were managed by his loyal men. At no time did he announce that he was converting the Republic into an empire. As a result, there is no official beginning for the Roman Empire; the best date is probably 27 B.C., for in that year Octavian laid the foundations of his system.

In 27 Octavian assumed control of an enormous provincial command, including Spain, Gaul, and Syria. Most of the legions were concentrated in these provinces; thus Octavian was the legal commander of most of the Roman army. Egypt was handled in a special manner; it was treated as a private possession of Octavian's and managed by his own appointee.

Along with this command (also in 27) the Senate conferred on Octavian the name Augustus, meaning "blessed" or "fortunate." This title brought with it no powers, but its semidivine overtones were useful to Augustus (as we shall now call him) in establishing his supremacy. In 23 he resigned the consulship but received two additional powers from the Senate. His imperium was extended to cover not only his provinces but the whole Roman world. He also obtained the authority of a tribune. As a patrician (by his adoption into Caesar's family), Augustus could not actually be a tribune. Yet his having the "power" of a tribune suggested that he was the patron and defender of the common people of Rome. This power also gave him the legal right to veto any actions and to offer legislation. He was usually called the *princeps*, an old republican

▸ The Ara Pacis (Altar of Peace) was built in Rome in 13 B.C. to celebrate the establishment of peace by Augustus. Relatives of the imperial family are portrayed in idealizations of their stations in life rather than in strict Roman realism.

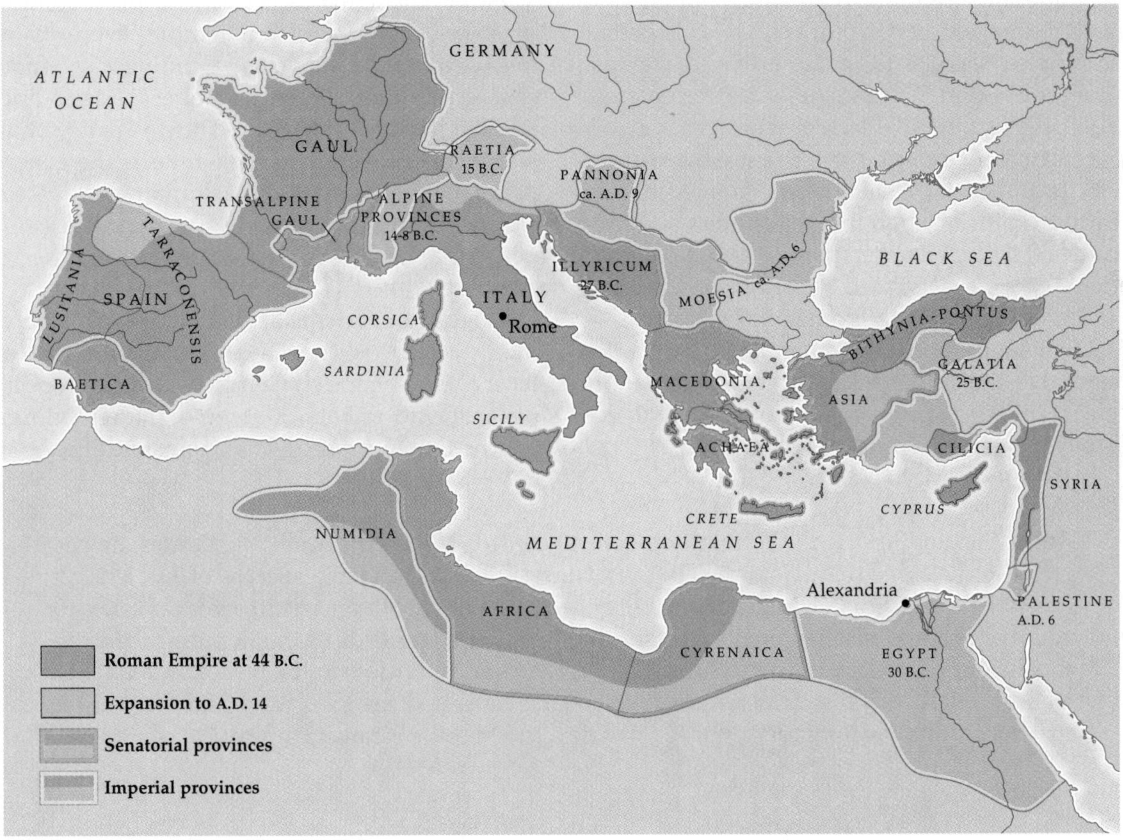

Map 4.5 THE ROMAN PROVINCES, 44 B.C.–A.D. 14

title denoting the senior ex-consul in the Senate. Modern writers often refer to the system Augustus established as the Principate.

AUGUSTUS, THE FIRST ROMAN EMPEROR

The Administration The long reign of Augustus from 27 B.C. to A.D. 14 established many abiding features of the Roman Empire. He provided a cash payment from the public treasury to soldiers who had served for 20 years, thus securing the loyalty of the legions to the state, not to their generals. He also made the Empire more secure by extending and solidifying the northern frontier (see Map 4.5). The provinces north of Italy now reached as far as the Rhine and Danube rivers. His control was nearly absolute, yet he did not install a reign of terror, and most people were relieved at the ending of the long period of civil war.

Augustus also created a force of soldiers stationed in Rome, known as the Praetorian Guard. This group of some 9000 men served as the city's police force and as Augustus' personal bodyguard, but after a few decades it came to play a decisive, and violent, role in the designation of new emperors.

Social Policy of Augustus Augustus also assumed the office of Pontifex Maximus, or high priest, and made attempts to revive the old Roman religion, probably as a device to promote political stability. He also grasped the possibilities of a ruler-cult. First he assigned Julius Caesar a place among the Roman gods and built a Temple to the Deified Julius. He also called himself

Divi Filius, or son of the divine Julius, though he was only the adopted son of Caesar. This verbal trick invited people to imagine that Augustus, though not divine, might some day become so. The poets Virgil and Horace, who wrote at his court, discreetly referred to Augustus as a future deity; and, in fact, Augustus was deified on his death, a political action that was imitated on the deaths of several later emperors who were considered to have ruled well. He also sponsored the building of temples to "Rome and Augustus"—a further suggestion, though not an offensive demand, that the emperor should be worshiped. It also became customary to make an offering to the Genius (protecting spirit) of the emperor.

Part of the religious revival was the rebuilding of scores of temples, but temples were by no means the only Augustan buildings; a famous saying was that "he found Rome made of brick and left it made of marble." The prosperity of the later years of Augustus' rule reflects the general peace that he brought to the Roman world. Freed of the expense of wars, Rome enjoyed a confidence that expressed itself in artistic and literary creativity.

Augustus also legislated in favor of the Roman family. To encourage the repopulation of Italy after the losses in the civil wars, he awarded special privileges to fathers of three or more children, and he issued a strong law against adultery.

Augustus died in A.D. 14. Through his careful control of the army and magistrates, he had given Rome three decades of healing after the civil wars, and the success of his work is shown by the fact that the state did not relapse into civil war after his death. He was Caesar's adopted son and also his final successor, the last of the warlords of the Republic. His personality seems to lack the panache of Caesar, who was invincible in the field and a talented man of letters, but his claim to greatness is that he ended the civil wars and formed the structure from which modern Europe has descended—the Roman Empire.

Recommended Reading

Sources

Julius Caesar. *War Commentaries.* Rex Warner (tr.). 1960. An unsurpassed textbook in political-military decision making.

Cicero. *Selected Political Speeches.* Michael Grant (tr.). 1977.

———. *Selected Works.* Michael Grant (tr.). 1960.

Livy. All surviving parts of his history of Rome are in four volumes published by Penguin (various translators). 1965–1982.

Plutarch. *Fall of the Roman Republic.* Rex Warner (tr.). 1972. Biographies of Caesar, Pompey, Cicero, and other leading politicians of the Republic.

Polybius. *The Rise of the Roman Empire.* Ian Scott-Kilvert (tr.). 1979.

Sallust. *Jugurthine War and War with Catiline.* S. A. Handford (tr.). 1963.

Studies

Badian, E. *Foreign Clientelae.* 1958. Classic study of the patron-client relationship at work in Roman foreign policy.

———. *Publicans and Sinners.* 1983. Together, this and the following book survey the reasons for Rome's acquisition of an empire and the financial administration that managed the regime.

———. *Roman Imperialism in the Late Republic.* 1971.

Dixon, S. *The Roman Mother.* 1988. On the role of women within the Roman family.

Errington, R. M. *The Dawn of Empire: Rome's Rise to World Power.* 1973.

Gelzer, Matthias. *Caesar: Politician and Statesman.* 1968. For more advanced students; contains precise references to ancient sources.

Gruen, Erich S. *The Hellenistic World and the Coming of Rome.* 1984. Full historical narrative, arguing against the view that Rome tried to make Eastern possessions adopt Roman ways.

———. *The Last Generation of the Roman Republic.* 1973. On the collapse of the Sullan system and the final struggle between Caesar and Pompey.

Habicht, C. *Cicero the Politician.* 1990. Concise treatment, placing Cicero within Roman politics; especially good for students.

Heurgon, Jacques. *The Rise of Rome to 264 B.C.* 1973. Good on the rise of the city and its earliest history.

Lintott, A. W. *Violence in the Roman Republic.* 1968.

Ogilvie, Robert M. *Early Rome and the Etruscans.* 1976. The interaction of the two cultures.

———. *The Romans and Their Gods in the Age of Augustus.* 1970. A brief, approachable discussion.

Richardson, Emeline. *The Etruscans: Their Art and Civilization.* 1964. Well illustrated.

Rose, H. J. *A Handbook of Latin Literature.* 1954. The best brief history, better for reference than for continuous reading.

Scullard, H. H. *From the Gracchi to Nero* (5th ed.). 1982. The best textbook for the central period of Roman history, with good references to sources.

Stockton, D. *The Gracchi.* 1979. The best modern study of the two who discovered and used popular support.

Syme, Ronald. *The Roman Revolution.* Originally 1939. Brilliant analysis of the passing of the Republic and the founding of the Empire by Augustus. For advanced students.

Taylor, L. R. *Party Politics in the Age of Caesar.* 1949. Analysis of the factions within the late Republic.

Ward, A. *Marcus Crassus and the Late Roman Republic.* 1977. The best study of the partner of Caesar and Pompey.

Warmington, B. H. *Carthage.* 1960. History and society of Rome's main rival.

Gaius Octavius, given the title "Augustus" by the Roman Senate, is portrayed as ruler and military commander in this idealized statue.

CHAPTER FIVE

THE EMPIRE AND CHRISTIANITY

THE history of the Roman Empire is one of remarkable continuity. The system of government devised by Augustus and maintained by his successors gave the Empire two centuries of solid prosperity. Historians call this the period of the *Pax Romana,* "the Roman Peace," and the Empire as a system of government remained an ideal in Europe for centuries. Its remains—stadiums, public baths, marketplaces, temples, official buildings—have inspired imitations down into our own times.

At the beginning of the third century, the Empire entered a period of crisis. Control of the army became the key to power, and emperors and would-be emperors followed one another in rapid succession. When order finally returned during the fourth century, the old Roman Empire was no more. In the East, the Byzantine Empire was formed; in the West, the Empire steadily declined, finally ceasing to be governed by Roman emperors in 476.

But even as antiquity was passing, ancient peoples were laying the basis for a new form of civilization. Their most important innovation was the development of a new set of religious beliefs—Christianity, which was destined to transform the life and culture of the Western heirs of the Roman Empire.

I. The Empire at Its Height

Three unifying elements preserved the Roman Empire that Augustus founded. First was the figure of the emperor, whom all subjects identified as the head of the regime. With some exceptions, the emperors maintained an active, personal ruling style until about A.D. 200. Second were the civil servants and city councils, who collected taxes and maintained urban life. Third was the army, both the ultimate security of the emperor himself and the protector of the frontiers. The three elements supported one another, and the failure of any one of them threatened the others and thus the fabric of the state (*see box*, below).

THE SUCCESSORS OF AUGUSTUS

The Julio-Claudian Dynasty The first emperor, Augustus, had no male heir. His last wife, Livia, was from an old patrician family and evidently persuaded him to adopt her son, Tiberius, and to designate him as his successor. She thus played a leading role in the shaping of the imperial dynasty.

After the death of Augustus in A.D. 14, the Senate recognized Tiberius as ruler and thus confirmed the principle of dynastic succession, establishing the fact that an empire, not a republic, now existed. The dynasty founded by Augustus, called the Julio-Claudians, reigned until A.D. 68. Much can be said against the rule of the Julio-Claudians. Tiberius was morbid, suspicious, and vengeful. His successor, Gaius (or Caligula), suffered from insanity. Claudius was gullible and was manipulated by his wives and assistants. Nero was one of the worst emperors, whose tyranny led to a rebellion in Gaul. When the revolt spread to Rome, he saw that he was doomed and killed himself.

Yet these emperors did maintain, and even expand, the heritage left by Augustus. Claudius, for example, saw to the conquest of southern Britain, which became a Roman province in 47. Moreover, the Empire remained at peace internally, and the provincial administration that Augustus had established continued to function effectively.

Imperial Administration The process of centralization of power in the person of the emperor and away from the Senate continued. From

Tacitus on the Powers of Augustus

The first emperor of Rome, Augustus, maintained that he had restored the Republic after years of civil war. The historian Tacitus, writing about A.D. 120, gave a different evaluation of his work.

"After Brutus and Cassius were killed, the state had no military force. [. . .] Even the party of Julius Caesar had no leader left but Augustus, who laid aside the title of Triumvir and called himself a consul. For controlling the people he contented himself with the rights of a tribune. When he had seduced the army with gifts, the people with distributions of food, and everyone with the pleasure of general calm, he began little by little to increase his authority and to gather to himself the powers of the senate, the magistrates, and the laws. No one opposed him, since the strongest men had fallen either in battle or through legalized executions, and the rest of the nobles, according to who was more ready to accept servitude, were awarded gifts and public offices; since they profited from the new arrangements, they preferred their present security to the previous uncertainties. The provinces, too, accepted this state of affairs, since the former government by the senate and people was suspect owing to the struggles among the powerful and the greed of local governors; the protection of the laws had been worthless, because the laws were constantly overturned by violence, intrigue, and finally outright bribery."

Tacitus, *Annals*, book 1, chap. 2, M. H. Chambers (tr.).

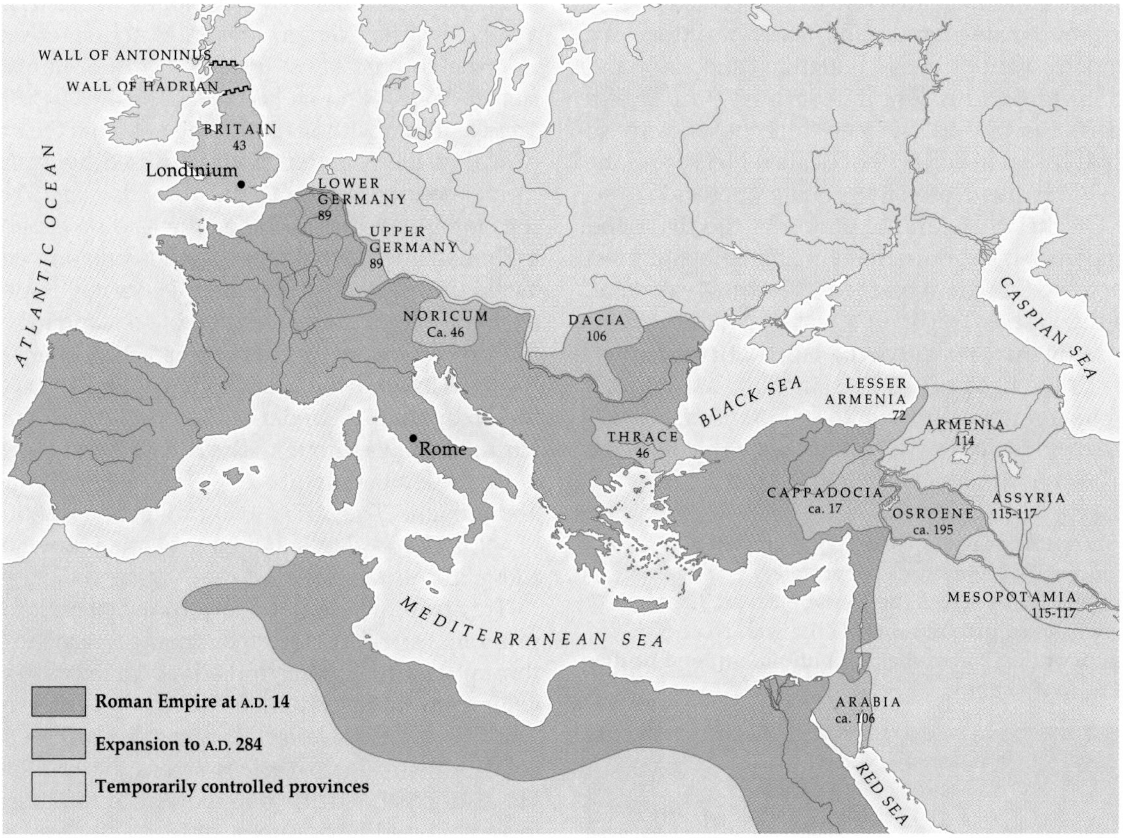

Map 5.1 **THE ROMAN EMPIRE, A.D. 14–284**

Tiberius onward, the emperor appointed magistrates directly, without the charade of having a single list of candidates "elected" by the people. Claudius turned many affairs of state over to his trusted assistants, usually Greeks who had been freed from slavery (thus called *freedmen*), who helped to found the bureaucracy that more and more ran the Empire.

Another factor that weakened senatorial power was the frequent interference in affairs of state by the Praetorian Guard, the emperor's bodyguard. The Guard first intervened in politics in 41, when it forced the Senate to recognize Claudius as emperor. It did the same for Nero in 54. This repeated invasion of civil authority by the Praetorian Guard was a step on the road toward militarization; within little more than a century the emperors were to become totally dependent for power on their ability to buy the good will of the soldiery. The army, which had kept the emperors secure, sometimes became a force beyond control.

The military played a significant role in the struggle over the succession after Nero's death in 68, as troops in various quarters of the Empire backed their own candidates for emperor. The year 69 is often called "the year of the four emperors" because in the course of the year four men claimed to be emperor. Vespasian finally stabilized the situation and emerged as sole ruler late in 69. He founded the Flavian dynasty (so called from his middle name, Flavius), which lasted through the reigns of his two sons.

THE FIVE GOOD EMPERORS

The Flavian dynasty ended in violence in 96, when a group of senators instigated the murder of the emperor Domitian, Vespasian's despotic son. The Senate then picked a quiet older senator, Nerva (96–98), to be the new emperor. Nerva, in turn, adopted an experienced military officer,

Trajan, and designated him as his successor. This system remained in use for nearly a century: An emperor would choose a qualified successor and adopt him as his son, thus ensuring a peaceful transfer of power. The men thus chosen were so capable that historians have called Nerva and the next four rulers the "five good emperors."

On the whole, in the period of the five good emperors the Empire remained stable and even expanded. In 116 it reached its farthest extension to the East as Trajan, in a war of conquest, temporarily marched down the Tigris-Euphrates valley to the head of the Persian Gulf; but he died while trying to return to Rome. Hadrian, his successor, decided to withdraw from this extreme eastern position.

In A.D. 113 the emperor Trajan erected a monumental column to celebrate his war against peoples living across the Danube River. These panels show preparations for the war. Note the figure of the river god at the bottom, under a bridge built for the army.

Hadrian continued the development of a frank autocracy. The Roman assemblies no longer met in order to pass laws. Instead, Hadrian himself issued laws—known as "decisions" (*constitutiones*)—often without bothering to obtain the approval of the Senate. He was advised by an informal council known as the "friends" (*amici*) of the emperor, which included the leading experts in Roman law. One of these, Salvius Julianus, collected the edicts that Roman praetors had issued over the centuries, in an attempt to standardize the procedures of civil law; this action pointed the way toward the great codification of law in the sixth century under the emperor Justinian. Hadrian's laws, though issued without any pretense of democratic process, were generally fair and humane. They tried to improve the condition of soldiers and slaves and gave women the same rights in court as men.

Trajan and Hadrian undertook a vast building program. Trajan erected many structures throughout the Empire and added an impressive column to the newly built Forum of Trajan, on which is carved a series of scenes recording episodes in wars against tribes across the Danube. He also expanded his new Forum by adding a group of buildings—shops, offices, a library—to the east of his column. Hadrian undertook various building projects in the provinces. Most famous is Hadrian's wall (much of it still stands) built across Britain to protect the frontier between the Roman province of Britain and the areas controlled by Celtic tribes to the north.

Hadrian arranged the succession of the next two emperors, Antoninus Pius (138–161) and Marcus Aurelius (161–180), who are the last of the "five good emperors." The rule of Antoninus was peaceful, and under the reign of Marcus Aurelius the Empire enjoyed its last years of prosperity. But in his final years a gathering storm broke in all its fury, and Marcus had to fight invasions by tribes on the Danube River and in the East. One campaign was especially disastrous, for the army returning from Asia Minor in the 160s brought with it a devastating plague that spread through much of Europe. This plague must have been one cause of the later weakening of Rome, but the nearly total lack of records prevents our knowing how many died.

Marcus abandoned the principle of adoption

▸ **The emperor Hadrian had this famous wall built across Britain to mark off the Roman Empire and keep foreign peoples out.**

and passed the throne to his worthless son, Commodus (180–192), whose extravagance and cruelty were reminiscent of Nero and Domitian. His murder on the last day of 192 opened a period of terrible instability, to which we shall return (p. 127).

ROMAN IMPERIAL CIVILIZATION

Economy In the first two centuries of the Empire, Italy and the provinces reached a level of prosperity and of flourishing population that Europe would not see again for a thousand years. The results of Roman censuses, which have partially survived, indicate that Italy at the death of Augustus contained about 7.5 million inhabitants. (In about 1500, the earliest date at which we can make a comparable estimate, the same area contained about 10 million people.)

Cities were a distinctive feature of settlement throughout the Empire. In the Western provinces, cities were, for the most part, small; to judge from the area enclosed by Roman walls, most towns contained only a few thousand residents. Yet they usually imitated Rome with temples, markets, arenas, courthouses, and other public buildings, and thus displayed an authentic urban character. In the East, cities were often much larger. Alexandria in Egypt is estimated to have had about 400,000 inhabitants; Ephesus in Asia Minor, 200,000; Antioch in Syria, 150,000. The size of the cities in the East is surely one reason why the economy in the Eastern part of the Empire was stronger than that in the Western part.

Largest of all the imperial cities, and a true wonder of the ancient world, was Rome. Estimates of its size generally suggest about 1 million inhabitants. Not until the eighteenth century would European cities again contain such a concentration of people; in the 1780s, for example, Paris held about 600,000 people. Roman civil engineering maintained, even under crowded conditions, acceptable standards of public hygiene

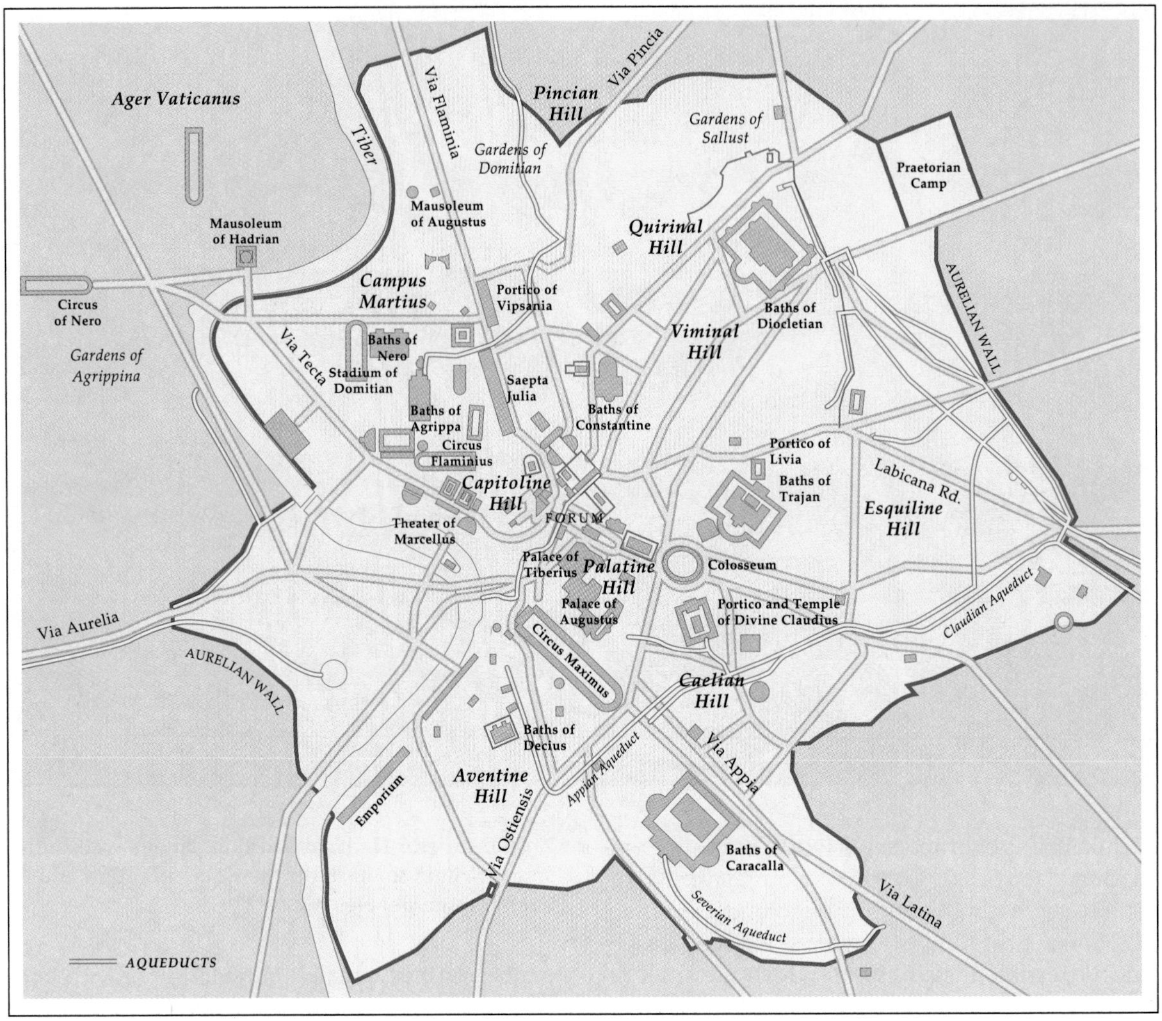

Map 5.2 THE CITY OF ROME IN THE EMPIRE

and supplied enormous quantities of pure water and food.

Agriculture still remained the basic support of the economy, supplying, according to rough estimates, more than 75 percent of the total product of the Empire. One important change in Italian agriculture in the last century of the Republic had been the triumph of the great slave-run estates, called *latifundia*, at the expense of small peasant farms. The owners of the big *latifundia* were wealthy senators and equestrians, even entrepreneurs from outside the traditional governing classes. Trimalchio, a freed slave who appears as a character in Petronius' novel, the *Satyricon*, boasted that he could ride from Rome to the area near Naples without leaving his own land.

The managers of these vast plantations favored varied forms of agriculture—the cultivation of vines, olives, and fruit, and the raising of large numbers of cattle, sheep, and goats. Only enough grain was cultivated to feed the resident staff of workers, most of them slaves. The great estates also supplied the cities with building stone, lumber, and firewood; huge quantities of wood were required, for example, to keep the Roman baths at comfortable temperatures. In the view of many historians, extensive deforestation and overgrazing led inevitably to erosion of the land and the loss of fertile topsoil—principal reasons for the economic decline of Roman Italy.

Even ancient peoples had the power to injure their environments.

In the provinces, the "Roman peace" favored the development of what had once been backward areas to the point where they threatened Italy's economic leadership. The wine market, for example, passed into the hands of Spanish cultivators in the second century, for Spanish wine was better than Italian and was cheaper to produce, thanks to lower labor costs. In some areas of industry, too, the provinces began to outrun Italian production. One of the main Italian industries was pottery, but by about A.D. 50 pottery made in Gaul had replaced Italian pottery even in Italy and had also taken over the market in the provinces and military camps. Thus Rome's success in establishing a commercial network created markets for products from the provinces and eventually contributed to Italy's own economic decline.

Social Conditions The upper class in Rome lived on a far higher scale, and was more widely separated from the common people, than the rich of Greece. The wealthy had running water tapped into their homes, slaves to tend them hand and foot, and elegant country villas for recreation. Hadrian's villa, or country retreat, near Rome was the size of a small city. These villas approached economic self-sufficiency, for slaves manufactured articles of light industry (clothing, leather goods, domestic utensils) on the farms.

▸ An arch built by the emperor Trajan at Beneventum. Some panels show sacrifices to the gods, and the whole was intended to commemorate Trajan's generosity to his people. Triumphal and commemorative arches were among the proudest monuments in Rome and have been imitated in many modern cities.

A modern feature of Roman cities was the existence of suburbs and resorts. Pompeii was a commercial town, but its neighbor Herculaneum was a residential suburb. Both towns, buried and thus preserved by the volcanic eruption of Mt. Vesuvius in 79, contain examples of the airy Roman house, built around a central open court, or atrium, and decorated with graceful wall paintings.

The workers of Rome had no such elegant housing, living rather in flimsy and inflammable apartments. They lacked running water, but a complex system of aqueducts gave easy access to water outside the home, and Rome always took pride in its enormous, cheap public baths. There were trade groupings in Rome for every kind of worker: fishermen, engineers, cobblers, silk workers, and so on. These city laborers had working conditions that were beyond the dreams of a Near Eastern peasant. They worked only about six or seven hours a day, and the Roman year contained about 160 holidays, to which the state added from time to time special days of celebration.

The major amusements for the people during days of leisure were public games, especially chariot races, which brought honor and wealth to the skilled charioteers, in arenas such as the huge Circus Maximus. Besides races, the Romans gave themselves over to brutal contests, which sometimes went on to death, between professional gladiators or between men and animals. The main arena for these spectacles was the grandiose Colosseum, begun by the emperor Vespasian in the 70s. It held about 50,000 spectators, and much of it still stands in central Rome, probably the one monument that most vividly recalls the classical city.

Rome was wealthy enough to support roughly half its population at public expense through free allotments of food, especially grain, which was the most common item in the diet. In the less prosperous years after 200 the cost of these subsidies was to place a heavy strain on the Empire's economy.

Social mobility became easier under the Empire. For example, some Greeks who had been freed from slavery enjoyed enviable careers as secretaries to emperors or as businessmen. The need for more troops opened new opportunities

▸ A well preserved apartment house (second to third century A.D.) in the city of Ostia, which served Rome as a port. The dwelling space is located over shops on the ground floor. The tradition of snack bars everywhere in Rome and Italy is an old one.

for provincials, who entered the Roman legions, especially during the second century and later; and even the Senate began to include men born in the provinces. In time the Empire became less "Roman," for in both manpower and economic strength the primacy of Italy was of the past.

Law A complex system of law and procedure was one of the chief cultural contributions of Roman civilization. Roman law had already developed under the Republic, but its growth under the Empire made it even more comprehensive. The assemblies, both that of the Centuries and that of the Tribes (see Chapter 4), issued laws mainly on large public issues, such as distributions of land or assignments of military commands overseas. The reshaping of laws that affected relations among citizens, private rights, and the like, was largely the work of individual magistrates.

Normally, cases came before a judge, who was a private citizen relying on the advice of other private citizens who were reputed to understand the law. These advisers were called jurists (*iurisprudentes* or *iurisconsulti*), and their opinions constantly influenced the growth of the law. Another impact on the law came from magistrates, especially praetors, who issued edicts that explained the principles by which they would interpret the law during their year in office; these edicts acquired the authority of tradition and ultimately passed into permanent law.

The Romans distinguished their own citizens from the other members of the Empire. Roman citizens were subject to the "civil law" (*ius civile*), or law applying to citizens; others were allowed to maintain many of their own customs, which came to form the *ius gentium*, or law of other nations. These two kinds of law were assigned, logically enough, to two magistrates for administration, the "urban praetor" (*praetor urbanus*) and the "traveling praetor" (*praetor peregrinus*). As the Empire grew and embraced more peoples, the *ius gentium* gradually displaced the *ius civile*.

The Romans' respect for their law is consistent with the remarkable cohesiveness that one sees throughout their society. In war they were often brutal, but then so were many others in all periods of history. Rome's achievement in designing and preserving a system of laws governing the behavior of citizens toward one another has served as a model for much of the law of Western Europe. Codes of law, as we have also observed, are a feature of several other ancient societies, but in richness and complexity the codifications of the late Roman Empire easily surpass all the rest.

Engineering and Architecture The Romans showed brilliance in the fields of engineering and construction. The most enduring monument to Roman civilization is the impressive network of roads found everywhere from Britain to Africa. Originally designed as highways for the rapid movement of legions, these roads became trade routes in more peaceful times and eliminated all barriers to travel. From the earliest times the Romans also built aqueducts that converged toward the cities, sloping down and carrying fresh water from the mountains; Rome's imposing system of sewers was constantly flushed by water from the aqueducts. The Romans placed more emphasis on personal cleanliness than any other civilization until modern times. Several emperors commissioned the building of immense public baths, of which the grandest of all were the Baths of Caracalla, built in the third century. The English city of Bath is named for the facilities that the Romans built there.

Roman temples, imitating those of the Greeks, were supported by columns, usually in the Corinthian style, crowned with a bell-like acanthus flower. Their temples had large interiors and were often completely walled at the rear, because Romans performed their ceremonies indoors. They were the first to grasp the possibilities of using arches and vaults on a large scale, thus giving their buildings a vastness that the Greeks could not achieve. They also invented concrete, which is inexpensive and can be laid by relatively unskilled labor. It can also be shaped into forms impossible in marble, and it is lighter in weight and can easily be supported in vaulted buildings. One of its most successful applications is the spacious Pantheon—built in the time of Augustus and then rebuilt under Hadrian—covered by a dome with a striking opening in the center. Sculpture and architecture coincided in triumphal arches, which often bear reliefs depicting the historical event that the arch commemorates.

▸ **The Sacred Way leads into the Roman Forum through the Arch of Titus, which was erected to celebrate the end of the great Jewish rebellion in A.D. 70. A triumphal procession would enter the Forum through this elegantly placed arch and parade up to the Temple of Jupiter on the Capitoline Hill.**

Literature in the Empire The leisure provided by Rome's prosperity encouraged the patronage of literature. In Rome, literature was far more the enjoyment of the upper classes than in Greece, where, for example, dramas were presented before 12,000 or more spectators. The most famous Latin poet, Virgil (70–19 B.C.), borrowed from Greek models, as Roman poets often did. His early poems, the *Bucolics* and *Georgics*, are polished hymns of praise to the Italian landscape, which reflect the style of Theocritus and Hesiod; but the gentle, human spirit of Virgil himself is always present. The best qualities of Virgil appear when he treats civilized emotions—mercy, compassion, and sadness; then his work echoes with a graceful melancholy.

These qualities appear in his patriotic epic, the *Aeneid*, which borrows and transforms materials from Homer. In this work Virgil narrates the wanderings of Aeneas, the Trojan whose descendants were the legendary founders of Rome. Leaving his native city after the fall of Troy, Aeneas reached Carthage and had a romance with its queen, Dido; but his sense of duty compelled him to abandon her in order to reach Italy and fulfill his destiny. Virgil's aim was to sing the glory of Rome and its salvation by Augustus after the civil wars of the late Republic.

A contemporary of Virgil's was Horace, whose *Odes*, *Epodes*, and *Satires* examine love, amusement, annoyance, contentment—in short, the feelings of everyday life. Now and then Horace makes an attempt at serious patriotic verse, but these poems are self-conscious and moralizing and do not speak with the real Horatian voice of gentle, amusing irony.

Juvenal, a more pungent satirist than Horace, wrote shortly after 100. He took as his motto "Indignation inspires my poetry" (*facit indignatio versum*). His poems denounce the excess of pride and elegance in Roman society. His language is colorful, often bitter and obscene. One of his richest and wisest satires concerns the vanity of human wishes. After reviewing the foolishness of human beings, Juvenal gives his advice in a famous epigram: One should pray for "a sound mind in a sound body" (*mens sana in corpore sano*).

Historians The histories of Rome written during the Republic were usually the work of men directly involved in politics. Under the Empire this changed, for political contest had almost vanished. It therefore seemed appropriate to look back on the Republic and write a final history of its politics and imperialism. Titus Livius, or Livy, undertook this task during the reign of Augustus, when the decisive political transformation occurred. Livy narrated Roman history from its legendary beginnings until 9 B.C. Because he usually drew on the work of earlier historians, he was sometimes unable to escape the influence of the myths that had clouded the history of the early Republic; thus he is at his best when he uses a good source such as Polybius.

Livy's *Roman History* is a kind of prose epic, filled with patriotism and admiration for the great men who had led Rome when the Republic was conquering the Mediterranean. Just as Virgil became the last Roman epic poet, so Livy was the last writer in Latin to attempt a full history of Rome. His work inspired many later writers who looked back at the Republic as the Golden Age of Rome; it was accepted as authoritative until soon after 1800, when historians began to be more skeptical about Roman tradition.

The leading Roman historian in accuracy and seriousness is Cornelius Tacitus (55?–120?). His first major work is the *Histories,* in which he treats Roman history from 69, the year of the four emperors, through the death of Domitian in 96, with emphasis on the analysis of character. Deeply influenced by satire, the dominant literary form of his age, Tacitus loved to fashion stinging epigrams aimed at members of the governing class, and he treated nearly all his main characters as selfish or corrupt. His disillusioned attitude was partly the result of his being an outsider, probably from southern Gaul; he saw Roman society through the cool eyes of a provincial who became a senator and even rose to the office of consul.

His other major work is the *Annals,* which covers the reign of the Julio-Claudian emperors from Tiberius through Nero. Tacitus looked back at the early Empire from the vantage point of a later period; and though he said he wrote "without anger or partisanship" (*sine ira et studio*),[1] he found little good to say about the first emperors and few modern critics would call him impartial.

II. Changes in Ancient Society

THE PERIOD OF CRISIS (192–284)

The Crisis of Leadership The centuries of the "Roman peace" ended with the death of the emperor Commodus in 192, and in the following years the political balance shifted to the military. During the third century dozens of emperors claimed the throne, but many of these men were really no more than political gamblers or warlords who for a short time purchased the loyalty of their soldiers. Thus two of the stabilizing elements of the Empire—the strong, effective emperor and the disciplined army—began to fall apart.

The Roman Senate, which had once been the inspiration and bulwark of the state, now had neither interest nor ability to intervene in affairs of state as the emperors assumed more and more dictatorial powers and governed through court favorites. The economy of the Empire, too, nearly collapsed during this period, largely because defense costs had risen as raiders plundered the wealth of the Empire on several frontiers. Moreover, the emperors had been supplying the inhabitants of Rome with free food and public games, or "bread and circuses," in the usual phrase—a fairly effective means of political domination, but a heavy drain on the economy. Adding to these financial problems was a shortage of silver, on which the imperial currency was based. The emperors resorted to depreciating the currency, but this forced people to hoard what silver

▸ The ancient Greek city Ephesus, on the coast of Turkey, remained prosperous in the Empire. T. Julius Celsus, consul in A.D. 92, endowed this magnificent library, which his son completed about 135.

[1]*Annals,* 1.1.

they had and actually drove more of the metal out of circulation.

A further problem was the increasing reluctance of people of independent means to hold civic offices, which paid no salary. Finally, the government was forced to compel people to take office, a step that pointed to the practice, which was to become common in the fourth century, of binding people to their occupations. This in turn led to the collapse of the third crucial element of stability in the state, the efficient administrators and civil servants. Many of the emperors during the century of crisis were men of little leadership; but some of them must have been among the most able rulers in the history of Rome, for otherwise the Empire would have totally disintegrated.

Slavery and its Dilemmas Like most other ancient states, Rome used slaves widely, but no earlier society had organized the institution of slavery to such a degree or used slaves in such large numbers. Ancient slavery, unlike slavery in the United States, was never restricted to members of a single ethnic group. Anyone might have the bad luck to be rounded up and forced into slavery. During the late Republic, the number of available slaves increased dramatically, as Rome overran Greece, Asia Minor, Spain, and Gaul. Julius Caesar reports in his *Gallic War* that he once sold 53,000 Gauls into slavery in a single day. One owner of a large estate mentioned in his will that he owned no fewer than 4116 slaves. Of the 7.5 million inhabitants of Italy at the death of Augustus, an estimated 3 million were slaves.

The mounting flood of cheap slaves allowed the expansion of the great plantations during the last century of the Roman Republic. In most places slaves lived in modest quarters and were more or less properly fed. On the other hand, in Sicily they were often turned loose without shelter to feed off the land.

Slaves were better treated in the cities, where they served as artisans, hairdressers, secretaries, and, of course, personal servants. Slaves from the East, Greeks in particular, commonly tutored the children of the free classes. Slaves supplied much of the entertainment in ancient society. Girls and boys who could sing, dance, or recite were highly valued; there was also active traffic in beautiful young slaves of both sexes, often for sexual purposes. Gladiators were slaves, and reputedly fought harder because of it. If they prevailed over an opponent, they might win their freedom; if they lost, they forfeited nothing more than a miserable existence.

Judged solely as an economic system, ancient slavery offered the Empire certain advantages. It permitted a calculated use of labor in relation to land and capital. But in the long run, the slave system of antiquity also had serious weaknesses, which we must include in the causes for the decline of the Empire in the West.

Rome declined in part because its economy could no longer support the army needed to defend the frontiers against invaders. Why was the economy not equal to the task? One principal reason was that the slave system could not resolve two problems that every economy must face: the creation of incentives, to ensure that workers will labor hard and well; and the recruitment of replacements for the aging and the dead.

Especially in the countryside, the principal incentive that bent slaves to their tasks was the dread of punishment. For this reason, they were best employed in work that required little skill, diligence, or effort. The association of slavery with physical labor drained work of its dignity and dampened interest in technological innovation. And, in the view of most historians, demoralized slaves were poor producers of children, even when they were allowed to marry. Why pass misery down the generations? And conquests ceased from the time of Hadrian, a fact that threatened the continued supply of slaves.

The Plight of the Poor Within the free population, the spread of the great estates in the last century of the Republic had driven many small cultivators off the land. Many drifted to the Roman metropolis, where free bread and circuses purchased their docility. In many provinces, too, rural depopulation and the abandonment of cultivated fields had become a major problem in the centuries after Augustus.

Faced with shrinking numbers of cultivators and taxpayers, the Roman government sought desperately to reclaim and resettle the abandoned fields. For example, Marcus Aurelius initiated a policy of settling foreigners on deserted lands within the Empire. The state also sought to attract free Roman cultivators back to the countryside. The free cultivator who settled on another's land was called a *colonus*, and the institution was called the *colonate*.

Roman policy toward the *coloni* and other free cultivators was ambivalent and shifting. In many cases the *colonus* was treated well, with a light and fixed rent that he paid to the landlord, or *dominus*. He could sell the land he improved or pass it on to his heirs, and he could depart from it at will. But by the fourth century the picture was much worse: The *colonus* was bound to the soil, as were his children after him, and he was subject to the personal jurisdiction of his lord.

The long-term interests of society dictated that resettlement within family-owned farms should be encouraged. On the other hand, the hard-pressed government could not overlook any source of revenue, and it often resorted to outrageous fiscal practices. It ruthlessly requisitioned food; it forced settlers to pay the taxes of their absent neighbors; and it subjugated settlers to the authority of their landlords, who could be held responsible for collecting from them services and taxes. By the fourth and fifth centuries, under conditions of devastating fiscal oppression, some peasants preferred to flee the Empire rather than face ruin at home.

CULTURAL DISINTEGRATION

The cultural system of classical antiquity, in spite of its intellectual appeal, had some crucial weaknesses. It spoke primarily to the privileged and the gifted, the elites of ancient society. Even as they failed to develop a technology that might have eased the labors of slaves and the poor, so also the intellectual leaders of the age could point to little meaning in the lives of the unfree, the unhealthy, the disadvantaged, those without property, those without talents.

Moreover, after the Augustan Age Roman civilization produced fewer original thinkers. A certain morose resignation pervades their writings. The emperor Marcus Aurelius, in his *Meditations*, expressed the Stoic virtue of resignation: "When necessity is there, why strain against it?" The earth was in decline, and history was approaching its term.

III. The Late Roman Empire

RESTORATION AND REFORM

The political crisis of the third century finally ended in 284 when Diocletian, a high army officer, seized the imperial throne. He was from the peasantry of Illyria and was a strong, ruthless man, who ruled through an authoritarian bureaucracy. Recognizing that the Empire was too large and too unstable to be directed by one man, Diocletian enlisted three corulers, forming the Tetrarchy (rule of four). Each of the four rulers was placed wherever he was needed.

In order to solve the financial crisis, Diocletian had every plot of land taxed at a certain amount, to be paid to the emperor's agents. Trades and professions were also taxed so that the burden would not fall solely on landowners. The cities in the Empire each had a local city council, or *curia*; the officials, called *curiales*, were personally responsible for the required tax and had to pay it

The Tetrarchs (Diocletian and his co-rulers), shown supporting each other: Diocletian and Maximian are on the right; Galerius and Constantius on the left. The heads on the swords are Germanic.

themselves if they could not collect it from others. Diocletian tried to hold back inflation with a famous Edict on Prices, which fixed a maximum price for nearly all goods. But natural economic forces led to further inflation, and he had to let the edict lapse after a few years.

Diocletian's severe rule stabilized the Empire, though it is hard to find in it much to praise. Many of his practices continued throughout the fourth century, especially his establishment of a despotism that resembled the ancient kingdoms of the Near East in its absolute monarchic rule.

Diocletian retired in 305, and soon afterward his system of shared rule broke down. Years of complex intrigue and civil war followed, as several leaders fought for the throne. One of the ruling circle was Constantius, the father of Constantine. When Constantius died in 306, Constantine began to fight for supreme power; in 324 he overcame the last opposition and was recognized as sole emperor of Rome. Thus 40 years after the accession of Diocletian, the Empire once again had a single ruler. In 330 Constantine renamed the old Greek city of Byzantium as New Rome and established it as his capital; popular usage gave it the name Constantinople.

CONSTANTINE AND THE BUREAUCRACY

By the end of his reign in 337 Constantine had set the pattern that remained throughout the fourth and later centuries. The whole state was now one rigid structure, almost one massive corporation that brutally discouraged individual initiative.

The economy was in virtual stagnation. Members of all trades and professions were grouped into *corpora*, or corporations, and to change professions was difficult. To make certain that the various day-to-day services would be performed,

Map 5.3 **THE EASTERN AND WESTERN EMPIRES IN 395**

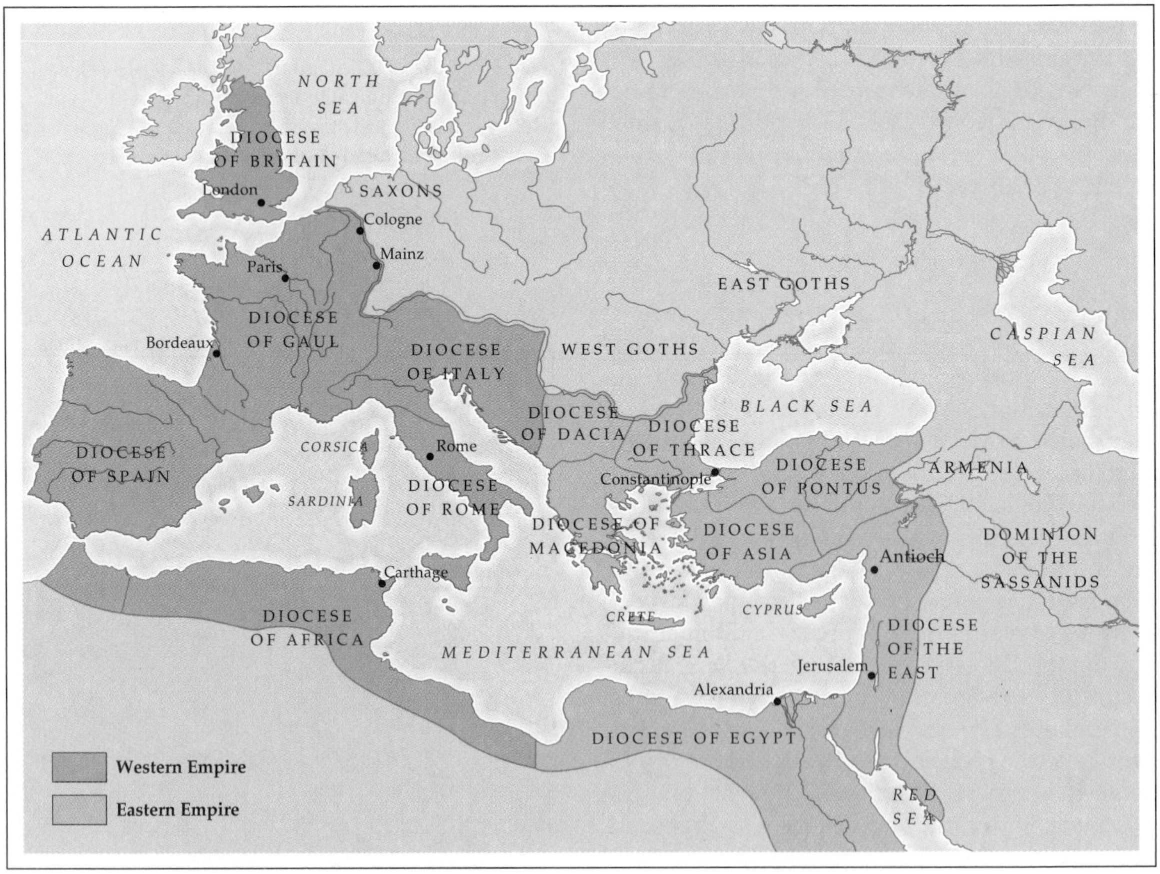

the state made professions hereditary. A small class of independent farmers clung to their existence, but the general trend was toward converting agricultural workers into near slaves. There was a deep gulf between the monarch's court and the common people. Even within the court the emperor stood apart from the rest, surrounded by ceremony. Fourth-century rulers wore expensive cloaks dyed in purple, and courtiers had to kiss a corner of the emperor's robe when approaching the throne. Diadems, the custom of kneeling before the emperor, and other marks of royalty became traditional and have remained so in European monarchies.

THE DECLINE OF THE WESTERN EMPIRE

After Constantine's death in 337, the chief administrative question for more than a century was whether one man could be strong enough to rule as sole monarch. For most of the time this proved impossible, and some kind of shared rule became common. On the death of Theodosius, in 395, the Empire was divided into an Eastern half and a Western half, with the dividing line just east of Italy.

In the last centuries of the Empire, society became more and more rigid; it did not, and perhaps could not, allow people to move freely from one class to another. As the central government weakened, local estates, usually called *villas*, became self-sufficient units resembling the later manors of the Middle Ages, with hunting lands and workshops that supplied the goods that the local population needed; they therefore became the main economic and political units of the Western Empire. At the same time, trade was declining because of a shortage of new markets and the constant threat of invasions along the frontiers. Moreover, a shortage of labor caused fertile lands to lie fallow and mines to remain unexploited.

The "Fall" of Rome? Such was the background for the dramatic turning point in history that is the end of the Western Empire. The formal end of the Western Empire is traditionally dated to 476, when a Germanic warlord deposed the youth whom we call the last Western emperor, Romulus Augustulus, and the Senate resolved not to try to name any further Western emperors. Modern readers inevitably think of this event in the terminology imposed by the historical masterpiece of Edward Gibbon—that is, as the "decline and fall" of the Empire. But, of course, no political structure as large as the Roman Empire really falls like a tree in a forest without further influence or legacy. Moreover, some emperors in Constantinople, notably Justinian in the sixth century, saw themselves as the head of the whole traditional Empire, West and East, and tried to reunite the two geographic parts.

Yet even though historians take care to speak of the transformation of the Empire rather than of its disappearance, there is no doubt that the

Chronology of the "Fall" of Rome

476 is known to all readers of history as the year of the fall of Rome, but the true chronology is more complex.

393	Theodosius I, ruling in Constantinople, installs his son Honorius as emperor in the West.
395	Death of Theodosius; the division of the Empire into Eastern and Western parts is maintained.
423	Death of Honorius in West; other Western emperors continue to be appointed.
474, June 24	Leo I, emperor in East, appoints Julius Nepos as emperor in West.
475	Nepos appoints Orestes, a former lieutenant of Attila the Hun, as Master of the Soldiers. Orestes insists that his young son, Romulus Augustus (or Augustulus), be recognized as Western emperor. Nepos flees to Salona in Dalmatia. Romulus is proclaimed emperor in Ravenna, October 31, but the act is without legal force, and Nepos continues to be recognized as official Western emperor.

476	The German warlord Odovacar (sometimes Odoacer) leads a rebellion against Orestes and kills him, August 28. He deposes Romulus in Ravenna (September 4) and exiles him with a pension to Campania. The Roman Senate sends an embassy to Zeno, the Eastern emperor (474–491), proclaiming that there is no further need for a Western emperor; but Zeno continues to recognize Nepos until his death.
480, April or May	Nepos is murdered in his villa at Salona.
about 520	Marcellinus, in his Latin *Chronicle* written in Constantinople, states that the Western Empire (Hesperium imperium) "perished" with the deposition of Romulus Augustulus in 476, thus establishing this date for the "fall" of Rome.

Empire in the West did pass away while the Eastern part, called the Byzantine Empire, survived for nearly another thousand years. The problem is to explain why the Western regions could not maintain themselves under a continuous government while no similar dissolution threatened the Eastern portion of the Empire.

Some historians have been enticed into trying to state the one great cause for the fall of Rome—and this may be an impossible quest. Gibbon, for example, blamed the destructive work of barbarism and religion. But to say that Rome declined because of invasions by Germans, Franks, and Goths only pushes the inquiry back one step: Why were these peoples able to defeat an Empire that had ruled the civilized world for centuries? And why did the Eastern part of the Empire not decline along with the Western?

Causes for the Fall Some historians suggest that the emperors unintentionally paved the way for the fall of Rome by exterminating possible political rivals in the upper class, thus weakening the group that could have supplied leadership for the state. Others have advanced an economic argument, saying that the Empire was bound to decline because it never really emerged from a domestic economy. But this second theory is hardly convincing, for some societies—admittedly much less complex than the Empire—have existed for many centuries with no more than a domestic economy. If there had been no convulsions and strains in the Empire, the production of goods and food could have continued more or less unchanged. Exhaustion of the soil and fluctuating cycles of rainfall and drought have also been proposed in order to explain Rome's economic depression, but there is little exact knowledge about the cycles of crops and weather conditions that would indubitably account for the fall of the Empire.

Others have suggested that the weakness of the Western Empire was due to a shortage of manpower. This explanation does have some merit, because the Eastern cities appear to have been more populous than the Western ones, and thus they had more strength and resilience. The numerical inferiority of the West became even more serious when the villas became self-sufficient units and there was no longer a centralized military system. It was much easier for outsiders to invade the Empire when they met haphazard resistance from local forces. The relocation of the capital to Constantinople moved the administrative center even farther from the Western provinces and probably accelerated the dissolution of the regions of Italy and Gaul.

But the shortage of manpower was not the only factor in the weakening of the Western Empire. Its physical geography doomed it to be more vulnerable to invasion than the Eastern Empire. Warlike peoples streamed along the Danube valley and through the terrain of Central Europe into the Western provinces, a less hazardous route than the journey south through the difficult mountains of the Balkans, Greece, and Asia Minor into the Eastern Empire.

Social Conditions and Decline Other conditions made the Western Empire less able to resist destructive invasions. In the late second and third centuries the emperors had deliberately increased the prestige of the army and depressed the Senate and the civil service. The creature that they fashioned soon began to rule them, for the armies and their leaders made and unmade emperors at will. The only way to preserve civilian control over the military machine would have been to entrust more responsibility to the Senate and maintain strong civil servants. But the emperors simply continued along the path of absolute coercion, stifling initiative and making the lower classes apathetic and resentful. These conditions gave citizens only slight motivation to defend their oppressive government; domination by invaders may have seemed not much worse than being in the grip of the Roman state.

One must also consider the large number of holidays and many forms of amusement within the city of Rome: To what degree did such luxuries contribute to the transformation of the Western Empire? There is evidence here and there that the masses in the city gradually lost their feelings of responsibility. For example, in

Map 5.4 THE RHINE FRONTIER OF THE ROMAN EMPIRE

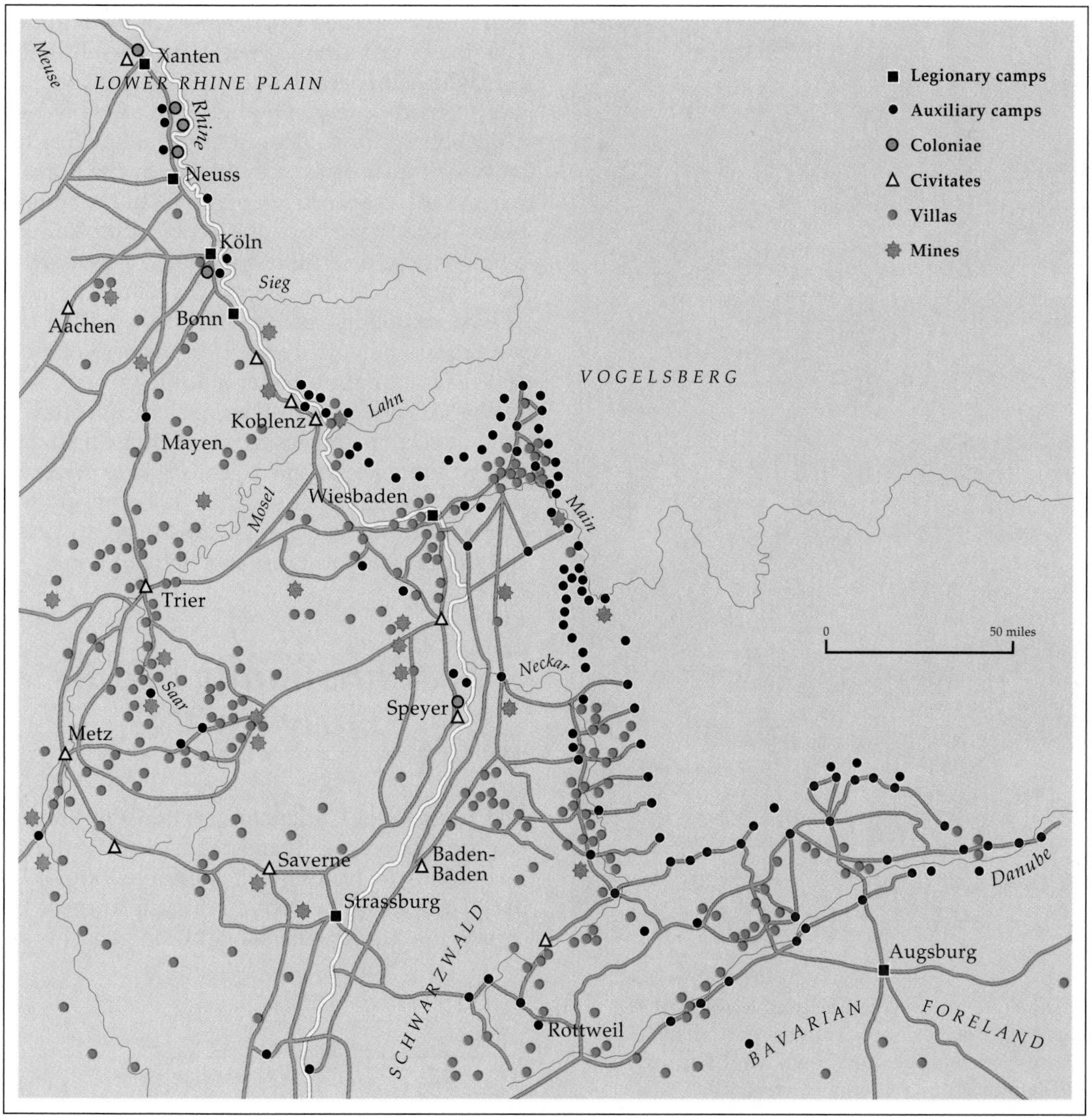

▸ **The emperor Constantine tried to increase his glory by commissioning colossal portraits of himself, such as the one shown here. The original full-length statue was some 40 feet tall.**

69, as Tacitus reports, the crowd cheered with pleasure as rival troops fought in the streets for the throne.[2] When the masses no longer had to exert more than minimal effort to survive, they abandoned the discipline and civic cooperation that had created the Empire. Public office was shunned, non-Italians supplied the troops, and appeals for traditional Roman firmness in danger found little response.

Finally, historians must take into account the great upheaval in ideas and faith. We cannot express this view in the language of science or statistics, but the new religion, Christianity, may also have weakened the defenses of the Empire. This thesis was first espoused by Edward Gibbon, who had rejected Catholicism in his own life and scorned Christianity. But even as we recognize Gibbon's prejudices, we must allow that he may have hit a part of the truth. In the Roman scheme the emperors, governors, and administrators stood far above the people, and Roman religion provided little spiritual compensation for a low rank in the world. The Christian faith offered something better: the message that all persons are potentially equal in the eyes of God and may hope for a better afterlife through salvation. As the Western Empire came under constant attack, the increasing number of Christians may have been less than eager to fight to preserve the old system. This spiritual rejection, as we might call it, worked along with the mighty pressures of invasion to cause the "fall" of Rome.

IV. Christianity and Its Early Rivals

The triumph of Christianity within the Roman Empire was one of the most remarkable cultural revolutions in history—all the more extraordinary since its values were opposed to those of classical thought, which sought the good life in

[2] *Histories*, 3.83.

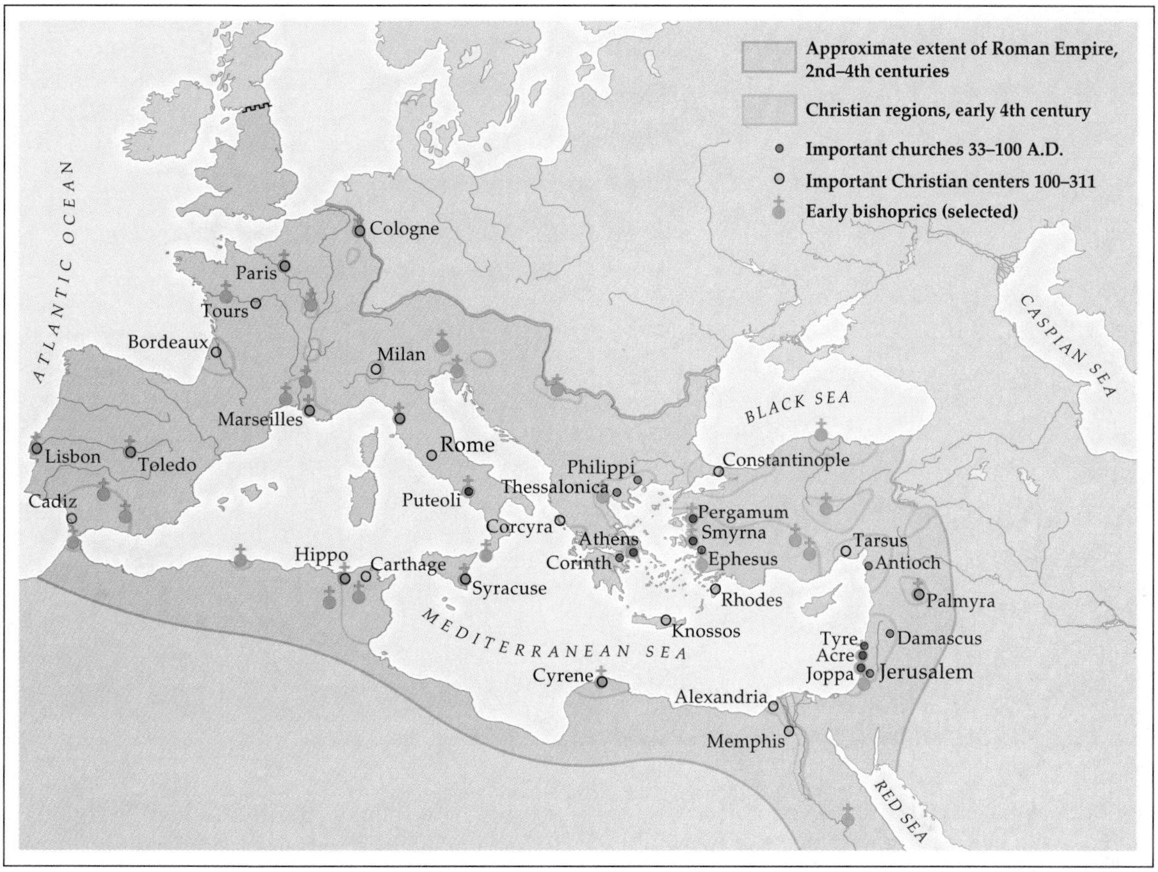

Map 5.5 **THE SPREAD OF CHRISTIANITY**

the present world. *Carpe diem*, "Seize the day," said Horace; there is no certainty about tomorrow. But classical values were failing to reach the disadvantaged, the subjugated, the losers. Small wonder that people sought a meaning for their existence in new religious movements.

THE MYSTERY RELIGIONS

One element of a spreading religious ferment under the Empire was the growing popularity of the so-called mysteries, which promised a blessed life after death to those who were initiated into secret (therefore "mysterious") rites. Through these rites, the believer attained a mystical identification with the renewing cycles of nature.

The oldest and most famous rites were held each fall at Eleusis, a day's walk from Athens. A drama-filled night culminated in the initiate's conviction that he or she would be given a lovely life after death by Demeter, the goddess of grain, just as she caused beautiful new grain to come forth from the apparently dead seed.

This hope for survival after death did not bring with it any expectation of a changed moral life, nor did initiation lead to membership in any kind of community of believers or "church," with one notable exception: the religion known as Mithraism. Mithras was originally a Persian god of light and truth and an ally of the good god, Ahura Mazda; he symbolized the daily triumph of life over death by bringing back the sun to the dark heavens. Initiation was open only to men, and Mithraism—with its emphasis on courage, loyalty, self-discipline, and victory—became especially popular in the Roman army.

When Christians began, around A.D. 30, to proclaim the good news (or "gospel") of the recent

▶ **A Mithraeum, or shrine to the savior god Mithras, with benches for worshipers. It was built in the second or third century within a large first-century apartment. On the altar, Mithras is shown sacrificing a bull to Apollo. Above this level was built the church of San Clemente in Rome.**

death and resurrection of their leader Jesus of Nazareth[3] throughout the Empire, many who responded thought they were hearing about the best "mystery" of all: A historical person had conquered death and promised a blessed afterlife to all who believed in him. Yet much early Christian literature was written to teach believers that Christianity was far more than a "mystery." The new faith demanded that every believer practice love and justice in new communities made up of Jew and Greek, slave and free, male and female, rich and poor, educated and ignorant.

This new religion hardly looked "religious." Christians had no temples or other holy places, no priests, no ordinary sacrifices, no oracles, no visible gods, no initiations; they made no pilgrimages, did not practice divination, would not venerate the emperor, and challenged the final authority of the father (or oldest male) in family life. No wonder Christians were accused of being atheists who undermined traditional society. The roots of these radical beliefs and practices are found in the long Judaic tradition and its sacred writings. Christians maintained that prophecies in the Hebrew Bible, which in the light of new revelation they began to call the *Old* Testament, had foretold the coming of Jesus as the Messiah, the deliverer of the Jewish people, and as the future lord of the world. Like the Jews, Christians emphasized their god's wish to create a community of men and women who practiced justice and mercy. All the first Christians were Jews, but they parted company with Jewish tradition by insisting that Jesus' life, his sacrificial death, and his resurrection all meant that God's community had become open to everyone from every background.

[3]"Jesus" was his name; after his death he was called *ho Christos*, "the anointed one" or the Messiah, by his followers; thus the names "Christ" and "Jesus Christ," though universally used, are not historically accurate; and "Jesus, called the Christ" is cumbersome.

THE JEWS IN THE ROMAN EMPIRE

The Jews had been favored subjects of the Persian Empire until Alexander's invasion of the East (334–323 B.C.) swept away Persian rule. In the Hellenistic Age they were governed, during the third century B.C., by the Ptolemies of Egypt and then by the Seleucid kings of Syria, who began to force Greek culture on them and finally outlawed the Jewish religion altogether. Pious Jewish nationalists responded under the leadership of Judas Maccabaeus with guerrilla warfare. This successful Maccabean Revolt (167–164 B.C.) is celebrated today with Hanukkah, the Festival of Lights. After a century of virtual independence, the Jews in Judea (the province created out of the Jewish kingdom of Judah) were brought under Rome's control by the arrival in Jerusalem of the Roman general Pompey in 63 B.C.

When Julius Caesar was at war with Pompey in 47 B.C., he was assisted by a Jewish force, and he rewarded the Jews with reduced taxes and exemption from military service. The Romans also agreed that Jews could not be called to court on the Sabbath and that they could continue to worship in their synagogues, even in Rome itself. Thus, despite the loss of their century-long freedom, the Jews enjoyed at least some measure of toleration.

Rome permitted client kings, local rulers who pledged loyalty to Rome, to rule Judea. The most notorious was Herod the Great (ruled 40–4 B.C.), hated by most Jews, whom he sought to win over by remodeling the Temple in Jerusalem into one of the wonders of the ancient world. Political weakness in the son who followed Herod forced Rome to begin direct rule in Judea through civil servants from Rome, usually called procurators, the most famous of whom was Pontius Pilate.

Constant quarrels between the Roman officers and the Jews reached a climax in A.D. 66, when Jerusalem burst into rebellion. This great Jewish War, as the Romans called it, lasted until 70, when the Romans demolished the Temple, except the Western Wall, at which Jews were allowed to pray once a year. Hoping to retain the favor of the Jews by respecting their god, the Romans did not at first try to suppress the Jewish faith itself; but they finally did attempt this after another Jewish rebellion (131–135). Nonetheless, Judaism retained its coherence and strength, assuring its people that God would one day send them their redeemer.

Jewish Factions The attractiveness of Hellenistic culture, combined with the insult of Roman occupation, led to a continuing crisis of identity among the Jews. After the Maccabean Revolt, three principal factions arose, each stressing the part of Jewish tradition that it considered most essential for the survival of the Jews as God's people.

First, the landed aristocracy and high priests formed the Sadducees, religious conservatives who rejected belief in an afterlife and in angels because they did not find such teaching in the Books of Moses (the Pentateuch, called the *Torah* by Jews). A second faction, the Pharisees, were pious middle-class lay people who taught the resurrection of the dead, believed in angels, and accepted gentile converts.[4] During the century following the Roman expulsion of the Jews from Jerusalem in 135, the spiritual heirs of the Pharisees, the great rabbis, organized their oral legal traditions, which updated the practice of the Torah, into a book called the Mishnah. This compendium became fundamental for all subsequent Jewish thought and was augmented in the East by an authoritative commentary (the Gemara) to form the Babylonian Talmud, or general body of Jewish tradition. A similar process in the West created the less elaborate Persian Talmud.

The third faction was the Essenes, who have drawn the most attention in recent years because of the astonishing discovery of the Dead Sea Scrolls, documents found from 1947 onward in 11 caves near the Dead Sea. Although scholarly debate continues, the consensus is that the writers were ascetic priests who settled at Qumran, 15 miles into the desert east of Jerusalem, after the Maccabean Revolt; they were evidently protesting against the leadership of the Temple by high priests whom they considered corrupt and unworthy.

---

[4]The Latin word *gentiles* (akin to *gens*: see p. 93) means "foreigners," those born to non-Jewish mothers.

These rolls and many fragments of leather have given historians an extraordinary view of the apocalyptic beliefs and strict practices of this protesting faction, which was active from about 150 B.C. to A.D. 70. The Essenes were convinced that evil in the world had become so powerful—even prevailing in the Temple—that only a cataclysmic intervention by God, which would soon arrive, could cleanse the world and open the way for righteousness to prevail.

▸ **The church of Santa Costanza in Rome, built in the early fourth century as a mausoleum for Constantia and Helena, daughters of the emperor Constantine, contains some of the oldest Christian mosaics. This scene from daily life shows workers bringing in the grape harvest.**

A certain "Teacher of Righteousness," the priestly champion of the forces of light, is thought to be the anonymous author of many of the scrolls; his opponent in Jerusalem, who he says serves the powers of darkness, is called the Wicked Priest. At least two God-anointed leaders are foreseen in the scrolls: the Messiah of David (a military commander) and the Messiah of Aaron (a high priest). The return of the "Teacher" is also predicted.

The relations of the Essenes at Qumran to Jesus and the first Christians remain much debated. The Essenes are never mentioned in the New Testament, the books of the Bible that record the life of Jesus. To be sure, in the spectrum of Jewish factions, these two groups could hardly have differed more widely. The Essenes were exclusive, hierarchic, priestly, and withdrawn from society. Jesus and his followers welcomed everyone; they were egalitarian, uninterested in sacrifices in the Temple, and wholly "in the world."

ORIGINS OF CHRISTIANITY

The modern historical investigation of Jesus of Nazareth has challenged scholars for two centuries. He seems to have been a charismatic Jewish teacher, yet he wrote nothing that we know of. His existence and his execution by the Romans are confirmed by such first- and second-century historians as Josephus, Tacitus, and Suetonius.

For details we must sift the writings of early converts, such as Saul of Tarsus (who did not know Jesus) or the authors of the Gospels (the first four books of the New Testament), which focus on Jesus' power over evil forces, his message of hope and moral demands, his healing miracles, and his radical inclusiveness (even lepers were welcomed into the faith). But ancient writers had little interest in presenting his biography in chronological order or in probing his inner life. We know almost nothing about his career as a youth and young adult apart from his being raised a Jew in Galilee; thus, despite the efforts of many, it is impossible to write a biography of Jesus.

As his followers recalled his career, Jesus was born of a virgin named Mary, betrothed but not yet married to a man named Joseph, in the last years of Herod the Great, at a date that modern scholarship sets about 4 B.C. At around age 30 he went to John the Baptist, an outspoken prophet, to be baptized—that is, to become purified through a ritual washing—and join his apocalyptic movement, which foresaw the coming end of the world. Soon afterward John was imprisoned, and Jesus began a program of itinerant teaching and healing, apparently rejecting John's apocalyptic message by proclaiming instead the "good news" that God's rule had already begun *before* the final judgment. Jesus affirmed the Pharisees' belief in resurrection, yet he urged his disciples to pray that God's will be done here on earth as it is in heaven, that God's kingdom should come to people here.

In the Sermon on the Mount, the summary of Jesus' basic principles recorded in the Gospel of Matthew, Jesus declared that when God rules, the poor, the meek, the pure in heart, the peacemakers, and the justice seekers will be honored. He said too that prayer and piety were matters of personal commitment, not public gestures to win society's acclaim.

With all other Jews he believed that God was a gracious, welcoming God. The related questions were: To *whom* is God gracious? and, therefore, Whom must I treat as my neighbor? As Jesus demonstrated by his fellowship at open meals, every person was potentially such a neighbor, especially a person in need.

Jesus' fellowship at meals reached its climax at his last supper at the time of Passover, a Jewish religious holiday. At this meal he urged his disciples to continue a ritual practice in memory of him, using bread and wine to symbolize the gift of his body and the sacrifice of his blood. The early Christians regularly did so, calling this meal the eucharist, or thanksgiving.

Christian sources state that Jesus was accused by the high priests in Jerusalem of blasphemy (he had challenged their authority in the Temple), of pretending to be God's Messiah and a king, and of opposing paying taxes to the Roman emperor. Apparently convinced that Jesus presented a serious threat to public order at the Passover, the Roman governor, Pontius Pilate, ordered his crucifixion, a horribly painful form of execution (about A.D. 30).

Jesus' followers became convinced that God raised him from the dead after three days and that this resurrection confirmed the truth of his deeds and words despite his rejection and persecution. The Christians further believed that he ascended bodily into heaven but would return to save his followers and establish his kingdom. Armed with this conviction, they began to convert other Jews to their faith; some converts, such as Stephen, the first Christian martyr, took the lead in extending the all-inclusive new movement to gentiles.

Paul and His Mission A Pharisee, Saul of Tarsus, known to us as Paul, became a leader in persecuting Jews who had become Christians. Then, about A.D. 33, on his way to Damascus to organize further persecutions, he saw on the road an apparition of the risen Jesus, who asked him to explain his hatred. Paul realized he had been given a special mission to the gentiles and became Christianity's tireless advocate, traversing the Roman world, organizing Christian communities of both Jews and gentiles, and advising their members through his letters. He was executed in Rome about A.D. 62 while planning a mission to Spain (see Map 5.6).

Paul became the best known of all the early Christian teachers. His letters, or epistles, written to give specific guidance to the congregations he founded, were widely circulated and then collected as part of the Christians' authoritative Scriptures. Luke devotes nearly half of the Acts of the Apostles to Paul's career as a courageous witness who fought with burning missionary fervor for his new lord.

Above all, Paul rejected the policy of some early Jewish Christians who wanted to restrict membership in the new faith to Jews or to gentiles who had become Jews through circumcision. In one of his tautly argued letters in the Bible's Book of Romans he asked: "Is God the God of the Jews only? Is he not also the God of the Gentiles? Yes, of the Gentiles also." By rejecting circumcision as a condition of membership, Paul helped firmly establish the Christian church on the basis of personal faith, not limited by ethnic identity, bloodlines, or observation of the Mosaic law.

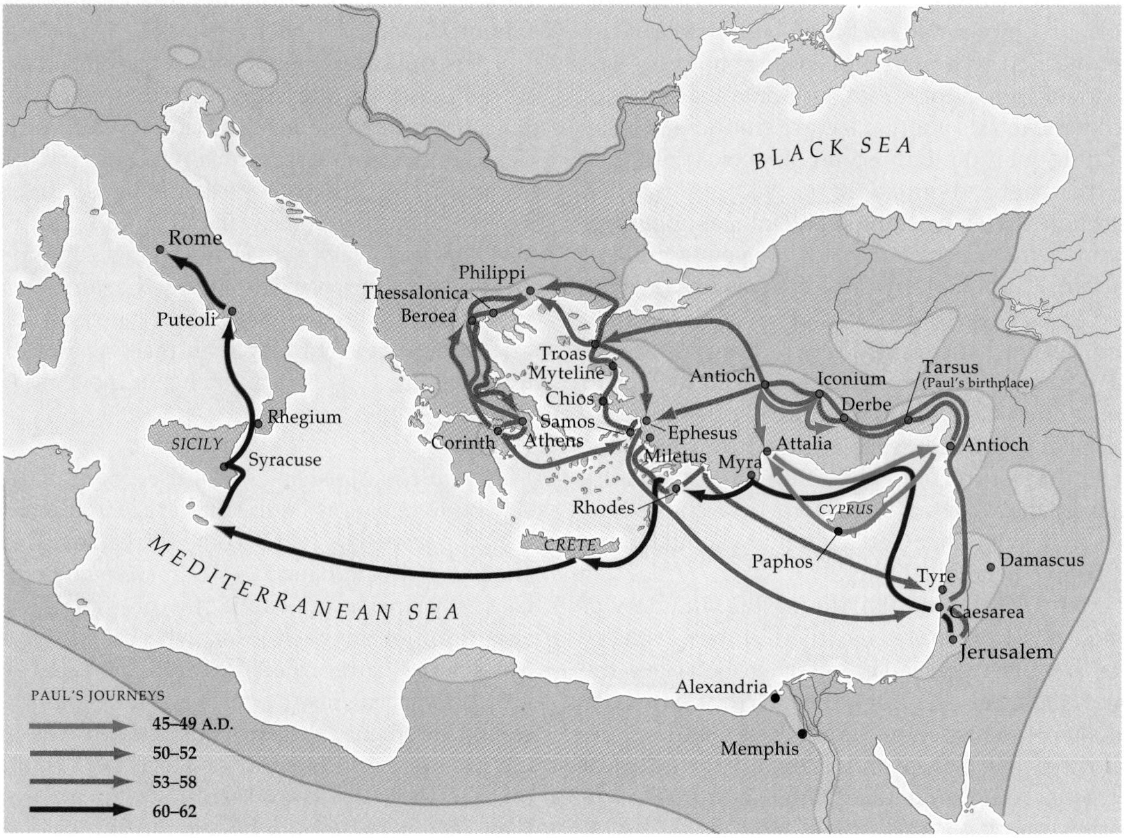

Map 5.6 THE JOURNEYS OF ST. PAUL

He and later Christian teachers saw themselves as the direct heirs of the Jewish tradition, from which they drew their concept of one God and their notions of creation and the early history of humanity. The first human beings, Adam and Eve, had disobeyed God, thus introducing sin and death into the world. By nature Adam was the founder of the human race; by grace—that gift by which God redeems sinners and gives them life after death—Jesus was its second founder, restorer, and redeemer.

Paul taught Christians to regard themselves as citizens of heaven and to begin living with one another in humility and love, in joyous expectation of their final destiny. The Christians were sure that God would soon consign their world's system of honor and shame based on violence, pride, and class discrimination to the trash heap of history. Paul also redefined the notion of the Messiah. For Jews, this leader would some day arrive and create another kingdom on earth. For Paul, the messianic age had begun with Jesus, interrupting the age of violence and death as the sign and promise of what the future would bring. Paul's vision of human freedom and a renewed human community characterized by mutual service is one of the most compelling social images in Western culture. Taking this message throughout the lands of the eastern Mediterranean, Paul and his successors brought converts by the thousands into the new church.

Persecutions Toward the many religious sects of the Empire, the Roman government adopted a general policy of toleration, seeking the blessings of all divine powers on the Empire. The Romans even paid for sacrifices to be performed on behalf of the Empire in the temple in Jerusalem. They asked only that veneration be shown on official occasions to the traditional gods and to the

The fourth-century sarcophagus of Junius Bassus, in classicizing style, showing Adam and Eve in Eden, with the threatening serpent.

deceased and deified emperors—little more than public patriotism. But the Christians, like the Jews before them, refused even this apparently small compromise with polytheism. As a result, many despised them as enemies of the human race.

Sporadic persecutions and long periods of peace marked the history of the Church—that is, the Christian community—into the fourth century. Then, in the period 303–313, came the Great Persecution under Diocletian and his successors, as the rulers sought to stamp out what they saw as a potential menace to the state. Their unsuccessful efforts testify to the widespread strength of Christianity. Moreover, the persecutions created a list of venerated Christian martyrs, which led to the cult of saints, thereafter an integral part of Christian piety.

An Emperor Becomes the Church's Patron One of the most surprising events in Roman history is the radical shift in the policy of the government toward the Christians initiated in 313 by the emperor Constantine. In the traditional story, first appearing around the period 318–320, Constantine had a dream on the evening before he was to fight a rival for supremacy over Italy in 312, at the Milvian Bridge near Rome. In the dream he was told to decorate the shields of his soldiers with the monogram of Christ: "In this sign you shall conquer." Constantine won the battle and thereafter recognized divine power in the name of Christ.

At what point Constantine personally converted to Christianity is debated. In any case, in

The fourth-century emperor Valentinian I shown as Christian ruler in a colossal statue from Barletta in southeast Italy. In one hand, he holds a (restored) orb to signify his imperial power; in the other, the cross to show his devotion to the Church. The portrait thus unites the two forces that sustained the later Empire.

313, at a conference held at Milan, Constantine ended the age of persecutions by extending complete freedom of worship to the Christians and ordering the return of their confiscated goods. Other favors followed: Churches could own property and enjoyed exemptions from certain taxes, and bishops were allowed to judge the legal disputes of the members of their congregations. Thus the Church acquired a privileged juridicial status that it would retain, in many Western lands, until the eighteenth and nineteenth centuries.

Just before his death in 337 Constantine received baptism from the bishop Eusebius of Nicomedia, but Christianity was not yet the official religion of the Empire. The emperor Julian, known as the Apostate, tried in the period 361–363 to restore the position of the traditional gods, but by then the wave of Christianity could not be turned back. In 392 Theodosius the Great forbade the practice of all religions except the form of Christianity recognized by the government, thus transforming in one move the character of both the Empire and Christianity. He reversed Rome's long-standing policy of religious toleration and changed the Church from a brave alternative society sharply critical of "this world" into a friend of worldly power; it thus began attracting some "converts" who sought personal gain rather than spiritual renewal.

BATTLES WITHIN CHRISTIANITY

Dogma and Heresies Usually, the Christian community did not bother to define matters of dogma or discipline until disputes threatened its internal unity. The losers in these disputes, if they did not amend their beliefs, were regarded as heretics (from the Greek word *hairesis*, meaning "choice"—that is, a wrong choice).

A heresy that threatened the character of the Christian revelation was that of Marcion of Sinope in Asia Minor (circa 150). He sought to reform Christianity by restricting it to the message of St. Paul alone. He therefore edited his version of the New Testament, which included and recognized as divine only the Gospel of Luke and the Epistles of Paul.

Another heresy was that of a bishop from Asia Minor, Montanus (about 170 to 200), who maintained that certain living believers were prophets who were continuously receiving direct inspiration from the Holy Spirit. Women were prominent among these prophets, and Montanus' ideas eventually won the allegiance of the great North African writer Tertullian. The movement forced Christians to ask: Who should rule the Christian congregations—teachers, who could only interpret texts from the past, or prophets, who might expect continuing new revelations.

Christians who accepted the standard doctrines of the Church branded the ideas of Marcion and Montanus as heresy. Since such heresies have vanished over the centuries, one might well ask: What is their historical importance? The answer is that they stimulated the early Church to redefine its positions. Out of the turmoil and disagreement, the Church emerged stronger, even though the price was sometimes the blunt suppression of sincerely held opinions.

Orthodox theologians of the second century answered Marcion by defining the canon of sacred writings to include, in effect, the modern Bible—the entire Old and New Testaments. And the Church answered Montanus by declaring that the age of divine inspiration had come to an end. All the truths needed for salvation, the Church now said, were complete with the work of St. John, the last inspired author (about 100), and no new revelations were needed. In the fourth century, too, the Church refused to accept as inspired certain other writings, calling them the Apocrypha (obscure or unclear writings).

The Government of the Church Evidence from the first century indicates that James, a brother of Jesus, was the recognized head of the Christians in Jerusalem. During this period, too, we meet the terms *deacon* (*diakonos*), *bishop* (*episkopos*, or "overseer"), and *elder* (*presbuteros*), which at first were nearly synonymous. Then, in the second century, the bishop became the elected leader of a group of elders (later called priests) and deacons (both men and women), who became responsible for collecting donations, distributing charities, and managing the Church's material affairs.

In the early generations of the Church women were often valued as leaders, as for example one Junia, mentioned in the Book of Romans by Paul as "outstanding among the apostles." Other

▸ **The finest mosaics in Europe are in Ravenna. This sixth-century group (below) depicts a line of saints and martyrs under some prophets. The top row shows scenes from the life of Jesus.**

gifted women served as teachers and coworkers with Paul, but as the Church came under patriarchal social pressures, women were limited to working as deaconesses and serving in orders of widows and virgins.

The bishops gained the right to appoint priests, define doctrine, maintain discipline, and oversee morals. This political structure gave Christianity a stable administration that no ancient mystery religion enjoyed. In the West, the number of bishops remained small; they thus obtained power over fairly large areas. Bishops in cities with the largest Christian communities—Rome, Alexandria, Antioch—became the most influential. Finally the bishop of Rome became the head of the Church in the West. The general name for a bishop was *papa*, or father, but eventually the bishop of Rome was the only one who could so call himself (in English, *pope*).

Donatists and Arians In 303, in proclaiming the last persecution of the Christians, Diocletian had ordered priests to surrender their sacred books. Those who did so were called *traditores* ("those who handed over" the Scriptures—thus our word *traitor*) and were hated by the more steadfast Christians. When the persecutions ended in 313, a party of North African Christians led by a bishop named Donatus declared that the traitors, even if repentant, had forever lost membership in the Church; all the sacraments they had ever administered—all baptisms, marriages, ordinations, and the like—were declared worthless.

Since the traitors were many, acceptance of the Donatist program would have brought chaos to the North African church.

The result was violent schism, which mounted on occasion to civil war. Refusing to accept the rule of traitors, the Donatists established their own bishops and hierarchy. In response, the more forgiving orthodox Church declared that the sacraments conferred grace on the recipients *ex opere operato*, simply "from the work having been performed," and that the spiritual state of the priests at the time did not matter. This remained the official Christian position until challenged during the Protestant Reformation of the Middle Ages.

Another major dispute arose about 320 when Arius, an Alexandrian priest, began to teach that Jesus was not coequal with God the Father but had been created by him at a moment in time: "There was a time when he [Jesus] was not." Arius' teachings raised a furor in Egypt and soon throughout the Empire. To restore peace, Constantine summoned the first "ecumenical" council (that is, one representing the entire inhabited world) of the Church, which met at Nicaea in Asia Minor in May 325. The council condemned Arius in the "Nicene Creed," which declared that Jesus was coeternal with the Father and of one substance with God. But not until the Council of Chalcedon of 451 was Jesus clearly defined as one person with two natures. As a human being, he was the son of Mary; as God, he was coequal with the Father and had reigned and would reign with him eternally. This definition has since remained the belief of orthodox Christians.

▶ **An early mosaic (circa 400) showing Christ holding a book and surrounded by apostles in Roman dress. Two women, perhaps saints, crown St. Peter and St. Paul, with the holy city of Jerusalem in the background. The commanding figure of Jesus resembles that of Jupiter in Roman art.**

The Church and Classical Culture Christian writers, although they were proclaimed enemies of pagan culture, had no choice but to be indebted to classical traditions. The basic grammars and texts, the authoritative models of argument and style, were all pagan. To defend the faith, Christian apologists had to master the art of rhetoric and use the arsenal of pagan learning. This Christian accommodation with pagan learning had decisive repercussions. Nearly all the texts of the great classical authors have reached us in copies made by Christians, who believed they were useful in education. Paradoxically, these outspoken enemies of pagan values actually preserved a rich cultural heritage that they sought to undermine.

THE FATHERS OF THE CHURCH

Christianity became the chief religion of Europe partly because it reached the people through the languages and thought of Greco-Roman civilization. Even before the birth of Jesus, Greek-speaking Jews in Alexandria had translated the Old Testament into Greek; this version, said to have been made by 72 scholars, is called the *Septuagint* (from the Latin *septuaginta*, meaning 70), and the authors of the New Testament referred to it and wrote in the common Greek of the day. On the basis of these sacred texts there came an ocean of commentary and persuasion by the so-called Fathers of the Church, the leading theologians of the second to fifth centuries.

Origen and Eusebius The most learned father writing in Greek was Origen (185?–253?), a priest in Alexandria. Both the volume and the profound scholarship of his writings were a wonder of late antiquity. He worked especially on the text of the Scriptures by comparing the original Hebrew and the Septuagint; he also wrote extensive commentaries on books of the Bible and a tract, *Against Celsus*, in which he answers the arguments of an elitist Aristotelian critic of the Christians.

Another highly influential Greek father was Eusebius of Caesarea (260?–340?). His most original work was a history of the Church, which became the model for later such histories. The most learned man of his time, he also wrote a *Chronicle* of universal history, which is one of our most important sources for ancient history in general.

The Latin Fathers Among the fathers who wrote in Latin was Ambrose, bishop of Milan from 374 to 397. His most important doctine was that the Church must be independent of the emperor and that bishops should have the right to chastise rulers. In 390 he excommunicated the emperor Theodosius after he had massacred the rebellious citizens of Thessalonica, forbidding him to receive the eucharist and thus placing him outside the body of the Church. Theodosius admitted his guilt and repented, and the popes of later centuries who struggled with secular officials owed much of their power to the resolute example of Ambrose.

Jerome (340?–420) succeeded Eusebius as the most learned Church father of his time. His translation of both the Old and the New Testaments into Latin, usually called the Vulgate version of the Bible, is probably the most influential book ever written in the Latin language. It became the medium through which the Judeo-Christian writings permeated the Latin-speaking nations of Europe and was the biblical text most often used during the Middle Ages.

Augustine Augustine (354–430), the best known of the fathers, was born in North Africa of a pagan father and a Christian mother and accepted Christianity under the influence of Ambrose in 387 (*see box*, p. 146). He became bishop of Hippo in North Africa in 395 and spent the remaining years of his long life writing, preaching, and administering his see.

In his voluminous writings Augustine had something to say about almost every question of Christian theology. He profoundly influenced, for example, Christian teachings on sexual morality and marriage. Like some of his pagan contemporaries, he believed that the world was already filled with people. "The coming of Christ," he wrote, "is not served by the begetting of children." He therefore urged all Christians to a life of celibacy, even though this would mean their own declining numbers: "Marriage is not expedient, except for those who do not have self-control." He banned all sexual activity for the unmarried. Within marriage, husband and wife

Augustine Is Brought to His Faith

St. Augustine describes how, after many struggles to overcome his lustful nature, he was inspired at age 31 to pick up and read in the New Testament; this was the critical moment in his conversion.

"And, not indeed in these words, but to this effect I spoke often to you: 'But you, O Lord, how long? Will you be angry forever? Do not remember against us the guilt of past generations.' I sent up these sorrowful cries—'How long, how long? Tomorrow, and tomorrow? Why not now? Why is there now no end to my uncleanness?'

"I was saying these things and weeping in the most bitter contrition of my heart, when I heard the voice of a boy or girl, I do not know which, coming from a neighboring house, chanting, and often repeating, 'Take up and read; take up and read.' Immediately my face changed, and I began to consider whether it was usual for children in any kind of game to sing such words; nor could I remember ever hearing anything like this. So, restraining the torrent of my tears, I rose up, interpreting it as nothing but a command from heaven to open the Bible, and to read the first chapter I saw. So I returned to where I had put down the apostles. I grasped it, opened it, and in silence read the first paragraph I saw—'Not in rioting and drunkenness, not in debauchery and lust, not in strife and envy; but let Jesus Christ be your armor, and give no more thought to satisfying bodily appetites' [Romans 13–14]. I read no further, I did not need to; for instantly, as the sentence ended—by a light of security that poured into my heart—all the gloom of doubt vanished."

St. Augustine, *Confessions*, VIII, 12, J. G. Pilkington (tr.), in *Basic Writings of Saint Augustine*, vol. 1, Random House (1948), p. 126, language modified.

should unite sexually only for procreation, and the pleasure they took even in this act, representing a triumph of passion over reason, was a small, though pardonable, sin.

In theological matters, Augustine was passionately interested in the operations of grace (see p. 140). He sought the work of grace in his own life, and the result was his *Confessions*, an intensely personal autobiography; it is both a record of his early life, when he was consumed by material and sexual passions, and a celebration of the providence that had guided him in his struggle toward God. This masterpiece of introspective analysis is a type of literature virtually unknown in the classical tradition.

Augustine distinguished between God the creator (the author of nature) and God the redeemer (the source of grace), and insisted that these two figures not be confused. God as creator had given humanity certain powers, such as intelligence superior to that of beasts, but those powers, injured by the original fall of Adam and Eve, are insufficient to earn salvation. Only through grace, which Jesus' sacrifice had earned, could humanity hope to be saved. Moreover, God had already decided on whom he would bestow grace; hence, even before we are born, we are all predestined either to heaven or to hell.

Augustine was consumed by the problem of sin—the breaking of God's law—and quarreled with Pelagius, a British monk, who argued that sin was only the result of a wrong choice and that people could achieve perfection, do good works, and thus attain salvation. For Augustine, sin descended from Adam into every human being, and doing any good works offered only a temporary reprieve: Humanity's salvation must await a glorious transformation at the end of time.

Augustine further believed that the whole course of human history might be redeemed by the power of grace. In his greatest work, *The City*

▸ The cathedral in Syracuse, Sicily. The interior, in powerful historical symbolism, shows a Doric temple to Athena (fifth century B.C.) with its original columns, now supporting the walls and roof of a Christian church built in the seventh century.

of God, he set out to show that there was order in history: Behind the manifold events of the past there was evident the hand of God, directing people through his grace to their destiny. Into this immense panorama, Augustine brought the sacred history of the Jewish Testament, the history of his own times, and the Christian expectation of resurrection. He held that the grace of God united the chosen in a form of community or city, which was set against the community of those joined by the love of earthly things. The city of God, in which live those chosen for salvation, was as yet invisible, and the elect who were its members should recognize that this present earth was not their true home. To Christians of his own troubled age and to those of later ages, Augustine held out the beckoning vision of a heavenly city, a celestial Jerusalem, where at last they would be at home with God.

Christians therefore felt able to ignore or transcend the "fall" of Rome—an event that the modern world sees as a possible model of its own fate. The transformation of the Empire, as it is better called, is a challenge and a warning to all who read history; it is also the recognized end of the ancient world and the beginning of a long period in which new nations would use the legacy of antiquity in their own development.

Recommended Reading

Sources

Ayer, Joseph Cullen. *A Source Book for Ancient Church History.* 1913.

Early Christian Writings: The Apostolic Fathers. M. Staniforth (tr.). 1968.

Suetonius. *Lives of the Caesars.* Robert Graves (tr.). 1972.

Tacitus. *Annals of Imperial Rome.* M. Grant (tr.). 1978.

———. *The Histories.* K. Wellesley (tr.). 1964. The two works give the history of the Empire in the first century A.D. by the leading Roman historian.

Studies

Barnes, T. D. *The New Empire of Diocletian and Constantine.* 1982. On the two most important late emperors.

Bradley, K. R. *Slaves and Masters in the Roman Empire.* 1988. On the relations between slaves and their owners.

Brown, Peter. *Augustine of Hippo: A Biography.* 1967.

———. *The World of Late Antiquity, A.D. 150–750.* 1971. Together, superb historical and cultural discussions.

Cross, Frank M. *The Ancient Library of Qumrân and Modern Biblical Studies.* 1976. A balanced introduction to the study of the Dead Sea Scrolls.

Daniélou, Jean, and Henri Marrou. *The First Six Hundred Years.* Vol. I of *The Christian Centuries,* L. J. Rogier and others (eds.). 1964. The most comprehensive study of the early Catholic Church.

Dodds, E. R. *Pagan and Christian in an Age of Anxiety: Some Aspects of Religious Experience from Marcus Aurelius to Constantine.* 1970. On the inner reasons for the great change of gods in the Roman Empire.

Frend, W. H. C. *The Rise of Christianity.* 1984. Now the most extensive single discussion.

Garzetti, Albino. *From Tiberius to the Antonines: A History of the Roman Empire, A.D. 14–192.* 1974. The best political narrative of this important period.

Gibbon, Edward. *The History of the Decline and Fall of the Roman Empire.* 6 vols. 1776–1788. Many modern editions, the best by J. B. Bury, 7 vols., 1896–1900.

Grant, Michael. *The Army of the Caesars.* 1974. Comprehensive discussion of the development of the Roman army in the Empire.

———. *The Fall of the Roman Empire: A Reappraisal.* 1976.

Hopkins, K. *Conquerors and Slaves.* 1978. Essays on the social and economic consequences of Roman imperialism.

Jones, A. H. M. *The Later Roman Empire, 284–602.* 1964. Encyclopedic narrative, with detailed citation of primary sources; for advanced students.

———. *The Decline of the Ancient World.* 1975. Essentially a shortened version of the foregoing.

Luttwak, *The Grand Strategy of the Roman Empire.* 1976. An original analysis by a professional strategist.

MacMullen, Ramsay. *Corruption and the Decline of Rome.* 1988. On the transformation of ideas and conduct in the Empire.

———. *Enemies of the Roman Order.* 1966. On the internal causes for the weakening of Rome.

———. *Paganism in the Roman Empire.* 1981.

Millar, Fergus (ed.). *The Roman Empire and Its Neighbors.* 1981. With chapters by various experts on the nations bordering on the Empire.

Millar, Fergus. *The Emperor in the Roman World.* 1977. Study of the emperor and the imperial bureaucracy.

Nock, Arthur Darby. *Conversion.* 1961. The best book on the reasons for the transition from paganism to Christianity, by a great scholar.

Raaflaub, K. A., and M. Toher (eds.). *Between Republic and Empire.* 1990. Essays on Augustus and the politics and culture of the Empire.

de Ste Croix, G. E. M. *The Class Struggle in the Ancient World.* 1981. A Marxist survey of Greco-Roman culture, concentrating largely on the Empire.

Syme, Ronald. *Tacitus.* 1958. Not only a study of the historian but also a microscopic analysis of the politics of the Empire. For advanced students.

Watson, G. R. *The Roman Soldier.* 1969.

Wells, C. *The Roman Empire.* 1984. A good modern account.

This twelfth-century silver reliquary from Aachen represents Charlemagne as emperor, saint, and protector of the Church. After his death, through all the subsequent medieval centuries, Charlemagne was remembered and viewed as the ideal Christian emperor.

CHAPTER SIX

The Making of Western Europe

THREE new civilizations fell heir to the Classical tradition after the fall of Rome. A separate religion marked each of them: Roman, or Catholic, Christianity in western Europe; Eastern, or Orthodox, Christianity in Asia Minor and eastern Europe; and Islam in the Middle East and North Africa. The new societies were predominantly peasant; although slavery remained important, it was no longer the principal basis for their economies.

The new cultures were dominated by the Christian and Muslim visions of an afterlife, visions that offered to even the humblest members of society a sense of individual dignity and destiny. All men and women could learn from Christianity and Islam that their lives, however hard and cruel, were not meaningless. God, they believed, had created them, and obedience to his will might earn them eternal life.

The age also witnessed a vast movement of peoples. Celts, Germans, Slavs, Arabs, and others shifted or enlarged the areas of their former settlements. The migrations permanently affected the composition of peoples in Europe and the Middle East. They also caused violent upheavals, but economies were slowly rebuilt, largely through innovations in agriculture that enabled peasants to cultivate areas that had not been efficiently farmed before. Medieval societies also built new economic institutions such as the large estate or manor, based in Europe on semifree or serf labor.

I. The New Community of Peoples

The civilization that took root in the west and north of Europe after the decline of the Roman Empire was unmistakably the direct ancestor of the modern Western world. Historians call the millennium between the fall of the Roman Empire and approximately 1500 *the Middle Ages*, or medieval period, of European history and have further divided this era into three distinct periods:

Early Middle Ages	500–1000
Central Middle Ages	1000–1350
Late Middle Ages	1350–1500

The Early Middle Ages witnessed the emergence of the first recognizably Western civilization from the shambles of the Roman Empire; this new civilization embraced both the former subjects of the Empire and peoples from beyond its borders. The Greeks and Romans called all these peoples *barbarians*[1] because of their unintelligible languages and strange customs. There was no single barbarian nation: These peoples were many and differed considerably in language and culture.

THE GREAT MIGRATIONS

Among the barbarian peoples were the Celtic tribes in northern Scotland (the Picts, the "painted ones," so called by the Romans from their habit of tattooing themselves) and in Ireland. (The common name for the Celtic Irish was, confusingly, Scots.) The Picts and Scots escaped the Roman domination that had befallen their cousins, the Britons and Gauls.

More numerous and more formidable than the Celts were the Germans, who were settled in a great arc that stretched from Scandinavia to the Black Sea. The Germans had long been exposed to Mediterranean influences and were culturally among the most advanced of the barbarian peoples. From about 350, Christianity spread among the Germans north of the Danube, but in its Arian form (see p. 144). Beyond this Germanic cordon lived the still pagan Slavic tribes, probably the most numerous of the barbarians.

Huns and Germanic Peoples Germanic tribes had for centuries challenged the Roman frontiers because their primitive, unproductive economies forced them to search constantly for new lands to plunder or settle. The Germans were attracted by the wealth and splendor of the Roman world, and the Romans admitted them into the Empire, even while resisting their armies. The barbarians came initially as slaves or prisoners of war, then as free peasants to settle on deserted lands, and finally as mercenary soldiers and officers. In the fourth century the barbarian penetration of the Empire was made more violent because the barbarians themselves were being invaded and forced southwestward by nomadic hordes from central Asia.

The nomads who sowed tumult in the barbarian world were the Huns, a people probably of Mongolian or Tatar origin. Perhaps in reaction to climatic changes and the desiccation of their pastures, the Huns swept out of their Asiatic homeland and terrorized western Europe. Their great chief Attila (433?–453), the "scourge of God" according to Christian writers, established his horde on the plain of the middle Danube and from there led them on raids into both Gaul and Italy. With Attila's death in 453, the Hunnic empire disintegrated, but the Huns had already given impetus to the great movement of peoples that marks the beginning of the Middle Ages.

The Visigoths (or West Goths) were the first of the Germanic tribes to be dislodged by the Huns. In 376 the emperor Valens admitted them into the Empire, but the starving barbarians soon rebelled at the high prices that Roman officials demanded for food. To put down the uprising, Valens led an expedition against them but was defeated by the Visigothic cavalry in the battle of Adrianople in 378. This battle ended the Romans' military advantage over the barbarians and showed the superiority of the mounted warrior (the prototype of the medieval knight) over the foot soldier. Continuing their westward movement, the Visigoths sacked Rome in 410 and crossed the Alps into Gaul, where in 418 they established the first

[1]The Greeks invented the word *barbaros* to imitate the strange sounds of unintelligible languages.

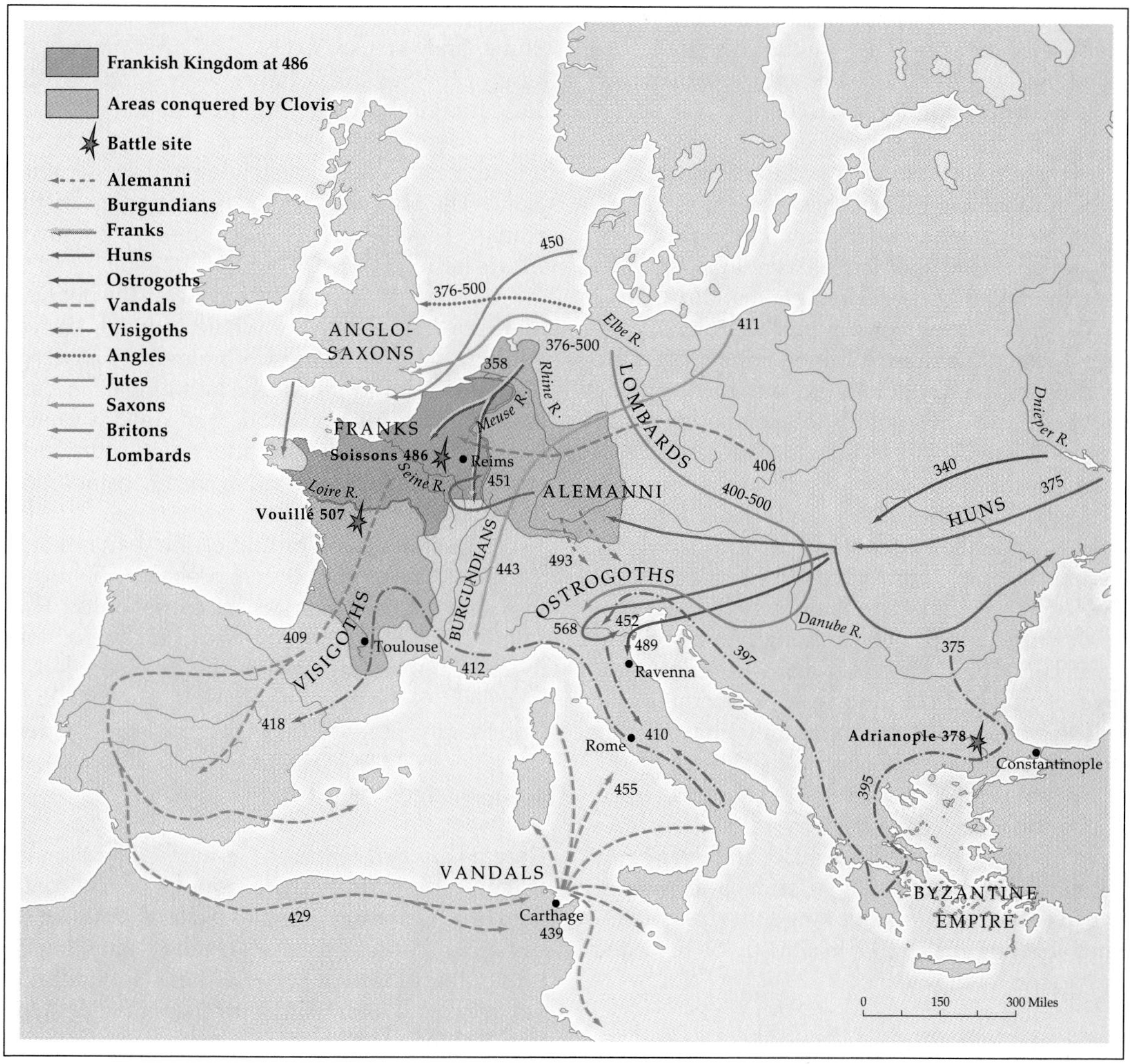

Map 6.1 INVASIONS, FOURTH THROUGH SIXTH CENTURIES

autonomous kingdom on Roman soil. At its height in the mid-fifth century the kingdom of the Visigoths extended from Gibraltar to the Loire River. Another Germanic people, the Franks, conquered the Visigothic kingdom in Gaul in the sixth century; and the Saracens[2] overpowered the surviving Visigothic kingdom in Spain in the eighth century.

Another Germanic people pushed by pressure from the Huns were the Vandals. The Vandals came from what is now eastern Germany and broke across the Rhine River into Gaul in 406. Perhaps 80,000 in number, they continued south through Spain and crossed to North Africa, where they established a permanent kingdom in 429. They were Arians and persecuted orthodox Christians. They became so powerful on the Mediterranean Sea that in 455 they were able to plunder Rome. This act, the cruelty involved in their religious persecutions, and their piracy in the Mediterranean earned the Vandals a reputation

[2]The name *Saracens* originally referred to Arabs living in the Sinai peninsula; in the Middle Ages the name was used to refer to Muslims in general.

for senseless violence, which the modern word *vandal* still reflects. The Vandal kingdom survived until the Byzantine emperor Justinian saw to its destruction in the sixth century.

The Burgundians, another Germanic tribe from eastern Europe, followed the Vandals into Gaul, probably in 411. These Germans established an independent kingdom in the valleys of the upper Rhône and Saône rivers in 443, which gave the region its permanent name, Burgundy.

The ease with which all these Germanic peoples invaded the Roman frontiers shows that the Empire had lost virtually all authority by the middle of the fifth century. The emperor Valentinian III was the last Roman to exercise any real power in the West and was followed by a series of feeble emperors. They were raised to the throne and then deposed or murdered by German officials, who were the effective rulers. One of these, Odovacar, deposed the last emperor in 476 (see p. 131). Although no more than a palace mutiny, this coup marks the final passage of power from Roman to German hands. Odovacar remained in control until he was overthrown in 493 by Theodoric, the leader of the Ostrogoths (eastern Goths). A shrewd ruler, Theodoric founded a kingdom in Italy that provided more than 30 years of peace and even some prosperity as Romans and Germans learned to live together. Although his kingdom was not destined for long survival, it may justly be regarded as the first medieval state.

Germanic Tribes in Gaul In the third and fourth centuries the Germanic tribes living just beyond the Roman frontier in the Rhine valley coalesced into two large federations, the Alemanni in the upper valley and the Franks in the lower valley. The Alemanni pushed beyond the Rhine into the middle of Gaul and founded a kingdom in 420. They give to both modern French and Spanish their names for Germany (*Allemagne, Alemania*). The Franks slowly penetrated into northern Gaul, moving across the valley of the Seine up to the Loire River. By the fifth century they had separated into two peoples: the Salian, or "salty," Franks, who occupied the lands from the shores of the British Channel to the Loire valley (excluding only Brittany); and the Ripuarian, or "river bank," Franks, whose history is wrapped in obscurity, but who seem to have settled between the Rhine and Meuse rivers. The first-mentioned king of the Salians, a figure who stands on the dark margin between legend and history, was called Merovech, and he gave his name to the first dynasty of Frankish kings, the Merovingians. The true founder of the kingdom of the Franks, however, was his putative grandson Clovis (481–511).[3]

Clovis' great accomplishment was the political unification of nearly the whole of Gaul, corresponding roughly to most of modern France. Already king of the Salians, he had himself elected king of the Ripuarians and thus ruled a united Frankish people. His sons added both Burgundy and Provence to the kingdom, nearly completing the conquest of Gaul.

No less important for unification than military force was Clovis' conversion, probably about 496, to Roman, rather than Arian, Christianity. This step facilitated his conquests and made possible the peaceful assimilation of the diverse peoples he ruled. As the first barbarians to accept Roman Christianity, the Franks became the "eldest daughter" of the Western Church and soon its acknowledged sword and champion.

Germans in Britain The Germanic invasions of Britain differed from the conquests on the continent. The Germans—Angles, Saxons, Jutes, even some Franks and Frisians—came in small bands under the authority of chiefs. These Germans did not settle and assimilate with the native peoples (the Britons) as they did in most other Roman provinces; they either exterminated the Britons or pushed them westward into Cornwall and Wales. In a search for safer homes, some Britons crossed the Channel to settle in the Roman province of Armorica, which therefore came to be called *Brittany*, or "little" Britain, as distinct from Great Britain, their former homeland. For a few decades in the early sixth century the Britons in Britain unsuccessfully rallied against the Germans under a king whom later sources call Arthur, but after 550 the Germans were triumphant

[3]His name is really a cognate of Louis; thus, by this historical oddity, all the long line of French kings named Louis are misnumbered.

▶ Baptism of Clovis I

Although this depiction of Clovis comes from a fourteenth-century manuscript, it suggests the continuing power of his image, and particularly the importance of his conversion and baptism, which is here commemorated some 800 years after the event. Even as the bishop performs the baptism, he is helped by an angel from above. Apart from its content, this miniature is a splendid example of the way the initial letters of chapters were decorated by medieval monks.

and imposed their language on the region. So sharp was the linguistic change thus enforced that modern English, apart from place names, shows little trace of the speech of the original Britons.

The Early Slavs The Slavic tribes living to the east of the Germans embarked on their own extensive migrations. In the fifth and sixth centuries some Slavic tribes pushed their settlements as far west as the Elbe River and as far north as the Baltic Sea; they are the ancestors of the modern West Slavs—the Poles, Czechs, and Slovaks. During the same years other Slavic tribes penetrated into the Balkan peninsula and Greece; their descendants are the modern South Slavs—the Serbs, Croats, Bulgarians, and Macedonians. Still other tribes moved east beyond the Dnieper River and north into the forest regions of Russia; they are the ancestors of the modern East Slavs—the Russians, Ukrainians, and Belarussians (or White Russians). No other Indo-European peoples came to occupy so extensive a geographic area as the Slavs, although distance inevitably weakened their ethnic and cultural unity.

GERMANS AND ROMANS

Historians have estimated, although on flimsy evidence, that the Germans who settled within the Roman Empire constituted no more than 5 percent of the total population. In the course of time, the Germanic chiefs and armies obtained perhaps a third of the territory of the former Empire. Most of the humble freemen (those who were not slaves) apparently settled as cultivators, obligated to pay rents and perform services to the owners of the property; but unlike the *coloni* in the Late Roman Empire, these freemen retained their liberty of movement. The Germans did not exterminate the Roman middle classes; rather, through intermarriage with Romans, the Germans adopted lives that made them almost indistinguishable from their Roman counterparts.

Historians no longer speak confidently, as they once did, of specifically Germanic contributions to medieval and Western civilization. Even before entering the Empire, many Germans, particularly those settled near the frontiers, had achieved a cultural level that resembled that of the Romans. Nonetheless, they arrived as invaders, and the destruction they wrought and their apparent reluctance to settle in cities accelerated the decline of urban life in the West. The centers of economic, social, and cultural life shifted to the countryside. This was a critical change, for cities had dominated the economy and culture of the Classical Mediterranean world.

GERMANIC SOCIETY

The Role of Women A sensitive indicator of social values in the study of any society is the status of women. The Roman historian Tacitus praises the Germans for their chastity and fidelity, but he notes that men "of high position" took several wives. German women, Tacitus also tells us, were mature at first marriage, and their husbands were their equals in age. To his surprise, the family of the groom paid a dowry to the bride, which was hers to keep and pass on to her heirs.

Women made essential contributions to the Germanic household at every social level. The free German male aspired to be a warrior; a wife who would tend his fields and watch over his flocks and herds during his absences enabled him to fight. The chief or king similarly looked for a wife who could collect his dues, pay his retainers, and manage his lands. Germanic women did these things, which slaves or freedmen had done in Classical society. The social importance of Germanic women was not, however, an unmixed benefit. According to Tacitus, they worked harder than the men. In a violent society they were often the prized booty for raiding expeditions and constant targets of abduction. Their life expectancy seems to have been shorter than that of males, and their resulting smaller number added to their social value.

▶ This small (8⅝ inches) ivory depiction of the Virgin was probably executed at Aachen, one of the capitals of Charlemagne, in the ninth century. Note that the Virgin holds spindles in her left hand; spinning was typically woman's work. But surprisingly, she also wears armor—gauntlets on her wrists and what look to be shoulder pieces. Though a woman doing woman's work, she is a militant, imperious figure, strikingly different from the motherly madonnas of later medieval art.

The Metropolitan Museum of Art.

Children The Germanic attitude toward children was also distinctive. The cultures of the Mediterranean world, based on literacy and learning, invested heavily in the education of the young. The illiterate Germans, by contrast, reared many children but invested little in their upbringing. Tacitus notes that the Germans, unlike the Romans, did not practice infanticide, though children of rich and poor were reared with equal indifference. This contrast in cultures helped ensure that the Germanic peoples would eventually overwhelm the Roman world through sheer numbers.

Social Structure The Germanic freemen owned land, and individual ownership existed as far back in their history as our knowledge goes. And individual ownership allowed some families to become richer than others. Germanic society was not egalitarian. Families with a common ancestry were linked together into kindreds (groups of near relatives; the common name for the Germanic kindred was the *Sippe*). The kindred fought, migrated, settled, and held certain forms of property (forests and wastelands) in common.

The kindred also adjudicated disputes among its members and avenged injuries done to them. Compensation was defined in money for loss of a person's life (his or her *Wergeld*, meaning basically "man money"), arm, eye, or nose. Since the circle of kin was frequently unable to protect its members, Germanic society often formed associations of self-help. Such an association was called by Tacitus a *comitatus* ("following"), in which young warriors would join the retinue of an established chief, follow him to battle, and fight under his leadership in return for his protection and a share of his booty. Another kind of self-help was provided by the guild, an association of equals, originally having no relation to economic life. Guild brothers sacrificed to the gods, feasted and drank together, and aided one another in danger.

Kindreds grouped together to form a tribe, a people, or a nation; members of a tribe always looked upon themselves, rightly or wrongly, as descendants from a common ancestor. Before the Germanic invasions of the Roman Empire, the tribes or peoples did not usually have kings; only the invasions, which required a continuing military command, made the king (who also served as chief priest) usual within Germanic society.

Law and Procedures Germanic laws were not written down until the sixth century, and reliance on oral tradition explains several peculiarities of Germanic institutions. To recall the ancient laws, the Germans consulted old, respected men of the community, who could remember what was done in the misty past. One of the most distinctive features of tribal government was its reliance on large councils or assemblies. The chief or king had only limited power and never made decisions alone; he always acted in an assembly or council of freemen who could help him recall the customs and aid him in making his judgments.

To confirm the making of contracts within the community, Germans (and the medieval world after them) relied heavily on symbolic gestures publicly performed. In conveying property, for example, the former owner would hand over a twig or a clod of earth to the new owner in the presence of witnesses. But since the memory of witnesses was often unreliable as a record of such agreements, the Germans also determined truth or falsehood, guilt or innocence, in disputes by investigating the character of the litigants or by appealing to magic. In a practice known as *compurgation*, 12 good men who typically knew nothing about the facts at issue would swear to the honest reputation and presumed innocence of the accused. Or the accused would undergo an *ordeal* (the word originally meant "judgment"), such as stepping barefoot over hot irons or immersing a hand in boiling water; if the feet or hand showed no severe burns, the accused was declared innocent. Sometimes two litigants would simply fight before the court on the assumption that God would not allow the innocent to be vanquished.

All these practices influenced the development of medieval law and government. The use of juries in trials, a common practice of Europe in the Middle Ages, was based on the assumption that the entire community, represented by sworn men, should determine when a law was violated. The medieval king, like his early Germanic predecessor, was also expected to make his major decisions with the advice of senior men, assembled in councils or parliaments (*see box*, p. 158).

Germanic Culture Since the Germans made little use of writing, their literature was preserved by oral transmission. Poetry, more easily memorized than prose, was the favored form of literary expression. The earliest surviving examples of Germanic poetry were not written down until the ninth century, but they still provide an authentic reflection of barbarian culture, testifying to a violent age. In the Anglo-Saxon epic *Beowulf*, the king of the Danes, Hrothgar, is powerless against the terrible monster Grendel; his plight illustrates the weakness of tribal kingship. Hrothgar must appeal for help to the hero Beowulf, a great warrior who offers the community its one hope of salvation.

Religion displayed an abiding sense of pessimism. The Germans saw nature as a hostile force controlled by two sets of gods. Minor deities, both good and bad, dwelt in groves, streams, fields, and seas, and directly affected human beings. Through incantations, spells, or charms, people tried to influence the actions of these spirits. Such magical practices strongly influenced popular religion and mixed with it a large element of superstition, which lasted through the Middle Ages and long beyond.

The higher gods lived in the sky and took a remote interest in human affairs. Chief among them was Woden or Odin, god of magic and victory, whom Tacitus equates with the Roman Mercury. Woden, his wife Friia or Frig, Thor the thunderer, Ti or Tyr the god of war—all give their names to days of the week in all Germanic

Tacitus on the Early Germans

The short book by Cornelius Tacitus,* Germania, *published in 98, is virtually the only surviving portrait of early Germanic society. In this passage Tacitus describes the customs of the Germans in government.

"On matters of minor importance only the chiefs deliberate, on major affairs the whole community; but, even where the people have the power to decide, the case is carefully considered in advance by the chiefs. Except in case of accident or emergency they assemble on fixed days. [. . .] When the mass so decide, they take their seats fully armed. Silence is then demanded by the priests, who on that occasion have also power to enforce obedience. [. . .] If a proposal displeases them, the people roar out their dissent; if they approve, they clash their spears.

"One can launch an accusation before the Council or bring a capital charge. The punishment varies to suit the crime. The traitor and deserter are hanged on trees, the coward, the shirker and the unnaturally vicious are drowned in miry swamps under a cover of wattled hurdles. The distinction in the punishment implies that deeds of violence should be paid for in the full glare of publicity, but that deeds of shame should be suppressed. Even for lighter offences the punishment varies. The man who is found guilty is fined so and so many horses or cattle. Part of the fine is paid to the King or State, part to the injured man or his relatives."

From Cornelius Tacitus, *Germania,* H. Mattingly (tr.), pp. 11–12.

▸ SUTTON HOO DRAGON
There were many metallic buckles and pins found at Sutton Hoo, the ship burial site of the East Anglian king Anna, who died in 654. Shown here is a dragon, made of gilt bronze and garnet. The body, extending from the head—with its jaws, teeth, and garnet eye—to the tail, is embellished in a style common at the time, with intricate beasts intertwined in long ribbon-like patterns.

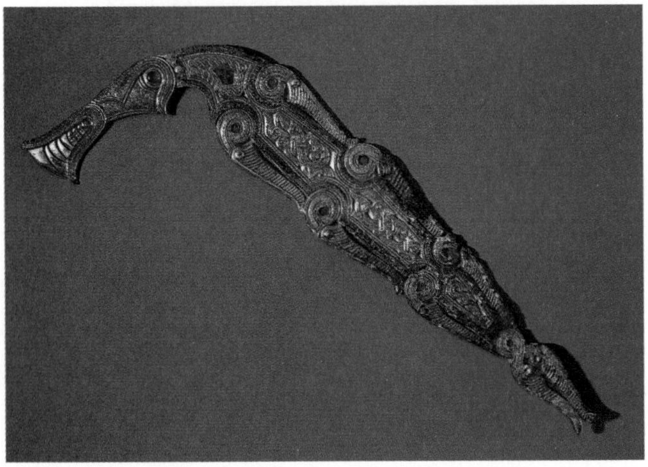

languages, including English. According to late Scandinavian myth, warriors who died in battle joined the following of Odin in a great banquet hall, Valhalla. But the entire company of gods and heroes was doomed to destruction by fire during a cosmic twilight when the ravaged earth would sink entirely into the sea. It is not known whether the early Germans shared this elaborate myth. They certainly shared in the exaltation of heroes and in a deep pessimism about humanity's ultimate fate.

Because they changed their homes so frequently, the Germans developed no monumental art—no temples, palaces, or large statues—before settling within the Empire. Their finest art was jewelry made from precious metals, often embodying forms of animals. This animal style, probably originating in the steppe region of eastern Europe and Asia, strongly influenced early medieval art; even the lettering and illuminations in the manuscripts of that epoch reflect some of its motifs.

The age after the Germanic invasions saw a near triumph of a nonliterate culture over the literate culture of the Roman aristocracy. The invaders were not alone responsible for the victory of this nonliterate culture, for the great, unlettered masses of the Empire surely shared many of the Germanic attitudes and practices; but the invasions did lend this vulgar culture a new strength and stability.

II. The New Economy, 500–900

The great achievement of the Early Middle Ages was the emergence of the single-family peasant farm as the basic unit of agricultural production. There were three reasons for this development. First, the declining supply of slaves induced many owners of villas to settle their slaves on these family farms. Second, changes in warfare, specifically the new supremacy of the mounted warrior, made fighting an expensive profession and converted many freemen into full-time cultivators. Finally, a series of technological innovations in agriculture aided the peasant in supporting himself, his family, and the new society.

AGRICULTURE

The most fertile agricultural region of Europe is the great alluvial plain that stretches from southeast England and France to the Urals. The peoples of the ancient world had not been able to farm it efficiently. The light plow of antiquity only scratched the heavy soils of the north, though it was suitable enough for the thin soil and dry climate in the Mediterranean, where only the surface needed to be pulverized to retain moisture. On the northern plain, however, the earth had to be cut deeply and turned to form the furrows needed to carry away excess water from the abundant rains. Thus a heavier, more powerful plow was needed. Most historians date the emergence of such a plow, simultaneously among the Germans and the Slavs, to the sixth century.

The development of the heavy plow was accompanied by other changes in farming techniques. The Mediterranean plow was dragged by two oxen, while the northern plow required as many as eight. Thus peasants in the north often kept oxen collectively and therefore needed to live in communities rather than in isolated individual settlements.

At the same time, new techniques allowed peasants to substitute the horse for the ox as a draft animal. The Romans had harnessed the horse with almost incredible inefficiency. The animal was bound to its load by pliant straps around the throat and belly that rewarded its best efforts with strangulation. Moreover, the load was bound so high on the horse's withers that the animal could not throw its full weight against the harness. In the ninth century northern Europeans developed a collar and harness that made efficient use of the horse as a draft animal. At about the same time there appeared the tandem harness, which permitted teams of horses to be hitched one behind the other, and the horseshoe, which gave the animal better traction and protected his sensitive hooves. By virtue of these devices the Early Middle Ages, in the words of one historian, "discovered horsepower."[4]

Northern Europeans also developed a new method of crop rotation: the three-field system, based on a triennial cycle and first documented in 763. The field was planted in winter wheat, then in a spring crop—oats, barley, peas, or beans—then permitted to lie fallow for a year. The older two-field system, based on the yearly alternation of winter wheat and fallow, continued to be used in Mediterranean lands, where spring crops were difficult to raise because rain was scarce in the spring and summer; but they grew well in the north because of the abundant year-round rainfall.

The three-field system kept a larger portion (two-thirds) of the soil under crops. It raised the productive efficiency of the peasant's labor by an even higher degree; the fallow, although it returned no crop, still had to be worked, and with a smaller fallow (one-third rather than one-half the land), the peasant had more time for productive labors. The spring crop restored fertility to the soil, provided a more varied diet for the people, and lessened the risk of total failure because

[4]Lynn T. White, Jr., *Medieval Technology and Social Change,* 1966, pp. 57–69.

BAD AND GOOD REGIMENT, CA. 1125
This manuscript illustration shows a typical medieval plow team of oxen. The heavy plow used on the plain of northern Europe included three indispensable parts: a colter or knife to cut the soil, a share or wedge to widen the breech and break up the clods, and a moldboard to lift the earth and turn the furrow.

two crops were planted in one year. The spring crop was often used for fodder and thus helped support a larger number of animals, which in turn provided manure for more abundant crops. For the first time the agricultural resources of the northern plain were used with some measure of efficiency.

These technological innovations were not victorious overnight; they spread through Europe at a glacial pace, but their eventual adoption profoundly affected the new Western civilization. They allowed northern Europe to support a denser population and established a tradition of technical innovation that has remained alive and unbroken to the present.

The Manor In the opening centuries of the Middle Ages, Europeans developed a new form of agricultural organization: the *manor*, or large estate. It differed from the Roman colonate above all in the status of the laborers. The owner of the Roman villa depended primarily on slaves or hired labor to work his lands, whereas the lord of the manor relied upon his *serfs*, as laborers dependent on the owner are called.

The manor was characteristic of southeast England, northern France, western Germany, and certain areas of the south, such as the Rhône and Po valleys. These were regions of fertile soil where grains were cultivated intensively. The manor, a tightly disciplined community of peasants organized under the authority of a lord, was therefore a fundamental unit of economic, political, and social organization.

The lands of most manors were divided into two roughly equal parts: the small farms that belonged to the peasants and the large demesne, or land owned by the lord that the peasants worked for him. All manors had extensive meadows, forests, and wastelands, where the lord hunted and the peasant grazed his animals or collected firewood. Forests and wastelands were usually part of the lord's demesne; the peasants would often have their own commons, a collectively owned meadow in which each resident had the right to graze a fixed number of animals. Many manors also had workshops that produced garments, tools, and other products needed by the community. Self-sufficiency, in other words, remained an ideal in manorial organization, although it was never completely realized.

The lord was the chief police officer and judge. He or his steward ran the court, which was an important source of revenues. The lord held the rights to operate the bakery, brewery, mill, and winepress on the manor and to sell the peasants salt or iron. He was also the chief military officer, recruiting soldiers from among the free peasants and leading them to war. For many peasants the manorial lord was the only government they ever directly confronted.

Most of the peasants inhabiting the manor were serfs; they, and their children after them, could not leave the land without the lord's permission. The defining element of serfdom was enforced labor. Men were usually obliged to work three days a week on the lord's land and to provide additional service at special times of the year, particularly at harvest. Women had to spend some time in the workshops producing cloth and clothing. The serfs paid, usually in goods, a yearly rental on their land and sometimes a small head tax to the lord. They also honored him with yearly gifts, such as eggs in the spring or a capon in the fall. When a serf died and his farm passed to a son, the family usually paid an inheritance tax, either the best animal or piece of furniture, to the lord. If a serf wished to marry someone outside the manor, he had to seek, and usually purchase, the lord's permission.

Although serfs lived harsh lives, their condition was still superior to that of the Roman slaves. Serfs had a moral right to their land, and they and their children could profit from the improvements they made on it. Moreover, the serfs' obligations were traditional and fixed and could not be raised.

THE EXCHANGE OF WEALTH

A new set of economic relations began to bind medieval society, relations largely defined by the flow of treasure—brooches, rings, plates, armor, and coins. The exquisite jewelry of the Early Middle Ages pleased the eye but also rewarded accomplishment, advertised status, and cemented the social structure. Kings gained treasure through pillage, gift, or tribute, and distributed the precious objects to their warriors and retainers.

The gift thus established a social bond between donor and recipient. Gifts made to churches that housed the bodies of saints placed these holy potentates under the obligation to bless and favor the donor. Finally, the flow of treasure defined social status. Even in death, the treasure buried with the king proclaimed his royalty to another world. The humble folk shared in this gift economy only by providing food to their rulers.

The gift economy all but replaced the market economy of the Classical Roman world. The Mediterranean above all had been a great commercial artery for the exchange of goods from the West for the spices and fine cloths of the Levant and for papyrus and grain from Egypt. By the seventh century the peasants and warriors of Western society no longer had the skill, or perhaps the desire, to maintain an economy based on commercial exports.

► VISIGOTHIC FIBULAE
Fibulae were decorative pins used to fasten clothes. These sixth-century Spanish examples are typical of the sophisticated metalwork practiced by medieval artisans. Gems set in gold and bronze reveal the outline of an eagle form, as well as a delight in pattern that was characteristic of the age.

III. The Leadership of the Church

The Church exercised an unrivaled leadership in the Early Middle Ages. This institution retained the Roman tradition of effective social organization and also kept alive the Classical tradition of literacy, rhetoric, and logic. One of history's great paradoxes is that the Church, so hostile to many values of the Classical tradition, was more effective than any other institution in ensuring their survival.

ORIGINS OF THE PAPACY

The papacy, the office through which one man governs the Roman Catholic Church, is the oldest living institution in the Western world; it is the only office that can trace its history back without interruption to the age of the Caesars. According to the traditional Catholic (and medieval) view, Jesus himself endowed the apostle Peter with supreme responsibility for his church.

> And I say unto thee, thou art Peter and upon this rock I will build my church, and the gates of hell shall not prevail against it.
>
> [MATT. 16:18]

In the Aramaic language that Jesus spoke, as well as in Greek and Latin, *Peter* and *rock* are the same words, implying that the Church was to be founded upon Peter. This play on words has been called the most momentous pun in history. Medieval tradition further held that Peter became the first bishop of Rome and was martyred there about the year 60.

The pronouncements of the Roman bishops were often accepted by the bishops of other churches with extraordinary reverence. In the second century Ignatius, bishop of Lyons, taught that beliefs accepted by the Roman bishops as orthodox should be considered orthodox by the entire Church. But in the third century Cyprian, bishop of Carthage, maintained that all bishops were equal in authority; there could be within the Church no "bishop of bishops."

It is hardly surprising that the church at Rome should have acquired preeminence. Rome was, after all, the city of the Caesars, the capital of the world, and the center of Latin culture; people were accustomed to seeking guidance from Rome. The Christian community there dated from apostolic times, and it had no Western rival in age, size, wealth, and talent.

Growth of Papal Primacy The idea of the absolute primacy of the pope, or bishop of Rome, gained support in the fourth and fifth centuries. The emperors, eager to use the Church as an ad-

▸ Pope Gregory the Great was one of the key figures in the transition from the ancient world to the Middle Ages. He is regarded—along with Jerome, Ambrose, and Augustine—as one (and the last) of the four fathers of the Latin Church. His efforts to defend Rome against the Lombards and to advance missionary work gave added prestige to the papal see.

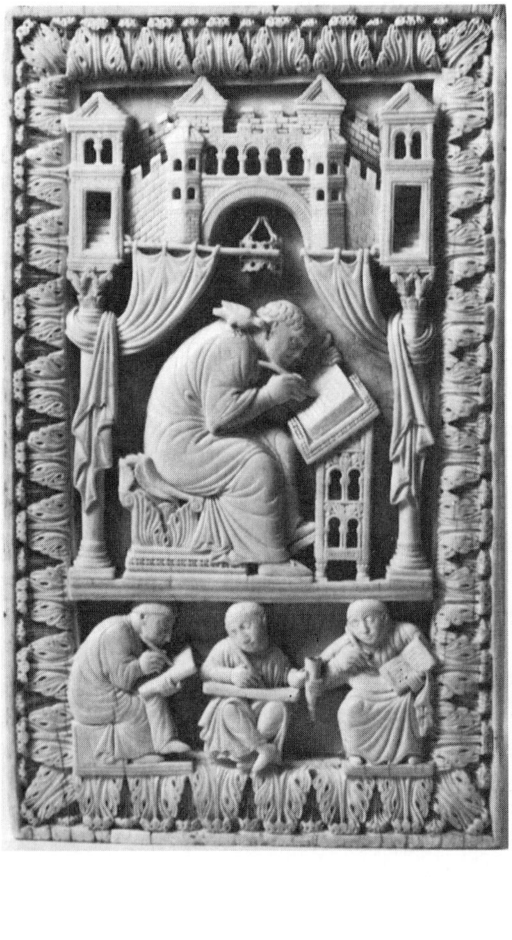

junct to their own imperial administration, favored the concentration of religious authority in Roman hands. The most effective promoter of the conception of Roman primacy was Pope Leo I (440–461). In numerous letters and sermons Leo identified the person of the living pope with the person of Peter, who was divinely commissioned to rule the Church. At the Council of Chalcedon in 451 (see p. 144) the bishops received the declaration of the papal legates with the words "Peter speaks through Leo." Although the popes were not exercising an autocracy over the Church, their prestige in the Western world was unrivaled.

Gregory the Great The popes increasingly assumed responsibility for the security of Italy and the defense of the Church. They negotiated with a sequence of invaders—Huns, Vandals, Ostrogoths, and Lombards—and repeatedly sought help from the distant and distracted Eastern emperors. The pope who best exemplifies the problems and accomplishments of the early medieval papacy is Gregory I (590–604).

When Gregory became pope, the Lombards (Germans who had entered Italy in 568) were plundering the Roman countryside and threatening Rome with destruction and starvation. Under these difficult conditions he maintained the productive capacity of the Church's estates, kept food coming to Rome, ransomed captives, aided widows and orphans, and organized the defense of the city. Gregory finally negotiated a truce with the Lombards in 598, although they continued to pose a threat to the security of Rome for more than a century.

Gregory was no less solicitous for the welfare of the entire Church. During his pontificate Gregory gave new momentum to missionary efforts and achieved some remarkable successes. He sent a monk named Augustine and 30 companions to bring Christianity to England, and these missionaries ultimately converted the Anglo-Saxons to Christianity. The Spanish Visigoths were also converted from Arian to Roman Christianity during Gregory's reign. By establishing a tradition of active involvement in the affairs of the world, to which most of his medieval successors would faithfully adhere, Gregory widened enormously the influence of the Roman see.

MONASTICISM

Even more effective than the papacy in shaping medieval civilization were the monks. The ascetic ideal of fleeing the world in order to devote oneself to worship is common to many religions. Beginning in the third century, monks—highly devout Christians who sought refuge in permanent prayer and isolation—began to live apart from humanity. The first to do so was St. Anthony, who lived a life of rigid asceticism in the desert of Egypt. But soon monks began to live and work together in cenobitic ("living in common") monasticism.

The monk who brought order into the movement, St. Benedict of Italy, founded a community at Monte Cassino in 529 and drew up a rule, or manual of conduct, for its members. The Benedictine rule referred to all the main problems of monastic life and was a constitution meant to be applicable to many individual communities; it is an example of the survival of Roman governmental genius in the service of the Church. The abbot was to be elected for life with full authority over the community, but he was to consult the

▶ St. Benedict Presenting His Rule
This fourteenth-century image depicts Saint Benedict presenting his rule to a group of nuns. His connection with female spirituality went back to his own lifetime, because his sister, Scholastica, was also devout and lived at a convent near Benedict's at Monte Cassino.

elder and even the younger monks. One of the most famous regulations required some manual labor, lending to it a dignity that both the Greeks and Romans had denied. "Idleness," said the regulation, "is the enemy of the soul."

The Role of the Monk The monks exerted an extraordinary influence on every level of medieval civilization. They were the most successful agriculturists of the age, first as farmers in their own right and then, gradually, as managers of ever larger estates; thus they set an example of good farming practices from which laypeople could benefit.

Monasteries came to play a major role in early medieval society and government. Powerful families often established monasteries on their lands. The abbots and abbesses were often closely related to these prominent laypeople, and they administered the monastery's lands and resources in the interest of their lay relatives. Monasteries, in other words, became integrated into the structures of local power.

Kings, too, relied heavily on monastic farms to supply food for their administrations and armies and often appropriated part of the monks' income to finance their own needs. Culturally, monks were almost the only people who were literate and learned. The Benedictine rule assumed that the monk could read; and the monasteries, although not expressly obliged to do so, maintained both libraries and schools for the training of young monks and, sometimes, lay children. The monks also organized *scriptoria,* or writing offices, in which manuscripts that were

▸ Plan of an Ideal Monastery, St. Gall, Switzerland, ca. 820
According to the rule of St. Benedict, a well-regulated monastic life centered around the liturgical hours, but also included a full range of physical activity. This plan for an ideal monastery from about 820 depicts the church and cloister at the center of a sprawling complex that also includes workshops for artisans, a school, and a hospital, as well as extensive agricultural lands.

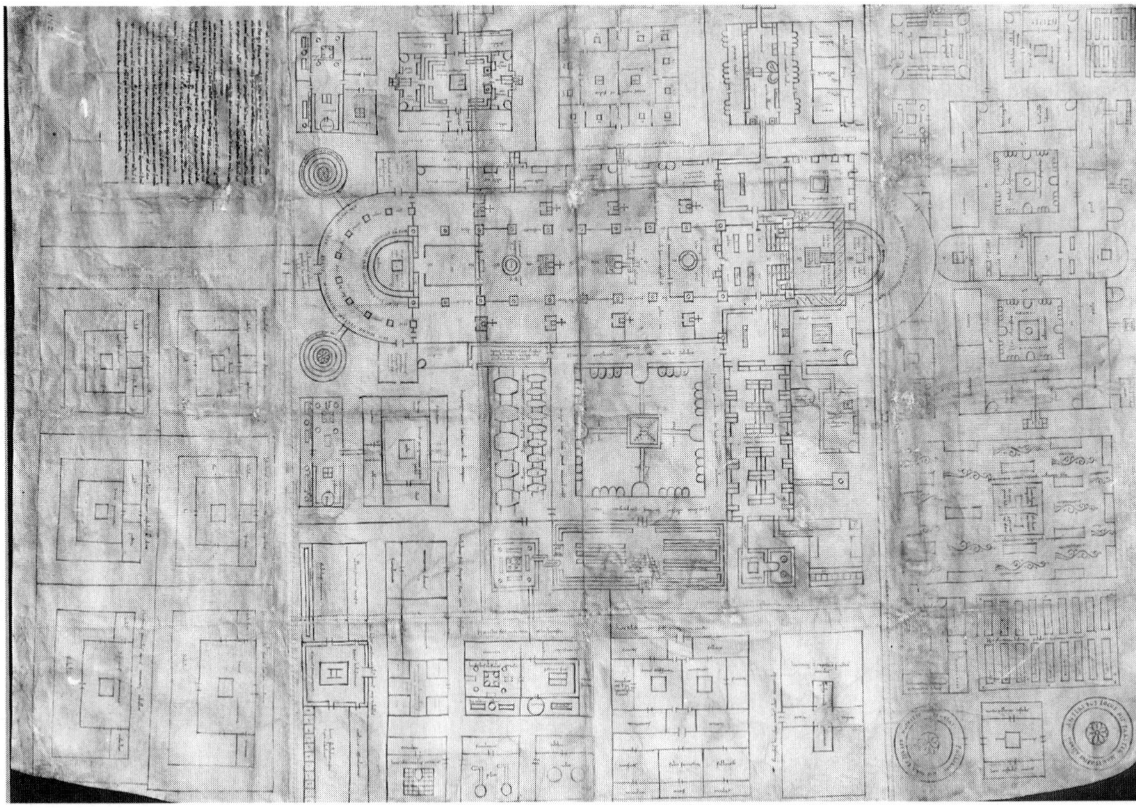

▸ **This Spanish manuscript illumination of daily life in the monastery shows that the writing of manuscripts was one of the monks' principal occupations. In addition, one of the monks is ringing the bells that marked the different services of the day and would have served to remind the surrounding countryside of the activities of the monastery.**

needed for liturgy or education were copied. The great bulk of the surviving Latin literary works of both pagan and Christian antiquity were preserved in copies made in monasteries. Sometimes monks decorated, or illuminated, the manuscript pages; manuscript illuminations are among the loveliest art forms that have come from the age. Because they maintained the schools and libraries, the monks were virtually the only intellectuals in society. Rulers recruited their counselors and officials from the monasteries, and nearly all the administrative records that have survived were written by monastic scribes. Finally, the monks, as holy men, were thought to ensure God's blessings for the world, and this helped

▸ **Centula Abbey, after Eleventh-Century Manuscript**
Centula Abbey, in northwestern France, was founded in 790 by Angilbert, a poet-scholar in Charlemagne's circle. This seventeenth-century engraving after a lost eleventh-century manuscript depicts the heart of a vast complex that included three churches (all known) and seven villages, and housed more than 300 monks.

support the morale of the troubled peoples of the Early Middle Ages.

Part of the monks' importance to society came from their communal organization, which enabled them to cope relatively effectively with the problems of a turbulent age. They could divide essential tasks among their members, assigning some monks to work the earth, others to arrange for the defense of the community, and still others to read and study. The community was also, in a real sense, immortal and could maintain continuity of effort over generations.

A second reason for the influence of monks on their society is that the ascetic temperament equipped monks to be powerful instruments of both economic and cultural change. Early medieval society was desperately poor. Like the people of every poor society, those of the Middle Ages hoped to shape a better future by saving and investing some part of the current, meager production. Grain uneaten and cattle not slaughtered meant more abundant harvests and larger herds the next year; whether the motivation that saved the grain or cattle was religious or economic hardly matters. Monks were the great savers and investors of the age, and their saving and investing may have influenced others to do the same.

Asceticism seems also peculiarly suited to an age of transition. The ascetic by his life calls into question the accepted attitudes of his age. The monks rejected both the Classical and barbarian systems of values and thus helped uproot or weaken such attitudes as the Classical aversion to physical labor and the barbarian love of violence. In so doing, they prepared the way for the elaboration of the new values and the new culture of the Central Middle Ages.

IV. The New Political Structures

THE FRANKISH EMPIRE

Clovis had established a strong Frankish kingdom in Gaul, but his Merovingian successors, known traditionally as the "do-nothing kings," showed the weaknesses of tribal monarchy. Unable to conceive of the kingdom as anything but a private estate, they divided and redivided their lands among their heirs. They showed no sense of political responsibility and relied primarily on violence to define their powers. The history of their reigns is largely a dismal story of intrigue and destructive feuds.

Yet amid the wars and rivalries the character of Frankish society was changing; the decisive shift was in the technique of making war. The

▶ Chi-Rho, *Book of Kells*

The Greek letters chi and rho, the first two letters of Christ's name, were frequently used as symbols of Christianity by early believers. This page, from the late eighth-century Irish manuscript *The Book of Kells,* is an example of the complex interlacing characteristic of Anglo-Saxon manuscript illumination in this period.

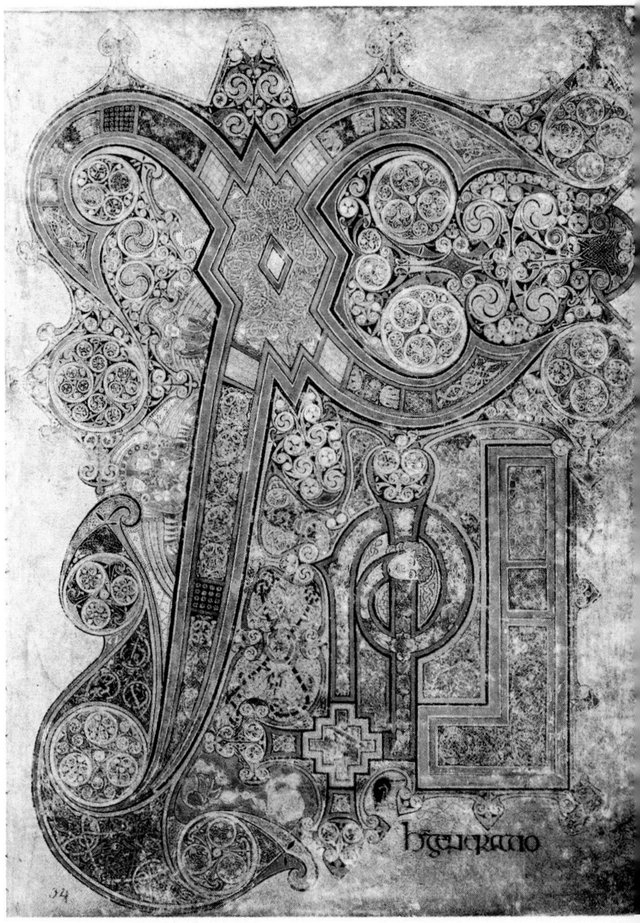

introduction of the stirrup, probably in the early eighth century, gave a final advantage to the mounted warrior over the foot soldier: He could now strike a hard blow without falling from his horse. This improvement confirmed the superiority, which had been evident for several centuries, of cavalry over infantry. Since horses were expensive, war became a preeminently aristocratic occupation; therefore a new functional and social division appeared in Frankish society. In the past most freemen had been both peasants and warriors. Now freemen who could not afford horses and arms—a majority of the population—became full-time peasants and serfs; those freemen who could afford the new implements of battle became full-time fighters and formed the new military aristocracy.

Because of the negligence of the Merovingian kings, their chief household official, known as the mayor of the palace, gradually took over the real powers of government. The mayor's functions were to manage the palaces and supervise the royal lands; he was also able to distribute the lands largely as he saw fit. Using this privilege, some of the mayors began to supply the aristocracy with the estates they needed to maintain expensive animals and arms. The mayors thus built a following among the new military aristocracy. One mayor, Pepin of Heristal, who already administered the eastern lands of the kingdom, gained control over the western lands in 687, thus unifying nearly the whole kingdom of Gaul under his rule.

Pepin's son and successor, Charles Martel, cultivated the support of the warrior aristocracy and gave substantial support to Christian missionaries. With the aid of these two groups, Charles began to extend Christianity and Frankish domination over the Germanic tribes settled beyond the Rhine River.

Charles's son, Pepin the Short, courted the allegiance of the other aristocracy of Frankish society, the great churchmen, by making a lasting alliance with the pope. The continuing support of the military aristocracy and the new sympathy of the ecclesiastical aristocracy enabled Pepin to effect a major constitutional change. In 751 an assembly of Frankish notables declared that the last Merovingian king, the feeble Childeric III, was not truly a king and recognized Pepin as their legitimate sovereign. In 754 Pope Stephen II visited Pepin's court, confirmed his coronation, and anointed him king. In return for these expressions of support Pepin defeated the Lombards, a Germanic people who had been harassing papal lands in Italy, and confirmed papal possession of the Patrimony of St. Peter (Rome and its environs). Later popes would repeatedly point to this Donation of Pepin as establishing the Papal States. By building strong Christian and Roman influences within his kingship, Pepin strengthened and transformed his reign. He bequeathed to his successors a monarchy founded on the support of great warriors and priests and dignified by association with the Christian and Roman past.

Charlemagne Pepin's son, Charles the Great, or Charlemagne (768–814), pursued the policies of his predecessors with unprecedented energy. His biographer, the court scholar Einhard, says that he was a large man, "seven times the length of his own foot," and that he delighted in physical exercise, particularly hunting, riding, bathing, and swimming. His taste for food and women seems to have been no less exuberant. Perhaps more remarkable in this man were his intellectual curiosity and alertness. He was probably illiterate; Einhard says that he kept tablets by his bed to practice forming letters at night though with "ill success." But Einhard also says that he spoke and understood Latin, comprehended Greek, and enjoyed the company of learned men (*see box,* p. 168). The vast empire Charlemagne built (called the "Carolingian" Empire from Carolus, his Latin name) was in large measure a personal accomplishment, a tribute to his abounding physical energy and intelligence.

Charlemagne's success as king depended on his success in waging long wars on every frontier. His chief concern was to spread Christianity and thus subservience to Frankish authority among pagan peoples. Where permanent conquest and conversion were not possible, the expeditions would still weaken neighboring enemies and prevent them from striking into the Frankish domains. At the pope's request he campaigned four times in Italy against the Lombards and against factions at Rome opposed to the pope. He suppressed the independent Bavarians and over-

Einhard on Charlemagne

The most important ruler of the Early Middle Ages was Charles the Great, or Charlemagne. A member of his court, Einhard, wrote his life and describes him as follows.

"Charles was large and strong, and of lofty stature; his height was seven times the length of his foot. In accordance with the national custom, he took frequent exercise on horseback and in hunting. He often practiced swimming, in which he was so skilled that none could surpass him. He was temperate in eating, and particularly so in drinking, for he hated drunkenness in anybody, much more in himself and in members of his household. While dining, he listened to reading or music. The subjects of the readings were the stories and deeds of older times; he was fond, too, of St. Augustine's books, and especially of 'The City of God.'

"Charles had the gift of ready and fluent speech, and could express himself with the utmost clearness. He was not satisfied with a command of only his native language, but studied foreign ones, and was such a master of Latin that he could speak it as well as his native tongue; but he could understand Greek better than he could speak it. He zealously cultivated the liberal arts, held those who taught them in great esteem, and conferred high honors on them. He also tried to write, and used to keep tablets under his pillow, so that in leisure hours he might train his hand to form the letters; but as he began his efforts late in life, he had poor success."

From Einhard, *Life of Charlemagne*, S. E. Turner (tr.) (shortened and modified).

came the Saxons after 33 years of fighting and thus brought them fully and finally into the community of Western peoples (*see box*, p. 169). These victorious wars added new territories to his empire (see Map 6.2).

On Charlemagne's fourth visit to Italy in 800, when he was praying before St. Peter's altar on Christmas night, Pope Leo III crowned him emperor of the Romans. The coronation of 800 added nothing to his possessions but still was of great symbolic importance. It confirmed the alliance of the papacy and the Frankish monarchy, and at a stroke created the alliance of Catholic states, Gaul and Italy, that defined the political axis of subsequent Western history and gave it its pronounced north-south orientation. It was a public declaration of the independence of the West, a final rejection of even a theoretical submission to the Eastern Empire that had become the heir of the Roman Empire. The coronation of 800 therefore marks the birth of Europe, for it proclaimed the complete political and cultural autonomy of the Western community of peoples.

Government The coronation added much to Charlemagne's dignity, and a grandiose imperial ideology developed around his person. The cult of the emperor played a vital role in preserving the unity of the empire because the government did not have the material force to hold it together. Charlemagne was presented to the people as the new David (the ideal king of the Old Testament), the new Augustus (the greatest of the pagan emperors), and the new Constantine (the champion of the Church). By presenting the emperor as a figure of such sanctity and brilliance, the government hoped to make rebellion against him unthinkable. Ideas might thus accomplish what armies could not do alone.

The emperor was, of course, the head of the government; and he was aided by several officials. The head of the palace clergy, the chief ecclesiastic of the realm, was the chaplain, who advised the emperor and the entire court in matters of conscience. The chaplain also supervised the chancery, or secretariat, where the official documents were written. The chief lay official was the count of the palace, who supervised the administration, judged cases that the emperor did not personally handle, and acted as regent during the emperor's frequent absences. Other officials included the chamberlain, who looked after the royal bedroom and treasury; the seneschal, who kept the palace in food and servants; and the constable, who cared for the horses.

At the local level the fundamental administrative unit was the county, which resembled in its extent the Roman provinces. The count was the administrator, judge, and military leader of the county. The county was further divided into small judicial units under a *vicarius*, who heard minor cases.

Charlemagne's chief administrative problem was to maintain an effective supervision and control over the local officials. He used three devices to resolve this problem. First, Charlemagne himself traveled widely to ascertain how the land was being administered and to hear appeals from the decisions of the counts. Second, he appointed special traveling inspectors, called *missi dominici*, to inspect a particular county every year. These men scrutinized the behavior of both the lay and the ecclesiastical officials, heard complaints, published imperial directives, and reported their findings to the emperor. Third, Charlemagne required that the important men of his realm, both laymen and ecclesiastics, attend a general assembly almost every year. There they reported on conditions in their local areas, advised the emperor on important matters, and heard his directives. Many of the imperial directives have survived. Divided into chapters (*capitula*), these informative records are known as *capitularies*.

To promote unity, Charlemagne also standardized weights, measures, and money throughout his empire. The monetary system came to be based on a single minted coin, the silver *denarius*, or penny. Twelve of these made a solidus, or shilling (although such a coin was not actually

Charlemagne Imposes Christianity on the Saxons

Charlemagne fought against the Saxons, a Germanic people, for about 30 years. After subduing them in 804 he made them Christians and imposed a kind of martial law, from which the following are some regulations.

"3. If anyone enters a church by violence and carries off anything in it by force or theft, or has burned the church itself, let him be punished by death.

"4. If anyone, out of contempt for Christianity, has despised the holy fast of Lent and has eaten flesh, let him be punished by death. But let the matter be considered by a priest, in case anyone has eaten flesh from necessity.

"5. If anyone has killed a bishop or priest or deacon, let him be punished by death.

"6. If anyone deceived by the devil has believed, in the manner of the pagans, that any man or woman is a witch and eats men, and on this account has burned the person, or has given the person's flesh to others to eat, or has eaten it himself, let him be punished by death.

"8. If any one of the race of the Saxons concealed among them has wished to hide himself unbaptized, and has scorned to come to baptism and has wished to remain a pagan, let him be punished by death.

"18. On the Lord's day no meetings and public judicial assemblies shall be held, unless in a case of great necessity or when war compels it, but all shall go to the church to hear the word of God, and shall be free for prayers or good works."

From *Capitulary for Saxony*, from *University of Pennsylvania Transactions and Reprints*, vol. VI, no. 5, 1900 (language modified).

Map 6.2 Frankish Empire under Charlemagne

The dates indicate the years when the regions were added to the empire. Marches were the frontier provinces (except Brittany, which was a maritime province) specially organized for the military defense of the empire. Magdeburg was the episcopal see that took the leadership in the conversion of the Danes and Slavs to Christianity. Aix-la-Chapelle, also called Aachen, was the capital of the empire. The tributary peoples were those beyond the frontiers of the empire over whom the emperor exercised a loose authority. They owed allegiance to him but were never integrated administratively into the empire.

minted), and twenty shillings made a pound. The Englishman who reckons prices in pounds, or the Italian in *lire*, still today uses terms of Carolingian origin.

Decline of the Empire Charlemagne passed on at his death to his single surviving son, Louis the Pious, a united and apparently strong empire. Louis, a weak and indecisive man, soon lost control over his own family, and his sons rebelled against him. After his death the three surviving sons partitioned the empire at the Treaty of Verdun in 843 and established their own kingdoms (see Map 6.3).

As the family of Carolingian rulers divided amid civil wars and partitions, the loyalty of the military aristocracy also waned. The new rulers conquered no new lands; so they had no new offices or properties with which to buy the loyalties of the aristocracy. The office of count, appointive under Charlemagne, became hereditary under his successors. The Carolingian rulers no longer summoned the great men of the realm to the yearly assemblies and no longer dispatched the *missi dominici* on their circuits. The institutional and moral bonds tying their central governments to the peripheral territories were thus broken or abandoned.

Map 6.3 **Partition of the Frankish Empire**

RENEWED INVASIONS

Under Charlemagne's weak successors invasions of the Frankish empire resumed, and centrifugal forces tore at the empire as well. To the south, Saracens from North Africa invaded Sicily and southern Italy in 827, attacked the valley of the Rhône in 842, and raided Rome in 846. Concurrently, from the East a new nomadic people, the Magyars, established themselves by about 895 in the valley of the Danube; and from this base for the next 50 years, they struck repeatedly into the areas that are now France, Germany, and Italy (see Maps 6.4 and 6.5).

The most wide-ranging of the new invasions were those mounted by the Northmen, or Vikings, who were Germanic tribes settled in Scandinavia. Their movements may be considered the last phase of the Germanic invasions begun in the fourth century. Several facts explain their invasions. The Vikings could not support a large population in the harsh northern climate, and they were familiar with the attractive wealth of the neighboring areas. The tribes were constantly at war with one another because there was no stable kingdom; a defeated chief, rather than become a vassal under his conqueror, often preferred to seek out new land overseas. The Vikings were skilled and versatile seamen whose explorations took them as far as a western territory they called Vinland, undoubtedly part of the North American continent. Iceland, settled as a result of these explorations, became a major center of medieval Scandinavian culture.

In England and on the continent the Vikings appeared first as merchants and pirates, then as conquerors and colonists. Vikings, chiefly Danes, began raiding England in 787; then in 866 a Danish army landed in eastern England and established a permanent settlement. The Vikings followed the same pattern on the continent. They attacked cities along the western coast of Europe, penetrated into the Mediterranean Sea, and invaded the valley of the Rhône. They sailed along the Russian river system to reach the Black Sea and raided Constantinople. In 911 the Viking Rollo secured from Charles the Simple, the king of France, the territory near the mouth of the Seine River, which became known as Normandy (from the name *Northmen*).

This new wave of invasion, though less dis-

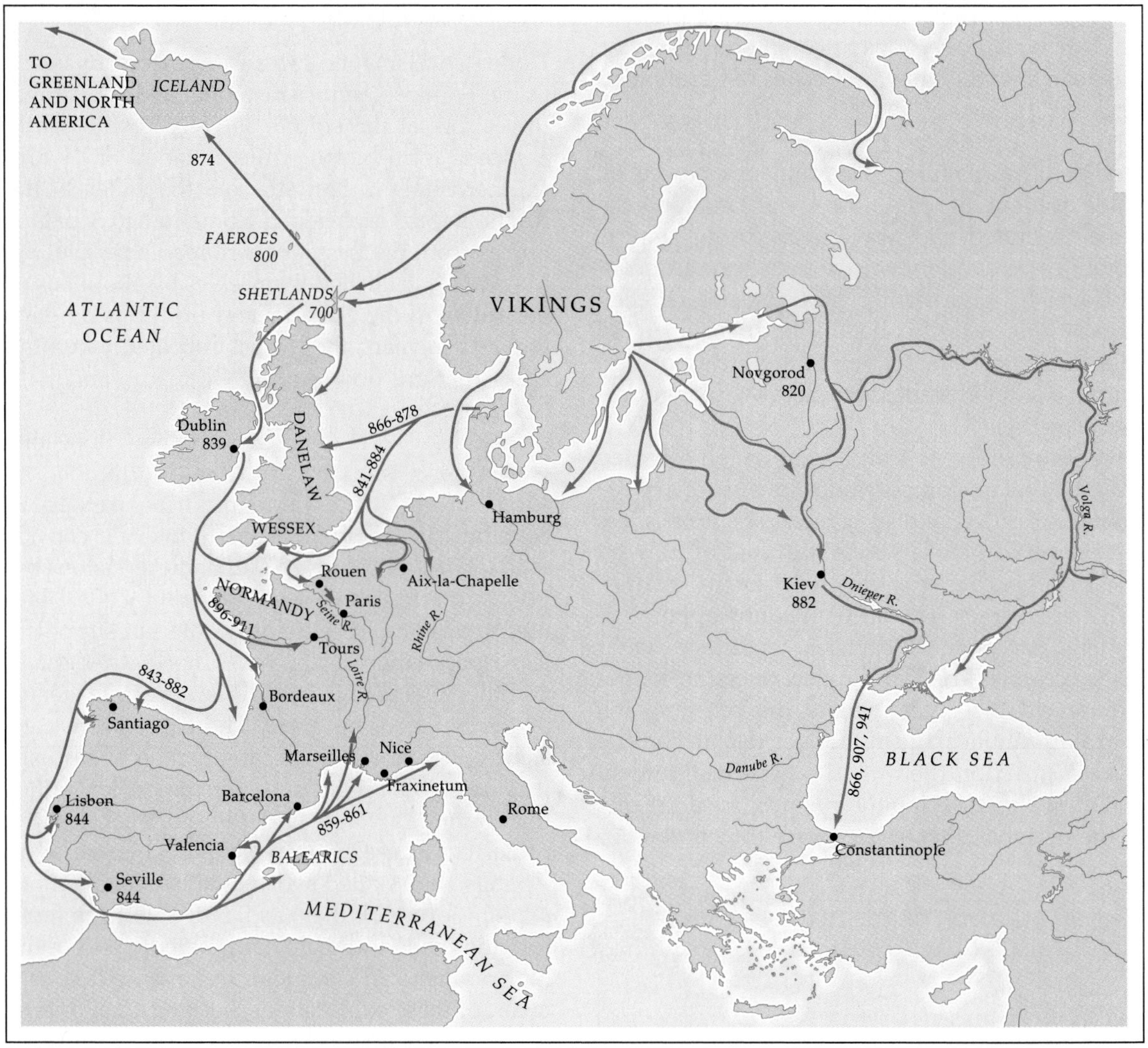

Map 6.4 Invasions of Northern Europe, Eighth through Ninth Centuries

ruptive than the great movements of peoples in the fourth and fifth centuries, opened for Western Europe a new dark age. Amid the violence, however, the work of Christianizing the pagan peoples continued. Missionaries in the tenth and eleventh centuries successfully converted the Magyars, Vikings, and Western Slavs (Poles and Czechs).

With their conversion to Christianity and simultaneous establishment of a stable kingdom, the Magyars, alone among the nomadic tribes that had invaded Europe, retained their linguistic and ethnic identity until the present as the modern Hungarians. From about the year 1000 neither Magyars nor Vikings nor Western Slavs represented a foreign or heathen threat to Christian Europe; rather, they had all become full partners in the community of Western peoples.

ANGLO-SAXON ENGLAND

The Germanic invasions in the fourth through sixth centuries divided England into more than 20 petty dynasties and kingdoms. They became fused into a single kingdom, but true political unity was not reached until after the Norman Conquest in 1066.

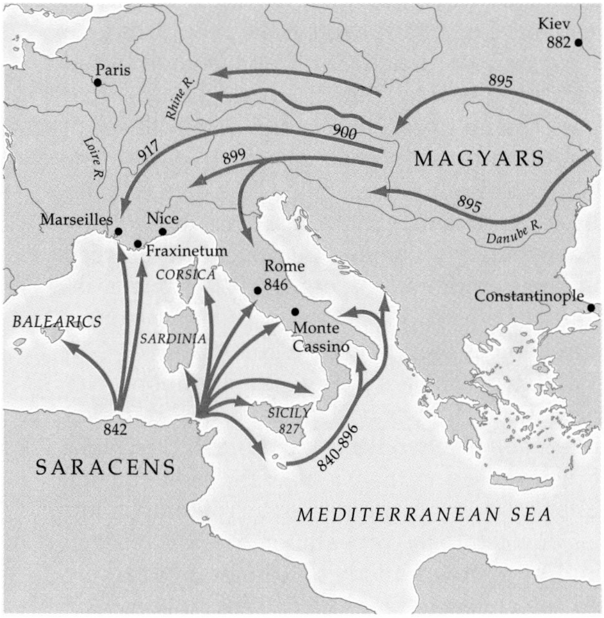

Map 6.5 INVASIONS OF SOUTHERN EUROPE, NINTH THROUGH TENTH CENTURIES

England achieved religious unity before political unity. Augustine and his fellow missionaries dispatched by Pope Gregory arrived in Kent in 597; but other Christian missionaries, especially the Irish, were already converting the island to a Christianity that differed from the Roman version.[5] Not until the late seventh century did Theodore of Tarsus, a monk from the Middle East who served as archbishop of Canterbury, complete the work of ecclesiastical unification. He reformed monastic education, held numerous councils, made the authority of Canterbury felt through the land, and helped give England one of the most vigorous and learned churches of the age.

Political unity came more slowly. The numerous petty dynasties coalesced into seven fairly stable kingdoms, traditionally known as the heptarchy: Northumbria, Mercia, East Anglia, Essex, Sussex, Kent, and Wessex (see Map 6.6). The first kings to exert a stable hegemony over England were the rulers of Northumbria in the seventh and eighth centuries. This was the golden age of Northumbrian culture; the monastery at Wearmouth-Jarrow then counted among its members Bede the Venerable, the greatest scholar of his day. But Northumbrian rule was short-lived, and by the late ninth century leadership passed to Egbert of Wessex and his successors.

Alfred the Great To the kings of Wessex fell the task of defending England against the Danes. The greatest of these kings was Alfred (871–899), the first king effectively to rule over the entire English people. After experiencing military defeats by the Danes in the early years of his reign, Alfred reorganized the defense of the kingdom. He reformed the militia to keep a larger and more mobile army in the field and built fortresses to defend the land and ships to defend the coast. His reforms proved successful. Before 880 several Danish chiefs received baptism as part of a treaty with Alfred, and in 886 the Danes agreed to confine themselves to a region in the north and east of England. This region, which the Danes continued to dominate for several generations, was later to be known as the *Danelaw*, in recognition of the fact that the Danish laws in force there dif-

Map 6.6 ANGLO-SAXON ENGLAND

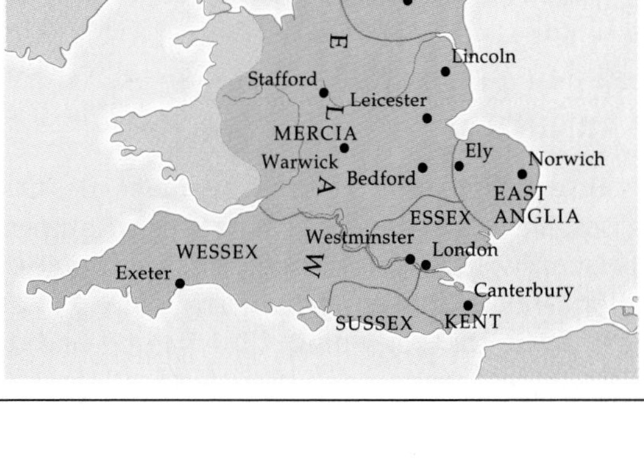

[5]Irish Christians set the date of Easter later than the Romans (reflecting later springs in the north), applied the tonsure (the haircut symbolizing clerical status) in their own way, and conceived differently the role and powers of the bishop.

fered from the English laws of other parts of the country.

Alfred also renewed intellectual activity; for example, he gathered a group of scholars and began a program of translating into Anglo-Saxon the works of several historians and theologians. During his reign an unknown author compiled a history of England known as the *Anglo-Saxon Chronicle.* Continued thereafter by various authors and now extant in several versions, the *Chronicle* is an indispensable source for the later Anglo-Saxon period in English history.

The English resurgence initiated under Alfred continued under his successors for almost a century. However, by 991 King Ethelred was unable to overcome renewed Danish advances and agreed to pay tribute to the Danes. The tax he imposed to meet the tribute was called the Danegeld. Its payment was a mark of weakness, but the Danegeld was still a national tax and shows that the kingdom remained united. In 1013 the Danish King Swein invaded and conquered England, which became a province in a great northern empire. His son Canute ruled Denmark, Norway, and England; but at his death in 1035 the empire disintegrated and Edward, a descendant of Alfred, became the king of England.

V. Letters and Learning

The great movement of peoples in the fourth and fifth centuries nearly destroyed the great Classical heritage of literature and learning. But the tradition of Classical learning did not entirely succumb. It survived in a peculiar context and for a peculiar purpose: to serve the Christian Church and to promote the interests of the Christian religion.

THE CHURCH AND CLASSICAL LEARNING

Because Christianity rebelled against Classical values, it is understandable that many prominent Christian writers condemned Classical literature as foolishness and an incitement to sin. Yet almost from the beginning Christianity had to make some accommodation to secular learning. Christianity was a religion founded on a book, the Bible. God had spoken to his people through the written word, and Christian theologians had to have the skill to read and interpret the sacred texts. The only way they could obtain this skill was to study at secular schools, because the Church had not yet established its own schools. The leaders of the Christian community, therefore, had to study under the same teachers, read the same authors, and master the same techniques of philosophical argument and rhetorical expression as their pagan neighbors.

Christian scholars preserved a tradition of literacy in the fifth and sixth centuries, but their output accurately reflects the difficult conditions of their times and the biases of their own mental outlook. An important part of their literary effort was devoted to the preparation of textbooks that would preserve a modicum of ancient learning and the ability to read the ancient authors. One of the most influential of these textbooks was the *Introductions to Divine and Human Readings* by a sixth-century Italian official and monk, Cassiodorus. In it he listed the religious and secular books that he thought a monk should copy and read. This book is about as appealing to modern readers as a library catalog, but it was carefully studied and helped to determine the holdings of medieval libraries.

Another sixth-century Italian Christian scholar, Boethius, translated several of Aristotle's treatises on logic from Greek into Latin; these translations were the main source of early medieval writers' limited but significant familiarity with Aristotelian logic. Boethius wrote on many other subjects as well and was most famed for his *Consolation of Philosophy,* a meditation on death that does not mention the Christian religion. The *Consolation* helped preserve the dignity of learning by showing the role that reason and philosophy play in solving human problems. Less elegant than the *Consolation,* but equally popular, were the *Etymologies* by Isidore, bishop of Seville, which were a vast encyclopedia of ancient learning, covering in 20 books subjects from theology to furniture and providing a rich source of Classical lore and learning for medieval writers.

Christian Writings Scholars also helped through original works to shape the character and interest of the age, especially by writing *exegeses*, or comments and interpretation, on the Bible. In this field the most important writer after St. Augustine was Pope Gregory. In his *Moralia in Job*, a commentary on the Book of Job, Gregory made extravagant use of allegory in explaining the biblical text and set the style for biblical exegesis in the medieval world.

Pope Gregory also taught readers about the lives of the saints and the miracles God wrought through them, notably through his *Dialogues*, a record of the lives and miracles of the holy men of Italy. Since Christians viewed history as a vast panorama illustrating and proclaiming God's miraculous providence, the study of history also evoked great interest among scholars. One of the most influential accounts was the *History of the Franks* by Gregory, bishop of Tours. Like many of the early medieval historians, Gregory began with Creation; he then recounted the history of the human race up to 591.

Modern readers are often surprised by the endless parade of miracles reported in medieval sources and slightly stunned by the apparent gullibility of the scholars who wrote such accounts, but we must view the miracles as did those who recorded them. For these writers the miraculous interventions of God leading his people to salvation gave purpose to human life and order to an otherwise chaotic world. In a universe shaped by the operations of grace, the miraculous was the natural and the expected.

Learning and Scholarship Scholarship on the continent sank to its lowest level in the seventh and early eighth centuries, but it flourished in Ireland in the seventh and England in the early eighth century. Scholars there enjoyed the relative shelter of an insular home. They had the zeal of new converts and a strong monastic system that supported the schools. Since they did not speak a language derived from Latin, they could learn a correct Latin in schools without being confused by related vernacular forms.

The finest English scholar was undoubtedly Bede the Venerable (673?–735), whose *Ecclesiastical History of the English People*, an account of the conversion of the English and the growth of their Church, established his fame even until today. His high sense of scholarship is evident in the careful way he collected and used documents and interviewed witnesses. As a faithful Christian, Bede accepted miracles, and the story of salvation is the principal theme of his history. But his belief that history was the unfolding of God's plan did not lead him to distort the material in his sources. He is a man whom any age would recognize as a scholar.

THE CAROLINGIAN RENAISSANCE

The Frankish rulers—Pepin, Charlemagne, and their successors—promoted learning within their domains in the movement known as the Carolingian Renaissance. These rulers were interested in learning for several reasons. In the sixth and seventh centuries, when the continent was divided among many small kingdoms, different styles of writing, known as *national hands* (Visigothic, Merovingian, Lombard, Beneventan, and so on), had developed; and numerous variant readings had slipped into such basic texts as the Bible and the Benedictine rule. The Latin grammar used by scholars had also absorbed many regional pecularities.

Literate persons in one part of Europe thus had great difficulty recognizing or reading a text written in another. The widespread decline in education had left few persons who could read at all. Furthermore, poorly educated priests could not properly perform the liturgy, on which God's blessings on the community were thought to depend; and variations in religious rituals were also growing. Both situations weakened the unity of the Church as well as the state.

Pepin and Charlemagne attempted to develop a standard curriculum, based on the same versions of the same texts and written in the same form of handwriting. They invited to court scholars from all over Europe for this purpose. To increase the supply of locally trained scholars, both Pepin and Charlemagne ordered all bishops and monasteries to establish schools to educate boys. Charlemagne himself set the example by founding a palace school for the sons of his own courtiers, but the school seems to have had little permanent impact on the intellectual life of the age.

One great achievement of this educational revival was a reform in handwriting. About the year 800, monks at the monasteries of Corbie and

Tours devised a new type of formal literary writing, a "book-hand," using lower-case letters and known as the Carolingian minuscule. Previously, the book-hands used for important texts had been based on various styles of capital letters only. But a book page written entirely in capitals is difficult to read rapidly; the eye is not aided in distinguishing letters by protrusions above and below the line. The Carolingian minuscule, the first book-hand based on lower-case letters, made rapid reading easier. In addition, more letters could be written on a page with this new script; thus more books were produced at less expense.

▸ The ninth-century manuscript illumination from the first Bible of Charles the Bald displays the Carolingian minuscule, which is the model for the lower-case letters used today in what printers call Roman type.

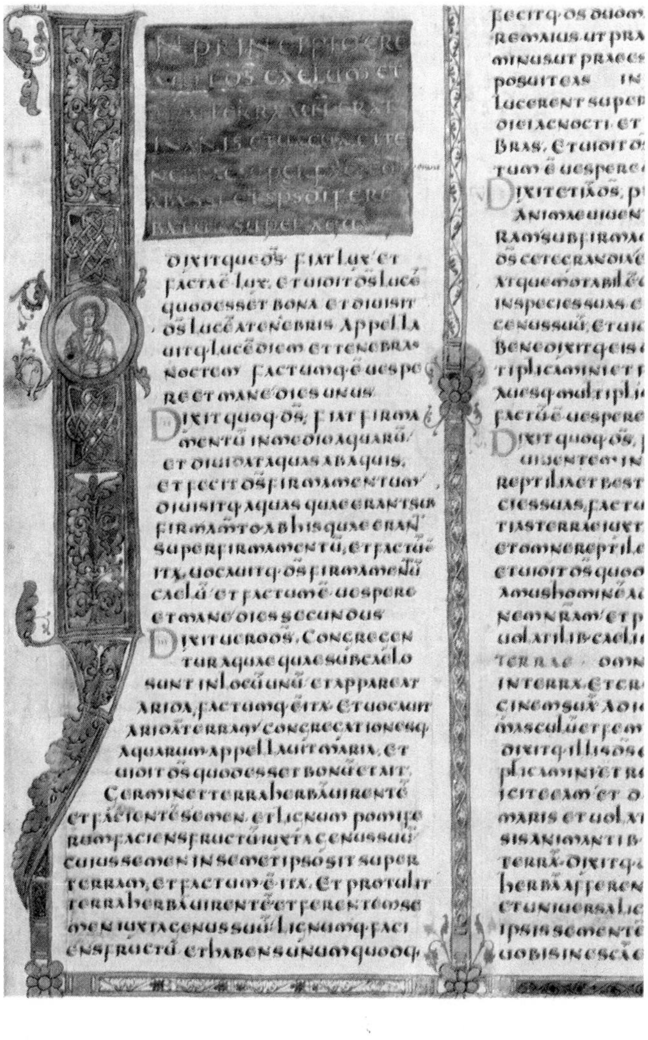

Use of this graceful new script eventually spread across Europe.

Another achievement of this educational revival was the development of a common scholarly language. Carolingian scholars perfected a distinctive language now known as Medieval Latin, which largely retained the grammatical rules of Classical Latin but was more flexible and open in its vocabulary, freely coining new words to express the new realities of the age. Medieval Latin was also clearly different from the vulgar, or Romance, Latin spoken by the people. The establishment of Medieval Latin as a distinct language of learning thus freed the Romance vernaculars to develop on their own. One of these vernacular languages is Old French, whose oldest surviving text dates from 842.[6]

The Latin created by the Carolingian scholars enabled travelers, administrators, and scholars to make themselves understood in all parts of Europe; and it continued to serve this function until the modern era. Even when it disappeared as an international language, it helped promote European unity. All the modern vernacular tongues of Europe developed under the strong influence of these scholars' Latin. One of the reasons why it is possible to translate quickly from one European language to another is that their learned vocabularies are in large measure based on common Latin models.

A further achievement of the educational revival was the standardization of important texts. Pepin "decorated all the churches of the Gauls with the songs of the Roman church"; that is, he sought to standardize the liturgy on the basis of Roman practice. Charlemagne continued this policy of standardization. He had the English scholar Alcuin of York, who served as a sort of minister of cultural affairs from about 783 until 794, prepare a new edition of Jerome's Vulgate translation of the Bible. This edition became the common biblical text for the entire Western Church. Charlemagne procured from Monte Cassino a copy of the Benedictine rule and had it

[6]At Strasbourg in 842, Charles the Bald and Louis the German, two of the sons of Louis the Pious, took an oath that was recorded in Latin, Old French, and German. The oath at Strasbourg not only preserves the oldest surviving text in Old French but also marks the first use of German in a formal legal document.

copied and distributed, so that monks everywhere would follow a standard code. He also initiated standardization into the school curriculum, based on the seven liberal arts. Alcuin divided the curriculum into the *trivium*, or verbal arts (grammar, rhetoric, and logic), and the *quadrivium*, or mathematical arts (arithmetic, astronomy, geometry, and music).

Carolingian scholars wrote lengthy educational tracts and huge quantities of didactic poetry, but little of their work can be considered

▶ **EZRA RESTORING THE BIBLE**
The image of Ezra restoring the Bible, in this eighth-century English manuscript, gives the work of the medieval monk an exalted self-justification. Here we see a biblical figure doing exactly what monks did—namely, writing and copying. In this case, Ezra was purifying the text of the Bible, and the implication was that monks were engaged in the same task. The vivid depiction of the bookshelves, with their open doors, and the table and stool are clearly an attempt to bring to life a scene from a monastery of the time.

notable for original thought or rhetorical grace. This is understandable. Most of the scholars were grammarians and educators, engaged in producing teachers' manuals, textbooks, and school exercises; they went back to the Latin classics to find models of correct grammar, usage, and vocabulary, but not for aesthetic satisfaction or philosophical insights. Their work was nonetheless of the greatest importance for the intellectual growth of Europe. The revived mastery of correct Latin equipped scholars of later generations to return to the Classical heritage and to recover from it philosophic and aesthetic values.

▶ PHILOSOPHY CONSOLING BOETHIUS, EARLY ELEVENTH CENTURY
In his *Consolation of Philosophy,* Boethius described the embodiment of philosophy as a mature woman who had grown as tall as the heavens, carrying a scepter and books. This image, from an eleventh-century manuscript, depicts philosophy as equal in height to the building whose solid facade and row of small windows may be the prison where Boethius wrote his famous work.

The Carolingian Renaissance made possible all subsequent renaissances in the history of Western thought. The establishment of Latin as a universal language permitted easy communication within Europe and made possible that vigorous and creative dialogue across linguistic frontiers on which the growth of Western scholarship has since depended. Even if the Early Middle Ages left no brilliant cultural monuments, it did lay the foundations on which the achievements of all subsequent periods of Western history have rested.

Recommended Reading

Sources

Colgrave, B. (ed.). *The Life of Bishop Wilfrid . . . , Two Lives of Saint Cuthbert . . . , Felix's Life of Saint Guthlac, and The Earliest Life of Gregory the Great.* 1985. An anthology of seventh- and eighth-century saints' lives, prime sources for social as well as Church history.

*Einhard. *The Life of Charlemagne.* 1962.

*Herlihy, David (ed.). *Medieval Culture and Society.* 1968.

Hillgarth, J. N. (ed.). *The Conversion of Western Europe, 350–750.* 1969.

*Mattingly, H. (tr.). *Tacitus on Britain and Germany. A Translation of the "Agricola" and the "Germania."* 1967.

Studies

*Baker, Derek (ed.). *Medieval Women.* 1981. Essays on both individual women and social movements concerning women.

Boussard, Jacques. *The Civilization of Charlemagne.* 1968.

Brown, Peter. *The Cult of the Saints. Its Rise and Function*

*Available in paperback.

in Latin Christianity. 1980. Locates its rise not in popular religion but in the power structures of late ancient society.

Burns, Thomas S. *A History of the Ostrogoths.* 1984. Based on archaeological as well as literary evidence.

Byock, Jesse. *Medieval Iceland.* 1988. The history of a society without a state.

The Cambridge Economic History of Europe. 1941–. Four volumes to date; the standard reference for all economic questions. A revised edition of Volume I (on agriculture) was published in 1966 and of Volume II (on trade) in 1987.

The Cambridge Medieval History, 1911–1936. Partially outdated but still a useful work of reference.

Campbell, James (ed.). *The Anglo-Saxons.* 1982. Essays presenting the latest archaeological and other research.

*Duby, Georges. *The Early Growth of the European Economy: Warriors and Peasants from the Seventh to the Twelfth Century.* Howard B. Clark (tr.). 1974. The early medieval economy viewed in terms of "gift and pillage."

*Dunbabin, Jean. *France in the Making: 843–1180.* 1985. On the formation of the political structure of France and the growth of a strong monarchy.

*Fell, Christine (and others). *Women in Anglo-Saxon England and the Impact of 1066.* 1984. Anglo-Saxon social history with women at its center.

*Fichtenau, Heinrich. *The Carolingian Empire.* P. Munz (tr.). 1963. An unsympathetic view of Charlemagne and his policies.

Fleckenstein, Josef. *Early Medieval Germany.* Bernard F. Smith (tr.). 1978. Germanic institutions from the migrations to the eleventh century.

Fossier, Robert (ed.). *The Cambridge Illustrated History of the Middle Ages, I: 350–950.* Janet Sondheimer (tr.). 1989. Essays by French scholars, including four on Eastern Europe. Full bibliographies; lavishly illustrated.

*Geary, Patrick. *Before France and Germany: The Creation and Transformation of the Merovingian World.* 1988. A comprehensive summary of recent research, stressing the importance of the Roman heritage for the growth of Frankish institutions.

Goffart, Walter. *Barbarians and Romans, A.D. 418–584: The Techniques of Accommodation.* 1980. A careful inquiry into the obscurities of barbarian settlement within the Empire.

———. *The Narrators of Barbarian History (A.D. 550–800): Iordanes, Gregory of Tours, Bede and Paul the Deacon.* 1988.

*Herrin, Judith. *The Formation of Christendom.* 1987. A survey of the development of the Christian world, from Constantine to the mid-ninth century, with particular emphasis on the Western debt to Byzantium.

Herwig, Wolfram. *History of the Goths.* Thomas J. Dunlap (tr.). 1988. Stresses the instability of Gothic tribal formations.

Horn, Walter W., and Ernest Born. *The Plan of St. Gall.* 1979. Reconstruction of the architecture and the life of a major Carolingian monastery.

James, Edward. *The Franks.* 1988.

———. *The Origins of France, 500–1000.* 1982. Community and authority in the Merovingian-Carolingian world.

Laistner, Max. *Thought and Letters in Western Europe: A.D. 500 to 900.* 1955. Basic guide to early medieval authors.

*Lawrence, C. H. *Medieval Monasticism: Forms of Religious Life in Western Europe in the Middle Ages* (2d ed.). 1989. On the Rule of Benedict, the rise of Cluny, and other topics.

*Moss, H. St. L. B. *The Birth of the Middle Ages: 395–814.* 1977. An older historical survey; solid, detailed narrative.

Musset, Lucien. *The Germanic Invasions: The Making of Europe, A.D. 400–600.* Edward and Columba James (trs.). 1975. Excellent survey.

*Reuther, Timothy (ed.). *The Medieval Nobility.* 1978.

Riché, Pierre. *Daily Life in the World of Charlemagne.* Jo Ann McNamara (tr.). 1975.

Sawyer, P. H. *Kings and Vikings: Scandinavia and Europe A.D. 700–1100.* 1984. Excellent summary of recent research on the Vikings.

Stenton, Frank. *Anglo-Saxon England.* 1971. Basic introductory text.

*Thrupp, Sylvia L. (ed.). *Early Medieval Society.* 1967. Essays emphasizing social development, the family, and commerce; modern sociological approaches.

*Wallace-Hadrill, J. M. *The Barbarian West.* 1962. Brief and readable essays.

Wemple, Suzanne Fonay. *Women in Frankish Society: Marriage and the Cloister, 500 to* 800. 1981. An important study of a neglected topic.

Wickham, Chris. *Early Medieval Italy: Central Power and Local Society 400–1100.* 1981. Mainly social history of the decline of unity within Italy after the fall of the Roman Empire.

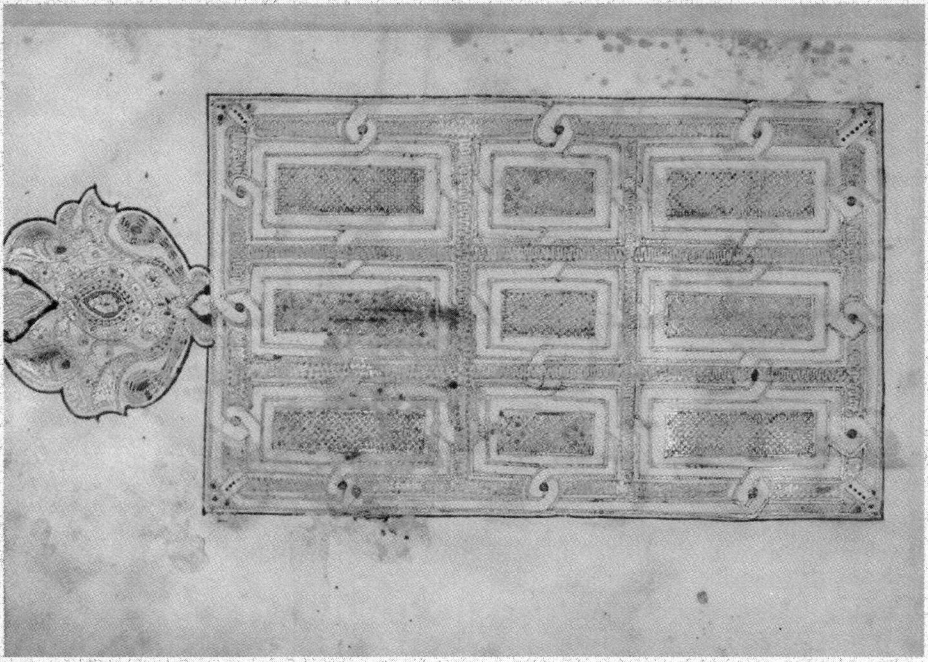

KORAN, NINTH THROUGH TENTH CENTURY
The Koran, the sacred book of Islam, in a ninth- or tenth-century printing. From the ninth century the design of sacred books followed specific forms that remained standard in Islamic art. Color and gilding are added not only as ornament but also to separate verses; the leafy projection to the left signals the beginning of a new chapter.

CHAPTER SEVEN

THE EARLY MEDIEVAL EAST

THE Early Middle Ages were a period of profound social and spiritual change in the East as well as in the West, as a new peasant economy replaced the slave systems that had principally supported ancient civilizations. The three leading civilizations of the East—Byzantine, Kievan, and Islamic—nonetheless differed greatly from the less developed societies of the West. The Roman Empire did not fall in the East, and Roman institutions lived on, as did the Hellenistic cultural heritage, based on the Greek language. The new religion of Islam grew up among a people, the Arabs, who (like the Germans in the West) had lived on the fringes of the Classical Mediterranean world. The expansion of Islam brought it into lands—Egypt, Palestine, Syria, Persia—that had ancient and rich traditions of literate culture. Islamic civilization, in turn, was deeply affected by the Hellenistic, Semitic, and Persian cultures that flourished in the areas it overran.

The East also surpassed the West in the number of cities that survived in the Byzantine and Islamic worlds. Even the Principality of Kiev, founded by a people now first appearing in history—the East Slavs—rapidly developed an urban culture. The cities in the East helped maintain commerce, governmental institutions, and high levels of learning. All these accomplishments gave the Eastern civilizations a marked superiority over contemporary Western societies in the Early Middle Ages.

I. The Byzantine Empire

The name *Byzantine* is, strictly speaking, a historical misnomer. The inhabitants of the Eastern Empire recognized no break between their civilization and that of Classical Rome. Throughout their history they called themselves *Romans,* even after Rome had slipped from their power and they had adopted Greek as their official language. Indeed, modern Western historians sometimes forget that the Roman Empire did not fall in the East until 1453.

Historians differ in the way they divide Byzantine history, but the following periodization probably enjoys the widest acceptance:

Early Byzantine Period	324–632
Middle Byzantine Period	632–1071
Late Byzantine Period	1071–1453

THE EARLY BYZANTINE PERIOD

Byzantine history begins when the emperor Constantine transferred the capital of the Roman Empire from the West to the East in 324. The emperor's motives were primarily military, for many powerful enemies were menacing the wealthy and populous Eastern provinces of the Empire.

Constantine chose as his new capital the site of the ancient Greek colony of Byzantium. The colony had been founded about 660 B.C.E. on a narrow peninsula that juts into the Sea of Marmara like a hand extended from Europe toward Asia. The official name of the rebuilt city was New Rome; however, it soon came to be called the City of Constantine, or Constantinople, after its founder.

The location of this capital influenced the character of Byzantium and the course of its history. The city stood at the intersection of two heavily

▸ **EMPEROR JUSTINIAN, RAVENNA**
The mosaics—patterns made from small chips of tinted glass backed with gold leaf—that cover the wall of the church of San Vitale in Ravenna are one of the greatest achievements of the Byzantine era. Here, the emperor Justinian is surrounded by both priests and warriors, emphasizing his power over the religious as well as the secular domain.

traveled trade routes: the overland highway from the Balkans to Asia Minor and the maritime route between the Black and Mediterranean seas. Moreover, the city at once acquired the aura of a Christian city, the capital of the Christian empire. Because of his close association with the emperor, the bishop of New Rome enjoyed the high status of patriarch, and in the entire Church only the bishop of Rome ranked above him.

The successors of Constantine had no intention of abandoning the powers of the old Roman Empire in either the West or the East. Thus they struggled continuously, if in vain, to restore the Empire to its former size, power, and glory. The emperor whose actions best illustrate this aim was Justinian (527–565).

Photo: Metropolitan Museum of Art, gift of J. Pierpont Morgan, 1917.

▸ This Byzantine gold cup, dating from the sixth or seventh century, was found at Durazzo in modern Albania. Four female figures in gold repoussé symbolize the cities of Rome, Cyprus, Alexandria, and Constantinople. The detail shows the figure of Constantinople. The representation of cities in allegorical form shows the prominence of urban centers in Byzantine thought and society.

Justinian the Great Historians have much information, or at least many allegations, about Justinian from the court historian Procopius. While the emperor lived, Procopius praised him in two histories: *On the Wars* recounts Justinian's victorious campaigns, and *On Buildings* describes his architectural achievements. But after Justinian's death, Procopius also wrote one of the most vicious efforts at character assassination in history. The *Secret History* paints Justinian, the empress Theodora, and several high officials of the court as monsters of public and private vice. Historians still have not satisfactorily reconciled the contradictory portraits left to us by the two-tongued Procopius.

Justinian's will was made strong by his ambitious wife Theodora and made effective by capable men in his service. Born about 500, Theodora became a famous actress and a celebrated courtesan before she was 20. She traveled through the cities of the empire, earning her way, according to Procopius, by skilled prostitution. In her early twenties she returned to Constantinople, mended her morals but lost none of her charm, and married Justinian. She was, in sum, an outsider, with no roots in the social establishment of the capital and no inclinations to respect its conventions.

Theodora's influence on her husband was decisive from the start. In 532, for reasons not entirely known, the popular factions of Constantinople rose in rebellion. Justinian panicked and planned to flee. But in a moving speech, as recorded by Procopius, Theodora urged her husband to choose death rather than exile. Justinian remained and crushed the uprising. The domestic peace that followed his victory freed him to pursue the three principal goals of his reign: the restoration of the Western provinces to the empire, the reformation of laws and institutions, and an ambitious program of splendid public works.

To restore imperial rule over the lost Western provinces, Justinian attacked the kingdoms of the Vandals, Ostrogoths, and Visigoths, and sought a precarious peace with the Persians beyond his eastern frontier. By 554 his troops had destroyed the Vandal kingdom in North Africa and established Byzantine rule there; had triumphed, at least for a while, over the Ostrogothic kingdom in Italy; and had forced the Visigoths in Spain to

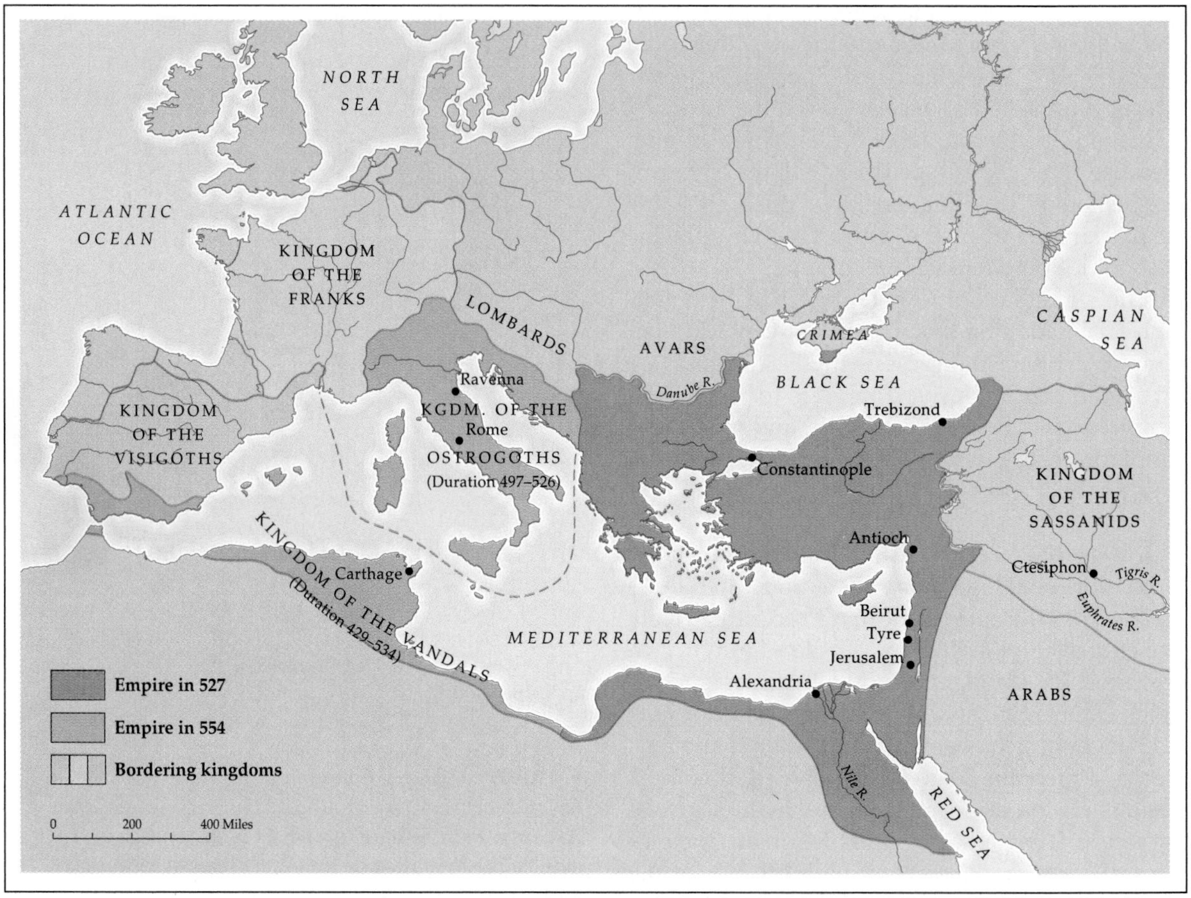

Map 7.1 Europe in the Age of Justinian

cede the southern tip of the peninsula (see Map 7.1). Justinian also sought to reconcile the Eastern and Western branches of the Church, which were bitterly divided over a theological question concerning the nature of Christ.[1] He had the pope abducted from Rome and taken to Constantinople, where he bullied him into accepting an unwelcome compromise. His coercive tactics did not bring union and peace to the Church and were bitterly resented by all the conflicting parties.

In 528 Justinian appointed a commission to prepare a systematic codification of Roman law. The result was the *Corpus Iuris Civilis* ("Body of Civil Law"). It consisted of four compilations: the *Codex Justinianus* (or "Law of Justinian"), an arrangement of the imperial edicts according to topics in an easily consulted order; the *Digest*, or *Pandects*, a summary of legal opinions; the *Institutes*, a textbook to introduce students to the reformed legal system (*see box*, p. 185); and the *Novellae*, a collection of new imperial edicts issued after 534.

It would be hard to exaggerate the importance of the *Corpus Iuris Civilis*. It has remained for all subsequent generations the largest and richest source of information concerning the legal institutions and thought of Roman antiquity. It profoundly influenced the canon law of the medieval and modern Church. The modern legal systems

[1]The Monophysite theory holds that Jesus has one nature, partly divine and partly human; he was not, in other words, simply true man. Condemned as heretical at the Council of Chalcedon (451), the belief remained strong in the East. The orthodox view is that Jesus has two natures, one human and one divine, and is both true God and true man.

of most Western countries are based on the principles of Roman law as preserved in the *Corpus*.[2]

The destruction caused by the rebellion in Constantinople gave Justinian the chance to start a rebuilding program, with the aim of making Byzantium reflect the physical splendor of Rome. The most spectacular of his many new churches, palaces, and public works was the great church of Hagia Sophia, or Holy Wisdom.

Justinian was remarkably successful in all his ambitious policies until the last years of his reign. Beginning in 542, terrible plagues repeatedly struck the imperial lands, while he waged a two-front war against the Persians to the east and the resurgent Ostrogoths on the western frontier. The strains on manpower left the empire everywhere on the defensive at his death.

[2]The British Commonwealth and the United States (except Louisiana) follow common law, based on cases decided in medieval England; but common law too was strongly influenced by Roman legal concepts.

Historians have tended to view Justinian's policies as unrealistic, excessively ambitious, and ultimately disastrous. Memories of ancient Roman greatness blinded him to the inadequacy of his own resources. Yet Hagia Sophia and the *Corpus Iuris Civilis* assure him a permanent and brilliant reputation in both the East and the West.

In the years following Justinian's death new invaders overwhelmed the frontiers and wrested from his successors most of the territorial acquisitions of his reign. These emperors could not recover the Western provinces of the old Roman Empire, and the Byzantine Empire, unable to remain a universal state, had to find its way as an Eastern, and exclusively Hellenic, empire.

THE MIDDLE BYZANTINE PERIOD

The reign of the emperor Heraclius (610–641) was pivotal in giving Byzantine policy and civilization their new Eastern orientation. His reign began amid repeated military disasters. The

From the **Institutes** *of Justinian*

The* Institutes, *published at the order of the emperor Justinian as part of his general restatement of Roman law, form a kind of introductory textbook to the whole study. Near the beginning of the work the compilers give this succinct definition of justice and of the differences among the "civil" law that applies to Roman citizens, "natural" law, and the "law of all nations." Note that the second and third classes are treated as partly identical. It was one of the great strengths of Roman law and administration to recognize and protect traditions of peoples whom the Romans brought into their Empire.

"Justice is the set and constant purpose which gives to every man his due. Jurisprudence is the knowledge of things divine and human, the science of the just and the unjust. [. . .] The law of nature is that which she has taught all animals; a law not peculiar to the human race, but shared by all living creatures, whether denizens of the air, the dry land, or the sea. Hence comes the union of male and female, which we call marriage; hence the procreation of children, for this is a law that we see even in the lower animals.

"The civil law of Rome, and the law of all nations, differ from each other thus. The laws of every people governed by statutes and customs are partly peculiar to itself, partly common to all mankind. Those rules which a state enacts for its own members are peculiar to itself, and are called civil law: those rules prescribed by natural reason for all men are observed by all people alike, and are called the law of nations. Thus the laws of the Roman people are partly peculiar to itself, partly common to all nations."

From *The Institutes of Justinian*, J. B. Moyle (tr.), 1896.

aggressive Persians took Antioch, Jerusalem, and Alexandria. By raising money through treasures donated by the churches, Heraclius strengthened the army and then boldly opened a successful war against the Persians in 622. In campaigns waged over six years Heraclius fought his way to the Persian capital of Ctesiphon, where the Persians agreed to a humiliating peace. Then a new menace arose. After the death of Muhammad, the founder of Islam, in 632, his Muslim followers from the Arabic world embarked on a tidal wave of conquests, overrunning most of the empire in scarcely more than 10 years.

At the same time that Heraclius was defending the empire against invaders, he was also reforming its administration. One of his predecessors had begun to give land to soldiers in exchange for military service. The military units and the provinces where they were settled were called *themes*. Heraclius and his successors extended this system to the navy and the entire empire. Soldiers and sailors, settled on their own farms and fighting in their own provincial army or navy, proved far more effective as both workers and warriors than the slaves, conscripts, and mercenaries on whom the empire had earlier relied. But a century elapsed before the Byzantines were able to take the offensive against the Muslims. The emperor Leo III (717–741) beat back a Muslim attack on Constantinople in 717 and 718 and then began a reconquest of Asia Minor.

▸ Agriculture
Cultivating their own plots was the principal work of Byzantine peasants. This manuscript illustration shows the various labors of digging, harvesting, and watering taking place in a fanciful landscape.

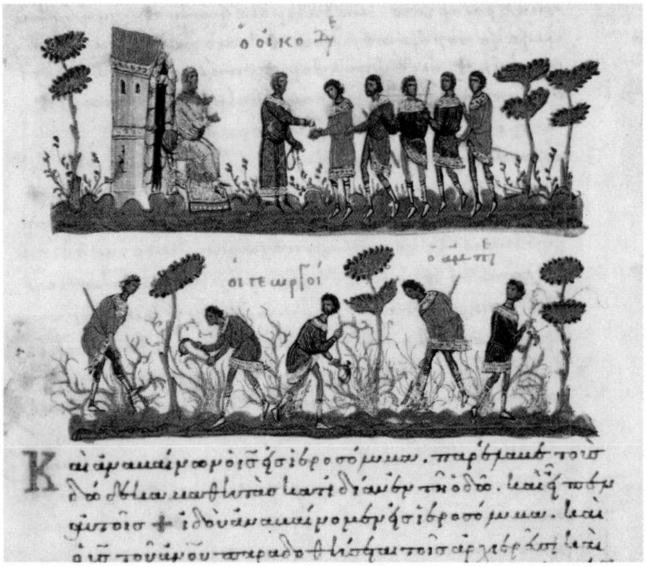

Leo introduced iconoclasm (image-breaking, from the Greek *eikón*, or "image") in the empire in 726 when he forbade the veneration of images within churches. Historians still do not agree about his motives. Iconoclasm may have been a legal pretext for obtaining land to support the army, by seizing the holdings of the monasteries, which strongly advocated the worship of images. Or it may have been an attempt to make Christianity more appealing to the Muslims whom he was seeking to conquer, by emulating the Islamic condemnation of the worship of images. Whatever the reasons, Leo's iconoclastic policy had a disastrous effect on relations with the West; it antagonized the popes and was a major factor in their decision to seek out a Frankish champion in the person of Pepin the Short (see p. 167). The veneration of images was restored in the Byzantine Empire between 784 and 813 and permanently after 843. But the iconoclastic policy helped to widen the cleavage between the Western and Eastern churches.

The military revival reached its height under the great warrior emperors of the ninth through eleventh centuries. They pushed the Muslims back into Syria and waged successful wars in southern Italy, the Balkan Peninsula, and the Caucasus. Their principal military accomplishment was in the Balkan Peninsula, where they defeated the nomadic people known as the Bulgars. The modern Bulgarians, who are entirely Slavic in language and culture, retain only the name of the original nomads.

BYZANTINE CIVILIZATION

The Byzantines adopted the assumptions of the Hellenistic world, especially of the Epicureans and Stoics, who had maintained that all people were one in nature and should be included in a single state. As there was one God, one true faith, and one universal Church, so there should be only one empire to rule all Christian peoples. The empire was thus given the sacred duty of aiding the salvation of the human race. The Byzantines

▶ **Iconoclast Whitewashing an Image of Christ, ca. 900**
Byzantine iconoclasts, protesting the worship of images and the leadership of a Latin pope, destroyed the decorations of numerous churches. This page from a Psalter illuminated around 900 depicts the obliteration through whitewashing of an icon of Christ.

believed that if the empire served this function, God would never permit its destruction. This idea gave the Byzantines the spirit they needed to resist for centuries a nearly continuous onslaught of invaders.

The Byzantines also believed that the emperor was a holy figure as the head of a state with a sacred function. Of course, a Christian emperor could not claim divinity; but the emperor lived surrounded by ceremony that imparted an aura of sanctity to his person; and the term *sacred,* used much as we use the word *public,* was liberally applied to his person, palace, and office.

Historians have traditionally used the term *caesaropapism* to describe the emperor's position in the Church. This term suggests that the emperor was both Caesar and pope, the true head of both Church and state. Recently, objections have been raised against the use of this term because the emperor's powers over the Church were restricted. He could not repeal the Nicene Creed or personally flout laws of Christian morality. He was not a priest and therefore could not say Mass or administer the sacraments.

Yet the emperor exercised a wide authority over ecclesiastical matters. He supervised the discipline of the Church, set the qualifications for ordinations, created bishoprics and changed their boundaries, investigated the monasteries and reformed them when necessary, and appointed patriarchs and at times forced their resignation. Even dogma was not beyond his influence. The emperor summoned councils, supervised their proceedings, and enforced their decisions. The clergy was largely limited in its functions to the performance of the sacred liturgy and the administration of the sacraments.

The Two Churches The Eastern Church developed and functioned under the supervision of the emperor. In the West, on the other hand, the collapse of central authority in the Roman Empire gave the clergy a position of leadership in secular affairs. These contrasting experiences in the Early Middle Ages deeply affected the character and spirit of the two major branches of Christianity. The differences between the two Churches clarify other contrasts in the history of the Eastern and Western peoples.

Both the Eastern Church and the Western Church considered themselves catholic (that is, universal) and orthodox (that is, holding true beliefs); the terms *Roman Catholic* and *Greek Orthodox* used to identify the Churches today are exclusively modern usages. The two Churches maintained nearly identical beliefs. Perhaps the principal, or at least the most famous, disagreement was, and still is, the *filioque* dispute (meaning "and from the son"), which concerns the relationship between members of the Trinity: the Father, Son, and Holy Spirit. The Eastern Church held, and still holds, that the Holy Spirit proceeds only from the Father, while the Western Church maintained that the Holy Spirit proceeds from the Father "and from the Son." The Eastern Church permitted, as the Western Church did not, divorce for reasons of adultery and the ordination of married men to the priesthood, although bishops had to be celibate.

The most significant difference between the two churches in liturgy was that the Eastern Church allowed the use of vernacular languages—Greek, Coptic, Ethiopian, Syriac, Armenian, Georgian, Slavonic, and others—in the liturgy. Liturgical usage added great dignity to these Eastern languages and stimulated their development. The East Slavs, for example, possessed a rich literature in Slavonic within a century after their conversion to Christianity. Western vernacular literature was much slower in developing. On the other hand, the toleration of many vernacular languages weakened the unity of the Eastern Church. An Eastern cleric using his own vernacular language could not easily communicate with clerics from other regions, whereas a Western cleric who used Latin could make himself understood anywhere in the West. Because of linguistic differences from their neighbors, Eastern churches tended to develop in isolation from one another. Moreover, the toleration of many vernacular languages made difficult the revival of Classical learning. In learning Latin, a Western cleric also acquired the ability to read the great Latin classics, while an Eastern cleric who did not know Greek was blocked from the Greek classics. Eastern cultures were thus deprived of one avenue of enrichment.

The Western and Eastern Churches also differed in their organization and relations with secular authority. In the Early Middle Ages the Western Church began to develop a centralized government under the papacy, a government often strong enough to defy secular rulers. By the late twelfth century the pope had become the absolute ruler of the Western Church, which he governed with the aid of an elaborate bureaucracy and a system of canon law common to the whole Western Church. The Eastern Church, however, remained thoroughly decentralized. It developed into a loose confederation of independent national churches that relied on secular authority to defend their temporal interests.

The close ties between Church and state in the East conferred advantages on both. The Church devoted itself to its essential functions of liturgical service and the administration of the sacraments; the state made full use of the great wealth and spiritual power of the Church. This was a critical advantage for rulers and peoples struggling to survive on the eastern frontier of Europe, where all resources had to be enlisted in the battle for existence. The East was largely spared and could have ill afforded the prolonged disputes between Church and state which marked Western history.

Yet the disputes between Church and state in the West, while often damaging and unseemly, served as a powerful stimulus to fruitful and original analyses of the nature of society and favored the emergence of a balance in which neither the king nor the Church exercised a monopoly of power. In the Byzantine Empire the withdrawal of the Church from temporal concerns established a pattern of Church-state relations that has lived on until the present. Even in our times, the divided Orthodox churches of eastern Europe have played a lesser role in secular political movements, such as the rejection of Communist rule, than the Catholic churches of Hungary, Poland, the Czech Republic, and Slovakia.

Byzantine Society The outstanding feature of Byzantine civilization, compared with that of Western Europe, was the continuing vitality of cities. At one time the Byzantine Empire included such great urban centers as Alexandria, Antioch, Beirut, Constantinople, Trebizond, and Tyre. At its peak under Justinian, Constantinople probably contained more than 300,000 inhabitants. The city had paved and illuminated streets and many splendid churches and palaces. Urban society was, however, marked by a wide division between rich and poor. The rich lived among magnificent surroundings in huge palaces; the poor, in sprawling slums. Crimes committed in broad daylight were commonplace.

Rural society consisted largely of peasants. Those who owned property assembled together, made decisions concerning the use of uncultivated or common lands, assumed (or were required to assume) collective responsibility for the payment of taxes, and elected judges and other officials to supervise the village government.

The Byzantine Empire was wealthy compared with other states of the age. One great source of wealth came from the commerce that passed through the ports and gates of Constantinople. The Rus and other Slavs from the north carried amber, fur, honey, slaves, wax, and wheat; Armenians and Syrians from the east brought clothing, fruit, glass, steel, and spices; merchants from the west contributed arms, iron, slaves, and wood. The vigorous commerce attracted large colonies of foreign merchants. The commercial importance of Byzantium is revealed in the prestige of its gold coin, the bezant. Its weight and purity were kept constant from the reign of Constantine to the late eleventh century; no other major system of coinage can match its record of stability.

Another source of wealth was the numerous active guilds. The *Book of the Prefect*, written about 950 and describing the duties of a city's chief administrative officer, mentions 21 professional and craft guilds; most of these made luxury products, especially silk cloth. Byzantine artisans were also famed for goldwork, cups, ivories, jewelry, and reliquaries, all of which were shipped everywhere in the known world. The government closely regulated prices and movement of goods and maintained state monopolies, particularly over silk products. The best silk, rich purple cloths, could not be exported.

The emperor, like his predecessors in the old Roman Empire, enjoyed absolute authority and governed with the aid of an elaborate civil service. Military affairs were entirely separated from civil administration and entrusted to masters of the soldiers directly responsible to the emperor. All these offices relied on a large professional bureaucracy. The offices were decentralized and simplified when Heraclius reformed the government in the seventh century and combined civil and military administrations on the local level under the generals who governed the themes (the military units and the provinces where they were settled). All justice flowed from the emperor, and he or his chief official could hear appeals from any local court in the empire.

There were great contrasts between the Byzantine government and Western governments of the same era. Even after Heraclius reformed the government, it continued to be served by a well-organized local administration and an elaborate bureaucracy. Western kingdoms, on the other hand, functioned with a rudimentary administration and without a professional civil service. The Byzantine government supported such refinements as an effective fiscal system, a state postal service, and even a secret police, ominously called the *agentes in rebus* ("those doing things"). Western governments had none of these. At a time when Western governments operated almost without a budget, the Byzantine government collected large revenues from the 10 percent tariff it imposed on trade and from the profit it received from the state monopolies. The government also employed skilled diplomats, who were celebrated by contemporary observers for their ability to keep enemies divided and their liberal use of bribes, tributes, and subsidies.

The bureaucracy was largely staffed by literate and trained laymen. Eunuchs were preferred for important positions in the government because it was believed that they would not be tempted by sexual intrigue and would have no wife or children to compete with the emperor for their loyalties. Eunuchs also performed managerial functions that in the West were assumed by queens and women of the court. The services of eunuchs thus had the social effect of restricting the influ-

▶ WOMEN WEAVING AND SPINNING
Textile production was an important industry in Byzantine culture. This manuscript illustration depicts a woman weaving on a simple rectangular frame and another who is spinning.

ence of women and led to the progressive seclusion of women within the inner reaches of the household, a tendency that set a model for the heirs of the Byzantine Empire.

Byzantine Culture Byzantine wealth supported a tradition of learning that benefited not only the clergy but also many laymen. There were three types of institutions of higher learning: A palace school trained civil servants in language, law, and rhetoric; a patriarchal school instructed priests in rhetoric and theology; and monastic schools taught young monks the mystical writings of the past. The poor people were dependent on their guild for what education they received.

Scholars used the Greek language almost exclusively after the sixth century. They composed school manuals, histories, saints' lives, biblical commentaries, and encyclopedias of ancient science and lore. Their greatest accomplishment, however, was the preservation of Classical Greek literature. With the exception of some few works preserved on papyri, virtually all the Western world possesses of Classical Greek authors has come down through Byzantine copies, most of which date from the tenth to the twelfth centuries.

The first flowering of artistic achievement occurred in the sixth century, when Justinian literally rebuilt Constantinople. Among his many buildings is the church Hagia Sophia, begun in 532 and completed in 537. As Procopius described it, its great dome seemed to float in the air, as if suspended by a chain from heaven. Hagia Sophia is one of the acknowledged architectural masterpieces of the world. Like other Byzantine churches, it was decorated with brilliant mosaics, but most of these were destroyed by the iconoclasts in the eighth and ninth centuries. Because of the iconoclastic movement, the richest examples of the early mosaics are not to be found in Constantinople and Asia Minor but rather in areas that were no longer under Byzantine rule in those centuries. San Vitale and Sant' Apollinare in Ravenna, Italy, are particularly noted for early Byzantine mosaics.

With the final rejection of iconoclasm in the middle of the ninth century, there was a resurgence of artistic endeavor. Byzantine artisans designed and decorated many churches throughout the empire. Their work is found in such places as Messina and Palermo in Sicily and Venice in

Italy. Artists were summoned to such distant places as Kiev to aid in the design, construction, and decoration of churches.

The mosaics make vividly concrete the Byzantine concepts of empire, emperor, and church. The emperor is always presented as the august figure that Byzantine ideology made of him (see plate on p. 182). Christ is never shown as suffering; he is, in other words, always God and never man. The reason for this seems to have been the close association that the figure of Christ bore to the living emperor. To show Christ as suffering would suggest that the emperor too might be a weak and vulnerable man. The mosaics have no sense of movement, admission of human frailty, or recognition of the reality of change. Operating within this picture of the world, the artists nevertheless portrayed their solemn figures with a rich variety of forms, garments, and colors. Byzantine mosaics may be static, but they are neither drab nor monotonous.

▸ INTERIOR OF HAGIA SOPHIA

Hagia Sophia, the monumental project of the emperor Justinian, is a lasting reminder of the power of the Byzantine Empire. The saucer-like dome, which rises 180 feet, is carried on four pendentives (the wedge-shaped supports that allow a circular dome to rest on a square structure) and is a notable achievement of Byzantine engineering.

DECLINE OF THE EMPIRE

The military power of the empire in its middle period was largely based on the system of themes, which created an army and navy of free peasant-warriors. But from the early tenth century these free peasant-warriors, apparently to escape mounting fiscal and military burdens, began to abandon their farms to more powerful neighbors. In the eleventh century many of them became serfs. The disintegration of the theme system reduced the military manpower and led to a rural aristocracy of landlords, which in turn weakened the strength of the central government.

The emperors tried to limit the size and number of great estates, but by the late eleventh century, their weaker successors rather sought to purchase the loyalty of the rural aristocracy by distributing imperial estates to them. The aristocracy was also gaining control over ecclesiastical lands, as the Church granted them entire monasteries to administer in the best interest of the monks and the Church. But, in fact, these concessions represented virtual gifts of monastic properties.

Socially, Byzantium was being transformed from a disciplined society of peasant-warriors under a strong central government to a society with a dependent peasantry, strong local landlords, and a weak central government. Thus in time of war the emperors had to seek outside help to compensate for the shrinking forces among their own subjects. To maintain control of the sea, essential to the security of Constantinople, they sought the support of the growing naval power of Venice. In 998 and 1082 they gave generous trading concessions to the Venetians, which were major steps in the growth of Italian (and Western) naval strength in the waters of the eastern Mediterranean. The problem of land defense was even more pressing. A new people, the Seljuk Turks, had recently emerged from the steppes to threaten the eastern frontiers.

The Seljuks The Byzantines gave the name *Turk* to a number of nomadic tribes that lived in the region east and north of the Caspian Sea (modern Turkestan) and had long threatened the settled Christian populations. In the eleventh century, members of one tribe, the Seljuks, penetrated beyond the eastern borders of the empire into Asia Minor. They shattered the largely mercenary army of the Byzantines and took the emperor Romanus himself captive at Manzikert in 1071.

As the Byzantine defenses broke down, Asia Minor lay open to the Seljuk forces. One Turkish chieftain, Suleiman, established himself and his warriors at Nicaea, only a few miles from Constantinople. He founded what eventually became the most powerful Turkish principality in Asia Minor: the Sultanate of Rum. The virtual loss of Asia Minor forced the Byzantine emperor to appeal to the West for help. This signaled the end of the Byzantine Empire as a great power in the East.

Schism with the West The second disaster of the eleventh century was the formal schism between the Eastern and Western branches of the Church. The schism was provoked not by major dogmatic differences but by rivalry, disputes, and snobbery. For years the popes at Rome and the patriarchs at Constantinople had been rivals in converting the Slavs and had been bitterly disputing jurisdiction over churches in southern Italy and Illyria (modern Albania and Croatia). Furthermore, the Byzantines resented the papal claim to primacy within the Church. Rome by this time appeared to them as a provincial town without an empire and subject territory, whereas they considered Constantinople, the seat of wealth and power, the more appropriate capital for the Church.[3]

Perhaps even more fundamentally, the rupture of relations reflected the breakdown in communications between the East and the West, which had begun when Justinian failed in the sixth century to reconcile the two branches of the Church within the old Roman Empire. After his reign the two halves of the Roman Empire ceased entirely to speak or understand a common language; misunderstandings came easily and were overcome with difficulty, and commercial and diplomatic contact between East and West became sporadic.

Personalities played a major role in the actual schism of 1054. A dedicated but rigid reformer, Cardinal Humbert of Silva Candida, led a papal delegation to Constantinople. Failing to secure satisfactory concessions from the Byzantine Patriarch Michael Cerularius, the papal legates deposited a bull of excommunication on the high altar of Hagia Sophia and left the city in anger. Cerularius, a haughty and ambitious prelate who

[3]In the tenth century the Byzantines told Liutprand, bishop of Cremona, that they, and not the residents of Rome, were the true Romans and that Rome was a town inhabited exclusively by "vile slaves, fishermen, confectioners, poulterers, bastards, plebeians, underlings."

welcomed a break with the Western Church and had labored to provoke it, publicly declared to the other Eastern patriarchs that the supporters of the pope were steeped in heresy and had taken themselves out of the true Church.

The schism of 1054 destroyed the hope for a united Christian Church, although only later centuries showed the full extent of the damage. Even today, more than 900 years after the event, adherents of the Western and Eastern traditions are trying to overcome the rift. Only in 1965 did the pope and the Greek patriarch formally remove the excommunications of 1054.

► Silk Textile

A splendid example of the quality of silk manufacture in Constantinople around the year 1000, this textile shows the eagle, an ancient symbol of power and victory, holding in its beak a ring while resting its claws on a row of pearls. This particular work of craftsmanship is said to have been used to transport the remains of St. Germain, who died in Ravenna in 448, back to Auxerre in France.

THE WESTERN DEBT TO BYZANTINE CIVILIZATION

The East Slavs were the direct heirs of Byzantine civilization, but Western peoples also owe a vast debt to this civilization. Above all, we owe our knowledge of Classical Greek writings to Byzantine scholars who preserved this literature and thus allowed Western scholars to study the most original thinkers of the ancient world. Neither the Western Renaissance nor modern European culture would have been the same without their contribution.

The very existence of the Byzantine Empire, guarding the eastern approaches to Europe, gave Western peoples a measure of immunity from the destructive incursions of Arabs, Persians, Turks, and others. The sophisticated Byzantine economy and government served as a kind of school of civilized practices from which less advanced Western peoples could learn new techniques and grasp the possibilities and rewards of civilized life.

II. The Principality of Kiev

During the Early Middle Ages the East Slavs, groups of people living in Eastern Europe, were converted to Eastern Christianity and gradually began forming societies based largely on the legacy of the Byzantine Empire and Eastern Christianity. Three modern Slavic peoples—the Russians, Ukrainians, and Belarussians—trace their ancestry directly to these East Slavs, and all regard the foundation of the first East Slavic state as the origin of their history. For this reason, it is inappropriate to call the East Slavic state *Russian*, since the Russians are not its exclusive heirs. In referring to these East Slavs we shall rather use a contemporary term, the *Rus*, a name of obscure origins that first referred to a dominant Viking tribe or group and then came to signify the entire people.

THE FOUNDATIONS OF KIEVAN RUS

Between the sixth and ninth centuries the East Slavs greatly expanded their area of settlement, and some tribes pushed to the east as far as the Volga River. There they met on the lower course of the river a Turkish-speaking people called the Khazars. The Khazars (or at least their upper classes) practiced Judaism; their obscure history has its own special fascination. Other Slavic tribes moved to the north nearly to the Baltic Sea. Two of their most important settlements were Kiev on the Dnieper River and Novgorod on Lake Ilmen, within easy access of the Baltic Sea.

In about 830, Vikings from Scandinavia penetrated into the lands of the East Slavs in quest of booty and profit. They also established trade routes that ran from the Baltic Sea over the rivers of eastern Europe to the Black Sea and thence to Constantinople, thus linking Scandinavia with Byzantium. Out of this encounter between Vikings and East Slavs emerged the first East Slavic state.

The most detailed and important source for the birth of the Rus state is the *Primary Chronicle* (*see box*, below). Many hands contributed to this work, which was not written down by East Slavs in its present form until 1117 or 1118, some 250 years after the events it describes. According to the *Primary Chronicle*, the Varangians, as the East Slavs called the Vikings, ruled Novgorod until the Slavic population rebelled against them and drove them back beyond the sea. Soon, however, the people of Novgorod began fighting among themselves. Unable to overcome their discord, they invited the Varangians to rule them once again. In response, a Varangian prince named Rurik, his two brothers, and "all the Rus," as the Varangians were called, came to govern Novgorod in 862. "On account of these Varangians," the *Primary Chronicle* explains, "the district of Novgorod became known as Russian land."

The *Primary Chronicle* goes on to say that Rurik soon left Novgorod and that his follower Oleg assumed authority in Novgorod and then Kiev. Oleg (873?–913) is thus considered the true

Literacy Comes to Rus

The* Russian Primary Chronicle, *narrating events of the ninth century, gives one version of how the Slavs became literate and developed texts of the Scriptures.

"When the Moravian Slavs and their princes were living in baptism, the Princes Rostislav, Svyatopolk, and Kotsel sent messengers to the Emperor Michael [Michael III of Byzantium], saying, 'Our nation is baptized, and yet we have no teacher to direct and instruct us and interpret the sacred scriptures. We understand neither Greek nor Latin. Furthermore, we do not understand written characters or their meaning. Therefore send us teachers who can make known to us the words of the scriptures and their sense.'

"The scholars suggested that there was a man in Salonika, by name Leo, who had two sons [Methodius and Constantine, the latter usually called Cyril], familiar with the Slavic tongue. The Emperor sent them into the Slavic country. When they arrived, they undertook to compose a Slavic alphabet, and translated the *Acts* and the Gospel. The Slavs rejoiced to hear the greatness of God extolled in their native tongue.

"Now some zealots began to condemn the Slavic books, contending that it was not right for any other nation to have its own alphabet apart from the Hebrews, the Greeks, and the Latins. When the Pope heard of this situation, he rebuked those who murmured against the Slavic books, saying, 'Let the word of the Scripture be fulfilled that "all nations shall praise God" (*Psalms* 71.17) and likewise that "all nations shall declare the majesty of God according as the Holy spirit shall grant them to speak" (cf. *Acts* 2.4).' "

From *Russian Primary Chronicle*, S. H. Cross (ed.), pp. 62–63 (condensed).

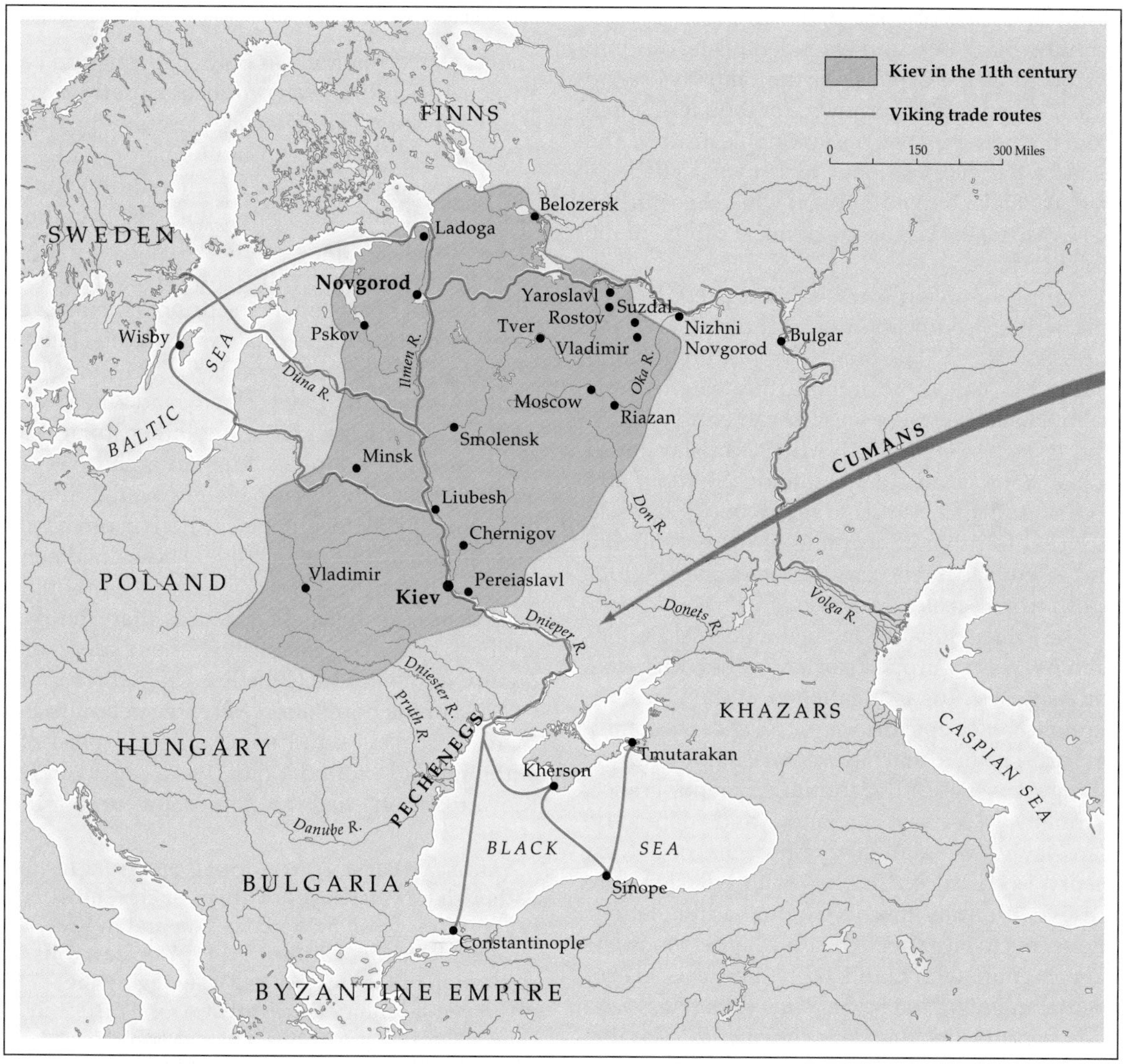

Map 7.2 PRINCIPALITY OF KIEV

founder of the Rus state because he united under his rule the two chief cities of Kiev and Novgorod. In 907 he led a fleet, allegedly containing 2000 ships, on a raid against Constantinople. The Byzantine emperor granted both tribute and trading concessions in order to purchase peace with the Rus. Oleg's successors completed the unification of the East Slavic tribes. This brought under their rule an area that stretched from the Baltic to the Black Sea and from the Danube to the Volga rivers. They also made war against the nomadic peoples of the steppes and strengthened commercial, diplomatic, and cultural ties with the Byzantine Empire. In 988 the ruler Vladimir converted to the Eastern form of Christianity and imposed baptism on his subjects. The East Slavs, the most numerous of all the Slavs, were thus brought within the Eastern cultural world.

Yaroslav the Wise The Principality of Kiev, as the federation of states based on Kiev is called (see Map 7.2), reached its height of power under Vladimir's son Yaroslav (1015–1054), who might well be termed the Slavic Justinian. Like Justinian, Yaroslav was a successful warrior, administrator, and builder. He defeated the Pechenegs, a nomadic people who roamed the grasslands south and east of Kiev and hampered contact with the Black Sea, and extended his territory to the north at the expense of the Finns (see Map 7.2). He won self-government for the Rus Church from the patriarch of Constantinople in 1037. The head of the independent Church was called the *metropolitan* and lived in Kiev, which became the ecclesiastical as well as the political capital of the East Slavs.

During his reign Yaroslav had prepared the first written codification of East Slavic law, the *Russkaia Pravda*. He built many churches and brought in skilled Byzantine artisans to decorate them. His masterpiece was the cathedral at Kiev. The *Primary Chronicle* says that Yaroslav loved books "and read them continually day and night," and that he wrote many books himself. He tried to promote learning in his principality and assembled many scribes to translate religious books from Greek into Slavic.

The Principality of Kiev maintained closer ties with Western Europe than any other Rus state for centuries. Rus is mentioned in the eleventh-century French epic the *Song of Roland*. The family of Yaroslav had marriage connections with the ruling dynasties of Byzantium, England, France, Germany, Norway, Poland, and Hungary. Yaroslav's own daughter Anna married King Henry I of France. Charters with her signature survive, carefully inscribed with Cyrillic letters; she seems to have been the only layperson in the French court who could write. She was instrumental in giving the name *Philip* to her son, who thus became the first French king to bear the name of an ancient Christian saint and apostle.

KIEVAN CIVILIZATION

The Kievan economy was both vigorous and balanced. Agriculture was productive on the fertile steppes. The *Primary Chronicle* describes peasants plowing with horses at a time when the less efficient oxen were the more common draft animals in the West. The Rus traded with the Scandinavians, the steppe peoples, the Muslims at Baghdad, and especially the Byzantines. Every year a great fleet of boats, led by the princes themselves, assembled at Kiev and floated down the Dnieper River to the Black Sea and across to Constantinople. Amber, fur, honey, slaves, and wheat were exchanged for silks, spices, and other luxuries of the East. In recent years Russian archaeologists excavating at Novgorod have uncovered numerous commercial documents written on birch bark that illuminate this lively trade. These documents indicate that the Rus merchants were less sophisticated in their business practices than the Byzantines, but they established the variety and quality of the products the Rus offered for trade.

Most of the population were free peasants, but there were slaves and some enserfed peasants. Although its foundations were agricultural, Kievan society had an important urban life.

▶ YAROSLAV PRESENTING MODEL OF CHURCH **Although now destroyed, a group of eleventh-century frescoes in St. Sophia Cathedral in Kiev once depicted the family of Prince Yaroslav. This re-creation of the frescoes in a drawing by the seventeenth-century Dutch artist A. V. Westervelt shows Yaroslav presenting a model of a church to Prince Vladimir.**

Within the many towns a wealthy aristocracy of princes, warriors, and great merchants rubbed shoulders with artisans, workers, and large numbers of destitute persons. The princes had to concern themselves with such social problems as the oppression of the poor, usury, and enslavement for debt.

Kiev in the eleventh century was one of the great cities of the age. The German chronicler Adam of Bremen considered Kiev a rival in size to Constantinople; the Metropolitan Hilarion described it as "glittering with grandeur"; another German chronicler, Thietmar of Merseburg, said it had 400 churches, 8 marketplaces, and unnumbered inhabitants. In 1124 a fire allegedly destroyed 600 churches. Kiev must have included 20,000 to 30,000 people—more people than any contemporary Western city.

The head of the Kievan government was the prince, who selected nobles, called *boyars*, to aid him in governing. In all important matters the prince sought advice from his boyars. The towns had large citizen assemblies, called *veches*, that the prince also consulted for advice. The government was thus based on a balance of monarchic, aristocratic, and popular elements. The prince, unlike the Byzantine emperor, was not the fountain of justice. Most cases were settled in popular courts from which there was no organized system of appeal, features that brought Kievan justice closer to the Germanic system than to the Byzantine. The limitations on princely autocracy imposed by the boyars and the *veches* make the Kievan period distinctive in Russian constitutional history.

The Influence of Christianity The central event in Kievan cultural development was the acceptance of Eastern Christianity in 988. The arrival of some Byzantine clergy in Kiev changed the character of its culture. They established a formal educational system primarily to train the clergy; but their schools were open to the sons of ruling families, and a number of women, too, were educated in convents. Monks, as the first scholars in Kiev, used a modification of the Greek alphabet that missionaries had devised years before to convert the Slavs. They employed this alphabet in the translations of parts of the Bible and other ecclesiastical writings. These works constituted the dominant body of contemporary literature, and their religious themes served as models for the native writers.

The literary masterpiece of the age is the *Primary Chronicle*. Its principal theme is the conversion of the Rus to Christianity and their battles against the pagan peoples who surrounded them. This work illustrates the East Slavs' sense of national identity and acceptance of the Christian scheme of history. Although the account is of questionable accuracy in its earliest passages, it remains a classic of medieval literature. Few Western chronicles of comparable age can equal it in the wealth of information and liveliness of narration.

The monks, of whom the Metropolitan Hilarion was perhaps the most gifted, also produced many sermons, doctrinal and devotional tracts, and lives of the saints. These histories and the *Primary Chronicle* provide the best picture of the society and culture of medieval Rus. The poetry of medieval Rus is represented by the short heroic epic the *Song of Igor's Campaign*.[4] The poem records an unsuccessful campaign that the Rus princes conducted against the pagan Polovtsi in 1185 and depicts with considerable feeling the tragic but necessary costs of battle against the people of the steppes.

Christianity also had an immense influence on architectural and artistic development. After the conversion the East Slavs built many churches based on Byzantine models. The familiar "onion" domes of Russian churches, for example, were a late effort to imitate in wood the domes on ecclesiastical structures at Constantinople. The East Slavs loved magnificence and splendor in their churches and liturgical services. They learned the art of painting from the Byzantines and decorated their churches with icons—painted or enameled representations of sacred personages, such as Christ, a saint, or an angel.

Christianity imparted to the East Slavs a sense of world history and of their own place in it. They came to view their country as Holy Rus, the de-

[4]The original manuscript was discovered about 1790 by Count Aleksey Musin-Pushkin but was destroyed during the Napoleonic invasion in 1812, when Moscow was burned. Those who accept its authenticity usually date its composition to 1187. The *Song* is available in a fine English translation by the distinguished novelist Vladimir Nabokov.

fender of the true faith, facing and fighting a sea of pagan barbarians. Even though many accomplishments of the Kievan era were not maintained in the succeeding periods of East Slavic history, the Russians, Ukrainians, and Belarussians themselves did not lapse into barbarism.

DECLINE OF THE PRINCIPALITY

Both internal and external troubles destroyed the peace of the land after Yaroslav's death. To select his successor Yaroslav had introduced an extraordinarily complex procedure known as the rota system. The entire land was considered to be the property of the ruling family, and the towns were ranked in order of their importance and allotted to the princes, or sons of the ruler, according to their position within the family. When the senior prince of Kiev died, each of the junior princes became ruler of the next greatest town; brothers were given preference over sons. This cumbersome system of succession led to a constant movement of princes, to frequent bickerings, and often to civil wars. The political history after the reign of Yaroslav becomes an involved and dismal story of unending princely quarrels.

These struggles left the people unable to resist the renewed menace of the steppe nomads. In 1061 the Cumans, a nomadic Turkish people, began harassing the frontier, and they eventually cut off Kiev from contact with the Black Sea. This sundering of the trade route to Constantinople was a disaster for commerce and culture because it deprived Kiev of contact with the Byzantine Empire and the Western world.

Pressure from the nomads pushed the area of East Slavic settlement to the north and west, where extensive forests offered protection from nomadic forays. This dispersal prepared the way for the eventual separation of the East Slavs into three culturally distinct peoples. The Rus of the north—soon to be called Russians—were forced into a kind of isolation, removed and remote from the major centers of civilization. A new city, Moscow (not mentioned in the sources until 1147), assumed the arduous task of forming a united Russian state. In 1169 the soldiers of a northern prince, Andrew Bogoliubsky of Suzdal, sacked Kiev. With the ruin of Kiev, perpetrated by the steppe nomads and by the Rus themselves, the first major chapter of East Slavic history closes.

III. Islam

Sometime about 610 in the Arabian town of Mecca, a merchant's son named Muhammad began to preach to the people, summoning them to repentance and reform. Gradually, he brought his teachings together to form a new system of religious belief that he called Islam. The explosive impact of his preaching must be reckoned as one of the most extraordinary events of world history. Within a century after Muhammad's death his followers had conquered and partially converted territories larger than the old Roman Empire. Even today Islam remains the faith of perhaps 600 million people, more than an eighth of the world's population.

THE ARABS

The Arabian peninsula, the homeland of the Arabs, profoundly influenced their culture and history. Its vast interior and northern regions are dominated by steppes, wastelands, and some of the hottest and driest deserts of the world. The Arabs, however, adapted to this harsh environment. They supported themselves by raising sheep and camels, animals that provided nearly all their necessities: meat, milk, wool, skins for clothes and tents, and fuel from dried camel dung. The Arabs were extremely proud of their family, race, language, skill, and way of life. The harsh environment and their fierce pride made them spirited, tenacious, and formidable warriors.

The Arabian peninsula was in a state of intense political and social ferment on the eve of Muhammad's appearance. The stronger political powers—the Persians, Byzantines, and Abyssinians across the Red Sea—tried repeatedly to subdue the Arabs but could not dominate them in their desert home. Religious ferment was no less explosive. Several prophets, preaching new religious beliefs, had gained followers in Arabia before Muhammad; and this indicates a growing dissatisfaction among the Arabs with their traditional paganism, which gave no promise of an afterlife and offered no image of human destiny and the role of the Arabs in it. Both Christianity and Judaism had won numerous converts, but neither one was able to gain the adherence of most Arabs. The Arabs awaited a man who by the force of his vision could fuse all these contending ideas—pagan, Christian, and Jewish—into a single, commanding, and authentically Arabian religion.

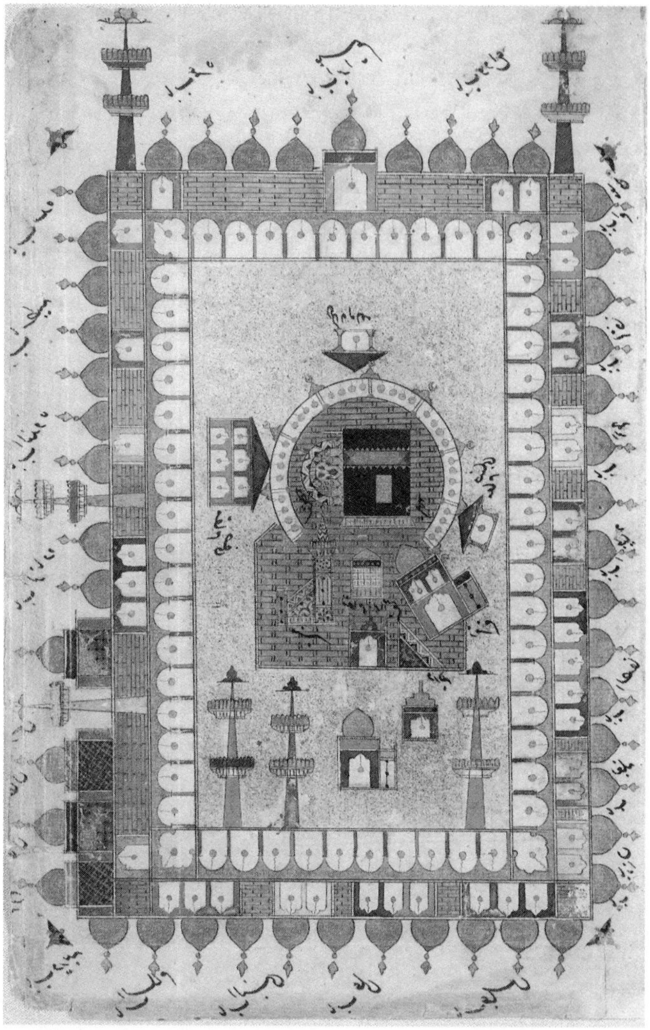

▸ **PILGRIMAGE GUIDE**
A sixteenth-century illustration of a pilgrimage guide written around 900, this picture shows the Kaaba at Mecca. The Kaaba, said to have been built by the Prophet Abraham, is the black rectangular building, surrounded by domed arcades.

MUHAMMAD

Historians have little information that is certain about the founder of Islam. Muhammad was born at Mecca about 570 or 571. His father died before his birth, and his mother died when he was 6. After being raised by his uncle, Muhammad worked as a camel driver in caravans. He may have been illiterate and may have had no direct knowledge of the Jewish and Christian Scriptures; but he did acquire a wide, if sometimes inaccurate, knowledge of the history and teaching of those two religions. About the age of 25 Muhammad married the widow of a rich merchant; thus freed from economic concerns, he gave himself to religious meditations in the desert outside Mecca.

In 610 Muhammad heard the voice of the angel Gabriel speaking to him, and he continued to receive such revelations in increasing frequency and length for the remainder of his life. After his first revelation from Gabriel, Muhammad began to preach publicly about personal moral reform, but only his wife and a small group of relatives initially accepted his teachings. The people of Mecca feared him because his strictures against paganism seemed to threaten the position of Mecca as a center of pilgrimages. Mecca possessed a renowned shrine containing the Kaaba, a sacred black stone that was the object of pagan worship. Rejected in his native city, Muhammad accepted an invitation to expound his ideas in Yathrib, a trading town 270 miles to the north, which he later renamed Medina.

Muhammad's emigration from Mecca to Yathrib is called the *hijra* and occurred in 622, which later became the year 1 of the Islamic calendar. The *hijra* was a turning point in Muhammad's career for two reasons: He became the political leader and governor of an important town, which gave him a base for the military expansion of the Islamic community; and his responsibilities as head of an independent town affected the character of his religious message. More and more, his message was concerned with public law, administration, and the practical problems of government.

Muhammad was more successful at Yathrib than he had been at Mecca in making converts. He told them that God ordered them to convert or conquer their neighbors; through enthusiastic proselytizing and war, the community of believers grew rapidly. With this support Muhammad marched against the Meccans, defeating them at

Badr in 624 and taking Mecca in 630. By his death in 632, Muhammad had given his religion a firm foundation on Arabian soil.

THE RELIGION OF ISLAM

Instructed by the angel Gabriel, Muhammad passed on to his followers the words or prophecies of Allah (from *al ilāh*, meaning "the God"). The collection of prophecies is known as the Koran; and Allah, in Islamic theology, is its true author. The Koran was written down in its present, official version in 651 and 652. The Koran imparts to the sympathetic reader a powerful mood, one of uncompromising monotheism, of repeated and impassioned emphasis upon the unity, power, and presence of Allah. The mood is sustained by constant reiterations of set formulas praising Allah, his power, knowledge, mercy, justice, and concern for his people (*see box*, below).

The chief obligation that Muhammad imposed upon his followers was submission (the literal meaning of *Islam*) to the will of Allah. Those who submit are Muslims. (*Muhammadan*, which suggests that Muhammad claimed divinity, is an inappropriate usage.) Muhammad was little concerned with the subtleties of theology; he was interested in defining for Muslims the ethical and legal requirements for an upright life. Unlike Christianity, Islam retained this practical emphasis; jurisprudence, even more than speculative theology, remained the great intellectual interest of Muslim scholarship. Also in contrast to Christianity, Islam did not recognize a separate clergy and church, for there was no need for specialized intermediaries between Allah and his people. Allah was the direct ruler of the faithful on earth; he legislated for them in the Koran and administered through Muhammad, the Prophet, and his successors, the caliphs. Church and state were not separate entities, at least in theory. There was only the single, sacred community of Allah.

The Koran on Christians and Jews

In the Koran, Muhammad proclaims that the faith of Islam also welcomes "the people of the Book"—that is, Christians and Jews who have the Bible as their sacred book—and that Islam is the fulfillment of these earlier faiths.

"Believers, Jews, Christians, and Sabaeans [of the kingdom of Saba in southwest Arabia]—whoever believes in Allah and the Last Day and does what is right—shall be rewarded by their Lord; they have nothing to fear or regret. To Moses We [that is, Allah] gave the Scriptures and after him We sent other apostles. We gave Jesus the son of Mary veritable signs and strengthened him with the Holy Spirit. And now that a Book [the Koran] confirming their Scriptures has been revealed to them by Allah, they deny it, although they know it to be the truth and have long prayed for help against the unbelievers.

"May Allah's curse be upon the infidels! Evil is that for which they have bartered away their souls. To deny Allah's own revelation, grudging that He should reveal His bounty to whom He chooses from His servants! They have incurred Allah's most inexorable wrath. An ignominious punishment awaits the unbelievers. The unbelievers among the People of the Book, and the pagans, resent that any blessings should have been sent down to you from your Lord. But Allah chooses whom He will for His mercy. His grace is infinite.

"Abraham enjoined the faith on his children, and so did Jacob, saying: 'My children, Allah has chosen for you the true faith. Do not depart this life except as men who have submitted to Him.' Say: 'We believe in Allah and that which is revealed to us; we believe in what was revealed to Abraham, Ishmael, Isaac, Jacob, and the tribes; to Moses and Jesus and the other prophets. We make no distinction between any of them, and to Allah we have surrendered ourselves. Your God is one God. There is no god but Him.' "

From *The Koran*, N. J. Dawood (tr.), 1968 (condensed).

Expansion of Islam The message of Islam exerted a powerful appeal to the Arabs. Compared with Christianity and Judaism, Islam was a starkly simple belief, easily explained and easily grasped. It was an effective fusion of religious ideas from Arabic paganism, Christianity, Judaism, and perhaps Zoroastrianism. Judaism influenced the legal code regulating diet and behavior. Judaism and Christianity provided the notion of prophecy, for Muhammad considered himself the last of a line of prophets that began with Abraham and included Jesus. More than that, the Bible tells that Abraham fathered Ishmael by Hagar, an Egyptian slave girl (Gen. 16–17), and Muslims believe that Ishmael was their ancestor and lies buried with Hagar in the Kaaba at Mecca. Christianity gave the concepts of Last Judgment, personal salvation, heaven and hell, charity to the poor and weak, and a universal religion. Christianity or perhaps Zoroastrianism suggested the figures of Satan and evil demons. Paganism contributed the veneration of the Kaaba and the requirement of pilgrimage to the sacred city.

Islam was therefore the fulfillment of religious ideas already familiar to the Arabs. Perhaps most important, Islam appealed strongly to the intense racial and cultural pride of the Arabs. The Koran was written in their native language, Arabic, and only in Arabic could Allah be addressed. Islam was seen as the final revelation, completing the message that God had partially conveyed through the Hebrew prophets and Jesus. The Arabs, a people who had hitherto played a negligible role in history, were given an important mission in life: to carry to the world the ultimate saving message. Even as Muhammad claimed to have supplanted Jesus as the supreme prophet, so the Arabs saw themselves as replacing the Jews as God's chosen people, with a sacred right to his holy places, including Jerusalem.

Allah instructed his followers to convert or conquer nonbelievers. Several factors aided the extraordinary expansion of Islam in the first century of its existence. Islam fused the once contending Arab clans and tribes into a unified and dedicated force. The Arabs, long familiar with camels, were masters of desert warfare. Their enemies, relying on horses, could not challenge them on desert terrain. Using the desert much as English imperialists later used the sea, the Arabs moved armies and supplies with facility across vast arid stretches, struck the enemy at places and times of their own choosing, and retreated to the safety of the desert when the odds turned against them. Moreover, the Arabs' immediate neighbors, the Byzantines and Persians, were mutually exhausted by their recurrent wars. Both empires included large Semitic populations that were linguistically and culturally related to the Arabs and, therefore, could comprehend the message of Islam.

The Arabs were able to make and hold their conquests through a unique combination of fanaticism and toleration. They were inspired to battle by the Prophet's promise of vast rewards to those who died in the Holy War against the nonbelievers and by the very real prospect of considerable booty if victory accompanied their efforts. The Prophet, however, also enjoined a policy of partial toleration toward Christians and Jews, who were both known as the "people of the Book." They were permitted to live under their own laws, but they paid a special tax for the privilege. Finally, because the Arabs did not have the numbers and the skills to govern all the territories they conquered, they opened the ranks of government to men from the newly conquered and converted peoples. This added stability to Islamic rule. The period of most rapid expansion of Islam followed Muhammad's death in 632 and coincided with the rule of the first four caliphs, as Muhammad's successors were called. Arabian forces seized the Byzantine provinces of Palestine and Syria, overran Persia, and conquered Egypt. By 661 Islam was firmly established as a world power. Islamic conquests continued under the caliphs of the Umayyad family, who were the first line of hereditary rulers. The Umayyads moved the capital from Mecca to Damascus. Under their rule the Muslims conquered North Africa and overran the kingdom of the Visigoths in Spain. After crossing the Pyrenees into the kingdom of the Franks, Muslim raiders were finally defeated by Charles Martel at Tours in 732. This battle, 100 years after Muhammad's death, marked the extent of the western advance and stabilized the frontier of Islam for the next several centuries (see Map 7.3).

The Schism As the territory under Islamic control grew to enormous size, powerful movements threatened and finally shattered Islamic unity.

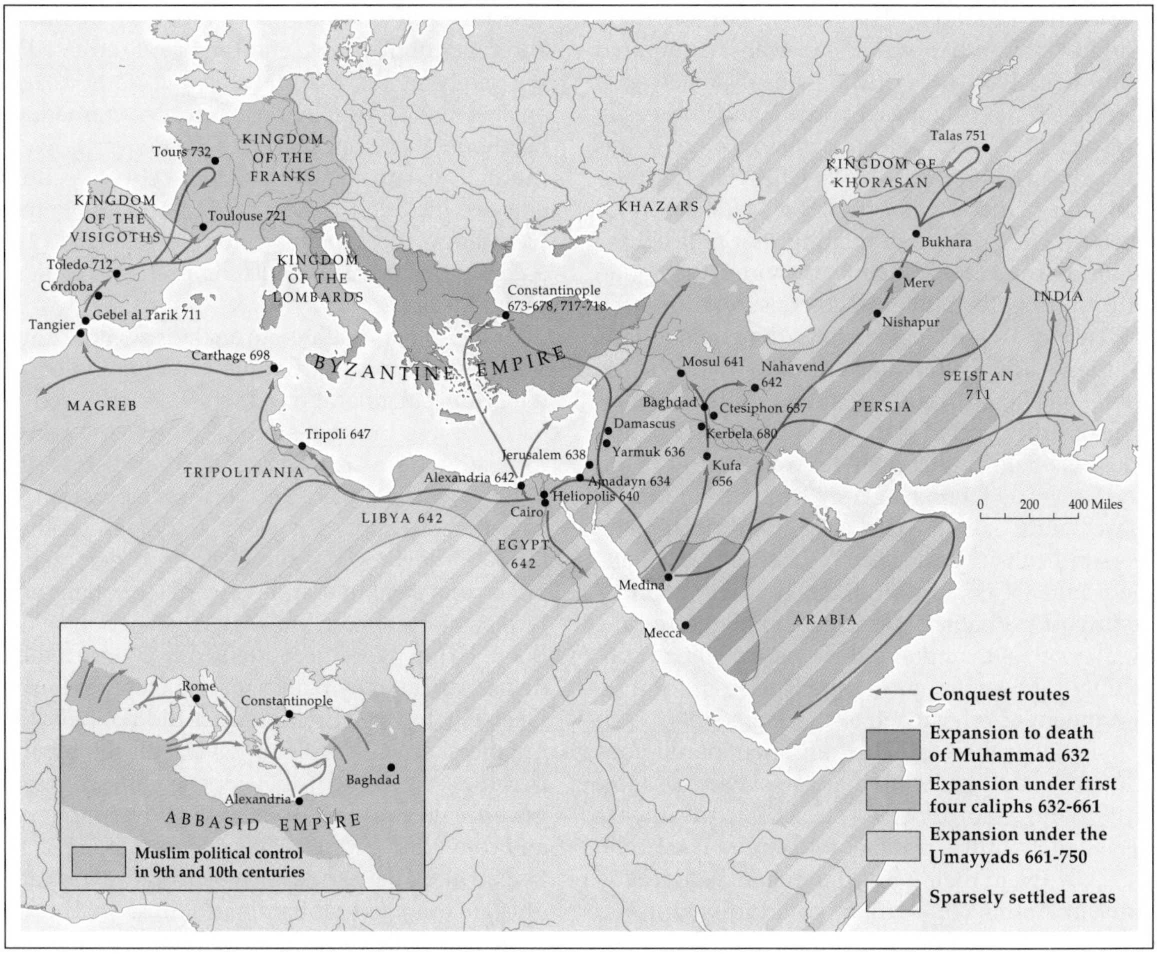

Map 7.3 **EXPANSION OF ISLAM**

Jealousies and frictions disturbed the relations among the various peoples who had accepted Islam, and religious divisions also appeared. Islam had been an open and fluid religion at the death of Muhammad, but scholars and teachers gradually elaborated a theology that a majority of the believers accepted as orthodox. The scholars based the new orthodoxy not only on the Koran but also on the Sunnas, or traditions, which were writings that purported to describe how the first companions of Muhammad or Muhammad himself dealt with various problems. Some Muslims, however, rejected the new orthodoxy of the *Sunnites,* as they came to be called. Those who opposed the Sunnites were called the *Shiites,* or schismatics.

This earliest schism was more a political than a religious protest. The Shiites maintained that only the descendants of Muhammad's son-in-law, Ali, who was the fourth caliph, could lawfully rule the Islamic community; therefore, beginning in the seventh century, they rejected the Umayyads (and later the Abbasids) as usurpers. Shiism soon became a cloak for all sorts of antagonisms, protests, and revolts. It struck deep roots among the mixed populations, reflecting the dissatisfactions of non-Arabs with Arab preponderance and channeling the antagonism between the poorer classes and their masters.

The growing social and religious dissensions finally broke the Umayyad caliphate. A descendant of one Abbas, the uncle of Muhammad, revolted against the Umayyads, captured Damascus, and ruthlessly massacred the caliph's family in 750. He thus founded the Abbasid dynasty. Only one member of the Umayyads escaped, Abdurrahman. He fled to Spain, where he set up an independent caliphate at Córdoba in 755. Other independent regimes soon arose: Morocco in 788, Tunisia in 800, eastern Persia in 820, and Egypt in 868. All became virtually independent under their local dynasties. The new Abbasid caliph moved the capital from Damascus to a new city, Baghdad. The power of Islam reached its highest point under the Abbasid dynasty, which endured until 1258. But the community of Islam was never again to be united.

ISLAMIC CIVILIZATION

Despite disunity, medieval Islamic civilization reached its peak of prosperity, refinement, and

▸ **ABU-ZAYD VISITING A MUSLIM VILLAGE**
This thirteenth-century illustration is a leaf from the *al-Hariri Magamat* (Assemblies of Entertaining Dialogues), a collection of tales set in various parts of the Muslim world. Here, the main character Abu-Zayd visits a lively village whose inhabitants carry on their daily tasks of spinning, agriculture, and worship.

▶ The remarkable series of rooms and courtyards that make up the Alhambra Palace in Granada are one of the supreme achievements of Islamic art. The delicate tracery, the elegant details, and the constant presence of running water create a mood of luxury and refinement that can still be experienced by the visitor today.

learning in the ninth and tenth centuries. This period inspired the tales of the *Arabian Nights*, through which the name of Caliph Harun al-Rashid became known throughout the world. These exotic stories, put into their present form in the fourteenth century, convey a glamorous and idealized, but not a false, picture of the luxurious life at Baghdad during its most splendid age. Harun's son Al-Mamun reigned even more splendidly than his father. He was also a patron of learning. Al-Mamun founded an observatory for the study of the heavens and established a "House of Wisdom" (sometimes referred to as the first Islamic institution of higher education), where translations were made and a library collected for the use of scholars.

Spain was a notable center of medieval Islamic civilization. The brilliance of Islamic-Spanish civilization is best reflected in three great architectural monuments: the mosque (now a cathedral) at Córdoba, the Alhambra Palace in Granada, and the Alcazar at Seville. Jewish communities in Spain, the most creative of Jewish communities in the West, contributed to the high quality of intellectual life. It was also in Spain that Western Christians came into intimate contact with Islamic learning and drew from it the greatest benefits.

As Islam expanded, it embraced numerous economic systems. The Bedouins in the Arabian peninsula, the Berbers in North Africa, and the Turkish people of Eurasia continued to have a pastoral economy. The majority of those living in Egypt, Persia, Sicily, and Spain lived from settled agriculture. The inhabitants of cities, especially those along the caravan routes that tied the Middle East to India and central Asia, relied on commerce.

Islam greatly improved communications through the imposition of a universal language, Arabic, and the obligation of at least one pilgrimage to Mecca ensured frequent travel. And Muhammad had been a merchant; Islamic law favored commerce, and Islam esteemed the merchant. Maritime commerce in the Mediterranean provided until the sixteenth century the chief commercial link among India, Egypt, and the West. A large collection of letters from Jewish merchants living in Cairo in the eleventh and twelfth centuries has survived and marvelously illuminates trade and many other aspects of social life in the medieval East.[5]

Commercial exchange stimulated agriculture within the world of Islam. Cultivators in Sicily and Spain adopted new plants from Asia, such as rice, and new techniques of cultivation, such as the irrigation of fields. Muslims from Persia to Spain practiced an agriculture remarkably advanced for the age. Trade also stimulated urban artisans to improve the quality of their products. The steel of Damascus, the leather of Córdoba, and the fine cotton, linen, and silk of many Eastern towns were desired and imitated in the West. These same products were shipped to India and Indonesia, where they were traded for spices and other products.

Medieval Islamic society was also distinguished by a vigorous urban life, concentrated in the cities of Damascus, Baghdad, Cairo, and Córdoba. According to travelers' reports, Damascus had 113,000 homes and 70 libraries. Baghdad surpassed all other cities in the number of palaces, libraries, and public baths. In all the major cities products from almost all parts of the known world could be purchased at the markets, or bazaars. The streets teemed with slaves, servants, artisans, merchants, administrators, and beggars. The aura of the Islamic cities was preeminently cosmopolitan.

A common religion ensured similarities in Islamic societies everywhere in the world. Religious law allowed the male Muslim to have as many as four legal wives and an unlimited number of concubines. In fact, only the rich could afford to have several wives. More important than polygyny in determining the position of women were the relative ease of divorce and the life of seclusion imposed on all women after puberty. Religious laws permitted the husband to dismiss

[5]They are called the *Geniza documents*. The geniza was a storeroom attached to a synagogue; records mentioning God's name (including merchants' letters) could not be destroyed and were stored in the geniza. The geniza of the Cairo synagogue was sealed up and not rediscovered until the nineteenth century. Its contents were then sold to collectors of Jewish documents and to libraries and thus dispersed throughout the world. For examples of these extraordinary records, see S. D. Goitein, *Letters of Medieval Jewish Traders*, 1973.

his wife almost at will and prohibited a woman from revealing her face except to her husband. These laws were not enforced everywhere with equal rigor and weighed primarily on women of the upper classes. Moreover, within the cities, at least in certain periods, women enjoyed relative freedom.

Because Islam recognized no distinction between church and state, the caliph was the supreme religious and civil head of the Muslim world. But he was not free to change the laws at will, since Allah had already provided all the laws his people needed; therefore, he was primarily a military chief and a judge. Among the Muslims the chief administrator on the local level was the *kadi*. He was primarily a judge, and his task was to see that the faithful lived according to the law of the Koran.

The Islamic conquests brought the Arabs into intimate contact with older and more accomplished civilizations than their own, particularly with the intellectual achievements of the Greeks, which they were eager to preserve. During the eighth and ninth centuries scholars translated into Arabic many Greek authors: Aristotle, Euclid, Archimedes, Hippocrates, and Galen. These works provided the foundations for Islamic learning and preserved the thought of these writers through a period when Greek texts were not being widely copied in the West.

Scholars were especially interested in astronomy, astrology, mathematics, medicine, and optics; and in these areas their writings exerted a great influence on the Western world. Al-Razi (known as Rhazes in the West) of Baghdad wrote some 140 medical treatises, including an admirable description of smallpox. Arabic mathematicians adopted their impressive numbering system from the Hindus but made the critical addition of the zero, which is itself an Arabic word. Italian merchants became familiar with the Arabic numbers shortly before the year 1200 and carried them back to the West. Arabic mathematicians also developed algebra. Astronomers and astrologers invented an improved astrolabe (which measures the angular declination of heavenly bodies above the horizon) and were able to improve the astronomical tables of antiquity.

Scholars also wrote philosophical and theological treatises. The most important Islamic philosopher was the Spaniard ibn-Rushd, or Averroës (1126?–1198), who wrote commentaries on Aristotle and exerted a profound influence on Christian as well as Islamic philosophy in the subsequent Middle Ages. Islamic philosophical speculations nourished intellectual life in the West in two ways: Western philosophers gained a much broader familiarity with the scientific and philosophical heritage of Classical Greece through translations made from the Arabic, chiefly in Spain; and Islamic philosophers explored issues central to religious philosophy much earlier than did Christian thinkers. What is the relation between faith and reason, between an all-powerful God and the freedom, dignity, and individuality of the human person? In posing these problems and in suggesting answers, the Muslims stimulated and enriched thought in the West.

▸ **This thirteenth-century Arab commentary on the *Geometry* of Euclid illustrates the proof of the Pythagorean theorem. Mathematics was one science in which the Arabs surpassed the Classical achievements.**

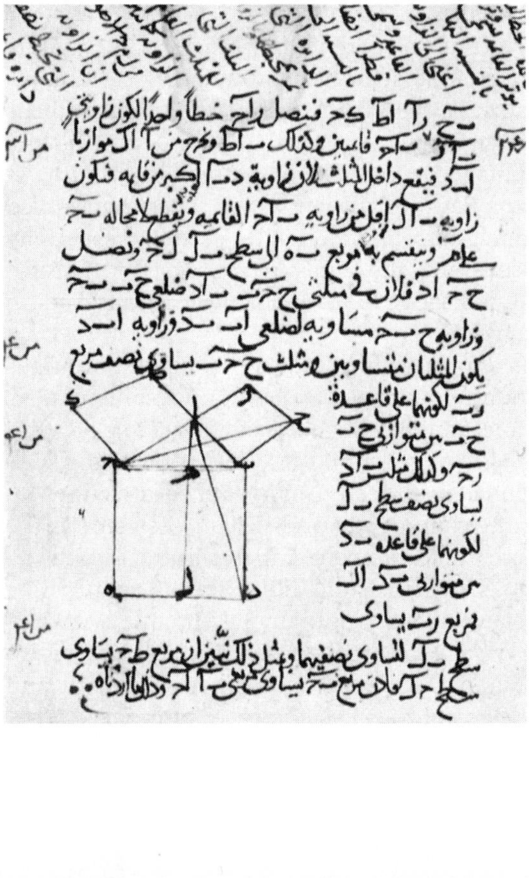

Photo: British Museum.

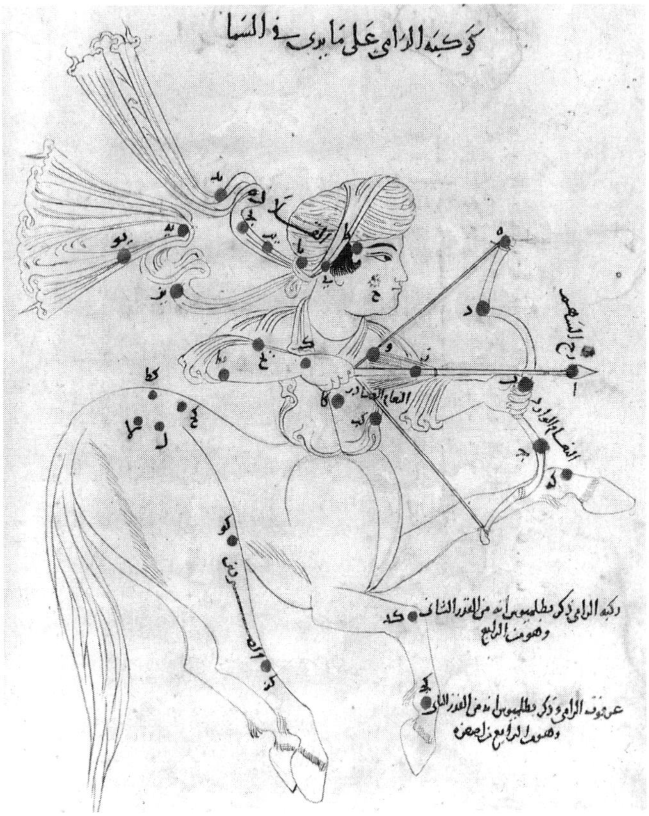

▶ FORMS OF THE FIXED STARS, CA. 1009–1010
One of the earliest examples of Islamic book illustration, this manuscript, written around 1009–1010, contains 75 drawings noting the forms of the fixed stars. Sagittarius, shown as an armed rider, is traced from the pattern of the constellation and indicates the sophistication of Muslim astronomy.

CHALLENGES TO MEDIEVAL ISLAMIC CIVILIZATION

The earliest indication of decline was the growing military weakness of the various Islamic states in the face of new invasions in the middle of the eleventh century. In the West, Christian armies embarked on the reconquest of the Iberian peninsula, and Christian fleets broke the Islamic domination of the western Mediterranean islands. The Christian offensive blends imperceptibly with the First Crusade, which wrested Jerusalem from Islamic control in 1099. At the same time in the East, Turkish nomads infiltrated the Abbasid caliphate in considerable numbers, and the Seljuks seized Baghdad in 1055. Turkish rulers gained supremacy in all the Eastern Islamic states over the next few centuries.

The Arabic economic base was also changing. By the thirteenth century, maritime and commercial supremacy on the Mediterranean Sea passed to Italians and other Westerners. Arabian coins largely disappeared from circulation in the West, documenting a headlong retreat from commerce. Simultaneously, the Islamic states were no longer supporting their warriors by salaries but by grants of land, which weakened central authority. The growing importance of an aristocracy of rural warriors seems to have brought a new militarism and rigidity into society.

To be sure, Islamic civilization continued to support some great cultural centers and to inspire some great artists and thinkers; but after the eleventh century it began to lose the qualities of openness, flexibility, and intellectual daring that had so distinguished it in the ninth and tenth centuries.

▸ MOSQUE AT CÓRDOBA, 784–990
Begun around 784, the Mosque at Córdoba was enlarged throughout the ninth and tenth centuries. The flexible plan of parallel aisles creates a complex visual forest of double-tiered arches that originally supported a wooden roof. This immense structure, with 850 columns and 19 aisles, was one of the largest buildings in the Islamic world.

THE WESTERN DEBT TO ISLAMIC CIVILIZATION

Almost every aspect of medieval Western life was influenced by Islamic civilization. Western farmers imitated Muslim techniques of irrigation and learned to grow many new plants, such as rice, citrus fruits, and peaches. Western merchants adopted the Arabic numbers, universally used in the West, and probably some Islamic forms of business partnerships. Muslim mathematicians made enormous contributions to the development of algebra. Western physicians, philosophers, and theologians were influenced by Islamic scholars. The stunning artistic monuments of Islam, such as the Alhambra Palace and the mosque at Córdoba, are still the wonder of travelers.

Yet the more remarkable aspect of the meeting of the two medieval civilizations, East and West, is really how little they affected one another in their basic cultural attitudes, apart from specific techniques and institutions. The medieval West was not much influenced by, and in fact poorly understood, the fundamental theology or the spirit of Islam. But it still enlisted many Islamic accomplishments in the service of its own civilization, a civilization that was to burst forth in spectacular form after the year 1000.

Recommended Reading

Sources

Cross, Samuel Hazard (ed.). *Russian Primary Chronicle: Laurentian Text.* O. P. Sherbowitz-Wetzor (tr.). 1968.

*Dmytryshyn, Basil. *Medieval Russia: A Source Book, 850–1700* (3rd ed.). 1991.

*Ibn, Khaldun. *The Mugaddimah: An Introduction to World History.* Franz Rosenthal (tr.). 1969. Reflections on societies and empires by a North African Muslim; written in the fourteenth century.

**The Meaning of the Glorious Koran.* M. Marmaduke Pickthall (tr.). 1948.

Procopius. *Secret History.* Richard Atwater (tr.). 1964. A scandal-filled history of Justinian's reign.

*Vernadsky, George (ed.). *Medieval Russian Laws.* 1964.

Zenkovsky, Serge A. (ed.). *Medieval Russia's Epics, Chronicles and Tales.* 1974. Includes sermons and saints' lives.

Studies

*Baynes, Norman H., and Henry Moss (eds.). *Byzantium: An Introduction to East Roman Civilization.* 1948. Elegant essays by leading scholars.

Fine, John V. A. *The Early Medieval Balkans. A Critical Survey from the Sixth to the Late Twelfth Century.* 1983. The only work of its kind in English.

*Geanakoplos, Deno J. *Byzantine East and Latin West: Two Worlds of Christendom in the Middle Ages and Renaissance.* 1966. The Western debt to Byzantium.

Goitein, S. D. *A Mediterranean Society: The Jewish Communities of the Arab World as Portrayed in the Documents of the Cairo Geniza.* 1967–. Portrayal of Jewish social life on the basis of the remarkable Geniza documents.

Grekov, B. D. *Kiev Rus.* Dennis Ogden (ed.). 1959. A Soviet interpretation.

Hodgson, Marshall G. *The Venture of Islam: Conscience and History in a World Civilization.* 1974. A lengthy examination of the traditional beliefs and values of Islam.

Hussey, J. M. *The Orthodox Church in the Byzantine Empire.* 1986.

*Lewis, Bernard. (ed.). *Islam from the Prophet Muhammad to the Capture of Constantinople.* Vol. 1: *Politics and War.* Vol. 2: *Religion and Society.* 1987. Collected essays.

Mango, Cyril. *Byzantium: The Empire of New Rome.* 1980. An introduction to the civilization of the Eastern Empire, with effective use of archaeological data.

Obolensky, Dimitri. *The Byzantine Commonwealth. Eastern Europe 500–1453.* 1971. Excellent general survey, dealing with politics, religion, art, and culture in general.

Ostrogorski, George. *History of the Byzantine State.* Joan Hussey (tr.). 1969. The basic reference for all matters of political history.

*Vasiliev, A. A. *History of the Byzantine Empire: 324–1453.* 1953–1959. Stronger on cultural matters than Ostrogorski; by a great Russian scholar.

Vernadsky, George. *A History of Russia.* 1946–1963. In five parts and six volumes, the most comprehensive history of early Russia by a single historian in any language.

*Von Grunebaum, Gustave E. (ed.). *Medieval Islam: A Study in Cultural Orientation.* 1966. By one of the great figures in Islamic studies.

*Available in paperback.

A medieval knight in armor.

CHAPTER EIGHT

Two Centuries of Creativity

THE present historical view of the Middle Ages recognizes the year 1000 as a watershed between two contrasting periods. Before 1000 Western civilization changed slowly, nearly imperceptibly. Europe's population remained small, and the economy overwhelmingly agricultural. Trade was sporadic, and the few towns that survived the repeated invasions played only a minor role in economic life. Governments tended to be weak and unstable. In art and literature, very few of the works produced would be regarded today as masterpieces.

After 1000 change came rapidly on virtually every level. Population, stagnant or declining since the last years of the Roman Empire, increased. People cleared and settled new lands and extended Europe's land frontiers in every direction. Commerce grew, and the resulting expansion of wealth restored vitality to the cities. Rulers reorganized their governments in an effort to adapt the institutions of feudalism to a more stable political environment. Western philosophers embarked on a reexamination of Christian theology, and the Church itself generated a major reform. Artists were once again productive, primarily in service to the Church.

As historians have come to appreciate the dimensions of these changes, they have reassessed the contribution of the Middle Ages to Western development. Many historians now speak of a medieval renaissance during the eleventh and twelfth centuries, which laid the foundations for the civilization we label "traditional Europe." In many respects this civilization lasted until the revolutionary upheavals of the eighteenth and nineteenth centuries, the beginning of the authentically modern world.

I. Economic and Social Changes

From the year 1000, European society showed many signs of growth in its human numbers and in its geographic area of settlement. Moreover, some of these people were earning their livings in novel ways, which sparked a revival of trade and a rebirth of urban life. Simultaneously, Europeans were creating new forms of social and political organization and of cultural expression.

THE BEGINNINGS OF EXPANSION

Europe's population in the Early Middle Ages, to about the year 1000, was small in absolute numbers and was not distributed evenly across the countryside. Rather, the people tended to cluster into crowded communities separated from one another by vast stretches of wilderness. Within these islands of population there is much evidence of overcrowding, even though there was little or no absolute growth. Peasant farms (the *mansi*), each intended for the support of a single family, often contained several by the ninth century.

Why did the population not spread out from these impacted settlements and clear new farms in the extensive surrounding wilderness? Many factors obstructed such an exodus; among them were the bonds of serfdom, the safety provided by close settlement in a period of invasions, the bonds of kinship, and a fear of the wilderness.

This pattern of settlement changes from about the year 1000. Peasants poured out of their older centers of settlement to newly opened frontiers, both within Europe and beyond its former borders. What had happened? There is some evidence that the climate became milder, perhaps encouraging the colonization of new lands. In addition, by the middle and late tenth century, the incursions of Vikings, Hungarians, and Saracens were waning, and the new security made the wilderness less intimidating. Beginning in the late tenth century many lords and princes began to encourage the settlement of the wilderness areas they controlled; others assumed leadership in the expansion of the external frontier. They offered land to new settlers under favorable terms and assured them protection in the work of colonization. Their interest in increased rents perhaps indicates that the warrior aristocracy of Europe could no longer live, as it had in the past, predominantly from royal gifts and pillage taken in the frequent wars. The Church, too, Europe's largest landlord, by the late tenth century actively sought to increase its own revenues from the land in the interest of supporting a celibate and reformed clergy.

The opening of new lands encouraged reproduction. Children became an asset to families engaged in the hard work of clearing land. More land in cultivation meant more food. For the first time since the fall of the Western Roman Empire, Europe's population gives evidence of sustained and substantial growth.

Frontiers In England, France, and Germany, the peasants leveled forests and drained marshes; in England and the Low Countries, they also won land from the sea by building dikes and draining marshes. German peasants and knights, looking for new lands to settle, pushed eastward beyond the former borders of the Frankish Empire (see Map 8.1) into territories that were thinly inhabited by Slavs, Prussians, Letts, and Lithuanians. Some Germans settled just beyond the Elbe River and established the Principality of Brandenburg. Other Germans advanced along the shores of the Baltic Sea at the same time that Swedes began to move across Finland. The Russian prince of Novgorod, Alexander Nevsky, defeated the Swedes on the Neva River close to the Baltic Sea in 1240 and repulsed the Germans at Lake Peipus in 1242. Although these defeats halted further advances in northeastern Europe, the Germans and Swedes retained control of the shores of the Baltic Sea. The Germans had by then pushed through the middle Danube valley and founded another principality: Austria. By the mid-thirteenth century the "drive to the east" had clearly spent its strength, but it had tripled the area of German settlement over what it had been in Carolingian times (see Map 8.1).

Settlers also moved into the Iberian peninsula (present day Spain and Portugal). In the mid-eleventh century the Christian kings, whose kingdoms were confined to the extreme north of

Map 8.1 **GERMAN MIGRATION EASTWARD**

the peninsula, began an offensive against the Muslims, who ruled most of Iberia. The Christians pushed south over two centuries, until they held most of the peninsula. The battle of Las Navas de Tolosa (in 1212), between an allied Christian army and an invading Muslim army from North Africa, confirmed this domination. By 1275 only the emirate of Granada remained under Muslim rule. The Christian kings actively recruited Christian settlers for the territories they reconquered and gave them land under favorable terms. The reconquest and resettlement of the peninsula, known as the *Reconquista,* proved lasting achievements; the Iberian frontier remained almost unchanged for the next 280 years, during which time Castile, Aragon, Portugal, and other states developed and flourished (see Chapter 9).

In Italy, too, pioneers pushed the Christian frontier to the south. From about 1015, knights from Normandy, initially serving as mercenaries, began fighting in southern Italy against Muslims, Byzantines, and local lords who had long been disputing dominion there. In 1124, now acting in their own name, they finally drove the Muslims and Byzantines from southern Italy and Sicily and united the two regions into the Kingdom of Naples and Sicily. European power swept over the sea as well as the land. The leaders were the maritime cities of Pisa and Genoa. In 1015 and 1016 fleets from Pisa and Genoa freed Sardinia from Islamic rule.

SOCIAL CHANGES

In many regions of Europe the expansion in settlement shifted the balance between the free and unfree classes. To attract settlers onto previously uncultivated lands, lords had to offer generous terms, frequently guaranteed in a written charter. Many landlords established free villages on their properties. The peasant who settled in a free village usually paid only a small fixed rent for the lands he cleared and was not required to labor for the landlord. He could leave the village at will, selling his lands and the house he had built at their market value. A runaway serf who resided in a free village for one year and one day without being claimed by his owner was thenceforth free.

The social conditions of the serfs also improved. Emancipation was considered a religiously meritorious act, and the period was one of marked religious enthusiasm. The increase in population eliminated the need for landlords to keep the entire labor force tied to the soil. Moreover, since the new frontiers attracted the serfs, only better terms, not brute force, could hold the laborers on the lord's land. Revived trade enabled some serfs to sell their produce at market; they could thus earn money with which to buy their freedom. Finally, serfdom bound landlords as well as serfs. Enterprising lords who wished to raise their rents or even change routines of cultivation were blocked by the custom, making servile obligations fixed and immutable. To reorganize their estates, to free their lands, to free themselves, the landlords had also to free their serfs.

By the early thirteenth century serfdom had almost disappeared in France, Spain, Italy, and western Germany, although some vestiges of it were to remain until the eighteenth century. In England serfdom also declined until the thirteenth century; but the growing cities of the continent created a large, profitable market for cereals, and English landlords were eager to produce for it. Rather than leasing out their estates, they continued to cultivate them directly. To find the necessary laborers, English lords maintained, or reimposed, conditions of serfdom over their peasants. But this Indian summer of English serfdom did not last much beyond the fourteenth century.

The changes in agriculture altered the character of noble life. Most landlords now rented their lands to peasants to cultivate; they were no longer direct cultivators but rent collectors. Since this new function did not require the constant supervision of their lands, the lords were free to live away from home for extended periods, perhaps traveling as pilgrims or crusaders to distant lands or mingling with their peers at the courts of great nobles. The new agricultural system, and the physical freedom it allowed the lords, permitted the growth of a courtly society, which in turn brought with it a rich lay culture.

Peasant Life Life continued to be very hard, of course, for the peasants of Western Europe, but there were some improvements. To judge from skeletons found in medieval churchyards and from other slight evidence, the incidence of violent death declined, and life expectancy was growing; by the thirteenth century the average newborn might expect to live as long as 40 years. But rural conditions continued to be taxing for women. In the typical peasant village, men continued to outnumber, and presumably to outlive, women.

Although most peasants no longer lived in packed settlements, they still saw a good deal of their fellows. Markets and market days became a characteristic feature of rural life in Europe. Peasants slowly grew accustomed to selling or exchanging their surplus produce, purchasing their needs, borrowing money, or simply sharing information with their neighbors at the markets. The influence of markets further stimulated the growth of cottage industries, especially in the vicinity of towns. Within their homes, after their agricultural tasks were accomplished, the peasants and their families spun yarn, wove cloth, brewed ale, cured leather, made wood products, and produced other commodities that they could exchange at the urban markets.

The rural Church acquired new importance, and it is to this period that the rural parishes of Europe (and the Christianization of the countryside) must be dated. Churches were built at an extraordinary pace. The parish priest was usually of peasant origin and was often assisted by a young cleric or clerics in training for the priesthood (there were no seminaries). Because the priest was frequently the only member of the community who could read, he aided the peasants in their contacts with merchants, tax collectors, and other representatives of the literate culture of the city. Sundays and feast days brought the people together for divine services and for boisterous celebrations too. Church councils repeatedly condemned dancing and singing in the churchyard, especially since the songs on such occasions tended to be bawdy, but the denunciations had scant effect.

The Rise of the Nobility The appearance of a hereditary nobility in the eleventh and twelfth centuries reflected a fundamental change in the structure of the elite family. In early medieval society the kindred—or set of relatives, even of important persons—traced their relationships through both males and females. Kindreds were formed, in other words, around a horizontal axis and did not extend far back in time. The kindred structure of the newly emerging nobility was much different. It placed exclusive emphasis on descent from, and relation through, males. And it pushed the line of descent through males far into the past, to the ancestor or founder of the line. It had, in other words, a vertical orientation. This set of male relatives descending through males from a common ancestor is called a *patrilineage*. (If, as was almost invariably the case until very recently, you bear your father's name, the same that his father bore, and so on up through the generations, then your surname recalls your own patrilineage. This custom reflects a tradition of family organization that has its origins among the nobility in the Central Middle Ages.)

Several factors contributed to the appearance of the noble patrilineage. The division of ancestral lands when there were many claimants threatened to destroy the economic base upon which the claimants' status depended, and to shore up their social position, the elite families sought to limit the number of heirs. The great families accordingly provided their daughters with dowries, but otherwise excluded them from a full share in the inheritance. They excluded

This enameled plate shows Count Geoffrey of Anjou, who died in 1151, holding a shield that depicts his family's new coat of arms.

younger sons as well. Often these sons were denied the chance to marry, unless they could win prizes in war or the hand of an affluent heiress. The family wealth was principally reserved for the support of the eldest son, and with him went the chief hope for the preservation of the lineage. To proclaim their identity and distinctiveness from the rest of society, the nobles adopted family names, which usually recalled the name of the revered founder or of the ancestral castle. They adopted other symbols of solidarity, such as coats of arms, mottoes, and sometimes fanciful genealogies.

To attract a suitable husband for a daughter, noble fathers had to offer ever larger dowries. Fathers were anxious to settle the future of their daughters as early as possible, even as they were requiring sons to marry late, if they were allowed to marry at all. Noble society, in which the patrilineage was the central institution, thus acquired certain peculiar features. Unattached young males abounded. They drifted from court to court as knights errant and were eager participants in tournaments, mock wars in which they hoped to win a prize that would make their fortunes. Or they wandered off on crusade to Europe's distant frontiers (see Chapter 10). The young women their own age would likely be married or deposited in convents. The interests of the firstborn male were not often the same as the good of all descendants, and the claims of the latter played upon parental consciences. Conflicts involving parents and siblings were commonplace in noble families.

THE REVIVAL OF COMMERCE

The European economy remained predominantly agricultural, although new forms of economic endeavor were emerging. Trade, which had dwindled to small importance in the Carolingian Age, became more vigorous. Most of the trade was local, between rural areas or between city and countryside, but there was also a dramatic rebirth of trade with regions beyond the European frontiers. Three trading zones developed based on the Mediterranean Sea in the south, the Baltic Sea in the north, and the overland routes that linked the two seas (see Map 8.2).

Venice, Pisa, and Genoa led this commercial expansion. In 998 and again in 1082 the Venetians received from the Byzantine emperors charters that gave them complete freedom of Byzantine waters. In the twelfth century Pisans and Genoese negotiated formal treaties with Islamic rulers that allowed them to establish commercial colonies in the Middle East and North Africa. Marseilles and Barcelona soon began to participate in the profitable Eastern trade.

In this Mediterranean exchange, the East

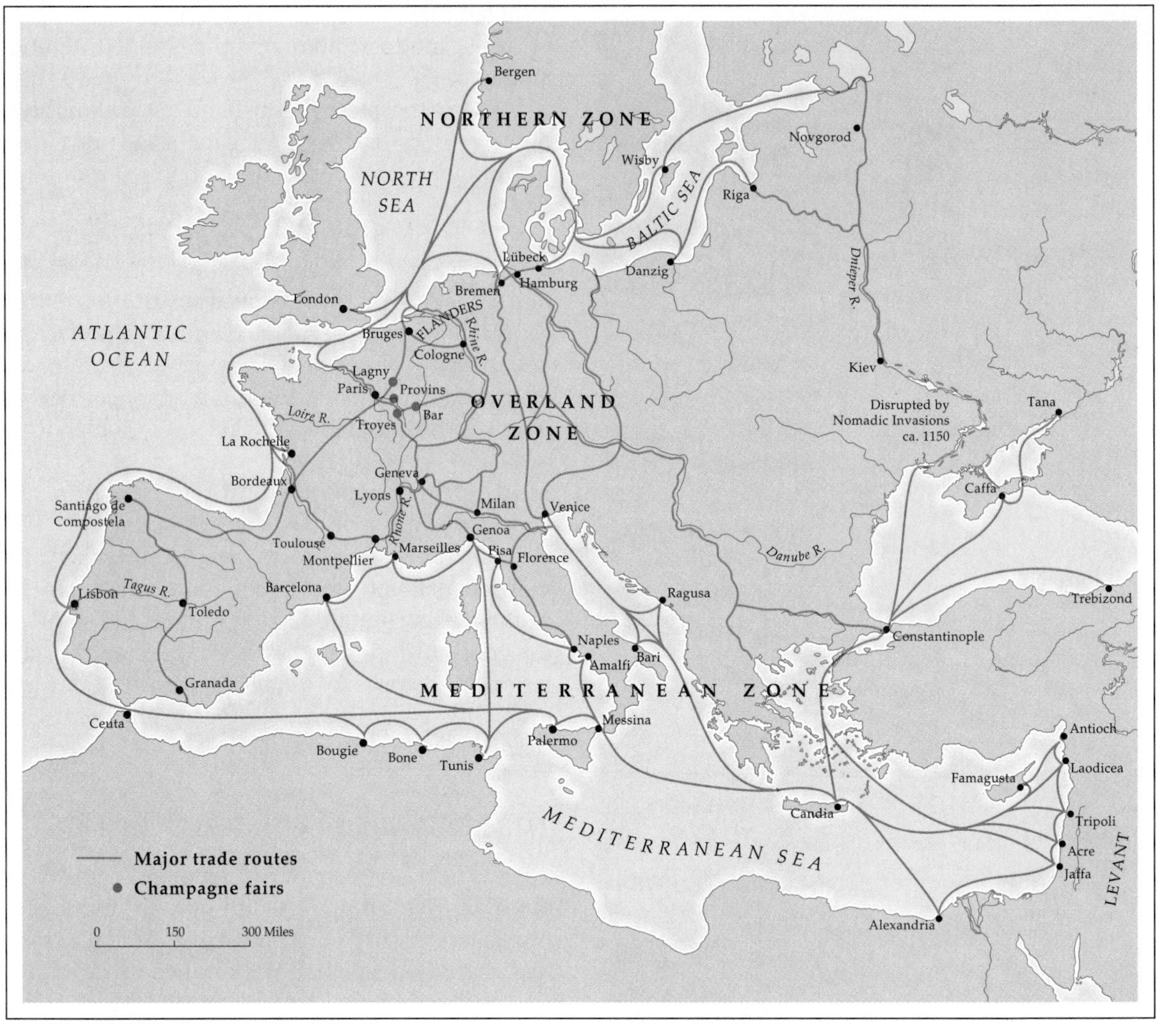

Map 8.2 MEDIEVAL TRADE ROUTES

shipped condiments, medicines, perfumes, dyes, paper, ivories, porcelain, pearls, precious stones, and rare metals such as mercury—all of which were known in the West under the generic name of *spices*. Eastern traders also sent a variety of fine linens and cottons (damask, muslin, organdy) as well as brocades and other silks. Western North Africa supplied animal skins, leather, cheese, ivory, and gold. Europe shipped wood and iron and products made from them (including entire ships), and grain, wine, and other agricultural commodities. By 1200 manufactured goods, especially woolen cloth woven in Flanders and finished in Italy, began to play an increasingly important role in the Mediterranean exchange. This cloth gave European merchants a product valued in the Eastern markets; with it they were able not only to pay for Eastern imports but also to generate a flow of precious metals into Europe.

Trade in northern Europe among the lands bordering the Baltic Sea linked the great ports of London, Bruges, Bergen, Cologne, Lübeck, and Novgorod with the many smaller maritime towns. The eastern Baltic regions sold grain, lumber and forest products, amber, and furs. Scandinavia supplied wood and fish. England provided raw wool and grains. Flanders was the great industrial area of the north, taking food and raw material for its excellent cloth.

The northern and Mediterranean trading

zones were joined by numerous overland routes. After 1100 the most active exchange between north and south was concentrated at six great fairs, held at various times of the year in the province of Champagne in France. Merchants could find at least one fair open no matter what time of year they came. They were guaranteed personal security at the fairs, low tariffs, and quick and fair justice. For two centuries the fairs remained the greatest markets in Europe.

THE REBIRTH OF URBAN LIFE

Although the towns in Western Europe were increasing in size and social complexity, their growth was very slow even in this age of economic expansion. Before 1200 probably no town in Western Europe included more than 30,000 inhabitants. These small towns, however, were assuming new functions.

In the Early Middle Ages the towns had been chiefly administrative centers, serving as the residence of bishops—or, much more rarely, of counts—and as fortified enclosures to which the surrounding rural population fled when under attack. (The original sense of the English word *borough* and of the German *Burg* is "fortress.") As the revival of trade made many of them centers of local or international exchange, permanent colonies of merchants grew up around the older fortresses. These merchant quarters were sometimes called a *faubourg* ("outside the fortress"). Many European towns, especially in the north, still show these two phases of their early history in their central fortress and surrounding settlements (see Map 8.3). By the thirteenth century some towns added to their administrative and commercial services a third function: They became centers of industrial production, especially of woolen cloth.

While growing in size, town populations, or at least their richest merchants, began demanding a greater measure of liberty from the bishop or lords who ruled them. They resented the cumbersome, expensive, and uninformed justice of the lord, who probably knew little about commercial needs, and they feared his powers to tax and to demand military service. The instrument by which the medieval townsmen sought to govern themselves was the *commune*, a permanent association created by the oath of its members and under the authority of several elected officials. Communes first appeared late in the eleventh century in northern Italy and Flanders, the two most heavily urbanized areas of Europe. Through force, persuasion, or purchase, many communes acquired from their lords charters

Map 8.3 **The Growth of Medieval Bruges**
Bruges (in modern Belgium) presents a fine example of the topographical dualism of many commercial towns of northern Europe. The town grew from two centers: the central fortress (A) and the merchants' settlement (B), gradually absorbing surrounding parishes and villages. The size of the late medieval walls conveys an accurate impression of the dimensions of medieval urban growth.

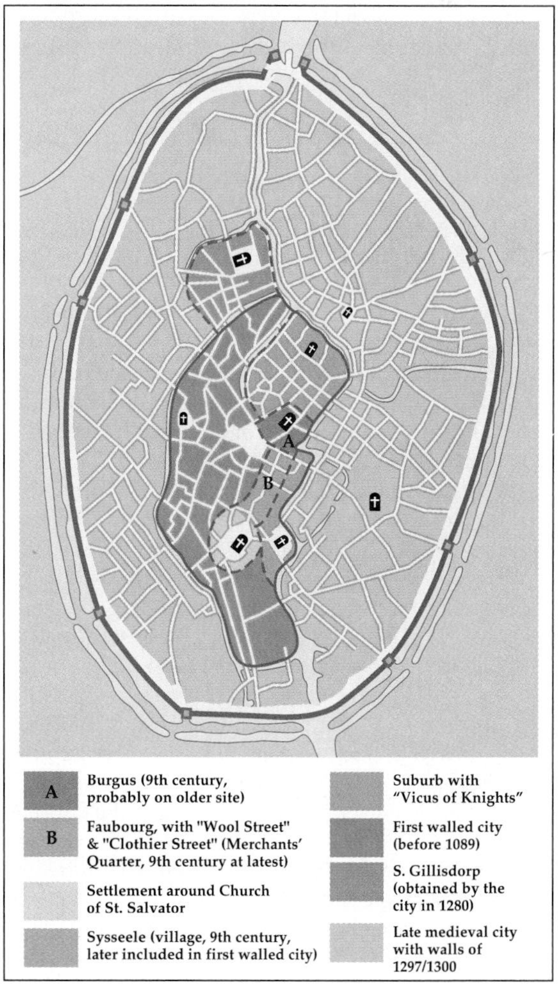

that set out their privileges and recognized their right to judge and tax themselves (*see box*, below).

Urban society also began to show considerable complexity. At the top of the social scale was a small aristocracy, usually referred to as *patricians*. In Italy this aristocracy included many nobles and great landlords from the countryside, who lived for part or all of the year in the towns. In contrast, in Flanders nobles and great landlords tended to keep to their rural estates, whence they viewed with disdain and fear the growing wealth of the towns. The powerful urban families in the north came chiefly from common origins, and most of them founded their fortunes upon commerce or the management of urban property. Social and cultural contrasts between town and countryside, then, were much sharper in the north than in Italy.

Below the patricians were the small merchants and shopkeepers, who were at first unspecialized in their economic interests. Most towns in the twelfth century still had only a single guild, or association of merchants. Soon after 1200, however, the guilds multiplied, showing an ever greater diversification in the commercial enterprises of the mercantile classes. At the same time the small merchants and shopkeepers were disputing, often with violence and soon with some success, the political domination of the patricians. Before the coming of industries the cities did not support a large class of artisans and workers. But here, too, the city presents a dynamic picture, and the commercial growth in the twelfth century was laying the basis for industrial expansion in the thirteenth.

Perhaps the most distinctive feature of urban society, even in the twelfth century, was the fluid division of the classes. Vertical social mobility was easier in the city than in any other part of the medieval world, the only possible exception

The Charter of Lorris

This charter was granted to the town of Lorris by King Louis VII in 1155 and was subsequently used as a model for other towns in northern France.

"1. Every one who has a house in the parish of Lorris shall pay as *cens* sixpence only for his house, and for each acre of land that he possesses in the parish.

"2. No inhabitant of the parish of Lorris shall be required to pay a toll or any other tax on his provisions; and let him not be made to pay measurage fee on the grain which he has raised by his own labor.

"4. No burgher shall pay toll on the road to Etampes, to Orléans, to Milly, or to Melun.

"5. No one who has property in the parish of Lorris shall forfeit it for any offense whatsoever, unless the offense shall have been committed against us or any of our *hôtes*.

"6. No person while on his way to the fairs and markets of Lorris, or returning, shall be arrested or disturbed, unless he shall have committed an offense on the same day.

"9. No one, neither we nor any other, shall exact from the burghers of Lorris any tallage, tax, or subsidy.

"16. No one shall be detained in prison if he can furnish surety that he will present himself for judgement.

"17. Any burgher who wishes to sell his property shall have the privilege of doing so; and, having received the price of the sale, he shall have the right to go from the town freely and without molestation, if he so desires, unless he has committed some offense in it.

"18. Any one who shall dwell a year and a day in the parish of Lorris, without any claim having pursued him there, and without having refused to lay his case before us or our provost, shall abide there freely and without molestation."

From B. Tierney, *The Middle Ages, I: Sources of Medieval History* (1992), pp. 191–192.

being the Church. The patrician class was always admitting new members, chiefly, wealthy recent immigrants from the countryside. The towns of the Middle Ages were much more efficient than rural society in recognizing, utilizing, and rewarding talent.

The dynamic towns of the Middle Ages, like the cities of the ancient world, shaped culture more than size alone might indicate. Urban commercial life required skill in calculations and a high level of literacy. The towns provided adept administrators who soon figured prominently in the governments of both Church and state. The urban milieu fostered new cultural attitudes, an approach to life based on exact observations and reasoned decisions.

II. Feudalism and the Search for Political Order

Europe in the eleventh and twelfth centuries enjoyed a higher degree of security and political order than it had in the chaotic tenth century; this security was in part responsible for the growth in population, expansion in trade, and changes in society that occurred during this era, while these developments in turn encouraged political stability. Stability was achieved above all through the set of institutions that is traditionally called the *feudal system.* However much they differed, the governments of England, France, the Holy Roman Empire, and other European states in this era may all be called *feudal.*

FEUDAL INSTITUTIONS

Feudalism and *feudal system* must be reckoned among the most abused and confusing terms in the historical vocabulary. These terms were unknown in the Middle Ages. Lawyers in the seventeenth century first devised them to denote the combination of laws and customs governing the kind of land tenure known as the *fief,* whose characteristics will be described shortly. Among reformers in the eighteenth century feudalism meant the unjustified privileges enjoyed by the nobles and the Church. Nineteenth-century socialists, especially Karl Marx, used the term *feudalism* to mean an economic system based upon serfdom; they considered it a stage in economic development that followed slavery and preceded capitalism. To Marxists today the essential feature of feudalism is that it exploits peasants by binding them to the soil and forcing them to pay rent or labor service to the landlords. On the other hand, many books treat feudalism as if it meant no more than decentralized and weak government, or simple chaos. In popular usage, *feudal* is often indistinguishable from *backward.*

Most non-Marxist scholars currently use *feudalism* in reference to systems of political and social, *not* economic, institutions. Large estates and serfdom were not central to the feudal system and are better referred to as the *manorial system.* Still, feudalism remains an elastic term and is used in both a narrow and a broad sense. In its restricted meaning, feudalism refers to a set of distinct social and political institutions, defined by contract, that established the relationship between two freemen of differing social station, a lord and his vassal of lower rank. In practice, both lord and vassal came from the upper echelons of society. Feudal institutions did not include the serfs, who could not enter into a contract, and they touched only remotely and rarely the poorer freemen. In its broad sense, *feudalism* refers to the society and government in which social and political institutions created by contract played a major role in defining relationships within the upper classes. Perhaps the most distinctive feature of feudal government is that the powerful men in society defined their political rights and obligations through individual contracts. In contrast, in the ancient Roman Empire the public law of the state defined the rights and obligations of all citizens, with only minor exceptions.

Following the guidance of the great French historian Marc Bloch, many scholars now divide the era of Western feudalism into two periods. The first feudal age, which lasted from the disappearance of Roman government in the West until about 1050 or 1100, witnessed among the free classes of Europe the spontaneous development of feudal practices out of the early medieval and post-Carolingian chaos. In the second feudal age, which spans the period from about 1050 to

1300, princes began self-consciously to use and manipulate these institutions to buttress their own authority.

The Feudal Milieu To understand the growth of feudalism, we must first recall the chaotic conditions prevailing in the Early Middle Ages, especially in the ninth and tenth centuries. In a milieu in which governmental authority counted for little, individuals had to seek their security through their own efforts. The freeman in search of protection had little recourse but to appeal to a neighbor stronger than himself. If the neighbor accepted, the two men entered by implied contract into a close, quasi-familial relationship. Like the bonds between father and son, the feudal relationship between the strong "lord" and the weak freeman was initially more ethical and emotional than legally binding. It remained so until the thirteenth century, when lawyers systematically began to clarify and define its legal implications.

In Celtic areas of Europe (Ireland, Scotland, Wales, Brittany) traditionally powerful clans could extend such protection; a true feudalism never developed in those lands. Similarly, among the South Slavs, the persistence of a social organization based on the clan made superfluous the creation of authentically feudal relationships. Northern Italy was also an exceptional area in the history of feudalism. Perhaps because of the early importance of towns there, the quest for security primarily favored the development of communal associations, in which social equals rather than lords and vassals were linked in what might be considered artificial families or clans. The power of the urban communes in northern Italy stunted, although it did not entirely suppress, the extension of feudal ties even in the countryside.

The true homeland of Western feudalism was the region between the Loire and the Rhine rivers. The institutions that developed there were subsequently exported to England in the Norman Conquest and to southern Italy, and they greatly influenced government and society in southern France, Spain, and Germany beyond the Rhine. In this region the family seems to have been too scattered or too weak to guarantee security for its members.

Vassalage The honorable personal bond between the lord and his man is called *vassalage*, a term that derives from a Celtic word meaning "boy" or "servant." Vassalage was created by an act of homage, the prospective vassal placing his hands within those of his lord (sometimes, too, a kiss was exchanged) and perhaps swearing an oath of fidelity. The "joining of hands" was the central act in the ceremony of homage.

Vassalage imposed obligations on both the vassal and his lord. The vassal owed his lord primarily loyalty (or, in its feudal term, *fealty*), which meant that he had to render aid and counsel, or material and moral help, to his lord. He had to perform military service in the lord's army and usually had to bring additional men in numbers proportionate to his wealth. As the duty of service became more precisely defined, military service became more a matter of law than of the heart. The vassal might be expected to serve, for example, 40 days a year in a local war and less time if the lord intended to fight in foreign lands. The vassal could not refuse this service, but if asked by the lord for more time than custom allowed, he could demand compensation or simply return home. The lord could also demand financial aid, and there were four occasions which required that the vassals provide money without question: the ransoming of the lord, the knighting of the lord's eldest son, the marriage of the lord's eldest daughter, and the lord's own departure on crusade. At other times the vassal still had to consider requests for financial aid but could grumble and, if the lord was weak enough, refuse.

The obligation of counsel required the vassal to give good advice, to keep the lord's secrets, and to help him reach true judgments in legal cases that came before his court. The ordinary work of the court was the adjudication of disputes among the vassals and the hearing of complaints brought by the lord against his men. Feudal custom held that a vassal could be judged only by his own peers, that is, his fellow vassals. By the thirteenth century many great feudal courts were claiming the right to hear appeals from the courts of the individual vassals. The acceptance of such appeals was one of the principal ways by which royal governments were able to

Investiture Scene, Fresco, Ferrande Tower, Pernes-les-Fontaines, France, ca. 1270
Kneeling before his overlord the king, a vassal offers homage and receives in return investiture in a fief—the roll of paper, which would have recorded the transaction in detail. As this thirteenth-century fresco from Pernes-les-Fontaines in France indicates, the ceremony takes place before witnesses.

strengthen their authority in the second feudal age.

The vassal's duties toward his lord were further complicated in the second feudal age by the development of multiple vassalage—acts of homage by the same man to several lords. In case of conflict among his different lords, whom should he serve? To escape this dilemma, feudal custom required that the vassal select one of his lords as his *liege*, that is, the one whom he would serve against all others. The growth of multiple vassalage and liege homage was itself a sign of the waning emotional content of the feudal relationship.

The lord, in turn, owed his vassal protection and maintenance, or military and material support. He had to come to his vassal's aid when requested, repel invaders from his possessions, and even help him if he was sued in another's court. In the formative period of feudalism the lord's obligation of material support was often carried out at his own table, but as vassals became more numerous and more distantly located and as great princes came to be included among them, sheer logistics prevented the lord from feeding all his men. Since a lord often had no cash revenues for making monetary compensations, he would distribute land as a form of payment for the vassal's allegiance. This concession of land was the fief. The granting of a fief superimposed upon the personal relationship of vassalage a second relationship, involving property, between the lord and his man. The close union of personal and property ties was, in fact, the most characteristic feature of the Western feudal relationship.

The Fief The lord granted the fief in a special ceremony called *investiture* (it usually immediately followed the act of homage), in which he extended to his vassal a clod of earth or sprig of leaves, symbol of the land he was receiving. In a strict juridical sense the fief was a conditional, temporary, and nonhereditary grant of land or other income-producing property, such as an office, toll, or rent. At the vassal's death, disability, or refusal to serve his lord, the fief at once returned to the lord who granted it. The juridical origins of the fief seem to go back to forms of ecclesiastical land tenure that grew up in the Early Middle Ages. Churches were canonically forbidden to sell or give away their property, but they could grant its "use" while retaining ownership over it. In Carolingian times the emperors took to ordering churches and monasteries to make such concessions to favored laymen. The true fief, however, involving only laymen and linked with vassalage, does not appear until after the Carolingian Age.

Although technically not inheritable, the fief became gradually assimilated to the allodium (property held in absolute ownership), which was unconditional, permanent, and hereditary. From the start lords had found it convenient to grant a fief to the adult son of a deceased vassal, since he could at once serve in his father's stead. The son had only to make a special payment (the "relief") to the lord to acquire the fief. Feudal custom also came to recognize the right of a minor son to inherit, but the lord retained the privilege—the right of wardship—of serving as the son's guardian or of appointing someone to fulfill that function. Feudal practice only reluctantly admitted daughters to the inheritance of a fief since they could not perform military service. Nevertheless, in most areas of Europe women did acquire a right of inheritance. Their lord, however, could select their husbands for them, inasmuch as their spouses had to assume the obligations of service. Initially, vassals were forbidden to sell the fief, grant it to a church, or otherwise transfer it in whole or in part. By the thirteenth century, however, fiefs were commonly sold or granted—but only with the lord's permission, which almost always had to be purchased.

The fief was the dominant form of land tenure in northern France and western Germany from the late ninth and tenth centuries. The Norman Conquest carried it to England in the eleventh. In the same period it became common in southern France, but it never entirely supplanted the allodium. It was still later in arriving in Spain, and in Italy its importance always remained restricted. The diffusion of the fief, even if slow and incomplete, had important social effects nonetheless. Because vassals could not dispose of their lands without the lord's consent, property relationships (and society, indirectly) remained fixed and stable for long periods. Moreover, the economic pressure superimposed upon the moral force of vassalage gave the princes of the age an effective means of retaining the loyalty of their dependents: The disloyal vassal not only violated the ethics of his times but also risked losing the lands that supported him.

Stages of Feudal Development Although there were significant local variations in the character and chronology of medieval feudal institutions, it remains possible to speak of certain broad stages of feudal development. In the ninth and tenth centuries Carolingian administration on the local level disintegrated. The power of the count waned, and the *vicarii* (who judged minor cases) disappeared. Authority in the countryside largely passed into the hands of petty lords, most especially the castellans, or holders of castles. The eleventh and twelfth centuries saw a remarkable upsurge in the construction of castles in Europe. To cite one example, in the Diocese of Florence in Italy only 2 castles are mentioned in the sources before 900, 11 before 1000, 52 before 1050, 130 before 1100, and 205 before 1200. The proliferation of these fortresses reflects both the violence of European life and the growing effort to find protection from it.

The castellans initially had no official status in the shadowy structure of the post-Carolingian state, but they dominated the communities that lived in or near their fortresses. The castellan was the judge, tax collector, and military leader, and he usually controlled the local church as well. Within the confines of these small societies the institutions of feudalism developed spontaneously. The castles with their lands constituted fairly stable units.

From about the year 1050, counts, dukes, and some few kings were attempting to integrate these castles into fairly centralized principalities, insisting that the petty nobles assume toward them the obligations of vassals and fief holders. The use of these feudal concepts and institutions to serve the interests of princely authority initiates the second feudal age—the age of the feudal principality.

In granting a fief, the lord gave his vassal all possible sources of revenue the land could produce, including, usually, the right to hold a court and to profit from its fines and confiscations. This contributed to another characteristic of feudal society, private justice (that is, the exercise of public powers by private individuals as a right associated with their tenure of land). Lords and vassals, in other words, at every level of the feudal pyramid, could tax, judge, and punish their dependents.

By the second feudal age lawyers were arguing that the king, as the font of all justice, had the right of hearing appeals from the courts of his chief vassals (as well as those "rear vassals" who stood lower on the feudal ladder) and could also accept cases directly, which his vassals had traditionally heard. The exertion of these royal prerogatives brought about the gradual but unmistakable decline of private justice.

The *Bayeux Tapestry*, reputedly woven by the wife of William the Conqueror, is a strip of linen 231 feet long and 20 inches wide depicting the Norman Conquest of England in 1066. In the portion shown here, William arrives at Pevensey (top); King Harold fights in the Battle of Hastings (bottom). The tapestry was completed toward the end of the eleventh century.

NORMAN AND ANGEVIN ENGLAND

We could use the history of any one of several principalities—the Duchy of Normandy, the County of Flanders, the Kingdom of Naples and Sicily, among others—to illustrate the political reorganization characteristic of the second feudal age. But England offers the best example of feudal concepts in the service of princes. The growth of feudalism in England was, in turn, intimately connected with the Norman Conquest of 1066, the central event of English medieval history.

The Norman Conquest Duke William of Normandy (1026–1087), the architect of the Conquest, is the epitome of the ambitious, energetic, and resourceful prince of the Central Middle Ages. A bastard who had to fight 12 years to make good his claim over his own Norman duchy, William early set his ambitions on the English crown. His claims were respectable, but not compelling. He was the first cousin of the last Saxon king, the childless Edward the Confessor, who allegedly had promised to make William heir to the throne. However, before his death, Edward selected the Saxon Harold Godwinson to succeed him, and his choice was supported by the Witan, the English royal council.

Edward died in 1066. William immediately recruited an army of vassals and adventurers to support his claim to the throne and gained a papal blessing for his enterprise, but unfavorable winds kept his fleet bottled up in the Norman ports for six weeks. Meanwhile Harold Hardrada, king of Norway, who also disputed Harold Godwinson's claim, invaded England with a Viking army but was shattered by the Saxons near York on September 28, 1066. That same day, the channel winds shifted and William landed in England. Harold Godwinson foolishly rushed south to confront him. Although his army was not, as was once thought, technically inferior to the Norman army, it was tired and badly in need of rest and reinforcements after the victory over the Vikings. At the Battle of Hastings on October 14, fatigue seems eventually to have tipped the scales of an otherwise even struggle. The Normans carried the day and left Harold Godwinson dead upon the field. Duke William of Normandy had won his claim to be king of England.

Although the exact importance of the Norman Conquest in English history is still disputed, most historians today believe that while the Norman Conquest did not radically alter the course of English development, it did add a new speed and decisiveness to changes already in evidence. For example, the Conquest oriented England away from Scandinavia and toward the continent and established a French-speaking aristocracy. Norman and continental influences, however, were growing well before 1066; Edward had been raised in Normandy, and Normans were familiar figures in the English court and Church. Nor did William radically change the political and social institutions of Anglo-Saxon England; rather, he built upon them.

The basic unit of local administration remained the shire under the supervision of the sheriff, who had primary responsibility for looking after the king's interests. The sheriff administered the royal estates, collected the taxes, summoned and led contingents to the national militia, and presided over the shire court. William left all these institutions of local government intact.

The real impact of the Conquest was felt at the upper levels of Anglo-Saxon society. The Saxon earls, as the great nobles were called, and most of the lesser nobles, or thanes, lost their estates, which William redistributed among his followers from the continent—his barons (a title of uncertain origin, now used to connote the immediate vassals of the king). William allotted land liberally but cautiously. He made up each fief from several blocks of land in different parts of the countryside, thus giving his followers adequate support to serve him but limiting their autonomy and opportunity to rebel. William redefined the relations between the king and the great men of the realm on the basis of essentially feudal concepts. He now insisted that all English land be considered a fief held directly or indirectly from the king. The barons had to serve the king, and the knights had to serve the barons or risk losing their estates.

In 1086 William conducted a comprehensive survey of the lands of England, the report of which was the *Domesday Book*, probably so called because its judgments in their finality resembled those to be made on the Last Day. It showed a population in England of about 1.1 million people. This survey, unique for its age among the European kingdoms, served two main purposes: It gave the king a clear record of his own holdings and those of his barons, and it enabled him to know how much service the land could support. In the Salisbury oath of 1086 every vassal had to swear loyalty to the king as the liege lord of all. Feudal concepts thus brought a greater precision to the obligations of English freemen toward their king and placed a new ethical and material force behind royal prerogatives.

To maintain close contact with his barons and vassals, William also took from the continent the institution of the great council, or Curia Regis. Essentially, it was an assembly of bishops, abbots, barons—in fact, anyone whom the king summoned. The great council fulfilled the feudal functions of giving the king advice and serving as his principal court in reaching judgments. It was a much larger assembly than the Saxon

Witan. However, as the great council could not be kept permanently in session, a small council, consisting of those persons in permanent attendance at the court whom the king wished to invite, carried on the functions of the great council between its sessions. The development of the great and small councils had major importance for English constitutional history. The great council was the direct ancestor of Parliament, while the small council was the source of the administrative bureaus of the royal government.

Angevin Kingship William was succeeded by his second son, William Rufus. One of England's worst kings, he terrorized his subjects and antagonized the Church. At his death in 1100 (probably from assassination), his younger brother, Henry I, became king. Henry began a series of administrative reforms, but a dispute over the succession at his death and a protracted civil war undermined his accomplishment. By 1154, however, a unified and pacified England passed to the rule of Henry II of Anjou (in France), grandson of Henry I and the first of the "Angevin" kings of England.

Through combined inheritances and his marriage to Eleanor of Aquitaine in 1152, Henry II ruled over a sprawling assemblage of territories that included, besides England, nearly the entire west of France from the English Channel to the Pyrenees Mountains (see Map 8.4). A man of great energy who carried to completion many of the reforms of Henry I, he ranks among the most gifted statesmen of the twelfth century and among the greatest kings of England.

It was in the sphere of English government and law that Henry II left a permanent mark. He made royal justice the common justice of the kingdom through the use of itinerant officials, or "justices in eyre" (that is, on journey), who were endowed with all the authority of the king himself. The itinerant justice traveled regularly to the courts of the shires, investigating and punishing crimes. Upon his arrival the justice would impound 12 "good men" and inquire of them under oath what crimes they had heard about since his last visit and whom they suspected of guilt. (This sworn inquest is the direct ancestor of the modern grand jury.) Those indicted by the 12 "good men" were still tried by the ancient ordeals of fire and water, which were retained until the Church condemned these procedures in 1215. Thereafter, the small, or petty, jury was used, as it is today, to judge guilt or innocence.

The itinerant justice did not forcibly interfere in civil disputes, but he did offer the services of the royal court in settling them. Barons receiving fiefs from the king had also been given the right to hold a court and judge the disputes of their own knights and dependents. Normally, therefore, litigants in a civil dispute appeared before a baronial court. But as a result of Henry's reforms, a litigant could purchase one of many royal writs, which ordered the sheriff to bring the case under the scrutiny of the royal court presided over by the justice in eyre. The great superiority of royal justice in civil matters was that it relied not on ordeals or duels but on sworn inquests or juries. These juries in civil cases were composed of "good men" from the neighborhood who were likely to know the facts at issue and were able to judge the truth or falsity of claims. Henry made no effort to suppress baronial courts, but the better justice offered by the royal courts left them with a progressively shrinking role in the juridical life of England.

In time the justices built up a considerable body of decisions, which then served as precedents in similar cases. The result was the gradual legal unification of the realm, the development, in other words, of a "common law" of England—common in that it applied to the entire kingdom and was thus distinct from the local customs by which cases were formerly decided. It differed from Roman law in that it represented not the will of the king or legislator but the principles, formed by custom, that were followed in deciding cases. This marks the beginnings of the tradition of common law, under which most of the English-speaking world continues to live.

Thomas Becket The judicial reforms of Henry II led him into a bitter conflict with the English Church, which maintained its own courts, called canonical courts. In Henry's opinion the penalties these courts meted out to the guilty were too mild to deter them from future crime, and in 1164 he claimed the right to retry before his royal courts clerics accused of crime. The archbishop of Canterbury, Thomas Becket, rejected this claim. He

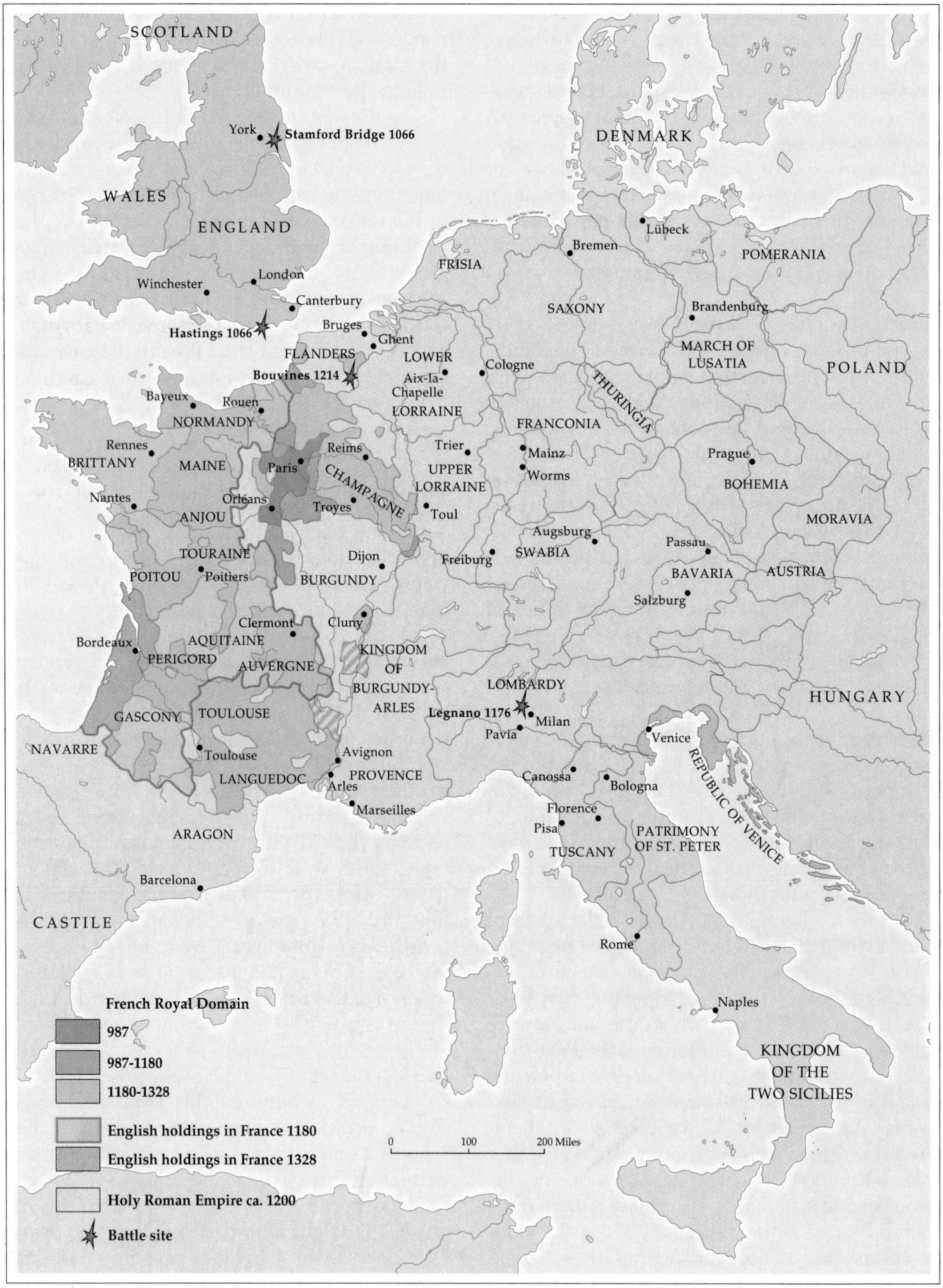

Map 8.4 **Medieval England, France, and Germany**

argued that both the Bible and canon law forbade what we now call "double jeopardy"—that is, a second trial and punishment for one crime.

Becket had been a warm personal friend of Henry's and had served him ably and faithfully as his chancellor, the chief official of the realm. Royal friendship and favor had brought him his election as archbishop of Canterbury in 1162. In the course of the six-year struggle between these former friends, Becket first submitted, then broke with Henry and fled to France, and then was reconciled once more in 1170. Yet a few months later he suspended the bishops that had supported the king. Henry, then in France, demanded in fateful rhetoric whether no man would free him of this pestilential priest. Four of the king's knights took the words to heart, journeyed to England, found Becket in his cathedral, and cut him down before the high altar on December 29, 1170. His death accomplished what his life could not. Henry revoked the objectionable reforms and performed an arduous personal penance for his unwise words.

Although Henry II was unable to dominate the Church, the English monarchy at his death in 1189 was the strongest in Europe. It remained for the thirteenth century to discover how the great power of the king might be managed and controlled.

CAPETIAN FRANCE

In France the pattern of feudal development was much different from that of England. Central government all but disappeared in the turmoil following the age of Charlemagne. What governmental functions could still be performed amid the chaos were carried out by counts, castellans,

This depiction of the murder of Thomas Becket in Canterbury in 1170 was completed within a few years of the event. That it should have appeared as a wall painting in the church of Sts. Giovanni and Paolo in Spoleto, Italy, hundreds of miles away from Canterbury, suggests the intensity of the European-wide reaction to the assassination.

and other lords of small territorial units. These factors alone would have made the rebuilding of an effective national monarchy considerably more difficult in France than in England; but, in addition, France was a much larger country, and its regions preserved considerable cultural diversity.

Nonetheless, the second feudal age did witness considerable changes in France. First, we can discern the emergence of several compact and effectively governed principalities, especially in the north—the Duchy of Normandy, the counties of Flanders and Champagne, the royal lands of the Île-de-France, and others. Second, the French kings sought with some success to establish a lord-vassal relation with the great dukes and counts who governed these principalities. The kings did not envision, and could not have achieved, the unification of the entire realm under their own direct authority. The goal of monarchical policy was rather a kind of federation of principalities bound together by a common fealty to the king on the part of distant dukes and counts.

Louis VI Subdues a Violent Baron

This selection describes the attempt of Louis VI (1108–37), a strong and honorable monarch, to keep the peace in his realm. It comes from **The Life of Louix VI**, *a chronicle by Suger, the head of a French monastery and a great admirer of the king. It is a good example of the chronicles that form one of the historian's basic sources for studying medieval history.*

"A king is obliged by virtue of his office to crush with his strong right hand the impudence of tyrants. For such men freely provoke wars, take pleasure in plunder, oppress the poor, destroy the churches, and give themselves free reign to do whatsoever they wish. . . .

"One such wicked man was Thomas of Marle. For while King Louis was busy fighting in the wars which we mentioned earlier, Thomas ravaged the regions around Laon, Reims, and Amiens. . . . Thomas devastated the region with the fury of a wolf. No fear of ecclesiastical penalty persuaded him to spare the clergy; no feeling of humility convinced him to spare the people. Everyone was slaughtered, everything destroyed. He snatched two prize estates from the nuns of Saint-John of Laon. And treating the two castles of Crécy-sur-Serre and Nouvion-Catillon as his own, he transformed them into a dragon's lair and a den of thieves, exposing the nearby inhabitants to the miseries of fire and plunder.

"Fed up with the intolerable afflictions of this man, the churchmen of France met together (on December 6, 1114) at a great council at Beauvais. There they passed a sentence of condemnation against the enemies of Jesus Christ. The venerable papal legate Cuno, bishop of Praeneste, was particularly moved by the numerous pleas of the church and the cries of the orphans and the poor. He drew the sword of Saint Peter against Thomas of Marle, and with the unanimous assent of the council, declared him excommunicated, ripped from him *in absentia* the titles and honors of knighthood, branded him a criminal, and declared him unworthy of being called a Christian.

"Heeding the wishes of so great a council, King Louis moved quickly against Thomas. Accompanied by his army and the clergy, he turned at once against the heavily defended castle of Crécy. There, thanks to his men at arms, or should we say on account of divine aid, Louis achieved swift victory. He seized the new towers as if they were no more than the huts of peasants; he drove out the criminals; he piously slaughtered the impious; and as for those who had showed no pity, he in turn showed no pity towards them. . . . Flushed by the success of his decisive victory, the king moved quickly against the other illegally held castle, Nouvion. . . ."

From C. W. Hollister et al., *Medieval Europe: A Short Source Book* (1992), pp. 207–208.

The Capetians In 987 the great nobles of France elected as their king Hugh Capet, whose descendants held the throne until 1792. Hugh was chosen primarily because his small possessions in the Île-de-France, which included Paris and the surrounding region, made him no threat to the independence of the nobles. He and his successors for the next century made no dramatic efforts to enlarge their royal authority, but they carefully nursed what advantages they had: the central location of their lands; the title of king, which commanded a vague prestige; and a close association with the Church, which gave them an avenue of influence extending beyond their own territory. They also pursued a remarkably prudent policy of consolidating control over their own lands, and they had the good luck to produce sons. For 200 years the kings crowned their sons during their own lifetime and thus built the tradition that the crown was theirs, not by election but by hereditary right.

The Capetian policy first bore fruit under Louis VI, the Fat (1108–1137). His aim was to be master of his own possessions, and he successfully reduced to obedience the petty nobles and castellans who had been disturbing his lands and harassing travelers seeking to cross them (*see box*, p. 228). By the end of his reign he had established effective control over the lands between the cities of Paris and Orléans. This gave him a compact block of territory in the geographic heart of France. Louis VI promoted the colonization of forests and wastelands by establishing free villages, and he courted the support of the town communes. The economic growth encouraged by the king added to his own fiscal resources. He staffed his administration with new men from the middle ranges of society at the expense of the older, entrenched, and unreliable nobility.

His son Louis VII married Eleanor of Aquitaine, heiress to the extensive lands of the Duchy of Aquitaine. This marriage promised to more than double the lands under direct royal control. But manifest incompatibility of character and Eleanor's failure to produce a male heir set the spouses feuding, and the marriage was annulled in 1152. Eleanor, or at least her possessions, proved irresistible to Henry II of England, who married her two months later, although he was her junior by some 10 years. The loss of her vast

▸ Eleanor of Aquitaine Effigy
Eleanor of Aquitaine bears comparison with other forceful female rulers of European history, such as Elizabeth I of England. She was a worthy consort for Henry II, one of the most powerful and innovative rulers of the Middle Ages, and is buried next to him. The site, a splendid French abbey, lies within the territories that Eleanor had inherited and added to the English kingdom. The crown and book in the effigy on her tomb are perfect symbols of the intelligence and power that characterized her life.

▶ **One of the castles that Richard I constructed to defend his Angevin holdings against attacks was the formidable Château Gaillard, upstream from Rouen.**

inheritance to the English monarchy was a major blow to the Capetian fortunes.

Louis VII's son by a later marriage, Philip II Augustus (1180–1226), set out to reclaim from the English the provinces of Aquitaine and Normandy. While King John of England dallied at home, French troops invaded Normandy and after an eight-month siege took the fortress of Château Gaillard, which Richard the Lion-Hearted had erected to defend the province. Normandy thus became part of the French royal domain (see Map 8.4). Finally, John bestirred himself to action. He organized a coalition of Philip's enemies, including Emperor Otto IV of Germany and the count of Flanders who, though Philip's vassal, viewed with considerable apprehension the growth of royal authority. Philip beat back the invading army at Bouvines in 1214, a victory that confirmed England's loss of Normandy and brought new prestige to the Capetian throne. It was convincing proof of the power the king now could wield.

Under Philip royal influence began to penetrate to the south of France. In 1208 Pope Innocent III declared a crusade against the Albigensian heretics of the south (see Chapter 9), who enjoyed the protection of many powerful nobles. Philip's vassals flocked to the pope's call, overwhelmed the counts of Toulouse and other prominent nobles, and seized much of their lands. The defeat of the southern nobility left a vacuum of power, which the king's authority soon filled.

Administration In addition to increasing his lands, Philip strengthened the administration of his own properties, the royal demesne, although he still made no effort to interfere directly in the governments of the kingdom's fiefs. On the local level the representative of the king—the French counterpart of the English sheriff—was the *prévôt*. About 1190, apparently in imitation of the English itinerant justices, Philip began to appoint a new official, the *bailli*, to oversee the work of the *prévôt*. The *bailli* supervised the collection of rents and taxes, the administration of justice, and all the king's interests within a certain prescribed circuit or area, but he never assumed the full range of functions and powers that the English justice in eyre had acquired. The central administration was also developing specialized bureaus, although less advanced than the English; the *Chambre de Comptes*, a special financial office, equivalent to the English Treasury, gradually assumed responsibility for the royal finances.

Louis VI and Philip Augustus made the French monarchy the unquestioned master in the Île-de-France, greatly enlarged the royal demesne, and insisted with considerable success that the great dukes and counts of the realm serve the king loyally. In France, as in England and widely in Europe, feudal practices did not necessarily mean weak government; on the contrary, the able and energetic princes of the age used these concepts and institutions to redefine the relationship between ruler and ruled in the interest of achieving a stronger central authority. The feudal system, as it was constructed in these principalities, was thus a major step toward a more ordered political life and toward the sovereign state of the early modern period.

THE GERMAN EMPIRE

In the tenth and eleventh centuries the German lands east of the Rhine show a pattern of political development very different from that of France or England. Whereas in France, after the collapse of the Carolingian Empire, power became fragmented among many petty lords and castellans, in Germany it came to be concentrated in certain relatively large territorial blocks. Saxony, Franconia, Swabia, and Bavaria—known as "Stem" duchies (from the German *Stämme*, meaning a distinct people, tribe, or ethnic group)—were originally districts of the Carolingian Empire that became independent political entities under powerful dukes. Because these duchies were close to the hostile eastern frontier, their inhabitants learned to appreciate the advantages of a unified leadership.

Moreover, in Germany the old idea of a Christian empire, which we have seen both in Byzantium and in the West under Charlemagne, retained considerable appeal. Perhaps because they were so close to the frontiers of Christendom, the German dukes considered themselves to be in a special way the champions of the Christian faith, and they mounted a missionary effort among the unconverted peoples. The dukes desired a leader who, like Charlemagne, would aid the Church against its foreign enemies while promoting its interests at home.

Otto I, The Great The last direct descendant of Charlemagne in Germany, a feeble ruler known as Louis the Child, died in 911. Recognizing the need for a common leader, the German dukes in 919 elected as king one of their number, Henry of Saxony. His descendants held the German monarchy until 1024. The most powerful of this line of Saxon kings, and the true restorer of the German Empire, was Otto I, the Great (936–973). Otto was primarily a warrior, and conquest was a principal foundation of his power. He routed the pagan Magyars near Augsburg in 955 and ended their menace to Christian Europe; he organized military provinces, or marches, along the eastern frontier and actively promoted the work of German missionaries and settlers beyond the Elbe River; and in 951 he marched into Italy.

Historians are not certain what exactly drew Otto to the south. Perhaps, like Charlemagne, he hoped to rescue the papacy from the clutches of the tumultuous Roman nobility, to which it had once again fallen victim. It does appear, at any rate, that Otto conceived of himself not just as a German king but as the leader of all Western Christians. He could not allow Italy, especially Rome, to remain in chaos or permit another prince to achieve a strong position there. In 962, during Otto's second campaign in Italy, Pope John XII gave formal recognition to Otto by crowning him Roman Emperor. The title gave him no new powers, but it did provide him high prestige.

The coronation of 962 not only marked the restoration of a "Roman" empire in the West (in fact, it was German) but also confirmed the close relations between Germany and Italy that lasted through the Middle Ages. Although the German emperors claimed to be the successors of the Caesars and of Charlemagne, and thus the titular leaders of all Western Christendom, their effective power never extended beyond Germany and Italy and the small provinces contiguous to them—Provence, Burgundy, and Bohemia. Government of his far-flung territories presented

▸ **Crown of the Holy Roman Empire, Tenth and Eleventh Centuries**
The crown of the Holy Roman Empire may originally have been given to Otto I by Pope John, but throughout the tenth and eleventh centuries various pieces were added by different emperors. It eventually consisted of eight panels, decorated with cloisonné enamels, which are hinged together with gold filigree and surrounded with jewels and pearls.

Otto with problems even more formidable than those that confronted the English and French kings. He distributed the Stem duchies among his relatives, in the poorly founded hope that they would be loyal to him, and placed great reliance upon the Church in both Germany and Italy, using its lands and officials as adjuncts to his own. He therefore insisted upon the right to nominate or approve the nominations of the great prelates of his empire—bishops, abbots, and popes. Control of Church offices and Church lands gave the emperor enclaves of power in the Stem duchies and in Italy, which no potential rival could match.

When Otto died in 973, his state was the strongest in Europe, but it was troubled by several difficulties. Foremost among them was the growing discontent of the Church with the imperial domination of ecclesiastical life. (This will be examined in the following section.) Reformers sought to liberate the Church from the emperor's tutelage, and they did succeed in undermining this source of imperial authority. But the reform did not end the efforts of the German kings to build a strong empire that would unite Germany and Italy and allow them to exercise a moral leadership over the whole of Western Europe.

Frederick I, Barbarossa The ruler who came closest to building a lasting foundation for the German Empire was Frederick I (1152–1190) of the House of Hohenstaufen. He was called *Barbarossa,* meaning "red beard." Large, handsome, gallant, and courageous, Frederick, like Charlemagne before him, gained a permanent place in the memories and myths of his people. He much resembles in his policies, if not quite in his achievements, the other great statesmen of the twelfth century—Henry II of England and Philip II of France. Frederick showed a broad eclecticism in his political philosophy. He claimed to be the special protector of the Church and therefore a holy figure. He called his empire the Holy Empire: This emphasis on the religious was retained in the later title, *Holy Roman Empire,* used after 1254 and until Napoleon abolished this German Empire in 1806. Frederick also introduced the new institutions and concepts of political feudalism to his government and effectively exploited ideas concerning the emperor's powers that the revived study of Roman law was providing.

Frederick pursued three principal goals. He hoped to consolidate a strong imperial domain consisting of Swabia, which he inherited; Burgundy, which he acquired by marriage; and Lombardy, which he hoped to subdue. These three contiguous territories would serve him much as the Île-de-France served the French king by giving him a central base of power from which he could dominate those more distant areas that he could not rule directly. In Germany he sought to force the great princes in the north and east to become his vassals. In Italy he claimed, as successor of the Caesars, to enjoy the sovereignty that Roman law attributed to the emperors.

Frederick's Italian ambitions disturbed the popes and the town communes, which from about 1100 had become the chief powers in the northern half of the peninsula. Both feared that a strong central government could be established only at the cost of their own independence. With active papal support the northern Italian towns, led by Milan, formed a coalition known as the Lombard League and defeated the imperial forces at Legnano in 1176. The Battle of Legnano not only marked the failure of Frederick's efforts to establish full sovereignty over the Lombard cities but also was the first time in European history that an army of townsmen had bested the forces of the established army under noble leadership. At the Peace of Constance in 1183 Frederick conceded to the towns almost full authority within their walls; the towns, in turn, recognized that their powers came from him, and they conceded to him sovereignty in the countryside. Frederick did not gain all that he had wished in Italy, but his position remained a strong one.

In Germany he was able to achieve a more resounding victory, this time over the powerful duke of Saxony, Henry the Lion, who had refused to aid him in his Italian war. Making effective use of feudal custom, Frederick summoned him in 1180 to face trial as a disloyal vassal. The court condemned Henry and confiscated his Saxon fief. With Henry humiliated and deprived of his lands, Frederick seemed to be the unchallenged master in Germany (see Map 8.4).

Frederick now wanted to advance the empire's prestige in Europe and sought out a position of leadership in the Third Crusade, as it is traditionally numbered. But the aged emperor drowned while trying to ford a small stream in Asia Minor, bringing to a pathetic end a crowded and brilliant career.

His successors proved unable to build upon, or even maintain, his accomplishments. The very extent of the lands they sought to dominate, and their great cultural diversity, worked against them. The chief powers in Italy, the pope and the towns, maintained their opposition to the establishment of a strong imperial government under German auspices. The heritage of the medieval empire was to be a divided Germany and Italy—divisions that would not be overcome until the nineteenth century.

III. The Reform of the Western Church

The Church, like lay government, experienced fundamental transformations in the eleventh and twelfth centuries, as it acquired characteristics it was to retain in large measure to the present day. The reform of the Church was the direct result of revolt against the traditional system of lay domination over ecclesiastical offices and lands.

MORAL CRISIS

After the disintegration of the Frankish Empire, a kind of moral chaos invaded the lives of the clergy. Since the fourth century the Church had demanded that its clergy remain celibate, but this injunction was almost completely ignored in the post-Carolingian period. Also rampant in the Church was the sin of simony—the buying or selling of offices or sacraments. Many bishops and even some popes purchased their high positions, and parish priests frequently sold their sacramental services (baptisms, Masses, absolutions of sins, marital blessings) to the people.

The constitution of the Western Church seems to have contributed to this moral breakdown. On the highest level the tradition of lay domination made the king or emperor effective head of the Church in all its temporal affairs. At the local level ecclesiastical offices and lands were largely under lay control. Landlords were considered to own churches built upon their property. They therefore could name the priests who served in them and profit from donations made to them, freely sell the offices they controlled, or distribute Church lands to their relatives and friends. The results were disastrous. The Church was flooded with unworthy men who were little concerned with their spiritual duties, and the pillaging of Church lands and revenues left many clerics without adequate livings. For these, simony was often an essential means of support.

EARLY ATTEMPTS AT REFORM

According to canon law, the bishops bore the chief responsibility for the moral conduct of the clergy. A few reforming bishops in the tenth and eleventh centuries tried to suppress clerical marriage and the simony of their priests, but they could make little headway. The powers of a single bishop were perforce limited to his own diocese and to his own lifetime, since he could not name his successor.

Monastic discipline was the focus of a more effective attempt at reform, the center of which was the monastery of Cluny in Burgundy, founded in 910. First, the monastery was placed directly under the pope (neither lay lords nor bishops could interfere in its affairs). While monasteries had formerly been autonomous communities, electing their own abbots and supervising their own affairs, the administration was now centralized under the abbot of Cluny. He retained authority over the many daughter houses his monks had founded or reformed and could visit them at will, freely correcting any abuses. The congregation of Cluny grew with extraordinary rapidity in the eleventh and twelfth centuries until it included no fewer than 1184 houses, which were spread from the British Isles to Palestine.

The restoration of the German Empire in 962 opened another avenue of ecclesiastical reform. Otto I and his successors repeatedly condemned clerical marriage, simony, and the unauthorized usurpation of Church lands. However, in the interests of their own authority, the emperor's actions were limited, as they were not willing to abandon their own traditional control over ecclesiastical offices and lands. Thus, their efforts did not satisfy a growing number of radical reformers who believed that complete freedom of the Church from lay domination was the only means to effect change. To win and defend this liberty, they looked for leadership to the long-degraded office of pope.

PAPAL REFORM

The first of the reforming popes—selected, ironically, by the emperor—was Leo IX (1049–1054). He traveled widely and presided at numerous councils, where he promulgated decrees ordering reforms, summoned suspect bishops, and deposed many of them. He was the first pope to make wide and regular use of papal legates or emissaries, who, like Charlemagne's *missi dominici*, traveled through Europe, inspecting, reprimanding, and reforming. For the first time lands distant from Rome were subject to the close supervision of the papacy.

Under Pope Nicholas II the movement toward ecclesiastical liberty took several forward strides. By allying himself with the Normans of southern Italy, Nicholas freed the papacy from military dependence on the German Empire. He was the first pope who expressly, if vainly, condemned the practice of "lay investiture"—that is, receiving churches and Church offices from laymen. In 1059 a Roman council reformed papal elections and defined the principles by which popes to this day have been elected.

Tradition required that the pope, like all bishops, be elected by the clergy and people of his diocese. In practice, however, the emperor named him, or in his absence the powerful noble families and factions of Rome did. However, the election procedures set up by the council of 1059 conferred this prerogative upon the cardinals, the chief clergymen associated with the Church at Rome, thereby ensuring that the College of Cardinals, and the reformers who controlled it, could maintain continuity of papal policy. (Even today all cardinals, no matter where they live in the world, hold a titular appointment to a church within the archdiocese of Rome.) Both the emperor and the Roman nobility were simultaneously deprived of one of their strongest powers.

GREGORY VII

The climax of papal reform came with the pontificate of Pope Gregory VII (1073–1085), who brought to his office a high regard for its powers and responsibilities and a burning desire for reform. With regard to Church matters Gregory asserted that the pope wielded absolute authority—that he could at will overrule any local bishop in the exercise of his ordinary or usual jurisdiction. His ideas on the relations of Church and state, however, are less than clear. According to some historians, he believed that all power on earth, including the imperial power, came from the papacy. According to others, Gregory held merely that the normal function of kings was far lower than the sacred authority of popes. This much at least is beyond dispute: Gregory believed that all Christian princes must answer to the pope in spiritually significant matters and that the pope himself had a weighty responsibility to guide them (*see box*, below).

The Investiture Controversy The major collision between the papacy and the Holy Roman Empire that occurred during the pontificate of Gregory VII is traditionally called the *Investiture Controversy*. The name suggests that the principal issue was the practice of great laymen, most notably the emperor, of "investing" bishops with ring and staff, the symbols of their spiritual office. More fundamentally, the struggle revolved around the claims of laymen to dispose of ecclesiastical offices and revenues by their own authority and in their own interests.

At a Roman council in 1075, Gregory, convinced that Emperor Henry IV had no sincere interest in reform, condemned lay investiture and excommunicated some of Henry's advisers. Henry reacted with unexpected fury; he summoned a meeting of imperial bishops and declared Gregory not the true pope but a false monk. Not one to pause in what he thought to be the work of God, Gregory, in turn, excommunicated Henry, deposed him, and freed his subjects from allegiance to him. These acts struck at the fundamental theory of the Christian empire, according to which the emperor was supreme head of the Christian people, responsible only to God.

Gregory's forceful appeal to spiritual power gained remarkable success in Germany. Henry's enemies leagued against him and demanded that

Gregory VII's "Dictates of the Pope"

This papal manifesto, drawn up under Pope Gregory VII's direction in 1075, was intended to guide papal officials in disputes with rulers or with bishops. It represents an extreme claim for papal supremacy both within the Church and within the world, and formed the basis for the papacy's position in the Investiture Controversy.

"1. That the Roman church was established by God alone.

"2. That the Roman pontiff alone is rightly called universal.

"3. That he alone has the power to depose and reinstate bishops.

"4. That his legate, even if he be of lower ecclesiastical rank, presides over bishops in council, and has the power to give sentence of deposition against them.

"7. That he alone has the right, according to the necessity of the occasion, to make new laws, to create new bishoprics, to make a monastery of a chapter of canons and vice versa, and either to divide a rich bishopric or to unite several poor ones.

"9. That all princes shall kiss the foot of the pope alone.

"12. That he has the power to depose emperors.

"13. That he has the right to transfer bishops from one see to another when it becomes necessary.

"14. That he has the right to ordain as a cleric anyone from any part of the church whatsoever.

"16. That no general synod may be called without his order.

"17. That no action of a synod and no book shall be regarded as canonical without his authority.

"18. That his decree can be annulled by no one, and that he can annul the decrees of anyone.

"19. That he can be judged by no one.

"22. That the Roman Church has never erred and will never err to all eternity, according to the testimony of the holy scriptures.

"24. That by his command or permission subjects may accuse their rulers.

"26. That no one can be regarded as catholic who does not agree with the Roman Church.

"27. That he has the power to absolve subjects from their oath of fidelity to wicked rulers."

From Hollister, *Medieval Europe: A Short Source Book* (1992), pp. 183–184.

the emperor be judged before an assembly of lords and prelates to be held at Augsburg in February 1077. They invited Gregory to preside, and he readily accepted. Henry resolved to fight spiritual weapons with spiritual weapons. He slipped across the Alps and intercepted Gregory, then on his way to Germany, at the Apennine castle of Canossa near Modena. He came in the sackcloth of a penitent, radiating contrition, pleading for absolution. Gregory, who doubted the sincerity of the emperor's repentance, refused for three days to receive him, while Henry waited in the snow. Finally, in the face of such persistence, Gregory the suspicious pope had to give way to Gregory the priest, who, like all priests, was obligated to absolve a sinner professing sorrow.

The incident at Canossa is one of the most dramatic events of medieval history. Through the centuries since, the picture of the supreme lay magistrate of Christendom begging forgiveness from the pope has symbolized a victory of spiritual over material power, a triumph of Church over state. The reality was more complex. Henry was the immediate victor. He had divided his opponents and stripped his German enemies of their excuse for rebelling. They named a rival emperor anyway, Rudolf of Swabia, but he was killed in battle in what seemed a divine judgment in Henry's favor. Gregory appears to have become unsure of himself after Canossa. He finally excommunicated Henry a second time in 1080 but was forced to flee Rome at the approach of an imperial army. Gregory died at Salerno in 1085 in apparent bitterness, avowing that his love of justice had brought him only death in exile.

After years of confused struggle pope and emperor settled the Investiture Controversy through the Concordat of Worms in 1122. They agreed that the emperor would no longer invest prelates with the symbols of their spiritual office, and the pope would allow the elections of imperial bishops and abbots to be held in the presence of the emperor or his representative. This clearly permitted the emperor to influence the outcome of elections. In addition, the emperor retained the right of investing prelates with their temporalities—that is, their imperial fiefs. In essence, the great bishops and abbots of the realm would have to be acceptable to both parties—worthy

▶ Holy Roman Emperor Henry IV is shown at Canossa on his knees, begging Pope Gregory for readmission to the church. Countess Matilda of Tuscany, a powerful supporter of the pope, appears on the right.

and religious men to please the Church and loyal and capable servants to please the emperor. This agreement at Worms established that major appointments in the Church ought to be made through consultation and compromise.

The Consolidation of Reform In the twelfth century the popes continued to pursue Gregorian ideals—reform, liberty, and centralization—and to consolidate past advances. In their struggle to be free of lay authority the reformers had insisted that certain persons—such as clerics, widows, orphans, crusaders, and other wards of the Church—should be judged only in ecclesiastical courts and that cases touching on sacrilege, heresy, marriage, testaments, contracts, and the like should also, because of their religious nature, be under ecclesiastical jurisdiction, no matter who the parties might be. A complex system of ecclesiastical courts thus developed according to this premise, and these paralleled and at times rivaled the courts of the kings. Judicial decisions from these ecclesiastical courts could be appealed to Rome.

Legal scholars at this time were compiling and clarifying the canons of the Church—the authoritative statements from the Bible, Church councils, Church fathers, and popes, which constituted the law of the Church. The compilation ultimately recognized as official and binding was the *Decretum*, put together by the Italian jurist Gratian about 1142. With systematic compilations came trained canon lawyers to comment upon, interpret, and apply the law.

Centralization gained in other ways. The popes came to exert a progressively tighter control over the canonization of saints, hitherto a local, informal matter. They also gained a stronger voice in the election of bishops, until finally papal approval was accepted as essential to a valid choice. In papal tithes imposed upon the clergy and in the administration of yearly payments made by many churches to Rome, the outlines of a centralized financial administration appear, though the structures remained rudimentary in the twelfth century.

The reform of the Church in the eleventh and twelfth centuries left an indelible mark on both religious and secular life in the West. The successful establishment of sacerdotal celibacy set the clergy apart from the laity to a degree unknown in the ancient or Eastern Church. At the same time the disputes between Church and state over their respective authority greatly stimulated fruitful speculations on the nature of Christian society. The Gregorian reform was based on the assumption that good men facing an evil world need not timidly flee it; rather, they can and should seek to correct its abuses and bring it closer to what God intended it to be. The reform thus helps mark the emergence of a new faith in human power and in the possible improvement of this present world.

IV. The Cultural Revival

The reorganization of European life in the eleventh and twelfth centuries affected institutions of learning and even the direction and methodology of Western thought. Its impact was notable in vernacular literature and even in art. The Western peoples entered upon a period of high creativity, which marked most forms of cultural expression.

THE RISE OF UNIVERSITIES

During the Central Middle Ages a new institution, the university, came to assume a role in the intellectual life of Europe, a role it has not since relinquished. The university ranks as one of the most influential creations of the medieval world.

Up to about 1050, monastic schools had dominated intellectual development in the West (see Map 8.5). But the monastic devotion to prayer, self-denial, and mystical meditation was not especially favorable to original thought, while the isolation of monasteries restricted the experiences of the monastic scholar and made difficult the exchange of ideas that intellectual progress requires.

Map 8.5 **Great Monastic Centers of Learning**

From about 1050 to 1200, the cathedral, or bishop's, school assumed the intellectual leadership in Europe. Traditionally, bishops had been obliged to provide for the education of their clergy. From the late eleventh century the growth of cities, the Gregorian emphasis on a trained clergy, the shock of the Investiture Controversy, and the stimulus of a more intimate contact with non-Christian areas all served to revitalize the long-moribund cathedral schools.

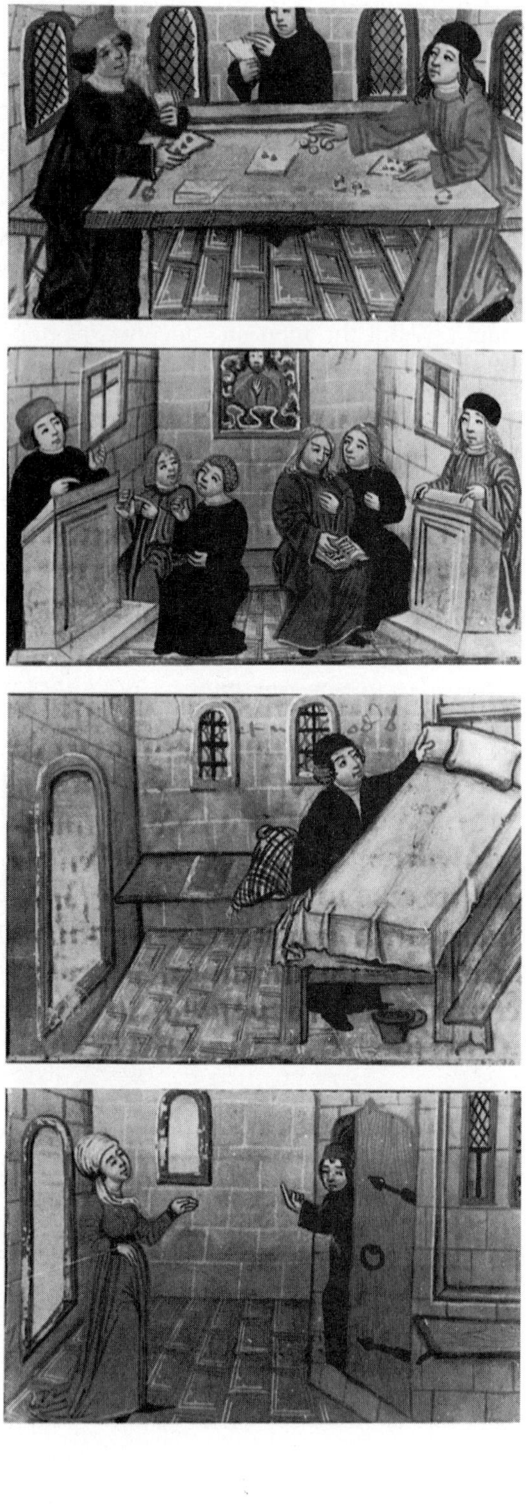

The cathedral schools were at first very fluid in their structure. The bishop's secretary, the chancellor, was usually in charge of the school and had the responsibility of inviting learned men, or "masters," to lecture to the students. Both masters and students roamed from town to town, seeking either the best teachers or the brightest (or best-paying) students and the most congenial atmosphere for their work. The twelfth century was the age of the wandering scholars, who have left us charming traces of their spirit or at least that of their more frivolous members in the form of "Goliardic" verses,[1] largely concerned with such unclerical subjects as the joys of wine, women, and song.

Townspeople frequently registered protests with the bishops or with the king against the students, whom they resented because of their boisterous ways and because their clerical status gave them immunity from the local police and courts. Riots involving town and gown were commonplace events. To impose some order on this flux, and to protect young students from incompetent or unorthodox teachers, the twelfth-century cathedral schools gradually insisted that masters possess a certification of their learning. The chan-

▶ The university as a community of scholars, teachers, and learners was a medieval innovation. Its structure was such that students exercised a degree of control that they rarely possess today. Since there were no salaries, professors relied upon tuition fees for their daily bread, and students could starve out unpopular teachers merely by refusing to attend their classes. However, in other aspects, student life then was much the same as it is today. These scenes from a fifteenth-century manuscript show students gambling, opposing each other in disputations (class debates), and engaging in other activities of dormitory life.

---

[1]The exact etymology of the word *Goliardic* remains unknown. It possibly derives from Goliath the Philistine, who was honored as a kind of antisaint by the boisterous students.

cellor awarded this "license to teach," the ancestor of all modern academic degrees.

The throngs of masters and students, many of them strangers to the city where they lectured and studied, eventually grouped themselves into guilds to protect their common interests. It was out of these spontaneously formed guilds of masters and students that the medieval university grew (*universitas* was a widely used Latin word for "guild"). The guild formed by the masters in Paris, for example, received a royal charter about 1200 and sanction from a papal bull in 1231. These documents confirmed the guild's autonomy and powers to license teachers. The University of Paris may thus claim to be the oldest of the northern European universities. From about 1200 we may also date the beginnings of the age of the university in European intellectual life.

The university in Italy sprang from slightly different origins. Even in the Early Middle Ages professional schools for the training of notaries, lawyers, and doctors survived in some Italian cities. The Italian schools, too, seem to have enjoyed rapid growth from the late eleventh century, and growth, in turn, led to the formation of guilds. Here, however, the students rather than the professors constituted the dominant "university." At the oldest of these schools, the University of Bologna, the students regulated discipline, established the fees to be paid to the professors, and determined the hours and even the content of the lectures.

Like all guilds, the university sought to protect and advance its "art" of thought and teaching and to preserve that art over generations through the appropriate training of the young. The ancient world, although it possessed several famous schools, had never developed a university system, in the sense of numerous institutions of higher learning, specifically organized for the pursuit and preservation of learning. The rise of the universities also marks the appearance in Western society of a social class professionally committed to the life of thought and to its transmission to future generations.

SCHOLASTICISM

In its broadest sense, Scholasticism refers to the teaching characteristic of the medieval schools,

▸ CASKET DEPICTING GRAMMAR, RHETORIC, AND MUSIC, CA. 1170
This chest, made around 1170, is decorated with enamel medallions representing the various courses of study that made up a medieval education: arithmetic, astronomy, dialectic, rhetoric, music, grammar, and natural philosophy.

that is, all the subjects taught in the four major branches of learning or faculties: the arts, canonical and Roman law, medicine, and theology. But in a narrower and perhaps more accurate sense, Scholasticism refers to theology, the medieval "queen of the sciences," in which the character and originality of Scholastic reasoning appear most clearly.

Theology had similarly dominated the monastic thought of the Early Middle Ages, but the monks had largely limited their interests to biblical interpretation, or exegesis. They sought in the sacred Scriptures four traditional levels of meaning (literal, moral, allegorical, and mystical) and wrote voluminous commentaries without constructing a rigorously logical system of theology.

The novelty of Scholasticism was its application of dialectic to Christian theology. Dialectic is the art of analyzing the logical relationships among propositions in a dialogue or discourse. The monastic theologian, through exegesis, wished to discover biblical truth; the Scholastic sought to learn how propositions of faith joined one another within a larger, consistent, and logically forceful theological system.

The first thinker to explore, although still not in rigorous fashion, the theological applications of dialectic was St. Anselm of Canterbury (1033–1109). Anselm defined his own intellectual interests as "faith seeking to understand"—in actuality, faith seeking to find logical consistency among its beliefs. In a work known as the *Proslogium* he tried to show that there is a necessary, logical connection between the traditional Judeo-Christian dogma that God is a perfect being and the dogma that he really exists. A perfect being must possess the perfection of existence. Otherwise, our concept of him would be absurd and unthinkable.

The Scholastic interest in dialectical relationships much resembles Classical Greek thought, with its eagerness to know the "whys" of things, to find order and consistency among statements accepted as true—with the important difference that the Scholastics initially sought order among propositions presented by faith. (Later they would take further propositions from the ancient pagan philosophers and even, to a limited degree, from their own observations.) From the time of Anselm, Scholastic thought assumed that the human intellect was powerful enough to probe the logical and metaphysical patterns within which even God had to operate.

Abelard Peter Abelard (1079–1142), a second father of Scholasticism, brought a new rigor and popularity to dialectical theology. Abelard came to Paris in the early years of its intellectual growth, and his brilliant teaching helped give that city its reputation as Europe's leading center of philosophical and theological studies.

Abelard's major contribution to the growth of Scholasticism was his book *Sic et Non* ("Yes and No"), the first version of which probably appeared in 1122. Using what became the Classical

Abelard's "Sic et Non"

Completed in 1138, Peter Abelard's* Sic et Non *("Yes and No") explained the techniques for reconciling divergent opinions in theology and law. His approach reflects the ambition of Scholasticism to bolster faith through reason.

"Among the many words of the holy fathers some seem not only to differ from one another but even to contradict one another. . . . Why should it seem surprising if we, lacking the guidance of the holy spirit, fail to understand them?

"Our achievement of understanding is impeded especially by unusual modes of expression and by the different significances that can be attached to one and the same word. We must also take special care that we are not deceived by corruptions of the text or by false attributions when sayings of the [Church] fathers are quoted that seem to differ from the truth or to be contrary to it; for many apocryphal writings are set down under names of saints to enhance their authority, and even the texts of the divine scripture are corrupted by the errors of scribes. If, in scripture, anything seems absurd, you are not permitted to say, 'The author of this book did not hold the truth,' but rather that the book is defective or that the interpreter erred or that you do not understand. But if anything seems contrary to truth in the works of later authors, the reader or auditor is free to judge, so that he may approve what is pleasing and reject what gives offense, unless the matter is established by certain reason or canonical authority.

"In view of these considerations we have undertaken to collect various sayings of the fathers that give rise to questioning because of their apparent contradictions. Assiduous and frequent questioning is indeed the first key to wisdom. For by doubting we come to inquiry; and through inquiring we perceive the truth."

From Tierney, *Sources of Medieval History*, pp. 172–175.

method of Scholastic argumentation, the posing of formal questions and the citation of authorities on both sides, Abelard assembled 150 theological questions. For each question he marshaled authorities from the Bible, Church councils, and Church fathers. In every case there was conflict. He made no effort to reconcile the discrepancies but left the authorities standing in embarrassing juxtaposition. His method was an ingenious retort to those who maintained that dialectic could make no contribution to Christian theology and that it was enough to hold fast to the ancient writings. *Sic et Non* implied that one must either enlist dialectic to reconcile the conflicts or concede that the faith was a tissue of contradictions (*see box*, p. 240).

In the early phases of the medieval intellectual revival, dialectic had to contend for supremacy with humanistic studies, which emphasized familiarity with the Classical authors and the ability to appreciate and write good Latin. Chartres, a small cathedral town near Paris, was the center of this twelfth-century humanism. But by the end of the century dialectic, as cultivated at Paris, predominated partly because it seemed to offer to the inquisitive men of the twelfth century a certain avenue to truth and a sound means for organizing the truths they had inherited. Another reason Scholastic dialectic could become dominant was that after the middle of the twelfth century, translators working chiefly in Spain and Sicily introduced European scholars to hitherto unknown works of Aristotle, as well as to the great commentary that the Muslim Averroës had written on them. Christian thinkers now had at their disposal the full Aristotelian corpus, and it confronted them with a thoroughly naturalistic and rationalistic philosophical system. Aristotle's philosophy was built on reason alone, and his assumptions drove Western scholars to examine his works and their own faith through dialectic. The difficult task of reconciling Aristotelian reason and nature with Christian revelation and divine grace remained the central philosophical problem of the thirteenth century.

VERNACULAR LITERATURE

Scholasticism reflected the cultural interests of only a small group of intellectuals in medieval society. What the broader masses of the people valued can be found in vernacular literature. Here, too, the themes treated and characters described largely reflect the life of the nobility, not that of the common people. But there is much reason to believe that this literature, or some oral version of it, was appreciated well beyond aristocratic circles. Townsmen and even peasants seem to have delighted in hearing of the doings of the great.

Of the vernacular literatures of Europe only Anglo-Saxon possesses a substantial number of surviving writings that antedate the year 1000. For most of the major languages of Europe an abundant tradition of literary work dates only from the eleventh and twelfth centuries. In forming the literary tastes of Europe, the Romance tongues (the vernacular languages descended from Latin) achieved a particular importance, especially the two great dialects of France, the langue d'oïl spoken north of the Loire River and the langue d'oc, or Provençal, used in the south. Castilian was slightly later in producing an important literature in Spain, and Italian, perhaps because of its similarity to Latin, did not emerge as a major literary language until the late thirteenth century.

There were three principal genres of vernacular literature: the heroic epic, troubadour lyric poetry, and the courtly romance. Heroic epics have survived in great abundance. The oldest and probably the best of them is the *Song of Roland*, which was composed in the langue d'oïl probably in the last quarter of the eleventh century. The subject of the poem is the ambush of the rear guard of Charlemagne's army under the command of Roland by the Basques at Roncesvalles in 778, but poetic imagination (or perhaps older legend) transformed this minor Frankish setback into a major event in the war against Islam.

With fine psychological discernment the poem examines the character of Roland. The qualities that make him a hero, his dauntless courage and uncompromising pride, are at war with the qualities required of a good vassal—obedience, loyalty, cooperation, and common sense. Roland is in serious danger but refuses for reasons of personal dignity to sound his horn in time for Charlemagne to return and save him and his men. By the time his pride relents and he does blow the horn, their deaths are ensured. The sensitive examination of the conflict between Roland's thoughtless if heroic individualism and the demands of the new feudal order gives this poem its stature as the first masterpiece of French letters.

The Troubadours Very different from the heroic epic is troubadour lyric poetry, initially written in the langue d'oc of the south. The novelty of this complex poetry is its celebration of women and of love. The heroic epic was written for the thoroughly masculine society of the battle camp. The troubadours sang at courts, in which women exerted a powerful influence. In a mobile age, when knights and nobles would be away for long periods on crusades and wars, their mothers, wives, and daughters administered their households and estates and achieved considerable social prominence. The women became the arbiters of what constituted "courtly manners"—proper behavior—in their households, and they surely influenced the literature that was heard within their walls.

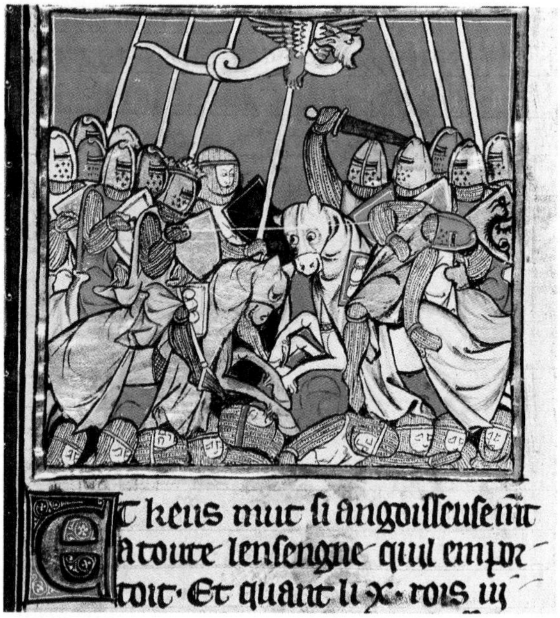

▶ **ARTHUR IN BATTLE**
Legend had it that anyone who found the Holy Grail, a cup from which Christ was reputed to have drunk, would achieve eternal happiness. In medieval romances this story became a metaphor for a chivalrous search for perfection. In this miniature from Robert de Boron's thirteenth-century *History of the Grail*, King Arthur—the only figure whose face we can see—battles 10 rebel kings during his quest.

▶ **HÉLOÏSE AND ABELARD, FROM *ROMAN DE LA ROSE***
Already a famous professor in Paris, Abelard began a secret relationship with Héloïse, and in revenge her relatives had him castrated. The two were then separated for decades, and their correspondence remains one of the most powerful human documents of medieval times. Despite the conventions of the day, Héloïse was clearly an equal partner in the relationship, as is indicated in this fifteenth-century depiction of the pair engaged in intense discussion.

The troubadour usually addressed a lady of superior social station, almost always someone else's wife, whom he had little chance of winning. Although she was not a likely means of sensual gratification, love for her did offer a hope for inward consolation; it could, if returned, elevate the poet's spirits and transform his world to eternal spring. Courtly love (at least as the troubadours present it) was not a dalliance but quite literally a way of salvation, a means of rescuing the lover from despondency and introducing him into an earthly paradise. This discovery and intensive exploration of the emotion of love represents one of the most influential creations of the medieval mind.

The courtly romance, which entered its great age after 1150, combines traits of both heroic epic and troubadour lyric poetry. It is narrative in form like the epic; but, like Provençal poetry, it allots a major role to women and love. Chrétien de Troyes, whose works probably date from shortly before 1182, is the author of the oldest surviving romances, those about King Arthur of Britain and his coterie of knights. Many of these tales are concerned with an analysis of the tensions that love, the rebellious emotion, creates in society. Western letters have since endlessly explored this theme.

ROMANESQUE ART

The conventional term used to describe the architectural and artistic style of this period is *Romanesque*. It means "of Roman origins" but is, like many terms applied to the Middle Ages, misleading. Artists in the Central Middle Ages did imitate Classical models, but not exclusively; they also drew on nearly every other artistic tradition to which they had access—barbarian, Byzantine, and Arab.

The proliferation of castles across the face of Europe stimulated the development of new techniques of construction. These fortresses were built on a progressively larger scale, in contrast to the castles of the Carolingian Age, and by the thirteenth century, builders were working entirely in stone. Crusaders returning from the East brought with them new concepts of fortress design and perhaps also a desire to render castle life more gracious. The crafting of tapestries, furniture, and glass benefited from the new importance of cities, the strength of markets, and the growing number of artisans. Although life about 1200 was still remarkably crude even for the rich, it was clearly becoming less so.

Art, however, remained in most of its forms the servant of the Church. The religious reform in the eleventh century brought with it a liturgical revival. The monks of the Cluniac monasteries were especially devoted to (and occasionally criticized for) sumptuous religious services. Liturgical needs stimulated the art of metalwork (which produced chalices and other sacred vessels), glassmaking, and the weaving of fine fabrics for the priests' vestments. Music, too, advanced. The Gregorian chant (named for Pope

▶ Pisa Cathedral, ca. 1063–1272

One of the finest architectural ensembles in the new Romanesque styles of the eleventh and twelfth centuries is the cathedral and its surrounding buildings in Pisa, Italy. Although the famous leaning tower, which is now slowly being restored to the vertical, is the best known of these buildings, the huge marble-clad cathedral was in fact regarded as the supreme achievement of the Pisans and was widely influential in church building throughout Italy.

Gregory the Great, but in fact representing the traditional plainsong of the Church of Rome) had become established as the common music of the Western Church in the Carolingian epoch. The eleventh and twelfth centuries witnessed the development of polyphonic music (part-singing). The coordination of the vocal parts in choral music also required systems of musical notation. A monk named Guido d'Arezzo is credited with giving names to the notes.

▸ **St. Etienne, Caen, Vaults, ca. 1115–1120**
St. Etienne, Caen, was begun by William the Conqueror in 1067 and is considered a superb example of Norman Romanesque architecture. It was originally supposed to have a wooden roof, but it was vaulted in stone between 1115 and 1120. Each section of the roof was held up by six ribs that met at the center and two arches, all of which rested on pillars at the side of the nave. The resultant pattern added to the sense of height and drew the eye ever upward toward heaven.

The most impressive artistic monuments left to us from the Romanesque period are the churches themselves. In engineering, the great achievement of the Central Middle Ages was the roofing of churches in stone. From about the year 1000, small stone-roofed churches began to appear, especially in southern Europe. At first the builders used the simple barrel, or tunnel, vault, but this design did not allow for windows because the roof would collapse if holes were put into the supporting sides of the tunnel. Engineers then developed and mastered the use of the groin vault, which is formed by the intersection of two barrel vaults. The area of intersection is called the bay, and the roof over the bay is supported at four points, not by the entire length of the lateral walls. Bays could be built next to bays, an entire church could be roofed with stone, windows could be easily cut, and the monotony of tunnel vaulting would be avoided.

Romanesque churches were decorated on the exterior with stone sculpture. Monumental sculpture had been a dead technique in the West since the end of the Roman Empire. Romanesque statues, which exist by the thousands, show a marked quality of antirealism, a refusal to allow visual accuracy to dominate portrayals. The artists were striving to present a world as seen by faith. Christ, for example, had to be shown larger than others, in keeping with his dignity. Demons and monsters, many drawn from the popular imagination, abound in Romanesque sculpture. While similar to Byzantine portrayals in its antirealism, Romanesque style, unlike the Byzantine, overflows with movement, tension, excitement, and the spirit of mystical exhilaration. Romanesque statuary documents the exuberant spirit of this age of reform and crusades, when people seemed convinced that God was actively at work among them, setting right the world.

► Tympanum of South Portal of St. Pierre, Moissac, ca. 1115–1135

The revival of sculpture is one of the noteworthy achievements of Romanesque art. Integrating architecture and sculpture, this tympanum (the semicircular space above a church portal) shows the Second Coming of Christ, attended by symbols of the evangelists and the kings of the world seated in rows divided by stylized clouds.

The eleventh and twelfth centuries were vigorously creative at every level of European life. By 1200 Europe was very different from the old, or "first," Europe of Charlemagne. Its economy was more diversified and productive, its society more complex, its government more effective, its religion more sensitive, and its thought and art more original and daring. But the very innovations of the age posed severe problems for European society. How could the new forms of economic endeavor be reconciled with the older hostility and suspicion toward a life of buying and selling? How could the rising power of monarchs be reconciled with the self-consciousness and self-interest of the nobility, reformed Church, and privileged towns? How could the new confidence in human reason and in nature, reinforced by familiarity with Aristotle, be synthesized with the older notions that nature was corrupt, human beings weak, and the afterlife the only hope? From about 1200 the West was trying to consolidate its recent advances and bring them into harmony with its older heritage. This effort at consolidation, reconciliation, and synthesis is the theme of Western history in the thirteenth century.

Recommended Reading

Sources

Anselm of Canterbury. *Basic Writings: Proslogium, Monologium, Gaunilon's On Behalf of the Fool, Cur Deus Homo.* S. W. Deane (tr.). 1962.

Chrétien de Troyes. *Yvain, The Knight of the Lion.* Burton Raffel (tr.). 1987. Recent translation of a great French romance.

Douglas, David C. (ed.). *English Historical Documents.* 1955. The largest available collection of translated sources bearing on English history.

Duby, Georges (ed.). *The Legend of Bouvines. War, Religion, and Culture in the Middle Ages.* Catherine Tihanyi (tr.). 1989. An anthology of contemporary and recent depictions of the great battle, with a commentary that sets the event and the legends in their cultural context.

Fitzneale, Richard. *The Course of the Exchequer.* Charles Johnson (tr.). 1950.

*Herlihy, David (ed.). *The History of Feudalism.* 1971.

John of Salisbury. *The Statesmen's Book.* John Dickinson (tr.). 1963.

Matthew Paris. *Chronicles. Monastic Life in the Thirteenth Century.* Richard Vaughan (ed.). 1984. Excerpts from an English chronicler with a worldview; a superb perspective on medieval monastic mentalities.

Oderic Vitalis. *The Ecclesiastical History.* Marjorie Chibnall (tr.). 1969–1980. Latin and English texts of a prolific Anglo-Norman monastic chronicler.

*Available in paperback.

Studies

Baldwin, John W. *The Government of Philip Augustus. Foundations of French Royal Power in the Middle Ages.* 1986. A mature look at the great French king.

Barlow, Frank. *Thomas Becket.* 1986. Balanced biography of the martyred archbishop.

Boswell, John. *Christianity, Social Tolerance and Homosexuality in Western Europe from the Beginning of the Christian Era to the Fourteenth Century.* 1980. A long and learned survey of the treatment of homosexuals in medieval Europe.

Brundage, James. *Law, Sex, and Christian Society in Medieval Europe.* 1987. Encyclopedic survey of the sexual and marital legislation of the Western Church.

*Bynum, Caroline Walker. *Holy Feast and Holy Fast: The Religious Significance of Food to Medieval Women.* 1987. The mystical meanings of women's food consumption in the Middle Ages.

Chenu, M. D. *Nature, Man, and Society in the Twelfth Century.* Jerome Taylor and Lester K. Little (trs.). 1968. Seminal essays on twelfth-century thought by a French Dominican.

Chibnall, Marjorie. *Anglo-Norman England, 1066–1166.* 1987.

———. *The World of Oderic Vitalis.* 1984. The cultural world of the Anglo-Norman historian.

Chrimes, Stanley B. *An Introduction to the Administrative History of Medieval England.* 1966. Clear and authoritative.

Cowdrey, H. E. J. *Popes, Monks and Crusaders.* 1984. Collected essays.

Dillard, Heath. *Women of the Reconquest. Women in Castilian Town Society, 1100–1300.* 1984. The status of women on the Spanish frontier, chiefly based on legal materials.

*Douglas, David C. *William the Conqueror: The Norman Impact upon England.* 1966. Outstanding among many biographies.

Duby, Georges. *The Chivalrous Society.* Cynthia Postan (tr.). 1977. Essays on feudal society by a prominent French medievalist.

———. *The Knight, the Lady and the Priest. The Making of Modern Marriage in Medieval France.* 1983.

*Dunbabin, Jean. *France in the Making, 843–1100.* 1987. From Carolingian to Capetian France.

Ennen, Edith. *The Medieval Town.* Natalie Fryde (tr.). 1979. By a German historian, now the best introductory survey available in English.

*Fawtier, Robert. *The Capetian Kings of France: Monarchy and Nation, 987–1328.* Lionel Butler and R. J. Adams (trs.). 1962.

Ferruolo, Stephen C. *The Origins of the University: The School of Paris and Their Critics, 1100–1215.* 1985. The universities as embodiments of a new educational ideal.

*Ganshof, François. *Feudalism.* P. Grierson (tr.). 1961. Standard introduction to feudal institutions.

Gold, Penny Schine. *The Lady and the Virgin: Image, Attitude and Experience in Twelfth Century France.* 1985. Women in image and reality.

Hallam, Elizabeth M. *Domesday Book through Nine Centuries.* 1986. The making, the uses, and the subsequent history of the great survey.

*Haskins, Charles H. *The Renaissance of the Twelfth Century.* 1927. A classic study.

*———. *The Rise of Universities.* 1957.

*Herlihy, David. *Medieval Households.* 1985.

*Kirshner, Jules, and Suzanne Wemple (eds.). *Women of the Medieval World.* 1986. Collected essays.

Poly, Jean-Pierre, and Eric Bournazel. *The Feudal Transformation, 900–1200.* 1990.

Reilly, Bernard F. *The Kingdom of Léon-Castilla under Alfonso VI, 1065–1109.* 1988.

*Southern, Richard W. *The Making of the Middle Ages.* 1955. Classic essay on twelfth-century culture.

*Tellenbach, Gerd. *Church, State and Christian Society at the Time of the Investiture Contest.* R. F. Bennett (tr.). 1970. Fine analysis of the issues involved in the Investiture Controversy.

GOD AS ARCHITECT OF THE UNIVERSE
The notion of God creating the universe as an architect was common during the Middle Ages. In this manuscript illumination, God is depicted holding a compass and literally measuring the structure of the physical world.

CHAPTER NINE

The Summer of the Middle Ages

THE thirteenth century (or, more precisely, the period between about 1200 and the Black Death of 1348 and 1349) has been traditionally considered the summer of the Middle Ages. It can claim many impressive achievements: a largely prosperous economy, which supported more people than Europe possessed at any other time during the Middle Ages; reasonably effective systems of government in the feudal monarchies; parliamentary institutions; Gothic cathedrals; the great works of Scholastic philosophy and theology; and the *Divine Comedy* of Dante Alighieri, one of the great masterpieces of Western literature. Moreover, these products of medieval genius seem to share a certain spirit: a sense of logic and order and a serene confidence, not only in divine grace and faith but also in human reason and effort. Thirteenth-century men and women believed that God had created a harmonious world and that they could describe its ordered structure in their philosophy, imitate it in their art, and use this knowledge to guide their earthly lives.

Today, as research probes ever deeper, we know that these favorable impressions of the era are not entirely accurate. Thirteenth-century society was less placid than the smiles of Gothic angels urge their admirers to believe. The population may have grown too large to be supported by available resources, and this may have been an important factor in provoking the plagues and famines that occurred beginning in the mid-fourteenth century. The prosperity of the rich often rested on the rampant misery of the poor; the aspirations toward a united and peaceful Europe did not dispel the specter of war; the status of Jews in the West deteriorated; and Scholastic theology did not quench the flames of intellectual and religious revolt. In sum, medieval society in the thirteenth century could not achieve permanent solutions to the many problems it confronted. But this ultimate failure should not prevent us from recognizing the accomplishments of the people of this era. They strove to build both an ordered society and ordered systems of thought, in which conflicts, social or intellectual, would be reconciled.

I. Economic Expansion

Population growth, land reclamations, and the expansion of external frontiers continued in the thirteenth century, though at a slackening pace after about 1250. Regional specialization in agricultural production also grew more pronounced. Southwest France (Gascony), for example, exported wine in large quantities to England and northern Europe. England itself, and soon Spain, supplied raw wool to the busy textile towns of Flanders and Italy. Peripheral areas—the Baltic lands beyond the Elbe River, Catalonia, Sicily, even parts of the Eastern Empire—delivered wheat to the more crowded central zones. Owners of agricultural land surrounding the towns usually devoted their fields to market farming. By raising what the natural endowment of their regions most favored, cultivators thus worked more productively. As peasants competed for land and workers for jobs, however, rents increased and wages fell while the profits of landowners and employers rose. In increasing measure, the prosperity of the propertied and business classes was coming to rest upon the deprivation and misery of the humble.

THE CITIES

Dramatic economic changes were also occurring in the cities.[1] Large-scale production, extensive trade, complex commercial and banking institutions, and the amassing of great fortunes became the commonplace features of urban economic and social life. Florence in 1252 began issuing gold florins—the first successful gold coinage in the West since ancient times. These urban centers pioneered many of the methods and show much of the spirit of modern business enterprises.

Medieval towns developed a new system of producing goods. With the exception of mines, construction sites, and such enterprises as the arsenal in Venice, most work was performed in the home or in small shops; little use was made of power, and there were no factories. Increased efficiency was achieved through finely dividing the process of production and through developing highly specialized skills. A merchant or manufacturer acquired the raw material, gave (or "put") it out in sequence to specialized artisans, and then sold the finished products. Usually called the *putting-out system*, this method of production remained characteristic of the Western economy until the Industrial Revolution of the late eighteenth century.

Wool Cloth Production The making of woolen cloth, the largest industry of the medieval town, well illustrates the complex character of thirteenth-century manufacturing. The raw wool—often coming from England, Spain, or North Africa—was first prepared by sorters, beaters, and washers. Then the cleaned and graded wool was carded, or combed. The next task, the spinning, was usually done by women who worked in their own homes with a distaff, a small stick to hold the wool, and a spindle, a weight to spin and twist the strands into thread. The spinning wheel, apparently first invented in Italy in the late thirteenth century, added speed and better quality to thread making.

Weavers, almost always men, wove the thread into broadcloths that were 30 yards in length and might contain 2000 to 3000 warp (lengthwise) threads. The cloth was then fulled—that is, washed and worked with special earths that caused the wool to mat. This was arduous work and was often done at a water-driven fulling mill. The giant cloth was then stretched on a frame, so that it would dry properly and shrink evenly. Next, the dry cloth was rubbed with teasels to raise the nap, and the nap was then carefully cut. Several times repeated, this last operation gave the cloth a smooth, almost silky finish, but it was extremely delicate work; one slip of the scissors could ruin the cloth and the large investment it represented. At various stages in this process the wool could be dyed—whether as unspun wool, thread, or woven cloth. Medieval people loved bright colors, and dyers used a great variety of animal, vegetable, and mineral dyes and special earths, such as alum, to fix the colors.

---

[1]We must, of course, recognize that the populations of towns everywhere in Europe remained small in comparison with the rural population. The largest medieval city seems to have been Paris, with a population of perhaps 210,000 in 1328. Few towns surpassed 40,000. In England in the fourteenth century only about 10 percent of the population lived in cities. In Flanders and certain regions of Italy, that figure may have reached 25 percent, but these areas were exceptions.

The medieval woolen industry thus came to employ a large, diversified labor force, which worked materials brought from all corners of the known world. Capital and labor were sharply divided; a few great entrepreneurs controlled huge masses of capital. In Florence in about 1300, the number of wool shops ranged between 200 and 300; they produced between 80,000 and 100,000 big broadcloths with a value surpassing 1.2 million gold florins. Over 30,000 persons earned their living from this industry.

THE GUILDS

To defend and promote their interests in a world still ruled by warriors and priests, the merchants and master artisans took to forming associations of self-help known as *guilds*. The first guilds were organized by merchants and appear about 1000. By the twelfth century both master artisans and merchants in special trades—for example, dealers in wool, spices, or silk—had organized their own independent guilds. A large industrial town such as Florence had more than 50 professional guilds.

Once a year the guild members met in their church or hall to elect permanent officials, or *consuls*. The consuls enforced the statutes, adjudicated disputes among the members, administered the properties of the guild, and supervised its expenditures. Equally important, the consuls regulated the methods of production in their trade in order to maintain the quality of the product and to protect the members from unfair competition. To this end they restricted the number of working hours and the number of employees that could be hired by any single master. Guilds might also aid those members who lost goods through fire or flood, and they supported the widows and educated the orphaned children of their deceased members. Banquets, public processions, and religious ceremonies enriched the social life of the membership. Many guilds assumed a further responsibility for the beauty and welfare of their town. They were among the principal donors to hospitals and charities, and they usually built and maintained their own church, or at least a chapel in the city cathedral.

One of the chief features of the guilds was the

▶ **YPRES GUILD HALL, CA. 1260–1380**
The Flemish towns were renowned for their textiles, and the economic importance of this manufacture is reflected by the size of the thirteenth-century cloth hall at Ypres (destroyed in World War I). Rows of arched windows and a central tower puncture the massive square edifice that functioned as the headquarters of the guild, as well as the place where goods were marketed.

apprenticeship system. The guilds stipulated what the apprentice had to be taught and what proof of skill he had to present to be admitted into the brotherhood of the trade, how long he had to work and learn in the shop of the master, and what the master had to give him by way of lodging, food, and pocket money. If, after finishing his training, the apprentice was too inexperienced or poor to open his own shop, he could work as a paid laborer, or journeyman, in the shop of an established master. By carefully saving his wages, the apprentice might eventually become a master in his own right and a member of the guild, but most medieval artisans continued to work as salaried laborers for their entire lives.

ITALIAN GRAIN MERCHANTS
This manuscript illustration shows Florentine grain merchants engaged in their trade and keeping their records in their shops. The manuscript itself noted the prices for grain between 1320 and 1335 that were set in the Or San Michele, the grain warehouse and market hall in Florence.

Only rarely did girls serve as apprentices, but Paris had five guilds composed exclusively or predominantly of women. Most wives and daughters helped their husbands and fathers in their labors. Many widows continued in their own name the trade of their deceased husbands. Women's contribution to the town economy was less visible than men's, but no less essential.

In protecting commercial skills under difficult conditions, offering a measure of insurance and social security to their members, and promoting education, the guilds played a crucial role in forming an environment favorable to commerce and manufacture.

BUSINESS INSTITUTIONS

The growth of trade and manufacturing stimulated the development of sophisticated commercial institutions. Christian ethics traditionally condemned the taking of usury (which then meant any interest or profit on a loan, however tiny); therefore, the medieval business community developed alternative instruments of credit.

Most important for properly commercial purposes was the bill of exchange, in essence a loan, but one that required repayment at a specified time in another place and currency. Thus a Florentine might borrow 100 pounds in Florence and agree to repay three months later in local money at a Champagne fair. He then bought goods in Florence, sold them in Champagne, and repaid the money. The rate of exchange between the currencies almost always concealed a substantial profit for the investor, but technically, he earned it for changing money, not for making the loan.

Partnerships and business associations were another important means of recruiting capital. At Venice, Genoa, and Pisa, overseas ventures were most often financed through special temporary partnerships. In its simplest form, an investor,

▶ WOMAN SELLING POULTRY

Women worked at many trades during the Middle Ages. They contributed significantly to luxury crafts such as silk spinning and weaving, but they were also a major presence in the marketplace selling such items as bread, beer, and poultry.

who remained at home, gave a sum of money to a merchant traveling abroad in return for a share of the eventual profits (usually three-quarters); the investor bore the entire loss if the ship sank or the venture failed. The partnership lasted only for the length of the specified voyage.

In the inland Italian towns a more permanent kind of partnership developed known as the *compagnia* (literally, "bread together," a sharing of bread). These earliest companies seem to have been partnerships among brothers. The sons of a deceased merchant, for example, might decide to leave their inheritance undivided and to trade together as a single company. By the thirteenth century such companies commonly included as partners persons who were not blood relatives but who could contribute capital and services, and they also accepted deposits from nonpartners in return for fixed yearly payments of interest that were called "gifts," lest they be considered usurious.

These companies performed a wide variety of functions and grew in size. They traded in any product that promised a profit, wrote bills of exchange, and fulfilled other banking services. From the late twelfth century they served the Roman Curia as papal bankers and were largely responsible for building and maintaining the financial system of the medieval papacy. They were also drawn into the risky business of extending loans to prelates and princes.

The most famous of such loans were those that the Bardi and Peruzzi Companies extended to King Edward III of England to fund the Hundred Years' War. The companies loaned approximately 900,000 and 600,000 florins, respectively, in 1338, to their eventual regret, as the English crown defaulted in 1342, leaving both companies bankrupt.

MEDIEVAL VIEWS OF ECONOMIC LIFE

The thinkers of the thirteenth century were coming to new and more favorable, if not exactly enthusiastic, views concerning wealth. Until then, the Church fathers had taught that difference in wealth in human society was a necessary evil arising out of sin. Sin had aroused concupiscence or greed and threatened to make social life a "war of all against all." Private property, defended by the power of the state, restrained greed and promoted peace. In contrast, Thomas Aquinas, the great thirteenth-century theologian, based his principal argument for private property on the practical advantages it supplied. Private property, he argued, provided incentive, ensured good care of belongings, and promoted peace and order. He thus gave property and wealth more dignity than the thinkers of an earlier age had accorded them.

Even commercial wealth was losing some of its ancient taint. As late as about 1150, canon lawyers had quoted with approval the aphorism that "rarely or never can a merchant be saved." By the thirteenth century, preachers in commercial cities were eloquently comparing merchants to Christ. After all, they, like Christ, lived by peaceful enterprise and not by violence. Nevertheless, the rich man could not use his wealth as his personal inclinations might dictate. Property could be private in possession, but it had to be used to promote the common good. The individual, in other words, was morally obligated to use his wealth to benefit the entire community, not just himself.

II. The States of Europe

Through its practices and institutions the thirteenth-century European economy acquired a more stable structure. Governments, too, were moving toward a new level of stability. Great laws helped define and fix governmental and legal procedures. They thus served to implant in the West a strong tradition of constitutionalism, a lasting belief that people should be governed by fixed and known procedures. The thirteenth century made one other lasting contribution to Western political development: the representative assembly. European princes extended to the great estates, or classes, of society—namely, the clergy, nobility, and eventually even the townsmen—the opportunity to hear and approve the major decisions of government. To make this participation possible, parliaments or assemblies of estates came to assume a recognized if still humble place among the institutions of government.

ENGLAND

At the death of Henry II in 1189, the English monarchy wielded exceptional authority, but neither in practice nor in theory was it clearly established within what limits, if any, royal powers should operate, or how, if at all, the great men of the realm might participate in government.

Henry's son and successor was Richard I, the Lion-Hearted. Although Richard had all the virtues of a model knight—boldness, military skill, stately bearing, even a flair for composing troubadour lyrics—he had none of the attributes of a good king. He loved battles and shunned conferences. In 1191 and 1192 he was off fighting in the Holy Land on the Third Crusade (see Chapter 10). Chivalry, which gave him his reputation, also took his life. He died in 1199 from a neglected wound received while besieging a castle in a minor war in southern France. Richard's presence in England was restricted to two visits, lasting less than 10 months, but the English government continued to function efficiently even in the absence of its chief—testimony to its fundamental strength.

Richard was succeeded by his younger brother John, who, rightly or wrongly, is considered a wicked king (significantly, no other English monarch has borne the name). While the towns and the common people supported him, he gratuitously antagonized his powerful subjects by his insolence and capricious cruelty. His reign is largely a record of humiliations suffered at the hands of the pope, Philip II of France, and his own barons.

In 1206 John brazenly tried to make a worthless favorite archbishop of Canterbury. The clergy of Canterbury appealed to Pope Innocent III, who selected for the office the learned, pious, and popular Stephen Langton. To force John to acquiesce, Innocent laid England under interdict in 1208. The interdict was a command to the English Church to go on strike. Priests were not to baptize babies, marry couples, or bury the dead in public ceremony. Parish bells were silenced, and the rhythm of life must have changed across England. But the Church's strike did not sway John at all. Only when he wanted papal support in his war against the French over the loss of Normandy did he finally submit in 1213. After his defeat by the French at Bouvines in 1214, John had to reap the bitter harvest that his long years of misrule at home and failures abroad had sown.

Magna Carta To meet the extraordinary expenses of war, the English kings had traditionally requested, and almost always received, special aids or contributions from their barons. But after Bouvines, when John's policies proved to be disastrous, the enraged barons refused further help. Encouraged by the Church, they took to arms. Their resistance was successful, and in June 1215

Excerpts from "Magna Carta"

"John, by the grace of God, king of England, lord of Ireland, duke of Normandy and Aquitaine, and count of Anjou, to the archbishops, bishops, abbots, earls, barons, justiciars, foresters, sheriffs, stewards, servants, and to all his bailiffs and faithful subjects, greetings. Know that we, out of reverence for God and for the salvation of our soul and those of all our ancestors and heirs, for the honour of God and the exaltation of the holy church, and for the reform of our realm . . . :

"[12] No scutage or aid shall be imposed in our kingdom unless by common counsel of our kingdom, except for ransoming our person, for making our eldest son a knight, and for once marrying our eldest daughter; and for these only a reasonable aid shall be levied. Be it done in like manner concerning aids from the city of London.

"[13] And the city of London shall have all its ancient liberties and free customs as well by land as by water. Furthermore, we will and grant that all other cities, boroughs, towns, and ports shall have all their liberties and free customs.

"[20] A free man shall not be amerced [subjected to a discretionary punishment] for a trivial offense except in accordance with the degree of the offense, and for a grave offense he shall be amerced in accordance with its gravity, yet saving his way of living; and a merchant in the same way, saving his stock-in-trade; and a villein shall be amerced in the same way, saving his means of livelihood—and none of the aforesaid amercements shall be imposed except by the oath of good men of the neighborhood.

"[21] Earls and barons shall not be amerced except by their peers, and only in accordance with the degree of the offense. . . .

"[30] No sheriff, or bailiff of ours, or anyone else shall take the horses or carts of any freeman for transport work save with the agreement of that freeman.

"[31] Neither we nor our bailiffs will take, for castles or other works of ours, timber which is not ours, except with the agreement of him whose timber it is.

"[38] No bailiff shall in future put anyone to trial upon his own bare word, without reliable witnesses produced for this purpose.

"[39] No free man shall be arrested or imprisoned or disseised or outlawed or exiled or in any way victimized, neither will we attack him or send anyone to attack him, except by the lawful judgment of his peers or by the law of the land.

"[54] No one shall be arrested or imprisoned upon the appeal of a woman for the death of anyone except her husband.

"[40] To no one will we sell, to no one will we refuse or delay right or justice.

"[52] If anyone has been disseised of or kept out of his lands, castles, franchises or his right by us without the legal judgment of his peers, we will immediately restore them to him: and if a dispute arises over this, then let it be decided by the judgment of the twenty-five barons who are mentioned below in the clause for securing the peace. . . .

"[61] . . . the barons shall choose any twenty-five barons of the kingdom they wish, who must with all their might observe, hold and cause to be observed, the peace and liberties which we have granted and confirmed to them by this present charter of ours, so that if we, or our justiciar, or our bailiffs or any one of our servants offend in any way against anyone or transgress any of the articles of the peace or the security, and the offense be notified to four of the aforesaid twenty-five barons, those four barons shall come to us, or to our justiciar if we are out of the kingdom, and, laying the transgression before us, shall petition us to have that transgression corrected without delay. And if we do not correct the transgression . . . within forty days . . . , the aforesaid four barons shall refer that case to the rest of the twenty-five barons. And those twenty-five barons together with the community of the whole land shall distrain and distress us in every way they can . . . until, in their opinion, amends have been made; and when amends have been made, they shall obey us as they did before."

at Runnymede the barons forced John to grant them the "Great Charter" (Magna Carta) of liberties, which was probably inspired, if not largely composed, by Archbishop Langton. The Magna Carta resembled oaths that English kings since Henry I had taken upon their coronation; it obligated the king to respect certain rights of his subjects. But no previous royal charter of liberties equaled it in length, explicitness, and influence (*see box*, p. 255).

The Magna Carta disappoints most modern readers. Unlike the American Declaration of Independence it offers no grand generalizations about human dignity and rights. Its 63 clauses, arranged without apparent order, are largely concerned with technical problems of feudal law—rights of inheritance, feudal relief, wardship, and the like. But it did establish, more clearly than any previous document, that the king ought not to disturb the estates of the realm—Church, barons, and all free subjects—in the peaceful exercise of their customary liberties. It thus guaranteed to the clergy the freedom to elect bishops and to make appeals to Rome, protected the barons against arbitrary exactions of traditional feudal dues, and confirmed for the men of London and other towns "all their liberties and free customs." To all freemen it promised access to justice and judgment by known procedures. Finally, the king could impose new taxes only with the common consent of the realm. While these concessions were certainly significant, the Magna Carta addressed the concerns of only the elite. The rights of the unfree classes, the serfs and villeins who constituted 80 percent of the population, are hardly mentioned.

The Magna Carta marked a major step toward constitutionalism, that is, toward government by recognized procedures that could be changed only with the consent of the realm. Of course, the barons and the bishops never anticipated that subjects other than themselves might be called upon to give consent, but this limitation in no way compromises the importance of the principle established. Future generations of Englishmen were to interpret the provisions of the Magna Carta in a much broader sense than its authors had intended. The document is of importance not only for what it said but also for what it allowed future generations to believe about the traditional relationship in England between authority and liberty.

Legal Reforms The powers and procedures of the royal government received a still clearer definition under Edward I (1272–1307). Pious without being weak, committed to crusading but also concerned with the welfare of his realm, Edward ranks as one of the most influential of medieval English kings. In 1284 he seized Wales and later gave it as an appanage (a province intended to provide "bread," or support) to his eldest son. (Since 1301 the heir presumptive to the English throne has borne the title Prince of Wales.) In a misguided effort to promote the unity of the realm, he expelled England's Jews in 1290. However, Edward left his strongest mark on English law and institutions.

Edward produced no systematic codification of English law, which remained based principally on custom and court decisions of the past, but he did seek to correct and enlarge the common law in certain critical areas and to give the system a new flexibility. He issued the first Statutes of the Realm, initiating a series in which all the public laws of England have since been entered. Edward's statutes required the barons to show by what warrant (*quo warranto*), or royal license, they exercised jurisdiction in their own courts; this marked an important step in the decline of baronial justice. His laws also limited the growth of mortmain, that is, land held by the Church. The statutes were especially important in determining the land law of England, regulating inheritance and defining the rights of lords, vassals, and the king when land changed hands through inheritance or purchase. Edward laid the foundations upon which the English (and eventually American) law of real estate rested for centuries. In enacting these statutes and in governing the kingdom, Edward also placed a new emphasis on securing the consent of his subjects through Parliament.

Parliamentary Origins Since the time of William the Conqueror the plenary meetings of the great council, or Curia Regis, had included the great barons, bishops, abbots, royal household officials—anyone whom the king wished to invite. During the reign of Henry III (1216–1272)

▶ **Magna Carta**

Originally agreed to in 1215 by King John, the Magna Carta (or Great Charter) was intended to settle disputes over the rights and privileges of England's nobility. The document itself was issued in sealed copies and sent throughout England, but it was successively modified during the thirteenth century. This example, which is one of only four that have survived, dates from 1297, when the charter was confirmed in final form.

these plenary sessions of the royal court grew more frequent and clearly more important, and came to be called *parliaments*. (The word means only "conversation" and, derivatively, an assembly where discussion occurs.) It also became customary, but by no means mandatory, to invite knights from the shires to these sessions. In 1265, during an abortive baronial rebellion against King Henry, the rebel leader Simon de Montfort summoned a parliament that included two knights elected from every shire and two townsmen or burgesses from every town. Edward followed him in this precedent.

Historians cannot assign an exact date for the division of Parliament into separate houses of Lords and Commons. The knights and burgesses seem to have met informally together since the time of Edward I, and these meetings gained official recognition at least from the reign of Edward III. Two unique features of the English Parliament helped enhance the influence of Commons. First, the lower aristocracy (that is, those knights who were not the tenants in chief or immediate vassals of the king) sat with the burgesses and learned to act together in their mutual interests. (On the continent the lower aristocracy and the townsmen sat as separate groups and rarely developed or supported common causes.) Second, though the bishops continued to sit in the House of Lords, they gradually became less interested in using Parliament as a vehicle for political representation. The bishops discussed Church affairs and approved grants of money to the king in their own convocations. The functions of the House of Lords were thus reduced, a fact that benefited the House of Commons.

Representation We now think of Parliament as a limitation on royal power, but it was not this at all in its earliest development. Parliament, as the assembly of the king's vassals, had the obligation merely of giving the king advice. In addition, the king found Parliament a valuable adjunct to his own administration, for it promulgated and enlisted support for his decisions, strengthened royal justice, and facilitated the collection of taxes. It was therefore in the king's interest to make the assembly broadly representative of the free classes. In summoning the Parliament of 1295 (this session would later be called the "model Parliament"), Edward cited a dictum taken from the Justinian Code: "What touches all, by all should be approved."

Parliament's role in the collection of taxes led to the development of a true system of representation. Feudal custom, the Magna Carta, and prudence had required that the king seek the consent of his subjects for new taxes. He could not ask all freeholders of the realm individually. He might seek the consent of the separate shires and the towns, but this was a slow and awkward process. Edward ingeniously simplified the procedure of consent. Through special writs, he ordered the shires and the towns to elect representatives and to grant them "full power" to grant him money. These representatives, gathered in Parliament, thus had authority to consent to taxes and to bind their electors back home. Paradoxically, the unique powers of the English king laid the basis for the eventual, unique powers of Parliament.

As the supreme feudal council, Parliament was also England's highest court (an honor the House of Lords retains today). The members attending its sessions would carry petitions or appeals from decisions made in lower courts; whereas a sheriff or shire court might have been subject to intimidation, Parliament would not be. By welcoming petitions, the king thus made his justice better known and respected throughout the realm. As with the U.S. Supreme Court, the decisions of Parliament determined the future policies of all English courts. The decisions were thus nearly the equivalent of legislation, and from them there was no appeal.

At Edward's death in 1307 the English constitution had acquired certain distinctive features. The constitution was not contained in a single written document but was defined by both custom and statute law. The king was the chief of the state, but it was recognized that the important men of the kingdom should have some participation in the decision-making processes, especially regarding taxes. Parliament gave this policy its practical implementation. The extraordinary continuity of these arrangements over centuries to come is testimony to the sound construction that the medieval English kings, lords, and commoners gave to their government.

FRANCE

In France, as in England, the thirteenth century was an age of constitutional consolidation. The successor of Philip Augustus, Louis VIII, ruled for only three years (1223–1226), but his reign was notable for several reasons. He was the first Capetian king not to be crowned in his father's lifetime; the Capetians had finally established that their claim to the monarchy was based on inheritance and not upon election. Louis VIII campaigned personally against the Albigensian heretics in southern France, and his victories prepared the way for the eventual inclusion of Toulouse and Languedoc in the royal domain (these were the last major additions to the royal lands until the late fifteenth century). He adopted the policy of supporting younger sons and brothers by granting them territories, the so-called appanages. This policy, continued by his successors, ultimately created powerful and troublesome princely lines in France.

St. Louis At Louis' death in 1226 the throne passed to Louis IX, St. Louis (1226–1270), one of the great figures of the thirteenth century. Louis was recognized as a saint even during his lifetime. He attended at least two Masses a day, was sternly abstemious in food and drink, often washed the feet of the poor and the wounds of lepers, and was scrupulously faithful to his wife, Margaret of Provence, who, like her husband, bore an aura of sanctity. However, his personal asceticism did not preclude a grand conception of royal authority. He added new pomp to court ceremonies and freely acted against the pope's wishes whenever the interests of the monarchy or his people seemed to require it. Three great ideals informed his policies as king: more effective justice within his kingdom, peace with its neighbors, and war against the Muslims, who still held Jerusalem (see Chapter 10).

Louis actively sought peace with his Christian neighbors. French monarchs had traditionally claimed some land south of the Pyrenees Mountains, and the Spanish kings of Aragon in turn claimed large areas of Languedoc in southern France (see Map 8.4). Rather than settling this dispute through war, Louis negotiated the Treaty of

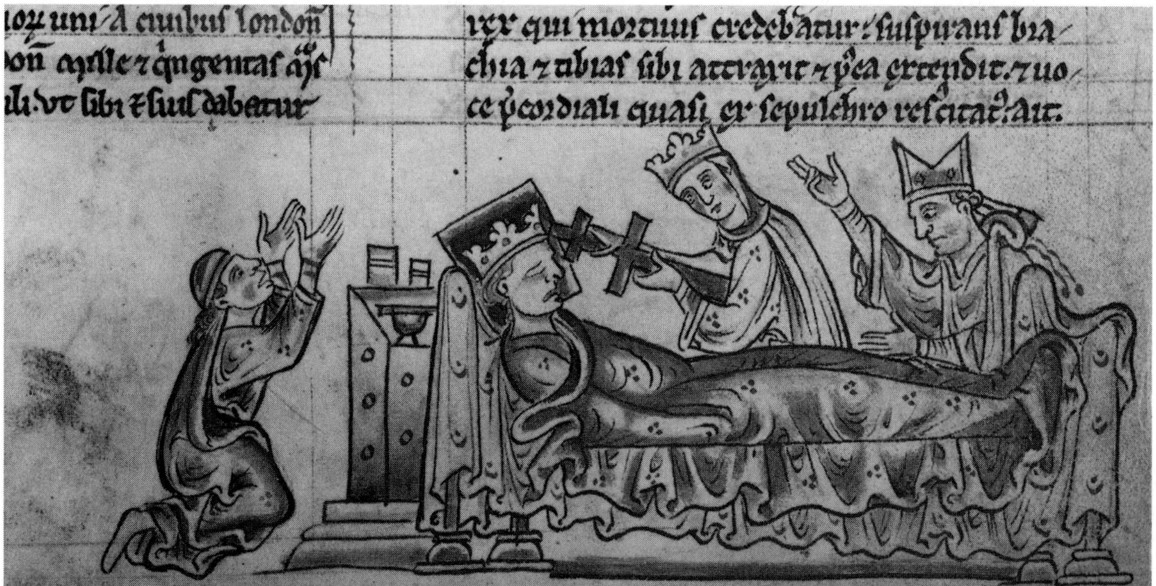

▶ Death of Louis IX

Louis IX of France died of the plague in Tunis during his Second Crusade. Attending his death bed in this manuscript illustration are his wife, Margaret of Provence, an unidentified bishop, and a mourner.

Corbeil (1258) with the Aragonese king, with each side renouncing its claims. This settlement defined the French-Spanish border for the next 200 years (see Map 9.1).

Peace with England was harder to attain. The English still held Aquitaine and Gascony and were not reconciled to the loss under King John of their extensive fiefs north of the Loire River. In the Treaty of Paris in 1259 Louis relinquished several territories that his troops had occupied along the borders of Gascony, and in return, King Henry III of England abandoned his claims to the lands that John had lost and agreed to perform liege homage to Louis for his fief of Gascony. The Treaty of Paris was unpopular in France; many believed that in ceding the Gascon borderlands Louis had given away more than the military situation warranted. Louis replied that these liberal terms might enable Henry's sons and his own to live thereafter in peace, as was proper for vassals and lords.

Legal Reforms In his own realm Louis made no attempt to extend the royal domain at the expense of his nobles or to deprive them of their traditional powers and jurisdictions, but he did expect them to be good vassals. He forbade wars among them, arbitrated their disputes, and insisted that his ordinances be respected; he was the first king to legislate for the whole of France. Although Louis did not suppress the courts of the great nobles, he and his judges listened to appeals from their decisions, so that royal justice would be available to all his subjects. The king liked to sit in the open under a great oak at Vincennes near Paris to receive personally the petitions of the humble. The prestige that the piety and fairness of his decisions lent to royal justice was his great contribution to its growth.

Map 9.1 Europe, ca. 1250

▸ **In this fourteenth-century manuscript illumination, St. Louis hears the pleas of his humble and defenseless subjects, chiefly women and a monk. Note the hanged felons in the left panel. The picture illustrates the abiding reputation for justice that St. Louis earned for the French monarchy.**

During Louis' reign jurists began to clarify and codify the laws and customs of France. The most important of these compilations was the Establishments of St. Louis, drawn up before 1273. It contained, besides royal ordinances, the civil and feudal customs of several northern provinces and seems to have been intended for the guidance of judges and lawyers. It was not an authoritative code, but it and other compilations helped bring a new clarity and system to French law. Also during his reign the Parlement of Paris—a tribunal rather than a representative assembly like the English Parliament—was confirmed by Louis as the highest court in France, a position it retained until 1789.

Philip IV Louis' successors were able to preserve the strength, but not the serenity, of his reign. His grandson Philip IV, the Fair (1285–1314), is perhaps the most enigmatic of the medieval French kings; neither contemporaries nor later historians have agreed on his abilities. To some, Philip has seemed capable and cunning; to others, phlegmatic and uninterested, content to leave the business of government almost entirely to his ministers. If Philip lacked the personal ability to rule, he at least had the capacity to select strong ministers as his principal advisers. They were usually laymen trained in Roman law and possessing a high opinion of royal authority. They considered the king to be not merely a feudal monarch who ruled in agreement with the magnates of his realm but rather an "emperor in his own land" whose authority was free from all restrictions (the root sense of *legibus solutus*, "absolute") and subject to no higher power on earth.

The greatest obstacle to the advance of Philip's power was Edward I of England, master of the extensive fief of Gascony. Philip's resolve to drive England from the continent resulted in intermittent wars from 1294 to 1302. To punish the English economically, Philip tried to block the importation of English wool into Flanders. The Flemish towns revolted. Philip marched against them but was overwhelmed at Courtrai in 1302 by the towns' militias. This defeat deprived Philip of all hope of expelling the English from the continent.

These costly wars had placed a heavy burden on the royal finances. To replenish the treasury, Philip confiscated all the property of the Jews and expelled them temporarily in 1306; he also imprisoned foreign merchants to extort money from them and from a military-religious order called the Knights Templars (see Chapter 10), which

▶ BATTLE OF THE GOLDEN SPURS
In 1302, Flemish peasants, who had rebelled because Philip IV of France attempted to block the importation of wool from England, defeated the king at the battle of Courtrai. It was said that after the battle 700 pairs of spurs were collected and displayed in the local cathedral, and some sense of the brutality of the fighting is conveyed by this illustration, with King Philip brandishing his sword at the center and the pile of bodies at the lower right.

he pressured the pope to suppress. Finally, Philip insisted on his right to demand from the Church "free gifts," which were actually taxes. The issue led to a protracted dispute with Pope Boniface VIII. In seeking to dominate these international powers—the Knights Templars and the Church itself—Philip showed his determination to become truly sovereign in his own lands.

In trying to achieve an absolute monarchy, Philip upset the delicate feudal equilibrium of the France of St. Louis. He left at his death a deeply disturbed France. The Flemish towns remained defiant, and the strained relation of the monarchy with its principal vassal, the king of England, threatened to produce a major war. Under Philip's successors, with the outbreak of the Hundred Years' War, France entered one of the darkest periods of its history.

THE IBERIAN KINGDOMS

The Christian *Reconquista* had achieved all but final victory by 1236 with only Granada still in Muslim hands. The principal challenge now was the consolidation of the earlier conquests under Christian rule and the achievement of a stable governing order.

The three major Christian kingdoms that emerged from the Christian offensive were Portugal, Castile (including León), and Aragon (including Catalonia and Valencia), but they were not really united within their own territories. The Christian kings had purchased the support of both old and new subjects through generous concessions during the course of the *Reconquista.* Large communities of Jews and Muslims gained the right to live under their own laws and elect their own officials, and favored towns were granted special royal charters, known as *fueros,* that permitted them to maintain their own forum, or court. Barcelona and Valencia in the kingdom of Aragon and Burgos, Toledo, Valladolid, and Seville in the kingdom of Castile were virtually self-governing republics in the thirteenth century. Among other groups, the military aristocracy was highly privileged. The magnates, particularly in Castile, the largest of the Iberian kingdoms, held much of their lands not as fiefs but as alods (properties in full title), which reinforced their independent spirit. The clergy, of course, formed still another powerful and privileged group. Moreover, the Iberian kings had to reckon with three wealthy religious orders of knights, which had been founded about 1200 to aid in the struggle against the infidel and that were now able to wield independent financial and military power.

To hold all these elements together under a common government was a formidable task, but the kings also retained real advantages. The tradition of war against the infidel gave kings a special prestige. And their rivals were too diverse and too eager to fight one another to be able to present a united challenge.

Sooner than other Western monarchs, the Iberian kings recognized the practical value of securing the consent of their powerful subjects to major governmental decisions, particularly regarding taxes. By the end of the twelfth century they were frequently calling representative assemblies, called *Cortes.* Although they never achieved the constitutional position of the English Parliament because there were too many of them, the Cortes were the most powerful representative assemblies in Europe during the thirteenth century.

In order to impose a stronger, essentially feudal sovereignty over their subjects, the Iberian kings set about systematizing the laws and customs of their realms, thus clarifying both their own prerogatives and their subjects' obligations. Alfonso X of Castile issued an encyclopedia of legal institutions, meant to instruct lawyers and guide judges. This code, known as the *Siete Partidas* ("Seven Divisions"), was thoroughly imbued with the spirit of Roman law and presented the king as the source of all justice. Alfonso was in no position to achieve a true absolutism in his government, but the code did serve to educate the people to the high dignity of kingship. Even more than in England and France, feudal government in the Iberian kingdoms rested on a delicate compromise between royal authority and private privilege, and this apparently fragile system worked tolerably well.

With the achievement of fairly stable governments the Iberian kingdoms were able to play a larger role in the affairs of Europe. Aragon in particular, with an opening on the Mediterranean Sea, made its power felt and seized Sardinia from the Genoese and Pisans in 1326. A seemingly invincible company of Catalan mercenaries besieged Constantinople (1302–1307) and then captured Athens and subjugated it to Catalan domination until 1388. The expansion of the Iberian kingdoms was to be a major theme in European history for the next several hundred years.

THE HOLY ROMAN EMPIRE

While the English, French, and Iberian kingdoms were moving toward greater unity under more centralized governments, the German and Italian territories of the Holy Roman Empire were disintegrating into a large number of small and virtually autonomous principalities. Frederick Barbarossa had negotiated an uneasy peace with the pope and the Italian towns in the last years of his reign, but the struggle was renewed soon after his death in 1190. Barbarossa's son Henry VI had married Constance, heiress to the Norman Kingdom of the Two Sicilies. Their son would thus have a legal claim to southern Italy as Constance's heir and a moral claim to the German throne. The prospect of Italian unification under German auspices disturbed both the papacy and the free cities of Lombardy. The towns feared the direct domination of the emperor, while the papacy believed that its liberty would not survive were it to be encircled by German lands. In his brief reign of seven years, however, Henry VI had little chance to effect "the union of the Kingdom with the Empire," as contemporaries called this fateful policy. It was a dream that was to elude his son, Frederick II, as well.

Frederick II Hohenstaufen Frederick II (1212–1250) is one of the most fascinating personalities

▶ FREDERICK II'S TREATISE ON FALCONRY

Frederick II was not only the dominant political leader of his age but also one of its most learned minds. He was an avid reader of Classical texts and apparently used Aristotle's *Historia Animalium* as a guide in one of his favorite pursuits, a study of birds. Illustrated here are a number of pages from his own copy of the treatise that he wrote on falconry.

of the Middle Ages. A contemporary called him *stupor mundi* ("wonder of the world"). Later historians have hailed him as the first modern ruler, the prototype of the cold and calculating statesman. Frederick spoke six languages, loved learning, patronized poets and translators, founded a university, and, after a fashion, conducted scientific experiments. He also corrected Aristotle by writing on the margins of his works in several places "It isn't so."

Several princes had contended for the German throne upon Henry VI's death, but the pope eventually crowned Frederick emperor in 1219 on the double promise that he would renounce his mother's inheritance of southern Italy and lead a crusade to Palestine. Frederick procrastinated on both agreements, creating lasting difficulties with the Church.

Emperor Frederick influenced German development in several fundamental ways. He established on the empire's eastern frontier a military-religious order, the Teutonic Knights, who eventually created the Prussian state; recognized Bohemia as a hereditary kingdom and Lübeck as a free imperial city; and issued the earliest charter of liberties to the Swiss cantons. (Later in the century, in 1291, the cantons entered into a "Perpetual Compact," or alliance, which marks the formal beginnings of the Swiss Confederation.) His most important policy, however, was to confer upon the German ecclesiastical princes and the lay nobles virtual sovereignty within their own territories. The emperor retained only the right to set the foreign policy of the empire, make war and peace, and adjudicate disputes between princes or subjects of different principalities. All other powers of government passed to the princes, and no later emperor could regain what Frederick gave away.

In Italy Frederick pursued a much different policy. For the government of the Kingdom of the Two Sicilies he relied upon a trained lay bureaucracy. He rigorously centralized his administra-

▶ Emperor Frederick II, in the ship showing the imperial eagles, watches his soldiers assaulting prelates on their way to a council summoned by Pope Gregory IX in 1241. This contemporary illustration of the emperor's sacrilegious behavior, taken from a manuscript, is a good example of the war of propaganda by which both pope and emperor sought to win public sympathy.

tion, suppressed local privileges, imposed a universal tax in money upon his subjects, recruited his army from all classes and from Muslims as well as Christians, and issued a constitution which, in the spirit of Roman law, interpreted all jurisdiction as stemming from the emperor.

While seeking to build a strong and centralized government in Italy, Frederick had to face the increasingly bitter opposition of the popes and the free cities of the north. Pope Gregory IX excommunicated him in 1227 because of his failure to lead an Eastern crusade. Frederick then departed on the crusade, but he preferred to negotiate rather than fight and made a treaty with the Muslims that guaranteed unarmed Christian pilgrims access to Jerusalem. The more militant among the Western Christians believed that this treaty was dishonorable. Frederick returned to Italy in 1229 and came to terms with Pope Gregory a year later.

The Lombard towns remained fearful of his designs and finally leagued against him. He defeated them in 1237, but his success once more awakened in Gregory fears of encirclement, and Frederick was again excommunicated. Both sides struggled to win the public sympathy of Europe, but the tide of history began to turn against Frederick. To break the power of the Lombard towns, he unsuccessfully besieged Parma in 1248. In 1250 death cut short his efforts to unify Italy under imperial auspices.

There are some historical figures whose careers seem to summarize a given epoch and to predict the one to come. Frederick is such a figure. In Germany he reinforced a political fragmentation that had become ever more pronounced since the eleventh century. In southern Italy he completed the constitutional reorganization that the Norman kings, his forebears, had begun. Above all he was perhaps the last emperor to take seriously the grand vision of a Christian empire.

III. The Church

Since the time of the Gregorian reform of the eleventh century, the papacy had sought to build in Europe a unified Christian commonwealth, one based on faith and on obedience to the pope, in which European princes and peoples might work out their salvation in fraternal peace. In the thirteenth century the Church came close to achieving this grand design, but it still had to face powerful challenges to both Christian unity and its own leadership.

THE GROWTH OF HERESY

From the fifth until nearly the eleventh century no major heresies had troubled the Western Church, a sure indication of intellectual and spiritual torpor. From about the year 1000, however, chroniclers begin to note with growing frequency the appearance of heretics and sporadic attempts to suppress them.

The spread of heresy in the eleventh and twelfth centuries was partially a reaction to abuses within the established Church. Angered by the wealth and moral laxity of the clergy, heretics rejected the claimed privileges of the official priesthood. But heresy also had social roots. The continuing increase of population brought many social dislocations in its wake. The young were too numerous for the positions and jobs left to them by the aged. Society was filled with young men, frustrated in their hopes for a career, and unmarriageable young women. The movement into new territories, the growth of towns, the appearance of new trades and industries—all created strong psychological tensions, which often found an outlet in heretical movements. Within the towns, for example, heresy offered a form of social protest to the urban poor. It held potential for rich townsmen, too, inasmuch as traditional Christianity had been highly suspicious of wealth, particularly when earned in the marketplace, and gave the rich merchant little assurance of reaching heaven. Nobles envied the property and power of the Church; to them, heresy offered a justification for seizing the wealth of a corrupt Church for themselves.

Heresy further had a particular appeal to women. Many could not marry because of the large dowry demanded and for the same reason could not enter a religious order, as this also required a monetary contribution. Without a firm and stable social niche, many women had cause for intense dissatisfaction with both Church and society. Many heretics made a special effort to recruit women, conducting schools for them and teaching them how to read the Scriptures at a time when the established Church largely ignored their needs.

This was also an age of spiritual tension. Many laypeople wanted a more mystical and emotional reward from religion but were denied such satisfaction because they were given no opportunity to study the Bible, to hear it read in the vernacular, or to be moved by sermons. These were the exclusive activities of monks. A principal effort of both the new heresies and the new movements within the Church was to break this monastic monopoly of the religious experience.

THE WALDENSIANS AND THE ALBIGENSIANS

Around 1170 a rich merchant of Lyons, Peter Waldo, adopted a life of absolute poverty and gave himself to preaching. He soon attracted followers, who came to be known as "the poor men of Lyons" or Waldensians. The Waldensians attacked the moral laxness of the clergy and denounced the sacraments they administered. This group was declared heretical by the Lateran Council of 1215, but the Church never succeeded in suppressing the movement.

Far more powerful in their own day, though not destined to survive the Middle Ages, were the Cathari, or Albigensians, named for the town of Albi in Languedoc. The Albigensians' religious attitudes were greatly influenced by Manicheanism, a belief that antedated Christianity. It continued to survive among various small sects in Asia Minor and the Balkans. The Albigensians, like the Manicheans, believed that two principles, or deities, a god of light and a god of darkness, were fighting for supremacy in the universe. The good person must help the god of light vanquish the evil god of darkness, who had created and ruled the material world. The true Albigensians led a life of rigorous asceticism. They abstained from sexual intercourse, since procreation replenished the earth, the domain of the god of darkness. Marriage they regarded as hypocrisy, and intercourse within it worse than any other sexual sin. They abstained from meat, since it was sexually reproduced. Because a sect that preached against marriage and procreation risked bringing about its own extinction, the Albigensians reached a practical compromise: Those who abided by these stringent regulations were the *Perfecti* (they formed the priesthood); those who did not live by this stern code were the believers.

The Albigensians, like the Waldensians, denied all value to the sacraments and priesthood of the established Church. They, of course, denied that Christ had ever taken on human flesh and saw no coming resurrection of the body. Their appeal came principally from their use of a vernacular Testament, from their willingness to preach in the vernacular to laypersons, and from their moral fervor. Eventually they developed a strong organization with councils and a hierarchy of *Perfecti* under a chief resembling a pope.

THE SUPPRESSION OF HERESY

The Church initially responded to the heretics by attempting to reconvert them. One of the first and greatest leaders supporting the policy of reconversion was a priest from Castile named Dominic, who began to preach among the Albigensians of Languedoc in about 1205. Dominic insisted that his followers—whose mission was to preach—live in poverty and support themselves by begging; they thus constituted a mendicant, or begging, order. This new Order of Preachers grew with amazing rapidity and was approved by the bishop of Toulouse in 1215 and shortly afterward by the pope. To prepare its members for their work, the Dominican Order stressed education and thus eventually became the intellectual arm of the medieval Church. It counted among its members Albertus Magnus, Thomas Aquinas, and many other important religious thinkers of the thirteenth century.

Reconversion through preaching, persuasion, and example remained, however, a slow and uncertain process. Moreover, canon law failed to provide an effective remedy against the powerful, organized heresies of the twelfth century. The law did give the bishop the right to try a suspected heretic before his own court, but a heretic protected by important men in the community was virtually immune to prosecution, inasmuch as the bishop often feared offending the lay powers of his diocese. The lack of any effective legal way of dealing with heretics led to frequent riots against them—the medieval equivalent of lynching—similar to the occasional massacres of Jews by anti-Semitic mobs.

By the early thirteenth century the Church began to suppress heresy systematically by force. Pope Innocent III, of whom more will be said later, favored peaceful solutions to heresy until his legate Peter of Castelnau, who had excommunicated the count of Toulouse for tolerating heresy, was murdered by one of the count's men. Innocent concluded that as long as the nobility of Languedoc abetted heresy, nothing short of force would be effective against it. He therefore proclaimed a crusade (1208–1229) against the Albigensians and the nobles who supported them. Knights from the north of France responded with zeal, but more out of greed for plunder than concern for orthodoxy. They defeated the nobles of Languedoc, but the problem of suppressing heresy remained.

The Inquisition In 1231 Pope Gregory IX instituted a special papal court to investigate and punish heresy. This was the famous papal Inquisition, which was to play a large and unhappy role in European history for the next several centuries. Through the Inquisition the popes sought to impose ordered and effective procedures upon the hunt for heretics. Like the English justices in eyre, the inquisitors were itinerant justices who visited the towns within their circuit at regular intervals. Strangers to the locale, they were not subject to pressures from the important men of the region. While the Inquisition was doubtless an improvement over riots and massacres, the procedures it adopted led to gross abuses. It accepted secret denunciations and, to protect the accusers, would not reveal their names to those denounced; at times it used evidence that was not even revealed to the accused. It denied the right of counsel and tortured stubborn heretics. The suspected heretics were, in fact, considered guilty before even being summoned to the Inquisition. They could confess and repent, with the likely consequence of a heavy penance and usually the confiscation of their property. But they had little chance to prove their innocence. As an ecclesiastical court, the Inquisition was forbidden to shed blood, but here too its procedures were novel: It delivered relapsed or unrepentant heretics to the secular authority with full knowledge that they would be put to death (*see box*, p. 268).

The weaknesses of this system soon became apparent. Secret procedures protected incompetent and even demented judges, who shocked and disgusted even their contemporaries with their savage zeal. In addition, the Inquisition could function only where it had the close cooperation of the secular authority. It was never established in areas (for example, England) where strong kings considered themselves fully competent to control heresy. (Kings characteristically equated religious and civil rebellion and considered heresy to be identical with treason; even Frederick II, in spite of his bitter dispute with the papacy, imposed the death penalty upon heretics.)

The number of heretics who were executed is not known exactly, but they were probably not more than several hundred. Fines, confiscations of property, and imprisonment were the usual punishments for all but the most obstinate heretics. There is no denying the unfortunate effect of the Inquisition upon the medieval papacy and Church, chiefly the association of the papacy with persecution and bloodshed.

THE FRANCISCANS

Crusades and the Inquisition could not alone preserve the unity of the medieval Church. A spiritual regeneration was needed; the Church had to reach laypeople, especially those living in towns, and provide them with a spiritual message they could comprehend. The Dominicans were the first religious order to undertake this task as their primary mission. A major role was also played by a contemporary of St. Dominic's, St. Francis of Assisi.

Francis (1182?–1226) is probably the greatest saint of the Middle Ages and possibly the most sensitive poet of religious emotion. He succeeded in developing a style of piety that was both faithful to orthodoxy and abounding in new mystical insights. Since most of Francis' life is screened by legend, it is nearly impossible to reconstruct the exact course of his spiritual development. He seems to have devoted his young manhood to a self-conscious search for happiness or, in the

The Techniques of the Inquisition

To combat heresy the Inquisition tried above all to get suspects to confess, repent, and thus save their souls. Bernard Gui, inquisitor at Toulouse in southern France between 1307 and 1323, left a vivid account of the psychological techniques used in interrogations.

"When a heretic is first brought up for examination, he assumes a confident air, as though secure in his innocence. I ask him why he has been brought before me. He replies, smiling and courteous, 'Sir, I would be glad to learn the cause from you.'

"I [Inquisitor]. You are accused as a heretic, and that you believe and teach otherwise than Holy Church believes.

"A [Answer]. (Raising his eyes to heaven, with an air of the greatest faith) Lord, thou knowest that I am innocent of this, and that I have never held any faith other than that of true Christianity. . . .

"I. I know your tricks. What the members of your sect believe you hold to be that which a Christian should believe. But we waste time in this fencing. Say simply, Do you believe in one God the Father, and the Son, and the Holy Ghost?

"A. I believe.

"I. Do you believe in Christ born of the Virgin, suffered, risen, and ascended to heaven?

"A. (Briskly) I believe.

"I. Do you believe the bread and wine in the mass performed by the priests to be changed into the body and blood of Christ by divine virtue?

"A. Ought I not to believe this?

"I. I don't ask if you ought to believe, but if you do believe.

"A. I believe whatever you and other good doctors order me to believe. . . .

"I. Will you then swear that you have never learned anything contrary to the faith which we hold to be true?

"A. (Growing pale) If I ought to swear, I will willingly swear.

"I. I don't ask you whether you ought, but whether you will swear.

"A. If you order me to swear, I will swear.

"I. I don't force you to swear, because as you believe oaths to be unlawful, you will transfer the sin to me who forced you; but if you will swear, I will hear it.

"A. Why should I swear if you do not order me to?

"I. So that you may remove the suspicion of being a heretic.

"A. Sir, I do not know how unless you teach me.

"I. If I had to swear, I would raise my hand and spread my fingers and say, 'So help me God, I have never learned heresy or believed what is contrary to the true faith.'

"Then trembling as if he cannot repeat the form, he will stumble along as though speaking for himself or for another, so that there is not an absolute form of oath, and yet he may be thought to have sworn. . . . Or he converts the oath into a form of prayer. . . . [And when further hard pressed he will appeal, saying] 'Sir, if have done amiss in aught, I will willingly bear the penance, only help me to avoid the infamy of which I am accused.' But a vigorous inquisitor might not allow himself to be worked upon in this way, but proceed firmly until he makes these people confess their error, or at least publicly abjure heresy, so that if they are subsequently found to have sworn falsely, he can, without further hearing, abandon them to the secular arm."

From H. C. Lea, *A History of the Inquisition of the Middle Ages*, vol. I: (1887), pp. 411–414.

troubadour terminology he favored, for perfect joy. He first tried the rowdy amusements of the city. But dissatisfaction lingered; a biographer, Thomas of Celano, relates that after a severe illness Francis wandered on a May morning out to the blossoming fields but did not feel his accustomed joy. He then became a knight, but contentment still eluded him. Finally, he turned to

This fresco from the basilica of St. Francis at Assisi, traditionally attributed to the Florentine painter Giotto, shows the saint preaching to the birds. He congratulates them on their bright plumage and bids them sing in praise of God. The implication is that if people too recognize God's providence over them, they will respond with gratitude and joy.

the religious life—instructed to do so, according to legend, by Christ himself—and adopted a life of poverty. Still, he believed that the test of true living, and indeed of true religion, ought to be joy: If all creatures, including human beings, recognized God's good providence over them, they would respond with joy. Joy would, in turn, ensure universal harmony in the world and bring a kind of golden age.

Disciples began to gather almost at once around the "little poor man" of Assisi. In 1208 Francis obtained papal approval for the formation of a new religious order. This Order of Friars Minor (Lesser Brothers) grew with extraordinary rapidity; within 10 years it included some 5000 members and spread from Germany to Palestine; before the end of the century it was the largest order in the Church. Although the problems of administering a huge order did not command Francis' deepest interests, he did write a brief rule for the Friars and shortly before his death gave them some further recommendations in a document known as his Testament, in which he stressed the importance of poverty and simplicity.

The success of the Friars Minor was an authentic triumph for the Church. Like the Dominicans, they carried their message primarily to laypeople in the growing towns, to the social classes where the heretics had hitherto won their greatest successes. Giving themselves to poverty and preaching, the Friars Minor came to include not only a second order of nuns but a third order of laypeople. Francis and his followers thus opened orthodox religion to delight in the natural world, to mystical and emotional experience, and to joy, which all people, they believed, including the ascetic and the pious, should be seeking.

PAPAL GOVERNMENT

In this period of social change and religious crisis the papacy faced serious obstacles in achieving its ideal of a unified, peaceful, and obedient European community. The pope of the thirteenth century whose reign best illustrates the aspirations and the problems of the medieval Church is Innocent III (1198–1216).

Innocent was somewhat ambiguous in defining his own powers. He once stated that God had given him "not only the universal Church, but the whole world to govern," yet he also declared to Philip II of France that he had no wish to "lessen or disturb the jurisdiction and power of the king." Although he seems to have been willing enough to leave the princes undisturbed in the routine exercise of government, he did insist that they obey him in matters concerning the rights of the Church, the peace and common interests of Christendom, and their own personal morality. He sought with vigor and with remarkable, if always partial, success to achieve three major goals: the unity of Christendom, the hegemony of the papacy over Europe, and the clarification of Christian discipline and belief.

Within Europe heresy was the greatest threat to Christian unity, and though he ordered the crusade against the Albigensians, Innocent primarily looked to the new mendicant orders to counter the appeal of the heretics. Beyond Europe he sought reunion with the Eastern Church. At first condemning the Fourth Crusade, which was directed against fellow Christians, Innocent came to consider the fall of Constantinople to the crusaders a providential act, meant to achieve unification of the Western and Eastern churches. From 1204 to 1261 an imposed union did hold the members of the Eastern Church, or at least some of them, in obedience to Rome, but the violence of the Western Europeans during the crusade sowed among the conquered a lasting hatred that frustrated later efforts at permanent union.

The pope also sought to exert his leadership over the princes of Europe in all spiritually significant affairs. Some of his efforts to bend kings to his will have already been mentioned, such as his struggle with King John to install Stephen Langton as archbishop of Canterbury. He also excommunicated Philip II of France for discarding his queen in order to cohabit with another woman. Innocent had occasion to reprimand the kings of Aragon, Portugal, Poland, and Norway. Indeed, no prior pope had scrutinized princely behavior with so keen an eye. Nevertheless, his interventions had uneven results, especially with regard to his dearest goal, the establishment of permanent peace among the European princes.

THE PAPACY IN THE THIRTEENTH CENTURY

Trained in canon law, Innocent wanted to bring a new order to Christian belief and government. In 1215 he summoned some 1500 prelates to attend the Fourth Lateran Council. The Lateran Council identified the sacraments as exactly seven and reaffirmed that they are essential to salvation; imposed an obligation of yearly confession and communion on the faithful; and defined the dogma of transubstantiation, according to which the priest, in uttering the words of consecration at Mass, annihilates the substance of bread and wine and substitutes for them the substance of Christ. Transubstantiation unambiguously affirmed the Mass as miracle and thus conferred a unique power on the Catholic priesthood. The council also pronounced on a wide variety of disciplinary matters: the qualifications for the priesthood, the nature of priestly education, the character of monastic life, the veneration of relics, and other devotional exercises.

Innocent's successors continued the work of codifying Church law. In 1234 Gregory IX published an authoritative collection of decretals (papal letters) to which additions were made in 1298 and 1314. Together with the *Decretum* of Gratian, these collections formed the Body of Canon Law, which in turn made up the finished constitution of the medieval Church.

Papal administration, and especially papal finances, continued to expand during the thirteenth century. Often desperate for funds to carry on their ambitious policies, the popes extracted substantial payments for appointments to office, imposed tithes (a tenth of income) upon the clergy, and sold exemptions and dispensations from the regulations of canon law. By the late thirteenth century the popes were clearly exploiting their spiritual powers for financial profit, and this was to prove a disastrous precedent.

Boniface VIII By the late thirteenth century the papacy was facing a rising challenge from the princes of Europe, who sought to dominate the churches within their own territories. Both Philip IV of France and Edward I of England had been taxing the clergy through the fiction of asking for, and always receiving, gifts, or subventions. In 1296, in the bull *Clericis laicos* (all solemn papal letters were called *bulls* because they were closed with a seal, or *bulla*, and they are usually identified by their first two words), Pope Boniface VIII forbade all clergy to make grants without papal permission. Such a restriction would have given the pope a powerful, if not controlling, voice in royal finances, which no king could tolerate. The English simply ignored the order, but Philip retaliated by forbidding all exports of coin from his realm to Rome. Boniface, surprised by the forceful reaction, dropped his demands a year later.

In 1301 Philip arrested for treason a French

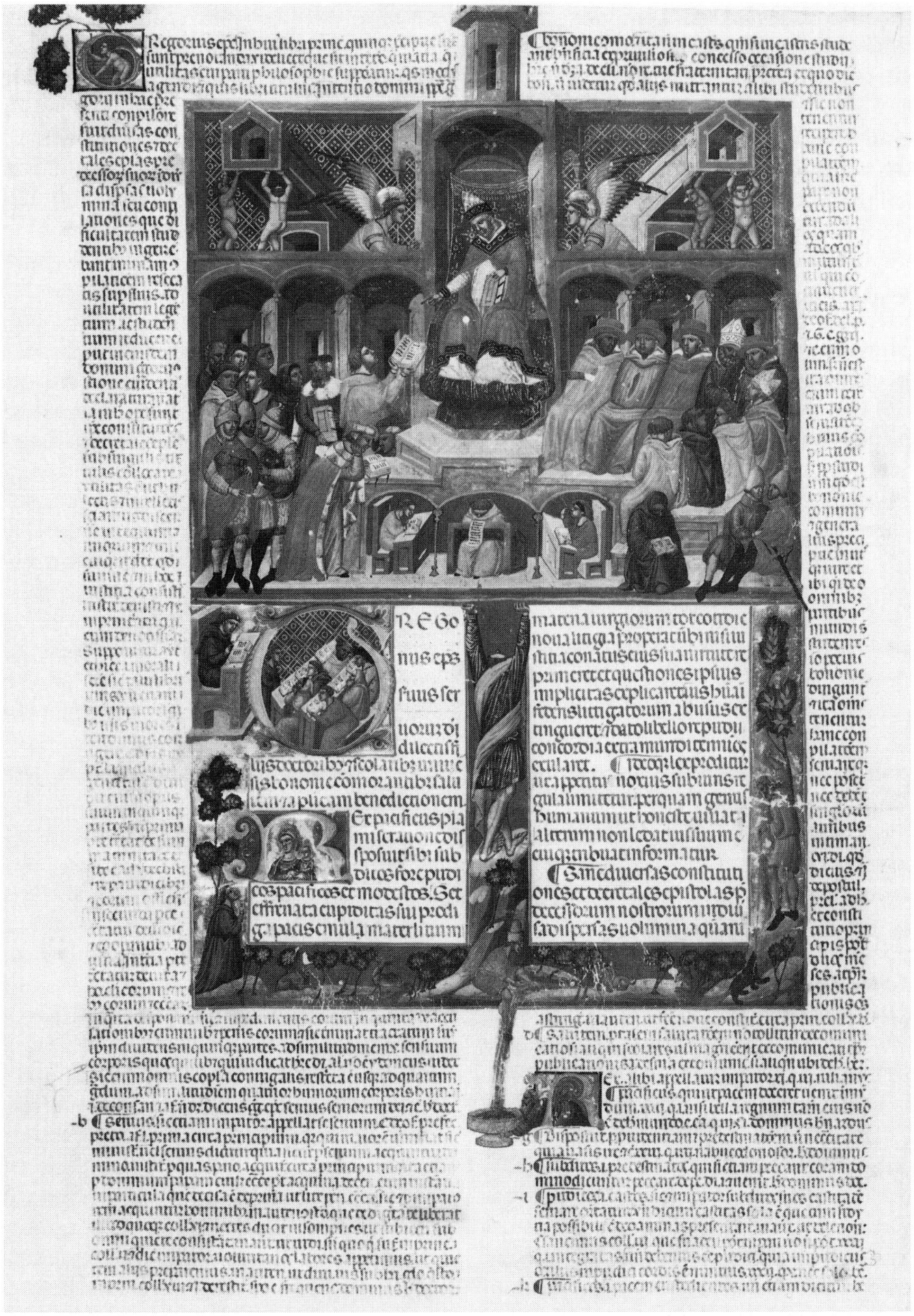

▸ GREGORY IX DECRETALS

One of the principal accomplishments of Pope Gregory IX was his sponsorship of an effort to bring together and update the basic decisions and rulings of the Church. The resulting collection is known as the decretals of Gregory IX, and it became the main source of canon law. In this miniature from a fourteenth-century manuscript of the decretals, Gregory sits at the center holding the book and surrounded by monks.

bishop who also happened to be a papal legate, thus striking directly at the sovereignty of the pope and the immunities of his representatives. Boniface reprimanded Philip for his behavior, but the king responded by circulating defamatory accusations against the pope. Naturally, Boniface felt that both his personal character and the papal authority were being threatened. He therefore issued the bull *Unam Sanctam*, which declared that Philip must submit to his authority or risk the loss of his immortal soul (*see box*, below). In no mood to accept a rebuff, Philip sent one of his principal advisers to Italy, who with the aid of a Roman faction opposed to Boniface broke into the papal palace at Anagni and arrested the pope. The citizens of Anagni rescued Boniface shortly afterward, but he died in Rome only a few months later. The vulnerability of the papacy had been clearly demonstrated.

The succeeding popes capitulated to the French king and even revoked *Unam Sanctam*. Philip's victory was complete when a Frenchman was elected pope in 1305. Clement V never reached Rome, settling instead in the French-speaking, though imperial, city of Avignon in 1309. For the next 68 years the popes lived within the shadow of the French monarchy.

The medieval papacy hoped to serve as the

Unam Sanctam

This statement of papal monarchy was issued by Pope Boniface VIII in 1302 to combat assertions of royal power by the kings of England and France against the authority of the universal Church. It did little, however, to deter the claims of such rulers to a growing sphere of authority.

"That there is one holy, Catholic and apostolic Church we are bound to believe and to hold, our faith urging us, and this we do firmly believe and simply confess; and that outside this Church there is no salvation or remission of sins. . . .

"We are taught by the words of the Gospel that in this Church and in her power there are two swords, a spiritual one and a temporal one. For when the apostles said 'Here are two swords' (Luke 22:38), meaning in the Church since it was the apostles who spoke, the Lord did not reply that it was too many but enough. Certainly anyone who denies that the temporal sword is in the power of Peter has not paid heed to the words of the Lord when he said, 'Put up thy sword into its sheath' (Matthew 26:52). Both then are in the power of the Church, the material sword and the spiritual. But the one is exercised for the Church, the other by the Church, the one by the hand of the priest, the other by the hand of kings and soldiers, though at the will and sufferance of the priest. One sword ought to be under the other and the temporal authority subject to the spiritual power. For, while the apostle says, 'There is no power but from God and those that are ordained of God' (Romans 13:1), they would not be ordained unless one sword was under the other and, being inferior, was led by the other to the highest things. . . . But that the spiritual power excels any earthly one in dignity and nobility we ought the more openly to confess in proportion as spiritual things excel temporal ones. Moreover we clearly perceive this from the giving of tithes, from benediction and sanctification, from the acceptance of this power and from the very government of things. For the truth bearing witness, the spiritual power has to institute the earthly power and to judge if it has not been good. . . .

"Therefore, if the earthly power errs, it shall be judged by the spiritual power, if a lesser spiritual power errs it shall be judged by its superior, but if the supreme spiritual power errs it can be judged only by God not by man. . . . Therefore we declare, state, define and pronounce that it is altogether necessary to salvation for every human creature to be subject to the Roman Pontiff."

From Hollister, *Medieval Europe: A Short Sourcebook* (1992), pp. 215–216.

vocal conscience of Europe. It was aided in this ambition by compelling theological and legal systems and by a huge administrative apparatus. But the growth of papal power weakened the bishop's ability to maintain the moral discipline of his clergy, and that permitted abuses to grow unchecked. Even the new intellectual rigor of Christian belief carried with it a certain risk for the spiritual life. Cold intellectualism or a narrow legalism might well threaten and dilute authentic piety—a problem the Church would encounter time and again.

IV. The Summer of Medieval Culture

Whereas the twelfth century was the period of discovery and creation in the cultural growth of the medieval world, the thirteenth century was an age of intellectual synthesis. As the statesmen of Europe tried to unite law and custom in ordered constitutional systems, the cultural leaders tried to bring earlier intellectual traditions into harmony.

THE MEDIEVAL SYNTHESIS

An appreciation of thirteenth-century culture requires an understanding of the ideas and values the period was seeking to combine. The Scholastics were trying to reconcile the fundamental assumptions of Aristotelian philosophy with the fundamental attitudes of Christianity: The former asserting that human reason could probe the structure of the universe unaided; the latter insisting on the necessity of divine revelation and grace.

In their attempt to reconcile these views, medieval intellectuals aimed at nothing less than uniting two historical and cultural experiences, for medieval civilization was itself the product of two quite different epochs. The violence and desperation of the late Roman and early medieval periods had implanted in the medieval mind a deep conviction that the natural powers of human beings were inadequate to control their destiny, that they needed help through grace. The experiences of society after 1000 had, on the other hand, bred a new confidence in human capabilities. Aristotelian philosophy lent intellectual force to what experience seemed to be teaching: that human beings could attain, through their own efforts, some measure of truth and fulfillment in this present world.

In seeking to reconcile faith and reason, medieval people were trying to extract the common denominator of truth from the vastly different experiences through which they had passed. They wanted to construct an open intellectual system that would give a place to all true values, wherever found, however they had been learned. The general nature of this effort at synthesis can be seen in three of the major achievements of the period: the Scholasticism of Thomas Aquinas, the Gothic cathedral, and the *Comedy* of Dante Alighieri.

THOMAS AQUINAS

The most gifted representative of Scholastic philosophy, and the greatest Christian theologian since Augustine, was St. Thomas Aquinas (1225?–1274), whose career well illustrates the character of thirteenth-century intellectual life. At 17 Thomas entered the new Dominican Order, perhaps attracted by its commitment to scholarship; he studied at Monte Cassino and Naples, and later, as a Dominican, at Cologne and Paris (see Map 9.2). His most influential teacher was another Dominican, Albertus Magnus, a German who wrote extensively on theological matters and questions of natural science, especially biology. Thomas was no intellectual recluse; he lectured at Paris and traveled widely across Europe, particularly on the business of his order and the Church.

In his short and active life Thomas produced a prodigious amount of writing: commentaries on biblical books and Aristotelian works, short essays on philosophical problems, and a lengthy compendium of Christian apologetics, the *Summa contra Gentiles*, which was probably intended for Dominican missionaries working to convert heretics and infidels. However, his most important work was one he did not live to finish. Divided into three parts on God, Man, and Christ, the *Summa Theologica* was meant to provide a com-

Map 9.2 MEDIEVAL UNIVERSITIES

prehensive introduction to Christian theology and to present a systematic view of the universe that would do justice to all truth, natural and revealed, pagan and Christian.

Thomas brought to his task a subtle and perceptive intellect, and his system (not unlike the feudal constitutions) rests upon several fundamental, delicate compromises. In regard to faith and reason, he taught that both are roads to a single truth. Reason is based ultimately on sense experience. It is a powerful instrument, but insufficient to teach people all that God wishes them to know. Nature is good, and humans can achieve some partial, temporary happiness in this life. But nature alone cannot carry them to ultimate fulfillment. Grace is still needed to bring nature to perfection and human beings to eternal salvation.

With respect to the fundamental structure of the universe, Thomas sought the common ground between two interpretations of reality, inherited from the ancient philosophers and called in the medieval schools *realism* and *nominalism*.

Though technically a moderate realist, Thomas argued that both interpretations were correct. Each object in the universe is autonomous and unique (the nominalist position), but it is also representative of general species or classes, which exist independently of the mind and which form a hierarchy or chain of being leading up to God (the realist position). To possess this double dimension of meaning, each object must be metaphysically a composite of two principles, one of which explains its unity with other objects and the other its individuality. In broadest terms, the principle of unity is "act," meaning the act of being, as it is ultimately in their being that objects resemble one another. The principle of individuation is "potency," which limits act and renders an object unique. Motion or change in the universe is essentially a transition from potency to act. Only God is unlimited, unindividuated Being—"pure act" in Thomas' definition. Only God cannot change, but He ultimately supports all change. In his proofs of God's existence, Thomas argued that instability, imperfection, and change, which we see all around us, point to the existence of an "unmoved mover," a principle of absolute perfection, stability, and power.

The *Summa* shows certain characteristic weaknesses of Scholasticism. Thomas affirmed that natural truth is ultimately grounded in observation, but, in fact, he observed very little. His critical distinction between act and potency, which he borrowed from Aristotle, was not founded on observation or experimentation. Many later thinkers found his system too speculative, too elaborate. Nonetheless, the *Summa* remains an unquestioned masterpiece of Western theology. It offers comment on an enormous range of theological, philosophical, and ethical problems, and consistently demonstrates openness, insight, and wisdom.

To be sure, Thomas' system fell under critical scrutiny even in the generation following his death. Among his early critics the most influential was a Scottish Franciscan, John Duns Scotus (1265?–1308). Drawing inspiration from St. Augustine, Duns Scotus affirmed that faith was logically prior to reason; that is, unless faith had first suggested to reason that spiritual beings—God and angels—could exist, reason would never have arrived at a concept of them. Once the mind accepted the idea of God from faith, it could then prove the necessity for God's existence. To Duns Scotus the proof of God's existence was not based, as with Aquinas, on the perception of change in the universe, for he did not trust the accuracy of sense observation; rather, it derived from an exclusively intellectual analysis of the concept of God as a necessary being.

THE GOTHIC CATHEDRAL

Artists as well as theologians were attempting to present a systematic view of the universe reflective of all truth. The artistic counterpart to the Scholastic *Summas* was the Gothic cathedral.

The word *Gothic* was coined in the sixteenth century as an expression of contempt for these supposedly barbarous medieval buildings. In fact, the Goths had disappeared some 500 years before any Gothic churches were built. As used today, *Gothic* refers to the style of architecture and art that initially developed in the royal lands in France, including Paris and its surroundings, from about 1150. The abbey church of Saint-Denis near Paris, built by the Abbot Suger in 1144, is usually taken as the first authentic example of the Gothic style. The early Gothic churches were almost all urban cathedrals and were characteristically dedicated to the Virgin Mary. In the thirteenth century the Gothic style spread widely through Europe and found special application in the large churches built by the Franciscan and Dominican orders.

Technically, three engineering devices helped stamp the Gothic style: the broken rather than rounded arch; ribbed vaulting, which concentrated support around the lines of thrust and gave the buildings a visibly delineated skeleton; and the flying buttress, an external support that allowed the walls to be made higher and lighter. The flying buttress also freed sections of the walls from the function of supporting the roof and therefore permitted the use of large areas for windows. Romanesque architects had pioneered all three devices, but the Gothic engineers combined them and used them with unprecedented vigor and boldness.

Innovations were also made in the statues that

AMIENS CATHEDRAL, CA. 1220–1236
Built between 1220 and 1236, Amiens Cathedral exemplifies the structure of a Gothic cathedral. The weight of the walls is supported by a system of buttresses and ribbed vaults, which allowed medieval builders to break up the walls with luminous areas of stained glass. The colored light that poured into these massive structures gave them an otherworldly majesty never before achieved.

In contrast to Romanesque sculpture, which overflows with great displays of emotion, Gothic sculpture evokes a sense of calm and orderly reality, as can be seen in the jamb figures on the central portal of Chartres Cathedral.

adorned the buildings. Romanesque sculpture often conveyed great emotion and power but did not reflect the visible world. Sculptors now wanted their works to emulate reality, or at least its handsomest parts (decorative foliage, for example, was carved with such accuracy that the botanical models can be identified). Their statues portray real and usually cheerful people, who subtly exert their own personalities without destroying the harmony of the whole.

The Gothic Spirit These magnificent churches with their hundreds of statues took decades to construct and decorate, and many were never completed. The builders intended that the churches provide a comprehensive view of the universe and instruction in its sacred history. One principal element of the Gothic aesthetic is a strong sense of order. The naked ribs and buttresses and the intricate vaulting constitute a spectacular geometry that instills in the viewer a vivid impression of intelligence and logical relationships. The churches, reflecting the structure of the universe, taught that God, the master builder, created and still governs the natural world with similar logic.

SAINTE-CHAPELLE, PARIS, INTERIOR, 1243–1248
Sainte-Chapelle, the private chapel attached to the French royal palace in Paris, was built between 1243 and 1248 to house relics brought back from the crusades by Louis IX. The building was deliberately intended to resemble a reliquary, and the enormous jewel-colored stained-glass windows make up three-quarters of its wall surface.

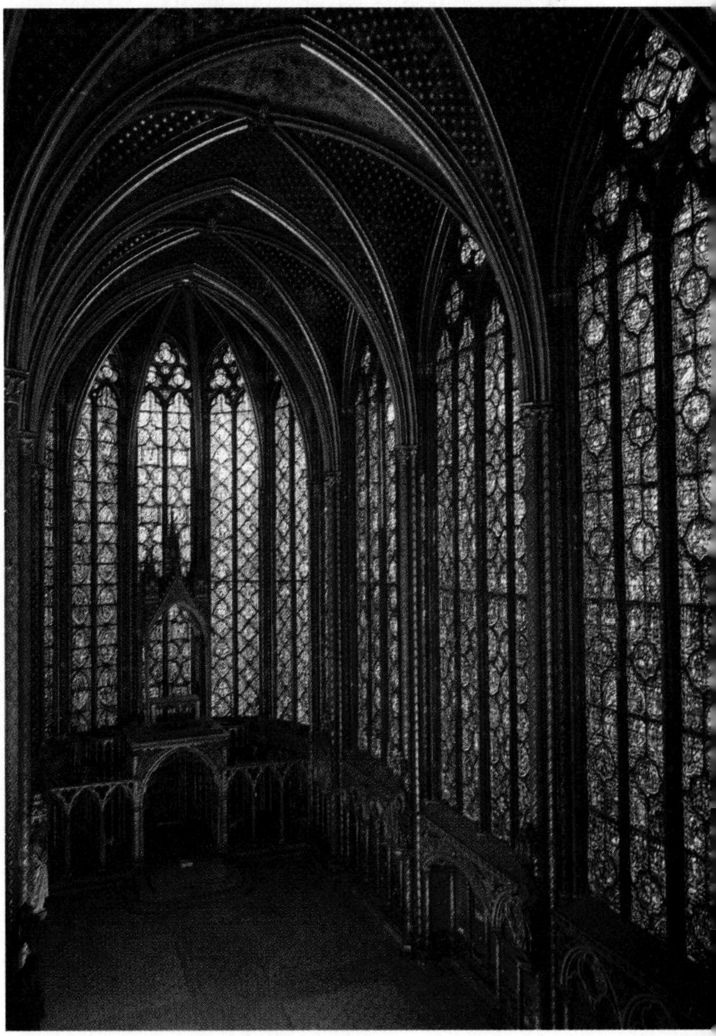

The most distinctive aspect of the Gothic style is its use of light in a manner unique in the history of architecture. Once within the church, the visitor has entered a realm defined and infused by a warm, colored glow. In Christian worship light is one of the most ancient, common, and versatile symbols. It suggests to the worshiper mystical illumination, spiritual beauty, grace, and divinity itself.

The impressions rendered by the architecture and the stained glass were further developed by the performance of the sacred liturgy. Here music was also enlisted to convey the sense of an intricate and sublime harmony in God's care of the world. Paris in the thirteenth century witnessed a marked development of polyphonic music; the choirmasters seem to have sought a musical style that would parallel the complexity and the harmony of the surrounding cathedral. Through architecture, sculpture, and music, the believer was encouraged to feel a universe permeated with the presence of God.

DANTE

Literary output in most vernacular languages grew continuously more abundant during the thirteenth century, except in English, which was retarded in its development by the continued dominance of a French-speaking aristocracy. Of several masterpieces the one that best summarizes the culture of the age is the *Comedy* of Dante Alighieri.

Dante was born in Florence in 1265. Little is known of his education, but he seems to have been immersed in scholarship. The *Comedy* is one of the most learned, and hence most difficult, poems of world literature.

Two experiences in Dante's life profoundly influenced his attitudes and are reflected in his works. In 1274, when (as he himself affirms) he was only nine years old, he fell deeply in love with a young girl named Beatrice. Much mystery surrounds her, but she seems to have been Beatrice Portinari, who later married into a prominent family and died in 1290. Dante could have seen her only rarely; we do not know if she ever returned his love. Still, in his youthful adoration of Beatrice he seems to have attained that sense of harmony and joy that the troubadours considered to be the great reward of lovers. In 1302 an experience of a much different sort shattered his life. For political reasons he was exiled from Florence. He spent the remaining years of his life wandering from city to city, a disillusioned, even bitter man. He died in 1321 and was buried at Ravenna.

The Comedy Dante composed his masterpiece from 1313 to 1321. He called it a *commedia* in conformity with the Classical notion that a happy ending made any story, no matter how serious, a comedy; the adjective *divine* was added to its title only after his death. The poem is divided into three parts, which describe the poet's journey through hell, purgatory, and heaven.

The poem opens with Dante "in the middle of the way of this our life." An aging man, he has grown confused and disillusioned; he is lost in a "dark forest" of doubt, harassed by wild animals, symbols of his own untamed passions. The theme of the poem is essentially Dante's rediscovery of a former sense of harmony and joy. Leading him back to his lost peace are two guides. The first, Virgil, who represents human reason, conducts Dante through hell and then up the seven-storied mountain of purgatory to the earthly paradise, the vanished Eden, at its summit. In hell Dante encounters people who have chosen as their supreme goal in life something other than the love of God—riches, pleasure, fame, or power. Virgil shows Dante that the good life cannot be built upon such selfish choices. Reason, in other words, can enable humans to avoid the pitfalls of egoistic, material existence. In fact reason can accomplish even more than that; for, as embodied by Virgil, it guides Dante through purgatory and shows him how to acquire the natural virtues that are the foundations of the earthly paradise—a full and peaceful earthly existence.

In the dignity and power given to Virgil, Dante shares the high regard for human reason characteristic of the thirteenth century. However, reason can take humans only so far. To enter heaven, Dante needs a new guide—Beatrice herself, representative of supernatural revelation and grace. She takes the poet through the heavenly spheres into the presence of God, "in Whom is our peace." The peace and joy of the heavenly court set the dominant mood at the poem's con-

▶ **A detail from a fourteenth-century manuscript copy of Dante's *Divine Comedy* illustrates the section of hell reserved for usurers. The Church regarded usury as one of man's many earthly sins that condemn him in the eyes of God. Dante appears four times in this scene, on three occasions accompanied by his bearded guide, Virgil.**

clusion, in contrast to the confusion and violence of the dark forest with which it had opened.

Like many other literary masterpieces, the *Comedy* has several dimensions of meaning. On a personal level, it summarizes the experiences of Dante's own life; it affirms that the youthful idealism and joy he had once so easily found were not proved false by age and bitter exile. The poem further reflects the great cultural issues that challenged his contemporaries—the relations between reason and faith, nature and grace, human power and the divine will. Dante, like Aquinas, was trying to combine two opposed views of human nature and its abilities to shape its own destiny. One, rooted in the very optimism of the twelfth and thirteenth centuries and in the more distant Classical heritage, affirmed that human beings were masters of themselves and the world. The other, grounded in the Judeo-Christian tradition, saw them, fundamentally, as lost children in a vale of tears. Both views had helped support human life and were therefore worth preserving. Dante's majestic panorama summarizes not only the medieval vision of the universe but also his estimation of what it meant to live a truly wise, truly happy, truly human life.

In the thirteenth century medieval civilization attained a new stability. Large-scale manufacture, long-range commercial exchanges, and sophisticated business practices gave the economy a dynamic aura. In political life, feudal governments consolidated and clarified their constitutional procedures, and parliaments and representative assemblies came to play a recognized role in the processes of government. Confronted with heresies that threatened its unity and dominance, the Church responded in part with crusades and the Inquisition, ultimately to its own detriment. At the same time, orthodox religion enjoyed an authentic spiritual renewal, of which Francis of Assisi was the chief inspiration. The papacy energetically sought to lead the Western princes as their guide and conscience, but secular entanglements and fiscal problems threatened and gradually diluted its moral authority.

In cultural life this was a period of magnificent synthesis. The masterpieces of the age aimed at bringing together all parts of the medieval heritage into an ordered whole that would offer people a comprehensive understanding of the universe and a wise formula for living.

Medieval society in the thirteenth century seemed close to resolving its principal problems, whether economic, political, or cultural. In fact, however, the relative prosperity and peace, along with the institutional stability and intellectual synthesis, were not to survive much beyond the year 1300. In the fourteenth century a new era of turmoil dawned for the medieval world. The close of the Middle Ages was a period of spectacular disasters and profound changes, which greatly altered the character of the civilizations in both Eastern and Western Europe.

Recommended Reading

Sources

*Alighieri, Dante. *The Divine Comedy.* Mark Musa (tr.).

Aquinas, Thomas. *Basic Writings.* Anton C. Pegis (ed.). 1945.

*Brown, Raphael (ed. and tr.). *The Little Flowers of St. Francis.* 1971. Legends collected in the early fourteenth century exemplifying the style of Franciscan piety.

Studies

*Abulafia, David. *Frederick II: A Medieval Emperor.* 1988.

Barraclough, Geoffrey. *The Origins of Modern Germany.* 1963. Classic interpretation of medieval German history.

*Bennett, Judith M. *Women in the Medieval English Countryside.* 1987. An assessment of women's changing status.

Bisson, Thomas. *Medieval Representative Institutions.* 1973. Introductory essays.

Boase, T. S. R. *Boniface VIII.* 1933. Standard biography of the controversial pope.

*Copleston, Frederick. *Aquinas.* 1955.

d'Avery, D. L. *The Preaching of the Friars: Sermons Diffused from Paris before 1300.* 1985.

Duby, Georges. *William Marshal: The Flower of Chivalry.* 1985. Sensitive biography of an Anglo-Norman lord.

———, and Philippe Aries (eds.). *A History of Private Life* (Vol. 2). 1988.

Epstein, Steven. *Wage Labor and Guilds in Medieval Europe.* 1991.

*Frisch, Teresa G. *Gothic Art, 1140–1450: Sources and Documents.* 1987.

*Hanawalt, Barbara. *The Ties That Bound: Peasant Families in Medieval England.* 1986. Peasant life sympathetically viewed.

*Heer, Friedrich. *The Medieval World: Europe, 1100–1350.* 1964. From an open to a closed medieval society.

*Herlihy, David. *Opera Muliebria: Women and Work in Medieval Europe.* 1990.

Hillgarth, J. M. *The Spanish Kingdoms, 1250–1516* (2 vols.). 1978. Spanish history across the Late Middle Ages.

Holt, J. C. *Magna Carta.* 1965. Gives useful guidance to an extensive literature.

Le Goff, Jacques. *Time, Work and Culture in the Middle Ages.* Arthur Goldhammer (tr.). 1980. Medieval culture studied through anthropological methods.

Little, Lester. *Religious Poverty and the Profit Economy in Medieval Europe.* 1978. Examines changes in economic attitudes in the thirteenth century.

Lyon, Bryce. *A Constitutional and Legal History of Medieval England* (2nd ed.). 1980.

*Available in paperback.

Mundy, John H. *Europe in the High Middle Ages.* 1973. A useful general survey.

Peters, Edward M. *Inquisition.* 1988. The Inquisition in fact and imagination.

Powicke, F. M. *The Thirteenth Century, 1216–1307.* 1953. Basic survey of English political history.

Reynolds, Susan. *Kingdoms and Communities in Western Europe 900–1300.* 1984. Medieval associations and their bondings.

*Strayer, Joseph R. *On the Medieval Origins of the Modern State.* 1973.

Von Simson, Otto. *The Gothic Cathedral: Origins of Gothic Architecture and the Medieval Concept of Order.* 1962. Interprets Gothic style primarily in terms of its use of light.

*Weinstein, Donald, and Rudolph M. Bell. *Saints and Society.* 1982. Statistical study of medieval saints.

WOMEN ASSISTING KNIGHTS
This manuscript illustration makes it clear that women took part in battles alongside the male crusaders. Here they wield picks and axes, and throw stones in a siege. Moreover, it is clear that the woman in the foreground, just behind the ladder, who does not cower behind a shield like the man on the ladder, is about to be killed by an arrow.

CHAPTER TEN

THE CRUSADES AND EASTERN EUROPE

THE peoples of Western Europe had remained fairly cut off from the East during the Early Middle Ages, an isolation that added to their economic and cultural stagnation. After the year 1000, however, the isolation began to break down. Western pilgrims and crusaders in large numbers visited the Christian holy places in the East and for some two centuries maintained the Latin Kingdom of Jerusalem, a colony in Palestine. Western merchants established contact with the principal ports of the eastern Mediterranean and Black seas. A vigorous trade developed across the Mediterranean, and Westerners once more came to enjoy the spices and other products of the East. In the thirteenth century some missionaries and merchants penetrated into central Asia, and a few traveled as far as China. These greatly enlarged geographic horizons made Europeans aware that rich and brilliant civilizations existed beyond their borders, and Westerners entered into intense military competition, close trade relations, and fruitful cultural exchanges with their Eastern neighbors. The East in these centuries was itself in a state of flux, as the three states that dominated the region in the Early Middle Ages—the Byzantine Empire, the Arab Caliphate, and Kievan Rus—gave way to new regimes. By the 1400s a new force, the Ottoman Empire, dominated the land bridge between Europe and Asia and presented the West with a formidable military challenge. As the Ottomans rose, the spiritual and cultural heritage of both Byzantium and Kievan Rus passed to a new Russian state that had its capital at Moscow. The contacts, the rivalries, and the economic and cultural exchanges that resulted from these changes have shaped the history of the peoples in these areas ever since.

I. The Crusades

In the eleventh century the Western peoples launched a series of armed expeditions to the East in an effort to free the Holy Land from Islamic rule. Known as crusades (because the armies' banner was a cross), these expeditions stimulated trade, encouraged the growth of towns, and contributed to the establishment of a stable political order in the West. But they could also be seen as costly failures, draining resources for what proved to be a temporary foothold in Palestine; they worsened relations not only with the Muslims but also with Eastern Christians; and they set in motion one of Europe's grimmest traditions when crusading zeal stimulated dreadful riots and pogroms against those most accessible infidels, the Jews.

Above all, the crusades reveal more dramatically than any other event the spirit of Western society in the eleventh and twelfth centuries: its energy, brash self-confidence, compelling faith, and frequent bigotry. At the same time as the expeditions helped acquaint the Western peoples with ideas and techniques of civilizations more sophisticated than their own, they also proved to be the initial phase in the expansion of the West—the massive exportation of European people and skills beyond the confines of their narrow continent.

ORIGINS

The origins of the crusades must be sought in a double set of circumstances: social and religious movements in the West and the political situation in the East. In the Christian West a favorite form of religious exercise was the pilgrimage, a personal visit to a place made holy through the life of Christ or one of his saints or the presence of a sacred relic. Common in the West since the fourth century, pilgrimages gained in popularity during the eleventh century as Europe experienced religious revival and reform. Bands of pilgrims, sometimes numbering in the thousands, set forth to visit the places sacred to their religion, and of these destinations, Palestine was the most holy.

The Turks This pilgrim traffic was threatened when the Seljuk Turks, Muslim nomads, overran much of the Middle East in the eleventh century. It does not appear that the Seljuks consciously sought to prevent the pilgrims from reaching Palestine, but they did impose numerous taxes and tolls on them, and many Christians became angry at the domination of the holy places of Palestine by a strong, aggressive Islamic power.

Even more daunting to the West was the possibility that the Christian empire of Byzantium would also be overrun. The Seljuks had crushed a Byzantine army at the Battle of Manzikert in 1071, and the road to Constantinople seemed wide open. The fall of Byzantium would remove the traditional barrier to Islamic advance toward the West and would be a major disaster for the Christian world. When, therefore, a delegation from the emperor of Byzantium requested the help of Pope Urban II in 1095, he resolved to appeal to the Western knights and princes to go to the aid of their fellow Christians in the East. Social and religious conditions in Europe helped ensure that Urban's summons would evoke a powerful response.

▸ CHRIST LEADING CRUSADERS
This fourteenth-century illustration from a manuscript on the Apocalypse captures an assumption that was common to all the crusaders—that their expedition was being led by Christ himself. On his magnificent charger, he leads into battle the troops carrying his symbol, the cross.

THE MOTIVES OF THE CRUSADERS

Religion The crusades were viewed by those who participated in them primarily as acts of religious devotion. Even before Urban made his appeal, the idea had gained currency in the West that God would reward those who fought in a good cause, that is, that wars could be holy. The crusaders also shared the beliefs expressed in the movement for Church reform that the good ought not simply to endure the evils of the world but should attempt to correct them. This active, confident spirit contrasted strongly with the resignation to evil and the withdrawal from the world recommended by most Christian writers of the Early Middle Ages.

► **MAKING COATS OF CHAIN MAIL**
This depiction of a craftsman making chain mail suggests the high skills and hard labor that were needed to bend the metal into elaborate shapes. Armor made of chain mail allowed the knight far greater freedom of movement, but it could be penetrated by the sharp thrust of a sword or arrow.

Expansion Social and economic motivations also contributed to the expeditions. The age of mass pilgrimages and crusades, from about 1050 to 1250, corresponds to the period in medieval history when the European population was growing most rapidly. The crusades may be considered one further example of the expanding Western frontier, similar in motivation and character to the Spanish *Reconquista* or the German push to the East. Of course, the crusades differed in at least one significant way from these other ventures. They were almost exclusively military expeditions of Europe's warrior classes; peasants did not settle in Palestine in significant numbers, as they did in the lands of Eastern Europe and in the Iberian peninsula.

Knighthood The younger sons of European knights were particularly sensitive to the pressures being created by an expanding population. Parental lands were often not large enough to provide support for younger sons. Pope Urban apparently believed that this land shortage created social problems, for he is reported to have told the knights of France in 1095: "This land which you inhabit is too narrow for your large population; nor does it abound in wealth; and it provides hardly enough food for those who farm it. This is the reason that you murder and consume one another." An additional problem was that knights were educated to do little but fight, and it was natural for them to place their chief hopes for wealth, honor, and social advance in war. The growth of the feudal principalities, the efforts of the Church to restrict fighting among Christians, and the resultant slow pacification of European society threatened to leave the knights poor, unhonored, and unemployed. "You should shudder, brethren," Urban is also reported to have told the knights, "you should shudder at perpetrating violence against Christians; it is less wicked to turn your sword against Muslims. . . . The possessions of the enemy will also fall to you, since you will claim their treasures as plunder."

War against the infidel thus offered constructive employment for Europe's surplus and often violent population of knights. In the following century St. Bernard of Clairvaux, whose preaching inspired thousands to join the Second Crusade, frankly affirmed that all but a few of the knights on the crusades were "criminals and sinners, ravishers and the sacrilegious, murderers, perjurers, and adulterers." To have them crusading in the East therefore brought a double benefit. As Bernard remarked, "Their departure makes their own people happy, and their arrival cheers those whom they are hastening to help. They aid both groups, not only by protecting the one but also by not oppressing the other." The crusades were thus, in one respect, a violent means of draining the violence from medieval life.

THE FIRST CRUSADE

In 1095, before a Church council assembled at Clermont in southern France, Pope Urban II urged the knights at the meeting to go to the East to aid their endangered Christian brothers and to free the Holy Land from its blasphemous masters. His sermon was intended for the upper classes, but its plea had sensational results at all levels of Western society. In northern France and the Rhineland influential preachers were soon rousing the people and organizing movements that historians now call the Popular Crusade. Bands of peasants and the poor (together with a few knights) set out for the East, miserably equipped and lacking competent leaders. They marched down the Rhine valley, attacking Jews as they went, and on through Hungary and Bulgaria to Constantinople. Emperor Alexius of Byzantium, who could only have been shocked at the sight

Map 10.1 THE EASTERN MEDITERRANEAN DURING THE EARLY CRUSADES
The effects of the first crusades on the Middle East can be seen in the territory the crusader kingdoms conquered and the expansion of the Byzantine Empire at the expense of the Seljuk Turks. Both of these newly Christian areas, won in the early 1100s, were to be regained by Muslims in the late 1100s and 1200s.

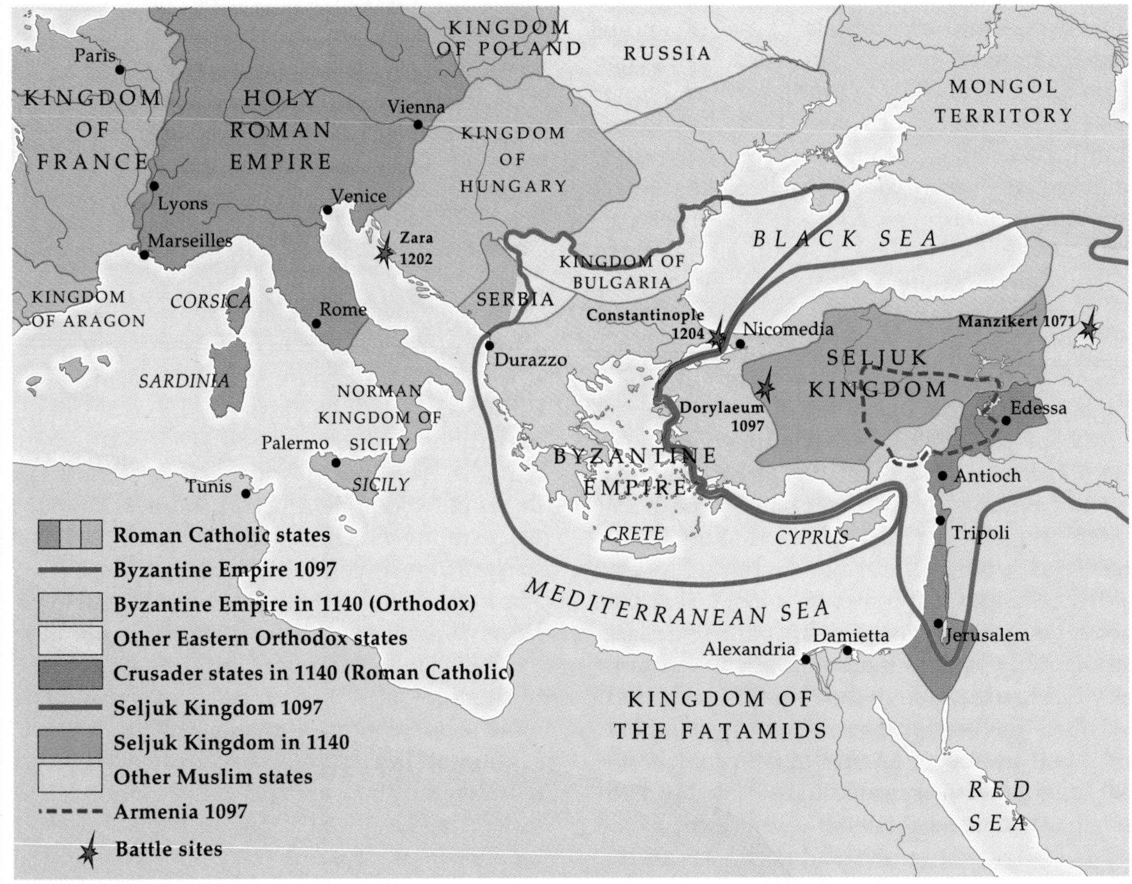

▸ **GODFREY APPROACHING THE GATE AT CONSTANTINOPLE**
This miniature illustration of a history of the expedition by one of its participants, William of Tyre, shows Godfrey of Bouillon, the leader of the First Crusade, entering Constantinople on his way to Jerusalem. In the lower half of the picture he approaches the city, and in the upper half he climbs a ladder over the walls.

of this hapless army, gave them transport across the Bosporus. The Turks at once cut them to pieces.

Far better organized was the official First Crusade, which was led by nobles. Robert of Normandy, son of William the Conqueror, headed a northern French army; Godfrey of Bouillon, his brother Baldwin, and Robert of Flanders commanded an army of Lotharingians and Flemings; Raymond of Toulouse led the men of Languedoc; and Bohemond of Taranto and his nephew Tancred marshaled the Normans of southern Italy. These four armies moved by various overland and sea routes to Constantinople (see Map 10.1) and arrived there in 1096 and 1097.

The Byzantines Although the leaders of the First Crusade had intended to conquer lands in the East in their own name, Emperor Alexius demanded from them an oath of fealty in exchange for provisioning the armies as they marched to Palestine. Grudgingly, they agreed, promising to regard the emperor as the overlord of any lands they might reconquer from the Turks. Subsequently, both the emperor and the Western leaders accused each other of violating the terms of the oath. The failure of the crusaders and the Byzantines to find a firm basis for cooperating ultimately weakened, although it did not defeat, the enterprise.

Victories In 1097 the crusaders entered the Seljuk Sultanate of Rum, achieving their first major victory at Dorylaeum. Baldwin then separated his troops from the main body and conquered Edessa, where he established the first crusader state in the East. The decisive victory of the First Crusade came in the battle for the port city of Antioch. After that, the road to Jerusalem was open. On July 15, 1099, the crusaders stormed the Holy City and slaughtered its population of Muslims, Jews, and eastern Christians.

Besides a high level of organizational skill and their own daring, the Westerners had a critical advantage because of the tumultuous political situation in the East. For all the brilliance of Islamic civilization, its leadership was in disarray. The rulers of the Holy Land, the Seljuk Turks, had only recently risen to power. They had not yet consolidated their rule and were still fighting

▸ **THE PILLAGE OF JERUSALEM BY ANTIOCHUS**
Although the crusades were conducted in the name of Christ, the behavior of their armies was no different from that of soldiers throughout the ages. In this scene in front of Jerusalem from a fifteenth-century manuscript, the commander Antiochus watches as his troops pile up the spoils they have looted from the Holy City.

the Fatimids, the ruling dynasty of Egypt, over the possession of Palestine. In addition, the ancient schisms among Islamic religious sects continued to divide and weaken the community. The inability of Muslims to present a united front against the crusaders was probably the decisive reason for the final success of the First Crusade.

THE KINGDOM OF JERUSALEM

The crusaders now had the problem of organizing a government for their conquered territory and its population of Muslims and Eastern and Western Christians. They chose as ruler Godfrey of Bouillon, but he died in 1100, and his younger brother Baldwin, the conqueror of Edessa, succeeded him.

Baldwin set out to strengthen his realm through the application of feudal concepts and institutions. He kept direct dominion over Jerusalem and its surroundings, including a stretch of coast extending from Gaza to Beirut. To the north, three fiefs—the County of Tripoli, the Principality of Antioch, and the County of Edessa—were made subject to his suzerainty (see Map 10.2). Although King Baldwin and his successors were able to exert a respectable measure of authority over all these lands, profound weaknesses undermined their power. For one thing, the kings were never able to push their frontiers to an easily defensible, strategic border, such as the Lebanese Mountains. Furthermore, their administration remained critically dependent on a constant influx of men and money from the European homeland. Many knights and pilgrims came, but relatively few stayed as permanent settlers. The Westerners constituted a foreign aristocracy, small in number and set over a people of largely

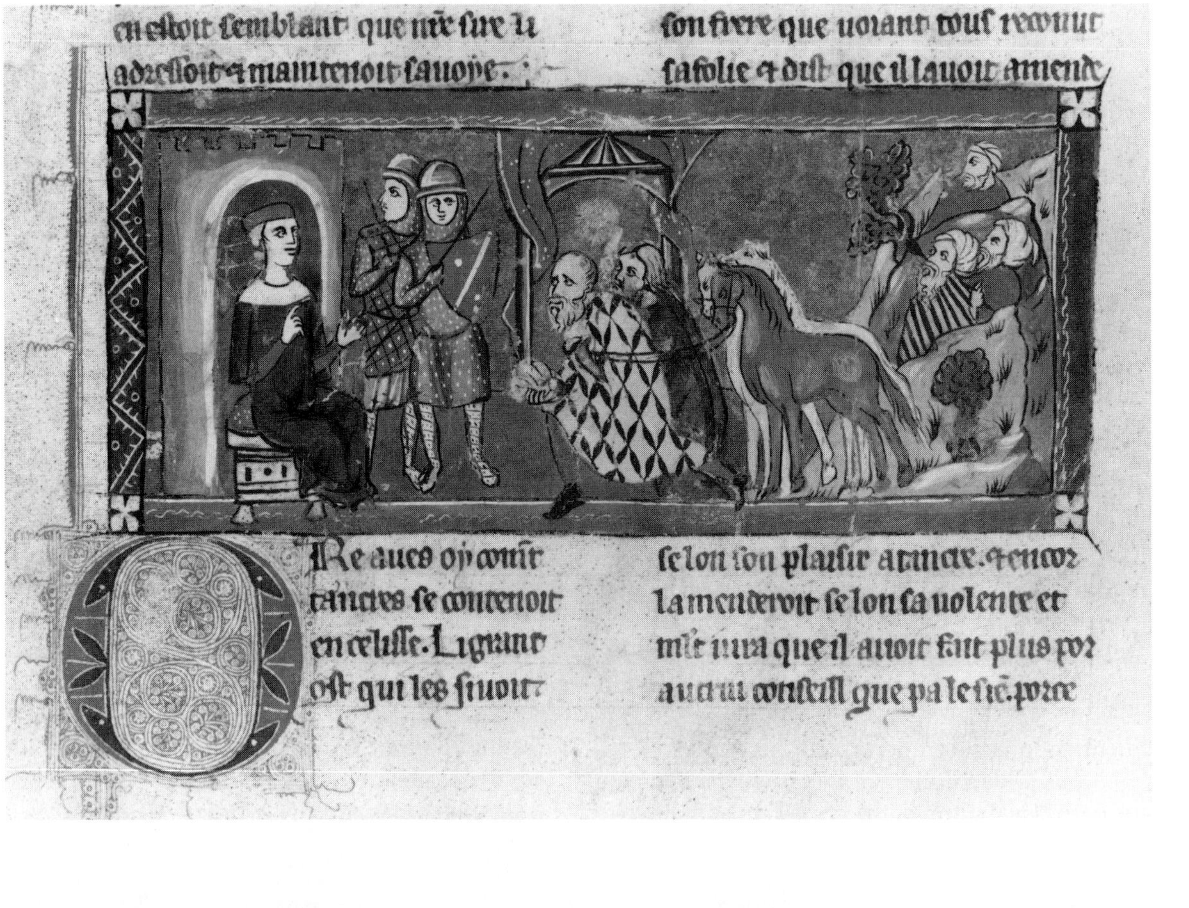

▸ **CITIZENS OF EDESSA IN HOMAGE TO BALDWIN I**
To emphasize the crusaders' triumph, this manuscript illustration shows Baldwin I, who captured Edessa in 1099, asserting his authority over the conquered Muslims. He sits on the left, with his knights next to him, and receives the homage and tribute of his new subjects.

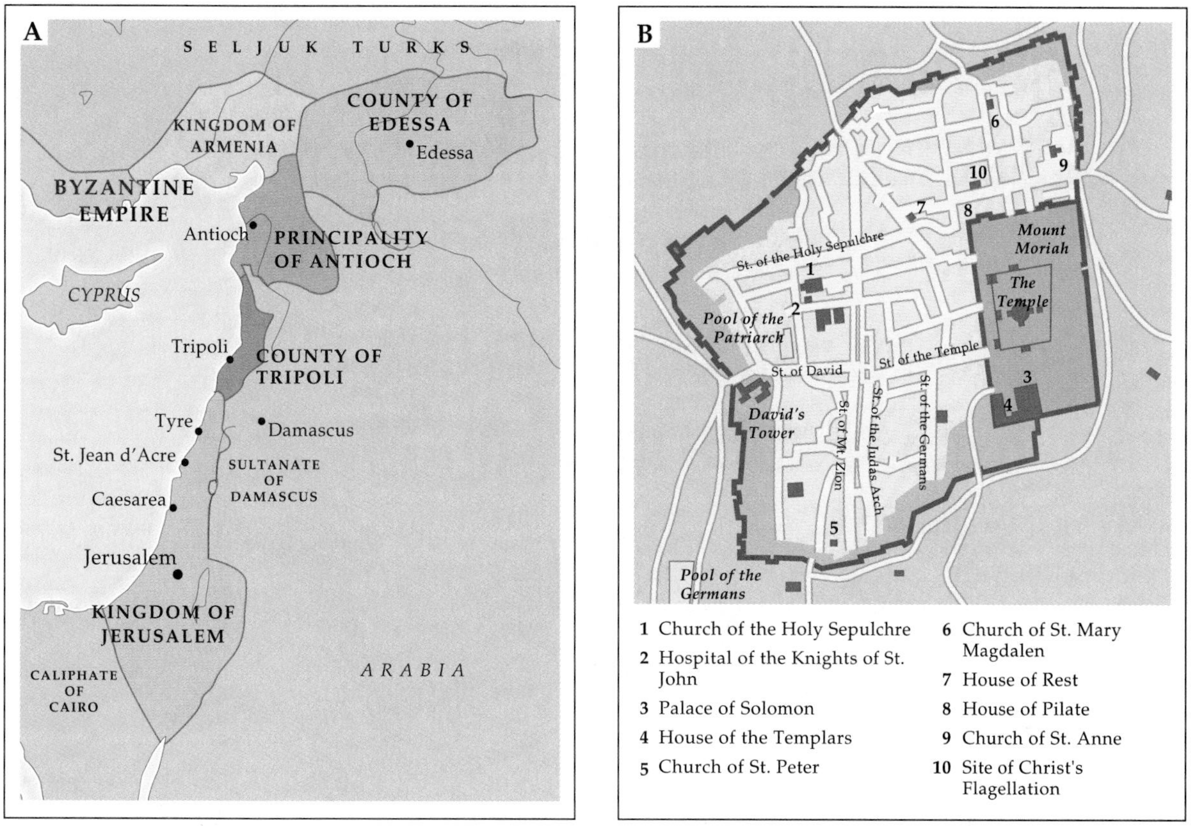

Map 10.2 **The Crusader States at Their Height**
For all the territory they covered, the crusader states proved vulnerable to reconquest from the East (A). Edessa was lost in less than 50 years, and even the fortified city of Jerusalem (B), captured in 1099, remained in Christian hands only until 1187.

different faith, culture, and sympathies. The wonder is not that the crusader states ultimately fell but that some of their outposts survived on the mainland of Asia Minor for nearly 200 years.

THE LATER CRUSADES

The Second Crusade Although historians have traditionally assigned numbers to the later crusades, these expeditions were merely momentary swells in the steady current of Western people and treasures to and from the Middle East. The recapture of the city of Edessa by the Muslims in 1144 gave rise to the Second Crusade (1147–1149). Two armies, led by King Louis VII of France and Emperor Conrad III of Germany, set out to capture Damascus to give the Kingdom of Jerusalem a more defensible frontier. However, they were soon forced to retreat ignominiously before superior Muslim forces.

The Third Crusade The capture of Jerusalem by the Muslim chief Saladin prompted the Third Crusade (1189–1192), which was the climax of the crusading movement and its greatest disappointment. Emperor Frederick Barbarossa and kings Philip II of France and Richard I, the Lion-Hearted, of England all marched to the East. (Frederick drowned while crossing through Asia Minor, and most of his forces turned back.) Although the crusaders captured Acre, the Third Crusade ended in a stalemate. The Kingdom of Jerusalem remained limited to a narrow strip of the coast from Acre to Jaffa, but unarmed Christian pilgrims were given the right to visit Jerusalem. These were paltry gains from so grand an effort.

In the thirteenth century the crusades lost their appeal to Western knights, though Louis IX of

▸ KNIGHTS IN COMBAT
This contemporaneous manuscript illustration is a splendid depiction, full of motion and action, of two knights jousting. The figure on the left is thought to be Richard the Lion-Hearted, battling with Saladin himself.

France did lead two futile expeditions to North Africa. The population expansion in Europe, which had helped lend strength to the earlier crusades, was already leveling off. Moreover, many Europeans were shocked when the popes tried to direct crusades against the Albigensian heretics in southern France and against political enemies such as Frederick II of Hohenstaufen. With dwindling support from the West, the Christians in 1291 lost Acre, their last outpost in Palestine. Repeatedly during the Late Middle Ages the popes attempted to organize crusades; many knights and princes vowed to participate, and some traveled east, but none gained a major victory.

RESULTS OF THE CRUSADES

In terms of their main professed goal, the crusaders gained a partial success but not a permanent one: They had Jerusalem for nearly a century and maintained outposts on the Palestinian coast for nearly two centuries. Meanwhile, Christian pilgrims in large numbers were able to visit the holy places in Palestine in moderate safety. Even after the loss of Acre the Westerners continued to hold Cyprus and Greece, conquered during the early crusades. When the Ottoman Turks, successors to the Seljuks, finally seized these last crusader territories, the Western peoples had already found new routes to the Far East and were in the midst of a far broader overseas expansion. The crusades thus strengthened the security of the West by slowing the Turkish advance across the Mediterranean Sea and into Europe.

Warfare The crusades exerted a powerful influence on military techniques. After their initial invasions the crusaders waged a largely defensive war, and they became particularly skilled in the art of constructing castles. The numerous remains of crusader castles in nearly all the Eastern lands reflect these advances in such features as the overhanging tower parapets, from which oil or missiles could be rained down on attackers, and in the angular castle entranceways that prevented the enemy from shooting directly at the gates. Islamic castles show a similar evolution toward a more advanced military design.

The foes continually copied each other, and the Ottoman Turks in particular adopted many Western technical skills. By the fifteenth century the Ottomans, originally landlocked nomads, had begun to build a fleet and challenge Western maritime supremacy in the eastern Mediterranean Sea. They also learned from Western technicians the new arts of firearms, specifically cannons, without which they probably could not have conquered their vast empire.

Finance The crusades presented enormous, unprecedented problems of financing and logistical support, and therefore they exerted a major stimulus on the growth of financial and governmental institutions in the West. In the early crusades each knight or soldier had usually provided his own support. He brought money with him (often acquired by selling or mortgaging his estates) and purchased supplies from the natives of the lands through which he marched. He replenished his funds through booty or gifts from his lord and eventually through estates granted him in Palestine. But as the crusader wars became largely defensive in character, the opportunity for booty declined and the armies could no longer live off the land; support had to come primarily from Europe, thus requiring permanent institutional arrangements by which a constant flow of money (and men) could be directed from Europe into Palestine.

Traditional sources of revenue were inadequate, so both the popes and the princes began to impose direct taxes on their lands and subjects. In 1188, for example, the pope authorized, and the princes collected, the so-called Saladin tithe, a direct tax of 10 percent imposed on all clerical and lay revenues so as to finance the Third Crusade. (Previously, European governments had made little use of direct taxes because they were difficult to assess and collect.) The imposition of the Saladin tithe and subsequent direct taxes required new institutional methods for assessment, collecting the moneys, and transferring the funds to where they were most needed. The crusades, in other words, helped the fiscal institutions of the governments of the West come of age.

One other financial course adopted by the papacy had great importance for the future. The popes allowed those Europeans who were too old or too weak to participate in the crusades to gain the spiritual benefits of crusading through monetary contributions, in return for which they were promised an *indulgence*—that is, a remission of punishment due for their sins. This practice was subsequently to become a major target of Church reformers and remained a central issue until the Reformation of the 1500s.

MILITARY-RELIGIOUS ORDERS

Templars Soon after the First Crusade a new kind of institution, the military-religious order, was founded to offer armed escorts and safe lodgings to pilgrims on their way to Palestine. Eventually it assumed a major role in supplying the settlers in the East with services, goods, defense, and means of communication. The military-religious orders combined the dedication, discipline, and organizational experience of monasticism with the military purposes of the crusade. The first of three great orders to emerge from the crusades was the Knights of the Temple, or Templars, founded some time before 1120 by a group of French knights. The knights took the three monastic vows of poverty, chastity, and obedience and, like monks, lived together in their own convents or communities. The Templars assumed a major role in the maintenance of safe routes between Europe and the crusader states and in the defense of the Kingdom of Jerusalem. The order also transported and guarded moneys in support of the Eastern war, and thus became the most important banking institution of the age until its suppression by the pope in 1312.

Hospitalers The Knights of the Hospital of St. John of Jerusalem, or Hospitalers, founded about 1130, enjoyed an even longer history. Never as numerous or as wealthy as the Templars, they

▶ **Hospitalers in Rhodes**
This fifteenth-century manuscript depiction of the capture of the island of Rhodes commemorates an event in 1306, when the Hospitaler knights attacked this fortress from the neighboring island of Cyprus. Wearing their distinctive tunic with its white cross, the Hospitalers swarmed through Rhodes, which they were to control until it was conquered by the Ottomans in 1522.

still made a major contribution to the defense of the Kingdom of Jerusalem. With the fall of Acre the knights moved their headquarters to Cyprus, then to Rhodes, and finally to Malta. As the Knights of Malta, they ruled the island until 1798. This "sovereign order" of the Knights of Malta survives today as an exclusively philanthropic confraternity and is an important arm of papal charities throughout the world.

Teutonic Knights About 1190, German pilgrims organized the Teutonic Knights to defend the roads to Palestine. These knights later transferred their headquarters to Venice, then to Transylvania (in modern Romania), and finally, in 1229, to Prussia, where they became the armed vanguard of the German eastward expansion and conquered for themselves an extensive domain along the shores of the Baltic Sea. In 1525 the last grand master, Albert of Hohenzollern, adopted Lutheranism and secularized the order and its territories. The German state of Brandenburg-Prussia eventually absorbed the lands, and also something of the militant spirit, of these crusading knights. The long history of these orders illustrates how organizational and military skills first acquired in the crusading movement continued to affect European life over the subsequent centuries.

ECONOMY

Historians still cannot draw up an exact balance sheet that registers accurately the economic gains and losses of these holy expeditions. Certainly the crusades were costly in blood and treasure. To support its armies, Europe exported large quantities of precious metals; the spoils of war and commercial profits undoubtedly brought some moneys back, but probably not enough to recoup the losses. Nevertheless, the crusades seem to have had a powerful and beneficial impact on the European economy, mainly by forcing into circulation moneys and treasures that hitherto had been hoarded in the West. Although there are no exact figures, both the volume of money and the speed of its circulation in Europe seem to have increased dramatically during this period. The new abundance of money stimulated commercial exchange and business investments and helped revive the Western economy, though the crusades were less significant in this respect than such influences as population growth and the settlement of new lands in Europe.

Trade The crusades also enlivened trade with the East. After the First Crusade most of the large

Western armies went to Palestine by water, creating a lucrative business for the maritime cities of the Mediterranean Sea, especially in Italy. The Italians poured much of their profit from transporting and provisioning crusaders into commercial enterprises, and they established merchant colonies in many Eastern ports. Moreover, the crusades greatly strengthened the market for Eastern condiments in Europe. Knights and other pilgrims—who had become familiar with sugar, spices, and similar products in the East—continued to want them when they returned home, and they introduced them to their neighbors.

The Western demand for spices promoted commerce not only on the Mediterranean Sea but also between the Middle East and East Asia. Furthermore, it had an impact that went beyond the narrowly commercial. In the Late Middle Ages political disruptions in central Asia and the high taxes imposed by the Turks and Egyptians hampered trade with the East, but the call for Eastern products continued to be strong within Europe. This situation ensured rich rewards to the navigators and nations who discovered surer, cheaper ways to import spices and other Eastern commodities, and thus provided a direct incentive for the geographic explorations and discoveries of the 1400s and 1500s.

In familiarizing Europeans with many new products, the crusades helped raise the standard of living in the West, and this, in turn, intensified the pace of economic activity. From the eleventh century on, Europeans seem to have worked harder, partly perhaps to gain for themselves some of the products and the amenities of life they had observed in the East. New commodities altered the popular appreciation of what was essential for a good life and prompted Europeans to work more energetically to satisfy their newly raised expectations.

RELIGION AND LEARNING

The Church As acts of piety the crusades inevitably affected the organization and practice of religion, although it is all but impossible to distinguish their impact from that of many other forces at work in the West. Their initial success added to the prestige of the popes who sponsored them, just as their subsequent failures undermined faith in papal leadership. Ecclesiastical finances and even canon law were influenced, as the Church sought to extend economic support and legal protection to both the crusaders and the families they left behind.

Scholarship It is difficult to assess exactly the importance of the crusades to the intellectual life of Europe. In one area of knowledge, geography, they did make important contributions. Starting from the crusader principalities in the East, first missionaries and then merchants penetrated deep into central Asia, and by the early thirteenth century they had reached China. Their reports, especially the memoirs of the Venetian Marco Polo at the close of the thirteenth century, gave Europe abundant information about East Asia and helped inspire Western navigators to seek new ways to penetrate beyond Islamic lands.

In other fields of knowledge the crusades seem to have brought little enlightenment. Most crusaders were rough warriors who had little interest in the subtleties of Islamic learning (*see box*, p. 295). However, the failure of these warriors to absorb new ideas from foreign cultures does not fully measure the cultural debt that the medieval West owes to Islam. Particularly through contacts in Spain and Sicily, Westerners learned new skills (the making of paper, perhaps the use of the compass) and new ideas that influenced the development of courtly love and scientific, philosophical, and religious thought in Europe. But it may also be true that by fomenting hatred against the infidel the crusades made Europeans less receptive to foreign ideas.

In the intellectual field as in all others, then, the crusades did not radically alter the course of medieval history, either in Christian or in Islamic societies; but they did powerfully reinforce existing tendencies and accelerate the pace of change on almost every level of life. Through the crusades Europeans learned about the geography of distant lands, became highly motivated to establish permanent and profitable contact with them, and acquired some experience in the conquest and administration of overseas territories. Appropriately, the crusades may be regarded as the initial chapter in the expansion of Europe.

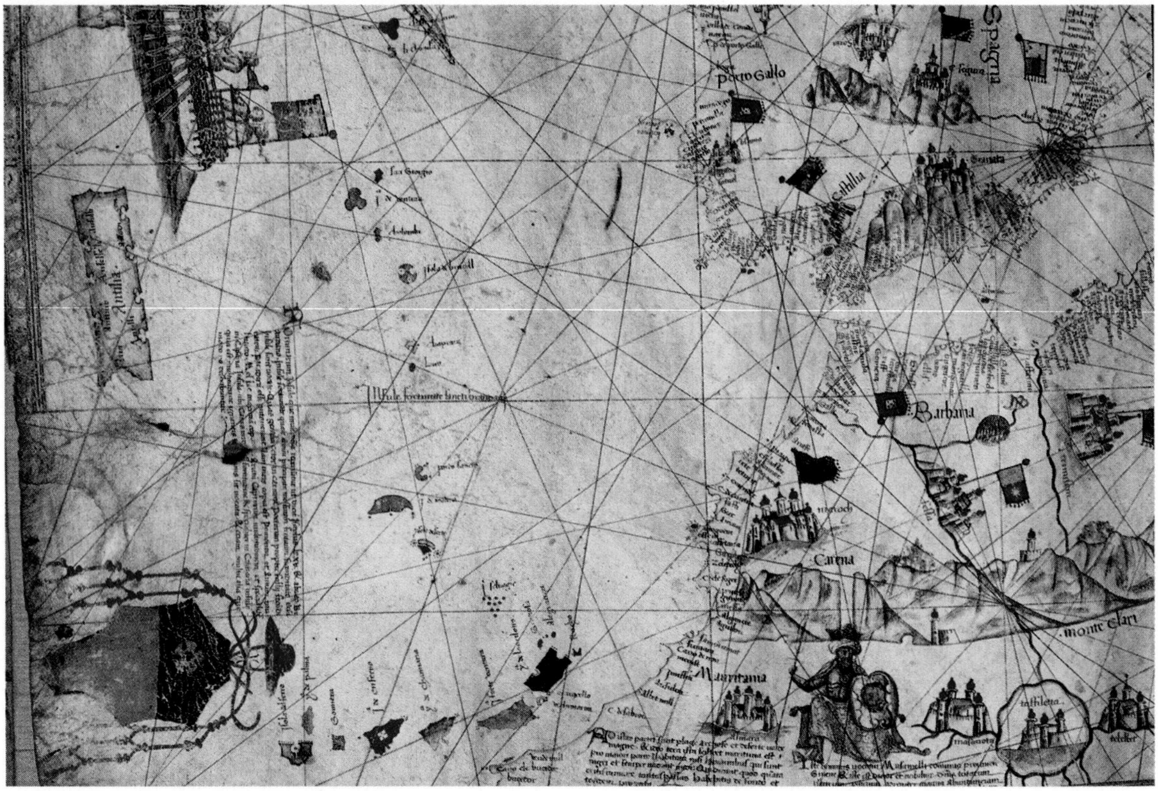

▸ **AN EARLY MAP OF THE WESTERN MEDITERRANEAN**
Cartography benefited as sea voyages multiplied, as Europeans gained increased knowledge of the world, and as they improved their skill in illustration. This map by the Italian cartographer Giovanni Benincasa describes in great detail the coasts of Portugal, Spain, and North Africa.

II. Byzantium and the Ascendancy of the Ottoman Empire

Although the Byzantine Empire survived its defeat by the Turks at Manzikert in 1071, from then until its demise in the mid-fifteenth century the empire's control was effective only in Greece, the Aegean, and the area around Constantinople. The Ottoman Turks eventually fell heir to Byzantium's former power and influence, and by the early sixteenth century they were the unquestioned masters of southeast Europe and the Middle East.

THE DECLINE OF BYZANTIUM

The beginning of the thirteenth century saw the launching of the Fourth Crusade and, unexpectedly, the subsequent fragmenting of the Byzantine Empire. The expedition was first planned as a campaign against Egypt, but the Venetian Doge Enrico Dandolo bargained the short-funded crusaders into capturing, in return for passage east, the Christian city of Zara in Dalmatia, which was opposing Venice in the Adriatic Sea. Then Alexius IV, a pretender to the Byzantine throne, hired the crusaders to seize Constantinople in return for money, military help in the Egyptian campaign, and the reunion of the Eastern and Western churches. The crusaders restored Alexius to the throne, but he could not honor his promises. In retaliation, the crusaders stormed and looted

Constantinople in 1204. They then divided the Byzantine Empire among themselves.

A Flemish nobleman assumed the office of emperor, although he ruled directly only a small parcel of territory surrounding Constantinople. The Venetians, by contrast, gained nearly half of all Byzantine possessions: This acquisition marked the foundation of a Venetian colonial empire that was to survive for centuries. Byzantine refugees from Constantinople set up an empire-in-exile, with its capital at Nicaea in Asia Minor. In 1261 the emperor of Nicaea, Michael III Paleologus, recaptured Constantinople, but neither he nor his successors could restore the shattered unity of the old Byzantine Empire.

The decline of the Byzantine Empire allowed the hitherto subject Balkan peoples to build independent kingdoms under Frankish princes and to aspire to dominate the area. First the Bulgarians in the thirteenth century, and then the Serbs in the fourteenth, created large Balkan empires. At the height of their powers these empires seemed destined to absorb the remnants of the Byzantine Empire, but by the fourteenth century it was the Ottoman Turks who presented the greatest menace to Byzantium.

Arabic and Frankish Medicine

Western accounts usually portray the Muslims whom the crusaders encountered in the Holy Land as barbarians. It is therefore instructive to read a view from the other side. Ousama Ibn Mounkidh, a twelfth-century Arab, here quotes the report of a doctor who had visited the crusader Franks; he sharply contrasts the medical expertise (and general humanity) of the two sides.

"They brought before me a knight with an abscess in his leg and a woman who was wasting away with a consumptive fever. I applied a little plaster to the knight; his abscess opened and took a turn for the better. The woman I forbade certain food and improved her condition.

"It was at this point that a Frankish doctor came up and said: 'This man is incapable of curing them.' Then, turning to the knight, he asked, 'Which do you prefer, to live with one leg or die with two?' 'I would rather live with one leg,' the knight answered. 'Bring a stalwart knight,' said the Frankish doctor, 'and a sharp hatchet.' Knight and hatchet soon appeared. I was present at the scene. The doctor stretched the patient's leg on the block of wood and then said to the knight, 'Strike off his leg with the hatchet; take it off at one blow.' Under my eyes the knight aimed a violent blow at it without cutting through the leg. He aimed another blow at the unfortunate man, as a result of which the marrow came from his leg and the knight died instantly.

"As for the woman, the doctor examined her and said, 'She is a woman in whose head there is a devil who has taken possession of her. Shave off her hair!' His prescription was carried out, and like her fellows, she began once again to eat garlic and mustard. Her consumption became worse. The doctor then said, 'It is because the devil has entered her head.' Taking a razor, the doctor cut open her head in the shape of a cross and scraped away the skin in the center so deeply that her very bones were showing. He then rubbed the head with salt. In her turn, the woman died instantly.

"After having asked them whether my services were still required, and receiving an answer in the negative, I came back, having learned from their medicine matters of which I had previously been ignorant."

Adapted from Brian Tierney, *The Middle Ages*, Vol. I: *The Sources of Medieval History*, 5th ed. (McGraw-Hill, 1992), p. 164.

▸ **VIEW OF VENICE**
This elaborate depiction of Venice in a fourteenth-century manuscript shows the buying and selling that was characteristic of the citizens of this commercial and maritime center. Particularly notable at the upper left are the four bronze horses that the Venetians brought back to the city after the capture and looting of Constantinople in 1204 during the Fourth Crusade. The horses were placed on the facade of the cathedral of St. Mark's, and they have remained there ever since.

THE FALL OF CONSTANTINOPLE

The Rising Threat Turkish communities and peoples had been assuming a large military and political role in the Middle East since the late tenth century. The Seljuk Turks had established the Sultanate of Rum in the late 1000s, and they dominated western Asia Minor for the next century and a half. This sultanate survived the attacks of the Western crusaders but was defeated by the far more formidable invasion of an Asiatic people, the Mongols, in the thirteenth century. The Ottoman Turks followed the Mongol invasions and took over the area of the Sultanate of Rum. They then established themselves at Gallipoli on the European side of the Straits in 1354, and soon their possessions completely surrounded Byzantine territory.

The Byzantine emperors, fearing the worst for their small and isolated realm, tried desperately but unsuccessfully to persuade the West that they needed military help against this threat. At the council of Florence in 1439 Emperor John VII even accepted reunion with Rome, largely on Roman terms, in return for aid, but he had no power to impose the reunion of the churches on his people; in fact, many Eastern Christians preferred Turkish rule to submission to the hated Westerners.

The Capture of the City The Ottomans were unable to mount a major campaign against Constantinople until 1453, when Sultan Mehmet II, the Conqueror, finally attacked by land and water. The city fell after a heroic resistance, and Emperor Constantine XI Paleologus himself, whose imperial lineage stretched back more than 1400 years to Augustus Caesar, died in this final agony of the Byzantine Empire.

The fall of Constantinople had very little military or economic effect on Europe and the Middle East. The Byzantine Empire had not been an effective barrier to Ottoman expansion for years, and Constantinople had dwindled commercially as well as politically. The shift to Turkish dominion did not, as historians once believed, substantially affect the flow of trade between the East and West. Nor did the Turkish conquest of the city provoke an exodus of Byzantine scholars and manuscripts to Italy. Scholars from the East, recognizing the decline and seemingly inevitable fall of the Byzantine Empire, had been emigrating to Italy since the late fourteenth century; the revival of Greek letters was well under way in the West by 1453.

Effects The impact of the fall was largely psychological; although hardly unexpected, it shocked the Christian world. The pope sought to launch a new crusade and received from the Western princes the usual promises but no armies. Venice waged a protracted and inconclusive war against the Turks (1463–1479). These military responses were less important in the long run, however, than the responses of Western merchants. The fall of Byzantium added to their incentives to find trade routes to East Asia that would bypass the Islamic waters of the Mediterranean.

Above all, the end of the Byzantine Empire had great symbolic importance for contemporaries and, perhaps even more, for later historians. In selecting Byzantium as his capital in 324, Constantine had founded a Christian Roman empire that could be considered the first authentically medieval state. For more than 1000 years this Christian Roman empire played a major political and cultural role in the history of both Eastern and Western peoples. In some respects, the years of its existence mark the span of the Middle Ages, and its passing symbolizes the end of an era.

► *Gentile Bellini*
MEHMET II
Mehmet II, here shown in a painting attributed to the Venetian artist Gentile Bellini, was the Conqueror of Constantinople in 1453.

EXPANSION OF THE OTTOMAN EMPIRE

The Ottomans took their name from Osman, or Othman (1290–1326), who founded a dynasty of sultans that survived for six centuries. Under Mehmet II (1451–1481), who from the start of his reign committed his government to a policy of conquest, the Ottomans began a century of expansion (*see box*, below). After the fall of Constantinople, which became his capital under the name of Istanbul (though the name was not

The Sultan Mehmet II

One of the first histories of the Ottomans by a westerner was written by an English schoolmaster named Richard Knolles and published in 1603. It is obvious that a great deal of research went into his work, which is marked by vivid portraits, such as this one of the Sultan Mehmet II, known as the Conqueror because of his capture of Constantinople, who had lived a century before Knolles wrote.

"He was of stature but low, square set, and strongly limbed; his complexion sallow and melancholy; his look and countenance stern, with his eyes piercing, and his nose so high and crooked that it almost touched his upper lip. He was of a very sharp and apprehending wit, learned especially in astronomy, and could speak the Greek, Latin, Arabic, Chaldee, and Persian tongues. He delighted much in reading of histories, and the lives of worthy men, especially the lives of Alexander the Great and Julius Caesar, whom he proposed to himself as examples to follow. He was of an exceeding courage, and a severe punisher of injustice. Men that excelled in any quality, he greatly favored and honorably entertained, as he did Gentile Bellini, a painter of Venice, whom he purposely caused to come from thence to Constantinople, to draw the lively counterfeit of himself (see plate above), for which he most bountifully rewarded him. He so severely punished theft, as that in his time all the ways were safe. He was altogether irreligious, and most perfidious, ambitious above measure, and in nothing more delighted than in blood: insomuch that he was responsible for the death of 800,000 men; craft, covetousness and dissimulation were in him accounted tolerable, in comparison of his greater vices. In his love was no assurance, and his least displeasure was death; so that he lived feared of all men, and died lamented of none."

Adapted by T. K. Rabb from Richard Knolles, *A Generall Historie of the Turkes,* as printed in John J. Saunders, (ed.), *The Muslim World on the Eve of Europe's Expansion* (Prentice-Hall, 1966), pp. 25–26.

officially adopted until 1930), Mehmet subjugated the Morea, Serbia, Bosnia, and parts of Herzegovina. He drove the Genoese from their Black Sea colonies, forced the khan of the Crimea to become his vassal, and fought a lengthy naval war with the Venetians. At his death the Ottomans were a power on land and sea, and the Black Sea had become a Turkish lake.

Early in the following century Turkish domination was extended over the heart of the Arab lands through the conquest of Syria, Egypt, and the western coast of the Arabian peninsula. (The Arabs did not again enjoy autonomy until the twentieth century.) With the conquest of the sacred cities of Mecca and Medina the sultan assumed the title of caliph, "successor of the Prophet," claiming to be Islam's supreme religious head as well as its mightiest sword.

Suleiman II The Ottoman Empire was brought to its height of power by Suleiman II, the Magnificent (1520–1566), who extended the empire in both the West and the East. In 1521 he took the citadel of Belgrade, which had hitherto blocked Turkish advance up the Balkan Peninsula toward Hungary, and the next year he forced the Hospitalers, after a six-month siege, to surrender the island of Rhodes, a loss that was a crippling blow to Western naval strength in the eastern Mediterranean.

Suleiman achieved his greatest victory by destroying the army of the king of Hungary at Mohacs in 1526 and taking over his kingdom. He then launched his most ambitious campaign, directed against Austria, the Christian state that now assumed chief responsibility for defending Europe's eastern frontiers. However, this effort, the high-water mark of Ottoman expansion into Europe, failed when Suleiman was unable to capture Vienna in 1529, and the frustrated sultan returned home, turning his attention toward the East. His armies overran Mesopotamia and completed the conquest of southern Arabia, and for the next two centuries the Ottoman Empire included all of southeastern Europe as well as the Middle East, Egypt, and Arabia (see Map 10.3).

Suleiman brought his empire fully into the diplomatic as well as the military struggles of Europe, taking shrewd advantage of the Europeans' rivalries. He hated Charles V who, as Holy Roman Emperor, similarly pretended to rule the world; and in 1525 he joined Francis I of France in an alliance directed against Charles, later negotiating a commercial treaty that further cemented cooperation between France and the Ottoman Empire. Through his alliance with France, Suleiman confronted Charles V with the possibility of a war on two fronts and prevented the formation of a common Christian crusade against himself, which the popes ceaselessly but vainly advocated.

OTTOMAN INSTITUTIONS

The Ottomans had expanded a small, landlocked community in western Asia Minor into a great empire. Several advantages account for this achievement, one of them being their geographic position. Set on the frontier between the Islamic and Christian worlds, the Ottomans could claim to be the chief warriors for the faith, and the resultant prestige won recruits and moral support from the more distant Islamic communities. Moreover, the Ottomans soon became a power in the political struggles of both Europe and the Middle East and were able to take advantage of favorable opportunities in both regions, even enlisting allies in one area to wage war in the other.

The intense rivalries among the Christian faiths also facilitated Ottoman expansion. Some Balkan Christians accepted papal supremacy, others adhered to the Eastern Orthodox traditions, and still others were regarded as heretics by both the Roman Catholics and the Orthodox. Often a Christian sect preferred the rule of the tolerant Ottomans to that of a rival Christian sect. In preserving peace among these dissident Christians, the Ottomans could serve as impartial referees, while Christians obviously could not.

Military and Administrative Skills A major advantage of the Ottomans in their remarkable ascendancy was their cultural heritage and treatment of the conquered. From their nomadic origins and their long experience as frontier fighters, they had preserved a strong military tradition. Their devout adherence to Islam, which

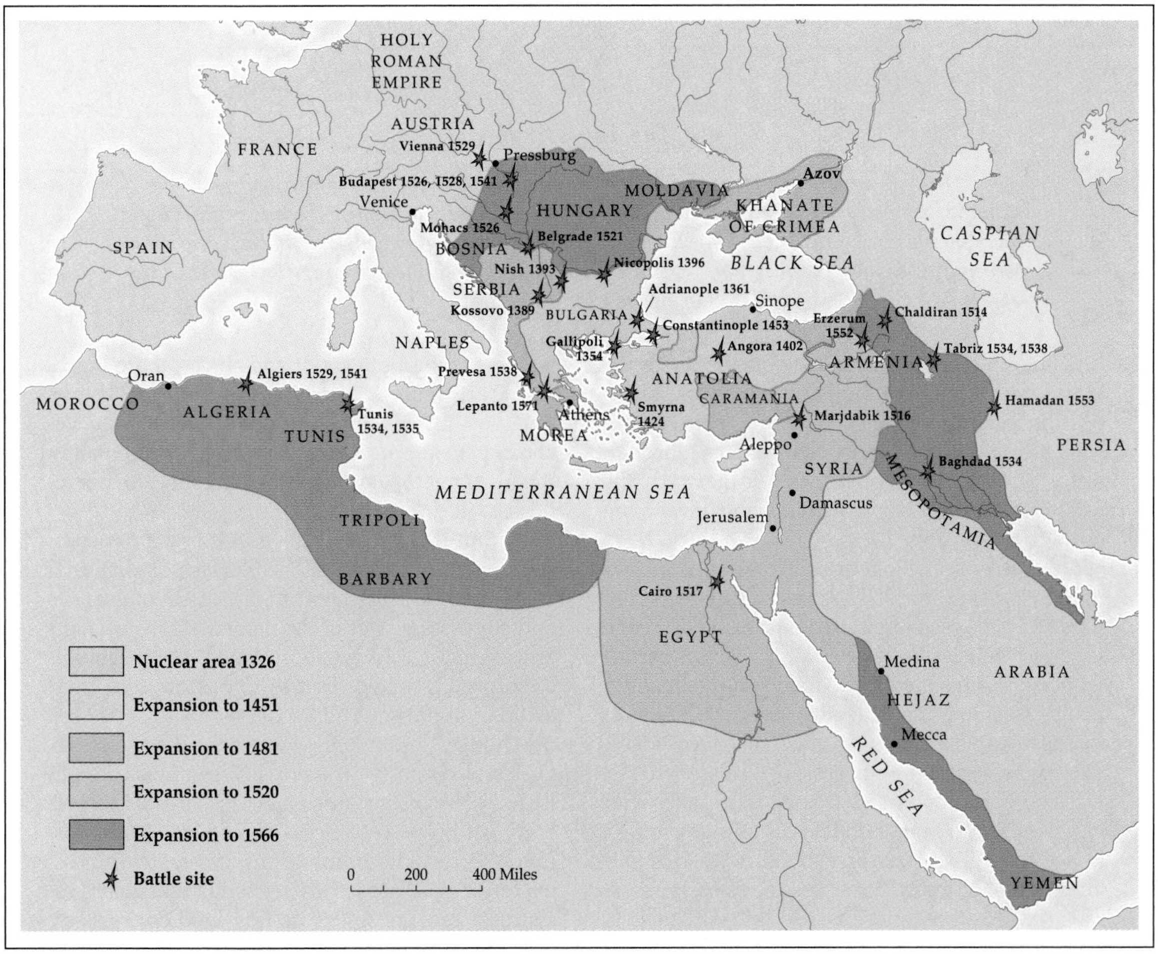

Map 10.3 THE OTTOMAN EMPIRE, 1300–1566
The stunning speed of Ottoman expansion, especially during the 1400s, raised the specter of a powerful enemy to the east that kept many Europeans fearful for centuries.

advocated holy wars against unbelievers, reinforced their aggressive tendencies; but they also showed a remarkable ability to organize conquered territories and gain the support, and to some degree even the loyalty, of the people they held in subjugation.

The Ottomans allowed the subject communities to live by their own laws under their own officials, requiring them only to pay taxes and supply men for the Ottoman army and administration. The conquests thus did not greatly disturb the society, economy, or culture of these communities, which were also able to play a role of considerable importance in the social and economic life of the Ottoman Empire. Trade, for example, which remained vigorous in the Black Sea and the eastern Mediterranean Sea, was still largely in the hands of Greeks, Armenians, and Jews. The Ottomans themselves remained aloof from commercial undertakings and confined their careers to government service and the army.

The Divan In the course of their enormous expansion the Ottoman sultans faced the formidable problem of developing military and administrative institutions strong enough to hold together their vast empire. Like all other medieval rulers, the sultan originally governed with the

The Janissaries

Most observers of the rise of the Ottomans emphasized their military skill, and particularly the discipline and effectiveness of their Janissaries, when explaining their successes. Typical was the Habsburg ambassador Ogier Ghiselin de Busbecq, who served in Constantinople from 1555 to 1562 and here describes passing through the city of Buda, now Budapest.

"At Buda, I made my first acquaintance with the Janissaries; this is the name by which the Turks call the infantry of the royal guard. The Turkish state has 12,000 of these troops, scattered through every part of the empire, either to garrison the forts or to protect the Christians and Jews from outrage and wrong.

"A garrison of Janissaries is always stationed in the citadel of Buda. The dress of the men consists of a robe reaching down to the ankles, while to cover their heads they employ a cowl, part of which contains the head, while the remainder hangs down and flaps against the neck. On their forehead is placed a silver-gilt cone of considerable height, studded with stones of great value.

"The Turkish monarch going to war takes with him over 20,000 camels and nearly as many mules, of which a great part are loaded with rice and other kinds of grain. They reserve their stores as much as possible, and a ration just sufficient to sustain life is daily weighed out to the Janissaries and other troops of the royal household. They take out a few spoonfuls of flour and put them into water, adding butter, salt and spices; these ingredients are boiled, and a large bowl of gruel is thus obtained. Of this they eat once or twice a day, according to the quantity they have, without any bread. Sometimes they have recourse to horseflesh.

"From this you will see that it is the patience, self-denial and thrift of the Turkish soldier that enable him to face the most trying circumstances and come safely out of the dangers that surround him. What a contrast to our men! Christian soldiers on a campaign refuse to put up with their ordinary food, and call for dainty dishes! It makes me shudder to think of what the results of a struggle between such different systems must be. On their side is vast wealth, experience in arms, a veteran soldiery, readiness to endure hardships, union, order, discipline, thrift and watchfulness. On ours are found luxurious habits, exhausted resources, broken spirits, a raw soldiery, greedy quarrels, no regard for discipline, drunkenness and debauchery. Can we doubt what the result must be?"

Adapted from John J. Saunders (ed.), *The Muslim World on the Eve of Europe's Expansion* (Prentice-Hall, 1966), pp. 20–22.

aid of a council of chosen advisers, which was called the *divan*. From the time of Mehmet the Conqueror, however, the sultan came to be considered too august to participate personally in the divan's deliberations. The function of presiding over the meetings of the divan fell to the grand vizier, who became the chief administrative official of the Ottoman state. The administration was divided into three major categories: civil, ecclesiastical, and military. The divan retained supreme responsibility over both the civil and the military branches; it supervised the collection of taxes and tribute, the conscription of soldiers, and the conduct of foreign affairs; it made recommendations to the sultan concerning peace, war, and other major decisions of state; and it also functioned as a court in disputes that were not religious in character.

Religion and the Army Religious affairs were administered by a class of judges trained in Islamic law, who constituted a special corps called the *ulema.* At their head, the sheikh-ul-Islam served as the supreme judge, after the sultan himself, in all matters of sacred law.

The army had two principal divisions: unpaid holders of fiefs granted by the sultan in exchange for military service; and paid soldiers, technically considered slaves, who remained permanently in the sultan's service. The holder of a fief was required to provide the military with armed men, the number being set in strict proportion to the revenue deriving from his estates. Among the paid soldiers the most important were those belonging to the highly trained, thoroughly professional, but legally unfree corps of the *Janissaries,* meaning "new troops." Slave armies had been common in Islamic states, but the Ottomans did not adopt the practice until the fifteenth century. According to the accounts of the earliest chronicles, Sultan Murad learned from a theologian in about 1430 that the Koran assigned him one-fifth of the booty captured by his army, including prisoners. Murad decided to convert his prisoners to Islam, teach them Turkish, and enlist them in a tough, well-disciplined military contingent, the Janissaries. Most medieval monarchs relied on mercenaries or poorly trained and poorly equipped feudal levies, composed of vassals with little enthusiasm for fighting, and feudal levies continued to make up the larger part of the Turkish army. But the Janissaries soon became an elite corps of professional fighters, dedicated to the sultan and to Islam, and were in large part responsible for Ottoman victories (*see box,* p. 300).

Local Government On the local level, the government of the empire was content to leave many administrative responsibilities to the self-governing communities of Christians and Jews and to the holders of fiefs, who collected taxes and mustered soldiers from those settled on their lands. Apart from the fiefs, the unit of local administration was the canton, or *kaza,* which was administered by a judge, or *qaid.* The cantons were grouped into departments and provinces, usually under the authority of a pasha, who was both a civil and a military official, since he bore the responsibility of leading the feudal levies of his provinces in time of war.

The Devshirme Some time in the fifteenth century a new system of recruiting slaves for the civil administration and the military was introduced—the *devshirme,* or levy of boys. In the *devshirme's* developed form, special commissioners every five years selected young boys from among the Christian population to be given special instruction in Turkish and converted to Islam. After their training they were examined and assigned either to the corps of Janissaries or to the palace administration. In the latter case they were given still more intensive training, and the most talented of them could aspire to the highest administrative offices of the empire. Even the grand vizier was usually a slave. Remarkably, in each generation the most powerful administrators were new to high position, with no family ties to the Turkish aristocracy and no reason to ally with them against the sultan's interests. This practice of recruiting slaves for the sultan's service is sometimes called the *fundamental institution of the empire,* for the sultan's power depended on its functioning properly.

THE SULTAN

The sultan united in his own person supreme civil, military, and religious authority. The way his power was defined was influenced by Byzantine views of imperial authority, which seem to have contributed to the pomp of court ceremony and the aura of sanctity surrounding the person of the sultan. Still more influential were Islamic traditions concerning governmental power, particularly the notion that the sultan was the successor of Muhammad, the legitimate ruler of all true believers. In a strict sense the sultan could not be an absolute ruler, for he was, like every member of the Islamic community, subject to the sacred law. But he was also the supreme judge of that law, and there was no way apart from revolution to challenge his decisions.

The early sultans devised a striking solution to a problem common to most medieval states: the peaceful transference of power from a ruler to his successor. From the fifteenth to the seventeenth century the Ottomans followed what has come to be called the law of fratricide. The sultan cohabited with numerous slave girls of the harem, who

▸ **SULEIMAN**

This portrait of Suleiman the Magnificent from a sixteenth-century Turkish manuscript suggests the ornate splendor that was associated with the awesome figure of the sultan. His court was famous for its lavish festivities and splendid costumes and decorations.

were selected much as were the male household slaves, and usually he fathered numerous progeny. He then picked one of the boys to be his successor. At the sultan's death, the designated heir had the right and obligation to put his brothers and half-brothers to death. (They were strangled with a silken bowstring in order to avoid the shedding of their imperial blood.) The religious judges allowed such massacres, because an uncontested succession was essential to the welfare of the empire.

THE LIMITS OF OTTOMAN POWER

In the sixteenth century Suleiman the Magnificent brought the Ottoman Empire to unprecedented heights of power, but already certain pressures were imposing limits on its expansion. One was geographical. The Ottomans had operated effectively in areas close to their homeland in Asia Minor, but the efficiency of their army and administration inevitably diminished with distance. The unsuccessful campaign against Austria proved that that region was already beyond their reach, and the Ottomans encountered similar walls to further advance in the Iranian plateau and the waters of the central Mediterranean. With the opening of trade routes around Africa and across the Atlantic, the Ottomans were no longer at the center of the civilized world and no longer the masters of movements east and west. Although they left the commerce of their empire largely in the hands of subject communities, they were well aware of the importance of trade, and Suleiman therefore sent a force to destroy Portuguese ships and trading stations in the Indian Ocean. The failure of this attack was an ominous sign for the empire, because the geographic discoveries of the 1400s and 1500s caused dislocations in east-west trade—a shift in trade routes, an increase in the stock of precious metal in Europe, rising inflation—and brought the Ottomans few benefits.

Within the empire there was also a deterioration in the quality of leadership. For reasons hard to explain, the sultans after Suleiman showed little of the energy and ability that had marked the earlier rulers of the House of Osman. Technical advance was continuing in the West, and it was critical for the empire to keep abreast of these changes. The great sultans had welcomed Western technicians and made use of their skills, especially in armament, but their successors after Suleiman seemed distinctly less interested in learning from the West. Declining efficiency was also evident in Ottoman government. The chanceries and secretariats kept precise and informative records in the 1400s, but they no longer did so in the late 1500s and seem to have been beset by mounting disorder. At the death of Suleiman in 1566, it is still much too early to speak of Ottoman decadence, but the fortunes of the Ottoman Empire were already past their height.

III. The Birth of Modern Russia

A great Russian historian, V. O. Kliuchevsky, once identified the principal theme in the history of the Russian people as colonization—the long, arduous, and ultimately successful struggle to settle and subdue the huge Eurasian plain that was their home.[1] The history of that struggle records defeats as well as victories. From the ninth to twelfth centuries, the center of Rus civilization had been Kiev, on the fringes of the southern steppe. Although the Rus of Kiev were able to maintain contacts across the steppes to the Black Sea and the Mediterranean world beyond, they could not resist forever the successive waves of invading steppe nomads. From the 1100s, Pechenegs and Cumans, followed by the still more terrible Mongols, mounted ever more destructive raids against the Rus settlements and cut off their contact with the Black Sea. Eventually the vulnerability of the steppe settlements forced many of the Rus to seek out safer homes in the forested regions to the north and west, where they formed new institutions and built a new civilization, the direct ancestor of the modern Russian state (*see box*, p. 304).

THE MONGOLS

The resurgence of the steppe nomads was the decisive reason for the decline of Kievan Rus, especially when the Mongols appeared on Europe's borders in the early 1200s. The Mongol chief Genghis Khan was amassing in Asia the largest empire the world has even known. In 1223 a Mongol army penetrated Eastern Europe in what seems to have been a reconnoitering expedition. The Mongols defeated the allied princes of Rus in a battle on the Kalka River (a tributary of the Don) but almost at once returned to the East, only to invade once again, in greater force, a few years later. From 1237 to 1241 a Mongol army conducted raids throughout Eastern Europe and established at Sarai, on the lower Volga River, the capital of a division of the Mongol Empire that came to be called the *Golden Horde.*

► COURT OF A MONGOL KING

The courts of the Mongol kings, as this illustration from a Persian manuscript suggests, were dazzlingly opulent. When Louis IX of France sent presents of liturgical objects (chalices and books), the Mongol king rejected the gift and suggested that a tribute of gold and silver would be more appropriate.

---

[1] *A History of Russia*, 1911, vol. 1, p. 2. This theory has interesting parallels to Frederick Jackson Turner's "frontier thesis" interpretation of American history.

The Birth of Christianity in Russia

Essential to the self-image of the Russian state was the belief that it was the heir of Byzantium and that its religion distinguished it from other Christian kingdoms. To emphasize this distinctiveness the monks of Kiev, writing* The Russian Primary Chronicle *around 1200, stressed the choice among alternative faiths when a Kievan prince, Vladimir (who was to become the first Russian saint) made the crucial decision to join the Greek church.

"Vladimir was overcome by lust for women. But Vladimir, though at first deluded, eventually found salvation. For at this time the Russes were ignorant pagans. The devil rejoiced. He knew not that the Prophet had said 'I will call those my people who are not my people.' (*Hosea*)

"Vladimir was visited by Bulgars of Mohammedan faith, who said, 'Though you are a wise and prudent prince, you have no religion. Adopt our faith, and revere Mahomet.' Vladimir inquired what was the nature of their religion. They replied that they believed in God, and that Mahomet instructed them to practice circumcision, to eat no pork, to drink no wine, and after death promised them complete fulfillment of carnal desires. Vladimir listened to them, for he was fond of women and indulgence. But circumcision and abstinence from pork and wine were disagreeable to him. 'Drinking,' said he, 'is the joy of the Russes. We cannot exist without that pleasure.'

"Then came the Germans as emissaries of the Pope. 'Our faith is the light. We worship God, who has made heaven and earth, the stars, the moon, and every creature, while your gods are only wood.' Vladimir inquired what their teaching was. They replied, 'Fasting according to one's strength. But whatever one eats or drinks is all to the glory of God.' Then Vladimir answered, 'Depart hence; our fathers accepted no such principle.'

"Then the Greeks sent a scholar, who exhibited to Vladimir a canvas on which was depicted the Judgement Day of the Lord, and showed him, on the right, the righteous going to their bliss in Paradise, and on the left, the sinners on their way to torment. Then Vladimir sighed and said, 'Happy are they upon the right, but woe to those upon the left!' The scholar replied, 'If you desire to take your place upon the right with the just, then accept baptism!' Vladimir took this counsel to heart, saying, 'I shall wait yet a little longer,' for he wished to inquire about all the faiths.

"[Vladimir then sought in marriage the sister of the Byzantine emperor, Anna, who was persuaded to go by the promise:] 'Through your agency God turns the land of Rus to repentance.' The Princess embarked on a ship, and set forth across the sea. By divine agency, Vladimir was suffering at that moment from a disease of the eyes, and could see nothing. The Princess declared that if he desired to be relieved of this disease, he should be baptized. When Vladimir heard her message, he said, 'If this proves true, then surely the God of the Christians is great,' and gave order that he should be baptized. The Bishop of Kherson, together with the Princess's priests, baptized Vladimir, and as the Bishop laid his hand upon him, he straightway received his sight. Upon experiencing the miraculous cure, Vladimir glorified God, saying, 'I have now perceived the one true God.' When his followers beheld this miracle, many of them were also baptized. After his baptism, Vladimir took the Princess in marriage."

Adapted from Harry J. Carroll, Jr., Ainslee T. Embree, Knox Mellon, Jr., Arnold Schrier, and Alastair M. Taylor (eds.), *The Development of Civilization: A Documentary History of Politics, Society, and Thought*, vol. I (Scott, Foresman, 1961), pp. 217–220.

The khans, or rulers, of the Golden Horde maintained suzerainty over the lands of what is now Ukraine and Belarus until the mid-1300s and over eastern Russia until the mid-1400s. The princes subject to the Golden Horde had to pay tribute to the khans and secure from them a charter, called *yarlik*, that confirmed them in office, but otherwise they could rule their own people.

As a result, despite the power they exercised over the East Slavs for centuries, the Mongols' influence on Slavic languages and cultures remained relatively slight.

Slavic Resettlement The nomad invasions and the formation of the Golden Horde had a devastating effect on the settlements in the southern steppes. A chronicler lamented that Kiev, once proudly known as the "mother of Rus cities," had only 200 houses left standing in the 1200s. Most of the Rus population sought more protected lands, and in the 1100s and 1200s three new areas of East Slavic settlement rose to prominence.

Some colonists moved west into the provinces of Galicia and Volynia along the upper Dniester River and became the ancestors of the modern Ukrainians and the Belorussians, or White Russians. After a short period of submission to the Mongols, these colonies fell under the political domination first of the grand dukes of Lithuania and then of the Polish kings. They developed their own literary languages and cultural traditions, and they were not politically reunited with their fellow East Slavs for centuries. (The province of Galicia, with a large Ukrainian population, remained under Polish or Austrian rule until 1944.)

Other colonists moved north into the vast and empty area ruled by the city of Novgorod, the region of Russia where Mongol rule lasted the shortest time. But the poor soil could not support a dense population. More important than these two areas was the third new center of settlement: the Russian "Mesopotamia," the lands between the upper Volga and Oka rivers, where dense forests offered both relative security from the nomads and a productive soil. Those who moved north to Novgorod and to the Russian Mesopotamia were the ancestors of the modern Great Russians, still the largest of the East Slavic peoples, and they formed the nucleus of a new Russian state.

Feudal Russia Historians call the period between the twelfth and fifteenth centuries the age of feudal Russia—the time when Russia was divided into many princely domains. Nearly all the small towns within Russian Mesopotamia had their own princes, their own citadels, or kremlins, and their own territories. All the princes were subject to the khan of the Golden Horde, but Mongol government remained limited to extracting tribute and granting *yarliks.* Russia lacked a central government.

In this feudal period, Russian economy, society, and culture acquired distinctive characteristics. With the exception of Novgorod, the towns of the north could not develop an active commerce with distant areas, as Kiev had, nor did they have much contact with Constantinople or other centers of learning. The Russian towns in the main were not commercial or industrial centers but rather served as fortresses to which the surrounding population could flee in times of danger. The economy was overwhelmingly agricultural, and the energy of the people was directed primarily to clearing the great forests. In social terms, most peasants remained free and their freedom was protected by their closeness to an expanding frontier, which offered them places of refuge if conditions at home deteriorated.

Art, which remained within the conventions of icon painting created by the Byzantines, was produced primarily for the Church. Architects as well as artists achieved remarkable delicacy, and Russia's supreme religious painter, Andrei Rublev (1370?–1430?), deserves to be recognized as one of the world's great artistic geniuses, even though few of his works survive.

THE RISE OF MOSCOW

In spite of the political differences that divided them, the Russians' religion and their submission to the Mongols preserved a sense of identity and unity among them, though it was long uncertain which of the many petty princes would take the leadership in building a politically united nation. One of the towns that seemed unlikely to achieve this hegemony was the new settlement of Moscow, which is mentioned in a chronicle for the first time in 1147. But its early obscurity proved an advantage because this small town was passed over by raiding nomads in search of richer plunder. Located on the Moskva River, Moscow also had other advantages. It was in the center of Russian Mesopotamia, close to the tributary rivers feeding the Volga River to the north and the Oka River to the south. The princes of Moscow could

▸ *Andrei Rublev*
Old Testament Trinity, 1410–1420
Andrei Rublev, one of the most influential Russian artists of the fifteenth century, worked within a Byzantine tradition of wall painting. His *Old Testament Trinity*, originally from a monastery, shows a reinterpretation of the standard Christian iconography: the three angels positioned around a dish represent God the Father, the Son, and the Holy Ghost.

pursue a "river policy" in their expansion, following the courses of streams in all directions and depending on this network of water routes to bind their state together. The region between the Volga and the Oka rivers also formed the geographic heart of European Russia and allowed the prince who ruled it to exploit opportunities in almost any part of Russia.

Moscow gained preeminence primarily through the talents of its early princes. Like other

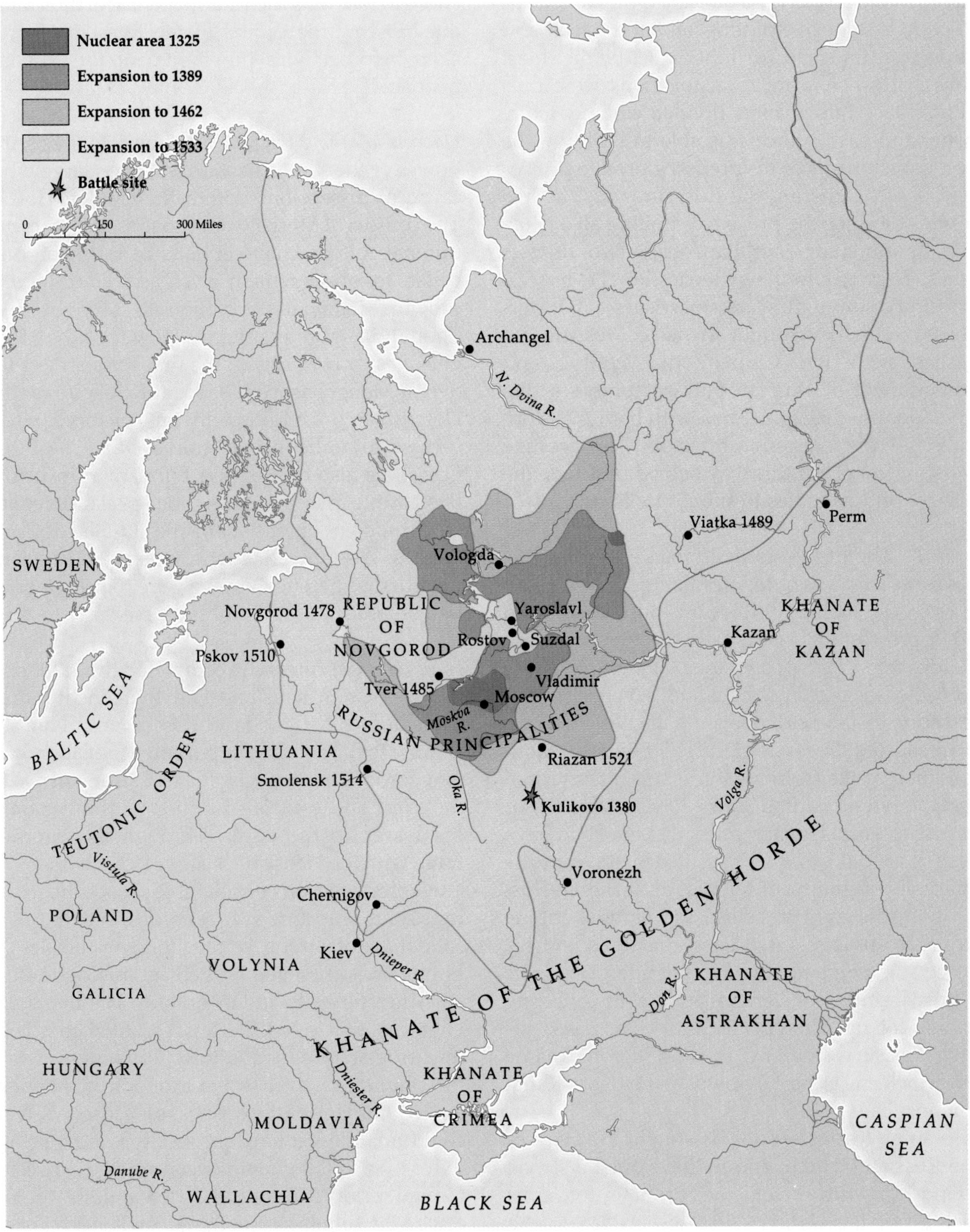

Map 10.4 THE RISE OF MOSCOW, 1325–1533
Despite its seeming backwoods location, Moscow was able to expand its power dramatically, especially in the reign of Ivan III (1462–1505), and to establish itself as the dominant force in Russia by the mid-1500s.

rulers in the area, they abandoned the disastrous Kievan system of splitting an inheritance and adopted primogeniture (inheritance by the eldest son) instead. A prince's acquisitions were thus kept intact rather than divided among many heirs, and each prince was able to build on the accomplishments of his predecessor. The princes set about "gathering the Russian land," as historians describe the process of uniting all of Russia, by pursuing simultaneously two distinct goals: They acquired new territories at every opportunity, through wars, marriages, and purchases; and they sought to make Moscow, together with the Church, the symbol and embodiment of Russian national unity—a distinct identity that contrasted with both the Mongols and the Western Christians. The prestige Moscow gained in this way helped persuade the princes of other cities to submit to its rule.

Ivan I The first Muscovite prince to raise this obscure little town to prominence was Ivan I (1328–1341). Chiefly through purchases from other princes but occasionally through conquest, he extended his possessions along the entire course of the Moskva River and won enclaves of territory to the north beyond the Volga River. Ivan courted the favor of the still powerful Mongol khan of the Golden Horde and often visited the khan in his capital on the lower Volga River. In return for his loyalty and gifts, the khan gave Ivan a special *yarlik* in 1328 that made him the chief representative of Mongol authority in Russia with the right to collect the Mongol tribute from all Russian lands. Thereafter Ivan and his successors permanently held the title *velikii kniaz* ("great prince," or "grand duke"). In collecting tribute for the Mongols, Ivan also increased his own treasury, thereby earning the nickname by which he is best known to history—Kalita ("moneybags").

Ivan no less determinedly sought the favor of the Russian Church, and he developed a strong friendship with Peter, the primate (or chief bishop) of the Church. Like his predecessor, a metropolitan of Kiev who had abandoned that decaying city, Peter had no fixed see but traveled throughout the new centers of Russian settlement. He visited Moscow frequently and by chance died there in 1326. His tomb became a national shrine, and his successors therefore chose Moscow as their permanent see, thus making Moscow the capital of the Russian Church even before it was the capital of the Russian people.

Decline of the Mongols By the late 1300s the power of the Mongols was declining, largely because of dissensions within the Golden Horde. The princes of Moscow now abandoned their traditional role as chief servants of the khan and began to present themselves as leaders of the growing national opposition to Mongol rule. Though far from ending the power of the Mongols, Prince Dmitri won the first Russian victory over a Mongol army in 1380, at Kulikovo on the Don River. In addition to this victory, which earned him the proud title *Donskoi* ("of the Don"), he also beat back a Lithuanian invasion. Dmitri thus made Moscow the special defender of Orthodoxy against both the infidel Mongols and the Western Christians, whom the Russians regarded as heretics, and he gave the city a prestige no other Russian city possessed.

Ivan III The ruler who completed the gathering of the Russian land and laid the constitutional foundations for modern Russia was Ivan III (1462–1505). His most important acquisition was Novgorod, a trading city that had strong ties with the West and controlled a huge if thinly populated area to the north. Through its vigorous trade with the Hanseatic League (see Chapter 11), Novgorod enjoyed considerable prosperity in the fourteenth and fifteenth centuries, but the consolidation of strong states along its borders—Lithuania and Poland as well as Muscovite Russia—threatened its independence. The merchant oligarchy that ruled the town wanted to accept the leadership of the Catholic Lithuanians, while the populace, which was Orthodox in religion, looked rather to the prince of Moscow. Ivan could not allow a territory so large and so close to his own to fall under the control of a powerful foreign prince. In 1471 he demanded and received the submission of the city; when it rebelled in 1478, he not only subdued the uprising but, as punishment, incorporated Novgorod and its territories into the Muscovite state. Ivan also took over the principalities of Yaroslavl, Perm, Rostov, and Tver. He ended the threat of Mongol rule over Russia by confronting an invading army at

▸ **Onion Domes at Kizhi**
Constructed entirely of wood, the remarkable churches of northern Russia, such as this eighteenth-century example from Kizhi, were made into magnificently elaborate structures even though they often served only small settlements. The onion domes were the characteristic symbol of the Russian Orthodox Church, and they were multiplied across the roofs of Russian churches.

the Oka River in 1480, though no battle was fought because neither side dared cross the river that separated them. When the enemy withdrew, over two centuries of Mongol rule in Russia quietly ended.

Under Ivan's successor Basil III, the principalities of Pskov, Riazan, and Smolensk were added; Moscow, which in 1462 had ruled some 15,000 square miles of territory, by the middle of the sixteenth century ruled 40,000 square miles, and the borders of the principality of Moscow included nearly all the areas settled by the Great Russians. The princes of Moscow now confronted beyond their frontiers not another Russian prince but foreign sovereigns. The reign of Ivan III thus began a new epoch in the relations between Russian and non-Russian peoples.

INSTITUTIONAL AND SOCIAL CHANGE

Ivan III refashioned Russian institutions to suit the newly achieved national unity. The ruler of all the Russians could no longer be considered a mere feudal prince, so Ivan adopted the title *tsar*, the Slavic equivalent of the Latin term *Caesar*, the traditional title of Roman and Byzantine emperors. Ivan also sought to depict himself as the successor of the Byzantine emperors. He adopted the Greek title *autokrator* ("autocrat") and introduced at his court the elaborate pomp and etiquette that had been characteristic of Byzantium. The Byzantine double-headed eagle became the seal and symbol of the new Russian Empire. Ivan also made his capital more splendid in appearance. Under the influence of his wife, Sophia Paleologus, who was the niece of the last Byzantine emperor and had been educated in Italy, he invited Italian artists to Moscow to help rebuild the Kremlin, the ancient citadel of the city. The Italians exerted considerable influence on Russian artistic style, especially Aristotele Fioravanti, who designed some of the Kremlin's most graceful churches and palaces.

Law Ivan was the first prince since the Kievan period to legislate for the whole of Russia. In 1497 he promulgated a new code of laws known as the *Sudebnik*, which was the first national legal code since the *Russkaia Pravda*, compiled by the Kievan Prince Iaroslav the Wise in the eleventh century. The new strength and splendor of the tsar inspired several monastic scholars to propose the idea that Moscow was the third Rome. The first Rome, they said, had fallen into heresy, and the second, Constantinople, had been taken by the infidel. Moscow alone, the capital of the one Orthodox ruler, preserved the true religion.

The Boyars In administering their state, the princes of Moscow had traditionally relied on the boyars, the hereditary nobles who were obliged to serve the prince in the army and the civil administration. Many boyars held vast estates, and their economic independence sometimes made them unreliable servants. Without directly attacking the boyars, Ivan created a new class of serving nobles who depended on the tsar's favor for their social position. He inaugurated a land grant called a *pomest'e*, which, like the Western fief, was made on condition of faithful service. The *pomeshchik*, as the holder of the grant was called, retained the property only so long as he fulfilled his obligations, and in the system's early days the land could not be inherited. This new class of officials acted as a counterpoise to the power of the boyars and as a major support of the tsar's authority.

Although Ivan's reforms were not completed until the reign of his grandson, Ivan IV, known as the Terrible—a tsar who brutally destroyed the old nobility of boyars and imposed on all landowners the status of servant to the tsar—Ivan III can be seen as the founder of the Russian state. He created a class of serving nobles; he finished the task of gathering the Russian land and unifying its people; he brought a united Russia to face the outside world; and he declared himself to be tsar, autocrat of Russia. Ivan III bequeathed to his successors one of the most characteristic institutions of modern Russia: its centralized, autocratic government.

Although Western Europe was spared the nomadic invasions that always threatened and frequently struck the Eastern peoples, it, too, sustained in the 1300s and 1400s a series of disastrous blows—famines, plagues, economic depression, and wars. These catastrophes caused profound dislocations in the society of the medieval West. The following two chapters examine this crisis, which transformed the medieval world and helped create the civilization of modern Western Europe.

Recommended Reading

Sources

The Chronicle of Novgorod. Robert Mitchell and Neville Forbes (trs.). 1914. Portrays social and political life of the principal commercial town of medieval Russia.

*De Villehardouin, Geoffrey, and Jean De Joinville. *Chronicles of the Crusades*. Margaret R. Shaw (tr.). 1963.

Howes, Robert Craig (ed. and tr.). *The Testaments of the Grand Princes of Moscow*. 1967.

William of Tyre. *A History of Deeds Done beyond the Sea*. Emily A. Babcock and A. C. Krey (trs.). 1943. One of the most important of the crusader chronicles.

Studies

Ashtor, Eliyahu. *Levant Trade in the Later Middle Ages*. 1982.

*Available in paperback.

Atiya, Azia S. *Crusade, Commerce and Culture.* 1962. An evaluation of the results of the crusades in European history.

Bartlett, Robert. *The Making of Europe: Conquest, Colonization and Cultural Change 950–1350.* 1993. An analysis of the effect on Europe of the outward movement of its peoples in the Late Middle Ages.

Billington, James H. *The Icon and the Axe: An Interpretive History of Russian Culture.* 1966.

Erdmann, Carl. *The Origin of the Idea of the Crusade.* Marshall W. Baldwin and Walter Goffart (trs.). 1977. Perceptive study by a German scholar of the idea that war could be holy.

Fennell, J. L. *Ivan the Great of Moscow.* 1963. A political biography.

*Halperin, Charles J. *Russia and the Golden Horde: The Mongol Impact on Medieval Russian History.* 1985.

Holt, P. M. *The Age of the Crusades. The Near East from the Eleventh Century to 1517.* 1986.

Housely, Norman. *The Later Crusades: From Lyons to Alcazar 1274–1580.* 1992.

Kedar, Benjamin Z. *Crusade and Mission. European Approaches toward the Muslims.* 1984. The shift in aims from conquest to conversion.

Mayer, Hans Eberhard. *The Crusades* (2d ed.). 1988. A standard account.

Merriman, Roger B. *Suleiman the Magnificent. 1520–1566.* 1966.

Meyendorff, John. *Byzantium and the Rise of Russia: A Study of Byzantine-Russian Relations in the Fourteenth Century.* 1981. Byzantine contributions to the rise of Muscovy.

Morgan, David. *The Mongols.* 1986. Emphasizes the impact of the Mongol conquests and empire on Eastern Europe.

Mylonas, George E. *The Balkan States: An Introduction to Their History.* 1947.

Riley-Smith, Jonathan. *The Crusades: A Short History.* 1987. Follows history of crusader states in some detail.

Runciman, Steven. *A History of the Crusades* (3 vols.). 1951–1954.

Setton, Kenneth M. (ed.). *A History of the Crusades.* (6 vols.) (2d ed.). 1969–1989. The most comprehensive history of the crusades.

———. *The Papacy and the Levant (1204–1571).* 1976–1978. The basic survey of papal relations with the East.

Vernadsky, George. *The Mongols and Russia.* 1953.

———. *Russia at the Dawn of the Modern Age.* 1959. Part of the author's monumental *History of Russia.*

Wittek, Paul. *The Rise of the Ottoman Empire.* 1971.

SIEGE OF MORTAIGNE

This manuscript illustration from the Hundred Years' War shows a city under siege by both land and sea. The French defender is using a crossbow; the English besiegers are using cannon as well as their famous longbows.

CHAPTER ELEVEN

THE WEST IN TRANSITION: ECONOMY AND INSTITUTIONS

THE vigorous expansion that marked European history from the eleventh to the thirteenth centuries came to an end in the 1300s. Plague, famine, and recurrent wars decimated populations and snuffed out their former prosperity. At the same time, feudal governments as well as the papacy struggled against mounting institutional chaos. But for all the signs of crisis the fourteenth and fifteenth centuries were not merely an age of breakdown. The failures of the medieval economy and its governments prompted change and drove the Western peoples to repair their institutions. By the late fifteenth century the outlines of a new equilibrium were emerging. In 1500 Europeans remained fewer in number than they had been in 1300, but they also had developed a more productive economy and a more powerful technology than they had possessed 200 years before. These achievements were to equip them for their great expansion throughout the world in the early modern period. Some historians refer to the fourteenth and fifteenth centuries as the "autumn of the Middle Ages," and their somber theme is the decline and death of a formerly great civilization. But the study of any past epoch requires an effort to balance the work of death and renewal. In few periods of history do death and renewal confront each other so dramatically as in the years between 1300 and 1500.

I. Population Disaster and Agricultural Change

The plagues and famines that struck European society in the fourteenth and fifteenth centuries profoundly affected economic life. Initially, they disrupted the established patterns of producing and exchanging goods and led directly to widespread hardship and depression. But the effects of the disruptions were not entirely negative; in reorganizing the economy under greatly changed demographic conditions, Europeans were able to make significant advances in the efficiency of economic production. To understand this paradox, we must see how the disasters affected the population of Europe.

DEMOGRAPHIC CATASTROPHE

A few censuses and other statistical records give us an insight into the size and structure of the European population in the 1300s. Nearly all these records were drawn up for purposes of taxation, and usually they survey only limited geographical areas—a city or a province. They are rarely complete even in limited areas and give us no reliable totals, but they still enable us to perceive with some confidence how the population was changing.

Almost every region of Europe from which we possess such records shows an appalling decline of population between approximately 1300 and 1450. Thus the population of Provence in southern France seems to have shrunk during the century after 1310 from between 350,000 and 400,000 to roughly one-third, or at most one-half, of its earlier size; only after 1470 did it again begin to increase. The city and countryside of Pistoia, near Florence, fell from about 43,000 people in the mid-thirteenth century to 14,000 by the early fifteenth. The nearby city and countryside of San Gimignano has not regained to this day the approximately 13,000 residents it had in 1332.

For the larger kingdoms of Europe the figures are less reliable, but they are similar. England had a population of about 3.7 million in 1347 and 2.2 million by 1377. By 1550 it had no more people than it had had in the thirteenth century. France by 1328 may have reached 15 million; it, too, was not again to attain this size for 200 years. In Germany, of some 170,000 inhabited localities named in sources before 1300, about 40,000 disappeared during the 1300s and 1400s. Since many of the surviving towns were also shrinking in size, the population loss was only greater.

Certain favored regions of Europe—the fertile lands surrounding Paris and the Po valley—did continue to attract settlers and maintain fairly stable populations, but they owed their good fortune more to immigration than to high birthrates or immunity from disease. It can safely be estimated that all of Europe in 1450 had no more than one-half, and probably only one-third, of the population it had had around 1300.

PESTILENCE

The great plague of the fourteenth century, known as the Black Death, provides a dramatic, but not a complete, explanation for these huge human losses. In 1347 a merchant ship sailing from Caffa in the Crimea to Messina in Sicily seems to have carried infected rats. A plague broke out at Messina, and from there it spread throughout Europe (see Map 11.1).

The Persistence of Plague The Black Death was not so much an epidemic as a pandemic, striking an entire continent. Yet it was not the first pandemic in European history. An earlier one had struck in 542, during the reign of Justinian (see Chapter 7). But this was the first in 800 years, and it erupted repeatedly during the century. A city was lucky if more than 10 years went by without an onslaught; the plague was raging in some part of Europe in almost every year (*see box*, p. 316). Barcelona and its province of Catalonia, for example, lived through this record of misery in the fourteenth century: famine, 1333; plague, 1347 and 1351; famine, 1358 and 1359; plague, 1362, 1363, 1371, and 1397.

Some of the horror of the plague can be glimpsed in this account by an anonymous cleric who visited the French city of Avignon in 1348:

> To put the matter shortly, one-half, or more than a half, of the people at Avignon are already dead. Within the walls of the city there are now more than

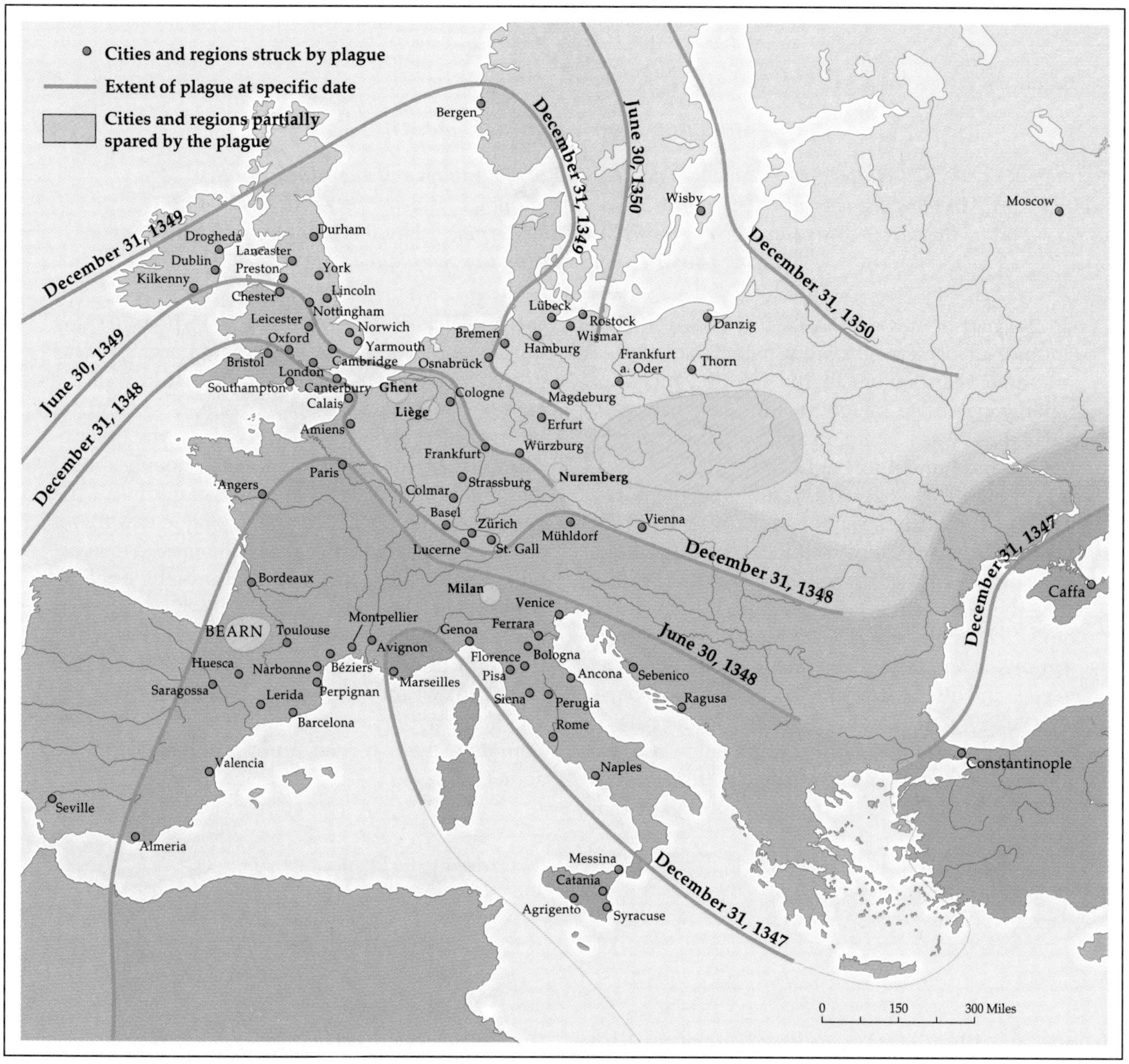

7,000 houses shut up; in these no one is living, and all who have inhabited them are departed. . . . On account of this great mortality there is such a fear of death that people do not dare even to speak with anyone whose relative has died, because it is frequently remarked that in a family where one dies nearly all the relations follow him. . . .[1]

Map 11.1 The Black Death
For all the impression that the plague spread almost instantly, this reconstruction of its progress reveals that, because it depended on Europe's poor travel conditions and died down each winter, it took three years to move from Sicily to Sweden.

Nature of the Disease Most historians identify the Black Death as the bubonic plague, but this makes it difficult to explain how the disease could have spread so rapidly and killed so many, since bubonic plague is more a disease of rats and small mammals than human beings. If bubonic plague is to spread to a human, a flea must bite an infected rat, pick up the infection, and carry it to a human host through a bite. The infection causes the lymphatic glands to swell, but recovery is not uncommon. Only if the infection travels

[1] *Breve Chronicon clerici anonymi*, quoted in Francis Aidan Gasquet, *The Black Death of 1348 and 1349*, 1908, p. 46.

Boccaccio on the Black Death

The following eyewitness description of the ravages of the Black Death in Florence was written by one of its most famous citizens, the writer Giovanni Boccaccio. This passage comes from his masterpiece,* The Decameron, *written during the three years following the plague.

"In the year of our Lord 1348, there happened at Florence a most terrible plague, which had broken out some years before in the Levant, and after making incredible havoc all the way, had now reached the west. There, in spite of all the means that art and human foresight could suggest, such as keeping the city clear from filth and the publication of copious instructions for preservation of health, it began to show itself in the spring. Unlike what had been seen in the east, where bleeding from the nose is the fatal prognostic, here there appeared certain tumors in the groin or under the arm-pits, some as big as a small apple, others as an egg, and afterwards purple spots in most parts of the body—messengers of death. To the cure of this malady neither medical knowledge nor the power of drugs was of any effect; whether because the disease was in its own nature mortal, or that the physicians (the number of whom, taking quacks and women pretenders into account, was grown very great) could form no just idea of the cause. Whichever was the reason, few escaped; but nearly all died the third day from the first appearance of the symptoms, some sooner, some later, without any fever or other symptoms. What gave the more virulence to this plague was that it spread daily, like fire when it comes in contact with combustibles. Nor was it caught only by coming near the sick, but even by touching their clothes. One instance of this kind I took particular notice of: the rags of a poor man just dead had been thrown into the street. Two hogs came up, and after rooting amongst the rags, in less than an hour they both turned around and died on the spot."

From Warren Hollister et al., *Medieval Europe: A Short Sourcebook* (2d ed.), McGraw-Hill, 1992, pp. 248–249.

through the bloodstream to the lungs, causing pneumonia, can the disease be spread directly from person to person. The real killer in the 1300s seems to have been pneumonic plague, which infects the lungs directly; it probably was spread through coughing and was almost always fatal.

In spite of the virulence of pneumonic plague, it is hard to believe that medical factors alone can explain the awesome mortalities. After all, Europeans had maintained close contact with the East, where the plague had been endemic, since the eleventh century, but not until 1347 and 1348 did it make serious inroads in Europe. In addition, pneumonic plague is a disease of the winter months, but the plagues of the 1300s characteristically raged during the summer and declined in the cooler weather of autumn. Some scholars think the weather of the age—it seems to have been unusually cool and humid—somehow favored the disease. Others argue that it was acute, widespread malnutrition that caused starvation and lower resistance to infections.

HUNGER

The second cause of the dramatic fall in population, hunger, was all too common. Even if famines were less lethal than the plague in their initial onslaught, they were likely to persist for several years. In 1315, 1316, and 1317 a severe famine swept the north of Europe; in 1339 and 1340 another struck the south. The starving people ate not only their reserves of grain but also most of the seed they had set aside for planting.

Only a remarkably good harvest could compensate for the loss of grain by providing both immediate food and sufficient seeds for future planting.

Why was hunger so widespread in the early fourteenth century? Some historians see the root of trouble in the sheer number of people the lands had to support by 1300. The medieval population had been growing rapidly since about 1000, and by 1300 Europe, so this analysis suggests, was becoming the victim of its own success. Parts of the continent were crowded, even glutted, with people. Some areas of Normandy, for example, had a population in the early fourteenth century not much below what they supported 600 years later. Thousands, millions even, had to be fed without chemical fertilizers, power tools, and fast transport. Masses of people had come to depend for their livelihood on unrewarding soils, and even in good years they were surviving on the margins of existence. A slightly reduced harvest during any one year took on the dimensions of a major famine.

Even though malnutrition does not directly worsen mortality from plague, it does raise the death rate from respiratory infections and intestinal ailments, which also reached epidemic proportions in the fourteenth century. Furthermore, illness is itself a major cause of malnutrition. Thus hunger, disease, and plague combined to create a grim balance between the numbers of people and the resources that supported them.

► The Triumph of Death

The great social disaster of the Black Death left few traces in the visual arts; perhaps people did not wish to be reminded of its horrors. One exception was the *Triumph of Death*, a mural painted shortly after 1348 in the Camposanto (cemetery) of Pisa in Italy. In this detail of the mural, an elegant party of hunters happens upon corpses prepared for burial. Note the rider who holds a handkerchief—scented, undoubtedly—to his nose, to ward off the foul odors.

ECONOMIC EFFECTS

What effects did the fall in population have on the economy of Europe? At first, the losses disrupted production. According to contemporaries, survivors of the plague often gave up toiling in the fields or looking after their shops; presumably, they saw no point in working for the future when it was so uncertain. But in the long run the results were not altogether negative. In agriculture, for example, the contraction of the population enabled the survivors to concentrate their efforts on better soils. Moreover, in both agriculture and industry the shortage of laborers was a challenge to landlords and entrepreneurs to save costs either by adopting productive measures that were less labor intensive or by increasing investment in labor-saving devices. Thus the decline in population eventually encouraged Europeans to find better techniques for making the most of available resources.

▶ **COLLECTING SILKWORMS AND PREPARING SILK**
One of the new industries that appeared in Europe in the fourteenth century was the raising of silkworms. Since the spinning of silk was a craft usually associated with women, this scene, from a fifteenth-century manuscript, shows a woman gathering silkworms from the mulberry bushes on which the worms lived, and from whose cocoons the silk threads were unwound.

AGRICULTURE

Perhaps the best indication of the changes in the European economy comes from the history of prices. This evidence is scattered and rarely precise, but it does reveal roughly similar patterns in prices all over Europe. The cost of most agricultural products—cereals, wine, beer, oil, and meat—shot up immediately after the Black Death and stayed high until approximately 1375 in the north and 1395 in Italy. High food prices in a time of declining population suggest that production was falling even more rapidly than the number of consumers.

The beginnings of an agricultural recovery are apparent in the early fifteenth century. With fewer Europeans to be fed, the demand for cereals (which had long dominated agriculture) lessened perceptibly and their prices declined; with fewer available workers, the cost of labor pushed steadily upward. Landlords had to compete with one another to attract scarce tenants to their lands and did so by offering lower rents and favorable terms of tenancy. The upward movement of wages and the downward price of cereals led to a concentration on commodities that would command a better price in the market or were less expensive to produce. Better wages in both town and country also enabled the population to consume a more varied and expensive diet. While the price of wheat fell, wine, beer, oil, butter, cheese, meat, fruit, and other foods remained relatively expensive, which indicates a strong market demand.

Enclosure One branch of agriculture that enjoyed a remarkable period of growth in the fifteenth century was sheep raising. Labor costs were low, since a few shepherds could guard thousands of sheep; and the prices for wool, skins, mutton, and cheese remained high. In England, landlords sought to take advantage of this situation by fencing large fields and converting them from plowland into sheep pastures and expelling the peasants or small herders who had formerly lived there; this process, called *enclosure,* continued for centuries and played an important role in English economic and social history.

By the middle of the fifteenth century, agricultural prices tended to stabilize, and this suggests that production had become more dependable. Farms enjoyed the advantages of larger size, better location on more profitable soil, and increased capital investments in tools and animals. Agriculture was now more diversified, which benefited the soil, lowered the risk of famine from the failure of a single staple crop, and provided more nourishment for the people. Europeans were consuming a healthier diet by the middle of the fifteenth century than their ancestors had 200 years before.

II. Depression and Recovery in Trade and Industry

Although agriculture was the main occupation of the age and also the area of economic activity most directly connected with plague and hunger, there were also profound consequences of the disasters of the 1300s for trade and industry. And here, as in agriculture, there was to be a recovery in the late 1400s that was to have a long-term effect on European history.

PROTECTIONISM

The movement of prices created serious problems for employers in cities. As the labor force contracted, wages in most towns surged to levels as much as four times higher than they had been before 1348. Although the prices of manufactured goods also increased, they did not rise as much as wages, and this worked to reduce profit margins. To offset these unfavorable tendencies, the employers sought government intervention. Between 1349 and 1351, England, France, Aragon, Castile, and other governments tried to fix prices and wages at levels favorable to employers. In enacting the Statute of Laborers, the English Parliament followed a policy typical of the age, forbidding employers to pay more than customary wages and requiring laborers to accept jobs at those wages. Such early experiments in a controlled economy failed. Price and wage ceilings set by law seem to have had little influence on actual prices.

A related problem for businesses was that competition grew as population fell and markets contracted. Traders tried to protect themselves by creating restricted markets and establishing monopolies. Guilds limited their membership, and some admitted only the sons of established masters. Cities, too, imposed heavy restrictions on the importation of foreign manufactures.

The Hanseatic League Probably the best example of this monopolizing trend is the association of northern European trading cities, the Hanseatic League. The league was a defensive association formed in the fourteenth century by the cities that dominated the commerce of the Baltic and North seas, with the aim of excluding foreigners from the Baltic trade. The cities initially sought this protection because the emperor was too weak to defend their interests. At its height, the Hanseatic League included about 70 or 80 cities, stretching from Bruges to Novgorod and led by Bremen, Cologne, Hamburg, and especially Lübeck. Maintaining its own treasury and fleet, the league supervised commercial exchange, policed the waters of the Baltic Sea, and negotiated with foreign princes. By the late fifteenth century, however, it began to decline and was unable to meet growing competition from the Dutch in northern commerce. Although never formally abolished, the Hanseatic League continued to meet—at lengthening intervals—only until 1669.

THE FORCES OF RECOVERY

Attempts to raise the efficiency of workers proved to be far more effective than wage and trade regulation in laying the basis for recovery. Employers were able to counteract high wages by

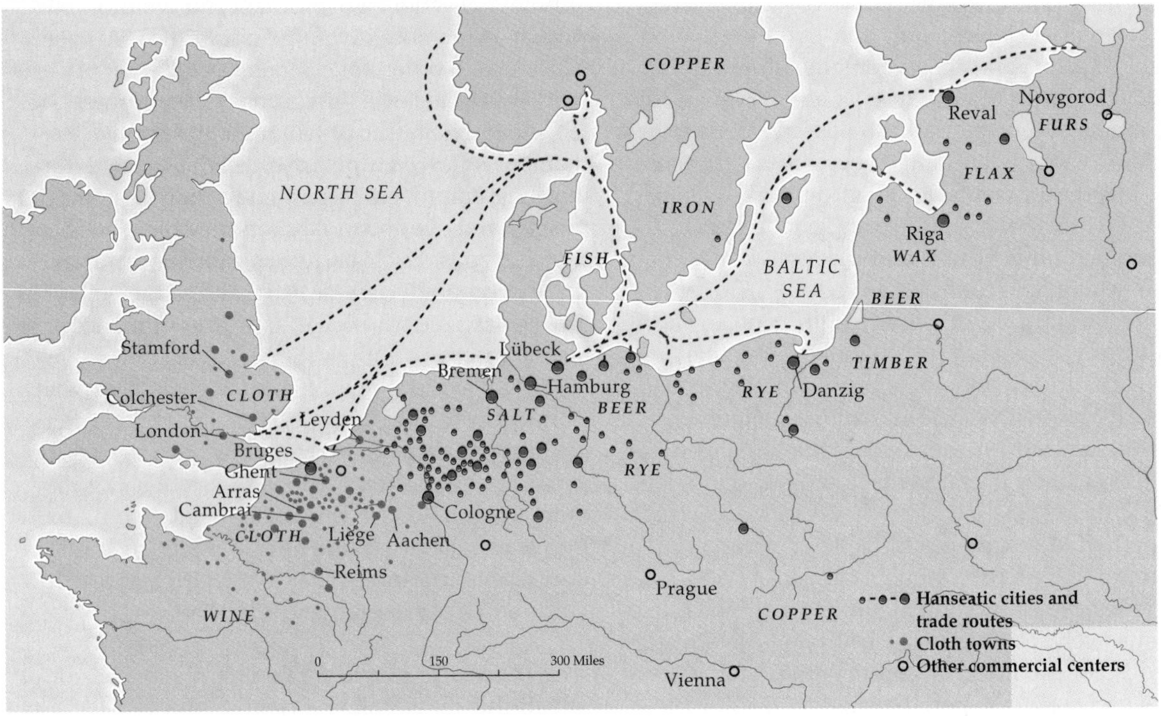

Map 11.2 THE HANSEATIC LEAGUE AND THE GOODS IT TRADED IN THE FOURTEENTH CENTURY **Even in the age of the Black Death, international trade remained vigorous in northern Europe. Its leaders were the cities of the Hanseatic League, which shipped a variety of commodities across the continent, though the most sought-after commodity was the cloth produced in England, the Netherlands, and northern France.**

adopting more rational methods of production and substituting capital for labor—that is, providing workers with better tools. Though largely inspired by hard times and labor shortages, most of the technical advances of the 1300s and 1400s—both in different industries and in business practices—led workers to practice trade more efficiently, and eventually this helped make Europe a richer community.

METALLURGY

Mining and metallurgy benefited from a series of inventions after 1460 that lowered the cost of metals and extended their use. Better techniques of digging, shoring, ventilating, and draining allowed mine shafts to be sunk several hundred feet into the earth, permitting the large-scale exploitation of the deep, rich mineral deposits of Central Europe. Some historians estimate that the output from the mines of Hungary, the Tyrol, Bohemia, and Saxony grew as much as five times between 1460 and 1530. During this period miners in Saxony discovered a method for extracting pure silver from the lead alloy in which it was often found—an invention that was of major importance for the later massive development of silver mines in America. Larger furnaces came into use, and huge bellows and trip-hammers, driven by waterpower, aided the smelting and working of metals. Simultaneously, the masters of the trade were acquiring a new precision in the difficult art of casting.

By the late fifteenth century, European mines were providing an abundance of silver bullion for coinage. Money became more plentiful, and this stimulated the economy. Exploitation also began in the rich coal deposits of northern Europe. Expanding iron production meant more and stronger pumps, gears and machine parts,

MINING, 1389
One does not normally associate miners with elegant decoration, but in this fourteenth-century manuscript, a miner provides the subject for the ornamentation of the capital M that starts the word *metalla* (metals). That the artist even considered such a subject is an indication of the growing importance of the industry in this period.

tools, and ironwares; such products found wide application in construction work and shipbuilding. And skill in metalworking contributed to two other inventions: firearms and movable metal type.

FIREARMS

Europeans were constantly trying to improve the arts of war in the Middle Ages, and one weapon they sought was a device to hurl projectiles with great force and accuracy. We do not know how they first learned that certain mixtures of carbon, sulfur, and saltpeter burn with explosive force and can be used to hurl boulders at an enemy. Firearms are first mentioned in 1328, and cannons were used in the early battles of the Hundred Years' War. At first, their effect was chiefly psychological: the thunderous roar, merely by frightening the enemy's horses, did far more damage than the usually inaccurate shots. Still, a breakthrough had been made, and cannons gained in military importance. Their development depended primarily on stronger, more precise casting and on proper granulation of the powder to ensure that the charge burned at the right speed and put its full force behind the projectile. With firearms, fewer soldiers could fight more effectively; capital, in the form of an efficient though expensive tool, was being substituted for labor.

PRINTING

The extension of literacy among laypeople and the greater reliance of governments and businesses on records created a demand for a cheap method of reproducing the written word. The introduction of paper from the East was a major step in reducing costs, for paper is far cheaper than parchment to produce. A substitute for the time-consuming labor of writing by hand was also necessary: Scribes and copiers were skilled artisans who commanded high salaries. To cut costs, printing was first tried by pressing woodcuts—inked blocks with letters or designs carved on them—onto paper or parchment. But these "block books" represented only a small advance over handwriting, for a separate woodcut had to be carved for each page. And the woodcuts were not durable; they tended to split after being pressed a number of times.

Gutenberg By the middle of the fifteenth century several masters were on the verge of perfecting the technique of printing with movable metal type. The first to prove this practicable was Johannes Gutenberg of Mainz, a former jeweler and stonecutter. Gutenberg devised an alloy of lead, tin, and antimony that would melt at a low temperature, cast well in the die, and be durable in the press; this alloy is still the basis of the printer's art. His Bible, printed in 1455, is the first major work reproduced through printing.

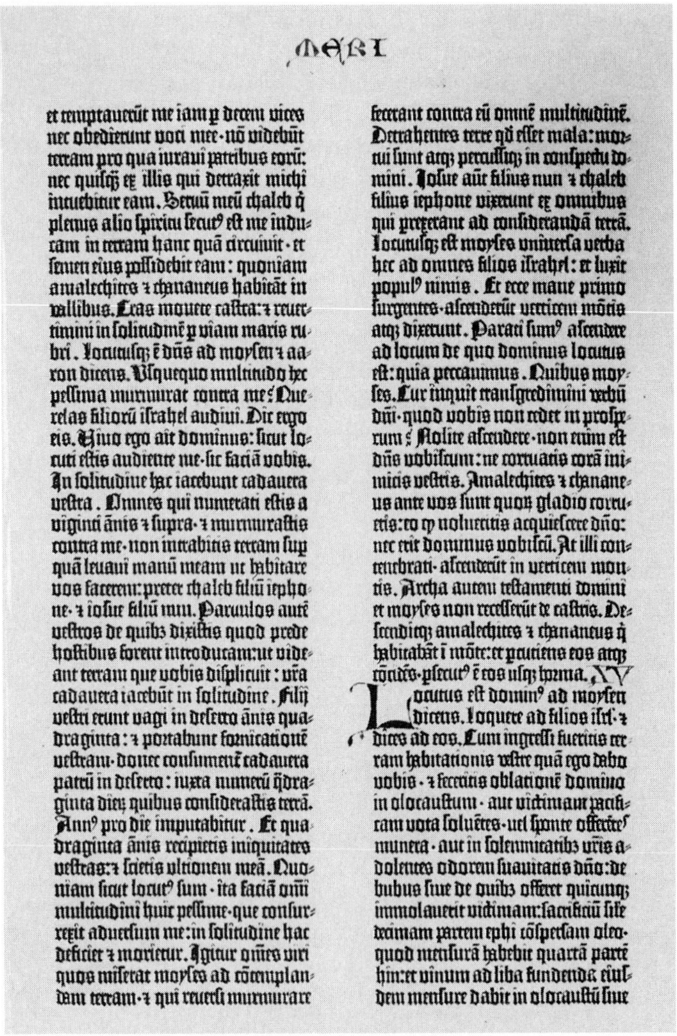

▶ **Gutenberg's Bible**

A page from Johannes Gutenberg's Bible marks one of the most significant technical and cultural advances of the fifteenth century: printing with movable type, a process that made possible a wider dissemination of literature and thought.

Aldus In spite of Gutenberg's efforts to keep the technique a secret, it spread rapidly. By 1500 some 250 European cities had presses (see Map 12.1). German masters held an early leadership, but Italians soon challenged their preeminence. The Venetian printer Aldus Manutius, in particular, published works that are minor masterpieces of scholarship and grace. Aldus and his fellow Italians rejected the elaborate Gothic typeface used in the north and developed their own *italic* type, modeled on the clear script they found in old manuscripts. They believed this was the style of writing used in ancient Rome, but in fact they were imitating the Carolingian minuscule script.

The immediate effect of the printing press was to multiply the output and cut the costs of books. It made information available to a much broader segment of the population, and libraries could store larger quantities of information at lower cost. Printing also helped disseminate and preserve knowledge in standardized form—a major contribution to the advance of technology and scholarship. Printing produced a revolution in what we would call *information technology*, and indeed it resembles in many ways the profound changes that computers are making in our own lives. Finally, printing could spread new ideas with unprecedented speed—a fact that was not fully appreciated, however, until the 1500s, when print became essential to the propaganda of religious reformers in the Protestant Reformation (see Chapter 13).

NAVIGATION

Ships People as well as ideas began to travel more easily in the fourteenth and fifteenth centuries. Before about 1325 there was still no regular sea traffic between northern and southern Europe by way of the Atlantic, but it grew rapidly thereafter. In navigation, the substitution of capital for labor meant the introduction of bigger ships, which carried more cargo with relatively smaller crews. Large ships were safer at sea; they could sail in uncertain weather, when smaller vessels had to stay in port; they could remain at sea longer; and they did not have to sail close to the coastline in order to replenish their supplies. Their voyages between ports could be more direct and therefore speedier.

The larger vessels required more sophisticated means of steering and navigation. Before 1300, ships were turned by trailing an oar over the side. This provided poor control, especially in sailing ships, which needed efficient steering to take advantage of shifting winds. Some time during the fourteenth century the stern rudder was developed, which enabled a captain to tack effectively against the wind and control his ship closely when entering or leaving ports. Voyages became quicker and safer, and the costs of maritime transport declined.

Instruments Ocean navigation also required a reliable means for estimating course and position, and here notable progress had been made in the late thirteenth century. Scholars at the court of King Alfonso X of Castile compiled the Alfonsine Tables, which showed with unprecedented accuracy the position and movements of the heavenly bodies. Using such tables, captains could take the elevation of the sun or stars with an astrolabe and calculate a ship's latitude, or position on a north-south coordinate. (They could not tell their longitude, or position on an east-west coordinate, until they could carry accurate clocks that could compare their time with that of a basic reference meridian, such as Greenwich in England. Until the 1700s, when the first accurate clocks immune to a ship's swaying were developed, navigators who sailed across the Atlantic could not tell how far they had traveled.)

The origin of the compass is unclear, but it was common on Mediterranean ships by the thirteenth century. By 1300, too, Mediterranean navigators sailed with maps of remarkable accuracy and used *portolani,* or port descriptions, which minutely described harbors, coastlines, and hazards. All these technical developments gave European mariners a mastery of Atlantic coastal waters and helped prepare the way for the voyages of discovery in the fifteenth century.

BUSINESS INSTITUTIONS

Banks The bad times of the fourteenth century also stimulated the development of more efficient business procedures. Merchant houses in the late fourteenth and fifteenth centuries were considerably smaller than those of the thirteenth century, but more flexible. The Medici bank of Florence, which functioned from 1397 until 1498, for example, was not a single monolithic structure; rather, it rested on separate partnerships, which established its various branches at Florence, Venice, Rome, Avignon, Bruges, and London. Central control and unified management were ensured by having the senior partners—members of the Medici family—in all the contracts; but the branches had autonomy, and most important, the collapse of one did not threaten others. This system of interlocked partnerships resembled a modern holding company.

Banking operations also grew more sophisticated. By the late 1300s "book transfers" had become commonplace; that is, a depositor could pay a debt without using coin by ordering the bank to transfer credit from his own account to his creditor's. At first the depositor had to give the order orally, but by 1400 it was commonly written, making it an immediate ancestor of the modern check.

Financial Practices Accounting methods also improved. The most notable development was the adoption of double-entry bookkeeping, which makes errors in arithmetic immediately evident and gives a clear picture of the financial position of a commercial enterprise. Although known in the ancient world, double-entry bookkeeping was not widely practiced in the West until the 1300s. In this, as in other business practices, Italy led the way, but these accounting techniques eventually spread to the rest of Europe.

Another financial innovation was the development of a system of maritime insurance, without which investors would have been reluctant to risk their money on expensive vessels. There

▶ EARLY BANKERS
This illustration from a printed Italian handbook, which gives instructions to merchants and is dated circa 1496, shows the interior of a bank or accounting house.

are references to the practice of insuring ships in the major Italian ports as early as 1318. In these first insurance contracts the broker bought the ship and cargo at the port of embarkation and agreed to sell them back at a higher price once the ship reached its destination. If the ship sank, it was legally the broker's and he assumed the loss. In the 1300s the leading companies of Florence abandoned the clumsy device of conditional sales and wrote explicit insurance contracts. By 1400 maritime insurance had become a regular item of the shipping business, and it was to play a major role in the opening of the Atlantic.

Insurance for land transport developed in the 1400s but was never common. The first life insurance contracts appeared in fifteenth-century Italy and were limited to particular periods (the duration of a voyage) or particular persons (a wife during pregnancy). But without actuarial tables, life insurance of this sort was far more of a gamble than a business.

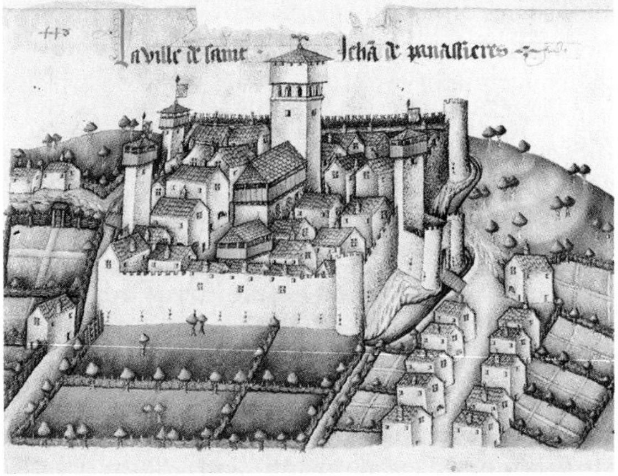

▸ **VIEW OF PANISSIÈRES, FROM A FIFTEENTH-CENTURY ARMORIAL**
As the population of Europe began to recover from the Black Death, one can see signs of expansion and prosperity in its most fertile regions. This fifteenth-century view of the town of Panissières, in the rich Loire valley in France, indicates that houses were again springing up and fields were being cultivated outside the walls of the fortified heart of the town.

THE ECONOMY IN THE LATE FIFTEENTH CENTURY

In the last half of the fifteenth century Europe had recovered fairly well from the economic blows of a hundred years before, and the revived economy differed greatly from what it had been. Increased diversification, capitalization, and rationalization aided production and enterprise in both countryside and city. Europe in 1500 was certainly a much smaller community than it had been in 1300. Possibly, too, the gross product of its economy may not have equaled the output of the best years of the thirteenth century. But in the end the population had fallen more drastically than production. After a century of difficult readjustment Europe emerged more productive and richer than it had been at any time in its history.

III. Popular Unrest

The demographic collapse and economic troubles of the fourteenth century deeply disturbed the social peace of Europe. European society had been remarkably stable and mostly peaceful from the Early Middle Ages until around 1300, and there is little evidence of uprisings or social warfare. The 1300s and 1400, however, witnessed numerous revolts of peasants and artisans against what they believed to be the oppression of the propertied classes.

RURAL REVOLTS

One of the most spectacular fourteenth-century rural uprisings was the English Peasants' War of 1381. This revolt originated in popular resentment against both the policies of the royal government and the practices of the great landlords. The royal government through the Statute of Laborers (1351) had sought to freeze wages and keep the workers bound to their jobs. Although this policy had little practical success, the mere effort to implement it aggravated social tensions, especially in the countryside, where it would have imposed a kind of serfdom on the peasants. Concurrent attempts to collect poll taxes (flat charges on each member of the population), which by their nature demanded less from the prosperous than the humble, crystallized resentment against the government. Rich landlords did nothing to help the situation by trying to revive many half-forgotten feudal dues, which had been allowed to lapse when rents were high in the thirteenth century.

Under leaders of uncertain background—Wat Tyler, Jack Straw, and a priest named John Ball—peasant bands, enraged by the latest poll tax, marched on London in 1381. They called for the abolition of serfdom, labor services, tithes, and other feudal dues, and demanded an end to the poll taxes. The workers of London, St. Albans, York, and other cities, who had similar grievances, rose in support of the peasants. After mobs burned the houses of prominent lawyers and royal officials, King Richard II, then aged 15, bravely met with the peasants in person and was able to placate them by promising to accept their demands. But as the peasants dispersed, the great landlords reorganized their forces and violently suppressed the last vestiges of unrest in the countryside; the young king also reneged on his promises.

The peasant uprising in England was only one of many rural disturbances between 1350 and 1450, including revolts near Paris and in Languedoc, Catalonia, and Sweden. There were also such disturbances in Germany in the fifteenth century and a major peasant revolt in 1524, which was to feed into the tensions of the early days of the Protestant Reformation.

▸ **FEBRUARY, *LES TRÈS RICHES HEURES*, 1413–1416**
The different labors of the 12 months of the year are depicted in this fifteenth-century book of hours commissioned by the French Duke of Berry. Despite the snowy, barren season, the rural laborers still have to work. They gather sticks and wood and then carry them to the distant village.

URBAN REVOLTS

The causes of social unrest within the cities were similar to those in the countryside. Governments controlled by the propertied classes tried to prevent wages from rising and workers from moving and also sought to impose a heavier share of the tax burden on the poorer segments of society. In the 1300s and early 1400s, Strassburg, Metz, Ghent, Liège, and Paris were all scenes of riots. Though not entirely typical, one of the most interesting of these urban revolts was the Ciompi uprising at Florence in 1378.

The Ciompi Florence was one of the wool-manufacturing centers of Europe; the industry employed probably one-third of the working population of the city, which shortly before the Black Death may have risen to 120,000 people. The wool industry, like most, entered bad times immediately after the plague. To protect themselves, employers cut production, thereby spreading unemployment. Since many of the employers were also members of the ruling oligarchy, they had laws passed limiting wages and manipulating taxation and monetary policy to benefit the rich. The poorest workers were denied their own guild and had no collective voice that could influence the government. In all disputes they were subject to the bosses' judges and the bosses' law.

▶ CLOTH MARKET IN BOLOGNA
The manufacture and marketing of textiles was one of the main sources of wealth for the cities of northern Italy. This scene, from a manuscript dated 1411, gives us a sense of what the cloth market in Bologna must have been like as merchants examined, bought, and sold various fabrics. But ordinary cloth workers like the Ciompi rarely shared in the wealth.

The poorest workers—mainly the wool carders, known as Ciompi—rose in revolt. They demanded, and for a short time got, several reforms. The employers would produce at least enough cloth to ensure work, they would refrain from monetary manipulations considered harmful to the workers, and they would allow the workers their own guild and representation in communal government. This was hardly power for the workers, but it was nevertheless intolerable to the ruling oligarchy. Because the Ciompi did not have the leaders to maintain a steady influence on government policy, the great families regained full authority in the city by 1382 and quickly ended the democratic concessions. Although the Ciompi revolt was short-lived and ultimately unsuccessful, the incident is one of the first signs of the urban class tensions that would be a regular disturbance in future centuries.

THE SEEDS OF DISCONTENT

Each of the social disturbances of the 1300s and 1400s was shaped by circumstances that were local and unique. Yet there were similarities in these social movements: for example, the fact that misery does not seem to have been the main cause of unrest. Indeed, the evidence suggests that the conditions of the working classes in both countryside and city were improving after the Black Death. The prosperity of the thirteenth century, which was chiefly a prosperity of landlords and employers, had been founded in part upon the poor negotiating position, and even exploitation, of the workers. The depopulation of the fourteenth century radically altered this situation. The workers, now reduced in number, were better able to bargain for lower rents, higher wages, and a fairer distribution of social benefits.

With the possible exception of the Ciompi, the people who revolted were rarely the desperately poor. In England, for example, the centers of the peasant uprising of 1381 were in the lower Thames valley—a region that was more fertile, more prosperous, less oppressed and with less serfdom than other parts of the kingdom. Also, the immediate provocation for the revolt was the imposition of a poll tax, and poll taxes (or any taxes) obviously do not alarm the truly destitute, whereas they do alarm people who have recently made financial gains and are anxious to hold on to them.

Causes of Revolt The principal goad to revolt in both town and country seems to have been the effort of the propertied classes to retain their old advantages and deny the workers their new ones. In the first decades after the Black Death, governments failed in their efforts to increase taxes and to peg rents, wages, and prices at levels favorable to landlords and employers; meanwhile, they spread hostility among the workers, who felt that their improving social and economic status was being threatened.

The impulse to revolt also drew strength from the psychological tensions of this age of devastating plagues, famines, and wars. The nervous temper of the times predisposed people to take action against real or imagined enemies. When needed, justifications for revolt could be found in Christian belief, for the Christian fathers had taught that neither the concept of private property nor social inequality had been intended by God. In a high-strung world many of these uprisings involved an emotional effort to attain the millennium, to reach that age of justice and equality that Christian belief saw in the past, expected in the future, and put off for the present.

A New Stability In the end, as labor became scarce, the rich had to offer favorable terms if they wanted tillers for their lands and workers for their shops. Thus, by about 1450, after a century of instability, a new equilibrium was emerging in European society, even if slowly and never completely. The humblest classes improved their lot and were fairly secure in their gains. Serfdom all but disappeared in the West; wages remained high and bread cheap. Life, of course, was still very hard for most workers, but it was better than it had been two centuries before. Perhaps reflective of better social conditions for the masses, the population once more began to grow, equipping Europe for its great expansion in the sixteenth century.

IV. The Governments of Europe

War was a frequent occurrence throughout the Middle Ages but was never so widespread or long-lasting as in the conflicts of the 1300s and 1400s. The Hundred Years' War between England and France is the most famous of these struggles, but there was fighting in every corner of Europe. The inbred violence of the age indicated a partial breakdown in governmental systems, which failed to maintain stability at home and peace with foreign powers.

THE FEUDAL EQUILIBRIUM

The governmental systems of Europe were founded on multiple partnerships that exercised power under feudal constitutions. The king enjoyed supreme dignity and even a recognized sacred character, but he was far from being an absolute ruler. In return for loyalty and service, he conceded a large share of the responsibility for government to a wide range of privileged persons and institutions: the great secular and ecclesiastical princes, the nobles, religious congregations, powerful military orders such as the Templars, free cities or communes, and even favored guilds such as the universities.

The growth of the feudal constitution in the eleventh and twelfth centuries had been a major step toward a more ordered political life, but it rested on a delicate equilibrium. To keep internal peace, which often meant international peace because of the confused borders of most feudal states, all members of the feudal partnership had to remain faithful to their obligations. This governmental system worked well until the early 1300s, but it could not sustain the blows it suffered during the period of social crisis. Governments had to be slowly rebuilt, though still along feudal lines and still based on shared authority. Nevertheless, many of the new governments that came to dominate the European political scene in the late 1400s conceded far more power to the senior partner in the feudal relationship, the king or prince.

DYNASTIC INSTABILITY

The forces that upset the equilibrium of feudal governments were many. One of the most obvious, itself rooted in the demographic instability of the age, was the failure of dynasties to perpetuate themselves. The Hundred Years' War, or at least the excuse for it, arose from the inability of the Capetian kings of France, for the first time since the tenth century, to produce a male heir in direct line. The English War of the Roses resulted from the uncertain succession to the crown of

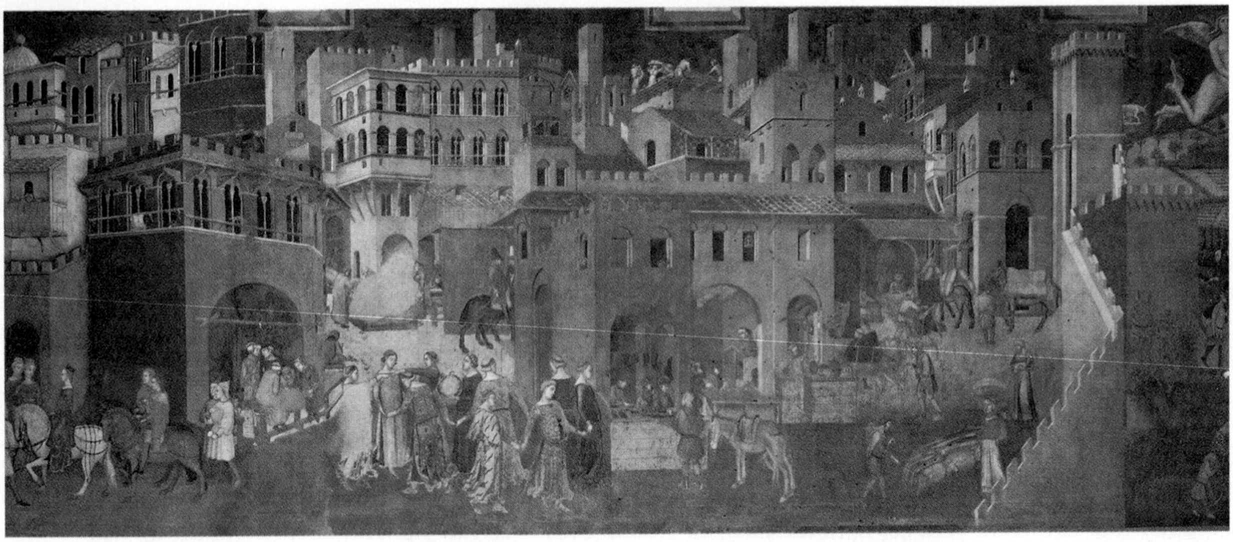

▸ *Ambrogio Lorenzetti*
The Peaceful City (detail from Good Government), 1338–1341
The effects of good government, seen in this idealized representation of the *Peaceful City*, by Ambrogio Lorenzetti, include flourishing commerce, dancing maidens, and lavish residences, as opposed to the protective towers of feudal warfare. This fresco in the city hall of Siena was a constant reminder to the citizens of the advantages of living in their city.

England and the claims of the two rival houses of Lancaster and York. In Portugal, Castile, France, England, Naples, Hungary, Poland, and the Scandinavian countries, the reigning monarchs of 1450 were not the direct, male, legitimate descendants of those reigning in 1300. Most of the founders of new lines had to fight for their positions.

FISCAL PRESSURES

War The same powerful economic forces that were creating new patterns of agriculture and trade were also reshaping the fiscal policies and financial machinery of feudal governments. War was growing more expensive, as well as more frequent. Better-trained armies were needed to fight for longer periods of time and with more complex weaponry. Above all, the increasing use of firearms was adding to the costs of war. To replace the traditional, undisciplined, unpaid, and poorly equipped feudal armies, governments came more and more to rely on mercenaries, who were better trained and better armed than the vassals who fought to fulfill their feudal obligations. Many mercenaries were organized into associations known as companies of adventure, whose leaders were both good commanders and businesssmen. They took their enterprise where the market was most favorable, sold their services to the highest bidder, and turned substantial profits. To hire mercenaries, and win battles, was increasingly a question of money.

Taxes While war went up in price, the traditional revenues upon which governments depended sank. Until the fourteenth century, the king or prince was expected to meet the expenses of government from ordinary revenues, chiefly rents from his properties; but his rents, like everyone else's, were falling in the Late Middle Ages. Governments of all types—monarchies, the papacy, cities—desperately sought to develop new sources of revenue. For example, the papacy, because it could not rely on the meager receipts from its lands, built a huge financial apparatus that sold ecclesiastical appointments, favors, and dispensations from normal canonical requirements; imposed tithes on ecclesiastical revenues; and sold remissions of sin known as *indulgences*. In France the monarchy established a monopoly over the sale of salt. In England the king at various times imposed direct taxes on hearths, individuals (the poll tax), and plow teams, plus a host of smaller levies. The Italian cities taxed a whole range of items from windows to prostitutes. Under acute fiscal pressures, governments scrutinized the necessities, pleasures, and sins of society to find sources of revenue; and surviving fiscal records indicate that, in spite of the disturbed times, they managed to increase their incomes hugely through these taxes. For example, the English monarchy never collected or spent more than £30,000 per year before 1336; thereafter, the budget rarely sank below £100,000 and at times reached £250,000 in the late fourteenth century.

This new reliance on extraordinary taxes had important political consequences. The most lucrative taxes were not limited to the ruler's own lands but extended over all the realm. Since he had no established right to these demands, he had to seek the consent of his subjects, and he therefore had to summon territorial or national assemblies of estates, such as Parliament in England or the Estates General in France, to grant new taxes. But these assemblies, in turn, often balked at the demands or offered taxes only in return for political concessions. Even in the Church many reformers maintained that a general council should have ultimate control over papal finances. The extraordinary expansion of governmental revenues thus raised profound constitutional questions in both secular and ecclesiastical governments.

FACTIONAL CONFLICTS

The nobility that had developed nearly everywhere in Europe also entered a period of instability in the Late Middle Ages. Birth was the main means of access to this class, and membership offered legal and social privileges—exemption from most taxes, immunity from certain juridical procedures (such as torture), and so forth. The nobles saw themselves as the chief counselors of the king and his principal partners in the conduct of government.

By the 1300s, however, the nobles had long since lost whatever economic homogeneity they might once have possessed. Their wealth was chiefly in land, and they, like all landlords, faced the problem of declining rents. They often lacked the funds needed for the new systems of agriculture, and they were further plagued by the continuing problem of finding income and careers for their younger sons. In short, the nobles were not immune from the acute economic dislocations of the times, and their class included men who lived on the brink of poverty as well as holders of enormous estates.

Factions To maintain their position, some of the nobles joined the companies of adventure to fight as mercenaries. Others hoped to buttress their sinking fortunes through marriage or by winning offices, lands, pensions, or other favors from governments. But as the social uncertainties intensified, the nobles tended to coalesce into factions, which disputed with one another over the control of government and the distribution of its favors. From England to Italy, factional warfare constantly disturbed the peace. A divided and grasping nobility added to the tensions of the age and to its violence.

Characteristically, a faction was led by a great noble house and included people of varying social station—great nobles in alliance with the leading house, poor knights, retainers, servants, sometimes even artisans and peasants. Some of the factions encompassed scores of families and hundreds of men and could almost be considered little states within a state, with their own small armies, loyalties, and symbols of allegiance in the colors or distinctive costumes (livery) worn by their members.

ENGLAND, FRANCE, AND THE HUNDRED YEARS' WAR

All the factors that upset the equilibrium of feudal governments—dynastic instability, fiscal pressures, and factional rivalries—helped to provoke the greatest struggle of the epoch, the Hundred Years' War.

Causes The issue over which the Hundred Years' War was supposedly fought was a dispute over the French royal succession. After more than 300 years of extraordinary good luck, the last three Capetian kings (the brothers Louis X, Philip

V, and Charles IV) failed to produce male heirs. With Charles's death in 1328, the nearest surviving male relative was his nephew King Edward III of England, son of his sister Isabella. But the Parlement of Paris—the supreme court of France—declared that women could not transmit a claim to the crown. In place of Edward, the French Estates chose Philip of Valois, a first cousin of the previous kings. Edward did not at first dispute this decision, and as holder of the French fiefs of Aquitaine and Ponthieu, he did homage to Philip.

More important than the dynastic issue was in fact the clash of French and English interests in Flanders, an area whose cloth-making industry relied on England for wool. In 1302 the Flemings had rebelled against their count, a vassal of the French king, and had remained virtually independent until 1328, when Philip defeated their troops and restored the count. At Philip's insistence, the count ordered the arrest of all English merchants in Flanders; Edward retaliated by cutting off the export of wool, which spread unemployment in the Flemish towns. The Flemings revolted once more and drove out the count. To give legal sanction to their revolt, they persuaded Edward to assert his claim to the French crown, which held suzerainty over Flanders.

The most serious point of friction, however, was the status of Aquitaine and Ponthieu. Edward had willingly performed ordinary homage for them, but Philip then insisted on liege homage, which would have obligated Edward to support Philip against all enemies. Edward did not believe that, as a king, he could undertake the obligations of liege homage to any man, and refused. Philip began harassing the frontiers of Aquitaine and declared Edward's fiefs forfeit in 1337. The attack on Aquitaine pushed Edward into supporting the Flemish revolt and was thus the main provocation for the Hundred Years' War.

Philip, a new king eager for glory, had clearly embarked on a dangerous adventure by harassing Aquitaine; and Edward, in supporting the Flemings, reacted perhaps too strongly. Their minimal concern for traditional obligations suggests that the war was mainly the result of a breakdown of the feudal constitution of medieval France in both its institutions and its spirit.

THE TIDES OF BATTLE

The French seemed to have a decisive superiority over the English at the outset of the war. The population of France was perhaps 15 million; England had between 4 and 7 million. But the war was hardly ever a national confrontation, because French subjects (Flemings, Gascons, Burgundians) fought alongside the English against other French subjects. The confused struggle may, however, be divided into three periods: initial English victories from 1338 to 1360; French resurgence, then stalemate, from 1367 to 1415; and a wild denouement with tides rapidly shifting from 1415 to 1453.

First Period The English never fully exploited their early victories, nor did the French ever manage to undo them. An English naval victory at Sluys in 1340 ensured English communications across the Channel and determined that France would be the scene of the fighting. Six years later Edward landed in France on what was more a marauding expedition than a campaign of conquest. Philip pursued the English and finally overtook them at Crécy, where the French knights attacked before their own forces could be fully marshaled and organized. The disciplined English, making effective use of the longbow, cut the confused French army to pieces. The victory also ensured the English possession of Calais, which they took in 1347. The scenario was repeated in 1356 at Poitiers when John II, who had succeeded Philip, attacked an English army led by Edward's son, the Black Prince, and suffered an even more crushing defeat. English victories, the Black Death, and mutual exhaustion led to the Peace of Brétigny in 1360. The English were granted Calais and an enlarged Aquitaine, and Edward, in turn, renounced his claim to the French crown.

Second Period But the French were not willing to allow so large a part of their kingdom to remain in English hands. In 1369, under John's successor, Charles V, they opened a second phase of the war. Their strategy was to avoid full-scale battles and wear down the English forces, and they succeeded. By 1380 they had pushed the English nearly into the sea, confining them to Ca-

Chronology of the Hundred Years' War

1328 Charles IV, last Capetian king in direct line, dies; Philip of Valois elected king of France as Philip VI; Philip defeats Flemings at Cassel; unrest continues in Flemish towns.

1329 Edward III of England does simple homage to Philip for continental possessions but refuses liege homage.

1336 Edward embargoes wool exports to Flanders.

1338 Philip's troops harass English Guienne; Edward, urged on by the Flemings, claims French crown; war begins.

1346 Major English victory at Crécy.

1347–1351 Black Death ravages Europe.

1356 Black Prince defeats French at Poitiers.

1358 Peasants' uprising near Paris.

1360 Peace of Brétigny; English gain major territorial concessions but abandon claim to French crown.

1369 Fighting renewed in France.

1370 Bertrand du Guesclin, constable of France, leads French resurgence.

1381 Peasants' Revolt in England.

1392 Charles VI of France suffers first attack of insanity; Burgundians and Armagnacs contend for power over king; fighting wanes as both sides exhausted.

1399 Henry IV of Lancaster takes English throne.

1415 Henry V wins major victory at Agincourt.

1420 Treaty of Troyes; Charles VI recognizes Henry V as legitimate heir to French crown; high-water mark of English fortunes.

1429 Joan of Arc relieves Orléans from English siege; Dauphin crowned king at Reims as Charles VII.

1431 Joan burned at the stake at Rouen.

1435 Peace of Arras; Burgundy abandons English side.

1436 Charles retakes Paris.

1453 Bordeaux falls to French; English retain only Calais on Continent; effective end of war, though no treaty is signed.

lais and a narrow strip of the Atlantic coast from Bordeaux to Bayonne. Fighting was sporadic from 1380 until 1415, with both sides content with a stalemate.

Third Period The last period of the war, from 1415 to 1453, was one of high drama and rapidly shifting fortunes. Henry V of England invaded France and shattered the French army at Agincourt in 1415. His success was confirmed by the Treaty of Troyes in 1420, an almost total French capitulation. King Charles VI of France declared his son the Dauphin (the future Charles VII) illegitimate, named Henry his successor and regent of France, and gave him direct rule over all French lands as far south as the Loire River (see Map 11.3). Charles also gave Henry his daughter Catherine in marriage.

The Dauphin could not accept this forced abdication, and from his capital at Bourges he led an expedition across the Loire River. The English drove his forces back and systematically took the towns and fortresses north of the river that were loyal to him. In 1428 they finally laid siege to Orléans, a city whose fall would have given them a commanding position in the Loire valley and would have made the Dauphin's cause desperate.

Map 11.3 THE HUNDRED YEARS' WAR

Because of their closeness to the continent and their naval power, the English were able to dominate northern France, the area which traditionally had been that kingdom's heartland. As a result, Joan of Arc's decisive victory came not in Paris but in Orléans on the Loire River—which proved to be a crucial boundary between the two sides.

JOAN OF ARC

The intervention of a young peasant girl, Joan of Arc, saved the Valois dynasty. Convinced that heavenly voices were ordering her to rescue France, Joan persuaded several royal officials, and finally the Dauphin himself, of the authenticity of her mission and was given command of an army. In 1429 she marched to Orléans and forced the English to raise the siege. She then escorted the Dauphin to Reims, the historic coronation city of France, where his crowning confirmed his legitimacy and won him broad support as the embodiment of French royalist sentiment. The tide had turned.

Joan passed from history as quickly and as dramatically as she had arrived. The Burgundians, allies of the English, captured her in 1430 and sold her to the English, who put her on trial for witchcraft and heresy (*see box*, p. 334). She was burned at the stake at Rouen in 1431. Yet Joan's commitment was one sign of an increasingly powerful feeling among the people. They had grown impatient with continuing destruction and had come to identify their own security with the expulsion of the English and the establishment of a strong Valois monarchy. This growing loyalty to the king finally saved France from its long agony. A series of French successes followed Joan's death, and by 1453 only Calais was left in English hands. No formal treaty ended the war, but both sides accepted the outcome: England was no longer a continental power.

► JOAN OF ARC, 1484

Surrounded by the clerics who had condemned her, Joan of Arc is bound to the stake in this scene from a manuscript that was prepared half a century after she was executed in 1431. Despite Joan's own preference for short hair and manly costume, she is here shown as a conventionally idealized female figure.

THE EFFECTS OF THE HUNDRED YEARS' WAR

Like all the disasters of the era, the Hundred Years' War accelerated change. It stimulated the development of firearms and the technologies needed to manufacture them, and it helped establish the infantry—armed with longbow, pike, or gun—as superior in battle to mounted knights.

Parliament The war also had a major effect on government institutions in England and France. The expense of fighting forced the kings on each side to look for new sources of revenue through taxation. In England the king willingly gave Parliament a larger political role in return for grants of new taxes. The tradition became firmly established that Parliament had the right to grant or refuse new taxes, to agree to legislation, to channel appeals to the king, and to offer advice on important decisions such as peace and war. The House of Commons gained the right to introduce all tax legislation, since the Commons, unlike the Lords, were representatives of shires and boroughs. Parliament also named a committee to audit tax records and supervise payments. Equally important, the Commons could impeach high royal officials, a crucial step in establishing the principle that a king's ministers were responsible to Parliament as well as to their royal master. By the end of the Hundred Years' War, Parliament had been notably strengthened at the expense of royal power.

French Government The need for new taxes had a rather different outcome in France, where it enhanced the power of the monarchs while weakening the Estates General, the national representative assembly. In 1343 Philip VI established a monopoly over the sale of salt, laying down in many areas of France how much it cost and how much each family had to consume. The tax on salt, called the *gabelle*, was to be essential to

The Trial of Joan of Arc

The records of the trial of Joan of Arc in Rouen in 1431 give us a rare opportunity to hear her directly, or at least the words a secretary heard. Whether recorded accurately or not, her testimony does give us a glimpse of her extraordinary spirit and determination.

"When she had taken the oath the said Jeanne was questioned by us about her name and her surname. To which she replied that in her own country she was called Jeannette. She was questioned about the district from which she came.

"She said she was born in the village of Domrémy. Asked if in her youth she had learned any craft, she saw yes, to sew and spin; and in sewing and spinning she feared no woman in Rouen.

"Afterwards she declared that at the age of 13 she had a voice from God to help her and guide her. And the first time she was much afraid. And this voice came towards noon, in summer, in her father's garden. Asked what instruction this voice gave her for the salvation of her soul, she said it taught her to be good and to go to church often; and the voice told her that she should raise the siege of the city of Orléans.

"Asked whether, when she saw the voice coming to her, there was a light, she answered that there was a great deal of light on all sides. She added to the examiner that not all the light came to him alone!

"Asked whether she thought she had committed a sin when she left her father and mother, she answered that since God commanded, it was right to do so. She added that since God commanded, if she had had a hundred parents, she would have gone nevertheless.

"Jeanne was admonished to speak the truth. Many of the points were read and explained to her, and she was told that if she did not confess them truthfully she would be put to the torture, the instruments of which were shown to her.

"To which Jeanne answered in this manner: 'Truly if you were to tear me limb from limb and separate my soul from my body, I would not tell you anything more; and if I did say anything, I should afterwards declare that you had compelled me to say it by force.' "

From *The Trial of Jeanne d'Arc*, as cited in Leonard Bernard and Theodore B. Hodges (eds.), *Readings in European History* (New York: Macmillan, 1958), pp. 181–182.

French royal finance until 1789. In gaining support for this and other taxes, Philip and his successors sought the agreement of regional assemblies of estates as well as the national Estates General. The kings' reliance on the local estates hindered the rise of a centralized assembly that could speak for the entire kingdom. By the reign of Charles VII, during the last stages of the war, the monarchy obtained the right to impose national taxes (notably the *taille*, a direct tax from which nobles and clerics were exempt) without the consent of the Estates General. By then, too, the royal government was served by a standing professional army—the first in any European country since the fall of the Roman Empire.

The War of the Roses Both England and France experienced internal dissension during the Hundred Years' War. After the death of Edward III in 1377, England faced over a century of turmoil, with nobles striving to maintain their economic fortunes through factional conflicts—that is, by preying on one another. In time, these conflicts led to a struggle between two factions, the Lancastrians and the Yorkists, over the throne itself, with all English nobles aligning themselves on one side or the other. The civil war that followed is known to historians as the War of the Roses (the Lancastrians' emblem was a red rose, the Yorkists' a white rose). It lasted some 35 years, ending in 1485, when Henry Tudor defeated the

Yorkists at Bosworth Field and came to the throne as Henry VII. By this time, prosperity had relieved the pressures on the English nobles, and the people in general, weary of war, welcomed the strong and orderly regime that Henry established.

Burgundy In France, too, the power of the monarchy was threatened by rival factions of nobles, the Armagnacs and the Burgundians. The Armagnacs wanted the war with England vigorously pursued, while the Burgundians favored accommodation. The territorial ambitions of the Burgundians also posed a threat to the French monarchy. King John the Good of France had granted the huge Duchy of Burgundy to his younger son, Philip the Bold, in 1363. Philip and his successors greatly enlarged their possessions in eastern France, the Rhône and Rhine valleys, and the Low Countries (see Map 11.3). They were generous patrons of literature and the arts, and they made their court at Dijon the most brilliant in Europe. The dukes seem to have sought to establish a Burgundian "middle kingdom" between France and the Holy Roman Empire; such a state would have affected the political geography of Europe permanently and undermined the position of the French monarch. But the threat vanished in 1477 when the last duke, Charles the Bold, was killed in battle with the Swiss at Nancy. His daughter and heir, Mary of Burgundy, could not hold her scattered inheritance together, and a large part of it came under French control.

The English and French States With the loss of most of its continental possessions, England emerged from the war geographically more consolidated. It was also homogeneous in its language (English now replaced French as the language of the law courts and administration) and more conscious of its cultural distinctiveness and national identity. Freed from its continental entanglements, England was ready for its expansion beyond the seas and for a surge in national pride and self-consciousness.

France never achieved quite the territorial consolidation of England, but with the expulsion of the English from his lands and the sudden disintegration of the Duchy of Burgundy, the French king was without a major rival among his feudal princes. The monarchy emerged from the war with a permanent army, a rich tax system, and no clear constitutional restrictions on its exercise of power. Most significantly, the war gave the French king high prestige and confirmed him as the chief protector and patron of the people.

In both France and England, government at the end of the Middle Ages was still decentralized and "feudal," if we mean by that term that certain privileged persons and institutions (nobles, the Church, towns, and the like) continued to hold and to exercise some form of private jurisdiction. They retained, for example, their own courts. But the king had unmistakably emerged as the dominant partner in the feudal relationship. Moreover, he was prepared to press his advantages in the sixteenth century.

▶ CHRISTINE DE PISAN PRESENTS POEMS TO ISABEAU OF BAVARIA
Christine de Pisan (1364–1430) was the author of several important historical and literary works, including a biography of King Charles V of France and *The Book of the Three Virtues*, a manual for the education of women. She is here depicted presenting a volume of her poems to the queen of France, who is surrounded by ladies in waiting and the symbol of the French royal family, the fleur-de-lis. It is significant that there were such scenes of elegance and intellectual life even amidst the chaos and destruction of the Hundred Years' War.

THE HOLY ROMAN EMPIRE

With the death of Emperor Frederick II of Hohenstaufen (1250), the Holy Roman Empire ceased to function as a major power in European affairs. The empire continued to link Germany and Italy, but real authority fell to the princes in Germany and the city republics in Italy. In 1273, after a tumultuous period known as the Interregnum, during which several rivals contended for the title, the princes chose as emperor Rudolf of Habsburg, the first of that long-enduring family to hold the office. Instead of rebuilding the imperial authority, Rudolf sought to advance the interests of his own dynasty and its ancestral possessions. His successors also tended to use the office of emperor for their own narrow dynastic advantage.

The most significant event of the fourteenth century was the issuance in 1356 of the Golden Bull, which essentially defined the constitution of the empire until 1806. Although issued by the pope, the bull reflected the interests of the leading German princes. The right of naming the emperor was given to seven electors—the archbishops of Mainz, Trier, and Cologne; the count palatine of the Rhine; the duke of Saxony; the margrave of Brandenburg; and the king of Bohemia. As the bull assigned the papacy no role in naming or crowning the emperor, it was a victory for imperial autonomy.

The Swiss An indication of the growing autonomy of regions within the empire was the emergence of the Swiss Confederation of cantons (districts), which won virtual independence in the Late Middle Ages. In the early 1200s Emperor Frederick II of Hohenstaufen had recognized the autonomy of two cantons, Uri and Schwyz, and had given them the responsibility of guarding the Saint Gotthard Pass through the Alps, the shortest route from Germany to Italy. The lands of the cantons were technically part of the ancient Duchy of Swabia, and in the late thirteenth century the Habsburg princes, seeking to consolidate their possessions in the duchy, attempted to subjugate the Swiss lands as well. To resist the Habsburg threat, the cantons of Uri, Schwyz, and Unterwalden joined in a Perpetual Compact in 1291. They formed the nucleus of what was eventually to become the 22 cantons of present-day Switzerland.

The Swiss had to fight for their autonomy, and they acquired a reputation as the best fighters in Europe. At the same time, their confederated system of government, which allowed each canton to run its own affairs, was a notable exception to the tendency, evident elsewhere in Europe, for central governments to grow stronger in the 1300s and 1400s.

THE STATES OF ITALY

Free cities, or communes, dominated the political life of central and northern Italy in the early fourteenth century. The Holy Roman Empire claimed a loose sovereignty over much of the peninsula north of Rome, and the papacy governed the area around Rome; but in fact most of the principal cities, and many small ones too, had gained the status of self-governing city-states.

However, the new economic and social conditions of the 1300s worked against the survival of the smaller communes. The economic contraction made it increasingly difficult for industries and merchant houses in the smaller cities to compete with their rivals in the larger ones. And the rising costs of war made it hard for small communes to defend their independence. In addition, all of Italian society, in both large and small towns, was deeply disturbed by factional strife that often made political order impossible.

In response to these pressures, two major tendencies became evident. Much stronger governments, amounting at times to despotisms, tended to replace the weak governments of free communes. And regional states, dominated politically and economically by a single metropolis, replaced the numerous, free, and highly competitive communes.

Milan Perhaps the most effective Italian despot was the ruler of Milan, Gian Galeazzo Visconti (1378–1402), who set about enlarging the Visconti inheritance of 21 cities in the Po valley. Through shrewd negotiations and opportune attacks, he secured the submission of cities to his east, which gave him an outlet to the Adriatic Sea. He then seized Bologna, purchased Pisa, and through a variety of methods was accepted as ruler of Siena, Perugia, Spoleto, Nocera, and Assisi. In the course of this advance deep into central Italy,

FAMILY TOWERS AT LUCCA
This fourteenth-century view of the Italian city of Lucca testifies to the violence of factional conflict within these cities. Each major family and its leading supporters built a defensible structure, topped by an identifiable tower. Here, in a large building that surrounded a central courtyard and had its own chapel, they could find refuge from rival families and factions.

Gian Galeazzo kept his chief enemies, the Florentines and the Venetians, divided, and he seemed ready to create a united Italian kingdom.

To establish a legal basis for his power, Gian Galeazzo secured from the emperor an appointment as imperial vicar in 1380 and then as hereditary duke in 1395. This made him the only duke in all Italy, and it seemed a step toward a royal title. He revised the laws of Milan, but the chief administrative foundation of his success was his ability to wring enormous tax revenues from his subjects. Gian Galeazzo was also a generous patron of the new learning of his day; and with his conquests, wealth, and brilliance, he seemed to be awaiting only the submission of the Florentines before adopting the title of king. But he died unexpectedly in 1402, leaving two minor sons, who were incapable of defending their inheritance.

Venice Even those states that escaped the despotism of a Gian Galeazzo moved toward stronger governments and the formation of territorial or regional states. In Venice the government came to be run by a small and closed oligarchy—a group of families that dominated the Council of Ten, the body that controlled the Venetian state. Its policies were geared to preserving oligarchic rule and suppressing opposition to the government.

Whereas Venice had long devoted its main energies to maritime commerce and overseas possessions, it could not now ignore the growth of territorial states on the mainland, which might threaten its agricultural imports or jeopardize its inland trade routes. From the early fifteenth century onward, Venice, too, initiated a policy of territorial expansion on the mainland. By 1405, Padua, Verona, and Vicenza had become Venetian dependencies.

Florence While retaining the trappings of republican government, Florence also came under stronger central control. In 1434 a successful banker named Cosimo de Medici established a form of boss rule over the city. His tax policies favored the lower and middle classes, and he also gained the support of the middle classes by appointments to office and other forms of political patronage. He made peace in Italy his supreme goal and started his family's brilliant tradition of patronage of learning and the arts.

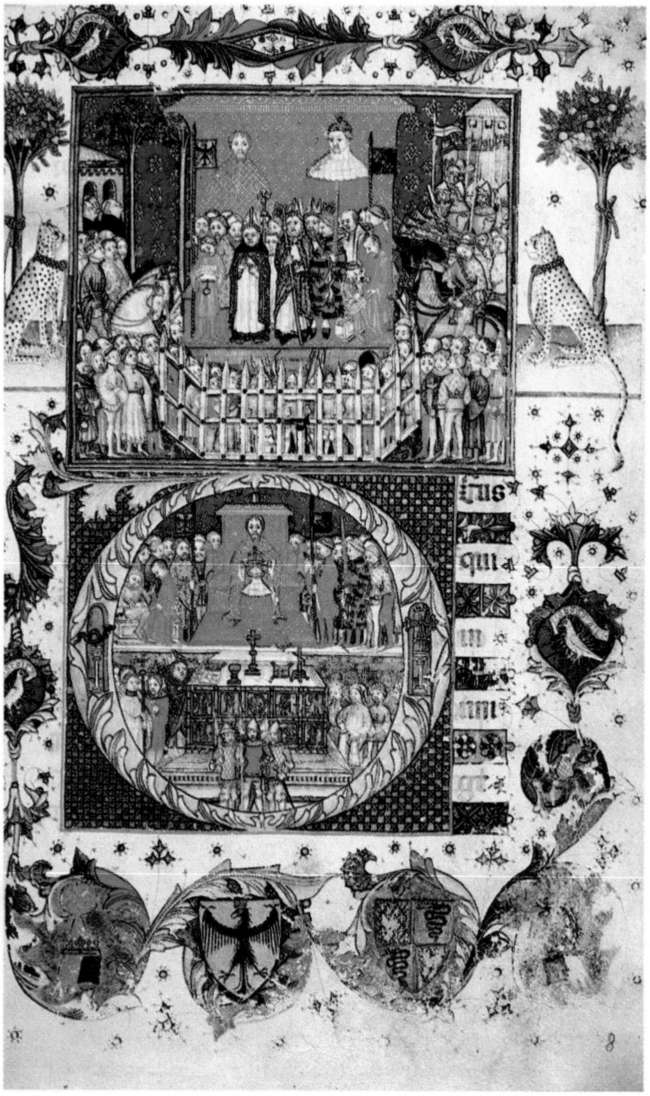

▸ INVESTITURE OF GIAN GALEAZZO VISCONTI, CA. 1395
This contemporary depiction of the investiture of Gian Galeazzo Visconti as duke of Milan is from a manuscript he commissioned to commemorate the occasion. The picture on top shows Visconti in a white cape seated next to the emperor's representative, who in the picture below places the diadem on the kneeling Visconti's head. The spectators come from all walks of life, including bishops and soldiers carrying cannon, but the ceremony itself takes place in front of an altar. The margins contain such Visconti family symbols as the eagle, the cheetah, and various fruit trees; and the entire manuscript leaf is a rich and colorful glorification of a central event in Visconti's life.

This tradition was enhanced by Cosimo's grandson, Lorenzo the Magnificent (1469–1492), who beat back the plots of other powerful Florentine families and strengthened centralized control over the city. Lorenzo's Florence came to set the style for Italy, and eventually for Europe, in the splendor of its festivals, the elegance of its social life, the beauty of its buildings, and the lavish support it extended to scholars and artists.

THE PAPAL STATES AND THE KINGDOM OF NAPLES

The popes were as concerned as the leaders of city-states to consolidate their rule over their possessions in central Italy, but they faced formidable obstacles because the papacy was now located in Avignon in southern France. The difficult terrain of the Italian Papal States—dotted with castles and fortified towns—enabled communes, petty lords, and plain brigands to defy papal authority. Continuing disorders discouraged the popes from returning to Rome, and their efforts to pacify their tumultuous lands were a major drain on papal finances. Even after its return to Rome in 1378 the papacy had difficulty maintaining authority. Not until the pontificate of Martin V (1417–1431) was a stable administration established, and Martin's successors still faced frequent revolts throughout the fifteenth century.

The political situation was equally confused in the Kingdom of Naples and Sicily. With papal support, Charles of Anjou, younger brother of St. Louis of France, had established a dynasty of Angevin rulers over the area. But in 1282 the people of Sicily revolted against the Angevins and appealed for help to the king of Aragon. For the next 150 years the Aragonese and the Angevins battled for dominion over Sicily and Naples. Then in 1435 the king of Aragon, Alfonso V, the Magnanimous, reunited Sicily and southern Italy and made the kingdom the center of an Aragonese empire in the Mediterranean. Alfonso sought to suppress the factions of lawless nobles and to reform taxes and strengthen administration. His efforts were not completely successful, for southern Italy and Sicily were rugged, poor lands and difficult to subdue; but he was at least able to overcome the chaos that had prevailed earlier. Alfonso thus extended to the Mediterra-

▸ *Benozzo Gozzoli*
Procession of the Three Kings to Bethlehem (detail)
This enormous fresco in the Medici palace in Florence, completed in 1459, gives place of honor in the biblical scene of the procession of the Magi to the future ruler of Florence, the ten-year-old Lorenzo de Medici, riding a white horse, and to his grandfather Cosimo de Medici, the founder of the dynasty's power, who is behind Lorenzo, also on a white horse.

nean the strengthening of central governments that took place elsewhere in Europe in the 1400s. The court he created at Naples was one of the most brilliant centers of art and literature of the age.

DIPLOMACY

By about 1450, Italy was no longer a land of numerous, tiny free communes. Rather, it was divided among five territorial states: the Duchy of Milan, the republics of Venice and Florence, the Papal States, and the Kingdom of Naples (see Map 11.4). To govern the relations among these states, the Italians conceived new methods of diplomacy. Led by Venice, they began to maintain permanent embassies at important foreign courts. Moreover, largely through the political sense of Cosimo de Medici, these states were able to pioneer a new way of preserving stability. The Peace of Lodi in 1454 ended a war between Milan, Florence, and Venice; and Cosimo sought to make the peace lasting by creating alliance systems that would balance one another. Milan, Naples, and Florence held one side of the balance; and Venice and the Papal States, the other. Each state felt sufficiently secure in its alliances to have no need to appeal to non-Italian powers for support. During the next 40 years, until the French

Map 11.4 THE ITALIAN STATES IN 1454
Five major states dominated Italy after the Peace of Lodi in 1454. For the next 40 years they maintained a balance of power among themselves, dominating the few independent areas—such as Siena, Genoa, Savoy—and a number of principalities too tiny to be shown on this map.

invaded the peninsula in 1494, the balance was occasionally rocked but never overturned, and it gave Italy an unaccustomed period of peace and freedom from foreign intervention. This system represents one of the earliest appearances in European history of a diplomatic balance of power maintaining international security and peace.

V. The Church

The Church as an institution also experienced major transformations in the 1300s and 1400s. It continued to seek a peaceful Christendom united in faith and obedience to Rome. But the international Christian community was in fact beset by powerful forces that undermined its cohesiveness and weakened papal authority and influence. Although the culmination of these disruptions did not come until the Reformation in the 1500s, the history of the previous two centuries made it clear that the institution was profoundly troubled.

THE AVIGNON EXILE

The humiliation of Pope Boniface VIII by the agents of Philip IV of France at Anagni in 1303 opened the doors to French influence at the Curia. In 1305 the College of Cardinals elected a French pope, Clement V, who because of the political disorders in the Papal States eventually settled at Avignon (1309). Though technically a part of the Holy Roman Empire, Avignon was in language and culture a French city. The popes who followed Clement expressed an intention to return to Rome but remained at Avignon, claiming that the continuing turmoil of central Italy would not permit the papal government to function effectively. These popes were skilled administrators who expanded the papal bureaucracy enormously—especially its fiscal machinery—but the long absence from Rome clearly harmed papal prestige.

FISCAL CRISIS

Like many secular governments, the papacy at Avignon faced an acute fiscal crisis. But unlike the major powers of Europe, its territorial base could not supply it with the funds it needed, because controlling the Papal States usually cost more money than they produced. The powers of appointment, dispensation, tithing, and indulgences were the only resources the papacy had, and it was thus drawn into the unfortunate practice of exploiting these powers for financial gain. Thus the popes insisted that candidates appointed to high ecclesiastical offices pay a special tax, which usually amounted to a third or a half of the first year's revenues. The popes also claimed the income from vacant offices and even sold future appointments to office when the incumbents were still alive. Dispensations, which were also sold, released a petitioner from the normal requirements of canon law. A monastery or religious house, for example, might purchase from the pope an exemption from the visitation and inspection of the local bishop. Tithes paid to the pope amounted to one-tenth of the revenues of ecclesiastical benefices or offices throughout Christendom. And indulgences, remissions of the temporal punishment for sin, were given in return for monetary contributions to the papacy.

These fiscal practices enlarged the popes' revenues, but they had deplorable results. Prelates who paid huge sums to Avignon tended to pass on the costs to the lower clergy. Parish priests, hardly able to live from their incomes, were more easily tempted to lower their moral standards. The flow of money to Avignon angered rulers and prompted demands for a halt to such payments and even for the confiscation of Church property. Dispensations gravely injured the authority of the bishops, since an exempt person or house all but escaped their supervision. The bishops were frequently too weak, and the pope too distant, to deal effectively with abuses on the local level. The fiscal measures thus helped sow chaos in many parts of the Western Church.

THE GREAT SCHISM

The end of the 70-year Avignon exile led to a controversy that almost split the Western Church. Pope Gregory XI returned reluctantly to Rome in 1377 and died there a short time later. The Roman people, fearing that Gregory's successor would once more remove the court to Avignon and

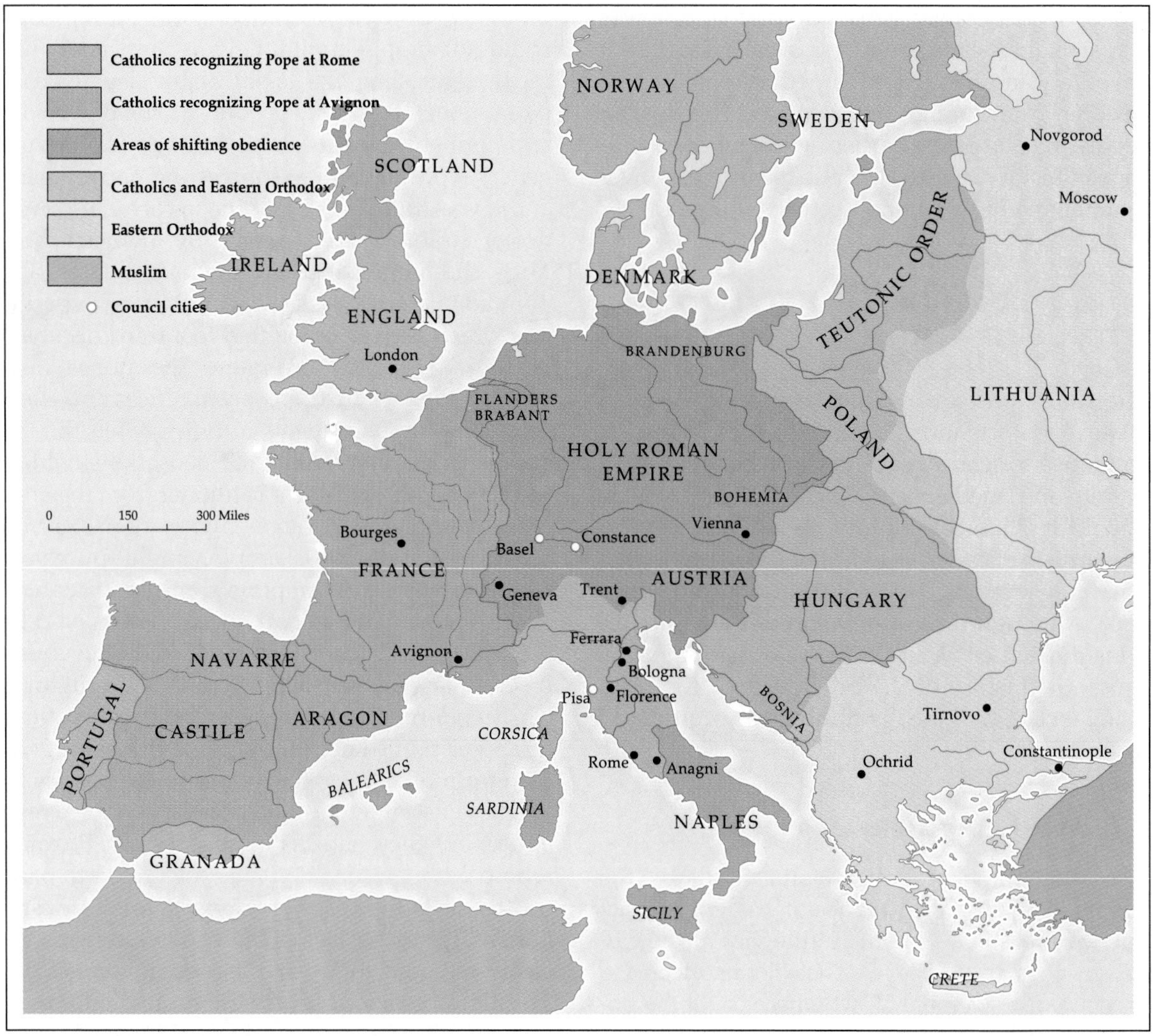

Map 11.5 **THE GREAT SCHISM 1378–1417**
The antagonisms in Europe during the Great Schism set neighboring regions against one another and created divisions from which the Church never fully recovered.

thereby deprive Rome of desperately needed revenues, agitated for the election of an Italian pope. Responding to this pressure, the College of Cardinals found a compromise candidate who satisfied both French and Italian interests, but the new pope, Urban VI (1378–1389), soon antagonized the French cardinals by seeking to limit their privileges and by threatening to pack the College with his own appointments. Seven months after choosing Urban, a majority of the cardinals declared that his election had taken place under duress and was therefore invalid; they then named a new pope, who returned to Avignon. Thus began the Great Schism of the West (1378–1417), the period when two, and later three, popes fought over the rule of the Church.

Christendom was now confronted with the spectacle of two pretenders to the throne of Peter, one in Rome and one in Avignon. Princes and peoples quickly took sides (see Map 11.5), and the troubles of the papacy multiplied. Each pope had his own court and needed yet more funds, both to meet ordinary expenses and to pay for policies that he hoped would defeat his rival. And since each pope excommunicated the other and those who supported him, everyone in

Christendom was at least technically excommunicated.

THE CONCILIAR MOVEMENT

Theologians and jurists had long speculated on who should rule the Church if the pope were to become heretical or incompetent; some concluded that it should be the College of Cardinals or a general council of Church officials. Since the College of Cardinals had split into two factions, each backing one of the rival popes, many prominent thinkers supported the theory that a general council should rule the Church. These conciliarists, as they were called, went further. They wanted the Church to have a new constitution to confirm the supremacy of a general council. Such a step would have reduced the pope's role to that of a limited monarch, but the need to correct numerous abuses, particularly in the fiscal support and morality of the clergy, lent strength to the idea that a general council should rule and reform the Church.

Pisa and Constance The first test of the conciliarists' position was the Council of Pisa (1409), convened by cardinals of both Rome and Avignon. This council asserted its supremacy within the Church by deposing the two popes and electing another. But this act merely compounded the confusion, for it left Christendom with three rivals claiming to be the lawful pope.

A few years later another council finally resolved the situation. Some 400 ecclesiastics assembled at the Council of Constance (1414–1418), the greatest international gathering of the Middle Ages. The council was organized in a new way, with the delegates voting as nations to offset the power of the Italians, who constituted nearly half the attendance. This procedure reflected the new importance of national and territorial churches. It enabled the assembled delegates immediately to depose both the Pisan pope and the pope at Avignon and to persuade the Roman pope to resign. In his stead they elected a Roman cardinal, who took the name Martin V. Thus the Great Schism was ended, and the Western Church was once again united under a single pope.

As the meetings continued, the views of the conciliarists prevailed. The delegates formally declared that a general council was supreme within the Church. To ensure continuity in Church government, the delegates further directed that new councils be summoned periodically.

The Revival of the Papacy In spite of this assertion of supremacy, the council made little headway in reforming the Church. The delegates, mostly great prelates, were the chief beneficiaries of the fiscal system and were reluctant to touch their own privileges and advantages. The real victims of the fiscal abuses, the lower clergy, were poorly represented. As a result, the council could not agree on a general program of reform—a failure that illustrated the fatal flaw in the vision of conciliar rule over the Church. The council was too large, too cumbersome, and too divided to maintain an effective ecclesiastical government. The restored papacy quickly reclaimed its position as supreme head of the Western Church (*see box*, p. 344).

The practical weaknesses of the conciliar movement were amply revealed at the Council of Basel (1431–1449). Because disputes broke out almost at once with the pope, the council deposed him and elected another, Felix V, to replace him. The conciliar movement, designed to heal the schism, now seemed responsible for renewing it. Recognizing the futility of its actions, the council at the death of Felix tried to rescue its dignity by endorsing the election of a new pope, Nicholas V, in 1449 and then disbanding. This action ended efforts to reform the Church by giving supreme authority to councils. But the idea of government by representation that they advanced was to have an important influence on later political developments in Europe.

Territorial Independence Although the popes remained suspicious of councils, they had much more serious rivals to their authority in the powerful lay princes, who were exerting ever tighter control over territorial churches. Both England and France issued decrees that limited papal powers within their kingdoms, and this policy was soon imitated in Spain and the stronger principalities of the Holy Roman Empire. Although such decrees did not establish national or territorial churches, they do document the decline of papal control over the international Christian community.

The Papacy Condemns Conciliarism

By 1460, the papacy was firmly back in command of the Church, and in that year, Pope Pius II issued a decree forbidding all further appeals above his head to a council. Decrees are known by their first Latin words, and it is appropriate that this angry denunciation of conciliarism should have been called "Execrabilis"—that is "execrable."

"The execrable and hitherto unknown abuse has grown up in our day, that certain persons, imbued with the spirit of rebellion, and not from a desire to secure a better judgment, but to escape the punishment of some offence which they have committed, presume to appeal from the pope to a future council, in spite of the fact that the pope is the vicar of Jesus Christ and to him, in the person of St. Peter, the following was said: 'Feed my sheep' [John 21:16] and 'Whatsoever thou shalt bound on earth shall be bound in heaven' [Matthew 16:18]. Wishing therefore to expel this pestiferous poison from the church of Christ and to care for the salvation of the flock entrusted to us, and to remove every cause of offence from the fold of our Savior, with the advice and consent of our brothers, the cardinals of the holy Roman church, and of all the prelates, and of those who have been trained in the canon and civil law, who are at our court, and with our own sure knowledge, we condemn all such appeals and prohibit them as erroneous and detestable."

From Warren Hollister et al., *Medieval Europe: A Short Sourcebook* (2d ed.), McGraw-Hill, 1992, p. 245.

THE REVIVAL OF ROME

When Martin V returned to Rome in 1417, the popes faced the monumental task of rebuilding their office and their prestige as both political and cultural leaders of Europe. They wanted Rome to be a major capital, a worthy home for the papacy, and not dependent on French rulers or culture as they had been for the past century. To this end, they adopted enthusiastically the new literary and artistic ideas of the Renaissance that were beginning to come out of Florence in the 1400s (see Chapter 12). The result was a huge rebuilding program that symbolized the restored authority of the popes. They sought, as one contemporary put it, "by the construction of grand and lasting buildings to increase the honor of the Roman Church and the glory of the Apostolic see, and widen and strengthen the devotion of all Christian people." One of the popes even proclaimed that if any city "ought to shine by its cleanliness and beauty, it is above all that which bears the title of capital of the universe." The building of a new St. Peter's Church in the 1400s was but the climax of this campaign of beautification, designed to assert a cultural supremacy that went along with the supremacy of the Pope's authority. At the same time, vigorous military campaigns in the Papal States subdued that difficult territory and established the papacy as a major Italian power.

It could be argued, however, that in identifying itself so closely with Rome and with Italian politics, the papacy became less universal. For all its splendor and its renewed control over the institution of the Church, it was failing to retain the spiritual allegiance of Europe, especially in the north. The popes may have succeeded in reshaping the Church into a powerful and centralized body, and in making Rome once again a cultural capital of the Western world, but the new cultural and intellectual forces that were at work in the 1400s were ultimately to undermine the centrality of the papacy to the life of Europe.

Recommended Reading

Sources

Council of Constance. Louise R. Loomis (tr.). 1961.

*Froissart, Jean. *The Chronicles of England, France, Spain and Other Places Adjoining.* 1961.

*Vespasiano da Bisticci. *Renaissance Princes, Popes and Prelates.* 1963.

Studies

Allmand, Christopher. *The Hundred Years War: England and France at War, c. 1300–1450.* 1988.

———. *Florentine Politics and Society, 1373–1378.* 1962.

Brucker, Gene A. *The Civic World of Early Renaissance Florence.* 1977. Important studies of Florentine politics and society from about 1300 to 1430.

Burne, Alfred H. *The Agincourt War: A Military History of the Latter Part of the Hundred Years War, from 1369 to 1453.* 1991.

De Roover, Raymond. *The Rise and Decline of the Medici Bank.* 1963.

Eisenstein, Elizabeth L. *The Printing Press as an Agent of Change in Early-Modern Europe* (2 vols.). 1979. Provocative interpretation of the place of printing in European history.

Gillingham, John. *The Wars of the Roses: Peace and Conflict in Fifteenth-Century England.* 1981. Readable political and military history.

Gottfried, Robert S. *The Black Death: Natural and Human Disaster in Medieval Europe.* 1983. With particular emphasis on the medical consequences.

Harvey, L. P. *Islamic Spain 1250–1500.* 1990. A survey of the one non-Christian territory in Western Europe and its steady decline.

Hatcher, John. *Plague, Population and the English Economy.* 1977. Economic effects of the great mortality in England.

*Hilton, Rodney. *Bond Men Made Free.* 1979. A study of peasant unrest in the Late Middle Ages.

*Hilton, Rodney, and T. H. Aston (eds.). *The English Rising of 1381.* 1987. Collected essays.

Kaeuper, Richard W. *War Justice and Public Order: England and France in the Late Middle Ages.* 1988.

Mallett, M. E., and J. R. Hale. *The Military Organization of a Renaissance State: Venice c. 1400 to 1617.* 1984.

*Mattingly, Garrett. *Renaissance Diplomacy.* 1964.

Miskimin, Harry A. *The Economy of Early Renaissance Europe, 1300–1460.* 1969.

———. *The Economy of Later Renaissance Europe, 1460–1600.* 1977.

Monahan, Arthur P. *Consent, Coercion and Limit: The Medieval Origins of Parliamentary Democracy.* 1987.

Oakley, Francis. *The Western Church in the Later Middle Ages.* 1979.

*Perroy, Edouard. *The Hundred Years' War.* 1965. An excellent survey.

Russell, J. C. *British Medieval Population.* 1948.

Seward, Desmond. *The Hundred Years War.* 1978. Short and readable.

Unger, Richard W. *The Ship in the Medieval Economy.* 1980. The evolution of medieval ship design.

Vaughan, Richard. *John the Fearless: The Growth of Burgundian Power.* 1979.

———. *Philip the Bold: The Formation of the Burgundian State.* 1979.

*Available in paperback.

National Gallery, London

Jan Van Eyck
PORTRAIT OF GIOVANNI ARNOLFINI AND HIS WIFE, 1434
The symbolism that permeates this depiction of a husband and wife has led to the suggestion that it is a wedding picture. The bed and seeming pregnancy are symbols of marriage, and the husband blesses his wife as he bestows the sacrament of marriage (for which the Church did not yet require a priest). On the back wall, the mirror reflects the witnesses attending the wedding. Van Eyck's use of the new medium of oil paint allowed him to reproduce vividly the texture of the fur-edged robe and the glimmer of the mirror's glass.

CHAPTER TWELVE

The West in Transition: Society and Culture

By 1300 the civilization of Europe appeared to have settled into stable and self-assured patterns. The division of society into the vast majority who labored, the knights and nobles who fought, and the clergy who prayed for the salvation of all seemed accepted and secure. If this was primarily a rural pattern, into which city dwellers did not easily fit, they were no more than a minor exception. The whole society shared assumptions about religious beliefs, about the appropriate way to integrate the heritage of the ancient world with faith, about the purposes of scholarship, and about the forms of literature and art; and this has led historians to describe the outlook of the age as "the medieval synthesis." But such moments of stability or apparent stability rarely last long. Within a few generations, major changes had overtaken European society, and profound doubts had arisen on such fundamental questions as the nature of religious faith, the authority of the Church, the aims of scholarship, the source of moral ideals, and the standards of beauty in the arts. As challenges to old ideas arose in each of these areas, there was an outpouring of creativity that has dazzled us ever since. Because those who sought new answers tended to look for guidance to what they considered a better past—the ancient world, or the early days of Christianity—and sought to revive those long-lost values, their efforts, and the times in which they lived, have been called an age of rebirth, or Renaissance.

I. Italian Society

In the fourteenth and fifteenth centuries the ideas that we associate with the Renaissance flourished mainly in Italy. Before looking at those ideas, therefore, we need to understand the elements that made Italy distinctive. What possibilities arose when, in the 1300s, the two major international powers that had dominated the peninsula for centuries—the pope and the emperor—turned their attention elsewhere and gave the Italians the opportunity to shape their own destinies?

CITIES

One basic social characteristic clearly distinguished Italy from most European areas: the number and size of its cities, particularly in the northern regions of Tuscany and the Lombard plain. In 1377, for example, only 10 percent of the people in England lived in urban centers with a population greater than 3200—a percentage fairly typical for most of northern Europe—whereas in Tuscany about 26 percent lived in urban centers. The cities were large. Venice, for instance, probably had 120,000 inhabitants in 1338, and despite the plagues of the next two centuries, the city had grown to 169,000 by 1563—a figure it was not to reach again until the twentieth century.

This remarkable urban concentration affected Italian culture. The large nonagrarian population depended for its support on a vigorous commerce and active urban industries. All levels of society participated in commerce, including the great landlords, nobles, and knights—classes that in northern Europe remained mainly on their rural estates. Moreover, success in urban occupations required a level of training higher than that needed in agriculture; therefore, many Italian cities supported public schools to assure themselves of an educated citizenry. Frequently even girls were given an elementary education, since literacy was a nearly essential skill for the wives of shopkeepers and merchants. Finally, many towns were politically independent and offered their affluent citizens the opportunity to participate in governmental decisions. To many great families, such participation was essential to the protection of their interests and required a mastery of the arts of communicating with their fellow citizens. In sum, Italian urban society in the fourteenth and fifteenth centuries was remarkably well educated and committed to active participation in the affairs of business and of government.

FAMILIES

The cities were populous, but the households within them tended to be small and unstable. The average household size in Florence in 1427 was only 3.8 persons, and in some other cities it was even smaller. The low numbers reflected the numerous deaths in a time of plagues, but marital customs also had an effect. For urban males tended to be much older than their brides when they married. In fifteenth-century Florence, men tended to postpone marriage until they were 30, and some did not marry at all. Economic factors—the lengthy apprenticeships men served in urban trades, their extended absences from home on commercial ventures, and their need to accumulate capital before starting a family—delayed and sometimes prevented marriage. Florentine women, on the other hand, were, on the average, less than 18 years old when they married for the first time; the modal (most common) age of first marriage for these women in 1427 was 15 years.

Gender Roles The result of this distinctive marriage pattern, when combined with high mortality, was that the pool of prospective grooms (men approximately 30 years old) was distinctly smaller than the pool of eligible young women (in their middle and late teens). A girl faced acute competition in the search for a husband; young women, in consequence, often entered marriage under unfavorable terms. Their families had to pay substantial dowries, and families with many daughters faced financial ruin. This was one reason why girls were married so young; their fathers or families were eager to settle their uncertain futures as soon as possible. Those who could not be married before the age of 20 had no honorable alternative but to enter a convent—which many did reluctantly. A contemporary saint, Bernardino of Siena, called the unwilling nuns "the scum and vomit of the world."

Given the wide age difference separating the spouses, urban marriages were not likely to last long before the death of the husband. Often, too, the young widow did not remarry. Florentine husbands typically tried to discourage their spouses from remarrying because widows, once remarried, might neglect the offspring of earlier unions. Thus the wills of Florentine husbands often gave their widows special concessions that would be lost on remarriage: use of the family home, the right to serve as guardians over their children, sometimes a pension. In general, after the death of a husband a woman tended to find herself suddenly in control of significant assets. The dowry that her family had paid at her marriage became her own property as a widow, and for the first time in her life she was freed from the male tutelage of a father, brother, or husband. Many widowed women relished this newfound freedom. At Florence in 1427, more than one-half of the female population, age 40 or over, were widowed. Thus the city teemed with mature women, many of them widows and some wealthy enough to influence urban culture.

Even while her husband lived, the Florentine woman was of great importance within the household. Men were likely to be occupied by affairs of business or politics, and the wife was responsible for running the household and bringing up the children. She was also usually destined for longer contact with her children. The average baby in Florence in 1427 was born to a mother of 26 and a father of 40. To many Florentines of the fourteenth and fifteenth centuries, the father was a distant figure, routinely praised but rarely intimately known; the mother dominated the formative years of the children. A friar named Giovanni Dominici, writing in the 1410s, complained that Florentine mothers were spoiling their children. They dressed them in elegant clothes and taught them music and dancing, but not rough games or sports. The result, Dominici implied, was an effeminization of Florentine culture because women, as crucial intermediaries between the generations, shaped the values and attitudes of the young. Thus the elegance and refinement that were essential attributes of Renaissance culture seem to have been nurtured within the bosom of the urban family.

Migration The short duration of urban marriage, the reluctance of many widows to remarry, and the commitment of many girls to the convent limited the number of pregnancies. In the countryside, men characteristically married in their middle twenties and took as brides women nearer in age to themselves. Rural marriages lasted longer, and couples had more children. The city thus ran a demographic deficit in relation to the countryside. This, too, had important social consequences. The city was forced to replenish its numbers by encouraging immigration from the countryside and small towns, and this promoted both physical and social mobility, because the city often attracted and rewarded skilled and energetic immigrants. Many of the leaders of the Renaissance—Boccaccio and Leonardo da Vinci, to name but two—came from rural or small-town origins to the city to meet its constant need for immigrants. The Renaissance city was highly successful in identifying the talented and in using its human capital to best effect.

Theories of Family Life The unstable character of the urban household and of human relations within it prompted much reflection on the family. Earlier, social thinkers had viewed the family in the abstract, in terms of humanity's ultimate destiny; they said it accorded with nature and was a training ground for faith and morality, but they did not examine how it functioned in the real world. In contrast, writers of the fifteenth century in Italy were concerned about the welfare, even the survival, of families. Foremost among them was the Florentine scholar, artist, and architect Leon Battista Alberti, who in the 1430s wrote a tract entitled *Four Books on the Family*. He suggested how children should be reared, wives chosen, domestic affairs managed, and friends cultivated—all to ensure the survival of threatened lineages. There were also many books on the education of children and attempts to reform schools, all of which showed a new awareness of the special psychology of children. And the artists of the period presented young people, even the infant Christ, not as miniature adults but authentically as children, looking and acting as children do. The playful baby angels known as *putti* appear in even the most solemn religious paintings. The very fragility of the Italian urban family thus seems to have inspired a deeper appreciation for the values of family life and the contributions that are made by every one of its members, even the youngest.

LIFE EXPECTANCY

A major reason for the instability of the urban family was the high mortality in Europe during the fourteenth and fifteenth centuries. The family memoirs of Florentine merchants, which record births and deaths, suggest that life expectancy from birth for these relatively affluent persons was 40 years in about 1300, dropping to only 18 years in the generation of the Black Death, and rising to 30 years in the fifteenth century as the plagues declined in virulence. (Today in the United States a newborn may be expected to survive for over 70 years.) To be sure, the high death rates attributable to plague were strongly "age specific"; that is, they varied considerably by age. The principal victims were the very young. In many periods, between a half and a third of the babies born never reached 15. Society swarmed with little children, but their deaths were common occurrences in almost every family.

The plague took a greater toll among young adults than among the aged. In effect, a person who survived one or more major epidemics had a good chance of living through the next onslaught. Thus a favored few did reach extreme old age, despite horrendous mortalities. But young adults always faced high risks of dying. Friars who entered the convent of Sta. Maria Novella at Florence in the last half of the fourteenth century, for example, lived an average of only 20 years after entering their order (which they usually did in their late teens). Although there are exceptions, the normal adult career was short.

Leadership of the Young For this reason, in every activity of life, the leaders of the 1300s and 1400s were often very young and were subject to rapid replacement. The young were not frustrated by the survival of their immediate elders, who in other times would have clung to the available jobs. There was far less of the generational tensions and conflicts that have disturbed modern societies. Indeed, the leaders of the age show psychological qualities that may be attributed, in part at least, to their youth: impatience and imagination; a tendency to turn quickly to violence; a love of extravagant gesture and display; and a rather small measure of prudence, restraint, and self-control. High mortality and a rapid turnover of leaders contributed to making this an age of opportunity, especially within cities. Early death created room at the top for the energetic and the gifted, especially in business and the arts, where birth mattered little and skill counted for much.

The power given to the young, the rapid replacement of leaders, the openings for talent, and the thin ranks of an older generation that might counsel restraint intensified the pace of cultural change. To be sure, poor communications hampered the spread of ideas. The quickest a person or a letter could travel on land was between 20 and 30 miles per day: To get to Bruges by sea from Genoa took 30 days; from Venice, 40 days. The expense and scarcity of manuscripts before the age of printing further restricted intellectual dialogue. Nevertheless, new generations pressed upon the old at a much more rapid rate than in our own society, and they brought with them new preferences and ideas—or at least a willingness to experiment—because the individual had his or her main chance early in life and passed early from the scene.

FLORENCE AND VENICE

The two chief sources of the new ideas and art of the Italian Renaissance were its richest cities, Florence and Venice. Both were governed by oligarchies of leading families, but it was their wealth rather than their political system that set them apart, because in one city the families were in constant competition, while in the other they ruled cooperatively.

Florence Florence by the mid-1300s was the principal banking center in Europe and one of the most important producers of luxury goods. Its silks, textiles, fine leather, and silver and gold ob-

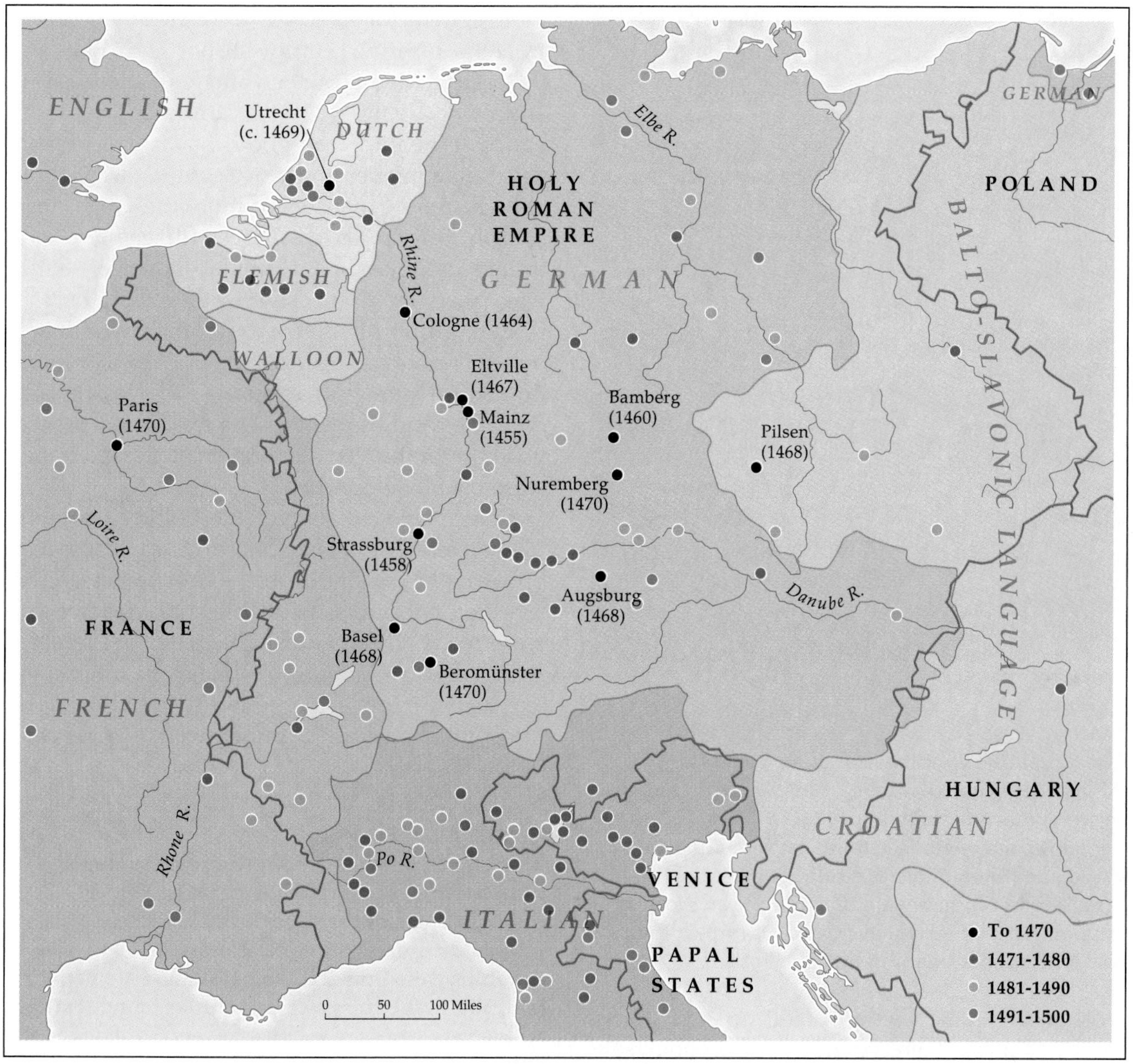

jects were much prized, and the training its guilds offered in design and craftsmanship was a major reason for the high skills of its artists. The florin, the city's gold coin, had international standing as one of the most reliable currencies of the time, and the broad contacts of its merchants gave Florence a cosmopolitan air. The citizens took special pride in the fame of two of their sons, Dante and Giotto, who during the first decades of the fourteenth century had become, respectively, the most famous poet and the most famous artist in Italy.

It was ironic that the Florentines should have taken credit for Dante, because he had been exiled from the city as a result of its vicious factional divisions. By the 1300s Florence had been a self-governing commune for two centuries, but it had rarely enjoyed political stability. It was ruled by a series of councils, whose members were drawn from the leading families. From time to time, however, as movements for wider representation

Map 12.1 THE SPREAD OF PRINTING BEFORE 1500 After its invention in the Rhineland, printing first spread along the rivers that were Europe's main highways. By 1500 it was concentrated mainly in southern Germany, the Netherlands, and northern Italy.

▸ *Giotto*
LAMENTATION
The Florentine Giotto di Bondone (1266?–1337) was the most celebrated painter of his age. He painted fresco cycles in a number of Italian cities, and this segment from one of them indicates the qualities that made him famous: the solid bodies, the expression of human emotion, and the suggestion of landscape, all of which created an impact that was without precedent in medieval art.

arose, such as the Ciompi revolt of 1378, places on the councils were opened to a broader segment of the citizenry—at times, as many as 20 percent of adult males may have been eligible for office. The volatile fortunes of the different groups did not give way to a more stable regime until the rich Medici banking family gained control of the city's government in 1434 and made sure that only people they favored were defined as eligible for government positions. Even amidst the disputes, however (and partly *because* of their competitive instincts), Florence's wealthy families eagerly provided the patronage that enabled this city of some 60,000 people to become one of Europe's most influential cultural centers in the fifteenth century.

Venice The city of Venice reached its greatest power and influence at the same time. Already independent for over 500 years, by 1400 it controlled a far-flung empire in northern Italy and the eastern Mediterranean and kept a large army and navy. Venice's wealth came from its dominance of the import of goods from Asia, notably spices like pepper and cloves, which were probably the most expensive commodities, per ounce, sold in Europe. Its wealthiest citizens also controlled its government; unlike Florence, Venice was ruled by a cohesive, rather than faction-ridden, group of some 150 families, who inherited this dominance from generation to generation. From among their number they elected the *doge*, the head of the government, who held that position for life. (To increase turnover, older men were usually elected.)

Venice enjoyed remarkable political stability. There were occasional outbursts of discontent, but usually the patricians—who stayed united, relied on informers, made decisions in secret, and were ready to punish troublemakers severely—were able to maintain an image of orderliness and justice in goverment. They were also careful to show a concern for public welfare. The chief

▸ *Antonio Natale*
VENICE ARSENAL
This eighteenth-century depiction of the huge complex that made up the Arsenal in Venice indicates some of the specialized buildings that formed the production line around the pools where the ships were built. At the back, hulls are being laid, and in the foreground, a ship is being scuttled. At the very front are the two towers that flanked the entrance gate to the Arsenal.

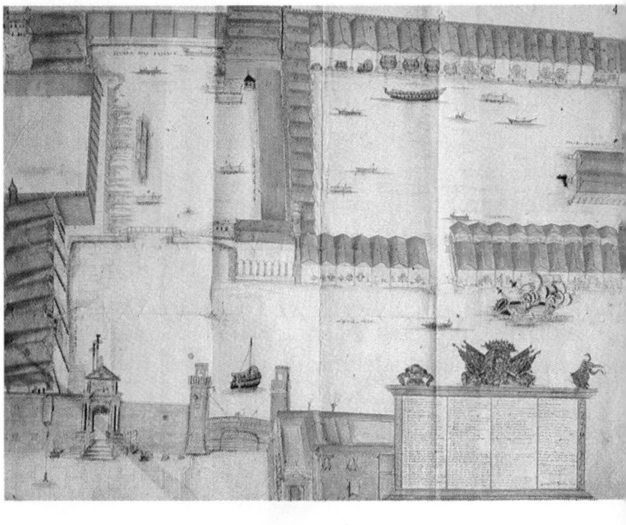

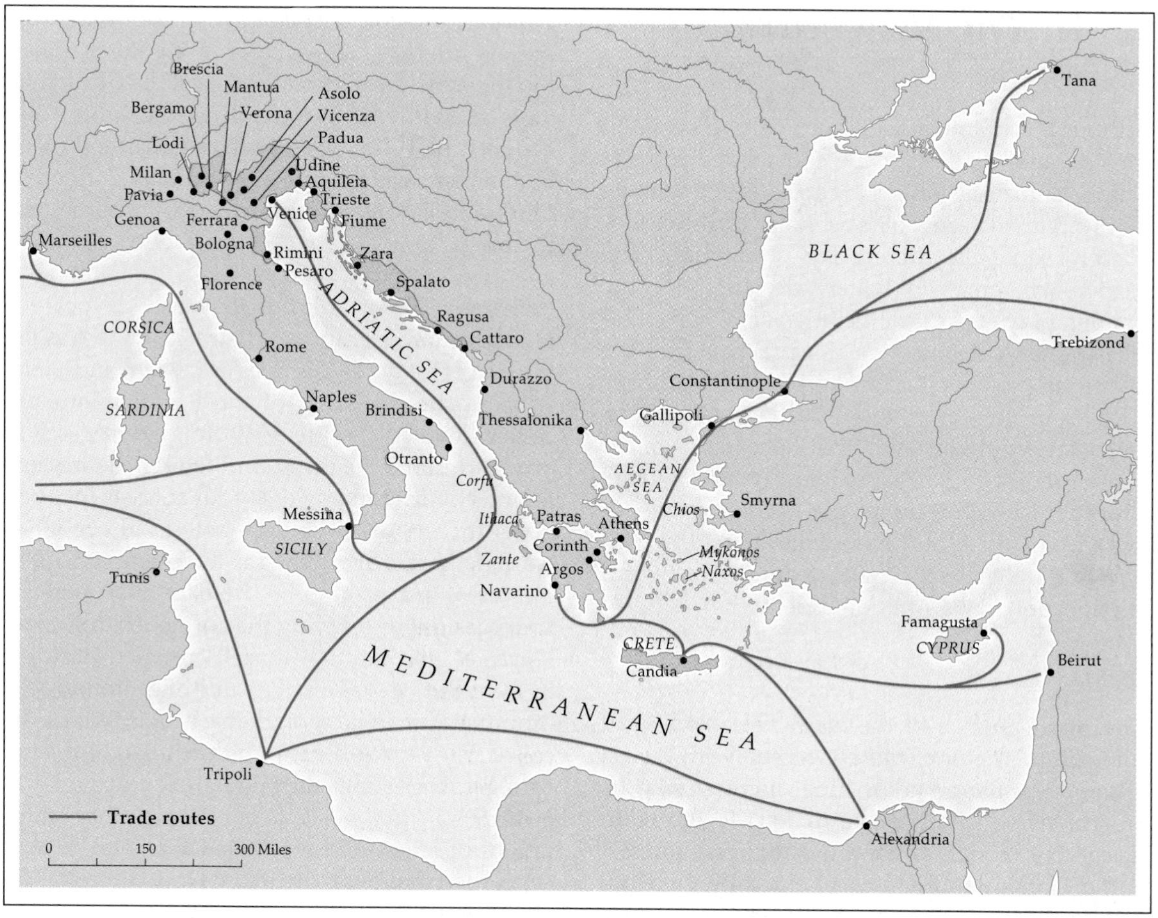

Map 12.2 THE VENETIAN EMPIRE IN THE 1400s
Thanks to its trade, Venice became a major power, controlling dozens of cities in northern Italy and the eastern Mediterranean.

support of the navy, for instance—an essential asset for a city that, though containing over 100,000 people, was built on a collection of islands in a lagoon—was a unique ship-building and arms manufacturing facility, the Arsenal. This gigantic complex, which employed over 5 percent of the city's adult population, was not only the largest industrial enterprise in Europe but also a crucial source of employment. The Arsenal could build a fully equipped warship, starting from scratch, in just one day, and the skills it required helped maintain Venice's reputation as a haven for the finest artisans of the day. Not only men but entire families came to work there; one visitor described a "hall where about 50 women were making sails for ships" and another where 100 women were "spinning and making ropes and doing other work related to ropes."

An institution like the Arsenal promoted economic and social stability by offering so many jobs and also helped improve the craftsmanship and skills of the city's artisans. In addition, because of its location and its easy openness to all who wished to trade, Venice was a meeting ground for Slavs, Turks, Germans, Jews, Muslims, Greeks, and other Italians. It was a favorite tourist spot for travelers and for pilgrims on the way to the Holy Land; it was a major center of the new international art of printing (see Map. 12.1); and it was famous for its shops and entertainments. By the mid-1400s, its coin, the ducat, was replacing the florin as a standard for all Europe; and its patrons, often interested in more earthy themes than the Florentines, were promoting a flowering of literature, learning, and the arts that made Venice a focus of Renaissance culture.

II. The New Learning

Although traditional forms of learning retained considerable vitality in the fourteenth and fifteenth centuries, medieval Scholasticism, with its highly refined forms of reasoning, did not adequately serve the literate lay population. The curriculum remained largely designed for the training of teachers and theologians, whereas increasingly the demand was for practical training in the arts of persuasion and communication: good speaking and good writing. Moreover, many laypeople believed that Scholastics failed to offer moral guidance. As Petrarch was to note, education should train people in the art of leading a wise, pious, and happy life. A central concern of the Renaissance was to develop a system of education that would do exactly that.

HUMANISM

One minor branch of the medieval educational curriculum, rhetoric, was concerned with the art of good speaking and writing. Increasingly, its practitioners in Italy began to turn to the Latin classics for models of good writing. This interest in the Classical authors was helped by the close relationship between the Italian language and Latin, by the availability of manuscripts, and by the presence in Italy of countless Classical monuments. It was rhetoricians who first began to argue, in the late thirteenth century, that education should be reformed to give more attention to the classics and to help people lead more moral lives.

These rhetoricians were to found an intellectual movement known as Humanism. The term *Humanism* was not coined until the nineteenth century. In fifteenth-century Italy, *humanista* signified a professor of humane studies or a Classical scholar, but eventually Humanism came to mean Classical scholarship—the ability to read, understand, and appreciate the writings of the ancient world. The aim of a humanist education was to train individuals in the classics, which offered models both of the wisdom a person needed to follow the right path in any situation and of the eloquence necessary to persuade others to that path. The modern use of the word *Humanism* to denote a secular philosophy that denies an afterlife has no basis in the Renaissance. Most Renaissance humanists read the Church fathers as avidly as they read pagan authors and believed that the highest virtues included piety. Humanism was far more an effort to enrich traditional religious attitudes than a revolt against them.

Petrarch The most influential early advocate of Humanism was Francesco Petrarca, known as Petrarch (1304–1374). He was a lawyer and cleric who practiced neither of those professions but rather devoted his life to writing poetry, scholarly and moral treatises, and letters. He became famous for his Italian verse—his sonnets inspired poets for centuries—but he sought above all to emulate Virgil by writing a Latin epic poem. A master of self-promotion, he used that work as the occasion for reviving the ancient title of "poet laureate" and having himself crowned in Rome in 1341. But he was also capable of profound self-examination. In a remarkable work, which he called *My Secret*—a dialogue with one of his heroes, St. Augustine—he laid bare his struggles to achieve spiritual peace despite the earthly temptations of fame and love. Increasingly, he became concerned that nowhere in the world around him could he find a model of virtuous behavior that he could respect. The leaders of the Church he considered poor examples, for they seemed worldly and materialistic. Convinced that no guide from his own times or the immediate past would serve, Petrarch concluded that he had to turn to the Church fathers and the ancient Romans to find worthy examples of the moral life (*see box*, p. 355).

How, then, could one be a good person? By imitating such figures from antiquity as Cicero and Augustine, who knew what proper values were and pursued them in their own lives, despite temptations and the distractions of public affairs. The period between their time and his own—which Petrarch regarded as the "middle" ages—he considered contemptible. His own world, he felt, would improve only if it tried to emulate the ancients, and in fact a central purpose of education ought to be to teach what they did and said. In particular, like the good rheto-

Petrarch on Ancient Rome

Petrarch was so determined to relive the experience of antiquity that he wrote letters to famous Roman authors as if they were acquaintances. In one letter, he even described Cicero coming to visit him. While he was passing through Padua in February 1350 he recalled that the city was the birthplace of the Roman historian Livy, and he promptly wrote to him.

"I only wish, either that I had been born in your time or you in ours. If the latter, our age would have benefited; if the former, I myself would have been the better for it. I would surely have visited you. As it is, I can merely see you reflected in your works. It is over those works that I labor whenever I want to forget the places, times, and customs around me. I am often filled with anger at today's morals, when people value only gold and silver, and want nothing but physical pleasures.

"I have to thank you for many things, but especially because you have so often helped me forget the evils of today, and have transported me to happier times. As I read you, I seem to be living with Scipio, Brutus, Cato, and many others. It is with them that I live, and not with the ruffians of today, among whom an evil star had me born. Oh, the great names that comfort me in my wretchedness, and make me forget this wicked age! Please greet for me those older historians like Polybius, and those younger than you like Pliny.

"Farewell forever, you unequalled historian!

"Written in the land of the living, in that part of Italy where you were born and buried, in sight of your own tombstone, on the 22nd of February in the 1350th year after the birth of Him whom you would have seen had you lived longer."

Petrarch, *Epistolae Familiares*, XXIV, 8. Passages selected and translated by Theodore K. Rabb.

rician he was, he believed that only by restoring the mastery of the written and spoken word that had distinguished the great Romans—an imitation of their style, of the way they had conveyed their ideas—could his contemporaries learn to behave like the ancients.

Boccaccio The program Petrarch laid out soon caught fire in Florence, the city from which his family had come and where he found influential friends and disciples. The most important was the poet and writer Giovanni Boccaccio (1313–1375). He became famous in Florence for a collection of short stories known as *The Decameron*, written between 1348 and 1351. It recounts how a group of young Florentines—seven women and three men—fled during the Black Death of 1348 to a secluded villa, where for 10 days each told a story. The first prose masterpiece in Italian, *The Decameron*'s frank treatment of sex and its vivid creation of ordinary characters make it one of the first major works in Western letters intended to divert and amuse rather than edify. But in his later years Boccaccio grew increasingly concerned with the teaching of moral values, and he became a powerful supporter of Petrarch's ideas.

THE CIVIC HUMANISTS

In the generation after Petrarch and Boccaccio, Humanism became a rallying cry for the intellectual leaders of Florence. They argued that, by associating their city with the revival of antiquity, Florentines would be identified with a distinctive vision that would become the envy of their rivals among the cities and states of Italy. And that was indeed what happened. The campaign for a return to the classics started a revolution in education that soon began to take hold throughout

Italy; the writing and speaking skills the humanists emphasized came to be in demand at every princely court (including that of the papacy); and the crusade to study and imitate the ancients transformed art, literature, and even political and social values.

Led by the chancellor of Florence, Coluccio Salutati (whose position, as the official who prepared the city's official communications, required training in rhetoric), a group of humanists began to collect ancient manuscripts and form libraries, so as to make accessible to scholars virtually all the surviving writings of Classical Latin authors. These Florentines also sought to reestablish in Italy a command of the Greek language, and in 1396 they invited the Byzantine scholar Manuel Chrysoloras to lecture at the University of Florence. In the following decades—troubled years for the Byzantine Empire—other Eastern scholars joined the exodus to the West, and they and Western visitors returning from the East brought with them hundreds of Greek manuscripts. By the middle of the fifteenth century Western scholars had both the philological skill and the manuscripts to establish direct contact with the most original minds of the Classical world and were making numerous Latin and Italian translations of Greek works. Histories, tragedies, lyric poetry, the dialogues of Plato, many mathematical treatises, and the most important works of the Greek fathers of the Church fully entered Western culture for the first time.

Salutati and his contemporaries and successors in Florence are often called *civic humanists*, because they stressed that participation in public affairs is essential for full human development. Petrarch had wondered whether individuals should cut themselves off from the larger world, with its corruptions and compromises, and focus only on what he called (using its Latin name) the *vita contemplativa*—the contemplative life—or try to improve that world through the *vita activa*—the active life. Petrarch's models had offered no clear answer. Cicero had suggested the need for both lives, but Augustine had been fearful of outside temptations. In the generations following Petrarch, however, the doubts declined, and the humanists argued that only by participating in public life, seeking higher ends for one's society as well as oneself, could an individual be truly virtuous. Republican government was the best form, they argued, because unless educated citizens made use of their wisdom for the benefit of all, their moral understanding would remain socially barren. These were lessons exemplified by the ancient classics, and thus in one connected argument the civic humanists defended the necessity of studying the ancients, the superiority of the active life, and the value of Florentine republican institutions.

HUMANISM IN THE FIFTEENTH CENTURY

As the humanist movement gained in prestige, it spread from Florence to other cities of Italy. Pope Nicholas V (1447–1455), for example, founded a library in the Vatican that was to become the greatest repository of ancient manuscripts in Italy. And princely courts, such as those of the Gonzaga at Mantua and the Montefeltro at Urbino, gained fame because of their patronage of humanists. Moreover, the influence of antiquity was coming to be felt in all areas of learning and writing. Literature was profoundly influenced by the ancients, as a new interest in Classical models reshaped the form and content of both poetry and drama, from the epic to the bawdy comedy. Purely secular themes, without religious purpose, became more common. And works of history grew increasingly analytic, openly acknowledging such ancients as Thucydides, Livy, and Tacitus as their inspiration.

Education Perhaps the most direct effect was on education itself. Two scholars from the north of Italy, Guarino da Verona and Vittorino da Feltre, succeeded in turning the diffuse educational ideas of the humanists into a practical curriculum. Guarino argued for a reform of traditional methods of education, and Vittorino brought the new methods to their fullest development in the various schools he founded, especially his Casa Giocosa ("Happy House") at Mantua. The pupils included boys and girls, both rich and poor (the latter on scholarships). All the students learned Latin and Greek, mathematics, music, and philosophy; in addition—because Vittorino believed that education should aid physical, moral, and social development—they were taught social graces, such as dancing and courteous manners, and received instruction in physical exercises like riding and fencing. Vittorino's school attracted pupils from all over Italy, and his methods were widely imitated.

Ultimately, a humanist education was to give the elite throughout Europe a new way of measuring social distinction. It soon became apparent that the ability to quote Virgil or some other ancient writer was not so much a sign of moral seriousness as a badge of superiority. What differentiated people was whether they could use or recognize the quotations, and that was why the new curriculum was so popular—even though it seemed to consist, more and more, of endless memorizations and repetitions of Latin texts.

New Standards of Behavior The growing admiration for the humanists and their teachings also gave an important boost to the patronage of arts and letters. In the age of gunpowder, it was no longer easy to claim that physical bravery was the supreme quality of noblemen. Instead, nobles began to set themselves apart not just by seeking a humanist education but by winning fame through the patronage of artists and writers whose praise made their benefactors famous. Thus a new image of gentlemanly behavior, which included the qualities that Guarino fostered—a commitment to refinement, taste, and elegance as well as to courage—became widely accepted. This new life style was to be summarized and promoted in a book, *The Courtier*, written in 1516 by Baldassare Castiglione, that became a manual of proper behavior for gentlemen and ladies for centuries. Castiglione's patron, duke Federigo Montefeltro of Urbino, even had his portrait painted sitting in his study reading a book, but dressed in armor.

► *Raphael*
BALDASSARE CASTIGLIONE
Raphael painted this portrait of his friend, the count Baldassare Castiglione, around 1514. Castiglione's solemn pose and thoughtful expression exude the dignity and cultivation that were described as essential attributes of the courtier in Castiglione's famous book on courtly behavior.

By the mid-1400s Humanism was a dominant intellectual force throughout Italy, and by the end of the century it was sweeping all of Europe, transmitted not only by its devoted adherents but also by a recent invention, printing, which made the texts of both humanists and ancients far more easily available. Dozens of new schools and universities were founded, and no court of any significance was without its roster of artists and writers familiar with the latest ideas. Even legal systems were affected, as the principles of Roman law (which tended to endorse the power of the ruler) were adopted in many countries. But in the late fifteenth century the revival of antiquity took a direction that qualified the commitment to the *vita activa* that had been the mark of the civic humanists. A new movement, Neoplatonism, brought to the fore the interest in spiritual values that was the heart of the *vita contemplativa*.

▸ *Joos van Wassenhove and Pedro Berruguete*
FEDERIGO DA MONTEFELTRO
This remarkable painting embodies the new ideal of the gentleman that emerged in the Renaissance. Federigo da Montefeltro was both one of the most notable warriors and one of the most distinguished patrons of learning of the age, and this portrait captures both sides of his princely image. Sitting in his study with his richly clothed son, Guidobaldo, Duke Federigo is reading a book but is also dressed in armor.

THE FLORENTINE NEOPLATONISTS

The turn away from the practical concerns of the civic humanists toward a renewed exploration of grand ideals of truth and perfection was a result of the growing interest in Greek as well as Roman antiquity—especially the works of Plato. A group of Florentine philosophers, active in the last decades of the fifteenth century and equally at home in Greek and Latin, led the way.

Ficino The most gifted of these Neoplatonists, as they are called—"new" followers of Plato—was the physician Marsilio Ficino. His career is a tribute to the cultural patronage of the Medici family, which spotted his talents as a child and gave him the use of a villa and library near Florence. In this lovely setting a group of scholars and statesmen met frequently to discuss philosophical questions. Drawn to the idealism of Plato, Ficino and his colleagues argued that Platonic ideas demonstrated the dignity and immortality of the human soul. To spread these views among a larger audience, Ficino translated into Latin all Plato's dialogues and the writings of Plato's chief followers. In his *Theologica Platonica* (1469), he made an ambitious effort to reconcile Platonic philosophy and the Christian religion.

Pico Another member of the group was Count Giovanni Pico della Mirandola, who thought he could reconcile all philosophies in order to show that there was a single truth that lay behind every quest for the ideal. In 1486 Pico sought to defend publicly, in Rome, some 900 theses that would show the essential unity of all philosophies. The pope, fearful that the theses contained several heretical propositions, forbade the disputation, but Pico's introductory "Oration on the Dignity of Man" remains one of the supreme examples of the humanists' optimism about the potential of the individual.

The message of both Ficino and Pico was founded on two essential assumptions. First, the entire universe is arranged in a hierarchy of excellence, with God at the summit. Second, each being in the universe, with the exception only of God, is impelled by "natural appetite" to seek perfection; it is impelled, in other words, to achieve—or at least to contemplate—the beauti-

ful. As Pico expressed it, man is unique in that he is placed in the middle of the universe, linked with both the spiritual world above and the material one below. His free will enables him to seek perfection in either direction; he is free to become all things. A clear ethic emerges from this scheme: The good life should be an effort to achieve personal perfection, and the highest human value is the contemplation of the beautiful.

Map 12.3 THE SPREAD OF UNIVERSITIES IN THE RENAISSANCE

A significant indication of the rising status accorded to learning, and the growing importance of education in general during the Renaissance, is the opening of major new universities. Even where earlier universities existed, as at Oxford, many new colleges were founded, and the number of graduates increased rapidly in the fifteenth and sixteenth centuries.

These writers believed that Plato had been divinely illumined and therefore that Platonic philosophy and Christian belief were two wholly reconcilable faces of a single truth. Because of this synthesis, and also its passionate idealism, Neoplatonic philosophy was to be a major influence on artists and thinkers for the next two centuries.

THE HERITAGE OF HUMANISM

Although its scholarship was often arid and difficult, fifteenth-century Italian Humanism left a deep imprint on European thought and education. The humanists greatly improved the command of Latin; they restored a large part of the Greek cultural inheritance to Western civilization; their investigations led to a mastery of other languages associated with great cultural traditions, most notably Hebrew; and they laid the basis of modern textual criticism. They also developed new ways of examining the ancient world—through archaeology, numismatics (the study of coins), and epigraphy (the study of inscriptions on buildings, statues, and the like), as well as through the study of literary texts. As for the study of history, while medieval chroniclers had looked to the past for evidence of God's providence, the humanists used the past to illustrate human behavior and provide moral examples. They also helped standardize spelling and grammar in vernacular languages; and the Classical ideals of simplicity, restraint, and elegance of style that they promoted helped reshape Western literature.

No less important was the role of the humanists as educational reformers. The curriculum they devised spread throughout Europe in the sixteenth century, and until our own century it continued to define the standards by which the lay leaders of Western society were trained. In the thirteenth century, learning was largely a monopoly of monks and Scholastics; during the Renaissance, the humanists introduced a narrow but still important segment of lay society to the intellectual treasury of the European past, both ancient and medieval. Simultaneously, they reinterpreted that heritage and enlarged the function of education and scholarship to serve human beings in their present lives by teaching them, as Petrarch recommended, the art of living wisely and well. Moreover, the fact that, regardless of religious and other divisions, men and women throughout Europe were steeped in the same classics meant that they thought and communicated in similar fashion. In spite of the continent's bitter conflicts, this common humanistic education helped preserve the fundamental cultural unity of the West.

III. Art and Artists in the Italian Renaissance

The most visible effect of Humanism and its admiration for the ancients was on the arts. Since the movement first took hold in Florence, it is not too surprising that its first artistic disciples appeared among the Florentines. They had other advantages. First, the city was already famous throughout Italy for its art, because the greatest painters of the late 1200s and 1300s, Cimabue (1240–1302) and his pupil Giotto (1276–1336), were identified with Florence. Giotto, in particular, had decorated buildings from Padua to Naples and thus gained a wide audience for the sense of realism and powerful emotion that he created; he became celebrated for an immediacy that had never been seen in the formal and restrained styles of earlier artists. Second, Florence was full of wealthy citizens who were ready to patronize art; and third, the city had a long tradition of excellence in the design of luxury goods such as silks and gold objects. Many leading artists of the 1400s and 1500s started their careers as apprentices to goldsmiths, in whose workshops they mastered creative techniques as well as aesthetic principles that informed their work when they turned to painting, sculpture, or architecture.

THREE FRIENDS

The revolution in these three disciplines was started by three friends, who were united by a determination to apply the humanists' lessons to art. They wanted to break with the styles of the immediate past and create paintings, statues, and buildings that would not merely imitate the glories of Rome but actually bring them back to life. All three went to Rome in the 1420s, hoping by direct observation and study of ancient master-

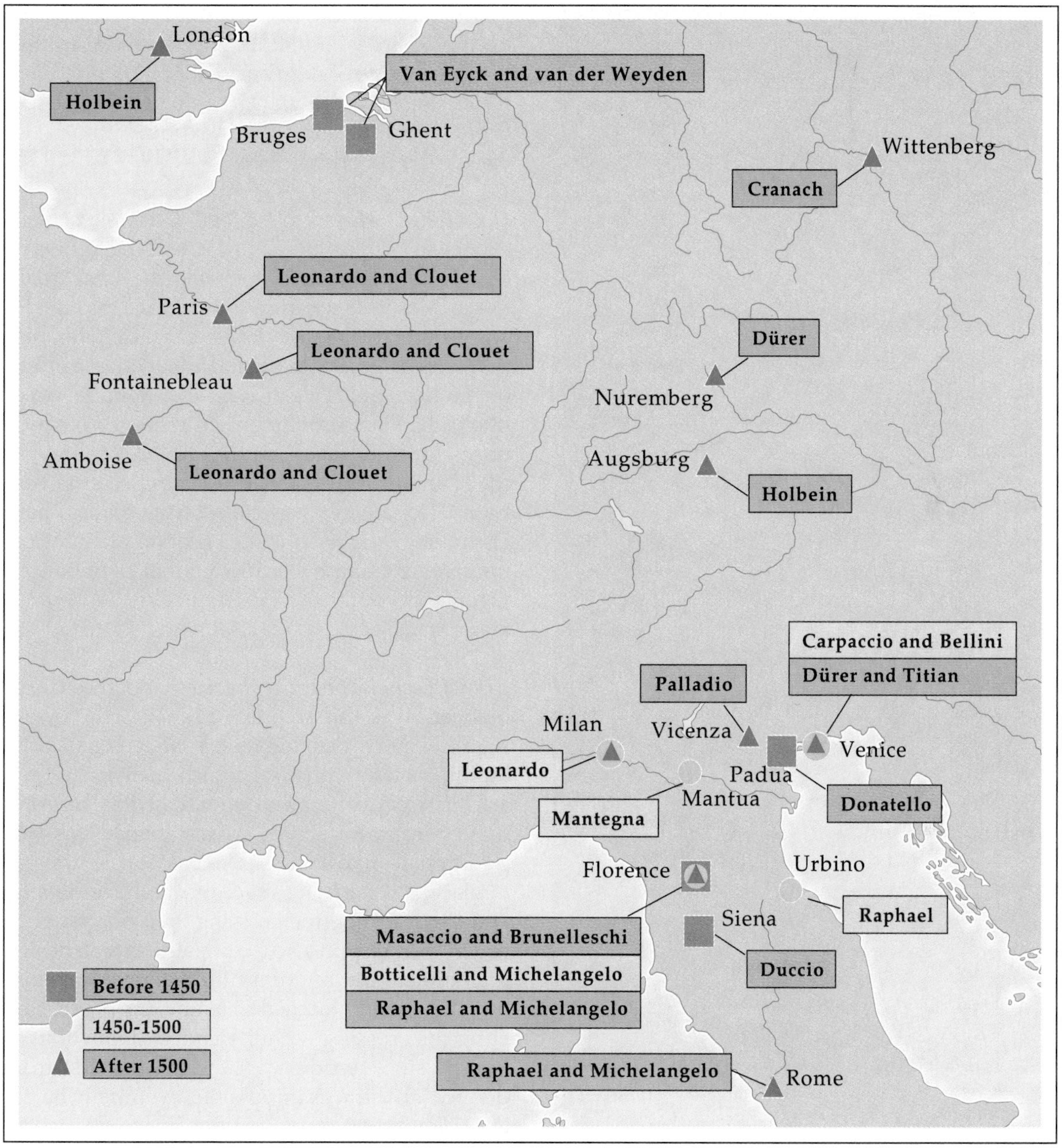

Map 12.4 **Major Centers of Renaissance Art**
From its beginnings in Florence, Renaissance art spread throughout Italy, while in northern Europe, after the pioneering work of Van Eyck, the Italian influence took hold mainly in Germany and France.

pieces to re-create their qualities and thus fulfill the humanists' goal of reviving the spirit of Classical times. The locals regarded the three as rather strange, for they went around measuring, taking notes, and calculating sizes and proportions. But the lessons they learned enabled them to transform the styles and purposes of art.

Masaccio The painter among the three, Masaccio (1401–1428), used the inspiration of the ancients to put a new emphasis on nature, on three-dimensional human bodies, and on perspective. In showing Adam and Eve, he not only depicted the first nudes since antiquity but showed them coming through a rounded arch that was the

▶ *Masaccio*
The Expulsion of Adam and Eve, ca. 1425
Masaccio shows Adam and Eve expelled from paradise through a rounded archway that recalls ancient architecture. Also indicative of the influence of Roman art is the attempt to create what we would consider realistic (rather than stylized) human beings and to portray them nude, displaying powerful, recognizable emotions. This was one of the paintings that made the Brancacci Chapel an inspiration to generations of artists.

pointed arch of the Middle Ages. The chapel he decorated in a Florentine church, the Carmine, became a place of pilgrimage for painters for centuries, for here the values of ancient art—especially its emphasis on the individual human figure—were reborn.

Donatello Masaccio's friend Donatello (1386–1466) was primarily a sculptor, and the figures he created in three dimensions had the same qualities as Masaccio's had in two. Once again the focus was on the beauty of the body itself, because that had been a notable and distinctive concern of the ancients. The interest in the nude, accurately displayed, transformed the very purpose of art, for it led to an idealized representation of the human form that had not been seen in centuries. Donatello's depiction of the biblical hero David shows him in contemplation after his triumph over Goliath. Because his story symbolized vigor and youth, the Florentines made David a favorite subject.

Brunelleschi The most spectacular of these three pioneers was the architect Brunelleschi (1377?–1446). For decades, his fellow citizens had been building a new cathedral, which, as a sign of their artistic superiority, was going to be the largest in Italy. Seen from above, it was shaped—as was traditional—like a cross. The basic structure was in place, but the huge space where the horizontal and vertical met, the crossing, had not yet been covered. In response to a competition for a design to complete the building, Brunelleschi, inspired by what he had learned in Rome, proposed covering the crossing with the largest dome built in Europe since antiquity. Although the first reaction was that it was impossible, eventually he got the commission. In an extraordinary feat of engineering, which required that he build the dome in rings, without using scaffolding, he erected a structure that became not only a fitting climax to the cathedral but also the hallmark of Renaissance Florence and an inspiration for all architects. And the symmetrical simplicity of his other buildings shaped a new aesthetic of harmony and balance that matched what Masaccio and Donatello accomplished in painting and sculpture. In all three, the imitation of ancient Rome inspired subjects and styles that broke decisively with their immediate medieval past.

During the remaining years of the 1400s, a succession of artists, not just in Florence but increasingly in other parts of Italy as well, built on the achievements of the pioneer generation. They experimented with perspective and the modeling of bodies and drapery, so as to recapture the ancients' mastery of depth, and they made close observations of nature. The sculptors created monumental figures, some on horseback, in imitation of Roman models. And the architects perfected the use of the rounded arches and symmetrical forms they saw in antique buildings. Subject matter also changed, as artists produced increasing numbers of portraits of their contemporaries and depicted stories out of Roman and Greek myths as well as traditional religious scenes. By the end of the 1400s, the leading Florentine painter of the day, Botticelli (1444?–1510), was presenting ancient subjects like the Birth of Venus, goddess of love, in exactly the way a Roman might have fashioned them.

▸ *Donatello*
DAVID, CA. 1430–1432
Like Masaccio, Donatello imitated the Romans by creating idealized nude bodies. His *David* has just killed and decapitated Goliath, whose head lies at his feet. Goliath's helmet recalls those worn by Florence's enemies, which makes this sculpture a work of patriotism as well as art. It happens also to have been the first life-size bronze figure cast since antiquity.

▸ *Brunelleschi*
DOME OF FLORENCE CATHEDRAL, 1420–1436
Brunelleschi's famous dome—the first built in Italy since the fall of the Roman Empire—embodied the revival of Classical forms in architecture. The contrast with the bell tower designed a century earlier by Giotto, with its suggestion of pointed Gothic arches, is unmistakable. The dome was a feat of engineering as well as design: Its 135-feet diameter was spanned without scaffolding, and Brunelleschi himself invented the machines that made the construction possible.

THE HIGH RENAISSANCE

The artists at work in the early years of the 1500s are often referred to as the generation of the High Renaissance. Four, in particular—Leo-

▸ *Sandro Botticelli*
BIRTH OF VENUS, CA. 1480
Sandro Botticelli was a member of the intellectual circle of Lorenzo de Medici, and this painting is evidence of the growing interest in Neoplatonism at the Medici court. The wistful, ethereal look on Venus' face reflects the otherworldliness that was emphasized by the Neoplatonists; moreover, their belief in the analogies that link all ideas suggests that Botticelli may have been implying that Venus resembled the Virgin Mary as a source of divine love. In depicting an ancient myth as ancient painters would have shown it, Botticelli represents the triumph of Renaissance ambitions, and the idealized beauty of his work helped shape an aesthetic standard that has been admired ever since.

▸ *Leonardo da Vinci*
MONA LISA, CA. 1503–1505
This is probably the most celebrated image in Renaissance art. The famous hint of a smile and the calm and solid pose are so familiar that we all too easily forget how striking it seemed at the time and how often it inspired later portraits. As in his *Last Supper*, however, Leonardo was experimenting with his materials, and the picture has therefore faded over the years.

nardo, Raphael, Michelangelo, and Titian—are thought of as bringing the new movement that had begun a hundred years before to a climax.

Leonardo The oldest, Leonardo (1452–1519), was the epitome of the experimental tradition. Always seeking new ways of doing things, whether in observing anatomy or designing fortifications, he was unable to resist the challenge of solving practical problems, even in his paintings. They are marvels of technical virtuosity, which make difficult angles, tricks of perspective, and bizarre geological formations look easy. His portrait of the *Mona Lisa,* for example, is famous not only for her mysterious smile but for the incredible rocky landscape in the background. Unfortunately, Leonardo also experimented with methods of painting; as a result, one of his masterpieces, the *Last Supper,* has almost completely disintegrated.

Raphael By contrast, Raphael (1483–1520) used the mastery of perspective and ancient styles that had been achieved in the 1400s to produce works of perfect harmony, beauty, and serenity. His paintings give an impression of utter relaxation, of an artist in complete command of his materials and therefore able to create sunny scenes that are

▶ *Raphael*
SCHOOL OF ATHENS
Painted in 1510 and 1511, this fresco celebrating the glories of Greek philosophy represents the triumph of the Renaissance campaign to revive antiquity. That the Classical setting and theme could have been accepted as appropriate for a wall of the Vatican suggests how completely Humanism had captured intellectual life. A number of the figures are portraits of artists whom Raphael knew: Plato, pointing to heaven at the back, has the face of Leonardo, and the notoriously moody Michelangelo broods, with his head on his arm, at the front.

▶ *Michelangelo*
THE CREATION OF MAN
Michelangelo worked on the ceiling of the Sistine Chapel in the Vatican from 1508 to 1512 and painted hundreds of figures. None has come to symbolize the rebirth associated with the Renaissance and the power of creative genius so forcefully as the portrayal of God extending a finger to bring the vigorous body of Adam to life. Tucked under God's other arm is the figure of Eve, ready to join Adam in giving birth to mankind.

balanced and at peace. His tribute to the ancient world, *The School of Athens*, places in a Classical architectural setting the great philosophers of Greece, many of whom are portraits of the artists of the day: Aristotle, for instance, has Leonardo's face. If the philosophers were the chief glory of Athens, Raphael seems to be saying, then the artists are the crowning glory of the Renaissance.

Michelangelo For Michelangelo (1475–1564), painting was but one means of expression. Equally at home in poetry, architecture, and sculpture, he often seems the ultimate embodiment of the achievements of his age. Yet there are few of Raphael's relaxed qualities in his work. He once said that no two of the thousands of figures he depicted were the same, and one might add that just about every one of them conveys the sense of latent strength, of striving, that was Michelangelo's signature. Although Adam, shown at the moment of his creation, has not yet received the gift of life from God, he already displays the vigor that Michelangelo gave to every human body. The same is true of his version of David, seemingly tranquil but showing his potential power in his massive, oversized hand. The sculptor relishes his ability to show the human being in full majesty, as an independent and potent individual.

Titian In Venice, the developments in art took a slightly different form. This was also a rich trading city, sophisticated, with broad international connections. But here Humanism was not so central, and the art—as befitted this most down-to-earth and cosmopolitan of Europe's cities—was more sensuous. The most famous Venetian painter, Titian (1482?–1576), depicted rich velvets, lush nudes, stormy skies, and dogs with wagging tails with a directness and immediacy that enable the viewer almost to feel them. His friend Aretino said of one of his pictures: "I can say nothing of the crimson of the garment nor of its lynx lining, for in comparison real crimson and real lynx seem painted, and these seem real." Titian was Europe's most sought-after portraitist, and to this day we can recognize the leading figures of his time, and sense their character, because of the mastery of his depictions.

STATUS AND PERCEPTION

The Artist as Craftsman To the generation of Masaccio, a painter was merely one of the many craftsmen in a city, not inherently more admired than a skilled leather finisher or mason. Like them, he was a member of a guild, he had to pass a carefully regulated apprenticeship, and he was subject to the rules that controlled his trade. Both Donatello and Brunelleschi were trained as goldsmiths, and the latter was even briefly imprisoned by his guild for not paying his dues while he was working—as an independent person, so he thought, and thus outside the guild structure—on the cathedral dome.

Given the Florentines' interest in gaining fame by beautifying their city, it was not surprising that the work of these artists should have at-

► *Titian*

Bacchanal, ca. 1518

The earthy realism of Venice contrasted sharply with the idealization common in Florentine art. The setting and even the sky seem more tangible, and Titian's lush nude in the foreground (who was to be much copied) is the essence of sensuality. It has been suggested that the painting represents the different stages of life, from the incontinent child through the vigorous youths and adults to the old man who has collapsed in the back.

tracted considerable attention. But it rarely occurred to anyone in the early 1400s—as Brunelleschi discovered from his guild—that they might deserve special respect or be considered anything more elevated than middle-class tradesmen. It was true that some of them were becoming famous throughout Italy, but would that lead to a change in their social status?

Humanism and the Change in Status The answer was that it did, and again the impetus came from the humanist movement. Three consequences of the revival of antiquity, in particular, began a reevaluation of the position of the artist. First was the recognition that the most vivid and convincing re-creations of the achievements of the ancient world were being produced in the visual arts. No letter written like Cicero's could compare with a painting, a statue, or a building as a means of bringing Rome back to life for all to see—as an open and public display of the virtues of Classical times.

A second influence was the humanists' new interest in personal fame. This had been an acceptable aspiration in antiquity, but during the Middle Ages spiritual concerns encouraged a disdain for worldly matters, and so it was a problem for Petrarch to admit that, like the ancients he admired, he wanted to be famous. In the book he called *My Secret* he struggled to justify his ambition, but he could never shake free of the guilt it aroused in him. For later humanists, the doubts receded, and the princes who valued their ideas eagerly accepted the notion that they should devote their lives to attaining fame. That was what nobles had won as warriors, but now there was a more reliable way to ensure that one's name lived forever.

The New Patrons That way was provided by the third of the humanists' lessons: that the truly moral person had to combine the contemplative with the active life. A prince, therefore, ought to cultivate the fine as well as the martial arts. No aristocratic court could be complete without its poets and painters, who sang their patron's praises while fashioning the masterpieces that not only brought prestige but also endured far longer than a brief human life. As a result, if a duke or a count wanted to be remembered, it was no longer enough to be a famous warrior; increasingly, it became essential to build a splendid new palace or have his portrait done by a famous painter. To be most like the virtuous heroes of Rome who were the society's ideal, he had to be a patron of culture as well as a vigorous leader. And this outlook was not confined to the males who now tried to unite artistic and military glory. Noble women, whose chief role had long been to offer an idealized object of chivalric devotion and who continued to struggle to gain access to education, occasionally won that struggle, and the result was a refined patronage that could be crucial in fashioning a princely image. Without Isabella d'Este, for example, the court in Mantua would not have achieved all the fame it won as a center of painting, architecture, and music. That both Leonardo and Titian did her portrait was a reflection not of her husband's importance but of her own independent contribution to the arts. Her rooms, surrounding a lovely garden, remain one of the wonders of the palace at Mantua and a worthy testimony to the fame she achieved as a patroness (*see box*, p. 369).

The effect of this new attitude was to transform the status of artists. They became highly prized at the courts of aristocrats, who saw them as extraordinarily effective image makers. Perhaps the most famous family of patrons in Italy, the Medici of Florence, were envied throughout Europe mainly because, for generations, they seemed always to be surrounded by the finest painters, sculptors, and architects of the age. Two of the Medici became popes, and they brought Raphael and Michelangelo to Rome, just as their ancestors had patronized Brunelleschi, Donatello, and Botticelli in Florence. The Church as an institution had been the main sponsor of art in the Middle Ages, but now it was the papacy in particular that promoted and inspired artistic production. In their determination to rebuild and beautify Rome as a worthy capital of Christendom, the popes gave such artists as Raphael and Michelangelo their most famous commissions—notably Michelangelo's Sistine Chapel within the Vatican. It was thus as a result of shifting patterns in the commissioning and buying of art that, as honored members of papal as well as princely courts, Renaissance artists created both a new aesthetic and a new social identity.

Isabella d'Este's Quest for Art

As the passion for art took hold, the great patrons of the Renaissance became relentless in their search for new works. None was more avid than Isabella d'Este (1474–1539), who became the wife of the Gonzaga prince of Mantua at the age of 16 and made her private suite of rooms (which she called her* studio*) a gathering place for artists, musicians, and poets for nearly 50 years. Her passion for art shines through her letters; in these extracts, she is pursuing both the Venetian painter Bellini and Leonardo da Vinci.

"*To an agent, 1502*: 'You may remember that many months ago we gave Giovanni Bellini a commission to paint a picture for the decoration of our studio, and when it ought to have been finished we found it was not yet begun. We told him to abandon the work, and give you back the 25 ducats, but now he begs us to leave him the work and promises to finish it soon. As till now he has given us nothing but words, tell him that we no longer care to have the picture, but if instead he would paint a Nativity, we should be well content, as long as he does not keep us waiting any longer.'

"*Two months later:* 'As Bellini is resolved on doing a picture of the Madonna and Child and St. John the Baptist in place of the Nativity scene, I should be glad if he would also include a St. Jerome; and about the price of 50 ducats we are content, but above all urge him to serve us quickly and well.'

"*Three years later, to Bellini himself:* 'You will remember very well how great our desire was for a picture painted by your hand, to put in our studio. We appealed to you for this in the past, but you could not do it on account of your many other commitments. [We recently heard you might be free,] but we have been ill with fever and unable to attend to such things. Now that we are feeling better it has occurred to us to write begging you to consent to painting a picture, and we will leave the poetic invention for you to make up if you do not want us to give it to you. As well as the proper payment, we shall be under an eternal obligation to you. When we hear of your agreement, we will send you the measurements of the canvas and an initial payment.'

"*In the meantime, in May 1504, she wrote to Leonardo da Vinci*: 'Hearing that you are staying in Florence, we have conceived the hope that something we have long desired might come true: to have something by your hand. When you were here and drew our portrait in charcoal, you promised one day to do it in color. Since it would be inconvenient for you to move here, we beg you to keep your good faith with us by substituting for our portrait a youthful Christ of about twelve years old, executed with that sweetness and soft ethereal charm which is the peculiar excellence of your art.'

"*Five months later she wrote again:* 'Some months ago we wrote to you that we wanted to have a young Christ, about twelve years old, by your hand. You replied that you would do this gladly, but owing to the many commissioned works you have on your hands, we doubt whether you remembered ours. Wherefore it has occurred to us to send you these few lines, begging you that you will turn to doing this little figure for us by way of recreation, which will be doing us a very gracious service and of benefit to yourself.' "

From D. S. Chambers (ed.), *Patrons and Artists in the Italian Renaissance* (London: Macmillan, 1970), pp. 128–130 and 147–148.

Vasari In the mid-1500s, a leading protégé of the Medici, an architect and painter named Giorgio Vasari (1511–1574), decided to try and figure out how and why it was that artists like him were being showered with privileges. He himself had been given the responsibility to design, build, and decorate a large new building in the center of the city for the government's offices—or, in

▸ *Benvenuto Cellini*
Salt Cellar for Francis I
Benvenuto Cellini, a Florentine goldsmith who challenged Giorgio Vasari's distinction between artisan and artist in his lively *Autobiography* (1562), executed this work for the French king Francis I in 1543. Juxtaposing allegorical images of the Earth and the Sea, which he presented as opposing forces, Cellini created figures as elegant as any sculpture and set them on a fantastic base of gold and enamel. His extraordinary skills indicate why so many Renaissance artists began their careers in goldsmiths' workshops.

Italian, Uffizi (now the main museum of Renaissance art in Florence). He had been knighted for his services, and he was a significant figure at the court ruled over by the Medici, who in 1530 had been named Grand Dukes of Tuscany. To understand his own good fortune, he looked to the past and wrote the first major work of what became, in his hands, a new field of study: the history of art.

Vasari put forward the idea that certain artists were filled with a special spirit, which he called genius, that set them apart from—and above—other people. The status artists had achieved was, in Vasari's account, richly deserved. They were appropriate courtiers, and even minor aristocrats, because of their genius and their fame. He wrote of them as if it were impossible to remember that, just a century before, they had been considered mere craftsman. Titian, for example, lived like a member of one of the finest families in Venice. He had a splendid house and was welcomed at the grandest occasions. Although he was in huge demand throughout Europe, he chose not to leave his native city. He might visit a king or an emperor, but he did not need to be attached to their court—as Botticelli was, for instance, to the Medici—in order to maintain his high standing. The acceptance of artists into the uppermost levels of society was one of the most remarkable transformations produced by the Italian Renaissance.

IV. The Culture of the North

North of the Alps the transformations of the 1300s and 1400s were not as dramatic as those that took place in Italy, but they were to have consequences after 1500 that were no less dramatic than the effects of Humanism, Neoplatonism, and the social changes of the south. This area of Europe did not have the many large cities and the high percentages of urban dwellers that were crucial to the humanist movement in Italy. Nor did the physical monuments and languages of northern Europe offer ready reminders of the Classical heritage. Humanism and the revival of Classical learning—with its literate, trained laity—did not come to the north until the last decade of the fifteenth century. But here, where the princely court rather than the city, and the knight rather than the merchant, dominated cultural life, there were other vital shifts in outlook.

CHIVALRY

In 1919 a Dutch historian, Johan Huizinga, described northern European culture in the 1400s and 1500s not as a renaissance but as the decline of medieval civilization. The stimulating book in which he made that argument, *The Waning of the Middle Ages*, focused primarily on the court of the dukes of Burgundy, who were among the wealthiest and most powerful princes of the north. Huizinga found tension and frequent violence in this society, with little of the serenity that had marked the thirteenth century. Instead, writers and artists seemed to have little grasp on reality and displayed deep emotional instability. Although many now consider Huizinga's interpretation exaggerated, his analysis clearly contains much that is accurate.

The poor grasp of reality that Huizinga noted is evident in the extravagant cultivation of the notion of chivalry. Militarily, the knight was becoming less important than the foot soldier armed with longbow, pike, or firearms. But the noble classes of the north continued to pretend that knightly virtues governed all questions of state and society; they discounted such lowly considerations as money, arms, number of forces, supplies, and the total resources of countries in deciding the outcome of wars. For example, before the Battle of Agincourt, one knight told the French King Charles that he should not use contingents from the Parisian townsfolk because that would give his army an unfair numerical advantage; the battle should be decided strictly on the basis of chivalrous valor.

Bravery and Display This was the age of the perfect knight and the "grand gesture." King John of Bohemia insisted that his soldiers lead him to the front rank of battle, so that he could strike at the enemy even though he was blind. The feats of renowned knights won the admiration of chroniclers but affected the outcome of battle hardly at all. And the reason for the foundation of new orders of chivalry—notably the Knights of the Garter in England and the Burgundian Knights of the Golden Fleece—was that these orders would reform the world by cultivating knightly virtues.

Princes rivaled one another in the sheer glitter of their arms and the splendor of their tournaments. They waged wars of dazzlement, seeking to confound rivals and confirm friends with spectacular displays of gold, silks, and tapestries. Court ceremony was marked by excess, as were the chivalric arts of love. A special order was founded for the defense of women, and knights frequently took lunatic oaths to honor their ladies, such as keeping one eye closed for weeks. Obviously people rarely made love or war in this artificial way. But they still drew satisfaction in dreaming about the possibilities for love and war if this sad world were only a perfect place.

THE CULT OF DECAY

Huizinga called the extravagant life style of the northern courts the "cult of the sublime," or the impossibly beautiful. But he also noted that both knights and commoners showed a morbid fascination with death and its ravages. Reminders of the ultimate victory of death and treatments of decay are frequent in both literature and art. One popular artistic motif was the *danse macabre*, or dance of death, depicting people from all walks of life—rich and poor, clergy and laity, good and bad—dancing with a skeleton. Another melancholy theme favored by artists across Europe was the Pietà—the Virgin weeping over her dead son.

This morbid interest in death and decay in an age of plague was not the result of lofty religious sentiment. The obsession with the fleetingness of material beauty in fact indicated how attached people were to earthly pleasures; it was a kind of inverse materialism. Above all, the gloom reflected a growing religious dissatisfaction. In the 1200s Francis of Assisi addressed death as a sister; in the fourteenth and fifteenth centuries people apparently regarded it as a ravaging, indomitable fiend. Clearly (as Petrarch, too, had noted) the Church was failing to provide consolation to many of its members, and a religion that fails to console is a religion in crisis.

The Devil Still another sign of the unsettled religious spirit of the age was a fascination with the devil, demonology, and witchcraft. The most enlightened scholars of the day argued at length about whether witches could ride through the air on sticks and about their relations with the devil. One of the more notable witch trials of Western history was held at Arras in 1460, when scores of people were accused of participating in a witches' sabbath, giving homage to the devil, and having sexual intercourse with him. In 1486 two inquisitors who had been authorized by the pope to prosecute witches published the *Malleus Maleficarum* (hammer of witches), which defined witchcraft as heresy and became the standard handbook for prosecutors. This fear of the devil and interest in occult arts among all levels of society were departures from the serene, confident religion of the thirteenth century.

Relics At the same time, there was a growing fascination with concrete religious images. The need to have immediate, physical contact with the objects of religious devotion added to the popularity of pilgrimages and stimulated the obsession with the relics of saints. These were usually fake, but they became a major commodity in international trade. Some princes accumulated collections of relics numbering in the tens of thousands.

Huizinga saw these aspects of northern culture as signaling the disintegration of the cultural synthesis of the Middle Ages. Without a disciplined and unified view of the world, attitudes toward war, love, and religion lost balance, and disordered behavior followed. This culture was not young and vigorous but old and dying. However, this concept of decadence must be used with caution. Certainly this was a psychologically disturbed world that had lost the self-confidence of the thirteenth century; but these supposedly decadent people, though dissatisfied, were also passionately anxious to find solutions to the tensions that unsettled them. We need to recall that passion when trying to understand the appeal and the power behind other cultural movements—lay piety, northern Humanism, and efforts for religious reform.

CONTEMPORARY VIEWS OF NORTHERN SOCIETY

Froissart Huizinga wrote about chivalric society from the perspective of the twentieth century. One of the best contemporary historians of that society was Jean Froissart (1333?–1400?) of Flanders, who traveled widely across England and the continent, noting carefully the exploits of valiant men. His chronicles, which survey the years 1325 to 1400, give the richest account of the first half of the Hundred Years' War, and he has no equal among medieval chroniclers for colorful, dramatic narration. Nonetheless, Froissart seems overly preoccupied with chivalric society; his narrative treats peasants and townspeople with contempt, or simply ignores them. Yet these emphases suited his purpose, which was, as he put it, to record the wars of his day, lest "the deeds of present champions should fade into oblivion."

Langland The works of two contemporary English writers give a broader picture of northern society in the fourteenth century. One of them, a poet known as William Langland, offered the viewpoint of the humbler classes. His *Vision of Piers Plowman*, probably written about 1360, is one of the most remarkable works of the age. The poem gives a loosely connected account of 11 visions, each of which is crowded with allegorical figures and is filled with spirited comment about the various classes of people, the impact of plague and war on society, and the failings of the Church.

Chaucer Geoffrey Chaucer (1340?–1400) came from a middle-class background; his father was a London vintner, and he himself was a soldier, diplomat, and government official. His *Canterbury Tales*, written in the 1390s, is the greatest work of imaginative literature of the late fourteenth century. It recounts the pilgrimage of some 30 persons to the tomb of St. Thomas Becket at Canterbury. For entertainment on the road, each pilgrim agrees to tell two stories. Chaucer's lively portraits provide a rich tapestry of English society, especially in its middle ranges. The stories also sum up the moral and social ills of the day. His robust monk, for example, ignores the Benedictine rule; his friar is more interested in donations than in the cure of souls; his pardoner knowingly hawks fraudulent relics; and the wife of Bath complains of prejudice against women. But Chaucer's picture remains balanced and good-humored; he praises the student of Oxford, who would gladly learn and gladly teach, and the rural parson, who cares for his flock while others search out benefices to the neglect of the faithful. Apart from the grace of his poetry, Chaucer had the ability to delineate character and spin a lively narrative. The *Canterbury Tales* is a masterly portrayal of human personalities and human behavior that can delight readers in any age.

THE FINE ARTS

The leaders of the transformation in both the style and the status of artists in the 1400s were mainly Italians. But there were also major advances in northern Europe. Indeed, oil painting—

on wood or canvas—was invented in the Netherlands, and its first great exponent, Jan Van Eyck, a contemporary of Donatello, revealed both the similarities and the differences between north and south. Van Eyck was less interested in idealization than the Florentines and more fascinated with the details of the physical world. One sees almost every thread in a carpet. But his portrait of an Italian couple, the Arnolfinis, is shot through with religious symbolism as well as a sly sense of humor about sex and marriage. The dog is a sign of fidelity, and the carving on the bedpost is of St. Margaret, the patron saint of childbirth; but the single candle is what newlyweds are supposed to keep burning on their wedding night, and the grinning carved figures behind their clasped hands are a wry comment on their marriage. The picture displays a combination of earthiness and piety that places it in a tradition unlike any that one finds in Italy (see p. 346).

Dürer The leading northern artist of the period of the High Renaissance was a German, Albrecht Dürer, who deliberately sought to blend southern and northern styles. He made two trips to Venice, and the results were clear in a self-portrait that shows him as a fine gentleman, painted in the Italian style. But he continued, especially in the engravings that made him famous, to emphasize the detailed depiction of nature and the religious purposes that were characteristic of northern art.

Dürer refused to break completely with the craft origins of his vocation. He knew, from his visits to Venice, that Italian painters could live like lords, and he was invited by the Holy Roman Emperor to join his court. But he preferred to remain in his home city of Nuremberg, earning his living more through the sale of his prints than from the stipends he was offered by patrons. Indeed, he became a highly successful entrepreneur, creating different kinds of prints for different markets—the elite liked elegant and expensive copper engravings, while others preferred cruder but cheaper woodcuts—and producing a best-seller in a book of illustrations of the Apocalypse. Working with his wife, who was a highly effective seller of his prints, he seemed as much engaged in business as in art.

▶ *Albrecht Dürer*
THE FOUR HORSEMEN
OF THE APOCALYPSE
The best-seller Dürer published in 1498, *The Apocalypse*, has the text of the biblical account of the apocalypse on one side and full-page woodcuts on the other. The four horsemen who will wreak vengeance on the damned during the final Day of Judgment are Conquest holding a bow, War holding a sword, Famine or Justice holding scales, and Death or Plague riding a pale horse and trampling a bishop.

MUSIC

Interestingly, the process that was at work in the visual arts had similar effects in music, which again had been created primarily for liturgical purposes in the Middle Ages. In the Renaissance, musicians became as prized as artists at princely courts, and their growing professionalism was demonstrated by the organists and choir singers hired by churches, the trumpeters employed by cities for official occasions, and the composers and performers who joined the households of the wealthy. Musical notation became standardized, and instruments became more diverse as old ones were improved and new ones—such as the viol, the oboe, and the clavichord—were invented.

Unlike the visual arts, the chief musical center of Europe around 1500 was in the Low Countries, not Italy. The choirmasters of cathedral towns like Bruges employed professional singers who brought the traditional choral form of four-part polyphony (that is, four different lines playing against one another) to new levels. This complex vocal harmony had no need of instrumental accompaniment; as a result, freed from their usual subservience to the voice, instruments could be developed in new ways. The greatest masters of the time, Guillaume Dufay and Josquin des Prez, excelled in secular as well as religious music, and theirs was one field of creativity in which new techniques and ideas flowed mainly from the north to Italy, not the other way around.

V. Scholastic Philosophy, Religious Thought, and Piety

In theology, Scholasticism retained its hold even as Humanism swept the literary world. But it was not the Scholasticism of the thirteenth century, of Thomas Aquinas, which asserted that human reason could construct a universal philosophy that did justice to all truths and reconciled all apparent conflicts among them. Nor did the traditional acceptance of ecclesiastical law continue, with its definition of Christian obligations and the Christian life in terms of precise rules of behavior rather than interior spirit. This style of thinking changed as the Scholastics of the 1400s and 1500s were drawn to analysis (breaking apart) rather than synthesis (putting together) in their examinations of philosophical and theological statements. Many of them no longer shared Aquinas' confidence in human reason, and they hoped to repair his synthesis or to replace it with new systems that, though less comprehensive, could at least be more easily defended in an age growing increasingly doubtful about reason. Piety changed too, as more and more Christian leaders sought ways of deepening interior, mystical experience.

THE "MODERN WAY"

The followers of Aquinas remained active in the schools, but the most original of the Scholastics in the fourteenth century took a different approach to their studies. They were known as *nominalists*, because they focused on the way we describe the world—the names (in Latin *nomina*) that we give to things—rather than on its reality. The nominalists denied the existence, or at least the knowability, of universal forms—"manness," "dogness," and the like. The greatest among them was the English Franciscan William of Ockham (1300?–1349?), and the fundamental principle of his logical analysis later came to be called *Ockham's razor*. It can be stated in various ways, but essentially it affirms that between alternative explanations for the same phenomenon, the simpler is always to be preferred.

Ockham On the basis of this "principle of parsimony," Ockham attacked the traditional focus of philosophy on ideal forms, which required Aquinas to argue that all individual beings had to be understood as reflections of their universal forms. The simplest way to explain the existence of any specific object, Ockham said, is just to affirm that it exists. The mind can detect resemblances among objects and form general concepts about them; these concepts can then be examined in coherent and logical ways. But they offer no certainty that Aquinas' ideal forms—the grand principles of unity like "manness" that all individual beings and objects reflect—actually exist.

The area of reality in which the mind functions is thus severely limited. The universe, as far as human reason can detect, is a collection of separate individual beings, not a hierarchy of ideal forms. The proper way to deal with this universe is by direct experience, not by speculating about ideal or abstract natures. This theology, based on observation and reason, was obviously rather limited. Ockham believed that one could still prove the existence of some necessary principles in the universe, but he thought human beings could know very little about the ultimate necessary principle, God.

Nominalist Theology Ockham and many of his contemporaries insisted on the total power of God and emphasized humanity's absolute dependence on him. God's freedom allowed him, if he chose, to reward vice or punish virtue. But if God was free to act in erratic ways, how could there be a stable system of dogma, a fixed theology or ethics? To escape this dilemma, the nominalists made a crucial distinction between the absolute and the ordained power of God. With his absolute power, God could act in any way he chose. But through a covenant, or agreement, God assures people that he will act in consistent and predictable ways. Given these assumptions, theology becomes the study not of metaphysics but of God's will and covenant regarding the human race.

Nominalists thus rejected Aquinas' high assessment of human powers and his confident belief in the ordered and knowable structure of the natural world. Living in a disturbed, pessimistic age, they reflected the crisis of confidence in natural reason and human capability that is a major feature of the cultural history of the north in these years.

Nominalists enjoyed wide popularity in the universities, and Ockhamite philosophy, in particular, came to be known as the *via moderna* ("modern way"). Although nominalists and humanists were frequently at odds, they did share a dissatisfaction with aspects of the medieval intellectual tradition, especially the speculative abstractions of medieval thought; and both advocated approaches to reality that concentrated on the concrete and the present and demanded a strict awareness of method.

SOCIAL AND SCIENTIFIC THOUGHT

Marsilius The belief of the nominalists that reality was to be found not in abstract forms but in concrete objects had important implications for social thought. Among social thinkers influenced by nominalism, the most remarkable was Marsilius of Padua, an Italian lawyer who served at the French royal court. In 1324 he wrote a book, *Defender of Peace*, which attacked papal authority and supported lay sovereignty within the Church. His purpose was obviously to endorse the independent authority of his patron, the king of France, who was engaged in a running battle with the pope. But his work had wider implications. Using nominalist principles, Marsilius argued that the reality of the Christian community, like the reality of the universe, consists of the aggregate of all its parts. The sovereignty of the Church thus belongs to its membership, which alone can define the collective will of the community.

Marsilius is sometimes described as one of the first theorists of the modern concept of sovereignty, and he certainly endorsed secular authority. He maintained that only regulations supported by force are true law, and that therefore the enactments of the Church do not bind because they are not supported by coercive force. The Church has no right to power or to property and is entirely subject to the sovereign will of the state, which is indivisible, absolute, and unlimited. *Defender of Peace* is noteworthy not only for its radical ideas but also for its reflection of the deep dissatisfactions in medieval society. Marsilius and others revealed a hostile impatience with the papal and clerical domination of Western political life. They wanted the guidance of the Church and the Christian community to rest with laypeople. In this respect at least, the book was a prophecy of things to come.

Nature In studies of nature, a few nominalists at Paris and Oxford in the fourteenth century took the first hesitant steps toward a criticism of the Aristotelian world system that had dominated European studies of physics since antiquity. At the University of Paris, for example, Jean Buridan proposed an important revision in Aristotle's theory of motion. If, as Aristotle had said, all objects are at rest in their natural state, what keeps an arrow flying after it leaves the bow? Aristotle had reasoned rather lamely that the arrow disturbs the air through which it passes and that it is this disturbance that keeps pushing the arrow forward.

But this explanation did not satisfy the nominalists. Buridan suggested that the movement of the bow lends the arrow a special quality of motion, an "impetus," which stays with it permanently unless removed by the resistance of the air. In addition, Buridan and other fourteenth-century nominalists theorized about the acceleration of falling objects and made some attempt to describe this phenomenon in mathematical terms. Although they were often inadequate or inaccurate, these attempts at new explanations started the shift away from an unquestioned acceptance of ancient systems (such as Aristotle's) that was to climax, 300 years later, in the scientific revolution.

The humanists also helped to prepare the way for scientific advance. Not only did they rediscover important ancient writers whose works had been forgotten, but their skills in textual and literary criticism taught people to look with greater precision at works inherited from the past. As more of the classics became available, it became apparent that ancient authors did not always speak in unison. Could they, therefore, always be correct? Furthermore, the idealism of Plato and the number mysticism of Pythagoras suggested that unifying forms and harmonies lay behind the disparate data of experience and observation. Once this assumption took hold, it was soon being argued that perhaps the cosmic harmonies might be described in mathematical terms.

STYLES OF PIETY

The natural world was never a central object of study in the fourteenth and fifteenth centuries, because theology remained the queen of the sciences. Within the world of faith, however, important changes began to take place as new forms of piety and religious practice appeared in order to meet the needs of laypeople. Where once praying for the salvation of the community had been considered the province of the clergy, it was now increasingly felt that each individual ought to take responsibility for seeking the favor of God.

Lay Mysticism and Piety One consequence was that mysticism—an interior sense of the direct presence and love of God—which previously had been characteristic only of monastic religious life, began to move out of the monasteries in the thirteenth century. The prime mission of the Franciscans and the Dominicans was preaching to the laity, and increasingly they were communicating some of the satisfactions of mystical religion. Laypeople wishing to remain in the outside world could join special branches of the Franciscans or Dominicans known as third orders. Confraternities, which were religious guilds founded largely for laypeople, grew up in the cities and, through common religious services and programs of charitable activities, tried to deepen the spiritual lives of their members. Humanism had strong overtones of a movement for lay piety. And hundreds of devotional and mystical works were written for laypeople to teach them how to feel repentance, not just how to define it. Translations of the Scriptures into vernacular languages also appeared, though the Church disapproved of such efforts and the high cost of manuscripts before the age of printing severely limited their circulation.

This growth of lay piety was, in essence, an effort to put at the disposal of all what hitherto had been restricted to a spiritual elite. Frightened by the disasters of the age, people hungered for emotional reassurance, for evidence of God's love and redeeming grace within them. Moreover, the spread of education among the laity, at least in the cities, made people discontented with empty forms of religious ritual.

FEMALE PIETY

The commitment to personal piety among the laity was particularly apparent among women. It is significant that, whereas male saints outnumbered females in the years between 1000 and 1150 by 12 to 1, in the years 1348 to 1500 the ratio dropped to 2.74 to 1. Moreover, the typical female saints of the later Middle Ages were no longer queens, princesses, and abbesses. They were mystics and visionaries, ordinary yet charismatic people who gained the attention of the Church and the world by the power of their message and the force of their own personalities. Catherine of Siena (1347–1380), for example, was the youngest of the 25 children of a humble Italian dyer. Her reputation for holiness attracted a company of followers from as far off as England, and she wrote (or dictated, for she probably couldn't write) devotional tracts that are monuments of Italian literature. Similar charismatic qualities made a simple Englishwoman, Margery Kempe, famous for her visions and her piety.

Women who out of poverty or preference lived a religious life outside convents became numerous, especially in towns. Some lived with their families, and others eked out a living on the margins of society. Still others lived in spontaneously organized religious houses—called Beguines in northern Europe—where they shared all tasks and property. The Church was suspicious of these women professing a religious life outside convents, without an approved rule. But the movement was too large for the Church to suppress or control. And many of them came to be particularly identified with one of the most powerful forms of lay piety in this period, mysticism.

▶ *Pisan Artist of XIV Century*
The Mystic Marriage of Catherine of Siena
Catherine of Siena was a nun who was known for her efforts to return the papacy to Rome. Part of the reason for her sainthood was that, like Joan of Arc, she experienced visions from an early age. She is shown here with her symbol, the lily, in a scene from one of her visions. About to enter into a mystic marriage with Christ, she is accepting the wedding ring directly from him. Note that in the Renaissance, wedding rings were often placed on the third finger.

THE MYSTICS

It was appropriate that one of the most active centers of the new lay piety should have been the Rhine valley, a region that was especially noted for its remarkable mystics. The most famous was the Dominican Meister Eckhart (1260?–1327?), a spellbinding preacher and a devoted student of Aquinas, who sought to bring his largely lay listeners into a mystical confrontation with God. Believers, he maintained, should cultivate the "divine spark" that is in every soul. To achieve this, they had to banish all thought from their minds and seek to attain a state of pure passivity. If they succeeded, God would come and dwell within them. Eckhart stressed the futility of dogma and, implicitly, traditional acts of piety. God is too great for such categories and cannot be moved by conventional piety.

Brethren of the Common Life Just as the nominalists argued for philosophical reasons that God is unknowable, so the mystics dismissed the value of formal knowledge and stressed the need for love and an emotional commitment to God and his attributes. Perhaps the most influential of them was Gerhard Groote of Holland. Groote wrote sparingly, exerting his influence over his followers largely through his personality. After his death in 1384 his disciples formed a religious congregation known as the Brethren of the Common Life. Taking education as their principal task, they founded schools in Germany and the Low Countries that imparted a style of lay piety known as the *devotio moderna* (modern devotion). Later reformers, such as Erasmus of Rotterdam and Martin Luther, were to be among their pupils.

Thomas à Kempis The richest statement of the *devotio moderna* appeared about 1425 in *The Imitation of Christ,* a small devotional manual attributed to Thomas à Kempis, a member of the Brethren of the Common Life. *The Imitation of Christ* says almost nothing about fasting, pilgrimages, or other traditional acts of private piety. Instead, it emphasizes interior experience as essential to religious life. The believer, it argued, needed only to emulate the life of Jesus. The book's ethical and social consciousness is also unusual. Powerful interior faith leads not to extreme acts of personal expiation but to highly ethical behavior: "First, keep yourself in peace, and then you shall be able to bring peace to others."

Features of Lay Piety The new lay piety was by no means a revolutionary break with the medieval Church, but it implicitly discounted the importance of many traditional institutions and practices. In this personal approach to God there was no special value in the monastic vocation. As Erasmus would later argue, what was good in monasticism should be practiced by every Christian. Stressing simplicity and humility, the new lay piety was reacting against the pomp and splendor that had come to surround popes and prelates and to mark religious ceremonies. Likewise, the detailed rules for fasts, abstinences, and devotional exercises; the cult of the saints and their relics; and the traffic in indulgences and pardons all seemed peripheral to true religious needs. Without the proper state of soul, these traditional acts of piety were meaningless; with the proper state, every act was worship.

This new lay piety, emerging as it did out of medieval religious traditions, was clearly a preparation for the reformations of faith that took place in the sixteenth century among both Protestants and Catholics. It helped produce a more penetrating faith at a time when the formal beliefs of the Middle Ages, for all their grandeur and logical intricacies, no longer fully satisfied the religious spirit and were leaving hollows in the human heart.

Although the *devotio moderna* was a religious movement and had little regard for humanist learning, it shared Humanism's distaste for the abstractions and intellectual arrogance of the Scholastics and the humanists' belief that a wise and good person will cultivate humility and maintain toward the profound questions of religion a "learned ignorance." Moreover, both movements addressed their message primarily to laypeople, in order to help them lead a higher moral life. The humanists, of course, drew their chief inspiration from the works of pagan and Christian antiquity, whereas the advocates of the new lay piety looked almost exclusively to Scripture. But the resemblances were close enough for scholars like Erasmus and Thomas More, writing in the early 1500s, to combine elements from both in the movement known as Christian Humanism.

MOVEMENTS OF DOCTRINAL REFORM

The effort to reform the traditions of medieval Christianity also led to open attacks on the religious establishment—fueled, of course, by antagonism toward the papacy and corruption in the Church and by the larger tensions of this troubled epoch. Above all, these attacks gained support because the Church remained reluctant to adapt its organization and teachings to the demands of a changing world.

Wycliffe The most prominent of the assaults of the 1300s was launched by an Englishman, John Wycliffe (1320?–1384), a clergyman who taught at Oxford University. He argued that the Church had become too remote from the people, and he wanted its doctrines simplified. To this end, he sought a more direct reliance on the Bible itself (which he suggested having translated into English so as to make it easier to understand) and less power for priests. Beyond his unease over the Church's remoteness from ordinary believers, he may have had political reasons (and thus support) for his stand. He was close to members of the royal court, who were increasingly resistant to papal demands and who were troubled that, in the midst of England's war with France, the papacy should have come under French influence when it moved from Rome to Avignon. In 1365 Wycliffe denounced the payment of Peter's pence, the annual tax given by English people to the papacy, and shortly thereafter he publicly denounced the papal Curia, monks, and friars for their vices.

Wycliffe argued that the Scriptures alone declared the will of God and that neither the pope and the cardinals nor the Scholastic theologians could tell Christians what they should believe. In particular, he questioned one of the central dogmas of the Church that emphasized the special power of the priest: *transubstantiation,* which asserts that priests at the Mass work a miracle when they change the substance of bread and wine into the substance of Christ's body and blood. Besides attacking the exalted position and privileges of the priesthood in such rites as transubstantiation, Wycliffe denied the authority of the pope and the hierarchy to exercise jurisdiction or to hold property. He claimed that the true Church was that of the predestined—that is, those whom God would save and were thus in a state of grace. Only these elect could rule the elect; therefore, popes and bishops who had no grace could have their properties removed and had no right to rule. Responsibility for ecclesiastical reform rested with the prince, and the pope could exercise only as much authority as the prince allowed.

The Lollards Many of Wycliffe's views were branded heretical, but even though he was forced to leave Oxford when he offended his protectors at the royal court, they did keep him unharmed until he died. His followers, mostly ordinary people who were known as Lollards—a name apparently derived from "lollar" (idler)—were not so lucky. They managed to survive as an underground movement in the countryside until the Protestant Reformation exploded more than a century later, but they were constantly hounded, and in 1428 the Church had Wycliffe's remains dug up, burned, and thrown into a river.

Hus An even harsher fate awaited Wycliffe's most famous admirer, a Bohemian priest named Jan Hus (1369–1415), who started a broad and even more defiant movement in his homeland. Hus was a distinguished churchman and scholar. He served as rector (the equivalent of president) of the Charles University in Prague, one of Europe's best-known institutions, and he was the main preacher at a fashionable chapel in Prague. Like Wycliffe, he argued that priests were not a holy and privileged group, set apart from laymen, but that the Church was made up of all the

Hus at Constance

A few weeks before he was executed, Jan Hus wrote to his Czech followers to tell them how he had responded to his accusers at the Council of Constance:

"Master Jan Hus, in hope a servant of God, to all faithful Czechs who love God: I call to your attention that the proud and avaricious Council, full of all abomination, condemned my Czech books having neither heard nor seen them; even if it had heard them, it would not have understood them. O, had you seen that Council which calls itself the most holy, and that cannot err, you would have seen the greatest abomination! I have heard it commonly said that Constance would not for thirty years rid itself of the sins which that Council has committed. That Council has done more harm than good.

"Therefore, faithful Christians, do not allow yourselves to be terrified by their decrees, which will profit them nothing. They will fly away like butterflies, and their decrees will turn into a spiderweb. They wanted to frighten me, but could not overcome God's power in me. They did not dare to oppose me with Scripture.

"I am writing this to you that you may know that they did not defeat me by any Scripture or any proof, but that they sought to seduce me by deceits and threats to recant and abjure. But the merciful Lord God, whose law I have extolled, has been and is with me, and I hope that He will be with me to the end and will preserve me in His grace until death.

"This letter was written in chains, in the expectation of death."

From Matthew Spinka (ed.), *The Letters of John Hus* (Manchester University Press, 1972), pp. 195–197.

faithful. To emphasize this equality, he rejected the custom of allowing the congregation at a Mass to eat the wafer that symbolized Christ's body but allowing only the priest to drink the wine that symbolized his blood. In a dramatic gesture, Hus shared the cup of wine with all worshipers, thus reducing the distinctiveness of the priest. His followers adopted a chalice, or cup, as the symbol of their movement.

Hus was not hesitant about defying the leadership of the Church. Denounced for the positions he had taken, he replied by questioning the authority of the pope himself:

> If a Pope is wicked, then like Judas he is a devil and a son of perdition and not the head of the Church militant. If he lives in a manner contrary to Christ he has entered the papacy by another way than through Christ.

In 1415 Hus was summoned to defend his views before the Church Council at Constance. Although he had been guaranteed safe passage if he came to answer accusations of heresy, the promise was broken. He was condemned, handed over to the secular authorities, and executed (*see box*, p. 379). But his followers, unlike the Lollards who stayed out of sight in England, refused to retreat in the face of persecution.

The Hussites A new leader, Jan Žižka, known as John of the Chalice, raised an army and led a successful campaign against the emperor, who was also king of Bohemia and the head of the crusade that was now mounted against the Hussites. The resistance lasted 20 years, outliving Žižka, but sustained by Bohemian nobles, and eventually the Hussites were allowed to establish a special church, the Utraquist Church, in which both cup and wafer were shared by all worshipers at Mass. But Hus's other demands, such as the surrender of all personal possessions by the clergy (an echo of St. Francis), were rejected. Those who tried to fight on for these causes were defeated in battle, and after a long struggle the resistance came to an end, having made only a minor dent in the unity of the Church.

The popular appeal of Wycliffe and Hus reflected the widespread dissatisfaction with official teachings in the late 1300s and 1400s—a dissatisfaction that Petrarch, too, had shown, although in his case there was no question of challenging traditional doctrine. Instead of trying to change the Church itself, he merely sought moral guidance elsewhere. And yet, when Wycliffe and Hus chose to risk an open confrontation, they demonstrated that reform ideas, advanced by charismatic leaders, could find a following among those who resented the authoritarian and materialistic outlook of the Church. At the same time, however, it became clear that such dissent could not survive without support from nobles, princes, or other leaders of society. Even with such help, the Hussites had to limit their demands; without it, they would have gained nothing. It was 100 years after Hus's death before a new reformer arose who had learned these lessons, and he was to transform Western Christianity beyond recognition.

Recommended Reading

Sources

*Brucker, Gene A. (ed.). *The Society of Renaissance Florence: A Documentary Study*. 1971.

*Cassirer, Ernst, P. O. Kristeller, and J. H. Randall, Jr. (eds.). *The Renaissance Philosophy of Man*. 1953. Selections from Petrarch, Ficino, Pico, and others.

*Chambers, David, and Brian Pullan (eds.). *Venice: A Documentary History. 1450–1630*. 1992.

Eckhart. *Meister Eckhart, a Modern Translation*. R. B. Blakney (tr.). 1956.

*Available in paperback.

Kempe, Margery. *The Book of Margery Kempe (1436)*. B. A. Windeatt (tr.). The autobiography of an extraordinary woman. 1985.

*Kohl, Benjamin G., and Ronald G. Witt (eds.). *The Earthly Republic: Italian Humanists on Government and Society*. 1978.

*Marsilius of Padua. *Defender of Peace*. Alan Gerwith (tr.). 1986.

Studies

*Baron, Hans. *The Crisis of the Early Italian Renaissance: Civic Humanism and Republican Liberty in the Age of Classicism and Tyranny*. 1966. Fundamental analysis of Florentine "civic humanism."

Becker, M. B. *Civility and Society in Western Europe. 1300–1600*. 1988.

*Berenson, Bernard. *The Italian Painters of the Renaissance*. 1968. Classic essays on the history of art.

Bergin, Thomas G. *Boccaccio*. 1981. Learned and readable.

Brucker, Gene A. *Renaissance Florence*. 1983. The standard introduction.

*Burckhardt, Jacob. *The Civilization of the Renaissance in Italy*. 1958. One of the pioneering works of European history, first published in 1860.

Clark, J. M. *The Great German Mystics: Eckhart, Tauler and Suso*. 1949.

Cole, Bruce. *The Renaissance Artist at Work: From Pisano to Titian*. 1983.

Crombie, Alistair C. *Medieval and Early Modern Science*. 1961.

Funkenstein, Amos. *Theology and the Scientific Imagination from the Middle Ages to the Seventeenth Century*. 1986.

*Goldthwaite, Richard A. *The Building of Renaissance Florence: An Economic and Social History*. 1980. Imaginative examination of the relations between society and architecture.

Grendler, Paul F. *Schooling in Renaissance Italy: Literacy and Learning. 1300–1600*. 1989. A recent survey.

Hanning, Robert W., and David Rosand (eds.). *Castiglione: The Ideal and the Real in Renaissance Culture*. 1983.

*Herlihy, David, and Christiane Klapisch-Zuber. *Tuscans and Their Families*. 1985. A study of a Florentine census of 1427.

Holmes, George. *Florence, Rome and the Origins of the Renaissance*. 1986.

*Huizinga, Johann. *The Waning of the Middle Ages*. 1954.

Hutchison, Jane C. *Albrecht Dürer: A Biography*. 1990.

*Keen, Maurice. *Chivalry*. 1984. Sympathetic survey of knightly culture.

Kent, F. W., and Patricia Simons (eds.). *Patronage, Art and Society in Renaissance Italy*. 1987. A collection of interesting essays.

Klapisch-Zuber, Christiane. *Women, Family and Ritual in Renaissance Italy*. 1985. Collected essays.

*Kristeller, Paul O. *Renaissance Thought and Its Sources*. 1979. By a leading historian of Renaissance thought.

Leff, Gordon. *William of Ockham*. 1975. Authoritative examination of a difficult philosopher.

Martines, Lauro. *The Social World of the Florentine Humanists*. 1963. The humanists examined in the light of their social background.

Rosand, David (ed.). *Titian, His World and His Legacy*. 1981.

Tobin, Frank. *Meister Eckhart: Thought and Language*. 1986.

Wilkins, Ernest Hatch. *Life of Petrarch*. 1961.

Lucas Cranach the Elder
LUTHER IN THE VINEYARD
This work of propaganda uses the biblical image of Christians toiling in the vineyard of the Lord to contrast the seriousness and fruitfulness of the Protestants on the left with the greed and destructiveness of the Catholics on the right. Luther himself rakes in the center, while Melanchthon at the far left goes to the source (the Bible) and draws from the well; meanwhile, on the right, bishops and monks ruin the crops, burn the wood, and fill the well with stones.

CHAPTER THIRTEEN

REFORMATIONS IN RELIGION

ALTHOUGH it may have seemed monolithic and all-powerful, the Roman Church in the fifteenth century was neither a unified nor an unchallenged institution. It had long permitted considerable variety in individual beliefs, from the analytic investigations of canon lawyers to the emotional outpourings of mystics. There were local saints, some of whom were recognized as holy only by a few villages; and for many Europeans the papacy remained a distant and barely comprehensible authority. To assume that its theological pronouncements were understood by the average illiterate Christian is to misrepresent the loose, fragmentary nature of the medieval Church. Moreover, doubts had been raised, by the political disputes and reform movements of the fourteenth and fifteenth centuries, about the central structure and doctrines of the Church. That the papacy had weathered these storms by 1500 indicated both how flexible and how powerful it was. What was to be remarkable in the years that followed was the sudden revelation of the Church's fragility, as a protest by a single monk snowballed into a movement that shattered the thousand-year unity of Western Christendom.

I. Piety and Dissent

DOCTRINE

The fundamental question all Christians face is: How can sinful human beings gain salvation? In 1500, the standard official answer was that the Church was an essential intermediary. Only through participation in its rituals, and particularly through the seven sacraments its priests administered—baptism, confirmation, matrimony, the eucharist, ordination, penance, and extreme unction—did the believer have access to the grace that God offered as an antidote to sin. But there was another answer, identified with distinguished Church fathers such as St. Augustine: People can be saved by their faith in God and love of him. This view emphasized inward and personal belief and focused on God as the source of grace.

The two traditions were not incompatible; for centuries they had coexisted without difficulty. Yet the absence of precise definition in many areas of Christian doctrine was a major problem for theologians, because it was often difficult to tell where orthodoxy ended and heresy began. The position taken by the papacy, however, had grown less inclusive and adaptable over the years; by 1500 it was stressing the outward and institutional far more than the inward and personal route to salvation. The aim of reformers for over a century had been to reverse this trend, and it remained unclear whether the change would be accomplished by reform from within or by a revolution and split in the Church.

FORMS OF PIETY

The root of the demand for change was the need of many laypeople for a more personal way of expressing their piety than official practices offered. Church rituals meant little, they felt, unless believers could cultivate an interior sense of the love and presence of God. They looked for nourishment, therefore, to those who emphasized religious individualism. Rejecting the theological subtleties of Scholasticism, they sought divine guidance in the Bible and the writings of the early Church fathers, especially St. Augustine. Lay religious fraternities dedicated to private forms of worship and charitable works proliferated in the cities, especially in Germany and Italy. The most widespread of them in Germany, the Brotherhood of the Eleven Thousand Virgins, consisted of laypeople who gathered together, usually in a church, to sing hymns. In the mid-fifteenth century, more than 100 such groups had been established in Hamburg, a city of slightly more than 10,000 inhabitants. Church leaders, unhappy about a development over which they had no control, had tried to suppress them but to no avail.

Savonarola The most spectacular outburst of popular piety around 1500 occurred in seemingly materialist Florence, which embraced Girolamo Savonarola, a zealous friar who wanted to banish the irreligion and materialism he saw everywhere about him. The climax of his influence came in 1496, when he arranged a tremendous bonfire in which the Florentines burned cosmetics, light literature, dice, and other such frivolities. Savonarola embodied the desire for personal renewal that had long been a part of Western Christianity but seemed to be gaining intensity in the 1400s. His attempts at reform eventually brought him into conflict with the papacy, which rightly saw him as a threat to its authority. The Church therefore denounced him and gave its support to those who resented his power in Florence. His opponents had the friar arrested in 1498 and then executed on a trumped-up charge of treason.

The widespread search for a more intense devotional life was a sign of spiritual vitality. But Church leaders in the age of Savonarola gave little encouragement to ecclesiastical reform and the evangelization of the laity. Only in Spain was there a deliberate attempt to eradicate abuses and encourage religious fervor, and there the leadership in the effort came not from Rome but from the head of the Spanish Church, Cardinal Francisco Ximenes. Elsewhere, the hierarchy reacted harshly when such movements threatened its authority.

THE LEGACY OF WYCLIFFE AND HUS

Such threats had arisen from time to time, notably at universities, where the basic method of

▶ *Anonymous*
THE MARTYRDOM OF SAVONAROLA, CA. 1500
This painting still hangs in the monastery of San Marco where Savonarola lived during his years of power. It shows the city's central square—a setting that remains recognizable to anyone who visits Florence today—where the bonfire of the "vanities" had been held in 1496, and where Savonarola was executed in 1498. The execution is depicted here as an event that the ordinary citizens of Florence virtually ignore as they go about their daily routines.

instruction, the disputation, encouraged the discussion of unorthodox ideas. At disputations, students learned by listening to arguments for and against standard views. It was not impossible for someone taking the "wrong" side in such a debate to be carried away and cross the line between a theoretical discussion and open dissent.

That is what had happened with the Englishman John Wycliffe, who taught at Oxford University in the late 1300s, and with the Bohemian Jan Hus, a professor at the University of Prague a few years later. They had demanded a simplification of doctrines, more reliance on the Bible, and less power for priests. Both had been condemned by the Church, and Hus had been burned at the stake in 1415. But their disciples had kept their ideas alive. Known in England as "Lollards," Wycliffe's followers managed to survive as an underground movement in the coun-

tryside. In Bohemia the Hussites had raised an army and won acceptance for their own church, which allowed worshipers greater participation in the Mass than did the Roman Church.

These protests revealed the extent of the dissatisfaction with official teachings. Charismatic leaders could find a following for unorthodox ideas if they could tap popular piety and resentment toward the Church. It was not easy for dissent to survive without support from nobles or princes; aristocrats had protected Wycliffe, and they had formed and led the Hussite army. Even without such patronage, however, the concerns persisted.

CAUSES OF DISCONTENT

By 1500 the spiritual authority of the papacy had been declining for more than two centuries. During the 70 years of the Babylonian captivity, when the pontiffs had lived in Avignon, they had seemed to be captives of the French monarchy rather than symbols of the universal Church. Far more demoralizing, the Great Schism that followed had threatened to undermine the unity of Western Christendom, as two and then three pretenders each claimed to be the true pope. The Council of Constance had closed this breach by 1418 but had also encouraged the conciliar movement. This attempt to subordinate papal power to the authority of Church councils ultimately failed, but it was yet another direct challenge to the pope's supremacy.

Secular Interests The papacy had also lost spiritual influence because of its secular interests. Increasingly, popes conducted themselves like princes. With skillful diplomacy and even military action, they had consolidated their control over the papal lands in the Italian peninsula. They had surrounded themselves with an elaborate court, had become patrons of the arts, and for a time had taken over the cultural leadership of Europe. This concern with political power and grandeur had eclipsed religious duties to the point that some popes used their spiritual powers to raise funds for their secular activities. The fiscal measures developed at Avignon, which furnished the papacy with income from appointments to Church offices and from various fees, had enlarged revenues but led to widespread abuses. High ecclesiastical offices could be bought and sold, and men (usually sons of nobles) were attracted to these positions by the opportunities they provided for wealth and power, not by a religious vocation.

Abuses were widespread at lower levels in the Church as well. Some prelates held several offices at a time and could not give adequate attention to any of them. The ignorance and moral laxity of the parish and monastic clergy also aroused antagonism. Even more damaging was the widespread impression that the Church was failing to meet individual spiritual needs because of its remoteness from the day-to-day needs of the average believer, its elaborate and incomprehensible system of canon law and theology, and its formal ceremonials. Above all, there was a general perception that priests and monks were profiting from their positions, exploiting the people, and giving minimal moral leadership or religious guidance in return.

Anticlericalism These concerns provoked anticlericalism (hostility to the clergy) and calls for reform which, except in the Spain of Cardinal Ximenes, went unheeded. For increasing numbers of deeply pious people, the growing emphasis on ritual and standardized practices seemed irrelevant to their personal quest for salvation. And their reaction was symptomatic of the broad commitment to genuine piety that was apparent, not only in the followers of Wycliffe, Hus, and Savonarola but in many segments of European society in the early 1500s.

POPULAR RELIGION

It was not only the educated elite and the city dwellers (a minority of Europe's inhabitants) who sought to express their faith in personal terms. The yearning for religious devotion among ordinary villagers, the majority of the population, was apparent even when the local priest—who was often hardly better educated than his parishioners—did little to inspire spiritual commitments. People would listen avidly to news of distant places brought by travelers who stopped at taverns and inns (a major source of information and ideas), and increasingly the tales they told were of religious upheaval. In addition, itinerant preachers roamed some regions, notably Central Europe, in considerable numbers, and they drew crowds when they started speaking—on street corners in towns or out in the fields—and described the power of faith. They usually urged direct communication between believers and God, free from ritual and complex doctrine. To the vast crowds they often drew, many of them seemed to echo the words of St. Augustine: "God and the soul I want to recognize, nothing else."

Equally important as a means of learning about and discussing the latest religious issues were the gatherings that regularly brought villagers together. Throughout the year, they would assemble to celebrate holidays—not only the landmarks of the Christian calendar like Christmas and Easter but also local festivals. Religion was always essential to these occasions. When, for example, the planting season arrived, the local priest would lead a procession into the countryside to bless the fields and pray for good crops. Family events, too, from birth to death, had important religious elements.

The Veillée The most common occasion when the community's traditional beliefs and assumptions were discussed, however, was the evening gathering—generally referred to by its French name, *veillée*, which means staying up in the evening. Between spring and autumn, when the weather was not too cold, a good part of the village came together at a central location after each day's work was done. There was little point in staying in one's own home after dark, because making a light with candles or oil was too expensive. Instead, sitting around a communal fire, people could sew clothes, repair tools, feed babies, resolve (or start) disputes, and discuss news. It was one of the few times when women were of no lesser status than men; the views they expressed were as important as any in shaping the common outlook of the villagers.

A favorite occupation at the *veillée* was listening to stories. Every village had its storytellers, who recounted wondrous tales of local history, of magical adventures, or of moral dilemmas, as the mood required. Biblical tales and the exploits

▶ *Hans Sebald Beham*
Church Festival, Woodcut, 1535
The celebration of the anniversary of a church's consecration was one of the most important holidays in a village. Not everyone, however, used this opportunity for spiritual ends, like the couple getting married in front of the church. Some overindulged at the tavern (lower right); some had a tooth extracted (center left); and some, as the chickens in the center and various couples in the scene suggest, used the occasion for pleasure alone. (Hans Sebald Beham, *Large Peasant Holiday*, 1535, Art Institute of Chicago.)

Peter Brueghel
THE PEASANT DANCE, CA. 1567
The most vivid images of life in the village during the sixteenth century were created by the Flemish artist Peter Brueghel. The different human types, and the earthiness of country life, are captured in scenes that show the villagers both at work and, as here, at ease and relaxed.

of Christian heroes like the Crusaders had always drawn an attentive audience. Now, however, in addition to entertainment and general moral uplift, peddlers and travelers who attended the *veillée* brought news of challenges to religious traditions. They told of attacks on the pope and Church practices, and of arguments for a simpler and more easily understood faith. This was how the ideas of religious reformers spread and how those with unorthodox views like the Lollards kept their faith alive. In some cases, the beliefs that were described made converts of those who heard them, and traveling preachers came to regard the gatherings at the *veillées* as ready-made congregations. They were usually far more knowledgeable, better trained, and more effective than local priests.

The response of the traditional Church to this challenge, after decades of indifference, was to insist that the local priest be better educated and more aware of what was at stake in the religious struggles of the day. As long as he had the support of the local authorities, he could make sure that his views dominated the *veillée* and that contrary beliefs were not expressed. Whichever way the discussions at these communal gatherings went, however, they demonstrated the power of popular piety in the tens of thousands of villages that dotted the European countryside.

THE IMPACT OF PRINTING

The expression of this piety received unexpected assistance from technology: the invention of a printing press with moveable type in the mid-1400s. At least a hundred years earlier, Europeans had known that by carving words and pictures into a wood block, inking them, and pressing the block onto paper, they could make an image that could be repeated on many sheets of paper. We do not know exactly when they discovered that they could speed up this cumbersome process and therefore change the text from page to page, if they used individual letters and put them together within a frame. We do know, however, that a printer named Johannes Gutenberg, who lived in the city of Mainz on the Rhine, was producing books this way by the 1450s. The technique spread rapidly (see table below) and made reading material available to a much broader segment of the population.

As a result, new ideas could travel with unprecedented speed. Perhaps a third of the trading and upper classes—townspeople, the educated, and the nobility—could read, but books could reach a much wider audience, because peddlers began to sell printed materials throughout Europe. They were bought everywhere and became favorite material for reading out loud at *veillées.* Thus people who had had little contact with written literature in the days of manuscripts now gained access to the latest ideas of the time.

Printing and Religion Printers were not slow to take advantage of the popular interest in books

Der Buchdrucker.

▸ *Jost Amman*
"THE PRINTER" FROM DAS STÄNDEBUCH (THE BOOK OF TRADES), 1568
This is the first detailed depiction of a printer's shop, showing assistants taking type from large wooden holders in the back, the press on the right, the pages being prepared and inked in the foreground, and finally the sheets of paper before and after they are printed. The caption notes that printing had been invented in the German city of Mainz.

THE SPREAD OF PRINTING THROUGH 1500

Number of towns in which a printing press was established for the first time, by period and country

Period	*German-*	*Italian-* *Speaking Areas*	*French-*	*Spain*	*England**	*Netherlands*	*Other*	*Total*
Before 1471	8	4	1	1	—	—	—	14
1471–1480	22	36	9	6	3	12	5	93
1481–1490	17	13	21	12	—	5	4	72
1491–1500	9	5	11	6	—	2	8	41
Total by 1500	56	58	42	25	3	19	17	220

*In order to try to control the printers, the English government ordered that they work only in London and at Oxford and Cambridge universities.

Adapted from Lucien Febvre and Henri-Jean Martin, *The Coming of the Book: The Impact of Printing 1450–1800,* translated by David Gerard, London, NLB, 1976, pp. 178–179 and 184–185.

by publishing almanacs filled with home-spun advice about the weather and nature that were written specifically for simple rural folk. Even the almanacs, however, carried religious advice; and, more importantly, translations of the Bible made it available to ordinary people in a language that, for the first time, they could understand. Books thus became powerful weapons in the religious conflicts of the day. Devotional tracts, lives of the saints, and the Bible were the most popular titles—often running to editions of around 1000 copies. They became means of spreading new ideas, and the ready markets they found reflected the general interest of the age in spiritual matters.

Printing clearly lessened laypeople's dependence on the clergy; whereas traditionally the priest had read and interpreted the Scriptures for his congregation, now people could consult their own copies. By 1522, 18 translations of the Bible had been published. Some 14,000 copies had been printed in German alone, enough to make it easy to buy in most German-speaking regions. The Church frowned on these efforts, and governments tried to regulate the numbers and locations of presses; but in the end it proved impossible to control the effects of printing.

PIETY AND PROTEST IN LITERATURE AND ART

The printing press broke the Church's monopoly over the public discussion of religious teachings. Authorities might be dismayed by, but could not totally prevent, the publication of writings that criticized doctrines or practices. Thus the most gifted satirist of the sixteenth century, the French humanist François Rabelais, openly ridiculed the clergy and the morality of his day. Rabelais was a monk (as well as a doctor), and he was deeply unhappy that traditional religious practices had diverged so far from the ideals of Jesus. He was most famous for his earthy bawdiness, but again and again he returned to clerical targets, as in this passage from his *Gargantua* (1533):

> "Don't monks pray to God for us?" "They do nothing of the kind," said Gargantua. "All they do is keep the whole neighborhood awake by jangling their bells.... They mumble over a lot of legends and psalms, which they don't in the least understand; and they say a great many paternosters ... without thinking or caring about what they are saying. And all that I call a mockery of God, not prayer."

Scurrilous broadsides no less stinging in tone became very popular during the religious disputes of the 1500s. These single sheets often contained vicious attacks on religious opponents and were usually illustrated by cartoons with obscene imagery. The broadsides were examples of par-

▸ *Hans Baldung Grien*

THE THREE AGES OF WOMAN AND DEATH, CA. 1510
The preoccupation with the transitoriness of life and the vanity of earthly things took many forms in the sixteenth century. Here the point is hammered home unmistakably, as the central figure—a young woman at the height of her beauty between infancy and old age—is reminded of the passage of time (the hourglass) and the omnipresence of death even as she admires herself in a convex mirror.

▸ *Matthias Grünewald*
The Temptation of St. Anthony, ca. 1510
This detail from a series of scenes Grünewald painted for the Isenheim Altar suggests the power the devil held over the imagination of sixteenth-century Europeans. The gentle, bearded St. Anthony is not seated in contemplation, as in Dürer's portrayal (see plate on p. 392). Instead, he is surrounded by the monsters the devil has sent to frighten him out of his faith. This was a favorite subject of the period, and provided artists like Bosch and Grünewald the opportunity to make vivid and terrifying the ordinary Christian's fear of sin.

tisan hostility, but their broader significance should not be ignored. Even the most lowly of hack writers could share with a serious author like Rabelais a sense of outrage at indifference in high places and a dismay with the lack of spiritual leadership of the time.

Art This emphasis on the importance of religious belief, so evident in European literature, also permeated the work of northern artists in the late fifteenth and early sixteenth centuries (see plates on p. 390 and above). The gruesome paintings of Hieronymus Bosch, for example, depicted the fears of devils and of hell that his contemporaries felt endangered them at all times. He put on canvas the demons, the temptations, the terrible punishments for sin that people considered as real as their tangible surroundings. Bosch's younger contemporary Matthias Grünewald conveyed the same mixture of terror and devotion. Like Bosch, he painted a frightening *Temptation of St. Anthony,* showing the travails of the saint who steadfastly resisted horrible attacks by the devil. These artists explored the darker side of faith, taking their inspiration from the fear of damnation and the hope for salvation—the first seen in the demons, the second in the redeeming Christ.

Dürer The most famous northern artist of this period was Albrecht Dürer, and it is significant that his fame began when he produced an illustrated edition of a biblical book, *The Apocalypse,* which describes God's punishment of sinners on the final Day of Judgment. The book became a best-seller and made Dürer a rich man. He was sought after throughout Europe, and he became known at all levels of society because he was a master of the art of the woodcut. Dürer enjoyed this medium more than painting because, as he noted, many copies could be sold quite cheaply, and his fame and his finances profited accordingly. His wife Agnes was a shrewd businesswoman who accompanied her husband on his travels and set up a stall to sell his works whenever she found a convenient marketplace. Dürer's subjects were largely religious—the life of Christ, portraits of saints, and scenes with the Virgin Mary—which ensured that they had the widest possible appeal.

The depth of piety conveyed by artists like Dürer reflected the temper of Europe. In art and literature, as in lay organizations and the continuing popularity of itinerant preachers, people showed their concern for individual spiritual values and their dissatisfaction with a Church that was not meeting their needs.

▸ *Albrecht Dürer*
ST. ANTHONY, ENGRAVING, 1519
The ease and mastery Dürer brought to the art of engraving made it as powerful and flexible a form as painting. Here the massive figure of the saint, deep in study, is placed in front of a marvelously observed city. The buildings display Dürer's virtuosity—their shapes echo the bulk and solidity of the figure—and they may have symbolized the temptations of city life for a saint who was revered for his solitary piety in the desert.

CHRISTIAN HUMANISM

No segment of society expressed the strivings and yearnings of the age more eloquently than the northern humanists. The salient features of the humanist movement in Italy—its theory of education, its emphasis on eloquence, its reverence for the ancients, and its endorsement of active participation in affairs of state—began to win wide acceptance north of the Alps in the late 1400s. But the northerners added a significant religious dimension to the movement by devoting considerable attention to early Christian literature: the Bible and the writings of the Church fathers. As a result, they have been called *Christian humanists*.

The first major center of humanism in the north was at the University of Heidelberg; but by the end of the fifteenth century the movement's influence, carried by the printing press, was European-wide. The northern humanists were particularly determined to probe early Christianity for the light it could throw on the origins and accuracy of current religious teachings. Indeed, northern humanism's broad examination of religious issues in the early 1500s helped create an atmosphere in which much more serious criticism of the Church could flourish.

The Christian humanists did not abandon the interest in classical authors or the methods for analyzing ancient texts, language, and style that had been developed by Italian humanism. But they put these methods to a new use: analysis of the Bible in order to explain more clearly the message of Jesus and his apostles, and thus to provide a better guide to true piety and morality. This deeply religious undertaking dominated the writings of the two most famous Christian humanists, one English and one Dutch.

MORE AND ERASMUS

More Sir Thomas More (1478–1535), a lawyer and statesman, was the central figure of English humanism. His reputation as a writer rests primarily on a short work, *Utopia*, published in Latin in 1516, which describes an ideal society on an imaginary island. In it, More condemned war, poverty, intolerance, and other evils of his day and defined the general principles of morality that he felt should underlie human society.

The first book of *Utopia* returns to the conflict between the *vita contemplativa* and the *vita activa* that Petrarch had emphasized, and asks whether a learned person should withdraw from the world to avoid the corruptions of politics or actively participate in affairs of state so as to guide policy. In his own career, More chose the latter path, with fatal results. The second, more famous book of *Utopia* leaves such practical issues aside and describes what an ideal commonwealth might be like. In political and social organization, Utopia is a carefully regulated, almost monastic community that has succeeded in abolishing private property, greed, and pride—and thus has freed its inhabitants from some of the worst sins of More's day. The Utopians have accomplished all this without Christianity, and More implies that a society based on Christian principles can attain even greater good. Well-designed institutions, education, and discipline are his answer to the fall of Adam and Eve: Weak human nature can be led to virtuousness only if severely curbed.

Deeply devout and firmly attached to the traditional Church, More entered public life as a member of Parliament in 1504. He rose high in government service, but eventually he gave his life for remaining loyal to the pope and refusing to recognize the decision of his king, Henry VIII, to reject papal authority and become head of the English Church. When Henry determined to break with Rome, he found it intolerable that this prominent political figure rejected his actions and would not compromise; and so, to discourage any further disobedience, Henry had him beheaded. More's last words revealed his unflinching adherence to the Christian principles he pursued throughout his life: "I die the King's good servant, but God's first."

Erasmus The supreme representative of Christian humanism was the Dutchman Desiderius Erasmus (1466?–1536). Erasmus early acquired a taste for ancient writers, and he determined to devote himself to classical studies. For the greater part of his life, he wandered through Europe, writing, visiting friends, and occasionally working for important patrons. He always retained his independence, however, for unlike More, he answered the question of whether a scholar should

▸ *Hans Holbein the Younger*
PORTRAIT OF ERASMUS, 1523
The leading portraitist of the age, Hans Holbein, painted his friend Erasmus a number of times. Here he shows the great scholar at work, possibly writing one of the many elegantly constructed letters that he sent to colleagues throughout Europe. The richness of the scene bears noting—the gold ring, the fine coat with a fur collar, and the splendid tapestry hanging over the paneled wall.

enter public life by avoiding the compromises that would be necessary in the service of a ruler.

Erasmus was so famous for his learning and his literary skills that he dominated the world of letters of his time. Constantly consulted by scholars and admirers, he wrote magnificently composed letters that reflected every aspect of the culture of his age. He became known throughout Europe, however, as a result of a little book, *The Praise of Folly* (1509), which was one of the first best-sellers created by the printing press. Some of it is gay, lighthearted banter that pokes fun at the author himself, his friends, and the follies of everyday life, and suggests that a little folly is essential to human existence. The book also points out that Christianity itself is a kind of folly, a belief in "things not seen." In many passages, though, Erasmus launches sharply satirical attacks against monks, the pope, meaningless ceremonies, and the many lapses from what he perceived to be the true Christian spirit.

The Philosophy of Christ At the heart of Erasmus' work was the message that he called the "philosophy of Christ." He believed that the life of Jesus and, especially, his teachings in the Sermon on the Mount should be models for Christian piety and morality. For the Church's ceremonies and for rigid discipline he had only censure: Too often, he said, they served as substitutes for genuine spiritual concerns. People lit thousands of candles for Mary but cared little about the humility she is supposed to inspire. They forgot that what counts is the spirit of religious devotion, not the form. By simply following the precepts of Jesus, he argued, a Christian could lead a life guided by sincere faith. Because of his insistence on ethical behavior, Erasmus could admire a truly moral man even if he was a pagan. "I could almost say, 'Pray for me, St. Socrates!' " he once wrote.

Erasmus believed that the Church had lost sight of its original mission. In the course of 15 centuries, traditions and practices had developed that obscured the intentions of its founder, and purity could be restored only by studying the Scriptures and the writings of the early Church fathers. Here the literary and analytic tools of the humanists became vitally important, because they enabled scholars to understand the meaning and intention of ancient manuscripts. Practicing what he preached, Erasmus spent 10 years preparing a new edition of the Greek text of the New Testament so as to correct errors in the Latin Vulgate, which was the standard version, and he revised it repeatedly for another 20 years.

But the calm, scholarly, and tolerant moderation Erasmus prized was soon left behind by events. The rising intensity of religious reformers and their opponents destroyed the effort he had led to cure the ills of the Church quietly, from within. Erasmus wanted a revival of purer faith, but he would never have dreamed of rejecting the traditional authority of the Church. As Europe entered an age of confrontation, he found it impossible to preserve a middle course between the two sides. Unable to choose, Erasmus was swept aside by revolutionary forces that he himself had helped build but that Martin Luther was to unleash.

II. The Lutheran Reformation

THE CONDITIONS FOR CHANGE

That a major religious conflict should have erupted in the Holy Roman Empire is not surprising. In this territory of fragmented government, with hundreds of independent local princes, popular piety was noticeably strong. Yet anyone who was unhappy with Church leadership had all the more reason to resent the power of bishops, because in the empire they were often also princes—such as the aristocratic bishop who ruled the important city of Cologne on the Rhine. There were few strong secular princes who could protect the people from the fiscal demands of the Church, and the popes therefore regarded the empire as their surest source of revenue.

This situation was made more volatile by the ambitions of the secular princes. Their ostensible overlord, the emperor, had no real power over them, and they worked tirelessly to strengthen their control over their subjects and to assert their independence from all outside authority. A number of them were in fact to see the religious upheavals of the 1500s as a means of advancing their own political purposes. Their ambitions help explain why a determined reformer, Martin Luther, won such swift and widespread support.

MARTIN LUTHER

Martin Luther (1483–1546) was born into a miner's family in Saxony in central Germany. The household was dominated by the father, whose powerful presence some modern commentators have seen reflected in his son's vision of an omnipotent God. The boy received a good education and decided to become a lawyer, a profession that would have given him many opportunities for advancement. But in his early twenties, shortly after starting his legal studies, he had an experience that changed his life. Crossing a field during a thunderstorm, he was thrown to the ground by a bolt of lightning, and in his terror he cried out to St. Anne that he would enter a monastery.

Luther as a Monk Although the decision may well have been that sudden, it is clear that there was more to Luther's complete change of direction than this one incident, however traumatic. A highly sensitive, energetic, and troubled young man, he had become obsessed with his own sinfulness, and he joined a monastery in the hope that a penitential life would help him overcome his sense of guilt. Once he became a monk, he pursued every possible opportunity to earn worthiness in the sight of God. He overlooked no means of discipline or act of contrition or self-denial, and for added merit he endured austerities, such as self-flagellation, that went far beyond normal requirements. But it was all to no avail: When called upon to officiate at his first Mass after his ordination in 1507, he was so terrified at the prospect of a sinner like himself administering the sacrament—that is, transforming the wafer and wine of the Mass into the body and blood of Christ—that he almost failed to complete the ritual.

Fortunately for Luther, his superiors took more notice of his intellectual gifts than of his self-doubts and in 1508 assigned him to the faculty of a new university in Wittenberg, the capital of Saxony. It was from his scholarship, which was excellent, and especially from his study of the Bible that he was able at last to draw comfort and spiritual peace.

This second crucial turning point in Luther's life, as important as the lightning bolt, occurred while he was preparing his university lectures. Until this point, which is known as "the experience in the tower," he could see no way that he, a despicable mortal, could receive anything but the fiercest punishments from a God of absolute

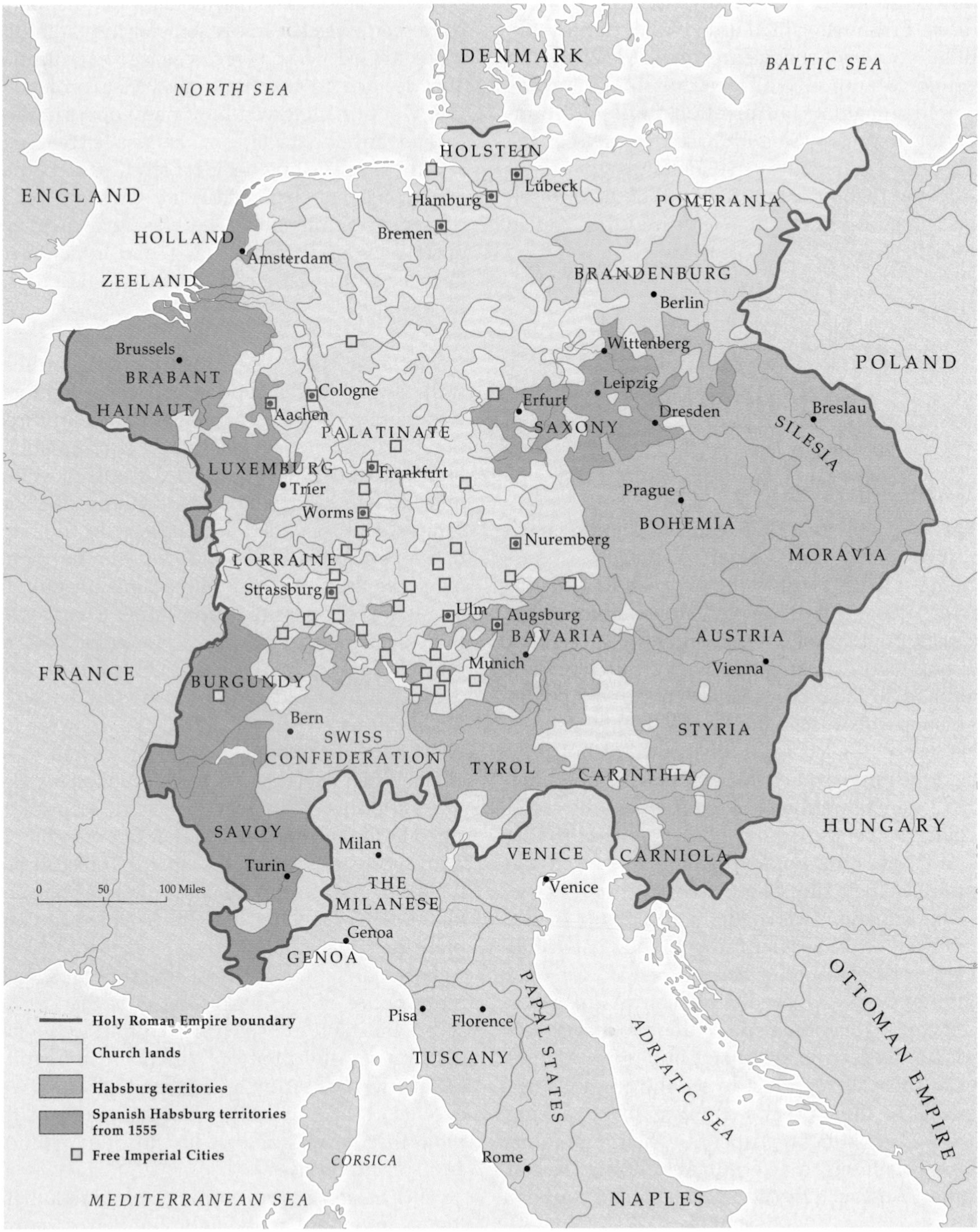

Map 13.1 THE EMPIRE IN THE AGE OF LUTHER

The fragmentation that divided the empire into dozens of distinct principalities, independent cities, and autonomous territories enabled Luther to find the political support that kept his religious reform alive.

justice. Now, however, he had an insight that led him to understand that he needed only to rely on God's mercy, a quality as great as divine justice (*see box*, below). The many advances in Luther's thinking thereafter came from this insight: that justification—which removes sin and bestows righteousness through a gift of grace—is achieved by faith alone.

THE INDULGENCE CONTROVERSY

In 1517 an event occurred that was ultimately to lead Luther to an irrevocable break with the Church. In the spring, a friar, Johann Tetzel, began to peddle indulgences a few miles from Wittenberg as part of a huge fund-raising effort to pay for the new Church of St. Peter in Rome. Originally, an indulgence had been granted to anyone going on a crusade. It was then extended to those who, though unable to join a crusade, gave enough money for a poor crusader to be able to reach the Holy Land. Indulgences released sinners from a certain period of punishment in purgatory before they went on to heaven and were justified doctrinally as a sort of credit that could be drawn from the treasury of merit built up by Jesus and the saints. But neither the doctrine nor the connection with money had been fully defined, and clerics had taken advantage of this vagueness simply to sell indulgences. Tetzel, an expert peddler, was offering complete releases from purgatory without bothering to mention the repentance that, according to Church teachings, was essential if a sinner was to be forgiven or absolved.

The 95 Theses The people of Wittenberg were soon flocking to Tetzel to buy this easy guarantee

Luther's "Experience in the Tower"

The following passage was written by Luther in 1545, at least 25 years after the experience it described. As a result, scholars have been unable to decide (a) whether the breakthrough was in fact as sudden as Luther suggests; (b) when it took place—possibly as early as 1512, five years before the indulgence dispute, or as late as 1519, when Luther was already under attack for his views; or (c) how it should be interpreted—as a scholar's insight, as a revelation from God, or as Luther's later crystallization into a single event of a process that had taken many years.

I wanted very much to understand Paul's Epistle to the Romans, but despite my determination to do so I kept being stopped by the one word, "the *righteousness* of God." I hated that word, because I had been taught to understand it as the active righteousness by which a just God punishes unjust sinners. The trouble was that, although I may have been an impeccable monk, I felt myself to be a sinner before God. As a result, not only was I unable to love, but I actually hated this just God, who punishes all sinners. And so I raged, yet I still longed to understand St. Paul.

At last, as I grappled with the words day and night, God had mercy on me, and I saw the connection between the words "the righteousness of God" and "The righteous shall live by faith" (Romans 1:17). I understood that the righteousness of God refers to the gift by which God enables the just to live—that is, by faith. A merciful God justifies us by faith, as it is written: "The righteous shall live by faith." At that point, I felt as if I had been reborn and had passed through open doors into paradise. The whole of Scripture took on new meaning. As I had previously hated the phrase, "the righteousness of God," so now I lovingly praised it.

Translation from the Latin by Theodore K. Rabb of Luther's Preface to the 1545 edition of his writings, in Otto Scheel (ed.), *Dokumente zu Luthers Entwicklung* (Tübingen: Mohr, 1929), pp. 191–192.

▶ *Jörg Breu*
ENGRAVING DEPICTING THE SALE OF INDULGENCES, CA. 1530
This would have been a familiar scene in Europe until Luther's attacks brought it to an end. The clerics on their fine horses on the right bring a cross and the papal bull, which is authenticated by the elaborate seals and ribbons that hang from it. The faithful put money in the barrel in the middle or hand it to the dispenser of certificates on the left, who sits near the large locked chest that will hold the revenues from the sales.

of salvation. For Luther, a man groping toward an evangelical solution of his own doubts, it was unforgivable that people should be deprived of their hard-earned money for spurious, worthless promises. On October 31, 1517, he published in Wittenberg 95 theses, or statements, on indulgences that he offered to debate with experts in Christian doctrine.

This was no revolutionary document. It merely described what Luther believed to be correct teachings on indulgences: that the pope could remit only the penalties that he himself or canon law imposed; that therefore the promise of a general pardon was damnable; and that every true believer shared in the treasury of merit left by Jesus and the saints, whether or not he or she obtained an indulgence. Within a few weeks the story was all over the empire that a monk had challenged the sale of indulgences. The proceeds of Tetzel's mission began to drop off; and other members of his order, the Dominicans, rallied to their brother by attacking his presumptuous critic, Luther, who happened to belong to a rival order, the Augustinians.

Luther Elaborates The controversy soon drew attention in Rome. At first, Pope Leo X regarded the affair as merely a monks' quarrel. But, in time, Luther's responses to the Dominicans' attacks began to deviate radically from Church doctrine, and by 1520 he had gone so far as to challenge the authority of the papacy itself in three pamphlets outlining his fundamental position.

In *An Address to the Christian Nobility of the German Nation*, Luther made a frankly patriotic appeal to his fellow Germans to reject the foreign pope's authority. The Church, he said, consisted of all Christians, including the laity; hence the nobles were as much its governors as the clergy, and they had a responsibility to remedy its defects. Indeed, Emperor Charles V had an obligation to call a council to end abuses. In *The Babylonian Captivity*, the most radical of the three works, Luther attacked the system of seven sacraments, the basis of the Church's authority, on the ground that only two are mentioned in the Bible. In *The Liberty of the Christian Man*, a less polemical work, he explained his doctrine of faith and justification by stressing that, although he did not reject good works, only the faith of the individual believer could bring salvation from an all-powerful, just, and merciful God. These three pamphlets had an overwhelming impact on Luther's fellow Germans. His emotional appeal to their resentment of Church power and their wish for a more personal faith made him, almost overnight, the embodiment of a widespread yearning for religious reform.

THE DIET OF WORMS

There could no longer be any doubt that Luther was breaking with the Church, and in 1520 Pope Leo X issued a bull excommunicating him. Luther publicly tossed the document into a bonfire, defending his action by calling the pope an Antichrist. In 1521 Emperor Charles V, who was officially the papacy's secular representative, summoned the celebrated monk to offer his defense against the papal decree at a Diet of the Empire (a meeting of princes, city leaders, and churchmen) at Worms, a city on the Rhine.

The journey across Germany was a triumphant progress for Luther, who now seemed a heroic figure. Appearing before the magnificent assembly dressed in his simple monk's robe, he offered a striking contrast to the display of imperial and princely grandeur. First in German and then in Latin, he made the famous declaration that closed the last door behind him: "I cannot and will not recant anything, since it is unsafe and wrong to go against my conscience. Here I stand. I cannot do otherwise. God help me. Amen." On the following day the emperor gave his reply: "A single friar who goes counter to all Christianity for a thousand years must be wrong."

Luther Protected Charles added legality to the papal bull by issuing an imperial edict calling for Luther's arrest and the burning of his works. At this point, however, the independent power of the German princes and their resentment of for-

▶ *Lucas Cranach the Elder*
PORTRAIT OF MARTIN LUTHER, 1525
One of the first faces made familiar by portraits, but not belonging to a nobleman, was Luther's. Cranach painted the reformer a number of times, so we can see what he looked like at various periods of his life. Luther here is in his early forties, a determined figure who four years earlier had made his stand at the Diet at Worms.

eign ecclesiastical interference came to the reformer's aid. The Elector Frederick III of Saxony, who had never met Luther and who was never to break with the traditional Church, nonetheless determined to protect the rebel who lived in his territory. He had him taken to the Wartburg castle, one of his strongholds, and here Luther remained for almost a year, safe from his enemies.

LUTHERAN DOCTRINE AND PRACTICE

While at the Wartburg, Luther, together with his friend Philipp Melanchthon, developed his ideas and shaped them into a formal set of beliefs that influenced most of the subsequent variations of Protestant Christianity. Codified in 1530 in a document known as the Augsburg Confession, these doctrines have remained the basis of Lutheranism ever since.

Luther's Debt to Nominalism It is important to realize that some of Luther's positions had roots in nominalism, the most influential philosophical and theological movement of the fourteenth and fifteenth centuries, which had flourished at his old monastery. Two nominalist teachings in particular left a lasting impression on Luther and later reformers. First, in opposition to Thomas Aquinas and the thirteenth-century attempts to unite reason and faith, the nominalists stressed the primacy of faith, the inadequacy of reason, and the unknowableness of God. Second, as a natural corollary to God's mystery, they emphasized his overwhelming power and majesty. Both of these beliefs were to reappear frequently in the reformers' writings.

Faith and the Bible The influence of nominalism is apparent in the two fundamental assertions of Luther's teachings. First, faith alone—not good works or the receiving of the sacraments—justifies the believer in the eyes of God and wins redemption. People themselves are helpless and unworthy sinners who can do nothing to cooperate in their own salvation; God bestows faith on those he chooses to save. Second, the Bible is the sole source of religious authority. It alone carries the word of God, and Christians must reject all other supposed channels of divine inspiration: Church tradition, commentaries on the Bible, or the pronouncements of popes and Church councils.

These two doctrines had far-reaching implications. According to Luther, all people are equally capable of understanding God's word as expressed in the Bible and can gain salvation without the help of intermediaries; they do not need a priest endowed with special powers or an interceding church. Luther thus saw God's faithful as a "priesthood of all believers," a concept totally foreign to the traditional Church, which insisted on the distinction between clergy and laity. The distinction disappeared in Luther's doctrines, because all the faithful shared the responsibilities formerly reserved for priests.

Sacraments and the Mass True to his reliance on biblical authority, Luther denied the efficacy of five of the sacraments. Only baptism and the eucharist are mentioned in Scripture; therefore they alone are the means by which God distributes grace. Moreover, the ceremony of the eucharist, or Lord's Supper, was now called *communion* (literally, "sharing") to emphasize that all worshipers, including the officiating clergy, were equal. Luther also reduced the distinctiveness of priests by abolishing the sacrament of confession and by giving them the right to marry.

Luther's teachings on the sacraments transformed the Mass, the ceremony that surrounds the eucharist, which had caused him such trouble when he first became a monk. According to traditional dogma, when the priest raises the wafer, the host, during the Mass and recites the words *Hoc est corpus meum* ("This is my body"), the sacrifice of Jesus on the cross is reenacted. The wafer and the wine retain their outward appearance, their "accidents," but their substance is transformed into the body and blood of Christ—in other words, transubstantiation takes place.

Luther asserted that the wafer and wine retain their substance as well as their accidents and undergo *con*substantiation at the moment the priest says "This is my body." The real presence of Christ and the natural substance *coexist* within the wafer and wine. Nothing suddenly happens; there is no miraculous moment. Instead, the believer is simply made aware of the real presence of God, who is everywhere at all times. Again, it is the faith of the individual, not the ceremony itself, that counts.

Luther further reduced the mystery of the Lord's Supper by allowing the congregation to drink the wine, which was reserved for the priest in the traditional ceremony. This change, which undermined the position of the priest, had been demanded by Hus. But Luther went further. He simplified services radically and gave ordinary people a greater role in worship by abolishing the use of Latin, processions, incense, and votive candles.

Translation of the Bible With the priest reduced in stature, it was vital to make God's word more readily available to the faithful, so that they could read or hear the Bible for themselves. To this end, Luther began the long task of translating the Bible. He was to complete the work in 1534, creating a text that is a milestone in the history of the German language. Families were encouraged to read Scripture on their own, and the reformed faith stimulated rising literacy among women as well as men. This was Luther's last major contribution to the religious changes of the sixteenth century. Although he was to live until 1546, henceforth the progress of the revolution he had launched would rely on outside forces: its popular appeal and the actions of political leaders.

THE SPREAD OF LUTHERANISM

It is usually said that Lutheranism spread from above, advancing only when princes and rulers helped it along. Although this view has some merit, it does not adequately explain the growth of the movement. The response to Luther's stand was immediate and widespread. Even before the Diet of Worms, preachers critical of the Church were drawing audiences in many parts of the Holy Roman Empire, and in 1521 there were waves of image smashing, reports of priests marrying, and efforts to reform and simplify the sacraments.

Soon there were congregations following Luther's teachings throughout the empire and neighboring countries. Broadsides and pamphlets fresh from the printing presses disseminated the reformer's message with breathtaking speed, and they stimulated an immediate response from thousands who welcomed the opportunity to renew their faith.

Radical Preachers As long as his own doctrines remained unaltered, Luther was naturally delighted to see his teachings spread. But from the start, people drew inferences that he could not tolerate. Early in 1522, for example, three men from the nearby town of Zwickau appeared in Wittenberg claiming to be prophets who enjoyed direct communication with God. Their ideas were both radical and, in Luther's eyes, damnable. When he returned from the Wartburg, therefore, he preached eight sermons to expose their errors—a futile effort, because the movement to reform the Church was now too dispersed to control. Capitalizing on mass discontent, radical preachers incited disturbances in the name of faith, and soon social as well as religious protest exploded, posing a new challenge for Luther as he struggled to keep his protest alive and under control.

DISORDER AND REVOLT

The first trouble arose in the summer of 1522, started by the weakest independent group in the empire, the imperial knights. The knights occupied a precarious position in the social hierarchy because their holdings rarely consisted of more than a single castle. They accepted no authority but the emperor himself, and they resented the growing power of cities and princes (rulers of large territories) in the empire.

Calling themselves true representatives of the imperial system—that is, loyal supporters of the emperor's authority, in contrast to the cities and princes who wanted to be more independent—and using Lutheranism as further justification, the knights launched an attack on one of the leading ecclesiastical rulers, the archbishop of Trier. The onslaught was crushed within a year, but the Lutherans' opponents could now suggest that the new religious teachings undermined law and order.

Peasant Revolt The banner of the new faith rose

over popular revolts as well. A peasant uprising began in Swabia in 1524 and quickly engulfed the southern and central parts of the empire. Citing Luther's inspiration, and especially his teaching that faith was all the individual needed, the peasants published a list of 12 demands in 1525. Admittedly, 10 of their grievances concerned social, not religious, injustices: They wanted an end to serfdom, tithes, and the restrictions and burdens imposed by their overlords, including prohibitions on hunting and fishing, excessive rents and services, and unlawful punishments. But they also had two religious aims: They wanted the right to choose their own pastors, and they refused to accept any authority other than Scripture to determine if their demands were justified.

Luther sympathized with the last two claims, and at first he considered the peasants' demands reasonable. But when it became apparent that they were challenging all authority, he ignored the oppressions they had suffered and wrote a vicious pamphlet, *Against the Rapacious and Murdering Peasants,* calling on the nobility to cut them down without mercy so as to restore peace. A few months later the rebels were defeated in battle, and thereafter Luther threw his support unreservedly on the side of the princes and the established political and social order. He also grew more virulent in his attacks on Catholics and Jews, and became as insistent as the Roman Church he was defying that his doctrines were not to be questioned.

LUTHERANISM ESTABLISHED

The advance of Lutheranism thus far had depended largely on its appeal to the ordinary believer, and it continued to enjoy wide support. But when Luther was forced to choose between the demands of his humblest followers and the authority of the princes who had protected him, he opted for the princes. It was a decision that enabled his movement to survive and may well have saved him from the fate of Hus—burned at the stake a century before because he defied po-

▶ CARTOON FROM LUTHERAN WOODCUT BROADSIDE

Vicious cartoons were a favorite device of religious propaganda during the Age of Religious Reformation. They were especially popular for an illiterate audience, which had to get the message from pictures. The more vivid the image, the easier it was to understand. Here the Protestants show the enemies of Luther as vicious animals. One theologian is a cat eating a mouse; another is a dog holding a bone.

litical as well as religious leaders. Had Luther not condemned the disorders, he would doubtless have been abandoned by the princes, and without their backing he and his followers could not have stood up to the traditional Church or been safe from the power of Charles V.

Luther's Conservatism One of the reasons the new set of beliefs could attract these princes was its conservatism. Any person who accepted the basic doctrines of justification by faith alone and Scripture as the sole authority could be accepted as a Lutheran. Consequently, the new congregations could retain much from the old religion: most of the liturgy, the sacred music, and, particularly important, a structured church that, though less hierarchical than before, was still organized to provide order and authority.

The Lutheran Princes Some rulers were swept up by the same emotions that moved their subjects, but others were moved by more material interests. Since the Church lost all its property when reform was introduced, princes could confiscate the rich and extensive ecclesiastical holdings in their domains. Furthermore, they now had added reason for flaunting their independence from Emperor Charles V, an unwavering upholder of orthodoxy. It was risky to adopt this policy, for Charles could strip a prince of his title. On the other side, if a prince promised to remain loyal to the Church, he could blackmail the pope into offering him almost as many riches as he could win by confiscation. Nevertheless, the appeal of the new faith eventually tipped the balance for enough princes to create a formidable party capable of resisting Charles's power. While they were attending an imperial Diet at Speyer in 1529, they signed a declaration "protesting" the Diet's decree that no religious innovations were to be introduced in the empire. Thereafter all who accepted religious reform, including the Lutherans, were known as Protestants; and adherents of the traditional Church, which was led from Rome and continued to claim that it was universal (or catholic), came to be known as Roman Catholics.

The following year, at another imperial Diet, the Lutheran princes announced their support of the Augsburg Confession, the official statement of Lutheran doctrines that had been prepared by Melanchthon and Luther. Charles V now threatened to use military force to crush the heresy, and in the face of this danger, the Lutherans formed a defensive league in 1531 at the small Saxon town of Schmalkalden. Throughout the 1530s this alliance consolidated Protestant gains, brought new princes into the cause, and, in general, amassed sufficient strength to deter Charles from immediate military action.

War over Religion The reform party became so solidly established that it negotiated with the pope on equal terms about the possibility of reconciliation in 1541, but the talks collapsed, and the chances for a reunification of Christendom evaporated. Not until 1546, the year of Luther's death, however, did open war begin. Then, after a brief campaign, Charles won a crushing victory over the Lutherans in 1547. But matters had advanced too far for their movement to collapse merely because of a single defeat on the battlefield. The new faith had won the devotion of a large part of the German people, particularly in the north and the east, farthest away from the center of imperial power. Some of the great cities of the south, such as Nuremberg, which had been centers of humanism, had also come over to the Lutheran side. By the 1550s Lutheranism had captured about half the population of the Empire.

The Catholic princes also played a part in ensuring the survival of the new faith. Fearful of Charles V's new power, they refused to cooperate in his attempt to establish his authority throughout the empire, and he had to rely on Spanish troops, who further alienated him from his subjects. The Lutherans regrouped after their 1547 defeat, and in 1555 the imperial Diet at Augsburg drew up a compromise settlement that exposed the decline of the emperor's power. Henceforth each prince was allowed to determine the religion of his own territory, Lutheran or Catholic. Religious uniformity was at an end, and the future of Lutheranism was secure.

The Heritage of Lutheranism The influence that this first Protestant Church was to exert on all of European life was immense. The idea that all believers were equal in the eyes of God inspired revolutionary changes in thought and society. It justified antimonarchical constitutional theories,

▸ **Engraving of the Diet of Augsburg, 1530**
At the Diet—the meeting of the princes and cities of the Holy Roman Empire—in Augsburg in 1530, the Lutherans presented to the emperor, Charles V, a statement, or "confession," of their faith. This "Confession of Augsburg" became the founding doctrine of the Lutheran church. It was rejected as heretical by Charles, but he could not suppress it. One of the Lutheran princes told him in 1530 that he would rather have his head cut off than attend a Catholic mass. And Charles was unable to crush such defiance.

it allowed people to feel that all occupations were equally worthy and that there was nothing wrong with the life of the merchant or even the moneylender, and it undermined the hierarchic view of the universe. One can easily overstate the notion that Lutheranism made people more self-reliant, because independent and pioneering behavior was far from new. Nevertheless, there is no question that, by condemning the traditional reliance on priests and the Church and by making individuals responsible for their own salvation, Luther did encourage his followers to act on their own. Yet the new faith had its most immediate effect on religious life itself: Before the century was out, the dissent started by Luther inspired a multitude of sects and a ferment of ideas without precedent in the history of Europe.

III. The Growth of Protestantism

ZWINGLIANISM

Hardly had Luther made his protest in 1517 when religious dissent in many different forms suddenly appeared. It was as if no more was needed than one opening shot before a volley of discontent broke out—testimony to the deep and widespread desire for individual piety of the times. The most influential of these new initiatives began in the Swiss city of Zurich.

Zwingli This new reformer, Ulrich Zwingli (1484–1531), was a priest, a learned humanist, and a disciple of Erasmus. The doctrines he began to develop between 1519 and 1522 were similar to Luther's. Like the Saxon reformer, Zwingli based his ideas entirely on Scripture and emphasized faith alone. He rejected the Church's role as the channel of God's grace to believers, the idea that the clergy should be celibate, and the belief in purgatory after death. Suspicious of any reliance on Church rituals, Zwingli, even more than Luther, wanted to simplify religious belief and practice. In his view, none of the sacraments bestowed grace; they were merely signs of grace already given. Thus, baptism is symbolic, not a ceremony that regenerates the recipient; and communion is no more than a memorial and thanksgiving for the grace given by God, who is present only symbolically—not in actuality, as Luther believed.

Despite his obvious debt to Luther, Zwingli's divergences were significant. When the two reformers met in 1529, hoping to iron out differences in order to present a united front, their inability to agree on a doctrine of communion kept them apart. Zwingli had founded a new form of Protestantism, more thoroughly dependent on the individual believer and more devoid of mystery and ritual than anything Luther could accept.

Zwingli held that people need constant correction to lead godly lives. Since he recognized no distinction between secular and religious authority, he established a tribunal of clergy and secular officials to enforce discipline among the faithful. They supervised all moral issues, from compulsory church attendance to the public behavior of amorous couples. The court could excommunicate flagrant transgressors, and it maintained constant surveillance—through a network of informers—to keep the faithful moral and godly.

Because Zwingli considered it vital for discipline that the faithful receive a continuing education, he founded a theological school and authorized a new translation of the Bible. He also insisted on lengthy sermons at each service. Worship was stripped bare, as were the churches, and preaching began to assume tremendous importance as a means of instructing believers and strengthening their faith. Zwingli also revived the ancient Christian practice of public confession of sin—yet another reinforcement of discipline.

Zwingli's Church Zwingli's ideas spread rapidly in the Swiss Confederation, helped by the virtual autonomy of each canton, or region. By 1529 a number of cantons had accepted Zwinglianism. As a result, two camps formed in the country, and a war broke out in 1531 in which Zwingli himself was killed. Thereafter the Swiss Confederation remained split between Catholics and reformers. Zwinglianism never grew into a major religion, but it had a considerable effect on later forms of Protestantism, particularly Calvinism.

THE RADICALS

Both Luther and Zwingli wanted to retain church authority, and both therefore insisted that infant baptism was the moment of entry into the church, even though this belief had no scriptural sanction. Some radical reformers, however, insisted on taking the Bible literally and argued that, as in biblical times, baptism should be administered only to mature adults who could make a conscious choice to receive grace, not to infants who could not understand what was happening. Soon these reformers were being called *Anabaptists* ("rebaptizers") by their enemies. The term is often applied to all radicals, though in fact it described only one conspicuous group.

Sects Diversity was inevitable among the radical reformers, most of whom refused to recognize church organization, rejected priests, and gave individual belief free rein, sometimes to the point of recognizing only personal communication with God and disregarding Scripture. Many groups of like-minded radicals formed small sects—voluntary associations which rarely included more than 100 or so adults—in an effort to achieve complete separation from the world and avoid compromising their ideals. They wanted to set an example for others by adhering fervently to the truth as they saw it, regardless of the consequences.

Some sects established little utopian communities, holding everything in common, including property and spouses. Others disdained all worldly things and lived only for the supreme ecstasy of a trance in which they made direct contact with God himself. Many, believing in the imminent coming of the Messiah, prepared themselves for the end of the world and the Day of Judgment.

PERSECUTION

Such variety in the name of a personal search for God was intolerable to major reformers like Luther and Zwingli, who believed that their own doctrines were the only means of salvation. Once these branches of Protestantism were firmly entrenched, they, like the Catholic Church, became deeply committed to the status quo and to their own hierarchies and traditions. The established reformers thus regarded the radicals' refusal to conform as an unmistakable sign of damnation; Heinrich Bullinger, Zwingli's successor, put it bluntly when he wrote that individual interpretation of the Bible allowed each man to carve his own path to hell. Indeed, Lutherans were just as ready as Catholics to persecute those who rejected their particular brand of salvation.

Münster The assault on the radicals began in the mid-1520s and soon spread through most of Europe. The imperial Diet in 1529 called for the death penalty against all Anabaptists, and indeed, most members of a group of more than 30 Anabaptist leaders who met to discuss their ideas in 1533 eventually met a violent death. Finally, in the northwest German city of Münster, a particularly fiery sect, inspired by a "prophet" named Melchior and known as Melchiorites, provoked a reaction that signaled doom even for less radical dissenters.

The Melchiorites had managed to gain considerable influence over the ordinary workers of Münster and over the craft guilds to which many belonged. They gained political control of the city early in 1534 and began to establish their "heavenly Jerusalem" on earth. They burned all books except the Bible, abolished private property, introduced polygamy, and, in an atmosphere of abandon and chaos, dug in to await the coming of the Messiah.

Here was a threat to society sufficient to force Protestants and Catholics into an alliance, and they captured the city and brutally massacred the Melchiorites. Thereafter the radicals were savagely persecuted throughout the empire. To survive, many fled first to Poland, then to the Low Countries and England, and eventually to the New World.

JOHN CALVIN

During the 1530s, Protestantism began to fragment. Neither Lutherans nor Zwinglians expanded much beyond the areas where their reforms had begun, radicals multiplied but gained few followers, and it might have seemed that the original energy had left the movement. In the early 1540s, however, a new dynamism and also a more elaborate and systematic body of doctrine were brought to Protestantism by a second-generation reformer, John Calvin (1509–1564). Born in Noyon, a small town in northern France, Calvin studied both law and the humanities at the University of Paris. In his early twenties he apparently had a shattering spiritual experience that he later called his "sudden conversion," an event about which he would say almost nothing else. Yet from that moment on, all his energy was devoted to religious reform.

In November 1533 Calvin was indicted by French Church authorities for holding heretical views, and after more than a year in hiding, he took refuge in the Swiss city of Basel. There in 1536 he published a little treatise, *Institutes of the Christian Religion*, outlining the principles of a new system of belief. He would revise and expand the *Institutes* for the remainder of his life, and it was to become the basis of Calvinism, the most vigorous branch of Protestantism in the sixteenth century.

Geneva Later in 1536 Calvin settled in Geneva, where, except for a brief period, he was to remain until his death and where he was to create a new church in the 1540s. The citizens of this prosperous market center had just overthrown their prince, a Catholic bishop. In achieving their independence, they had allied with other Swiss cities, notably Bern, a recent convert to Zwinglianism. Rebels who, with the help of Protestants, had just freed themselves from an ecclesiastical over-

lord were understandably receptive to new religious teachings, and they welcomed the beliefs that Calvin proclaimed.

▸ **An Engraving of the Army from Bern Invading a Neighboring Province in 1536, from Johannes Stumpf's Chronicle, 1548**
These are the soldiers who helped Geneva win its independence from the bishop who was the city's ruler. The Bernese also encouraged the acceptance of Protestantism, which John Calvin was soon to help establish in Geneva.

CALVINISM

Outwardly, Calvinism seemed to have much in common with Lutheranism. Both emphasized people's sinfulness, lack of free will, and helplessness; both rejected good works as a means of salvation; both accepted only two sacraments, baptism and communion; both regarded all occupations as equally worthy in the sight of God; both strongly upheld established political and social authority; and both leaned heavily on St. Paul and St. Augustine in their views of faith, people's weaknesses, and God's omnipotence. But the emphases in Calvinism were very different.

Predestination In arguing for justification by faith alone, Luther assumed that God can predestine a person to be saved but rejected the idea that damnation can also be preordained. Calvin's faith was much sterner. He recognized no such distinction: If people are damned, they should praise God's justice, because their sins certainly merit such a judgment; if people are saved, they should praise God's mercy, because their salvation is not a result of their own good deeds. Either way, the outcome is predestined, and nothing can be done to affect an individual's fate. It is up to God to save a person; he then perseveres in his mercy despite the person's sins; and finally, he alone decides whether to receive the sinner into the small band of saints, or elect, whom he brings into heaven. Calvin's was a grim but powerful answer to the age-old Christian question: How can sinful human beings gain salvation?

Calvin believed that our behavior here on

earth, whether good or bad, is no indication of our fate. He did suggest that someone who is to be saved by God is likely to be upright and moral, but such conduct is not necessarily a sign of salvation. However, because we should try to please God at all times, and because our communities ought to be fitting places for the elect to live, we must make every effort to lead lives worthy of one of the elect.

Morality and Discipline Calvin therefore developed a strict moral code for the true believer that banned frivolous activities, like dancing, in favor of constant self-examination, austerity, and sober study of the Bible. To help the faithful observe such regulation, he reestablished public confessions, as Zwingli had, and required daily preaching. He made services starkly simple: Stripped of ornaments, worship concentrated on uplifting sermons and the celebration of communion. His doctrine of communion occupied a middle ground between Luther's and Zwingli's. He rejected Zwingli's interpretation, saying instead that Christ's body and blood were actually and not just symbolically present. But unlike Luther, he held that they were present only in spirit and were consumed only spiritually, by faith.

To supervise the morals of the faithful and ensure that the community was worthy of the elect, Calvin gave his church a strict hierarchical structure. It was controlled by church officials called deacons and by lay elders, who were able to function even in the hostile territories where many Calvinists found themselves. A body of lay elders called the *consistory* served as the chief ecclesiastical authority. They enforced discipline and had the power of excommunication, though they always worked with local officials, who imposed the actual punishments for failures in religious duties.

Church Organization Calvin's system produced a cohesiveness and organization achieved by no other Protestant church. The *Institutes* spelled out every point of faith and practice in detail—an enormous advantage for Calvin's followers at a time when new religious doctrines were still fluid. The believer's duties and obligations were absolutely clear, as was his or her position in the very carefully organized hierarchy of the church. In France, for example, there was a small community (or cell) in each town, a governing synod (or council) in each local area, a provincial synod in each province, and a national synod at the top of the pyramid. Tight discipline controlled the entire system, with the result that Calvinists felt themselves to be setting a moral and religious example that all the world would eventually have to follow. They were part of a very privileged community from whom the elect would be drawn. Thus they could be oppressive when they had power, yet holy rebels when they were a minority. After all, since they were freed of responsibility for their own salvation, they were acting selflessly at all times. Like the children of Israel, they had a mission to live for God, and this sense of destiny was to be one of Calvinism's greatest strengths.

Preachers from Geneva traveled through Europe to win adherents and organize the faithful wherever they could. In 1559 the city opened a university for the purpose of training preachers, because Calvin regarded education as an essential means of instilling faith. From Geneva flowed a stream of pamphlets and books, which strengthened the faith of all believers and made sure that none who wished to learn would lack the opportunity. A special target was Calvin's homeland, France, where his preachers had their first successes, especially in the cities. Calvinism also won important support in the nobility, notably among women aristocrats who often influenced their families to adopt the new beliefs.

By 1564, when Calvin died, his church was well established: more than a million adherents in France, where they were called Huguenots; the Palatinate converted; Scotland won; and considerable groups of followers in England, the Low Countries, and Hungary. Despite its severity, Calvin's coherent and comprehensive body of doctrine proved to have wide appeal in an age of piety that yearned for clear religious answers. To whom, however, did it appeal?

The Appeal of Calvinism When those who adopted the new faith explained their conversion, they usually did so in terms of a slow or sudden revelation—God had finally shown them the truth. But historians have noted that there were certain groups who seemed especially open to Protestant, and particularly Calvinist, teachings. All the reformed faiths did particularly well in cities, and it has been suggested that the long history of independence among townspeople made them more inclined to challenge traditional authorities. In addition, they tended to be more literate, and thus were drawn to beliefs that emphasized reading the Bible for oneself. And Calvinism put an emphasis on sobriety, discipline, and communal responsibility that would have appealed strongly to the increasingly self-confident merchants and artisans of the cities. That the Calvinists were also successful in the areas of southern France farthest away from central authority in Paris only reinforces the connection with an inclination toward independence and self-reliance.

Geneva itself became a determinedly independent place—the only city in Europe that successfully resisted becoming part of a territorial state and remained an autonomous political force during the two centuries following Calvin's death. Because of the dominance of Calvinism, morals were strictly supervised, and there was an aura of public discipline that all visitors noted. At the same time, artisans and merchants made Geneva an important economic center, and the university achieved an international reputation. Gradually in the seventeenth century the atmosphere of austerity softened, but the city continued to be seen as a model community for all Calvinists.

Women and Reform Cities were not the only centers of religious reform. In some parts of Europe, such as Scotland, new beliefs flourished outside towns because they won political support. But in all areas, the importance of women to the spread of Protestantism was unmistakable. Calvin's earliest significant converts were aristocratic women, whose patronage helped his faith take root at the highest levels of society. Like the literate women of the cities, they saw in its message an opportunity to express themselves and to work for others in ways that had not been possible before. They were often the main readers of the Bible in family gatherings; they took the lead in demanding broader access to education, especially for girls; and they were regularly prominent in radical movements.

One theologian who despaired at the results of Luther's translation of the New Testament reserved his most bitter complaints for the women who were studying the Bible for themselves. And the results were apparent not only among the literate. The records of the Inquisition, the Catholic tribunal charged with rooting out heresy, are full of the trials and executions of women who were martyrs for their beliefs and who died defending doctrines they had learned from preachers or other women. Again and again, they rejected the authority of priests and asserted their right to individual faith. It was determination like this that enabled the Reformation to establish itself and to spread until it posed a major challenge to the traditional Church (*see box,* p. 410).

IV. The Catholic Revival

REFORM AND COUNTER REFORM

Those with Protestant sympathies usually refer to the Catholic revival that started in the 1530s as the Counter Reformation, implying that the Roman Church acted only as a result of criticisms by Luther and others. Catholic historians call it the Catholic Reformation, implying that the movement began within the Church and was not merely a reaction to Protestantism. There is justification for both views. Certainly the papacy was aware of its loss of control over millions of Christians, but a great deal of the effort to put the Catholic Church's house in order was a result of deep faith and a determination to purify the institution for its own sake.

Although a major effort was certainly needed, and serious problems had to be addressed, one must not forget that there was a vast reserve of loyalty and affection that the Church could draw on. Many more Europeans remained Catholic in the long run than converted to Protestantism. They took comfort from tradition and from priests who, rather than demanding that believers achieve salvation on their own, offered the Church's mediation, beautiful ceremonies, and rituals to help people overcome their sins. Catholicism had a long history of charity for the

The Trial of Elizabeth Dirks

In radical groups, women often occupied central roles they never achieved in the larger churches. Since the most important attributes of a believer in these groups were faith, commitment, and the presence of the holy spirit, there was frequently an egalitarianism not found elsewhere in sixteenth-century society. Thus it was that the radical "teacher" (or leader) whom the Inquisition in the Netherlands interrogated in January 1549 was a woman named Elizabeth Dirks. Her replies give us a vivid sense of the beliefs the Reformation was stimulating among ordinary people—though in this case they were put forward with a clarity and a conviction that would lead to Elizabeth's execution two months later.

Examiner: We understand you are a teacher and have led many astray. Who are your friends?

Elizabeth: Do not press me on this point. Ask me about my faith and I will answer you gladly.

Examiner: Do you not consider our Church to be the house of the Lord?

Elizabeth: I do not. For it is written that God said "I will dwell with you."

Examiner: What do you think of our mass?

Elizabeth: I have no faith in your mass, but only in the word of God.

Examiner: What do you believe about the Holy Sacrament of the Eucharist?

Elizabeth: I never in my life read in Scripture about a Holy Sacrament, but only of the Supper of the Lord.

Examiner: You speak with a haughty tongue.

Elizabeth: No. I speak with a free tongue.

Examiner: Do you not believe that you are saved by baptism?

Elizabeth: No: all the water in the sea cannot save me. My salvation is in Christ, who commanded me to love my God and my neighbor as myself.

Examiner: Do priests have the power to forgive sins?

Elizabeth: How should I believe that? Christ is the only priest through whom sins are forgiven.

As torture was applied:

Examiner: You can recant everything you have said.

Elizabeth: No, I will not, but I will seal it with my blood.

Adapted from Thieleman von Bracht, *The Bloody Theater or Martyr's Mirror*, Daniel Rupp (trans.) (Lancaster, Pa.: David Miller, 1837), pp. 409–410.

poor, and this was strengthened during the sixteenth century. For ordinary Christians, the familiarity, support, and grandeur they found in the Church were often more than enough reason to resist the appeals of reformers.

CRISIS AND CHANGE IN THE CHURCH

Yet there was no doubt that the first half of the sixteenth century was the lowest point in the history of the Catholic Church and that few would have expected the recovery that followed. By 1550 many areas of Europe had been lost to the Protestants, and even in regions that were still loyal, the papacy was able to exercise little control. The French Church, for example, had a well-established tradition of autonomy, exemplified by the right France's kings had had since 1516 to make ecclesiastical appointments. In Spain, too, the monarchy retained its independence and even had its own Inquisition. In the Holy Roman Empire, those states that had rejected Protestantism gave the pope no more than token allegiance.

Moreover, there was still no comprehensive

definition of Catholic doctrine on justification, salvation, and the sacraments. Worse yet, the Church's leadership was far from effective. Although one pope, Leo X, had attempted to correct notorious abuses such as simony, the sale of church offices, in the early sixteenth century, Rome simply did not have the spiritual authority to make reform a vital force in the Catholic Church.

Paul III The situation changed with the pope elected in 1534: Paul III, a man not renowned for saintliness but a genius at making the right decisions for the Church. By the end of his reign, in 1549, the Catholic revival was under way. The heart of Paul's strategy was his determination to assert papal responsibility throughout the Church. Realizing that uncertainties in Catholic doctrine could be resolved only by a reexamination of traditional theology, he decided within a few months of taking office to call a Church council for that purpose, despite the danger of rekindling the conciliar movement. It took 10 years to overcome resistance to the idea, but in the meantime Paul attacked abuses throughout the

▸ *Titian*
Pope Paul III and His Nephews, Alessandro and Ottavio Farnese, 1546
The psychological tension Titian created in this family portrait is extraordinary. The shrewd 77-year-old pope who had launched the Church's vigorous response to Protestantism looks benignly on Ottavio, whose seemingly calculated gesture of deference hints at the aggressiveness that was soon to cause a major family quarrel over land and money. And Cardinal Alessandro, standing apart, was already a famous patron of art with little concern for Church affairs. Perhaps because of its revelation of character, the painting was never finished.

Church, disregarding both vested interests and tradition. He aimed his campaign at all levels of the hierarchy, undeterred by powerful bishops and cardinals long used to a lax and corrupt regime. In addition, he founded a Roman Inquisition, a decision that reflected the era's growing reliance on persecution as a means of destroying dissent.

Paul realized that, in the long run, the revival of Catholicism would depend on whether his successors maintained his efforts. During his 15-year reign, therefore, he made a series of superb appointments to the College of Cardinals (the body that elects the popes); the result was the creation of possibly the most illustrious College in history. Many of its members were famous for their piety, others for their learning. They came from all over Europe, united by their devotion to the Church and their resolve to see it once again command admiration and reverence. The result of Paul's farsighted policy was to be a succession of popes through the early seventeenth century who would fully restore the atmosphere of spirituality and morality that had long been missing from the papacy.

THE COUNCIL OF TRENT

The ecumenical, or general, council of Church leaders called by Paul finally assembled at Trent, a northern Italian city, in 1545, and met irregularly until the delegates managed to complete their work in 1563. The council's history was one of stormy battles between various national factions. The non-Italians pressed for decentralization of religious authority; the Italians, closely tied to the papacy, advocated a consolidation of power. For both sides, the divisions were political as well as ecclesiastical, because at issue was the independence not only of bishops but also of local princes and kings. A large majority of the delegates were Italians, however, and their conclusions almost always reinforced the dominance of the pope. The threat of a revival of conciliarism never materialized.

Doctrine In keeping with Paul's instructions, the Council of Trent gave more of its time to the basic issue of Church doctrine than to the problem of reform. Nearly all its decisions were intended to establish clear definitions of practice and belief, and to bring to an end long-standing theological uncertainties or differences of opinion. The main sources for these decisions were the interpretations put forward by Thomas Aquinas, who now became the central theologian of the Catholic Church. At the same time, Trent's decrees were designed to affirm precisely those teachings that the Protestants had rejected. Catholicism from then on would be committed primarily to the outward, sacramental heritage of Christianity. In this view, the Bible is not the exclusive authority for the believer: Church tradition holds an equal place in establishing religious truth. Human will is free, good works as well as faith are a means of salvation, all seven sacraments are channels of grace, and Christ's sacrifice is reenacted in every Mass. The Council of Trent endorsed the special position of the priest and insisted that God be worshiped with appropriately elaborate ceremonies and rites.

These were the principal decisions at Trent, but hundreds of minor matters were also settled: For the first time, the priest's presence was declared to be essential at the sacrament of marriage, a further reinforcement of his importance; the Vulgate, the Latin translation of the Bible prepared chiefly by St. Jerome, was decreed to be a holy text, a decision which rebutted humanists and other scholars who had found mistranslations of Greek and Hebrew in Jerome's work; and in direct contrast to the Protestants, gorgeous ritual was heavily stressed, which encouraged artists to beautify church buildings and ceremonies.

Restoring the Church The achievement of the council was to adjust the Church to the world. Many ordinary people, troubled by the stern self-denial and predestination taught by most Protestant churches and sects, preferred the traditional comfort and support Catholicism had long offered. They were ready to champion their old faith as soon as its leadership restored its sense of purpose by removing abuses and defining doctrines. And the new discipline of the Church was apparent in the council's effort to deal with morality as thoroughly as with belief. When it gave its approval to the Inquisition and to the "Index of Forbidden Books," which informed all Catholics of the heretical works they were not allowed to read, the council signaled the determination of the Church to recover the ground it had lost.

▸ *Titian*
THE COUNCIL OF TRENT, CA. 1564
The splendor of the gathering of representatives of the Catholic Church from all of Europe is conveyed by this scene, attributed to Titian. The ranks of bishops in their miters, listening to one of their number address the assembly from the pulpit on the right, visibly embodied a Church putting itself in order as it faced the challenge of Protestantism.

THE AFTERMATH OF TRENT

The new atmosphere of dedication swept through the Catholic Church, inspiring thinkers and artists throughout Europe to lend their talents to the cause. In many ways, Baroque art was to be the genre of the Counter Reformation: Painters, architects, and musicians caught up by the new moral fervor in Catholicism expressed their faith in brilliant and dramatic portrayals of religious subjects and in churches that were designed to dazzle the observer in a way that most Protestants could not allow.

This artistic outpouring was, of course, far more than a reflection of the decisions of a few hundred prelates assembled in a council. It was also one of many indicators of the new vigor of Catholicism. In France the new generation of Church leaders who appeared in the late sixteenth century was distinguished for its austerity, learning, and observance of duties. The inheritors of the traditional Scholastic philosophy multiplied, and in the late sixteenth and early seventeenth centuries they were to become influential throughout Europe.

Women in the Church Moreover, the crucial contribution to Protestantism of its women adherents was echoed in the revival of Catholicism. There was a remarkable flowering of new religious orders for women in the sixteenth and seventeenth centuries, many of which became identified with charitable works. Since one of the most important ways the Church set about winning back the faithful was by expanding its philanthropic activities—through new hospitals and expanded assistance to the poor, to orphans, and to other unfortunates—its female orders played an essential role in the Counter Reformation. And nowhere was their devout spirituality more apparent than in Spain, the most fiercely Catholic of all European countries.

The Spaniards expressed their religious passion in many ways—by insisting on converting the native peoples they conquered overseas, by giving great power to the Inquisition that guarded orthodoxy from large Muslim and Jewish communities at home, by encouraging lay as well as clerical piety, and by founding the most famous new order of the age, the Jesuits (see below). But no indication of their devotion was as distinctive as the great flowering of mysticism, which was most famously represented by St. Teresa (1515–1582).

St. Teresa The mystic seeks to worship God directly and immediately, in an encounter that usually takes place in a trance and without the intervention of a priest. Because this is an entirely personal religious experience, which does not require the mediation of the Church, it has always been looked on with suspicion by the authorities. St. Teresa was no exception. As a rich and spoiled young girl, she had led a rather loose life, and her concerned father had sent her to a convent to instill some discipline. Perhaps because the family had only recently converted from Judaism, considerable attention was also given to Teresa's religious education. She later recalled a time when, after reading the lives of saints, she decided to become a martyr for Christ. She set out with her brother for North Africa, where she was determined to die fighting Muslims but was caught by an uncle. Of more lasting effect were the visions of God she began to have, which gradually convinced her that she had a special religious mission (*see box,* p. 415).

Church authorities became worried when, after becoming a nun, Teresa began to attract a following as a spiritual adviser to a number of women in her native city of Avila. Some churchmen suggested that her visions were the work of the devil, not God. After many examinations, however—and finally an interview with the king of Spain himself, who was deeply impressed by her holiness—the doubts evaporated. Teresa founded a strict new order of nuns and traveled all over Spain establishing convents. She soon became a legendary figure and was made a saint only 40 years after her death. To Spaniards she has remained a heroine, the subject of many affectionate stories. Once, when her carriage got stuck in the mud, she apparently looked heavenward and said: "If this is the way you treat your friends, God, no wonder you have so few of them." Above all, she came to embody the deep religious devotion of Counter Reformation Spain.

The Papacy The most conspicuous embodiments of the new energy of the Church, however, were the popes themselves. Paul III's successors used their personal authority and pontifical resources not to adorn their palaces but to continue the enormous cleansing operation within the Church and to lead the counterattack against Protestantism. If a king or prince refused to help, the popes would try to persuade one of his leading subjects (for example, the Guise family in France and the dukes of Bavaria in the empire) to organize the struggle. Their diplomats and agents were everywhere, ceaselessly urging Catholics to stamp out Protestantism wherever it was found. And the pontiffs insisted on strict morality so as to restore their reputation for piety and to set a proper example to the faithful: One pope even ordered clothes painted on the nudes in Michelangelo's *Last Judgment* in the Sistine Chapel.

With the leaders of the Church thus bent on reform, the restoration of the faith and the reconquest of lost souls could proceed with maximum effect. And the popes had at their disposal a religious order established by Ignatius Loyola in 1540 specifically for these purposes: the Society of Jesus.

IGNATIUS LOYOLA

The third of the great religious innovators of the sixteenth century, after Luther and Calvin, was Ignatius Loyola (1491–1556); unlike his predecessors, however, he sought to reform the Catholic Church from within.

Loyola was the son of a Basque nobleman, raised in the chivalric and intensely religious atmosphere of Spain, and he was often at the court of Ferdinand of Aragon. In his teens he entered the army, but when he was 30, a leg wound ended his military career. While convalescing, he was deeply impressed by a number of popular

St. Teresa's Visions

These two are among the most famous passages from the autobiography St. Teresa began writing in 1562, when she was 47 years old. The book is essentially the story of a spiritual journey, as a restless young woman gains purpose and strength through mystical visions and unwavering faith. Her account of a mystical transport in the second passage quoted here was the inspiration for a famous sculpture by Gian Lorenzo Bernini, The Ecstasy of St. Teresa, *in the seventeenth century.*

I: One day, when I was at prayer, the Lord was pleased to reveal to me nothing but His hands, whose beauty was so great as to be indescribable. This made me very fearful. A few days later I also saw the Divine face. On St. Paul's Day, I saw a complete representation of his sacred Humanity. If there were nothing else in Heaven to delight the eyes but the extreme beauty of the glorified bodies there, that alone would be the greatest bliss. If I were to spend years and years imagining how to invent anything so beautiful, I could not do it. In its whiteness and radiance, it exceeds all we can imagine. It is a soft whiteness which, without wearying the eyes, causes them the greatest delight. By comparison with it, the brightness of our sun seems quite dim.

II: It pleased the Lord that I sometimes saw beside me an angel in bodily form. He was not tall, but short, and very beautiful, his face aflame. In his hands I saw a long golden spear, and at the end of the iron tip I seemed to see a point of fire. With this he seemed to pierce my heart several times. When he drew it out, he left me completely afire with a great love for God. During the days when this continued, I went about as if in a stupor.

From E. Allison Peers, *The Life of Teresa of Jesus* (London: Sheed & Ward, 1944; reprinted New York: Doubleday, 1960), pp. 258–260 and 273–274.

lives of the saints he read, and soon his religious interests began to take shape in chivalric and military terms. He visualized Mary as his lady, the inspiration of a Christian quest in which the forces of God and the devil fight in mighty battle. This was a faith seen from the perspective of the knight, and though the direct parallel lessened as Loyola's thought developed, it left an unmistakable stamp on his future work.

In 1522 Loyola gave up his knightly garb and swore to go on a pilgrimage to Jerusalem. He retired to a monastery for 10 months to absolve himself of the guilt of a sinful life and to prepare spiritually for the journey to the Holy Land. At the monastery he had a momentous experience that, like Luther's and Calvin's, dominated the rest of his life. According to tradition, he had a vision lasting eight days, during which he saw in detail the outline of a book, the *Spiritual Exercises,* and a new religious order, the Society of Jesus.

***The* Spiritual Exercises** The first version of the *Spiritual Exercises* certainly dated from this period, but like Calvin's *Institutes,* it was to be thoroughly revised many times. The book deals not with doctrines or theology but with the discipline and training necessary for a God-fearing life. Believers must undertake four weeks of contemplation and self-examination that culminate in a feeling of union with God, in which they surrender their minds and wills to Christ. If successful, they are then ready to submit completely to the call of God and to pursue the Church's commands without question.

The manual was the heart of the organization of the Society of Jesus, and it gave those who followed its precepts (known as Jesuits) a dedication and determination that made them seem the Church's answer to the Calvinists. But while the end might be similar to Luther's and Calvin's—the personal attainment of grace—the method,

Map 13.2 RELIGIOUS DIVISIONS IN EUROPE AT THE END OF THE SIXTEENTH CENTURY
By the late sixteenth century, the division of Europe into distinct areas, each committed primarily to one church, was virtually complete. Now that they were solidly established, the major faiths became associated with universities that elaborated and promoted their beliefs.

with its emphasis on individual effort and concentration, could not have been more different. For the *Spiritual Exercises* emphasize that believers can *act* for themselves; they do not have to depend on faith alone to gain salvation, as Protestants assert. One can prepare for grace through a tremendous act of will and not depend solely on a gift from God. Loyola makes immense demands precisely because he insists that the will is free and that good works are efficacious.

Loyola's Followers During the 16 years after he left the monastery, Ignatius led a life of poverty and study. Though lame, he traveled to Jerusalem and back barefoot in 1523–1524, and two years later he found his way to the University of Alcalá, where he attracted his first disciples, three fellow students. Suspected by the Inquisition of being rather too independent in their beliefs, the little band walked to Paris, where they were joined by six more disciples. Ignatius now decided to return to the Holy Land, but the companions found themselves unable to travel beyond Venice because of war. Instead, they preached in the streets, visited the poor and the sick, urged all who would listen to rededicate themselves to piety and faith, and in 1537 achieved ordination as priests. Their activities were beginning to take definite shape, and so they decided to seek the pope's blessing for their work. They saw Paul III in 1538, and two years later, despite opposition from those who saw it as a threat to the authority of local bishops, the pope approved a plan Ignatius submitted for a new religious order that would owe allegiance only to the papacy.

THE JESUITS

The Society, or Company, of Jesus had four principal functions: preaching, hearing confessions, teaching, and founding and maintaining missions. The first two were the Jesuits' means of strengthening the beliefs of individual Catholics or converting Protestants. The third became one of their most effective weapons. Loyola, much influenced by the Christian humanists he had encountered, was convinced of the tremendous power of education. The Jesuits therefore set about organizing the best schools in Europe and were so successful that some Protestants sent their children to the Society's schools despite the certainty that the pupils would become committed Catholics. The instructors followed humanist principles and taught the latest ideas, including the most recent advances in science. The Jesuits' final activity, missionary work, brought them their most spectacular successes among both non-Christians and Protestants.

► *Peter Paul Rubens*
THE MIRACLE OF ST. IGNATIUS, 1619
Loyola quickly became one of the major heroes of the Catholic revival. Within less than 60 years of his death (1556), he was to become a saint of the Church. He became one of the heroes of Baroque art, as is apparent in this painting by Peter Paul Rubens, which creates a powerful image that represents Loyola at the moment when he cures a man and a woman who have been possessed by the devil.

A number of qualities combined to make the Jesuits extraordinarily effective in winning converts and turning Catholics into militant activists. First, the order demanded very high intellectual abilities. It selected recruits carefully (turning many applicants away) and gave them a superb education. Jesuits were famous for their knowledge of Scripture and traditional teachings and their ability to out-argue opponents. In addition, they were trained to be highly effective preachers and excellent educators. And their discipline, determination, and awareness of the contemporary world soon won them a fearsome reputation. They had no equal in the forcefulness with which they advanced the aims of the Council of Trent and the papacy.

There is every reason to regard the Jesuits as the striking arm of the Counter Reformation; indeed, their organization was to some extent modeled on the medieval military orders. A Jesuit at a royal court was often the chief inspiration for a ruler's militant support of the faith, and in many areas the Society was the main conqueror of rival beliefs—for example, in Poland, where Jesuits in the late sixteenth century led a campaign that eradicated widespread Protestantism and created a devotedly Catholic country. Yet it must be noted that in an age that took persecution for granted, the Jesuits always opposed execution for heresy; they far preferred to win a convert than to kill a heretic. Their presence was soon felt all over the world: As early as the 1540s, one of Loyola's first disciples, Francis Xavier, was conducting a mission to Japan. Despite the many enmities they aroused by their single-mindedness and their self-assurance, their unswerving devotion was a major reason for the revival of the Roman Church.

CHRONOLOGY OF THE REFORMATION AND COUNTER REFORMATION

1517	Luther's protest begins: the 95 Theses on indulgences.
1521	Diet of Worms: Luther condemned by Emperor Charles V.
1524–1525	Peasants' Revolt in Germany. Zürich adopts Zwingli's Reformation.
1531	Protestant League of Schmalkalden formed in Germany. Death of Zwingli. King Henry VIII proclaims himself head of the Church of England.
1534	Paul III becomes pope. Anabaptists take over the city of Münster in Germany.
1535	Thomas More executed for not accepting Henry VIII as head of the Church of England.
1536	Calvin comes to Geneva; first edition of his *Institutes*. Death of Erasmus.
1540	Pope Paul III approves the Jesuit Order.
1541	Calvin settles in Geneva permanently.
1545	Council of Trent begins.
1546	Death of Luther.
1556	Death of Loyola.
1559	First "Index of Forbidden Books" published. Execution of Protestants after Inquisition trials in Spain.
1564	Publication of the Decrees of the Council of Trent. Death of Calvin.

RELIGION AND POLITICS

As a revived Catholic Church confronted the Protestants, religious warfare of unprecedented ferocity erupted throughout Europe (see Chapter 15). More people seemed to feel more passionately about faith than at any other time in Western history. But the conflict would not have continued as long as it did without the armies and resources provided by princes and monarchs. Both sides drew crucial support from rulers who were determined either to suppress any sign of heresy (that is, any faith other than their own) in their territories or to overthrow heretical regimes in neighboring lands. The struggle over religion was, for these rulers, a means of establishing their authority in their own realms and a justification for aggression abroad.

The strong connection between politics and belief, and its dire consequences, was the result of a transformation that was almost as far-reaching as the Reformation itself. Just as Western Christianity was changed forever in the sixteenth century, so too were the power and the ambition of the territorial state. At the same time as a handful of reformers, building on powerful social and intellectual forces, reshaped religious structures and practices, a handful of political leaders—building on no less powerful military, social, and economic forces—created armies, systems of taxation, and bureaucratic organizations that reshaped the structures and practices of central governments throughout Europe.

Recommended Reading

Sources

*Calvin, John. *On God and Political Duty.* J. T. McNeill (ed.). 1950.

*Erasmus, Desiderius. *Essential Works of Erasmus.* W. T. H. Jackson (ed.). 1965.

Loyola, Ignatius. *The Spiritual Exercises of St. Ignatius.* R. W. Gleason (ed.). 1964.

*Luther, Martin. *Martin Luther: Selections from His Writings.* John Dillenberger (ed.). 1961.

Studies

*Bainton, Roland H. *Here I Stand: A Life of Martin Luther.* 1955. A classic biography in English, with many quotations from Luther's writings.

Bangert, William. *A History of the Society of Jesus.* 1972. The best basic history in English of the work of Loyola and the Jesuits.

*Bossy, John. *Christianity in the West. 1400–1700.* 1985. An overview of the religious history of Europe by one of the leading historians of Catholic thought and practice.

*Bouwsma, William J. *John Calvin: A Sixteenth-Century Portrait.* 1988. The standard biography.

*Davis, Natalie Zemon. *Society and Culture in Early Modern France.* 1975. A collection of essays about popular beliefs and attitudes, particularly on religious matters, during the sixteenth century.

Delumeau, Jean. *Catholicism between Luther and Voltaire: A New View of the Counter-Reformation.* 1977. The standard introduction.

Hillerbrand, Hans J. (ed.). *Radical Tendencies in the Reformation: Divergent Perspectives.* 1986. Important essays on the emergence of radical ideas and sects in the Reformation.

*Huizinga, Johan. *Erasmus and the Age of Reformation.* 1957. A warm and sympathetic biography, beautifully written.

*Kenny, Anthony. *Thomas More.* 1983. An excellent brief introduction to the life and work of the humanist-statesman.

Kittelson, James M. *Luther the Reformer: The Story of the Man and His Career.* 1986. The best introduction to Luther's life and thought.

Moeller, Bernd. *Imperial Cities and the Reformation.* H. C. E. Midelfort and M. U. Edwards (trs.). 1972. Three stimulating essays about the special role of cities in establishing the Reformation in Germany.

Po-chia Hsia, R. (ed.). *The People and the German Reformation: Approaches in the Social History of Religion.* 1988. A set of essays that reflects recent trends in the social interpretation of the Reformation.

Scribner, Robert. *For the Sake of Simple Folk: Popular Propaganda for the German Reformation.* 1981. A path-breaking analysis of how the Reformation was spread.

Scribner, Robert, and Gerhard Benecke (eds.). *The German Peasant War of 1525: New Viewpoints.* 1979. A stimulating set of essays about the social upheaval that accompanied the Reformation.

*Weber, Max. *The Protestant Ethic and the Spirit of Capitalism.* Talcott Parsons (tr.). 1958. Originally published in 1904 and 1905, this study of the way in which the Reformation helped create the modern world has influenced much of the historical thinking about the Reformation.

Williams, George H. *The Radical Reformation.* 1962. The most comprehensive account of the sects and their founders.

*Available in paperback.

National Gallery, London

Hans Holbein the Younger
THE AMBASSADORS, 1533
Hans Holbein the Younger's *The Ambassadors* shows the worldliness that was expected of diplomats (many of whom were also soldiers) in the sixteenth century. The two men are surrounded by symbols of the skills, knowledge, and refinement their job required—geography, mathematics, literature, and music. But despite this emphasis on material concerns, Holbein reminds us (in the optically distorted skull across the bottom of the painting) that death and spiritual needs cannot be forgotten.

CHAPTER FOURTEEN

ECONOMIC EXPANSION AND A NEW POLITICS

EUROPE in 1400 was a poor, technologically backward, and politically disorganized area compared to the realms of the Indian moguls or Chinese emperors. And yet within little more than a century, Europeans were expanding aggressively into Asia and the Americas. Their numbers were growing, their economy was booming, their technological advances were making possible the creation of new markets and new empires, and their political leaders were developing structures of government and authority more elaborate than any that had been seen since the fall of the Roman Empire. The emergence of this new world power was one of the most astonishing transformations in Western history, and historians have long debated its causes. Their suggestions have ranged from the personal (the initiatives of specific kings, entrepreneurs, or explorers) to the abstract (such forces as demographic change or a gradual warming of the climate). Like the fall of the Roman Empire, however, this was so profound a reshaping of Europe that one cannot suggest a single comprehensive explanation. Indeed, it is only by looking at the individual changes in some detail that one can understand how far-reaching was the reordering that had taken place by the late sixteenth century.

I. Expansion at Home

POPULATION INCREASE

It was during the last third of the fifteenth century that signs of change appeared in the demographic, economic, and political history of Europe. Some have argued that the root cause lay in politics: Because assertive regimes restored order and authority in a number of states, confidence rose, trade quickened, and populations grew. Others regard either economic or demographic advance as the source of change. In fact, it is clear that all three were connected and that all three reinforced one another. Thus, although we are not certain why the number of Europeans began to increase after more than 100 years of decline, we can see the effects of the increase in many areas of life.

Exact measurements are not possible, but it seems likely that the loss of population that began with the Black Death in the 1340s had run its course by the 1460s. Plagues, though recurrent, began to take less of a toll (perhaps because immunities developed); bad harvests became less frequent (perhaps because of a warming climate); and families were thus able to produce more surviving children. As a result, Europe's population rose by some 50 percent between 1470 and 1620. And cities expanded even faster: London had fewer than 50,000 inhabitants in the early sixteenth century but over 200,000 a hundred years later. There was also extensive reoccupation of marginal farmland, which had been abandoned in the fourteenth and fifteenth centuries because a shrinking population had provided no market for its produce. Now there were more mouths to feed, and the extra acres again became profitable.

Consequences of the Increase The rise in population was followed by a staggering jump in food prices. By the early 1600s wheat cost approximately five times more than in the late 1400s, an increase that far outpaced the movement of prices in general. It is not surprising, therefore, that this period witnessed the first wave of enclosures in England: Major landowners put up fences around common tilling or grazing ground, traditionally open to all the animals of the locality, and reserved it for their own crops or their sheep, whose wool was also in increasing demand. By 1600 about one-eighth of England's arable land had been enclosed. The only answer, when changes like these made a village incapable of supporting its growing population, was for people to move to towns and cities.

ECONOMIC GROWTH

As markets began to grow in response to population pressures, the volume of trade also shot upward; commercial profits thus kept pace with those of agriculture. Customs receipts rose steadily, as did the yield of tolls from ships entering the Baltic Sea, one of the main routes of European trade. In many areas, too, shipbuilding boomed. This was the heyday of the English cloth trade and the great Spanish sheep farms, of the central German linen industry and the northern Italian silk industry. Printing became a widespread occupation, and gun making and glassmaking also expanded rapidly. Glassmaking had a major effect on European society because the increasing use of windows allowed builders to divide houses into small rooms, thus giving many people a little privacy for the first time.

Leading financiers who invested in the growing volume of trade accumulated large fortunes. For centuries the Italians had been in the vanguard of economic advance, but in the sixteenth century firms of other nations were achieving international prominence. The most successful of the new enterprises was run by a family descended from a fourteenth-century weaver, Johannes Fugger of Augsburg. The sixteenth-century Fuggers financed the Spanish King Charles I's quest for the throne of the Holy Roman Empire and his later wars after he became the Emperor Charles V. Great bankers were thus often closely allied with monarchs, and like all merchants, they gained from the mounting power of central governments. Rulers encouraged commerce in the hope of larger revenues from customs duties and taxes, and they gave leading entrepreneurs valuable privileges. Such alliances were eventually the undoing of some firms, which were ruined when kings went bankrupt, but until the late sixteenth century, Italian and German bankers controlled Europe's finances.

Almost every level of commercial activity offered opportunities for advancement. The guild system expanded in the sixteenth century to incorporate many new trades, and the structure of merchant enterprises became more elaborate. The idea took hold that a business firm was an impersonal entity—larger than the person who owned it—with an identity, legal status, permanence, and even profits that were not the same as those of its members. Here was yet another indication of the changes taking place in economic affairs.

INFLATION AND SILVER

The surest sign of growth, however, was the slow inflation of prices, which began around 1500 after some 150 years of either stagnant or falling prices. By modern standards, the increase was tiny—1 or 2 percent a year, totaling 75 percent in Spain by 1600 and slightly less elsewhere in Europe—but it prompted bitter protests from those who thought a loaf of bread had a "just" price and that any increase was mere exploitation by the baker. In general, however, the modest inflation was an indication that demand was rising, and it not only boosted profits but also reduced people's debts (because the amount that had been borrowed was worth less each year).

Silver Imports A major reason for the inflation was the growth of the population, but it was also propelled by the huge quantities of silver the Spaniards imported from the New World, which made money more readily available (see accompanying table). Most of the silver passed from Spain to the Italian and German merchants who financed Spanish wars and controlled the American trade, and it thus affected all of Europe. Other sources of supply, notably silver mines in Austria, were appearing at this time; but the flow of New World silver was the main reason for the end of the crippling shortage of precious metals

▶ *Anonymous French Miniature*
Merchants Clearing Accounts
This sixteenth-century depiction of a group of people in a fine house calculating accounts gives a sense of the increasingly complicated exchanges that became necessary as commerce expanded. Books had to be checked and moneys counted, and it is noteworthy that the transactions involve the monk on the left and the woman holding her purse on the right.

Imports of Treasure to Spain from the New World, 1511–1600

Decade	*Total Value**
1511–1520	2,626,000
1521–1530	1,407,000
1531–1540	6,706,000
1541–1550	12,555,000
1551–1560	21,437,000
1561–1570	30,418,000
1571–1580	34,990,000
1581–1590	63,849,000
1591–1600	85,536,000

*In ducats.

Source: Adapted from J. H. Elliott, *Imperial Spain, 1469–1716* (New York, 1964), p. 175.

and, hence, of coins that had plagued Europe for centuries. By the middle of the seventeenth century, the continent's holdings in gold had increased by one-fifth and, more important, its stock of silver had tripled.

With money circulating more freely and markets growing, the profits of traders and financiers improved dramatically. They could invest more widely (for example, in overseas ventures), and they could achieve new levels of wealth.

THE COMMERCIAL REVOLUTION

As the volume of trade rose, new mechanisms for organizing large-scale economic activity were put in place—a process that has been called Europe's *commercial revolution.* Bookkeepers devised new, standardized principles for keeping track of a firm's accounts, bankers created elaborate systems of agents and letters of credit to transfer funds across large distances, merchants developed more effective means of forming broad partnerships that were capable of major investments and of ensuring against losses, and governments gave increased support to new ventures and to the financial community in general. Essential to these activities was an attitude and a way of conducting business that is known as *capitalism.*

Capitalism Capitalism was both a product of economic change and a stimulus to further change. It is often thought of as a system, but it refers primarily to the distinct outlook and kinds of behavior displayed by certain people as they make, buy, and sell goods. At its root capitalism means the accumulation of capital—that is, tangible wealth—for its own sake. In practice, this requires taking risks and also reinvesting whatever one earns so as to enlarge one's profits. Those who undertook long-distance trade had many capitalist traits: They took great risks, and they were prepared to wait months and even years in order to make as large a financial gain as possible. Similarly, bankers were prepared to lend their capital, despite the danger that the loan might not be repaid, in the hope of profit; and if

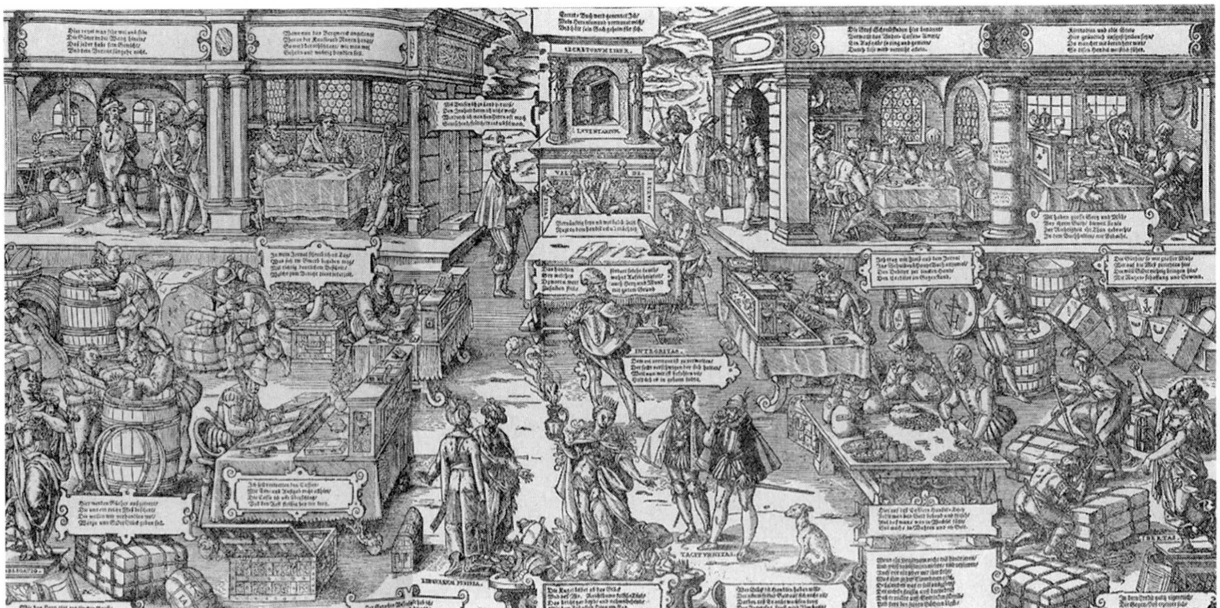

▸ *Jost Amman*
ALLEGORY OF TRADE, WOODCUT
This late-sixteenth-century celebration of the world of the merchant shows, around the sides, the shipping of goods, the keeping of accounts, and the exchange of money that were transforming economic life. In the center, the virtues of the merchant are symbolized: integrity (a man looking over his shoulder), taciturnity (two men on his right), and a knowledge of languages (two men in turbans) in front of judiciousness on a throne and a book representing invention.

The Metropolitan Museum of Art

they succeeded, they continually plowed their earnings back into their businesses to make them ever larger. The fortunes that these capitalists accumulated, and the desire for worldly riches that they displayed, became an essential stimulus to economic growth. Far from the rural world where food was grown primarily for survival, not for profit, they were forging a new way of thinking about money and wealth. Although their outlook had existed before, only in the sixteenth century did it come to dominate Europe's economy. As a result, traditional religious prohibitions on the charging of interest began to weaken, and materialist ambitions became more open and accepted.

Unease over this new outlook did not disappear. Shakespeare's play *The Merchant of Venice*, written in the 1590s, attacked the values that capitalism was coming to represent. He contrasted unfavorably the quest for profit with more traditional commitments, such as charity and mercy. And his choice of Venice as a setting was appropriate because the large empire this city built in the eastern Mediterranean was mainly the result of a single-minded pursuit of trade. But criticism had no effect. The spread of capitalism was now irresistible.

► *Petrus Christus*
St. Eligius as a Goldsmith, 1449
Goldsmiths played a vital financial role in the early days of capitalism. Because of the value of the merchandise they made and sold, their shops—like the one here, with customers looking in the window, as one can see in the convex mirror on the right—were sources of capital as well as goods. In addition to providing such items as the ring he is handing to the young woman, the goldsmith might well have provided investments for the traders in his city.

SOCIAL CHANGE: THE COUNTRYSIDE

Not everyone shared in the new prosperity of the sixteenth century. Landowners, food producers, artisans, and merchants benefited most from the rising population and could amass fortunes. Tenants who were able to harvest a surplus beyond their own needs did well, because for a while rents did not keep pace with food prices. But the wages of ordinary laborers lagged miserably. By the early seventeenth century, a laborer's annual income had about half the purchasing power it had had at the end of the fifteenth century, a decline that had its most drastic impact in Eastern Europe, where serfdom reappeared.

In the West, the large numbers of peasants who were forced off the land as the population rose turned to begging and wandering across country, often ending up in towns, where crime became a serious problem. Peasant uprisings directed at tax collectors, nobles, or food suppliers were almost annual affairs in one region or another of France after the mid-sixteenth century, and in England the unending stream of vagrants gave rise to a belief that the country was overpopulated. The extreme poverty was universally deplored, particularly as it promoted crime and disorder.

▸ *Hieronymus Bosch*
THE PRODIGAL SON, CA. 1516
Usually known for his horrific paintings of devils and monsters, Bosch here creates a realistic scene of his time to illustrate the biblical story of the prodigal son. He shows the son as one of the many poor peddlers, in torn clothes and ill-matching shoes, who roamed the European countryside. The house he is leaving is hardly in better condition, with holes in the roof and a broken shutter; and the residents show in various ways their indifference to his departure.

Relief of Distress Nobody could understand, much less control, the forces that were transforming society. Some governments tried to relieve the economic distress, but their efforts were not always consistent. English legislation in the sixteenth century, for example, treated beggars sometimes as shirkers who should be punished and at other times as unfortunates who needed to be helped. Not until the enactment of the English Poor Law of 1601, which provided work for the poor, did the more compassionate view begin to prevail. In the years that followed, governments in a number of countries began to create institutions that offered basic welfare benefits.

The traditional source of food for the hungry and care for the ill, the monastery, had lost its importance because of the Reformation and because governments were now considered responsible for the needy. Among the remedies they offered were the workhouses established by the English Poor Law where, although conditions could be horrible, the destitute could at least find work, food, and shelter. Other governments founded hospitals, often staffed by nuns, which were especially important as places that looked after abandoned women or children. But these institutions were few and far between, and it was exceptional for a poor person to find such relief. The conditions were especially harsh for women forced off the land, because few trades were open to them even if they got to a town; their choice might be either continued vagrancy or prostitution.

SOCIAL CHANGE: THE TOWN

Vagrancy was only one of the signs that Europeans were witnessing the beginnings of modern urbanization with all its dislocations. Major differences also developed between life in the country and life in the town. Rural workers may have led a strenuous existence, but they escaped the worst hazards of their urban counterparts. Whole sections of most large cities were controlled by the sixteenth-century equivalent of the underworld, which offered sanctuary to criminals and danger to most citizens. Plagues were much more serious in towns—the upper classes soon learned to flee to the country at the first sign of disease—and famines more devastating because of the far poorer sanitation in urban areas and their remoteness from food supplies.

New Opportunities Nevertheless, it was in towns and cities that the economic advances of the age were most visible. As cities grew, they stimulated construction, not only of houses but also of public buildings and city walls. Anyone skilled in bricklaying, in carpentry, or even in carrying heavy loads found ready employment. Townsfolk needed endless services, from sign painting to the transportation of books, which created jobs at all levels. Given the demand for skills, guilds increasingly allowed the widows of members to take over their husbands' trades, and women shopkeepers were not uncommon. Nobody would have been taken aback, for example, to see an artisan's daughter or wife (like Agnes Dürer, the wife of the famous German artist) take charge of a market stall or a shop. In some trades, such as oil making and baking, women were often essential to production as well as sales, and

▶ *Pieter Brueghel the Elder*
CARNIVAL AND LENT, 1559
This detail from a huge scene shows one of the customary practices during the season of Lent: giving alms to the poor. Beggars were a common subject for Brueghel, who used them to convey a vivid sense of the appearance and behavior of the unfortunate as well as the more comfortable members of his society.

there is also evidence of their growing importance as the keepers of the paperwork and the accounts in family businesses. The expansion of opportunity in the cities, in other words, had social as well as economic consequences.

At the top levels of society—at princely courts and in royal administrations, in the law, among the leaders of the burgeoning cities, and in growing empires overseas—the economic expansion enabled ambitious families to win fortunes and titles and to found new aristocratic dynasties. The means of advancement varied. Once a family had become rich through commerce, it could buy the lands that, in Protestant countries, rulers had confiscated from the Church, or the offices that many governments sold to raise revenue and build bureaucracies. In addition, the New World offered the possibility of acquiring vast estates. Since the possession of land or high office was the key to noble status, the newly rich were soon able to enter the ranks of the nobility. The long boom in commerce thus encouraged a broad spectrum of social change. By the 1620s, when the upward trend of the economy came to an end, a new aristocracy had been born that was destined to dominate Europe for centuries.

II. Expansion Overseas

THE PORTUGUESE

Long before Europe's demographic and economic recovery began in the late fifteenth century, pioneer explorers had taken the first steps that were to lead to the creation of huge empires overseas. Taking farther the voyages beyond Europe of the crusaders and such travelers as Marco Polo, sailors had been inching around Africa seeking a route to the Far East. The riches in goods and lands they eventually found would help fuel the boom of the sixteenth century. But there was little expectation of world-shattering consequences among the Portuguese who began these voyages in the 1410s.

Henry the Navigator The Portuguese lived in an inhospitable land whose seafarers had always been essential to the country's economy. The need for better agricultural opportunities had long turned their eyes toward Atlantic islands like the Canaries and the territories held by the Muslims (Moors) in North Africa. But this ambition had to be organized into a sustained effort if it was to achieve results, and in the early fifteenth century Prince Henry the Navigator, a younger son of the king, undertook that task.

Henry participated in the capture of the North African port of Ceuta from the Muslims in 1415, a crusading expedition that only whetted his appetite for more such victories. At Ceuta he probably heard stories about lost Christians and mines of gold somewhere in the interior of Africa. A mixture of motives—profit, religion, and curiosity—spurred him on; and in 1419 he began patronizing sailors, mapmakers, astronomers (because their contributions to celestial navigation were vital), shipbuilders, and instrument makers who were interested in discovery. They were mainly Italians, and their aim was not merely to make contact with Africans but to find an alternative route to India and the Far East around Africa (in order to avoid the Ottoman Empire, which was coming to dominate the eastern Mediterranean). The early adventurers did not succeed, but during their gradual advance down the West African coast, they opened a rich new trade in ivory, gold, and slaves.

To India and Beyond Then, in 1488, a Portuguese captain, Bartholomeu Dias, returned to Lisbon after making a landfall on the east coast of Africa, beyond the Cape of Good Hope, which previously no one had been able to pass. The way to India now seemed open, but before the Portuguese could send out their first expedition, the news arrived that a sailor employed by the Spaniards, one Christopher Columbus, had apparently reached India by sailing west. To avoid conflicting claims which might interfere with their trade, Portugal and Spain signed the Treaty of Tordesillas in 1494. This gave Portugal possession of all the lands to the east of an imaginary line about 300 miles west of the Azores, and Spain a monopoly of everything to the west. Portugal thus kept the only practical route to India (as well as the rights to Brazil, which one of her sailors may already have discovered). Three years later Vasco da Gama took the first Portuguese fleet across the Indian Ocean.

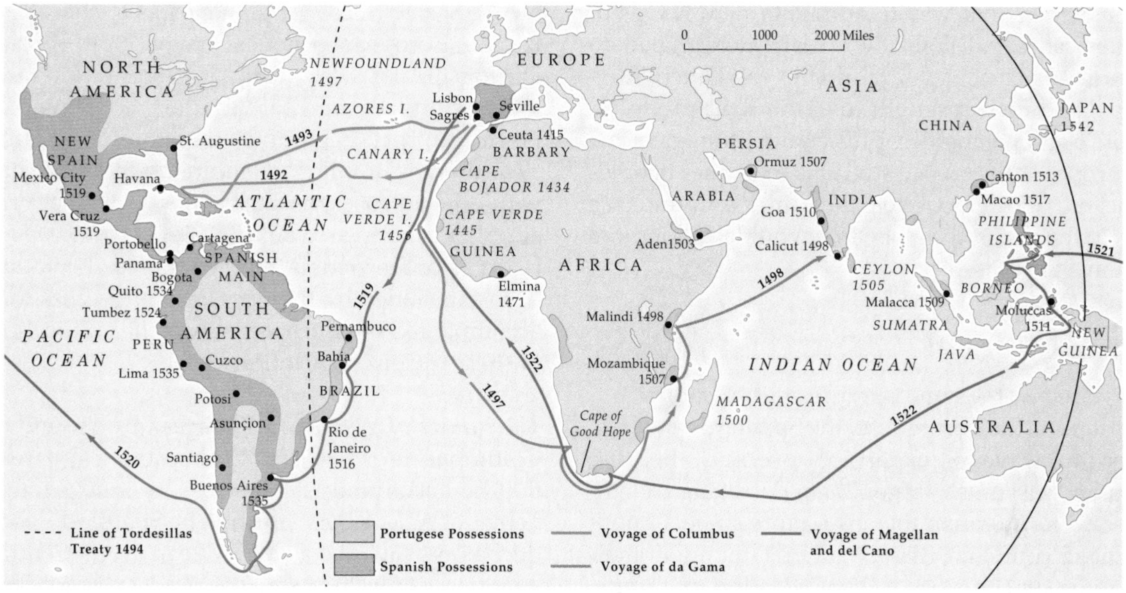

Map 14.1 **EXPLORATION AND CONQUEST IN THE FIFTEENTH AND SIXTEENTH CENTURIES**
The division of the world between the Portuguese and the Spaniards led to distinct areas of exploration and settlement, demarcated by the line that both sides accepted at the Treaty of Tordesillas.

At first, he found it hard to trade, because the Arabs, who had controlled these waters for centuries, tried to keep out all rivals. Within 14 years, however, the Portuguese merchants had established themselves. The key to their success was naval power, for their ship designers had learned to combine their old square sails, which provided speed, with the Arabs' lateen sails, which increased maneuverability. The Portuguese were also the first to give their fleets effective fire power, realizing that cannon, not soldiers, won battles at sea. In addition, they deployed their ships in squadrons rather than individually, a tactic that further increased their superiority. The result was overwhelming military success. A series of victories reduced Arab naval strength, and bombardments quieted stubborn cities. By 1513 Portugal's trading posts extended beyond India to the rich Spice Islands, the Moluccas.

The Portuguese Empire The empire Portugal created remained dependent on sea power, not overseas colonies. Except in Brazil, which was virtually unpopulated and where the settlers were able to establish huge estates worked by slave labor, the Portuguese relied on a chain of small trading bases that stretched from West Africa to China. They supplied and defended these bases, which usually consisted of little more than a few warehouses and a fort, by sea; and they tended to keep contacts with the local people to a minimum, so as to maintain friendly relations and missionary and trading rights. The one exception to the isolation was a result of the small numbers of women who traveled to the settlements from Portugal: In these early years there were more marriages with local women than there were in other European empires. But even though their effort remained relatively small-scale, the Portuguese soon began to profit from their explorations—between 1442 and 1446 almost 1000 slaves were brought home from Africa—and in the sixteenth century their wealth grew as they became major importers of luxuries from the East, such as spices, which were in great demand as medicines, preservatives, and tasty delicacies.

By dominating commerce with the Oriental civilizations, which were not only richer but also more sophisticated than their own, Portugal's merchants controlled Europe's most valuable trade. But their dominance was to last less than a century, for their success spurred a competition for empire that was to stimulate new waves of overseas expansion. First Spain determined to emulate her neighbor; and later the Dutch, English, and French sought to outdo their predecessors and one another. This competition gave the Europeans the crucial stimulus that other peoples lacked, and it projected them into a dominance over the rest of the globe that would last for more than 450 years.

THE SPANIARDS

Inspired by the same centuries-old crusading ambitions as the Portuguese, the Spaniards rode the second wave of expansion overseas. Because Spain was much larger than Portugal, and directed its attention toward a more sparsely populated continent, the Spaniards founded their empire on conquest and colonization, not trade. But they got their start from a stroke of luck.

Columbus Christopher Columbus—an experienced Genoese sailor who was widely read, well versed in Atlantic sailing, and familiar with the leading geographers of his day—seems to have believed (we do not know for certain because he was a secretive man) that Asia lay only 3500 miles beyond the Canary Islands. Thus convinced that sailing west across the Atlantic to the Far East was perfectly feasible, Columbus took his proposal in 1484 to the Portuguese government, which refused to underwrite the venture. With a mystic belief in his own destiny, he persisted, gained the financial backing and blessing of Ferdinand V and Isabella I of Spain, and set sail in 1492. He was an excellent navigator (one of his discoveries on the voyage was the difference between true and magnetic north), and he kept his men going despite their horror of being so long at sea without sight of land. After 33 days he reached the Bahamas. He was disappointed that he found no Chinese or Japanese as he investigated Cuba and the west coast of Hispaniola (today's Haiti), but he was certain that he had reached Asia, even though the few natives he saw did not resemble those whom travelers such as Marco Polo had described.

Columbus crossed the Atlantic Ocean three more times, but he made no other significant discoveries. Yet he did also start the tradition of violence against local people that was to characterize the European conquest of the New World. During his first stay in the Caribbean, his men killed some of the natives they encountered. From the very beginning, therefore, it became clear that the building of empires in the Americas would be a process of destruction as well as creation, of cruelty as well as achievement (*see box, p. 431*). For the victims, the legacy of the brutality, soon intensified by the devastating diseases that accompanied the Europeans, was the eradication of their ancient civilizations.

The Limits of Westward Voyages By the end of Columbus' life in 1506, it was becoming apparent that he had found islands close by a new continent, not Asia. When, in 1513, the Spaniard Vasco de Balboa saw the Pacific Ocean from Central America, some thought that an easy westward passage to the riches of East Asia might still be found. But the last hope of a quick journey was dashed in 1522, when the one surviving ship from a fleet of five that had set out under Ferdinand Magellan three years before returned to Spain after the ordeal of having sailed around the world.

▶ WOODCUT OF COLUMBUS
This picture, by a contemporary, shows King Ferdinand, back in Spain, pointing to Columbus' three ships and the natives greeting the explorer in the New World.

Two Views of Columbus

The following two passages suggest the enormous differences that have arisen in interpretations of the career of Christopher Columbus. The first, by Samuel Eliot Morison, a historian and a noted sailor, represents the traditional view of the explorer's achievements that held sway until recent years. The second, by Kirkpatrick Sale, a writer and environmentalist, indicates how radically the understanding of the effects of exploration has changed in recent years.

1. "Columbus had a Hellenic sense of wonder at the new and strange, combined with an artist's appreciation of natural beauty. Moreover, Columbus had a deep conviction of the sovereignty and the infinite wisdom of God, which enhanced all his triumphs. One only wishes that the Admiral might have been afforded the sense of fulfillment that would have come from foreseeing all that flowed from his discoveries. The whole history of the Americas stems from the Four Voyages of Columbus, and as the Greek city-states looked back to the deathless gods as their founders, so today a score of independent nations unite in homage to Christopher the stout-hearted son of Genoa, who carried Christian civilization across the Ocean Sea."

From S. E. Morison, *Admiral of the Ocean Sea: A Life of Christopher Columbus* (Boston: Little, Brown, 1942), pp. 670–671.

2. "For all his navigational skill, about which the salty types make such a fuss, and all his fortuitous headings, Admiral Colón [Christopher Columbus] could be a wretched mariner. The four voyages, properly seen, quite apart from bravery, are replete with lubberly mistakes, misconceived sailing plans, foolish disregard of elementary maintenance and stubborn neglect of basic safety—all characterized by the assertion of human superiority over the natural realm. Almost every time Colón went wrong it was because he had refused to bend to the inevitabilities of tide and wind and reef or, more arrogantly still, had not bothered to learn about them.

"Many of those who know well the cultures that once existed in the New World have reason to be less than enthusiastic about [the 1992 celebrations of] the event that led to the destruction of much of that heritage and the greater part of the people who produced it; others are planning to protest the entire goings-on as a wrongful commemoration of an act steeped in bloodshed, slavery and genocide."

Kirkpatrick Sale, *The Conquest of Paradise: Christopher Columbus and the Columbian Legacy* (New York: Knopf, 1990), pp. 209–210 and 362.

Magellan's 98-day crossing of the Pacific was the supreme accomplishment of seamanship in the age of discovery. But the voyage persuaded the Spaniards that Portugal had the fastest route to the East, and in 1529 they renounced all attempts to trade with the Spice Islands. Spain could now concentrate on the Americas, those unexpected continents that were to become not an obstacle on the way to the Spice Islands but possessions of unbelievable richness.

The Conquistador Volunteers for empire building were amply available. When the last Muslim kingdom in southern Spain was conquered by the Castilians in 1492, soldiers with long experience of military service found themselves at loose ends. Many were the younger sons of noble families, who were often kept from inheriting land because Spanish law usually allowed only the eldest son to inherit. The prospect of unlimited land and military adventure across the Atlantic appealed to them, as it did to ambitious members of Castile's lower classes, and thus the conquistador, or conqueror, was born. There were not many of them—fewer than 1000—but they overran much of the Americas in search of wealth and glory.

The first and most dramatic of these leaders was Hernando Cortés, who in 1519 landed on the Mexican coast and set out to overcome the rich Aztec civilization in the high plateau of central Mexico. His army consisted of only 600 troops, but in two years, with a few reinforcements, he had won a complete victory. Guns alone made no important difference because Cortés had only 13 muskets and some unwieldy cannon. More effective were his horses, his manipulation of the Aztecs' beliefs (especially after he murdered their ruler) to make them regard him as more powerful than he was, and the unshakable determination of his followers. The conquest of the Mexican Mayas also began under Cortés, while the Incas of Peru fell to Francisco Pizzaro. Other conquistadors repeated these successes throughout Central and South America. By 1550 the conquest was over, and the military leaders gave way to administrators who began organizing the huge empire they had won.

THE FIRST COLONIAL EMPIRE

The Spanish government established in the New World the same pattern of political administration that it was setting up in its European territories. Representatives of the throne, viceroys, were sent to administer each territory and to impose centralized control. They were advised by the local *audiencia*, a kind of miniature council that also acted as a court of law, but the ultimate authority remained in Spain.

Real growth did not begin, however, until women pioneers came out to the settlements. In this empire, unlike Portugal's, intermarriage was strongly discouraged. Indeed, the indigenous peoples were treated with a brutality and disdain that set a dismal model for overseas empires. Not only was their labor cruelly exploited (both on farms and especially in silver mines that the Spaniards discovered, where working conditions were dreadful) and not only were families split apart so that men could be put to work, but local beliefs and traditions were actively suppressed (though many survived despite the oppression). Over the years, there was to be increased intermarriage between Europeans and natives, and the creation of a more united society, but this took centuries to achieve. In the early days, only a few humane voices were raised, mainly by Spanish clergymen, to denounce the oppression. That they were ignored was only one indication of the indifference shown by Europe's colonizers to the well-being of other peoples as the empires were built.

For Spain's neighbors, the colonies were an object of envy because of their mineral wealth. In 1545 a major vein of silver was discovered at Potosí, in Bolivia, and from those mines came the treasure that made fortunes for the colonists, sustained Spain's many wars, and ultimately enriched much of Europe. For the balance of the sixteenth century, however, despite the efforts of other countries, Portugal and Spain remained the only conspicuous participants in Europe's overseas expansion.

THE LIFE OF THE SETTLERS

It took a great deal of determination to board one of the ships that set off across the oceans from Europe. Life at sea offered discomfort and peril: horrible overcrowding, inadequate and often rotting food, disease, dangerous storms, poor navigation, and threats from enemy ships. One cannot determine numbers precisely, but it has been estimated that in some decades of the sixteenth and seventeenth centuries, fewer than two-thirds of those who embarked reached their destination. And their troubles did not end when they came off the ships. Unfamiliar countries, famine, illness, and attacks by natives and European rivals made life precarious at best. Although 5000 people sailed for Virginia between 1619 and 1624, for instance, disease and massacre kept the colony the same size at the end of that period—about 1000 inhabitants—as it had been at the beginning. And yet, despite the difficulties and dangers, people found reasons to keep coming.

The Aims of the Colonists For a few leaders, like the Spanish minor nobles known as *hidalgos* who commanded most of Spain's first missions, the attraction was partly adventure, partly the chance to command a military expedition of con-

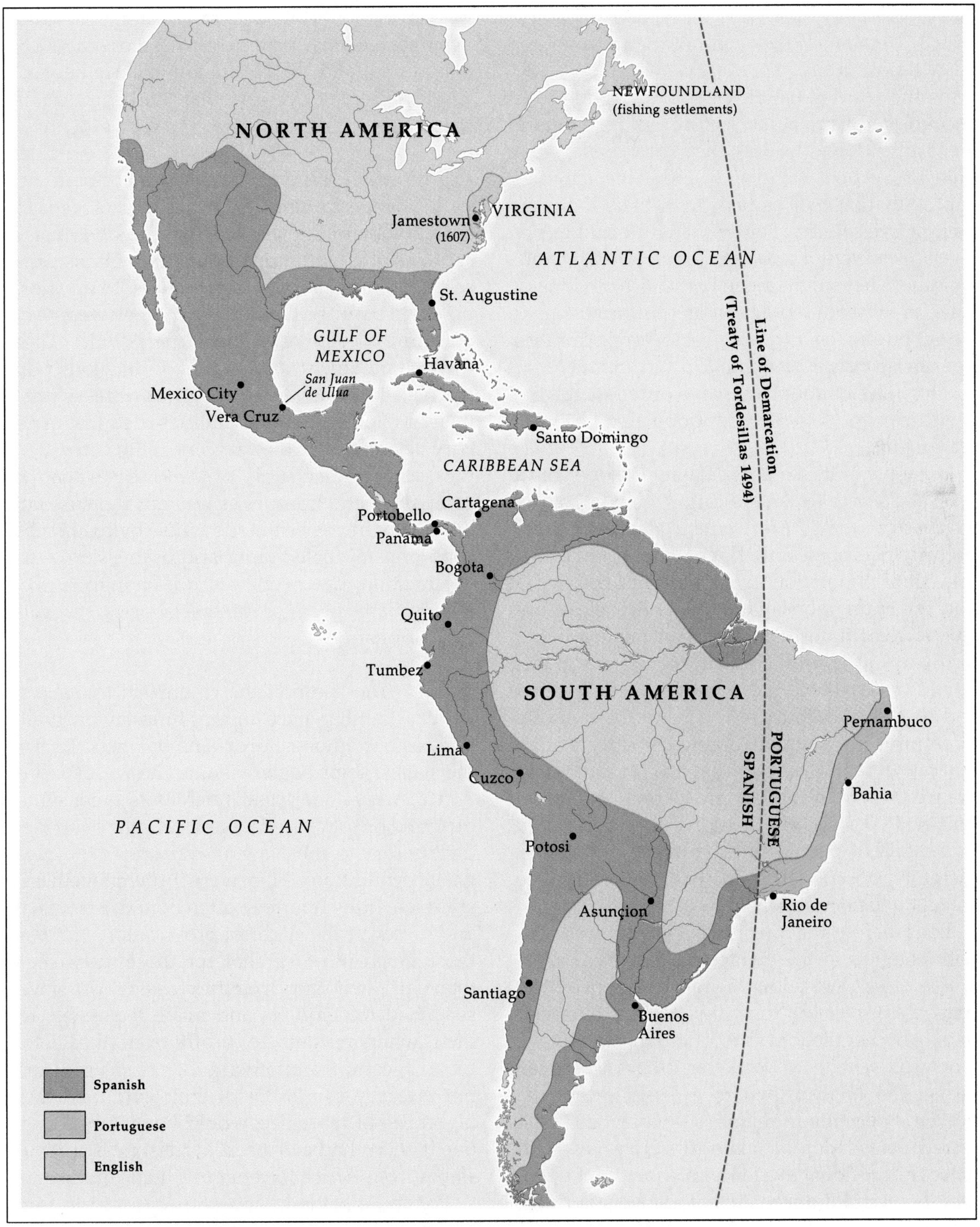

Map 14.2 EMPIRE AND SETTLEMENT IN THE AMERICAS, 1493–1610
The leadership of the Spaniards in expanding into the New World during the century following the voyages of Columbus is apparent from the territories they dominated. The much smaller area controlled by the Portuguese, the tentative activities of the English in Virginia, and the occasional settlements of fishermen in Newfoundland, paled by comparison with the Spanish empire.

quest, and partly the hope of making a fortune which seemed unlikely at home. For another fairly small group, the clergy, the aim was to bring the word of God to people who had never encountered Christianity before. As for government officials and traders, they were usually just following orders, bringing overseas the activities and skills that had earned them their living in their native country. For these middle and upper levels of society, moreover, survival was rarely an issue: They might die in battle or from illness, and life may not have been as comfortable as it would have been at home, but the opportunities to exercise power or to make a fortune were far greater. The outlook was very different for the vast majority of those who populated the new settlements.

For most of the settlers, leaving Europe was a fairly desperate act, an indication that almost any alternative seemed preferable to the bleak prospects in their homeland. If it had not been for the growth of population in the sixteenth century—and the many thousands it made homeless, unable to remain in their villages or make a living in towns—it is unlikely that enough emigrants would have been found to do the work in ports and on the land that was crucial to the building of empires in Asia and America. It is significant that fewer people moved from a rich country like France than from the less prosperous Spain and Portugal. Despite the pressures that persuaded thousands of people to leave their homelands, therefore, additional means had to be found to populate the empires.

Long before the English colonized Australia with convicts in the eighteenth century, for example, they were taking people out of prison to send them overseas to places desperate for settlers. Another tactic was to offer land to anyone who was willing to work for others for seven years. The English, and to a lesser extent the French, permitted religious minorities who feared persecution at home to start a new and more independent existence in America. In general, powerful inducements like poverty or persecution were needed to drive Europeans to accept the hazards of the journey and the subsequent struggles of the pioneer. Some settlers, such as the religious refugees, set out as families, but usually many more men than women made the voyage. In a society suspicious of single females, women had far more to risk by emigrating, and the chronic imbalance between genders became yet another hardship of life overseas.

Exploitation When even distress at home provided too few volunteers, the colonizers relied on force to obtain the workers they needed. Just as captains often kidnapped men for a ship's crew, so, too, did the suppliers of settlers. Many woke up at sea surprised to find where they were. And once in the colonies, wage earners could expect their employment to be harsh. Indigenous populations, however, faced the most ruthless treatment: In South America millions died (estimates vary between 25 and 90 percent of the native peoples) as a result mainly of the diseases that accompanied the Europeans, though the susceptibility may have been made worse by the terrible conditions of forced labor and oppression. Even exploitation, however, was not enough to feed the insatiable need for miners, laborers, servants, and farmhands.

Slaves The solution the colonizers found was slavery, familiar since ancient times but virtually nonexistent among Europeans by 1500. To find the slaves, ships began visiting the west coast of Africa, where the local inhabitants were either captured or purchased from local rulers and then transported to the New World under the most ghastly conditions. They were thrown together in cramped, filthy quarters, often bound, barely fed, and beaten at the slightest provocation. Nor was there much improvement for those—often less than half—who survived the crossing. The slaves sustained the empires and made it possible for their white masters to profit from the silver, tobacco, cotton, and other goods they produced; but the grim conditions of their lives, and their high rates of mortality, would have wiped them out if there had not been a constant stream of slaves from Africa to replenish their numbers.

For those settlers who reaped rewards from the mines and the agricultural products of America, or from the trade with Europe that enriched all the colonies, the hardships did not last long. They created flourishing cities and universities, and made huge fortunes. Their commercial net-

works began to link the entire world together for the first time in history. But for the many who struggled to expand these empires, life on the frontier, despite the promise of new opportunities, remained hard and dangerous for centuries. And for the slaves, there was not the slightest improvement in conditions or even hope of improvement, until revolts and civil wars finally abolished slavery in the nineteenth century.

Slave Ship
This picture, made aboard a slave ship, shows the dangerously crowded conditions in which Africans were brought to the New World. It is small wonder that so many of them died of disease even before the end of this miserable voyage.

III. The Centralization of Political Power

THE "NEW MONARCHS"

The economic and social transformations that began around 1500 gained important support from the actions of central governments. Especially in England, France, and Spain, rulers gave vital encouragement to the growth of trade, overseas expansion, and attempts to relieve social distress. At the same time, the growing prosperity of the age enhanced the tax revenues that were essential to their power. Both of these mutually reinforcing developments had long-term effects, but it could be argued that the creation of well-organized states, built around strong central governments, was even more decisive than the economic boom in shaping the future of Western Europe.

The rulers of England, France, and Spain in the late fifteenth and early sixteenth centuries were especially successful in accumulating and centralizing power, and historians have therefore called them "new monarchs." The reigns of

Henry VII, Louis XI, and Ferdinand and Isabella, in particular, have come to be regarded as marking the end of more than a century of political fragmentation. They set in motion a revival of royal authority that eventually weakened all rivals to the crown and created the bureaucracies characteristic of the modern state.

TUDOR ENGLAND

The English monarchs had relied for centuries on local cooperation to run their kingdom. Unlike other European countries, England contained only 50 or 60 families who were legally nobles out of a population of perhaps 2.5 million. But many other families, though not technically members of the nobility, had large estates and were dominant figures at the parish, county, and even national levels. They were known as *gentry*, and it was from their ranks that the crown appointed the local officers who administered the realm—notably the justices of the peace (usually referred to as JPs). These voluntary unpaid officials served as the principal public servants in the more than 40 counties of the land.

For reasons of status as well as out of a feeling of responsibility, the gentry had always sought such appointments. From the crown's point of view, the great advantage of the system was its efficiency: Enforcement was in the hands of those who could enforce. As a "great man" in his neighborhood, the justice of the peace rarely had trouble exerting his authority. Thus, the king had at his disposal an administrative structure without rival in Europe because, unlike other rulers, he could count on the cooperation of the leaders of each locality. Since the gentry had been given so much responsibility, they had developed a strong sense of duty over the centuries, and the king had increasingly sought their advice.

Parliament and Common Law In the sixteenth century an institution that had developed from this relationship, Parliament, began to take on a general importance as the chief representative of the country's wishes; it was increasingly considered to be the only body that could give a ruler's actions a wider sanction than he could draw from his prerogatives alone. Although Parliament remained subordinate to the crown for a long time, England's kings already realized that they could not take such measures as raising extraordinary taxes without its consent.

Just as Parliament served to unify the country, so too did another ancient institution: the common law. This was a system of justice based on precedent and tradition that was the same, or "common," throughout England. In contrast to the Roman law that prevailed on the continent, common law grew out of the interpretations of precedent made by individual judges and the decisions of juries. A court could be dominated by local leaders, but in general this was a system of justice, administered by judges who traveled from area to area, that helped bind England together. Like Parliament, the common law would eventually be regarded by opponents of royal power as an independent source of authority with which the crown could not interfere. In the late 1400s, however, it was an important help to a king who was trying to overcome England's political fragmentation and forge a more unified realm.

HENRY VII

Henry VII (1485–1509), who founded the Tudor dynasty, came to the throne as a usurper in the aftermath of more than 30 years of civil conflict, the Wars of the Roses. England's nobles had caused chaos in these wars, and they had consistently ignored the wishes of the monarchy. The situation hardly looked promising for a reassertion of royal power. Yet Henry both extended the authority of the crown and restored order with extraordinary speed.

Finance His first concern was finance, because he knew that unless he had sufficient funds to run his government, his ability to control the nobles would remain uncertain. At the same time, he was aware that extra taxes were the surest way to alienate subjects who expected a king to "live of his own," that is, from the income his lands provided, from customs duties, and from the contributions he received at special times, such as the marriage of his daughter. It is a testimony to the care with which Henry nurtured his revenues that by the end of his reign he had paid off the crown's debts and accumulated a substantial reserve. His success came, first, from increases in the profits of justice—fees and fines—which also cowed unruly subjects. In addition, he improved his returns by putting collection and supervision of revenue in the hands of a small, efficient group of officials in his own household. Above all, it was by careful management, and avoidance of foreign entanglements, that he was able to "live of his own."

Restoring Order Where domestic order was concerned, the revival of royal authority was largely due to the energy of the king and his chief servants. Henry increased the powers of the justices of the peace, thus striking severely at the independence attained by leading nobles during the previous two centuries. Under his leadership, too, the royal Council became a far more active and influential body. Leading officials not only exercised executive powers but also resumed hearing legal appeals—a policy that further undermined the independence of gentry and nobles, who could dominate proceedings in local common law courts. When the royal councillors sat as a court (known as Star Chamber from the decorations on the ceiling of the room where they met), there was no jury, local lords had no influence, and decisions were quick and fair. Eventually, Star Chamber and other so-called royal courts (which derived their jurisdiction from the authority of the king himself) came to be seen as threats to England's traditional common law. Under the Tudors, however, they were accepted as highly effective means of restoring order and asserting the power of the central government.

HENRY VIII AND HIS SUCCESSORS

The first Tudor was a conservative, building up his authority and finances by applying vigorously the traditional methods and institutions that were available to a king. The young man who followed him on the throne, Henry VIII (1509–1547), was an arrogant, dazzling figure, a strong contrast to his careful father. In 1513 he removed a long-standing threat from England's north by inflicting a shattering defeat on an invading Scots army at Flodden. With his prestige thus enhanced, he spent the next 15 years taking little part in European affairs and consolidating royal power at home with the capable assistance of his chief minister, Cardinal Thomas Wolsey.

The Divorce This successful continuation of Henry VII's policies ended in 1529 when Wolsey fell from power, ruined by the king's wish for a divorce from his wife, who had failed to produce a male heir to continue the dynasty. Henry had married his brother's widow, Catherine of Aragon, under a special papal dispensation from the biblical law that normally prohibited a union between such close relatives. Obsessed with dynastic continuity—and infatuated with a young lady at court, Anne Boleyn—Henry urged Wolsey to ask the pope to declare the previous dispensation invalid. Under ordinary circumstances there would have been no trouble, but at this moment the pope was in the power of Charles V, the Holy Roman Emperor, who was also Catherine's nephew. When Wolsey's efforts to get papal approval for the divorce failed, Henry dismissed him and accused him of treason.

For three years thereafter the king kept trying to get the Church to grant him the divorce. He called Parliament and gave it free rein to express bitter anticlerical sentiments, he sought opinions in European universities in favor of the divorce, he attacked his own clergy for having bowed to Wolsey's authority, and he even extracted a vague recognition from the clergy of his position as "supreme lord" of the Church. Finally, he placed his confidence in Thomas Cromwell, a former servant of Wolsey's and, like Wolsey, a talented man from a humble background who had risen rapidly in royal service. Cromwell suggested a radical but simple solution: that Henry break with the pope, declare himself supreme head of the Church, and divorce Catherine on his own authority. The king agreed, thus unleashing a revolution that dramatically increased the powers of the royal government. At the same time, although he himself had written a book attacking Martin Luther, Henry established the Reformation in England. By identifying his kingdom with Europe's Protestants, in opposition to the Catholics, Henry gave his subjects an emotional cause that eventually stimulated a sense of national pride.

The Reformation Parliament The instrument chosen to accomplish the break with Rome was Parliament, the only body capable of giving the move legal sanction and an aura of national approval. Henry called the assembly in 1529 and did not dissolve it until 1536. During its sessions it acted on more matters of importance than a Parliament had ever considered before. It forbade litigants from making ecclesiastical appeals to Rome, thus allowing Henry to obtain his divorce and remarry, and in 1534 it took the decisive step: It declared the king supreme head of the Church in England, thus bringing to an end over 1000 years of papal supremacy (*see box,* below). Royal power gained enormously from these acts, but so, too, did the stature of Parliament, thanks to its new responsibilities and the length of its sessions.

Previously, election to Parliament had been considered a chore by the townsmen and landed gentry in the House of Commons, who found the expense of unpaid attendance and the time it took more irksome than did the wealthy nobles in the House of Lords (so named during Henry VIII's reign). But this attitude began to change in the 1530s as members of the Commons, returning to successive sessions, came to know one another and to regard themselves as guardians of Parliament's traditions and privileges. Eventually, they were to make the Commons the dominant house in Parliament.

Royal Power Following his successful suggestion for solving Henry's conflict with Rome, Thomas Cromwell became the king's chief minister. He was a tireless bureaucrat, who reorganized the administration of the country into six departments, each with specific functions, and took the chief executive position, the secretaryship. At the same time, a Privy Council, consisting of the king's principal advisers, was created to coordinate and direct royal administration.

The principal beneficiary of the events of the 1530s was the crown. Royal income rose markedly when Henry became head of the English Church and took over the ecclesiastical fees that previously had gone to the pope. He gained an even larger windfall when he dissolved all Eng-

Henry VIII Claims Independence from the Pope

One of the crucial acts of Parliament through which Henry VIII made the Church of England independent of Rome was the so-called Act in Restraint of Appeals, which became law in 1533. This law forbade Englishmen from appealing court decisions to Rome, which they had been allowed to do when the pope was accepted as the supreme authority. To justify this action, the preamble of the act made a claim for the independence of England and the authority of the king that was typical of the new monarchs of the age.

"Where by divers sundry old authentic histories and chronicles it is manifestly declared that this realm of England is an empire, governed by one supreme head and king, having the dignity and royal estate of the imperial crown of the same, unto whom a body politic be bound and owe next to God a natural and humble obedience; he being also furnished by the goodness of Almighty God with whole and entire power, preeminence, authority, prerogative and jurisdiction to render justice and final determination in all causes, debates and contentions, without restraint to any foreign princes, [and] without the intermeddling of any exterior person, to declare and determine all such doubts. In consideration whereof the King's Highness, his Nobles and Commons, enact, establish and ordain that all causes, already commenced or hereafter coming into contention within this realm or within any of the King's dominions, whether they concern the King our sovereign lord or any other subject, shall be from henceforth heard, examined, discussed, finally and definitely adjudged and determined within the King's jurisdiction and authority and not elsewhere."

From 24 Henry VIII, c. 12, as printed in *Statutes of the Realm,* 11 vols. (London, 1810–1828), vol. III, pp. 427–429.

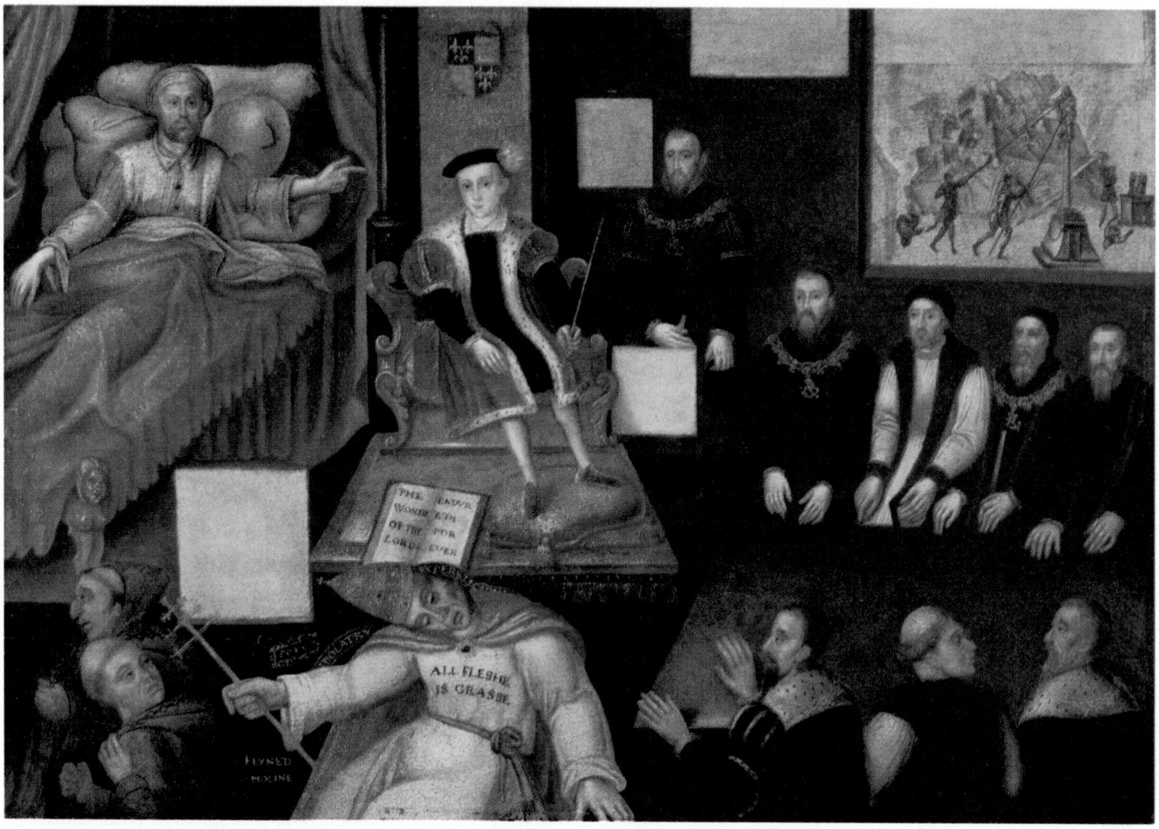

▸ *Unknown Artist*
Edward VI and the Pope
The anti-Catholic feelings that began to grow in England during the reign of Edward VI are expressed in this painting. The young king sits on his throne. His father, Henry VIII, who started the Reformation in England, points to him as the victor over Catholicism. The crushing of the old faith is symbolized by Christ's conquering of the pope and monks (below) and the destruction of Roman churches and images (through the window).

lish monasteries and confiscated their immensely valuable lands, which were sold over the next few decades. The result was that fortunes were made by speculators, and new families rose to prominence as major landowners.

For all the stimulus he gave to parliamentary power, Henry now had a much larger, wealthier, and more sophisticated administration at his disposal; and he left no doubt where ultimate authority lay. He did not establish a standing army, as some of the continental kings did, because he had no need for one. He was fully capable of intimidating ambitious nobles or crushing such uprisings as a 1536 revolt against the Reformation.

The English Church Where doctrine and the structure of the Church were concerned, Henry was a conservative; he allowed few changes in dogma or liturgy and seems to have hoped that he could simply continue the old ways, changing only the person at the head of the institution. He tried to restrain the spread of Reformation beliefs, which travelers and books brought into England from the continent, and he persecuted heresy. But it proved impossible to do no more than expel the papacy. Although many English men and women clung to tradition, others were drawn to the new religious ideas, and they pressured Henry to accept Protestant doctrines. Followers of the fourteenth-century reformer John Wycliffe, known as Lollards, had kept his ideas alive, and they now joined forces with Protestants inspired by continental reformers to demand services in English and easier access to Scripture. New translations of the Bible appeared in the 1530s, as did echoes of the opposition to clerical privilege that had swept Protestant areas on the continent. Perhaps realizing that the pressure would only grow, Henry had his son, Edward, tutored by a committed reformer.

Edward VI and Mary I During the reign of that son, Edward VI (1547–1553), who died while still a minor, the nobility attempted to regain control of the government. There was a relaxation of central authority, and the Reformation advanced rapidly. But Edward's half-sister, Mary I, reestablished Roman Catholicism as England's official religion when she became queen in 1553, forcing many of her subjects into exile and provoking two major revolts during her five-year reign. Royal power, however, was now strong enough to survive both the nobles' ambitions and the revolts. The revival of the nobles was short-lived, and Mary's death, in 1558, brought an end to the reversal of religions. She was succeeded by Henry VIII's last surviving child, Elizabeth, who demonstrated that the growth of the monarchy's authority had been but briefly interrupted under Edward and Mary.

VALOIS FRANCE

The rulers of France in the fifteenth century, unlike their English counterparts, lacked a well-formed organization for local government. Aristocrats dominated many regions, particularly those farthest from Paris, and great nobles had become virtually independent rulers. They had their own administrations and often their own courts and taxation, leaving the crown little say in their affairs. The size of the kingdom also placed restraints on royal power; it took more than a week to travel from Paris to the remoter parts of the realm—almost double the time for the equivalent English journey. Delays of this nature inevitably hampered central authority.

The monarchy had tried to resolve the problem of ruling distant provinces by granting to close relatives large blocs of territory that the crown seized or inherited. Theoretically, these relatives would devote full attention to their lands and execute royal wishes more effectively than the king could from Paris. In practice, however, an ambitious family member often became just as difficult to handle as any powerful noble. After 1469 the crown kept control over such acquisitions—an indication that it now had the resources to exercise authority even in areas far from the capital.

Royal Government The administrative center of the government in Paris was the royal council and its chief departments: the Chancery, which had charge of all formal documents, and the Treasury. The greatest court of law in the land was the Parlement of Paris, which had remained a judicial body, unlike the English Parliament, and whose members were appointed by the crown. As the central administration grew in the fifteenth and early sixteenth centuries, various provinces received their own parlements, a recognition of the continuing strength of the demand for local autonomy. But there was a countervailing force: the dominance of Roman law, which (unlike England's common law) was based on royal decree and which allowed the monarch to govern by issuing ordinances and edicts. These had to be registered by the parlements in order to take effect, but usually that was a formality.

Representative assemblies, known as Estates, also challenged the power of the throne. A number of provinces had such Estates, and they had to approve the level of taxation and other royal policies. But France's chief representative body, the Estates General—consisting of clergy, nobles, and townsmen from every region—never attained the prestige of the English Parliament and was never able to bind the country together or function as an essential organ of government.

For all the threats from nobles and assemblies, therefore, French kings had a degree of independence that English monarchs did not achieve, most notably in one critical area: finances. For centuries they had supplemented their main sources of income, from lands and customs duties, with special levies in the form of a sales tax (*aide*), a hearth tax (*taille*), and a salt tax (*gabelle*). Consequently the average French family that was subject to taxation (all nobles and many towns were exempt) usually bore a heavier burden than its English counterpart. In earlier days the consent of the localities had been required before such levies could be raised, but after 1451 the taxes could be collected on the king's authority alone, although he still had to negotiate the exact rate with provincial Estates and be careful not to go beyond what would seem reasonable to his subjects.

The Army The most decisive source of power available to the French king (unlike the English king) was his standing army. The upkeep of the troops accounted for more than half the royal expenditures in Louis XI's reign, mainly because their numbers grew as revenues increased. In the 1480s a force probably larger than 15,000 men, chiefly professional mercenaries and military-minded nobles, was held in permanent readiness every campaigning season from spring to fall. Because of the rising costs that were associated with the development of gunpowder weapons, only the central government could afford to maintain such an army. And the troops had to be billeted in various provinces, with support from the local Estates. As a result, the entire French population eventually bore the indirect burden of heavier taxation, while many regions of France had direct contact with royal soldiers. Although frequently short of pay, the troops were firmly under royal control and hence a vital device—rarely used, but always a threat—in the strengthening of royal authority.

LOUIS XI AND CHARLES VIII

When Louis XI (1461–1483) began his reign, he faced a situation as unpromising as that of Henry VII at his succession, for the country had just emerged from the Hundred Years' War and royal authority was generally ignored. English troops, which had been in France for most of the war, had finally departed in the 1450s; but a new and equally dangerous menace had arisen in the east: the conglomeration of territories assembled by successive dukes of Burgundy.

Burgundy By the 1460s this duke, though a vassal of the French crown in his southern holdings, was among the most powerful lords in Western Europe. He ruled a loosely organized dominion that stretched from the Low Countries to the Swiss Confederation, and his Burgundian capital, Dijon, had become a major cultural and political center. In 1474 Louis XI put together a coalition against Duke Charles the Bold, who had been at war with him for some seven years, and in 1477 Charles was killed in battle with the French king's Swiss allies. Louis then reannexed the duchy of Burgundy itself; but Mary, the duke's daughter, retained the Low Countries, which would later form part of the inheritance of her grandson, the Holy Roman Emperor Charles V.

Diplomacy The Burgundian lands added considerably to Louis' sphere of authority. His masterly maneuvering in the tortuous diplomacy of his day soon won him other territories; he was appropriately nicknamed "the Spider" because the prizes he caught in his web were the result of waiting or shrewd negotiation rather than victories on the battlefield. Such was the case at the beginning of his reign when, by a typical combination of force and fraud, he pried two provinces on his southern border away from Spain. Simple luck enlarged his realm as well: In 1481 he inherited the three large provinces of Anjou, Maine, and Provence. The result was that by the end of his reign, though government procedures had not noticeably changed, royal power had penetrated into massive areas where previously it had been unknown.

The Invasion of Italy Louis XI's son and successor, Charles VIII (1483–1498), was equally dedicated to increasing the territories under the Valois dynasty's command. In 1494, he led an army into Italy at the request of the duke of Milan, who was afraid of being attacked by Florence and Naples. After some initial successes the French settled into a prolonged struggle with the Habsburgs for control of the rich Italian peninsula. The conflicts lasted for 65 years, ending in defeat for the French. Although the Italian wars failed to satisfy the territorial ambitions of Charles and his successors, they provided an outlet and distraction for the restless French nobility and gave the monarchs, as commanders in time of war, an opportunity to consolidate royal power at home.

THE GROWTH OF GOVERNMENT POWER

After Charles VIII's reign, France's financial and administrative machinery grew in both size and

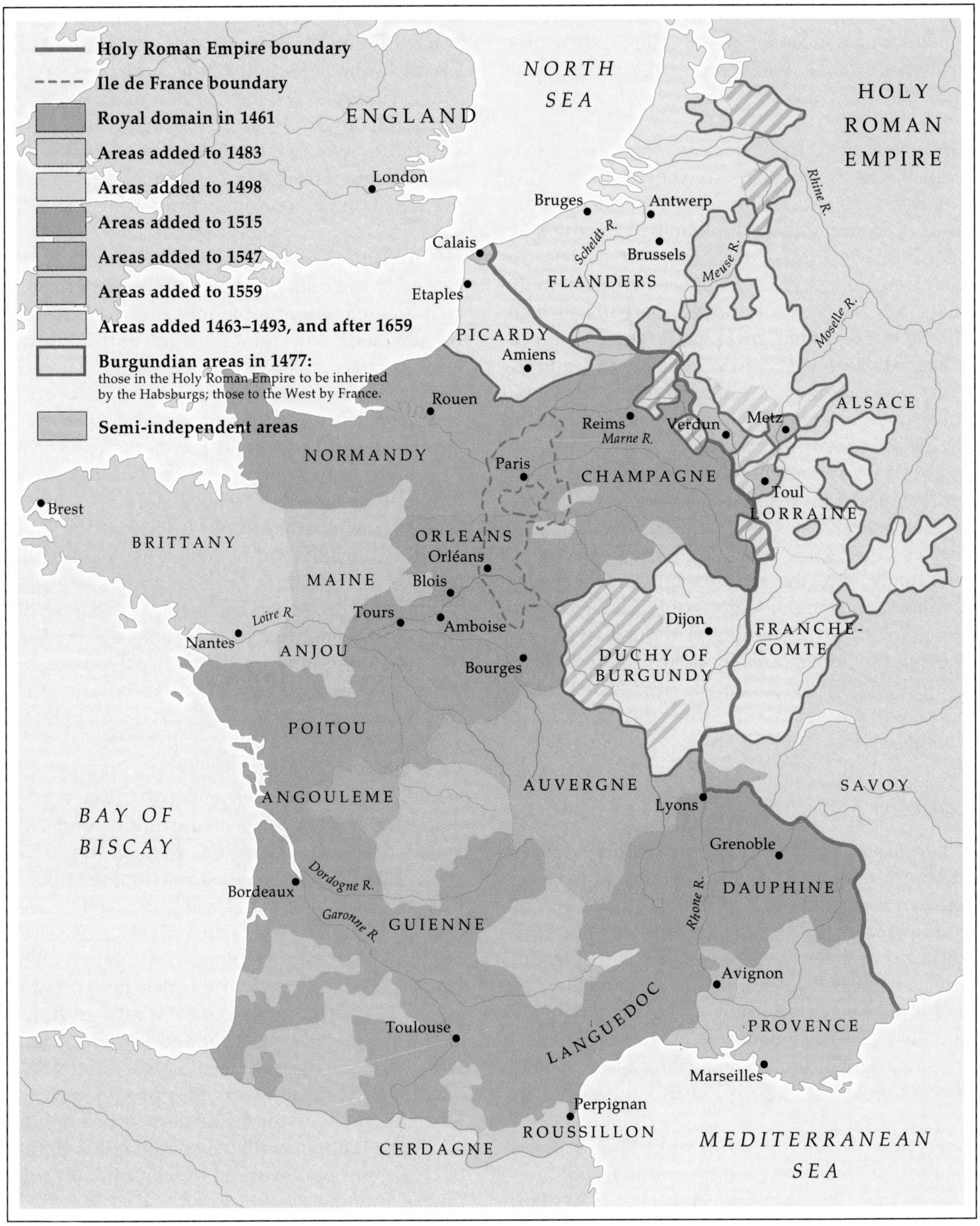

Map 14.3 FRANCE IN THE FIFTEENTH AND SIXTEENTH CENTURIES
This map shows in detail the successive stages whereby the monarchy extended its control throughout France.

effectiveness, largely because of the demands of the Italian wars. There was rarely enough money to support the adventure; the kings therefore relied heavily on loans from bankers, who sometimes shaped France's financial policies. At the same time, the crown made a determined effort to increase traditional royal revenues.

Taxes France was a rich country of 15 million people with the most fertile land in Europe; yet the financial needs of the monarch always outstripped his subjects' ability to pay. Nobles, many towns, royal officeholders, and the clergy were exempt from the *taille* and the *gabelle.* Thus the bulk of the taxes had to be raised from the very classes that had the least to give. Other means of raising revenue were therefore needed to supplement royal income. One solution was the sale of offices. Positions were sold in the administration, the parlements, and every branch of the bureaucracy to purchasers eager to obtain both the tax exemption and the considerable status (sometimes a title of nobility) that the offices bestowed. From modest and uncertain beginnings under Louis XII (1498–1515), the system widened steadily; by the end of the sixteenth century, the sale of offices provided the crown with one-twelfth of its revenues.

Many other rulers were adopting this device, and everywhere it had similar effects: It stimulated social mobility, creating dynasties of noble officeholders and a new administrative class; it caused a dramatic expansion of bureaucracies; and it encouraged corruption. The system spread most rapidly, and the effects were most noticeable in France, where the reign of Francis I (1515–1547) witnessed a major increase in the government's power as its servants multiplied. Francis tried hard to continue the expansion of royal control by launching expeditions into Italy, but in fact, he contributed more to the development of the crown's authority by his actions at home.

The Church One of the most remarkable of Francis' accomplishments was the power he gained over his formidable rival, the Church. He was highly successful in his Italian campaigns early in his reign, and he used the power he attained in Italy to persuade the pope in 1516 to give the crown the right to appoint all of France's bishops and abbots. According to this agreement, the income a bishop earned during his first year in office still went to the Vatican, but in effect, Francis now controlled the French Church. Its enormous patronage was at his disposal, and he could use it to reward servants or raise money. Since he had reached an agreement with the pope, he did not need to break with Rome in order to obtain the authority over the clergy that Henry VIII was soon to achieve in England.

▸ *Anonymous Miniature*
FRANCIS I AND HIS COURT, FROM THE MANUSCRIPT OF ANTOINE MACAULT'S TRANSLATION OF DIODORUS SICULUS, CA. 1532
The splendor and the patronage of learning for which the "new monarchs" were known are evoked by this tiny painting of the French king. He sits at a table with his three sons, surrounded by his courtiers and listening to the author reading the very manuscript (a translation of an ancient Greek historian) that this picture illustrates.

The Advance of Centralization In the 1520s Francis also began a major reorganization of the government. He legalized the sale of offices, and the purchasers gradually replaced local nobles as the administrators of the various regions of France. He also formed an inner council, more manageable than the large royal council, to act as the chief executive body of the realm. As part of this streamlining, in 1523 all tax-gathering and accounting responsibilities were centralized in one agency. Against the parlements, meanwhile, the king invoked the *lit de justice*, a prerogative that allowed him to appear in person before an assembly that was delaying the registration of any of his edicts or ordinances and declare them registered and therefore law. The Estates General was no threat because it did not meet between 1484 and 1560.

By the end of Francis' reign, royal power was stronger than ever before; but signs of disunity had begun to appear that would intensify in the years to come. The Reformation was making gains in the Holy Roman Empire, and one of its movements, Calvinism, was soon to cause religious divisions and social unrest in France. As the reign of Francis' son Henry II (1547–1559) came to a close, the Italian wars finally ended in a French defeat, badly damaging royal prestige. The civil wars that followed came perilously close to destroying all that France's kings had achieved during the previous 100 years.

UNITED SPAIN

The Iberian peninsula in the mid-fifteenth century was divided into three very different kingdoms. Portugal, with some 1.5 million inhabitants, was in the midst of its overseas expansion. Castile, in the center, with a population of more than 8 million, was the largest and richest area. Sheep farming was the basis of its prosperity, and its countryside was dominated by powerful nobles. Castile was the last kingdom still fighting Muslims on its southern frontier, and in this ceaseless crusade the nobles played a leading part. They had built up both a great chivalric tradition and considerable political strength as a result of their exploits, and their status was enhanced by the religious fervor that the long struggle had inspired. The third kingdom, Aragon, approximately the same size as Portugal, consisted of three areas: Catalonia, the heart of the kingdom and a great commercial region centered on the city of Barcelona; Aragon itself, which was little more than a barren hinterland to Catalonia; and Valencia, a farming and fishing region south of Catalonia along the Mediterranean coast.

In October 1469, Isabella, future queen of Castile, married Ferdinand, future king of Sicily and heir to the throne of Aragon. Realizing that the marriage would strengthen the crown, the Castilian nobles opposed the union, precipitating a 10-year civil war. But the two monarchs emerged victorious, and they created a new political entity: the Kingdom of Spain. They and their successors were to be as effective as the kings of England and France in centralizing power and establishing royal control over their realms.

FERDINAND AND ISABELLA

When Ferdinand and Isabella jointly assumed the thrones of Castile in 1474 and Aragon five years later, they made no attempt to create a monolithic state. Aragon remained a federation of territories, administered by viceroys who were appointed by the king but who allowed local customs to remain virtually intact. The traditions of governing by consent and preserving the subjects' rights were particularly strong in this kingdom, where each province had its own representative assembly, known as the Cortes. Ferdinand left the system untouched, but he did make the viceroys a permanent feature of the government and created a special council for Aragonese affairs, through which he controlled the kingdom. In Castile, however, the two monarchs were determined to assert their superiority over all possible rivals to their authority. Their immediate aims were to restore the order in the countryside that had been destroyed by civil war, much as it had been in England and France, and to reduce the power of the nobility.

The first objective was accomplished with the help of the Cortes of Castile, an assembly dominated by urban representatives who shared the wish for order because peace benefited trade. The Cortes established special tribunals to pursue and try criminals, and by the 1490s it had succeeded in ending the widespread lawlessness in the kingdom.

The Centralization of Power To reinforce their authority, Ferdinand and Isabella sharply reduced the number of great nobles in the royal council and overhauled the entire administration, particularly the financial agencies, applying the principle that ability, rather than social status, should determine appointments. As the bureaucracy spread, the *hidalgo*, a lesser aristocrat who was heavily dependent on royal favor, became increasingly important in government. Unlike the great nobles, whose enormous wealth was little affected by reforms that reduced their political role, the *hidalgos* were hurt when they lost their tax exemptions. The new livelihood they found was in the service of the crown, and they became essential figures in the centralization of power in Castile as well as in the overseas territories.

The monarchs achieved greater leverage over their nobles in the 1480s and 1490s, when they gained control of the aristocracy's rich and powerful military orders. These organizations, which served almost as independent armies, run by Castile's most important aristocratic families, gave allegiance primarily to their own elected leaders. To take over their leadership required assertiveness and determination, especially by Isabella, Castile's inherited ruler. At one point she rode on horseback for three straight days in order to get to one of the order's elections and control the outcome. The great nobles could not be subdued completely; nor did the king and queen wish to destroy their power, because they were essential servants of the crown, especially in the army and in the higher levels of government. But like the kings of England and France, Ferdinand and Isabella wanted to reduce the nobles' autonomy to a level that did not threaten central authority, and for that reason it was crucial that they overcame the independence of the military orders by 1500.

The Church The rulers also succeeded in weakening Spain's bishops and abbots, who were as strong and wealthy as leading nobles. When Ferdinand and Isabella finally destroyed the power of the Muslims in southern Castile in 1492, the pope granted the monarchy the right to make major ecclesiastical appointments in the newly won territory, and this right was extended to the New World shortly thereafter. During the reign of Ferdinand and Isabella's successor, Charles I, the monarchy gained complete control over Church appointments, making Spain more independent of Rome than any other Catholic state.

Royal Administration Mastery over the towns and the Cortes of Castile proved easy to achieve. Where local rule was concerned, a minor royal officials, the *corregidor*, was given new powers and a position of responsibility within the administrative hierarchy. He was usually a *hidalgo*, and he became the chief executive and judicial officer in his region, rather like the justice of the peace in England; he also supervised town affairs. No major local decisions, such as the number of soldiers to be sent to the army, could be made without his (and hence royal) approval. The Cortes did not seriously restrict the crown because Spanish taxes, like French, could be raised without consent. The Castilian assembly met frequently and even provided additional funds for foreign wars, but it never challenged royal supremacy during this reign.

The king and queen supervised the system of justice directly, hearing cases personally once a week. As was true of most Roman law systems, all law was considered to come from the throne, and the monarchs had full power to overrule the decisions of local courts, often run by nobles. Centralized judicial machinery began to appear, and in a few decades Castilian law was organized into a uniform code—always a landmark in the stabilization of a state. The code remained in effect for centuries and was a tribute to the determination and effectiveness with which the crown had centralized its dominions.

Revenues Considering the anarchy at the start of their reign and the absence of central institutions, Ferdinand and Isabella performed greater wonders in establishing royal power than did any of the other new monarchs. A good index of the effectiveness of their growing bureaucracy is the increase in their revenues. As soon as the main administrative reforms were completed in the 1490s, the yield of the sales tax (the *alcabala*), which was the mainstay of royal income, began to rise dramatically. Total annual revenue is estimated to have soared from 80,000 ducats in 1474 to 2.3 million by 1504, the year Isabella died.

Religion Religious affairs, too, helped in the consolidation of royal authority. After the civil wars in Castile ended in 1479, the two monarchs sought to drive the Muslims from southern Castile. The reasons for the aggressive policy were clear: First, it complemented the drive for centralized power; second, war was a traditional interest for ambitious rulers, and it helped keep restless nobles occupied; and finally, the crusade stimulated the country's religious fervor, which in turn promoted enthusiasm for its rulers.

The religious zeal aroused by the fight with the Muslims intensified Spaniards' loyalty toward their rulers, and it is not surprising that the monarchy sought religious uniformity as a means of strengthening political uniformity. Nor did the campaign come to an end when the last Muslim stronghold in the south, Granada, capitulated in 1492. Later that year, all Jews were expelled from Spain. Some 150,000 of the country's most enterprising people—including prominent doctors, government officials, and other leaders of economic and cultural life—departed overnight. For rulers who sought all means to win their subjects' loyalty, there was much to be gained by targeting a visible and often persecuted minority; it was a popular move, and it stimulated the religious passion that helped sustain the crown's authority. The campaign against the Jews thus went hand in hand with the other efforts to extend royal power.

The Inquisition The same drive to consolidate their strength had prompted Ferdinand and Isabella to obtain permission from the pope in 1478 to establish their own Inquisition. Since 1483 this body had been run by a royal council and given a mandate to root out Marranos and Moriscos—Jews and Muslims who, usually under coercion, had pretended to accept Christianity but, in fact, retained their original beliefs. After the fall of Granada, the Spanish Church attempted to convert the conquered Muslims, and in 1502 those who had not accepted Christianity were expelled from the country. Nonetheless suspected Moriscos and Marranos kept the Inquisition busy. The persecution welded the country into a religious unity that paralleled and supported the political centralization achieved by the monarchy. Religious policy was thus as much an instrument of political power as it was of ideological conformity.

FOREIGN AFFAIRS

The fall of Granada extended Spain's dominion southward, but there were also lands to be captured to the north and east. This undertaking was Ferdinand's responsibility, because men took command in war, and he focused on foreign affairs during the 12 years he ruled on his own after Isabella's death in 1504. His first success had come in 1493, when he regained the two provinces on the French border that Louis XI had taken 30 years before. Two years later, fearful that France's Italian invasion might threaten his Kingdom of Sicily, Ferdinand entered the war in Italy.

His achievements in the next two decades were due to a combination of military and diplomatic skills unusual even among the highly capable rulers of the age. A reorganization of Spain's standing army made it the most effective in Europe, and it soon achieved a commanding presence in Italy: By 1504 it had conquered Naples, and Spain had become a major power in the peninsula. Ferdinand also founded the finest diplomatic service of the sixteenth century, centered on five permanent embassies: at Rome, Venice, London, Brussels, and the Habsburg court. The ambassadors' reports and activities made him the best-informed and most effective maneuverer in the international politics of his reign.

Thus by the time of his death in 1516, the united Spain that he and Isabella created had gained both territory and authority at home and international power abroad. The successor to the throne inherited a monarchy fully as dynamic and as triumphant over its rivals as those of England and France.

CHARLES V, HOLY ROMAN EMPEROR

To bolster their dynasty, Ferdinand and Isabella had married their children to members of the leading families of Europe. Their daughter Joanna became the wife of the Habsburg Archduke Philip of Austria, and her son Charles became in turn heir to both the royal throne of Spain and the Habsburg dukedom.

The Revolt of the Communes Early in his reign as King of Spain, however, Charles (1516–1556) had to withstand a major onslaught on the crown's position. Educated in Flanders, he spoke no Castilian, and when he arrived in Spain late in 1517, he soon aroused the resentment of the local nobility, particularly when members of the large Flemish entourage he brought with him were given positions in the government. The young king stayed for two and a half years, during which time he was elected emperor of the Holy Roman Empire (1519). This enhanced his prestige, but it also intensified his subjects' fears that he would become an absentee ruler with little interest in their affairs. The Cortes, in particular, showed open hostility when Charles requested additional tax funds so that he could leave the country with Spanish troops to pursue his Europe-wide ambitions. As soon as he left in 1520, revolts began to break out in Spain's towns, and the risings of these communes racked the country for two years. The troubles Charles now endured were among the first of many major clashes during the next 150 years between the traditional dynastic aims of the leading European monarchs and the jealous sense of distinctiveness felt by their subjects.

Fortunately for the crown, the communes lacked clear aims; their resentments and hopes were deep but vague. They wanted to reverse the growth of royal power and to restore their traditional autonomy—a grievance that central governments were bound to encounter as they extended their authority. To this end, the communes asked for the removal of Flemish royal officials and a reduction in taxation, and at first they had the strong sympathy of the Spanish nobles, who particularly disliked the foreign ruler. But the movement soon revealed other aims, with social overtones: The communes launched attacks on the privileged orders of society, especially the nobility, and this lost the revolt its only chance for success. For the nobles now turned against the communes and defeated them in battle even before Charles returned to Spain.

Imperial Ambitions The king took warning from the uprisings and made sure that his administration was now kept entirely in Spanish hands. As calm returned, his subjects could channel their energies into imperial missions overseas, where the conquest of Mexico was under way, and against the Ottoman Turks in the Mediterranean. As in France, foreign excursions brought a monarch peace at home.

The one notable extension of royal power during Charles's reign was the large empire Spaniards were establishing in Central and South America. Closer to home, however, there was little that gave him or his Spanish subjects cause for pleasure. As Holy Roman Emperor, Charles was the official ruler of almost all of continental Europe west of Poland and the Balkans, with the major exception of France; and although his real power in the Empire was limited, he was almost ceaselessly at war defending his territories. In the Spaniards' view, most of the wars helped Charles's ambitions as emperor and were thus irrelevant to Spain. As far as they were concerned, aside from the widening acquisitions in the New World, Charles did little to further the expansion started by Ferdinand and Isabella.

Royal Government The recurrent crises and wars outside of Spain kept Charles away from his kingdom for more than two-thirds of his 40-year reign. He relied, during these absences, on a highly talented administrator, Francisco de los Cobos, who shaped and clarified the government's policies. De los Cobos confirmed the supremacy of the crown by enlarging the bureaucracy and elaborating the system of councils that Ferdinand and Isabella had begun. In the 1520s this structure, which was to survive for centuries, received its final form.

There were two types of council. One was responsible for each of the departments of the government: finance, war, the Inquisition, and so on. The other supervised each of the territories ruled by the crown: Aragon, Castile, Italy, the Indies, and (later in the century) the Low Countries. At the head of this system was the Council of State, the principal advisory group, consisting of leading officials from the lower councils. All these councils reported to the king or to his chief ministers, but since each one controlled its own bureaucracy, they were perfectly capable of running the empire in the monarch's absence.

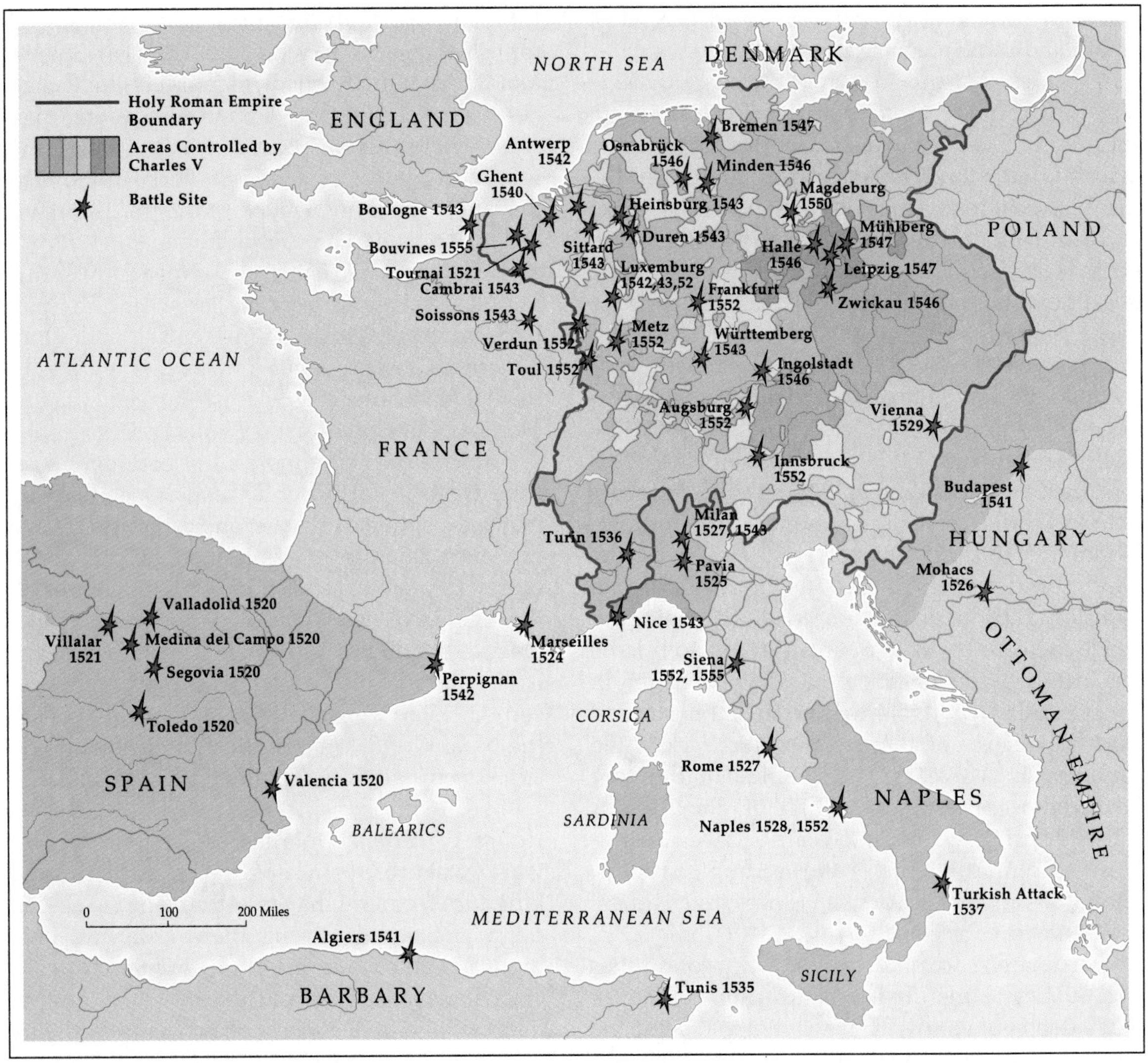

Map 14.4 THE EMPIRE OF CHARLES V
This map indicates both the vastness of Charles's empire and the extent of the fighting in which he became involved. Almost every battle his troops fought—against Spanish communes, German Protestants, the Turks, and the French—is included so as to show the full measure of the emperor's never-ending ordeal.

What emerged was a vast federation, with Castile at its heart but with the parts, though directed from the center, allowed considerable autonomy. A viceroy in every major area (there were nine altogether from Naples to Peru) ran the administration under the supervision of the *audiencia*—the territorial council—and while on the whole these officials were left to do as they wished, they had to report to Castile in minute detail at regular intervals and refer major decisions to the central government.

The Bureaucracy Although corruption was widespread and slow communications (it took over eight months to send a message from Castile to Peru) made the system unwieldy, the centralization gave the monarch the power he wanted. The huge bureaucracy was carefully staffed with *hidalgos* and townsmen, while great nobles were given viceroyalties or high army posts. Some local initiative was allowed, but through the hierarchy of loyal servants the crown could exercise full control. As a result, Spain's administrative machine was one of the most remarkably detailed (if not always efficient) structures ever devised for ruling so vast an empire.

THE FINANCIAL TOLL OF WAR

The only serious strain on Charles's monarchy was financial, the result of the Habsburgs' constant wars. A large portion of the money for the fighting came from Italy and the Low Countries, but Spain had to pay a growing share of the costs. During the sixteenth century, the Spaniards increasingly resented the siphoning away of their funds into foreign wars. It was the tragedy of their century of glory that so much of the fantastic wealth they discovered in South America was exported for hostilities that brought them little benefit.

The burden was by no means equally distributed. The more independent Cortes of Aragon was able to prevent substantial increases in taxation, which meant that Castile had to assume the brunt of the payments. To some extent this was balanced by a monopoly of trade with the New World that was granted to the inhabitants of Castile, but in the next century the basic inequality among different Spanish regions would lead to civil war.

New World Trade Charles's finances were saved from disaster only by the influx of treasure—mainly silver—from America. Approximately 40 percent of the bullion went into the royal coffers, while the rest was taken by merchants (mainly Genoese) in the Castilian port of Seville, which was the only city where ships carrying goods to and from America were permitted to load and unload. Charles was receiving some 800,000 ducats' worth of treasure each year by the end of his reign. Unfortunately, it was always mortgaged in advance to the Italian and German bankers whose loans sustained his armies.

The country and the monarchy faced increasing difficulties as the wars continued for more than a century and a half. Seville's monopoly on shipping prevented the rest of the nation from gaining a share of the new wealth, and foreigners—notably the Italian and German financiers—came to dominate its economy and its commerce. Spain was squeezed dry by the king's financial demands, yet he only just kept his head above water. In 1557, early in the reign of Charles's successor, Philip II, the monarchy had to declare itself bankrupt, a self-defeating evasion of its mammoth debts that it had to repeat seven times in the next 125 years. There has never been a better example of the way that ceaseless war can sap the strength of even the most formidable nation.

IV. The Splintered States

THE HOLY ROMAN EMPIRE

If in England, France, and Spain the authority of kings had begun to replace that of the local lord, to the east of these three kingdoms such centralization advanced fitfully and only within small states. Especially in the largest of these territories, the Holy Roman Empire, weak institutions prevented the emergence of a strong central government. Members of the leading family of Central Europe, the Habsburgs, had been elected to the imperial throne since the thirteenth century, but they lacked the authority and machinery to halt the fragmentation of this large territory; indeed, except for their own personal domain in the southeast of the empire, they ruled most areas and princes in name only. In addition to about 2000 imperial knights, some of whom owned no more than four or five acres, there were 50 ecclesiastical and 30 secular princes, more than 100 counts, some 70 prelates, and 66 cities, all virtually independent politically though officially subordinate to the emperor.

Local Independence The princes, whose territories comprised most of the area of the Holy Roman Empire, rarely had any trouble resisting the emperor's claims; their main concern was to increase their own power at the expense of their subjects, other princes, and the cities. The cities themselves also refused to remain subordinate to a central government. In 1500, 50 of them contained more than 2000 inhabitants—a sizable number for this time—and 20 had over 10,000. Their wealth was substantial because many were situated along a densely traveled trade artery, the

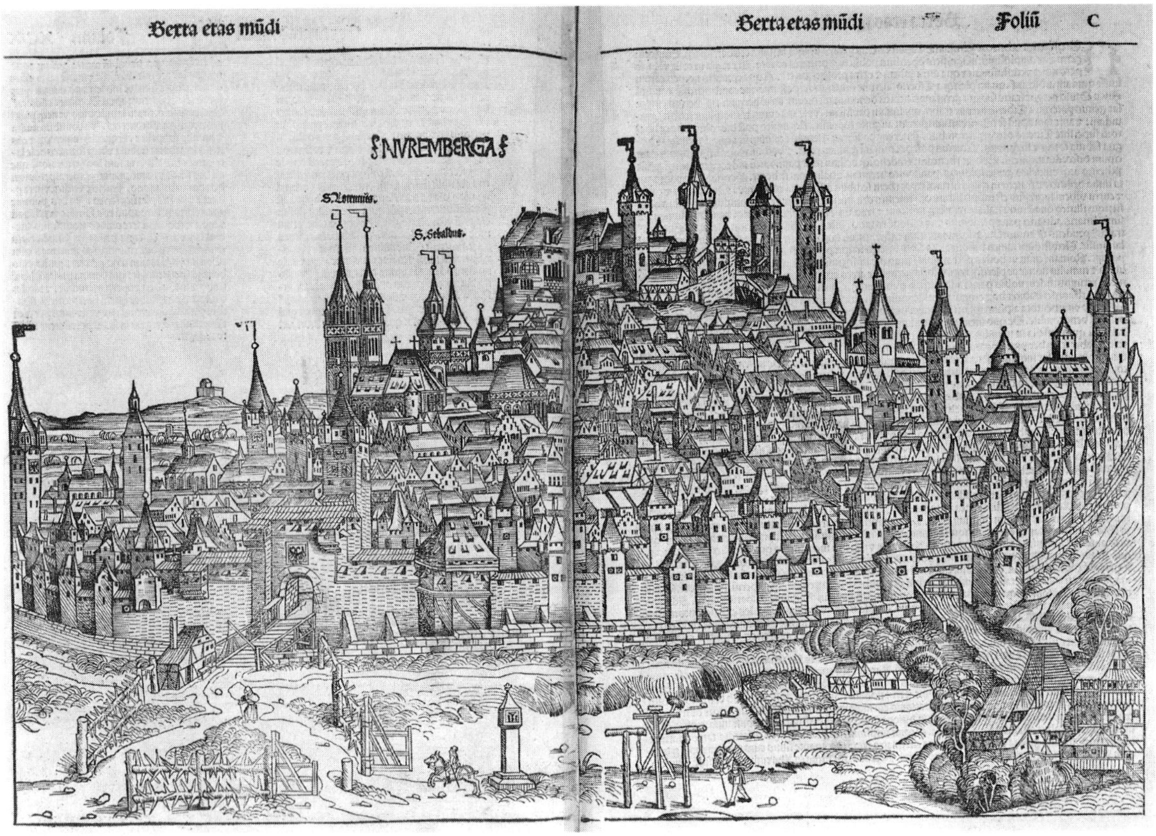

▶ *Hartmann Schedel*
The Nuremberg Chronicle, 1493
This lavishly illustrated book, a history of the world since the creation, is one of the earliest masterpieces of the printer's art. It took about four years to produce and contains dozens of elaborate woodcuts, most of which are recognizable views of European cities. This one depicts the proud and independent German city where the book was printed, Nuremberg, a major center of art and craftsmanship.

Rhine River, and many were also political powers. But their fierce independence meant that the emperor could rarely tap their wealth or the services of their inhabitants.

The only central institution alongside the emperor was the Diet, which consisted of three assemblies: representatives of the cities, the princes, and the electors (the seven princes, including three archbishops, who elected each new emperor). Given this makeup, the Diet became in effect the instrument of the princes; with its legislation they secured their position against the cities and the lesser nobility within their own domains.

By the end of the fifteenth century, most of the princes had achieved considerable control over their own territories. Their success paralleled the accomplishments of monarchs in England, France, and Spain except that the units were much smaller. Although the Habsburgs tried to develop strong central authority, they exercised significant control only over their personal domain, which in 1500 consisted of Austria, the Low Countries, and Franche-Comté. To the rulers of other states of the empire, they were feudal overlords in theory but powerless in practice.

Attempts at Centralization Nevertheless, the need for effective central institutions was recognized in the late fifteenth century, especially in the west and southwest of the Holy Roman Empire. In 1495 the emperor created a tribunal to settle disputes between local powers. Controlled and financed by the princes, the chief beneficiaries of its work, it made considerable headway toward ending the lawlessness that had marked the fifteenth century—an achievement similar to the restoration of order in France, Spain, and England at the same time. The tribunal's use of Roman law had a wide influence on legislation and justice throughout the empire, but again only to the advantage of the princes, who interpreted its endorsement of a leader's authority as referring only to themselves.

Other attempts at administrative reform had little effect, as ecclesiastical and secular princes tightened their hold on the multitude of territories that constituted the empire. The religious dissensions of the Reformation worsened the rivalries, dividing the empire and making Charles V no more than the leader of one party, incapable of asserting his authority over his opponents. The sheer number of Charles's commitments repeatedly diverted him, but even when he won decisive military victories, he could not break the empire's long tradition of local independence. His dream had been to revive the sweeping imperial grandeur of an Augustus or a Charlemagne, and his failure brought to an end the thousand-year ambition to restore in Europe the power of ancient Rome.

▶ *Titian*
CHARLES V AT THE BATTLE OF MÜHLBERG, 1548
Because a statue of an ancient Roman emperor showed him in this pose, it was thought in the sixteenth century that a ruler appeared at his most magnificent on a horse and in full armor. Equestrian sculptures appeared in the fifteenth century, but this portrait is the first such painting. Titian created a heroic Charles V, even though the emperor had not been present at the military victory of the previous year that the picture celebrates.

▶ *Christoph Paudiss*
PEASANTS IN A HUT
The sadness in the eyes of these two figures, even in a relaxed moment—the old man smoking a pipe, the boy playing the bagpipes—reflects the hardships of the peasants who were at the lowest level of European society and in eastern Europe were bound to the land as serfs.

EASTERN EUROPE

Hungary In the late fifteenth century, the dominant force in Eastern and Central Europe was the Kingdom of Hungary, ruled by Matthias Corvinus (1458–1490). He was in the mold of the other new monarchs of the day: He restrained the great nobles, expanded and centralized his administration, dramatically increased the yield of taxation, and established a standing army. The king's power thus grew spectacularly both at home and abroad. He gained Bohemia and some German and Austrian lands, and he made Vienna his capital in 1485.

Immediately after Matthias' death, however, royal authority collapsed. To gain Habsburg recognition of his right to the throne, his successor Ladislas II (1490–1516) gave up the conquests of Austrian and German territories and married his children to Habsburgs. This retreat provided the nobles of Hungary with an issue over which to reassert their position. First, by refusing the king essential financial support, they forced him to dissolve the standing army. Then, following a major peasant revolt against increasing repression by landowners, the nobles imposed serfdom on all peasants in 1514 at a meeting of the Hungarian Diet, the governing body, which was controlled by the aristocracy. Finally, they became the major beneficiaries of the conquest of Hungary by the Ottoman Empire over the next 30 years. That empire always supported any local leader who promised allegiance to Constantinople; by affirming loyalty to their new masters, the nobles were able to strengthen their power at the expense of both the old monarchy and the peasantry. By the middle of the sixteenth century, a revival of central authority had become impossible.

The Fragmentation of Poland Royal power in Poland began to decline in the 1490s, when the king was forced to rely on the lesser nobles to help him against the greater nobility. In return, he issued a statute in 1496 that strengthened the lower aristocrats against those below them, the townsmen and the peasants. The latter became virtual serfs, forbidden to buy land and deprived of freedom of movement. Once that was accomplished, the nobles united against the king. In 1505 the national Diet, consisting only of nobles, was made the supreme body of the land, and shortly thereafter it established serfdom officially. Since no law could now be passed without the Diet's consent, the crown's central authority was severely limited.

Royal and noble patronage produced a great cultural flowering around 1500 in Poland, which became an active center of Renaissance humanism and scholarship, most famously represented by the astronomer Nicolaus Copernicus. Yet the monarchy was losing influence steadily, as was revealed by the failure of its attempts to found a standing army. At the end of Sigismund II's reign (1548–1572), his kingdom was the largest in Europe; but his death ended the Jagellon dynasty, which had ruled the country for centuries. The Diet immediately made sure that succession to the crown, which technically had always been elective and in the hands of the nobles, would now depend entirely on their approval. Thus the aristocracy confirmed both its own dominance and the ineffectiveness of royal authority.

The Aristocracy The political and social processes at work in Eastern and Central Europe thus contrasted starkly with developments in England, France, and Spain in this period. Nevertheless, although the trend was toward fragmentation in the East, one class, the aristocracy, did share the vigor and organizational ability that in the West was displayed by kings and queens. To that extent, therefore, the sense of renewed vitality in Europe during these years, spurred by economic and demographic growth, was also visible outside the borders of the new monarchies. But where nobles dominated, countries lost ground in the fierce competition of international affairs.

The Ottomans Only in one state in Eastern Europe was strong central authority maintained in the sixteenth century: the Ottoman Empire. From his capital in Constantinople the sultan exercised unparalleled powers throughout the eastern Mediterranean and North Africa. He had a crack army of more than 25,000 men, who stood ready to serve him at all times, and within his domains his supremacy was unquestioned. He was both spiritual and temporal head of his empire, completely free to appoint all officers, issue laws, and raise taxes. But these powers, geared to military conquest and extending over enormous territories, never became a focus of cohesion among the disparate races of the Balkans, the Middle East, and North Africa, because the sultan left authority in the hands of local nobles and princes as long as his ultimate sovereignty was recognized. Whenever questions of loyalty arose (as they did sporadically in the Balkans), they revealed that the authority of the central government rested on its military might. That was more than enough, though, to prevent any serious challenges to the power of the Ottomans until they began to lose ground to the Habsburgs in the eighteenth century.

The first signs of weakening at the center began to appear after the death in 1566 of the sultan whose conquests brought the empire to its largest size, Suleiman the Great. Suleiman had gained control of the Balkans with a victory at Mohacs in 1526, and he had even briefly laid siege to Vienna in 1529. Under his successors, the determined exercise of authority that had marked his rule began to decline; and harem intrigues, corruption at court, and the loosening of military discipline became increasingly serious. Yet the Ottomans remained an object of fear and hostility throughout the West—a constant threat to Central Europe from the Balkans and, despite naval setbacks, a formidable force in the eastern Mediterranean.

ITALY

Italy, the cultural and economic leader of Europe, had developed a unique political structure during the Renaissance. In the fifteenth century the five major states—Naples, the Papal States, Milan, Florence, and Venice—established a balance among themselves that was preserved without serious disruption from the 1450s to the 1490s. This long period of peace was finally broken in 1494, when Milan, abandoning a long tradition of the Italians settling problems among themselves, asked Charles VIII of France to help protect it against Florence and Naples. Thus began the Italian wars, which soon revealed that these relatively small territories were totally incapable of resisting the force that newly assertive monarchies could bring to bear.

Venice and Florence had long been regarded by Europeans as model republics—reincarnations of Classical city-states and centers of freedom governed with the consent of their citizens. In truth, Venice was controlled by a small merchant oligarchy and Florence by the Medici family, but the image of republican virtue was still widely accepted. Indeed, the political stability Venice had maintained for centuries was the envy of Europe. Tourists came not only to enjoy its many relaxations and entertainments but also

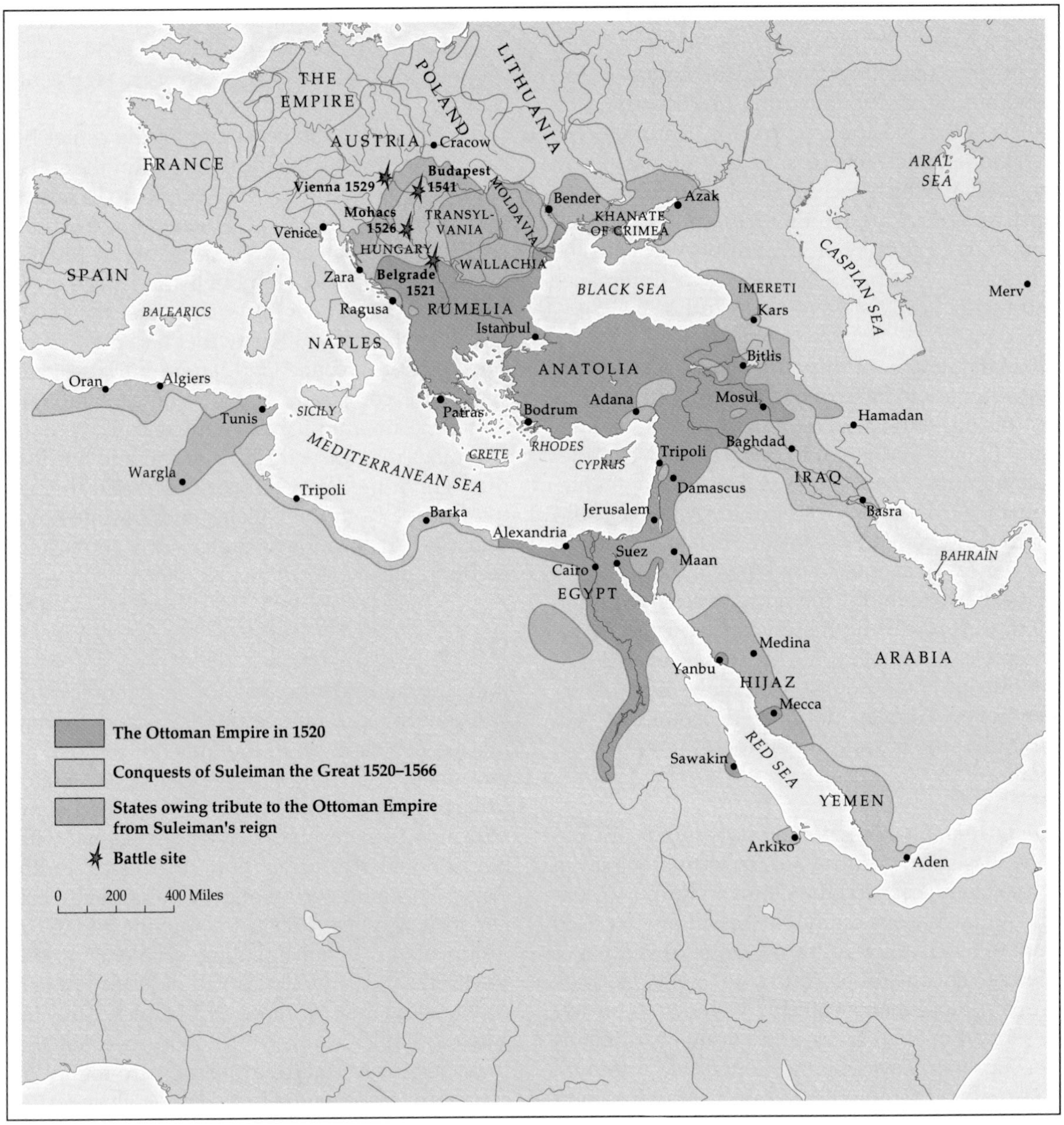

Map 14.5 THE GROWTH OF THE OTTOMAN EMPIRE UNDER SULEIMAN THE GREAT, 1520–1566
The remarkable conquests of the Ottomans in North Africa, the Middle East, and the Balkans terrified the rulers of Central and Eastern Europe. Only the failure of the siege of Vienna in 1529 halted the advance into Europe.

to marvel at the institutions that kept the city calm, powerful, and rich. Venice's leaders, elegant patricians who patronized some of the most sought-after artists of the sixteenth century, such as Titian, were thought of as the heirs of Roman senators. Throughout Europe, the Italians were regarded as masters not only of politics but also of culture and manners.

► *Titian*
THE VENDRAMIN FAMILY, 1547
The magnificence of the patrician families who ruled Venice is celebrated in this group portrait. Ostensibly, they are worshiping a relic of the true cross, but in fact they are displaying the hierarchy that rules their lives. Only men appear, dominated by the head of the family and his aged father, followed by his eldest son and heir, all of whom convey an image of wealth and power.

The Italian Wars It was a considerable shock, therefore, when the Italian states crumbled before the onslaught of French and then Spanish and Habsburg armies. Charles VIII's invasion led to the expulsion of the Medici from Florence in 1494 and the establishment of a new Florentine republic, but in 1512 the family engineered a return to power with the help of Ferdinand of Aragon, and eventually the Habsburgs set up the Medici as hereditary dukes of Tuscany. Ferdinand annexed Naples in 1504, and Emperor Charles V ultimately took over Milan. When the fighting ended in 1559, the Habsburgs controlled Italy and would do so for the next century. Only Venice, Tuscany under the Medici, and the Papal States remained relatively independent—though Venice was no longer a force in European affairs after a series of defeats. The one major local beneficiary of the Italian wars was the papacy, as Julius II (1503–1513), known as the Warrior Pope, carved out a new papal territory in central and eastern Italy by force of arms.

The critical lesson of these disastrous events was that small political units could not survive in an age when governments were consolidating their authority in large kingdoms. No matter how brilliant and sophisticated, a compact city-state could not withstand such superior force. Italy's cultural and economic prominence faded only slowly, but by the mid-sixteenth century, except for the papacy, the international standing of its states was fading.

V. The New Statecraft

INTERNATIONAL RELATIONS

The Italian states of the fifteenth century, in their intensive political struggles and competition with one another, developed various new ways of pursuing foreign policy. During the Italian wars these techniques spread throughout Europe and caused a revolution in diplomacy. Any state hoping to play a prominent role in international affairs worked under a serious disadvantage if it did not conform. The Italians' essential innovation was the resident ambassador. Previously rulers had dispatched ambassadors to other states only for specific missions, such as to arrange an alliance, declare war, or deliver a message; but from the sixteenth century on, important states maintained representatives in every major capital or court at all times. The permanent ambassador could keep the home government informed of the latest local and international developments and could also move without delay to protect his country's interests. The Venetians, in particular, were masters of the new diplomacy. Leading patricians served as ambassadors, and they sent home brilliant political analyses that have remained crucial sources for historians ever since.

The New Diplomacy As states established embassies, procedures and organization became more sophisticated: A primitive system of diplomatic immunities (including freedom from prosecution for ambassadors and their households) evolved, formal protocol developed, and embassy officials were assigned different levels of responsibility and importance. Many advances were still to come, but by 1550 the outlines of the new diplomacy were already visible—yet another reflection of the growing powers and ambitions of central governments.

The great dividing line between older arrangements and the new diplomacy was the Italian wars, a Europe-wide crisis that involved rulers as distant as the English King Henry VIII and the Ottoman Sultan Suleiman II. Gradually all states recognized that it was in everybody's interest not to allow one power to dominate the rest. In later years this prevention of excessive aggression was to be known as the balance of power, but by the mid-sixteenth century the idea was already affecting alliances and peace treaties.

MACHIAVELLI AND GUICCIARDINI

As the Italian wars unfolded, political commentators began to seek theoretical explanations for the new authority and aggressiveness of rulers and the collapse of the Italian city-states. Turning from arguments based on divine will or contractual law, they treated effective government as an end in itself. The first full expression of these views came from the Italians, the pioneers of the methods and attitudes that were revolutionizing politics. When their small states proved unable to resist the superior forces of France and Spain, just as the ancient Greek city-states had succumbed to Macedonia and then to Rome, the Italians naturally wanted to find out why. The most disturbing answer was given by an experienced diplomat, Niccolò Machiavelli, who was exiled when the Medici took control of Florence in 1512. Barred from politics and bitter over the collapse of Italy, he set about analyzing exactly how power is won, exercised, and lost.

Machiavelli The result, *The Prince*, is one of the few radically original books in history. To move from his predecessors to Machiavelli is to see legal and moral thought transformed. Machiavelli swept away conventions as he sought, in an age of collapsing regimes, to understand how states function and how they affect their subjects. If he came out of any tradition, it was the Renaissance fascination with method that had produced manuals on cooking, dancing, fencing, and manners. But he wrote about method in an area that had never previously been analyzed in this way: power.

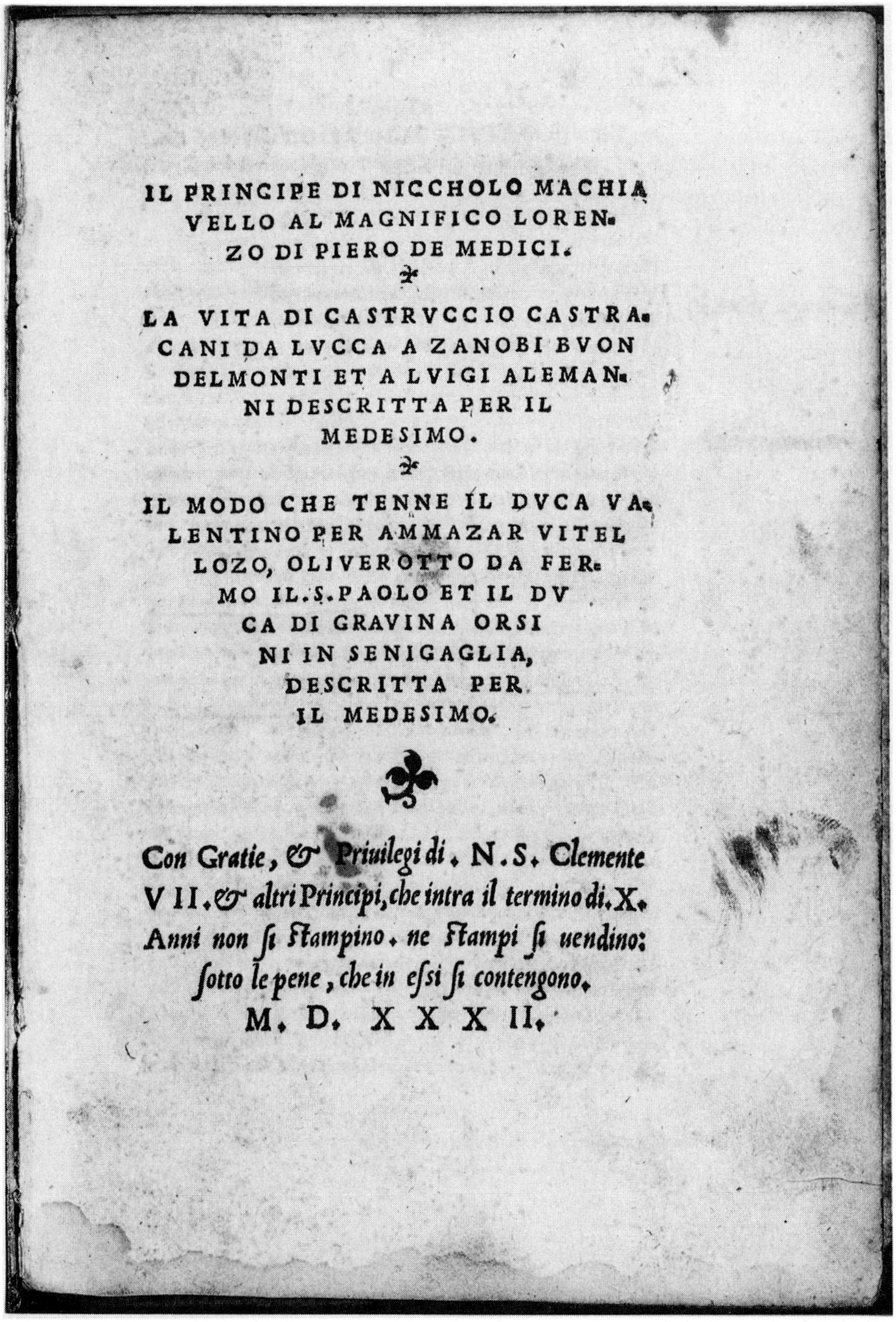

IL PRINCIPE DI NICCHOLO MACHIA
VELLO AL MAGNIFICO LOREN.
ZO DI PIERO DE MEDICI.

LA VITA DI CASTRVCCIO CASTRA.
CANI DA LVCCA A ZANOBI BVON
DELMONTI ET A LVIGI ALEMAN.
NI DESCRITTA PER IL
MEDESIMO.

IL MODO CHE TENNE IL DVCA VA.
LENTINO PER AMMAZAR VITEL
LOZO, OLIVEROTTO DA FER.
MO IL.S.PAOLO ET IL DV
CA DI GRAVINA ORSI
NI IN SENIGAGLIA,
DESCRITTA PER
IL MEDESIMO.

Con Gratie, & Priuilegi di. N.S. Clemente
VII. & altri Principi, che intra il termino di. X.
Anni non si stampino. ne stampi si uendino:
sotto le pene, che in essi si contengono.
M. D. X X X II.

▶ TITLE PAGE OF THE FIRST EDITION OF NICCOLÒ MACHIAVELLI'S THE PRINCE, 1532
This deceptively simple and elegant title page begins the brief but revolutionary book by which Machiavelli is usually remembered. It remained unpublished for nearly 20 years after it was written (and for 5 years after its author's death), probably because of concern over the stir it would cause. And indeed, within 25 years of appearing in print, *The Prince* was deemed sufficiently ungodly to be added to the index of books that Catholics were forbidden to read.

Machiavelli showed not why power does or should exist but how it works. In the form of advice to a prince and without reference to divine, legal, or natural justification, the book explains what a ruler needs to do to win and maintain complete control over his subjects. Machiavelli did not deny the force of religion or law; what concerned him was how they ought to be *used* in the tactics of governing—religion for molding unity and contentment, and devotion to law for building the ruler's reputation as a fair-minded person. *The Prince* outlines the methods to be used by conquerors or legitimate heirs, as well as the proper ways to deal with insurrection and the many other problems that rulers encounter. Fear and respect are the bases of their authority, and they must exercise care at all times not to relax their control over potential troublemakers or over their image among the people.

Very few contemporaries of Machiavelli dared openly to accept so harsh a view of politics, but he did not hesitate to expand his analysis in his other masterpiece, the *Discourses*. This book developed a cyclical theory of every government moving inexorably from tyranny to democracy and back again. His conclusion, drawn particularly from a study of Roman history, is that healthy government can be preserved only by the active participation of all citizens in the life of the state. And the state in turn, he suggested, is the force that keeps people civilized. As he put it in the *Discourses*, "Men act rightly only when compelled. The law makes men good." But there were better and worse states. Machiavelli took the Roman Republic as his ideal, and it was this model, together with his Italian patriotism (rather than his cynicism), that was largely responsible for his long-lasting influence on European political thought.

Guicciardini The *History of Italy*, written in the 1530s by another Florentine, Francesco Guicciardini, was the first major work of history to rely heavily on original documents rather than secondhand accounts. If the conclusions he reached seem dauntingly cynical—he attributed even less to underlying historical forces than did Machiavelli, and like Thucydides, he argued dispassionately that fate determines everything—the reasons for his pessimism are not far to seek. The actions of rulers during his generation hardly gave much room for optimism, and shrewd observers like Machiavelli and Guicciardini must therefore have found it difficult to avoid pessimism about public events.

It was appropriate that the political theorists of the sixteenth century should have emphasized the obsession with power that dominated the age in which they lived. The relentless pragmatism and ambition of kings and princes as they extended their authority both at home and abroad reshaped institutions and governments throughout Europe. Given the assertiveness of these rulers and the rising fanaticism generated by religious dispute, it is not surprising that there should have begun in the mid-sixteenth century a series of wars of a ferocity and destructiveness that Europe had never before seen.

Recommended Reading

Sources

*Guicciardini, Francesco. *The History of Italy and Other Selected Writings.* Cecil Grayson (tr.). 1964.

*Machiavelli, Niccolò. *The Prince* and the *Discourses.* Luigi Ricci (tr.). 1950.

*Parry, J. H. (ed.). *The European Reconnaissance: Selected Documents.* 1968.

Studies

Bonney, Richard. *The European Dynastic States 1494–1660.* 1991. An excellent overview.

Cipolla, Carlo M. *Guns, Sails, and Empires: Technological Innovation and the Early Phases of European Expansion 1400–1700.* 1965. This is a lively study of the reasons the expansion succeeded, with particular emphasis on weaponry.

*Crosby, Alfred W. *The Columbian Exchange: Biological and Cultural Consequences of 1492.* 1972. A fascinating study of plants, diseases, and other exchanges between the Old World and the New World.

*Elliott, J. H. *The Old World and the New 1492–1650.* 1970. A survey of the impact on Europe of the overseas discoveries.

Gilbert, Felix. *Machiavelli and Guicciardini: Politics and History in Sixteenth-Century Florence.* 1965. The standard account of the birth of new ideas in political theory and history.

*Jeannin, Pierre. *Merchants of the 16th Century.* Paul Fittingoff (tr.). 1972. A lucid introduction to sixteenth-century economic life.

*Kamen, Henry. *Spain 1469–1714: A Society of Conflict.* 1983. A clear and compact survey that gives a comprehensive account of Spanish history.

*Knecht, R. J. *French Renaissance Monarchy: Francis I & Henry II.* 1984. A lively introduction, with illustrative documents, to the development of governmental powers in France in the sixteenth century.

———, *Renaissance Warrior and Patron: The Reign of Francis I.* 1994.

*Mattingly, Garrett. *Renaissance Diplomacy.* 1971. An elegant account of the changes that began in international relations during the fifteenth century.

*Rady, Martin. *The Emperor Charles V.* 1988. An excellent overview, with illustrative documents, of the reign of the most powerful ruler in Europe.

*Rice, Eugene F., Jr. *The Foundations of Early Modern Europe, 1460–1559.* 1970. One of the best short surveys of the period, with three pages of suggested readings.

Scammell, G. V. *The First Imperial Age: European Overseas Expansion c. 1400–1715.* 1989. The best recent survey.

Scarisbrick, J. J. *Henry VIII.* 1968. A detailed but vivid biography of one of the most forceful of the new monarchs.

*Skinner, Quentin. *Machiavelli.* 1981. An excellent brief introduction to the man and his thought.

Strauss, Gerald. *Law, Resistance and the State.* 1986. A suggestive exploration of the development of legal and political thought.

Wilford, John Noble. *The Mysterious History of Columbus: An Exploration of the Man, the Myth, the Legacy.* 1991. A judicious account, both of Columbus' career and of the ways it has been interpreted.

*Williams, Penry. *The Tudor Regime.* 1981. The most recent comprehensive assessment of the workings of England's government.

*Wrigley, E. A. *Population and History.* 1969. An introduction to the methods and findings of historical demography by one of the pioneers of the field.

*Available in paperback.

Francois Dubois
THE MASSACRE OF ST. BARTHOLOMEW'S DAY
Although it makes no attempt to depict the massacre realistically, this painting by a Protestant does convey the horrors of religious war. As the victims are hanged, disemboweled, decapitated, tossed from windows, bludgeoned, shot, or drowned, their bodies and homes are looted. Dubois may have intended the figure dressed in widow's black, and pointing at a pile of corpses near the river at the back, to be a portrait of Catherine de Medici, who many thought inspired the massacre.

CHAPTER FIFTEEN

WAR AND CRISIS

IN the wake of the rapid and bewildering changes of the early sixteenth century—the Reformation, the rises in population and prices, the overseas discoveries, and the dislocations caused by the activities of the new monarchs—Europe entered a period of fierce upheaval. Such radical alterations were taking place in so many elements of society that conflict became inevitable. Many people, often led by nobles who saw their power dwindling, revolted against their monarchs. The poor launched hopeless rebellions against their social superiors. And the two religious camps struggled relentlessly to destroy each other. From Scotland to Russia, the century following the Reformation, from about 1560 to 1660, was dominated by warfare; and the constant military activity had widespread effects on politics, economics, society, and thought. The fighting was, in fact, a crucial element in the long and painful process whereby Europeans came to terms with the revolutions that had begun about 1500. Almost imperceptibly, fundamental economic, political, social, and religious changes took root; and troubled Europeans found ways to accept their altered circumstances.

I. Wars of Religion in the Age of Philip II

Although many other issues were involved in the wars that plagued Europe from the 1560s to the 1650s, religion was the burning motivation, the one that inspired fanatical devotion and the most vicious hatred. A deep conviction that heresy was dangerous to society and hateful to God made Protestants and Catholics treat one another brutally. Even the dead were not spared: Corpses were sometimes mutilated to emphasize how dreadful their sins had been. These emotions gave the fighting a brutality and a relentlessness that was unprecedented in European history.

National Gallery, London

▶ *El Greco*
THE DREAM OF PHILIP II, 1578
Characteristic of the mystical vision of El Greco is this portrayal of the devout, black-clad figure of Philip II. Kneeling alongside the doge of Venice and the pope, his allies in the victory of Lepanto over the Turks, Philip adores the blazing name of Jesus that is surrounded by angels in heaven, and he turns his back on the gaping mouth to hell.

THE CRUSADES OF PHILIP II

During the second half of the sixteenth century, international warfare was ignited by the leader of the Catholics, Philip II of Spain (1556–1598), the most powerful monarch in Europe. He ruled the Iberian peninsula, much of Italy, the Netherlands, and a huge overseas empire; but his main obsessions were the two enemies of his church, the Muslims and the Protestants. Against the Muslims in the Mediterranean area, Philip's campaigns seemed to justify the financial strains they caused. In particular, his naval victory at Lepanto, off the Greek coast, in 1571 made him a Christian hero at the same time as it reduced Muslim power. But elsewhere he fared less well.

Philip tried to prevent a Protestant, Henry IV, from succeeding to the French crown, and after he failed, he continued to back the losing side in France's civil wars even though Henry converted to Catholicism. Spain's policy toward England was similarly ineffective. After the Protestant Queen Elizabeth I came to the throne in 1558, Philip remained uneasily cordial toward her for about 10 years. But relations deteriorated as England's sailors and explorers threatened Philip's wealthy New World possessions. Worse, in 1585 Elizabeth began to help the Protestant Dutch who were rebelling against Spanish rule.

The Armada Philip decided to end all these troubles with one mighty blow: In 1588 he sent a mammoth fleet—the Armada—to the Low Countries to pick up a Spanish army, invade England, and crush his Protestant enemies. By this time, however, English mariners were among the

▸ *Anonymous*
THE ARMADA
This depiction suggests the sheer splendor of the scene as Philip II's fleet sailed through the channel on its way to invading England. The opposing ships were never this close, but the colorful flags (red cross English, yellow cross Spanish) and the elaborate coats of arms must have been dazzling. The firing cannon and the sinking ship remind us that, amidst the display, there was also death and destruction.

best in the world; and their ships, which had greater maneuverability and fire power than the Spaniards', made up in tactical superiority what they lacked in size. After several skirmishes, the English set fire to a few of their own vessels with loaded cannons aboard and sent them drifting toward the Spanish ships, anchored off Calais. The Spaniards had to raise anchor in a hurry, and some of the fleet were lost. The next day the remaining Spanish ships retreated up the North Sea. The only way home was around Ireland; and wind, storms, and the pursuing English ensured that less than half the fleet reached Spain safely. This shattering reversal was comparable in scale and unexpectedness only to Xerxes' disaster at Salamis over 2000 years earlier.

THE DUTCH REVOLT

Philip's most serious reversal was the revolt of the provinces he inherited from his father, the Emperor Charles V, in the Netherlands. Here his single-mindedness provoked a fierce reaction that grew into a successful struggle for independence—the first major victory in Western Europe by subjects resisting their monarch's assertions of authority.

Causes of Revolt The original focus of opposition was Philip's reorganization of the ecclesiastical structure so as to gain control over the country's Catholic Church, a change that deprived the aristocracy of important patronage. At the same time, the billeting of troops aroused the resentment of ordinary citizens. In this situation, the local nobles, led by William of Orange, warned of mass disorder, but Philip kept up the pressure:

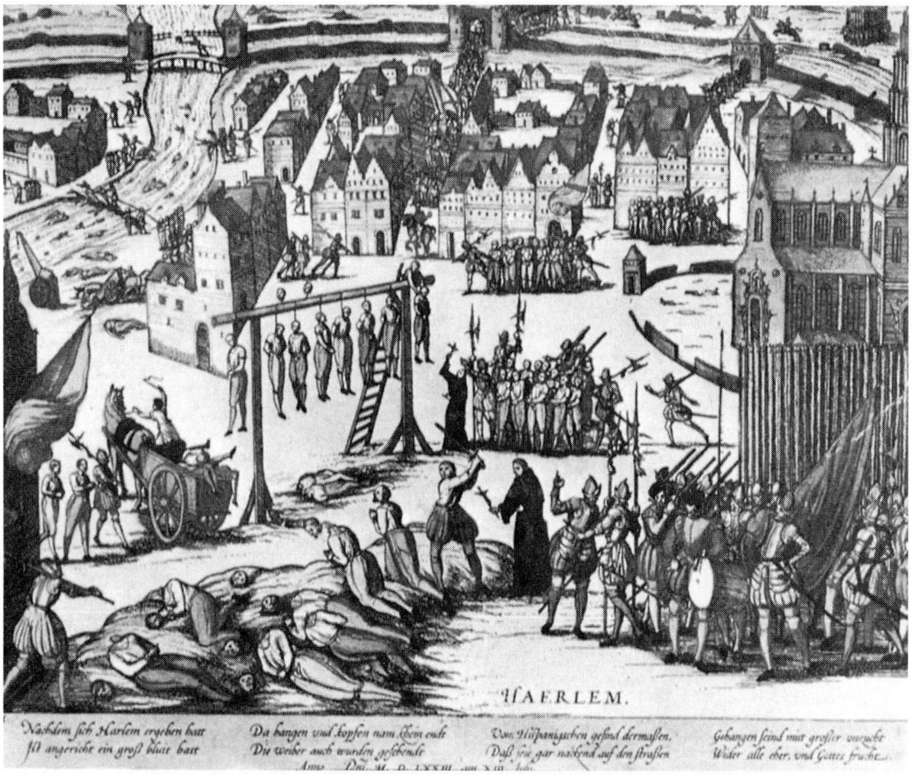

▸ *Anonymous*

ENGRAVING OF THE SPANIARDS IN HAARLEM

This engraving was published to arouse horror at Spanish atrocities during the Dutch revolt. As the caption indicates, after the Spanish troops (on the right) captured the city of Haarlem, there was a great bloodbath (*ein gross bliut batt*). Blessed by priests, the Haarlemites were decapitated or hung, and then tossed in a river so that the city would be cleansed of them. The caption states that even women and children were not spared.

He put the Inquisition to work against the Calvinists, who had begun to appear in the Netherlands, and also summoned the Jesuits to combat the heretics. These moves were disastrous because they further undermined local autonomy and made the Protestants bitter enemies of the king.

Philip's aggressiveness provoked violence in 1566: Although the Protestants were still a tiny minority, they formed mobs in a number of cities, assaulted Catholics, and sacked churches. In response, Philip tightened the pressure, appointing as governor the ruthless duke of Alba, whose Spanish troops were now used to suppress heresy and treason. Protestants were hanged in public, rebel groups were hunted down, and two nobles who had been guilty of nothing worse than demanding that Philip change his policy were executed.

Organized revolt broke out in 1572, when a small group of Dutch sailors flying the flag of William of Orange seized the fishing village of Brill, on the North Sea. The success of these "sea beggars," as the Spaniards called them, stimulated uprisings in towns throughout the Low Countries. The banner of William of Orange became the symbol of resistance, and under his leadership full-scale rebellion erupted. By 1576, when Philip's troops mutinied and rioted in Antwerp, 16 out of the 17 provinces in the Netherlands had united behind William. The next year, however, Philip offered a compromise to the Catholic nobles, and the 10 southern provinces returned to Spanish rule.

The United Provinces In 1579 the remaining seven provinces formed the independent United

Provinces. Despite the assassination of William in 1584, they managed to resist Spain's army for decades, mainly because they could open dikes, flood their country, and thus drive the invaders back. Moreover, Philip was often diverted by other wars and, in any case, never placed total confidence in his commanders. The heart of the resistance was the Calvinists, who (though still a minority) had the most to lose: They sought freedom for their religion as well as for their country. William never showed strong religious commitments, but his son, Maurice of Nassau, a brilliant military commander who won a series of victories in the 1590s, embraced Calvinism and helped make it the country's official religion. Unable to make any progress, the Spaniards agreed to a 12-year truce in 1609, but they did not recognize the independence of the United Provinces until the Peace of Westphalia in 1648. The new state demonstrated that warfare could have positive effects in this period: It could unite a people and give them the means to achieve dignity and full autonomy.

► *Pieter Brueghel the Elder*
THE MASSACRE OF THE INNOCENTS, CA. 1560
Probably to avoid trouble, Brueghel hid his critique of the Spanish rulers of the Netherlands in this supposed portrayal of a biblical event. It would have been clear to anyone who saw it, however, that this was a scene of Spanish cruelty toward the local inhabitants in the harsh days of winter, as soldiers tear babies from their mothers and kill them.

CIVIL WAR IN FRANCE

The warfare that religion inspired had no such redeeming effects in France. By the 1550s Calvinism was widespread among the peasants and in the towns of the south and southwest, and its leaders had virtually created a small semi-independent state. To meet this threat, a great noble

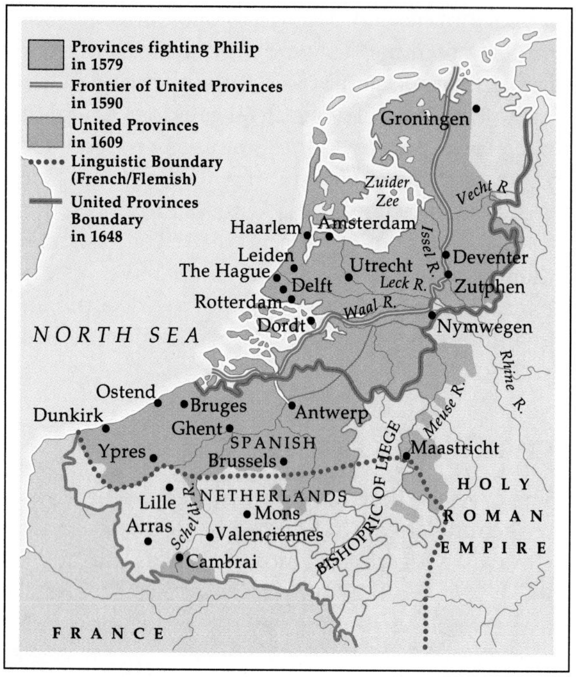

Map 15.1 THE NETHERLANDS, 1579–1609
The 17 provinces making up the Netherlands, or the Low Countries, were detached from the Holy Roman Empire when Charles V abdicated in 1556. As the map indicates, their subsequent division into two states was determined not by the linguistic difference between French-speaking people of the south and Dutch-speaking people of the north but rather by geography. The great river systems at the mouth of the Rhine eventually proved to be the barriers beyond which the Spaniards could not penetrate.

family, the Guises, assumed the leadership of the Catholics; and in response the Bourbons, another noble family, championed the Calvinists, about a twelfth of the population. Their struggle split the country apart.

It was ominous that in 1559—the year that Henry II, France's last strong king for a generation, died—the Calvinists (known in France as Huguenots) organized their first national synod, an indication of impressive strength. During the next 30 years, the throne was occupied by Henry's three ineffectual sons. The power behind the crown was Henry's widow, Catherine de Medici (see the genealogical table below), who tried desperately to preserve royal authority. But she was often helpless because the religious conflict intensified the factional struggle for power between the Guises and the Bourbons, both of whom were closely related to the monarchy and hoped one day to inherit the throne.

The Wars Fighting started in 1562 and lasted for 36 years, interrupted only by short-lived peace agreements. Catherine switched sides whenever one party became too powerful; and she may have approved the notorious massacre of St. Bartholomew's Day—August 24, 1572—which started in Paris, spread through France, and destroyed the Huguenots' leadership. Henry of Navarre, a Bourbon, was the only major figure who escaped. When Catherine switched sides again and made peace with the Huguenots in 1576, the Guises formed the Catholic League,

THE KINGS OF FRANCE IN THE SIXTEENTH CENTURY

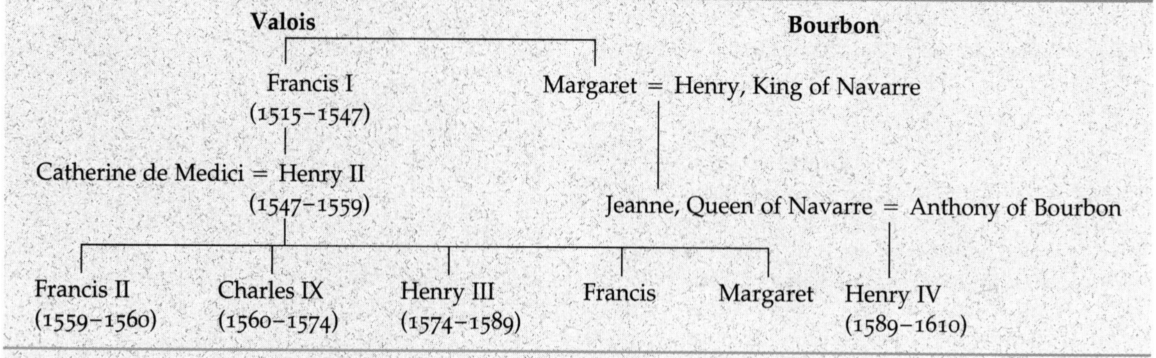

which for several years dominated the eastern half of the country. In 1584 the league allied with Spain's Philip II to attack heresy in France and deny the Bourbon Henry's legal right to inherit the throne.

The defeat of the Armada in 1588 proved to be the turning point in the French civil wars, for the duke of Guise lost his principal support, Spain, and was soon assassinated. Within a few months Henry of Navarre inherited the throne as Henry IV (1589–1610), though he had few advantages as he began to reassert royal authority. The Huguenots and Catholics ran almost independent governments in large sections of France. The Catholic League was in command of the east, including the capital, Paris; the Huguenots dominated the south and southwest, remote from the central government. In addition, the royal administration was in a sorry state because the crown's oldest rivals, the great nobles, could now resist all outside interference in their domains.

Peace Restored Yet largely because of the assassination of the duke of Guise, Henry IV was able to restore order. The duke had been a forceful leader, a serious contender for the throne. His replacement was a Spanish candidate for the crown who had little chance of success. The distaste for a possible foreign ruler, combined with war weariness, destroyed much of the support for the Catholic League, which finally collapsed as a result of revolts against it in eastern France in the 1590s. These uprisings, founded on a demand for peace, increased in frequency and intensity after Henry IV renounced Protestantism in 1593 in order to win acceptance by his Catholic subjects. The following year Henry had himself officially crowned, and all of France rallied to the king as he beat back a Spanish invasion—Spain's final, rather weak, attempt to put its own candidate on the throne.

When Spain finally withdrew and signed a peace treaty in 1598, the fighting came to an end. To complete the reconciliation, Henry issued (also in 1598) the Edict of Nantes, which granted limited toleration to the Huguenots. Although it did not create complete religious liberty, the edict made Calvinist worship legal, protected the rights of the minority, and opened public office to Huguenots.

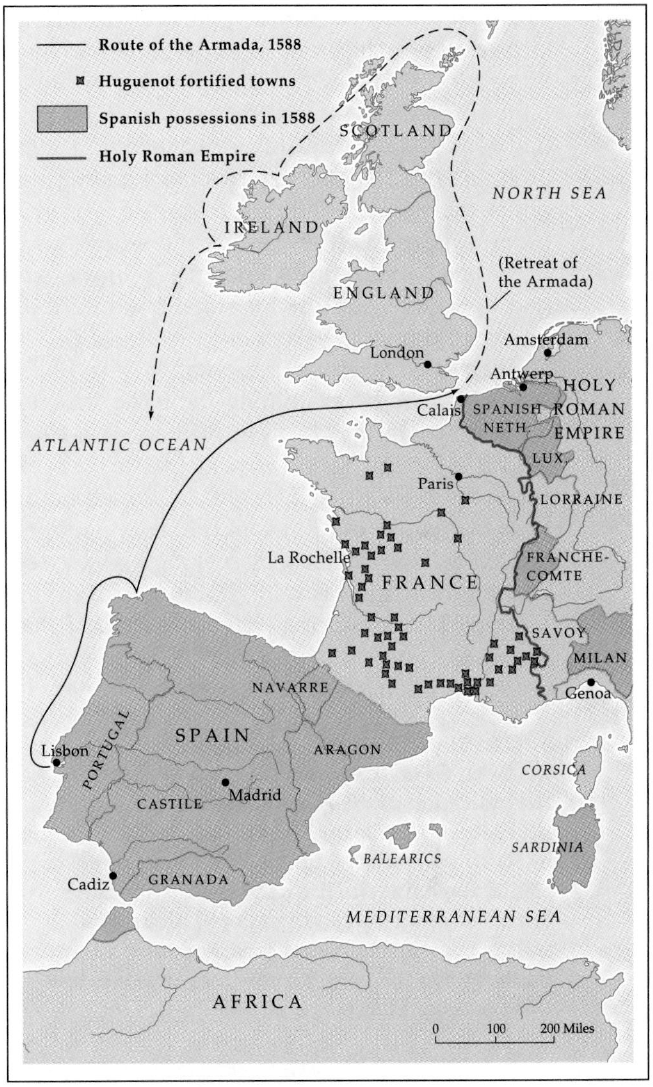

Map 15.2 CATHOLIC AND PROTESTANT POWERS IN THE LATE SIXTEENTH CENTURY
The heart of the Catholic cause in the wars of religion was the Spain of Philip II. Spanish territories surrounded France and provided the route to the Netherlands where the Protestant Dutch had rebelled against the Spaniards. The Armada was launched to help that cause by crushing the ally of the Dutch, Protestant England. In the meantime, the surrounded French had problems of their own with the Huguenots, who protected their Protestantism in a network of fortified towns.

Political Thought But the effects of decades of strife could not be brushed aside. A basic change in political thought, for example, was an inevitable response to the civil wars. The Huguenots had found ways to justify resistance to a monarch, and the Catholics used a similar justification when they were fighting the king. Even when order was restored, however, the advocates of peace and national unity, known as *politiques*, still had to argue forcefully for stability and a more powerful central government.

Their most famous representative, Jean Bodin, made his case by examining the basic structure of the state, and his analysis influenced political theorists for centuries. His principal work is *The Six Books of the Republic* (1576), in which he defines the nature and limits of the sovereignty exercised by governments. By seeking a balance between power and restraint, Bodin hoped to find a principle for restoring order in an age of shattering upheaval. But in the process, he also exposed the dilemma that has been the primary focus of political theory ever since: control versus freedom, the need for authority and yet the equal need for subjects' rights.

II. War and International Crisis

THE THIRTY YEARS' WAR

In the Holy Roman Empire, religious hatreds were especially disruptive because the empire lacked a central authority and unifying institutions. Small-scale fighting broke out repeatedly after the 1550s, always inspired by religion. And though in most of Western Europe the first two decades of the seventeenth century were a time of relative peace, which seemed to signal a decline of conflict over faith, in the empire the stage was being set for the bloodiest of all the wars fired by religion.

Known as the Thirty Years' War, this ferocious struggle began in the Kingdom of Bohemia in 1618 and continued until 1648. The principal battleground, the empire, was ravaged by the fighting, which eventually involved every major ruler in Europe. At first it was a renewed struggle between Protestants and Catholics, but eventually it became a fight among political rivals who were eager to take advantage of the fragmentation of

▶ "THE HANGING TREE," ENGRAVING FROM JACQUES CALLOT'S MISERIES OF WAR, 1633
An indication of the growing dismay over the brutality of the Thirty Years' War was the collection of 16 prints produced by the French engraver Callot, depicting the life of the soldier and the effects of armies on civilian populations. His soldiers destroy, loot, and rape, and only a few of them receive the punishments they deserve, like this mass hanging.

Ifrael ex. Cum Priuil. Reg.

A la fin ces Voleurs infames et perdus ,
Comme fruits malheureux a cet arbre pendus

Monfrent bien que le crime (horrible et noire engeance)
Eff luy mefme inftrument de honte et de vengeance ,

Et que ceft le Deftin des hommes vicieux
Defprouuer toft ou tard la iuftice des Cieux . 1)

the empire to advance their own ambitions. As the devastation spread, international relations seemed to be sinking into total chaos; but the chief victims were the Germans, who, like the Italians in the sixteenth century, found themselves at the mercy of well-organized states that used another country as the arena for settling their quarrels.

The First Phase, 1618–1621 The immediate problem was typical of the situation in the empire. In 1609 Emperor Rudolf II promised toleration for Protestants in Bohemia, one of his own domains. When his cousin Ferdinand, a pious Catholic, succeeded to the Bohemian throne in 1617, he refused to honor Rudolf's promise, and the Bohemians rebelled in 1618. Since the crown was elective, they declared Ferdinand deposed, replacing him with the leading Calvinist of the empire, Frederick II of the Palatinate. Frederick accepted the crown, an act of defiance whose only possible outcome was war.

The first decade or so of the war was a time of victories for the Catholics, and in particular the Habsburgs. Ferdinand became emperor (1619–1637), and the powerful Catholic Maximilian of Bavaria put an army at his disposal. Within a year the imperial troops won a stunning victory over the Bohemians at the Battle of the White Mountain. Leading rebels were executed or exiled, and Ferdinand II confiscated all of Frederick's lands. Maximilian received half as a reward for his army, and the remainder went to the Spaniards, who occupied it as a valuable base for their struggle with the Dutch. In this first round, the Catholic and imperial cause had triumphed.

F
Hie sicht man die 12. Köpff auff den Prager Bruckenthurn aufgesteckt

► "HEADS OF THE BOHEMIAN REBELS," ENGRAVING FROM MATHÄUS MERIAN, THEATRUM EUROPAEUM, CA. 1630

Since the scene had not changed when the engraving was made, this illustration is probably a fairly accurate representation of the punishment in 1621 of the leaders of the Bohemian rebellion. Twenty-four rebels were executed, and the heads of twelve of them were displayed on long poles at the top of the tower (still standing today) on the bridge over Prague's river. The heads were kept there for 10 years.

The Second Phase, 1621–1630 When the truce between the Spaniards and the Dutch expired in 1621, and warfare resumed in Germany as well as in the Netherlands, the Protestants made no progress for 10 years. A new imperial army was raised by Albrecht von Wallenstein, a minor Bohemian nobleman and remarkable opportunist who had become one of the richest men in the empire. In 1624 Wallenstein, realizing that the emperor remained weak because he lacked his own army, offered to raise a force if he could billet it and raise its supplies wherever it happened to be stationed. Ferdinand agreed, and by 1627 Wallenstein's army had begun to conquer the northern region of the empire, the last major center of Protestant strength. To emphasize his supremacy, Ferdinand issued the Edict of Restitution in 1629, ordering the restoration to Catholics of all the territories they had lost to Protestants since 1552.

But these Habsburg successes were more apparent than real, because it was only the extreme disorganization of the empire that permitted a mercenary captain like Wallenstein to achieve such immense military power. Once the princes realized the danger he posed to their independence, they united (Catholic as well as Protestant) against the Habsburgs, and in 1630 they made Ferdinand dismiss Wallenstein by threatening to keep his son from the imperial succession. The emperor's submission proved fatal to his cause, for Sweden and France were preparing to unleash new aggressions against the Habsburgs, and Wallenstein was the one military leader who might have been able to beat back the onslaught.

The Third Phase, 1630–1632 The year 1630 marked the beginning of a change in fortune for the Protestants and also a drift toward the purely political aim (of resisting the Habsburgs) that was coming to dominate the war. Although France's king was a Catholic, he was ready to join with Protestants against other Catholics so as to undermine Habsburg power. Early in 1630 the French attacked the duke of Savoy, a Habsburg ally, and occupied his lands. Then, in 1631, they allied with Gustavus Adolphus of Sweden, who, dismayed by Ferdinand's treatment of Protestants and fearing a Habsburg threat to Swedish lands around the Baltic Sea, had invaded the empire in 1630. The following year Gustavus destroyed an imperial army at Breitenfeld in one of the few decisive battles of the war. The tide had turned against the Habsburgs.

Ferdinand hastily recalled Wallenstein, whose troops met the Swedes in battle at Lützen in 1632. Although Gustavus' soldiers won the day, he himself was killed, and his death saved the Habsburg dynasty from being destroyed by Sweden. Nothing, however, could restore Ferdinand's former position. The emperor was forced by the princes to turn against Wallenstein once more; A few months later he had him assassinated. The removal of the great general marked the end of an era, for he was the last leader in more than two centuries who was capable of establishing unified authority in what is now Germany.

The Fourth Phase, 1632–1648 Gustavus' success opened the final phase of the war, as political ambitions—the quest of the empire's princes for independence, and the struggle between the Habsburgs and their enemies—almost completely replaced religious aims. The Protestant princes began to raise new armies, and by 1635 Ferdinand had to make peace with them. In return for their promise of assistance in driving out the Swedes, Ferdinand agreed to suspend the Edict of Restitution and to grant amnesty to all but Frederick of the Palatinate and a few Bohemian rebels. Ferdinand was renouncing most of his ambitions, and it seemed that peace might return at last.

But the French could not let matters rest. In 1635 they finally declared war on Ferdinand. For the next 13 years, the French and Swedes rained unmitigated disaster on Germany. Peace negotiations began in 1641, but not until 1648 did the combatants agree to lay down arms and sign the treaties of Westphalia. Even thereafter the war between France and Spain, pursued mainly in the Spanish Netherlands, continued for another 11 years; and hostilities around the Baltic among Sweden, Denmark, Poland, and Russia, which had started in 1611, did not end until 1661.

The Effect of War The wars and their effects (such as the diseases spread by armies) killed off over a third of Germany's population. The conflict caused serious economic dislocation because a number of princes—already in serious financial straits—sharply debased their coinage. This worsened the continentwide trade depression that had begun around 1620 and had brought the great sixteenth-century boom to an end, causing the first drop in prices since 1500. Few contemporaries perceived the connection between war and economic trouble, but nobody could ignore the drain on men and resources or the destructive effects of the conflict.

THE PEACE OF WESTPHALIA

By the 1630s it was becoming apparent that the fighting was getting out of hand and that it would not be easy to bring the conflicts to an end. There had never been such widespread or devastating warfare, and many diplomats felt that the settlement had to be of far greater scope than any negotiated before. And they were right. When at last the treaties were signed in 1648, after seven years of negotiation in the German province of Westphalia, a landmark in international relations was passed—remarkable not

▶ *Jan Asselyn*
THE BATTLE OF LÜTZEN
Although it is not an accurate rendition of the scene, this painting of Gustavus Adolphus (the horseman in a brown coat with sword raised) shot by a gunman in red does give the flavor of seventeenth-century battle. Because of the chaos, the smoke, and the poor visibility that often obscured what was happening, Gustavus' escort did not notice when he was in fact hit by a musket shot that shattered his left arm and caused his horse to bolt. Further shots killed him, and not until hours after the battle was his seminaked body found, stripped of its finery.

only because it brought an anarchic situation under control but because it created a new system for dealing with wars.

The most important innovation was the gathering at the peace conference of all the participants in the Thirty Years' War, rather than the usual practice of bringing only two or three belligerents together. The presence of ambassadors from Bavaria, Brandenburg, Denmark, France, the Holy Roman Empire, Saxony, Spain, Sweden, Switzerland, and the United Provinces made possible, for the first time in European history, a series of all-embracing treaties that dealt with nearly every major international issue at one stroke. Visible at the meetings was the emergence of a state system. These independent states recognized that they were creating a mechanism for controlling their relations with one another. Although some fighting continued, the Peace of Westphalia in 1648 became the first comprehensive rearrangement of the map of Europe in modern times.

The Peace Terms The principal beneficiaries were France and Sweden, the chief aggressors during the last decade of the war. France gained the provinces of Alsace and Lorraine, and Swe-

Gerard Terborch
THE PEACE OF WESTPHALIA, 1648
The artist was an eyewitness to this scene, the formal signing of peace between the United Provinces and Spain in Münster on May 15, 1648. The two leaders of the Spanish delegation on the right put their hands on a Bible as they swear to uphold the terms of the treaty, and the Dutch on the left all raise their hands as they declare "So help me God." Terborch himself, dressed in brown, is looking out at the viewer on the far left.

den obtained extensive territories in the Holy Roman Empire. The main loser was the House of Habsburg, since both the United Provinces and the Swiss Confederation were recognized as independent states, and the German princes, who agreed not to join an alliance against the emperor, were otherwise given almost complete independence.

The princes' autonomy was formally established in 1657, when they elected as emperor Leopold I, the head of the House of Habsburg, in return for two promises. First, Leopold would give no help to his cousins, the rulers of Spain; and second, the empire would be a state of princes, in which each ruler would be free from imperial interference. This freedom permitted the rise of Brandenburg-Prussia and the growth of absolutism—the belief that the political authority of the ruler was unlimited—within the major principalities. Moreover, the Habsburgs' capitulation prepared the way for their reorientation toward the east along the Danube River—the beginnings of the Austro-Hungarian Empire.

The Effects of Westphalia For more than a century, the settlement reached at Westphalia was regarded as the basis for all international negotiations. Even major new accords, such as the one that ended yet another series of wars in 1713, were seen mainly as adjustments of the decisions of 1648. In practice, of course, multinational conferences were no more effective than brief, limited negotiations in reducing tensions among states. Wars continued to break out, and armies grew in size and skill. But diplomats did believe that international affairs were under better control and that the chaos of the Thirty Years' War had been replaced by something more stable and more clearly defined.

This confidence was reinforced as it became clear after 1648 that armies were trying to improve discipline and avoid the excesses of the previous 30 years. As religious passions waned, combat became less vicious and the treatment of civilians became more orderly. On battlefields, better discipline reduced the casualty rate from 1 death per 3 soldiers in the 1630s to 1 death in 7, or even 1 in 20, during the early 1700s. And the aims of war also changed significantly.

Changed International Relations The most obvious differences after the Peace of Westphalia were that France replaced Spain as the continent's dominant power and that northern countries—especially England and the Netherlands,

Map 15.3 TERRITORIAL CHANGES. 1648–1661
This map shows the territorial changes that took place after the Thirty Years' War. The treaties of Westphalia (1648) and the Pyrenees (1659) arranged the principal transfers, but the settlements in the Baltic were not confirmed until the treaties of Copenhagen, Oliva (both 1660), and Kardis (1661).

where growth in population and in commerce resumed more quickly than elsewhere—took over Europe's economic leadership. But behind this outward shift a more fundamental transformation was taking place. What had become apparent in the later stages of the Thirty Years' War was that Europe's states were prepared to fight only for economic, territorial, or political advantages. Dynastic aims were still important, but supranational goals like religious causes could no longer determine a state's foreign policy.

The Thirty Years' War was the last major international conflict in Europe in which two religious camps organized their forces as blocs. After 1648 such connections gave way to more purely national interests. This shift marked the decisive stage of a process that had been under way since the Late Middle Ages: the emergence of the state as the basic unit and object of loyalty in Western civilization. That it had taken a major crisis, a descent into international anarchy, to bring about so momentous a change is an indication of how profoundly the upheavals of the mid-seventeenth century affected European history. Indeed, the reshaping of the relations among Europe's states for centuries to come that was achieved at Westphalia is but one example of the multiple military and political consequences of this age of crisis.

III. The Military Revolution

WEAPONS AND TACTICS

The constant warfare of the sixteenth and seventeenth centuries brought about dramatic changes in the ways battles were fought and armies were organized. Gunpowder, which had been used occasionally and to little effect since the 1330s, now came to occupy a central place in warfare. The result was not only the creation of a new type of industry, cannon and gun manufacture, but also a transformation of tactics. Individual castles could no longer be defended against explosives; even towns had to build heavy and elaborate fortifications if they were to resist the new fire power. Sieges became complicated, expensive operations, whose purpose was to bring explosives right up to a town wall so that it could be blown up. This required an intricate system of trenches, because walls were built in star shapes so as to multiply angles of fire and make any approach dangerous. Although they became increasingly costly, sieges remained essential to the strategy of warfare until the eighteenth century.

Tactics In open battles, the effects of gunpowder were equally expensive. The new tactics that appeared around 1500, perfected by the Spaniards, relied on massed ranks of infantry, organized in huge squares, that made the traditional cavalry charge obsolete. Interspersed with the gunners were soldiers carrying pikes. They fended off horses or opposing infantry while the men with guns tried to mow the enemy down. The squares with the best discipline usually won, and for over a century after the reign of Ferdinand of Aragon, the Spaniards had the best army in Europe. Each square had about 3000 troops, and to maintain enough squares at full strength to fight all of Spain's battles required an army numbering approximately 40,000. The cost of keeping that many men clothed, fed, and housed, let alone equipped and paid, was enormous. But worse was to come: New tactics emerged in the early seventeenth century that required even more soldiers.

Since nobody could outdo the Spaniards at their own methods, a different approach was developed by their rivals. The first advance was made by Maurice of Nassau, who led the Dutch revolt against Spain from the 1580s. He relied not on sheer weight and power but on flexibility and mobility. Then Sweden's Gustavus Adolphus, one of the geniuses of the history of warfare, found a way to achieve mobility on the field without losing power. His main invention was the salvo: Instead of having his musketeers fire one row at a time, like the Spaniards, he had them all fire at once. What he lost in continuity of shot he gained in a fearsome blast that, if properly timed, could shatter enemy ranks. Huge, slow-moving squares were simply no match for smaller, faster units that riddled them with well-coordinated salvos.

THE ORGANIZATION AND SUPPORT OF ARMIES

These tactical changes brought about steady increases in the size of armies, because the more units there were, the better they could be placed on the battlefield. Although the Spanish army hardly grew between 1560 and 1640, remaining at 40,000 to 60,000 men, the Swedes had 150,000 by 1632; and at the end of the century, Louis XIV considered a force of 400,000 essential to maintain his dominant position in Europe.

This growth had far-reaching consequences. One was the need for conscription, which Gustavus introduced in the late 1620s. At least half his army consisted of his own subjects, who were easier to control than foreign mercenaries. Because it also made sense not to disband such huge forces each autumn, when the campaigning season ended, most armies were kept permanently ready. The need to maintain so many soldiers the year round caused a rapid expansion of supporting administrative personnel. Taxation mushroomed. All levels of society felt the impact but especially the lower classes, who paid the bulk of the taxes and provided most of the recruits. To encourage enlistment, rulers made military service as attractive as possible—a task made easier by the problems many people faced in finding regular meals, clothing, housing, and wages. Social distinctions were reduced; an able young man could rise high in the officer corps, though the top ranks were still reserved for nobles. Even the lower echelons were given important responsibilities because the new system of small, flexible units gave considerable initiative to the junior officers who led them.

New Ranks Other changes followed. Maneuverability on the field demanded tighter discipline, which was achieved by the introduction of drilling and combat training. The order of command was clarified, and many ranks familiar today—major, colonel, and the various levels of general—appeared in the seventeenth century. The distinctions were reinforced by uniforms, which became standard equipment. These developments created a sense of corporate spirit among military officers, an international phenomenon that was to occupy an important place in European society for three centuries.

THE LIFE OF THE SOLDIER

For the average soldier, who was now a common sight in Europe, life in the army began with recruitment. Some genuinely wanted to join up. They had heard stories of adventure, booty, and comradeship, and they were tempted by free

▶ *Anonymous Engraving after Jacques de Gheyn*
WAFFENHANDLUNG
The expansion of armies and the professionalization of war in the seventeenth century were reflected in the founding of military academies and the growing acceptance of the notion that warfare was a science. There was now a market for published manuals, especially if they had illustrations like this one, which shows how a pikeman was supposed to crouch and hold his weapons (stabilizing his pike against his foot) when facing a cavalry charge.

Map 15.4 AREAS OF FIGHTING, 1618–1660
The endemic fighting of this age of crisis engulfed most of Central Europe and involved soldiers from every country.

food and clothing. But in many cases the "volunteers" did not want to go, for they had also heard of the hardship and danger. Unfortunately for them, recruiting officers had quotas, and villages had to provide the numbers demanded of them. Community pressure, bribery, enlistment of drunken men, and even outright kidnapping helped fill the ranks.

Joining an army did not necessarily mean cutting oneself off from friends or family. Men from a particular area enlisted together, and in some cases, wives came along. There were dozens of jobs to do aside from fighting, because soldiers needed cooks, laundresses, peddlers, and other tradespeople. It has been estimated that an army in the field might need five people for every soldier. The large majority of the troops, though, were on their own. For companionship, they looked to camp followers or the women of the town they were occupying. Few barracks had been built, and therefore, unless they were on the march or out in the open on a battlefield, they were housed (or billeted) with ordinary citizens. Since soldiers almost never received their wages on time—delays could be as long as a year or more—they rarely could pay for their food and housing. Local civilians therefore had to supply their needs, or risk the thievery that was universal. It was no wonder that the approach of an army was a terrifying event.

Military Justice Officially, there were severe penalties for misbehavior—imprisonment, flogging, or, for crimes like desertion, execution. Yet discipline, though harsh, was only occasionally

► *Sebastian Vrancx*
A Military Camp
Vrancx was himself a soldier, and the many military scenes he painted during the Thirty Years' War give us a sense of the life of the soldier during the many months when there were no campaigns or battles. Conditions could be grim, but there were many hours when one could simply nap, chat, or play dice.

enforced, because men were needed for combat and it was easy to slip away from an army. Troops had their own law and courts, but the main goal of their officers was to maintain an effective fighting force. And disputes with civilians rarely ended in a judgment against a soldier. Punishments were rare even for corruption at an army's upper levels (for instance, when officers who were paid to raise troops listed phantom recruits and kept their wages).

Discomforts The relatively light legal restrictions did not mean that military life was easy. Soldiers suffered constant discomfort. A garrison might be able to settle into a town in reasonable conditions for a long stretch; but if it was besieged, it became hungry, fearful, and vulnerable. Days spent on the march could be grim, exhausting, and uncertain; and even in camps soldiers were often filthy and wet. Real danger was not common, though it was intense during battles and occasionally during sieges. Even a simple wound could be fatal, because medical care was generally appalling. Yet the most persistent discomfort for the soldier was boredom. Sieges dragged, and even the hard labor of digging trenches or dragging cannons must have been a relief from the tedious waiting. Despite traditional recreations—drink, gambling, and the brawls common among soldiers—the attractions were limited; and most military men had few regrets when they returned to civilian life.

IV. Revolution in England

In the 1640s and 1650s the growing burdens of war and taxation, and the mounting assertiveness of governments, sparked upheavals throughout Europe that were the equivalent in domestic politics of the crisis in international relations. In country after country, people rose up in vain attempts to restore the individual and regional autonomies that were being eroded by powerful central governments. Only in England, however, did the revolt become a revolution—an attempt to overturn the social and political system and create a new structure for society.

ELIZABETH I

Before 1630, no such eruption could have been foreseen. With few wars, and those largely at sea, England was less affected than other countries by the fighting of the age. In addition, the people were united by such common bonds as the institution of Parliament and a commitment to the international Protestant cause that was carefully promoted by Queen Elizabeth I (1558–1603).

Elizabeth is an appealing figure because she combined shrewd hardheadedness and a sense of the possible with a disarming appearance of frailty. Her qualities were many: her dedication to the task of government; her astute choice of advisers; her civilizing influence at court, where she encouraged elegant manners and the arts; her tolerance of religious dissent as long as it posed no political threat; and her ability to feel the mood of her people, to catch their spirit, to inspire their enthusiasm. Although social, legal, and economic practices usually subordinated women to men in this age, inheritance was respected; thus a determined woman with a recognized claim to authority could win complete acceptance. Elizabeth was the most widely admired and most successful queen of her time, but she was by no means alone: Female rulers also shaped the histories of France, Sweden, and the southern Netherlands in the sixteenth and seventeenth centuries.

Royal Policy Elizabeth could be indecisive, notably where the succession was concerned. Her refusal to marry caused serious uncertainties, and it was only the shrewd planning of her chief minister, Robert Cecil, that enabled the king of Scotland, James Stuart, to succeed her without incident in 1603. Similar dangers arose from her indecisive treatment of England's remaining Catholics. They hoped that Mary Queen of Scots, a Catholic, would inherit the throne; and since she was next in line, they were not above plotting against Elizabeth's life. Eventually, in 1587, Elizabeth had Mary executed and the plots died away. But her reluctance to take firm positions was also apparent in her choice of advisers. Some advocated caution, inaction, and discretion in international affairs; whereas others favored an aggressive foreign policy. Yet Elizabeth showed

Queen Elizabeth's Armada Speech

Elizabeth's ability to move her subjects was exemplified by the speech she gave to her troops as they awaited the fight with the Spanish Armada. She understood that they might have doubts about a woman leading them in war, but she turned that issue to her own advantage in a stirring cry to battle that enhanced her popularity at the time and her legendary image thereafter.

"My loving People: We have been persuaded by some that are careful of our safety, to take heed how we commit ourselves to armed multitudes, for fear of treachery; but I assure you, I do not desire to live to distrust my faithful and loving people.

"Let tyrants fear; I have always so behaved myself, that, under God, I have placed my chiefest strength and safeguard in the loyal hearts and good will of my subjects, and therefore I am come amongst you, as you see, at this time, not for my recreation . . . but being resolved in the midst and heat of the battle, to live or die amongst you all, to lay down for my God, and for my kingdoms, and for my people, my honour and my blood, even in the dust.

"I know I have the body of a weak and feeble woman; but I have the heart and stomach of a king, and of a king of England too; and think foul scorn that . . . Spain, or any prince of Europe should dare to invade the borders of my realm; to which rather than any dishonour shall grow by me, I myself will take up arms, I myself will be your general, judge, and rewarder of every one of your virtues in the field. . . . By your concord in the camp, and your valour in the field, we shall shortly have a famous victory over those enemies of my God, of my kingdoms, and of my people."

From Walter Scott (ed.), *A Collection of Scarce and Valuable Tracts, on the Most Interesting and Entertaining Subjects: but Chiefly Such as Relate to the History and Constitution of these Kingdoms*, vol. I (London, 1809), pp. 429–430.

great skill in balancing the contrasting viewpoints, and her adroit maneuvering assured her of her ministers' loyalty at all times.

She also inspired the devotion of her subjects by traveling throughout England to make public appearances: by brilliant speeches (*see box, above*); and by shaping her own image, even regulating how she was to be depicted in portraits. She thus retained her subjects' allegiance despite the profound social changes that were eroding traditional patterns of deference and order. England's nobility, for instance, no longer dominated the military and the government; nearly all Elizabeth's ministers were new in national life, and the House of Commons was beginning to exert more political influence within Parliament than the House of Lords. The nobles, less directly involved in commerce, did not benefit as much as other sections of society from England's rising prosperity; and in general they were losing their hold over the power, wealth, and goverment of the country.

The Gentry The gentry, the new group that joined the nobles at the head of society, ranged from people considered great in a parish or other small locality to courtiers considered great throughout the land. There were never more than 60 nobles during Elizabeth's reign, but the gentry may have numbered close to 20,000 by the time she died. Most of these gentry were doing well economically, profiting from their agricultural holdings as well as from crown offices. A number also became involved in industrial activity, and hundreds invested in new overseas trading and colonial ventures. The gentry's participation in commerce made them unique among the landed classes of Europe, whose members were tradi-

▶ *William Segar* (attrib.)
PORTRAIT OF ELIZABETH I, 1585
Elizabeth I was strongly aware of the power of propaganda, and she used it to foster a dazzling public image. Legends about her arose in literature. And in art she had herself portrayed in the most elaborate finery imaginable. Here, she is every inch the queen, with her magnificent dress, the trappings of monarchy, and the symbol of virginity, the ermine.

tionally contemptuous of business affairs, and it testified to the enterprise and vigor of England's social leaders. Long important in local administration, they flocked to the House of Commons to express their views of public matters. Their ambitions eventually posed a serious threat to the monarchy, especially when linked with the effects of rapid economic change.

Economic Advance In Elizabeth's reign, thanks to a general boom in trade, England's merchants, helped by leading courtiers, began to transform the country's economy. They opened commercial links throughout Europe and parts of Asia and began English expansion overseas. At home, there was significant industrial development. Mining and manufacture developed rapidly, and shipbuilding became a major industry. The production of coal increased 14-fold between 1540 and 1680, creating fortunes and an expertise in industrial techniques that took England far ahead of its neighbors.

The economic vigor and growth that ensued gave the classes that benefited most—gentry and merchants—a cohesion and a sense of purpose that made it dangerous to oppose them when they felt their rights infringed. They increasingly regarded themselves as the leaders of the nation, second only to the nobility. They wanted respect for their wishes, and they bitterly resented the economic interference and political high-handedness of Elizabeth's successors.

The Puritans Heightening this unease was the sympathy many of the gentry felt toward a small but vociferous group of religious reformers, the Puritans. Puritans believed that the Protestant Anglican Church established by Elizabeth was still too close to Roman Catholicism, and they wanted further reductions in ritual and hierarchy. Elizabeth refused, and although she tried to avoid a confrontation, in the last years of her reign she had to silence the most outspoken of her critics. As a result, the Puritans became a disgruntled minority. By the 1630s, when the government tried to repress such religious dissent more vigorously, there were many in England, non-Puritan as well as Puritan, who felt that the monarchy was leading the country astray and was ignoring the wishes of its subjects. Leading parliamentarians in particular soon came to believe that major changes were needed to restore good government in England.

PARLIAMENT AND THE LAW

The place where the gentry made their views known was Parliament, the nation's supreme legislative body. Three-quarters of the House of Commons consisted of gentry. They were better educated than ever before, and nearly half of them had legal training. Since the Commons had to approve all taxation, the gentry had the leverage to pursue their grievances.

The monarchy was still the dominant force in

the country when Elizabeth died in 1603, but Parliament's demand to be heard was gathering momentum. Although the queen had been careful with money, in the last 20 years of her reign her resources had been overtaxed by war with Spain and an economic depression. Thus she bequeathed to her successor, Scotland's James Stuart, a huge debt—£400,000, the equal of a year's royal revenue—and the struggle to pay it off gave the Commons the means to seek changes in royal policy.

James I Trouble began in the reign of James I (1603–1625), who had a far more exalted view of his own powers than Elizabeth had had and who did not hesitate to tell his subjects, in the most tactless way, that he considered his authority almost unlimited. As a result, gentry opposed to royal policies dominated parliamentary proceedings, and they engaged in a running battle with the king. They blocked the union of England with Scotland that James sought. They drew up an "Apology" explaining his mistakes and his ignorance, as a Scotsman, of English traditions. They forced two of his ministers to resign in disgrace. And they wrung repeated concessions from him, including the unprecedented right for Parliament to discuss foreign policy.

Law The Commons used the law to justify their resistance to royal power. The basic legal system of the country was the common law—justice administered on the basis of precedents and parliamentary statutes, and relying on the opinions of juries. This system stood in contrast to Roman law, prevalent on the continent, where royal edicts could make law and decisions were reached by judges without juries. Such practices existed in England only in a few royal courts of law, such as Star Chamber, which, because it was directly under the crown, came to be seen as an instrument of repression.

The common lawyers, whose leaders were also prominent in the Commons, resented the growing business of the royal courts and attacked them in Parliament. Both James and his successor were accused of pressuring judges, particularly after they won a series of famous cases involving a subject's right to criticize the monarch. Thus the crown could be portrayed as disregarding not only the desires of the people but the law itself. The king still had broad powers, but when he exercised them contrary to Parliament's wishes, his actions seemed to many to be taking on the appearance of tyranny.

RISING ANTAGONISMS

The confrontation between Parliament and king grew worse during the 1620s, especially in the reign of James's son, Charles I (1625–1649). At the Parliament of 1628–1629, the open challenge to the crown reached a climax in the Petition of Right, which has become a landmark in constitutional history. The petition demanded an end to imprisonment without cause shown, to taxation without the consent of Parliament, to martial law in peacetime, and to the billeting of troops among civilians. Charles agreed, in the hope of gaining much-needed subsidies, but then broke his word. To many, this betrayal seemed to threaten Parliament's essential role in government alongside the king. Seeking to end discussion of these issues in the Commons, Charles ordered Parliament dissolved, but with great daring, two members denied the king even this hallowed right by holding the speaker of the House in his chair while they passed a final angry resolution denouncing Charles's actions.

Resentful subjects were clearly on the brink of openly defying their king. Puritans, common lawyers, and disenchanted country gentry had taken over the House of Commons; and Charles avoided further trouble only by refusing to call another session of Parliament. This he managed to do for 11 years, all the while increasing the repression of Puritanism and using extraordinary measures (such as reviving crown rights to special taxes that had not been demanded for a long time) to raise revenues that did not require parliamentary consent. But in 1639, the Calvinist Scots took up arms rather than accept the Anglican prayer book, and the parliamentarians had their chance. To raise funds for an army to fight the Scots, Charles had to turn to Parliament, which demanded that he first redress its grievances. When he resisted, civil war followed.

CIVIL WAR

The Parliament that met in 1640 began with a two-hour speech by John Pym, a prominent critic of the monarch, who outlined long-standing grievances against both church and government. Charles refused to change his policies, the Commons refused to grant a subsidy, and the king angrily dissolved the session. But there was no way to pay for an army without taxes. By the summer of 1640, the Scots occupied most of northern England, and Charles had to summon a new Parliament. This one sat for 13 years, earning the appropriate name of the Long Parliament.

In its first year, the House of Commons abolished the royal courts, such as Star Chamber, and made mandatory the writ of habeas corpus (which prevented imprisonment without cause shown); it declared taxation without parliamentary consent illegal; and it ruled that Parliament had to meet at least once every three years. Meanwhile, the Puritans in the Commons prepared to reform the church. Oliver Cromwell, one of their leaders, demanded abolition of the Anglican Book of Common Prayer and strongly attacked the institution of episcopacy. The climactic vote came the next year when the Commons passed a Grand Remonstrance, which outlined for the king all the legislation they had passed and asked that bishops be deprived of votes in the House of Lords.

The Two Sides This was the prelude to a more revolutionary Puritan assault on the stucture of the Church, but in fact the Grand Remonstrance passed by only 11 votes. A moderate group was detaching itself from the Puritans, and it was to become the nucleus of a royalist party. The nation's chief grievances had been redressed, and there was no longer a uniform desire for change. Still Charles misjudged the situation and tried to arrest five leaders of the Commons, supposedly for plotting treason with the Scots. But Parliament resisted, and the citizens of London, openly hostile to Charles, sheltered the five. England now began gradually to split in two. By late 1642 both the royalists and the antiroyalists had assembled armies, and the Civil War was under way.

What made so many people overcome their habitual loyalty to the monarchy? We know that the royalists in Parliament were considerably younger than their opponents, which suggests that it was long experience with the Stuarts and nostalgia for Elizabeth that created revolutionaries. Another clear divide was regional. The south and east of England were primarily antiroyalist, while the north and west were mostly royalist. This indicated that the more cosmopolitan areas, closer to the continent and also centers of Puritanism, were largely on Parliament's side. The decision was often a personal matter: A prominent family and its locality chose one side because its rival, a nearby family, had chosen the other. The Puritans were certainly antiroyalist, but they were a minority in the country and influential in the House of Commons only because they were so vociferous and determined. Like all revolutions, this one was animated by a small group of radicals (in this case, Puritans) who alone kept the momentum going.

Independents and Presbyterians As the fighting began, a group among the Puritans known as Independents urged that the Anglican Church be replaced by a congregational system, in which each local congregation, free of all central authority, would decide its own form of worship. The most important leader of the Independents in Parliament was Oliver Cromwell. Opposed to them, but also considered Puritans, were the Presbyterians, who wanted to establish a strictly organized Calvinist system, like the one in Scotland, where local congregations were subject to centralized authority, though laypeople did participate in church government. Since both the Scots, whose alliance was vital in the war, and a majority of the Puritans in the Commons were Presbyterians, Cromwell agreed to give way, but only for the moment. There was also a quarrel over the goals of the war because the antiroyalists were unsure whether they ought to defeat Charles completely. This dispute crossed religious lines, though the Independents were in general more determined to force Charles into total submission, and eventually they had their way.

As the fighting continued, Cromwell persuaded the Commons to allow him to reorganize the antiroyalist troops. His New Model Army—whipped to fervor by sermons, prayers, and the singing of psalms—became unbeatable. At Naseby in 1645, it won a major victory, and a year later Charles surrendered. The next two years were chaotic. The Presbyterians and Independ-

▶ *Anonymous*
ENGRAVING OF THE EXECUTION OF CHARLES I
This contemporary Dutch engraving of the execution of Charles I shows the scaffold in front of the Banqueting House in Whitehall—a building that still can be seen in London. On the far right of the scaffold, the executioner displays the severed head for the crowd.

ents quarreled over what to do with the king, and finally Civil War resumed. This time the Presbyterians and Scots backed Charles against the Independents. But even with this alliance the royalists were no match for the New Model Army; Cromwell soon defeated his opponents and captured the king.

The King's Fate At the same time, in 1647, the Independents abolished the House of Lords and removed all Presbyterians from the House of Commons. This "Rump" Parliament tried to negotiate with Charles but discovered that he continued to plot a return to power. With Cromwell's approval, the Commons decided that their monarch, untrustworthy and a troublemaker, would have to die. A trial of dubious legality was held, and though many of the participants refused to sign the death warrant, the "holy, anointed" king was executed by his subjects in January 1649, to the horror of all Europe and most of England.

ENGLAND UNDER CROMWELL

Oliver Cromwell was now master of England. The republic established after Charles's execution was officially ruled by the Rump Parliament, but a Council of State led by Cromwell controlled policy with the backing of the army. And they had to contend with a ferment of political and social ideas. One group, known as the Levellers, demanded the vote for nearly all adult males and parliamentary elections every other year. The men of property among the Puritans, notably Cromwell himself, were disturbed by the egalitarianism of these proposals and insisted that only men with an "interest" in England—that is, land—should be qualified to vote.

Radical Ideas Even more radical were the Diggers, a communistic sect that sought to implement the spirit of primitive Christianity by abolishing personal property; the Society of Friends, which stressed personal inspiration as the source of faith and all action; and the Fifth Monarchists, a messianic group who believed that the "saints"—themselves—should rule because the Day of Judgment was at hand. People of great ability, such as the famous poet John Milton, contributed to the fantastic flood of pamphlets and suggestions for reform that poured forth in these years, and their ideas inspired future revolutionaries. But at the time, they merely put Cromwell on the defensive, forcing him to maintain control at all costs.

Cromwell's Aims Cromwell himself fought for two overriding causes: religious freedom (except for the Anglican and Catholic churches) and constitutional government. But he achieved neither, and he grew increasingly unhappy at the Rump Parliament's refusal to enact reforms. When the assembly tried to prolong its own existence, he dissolved it in 1653 (the final end of the Long Parliament), and during the remaining five years of his life he tried desperately to lay down a new constitutional structure for his government. Cromwell always hoped that Parliament itself would establish the perfect political system for England, but he refused to influence its proceedings. The result was that he ignored the realities of politics and could never put his ideals into practice.

Cromwell was driven by noble aspirations, but in the end he had to rule by military dictatorship. From 1653 on he was called lord protector and ruled through 11 major generals, each responsible for a different district of England and supported by a tax on the estates of royalists. To quell dissent, he banned newspapers, and to prevent disorder, he took such measures as enlisting innkeepers as government spies.

Cromwell was always a reluctant revolutionary; he hated power and sought only limited ends. Some revolutionaries, like Lenin, have a good idea of where they would like to be carried by events; others, like Cromwell, move painfully, hesitantly, and uncertainly to the extremes they finally reach. It was because he sought England's benefit so urgently and because he considered the nation too precious to abandon to irreligion or tyranny that Cromwell remained determinedly in command to the end of his life.

The End of the Revolution Gradually, more traditional political forms reappeared. The Parliament of 1656 offered Cromwell the crown, and

Oliver Cromwell's Aims

When Parliament in late 1656 offered to make Oliver Cromwell the king of England as a way of restoring political stability, he hesitated before replying. He soon came to realize, however, that this was a solution that went against his deepest principles. When he finally came to Parliament with his reply on April 13, 1657, he turned down the offer of a crown and explained in a long speech—from which a passage follows—why he felt it would be wrong to reestablish a monarchy in England.

"I do think you ought to attend to the settling of the peace and liberties of this Nation. Otherwise the Nation will fall in pieces. And in that, so far as I can, I am ready to serve not as a King, but as a Constable. For truly I have, before God, often thought that I could not tell what my business was, save comparing myself to a good Constable set to keep the peace of the parish. And truly this hath been my content and satisfaction in the troubles I have undergone. . . . I was a person who, from my first employment, was suddenly lifted up from lesser trusts to greater. . . . The Providence of God hath laid aside this Title of King; and that not by sudden humor, but by issue of ten or twelve years Civil War, wherein much blood hath been shed. I will not dispute the justice of it when it was done. But God in His severity hath eradicated a whole Family, and thrust them out of the land. And God hath seemed providential not only in striking at the family but at the Name [of king]. It is blotted out. God blasted the very Title. I will not seek to set up that which Providence hath destroyed, and laid in the dust: I would not build Jericho again."

From Thomas Carlyle (ed.), *Oliver Cromwell's Letters and Speeches* (London, 1908), vol. III, pp. 230, 231, and 235.

though he refused, he took the title of "His Highness" and ensured that the succession would go to his son. Cromwell was monarch in all but name, yet only his presence ensured stability (*see box*, p. 484). After he died, his quiet, retiring son Richard proved no match for the scheming generals of the army, who created political turmoil. To bring an end to the uncertainty, General George Monck, the commander of a well-disciplined force in Scotland, marched south in 1660, assumed control, and invited the son of Charles I, Charles II, to return from exile and restore the monarchy.

Only the actions taken during the first months of the Long Parliament—the abolition of royal courts, the prohibition of taxation without parliamentary consent, and the establishment of the writ of habeas corpus—persisted beyond the revolution. Otherwise, everything seemed much the same as before: Bishops and lords were reinstated, religious dissent was again repressed, and Parliament was called and dissolved by the monarch. But the tone and balance of political relations had changed for good.

Henceforth the gentry could no longer be denied a decisive voice in politics. In essence, this had been their revolution, and they had succeeded. When in the 1680s a king again tried to impose his wishes on the country without reference to Parliament, there was no need for another major upheaval. A quiet bloodless coup reaffirmed the new role of the gentry and Parliament. Thus a new settlement was reached after a long period of growing unease and open conflict. The crisis had been resolved, and the English settled into a system of rule that with only gradual modification remained in force for some two centuries.

V. Revolts in France and Spain

THE FRANCE OF HENRY IV

In the 1590s Henry IV resumed the strengthening of royal power that had been interrupted by the civil wars that had begun in the 1560s. He mollified the traditional landed aristocracy, known as the nobility of the sword, with places on his Council of Affairs and large financial settlements. The principal bureaucrats, known as the nobility of the robe, controlled the country's administration, and Henry made sure to turn their interests to his benefit. Since all crown offices had to be bought, he used the system both to raise revenues and to guarantee the loyalty of the bureaucrats. He not only accelerated the sales of offices but also invented a new device, an annual fee known as the *paulette*, which ensured that an officeholder's job would remain in his family when he died. This increased royal profits (by the end of Henry's reign in 1610, receipts from the sales accounted for one-twelfth of crown revenues), and also reduced the flow of newcomers and thus strengthened the commitment of existing officeholders to the crown.

By 1610 Henry had imposed his will throughout France, and he was secure enough to plan an invasion of the Holy Roman Empire. Although he was assassinated as he was about to join his army, his heritage, especially in economic affairs, long outlived him. France's rich agriculture may have had one unfortunate effect—successful merchants abandoned commerce as soon as they could afford to move to the country and buy a title of nobility (and thus gain exemption from taxes)—but it did ensure a solid basis for the French economy. Indeed, agriculture suffered little during the civil wars, though the violence and the rising taxes did cause uprisings of peasants (the main victims of the tax system) almost every year from the 1590s to the 1670s.

Mercantilism By restoring political stability Henry ended the worst economic disruptions, but his main legacy was the notion that his increasingly powerful government was responsible for the health of the country's economy. This view was justified by a theory developed mainly in France: mercantilism, which became an essential ingredient of absolutism. Mercantilism was more a set of attitudes than a systematic economic theory. Its basic premise—an erroneous one—was that the world contained a fixed amount of wealth and that each nation could enrich itself only at the expense of others. To some thinkers, this meant hoarding bullion (gold and

▸ *Anonymous*
THE SEINE FROM THE PONT NEUF, CA. 1635
Henry IV of France, celebrated in the equestrian statue overlooking the Seine that stands in Paris to this day, saw the physical reshaping of his capital as part of the effort to restore order after decades of civil war. He laid out the first squares in any European city, and under the shadow of his palace, the Louvre, he built the Pont Neuf (on the right)—the first open bridge (without houses on it) across the Seine.

silver); to others, it required a favorable balance of trade—more exports than imports. All mercantilists, however, agreed that state regulation of economic affairs was necessary for the welfare of a country. Only a strong, centralized government could encourage native industries, control production, set quality standards, allocate resources, establish tariffs, and take other measures to promote prosperity and improve trade. Thus mercantilism was as much about politics as economics and fitted in perfectly with Henry's restoration of royal power. In line with their advocacy of activist policies, the mercantilists also approved of war. Even economic advance was linked to warfare in this violent age.

LOUIS XIII

Unrest reappeared when Henry's death left the throne to his nine-year-old son, Louis XIII (1610–1643). The widowed queen, Marie de Medicis, served as regent and soon faced revolts by Calvinists and disgruntled nobles. In the face of these troubles, Marie summoned the Estates General in 1614. This was their last meeting for 175 years, until the eve of the French Revolution; and the weakness they displayed, as various groups within the Estates fought one another over plans for political reform, demonstrated that the monarchy was the only institution that could unite the nation. The session revealed the impotence of those who opposed royal policies, and Marie brought criticism to an end by declaring her son to be of age and the regency dissolved. In this absolutist state, further protest could be defined as treason.

Richelieu For a decade, the monarchy lacked energetic direction; but in 1624, one of Marie's favorites, Armand du Plessis de Richelieu, a churchman who rose to be a cardinal through her favor, became chief minister and took control of the government. Over the next 18 years, this ambitious and determined leader resumed Henry IV's assertion of royal authority (*see box*, p. 487).

The monarchy had to manage a number of vested interests as it concentrated its power, and Richelieu's achievement was that he kept them under control. The strongest was the bureaucracy, whose ranks had been swollen by the sale of office. Richelieu always paid close attention to the views of the bureaucrats, and one reason he had such influence over the king was that he acted as the head and representative of this army of royal servants. He also reduced the independence of traditional nobles by giving them positions in the regime as diplomats, soldiers, and officials without significant administrative responsibility. Finally, he took on the Huguenots in a military campaign that led to the capture of their chief bastion, the port of La Rochelle, in 1628. Following the victory he abolished most of the guarantees in the Edict of Nantes and ended the Huguenots' political independence.

Royal Administration Under Richelieu the sale of office broke all bounds: By 1633 it accounted for approximately one-half of royal revenues. Ten years later more than three-quarters of the crown's direct taxation was needed to pay the salaries of the officeholders. It was a vicious circle, and the only solution was to increase the taxes on the lower classes. As this financial burden grew, Richelieu had to improve the government's control over the realm to obtain the revenue he needed. He increased the power of the *intendants,* the government's chief agents in the localities, and established them (instead of the nobles) as the principal representatives of the monarchy in each province of France. Unlike the nobles, the *intendants* depended entirely on royal favor for their position; and so it was with enthusiasm that they recruited for the army, arranged billeting, supervised the raising of taxes, and enforced the king's decrees. They soon came to be hated figures, both because of the rising taxes and because they threatened the power of the nobles. The result was a succession of peasant uprisings, often led by local notables who resented the rise of the *intendants* and of royal power.

POLITICAL CRISIS

France's foreign wars made the discontent worse, and it was clear that eventually the opponents of the central government would reassert themselves. But the amassing of centralized power by the crown had been so successful that when trou-

Richelieu on Diplomacy

The following passages are taken from a collection of the writings of Cardinal Richelieu that was put together after his death and published in 1688 under the title* Political Testament. *The book is presented as a work of advice to the king and summarizes what Richelieu learned of politics and diplomacy as one of Europe's leading statesmen during the Thirty Years' War.

"One cannot imagine how many advantages States gain from continued negotiations, if conducted wisely, unless one has experienced it oneself. I admit I did not realize this truth for five or six years after first being employed in the management of policy. But I am now so sure of it that I dare say boldly that to negotiate everywhere without cease, openly and secretly, even though one makes no immediate gains and future gains seem unlikely, is absolutely necessary for the good of the State. . . . He who negotiates all the time will find at last the right moment to achieve his aims, and even if he does not find it, at least it is true that he can lose nothing, and that through his negotiations he knows what is happening in the world, which is of no small consequence for the good of the State. . . . Important negotiations must not be interrupted for a moment. . . . One must not be disheartened by an unfortunate turn of events, because sometimes it happens that what is undertaken with good reason is achieved with little good fortune. . . . It is difficult to fight often and always win. . . . It is often because negotiations are so innocent that one can gain great advantages from them without ever faring badly. . . . In matters of State one must find an advantage in everything; that which can be useful must never be neglected."

From Louis André (ed.), *Testament Politique* (Paris, 1947), pp. 347–348 and 352. Translated by T. K. Rabb.

ble erupted, in a series of revolts known as the Fronde (or "tempest"), there was no serious effort to reshape the social order or the political system. The principal actors in the Fronde came from the upper levels of society: nobles, townsmen, and members of the regional courts and legislatures known as parlements. Only occasionally were these groups joined by peasants, and there was little foretaste of the revolution that was to overtake France in 1789.

Mazarin The death of Louis XIII, in 1643, followed by a regency because Louis XIV was only five years old, offered an opportunity to those who wanted to reverse the rise of absolutism. Louis XIII's widow, Anne of Austria, took over the government and placed all the power in the hands of an Italian, Cardinal Giulio Mazarin. He used his position to amass a huge fortune, and he was therefore a perfect target for the anger caused by the encroachment of central government on local authority

Early in 1648 Mazarin sought to gain a respite from the monarch's perennial financial trouble by withholding payment of the salaries of some royal officials for four years. In response, the members of various institutions in Paris, including the Parlement, drew up a charter of demands. They wanted the office of *intendant* abolished, no new offices created, power to approve taxes, and enactment of a habeas corpus law. The last two demands reflected what the English Parliament was seeking at this very time, but the first two were long-standing French grievances.

THE FRONDE

Mazarin reacted by arresting the Paris Parlement's leaders, thus sparking a popular rebellion in the city that forced him and the royal family to flee from the capital—an experience the young Louis XIV never forgot. In 1649, Mazarin promised to redress the parlementaires' grievances, and he was allowed to return to Paris. But the trouble was far from over; during that summer uprisings spread throughout France, particularly among peasants and in the old Huguenot stronghold, the southwest.

For the next three years there was political chaos, mainly as a result of intrigues and shifting alliances among the nobility. As it became clear that the perpetual unrest was producing no results, Mazarin was able to take advantage of the disillusionment among the nobles and the parlementaires to reassert the position of the monarchy. He used military force and threats of force to subdue Paris and most of the rebels in the countryside, and he brought the regency to an end by declaring the 14-year-old Louis of age in 1652. Although peasants continued their occasional regional uprisings for many years to come, the Fronde was over and the crown was established as the basis for order in the realm. As surely as England, France had surmounted its crisis and found a stable solution for long-standing conflicts.

SOURCES OF DISCONTENT IN SPAIN

For Spain the crisis that swept much of Europe in the mid-seventeenth century—with revolt in England and France, and war in the empire—meant the end of the country's international power. Yet the difficulties the monarchy faced had their roots in the sixteenth century. Philip II (1556–1598) had already found it difficult to hold his sprawling empire together, despite his elaborate bureaucracy. Obsessively suspicious, he maintained close control over all administrative decisions, and government action was therefore agonizingly slow. Moreover, the bureaucracy was run by Castilian nobles, who were resented as outsiders in other regions of the empire. And the standing army, though essential to royal power, was a terrible financial drain.

Philip did gain wide admiration in Spain for his devoutness. He persecuted heresy, encouraged the Inquisition, and for a while was even suspicious of the great flowering of Spanish mysticism, led by St. Teresa. Philip's commitment to religion undoubtedly promoted political cohesion, but the economic strains caused by relentless religious warfare eventually undermined Spanish power.

Economic Difficulties Spain was a rich country in Philip's reign, but the most profitable activities were monopolized by limited groups. Because royal policy valued convenience above social benefit, the city of Seville (dominated by foreign bankers) received a monopoly over shipping to and from the New World; and other lucrative

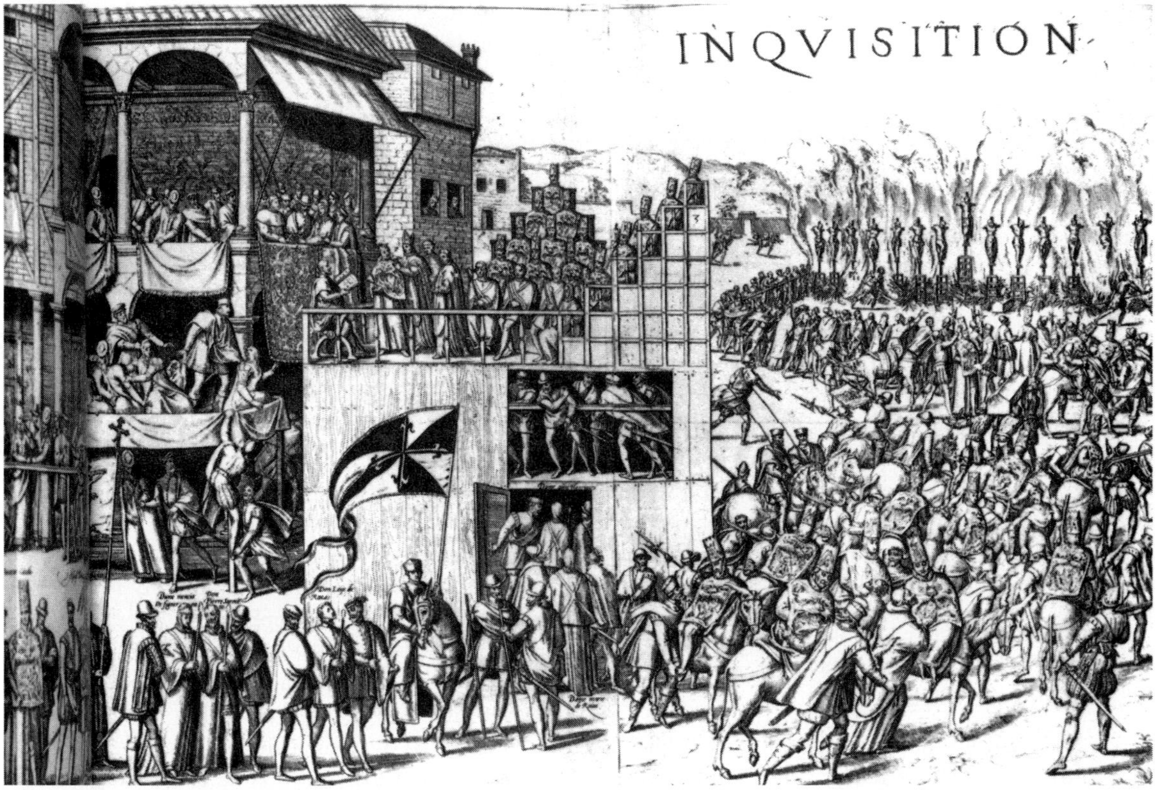

▸ *Anonymous Engraving*
THE SPANISH INQUISITION, 1560
The burning of heretics was a major public event in sixteenth-century Spain. Aimed mainly at people who practiced Judaism or Islam secretly, and in a few cases at Protestants, the Inquisition's investigations usually led to imprisonment or lesser punishments. The occasional executions of those who determinedly refused to accept Catholic teachings, even after torture, were carried out by secular authorities, and they attracted huge crowds.

pursuits, such as wool and wine production, were also controlled by a small coterie of insiders. The only important economic activities that involved large numbers of Spaniards were shipping and the prosperous Mediterranean trade, centered in Barcelona, which brought wealth to much of Catalonia.

Thus the influx of silver into Spain was not profitably invested within the country. Drastically overextended in foreign commitments, Philip had to declare himself bankrupt three times. For a while it seemed that the problems might ease because there was peace during the reign of Philip's son, Philip III (1598–1621). But, in fact, Philip III's government was incompetent and corrupt, capable neither of dealing with the serious consequences of the spending on war nor of broadening the country's exports beyond wool and wine. And when the flow of treasure from the New World began to dwindle after 1600, the crown was deprived of a major source of income that it was unable to replace (see table below).

IMPORTS OF TREASURE TO SPAIN FROM THE NEW WORLD, 1591–1660

Decade	*Total Value**
1591–1600	85,536,000
1601–1610	66,970,000
1611–1620	65,568,000
1621–1630	62,358,000
1631–1640	40,110,000
1641–1650	30,651,000
1651–1660	12,785,000

*In ducats.

Adapted from J. H. Elliott, *Imperial Spain 1469–1716*, New York, 1964, p. 175.

The decline was caused partly by a growing use of precious metals in the New World colonies but also by the depletion of the mines.

In the meantime, tax returns at home were shrinking. The most significant cause of this decrease was a drop in the population of Castile and Aragon as a result of severe plagues—from 10 million in 1600 to 6 million in 1700. No other country in Europe suffered a demographic reversal of this proportion during the seventeenth century. In addition, sheep farming took over huge tracts of arable land, and Spain had to rely increasingly on the importation of expensive foodstuffs to feed its people.

When Spain resumed large-scale fighting against the Dutch and French under Philip IV (1621–1665), the burdens became too much to bear. The effort to maintain the commitment to war despite totally inadequate finances was to bring the greatest state in Europe to its knees.

REVOLT AND SECESSION

The final crisis was brought about by the policies of Philip IV's chief minister, the count of Olivares. His aim was to unite the realm so that all the territories shared equally the burden of maintaining Spanish power. Although Castile would no longer dominate the government, it would also not have to provide the bulk of the taxes and army. Olivares' program was called the Union of Arms, and while it seemed eminently reasonable, it caused a series of revolts in the 1640s that split Spain apart.

The reason was that Castile's dominance had made the other provinces feel that local independence was being undermined by a centralized regime. They saw the Union of Arms, imposed by Olivares, as the last straw. Moreover, the plan appeared at a time when Spain's military and economic fortunes were in decline. France had declared war on the Habsburgs in 1635, the funds to support an army were becoming harder to raise, and in desperation Olivares pressed more vigorously for the Union of Arms. But all he accomplished was to provoke revolts against the Castilians in the 1640s by Catalonia, Portugal, Naples, and Sicily. By 1641 both Catalonia and Portugal had declared themselves independent republics and placed themselves under French protection. Plots began to appear against Olivares, and Philip dismissed the one minister who had understood Spain's problems but who, in trying to solve them, had made them worse.

The Revolts The Catalonian rebellion continued for another 11 years, and it was thwarted in the end only because the peasants and town mobs transformed the resistance to the central government into an attack on the privileged and wealthy classes. When this happened, the Catalan nobility abandoned the cause and joined the government side. About the same time, the Fronde forced the withdrawal of French troops from Catalonia. When the last major holdout, Barcelona, fell to a royal army in 1652, the Catalan nobles could regain their rights and powers, and the revolt was over.

The Portuguese had no social upheaval; as a result, though not officially granted independence from Spain until 1668, they defended their autonomy easily and even invaded Castile in the 1640s. But the revolts that the people of Sicily and Naples directed at their Castilian rulers in 1647 took on social overtones. In Naples the unrest developed into a tremendous mob uprising, led by a local fisherman. The poor turned against all the representatives of government and wealth they could find, and chaos ensued until the leader of the revolt was killed. The violence in Sicily, the result of soaring taxes, was aimed primarily at government officials. In both Naples and Sicily, however, a forceful response enabled the government to regain control within a few months.

The effect of all this unrest was finally to end the Spanish government's international ambitions and thus the worst of its economic difficulties. Like England and France, Spain found a new way of life after its crisis, as a stable second-level state, heavily agricultural, run by its nobility.

VI. Political Change in an Age of Crisis

THE UNITED PROVINCES

The Dutch did not escape the struggles against the power of centralized governments that created an atmosphere of crisis in much of Europe

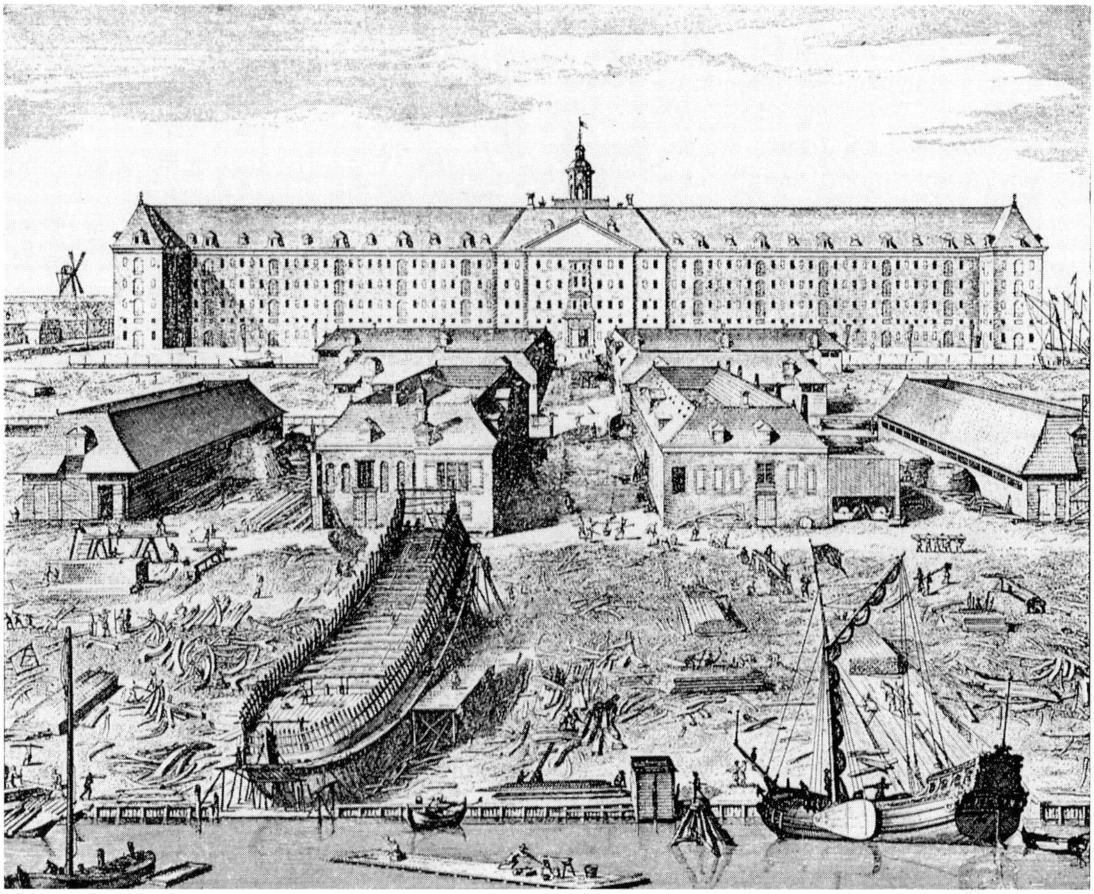

▸ *Anonymous*
Engraving of a Dutch Shipyard
The Dutch became the best shipbuilders in Europe in the seventeenth century; the efficiency of their ships, which could be manned by fewer sailors than those of other countries, was a major reason for their successes in trade and commerce.

during the middle decades of the seventeenth century. Despite the remarkable fluidity of their society, the Dutch, too, became embroiled in a confrontation between a ruling family seeking to extend its authority and citizens defending the autonomy of their local regions. The outcome determined the structure of their government for over a century.

The United Provinces were unique in a number of ways. Other republics existed in Europe, but they were controlled by small oligarchies; the Dutch, who had a long tradition of a strong representative assembly, the Estates General, had created a nation in which many citizens participated in government through elected delegates. Although powerful merchants and a few aristocrats close to the House of Orange did create a small elite, the social differentiation was less than elsewhere in Europe. The resulting openness and homogeneity underlay the economic mastery and cultural brilliance of the United Provinces.

Commerce and Tolerance The most striking accomplishment of the Dutch was their rise to supremacy in the world of commerce. Amsterdam displaced Antwerp as the continent's financial capital and gained control of the trade of the world's richest markets. In addition, the Dutch rapidly emerged as the cheapest international shippers. As a result, by the middle of the seventeenth century they had become the chief carriers of European commerce.

The openness of Dutch society permitted the freest exchange of ideas of the time. The new state gave refuge to believers of all kinds, whether extreme Protestant radicals or Catholics who wore their faith lightly, and Amsterdam became the center of a brilliant Jewish community. This freedom attracted some of the greatest minds in Europe and fostered remarkable artistic creativity. The energy that produced this outpouring reflected the pride of a tiny nation that was winning its independence from Spain.

Two Political Parties Yet there was a basic split within the United Provinces. The two most urbanized and commercial provinces, Holland and Zeeland, dominated the Estates General because they supplied a majority of its taxes. Their representatives formed a mercantile party, which advocated peace abroad so that their trade could flourish unhampered, government by the Estates General so that they could make their influence felt, and religious toleration so that their cities could attract enterprising people of all faiths. In opposition to this mercantile interest was the House of Orange: the descendants of William of Orange, who sought to establish their family's leadership of the Dutch. They were supported by the more rural provinces and stood for war because their authority and popularity derived from their command of the army, for centralized power to enhance the position of the family, and for the strict Calvinism that was upheld in the rural provinces.

The differences between the two factions led Maurice of Nassau to use religion as a pretext for executing his chief opponent, Jan van Oldenbarneveldt, the main representative of the province of Holland, in 1618. Oldenbarneveldt opposed war with Spain, and his removal left the House of Orange in full control of the country. Maurice resumed the war in 1621, and for more than 20 years, his family remained in command, unassailable because it led the army in wartime. Not until 1648—when a new leader, William II, tried to prolong the fighting—could the mercantile party reassert itself by insisting on peace. As a result, the Dutch signed the Treaty of Westphalia, which officially recognized the independence of the United Provinces. It now seemed that Holland and Zeeland had gained the upper hand. But their struggle with the House of Orange continued (there was even a threat by Orange troops to besiege Amsterdam) until William II suddenly died in 1650, leaving as his successor a baby son, William III.

Jan De Witt The mercantile interest now assumed full power, and Jan De Witt, the representative of the province of Holland, took over the government in 1653. De Witt's aims were to leave as much authority as possible in the hands of the provinces, particularly Holland; to weaken the executive and prevent a revival of the House of Orange; to pursue trading advantage; and to maintain peace so that the economic supremacy of the Dutch would not be endangered. For nearly 20 years, he guided the country in its golden age. But in 1672 French armies overran the southern provinces, and De Witt lacked the military instinct to fight a dangerous enemy. The Dutch at once turned to the family that had led them to independence; a mob murdered De Witt; and the House of Orange, under William III, resumed the centralization that henceforth was to characterize the political structure of the United Provinces. The country had not experienced a midcentury upheaval as severe as those of its neighbors, but it had nevertheless been forced to endure unrest and violence before the form of its government was securely established.

SWEDEN

The Swedes, too, settled their political system in the mid-seventeenth century. In 1600 Sweden, a Lutheran country of a million people, was one of the backwaters of Europe. A feudal nobility dominated the countryside, a barter economy made money almost unknown, and both trade and towns were virtually nonexistent. Moreover, the country lacked a capital, central institutions, and government machinery. The royal administration consisted of the king and a few courtiers; other officials were appointed only to deal with specific problems as they arose.

Gustavus Adolphus (1611–1632) transformed this situation. He won over the nobles by giving them dominant positions in a newly expanded bureaucracy, and he reorganized his army. Thus equipped both to govern and to fight, Gustavus embarked on a remarkable series of conquests abroad. By 1629 he had made Sweden the most powerful state in the Baltic area. He then entered the Thirty Years' War, advancing victoriously through the Holy Roman Empire until his death, in 1632, during the showdown battle with Wallenstein. Although without their general the Swedes could do little more than hang on to the gains they had made, they were now a force to be reckoned with in international affairs.

Government and Economy The system of government that Gustavus and his chief adviser, Axel Oxenstierna, established was to be the envy of other countries until the twentieth century. At the heart of the system were five administrative departments, each led by a nobleman, with the most important—the Chancellery, for diplomacy and internal affairs—run by Oxenstierna. An administrative center emerged in Stockholm, and the new bureaucracy proved that it could run the nation, supply the army, and implement policy even during the last 12 years of Gustavus' reign, when the king himself was almost always abroad.

A major cause of Sweden's amazing rise was the development of the domestic economy, stimulated by the opening up of copper mines and the development of a major iron industry. The country's traditional tar and timber exports were also stepped up, and a fleet was built. By 1700 Stockholm had become an important trading and financial center, growing in the course of the century from fewer than 5000 to more than 50,000 inhabitants.

The Nobles The one source of tension amidst this remarkable progress was the position of the nobles. After Gustavus died, they openly challenged the monarchy for control of government and society. Between 1611 and 1652 they more than doubled the proportion of land they owned in Sweden, and much of this growth was at the expense of the crown, which granted away or sold lands to help the war effort abroad. Both peasants and townspeople viewed these developments with alarm, because the nobility usually pursued its own rather than public interests. The concern intensified when, in 1648, the nobles in neighboring Denmark took advantage of the death of a strong king to gain control of the government. Two years later the showdown came in Sweden.

Political Confrontation The monarch now was Gustavus' daughter Christina, an able but erratic young queen who usually allowed Oxenstierna

CHRONOLOGY OF AN AGE OF CRISIS, 1618–1660

1618	Revolt in Bohemia, beginning of Thirty Years' War.
1621	Resumption of war between Spanish and Dutch.
1629	Edict of Restitution—high point of Habsburg power.
1630	Sweden enters war against Habsburgs.
1635	France declares war on Habsburgs.
1639	Scots invade England.
1640	Revolts in Catalonia and Portugal against Spanish government.
1642	Civil War in England.
1647	Revolts in Sicily and Naples against Spanish government.
1648	Peace of Westphalia ending Thirty Years' War. Outbreak of Fronde in France. Coup by nobles in Denmark. Revolt of Ukraine against Poland. Riots in Russian cities.
1650	Constitutional crisis in Sweden. Confrontation between William of Orange and Amsterdam in Netherlands.
1652	End of Catalan revolt.
1653	End of Fronde.
1655	War in Baltic region.
1659	Peace of the Pyrenees between France and Spain.
1660	End of English revolution. Treaties ending war in Baltic.

to run the government. For some time, she had hoped to abdicate her throne, become a Catholic, and leave Sweden—an ambition she fulfilled in 1654. She wanted her cousin Charles recognized as her successor, but the nobles threatened to create a republic if she abdicated. The queen therefore summoned the Riksdag, Sweden's usually weak representative assembly, in 1650; she encouraged the townspeople and peasants to raise their grievances and allowed them to attack the aristocracy. Very soon these groups were demanding the return of nobles' lands to the crown, freedom of speech, and real power; and under this pressure the nobility gave way and recognized Charles X as successor to the throne.

The political upheaval of 1650 was short-lived. Once Christina had her way, she turned her back on the Riksdag and rejected the demands of the lower estates. Only gradually did power shift away from the great nobles toward a broader elite of lesser nobles and bureaucrats, but the turning point in Sweden, as elsewhere, was during the crisis years of the mid-seventeenth century.

EASTERN EUROPE AND THE "CRISIS"

In Eastern Europe, too, long-term patterns became clear in this period. The limits of Ottoman rule were reconfirmed when an attack on Vienna failed in 1683. Poland's weak central government lost all claim to real authority when it proved unable to stop a group of nobles in the rich province of the Ukraine, who rebelled in 1648, from switching allegiance from the king of Poland to the tsar in Moscow. And in Russia, following a period of disorder known as the Time of Troubles (1584–1613), the new Romanov dynasty began consolidating its power. The nobility was won over, the last possibilities for escaping serfdom were closed, the legal system was codified, the church came under the tsar's control, and the revolts that erupted against these changes between 1648 and 1672 were brutally suppressed. As elsewhere in Europe, long-standing conflicts between centralizing regimes and their opponents were resolved, and a new political system, supported by the government's military power, was established for centuries to come.

Because these struggles were so widespread, historians have called the midcentury period an age of "general crisis." In country after country, people tried to resist the growing ambitions of central governments. These confrontations reached crisis proportions in almost all cases during the 1640s and 1650s, and then subsided, at the very time that the anarchy of warfare and international relations seemed to be getting out of hand, only to be resolved by the Peace of Westphalia. As a result, the sense of settlement after 1660 contrasted sharply with the turmoil of the preceding decades. Moreover, the progression in politics from turbulence to calm had its analogies in the cultural and social developments of the sixteenth and seventeenth centuries.

Recommended Reading

Sources

Bodin, Jean. *On Sovereignty.* Julian H. Franklin (ed. and tr.). 1992. An abridgment of Bodin's *Six Books of the Republic.*

*Franklin, Julian H. (ed. and tr.). *Constitutionalism and Resistance in the Sixteenth Century: Three Treatises by Hotman, Beza, & Mornay.* 1969. Three of the most radical tracts of the period, each justifying rebellion.

Kossmann, E. H., and A. E. Mellink. *Texts Concerning the Revolt of the Netherlands.* 1974. A collection of Spanish and Dutch documents which reveal the different political and religious goals of the two sides.

Studies

*Aston, Trevor (ed.). *Crisis in Europe 1560–1660: Essays from Past and Present.* 1965. This is a collection of the essays in which the "general crisis" interpretation was initially put forward and discussed.

*Available in paperback.

Brummett, Palmira. *Ottoman Seapower and Levantine Diplomacy in the Age of Discovery.* 1993.

*DeVries, Jan. *The Economy of Europe in an Age of Crisis, 1600–1750.* 1976. The standard introduction to the economic history of the period.

*Elliott, J. H. *Richelieu and Olivares.* 1984. A comparative study of the two statesmen who dominated Europe in the 1620s and 1630s, this book also analyzes the changing nature of political authority.

*Forster, Robert, and Jack P. Green (eds.). *Preconditions of Revolution in Early Modern Europe.* 1972. An excellent series of essays on resistance to central governments, and its causes, in a number of European countries.

*Hale, J. R. *War and Society in Renaissance Europe 1450–1620.* 1985. A vivid account of what it meant to be a soldier.

Hellie, Richard. *Enserfment and Military Change in Muscovy.* 1971. This study shows the links between military affairs and social change in Russia during the early modern period.

Hirst, Derek. *Authority and Conflict: England, 1603–1658.* 1986. The most recent survey of the revolution and its origins.

Lupinin, N. B. *Religious Revolt in the Seventeenth Century: The Schism of the Russian Church.* 1984. A thorough account of a major feature of Russia's crisis in this period.

Maczak, Antoni, Henryk Samsonowitz, and Peter Burke (eds.). *East-Central Europe in Transition: From the 14th to the 17th Century.* 1985. Essays on the history of Eastern Europe in this period.

*Mattingly, Garrett. *The Armada.* 1959. This beautifully written book, which was a best-seller when it first appeared, is a gripping account of a major international crisis.

Moote, A. Lloyd. *The Revolt of the Judges: The Parlement of Paris and the Fronde 1643–1652.* 1971. This is the most detailed account of the causes of the Fronde and its failures.

*Palliser, D. M. *The Age of Elizabeth: England under the Later Tudors 1547–1603.* 1983. A comprehensive history of English society and government.

Parker, Geoffrey. *The Dutch Revolt.* 1977. This brief book gives a good introduction to the revolt of the Netherlands and the nature of Dutch society in the seventeenth century.

———. *The Military Revolution: Military Innovation and the Rise of the West, 1500–1800.* 1988. The most recent history of the transformation of warfare in this period.

———. *The Thirty Years' War.* 1984. The most up-to-date history of the war.

Pierson, Peter. *Philip II of Spain.* 1975. A clear and lively biography of the dominant figure of the second half of the sixteenth century.

*Rabb, Theodore K. *The Struggle for Stability in Early Modern Europe.* 1975. An assessment of the "crisis" interpretation, including extensive bibliographic references.

Roberts, Michael. *Gustavus Adolphus and the Rise of Sweden.* 1973. This is the best biography of the Swedish king, emphasizing especially his military and administrative achievements.

Salmon, J. H. M. *Society in Crisis: France in the Sixteenth Century.* 1975. A clearly written overview, focusing mainly on the religious wars and Henry IV.

*Skinner, Quentin. *The Foundations of Modern Political Thought.* 1978. The standard account of the political theories of the fifteenth and sixteenth centuries.

Stone, Lawrence. *The Causes of the English Revolution, 1529–1642.* 1972. A short but comprehensive assessment of the reasons for the outbreak of the seventeenth century's most far-reaching revolution.

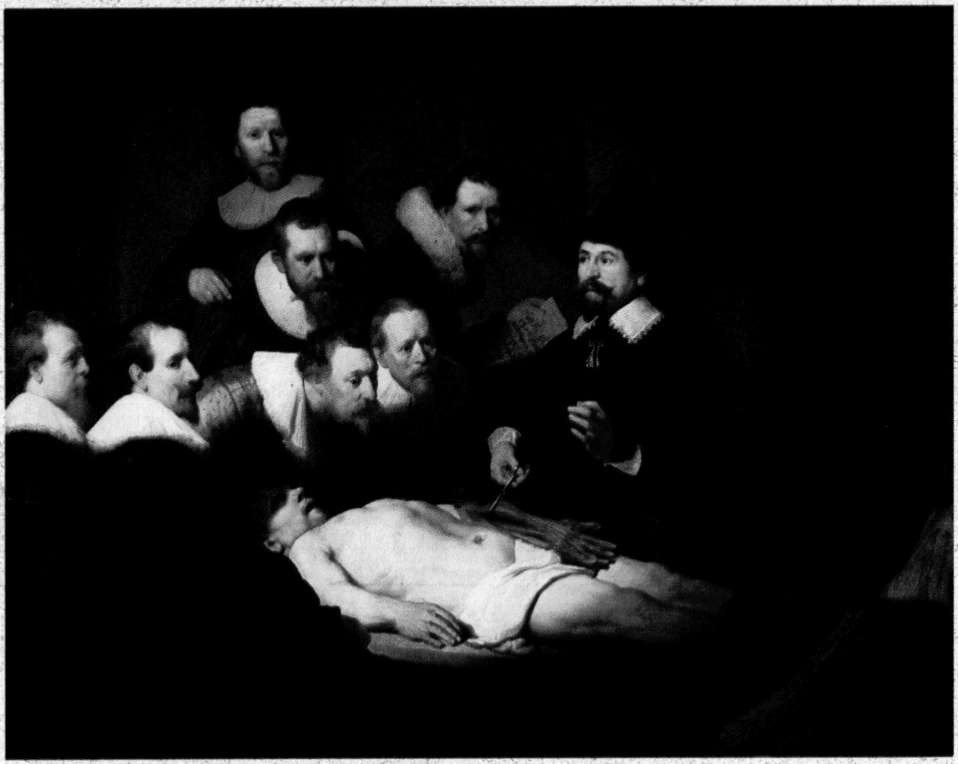

Rembrandt van Rijn
THE ANATOMY LESSON OF DR. NICOLAAS TULP (1632)
Among the many representations of the public anatomy lessons so popular in seventeenth-century Holland, the most famous is one of Rembrandt's greatest paintings, *The Anatomy Lesson of Dr. Nicolaas Tulp.*

CHAPTER SIXTEEN

CULTURE AND SOCIETY IN THE AGE OF THE SCIENTIFIC REVOLUTION

OF all the many changes of the sixteenth and seventeenth centuries, none had a more far-reaching impact than the scientific revolution. By creating a new way of understanding how nature worked—and by solving long-standing problems in physics, astronomy, and anatomy—the theorists and experimenters of this period convinced their contemporaries that they had discovered new knowledge. They were not merely adapting the ideas of the revered figures of Greece and Rome; they had gone further than the ancients. Although their revolution began with disturbing questions but few clear answers about traditional ideas, they ended up by offering a promise of certain knowledge and truth that was eagerly embraced by a society that had been racked by decades of religious and political turmoil and the horrors of war. Indeed, it is remarkable how closely intellectual and cultural patterns paralleled the progression from struggle and uncertainty to stable resolution that marked the political developments of these years. In international and domestic politics a series of clashes grew ever more intense until, following a major crisis in the mid-seventeenth century, Europe's states were able to create more settled conditions. Similarly, in the realms of philosophy and the study of nature, a long period of searching, anxiety, and dispute (epitomized by the confrontation of one scientist, Galileo Galilei, with traditional authority) was resolved in the mid-seventeenth century by scientists whose discoveries and self-assurance helped restore a sense of order in intellectual life. And in literature, the arts, and social relations, a time of insecurity and doubt gave way to an atmosphere of confidence and calm.

I. The Scientific Revolution

ORIGINS OF THE SCIENTIFIC REVOLUTION

The Importance of Antiquity Until the sixteenth century, the study of nature in Europe was inspired by the ancient Greeks. Their work shaped subsequent research in three main fields: Aristotle in physics, Ptolemy in astronomy, and Galen in medicine. The most dramatic advances during the scientific revolution came in these fields, to some extent because it was becoming evident that the ancient theories could not account for new observations without highly complicated adjustments.

For instance, Aristotle's belief that all objects in their natural state are at rest created a number of problems, such as explaining why an arrow kept on flying after it left a bow. Similarly, Ptolemy's picture of the heavens, in which all motion was circular around a central earth, did not readily explain the peculiar motion that observers noticed in some planets, which at times seemed to be moving backward. And Galen's anatomical theories were often shown by dissections to be wrong.

Still, it is not likely that scientists (who in the sixteenth and seventeenth centuries were still known as "natural philosophers," or seekers of wisdom about nature) would have abandoned their cherished theories—they far preferred making adjustments to accepted theories than beginning anew—if it had not been for other influences at work in this period. One such stimulus to rethinking was the humanists' rediscovery of a number of previously unknown ancient scientists, who had not always agreed with the theories of Aristotle or Ptolemy. A particularly important rediscovery was the work of Archimedes, whose writings on dynamics helped inspire new ideas in physics.

"Magic" Another influence was a growing interest in what we now dismiss as "magic," but which at the time was regarded as a serious intellectual enterprise. There were various sides to magical inquiry. Alchemy was the belief that matter could be understood and transformed by mixing substances and using secret formulas. A famous sixteenth-century alchemist, Paracelsus, suggested that metals as well as plants might have medicinal properties, and he helped demonstrate that mercury (if carefully used) could cure syphilis. Another favorite study was astrology, which suggested that natural phenomena could be predicted if planetary movements were properly interpreted.

What linked these "magical" beliefs was the conviction that the world could be understood through simple, comprehensive keys to nature. The theories of Neoplatonism—an influential school of thought during the Renaissance, based

▸ *Peter Brueghel*
THE ALCHEMIST, ENGRAVING
This down-to-earth portrayal, typical of Brueghel's art, shows the alchemist as an undisciplined figure. He is surrounded by a chaos of instruments and half-finished experiments, and his helpers resemble witches. Like Brueghel, most people thought it unlikely that this disorganized figure would make a major contribution to the understanding of nature.

on Plato's belief that truth lay in essential but hidden "forms"—supported this conviction, as did some of the mystical ideas that attracted attention at the same time. One of the latter, derived from a system of Jewish thought known as *cabala*, suggested that the universe might be built around magical arrangements of numbers. The ancient Greek mathematician Pythagoras had also suggested that numerical patterns might connect all of nature, and his ideas now gained new attention. For all its irrational elements, it was precisely this interest in new and simple solutions for long-standing problems that made natural philosophers capable, for the first time, of discarding the honored theories they had inherited from antiquity, trying different ones, paying greater attention to mathematics, and eventually creating an intellectual revolution.

Observations, Experiments, and Instruments Two other influences deserve mention. The first was Europe's fascination with technological invention. The architects, navigators, engineers, and weapons experts of the Renaissance were important pioneers of a new reliance on measurement and observation that affected not only how domes were built or heavy cannon were moved but also how problems in physics were addressed. A second, and related, influence was the growing interest in experiment among anatomists. In particular, the medical school at the university of Padua became famous for its dissections and direct observations of nature; many leading figures in the scientific revolution were trained there.

It was not too surprising, therefore, that important new instruments were invented in the sixteenth and seventeenth centuries which helped make scientific discovery possible: the telescope, the vacuum pump, the thermometer, the barometer, and the microscope. These instruments encouraged the development of a scientific approach that was entirely new in the seventeenth century: It did not go back to the ancients, to the practitioners of magic, or to the engineers. It was to be pioneered by the Englishman Francis Bacon (1561–1626—see p. 505) and consisted of the belief that in order to make nature reveal its secrets, it had to be made to do things it did not do normally: In Bacon's phrase, one had to "twist the lion's tail." What this meant was that one did not simply observe phenomena that occurred normally in nature—for instance, the way a stick seems to bend when it is placed in a glass of water—but created conditions that were *not* normal. With the telescope, one saw secrets hidden to the naked eye; with the vacuum pump, one could understand the properties of air.

THE BREAKTHROUGHS

The earliest scientific advances came in anatomy and astronomy, and by coincidence they were announced in two books published in 1543, which was also the year when the earliest printed edition of Archimedes appeared. The first book, *The Structure of the Human Body* by Andreas Vesalius (1514–1564), a member of the Padua faculty, pointed out errors in the work of Galen, the chief authority in medical practice for over a thousand years. Using dissections, Vesalius produced anatomical descriptions that opened a new era of careful observation and experimentation in studies of the body.

Copernicus The second book, *On the Revolutions of the Heavenly Spheres* by Nicolaus Copernicus (1473–1543), a Polish cleric who had studied at Padua, had far greater consequences. A first-rate mathematician, he felt that the calculations of planetary movements under Ptolemy's system had grown too complex. In Ptolemaic astronomy, the planets and the sun, attached to transparent, crystalline spheres, revolved around the earth. All motion was circular, and irregularities were accounted for by epicycles—movement around small revolving spheres that were attached to the larger spheres. Influenced by Neoplatonic ideas, Copernicus believed that a simpler picture would reflect more accurately the true structure of the universe. In good Neoplatonic fashion, he argued that the sun, as the most splendid of celestial bodies, ought rightfully to be at the center of an orderly and harmonious universe. The earth, no longer immobile, would thus circle the sun.

Copernicus' system was, in fact, scarcely simpler than Ptolemy's—the spheres and epicycles were just as complex—and he had no way of demonstrating the superiority of his theory. But he was such a fine mathematician that his suc-

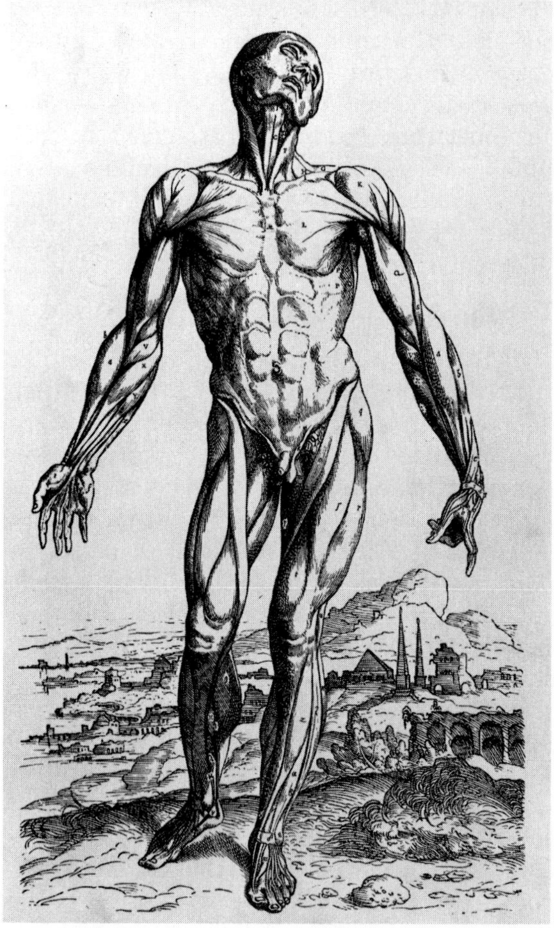

▸ *Titian* (attrib.)
ENGRAVING ILLUSTRATING ANDREAS VESALIUS, THE STRUCTURE OF THE HUMAN BODY (1543)
Almost as remarkable as the findings themselves were these illustrations of the results of Vesalius' dissections. Traditionally, professors of anatomy read from textbooks to their students while lowly barber-surgeons cut up a cadaver and displayed the parts being discussed. Vesalius did his dissections himself, and thus could observe directly such structures as the musculature. Here his illustrator displays the muscles on a gesturing figure and places it in a stretch of countryside near Padua, where Vesalius taught.

cessors found his calculations of planetary motions indispensable. His ideas thus became part of intellectual discussion, drawn on when Pope Gregory XIII decided to reform the calendar in 1582. The Julian calendar, in use since Roman times, counted century years as leap years, thus adding extra days that caused Easter—whose date is determined by the position of the sun—to drift farther and farther away from its normal occurrence in late March. The reform produced the Gregorian calendar, which we still use. Ten days were simply dropped: October 5, 1582, became October 15; and since then only one out of every four century years has been counted as a leap year (1900 had no February 29, but 2000 will have one). The need for calendar reform had been one of the motives for Copernicus' studies, which thus proved useful even though his theories remained controversial.

Theories in Conflict The effect of *Revolutions* for more than half a century was to cause growing uncertainty, as the scholarly community argued over the validity of the new ideas and the need to abandon the old ones. The leading astronomer of the period, the Dane Tycho Brahe (1546–1601), produced the most remarkable observations of the heavens before the invention of the telescope by plotting the paths of the moon and planets every night for decades. But the only theory he could come up with was an uneasy compromise between the Ptolemaic and Copernican systems. There was similar indecision among anatomists, who admired Vesalius but were not ready to discard Galen. As late as 1600 or so, it seemed that scientists were creating more problems than answers. But then two brilliant discoverers—Johannes Kepler (1571–1630), a German disciple of Brahe, and Galileo Galilei, an Italian professor of mathematics—made major advances on the work of Copernicus and helped resolve the uncertainties that had arisen in the field of astronomy.

KEPLER AND GALILEO

Kepler Like Copernicus, Kepler believed that only the language of mathematics could describe the movements of the heavens. He was a famous astrologer and an advocate of magical theories, but he was also convinced that Copernicus was right. He threw himself into the task of confirming the sun-centered (heliocentric) theory, and by studying Brahe's observations, he discovered three laws of planetary motion (published in 1609 and 1619) that opened a new era in astronomy.

Kepler was able to prove that the orbits of the planets are ellipses and that there is a regularity, based on their distance from the sun, that determines the movements of all planets. So revolutionary were these laws that few astronomers accepted them until Isaac Newton used them 50 years later as the basis for a new system of the heavens.

Galileo A contemporary of Kepler's, the Italian Galileo Galilei (1564–1642) took these advances a stage further when he became the first to perceive the connection between planetary motion and motion on earth. His studies revealed the importance to astronomy not only of observation and mathematics but also of physics. Moreover, he was the first to bring the new understanding of the universe to the attention of a reading public beyond the scholarly world. Galileo's self-consciousness about technique, argument, and evidence marks him as one of the first investigators of nature to approach his work in essentially the same way as a modern scientist.

Physics The study of motion inspired Galileo's most fundamental scientific contributions. When he began his investigations, the Aristotelian view that a body is naturally at rest and needs to be pushed constantly to keep moving dominated the study of dynamics. Galileo broke with this tradition, developing instead a new type of physical explanation that was perfected by Isaac Newton half a century later. Much of Galileo's work was based on observation. From watching how workers at the Arsenal in Venice used pulleys and other devices to lift huge weights, he gained insights into physics; adapting a Dutch lens maker's invention, he built himself a primitive telescope that was essential to his studies of the heavens; and his seemingly mundane experiments, such as swinging a pendulum or rolling balls down inclined planes, were crucial means of testing his theories. Indeed, it was by moving from observations to abstraction that Galileo arrived at the first wholly new way of understanding motion since Aristotle: the principle of inertia.

This breakthrough could not have been made by observation alone. For the discovery of inertia depended on mathematical abstraction, the ability to imagine a situation that cannot be created experimentally: the motion of a perfectly smooth ball across a perfectly smooth plane, free of any outside forces, such as friction. Galileo's conclusion was that "any velocity once imparted to a moving body will be rigidly maintained as long as external causes of acceleration and retardation are removed. . . . If the velocity is uniform, it will not be diminished or slackened, much less destroyed." This insight overturned the Aristotelian view. Galileo had demonstrated that only mathematical language could describe the underlying principles of nature.

Astronomy Galileo's most celebrated work was in astronomy. He first became famous in 1610, when he published his discoveries with the telescope that Jupiter has satellites and the moon has mountains. Both these revelations were further blows to traditional beliefs, which held that the earth is changing and imperfect while the heav-

► *Galileo Galilei*
THE MOON, 1610
This sketch of the moon's surface appeared in Galileo's *Starry Messenger* (1610). It shows what he had observed through the telescope and had interpreted as proof that the moon had a rugged surface because the lighted area within the dark section had to be mountains. These caught the light of the setting sun longer than surrounding lower terrain and revealed, for example, a large cavity in the lower center of the sketch.

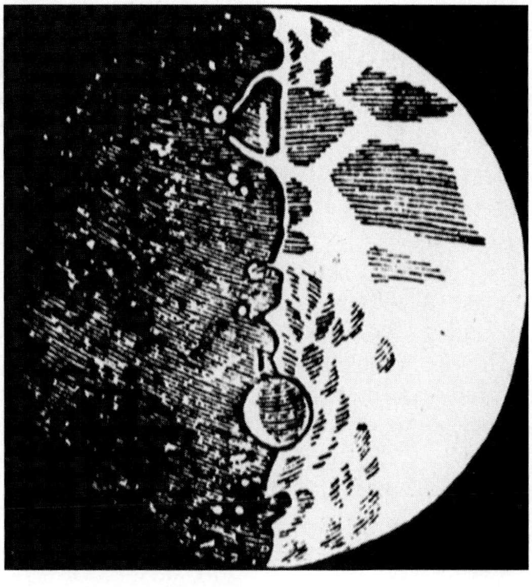

ens are immutable and unblemished. Now, however, it seemed that other planets had satellites, just like the earth, and that these satellites might have the same rough surface as the earth.

This was startling enough, but Galileo also argued that the principles of terrestrial physics could be used to explain phenomena in the heavens. He calculated the height of the mountains on the moon by using the geometric techniques of surveyors, and he described the moon's secondary light—seen while it is a crescent—as a reflection of sunlight from the earth. Galileo was treating his own planet simply as one part of a uniform universe. Every physical law, he was saying, is equally applicable on earth and in the heavens, including the laws of motion. As early as 1597 Galileo had admitted (in a letter to Kepler) that some of his discoveries in physics could be explained only if the earth were moving, and during the next 30 years he became the most famous advocate of Copernicanism in Europe (*see box*, below).

Galileo made a powerful case. Why, he asked, was it necessary to say that the entire universe revolved around the earth when all celestial motions could be explained by the rotation of a single planet, the earth? When academic and religious critics pointed out that we would feel the earth moving, or that the Bible said Joshua made the sun stand still, he reacted with scorn. In response to religious objections, he asserted that "in discussions of physical problems we ought to begin not from the authority of scriptural passages, but from sense experience and necessary demonstrations."

Conflict with the Church For all the brilliance of his arguments, Galileo was now on dangerous ground. Although traditionally the Catholic Church had not concerned itself with investigations of nature, in the early seventeenth century the situation was changing. The Church was deep in the struggle with Protestantism, and it responded to the challenge to its authority by try-

Galileo and Kepler on Copernicus

In 1597 Kepler sent Galileo a copy of his* New Astronomy, *which argued for the Copernican theory of the heavens and asked the Italian for his opinion. The exchange of letters that followed, with Galileo cautious and Kepler urging him on, reflects an age when the new ideas were not yet proved and also gives a hint, in Kepler's last comments, of the troubles that lay ahead.

Galileo to Kepler: "Like you, I accepted the Copernican position several years ago. I have written up many reasons on the subject, but have not dared until now to bring them into the open. I would dare publish my thoughts if there were many like you; but, since there are not, I shall forbear."

Kepler's Reply: "I could only have wished that you, who have so profound an insight, would choose another way. You advise us to retreat before the general ignorance and not to expose ourselves to the violent attacks of the mob of scholars. But after a tremendous task has been begun in our time, first by Copernicus and then by many very learned mathematicians, and when the assertion that the Earth moves can no longer be considered something new, would it not be much better to pull the wagon to its goal by our joint efforts, now that we have got it under way, and gradually, with powerful voices, to shout down the common herd? Be of good cheer, Galileo, and come out publicly! If I judge correctly, there are only a few of the distinguished mathematicians of Europe who would part company with us, so great is the power of truth. If Italy seems a less favorable place for your publication, perhaps Germany will allow us this freedom."

From Giorgio de Santillana, *The Crime of Galileo* (Chicago: University of Chicago Press, 1955), pp. 11 and 14–15.

ing to control potentially questionable views. And Galileo's biting sarcasm toward other scientists antagonized Jesuit and Dominican astronomers. These two orders were the chief upholders of orthodoxy in the Church. They referred Galileo's views to the Inquisition and then guided the attack on Copernicanism by seeking to condemn the brilliant advocate who had made the theory famous throughout Europe.

In 1616 the Inquisition forbade Galileo, within certain limits, to teach the heretical doctrine that the earth moves. When one of his friends was elected pope in 1623, however, Galileo thought he would be safe in writing a major work on astronomy, as long as he remained within the limits set in 1616. The result was Galileo's masterpiece, the *Dialogue on the Two Great World Systems*, published in 1632 (with the approval, probably accidental, of the Church). A marvelously witty, elegant book, the *Dialogue* is one of the few monuments in the history of science that the layperson can read with pleasure. And so it was intended. Galileo wrote it in Italian, not the Latin that had always been used for scholarly works, because he wanted it to reach the widest possible audience.

In April 1633 he was brought before the Inquisition for having defied the order not to teach Copernicanism. To establish their case, his accusers used a forged document that suggested the 1616 limits were stricter than they were. In a trial that has caused controversy ever since, the aged astronomer, under threat of torture, abjured the "errors and heresies" of believing that the earth moved. But he did not remain docile for the remainder of his life, though he was kept under house arrest and progressively lost his eyesight. He had his principal work on physics, the *Two New Sciences*, published in tolerant Holland in 1638, while many of his letters ridiculed his opponents.

Galileo's Legacy Galileo's condemnation discouraged further scientific activity by his compatriots. Italy had been a leader of the new investigations, but now major further advances were to be made by the English, Dutch, and French. Yet this shift showed merely that the rise of science, once begun, could not be halted for long. By the late 1630s no self-respecting astronomer could deny the correctness of the Copernican theory.

The new studies of nature may have started out by causing tremendous bewilderment, as scientists struggled with the ideas of pioneers like Copernicus and Vesalius. But in the end these investigations created a renewed sense of certainty about the physical world that was to have a far-reaching influence. And this was true not only in physics and astronomy but also in anatomy, where, in 1628, another genius of the scientific revolution, the English doctor William Harvey, revolutionized the understanding of the human body when he identified the function of the heart and proved that the blood circulates.

ISAAC NEWTON

The culmination of the scientific revolution was the work of Isaac Newton (1642–1727), who made decisive contributions to mathematics, physics, astronomy, and optics and brought to a climax the changes that had begun with Copernicus. He united physics and astronomy in a single system to explain all motion, he helped transform mathematics by the development of the calculus, and he established some of the basic laws of modern physics.

Part of the explanation of his versatility lies in the workings of the scientific community at the time. Newton was a retiring man who nevertheless got into fierce arguments with such prominent contemporaries as the learned German scholar and scientist Wilhelm von Leibniz, who was working on the calculus. If not for his active participation in meetings of scientists at the recently founded Royal Society of London (see p. 509) and the effort he had to make to demonstrate his views to his colleagues, Newton might never have pursued his researches to their conclusion. He disliked the give-and-take of these discussions, but he felt forced in self-justification to prepare some of his most important papers for the Royal Society. Such institutions were now being established throughout Europe to promote the advance of science, and their creation indicates how far the scientific community had come since the days of Copernicus, who had worked largely in isolation.

The Principia Newton's masterpiece, *The Mathematical Principles of Natural Philosophy* (1687)—usually referred to by the first word of its Latin title, the *Principia*–was the last widely influential book to be written in Latin, the traditional language of scholarship. Latin was still useful to Newton, who wanted as many experts as possible to read the book because he was seeking to refute the approach to science associated with the widely admired French philosopher and mathematician René Descartes (see p. 506). In contrast to Descartes, who emphasized the powers of the mind and pure reason in investigating nature, Newton felt that mere hypotheses, constructions of logic and words, were not the tools of a true scientist. As he put it in a celebrated phrase, "*Hypotheses non fingo*" ("I do not posit hypotheses"), because everything he said was proved by experiment or by mathematics.

The most dramatic of Newton's findings was the solution to the ancient problem of motion. Building on Galileo's advances and overturning Aristotle's theories once and for all, Newton defined his system in three laws: first, in the absence of force, motion continues in a straight line; second, the rate of change of the motion is determined by the forces acting on it (such as friction); and third, action and reaction between two bodies are equal and opposite. To arrive at these laws, he defined the concepts of mass, inertia, and force in relation to velocity and acceleration as we know them today.

Newton extended these principles to the entire universe by demonstrating that his laws govern the motions of the moon and planets too. Using the concept of gravity, he provided the explanation of the movement of objects in space that is the foundation for current space travel. There is a balance, he said, between the earth's pull on the moon and the forward motion of the satellite, which would continue in a straight line were it not for the earth's gravity. Consequently the moon moves in an elliptical orbit in which neither gravity nor inertia gains control. The same pattern is followed by the planets around the sun (as Kepler had shown).

The Influence of Newton It was largely on the basis of the uniformity and the systematic impersonal forces Newton described that the view of the universe as a vast machine gained ground. According to this theory, all motion is a result of precise, unvarying, and demonstrable forces. There is a celestial mechanics just like the mechanics that operates on earth. It was not far from this view to the belief that God is a great watchmaker who started the marvelous mechanism going but intervenes only when something goes wrong and needs repair. The general philosophical implication that the world was stable and orderly was as important as the specific discoveries in making Newton one of the idols of his own and the next centuries. The educated applauded Newton's achievements, and he was the first scientist to receive a knighthood in England. Only a few decades after the appearance of the *Principia*, the poet Alexander Pope summed up the public feeling:

> Nature and nature's law lay hid in night;
> God said, "Let Newton be!" and all was light.

So overpowering was Newton's stature that in physics and astronomy the remarkable advances of 150 years slowed down for more than half a century after the publication of the *Principia*. There was a general impression that somehow Newton had done it all, that no important problems remained. There were other reasons for the slowdown—changing patterns in education, an inevitable lessening of momentum—but none was so powerful as the reverence for Newton, who became the intellectual symbol of his own and succeeding ages.

A NEW EPISTEMOLOGY

Galileo had stressed that his discoveries rested on a way of thinking that had an independent value, and he refused to allow traditional considerations, such as common sense or theological teachings, to interfere with his conclusions. Scientists were now moving toward a new epistemology, a new theory of how to obtain and verify knowledge. They stressed experience, reason, and doubt; they rejected all unsubstantiated authority; and they developed a revolutionary way of determining what was a true description of physical reality.

The process the scientists said they followed,

after they had formulated a hypothesis, consisted of three parts: first, observations; second, a generalization induced from the observations; and third, tests of the generalization by experiments whose outcome could be predicted by the generalization. A generalization remained valid only as long as it was not contradicted by the experiments specifically designed to test it. The scientist used no data except the results of strict observation—such as the time it took balls to roll down Galileo's inclined planes, or the path Kepler saw the plants following—and scientific reasoning was confined to the perception of the laws, principles, or patterns that emerged from the observations. Since measurement was the key to the data, the observations had a numerical, not a subjective, value; and the language of science naturally came to be mathematics.

In fact, scientists rarely reach conclusions in the exact way this idealized scheme suggests. Galileo's perfectly smooth balls and planes, for instance, did not exist, but Galileo understood the relevant physical theory so well that he knew what would have happened if one had rolled across the other, and he used this "experiment" to demonstrate the principle of inertia. In other words, experiments as well as hypotheses can occur in the mind; the essence of scientific method still remains a special way of looking at and understanding nature.

▸ *Anonymous*
Portrait of Isaac Newton
The increasingly common portraits of scientists in the seventeenth century—Descartes was even painted by one of the leading artists of his age, Frans Hals—testify to their growing fame. In this case, the intensity of Newton's gaze hints at the power of scientific insight that contemporaries thought he embodied.

THE WIDER INFLUENCE OF SCIENTIFIC THOUGHT

The principles of scientific inquiry received attention throughout the intellectual community only gradually; it took time for the power of the scientists' method to be recognized. For decades, as Galileo found out, even his fellow astronomers continued to use what he would have considered irrelevant criteria, such as the teachings of the Bible, in judging scientific work. If the new methods were to be accepted, then their effectiveness would have to be demonstrated to more than a few specialists. This wider understanding was eventually achieved by midcentury as much through the efforts or ardent propagandizers like Francis Bacon as through the writings of the great innovators themselves. Gradually, they were able to convince a broad, educated public that science, after first causing doubts by challenging ancient truths, now offered a promise of certainty that was not to be found anywhere else in an age of general crisis.

BACON AND DESCARTES

Bacon Although he was not an important scientist himself, Francis Bacon was the greatest of science's propagandists, and he inspired a whole generation with his vision of what it could accomplish for humanity. His description of an ideal society in the *New Atlantis*—published in

1627, the year after his death—is a vision of science as the savior of the human race. It predicts a time when those doing research at the highest levels will be regarded as the most important people in the state and will work on a vast government-supported project to gather all known facts about the physical universe. By a process of gradual induction, this information will lead to universal laws that, in turn, will enable people to improve their lot on earth.

Bacon's view of research as a collective enterprise inspired a number of later scientists, particularly the founders of the Royal Society of London. By the mid-seventeenth century, his ideas had entered the mainstream of European thought, an acceptance that testified to the broadening interest in science.

Descartes The Frenchman René Descartes (1596–1650) made the first concentrated attempt to apply the new methods of science to theories of knowledge, and, in so doing, he laid the foundations for modern philosophy. The impulse behind his work was his realization that for all the importance of observation and experiment, people can be deceived by their senses. In order to find some solid truth, therefore, he decided to apply the principle of doubt—the refusal to accept any authority without strict verification—to all knowledge. He began with the assumption that he could know unquestionably only one thing: that he was doubting. This allowed him to proceed to the observation "I think, therefore I am," because the act of doubting proved he was thinking, and thinking, in turn, demonstrated his existence.

The heart of his philosophy was his statement that whatever is clearly and distinctly thought must be true. This was a conclusion drawn from the proof of his own existence, and it enabled him to construct a proof of God's existence. We cannot fail to realize that we are imperfect, he argued, and we must therefore have an idea of perfection against which we may be measured. If we have a clear idea of what perfection is, then it must exist; hence there must be a God.

This proof may have served primarily to show that the principle of doubt did not contradict religious belief, but it also reflected the emphasis on the power of the mind in his great work, *Discourse on the Method of Rightly Conducting the Reason and Seeking Truth in the Sciences* (1637). Thought is a pure and unmistakable guide, and only by reliance on its operations can people hope to advance their understanding of the world.

Descartes developed this view into a fundamental proposition about the nature of the world—a proposition that philosophers have been wrestling with ever since. He stated that there is an essential divide between thought and extension (tangible objects) or, put another way, between spirit and matter. Bacon and Galileo had insisted that science, the study of nature, is separate from and unaffected by faith or theology, the study of God. But Descartes turned this distinction into a far-reaching principle, dividing not only science from faith but even the reality of the world from our perception of that reality. There is a difference, in other words, between a chair and how we think of it as a chair.

The Influence of Descartes The emphasis Descartes placed on the operations of the mind gave a new direction to epistemological discussions. A hypothesis gained credibility not so much from external proofs as from the logical tightness of the arguments used to support it. The decisive test was how lucid and irrefutable a statement appeared to be to the thinking mind, not whether it could be demonstrated by experiments. Descartes thus applied what he considered to be the methods of science to all knowledge. Not only the phenomena of nature but all truth had to be investigated according to what he regarded as the strict principles of the scientist.

At the same time, his insistence on strict definitions of cause and effect helped create a general scientific and intellectual theory known as *mechanism*. In its simplest form, mechanism holds that the entire universe, including human beings, can be regarded as a complicated machine and thus subject to strict physical principles. The arm is like a lever, the elbow is like a hinge, and so on. Even an emotion is no more than a simple response to a definable stimulus. This view was to influence philosophers for generations.

Descartes' contributions to the scientific research of his day were theoretical rather than experimental. In physics, he was the first to perceive the distinction between mass and weight; and in mathematics, he was the first to apply algebraic notations and methods to geometry, thus founding analytic geometry. Above all, his emphasis on the principle of doubt undermined forever such traditional assumptions as the belief in the hierarchical organization of the universe. And the admiration he inspired indicated how completely the methods he advocated had captured his contemporaries' imagination.

BLAISE PASCAL

At midcentury only one important voice still protested against the new science and, in particular, against the materialism of Descartes. It belonged to a Frenchman, Blaise Pascal, a brilliant mathematician and experimenter. Before his death at the age of 39 in 1662, Pascal's investigations of probability in games of chance produced the theorem that still bears his name, and his research in conic sections helped lay the foundations for integral calculus. He also helped discover barometric pressure and invented a calculating machine. In his late twenties, however, Pascal became increasingly dissatisfied with scientific research, and he began to wonder whether his life was being properly spent. His doubts were reinforced by frequent visits to his sister, a nun at the Abbey of Port-Royal, where he came into contact with a new spiritual movement within Catholicism known as *Jansenism.*

Jansenism, which insisted that salvation was entirely in the hands of an all-powerful God and that unswerving faith was the only path to salvation, was not a particularly popular movement. But it guided the nuns at Port-Royal; and Pascal was profoundly impressed by their piety, asceticism, and spirituality. Moved by a growing concern with faith, Pascal had a mystical experience in November 1654 that made him resolve to devote his life to the salvation of his soul. He adopted the austere doctrines of Jansenism, and wrote a series of devastating critiques of the more worldly Jesuits, accusing them of irresponsibility and, as he phrased it, of placing cushions under sinners' elbows.

***The* Pensées** During the few remaining years of his life, Pascal put on paper a collection of reflections—some only a few words long, some many pages—that were gathered together after his death and published as the *Pensées* (or "reflections"). These writings revealed not only the beliefs of a deeply religious man but also the anxieties of a scientist who feared the growing influence of science. He did not wish to put an end to research; he merely wanted people to realize that the truths uncovered by science were limited and not as important as the truths perceived by faith. As he put it in one of his more memorable *Pensées,* "The heart has its reasons that reason cannot know."

Pascal was warning against the replacement of the traditional understanding of humanity and its destiny, gained through religious faith, with the conclusions reached by the methods of the scientists. The separation between the material and the spiritual would be fatal, he believed, because it would destroy the primacy and even the importance of the spiritual. Pascal's protest was unique, but the fact that it was put forward at all indicates how high the status of the scientist and his methods had risen by the 1650s. Just a quarter-century earlier, such a dramatic change in fortune would have been hard to predict. But now the new epistemology, after its initial disturbing assault on ancient views, was offering one of the few promises of certainty in an age of upheaval and general crisis. In intellectual matters as in politics, turmoil was gradually giving way to assurance.

SCIENCE INSTITUTIONALIZED

There were many besides Bacon who realized that scientific work should be a cooperative endeavor and that information should be exchanged among all its practitioners. A scientific society founded in Rome in 1603 made the first major effort to apply this view, and it was soon followed up in France, where in the early seventeenth century a friar named Marin Mersenne became the center of an international network of correspondents interested in scientific work. He also spread news by bringing scientists together for discussions and experiments. Contacts that were developed at these meetings led eventually to a more permanent and systematic organization of scientific activity.

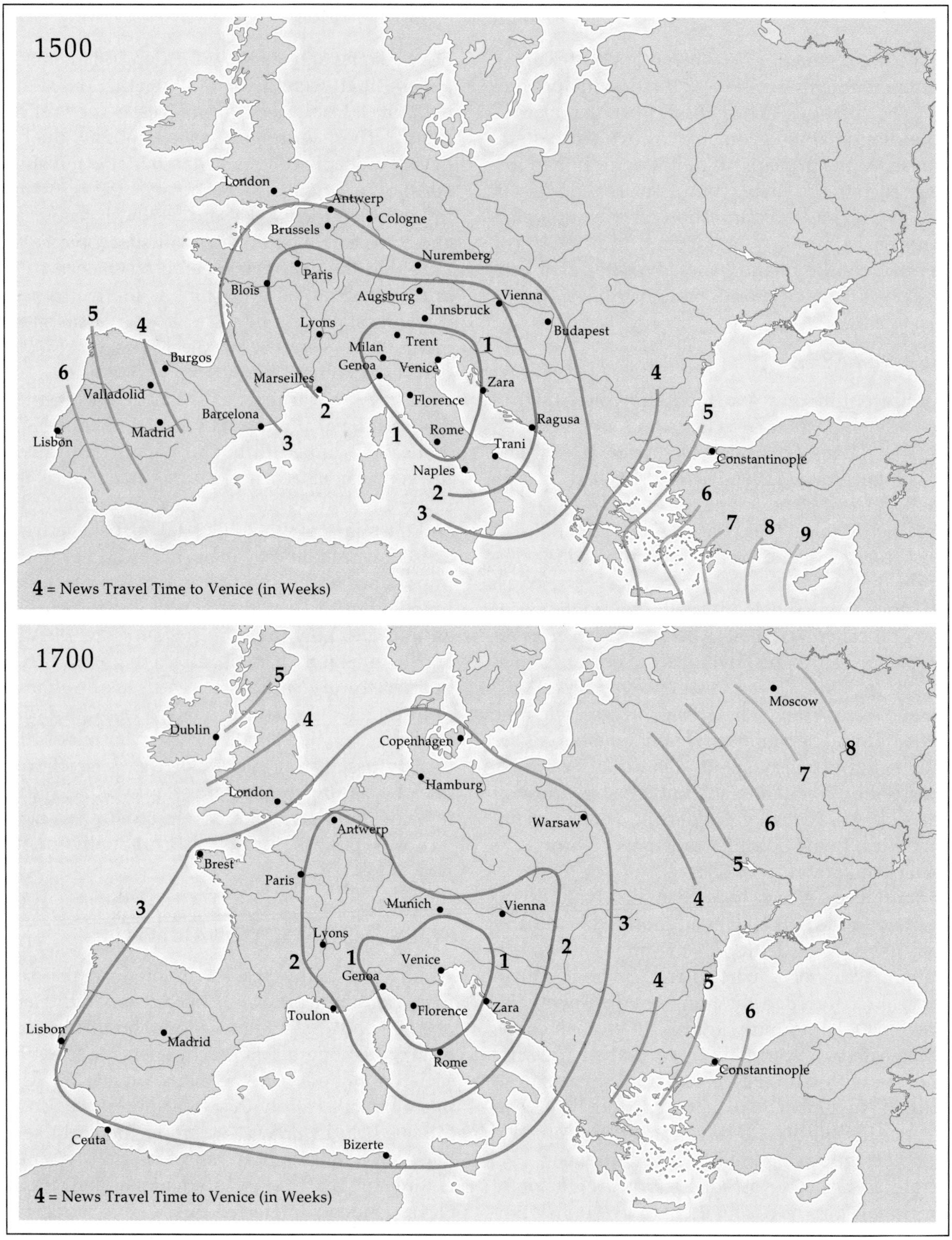

Map 16.1 Speed of News Traveling to Venice in 1500 and 1700

Although the dramatic advances in communications lay in the future, by 1700 improved roads and canals and more efficient shipping did bring about significant advances in the distance news could travel in two or three weeks.

The Royal Society In England, the first steps toward such organization were taken at Oxford during the Civil War in the 1640s, when the revolutionaries captured the city and replaced those at the university who taught traditional natural philosophy. A few of the newcomers formed what they called the Invisible College, a group that met to exchange information and discuss one another's work. The group included only one first-class scientist, the chemist Robert Boyle; but in 1660 he and 11 others formed an official organization, the Royal Society of London for Improving Natural Knowledge, with headquarters in the capital. In 1662 it was granted a charter by Charles II—the first sign of a connection with political authority that not only boosted science but also indicated the growing presence of central governments in all areas of society.

The Royal Society's purposes were openly Baconian. Its aim for a few years—until everyone realized it was impossible—was to gather all knowledge about nature, particularly if it had practical uses. For a long time the members offered their services for the public good, helping in one instance to develop the science of social statistics ("political arithmetic," as it was called) for the government. Soon, however, it became clear that the society's principal function was to serve as a headquarters and clearing center for research. Its secretaries maintained an enormous correspondence to encourage English and foreign scholars to send in news of their discoveries. And in 1665 the society began the regular publication of *Philosophical Transactions*, the first professional scientific journal.

Imitators were soon to follow. In 1666 Louis XIV gave his blessing to the founding of a French Royal Academy of Sciences, and similar organi-

▶ *Charles-Nicolas Cochin*
THE ACADÉMIE ROYALE DES SCIENCES, PARIS, ENGRAVING, 1698
This celebration of the work done by one of the first scientific societies suggests the variety of research that these organizations promoted. In contrast to the students of theology who merely read books (as we see through the arch on the right), the geographers, engineers, astronomers, physicists, and anatomists of the scientific academy examine the real world.

zations were established in Naples and Berlin by 1700. Membership in these societies was limited and highly prized, a sign of the glamour that was beginning to attach itself to the new studies. By the 1660s there could be no doubt that science, secure in royal patronage, had become a model for all thought. Its practitioners were extravagantly admired, and throughout intellectual and high social circles, there was a scramble to apply its methods to almost every conceivable activity.

The Wider Appeal of Science Descartes himself had applied the ideas of science to philosophy in general; Bacon had put them at the service of social thought. But the applications were not only on these high levels. Formal gardens were designed to show the order, harmony, and reason that science had made such prized qualities. And methods of fortification and warfare were affected by the principles of the new investigations, such as the need for accurate measurement.

As the scientists' activities became more popular and fashionable, even aristocrats began to spend time playing at science. Herbariums and small observatories were added to country estates, and parties featured an evening of star gazing. Science also fascinated the general populace. Among the most eagerly anticipated occasions in seventeenth-century Holland was the public anatomy lesson. The body of a criminal would be brought to an enormous hall that was packed with students and a fascinated public. A famous surgeon would dissect the cadaver, announcing and displaying each organ as he removed it.

On the whole, the reverence for science and its methods did not develop from an understanding of its actual accomplishments or its potential consequences. Rather, it was caused by the fame of the spectacular discoveries that had offered new and convincing solutions to centuries-old problems in astronomy, physics, and anatomy. Here was a promise of certainty and order in a world that otherwise was bedeviled by conflict and doubt. As a result, the protests of Pascal could be ignored, and the new discipline could be given unblemished admiration. The entire world was coming to be viewed through the scientist's eyes—a striking achievement for a recently minor member of the intellectual community—and the qualities of regularity and harmony associated with science began to appear in the work of artists and writers.

II. Literature and the Arts

We have seen that the late sixteenth and early seventeenth centuries were a time of political turbulence, culminating in a general crisis in the mid-seventeenth century from which a more settled Europe emerged. Not only did the development of science follow a similar pattern—with decades of uncertainty as old truths were challenged, followed by a new sense of assurance in the mid-seventeenth century—but so too did the concerns of literature and the arts.

MANNERISM

One response that was provoked by the upheavals of the sixteenth century was the attempt to escape reality, an effort that was echoed by some of the painters of the age, known as Mannerists. The Mannerists and their patrons cultivated artificial and esoteric images of the world; they undermined perspective, distorted human figures, and devised unnatural colors and lighting to create startling effects.

El Greco Mannerism was embodied in El Greco (1541–1614), a Greek who was trained in Italy and settled in Spain. His compelling and almost mystic canvases created an otherworldly alternative (reminiscent of St. Teresa's visions) to the troubles of his time. El Greco's elongated and often agonized human beings, cool colors, and eerie lighting make him one of the most distinctive painters in the history of art (see p. 462). Increasingly after 1600, though, painters were to reject the Mannerists' flight from reality; eventually the arts, too, were to reflect the sense of settlement that descended over European civilization in the mid-seventeenth century.

MICHEL DE MONTAIGNE

In the world of literature, the concerns of the age were most vividly expressed by the Frenchman

Michel de Montaigne (1533–1592). Obsessed by the death he saw all around him and determined to overcome his fears, he retired in 1570 to his country home in order to "essay," or test, his innermost feelings by writing short pieces of prose even about subjects he did not fully comprehend. In the process he created a new literary form, the essay, that also helped shape the modern French language. But his chief influence was philosophical: He has inspired the search for self-knowledge ever since.

At first Montaigne's anxieties led him to the radical doubt about the possibility of finding truth that is known as *Skepticism*; this inspired the total uncertainty of his motto *"Que sais-je?"* ("What do I know?"). Eventually, however, Montaigne struggled toward a more confident view, taking as his model the ancient saying "Know thyself." By looking into one's own person, one can find values that hold true at least for oneself, and these will reflect the values of all humanity. Montaigne came close to a morality without theology, because good and self-determination were more important to him than doctrine, and he saw everywhere religious people committing inhuman acts. Trying to be an angel is wrong, he said; being good is enough.

Neostoicism A more general application of some of these ideas was a theory known as *Neostoicism*, inspired by the ancient Stoics' emphasis on self-knowledge and a calm acceptance of the world. The most influential of the Neostoics, a Dutch writer named Justus Lipsius, argued that public leaders ought to be guided by profound self-examination. Lipsius urged rulers to be restrained and self-disciplined, and he was much admired by the kings and royal ministers of the seventeenth century.

CERVANTES AND SHAKESPEARE

Cervantes In Spain the disillusionment that accompanied the political and economic decline of Europe's most powerful state was perfectly captured by Miguel de Cervantes (1547–1616). He was heir to a brilliant satirical tradition that had already produced in the sixteenth century the writings of Erasmus and Rabelais. Cervantes saw the wide gap between the hopes and the realities of his day—in religion, in social institutions, in human behavior—and made the dichotomy the basis of scathing social satire in his novel *Don Quixote*.

At one level, Cervantes was ridiculing the excessive chivalry of the Spanish nobility in his portrayal of a knight who was ready to tilt at windmills, though he obviously admired the sincerity of his well-meaning hero and sympathized with him as a perennial loser. On another level, the author brought to life the Europe of the time—the ordinary people and their hypocrisies and intolerances—with a liveliness rarely matched in literature. His view of that society, however, was far from cheery. "Justice, but not for my house," says Don Quixote. Cervantes avoided politics, but he was clearly directing many of his sharpest barbs at the brutality and disregard for human values that were characteristic of his fanatical times. And in England another towering figure was grappling with similar problems.

Shakespeare For the English-speaking world, the most brilliant writer of this and all other periods was William Shakespeare (1564–1616), whose characters bring to life almost every conceivable mood: searing grief, airy romance, rousing nationalism, uproarious humor. Despite his modest education his imagery shows a familiarity with subjects ranging from astronomy to seamanship, from alchemy to warfare. It is not surprising, therefore, that some have doubted that one man could have produced this amazing body of work.

Shakespeare started writing in the 1590s, when he was in his late twenties, and continued until his death in 1616. During most of this time, he was also involved with a theatrical company, where he often had to produce plays on short notice. He thus had the best of all possible tests—audience reactions—as he gained mastery of theatrical techniques.

Shakespeare's plays made timeless statements about human behavior: love, hatred, violence, sin. Of particular interest to the historian, however, is what he tells us about attitudes that belong especially to his own era. For example, the conservatism of his characters is quite clear. They believe firmly in the hierarchical structure of society, and throughout the long series of historical plays, events suggest that excessive ambition does not pay. Again and again, legality and stability are shown as fundamental virtues amidst turbulent times. Shakespeare's expressions of patriotism are particularly intense; when in *Richard II* the king's uncle, John of Gaunt, lies dying, he pours out his love for his country in words that have moved the English ever since:

> This royal throne of kings, this scepter'd isle,
> This earth of majesty, this seat of Mars,
> This other Eden, demi-paradise, . . .
> This happy breed of men, this little world,
> This precious stone set in the silver sea, . . .
> This blessed plot, this earth,
> this realm, this England.
>
> *RICHARD II*, ACT 2, SCENE 1

As in so much of the art and writing of the time, instability is a central concern of Shakespeare's plays. His four most famous tragedies—*Hamlet, King Lear, Macbeth,* and *Othello*—end in disillusionment: The heroes are ruined by irresoluteness, pride, ambition, or jealousy. Shakespeare was exploring a theme that had absorbed playwrights since Euripides—the fatal flaws that destroy the great—and producing dramas of revenge that were popular in his day; but the plays also demonstrate his deep understanding of human nature. Whatever one's hopes, one cannot forget human weakness, the inevitability of decay, and the constant threat of disaster. The contrast appears with compelling clarity in a speech delivered by Hamlet:

> What a piece of work is man! How noble in reason! how infinite in faculties! in form and moving how express and admirable! in action how like an angel! in apprehension how like a god! the beauty of the world, the paragon of animals! And yet to me what is this quintessence of dust? Man delights not me.
>
> *HAMLET*, ACT 2, SCENE 2

Despite such pessimism, despite the deep sense of human inadequacy, the basic impression Shakespeare gives is of immense vigor, of a restlessness and confidence that recall the many achievements of the sixteenth century. Yet a sense of decay is never far absent. Repeatedly, people seem utterly helpless, overtaken by events they cannot control. Nothing remains constant or dependable, and everything that seems solid or reassuring, be it the love of a daughter or the crown of England, is challenged. In this atmosphere of ceaseless change, where landmarks easily disappear, Shakespeare conveys the tensions of his time.

THE BAROQUE: GRANDEUR AND EXCITEMENT

After 1600, the arts began to move toward the assurance and sense of settlement that was descending over other areas of European civilization. A new style, the Baroque, sought to drown the uneasiness of Mannerism in a blaze of grandeur. Passion, drama, mystery, and awe were the qualities of the Baroque: Every art form—from music to literature, from architecture to opera—had to involve, arouse, and uplift its audience.

The Baroque style was closely associated with the Counter Reformation's emphasis on gorgeous display in Catholic ritual. The patronage of leading Church figures made Rome a magnet for the major painters of the period. Elsewhere, the Baroque flourished primarily at the leading Catholic courts of the seventeenth century, most notably the Habsburg courts in Madrid, Prague, and Brussels. Few periods have conveyed so strong a sense of grandeur, theatricality, and ornateness.

Caravaggio The artist who first shaped the new aesthetic, Caravaggio (1571–1610), lived most of his life in Rome. Although he received commissions from high Church figures and spent time in a cardinal's household, he was equally at home among the beggars and petty criminals of Rome's dark back streets. These ordinary people served as Caravaggio's models, which shocked those who felt it inappropriate for such humble characters to represent the holy figures of biblical scenes. Yet the power of Caravaggio's paintings—their depiction of highly emotional moments, and the drama created by their sharp contrasts of light and dark—made his work much prized. He had to flee Rome after he killed someone in a brawl, but he left behind a body of work that influenced an entire generation of painters.

National Gallery, London

▸ *Caravaggio*
THE SUPPER AT EMMAUS, CA. 1597
By choosing moments of high drama and using sharp contrasts of light, Caravaggio created an immediacy that came to be one of the hallmarks of Baroque painting. This is the moment during the supper at Emmaus when his disciples suddenly recognized the resurrected Christ. The force of their emotions and their almost theatrical gestures convey the intensity of the moment, but many at the time objected to the craggy, tattered appearance of the disciples. These were not idealized figures, as was expected, but ordinary people at a humble table.

Rubens Among those who came to Rome to study Caravaggio's art was Peter Paul Rubens (1577–1640), the principal ornament of the brilliant Habsburg court at Brussels. His major themes typified the grandeur that came to be the hallmark of Baroque style: glorifications of great rulers and also of the ceremony and mystery of Catholicism. Rubens' secular paintings convey enormous strength; his religious works overwhelm the viewer with the majesty of the Church and excite the believer's piety by stressing the power of the faith.

Velázquez Other artists glorified rulers through idealized portraiture. The greatest court painter of the age was Diego Velázquez (1599–1660). His portraits of members of the Spanish court depict rulers and their surroundings in the stately atmosphere appropriate to the theme. Yet occasionally Velázquez hinted at the weakness of an ineffective monarch in his rendering of the face, even though the basic purpose of his work was always to exalt royal power. And his celebration of a notable Habsburg victory, *The Surrender of Breda,* managed to suggest the sadness and emptiness as much as the glory of war.

Bernini GianLorenzo Bernini (1598–1680) brought to sculpture and architecture the qualities that Rubens brought to painting, and like Ru-

▸ *Peter Paul Rubens*
THE DESCENT FROM THE CROSS, 1612
This huge altarpiece was one of the first pictures Rubens painted after he returned to his native Antwerp, after spending most of his twenties developing his art in Italy. The ambitious scale, the strong emotions, the vivid lighting, and the dramatic action showed the artist's commitment to the Baroque style that had recently evolved in Italy, and the powerful impact of the altarpiece helped make him one of the most sought-after painters of the day.

bens he was closely associated with the Counter Reformation. Pope Urban VIII commissioned him in 1629 to complete both the inside and the outer setting of the basilica of St. Peter's in Rome. For the interior Bernini designed a splendid papal throne that seems to float on clouds beneath a burst of sunlight, and for the exterior he created an enormous plaza, surrounded by a double colonnade, that is the largest such plaza in Europe. Similarly, his dramatic religious works reflect the desire of the Counter Reformation popes to electrify the faithful. The sensual and overpowering altarpiece dedicated to the Spanish mystic St. Teresa makes a direct appeal to the emotions of the beholder that reveals the excitement of Baroque at its best.

▶ *Diego Velázquez*
THE SURRENDER OF BREDA, 1635
The contrasting postures of victory and defeat are masterfully captured by Diego Velázquez in *The Surrender of Breda*. The Dutch soldiers droop their heads and lances, but the victorious Spaniards hardly show triumph, and the gesture of the victorious general, Ambrogio Spinola, is one of consolation and understanding.

Music The seventeenth century was significant, too, as a decisive time in the history of music. New instruments, notably in the keyboard and string families, enabled composers to create richer effects than had been possible before. Particularly in Italy, which in the sixteenth and seventeenth centuries was the chief center of new ideas in music, musicians began to explore the

GianLorenzo Bernini

St. Peter's Square and Church, Rome

The magnificent circular double colonnade that Bernini created in front of St. Peter's is one of the triumphs of Baroque architecture. The church itself was already the largest in Christendom (markers in the floor still indicate how far other famous churches would reach if placed inside St. Peter's), and it was topped by the huge dome Michelangelo had designed. The vast enclosed space that Bernini built reinforced the grandeur of a church that was the pope's own.

▸ *GianLorenzo Bernini*
THE ECSTASY OF ST. TERESA, 1652
Bernini's sculpture is as dramatic an example of Baroque art as the paintings of Caravaggio. The moment that St. Teresa described in her autobiography when she attained mystic ecstasy, as an angel repeatedly pierced her heart with a dart, became in Bernini's hands the centerpiece of a theatrical tableau. He placed the patrons who had commissioned the work on two walls of the chapel that houses this altarpiece, sitting in what seem to be boxes and looking at the stage on which the drama unfolds.

potential of a form that first emerged in these years: the opera. Drawing on the resources of the theater, painting, architecture, music, and the dance, an operatic production could achieve splendors that were beyond the reach of any one of these arts on its own. The form was perfectly attuned to the courtly culture of the age, to the love of display among the princes of Europe, and to the Baroque determination to overwhelm one's audience.

The dominant figure in seventeenth-century music was the Italian Claudio Monteverdi (1567–1643), one of the most innovative composers of all time. He has been called with some justification the creator of both the operatic form and the orchestra. His masterpiece *Orfeo* (1607) was a tremendous success, and in the course of the next century operas gained in richness and complexity, attracting composers, as well as audiences, in ever increasing numbers.

CLASSICISM: GRANDEUR AND RESTRAINT

Classicism, the other major style of the seventeenth century, attempted to recapture (though on a much larger scale than Renaissance imitations of antiquity) the aesthetic values and the strict forms that had been favored in ancient Greece and Rome. Like the Baroque, Classicism aimed for grandiose effects, but unlike the Baroque, it achieved them through restraint and discipline within a formal structure. The gradual rise of the Classical style in the seventeenth century echoed the trend toward stabilization that was taking place in other areas of intellectual life and in politics.

Poussin The epitome of disciplined expression and conscious imitation of Classical antiquity is the work of Nicolas Poussin (1594–1665), a French artist who spent much of his career in Rome. Poussin was no less interested than his contemporaries in momentous and dramatic subjects, but the atmosphere is always more subdued than in the work of Velázquez or Rubens. The colors are muted, the figures are restrained, and the settings are serene. Peaceful landscapes, men and women in togas, and ruins of Classical buildings are features of his art.

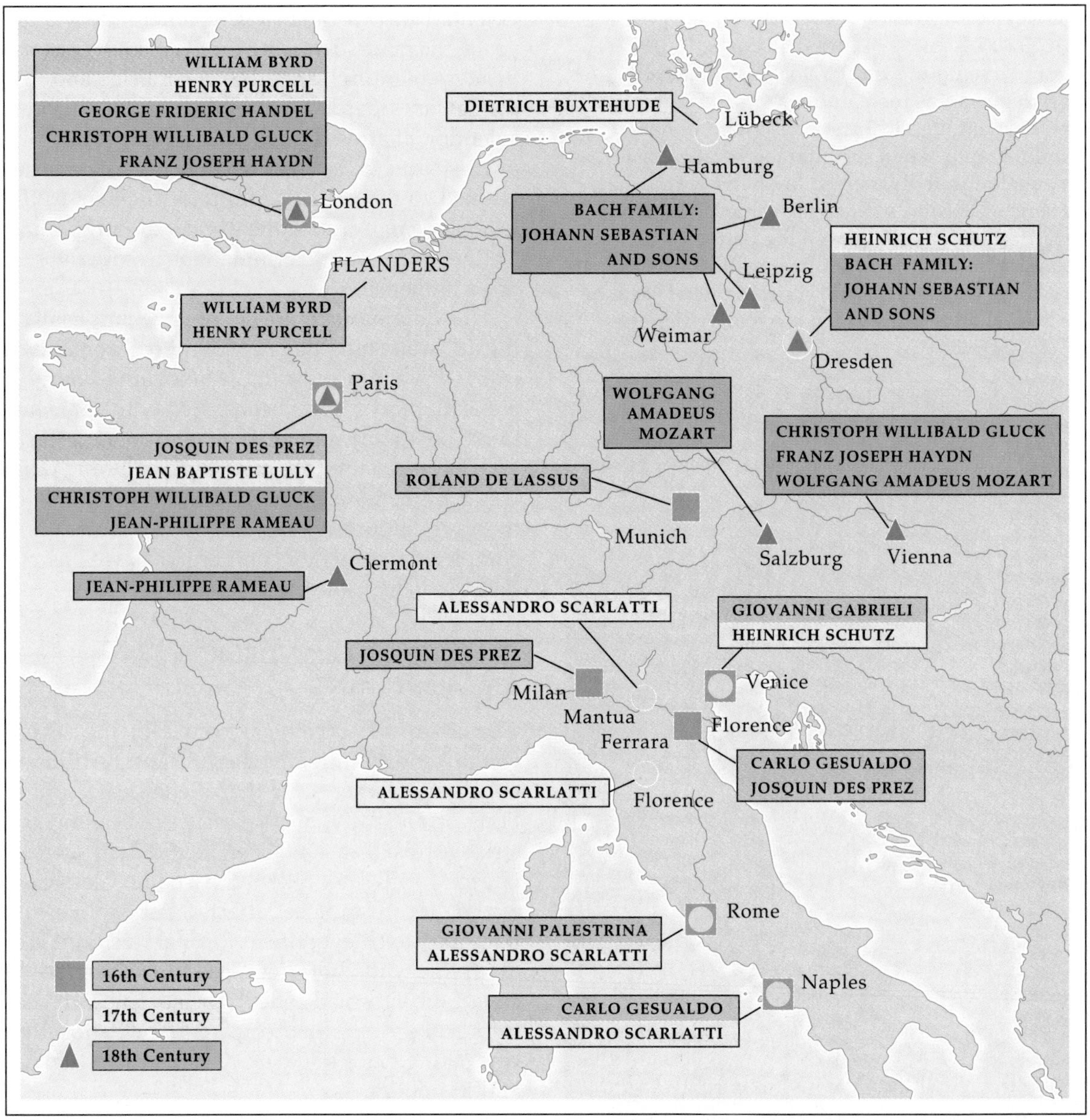

Map 16.2 CENTERS OF MUSIC, 1500–1800
This map indicates the shifting centers of new ideas in music from Flanders and Italy in the sixteenth century; to Italy in the seventeenth; and on to Germany, England, and France in the eighteenth.

The Dutch In the United Provinces different forces were at work, and they led to a style that was much more intimate than the grandiose outpourings of a Rubens or a Velázquez. Two aspects of Dutch society, Protestantism and republicanism, had a particular influence on its painters. The Reformed Church frowned on religious art, which reduced the demand for paintings of biblical scenes. Religious works therefore tended to express personal faith. And the absence of a court meant that the chief patrons of art were sober merchants, who were far more interested in precise, dignified portraits than in ornate displays. The result, notably in the profound and moving works of Rembrandt, was a compelling art whose beauty lies in its calmness and restraint.

Rembrandt Rembrandt van Rijn (1606–1669) explored an amazing range of themes, but he was particularly fascinated by human character, emotion, and self-revelation. Whether children or old people, simple servant girls or rich burghers, his subjects are presented without elaboration or idealization; always the personality speaks for itself. Rembrandt's most remarkable achievement in portraiture—and one of the most moving series of canvases in the history of art—is his depiction of the changes in his own face over his lifetime. The brash youth turns into the confident, successful, middle-aged man, one of the most sought-after painters in Holland. But in his late thirties the sorrows mounted: He lost his beloved wife, and commissions began to fall off. Sadness fills the eyes in these pictures. The last portraits move from despair to a final, quiet resignation as his sight slowly failed. Taken together, these paintings bear comparison with Montaigne's es-

▶ *Nicolas Poussin*
The Inspiration of the Epic Poet, ca. 1628
Whereas Baroque art emphasized emotion, the Classical style sought to embody reason. Poussin, the leading Classical artist of his time, believed that painting, like poetry, had to elevate the minds of its audience. The poet was thus a particularly apt subject for him—a noble and serious theme that could be presented as a scene from antiquity, with formal figures, muted colors, and ancient symbols like the laurel wreath. Poussin's views became the official doctrine of the academy of art founded in France with royal approval, and they influenced generations of painters.

▸ *Rembrandt*
SELF-PORTRAIT WITH PALETTE, 1660
Over 60 self-portraits by Rembrandt have survived; though all are penetrating explorations of human character, those from his last years are especially moving. We see him here in his mid-fifties with the tools of his trade. Adapting Caravaggio's interest in light, he uses different shades of brown and the illumination of the face to create a somber and reflective mood. The very act of thinking is captured in this canvas, not to mention the full life that is etched in Rembrandt's wrinkles.

says as monuments to the exploration of one's own spirit—a searching appraisal that brings all who see it to a deeper understanding of human nature.

One could argue that Rembrandt cannot be fitted into either of the dominant styles of his time. Except for his powerful use of light, his work is far more introspective than most of the Baroque. Nor did he adopt the forms of antiquity, as did Poussin and other Classical painters. Yet, like the advocates of Classicism, Rembrandt in his restraint seemed to anticipate the art of the next generation. After his death in 1669, serenity, calm, and elegance became the watchwords of European painting. An age of repose and grace was succeeding a time of upheaval as surely in the arts as in other spheres of life.

Drama By the middle of the seventeenth century, the formalism of the Classical style was also being extended to literature, especially drama. This change was most noticeable in France, but it soon moved through Western Europe, as leading critics insisted that new plays conform to the structure laid down by the ancients. In particular, they wanted the three Classical unities observed: unity of place, which required that all scenes take place without change of location; unity of time, which demanded that the events in the play occur within a 24-hour period; and unity of action, which dictated simplicity and purity of plot.

Corneille The work of Pierre Corneille (1606–1684), the dominant figure in the French theater during the midcentury years, reflects the rise of Classicism. His early plays were complex and involved, and even after he came into contact with the Classical tradition, he did not accept its rules easily. His masterpiece *Le Cid* (1636), based on the legends of a medieval Spanish hero, technically observed the three unities, but only by compressing an entire tragic love affair, a military campaign, and many other events into one day. The play won immediate popular success, but the critics, urged on by the royal minister Cardinal Richelieu, who admired the regularity and order of Classical style, condemned Corneille for imperfect observance of the three unities. Thereafter he adhered to the Classical forms, though he was never entirely at ease with their restraints.

Passion was not absent from the Classical play; the works of Jean Racine (1639–1699), the model Classical dramatist, generate some of the most intense emotion ever seen on the stage. But the exuberance of earlier drama was disappearing. Nobody summed up the values of Classicism better than Racine in his eulogy of Corneille:

> You know in what a condition the stage was when he began to write. . . . All the rules of art, and even those of decency and decorum, broken everywhere. . . . Corneille, after having for some time sought the right path and struggled against the bad taste of his day, inspired by extraordinary genius and helped by the study of the ancients, at last brought reason upon the stage.
>
> Paul Mesnard (ed.), *Oeuvres de J. Racine*, IV (1886), p. 366, translated by T. K. Rabb

This was exactly the progression—from turbulence to calm—that was apparent throughout European culture in this period.

III. Social Patterns and Popular Culture

POPULATION TRENDS

The sixteenth-century rise in Europe's population was succeeded by a period of decline that in most areas lasted long after the political and intellectual upheavals subsided. The rise had been fragile, because throughout these centuries only one child in two reached adulthood. Each couple had to give birth to four children merely to replace themselves, and since they had to wait until they were financially independent to marry—usually in their mid-twenties—they rarely had the chance to produce a big family. Women in this period lost the capacity to bear children in their late thirties, and on the average, therefore, a woman had some 12 years in which to give birth to four children to maintain the population. Because lactation delayed ovulation, the mean interval between births was almost two and a half years, which meant that most couples were only just capable of raising two adults. As soon as there was outside pressure—such as plague, famine, or war—population growth became impossible.

The worst of these outside pressures in the seventeenth century was the Thirty Years' War, which alone caused the death of more than 5 million people. It also helped plunge Europe into a debilitating economic depression, which, in turn, decreased the means of relieving famine. Disasters of such magnitude could not easily be absorbed. Only when better times returned could population increase resume. Because they led in economic recovery, England and the Netherlands experienced a demographic revival long before their neighbors; indeed, the rise in their numbers, which began in the 1660s, accounted for almost all of the slight population increase the whole of Europe was able to achieve in this difficult century.

SOCIAL STATUS

The determinants of status in modern times—wealth, education, and family background—were viewed rather differently in the seventeenth century. Wealth was significant chiefly to merchants, education was important mainly among professionals, and background was vital primarily to the nobility. But in this period the signifi-

EUROPE'S POPULATION, 1600–1700, BY REGIONS

Region	*1600**	*1700*	*Percentage Change*
Spain, Portugal, and Italy	23.6	22.7	− 4
France, Switzerland, and Germany	35.0	36.2	+ 3
British Isles, Low Countries, and Scandinavia	12.0	16.1	+34
Total	70.6	75.0	+ 6

*All figures are in millions.

Source: Jan de Vries, *The Economy of Europe in an Age of Crisis, 1600–1750*, Cambridge, 1976, p. 5.

cance of these three social indicators began to shift. Wealth became a more general source of status, as ever-larger numbers of successful merchants bought offices, lands, and titles that allowed them to enter the nobility. Education was also becoming more highly prized; throughout Europe attendance at institutions of higher learning soared after 1550, bringing the sons of artisans as well as nobles to universities. And although background was being scrutinized ever more defensively by old-line nobles, who regarded family lineage as the only criterion for acceptance into their ranks, their resistance to change was futile as the "new" aristocrats multiplied.

In general, it was assumed that everyone occupied a fixed place in the social hierarchy and that it was against the order of nature for someone to move to another level. The growing social importance of wealth and education, however, indicates that mobility was possible. Thanks to the expansion of bureaucracies, it became easier to move to new levels, either by winning favor at court or by buying an office. High status conferred important privileges: Great landowners could demand services and fees from their tenants; those with political rights in cities, nobles, and bureaucrats were often exempt from taxes; and courtiers controlled portions of the vast patronage that the government disbursed. At each level, however, women were always considered subordinate: In many countries, even the widows of aristocrats could not inherit their husbands' estates; an abbess could never become prominent in Church government; and the few women allowed to practice a trade were excluded from the leadership of their guild. Nevertheless, there were businesswomen and female artists, writers, and even scientists among the growing numbers of successful self-made people in this period.

MOBILITY AND CRIME

The Peasant The remarkable economic advances of the sixteenth century helped change attitudes toward wealth, but they brought few benefits to the lower levels of society. Peasants throughout Europe were, in fact, entering a time of increasing difficulty at the end of the sixteenth century. Their taxes were rising rapidly, but the prices they got for the food they grew were stabilizing. Moreover, landowners were starting what has been called the "seigneurial reaction"—making additional demands on their tenants, raising rents, and squeezing as much as they could out of the lands they owned. The effects of famine and war were also more severe at this level of society. The only escapes were to cities or armies, both of which grew rapidly in the seventeenth century. Many of those who fled their villages, however, remained on the road, part of the huge bodies of vagrants and beggars who were a common sight throughout Europe.

A few of those who settled in a town or city improved their lot, but for the large majority, poverty in cities was even more miserable and hungry than poverty on the land. Few could become apprentices, and day laborers were poorly paid and usually out of work. As for military careers, armies were carriers of disease, frequently ill fed, and subject to constant hardship.

Crime For many, therefore, the only alternative to starvation was crime. One area of London in the seventeenth century was totally controlled by the underworld. It offered refuge to fugitives and was never entered by respectable citizens. Robbery and violence—committed equally by desperate men, women, and even children—were common in most cities. As a result, social events like dinners and outings, or visits to the theater, took place during the daytime because the streets were unsafe at night.

If caught, Europe's criminals were treated harshly. In an age before regular police forces, however, catching them was difficult. Crime was usually the responsibility of local authorities, who depended on part-time officials (known in England as *constables*) for law enforcement. Only in response to major outbreaks, such as a gang of robbers preying on travelers, would the authorities recruit a more substantial armed band (rather like a posse in the American West) to pursue criminals. If such efforts succeeded in bringing offenders to justice, the defendants found they had few rights, especially if they were poor, and that punishments were severe. Torture was a common means of extracting confessions; various forms of maiming, such as chopping off a hand or an ear, were considered acceptable

▸ *Artemisia Gentileschi*
JUDITH SLAYING HOLOFERNES, CA. 1620
Women artists are rare in the seventeenth century because they were not allowed to become apprentices. But Artemisia (1593–1652) was the daughter of a painter who happened to be a friend of Caravaggio, and she had the opportunity to become a gifted exponent of Baroque style. Known throughout Europe for her vivid portrayals of dramatic scenes (she painted the murder of Holofernes by the biblical heroine Judith at least five times), she practiced her chosen profession with considerable success, despite the trauma of being raped at 17 by a friend of her father's—an act of violence that may be reflected (and avenged) in this painting.

penalties; and repeated thefts could lead to execution.

Society's hierarchical instincts were apparent even in civil disputes, where nobles were usually immune from prosecution and women often could not start a case. If a woman were raped, for example, she had to find a man to bring suit. In one famous case in Italy, a girl's father sued the rapist because it was *his* honor that had been damaged by the attack.

CHANGE IN THE VILLAGE

Over three-quarters of Europe's population still lived in small village communities, but their structure was not what it once had been. In Eastern Europe, peasants were being reduced to serfdom; in the West—our principal concern—familiar relationships and institutions were changing.

The essence of the traditional village had been its isolation. Cut off from frequent contact with the world beyond its immediate region, it had been self-sufficient and closely knit. Everyone knew everyone else, and mutual help was vital for survival. There might be distinctions among villagers—some more prosperous, others less so—but the sense of cohesiveness was powerful. It extended even to the main "outsiders" in the village, the priest and the local lord. The priest was often indistinguishable from his parishioners: almost as poor and sometimes hardly more literate. He adapted to local customs and beliefs, frequently taking part in semipagan rituals so as to keep his authority with his flock. The lord could be exploitative and demanding; but he considered the village his livelihood, and he therefore kept in close touch with its affairs and did all he could to ensure its safety, orderliness, and well-being.

Forces of Change The main intrusions onto this scene were economic and demographic. As a result of the boom in agricultural prices during the sixteenth century, followed by the economic difficulties of the seventeenth, differences in the wealth of the villagers became more marked. The richer peasants began to set themselves apart from their poorer neighbors, and the feeling of village unity began to break down. These divisions were exacerbated by the rise in population during the sixteenth century, which strained resources and forced the less fortunate to leave in search of better opportunities in cities, and by the pressures of "seigneurial reaction," plague, and famine during the more difficult times of the seventeenth century.

Another intrusion which undermined the traditional cohesion of the community was the increased presence of royal officials. For centuries, elected councils, drawn from every part of the population, had run village affairs throughout Europe. In the late seventeenth century, however, these councils began to disappear as outside forces—in some cases a nearby lord, but more often government officials—asserted their control over the localities. Tax gatherers and army recruiters were now familiar figures throughout Europe. Although they were often the target of peasant rebellions, they were also welcomed when, for example, they distributed food during a famine. Their long-term influence, however, was the creation of a new layer of outside authority in the village, which was another cause of the division and fragmentation that led many to flee to the city.

As these outside intrusions gathered force, the interests of the local lord, who traditionally had defended the village's autonomy and had offered help in times of need, also changed. Nobles were beginning to look more and more to royal courts and capital cities, rather than to their local holdings, for position and power. The natural corollary was the "seigneurial reaction," with lords treating the villages they dominated as sources of income and increasingly distancing themselves from the inhabitants. Their commitment to charitable works declined, and they tended more and more to leave the welfare of the local population to church or government officials.

CITY LIFE

As village life changed, the inhabitants who felt forced to leave headed for the city—an impersonal place where, instead of joining a cohesive population, they found themselves part of a mingling of peoples that was breaking down the isolation of local areas. The growing cities needed ever wider regions to provide them with food

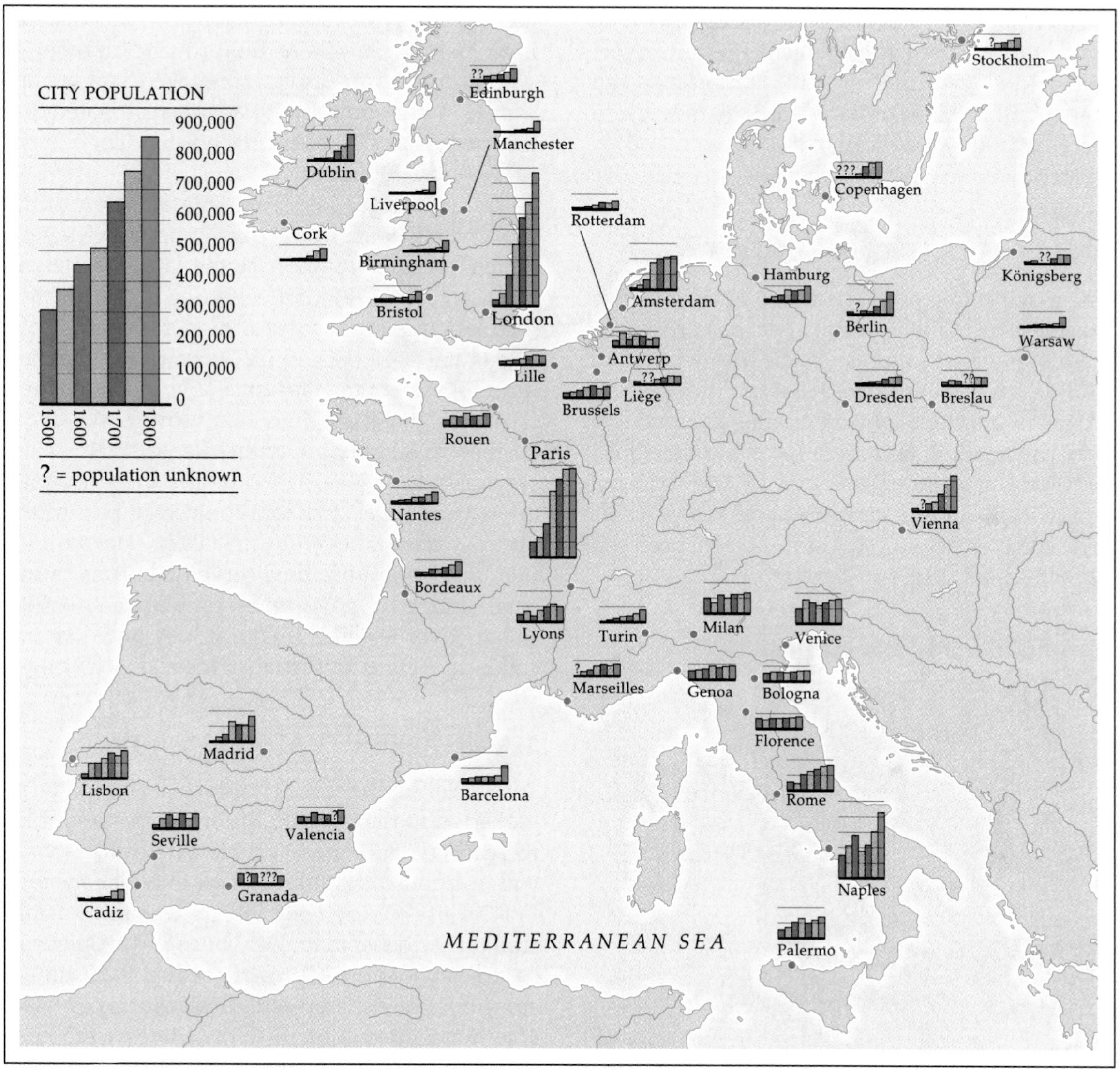

Map 16.3 **The Growth of Cities, 1500–1800**
In addition to the remarkable rise in the population of Europe's cities, particularly after 1550, this map reveals the northward shift in the distribution of the largest cities: in 1500, three of the four largest were in Italy; in 1700, only one.

and goods, and they attracted the many who could not make ends meet in the countryside. Long-distance communications became more common, especially as localities were linked into national market and trade networks, and in the cities the new immigrants met others from distant villages.

There was no question that a city was far a more chaotic place than a rural community. Even if one of its areas, such as a parish, seemed distinct and even cohesive—some parishes, for example, were associated with a single trade—urban society in general was fragmentary and disorganized. A city's craft guilds gave structure to artisans and shopkeepers, regulating their lives and providing welfare, but less than half the population could join a guild. The rest did odd jobs or turned to crime.

The chief attraction of cities was the wide variety of economic opportunity: for women, in such areas as selling goods and processing food;

for men, in construction, on the docks, and in delivery services. But employment was unpredictable, and citizens did not have community support to fall back on in hard times as they did in the village. Even the forms of recreation and enjoyment were different in the city.

POPULAR CULTURE IN THE CITY

One major difference between country and town was the level of literacy. Only in urban areas were there significant numbers of people who could read: It has been estimated that in cities perhaps a third of adult males were literate by 1700. Not only was reading necessary for commerce but it had been strongly encouraged by the Reformation, with its insistence that the faithful read the Bible for themselves. This stimulus ensured that literacy also rose among women, who increasingly became pupils at the growing number of schools in Europe (though they were still not admitted to universities). It has been estimated that as many as 20 percent of the adult women in cities were able to read.

These changes had a notable effect on urban life. There was now a readership for newspapers, which became common in the late seventeenth century, as did the coffeehouses in which they were often read. Theater and opera became popular entertainments, with women for the first time taking stage roles and able to obtain performances for plays they had written. When the English royal official Samuel Pepys hired a new servant in the 1660s, he made sure she could play an instrument so that she could take part in the family's musical evenings. Sales of books multiplied, often because they served a popular audience, and they gave wide circulation to traditional favorites like travel stories and lives of saints as well as to the latest ideas of science.

MAGIC AND RITUALS

Although in the countryside cultural patterns looked different—with lower literacy, simpler recreations, and more visible religiosity—there was one area of popular culture in which the outlook of the city and the village was remarkably similar: the belief in magic. The townspeople may have seemed more sophisticated, but the basic assumption they shared with their country cousins was that nature and their own lives were controlled by mysterious forces, and there was little they could do to ensure their own well-being. The world was full of spirits, and all one could do was

▶ *Anonymous Woodcut*
THE NEWSVENDOR
The ancestor of the regularly published newspaper was the occasional single sheet describing the latest news or rumors. Printers would produce a few hundred copies and have them sold by street vendors whenever they had an event of some importance to describe: a battle, the death of a ruler, or some fantastic occurrence like the birth of a baby with two heads. As cities and the potential readership grew, the news sheets expanded; by the seventeenth century they had distinctive names and began to appear every week.

encourage the good, defend oneself against the evil, and hope that the good would win. Nothing that happened—a calf dying, lightning striking a house—was accidental. Everything had a purpose. Any unusual event was an omen, part of a larger plan, or the action of some unseen force.

"Charivari" To strengthen themselves against trouble, people used whatever help they could find. They organized special processions and holidays to celebrate good times such as harvests, to lament misfortunes, to complain about oppression, or to poke fun at scandalous behavior. These occasions, known as "rough music" in England and "charivari" in France, often used the theme of "the world turned upside down" to make their point. In the set pieces in a procession, a fool might be dressed up as a king, a woman might be shown beating her husband, or a tax collector might appear hanging from a tree. Whether ridiculing a dominating wife or lamenting the lack of bread, the community was expressing its solidarity in the face of difficulty or distasteful behavior through these rituals. It was a way of letting off steam and declaring public opinion.

The potential for violence was always present at such gatherings, especially when religious or social differences became entangled with other resentments. The viciousness of ordinary Protestants and Catholics toward one another—it was not uncommon for one side to mutilate the dead bodies of the other—revealed a frustration and aggressiveness that was not far below the surface. When food was scarce or new impositions had been ordered by their rulers, peasants and townspeople needed little excuse to show their anger openly. Women took the lead, not only because they had firsthand experience of the difficulty of feeding a family but also because troops were more reluctant to attack them. This tradition was still alive in 1789, in the early days of the French Revolution, when a band made up primarily of women marched from Paris to the royal court at Versailles to demand bread.

The Belief in Magic Ordinary people also had other outlets for their frustrations. Recognizing their powerlessness in the face of outside forces, they resorted to their version of the magic that the literate were finding so fashionable at this very time. Where the sophisticated patronized astrologers, paying handsomely for horoscopes and advice about how to live their lives, the peasants and the poor consulted popular almanacs or sought out "cunning men" and wise women for secret spells, potions, and other remedies for their anxieties. Even religious ceremonies were thought of as being related to the rituals of the magical world, in which so-called white witches—the friendly kind—gave assistance when a ring was lost, when a new bride could not become pregnant, or when the butter would not form out of the milk.

WITCHCRAFT

Misfortunes, in other words, were never just plain bad luck; rather, there was intent behind everything that happened. Events were *willed*, and if they turned out badly, they must have been willed by the good witch's opposite, the evil witch. Such beliefs often led to cruel persecutions of innocent victims—usually helpless old women, able to do nothing but mutter curses when taunted by neighbors and easy targets if someone had to be blamed for unfortunate happenings.

This quest for scapegoats naturally focused on the most vulnerable members of society, such as Jews or, in the case of witches, women. Accusations were often directed at a woman who was old and alone, with nobody to defend her. She was feared because she seemed to be an outsider, or not sufficiently deferential to her supposed betters. It was believed that witches read strange books and knew magic spells, an indication of what many regarded as inappropriate and dangerous levels of literacy and learning for a woman.

Witch-hunts In the sixteenth and seventeenth centuries, the hunt for witches intensified to levels never previously reached. This has been called the era of "the great witch craze," and for good reason. There were outbursts in every part of Europe, and tens of thousands of the accused were executed. Dozens of men, most of them clerics, made witch-hunting a full-time profession, and persuaded civic and other government au-

▸ *Hans Baldung Grien*
WITCHES, WOODCUT
This woodcut, by the German artist Grien, shows the popular image of witches in early modern Europe. One carries a potion while flying on a goat. The others put together the ingredients for a magic potion in a jar inscribed with mystical symbols. The fact that witches were thought to be learned women who could understand magic was another reason they were feared by a Europe that expected women to be uneducated.

thorities to devote their resources to stamping out this threat to social and religious stability. Suspects were almost always tortured, and it is not too surprising that they usually "confessed" and implicated others as servants of the devil. The practices that were uncovered varied—in some areas witches were said to dance with the devil, in others to fly on broomsticks, in others to be possessed by evil spirits who could induce dreadful (and possibly psychosomatic) symptoms—but the punishment was usually the same: burning at the stake. And the hysteria was infectious. One accusation could trigger dozens more until entire regions were swept with fear and hatred.

FORCES OF RESTRAINT

By the middle of the seventeenth century the wave of assaults on witches was beginning to recede (*see box*, below). Social and political leaders came to realize how dangerous to authority campaigns against witches could become, especially when accusations were turned against the rich and privileged classes. Increasingly, therefore, cases were not brought to trial, and when they were, lawyers and doctors (who approached the subject from a different point of view than the clergy) cast doubt on the validity of the testimony. Gradually, excesses were restrained and control was reestablished; by 1700 there was only a trickle of new incidents.

The decline in accusations of witchcraft reflected not only the more general quieting down of conflict and upheaval in the late seventeenth century but also the growing proportion of Europe's population that was living in cities. Here, less reliant on the luck of good weather, people could feel themselves more in control of their own fates. If there were unexpected fires, there were fire brigades; if a house burned down, there might even be insurance—a new protection for

A Witness Analyzes the Witch Craze

Although for most Europeans around 1600 witchcraft was real—a religious problem caused by the devil—there were a few observers who were beginning to think more analytically about the reasons for the rapid spread of accusations. One such observer was a clergyman named Linden, who was attached to the cathedral of the great city of Trier in western Germany. His description of a witch-hunt in the Trier region ignored the standard religious explanations.

"Inasmuch as it was popularly believed that the continued sterility of many years was caused by witches, the whole area rose to exterminate the witches. This movement was promoted by many in office, who hoped to gain wealth from the persecution. And so special accusers, inquisitors, notaries, judges, and constables dragged to trial and torture human beings of both sexes and burned them in great numbers. Scarcely any of those who were accused escaped punishment. So far did the madness of the furious populace and the courts go in this thirst for blood and booty that there was scarcely anybody who was not smirched by some suspicion of this crime. Meanwhile, notaries, copyists and innkeepers grew rich. The executioner rode a fine horse, like a noble of the court, and dressed in gold and silver; his wife competed with noble dames in the richness of her array. A direr pestilence or a more ruthless invader could hardly have ravaged the territory than this inquisition and persecution without bounds. Many were the reasons for doubting that all were really guilty. At last, though the flames were still unsated, the people grew poor, rules were made and enforced restricting the fees and costs of examinations, and suddenly, as when in war funds fail, the zeal of the persecutors died out."

From George L. Burr (ed.), "The Witch Persecutions," *Translations and Reprints from the Original Sources of European History*, III (Philadelphia: University of Pennsylvania, 1902), pp. 13–14.

individuals that was spreading in the late 1600s. A process that has been called the "disenchantment" of the world—growing skepticism about spirits and mysterious forces, and greater self-reliance—was under way.

Religious Discipline The churches played an important part in the suppression of the traditional reliance on magic. In Catholic countries the Counter Reformation produced better-educated priests who were trained to impose official doctrine instead of tolerating unusual local customs. Among Protestants, ministers were similarly well educated and denounced magical practices as idolatrous or superstitious. And both camps treated passion and enthusiasm with suspicion. Habits did not change overnight, but gradually ordinary people were being persuaded to abandon old fears and beliefs.

Even at the level of popular culture, therefore, Europeans had reason to feel, by the late seventeenth century, that a time of upheaval and uncertainty was over. A sense of confidence and orderliness was returning, and in intellectual circles the optimism seemed justified by the achievements of science. In fact, there arose a scholarly dispute around 1700, known as "the battle of the books," in which one side claimed, for the first time, that the "moderns" had outshone the "ancients." Using the scientists as their chief example, the advocates of the "moderns" argued—in a remarkable break with the reverence for the past that had dominated medieval and Renaissance culture—that advances in thought were possible and that one did not always have to accept the superiority of antiquity. Such self-confidence made it clear that, in the world of ideas as surely as in the world of politics, a period of turbulence had given way to an era of renewed assurance and stability.

Recommended Reading

Sources

*Drake, Stillman (tr. and ed.). *Discoveries and Opinions of Galileo.* 1957. The complete texts of some of Galileo's most important works.

*Hall, Marie Boas (ed.). *Nature and Nature's Laws: Documents of the Scientific Revolution.* 1970. A good collection of documents by and about the pioneers of modern science.

Studies

Braudel, Fernand. *Capitalism and Material Life 1400–1800.* Miriam Kochan (tr.). 1973. A classic, pioneering study of the structure of daily life in early modern Europe.

*Burke, Peter. *Popular Culture in Early Modern Europe.* 1978. A lively introduction to the many forms of expression and belief among the ordinary people of Europe.

*Butterfield, Herbert. *The Origins of Modern Science.* 1949. An elegantly written history of the scientific revolution that conveys its excitement.

Drake, Stillman. *Galileo.* 1980. The standard biography of a central figure in the scientific revolution.

Frame, Donald M. *Montaigne: A Biography.* 1965. The best biography of this influential thinker.

*Ginzburg, Carlo. *The Cheese and the Worms: The Cosmos of a Sixteenth-Century Miller.* John and Ann Tedeschi (trs.). 1980. A remarkable account, focusing on the beliefs of a man who lived in a small northern Italian town, which brings to life the extraordinary variety of the popular culture of the time.

*Gutmann, Myron P. *Toward the Modern Economy: Early Industry in Europe 1500–1800.* 1988. A clear survey of recent work on economic development in this period.

*Hibbard, Howard, *Bernini.* 1965. A graceful account of the life and work of the artist who was the epitome of the Baroque.

*Krailsheimer, Alban. *Pascal.* 1980. The best brief biography, with good discussions of the life, the science, and the turn to religion.

*Available in paperback.

*Kuhn, Thomas S. *The Structure of Scientific Revolutions.* 1962. A suggestive interpretation of the reasons the scientific revolution developed and took hold.

*Ladurie, Emmanuel Le Roy. *The Peasants of Languedoc.* John Day (tr.). 1966. A brilliant evocation of peasant life in France in the sixteenth and seventeenth centuries.

*Levack, Brian P. *The Witch-Hunt in Early Modern Europe.* 1987. An excellent survey of the belief in witchcraft and its consequences.

Maland, David. *Culture and Society in Seventeenth-Century France.* 1970. This survey of art, drama, and literature contains a good discussion of the rise of Classicism.

Palisca, Claude. *Baroque Music.* 1968. The best survey of this period in the history of music.

*Popkin, Richard H. *The History of Scepticism from Erasmus to Descartes.* 1964. Taking one strand in European thought as its subject, this lively study places both Montaigne and Descartes in a new perspective.

Rabb, Theodore K. *Renaissance Lives.* 1993. Brief biographies of 15 people, both famous and obscure, who lived just before and during this period.

*Shearman, John. *Mannerism.* 1968. The best short introduction to a difficult artistic style.

Tapié, V. L. *The Age of Grandeur: Baroque Art and Architecture.* A. R. Williamson (tr.). 1960. Although concentrating primarily on France and Austria, this is the most comprehensive survey of this period in art.

*Thirsk, Joan. *Economic Policy and Projects: The Development of a Consumer Society in Early Modern England.* 1978. A fascinating study of changing social and economic patterns.

*Thomas, Keith. *Religion and the Decline of Magic.* 1976. The most thorough account of popular culture yet published, this enormous book, while dealing mainly with England, treats at length such subjects as witchcraft, astrology, and ghosts in a most readable style.

*Westfall, Richard S. *The Construction of Modern Science: Mechanisms and Mechanics.* 1971. A cogent analysis of a central theme in the history of the scientific revolution.

———. *Never at Rest: A Biography of Isaac Newton.* 1980. The best introduction to the life and work of the great scientist.

White, Christopher. *Rembrandt and His World.* 1964. A brief but wide-ranging introduction to the artist's work and life.

———. *Rubens and His World.* 1968. As good on Rubens as the previous title is on Rembrandt.

LOUIS XIV AND HIS FAMILY
Louis XIV (seated) is shown here in full regal splendor surrounded by three of his heirs. On his right is his eldest son, on his left is his eldest grandson, and, reaching out his hand, his eldest great-grandson, held by his governess. All three of these heirs died before Louis, and thus they never became kings of France.

CHAPTER SEVENTEEN

THE EMERGENCE OF THE EUROPEAN STATE SYSTEM

THE acceptance of the strong central governments that emerged out of the crisis of the mid-seventeenth century was a victory not merely for kings but for an entire way of organizing political structures. As a result of huge increases both in the demands of warfare and in the availability of resources, bureaucracies had mushroomed, and their presence was felt throughout Europe. Yet no central administration, however powerful, could function without the support of the nobles who ruled the countryside. Regional loyalties had dominated European society for centuries, and only a regime that drew on those loyalties could hope to maintain the support of its subjects. The political structures that were developed during the century following the 1650s were therefore as much the work of a nobility that had long been accustomed to exercising authority, but was now prepared to find new ways of exerting its influence, as they were the product of ambitious princes. There were conflicts between monarchs and their subjects, to be sure, but it was clear to the leaders of society during the century following the crisis of the 1640s and 1650s that state building required a common effort to create political, social, military, financial, and religious structures that would enable governments to function more effectively. The result was the emergence of a set of institutions and practices that have remained essential to the functioning of the modern state ever since.

I. The Creation of Absolutism in France

VERSAILLES

The setting in which a central government operated often told a great deal about its power and its methods. Philip II in the late sixteenth century had created, at the Escorial outside Madrid, the first isolated palace that controlled a large realm. A hundred years later, the French King Louis XIV (1643–1715) created at Versailles, near Paris, a far more elaborate court as the center of an even larger and more intrusive bureaucracy than Philip's. It was as if the isolation of government and the exercise of vast personal power went hand in hand.

The king moved the court out of the capital in the 1680s and eventually, at a cost of half a year's royal income, transformed a small château his father had built at Versailles, 12 miles from Paris, into the largest building in Europe. There he could enjoy in peace the splendor and the daily round of ceremonies, centered on himself, which exalted his majesty. His very name, "Sun King" was a means of self-aggrandizement, symbolized by coins that showed the rays of the sun falling first on Louis and then by reflection onto his subjects, who thus owed life and warmth to their monarch.

Louis himself was almost never alone. Every nobleman of any significance in France spent time each year at Versailles, not only to maintain access to royal patronage and governmental af-

THE PALACE OF VERSAILLES IN 1668
This painting shows Versailles not long before Louis decided to move there; he was soon to begin an enormous expansion into the gardens at the back which more than doubled the size of the buildings. In this scene, the royal coach, with its entourage, is just about to enter the château.

fairs but also to demonstrate the countrywide support for the system of rule Louis was developing. Historians have called this process the domestication of the aristocracy, in which great lords who had once drawn their status primarily from their lineage or their lands came to regard service to the throne as the best route to power. But the benefits cut both ways. The king gained the services of qualified and influential administrators, and they gained privileges and rewards without the uncertainties that had accompanied their traditional resistance to central control.

Absolutism The belief that the monarch was absolute—that all power emanated from his unlimited authority—was based on a widely held theory known as the divine right of kings. This theory, which derived from the fact that kings were anointed with holy oil at their coronations, had long asserted that the monarch was God's representative on earth. Taken to an extreme, as it was at Versailles, this view justified absolute power and regarded treason as blasphemy. The leading advocate of the theory, Bishop Bossuet, called Louis God's lieutenant and argued that the Bible itself endorsed absolutism. In reality, the king worked in close partnership with the nobles to maintain order, and he often (though not always) felt obliged to defend their local authority as a reinforcement of his own power. Nevertheless, the very notion that the king not only was supreme but could assert his will with armies and bureaucracies of unprecedented size gave absolutism both an image and a reality that set it apart from previous systems of monarchical rule. This was, at last, a force that could hold together and control the increasingly complex interactions of regions and interest groups that made up a state.

Court Life The visible symbol of Louis' absolutism was his court at Versailles. Here the leaders of France assembled, and around them swirled the most envied social circles of the time. From the court emanated the policies and directives that increasingly affected the lives of the king's subjects and also determined France's relations with other states.

At Versailles, too, French culture was shaped by the king's patronage of those artists and writers who appealed to the royal taste. For serious drama and history, Louis turned to the playwright and writer Racine (1639–1699); for comedy, to the theatrical producer and playwright Molière (1622–1673); and for opera and the first performances of what we now call ballet, to the composer Lully (1632–1687). Moreover, all artistic expression, from poetry to painting, was regulated by royal academies that were founded in the seventeenth century; backed by the king's authority, they laid down rules for what was acceptable in such areas as verse forms or architectural style. When the famous Italian sculptor and architect Bernini, for example, came to Paris to design part of a royal palace and fashion a sculpture of the king, both works were rejected as overly ornate. Official taste was all that counted. The dazzling splendor of Versailles had to be achieved in strict conformity to rules of dignity and gravity that were considered the only means of exalting the king. Yet everything was done on a scale and with a magnificence that no other European ruler could match, though many tried.

Paris and Versailles The one alternative to Versailles as a center of society and culture was Paris, and indeed it has been suggested that the split between the court and the capital was one of the divisions between government and people that was eventually to lead to the French Revolution. A particularly notable difference was in the role of women. Versailles was overwhelmingly a male society. Women achieved prominence only as royal mistresses in Louis' early years, or as the creators of a rigidly pious atmosphere in his last years. They were also essential to the highly elaborate rituals of civility and manners that developed at Versailles. But they were allowed no independent initiative in social or cultural matters. In Paris, by contrast, women established and dominated the salons that promoted easy conversation, a mixture of social backgrounds, and forms of expression—political discussion and ribald humor, for example—that were not acceptable at the staid and sober court. Yet the contrasts were not merely between the formalities of a palace and the relaxation of a salon. Even before the king moved to Versailles, he banned as improper one of Molière's comedies, *Tartuffe*, which mocked excessive religious devoutness. It took

▸ *Antoine Watteau*
FÊTE IN THE PARK, 1718
The luxurious life of the nobility during the eighteenth century is captured in this scene of men and women in fine silks, enjoying a picnic in a lovely park setting.

five years of reworking by Molière before Louis would allow the play to be performed (1669), and it then became a major hit in Paris; significantly, though, it was never to be a favorite at court.

GOVERNMENT

Absolutism was not merely a device to satisfy royal whims, for Louis was a gifted administrator and politician who used his power for state building. In creating or reorganizing government institutions, he strengthened his authority at home and increased his ascendancy over his neighbors. The most durable result of the absolutist regime he commanded was that the French state won control over three crucial activities: the use of armed force, the formulation and execution of laws, and the collection and expenditure of revenue. These functions, in turn, depended on a centrally controlled bureaucracy responsive to royal orders and efficient enough to carry them out in distant provinces over the objections of local groups.

Although it was impossible to suppress all vested interests and local loyalties, an absolute monarch's bureaucracy was supposed to be insulated from outside pressure by the king's power to remove and transfer appointees. This independence was also promoted by training programs, improved administrative methods, and the use of experts wherever possible—both in the central bureaucracy and in provincial offices. Yet the system could not have functioned without the cooperation of local aristocrats, who were encouraged to use the power and income they derived from official positions to strengthen central authority.

Louis as King At the head of this structure, Louis XIV carried off successfully a dual function that few monarchs had the talent to sustain: He was both king in council and king in court. Louis the administrator coexisted with Louis the courtier, who hunted, cultivated the arts, and indulged in huge banquets. In his view, the two roles went together, and he held them in balance. Among his numerous imitators, however, the easier side of absolutism, court life, consumed an excessive share of a state's resources and became an end in itself. The effect was to give prestige to the leisure pursuits of the upper classes while sapping the energies of influential figures. Louis was one of the few who avoided sacrificing affairs of state to regal pomp.

Like court life, government policy under Louis XIV was tailored to the aim of state building. As he was to discover, there were limits to his absolutism; the resources and powers at his disposal were not endless. But until the last years of his reign, they served his many purposes extremely well (*see box,* below). Moreover, Louis had superb support at the highest levels of his administration—ministers whose viewpoints differed but whose skills were carefully blended by their ruler.

Colbert and Louvois The king's two leading advisers until the late 1680s were Jean-Baptiste Colbert and the marquis of Louvois. Colbert was a financial wizard who regarded a mercantilist policy as the key to state building. He believed that the government should give priority to increasing France's wealth. As a result, he felt that the chief danger to the country's well-being was the United Provinces, Europe's great trader state, and that royal resources should be poured into the navy, manufacturing, and shipping. By contrast, Louvois, the son of a military administrator, consistently emphasized the army as the foundation of France's power. He believed that the country was threatened primarily by land—by the Holy Roman Empire on its flat, vulnerable northeast frontier—and thus that resources should be allocated to the army and to border fortifications.

Louis XIV on Kingship

From time to time, Louis XIV put on paper brief accounts of his actions: For example, he wrote some brief memoirs in the late 1660s. These reflections about his role as king were intended as a guide for his son and indicate both his high view of kingship and the seriousness with which he approached his duties. The following are extracts from his memoirs and other writings.

"Homage is due to kings, and they do whatever they like. It certainly must be agreed that, however bad a prince may be, it is always a heinous crime for his subjects to rebel against him. He who gave men kings willed that they should be respected as His lieutenants, and reserved to Himself the right to question their conduct. It is His will that everyone who is born a subject should obey without qualification. This law, as clear as it is universal, was not made only for the sake of princes: it is also for the good of the people themselves. It is therefore the duty of kings to sustain by their own example the religion upon which they rely; and they must realize that, if their subjects see them plunged in vice or violence, they can hardly render to their person the respect due to their office, or recognize in them the living image of Him who is all-holy as well as almighty.

"It is a fine thing, a noble and enjoyable thing, to be a king. But it is not without its pains, its fatigues, and its troubles. One must work hard to reign. In working for the state, a king is working for himself. The good of the one is the glory of the other. When the state is prosperous, famous, and powerful, the king who is the cause of it is glorious; and he ought in consequence to have a larger share than others do of all that is most agreeable in life."

From J. M. Thompson, *Lectures on Foreign History, 1494–1789* (Oxford: Blackwell, 1956), pp. 172–174.

FOREIGN POLICY

Louis tried to balance these goals within his overall aims—to expand France's frontiers and to assert his superiority over other European states. Like the magnificence of his court, his power on the international scene served to demonstrate "la gloire" (the glory) of France. But his effort to expand that power prompted his neighbors to form coalitions and alliances of common defense, designed to keep him in check. From this response was to emerge the concept of a state system and the notion of a balance of power among the states of Europe.

In his early years Louis relied heavily on Colbert, who moved gradually toward war with the Dutch when all attempts to undermine their control of French maritime trade failed. But the war (1672–1678) was a failure, and so the pendulum swung toward Louvois. In the early 1680s Louis adopted the marquis' aims and asserted his right to a succession of territories on France's northeast border. No one claim seemed important enough to provoke his neighbors to military action, especially since the Holy Roman Emperor, Leopold I, was distracted by a resumption in 1682 of war with the Turks in the East. The result was that France was able to annex large segments of territory until, in 1686, a league of other European states was formed to restrain Louis' growing power (see Map 17.1).

Map 17.1 THE WARS OF LOUIS XIV
***A.* Louis XIV's aggressive aims took his troops to many areas of Europe.**
***B.* The main conflict was on France's eastern border, where Louis made small but significant gains.**

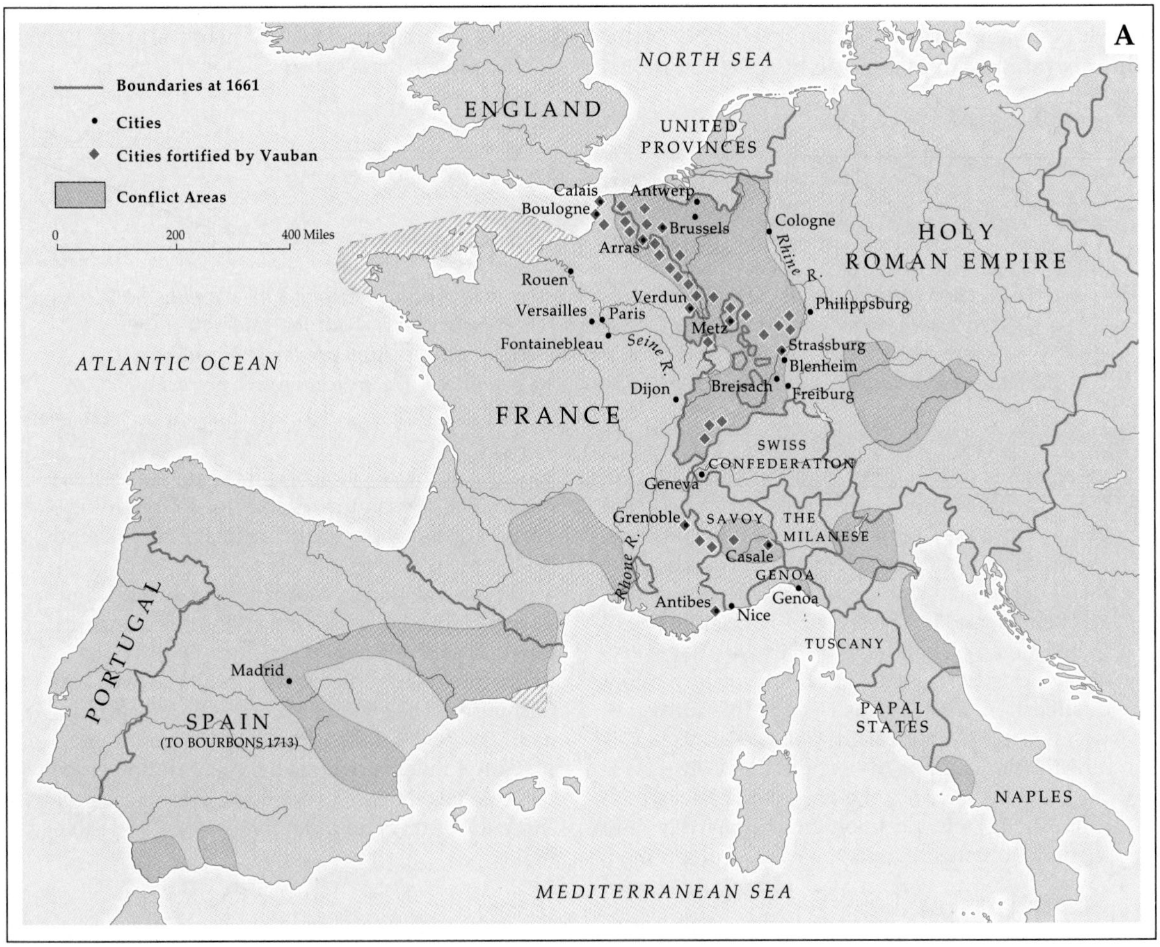

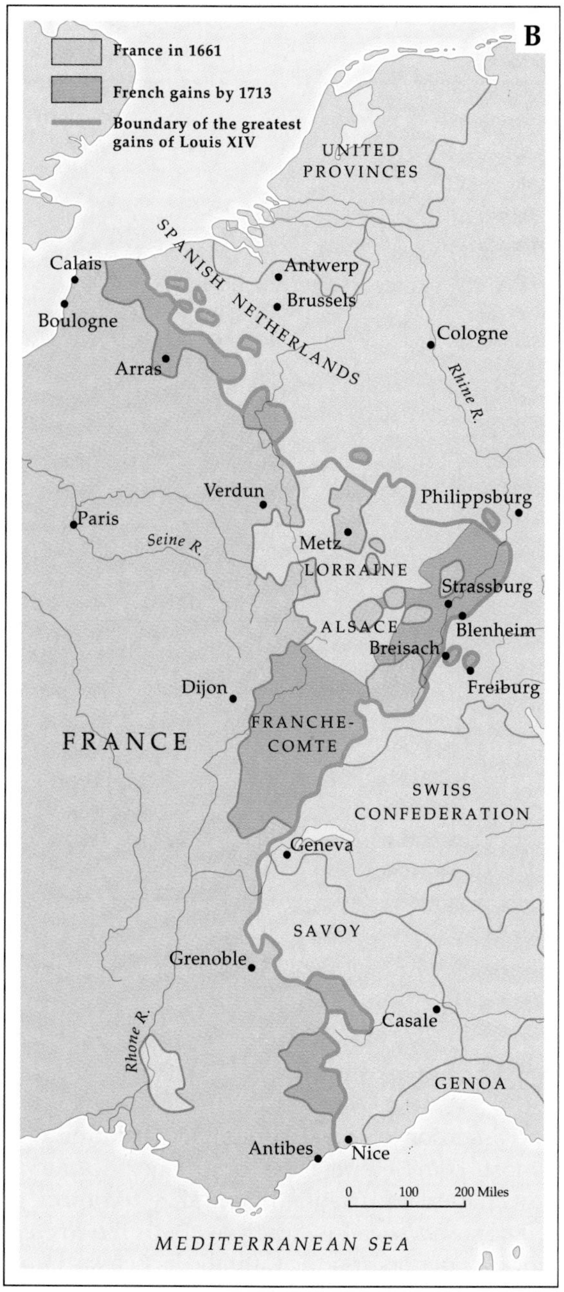

Louis versus Europe The leaders of the league were William III of the United Provinces and Emperor Leopold. Leopold was prepared to join the struggle because, even though his war with the Turks was to continue until 1699, the fighting turned in his favor after 1683, when his troops broke a Turkish siege of Vienna. And six years later William became a far more redoubtable foe when he gained the English throne. The league finally went to war to put an end to French expansion in 1688, and when Louis began to lose the territories he had gained in the 1680s, he decided to seek peace and remove Louvois from power in 1690, though the war did not end until 1697. But the respite did not last long. Four years later France became involved in a bitter war that brought famine, wretched poverty, and humiliation. Louis was now seeking the succession to the Spanish throne for his family, with no regard for the terrible consequences of the fighting. This final, ruinous enterprise revealed both the new power of France and its limits. By launching an all-out attempt to establish his own and his country's supremacy in Europe, Louis showed that he felt capable of taking on the whole of the continent; but by then he no longer had the economic and military base at home or the weak opposition abroad to ensure success.

Economic strains had begun to appear in the 1690s, when shattering famines throughout France reduced tax revenues and the size of the work force, even as enemies began to unite abroad. Louis had the most formidable army in Europe—400,000 men by the end of his reign—but both William and Leopold believed he could be defeated by a combined assault, and they led the attack in the final showdown when the Habsburg king of Spain, Charles II, died without an heir in 1700.

There were various possible claimants to the Spanish throne, and Charles himself had changed his mind a number of times, but at his death his choice was Philip, Louis XIV's grandson (see the genealogical table on p. 540). Had Louis been willing to agree not to unite the thrones of France and Spain and to allow the Spanish empire to be opened (for the first time) to foreign traders, Charles's wish might well have been respected. But Louis refused to compromise, and in 1701 William and Leopold created the so-called Grand Alliance, which declared war on France the following year. The French now found themselves fighting virtually all of Europe in a war over the Spanish succession, not only at home but also overseas, in India, Canada, and the Caribbean.

Led by two brilliant generals—the English-

THE SPANISH SUCCESSION, 1700

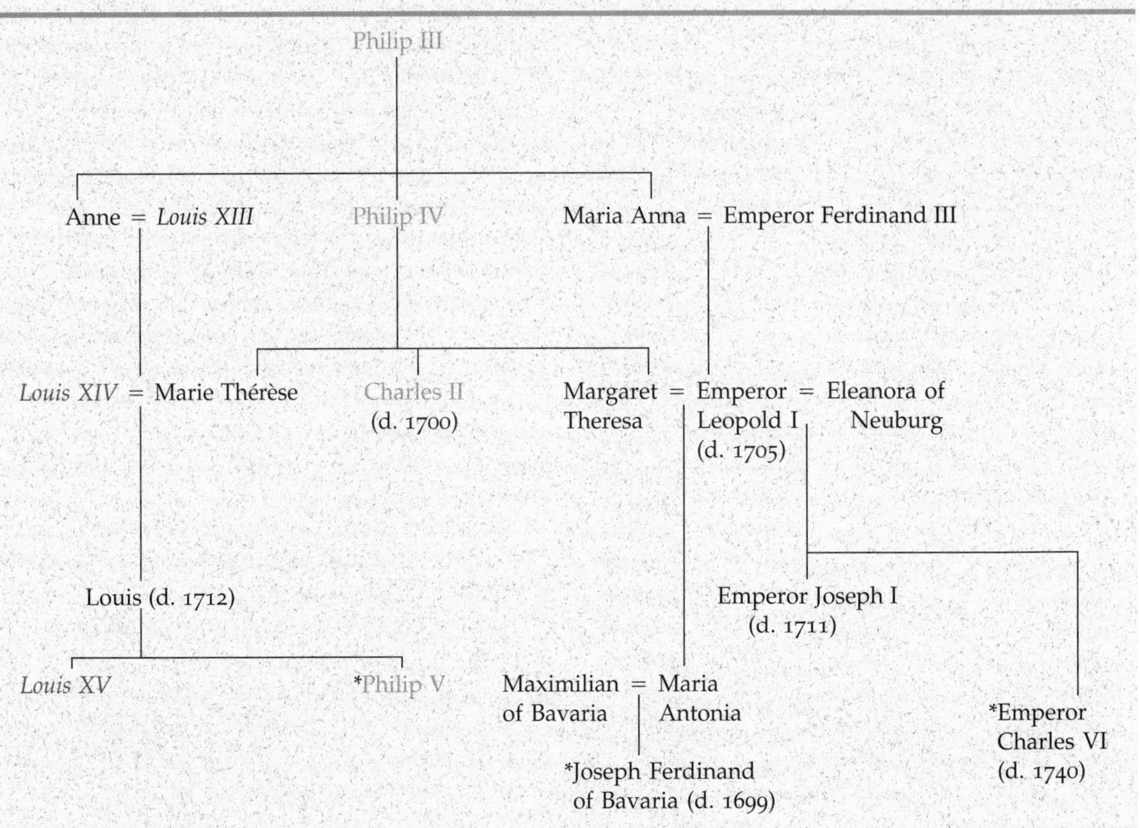

Note: Names in blue = Kings of Spain; Names in red = Kings of France.
*People designated at various times as heirs of Charles II.

man John Churchill, duke of Marlborough, and the Austrian Prince Eugène—the Grand Alliance won a series of smashing victories. France's hardships were increased by a terrible famine in 1709. Although the criticism of his policies now became fierce, and dangerous rebellions erupted, the Sun King retained his hold over his subjects. Despite military disaster he was able to keep his nation's borders intact and the Spanish throne for his grandson (though he had to give up the possibility of union with France and end the restrictions on trade in the Spanish empire) when peace treaties were signed at Utrecht in 1713 and 1714. When it was all over, Louis' great task of state building, both at home and abroad, had withstood the severest of tests: defeat on the battlefield.

DOMESTIC POLICY

The assertion of royal supremacy at home was almost complete by the time Louis came to power, but he extended centralized control to religion and social institutions. Both the Protestant Huguenots and the Catholic Jansenists interfered with the spiritual and confessional uniformity that Louis considered essential in an absolutist state. As a result, pressures against them mounted steadily. In 1685 Louis revoked the Edict of Nantes, now almost a century old, which had granted Protestants limited toleration, and he forced France's 1 million Huguenots either to leave the country (four-fifths did) or to convert to Catholicism. This was a political rather than a religious step, taken to promote unity despite the economic consequences that followed the departure of a vigorous and productive minority.

Jansenism was more elusive. It had far fewer followers, and it was a movement that emphasized spiritual values within Catholicism. But the very fact that it challenged the official Church emphasis on ritual and was condemned by Rome made it a source of unrest. Even more unsettling was its success in gaining support among the magistrate class—the royal officers in the parlements, who had to register all royal edicts before they became law. The Parlement of Paris was the only governmental institution that offered Louis any real resistance. The issues over which it caused trouble were usually religious, and the link between parlementaire independence and Jansenism gave Louis more than enough reason for displeasure. He razed the Jansenists' headquarters, the Abbey of Port-Royal, and persuaded the pope to issue a bull condemning Jansenism. He was prevented from implementing the bull—over parlementaire opposition—only by his death in 1715.

Control and Reform The drive toward uniformity that prompted these actions was reflected in all of domestic policy. Louis kept in check what little protest arose in the parlements and either forbade or overruled their efforts to block his decrees; major uprisings by peasants in central France in the 1690s and 1700s were ruthlessly suppressed, as were all disturbances; Parisian publishers came under bureaucratic supervision; and the *intendants*, the government's chief provincial officers, were given increased authority, particularly to supply the ever-growing money and recruitment needs of the army.

At the outset of his rule, Louis used his power to improve France's economy. In this, he followed a pattern familiar from earlier monarchs' reigns: an initial burst of reform measures designed to cure the country's economic ills, which were gradually forgotten because foreign policy demanded instant funds. In the early years, under Colbert's ministry, major efforts were made to stimulate manufacturing, agriculture, and home and foreign trade. Some industries, notably those involving luxuries, like the silk production of Lyons, received considerable help and owed their prosperity to royal patronage. Colbert also tried, not entirely effectively, to reduce the crippling effects of France's countless internal tolls. These were usually nobles' perquisites, and they could multiply the cost of goods shipped any distance. The government divided the country into a number of districts, within which shipments were to be toll-free, but the system never removed the worst abuses. Louis also tried to boost foreign trade, at first by financing new overseas trading companies and later by founding new port cities as naval and commercial centers. He achieved notable success only in the West Indies, where sugar plantations became a source of great wealth.

THE CONDITION OF FRANCE

Louis' success in state building was remarkable, and France became the envy of Europe. Yet ever since the Sun King's reign, historians have recalled the ruination caused by famine and war during his last years and have contrasted his glittering court with the misery of most French people. Taxes and rents rose remorselessly, and in many regions the hardships were made worse by significant declines in the population. Particularly after the famines of the 1690s and 1709, many contemporaries remarked on the dreadful condition of France's peasants.

The reign of Louis XIV can thus be regarded as the end of an era in the life of the lower classes. By pushing his need for resources to its limits, he inflicted a level of suffering that was not to recur, because governments increasingly came to realize that state building depended on the welfare and support of their people. In the eighteenth century, though there was still much suffering to come, the terrible subsistence crises, with their cycles of famine and plague, came to an end, largely because of official efforts to distribute food in starving areas and to isolate and suppress outbreaks of plague. Thus, although the hand of the central government was heavier in 1715 than a hundred years before, it was becoming more obviously a beneficent as well as a burdensome force. And the Counter Reformation Church, growing in strength since the Council of Trent, also had a more salutary influence as religious struggles died away, for it brought into local parishes better-educated and more dedicated priests who, as part of their new commitment to service, exerted themselves to calm the outbreaks of witchcraft and irrational fear that had swept the countryside for centuries. Despite the strains Louis had caused, therefore, his absolutist authority was now firmly in place and could ensure a dominant European role for a united and powerful France.

FRANCE AFTER LOUIS XIV

Although the Sun King created a model for absolutism in partnership with his nobility, the traditional ambitions of the nobles reasserted themselves after he died in 1715, leaving a child as his heir. The duke of Orléans, Louis XIV's nephew, who became regent until 1723, was committed to giving authority to the aristocracy. He also restored the parlements to political power and replaced royal bureaucrats with councils composed of leading members of the nobility. The scheme was a failure because the councils were unable to govern effectively. The parlements, however, would never again surrender their power to veto royal legislation. They became a rallying point for those who opposed centralization and wished to limit the king's powers.

Finance was also a serious problem for the government, because of the debts left by Louis XIV's wars. A brilliant Scottish financier, John Law, suggested an answer: a government-sponsored central bank that would issue paper notes,

▶ *P. D. Martin*
PROCESSION AFTER LOUIS XV'S CORONATION AT RHEIMS, 1722
This magnificent scene, in front of the cathedral where French kings traditionally were crowned, gives one a sense of the throngs who came to celebrate the day in 1722 when Louis XV officially came of age and received his crown. Paintings depicting royal virtue were erected around the cathedral, and Louis himself (in red on a white horse just to the right of center) was preceded by a flag covered with his symbol, the fleur-de-lis. The other flags remind us that this was an occasion for international pageantry.

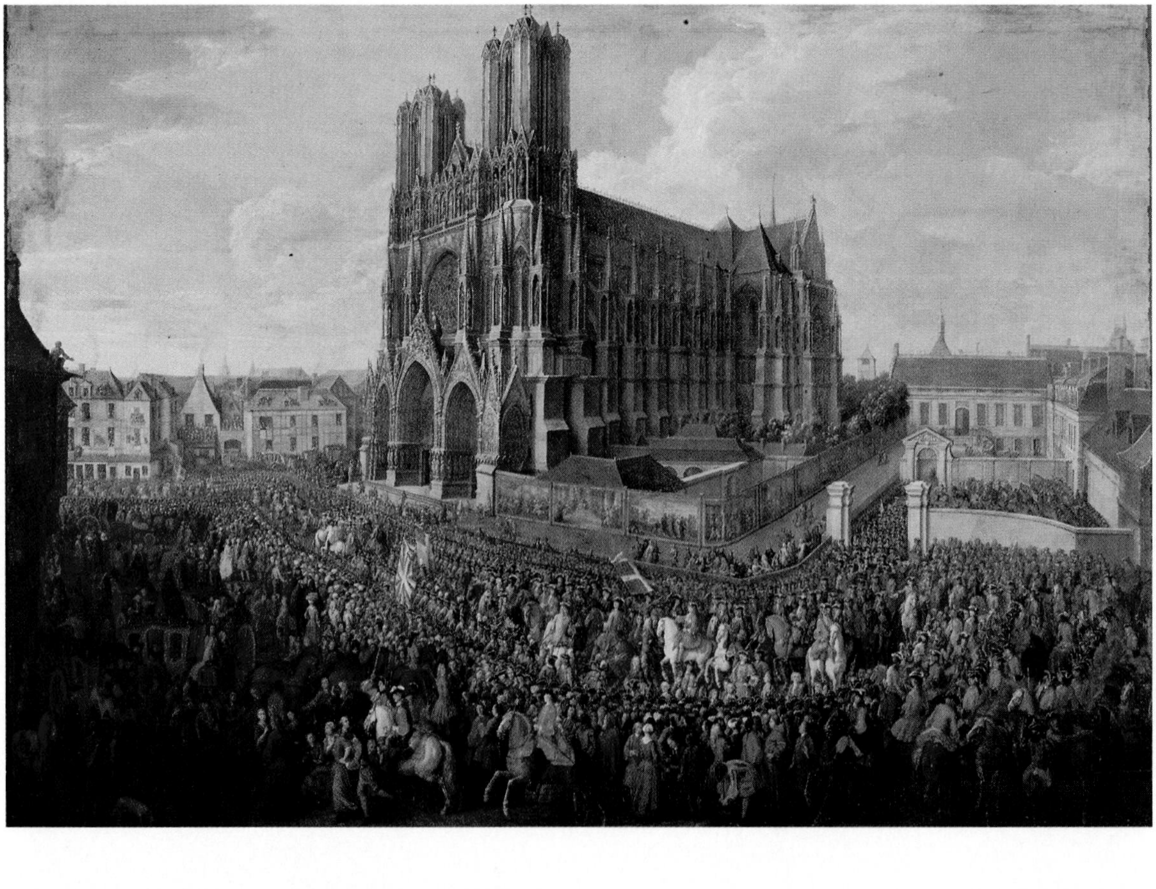

expand credit, and encourage investment in a new trading company for the French colonies. By tying the bank to this company, the Company of the Occident, a venture that promised subscribers vast profits from the Louisiana territory in North America, Law set off an investment boom. But the public's greed soon pushed prices for the company's stock to insanely high levels. A bust was inevitable, and when it came, in 1720, the entire scheme of bank notes and credit collapsed.

Fleury The same political and financial problems were to plague France, in different forms, throughout the eighteenth century, until the leaders of the French Revolution sought radical ways to solve them in the 1790s. Yet the uncertainties of the regency did give way to a long period of stability after 1726, when Louis XV gave almost unlimited authority to his aging tutor and adviser, Cardinal Fleury. Cautious, dedicated to the monarchy, and surrounded by talented subordinates, Fleury made absolutism function quietly and effectively, and enabled France to recover from the setbacks that had marked the end of Louis XIV's reign. Fleury's tenure coincided with abundant harvests, slowly rising population, and increased commercial activity.

Political Problems Fleury was able to contain the ambitions of the governing class. When he died in 1743 at the age of 90, these pressures exploded. War hawks immediately plunged France into the first of several unsuccessful wars with its neighbors that strained French credit to the breaking point. At home royal authority likewise deteriorated. Having no one to replace Fleury as unofficial prime minister, Louis XV put his confidence in a succession of advisers, some capable and some mediocre. But he did not back them when attacks from factions at court became uncomfortable. Uninterested in government, the king avoided confrontations and neglected affairs of state, devoting his energy instead to the pleasures of the hunt and court ceremony.

Although Louis XV provided weak leadership, France's difficulties were not simply personal but rather structural. The main problems—special privileges, political power, and finance—posed almost impossible challenges. Governments that levy new taxes arbitrarily seem despotic, even if the need for them is clear and the distribution equitable. One of France's soundest taxes was the *vingtième*, or twentieth, which was supposed to tap the income of all parts of French society roughly equally. The nobility and clergy, however, all but evaded the tax. Naturally, aggressive royal ministers wanted to remedy that situation. In the 1750s, for example, an effort was made to put teeth into the *vingtième*'s bite on the clergy's huge wealth. But the effort merely ruined the career of the capable royal official who devised it. The clergy resisted furiously; and the parlements joined the attack against the "despotism" of a crown that would arbitrarily tax its subjects. Thus the privileged groups not only blocked reforms but also made the monarch's position more difficult by taking up opposition and a rhetoric of liberty as they fought to limit royal absolutism.

Despite the demands of these special interests, the eighteenth century was a time of notable advance for Europe's most populous and wealthy state. As we will see, France in this period experienced remarkable expansion in population, in the rural economy, in commerce, and in empire building. No one knew at the time that the failures of reforming royal ministers in the mid-1700s foretold a stalemate that would help bring the old regime crashing down.

II. The Creation of Absolutism outside of France

THE HABSBURGS AT VIENNA

The pattern set at Versailles was repeated at the court of the Habsburg Leopold I, the Holy Roman Emperor (1658–1705). Heir to a reduced inheritance that gave him control over only Bohemia, Austria, and a small part of Hungary, Leopold still maintained a splendid establishment. His plans for a new palace, Schönbrunn, that was to have outshone Versailles were modified only because of a lack of funds. And his promotion of the court as the center of all political and social life turned Vienna into what it had never been before: a city for nobles as well as small-time traders.

Nevertheless, Leopold did not display the pretensions of the Sun King. He was a younger son and had come to the throne only because of the death of his brother. Indecisive, retiring, and deeply religious, he had no fondness for the bravado Louis XIV enjoyed. He was a composer of some talent, and his patronage laid the foundation for the great musical culture that was to be one of Vienna's chief glories. But he did inherit considerable royal authority, which he sought to expand—though unlike Louis XIV he relied on a small group of leading nobles to devise policy and run his government.

Government Policy The Thirty Years' War that ended in 1648 had revealed that the elected head of the Holy Roman Empire could no longer control the princes who nominally owed him allegiance. In his own dominions, however, he could maintain his control with the cooperation of his nobility. The Privy Council, which in effect ran Leopold's domain, was filled largely with members of aristocratic families, and his chief advisers were always prominent nobles. To make policy, he carefully consulted each of his ministers and then, even when all of them agreed, came to decisions with agonizing slowness.

Unlike the other courts of Europe, Schönbrunn did not favor only native-born aristocrats. The leader of Austria's armies during the Turks' siege of Vienna in 1683 was Charles, duke of Lorraine, whose duchy had been taken over by the French. His predecessor as field marshal had been an Italian, and his successor was to be one of the most brilliant soldiers of the age, Prince Eugène of Savoy. They became members of the Austrian nobility only when Leopold gave them titles within his own dominions, but they all fitted easily into the aristocratic circles that controlled the government and the army.

Eugène Prince Eugène (1663–1736) was a spectacular symbol of the aristocracy's continuing dominance of politics and society. A member of one of Europe's most distinguished families, he had been raised in France but found himself passed over when Louis XIV awarded army commissions, perhaps because he had been intended for the Church. Yet he was determined to have a military career, and he volunteered to serve the Austrians in the war with the Turks that, following the siege of Vienna, was to expand Habsburg territory in the Balkans by the time peace was signed in 1699 (see Map 17.2). Eugène's talents quickly became evident: He was field marshal of Austria's troops by the time he was 30. Over the next 40 years, as intermittent war with the Turks continued, he became a decisive influence in Habsburg affairs. Though foreign-born, he was the minister primarily responsible for the transformation of Vienna's policies from defensive to aggressive.

Until the siege of Vienna by the Turks in 1683, Leopold's cautiousness kept Austria simply holding the line, both against Louis XIV and against the Turks. In the 1690s, however, he tried a bolder course at Eugène's urging and in the process laid the foundations for a new Habsburg empire along the Danube River: Austria-Hungary. He helped create the coalition that defeated Louis in the 1700s, intervened in Italy so that his landlocked domains could gain an outlet to the sea, and began the long process of pushing the Turks out of the Balkans. Leopold did not live to see the advance more than started, but by the time of Eugène's death, the Austrians' advances against the Turks had brought them within a hundred miles of the Black Sea.

Yet the local power of the aristocracy tempered the centralization of Leopold's dominions. Louis XIV supported his nobles if they worked for him; Leopold, by contrast, gave them influence in the government without first establishing control over all his lands. The nobility did not cause the Habsburgs as much trouble as they had during the Thirty Years' War, but Leopold had to limit his ambitions outside Austria. Moreover, as Austrians came increasingly to dominate the court, the nobles of Hungary and Bohemia reacted by clinging stubbornly to their local rights. Thus Leopold's was an absolutism under which the nobility retained far more autonomous power—and a far firmer base of local support—than was the case in France, despite the centralization he achieved during his reign.

THE HABSBURGS AT MADRID

In Spain the Habsburgs had little success in state building either at home or abroad. The king,

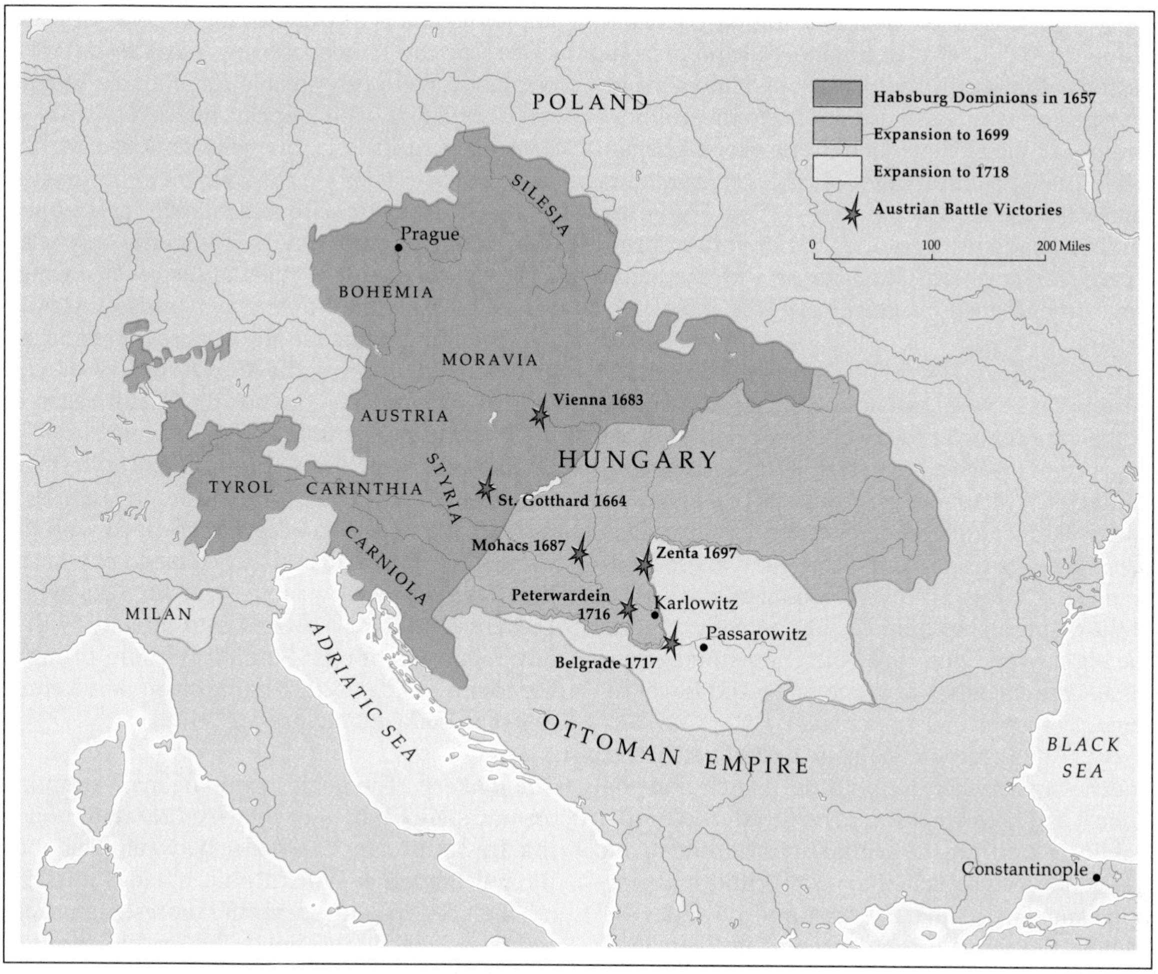

Map 17.2 THE AUSTRIAN EMPIRE, 1657–1718
The steady advance of the Habsburgs into the Balkans was marked by a succession of victories; their gains were confirmed by treaties with the Turks at Karlowitz (1699) and Passarowitz (1718).

Charles II (1665–1700), was a sickly man, incapable of having children; and the War of the Spanish Succession seriously reduced the inheritance he left. Both the southern Netherlands and most of Italy passed to the Austrian Habsburgs, and Spain's overseas possessions often paid little notice to the homeland.

The Spanish nobility was even more successful than the Austrian in turning absolutism to its advantage. In 1650 the crown had been able to recapture Catalonia's loyalty only by granting the province's aristocracy virtual autonomy, and this pattern recurred throughout Spain's territories. Parasitic, unproductive nobles controlled the regime, often for personal gain. The country fell into economic and cultural stagnation, subservient to a group of powerful families, with its former glory visible in the eighteenth century only in its strong navy.

THE HOHENZOLLERNS AT BERLIN

The one new power that emerged to prominence during the age of Louis XIV was Brandenburg-Prussia, and here again state building was made possible by a close alliance between a powerful ruler and his nobles. Frederick William of Hohenzollern (1640–1688), known as the "great elector," ruled scattered territories that stretched 700 miles from Cleves, on the Rhine, to a part of Prussia on the Baltic. That so fragmented and disconnected a set of lands could be shaped into a major European power was a testimony to the political abilities of the Hohenzollerns. The process began when, taking advantage of the uncertainties that followed the Thirty Years' War, Frederick William made his territories the dominant principality in northern Germany and at the same time strengthened his power over his subjects.

Foreign Policy His first task was in foreign affairs, because when he became elector, the troops of the various states that were fighting the Thirty Years' War swarmed over his possessions at will. Frederick William realized that by determination and intelligent planning, even a small prince could emerge from these disasters in a good position *if* he had an army. With some military force at his disposal, he could become a useful ally for the big powers, who could then help him against his neighbors; while at home he would have the strength to crush his opponents.

By 1648 Frederick William had 8000 troops, and he was backed by both the Dutch and the French as a possible restraint on Sweden in northern Europe during the negotiations leading to the treaty of Westphalia in that year. Without having done much to earn new territory, he did very well in the peace settlement, and he then took brilliant advantage of wars around the Baltic in the 1650s to confirm his gains by switching sides at crucial moments. In the process, his army grew to 22,000 men, and he began to use it to impose his will on his own lands. The fact that the army was essential to all Frederick William's successes—both at home and abroad—was to influence much of Prussia's and thus also Germany's subsequent history.

Domestic Policy The role of the military in establishing the elector's supremacy was apparent throughout Brandenburg-Prussia's society. In 1653 the Diet of Brandenburg met for the last time, sealing its own fate by giving Frederick William the right to raise taxes without its consent. The War Chest, the office in charge of financing the army, took over the functions of a treasury department and collected government revenue even when the state was at peace. The implementation of policies in the localities was placed in the hands of war commissars—who originally were responsible for military recruitment, billeting, and supply in each district of Brandenburg-Prussia, but who now became the principal agents of all government departments.

Apart from the representative assemblies, Frederick William faced real resistance only from the long-independent cities of his realm. Accustomed to going their own way because authority had been fragmented in the empire for centuries, and especially during the Thirty Years' War, city leaders were dismayed when the elector began to intervene in their affairs. Yet once again sheer intimidation swept opposition aside. The last determined effort to dispute his authority arose in the rich city of Königsberg, which allied with the Estates General of Prussia to refuse to pay taxes. But this resistance was crushed in 1662, when Frederick William marched into the city with a few thousand troops. Similar pressure brought the towns of Cleves into submission after centuries of proud independence.

The Junkers The nobles were the main supporters and beneficiaries of the elector's state building. It was, in fact, an alliance between the nobility and Frederick William that made it possible for the Diet, the cities, and the representative assemblies to be undermined. The leading families saw their best opportunities for the future in cooperation with the central government, and both in the representative assemblies and in the localities, they worked to establish absolutist power—that is, to remove all restraints on the elector. The most significant indicator of the nobles' success was that by the end of the century, two tax rates had been devised, one for cities and one for the countryside, to the great advantage of the latter.

Not only did the nobles staff the upper levels of the elector's army and bureaucracy, but they also won new prosperity for themselves. Particularly in Prussia, the support of the elector enabled them to reimpose serfdom and consolidate their land holdings into vast, highly profitable estates. This was a major grain-producing area, and they made the most of its economic potential. To maximize profits, they eliminated intermediaries not only by growing but also by distributing their produce themselves. Efficiency became their hallmark, and their wealth was soon famous throughout the Holy Roman Empire. Known as Junkers (from the German for young lord, *jung herr*), these Prussian entrepreneurs were probably the most successful group of European aristocrats in pursuing economic and political power.

Frederick III Unlike Louis in France, Frederick William had little interest in court life. The Berlin court became the focus of society only under his son, Elector Frederick III, who ruled from 1688. The great elector himself was more interested in organizing his administration, increasing tax returns, building his army, and imposing his authority at home and abroad. He began the development of his capital, Berlin, into a cultural center—he founded what was to become one of the finest libraries in the world, the Prussian State Library—but this was never among his prime concerns. His son, by contrast, had little interest in state building, but he did enjoy princely pomp and he encouraged the arts with enthusiasm.

Frederick III lacked only one attribute of royalty: a crown. When Emperor Leopold I, who still had the right to confer titles in the empire, needed Prussia's troops during the War of the Spanish Succession, he gave Frederick, in return, the right to call himself "king in Prussia," and the title soon became "king of Prussia." At a splendid coronation in 1701, Elector Frederick III of Brandenburg was crowned King Frederick I, and thereafter his court could feel itself the equal of the other monarchical settings of Europe.

Frederick determinedly promoted social and cultural glitter. He made his palace a center of art and polite society to compete, he hoped, with Versailles. A construction program beautified Berlin with new churches and huge public buildings. He also established an Academy of Sciences and persuaded the most famous German scientist and philosopher of the day, Gottfried Wilhelm von Leibniz, to become its first president. All these activities obtained generous support from state revenues, as did the universities of Brandenburg and Prussia. By the end of his reign in 1713, Frederick had given his realm a throne, celebrated artistic and intellectual activity, and an elegant aristocracy at the head of social and political life.

PETER THE GREAT AT ST. PETERSBURG

One of the reasons the new absolutist regimes of the late seventeenth and eighteenth centuries seemed so different from their predecessors was that many of them consciously created new settings for themselves. Versailles, Schönbrunn, and Berlin were all either new or totally transformed sites for royal courts. But only one of the autocrats of the period went so far as to build an entirely new capital: Tsar Peter I (the Great) of Russia (1682–1725), who named the new city St. Petersburg after his patron saint.

The Tsar's Rule None of the state-building rulers of the period had Peter's terrifying energy or ruthless determination to exercise absolute control. This he made clear when he destroyed ecclesiastical independence in one stunning gesture: He simply did not replace the patriarch of the Russian Church when he died in 1700. The government took over the monasteries, using their enormous income for its own purposes, and appointed a procurator (at first an army officer) to supervise all religious affairs. The church was, in effect, made a branch of government.

In ruling, Peter virtually ignored the Duma, the traditional advisory council, and concentrated instead on his bureaucracy. He carried out change after change until he had created an administrative complex many times larger than the one he had inherited. In this effort he determinedly copied Western models—notably Prussia, where nobles ran the bureaucracy and the army, and Sweden, where a complex system of government departments had been created. Peter organized his administration into similar departments: Each had either a specialized function, such as finance, or responsibility for a geographic area, such as Siberia. The result was an elaborate but unified hierarchy of authority, rising from local agents of the government through provincial officials up to the staffs and governors of 11 large administrative units and finally to the leaders of the regime in the capital. Peter began the saturating bureaucratization that characterized Russia from that time on.

Russian Society The tsar's policies laid the foundations for a two-class society that persisted until the twentieth century. Previously, a number of ranks had existed within both the nobility and the peasantry, and a group in the middle was seen sometimes as the lowest nobles and sometimes as the highest peasants. Under Peter such mingling disappeared. All peasants were reduced to one level, subject to a new poll tax, military conscription, and forced public work, such as the building of St. Petersburg. Below them were serfs, whose numbers were increased by legislation restricting their movement. Peasants had a few advantages over serfs, such as the freedom to move, but their living conditions were often equally dreadful. Serfdom itself spread throughout all areas of Peter's dominions and became essential to his state building, because on royal lands as well as the estates of the nobles, serfs worked and ran the agricultural enterprise that was Russia's economic base.

At the same time, Peter created a single class of nobles by substituting status within the bureaucracy for status within the traditional hierarchy of titles. In 1722 he issued a table of bureaucratic ranks that gave everyone a place according to the office he held. Differentiations still existed, but they were no longer unbridgeable, as they had been when family was the decisive determinant of status. The result was a more controlled social order and greater uniformity than in France or Brandenburg-Prussia. The Russian aristocracy was the bureaucracy, and the bureaucracy the aristocracy.

▶ PETER THE GREAT AT ST. PETERSBURG
In the eighteenth century Peter the Great of Russia outstripped the grandeur of other monarchs of the period by erecting an entirely new city for his capital. St. Petersburg was built by forced labor of the peasants under Peter's orders; they are shown here laying the foundations for the city.

The Nobility But this was not a voluntary alliance between nobles and government, such as existed in the West; in return for his support and his total subjection of the peasantry, Peter *required* the nobles to provide officials for his bureaucracy and officers for his army. When he began the construction of St. Petersburg, he also demanded that the leading families build splendid mansions in his new capital. In effect, the tsar offered privilege and wealth in exchange for conscription into public service. Thus there was hardly any sense of partnership between nobility and throne: The tsar often had to use coercion to ensure that his wishes were followed.

On the other hand, Peter did a good deal to build up the nobles' fortunes and their ability to control the countryside. It has been estimated that by 1710 he had put under the supervision of great landowners more than 40,000 peasant and serf households that had formerly been under the crown. And he was liberal in conferring new titles—some of them, such as count and baron, copies of German examples.

Western Models In creating an aristocratic society at his court, Peter mixed imitations of what he admired in the West with native developments. He sought to apply Western models because he felt that Russia had much to learn from the advances its neighbors had made. To observe these achievements at firsthand, Peter traveled secretly through France, England, and the Netherlands in 1697 and 1698, paying special attention to economic, administrative, and military practices (such as the functioning of a Dutch shipyard). Many of his initiatives derived from this journey, including his importation of Western court rituals and his founding of an Academy of Sciences in 1725. Italian artists were brought to Russia, along with Scandinavian army officers, German engineers, and Dutch shipbuilders, not only to apply their skills but also to teach them to the Russians. St. Petersburg, the finest example of a city built in eighteenth-century Classical style, is mainly the work of Italians. But gradually, the Russians took over their own institutions—military academies produced native officers, for example—and by the end of Peter's reign the nobles had little need of foreign experts to help run the government. Peter the Great had laid the foundations for the aristocratic society that would rule his people for 200 years.

The purpose of these radical internal changes was to assert the tsar's power both at home and abroad. Peter established a huge standing army, more than 300,000 strong by the 1720s, and imported the latest military techniques from the West. One of Peter's most cherished projects, the creation of a navy, had limited success, but there could be no doubt that he transformed Russia's capacity for war and its position among European states. He extended Russia's frontier to the south and west, beginning the destruction of Sweden's empire at the battle of Poltava in 1709 and following this triumph by more than a decade of advance into Estonia, Livonia, and Poland. The very vastness of his realm justified Peter's drive for absolute control, and by the time of his death he had made Russia the dominant power in the Baltic and a major influence in European affairs.

III. Alternatives to Absolutism

THE TRIUMPH OF THE GENTRY IN ENGLAND

The absolutist regimes provided one model of political and social organization, but an alternative model—equally committed to uniformity, order, and state building—was also created in the late seventeenth century: governments dominated by aristocrats or merchants. The contrast between the two was noted by contemporary political theorists, especially opponents of absolutism, who compared France unfavorably with England. And yet the differences were often less sharp than the theorists suggested, mainly because the position of the aristocracy was similar throughout Europe.

England's King Charles II (1660–1685), for example, seemed to have powers similar to those of his father, Charles I. He still summoned and dissolved Parliament, he made all appointments in the bureaucracy, and he signed every law. But he no longer had royal prerogative courts like Star Chamber, he could not arrest a member of

Parliament, and he could not create a new seat in the Commons. Even two ancient prerogatives, the king's right to dispense with an act of Parliament for a specific individual or group and his right to suspend an act completely, proved to be empty when Charles II tried to exercise them. Nor could he raise money without parliamentary assent: Instead, he was given a fixed annual income, financed by a tax on beer.

The Gentry and Parliament The real control of the country's affairs had by this time passed to the group of substantial landowners known as the *gentry*. In a country of some 5 million people, perhaps 15,000 to 20,000 families were considered gentry—leaders of the various localities throughout England, though they had neither titles of nobility nor special privileges. They represented about 2 percent of the population, a proportion that was probably not much different from the percentage of titled and privileged nobles in the populations of other states.

The gentry were distinguished from the nobles of other countries by the right they had won in England's civil war to determine national policy through Parliament. Whereas in France, Austria, Brandenburg-Prussia, and Russia nobles depended on the monarch for power and were subservient to him, the English revolution had made the gentry an independent force. Their authority was now hallowed by custom, upheld by law, and maintained by the House of Commons, a representative assembly that was both the supreme legislature and the body to which the executive government was ultimately responsible.

Not all the gentry took a continuing, active interest in affairs of state, and no more than a few of their number sat in the roughly 500-member House of Commons. Even the Commons did not exercise a constant influence over the govern-

THE ENGLISH SUCCESSION FROM THE STUARTS TO THE HANOVERIANS

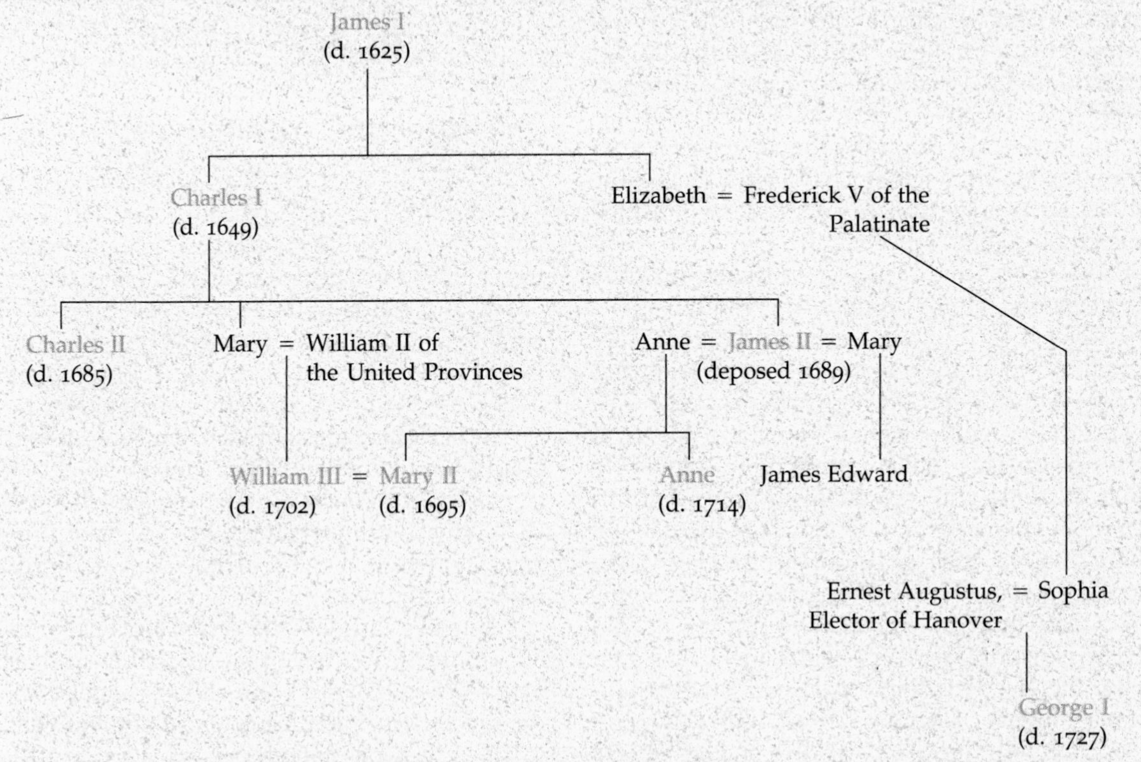

Note: Names in blue = Monarchs of England.

ment; nevertheless, the ministers of the king had to be prominent representatives of the gentry, and they had to be able to win the support of a majority of the members of the Commons. Policy was still set by the king and his ministers. But the Commons had to be persuaded that the policies were correct; without parliamentary approval, a minister could not long survive.

The Succession Despite occasional conflicts, this structure worked relatively smoothly throughout Charles II's reign. But the gentry feared that Charles's brother, James, next in line for the succession and an open Catholic, might try to restore Catholicism in England. To prevent this, they attempted in 1680 to force Charles to exclude James from the throne. But in the end the traditional respect for legitimacy, combined with some shrewd maneuvering by Charles, ensured that there would be no tampering with the succession.

Soon, however, the reign of James II (1685–1688) turned into a disaster. Elated by his acceptance as king, James rashly attempted the very encouragement of Catholicism that the gentry feared. This was a direct challenge to the gentry's newly won power, and in the fall of 1688, seven of their leaders—including members of some of the oldest families in the realm—invited the Protestant ruler of the United Provinces, William III, to invade the country and take over the throne. Although William landed with an army half the size of the king's, James, uncertain of his support, decided not to risk battle and fled to exile in France.

► *Sir Joshua Reynolds*
LADY SMITH AND HER CHILDREN
The quiet serenity and assurance of England's gentry in the eighteenth century is apparent in all their portraits, whether the head of the household is present or, as in this case, only his wife and children.

William and Mary The new king gained what little title he had to the crown through his wife, Mary (see the genealogical table on p. 550), and the couple were proclaimed joint monarchs by Parliament early in 1689. The Dutch ruler had taken the throne primarily to bring England into his relentless struggles against Louis XIV, and he willingly accepted a settlement that confirmed the essential position of Parliament in the government. A Bill of Rights settled the future succession to the throne, defined Parliament's powers, and established basic civil rights; an Act of Toleration put an end to all religious persecution, though members of the official Church of England were still the only people allowed to vote, sit in Parliament, hold a government office, or attend a university; and in 1694 a statute laid down that Parliament had to meet and new elections had to be held at least once every three years.

Despite the restrictions on his authority, William exercised strong leadership following this so-called Glorious Revolution.* He guided England into a new, aggressive foreign policy, picked the ministers favorable to his aims, and

*It got its name because it was bloodless and confirmed the supremacy of Parliament once and for all.

never let Parliament sit when he was out of the country to pursue the war or to oversee Dutch affairs. In his reign, too, the central government grew significantly, creating new positions, new powers, and new opportunities for political patronage. But unlike James, William recognized his limits. He tried to have the Bill of Rights reversed and a standing army established, but he gave up when these efforts provoked major opposition. By and large, therefore, the gentry were content to let the king rule as he saw fit. For they had shown by their intervention in 1688 that ultimately they controlled the country.

POLITICS AND PROSPERITY

The political system in England now reflected the social system: A small elite controlled both the country's policy and its institutions. This group was far from united, however, as was apparent when a party system began to appear in Parliament during Charles II's reign. On one side were the Whigs, who opposed royal prerogatives and Catholicism and were largely responsible for the attempt to exclude James II from the throne. Their rivals, the Tories, stood for the independence and authority of the crown and favored a ceremonial and traditional Anglicanism.

Party Conflict Because the Whigs had been the main advocates of the removal of James II, they controlled the government for most of William III's reign. They supported his war against Louis XIV (1689–1697), since France harbored both James and his followers, the romantic but ill-fated Jacobites, who kept trying to restore James's line to the throne. This was a relatively nonpartisan issue, but the Tories and Whigs still competed fiercely for voters. Because the qualification for voting—owning land worth 40 shillings a year in rent—had become less restrictive as a result of inflation (which made 40 shillings a fairly modest sum) and was not to be raised to a higher minimum until the late 1700s, England now had what would be its largest electorate before the 1860s. Almost 5 percent of the population (more than 15 percent of adult males) could vote, and although results were usually determined by powerful local magnates, fierce politicking was common. And in the election of 1700 there was a major upset: The Tories won by opposing a resumption of war against Louis XIV, who seemed to have been contained since the end of the previous war in 1697.

Within two years, however, and despite William's death in 1702, England was again at war with France, this time over the Spanish succession; and soon the Whigs were again in control of the government. The identification of the parties with their attitude toward war continued until 1710, when weariness over the fighting brought the Tories back into power. They persuaded Queen Anne, William's successor, to make peace with France at Utrecht in 1713; and it was only because the Tories made the mistake of negotiating with the rebel Jacobites after Anne died in 1714 without an heir that they lost power. Anne's successor was a German prince, the elector of Hanover, who founded the new Hanoverian dynasty as George I (1714–1727). Since they firmly supported his succession, the Whigs regained control of the government when George came to the throne. They then entrenched themselves, and under the leadership of Robert Walpole, they began almost a century of political ascendancy.

The Sea and the Economy At the same time, England was winning for itself unprecedented prosperity and laying the foundations of its world power. Its navy made it the premier force on the sea, the decisive victor over France during the worldwide struggle of the early eighteenth century. Overseas, new colonies were founded, and the empire expanded steadily. When England and Scotland joined into one kingdom in 1707, the union created a Great Britain ready to exercise a worldwide influence.

The economic advances were equally remarkable. A notable achievement was the establishment of the Bank of England in 1694. The bank was given permission to raise money from the public and then lend it to the government at a favorable 8 percent interest. Within 12 days its founders raised more than a million pounds, demonstrating not only the financial security and stability of England's government but also the commitment of the elite to the country's political structure. London was becoming the financial capital of the world, and British merchants were gaining control over maritime trade from East Asia to North America. Significantly, the benefits of this boom also helped the lower levels of society.

English Society There is little doubt that with the possible exception of the Dutch, ordinary English people were better off than their equivalents elsewhere in Europe. Compared with the sixteenth century, there was little starvation. The system of poor relief may often have been inhumane in forcing the unfortunate to work in horrifying workhouses, but it did provide them with the shelter and food that they had long lacked. It is true that thousands still found themselves unable to make a living in their home villages each year and were forced by poverty to take to the roads. And the many who ended up in London hardly improved their situation. The stream of immigrants was driving the capital's population toward half a million, and the city contained frightful slums and miserable crime-ridden sections. Even a terrible fire in London in 1666 did little to improve the appallingly crowded living conditions because the city was rebuilt much as before, the only notable additions being a series

▸ *William Hogarth*
The Polling, 1754
Despite the high reputation of the polling day as the central moment in the system of representative government, Hogarth's depiction of it in this scene suggests how corrupt and disheveled the process of voting was. The sick and the foolish are among the mob of voters; the central figure looks bewildered as he is told what to do; on the right a bloated official cannot decide whether a voter should be allowed to take his oath on the Bible with a wooden hand; and all ignore the distress of Britannia, the symbol of Britain, in her coach on the left.

The Metropolitan Museum of Art

▸ *Samuel Scott*
THE BUILDING OF WESTMINSTER BRIDGE, CA. 1742
The elegance, but not the squalor, of city life in the eighteenth century is suggested by this view of Westminster.

of splendid churches. But the grimness should not be overdrawn.

After more than a century of inflation, the laborer could once again make a decent living, and artisans were enjoying a growing demand for their work. Higher in the social scale, more men had a say in the political process than before, and more found opportunities for advancement in the rising economy—in trade overseas, in the bureaucracy, or in the expanding market for luxury goods. It has been estimated that in 1730 there were about 60,000 adult males in what we would recognize as the professions. England also had better roads than any other European country and a more impartial judicial system.

Yet none of these gains could compare with those that the gentry made. In fact, many of the improvements, such as fair administration of justice, were indirect results of what the upper classes had won for themselves. The fruits of progress clearly belonged primarily to the gentry.

ARISTOCRACY IN THE UNITED PROVINCES, SWEDEN, AND POLAND

In the Dutch republic, the succession of William III to the offfice of Stadholder in 1672 seemed to be a move toward absolutism. As he led the successful resistance to Louis XIV in war (1672–1678), he increasingly concentrated government in his own hands. Soon, however, the power of merchants and provincial leaders in the Estates General reasserted itself. William did not want to sign a peace treaty with Louis when the French invasion failed. He wanted instead to take the war into France and reinforce his own authority by keeping the position of commander in chief. But the Estates General, led by the province of Holland, ended the war.

A decade later it was only with the approval of the Estates General that William was able to seek the English throne, and he had to leave the representative assemblies that governed the two countries separate. When William died without an heir, his policies were continued by his close friend Antonius Heinsius, who held the same position of grand pensionary of Holland that Jan de Witt had once occupied; but the government was in effect controlled by the Estates General.

This representative assembly now had to preside over the decline of a great power. In finance and trade, the Dutch were gradually overtaken by the English, while in the war against Louis XIV, they had to support the crippling burden of maintaining a land force, only to hand command over to England. Within half a century Frederick II of Prussia was to call the republic "a dinghy boat trailing the English man-of-war."

Dutch Society The aristocrats of the United Provinces differed from the usual European pattern. Instead of ancient families and bureaucratic dynasties, they boasted merchants and mayors. The prominent citizens of the leading cities were the backbone of the Dutch upper classes. Moreover, social distinctions were less prominent than in any other country of Europe. The elite was composed of hard-working financiers and traders, richer and more powerful but not essentially more privileged or leisured than those farther down the social ladder. The inequality discussed in much eighteenth-century political writing—the special place nobles had, often including some immunity from the law—was far less noticeable in the United Provinces. There was no glittering court, and although here as elsewhere a small group controlled the country, it did so for largely economic ends and in different style.

Sweden The Swedes created yet another nonabsolutist model of state building. Here the nobles emerged from a long struggle with the king as the country's dominant political force. During the reign of Charles XI (1660–1697) the monarchy was able to force the great lords to return to the state the huge tracts of land they had received as rewards for loyalty earlier in the century. Since Charles stayed out of Europe's wars, he was able to conserve his resources and avoid relying on the nobility as he strengthened the smoothly running bureaucracy he had inherited from Gustavus Adolphus.

His successor, Charles XII (1697–1718), however, revived Sweden's tradition of military conquest. He won land from Peter the Great, but then made the fatal decision to invade Russia. Defeated at the battle of Poltava in 1709, Charles had to retreat and watch helplessly as the Swedish empire was dismembered. By the time he was killed in battle nine years later, his neighbors had begun to overrun his lands, and in treaties signed from 1719 to 1721, Sweden reverted to roughly the territory it had had a century before.

Naturally the nobles took advantage of Charles XII's frequent absences to reassert their authority. They ran Sweden's highly efficient government while he was campaigning and forced his successor, Queen Ulrika, to accept a constitution that gave the Riksdag effective control over the country. The new structure was consciously modeled on England's political system, and the nobility came to occupy a position like England's gentry—leaders of society and the shapers of its politics. A splendid court arose, and Stockholm became one of the more elegant and cultured aristocratic centers in Europe.

Warsaw fared less well. In fact, the strongest contrast to the French political and social model in the late seventeenth century was Poland. The sheer chaos and disunity that plagued Poland until it ceased to exist as a state in the late eighteenth century were the direct result of continued dominance by the old landed aristocracy, which blocked all attempts to centralize the government. There were highly capable kings in this period—notably John III, who achieved Europe-wide fame by relieving Vienna from the Turkish siege in 1683. These monarchs could quite easily gather an enthusiastic army to fight, and fight well, against Poland's many foes: Germans, Swedes, Russians, and Turks. But once a battle was over, the ruler could exercise no more than nominal leadership. Each king was elected by the assembly of nobles and had to agree not to interfere with the independence of the great lords, who were growing rich from serf labor on fertile lands. The crown had neither revenue nor bureaucracy to speak of, and so the country continued to resemble a feudal kingdom, where power remained in the localities.

CONTRASTS IN POLITICAL THOUGHT

The intensive development of both absolutist and antiabsolutist forms in the seventeenth century stimulated an outpouring of ideas about the nature and purposes of government. Two Englishmen, in particular, developed theories about the basis of political authority that have been influential ever since.

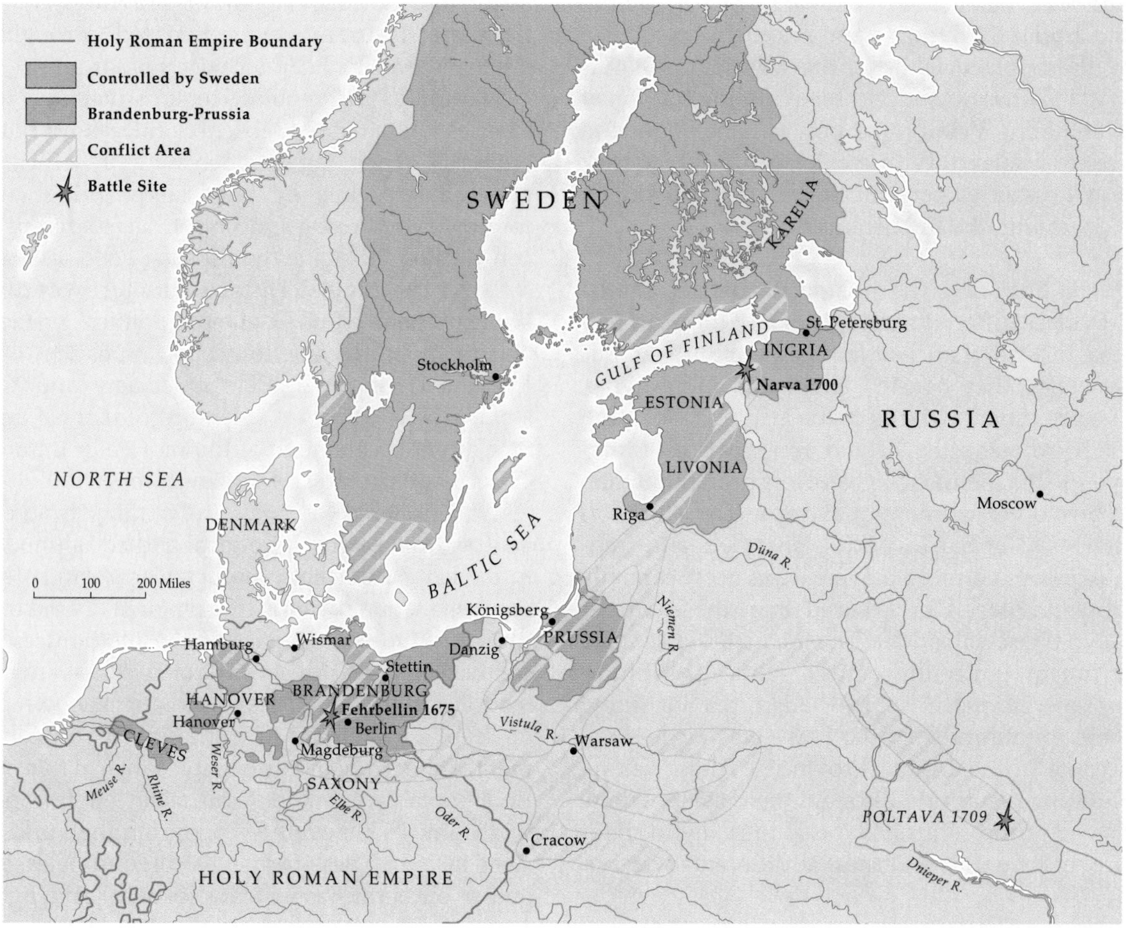

Map 17.3 **CONFLICT IN THE BALTIC AREA, 1660–1721**
The fighting around the Baltic eventually destroyed Sweden's power in northern Europe; the new powers were to be Brandenburg-Prussia and Russia.

Hobbes A story has it that Thomas Hobbes, a brilliant scholar from a poor family who earned his livelihood as the tutor to aristocrats' sons, once picked up a copy of Euclid's *Elements* and opened the book in the middle. The theorem on that page seemed totally without foundation, but it rested on a proof in the preceding theorem. Working his way backward, Hobbes discovered himself finally having to accept no more than the proposition that the shortest distance between two points is a straight line. He thereupon resolved to use the same approach to analyze political behavior. The story is probably apocryphal because as a young man Hobbes was secretary to Francis Bacon, who doubtless gave him a taste for science. Yet it does capture the essence of his masterpiece, *Leviathan* (1651), which began with a few premises about human nature from which Hobbes deduced major conclusions about political forms.

Hobbes's premises, drawn from his observation of the strife-ridden Europe of the 1640s and 1650s, were stark and uncompromising. People, he asserted, are selfish and ambitious; consequently, unless they are restrained, they fight a perpetual war with their fellows. The weak are more cunning and the strong more stupid. Given these unsavory characteristics, the state of nature—which precedes the existence of society—is a state of war, in which life is "solitary, poor, nasty, brutish, and short." Hobbes's conclusion was that the only way to restrain this instinctive aggressiveness is to erect an absolute and sovereign power that will maintain peace. Everyone should submit to the sovereign because the alternative is the anarchy of the state of nature. The moment of submission is the moment of the birth of orderly society.

In a startling innovation, Hobbes suggested that the transition from nature to society is accomplished by a contract that is implicitly accepted by all who wish to end the chaos. The unprecedented feature of the contract is that it is not between ruler and ruled; it is binding only on the ruled. They agree among themselves to submit to the sovereign; the sovereign is thus not a party to the contract and is not limited in any way. A government that is totally free to do whatever it wishes is best equipped to keep the peace, and peace is always better than the previous turmoil.

The power of Hobbes's logic, and the endorsement he seemed to give to absolutism, made his views enormously influential. But his approach also aroused hostility. Although later political theorists were deeply affected by his ideas, many of Hobbes's successors denounced him as godless, immoral, cynical, and unfeeling. It was dislike of his message, not weaknesses in his analysis, that made many people unwilling to accept his views.

Locke John Locke, a quiet Oxford professor who admired Hobbes but sought to soften his conclusions, founded his political analysis in a general theory of knowledge. Locke believed that at birth a person's mind is a *tabula rasa*, a clean slate; nothing, he said, is inborn or preordained. As human beings grow, they observe and experience the world. Once they have gathered enough data through their senses, their minds begin to work on the data. Then, with the help of reason, they perceive patterns, discovering the order and harmony that permeate the universe. Locke was convinced that this underlying order exists and that every person, regardless of individual experi-

Locke on the Origins of Government

The heart of John Locke's* Second Treatise of Civil Government, *written in the mid-1680s before England's Glorious Revolution but published in 1690, is its optimism about human nature—as opposed to Hobbes's pessimism. In this passage Locke explains why, in his view, people create political systems.

"If man in the state of nature be so free, if he be absolute lord of his own person and possessions, equal to the greatest, and subject to nobody, why will he part with his freedom, and subject himself to the dominion and control of any other power? To which it is obvious to answer, that though in the state of nature he hath such a right, yet the enjoyment of it is very uncertain, and constantly exposed to the invasions of others. This makes him willing to quit this condition, which, however free, is full of fears and continual dangers; and it is not without reason that he seeks out and is willing to join in society with others, who have a mind to unite, for the mutual preservation of their lives, liberties, and estates, which I call by the general name, property. The great and chief end, therefore, of men's putting themselves under government, is the preservation of their property.

"But though men when they enter into society give up the equality, liberty, and power they had in the state of nature into the hands of society; yet it being only with an intention in every one the better to preserve himself, his liberty, and property, the power of the society can never be supposed to extend further than the common good. And all this to be directed to no other end but the peace, safety, and public good of the people."

From John Locke, *The Second Treatise of Civil Government*, Thomas P. Peardon (ed.) (Indianapolis: Bobbs-Merrill, 1952), Chapter IX, pp. 70–73.

ences, must reach the same conclusions about its nature and structure.

When Locke turned his attention to political thought, he put into systematic form the views of the English gentry and other antiabsolutists throughout Europe. The *Second Treatise of Civil Government*, published in 1690, was deeply influenced by Hobbes. From his great predecessor Locke took the notions that a state of nature is a state of war and that only a contract among the people can end the anarchy that precedes the establishment of civil society. But his conclusions were decidedly different.

Using the principles of his theory of knowledge, Locke asserted that the application of reason to politics demonstrates the inalienability of the three rights of an individual: life, liberty, and property. Like Hobbes, he believed that there must be a sovereign power, but he argued that it has no power over these three natural rights of its subjects without their consent. Moreover, this consent—for levying taxes, for example—must come from a representative assembly of men of property, such as the English Parliament.

The affirmation of property as one of the three natural rights (it was changed to "the pursuit of happiness" in the more egalitarian American Declaration of Independence) is significant. Here Locke revealed himself as the spokesman of the gentry. Only people with a tangible stake in their country have any right to control its destiny, and that stake must be protected as surely as their life and liberty. The concept of liberty remained vague, but it was taken to imply the sorts of freedom, such as freedom from arbitrary arrest, that were outlined in the English Bill of Rights. All Hobbes allowed a person to do was protect his or her life. Locke permitted the overthrow of the sovereign power if it infringed on the subjects' rights—a course the English followed with James II and the Americans with George III.

Locke's prime concern was to defend the individual against the state, a concern that has remained essential to liberal thought ever since (*see box*, p. 557). But it is important to realize that Locke's emphasis on property served the elite better than the mass of society. With Locke to reassure them, the upper classes put their stamp on eighteenth-century European civilization.

IV. The State in the Eighteenth Century

STATE BUILDING

It sometimes seems as if international competition was the main preoccupation of eighteenth-century rulers. But, in fact, competition among states went hand in hand with internal state building. Conflict with rival powers compelled rulers to assert their sovereignty as forcefully as possible within their own borders in order to expand their revenues, armies, and bureaucracies. With the exception of Britain, countries where absolutism failed to develop—such as Sweden and the Netherlands—lost international influence. And Poland was partitioned three times by Russia, Austria, and Prussia, until in 1795 it ceased to exist as a sovereign state. The political consolidation of the eighteenth century, and the state system that was created, put a premium on military and economic power. In the process, the basic map of modern Europe emerged and the centralized character of the major states was confirmed.

The relationship between international rivalry and internal development is well illustrated by Prussia and Austria. In the mid-eighteenth century these two powers were vying to dominate Central Europe, and they instituted reforms so as to wage their struggle more effectively. Each was governed by absolute rulers who built their states by increasing the size of their armies, collecting larger revenues, and developing bureaucracies for their war effort. It did not seem to matter whether the ruler was a modern pragmatist like Frederick II of Prussia or a pious traditionalist like Maria Theresa of Austria. In their own way both understood the demands of the state system.

THE PRUSSIA OF FREDERICK WILLIAM I

Prussia's Frederick William I (1713–1740) was relentless in his pursuit of a strengthened absolutism at home and European-wide influence abroad. Strikingly different from his refined father, this spartan ruler approached affairs of state as all business and little pleasure. He disdained court life, dismissed numerous courtiers, and cut the salaries of those who remained. Uncluttered by royal ceremonies, his days were regulated in timetable fashion as he attempted to supervise everything himself.

The Emphasis on the Military It has been said that Frederick William I organized his state to serve his military power. During his reign the army grew from 38,000 to 83,000, making it the fourth largest in Europe, behind France, Russia, and Austria. While still relying on foreign mercenaries for one-third of his troops, he also instituted a form of conscription. And all his soldiers had to undergo intensive drilling and wear standardized uniforms. Determined to build an effective cadre of professionals, he forbade his subjects to serve in foreign armies and compelled the

Map 17.4 THE EXPANSION OF RUSSIA AND THE PARTITION OF POLAND
All three of the powers in Eastern Europe—Prussia, Russia, and Austria—gained territory from the dismemberment of Poland. At the same time, Russia was expanding to the south and east.

sons of nobles to attend cadet schools to learn martial skills and attitudes.

In this military state Frederick William I was the number one soldier. A colorful commander in chief, he maintained a personal regiment of towering grenadiers and always wore a uniform, declaring that he would be buried in it. But he did not intend to die in battle. For all his involvement with military life, he avoided committing his army to battle, and he therefore passed it on intact to his son, Frederick II.

The process of centralization kept pace with the growth of the army. In 1723 a government superagency was created; called the General Directory of Finance, War, and Domains, it united the administration of all functions except justice, education, and religion. Its main task was to coordinate the collection of revenue, expenditures (mostly military), and local administration. The king also put resources into education so as to give the population the basic instruction they needed to serve the state. He made education compulsory for all children where schools existed, and where there were none, he instructed local communities and parents to set them up, though he made no attempt to enforce these decrees. The educational policy was thus more theoretical than practical and had few social consequences. Teachers, for example, were often clergy who held their jobs as sidelines. Uninterested in intellectual pursuits for their own sake, the king allowed the universities to decline; they did not fit his relentless vision of how to build his state.

FREDERICK THE GREAT

Frederick William I's most notable triumph, perhaps, was the grooming of his successor. This was no mean task. Frederick II (1740–1786) seemed opposite in temperament to his father and little inclined to follow in his footsteps. The father was a God-fearing German Protestant. The son disdained German culture and was a deist (see p. 611). Sentimental and artistically inclined, Frederick II was a composer of music who played the flute, wrote poetry, and greatly admired French culture. He even wrote philosophical treatises and corresponded with leading European intellectuals.

Since the Prussian monarchy was mobilizing all its subjects for the tasks of state building, however, the young prince was not exempted. On the contrary, he was forced to work at all levels of the state apparatus so as to experience them directly, from shoveling hay on a royal farm to marching with the troops. The father trained his son for kingship, reshaping his personality, giving him a sense of duty, and toughening him for leadership. Despite Frederick's prolonged resistance, this hard apprenticeship succeeded. In the end, as a modern psychiatrist would put it, the prince identified with the aggressor.

Frederick's Rule When he assumed the throne in 1740, Frederick II was prepared to lead Prussia in a ruthless struggle for power and territory. While his intellectual turn of mind caused him to agonize over moral issues and the nature of his role, he never flinched from exercising power. He did, however, attempt to justify absolutism at home and aggression abroad. He claimed undivided power for the ruler, not because the dynasty had a divine mission but because only absolute rule could bring results. The monarch, he stated, was the first servant of the state. In the long run, he hoped, an enlightened monarch might lead his people to a more rational and moral existence. Some of these objectives, such as religious toleration and judicial reform, could be reached immediately, and in implementing them Frederick gained a reputation as an "enlightened" absolutist.

But these were minor matters. The paramount issue, security, provided the best justification for absolutism. Success here required Prussia to improve its vulnerable geographic position by acquiring more territory, stronger borders, and the power to face other European states as an equal. Until that was achieved, Frederick would not consider the domestic reforms that might disrupt the flow of taxes or men into the army, or provoke his nobility. The capture of territory was his most singular contribution to the rise of Prussia and what earned him his title of Frederick the Great.

By coincidence, the year 1740, when Frederick II came to the throne, was the year when a suitable task for his army presented itself—an attack on the Habsburg province of Silesia. Prussia had no claim to the province; it was simply a wealthy neighboring domain that would expand Prussia's territory and that the Habsburgs were un-

▸ *E. F. Cunningham*
THE RETURN OF FREDERICK II FROM A MANEUVRE, 1787
Were it not for the richly embroidered saddle cover and the fine white horse, it would be hard to spot Frederick the Great among his officers. Nor is there anything to indicate that the two men on the black and brown horses behind him are his son and grandson. This sober evocation of a king as a professional soldier contrasts strikingly with earlier glorifications (see plate on p. 451).

able to defend. Yet the conquest of Silesia brought to a new level the state building begun in Prussia by the great elector in 1648; the reaction also shaped state building in the Habsburg empire.

THE HABSBURG EMPIRE UNDER ATTACK

The Habsburg empire in the eighteenth century was like a dynastic holding company uniting diverse territories under one crown: Austria, Bohemia, Hungary, and other possessions like the Austrian Netherlands, Lombardy, and Tuscany. The emperors hoped to integrate Austria, Bohemia, and Hungary into a Catholic, centralized, German-speaking superstate. But the traditional representative assemblies in these provinces resisted such centralization.

International Rivalry and War In the reign of Charles VI (1711–1740), yet another problem complicated the destiny of this multinational empire, for his only heir was his daughter, Maria Theresa. In 1713 Charles drafted a document known as the Pragmatic Sanction, declaring that all Habsburg dominions would pass intact to the eldest heir, male or female; and for the next 25 years he sought recognition of the Pragmatic Sanction from the European powers. By making all kinds of concessions and promises, he won this recognition on paper. But when he died in 1740, his daughter found that the commitments were worthless: The succession was challenged by force from several sides. Concentrating on diplomacy alone, Charles had neglected the work of state building, leaving an empty treasury, an inadequately trained army, and an ineffective bureaucracy.

In contrast to Austria, Prussia had a full treasury, a powerful army, and a confident ruler, Frederick II, who seized the Habsburg province of Silesia without qualm. His justification was simply "reasons of state" combined with the Habsburgs' faltering fortunes. And Maria Theresa had her hands more than full, because the French declared war on her to support their ally Bavaria's claim to the Habsburg throne. Meanwhile, Spain hoped to win back control of Austria's Italian possessions. Worse yet, Maria Theresa faced a rebellion by the Czech nobles in Bohemia. Her position would probably have been hopeless if Hungary's Magyar nobles had followed suit. But Maria Theresa promised them autonomy within the Habsburg empire, and they offered her the troops she needed to resist the invaders.

In the War of Austrian Succession (1740–1748) that followed, Maria Theresa learned the elements of state building. With her Hungarian troops and with financial help from her one ally, Britain, she fought her opponents to a stalemate. Frederick's conquest of Silesia proved to be the only significant territorial change produced by this major war. Even for England and France, who fought the war mainly in their overseas colonies, it was a standoff. But Maria Theresa now regarded the recovery of Silesia and the humiliation of Prussia as esential. These aims, in turn, required determined state building within Habsburg domains.

MARIA THERESA

The woman whose authority was established not by her father's negotiations but by force of arms was a marked contrast to her archenemy, Frederick. The Prussian king was practical and irreligious; Maria Theresa was moralistic and pious. While Frederick barely tolerated a loveless marriage, the Habsburg ruler enjoyed a happy domestic life, bearing numerous children and taking great personal interest in their upbringing. Her personality and her ruling style were deceptively traditional, for she was a shrewd innovator in the business of building and reasserting the power of her state.

Unlike Frederick, or for that matter her own son and successor, Joseph II, Maria Theresa had a strong regard for her dynasty. In this respect her being a woman made no difference to the policies or government of the empire. She believed in the divine mission of the Habsburgs and conscientiously attended to the practical needs of her realm. It was because she put the state's interests first that this most pious of Catholic sovereigns—who disdained religious toleration and loathed atheists—felt obliged to reform the Church. Responding to waste and self-interest in her monasteries, she forbade the founding of new establishments. She also abolished the clergy's exemptions from taxes, something the French king found impossible to do.

A new bureaucratic apparatus was constructed on the models of French and Prussian absolutism. In Vienna, reorganized central ministries recruited staffs of experts. In the provinces, new agents were appointed who were largely divorced from feudal and local interests, though some concession did have to be made to the regional traditions of the Habsburg realm. The core domains (excluding Hungary and the Italian possessions) were reorganized into 10 provinces, each subdivided into districts directed by royal officials. With the help of these officials, the central government could wrest new taxes from the local diets. Meanwhile, Maria Theresa brought important nobles from all her domains to Vienna to participate in its social and administrative life. She also reformed the military, improving the training of troops and establishing academies to produce a more professional officer corps. Thus did international needs help shape domestic political reforms.

THE GROWTH OF STABILITY IN GREAT BRITAIN

It was not only absolutists who strengthened their states. Britain, too, expanded its government and its international power in the eighteenth century. This was the work not so much of a monarch as of the "political nation"—the landowners and leading townsmen who made up about 5 percent of the population of Great Britain yet who elected almost all the members of Parliament. Their control of the nation was symbolized

▸ *M. van Meytens*
Maria Theresa and Her Family, 1750
Although the setting is just as splendid, the portrayal of Maria Theresa with her husband and 11 of her 16 children suggests a domesticity that is absent from Louis XIV's family portrait of half a century before (see chapter opening plate on p. 532).

by the fact that the distribution of the 558 seats in the House of Commons bore little relation to the size of constituencies. In 1793, for example, 51 English and Welsh boroughs, which contained fewer than 1500 voters, elected 100 members of Parliament, nearly a fifth of the Commons. Many of these districts were safely in the pocket of a prominent local family; and election campaigns elsewhere were often determined by bribery, influence, and intimidation. On a national scale, loose party alignments did exist. The Whigs wanted a strong Parliament and generally preferred commercial to agricultural interests. The Tories usually supported the king and policies that favored large landholders. But the realities of politics were based on small factions within these larger groups, and politics revolved around the control of patronage and office.

As the financial and military needs and capabilities of the government expanded, Parliament now created a thoroughly bureaucratized state. Britain had always prided itself on having a smaller government and lower taxes than its neighbors, largely because, as an island, it had avoided the need for a standing army. All that now came to an end. Starting with the struggle against Louis XIV, wars required constant increases in resources, troops, and administrators. A steadily expanding navy had to be supported, as did an army that reached almost 200,000 men by the 1770s. Before the 1690s, public expenditures rarely amounted to £2 million a year; by the 1770s, they were almost £30 million, and most of that was spent on the military. In this period, as a result, Britain's fiscal bureaucracy more than tripled in size. The recruiting officer became a regular sight, and so too did the treasury men who were imposing increasingly heavy tax burdens.

Unlike their counterparts on the continent, however, the wealthier classes in Britain paid considerable taxes to support this state building, and they maintained more fluid relations with other classes. The landed gentry and the commercial class, in particular, were often linked by

▸ NEW GALLOWS AT THE OLD BAILEY, ENGRAVING
It was an indication of the severity of English criminal justice that the gallows erected near the chief court in London, the Old Bailey, in the mid-eighteenth century were specially constructed so that 10 condemned criminals, both men and women, could be executed at once.

▸ **William Pitt in the Commons**
William Pitt the younger is shown here addressing the House of Commons. Like his father during the Seven Years' War, Pitt provided firm leadership against France in the 1790s.

marriage and by financial or political associations. Even great aristocrats sometimes had close ties with the business leaders of London. For the lower levels of society, however, the barriers were as high as they had ever been. For all of Britain's prosperity, the lower third of society remained poor and often desperate. As a result, despite the severity of the system of justice and the frequency of capital punishment, crime was endemic in both country and town. The eighteenth century was the heyday of that romantic but violent figure, the highwayman.

The Age of Walpole The first two rulers of the Hanoverian dynasty, George I (1714–1727) and George II (1727–1760), could not speak English fluently. The language barrier and their concern for their German territory of Hanover left them often uninterested in British politics, and this was one reason Parliament grew in authority. Its dominant figure for over 20 years was Sir Robert Walpole, who rose to prominence because of his skillful handling of fiscal policy during the panic following the collapse of an overseas trading company in 1720. This crash, known as the South Sea Bubble, resembled the failure of John Law's similar scheme in France, but it had less effect on government finances. Thereafter, Walpole controlled British politics until 1742, mainly by dispensing patronage liberally and staying at peace.

Many historians have called Walpole the first prime minister, though the title was not official. He insisted that all ministers inform and consult with the House of Commons as well as with the king, and he himself continued to sit in Parliament in order to recruit support for his decisions. Not until the next century was it accepted that the Commons could force a minister to resign. But Walpole took a first step toward ministerial responsibility and thus shaped the future structure of British government.

In Great Britain as in France, the economic expansion of the eighteenth century increased the wealth and the social and political weight of the commercial and financial middle class. Although Londoners remained around 11 percent of the population, the proportion of the English who lived in other sizable towns doubled in the eighteenth century; and by 1800 some 30 percent of the country's inhabitants were urbanized. Walpole's policy of peace pleased the large landlords but angered this growing body of merchants and businesspeople, who feared the growth of French commerce and colonial settlements. They found their champion in William Pitt, later earl of Chatham, the grandson of a man who had made a fortune in India. Eloquent, self-confident, and infused with a vision of Britain's imperial destiny, Pitt began his parliamentary career in 1738 by attacking the timid policies of the government and demanding that France be driven from the seas. Although Walpole's policies continued even after his resignation in 1742, Pitt's moment finally came in 1758, when Britain became involved in the Seven Years' War (see p. 569). This conflict was to be a testing time throughout Europe for the advances of the previous century in state building and the development of the international system.

V. The International System

While rulers built up their states by enlarging their bureaucracies, strengthening governmental institutions, and expanding their resources, they also had to consider how best to deal with their neighbors. In an age that emphasized reasoned and practical solutions to problems, there was hope that an orderly system could be devised for international relations. If the reality fell short of the ideal, there were nevertheless many who thought they were creating a more impersonal and organized structure for diplomacy and warfare.

DIPLOMACY AND WARFARE

One obstacle to the creation of an impersonal international system was the continuing influence, in eighteenth-century diplomacy, of traditional dynastic interests. Princes and their ministers tried to preserve a family's succession, and they arranged marriages to gain new titles or alliances. Part of the reason that those perennial rivals, Britain and France, remained at peace for nearly 30 years until 1740 was that the rulers in both countries felt insecure on their thrones and thus had personal motives for not wanting to risk aggressive foreign policies.

Gradually, however, dynastic interests gave way to policies based on a more impersonal conception of the state. Men like Frederick II of Prussia and William Pitt of Britain tried to shape their diplomacy to what they considered the needs of their states. "Reasons of state" centered on security, which could be guaranteed only by force. Thus the search for defensible borders and the weakening of rivals became obvious goals. Eighteenth-century statesmen believed that the end (security and prosperity) justified the means (the use of power). Until a country was completely invulnerable, its leaders felt justified in using the crudest tactics in dealing with its neighbors.

The Diplomatic System If there was any broad, commonly agreed principle at work, it was that hegemony, or domination by one state, had to be resisted because it threatened international security. The concern aroused by Louis XIV's ambitions showed the principle at work, when those whom he sought to dominate joined together in order to frustrate his designs. Their aim was to establish equilibrium in Europe by a balance of power, with no single state achieving hegemony. From the War of Spanish Succession until the rise of Napoleon, that balance was maintained, though the means could be unsavory.

The diplomats who were responsible for implementing "reasons of state" and the balance of power knew there were times when they had to deceive. They might fabricate a claim to a province or a princely title, and it was known that ambassadors were spies by vocation. They offered the bribes that were a part of foreign policy and negotiated treaties that they sometimes expected their prince to violate. Yet there was also a more stabilizing side to diplomacy: The eighteenth century marks its growth as a serious profession, parallel to the rationalization of the state itself. Foreign ministries were staffed with experts and clerks, and kept extensive archives, while the heads of the diplomatic machine, the

▶ ENGRAVING FROM THE WESTMINSTER MAGAZINE, 1774
Political cartoons were standard fare in eighteenth-century newspapers and magazines. This one shows a weeping king of Poland and an angry Turk (who made no gains) after Poland was carved up in 1772 by Frederick the Great, the Austrian emperor, and the Russian empress. Louis XV sits by without helping his ally Poland, and all are urged on by the devil under the table.

ambassadors, were stationed in permanent embassies abroad. This routinized management of foreign relations helped foster a sense of collective identity among Europe's states despite their endless struggles. Linguistically and socially, diplomats gave a sugar coating to international relations. French was now the common language of diplomacy; by 1774 even a treaty between Turks and Russians was drafted in that language. And socially the diplomats were aristocratic and cosmopolitan. Regardless of the ruler they served, all ambassadors saw themselves as members of the same fraternity.

In general, the great powers dominated international agreements, usually at the expense of the smaller states. For example, Prussia, Austria, and Russia satisfied their territorial ambitions by agreeing to partition Poland among themselves. Ignoring the Poles, they declared in 1772 that "whatever the limits of the respective claims, the acquisitions which result must be exactly equal." Resolving disputes by negotiation could be as amoral as war.

ARMIES

Despite the settlement of some conflicts by diplomacy, others led to war. If Britain emphasized its navy, on the continent the focus of bureaucratic innovation and monetary expenditure was the standing army, whose growth was striking. France set the pace. After 1680 the size of its forces never fell below 200,000. In Prussia the army increased in size from 39,000 to 200,000 men between 1713 and 1786. But the cost, technology, and tactics of these armies served to limit the devastation of eighteenth-century warfare. The expenses led rulers to husband their armies carefully. Princes were quick to declare war but slow to deploy their armies at full strength or commit them to battle. And casualties also became less numerous as discipline improved and the ferocity that had been caused by religious passions died away.

Tactics and Discipline The techniques of building and besieging fortifications continued to preoccupy military planners, even though the impregnable fortresses that the French engineer Sebastian Vauban had built to protect France's northeastern border were simply bypassed by the English general Marlborough when he pursued the French army in the War of the Spanish Succession. The decisive encounter was still the battle between armies, where the majority of the troops—the infantry—used their training to

▸ *L. N. van Blarenberghe*
THE BATTLE OF FONTENOY, 1745
This panorama shows the English and Dutch assaulting the French position in a battle in present-day Belgium. The French lines form a huge semicircle from the distant town to the wood on the left. The main attacking force in the center, surrounded by gunfire, eventually retreated, and news of the victory was brought to Louis XV, in red on the right, by a horseman in blue who is doffing his hat.

maneuver and fire in carefully controlled line formations. The aim of strategy was not to annihilate but to nudge an opposing army into abandoning its position in the face of superior maneuvers. This improved organization also served to reduce brutality. Better supplied by a system of magazines, more tightly disciplined by constant drilling, troops were less likely to desert or plunder than they had been during the Thirty Years' War.

As these military practices took hold, some encounters were fought as if they were taking place on a parade ground, and pitched battles in open fields were increasingly avoided. Even important victories might be nullified if a winning army returned to its home bases for winter camp. And no victor ever demanded unconditional surrender. The same was true of naval battles. Commanders were cautious in combat and rarely pursued a defeated squadron.

The officer corps of the military were generally the preserve of the European nobility, though they also served as channels of upward social mobility for wealthy sons of middle-class families who purchased commissions. In either case, the officer ranks tended to be filled by men who lacked the professional training for effective leadership. Officers were likely to be long on martial spirit but short on technical skills. The branches of service that showed the most progress were the artillery and the engineers, in which competent middle-class officers played an unusually large role.

A final limit on the scale of war in the eighteenth century was the inherent weakness of coalitions, which formed whenever a general war erupted. On paper these alliances looked formidable. On the battlefield, however, they were hampered by primitive communications and lack of mobility even at the peak of cooperation. Moreover, the partnerships rarely lasted very long. The competitiveness of the state system bred distrust among allies as well as enemies. Sudden abandonment of coalitions and the negotiation of separate peace treaties mark the history of almost every major war.

THE SEVEN YEARS' WAR

The pressures created by the competition of states, dynasties, and empires finally exploded in midcentury in a major war, the Seven Years' War (1756–1763). Its roots lay in a realignment of diplomatic alliances that began at Austria's prodding. Previously, the Bourbon-Habsburg rivalry had been the cornerstone of European diplomacy. But by the 1750s two other sets of antagonisms had taken over: French competition with the British in the New World and Austria's vendetta against Prussia over Silesia. For Austria, the rivalry with Bourbon France was no longer important. Its position in the Holy Roman Empire depended now on humbling Prussia. France was not yet concerned over Prussia, but French hostility to Austria had lessened. Austria was therefore free to lead a turnabout in alliances—a diplomatic revolution—in order to forge an anti-Prussian coalition with France and Russia. Russia was the key. Aside from her personal loathing of Frederick II, the pious Empress Elizabeth of Russia saw him as an obstacle to Russian ambitions

▸ ENGRAVING OF A MILITARY ACADEMY, FROM H. F. VON FLEMING, VOLKOMMENE TEUTSCHE SOLDAT, 1726
This scene, of young men studying fortifications and tactics in a German academy, would have been familiar to the sons of nobles throughout Europe who trained for a military career in the eighteenth century.

in Eastern Europe. Geographical vulnerability also made Prussia an inviting target, and so the stage was set for a diplomatic revolution.

Prussia was active in trying to compensate for that vulnerability. But its countermoves only alienated the other powers. Frederick sought to stay out of the Anglo-French rivalry by coming to terms with both these states. He had been France's ally in the past, and he now sought to negotiate a treaty with England. England—seeking to protect the royal territory of Hanover—willingly signed a neutrality accord, the Convention of Westminster, with Prussia in January 1756. Frederick had no intention of repudiating his friendship with France, but to the French—who had not been informed in advance of these negotiations—the Convention seemed an insult, if not an actual betrayal. The accord with France's mortal enemy, England, seemed the act of an untrustworthy ally. France overreacted, turned against Prussia, and thus fell into Austria's design (*see box*, p. 571). Russia too considered the Convention of Westminster a betrayal by *its* supposed ally England. English bribes and diplomacy could no longer keep Russia from actively joining Austria to plan Prussia's dismemberment.

Map 17.5 PRUSSIA AND THE AUSTRIAN EMPIRE, 1721–1772
The steady territorial advances of Prussia had created a major power in northern and Eastern Europe, alongside the Austrian Empire, by the time of the first partition of Poland in 1772.

Maria Theresa in Vehement Mood

The animosities and ambitions that shaped international relations in the eighteenth century were exemplified by the Empress Maria Theresa. Her furious reaction to the event that destroyed Europe's old diplomatic system—England's signing of the Convention of Westminster with Maria Theresa's archenemy, Frederick the Great—suggests how deep were the feelings that brought about the midcentury conflagration. After learning the news and deciding (in response) to ally herself with France, she told the British ambassador on May 13, 1756, exactly where she stood.

"I have not abandoned the old system, but Great Britain has abandoned me and the system, by concluding the Prussian treaty, the first intelligence of which struck me like a fit of apoplexy. I and the king of Prussia are incompatible; and no consideration on earth will ever induce me to enter into any engagement to which he is a party. Why should you be surprised if, following your example in concluding a treaty with Prussia, I should now enter into an engagement with France?

"I am far from being French in my disposition, and do not deny that the court of Versailles has been my bitterest enemy; but I have little to fear from France, and I have no other recourse than to form such arrangements as will secure what remains to me. My principal aim is to secure my hereditary possessions. I have truly but two enemies whom I really dread, the king of Prussia and the Turks; and while I and Russia continue on the same good terms as now exist between us, we shall, I trust, be able to convince Europe, that we are in a condition to defend ourselves against those adversaries, however formidable."

From William Coxe, *History of the House of Austria*, vol. III (London: Bohn, 1847), pp. 363–364.

The Course of War Fearing encirclement, Frederick gambled on a preventive war through Saxony in 1756. Although he easily conquered the duchy, his plan backfired, for it activated the coalition that he dreaded. Russia and France met their commitments to Austria, and a combined offensive against Prussia began.

For a time Frederick's genius as a general brought him success. His forces won a spectacular victory at Rossbach in late 1757 over a much larger French-Austrian army. Skillful tactics and daring surprise movements would bring other victories, but strategically the Prussian position was shaky. Frederick had to dash in all directions across his provinces to repel invading armies whose combined strength far exceeded his own. Each successive year of the war, he faced the prospect of Russian attacks on Brandenburg in the north and Austrian thrusts from the south through Silesia and Saxony. Disaster was avoided mainly because the Russian army returned east for winter quarters regardless of its gains, but even so, the Russians occupied Berlin. On the verge of exhaustion, Prussia at best seemed to face a stalemate with a considerable loss of territory; at worst, the war would continue and bring about a total Prussian collapse. But the other powers were also war-weary, and Frederick's enemies were becoming increasingly distrustful of one another.

In the end, Prussia was saved by one of those sudden changes of reign that could cause dramatic reversals of policy in Europe. In January 1762 Empress Elizabeth died and was replaced temporarily by Tsar Peter III, a passionate admirer of Frederick. He quickly pulled Russia out of the war and returned Frederick's conquered eastern domains of Prussia and Pomerania. In Britain, meanwhile, William Pitt was replaced by the more pacific earl of Bute, who brought about a reconciliation with France; both countries then ended their insistence on the punishment of Prussia. Austria's coalition had collapsed.

The terms of the Peace of Hubertusburg (1763), settling the continental phase of the Seven Years' War, were therefore surprisingly favorable to Prussia. Prussia returned Saxony to Austria but paid no compensation for the devastation of the duchy, and the Austrians recognized Silesia as Prussian. In short, the status quo was restored. Frederick could return to Berlin, his dominion preserved partly by his army but mainly by luck and the continuing fragility of international alliances.

If, amidst the state building of the eighteenth century, many of Europe's regimes were able quite easily to sustain a major war even if it brought about few territorial changes, that was not simply because of the expansion of government and the disciplining of armies. It was also the result of remarkable economic advances and the availability of new resources that were flowing into Europe from the development of overseas empires. In politics, this was primarily an age of consolidation; in economics, it was a time of profound transformation.

Recommended Reading

Sources

*Hobbes, Thomas. *Leviathan.* 1651. Any modern edition.

*Locke, John. *Second Treatise of Civil Government.* 1690. Any modern edition.

Luvvas, J. (ed.). *Frederick the Great on the Art of War.* 1966.

Saint-Simon, Louis. *Historical Memoirs.* Lucy Norton (ed. and tr.). 2 vols. 1967 and 1968. Lively memoirs of the court at Versailles.

Studies

*Alexander, John T. *Catherine the Great: Life and Legend.* 1988.

Anderson, M. S. *Historians and Eighteenth-Century Europe, 1715–1789.* 1979. Past and current viewpoints on a number of fundamental issues.

Baxter, S. B. *William III and the Defense of European Liberty 1650–1702.* 1966. A solid and straightforward account of the career of the ruler of both England and the Netherlands.

*Behrens, C. B. A. *Society, Government, and the Enlightenment: The Experience of Eighteenth-Century France and Prussia.* 1985.

*Available in paperback.

Brewer, John. *The Sinews of Power: War, Money and the English State. 1688–1783.* 1989. The work that demonstrated the importance of the military and the growth of bureaucracy in eighteenth-century England.

——— and John Styles (eds.). *An Ungovernable People: The English and Their Law in the Seventeenth and Eighteenth Centuries.* 1980. A rich collection of essays on crime and the administration of justice.

*Carsten, F. L. *The Origins of Prussia.* 1954. The standard account of the background to the reign of the great elector, Frederick William, and the best short history of his accomplishments and the rise of the Junkers.

Corvisier, André. *Armies and Societies in Europe, 1494–1789.* 1979. A comparative study, strongest on the French army.

Duffy, Christopher. *The Army of Frederick the Great.* 1974. A comprehensive account of everything from recruitment to tactics.

*Goubert, Pierre. *Louis XIV and Twenty Million Frenchmen.* Anne Carter (tr.). 1970. This is not so much a history of the king's reign as a study of the nature of French society and politics during Louis' rule.

Hatton, R. N. *Charles XII of Sweden.* 1968. A thorough and well-written biography that does justice to a dramatic life.

*———. *Europe in the Age of Louis XIV.* 1969. A beautifully illustrated and vividly interpretive history of the period that Louis dominated.

Hay, D., P. Linebaugh, and E. P. Thompson. *Albion's Fatal Tree: Crime and Society in Eighteenth-Century England.* 1975. A pioneering study.

*Henshall, Nicholas. *The Myth of Absolutism: Change and Continuity in Early Modern European Monarchy.* 1992. A comparison, mainly of England and France, which argues that the term *absolutism,* a later invention, ignores the emphasis on tradition and continuity during the 1660–1789 period.

*Holmes, Geoffrey. *The Making of a Great Power: Late Stuart and Early Georgian Britain, 1660–1722;* and *The Age of Oligarchy: Pre-industrial Britain, 1722–1783.* 1993. The best detailed survey.

Linebaugh, Peter. *The London Hanged: Crime and Civil Society in the Eighteenth Century.* 1991. A detailed study of crime and criminals.

Mettam, Roger. *Power and Faction in Louis XIV's France.* 1988. An analysis of government and power under absolutist rule.

*Plumb, J. H. *The Growth of Political Stability in England, 1675–1725.* 1969. A brief, lucid survey of the developments in English politics that helped create Britain's modern parliamentary democracy.

———. *Sir Robert Walpole* (2 vols). 1956–1961. A masterly biography.

Raeff, Marc. *The Well-Ordered Police State: Social and Institutional Change through Law in the Germanies and Russia, 1600–1800.* 1983.

Rowen, Herbert H. *The King's State: Proprietary Dynasticism in Early Modern France.* 1980. An incisive study of the origins and elaboration of the theory by which Louis XIV ruled France.

Shennan, J. H. *Louis XIV.* 1986. A good introduction to the king and his reign.

Stoye, John. *The Siege of Vienna.* 1964. An exciting account of the last great threat to Christian Europe from the Turkish empire.

*Sumner, B. H. *Peter the Great and the Emergence of Russia.* 1950. This short but comprehensive book is the best introduction to Russian history in this period.

*Tuck, Richard. *Hobbes.* 1989. A clear and compact introduction to Hobbes's thought.

Weigley, R. F. *The Age of Battles: The Quest for Decisive Warfare from Breitenfeld to Waterloo.* 1991. The best military history of the age.

The docks of Marseilles in Southern France.

CHAPTER EIGHTEEN

THE WEALTH OF NATIONS

IN the early eighteenth century the great majority of Europe's people still lived directly off the land. With a few regional exceptions, the agrarian economy remained "immobile": It seemed to have no capacity for dramatic growth. People were aided in their labors by animals, wind, and water, but their technology, social arrangements, and management techniques offered little prospect of improvement. Several new developments, however, were about to touch off a remarkable surge of economic advance. The first sign of this new situation was the sustained growth of Europe's population, which depended in turn on an expansion of the food supply. While changes in agrarian output on the continent were modest but significant, in England innovations in the control and use of land dramatically increased food production and changed the entire structure of rural society.

The exploitation of overseas colonies provided another critical stimulus for European economic growth. Colonial trade in slaves, sugar, tobacco, and other raw materials radiated from port cities like London and Bristol in England and Bordeaux and Nantes in France. An infrastructure of supportive industries and processing facilities developed around these ports and fed trade networks for the reexport across Europe of finished colonial products. The colonies, in turn, offered new markets for goods manufactured in Europe, such as cotton fabrics.

The growing demand for cotton cloth at home and abroad touched off an urgent drive among English textile merchants for changes in the organization and technology of production. It was in English cotton manufacturing that dramatic structural change heralded the economic transformation known as industrialization. By the start of the nineteenth century, fundamental changes in the methods of raising food and producing goods were well under way in Britain and were beginning to spread to the continent. This chapter explores the character of economic development, the impediments to that process, and some of the consequences of the economic transformations that began in the eighteenth century.

I. Demographic and Economic Growth

A NEW DEMOGRAPHIC ERA

In the relationship between people and the land, between demography and agriculture, European life before the eighteenth century showed little change. Levels of population seemed to flow like the tides, in cyclical or wave-like patterns. Population might increase substantially over several generations, but eventually crop failures or the ravages of plague and other contagious diseases would drive the level of population down once again. In extreme cases, a lack of able-bodied workers led to the abandonment of land, and entire villages disappeared altogether. Such dramatic population losses had last occurred in seventeenth-century Germany, Poland, and Mediterranean Europe (the southern parts of Italy, Spain, and France).

For centuries Europe's population had been vulnerable to subsistence crises. Successions of poor harvests or crop failures might leave the population without adequate food and would drive up the price of grain and flour beyond what the poorest people could afford. If actual starvation did not carry them off, undernourishment made people more vulnerable than usual to disease. Such crises could also set off a chain of side effects, from unemployment to pessimism, that made people postpone marriage and childbearing. Thus subsistence crises could drive down the birthrate as well as drive up the death rate, causing in combination a substantial loss in population.

Population Growth A new era in Europe's demography began around 1730, and by 1800 Europe's population had grown by at least 50 percent and probably by more. (Since the first censuses were not taken until the early nineteenth century, all population figures prior to that time are only estimates.) During the eighteenth century (which is considered, demographically, to have begun around 1730), Europe's estimated population jumped from about 120 million to about 180 or 190 million. Europe had probably never before experienced so rapid and substantial an increase in the number of its people. Prussia and Sweden may have doubled their populations, while Spain's grew from 7.5 million to about 11.5 million. Even higher growth rates in England and Wales raised the population there from an estimated 5 million people in 1700 to more than 9 million in 1801, the date of the first British census. The French, according to the best estimates, numbered about 19 million at the death of Louis XIV in 1715, and probably about 26 million in 1789. France was the most densely populated large nation in Europe in the late eighteenth century and, with the exception of the vast Russian Empire, the most populous state, which no doubt helps to explain its remarkable military preponderance in the revolutionary and Napoleonic eras.

Europe's population growth of the eighteenth century continued and indeed accelerated during the nineteenth century, thus breaking once and for all the tide-like cycles and "immobility" of Europe's demography. What caused this fundamental transformation in the underlying structure of European history?

Death Rates and Birthrates There are two possible explanations for rapid population growth: a fall in death rates or a rise in birthrates. The consensus among historians is that a decline in mortality rates, rather than a rise in birthrates, accounts for most of the population growth in the eighteenth century, although England seems to have been an exception. Declines in the death rate did not occur because of improvements in medical science or hygiene, which became important factors in driving down mortality only in the late nineteenth century. Instead, Europe was beginning to enjoy a stabler and better food supply, perhaps owing to a mild improvement in average climate compared with that of the seventeenth century, which some historians regard as a "little ice age" of unusually cold and wet weather. The opening of new agricultural land in Poland, Hungary, and Russia helped increase Europe's food supplies, as did incremental advances in transportation networks (which made it easier to move regional grain surpluses to where they were most needed) and agrarian changes in England (to be discussed below).

Europe's population remained extremely vul-

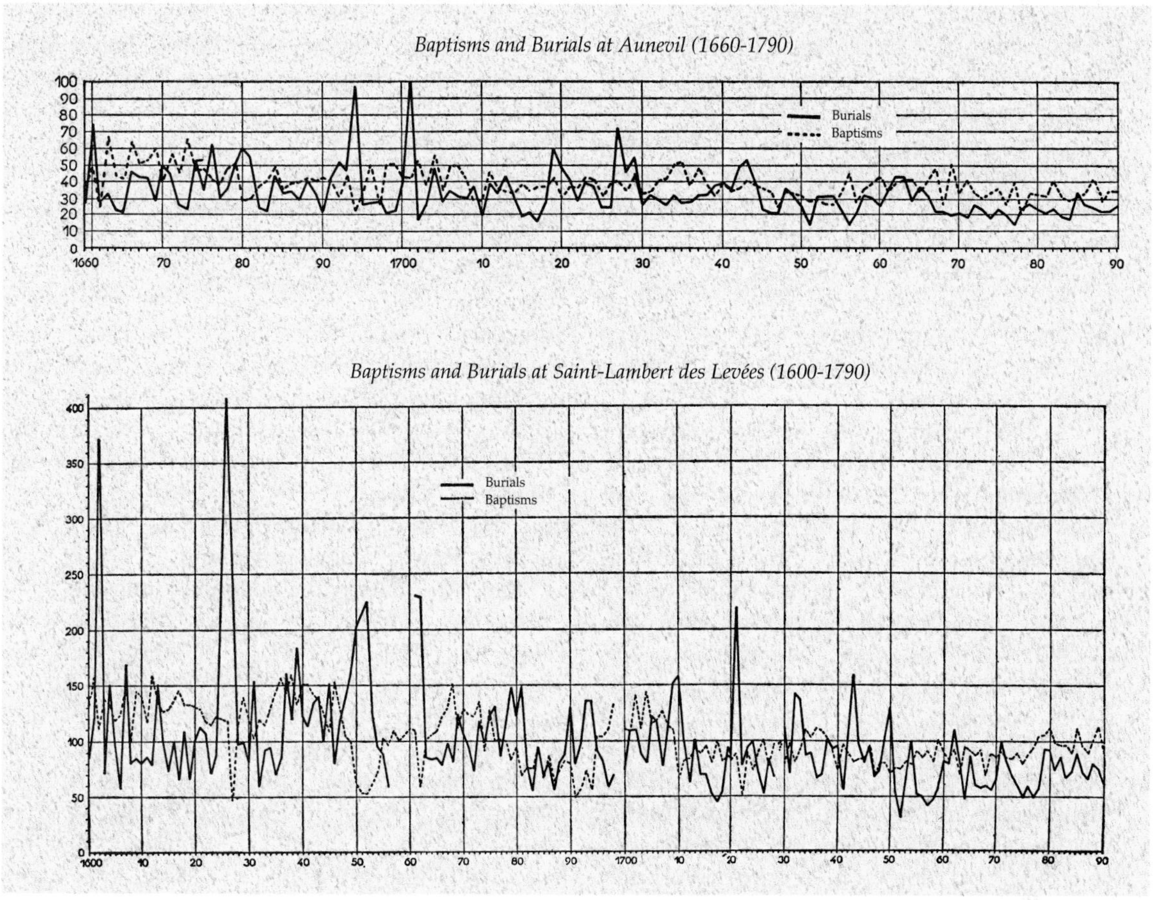

In these two French parishes, the seventeenth century came to a close with severe food shortages and sharp surges of mortality. In a more favorable economic climate, by contrast, the later eighteenth century brought an almost consistent annual surplus of births over deaths.

nerable to disease. Endemic diseases such as tuberculosis, typhoid, and malaria still ravaged the populations of many regions. Periodic epidemics of dysentery (which attacked the digestive system), influenza (lethal to the respiratory systems of the elderly), typhus (a lice-borne disease that flourished in the conditions of poverty), and smallpox (which assaulted rich and poor alike) continued to take their toll. But a better-nourished population could perhaps stand up to those assaults with greater success.

With the exception of England, in most regions of Europe birthrates do not seem to have increased in the eighteenth century. A high average age at marriage, with women typically well into their twenties and men in their mid- to late twenties, served to check population growth. Since the birth of illegitimate children remained relatively rare, late marriages kept women from becoming pregnant during some of their most fecund years; they therefore had fewer babies altogether. In England, however, where greater geographic mobility and economic opportunities may have encouraged young couples to start families earlier, the average age at marriage came down and birthrates increased, helping to explain Britain's explosive population growth.

PROFIT INFLATION: THE MOVEMENT OF PRICES

The population grew in eighteenth-century Europe in tandem with an increasing pace and scale of economic activity. Europe's overall wealth expanded, though not steadily and consistently. While the economy experienced periods of fluctuation, of growth and decline, the long-term, or secular, trend was positive, compared with the stagnation and economic difficulty that prevailed (outside of England) during the "long seventeenth century," until roughly 1730. Scholars have made particularly rigorous studies of the economic cycles in France as revealed through the history of prices, and there is reason to believe that economies elsewhere in Europe behaved comparably to France's.

During the first decades of the eighteenth century, prices generally remained stable, perpetuating the long depression of the seventeenth century and no doubt reflecting the exhaustion of the European states from the War of the Spanish Succession. As with Europe's demographic growth, significant economic growth began around 1730 and lasted up until the peace settlements that followed the Napoleonic wars in 1815. Inflation in prices dominated the era. Since French money was kept stable after 1726, the upward movement of prices must be attributed to other causes. Primarily, the rise in prices reflected the stimulus and pressures of a growing population in France and a growing demand for food, land, goods, and employment.

Gently rising prices and gradual, mild inflation usually stimulate the economy—unlike sharp spikes of inflation that create hard times. This nearly century-long cycle of "profit inflation" generated economic growth. There were of course periodic reversals or countercyclical trends. In France, for example, prosperity leveled off around 1770, ushering in two decades of falling profits, unemployment, and hard times. The difficulties were compounded by a succession of crop failures and sharply rising grain prices in 1788–1789—coincident with the outbreak of the French Revolution. After the 1790s, however, profit inflation resumed until the end of the Napoleonic era.

The Impact of Inflation Over the long term, the inflation did not affect all products, all sectors of the economy, or all segments of society equally. Prices in France between 1726 and 1789 increased by an average of about 65 percent. The cost of grains, the basic food for the poor, rose slightly more than the average and considerably more than other agricultural products, such as wine and meat. Rents rose sharply, suggesting a shortage of available land; in relation to averages for the decade of the 1730s, money rents had grown by 98 percent in the 1780s. Real wages, on the other hand, increased by a meager 22 percent in the same period, which points to a glut of workers competing for employment and to hard times for many wage earners.

These differentials had important social and economic effects. High rents in the countryside and low wages in the city took wealth from the poor and delivered it to the landlord and employer. Inflation helped drive many tenants from the soil, to the advantage of their better-off neighbors, who were eager to expand their holdings. In the city, inflation enabled merchants and manufacturers to sell goods for more and pay workers relatively less. Finally, inflation hurt the French government because its revenues did not grow as fast as its expenditures. Since a portion of French lands owned by the nobles and the Church was exempt from the land tax, the government relied heavily on sales and excise taxes that weighed on ordinary consumers. This inadequate and regressive tax base eventually contributed to a financial crisis for the French monarchy in the 1780s.

PROTOINDUSTRIALIZATION

Agriculture alone could not ensure economic growth in a heavily populated country like England, France, or the Netherlands. The excess of people to land in such countries meant that many rural people could not actually earn their livelihood in agriculture. One solution for needy families was domestic manufacturing. Traditionally, artisans in urban guilds manufactured the cloth fabrics used by Europeans, but textiles could also be produced through the putting-out system, whereby merchants distributed raw materials like wool or flax to rural households. Men and women would spin the raw material into yarn on hand-powered spinning machines; rural weavers working on looms in their cottages would then weave the yarn into cloth.

Protoindustrialization is the name historians

give to a type of economic development that occurred before the rise of the factory system in the late eighteenth century. In this phase, the volume of domestic rural manufacturing increased under the putting-out system, as more rural families devoted more time to industrial work—primarily spinning, weaving, or finishing textiles. A "thickening of the countryside" (a growth in population and in the pace of economic activity) occurred under protoindustrialization. This trend was particularly noticeable in certain regions of the Netherlands, Belgium, the Rhineland, France, and England, where the towns remained sources of capital, materials, and marketing services, but where merchants employed labor in the countryside.

Protoindustrialization had important economic, social, and demographic repercussions. Economically, it strengthened marketing networks, spurred capital accumulation that could be reinvested in production, generated additional revenue for needy rural families, and thereby increased their demand for products and services. Socially, it familiarized rural inhabitants with industrial processes and cash relationships. Demographically, it may have loosened restraints on marriages and births, which in turn might have led to increased immigration into the cities and thus to urban growth. On the other hand, protoindustrialization did not lead to significant technological improvements or to marked advances in productivity; it could not sustain continuous economic growth.

► In contrast to textile work, common artisanal trades such as shoemaking, tailoring, dressmaking, furniture making, and food services would continue to be conducted in small workshops down through the nineteenth century.

II. The New Shape of Industry

The transformation of manufacturing hinged above all on increasing the productivity of labor. This could occur through two kinds of innovations: the development of more efficient tools and machines, and the exploitation of new sources of energy. Economists call this process *factor substitution*, whereby capital, represented by the new tools and machines, is substituted for the skills or power of workers. In certain sectors of industry, the new tools were cheap and simple enough to be used by artisans in the home or in small workshops. But the growing complexity of machinery, especially when coupled with new sources of power, called into being a new social institution: the factory.

TOWARD A NEW ECONOMIC ORDER

In analyzing any economic system—traditional or modern, capitalist or socialist—economists distinguish between performance and structure. Performance is measured by output: the total or gross product, and the amount produced per individual in the community. This per capita productivity is, in fact, the best measure of an economy's performance. A particularly distinctive feature of an industrial economy is its capacity for sustained growth. Structure refers to all those characteristics of a society that support or affect performance. Economic, legal, and political institutions; tax policies; technology; demographic movements; even culture and ideology—all make up the structure underlying the economy.

Industrialization required innovations in technology, which dramatically raised per capita productivity. But new technology alone does not entirely explain the advent of industrialism. Social structure itself influences technological development in any age. To ask why dramatic change occurred in industry is thus to pose two deeper questions: What were the structural obstacles to technological innovation and entrepreneurship in traditional European society? And what structural changes in that society, from the late eighteenth century onward, promoted and rewarded innovation?

Impediments to Economic Innovation One major obstacle to innovation was the small size of most European markets, which were cut off from one another by physical barriers, political frontiers, tariff walls, and different laws, moneys, and units of measurement. Small markets slowed the growth of specialized manufacture and limited the mobility of capital and labor. Similarly, the highly skewed distribution of wealth typical of many European communities distorted the structure of demand. In many countries, a narrow aristocracy absorbed most disposable income, and the economy organized itself largely to serve the wealthy few. Catering to the desires of the rich, the economy produced expensive luxury goods, often exquisite in quality and workmanship but always in small quantities. Such small markets and skewed demand dampened the incentive to manufacture an abundance of relatively cheap goods.

Also crucial to the industrializing process was the question of property rights and privileges—whether they would encourage a high rate of return on innovation or impede it. Many institutions in traditional Europe worked against innovation. For instance, through feudal or seigneurial rents and tolls, lords throughout Europe collected payments for which they rendered no service in return. Increased production was thus likely to benefit these parasites as much as the entrepreneurs. In the towns, the guilds presented a major obstacle to economic innovation. Guild regulations, or government regulation of the economy enforced by the guilds, prescribed the techniques to be used in production and often dictated the terms and conditions under which goods could be sold, apprentices taken on, or workers hired. Out of simple self-interest, given their stake in existing arrangements, the guilds favored traditional technology and managerial techniques.

Governments, too, helped sustain these restrictive practices, principally by exploiting them for their own fiscal benefit. Governments typically collected substantial fees from guilds and other privileged institutions and groups. They also restricted economic activity by licensing monopoly companies with exclusive rights to trade in certain regions, such as the East Indies, or to manufacture certain products, such as fine por-

Laissez-Faire Ideology

At the heart of Adam Smith's laissez-faire ideology was a belief that individual self-interest is the motor of economic progress, a notion epitomized in this selection by Smith's reference to the "invisible hand." By the same token, each region or country should pursue what it does best, an argument against protective tariffs for domestic industry.

"Every individual is continually exerting himself to find out the most advantageous employment for whatever capital he can command. . . . But it is only for the sake of profit that any man employs a capital in the support of industry; and he will always, therefore, endeavor to employ it in the support of that industry of which the produce is likely to be of the greatest value, or to exchange for the greatest quantity either of money or of other goods. . . . [In so doing] he generally neither intends to promote the public interest, nor knows how much he is promoting it . . . he intends only his own security; and by directing that industry in such a manner as its produce may be of the greatest value, he intends only his own gain. [But] he is in this, as in many other cases, led by an invisible hand to promote an end which was not part of his intention. By pursuing his own interest he frequently promotes that of the society more effectually than when he really intends to promote it.

"What is the species of domestic industry which his capital can employ, and of which the produce is likely to be of the greatest value, every individual, it is evident, can, in his local situation, judge much better than any statesman or lawgiver can do for him. . . . To give the monopoly of the home market to the produce of domestic industry, in any particular art or manufacture, is in some measure to direct private people in what manner they ought to employ their capitals, and must, in almost all cases, be either a useless or hurtful regulation. If the produce of domestic can be brought there as cheaply as that of foreign industry, the regulation is evidently useless. If it cannot, it must generally be hurtful. . . . If a foreign country can supply us with a commodity cheaper than we ourselves can make it, better buy it from them with some part of the produce of our own industry."

From A. Smith, *An Inquiry into the Nature and Causes of the Wealth of Nations* (1776), Book IV, Ch. II.

celain. With assured markets and profits, these companies were not likely to assume the risks of new ventures, and they blocked others from doing so. Cultural attitudes may also have discouraged entrepreneurial efforts. Many persons, particularly in the aristocratic classes, still regarded money made in trade or manufacture as somehow tainted. The highest aspiration of a successful businessperson seems often to have been the purchase of a noble title.

Adam Smith Although these institutions and attitudes still marked European life in the eighteenth century, they were subject to ever sharper criticisms. From midcentury on, certain French social thinkers denounced guild control of production in the towns and economic privilege and monopoly in all forms. But the seminal work in this new school of economic thought was *The Wealth of Nations* (1776) by the Scottish philosopher Adam Smith (*see box*, above). Smith believed that economic progress required that each individual be allowed to pursue his or her own self-interest freely, without restriction by guilds, the state, or tradition. He argued that on all levels of economic activity—from the manufacturing process to the flow of international trade—a natural division of labor should be encouraged. High tariffs, guild restrictions, mercantilist restraints on free trade all artificially obstructed economic activity. Smith became a founding father of *laissez-faire* economic theory, meaning in effect: let individuals freely pursue their own economic interests—a battle cry that would be taken up vigorously by businesspeople and factory owners in the nineteenth century.

Such arguments slowly affected policy. Guilds were already growing weaker in most towns and were relatively powerless in towns of recent growth, like Manchester and Birmingham in England, where new industries such as cotton manufacturing escaped guild supervision altogether. This trend reached its culmination when the government of revolutionary France permanently dissolved all guilds and restrictive trade associations in 1791. Similarly, the British Parliament revoked the laws regulating apprenticeships in the 1790s. Legally and socially, the entrepreneur was winning greater freedom.

THE ROOTS OF ECONOMIC TRANSFORMATION IN ENGLAND

Of all the nations of Europe, England was the first to develop a social structure strongly supportive of innovation and economic growth. England's advantages were many, some of them deeply rooted in geography and history. This comparatively small realm contained an excellent balance of resources. The plain to the south and east, which contained the traditional centers of English settlement, was fertile and productive. The uplands to the north and west possessed rich deposits of coal and iron, and their streams had powered flour mills since the Middle Ages.

Proximity to the sea was another natural advantage. No part of the island kingdom was distant from the coast. At a time when water transport offered the sole economical means for moving bulky commodities, the sea brought coal close to iron, raw materials close to factories, and products close to markets. Above all, the sea gave Britain's merchants access to the much wider world beyond their shores.

Efficiency of transport was critical in setting the size of markets. During the eighteenth century, Britain witnessed a boom in the building of canals and turnpikes by private individuals or syndicates. By 1815 the country possessed some 2600 miles of canals linking rivers, ports, and other towns. In addition, there were few institutional obstructions to the movement of goods. United under a strong monarchy since the Middle Ages, Britain was free of internal tariff barriers, unlike prerevolutionary France, Germany, or Italy. Merchants everywhere counted in the same money, measured their goods by the same standards, and conducted their affairs under the protection of the common law.

The English probably had the highest standard of living in Europe and generated strong consumer demand for manufactured goods. English society was less stratified than that on the continent, the aristocracy powerful but much smaller. Primogeniture (with the family's land going to the eldest son) was the rule among both the peers (the titled members of the House of Lords) and the country gentlemen or squires. Left without lands, younger sons had to seek careers in other walks of life, and some turned toward commerce or manufacturing. They frequently recruited capital for their ventures from their landed fathers and elder brothers. English religious dissenters, chiefly Calvinists and Quakers, formed another pool of potential entrepreneurs; denied careers in government because of their religion, many turned their energies to business enterprises.

British Financial Management A high rate of reinvestment is critical to any takeoff into industrialization; reinvestment, in turn, depends on the skillful management of money by both individuals and public institutions. Here again, Britain enjoyed advantages. Early industrial enterprises could rely on Britain's growing banking system to meet their capital needs. In the seventeenth century the goldsmiths of London had assumed the functions of bankers. They accepted and guarded deposits, extended loans, transferred upon request credits from one account to another, and changed money. In the eighteenth century banking services became available beyond London; the number of country banks rose from 300 in 1780 to more than 700 by 1810. English businesspeople were familiar with bank notes and other forms of commercial papers, and their confidence in paper facilitated the recruitment and flow of capital.

The founding of the Bank of England in 1694 marked an epoch in the history of European finance. The bank took responsibility for managing

England's public debt, sold shares to the public, and faithfully met the interest payments due to the shareholders, with the help of government revenue (such as the customs duties efficiently collected on Britain's extensive foreign trade). When the government needed to borrow, it could turn to the Bank of England for assistance. This stability in government finances ensured a measure of stability for the entire money market and, most important, held down interest rates in both the public and private sectors. In general, since the "Glorious Revolution" of 1688, England's government had been sensitive to the interests of the business classes, who in turn had confidence in the government. Such close ties between money and power facilitated economic investment.

THE CONTOURS OF THE FRENCH ECONOMY

Structural obstacles to economic growth were more deeply entrenched in France than in England. The kingdom of France in the early modern period did not form a single national market; rather, it was a federation of regional markets. France was large, and transportation grew more expensive with distance. Inadequate waterways and miserable roads (except for some military highways built during Louis XIV's reign) acted as a restraint on trade. In 1664 Louis' minister Colbert had created an area of free trade in the monarchy's central provinces, but beyond this zone, internal tolls and tariffs at provincial borders burdened commerce. Guilds and other forms of monopoly held back commercial innovation, but they protected their interests by paying fees to the monarchy in return for their privileges. Differences in provincial legal systems and in weights and measures further complicated and slowed exchange. As the writer Voltaire sarcastically remarked, the traveler crossing France by coach changed laws as frequently as horses.

Despite these obstacles, the French economy was far from stagnant during the eighteenth cen-

► Incremental improvements in road and water transportation facilitated economic growth in the eighteenth century. In France the government enlisted peasants periodically to work on the upkeep of major highways under a system of forced labor known as the royal *corvée*.

tury, as we have seen. Indeed the government improved communications arteries by building canals that linked rivers in northern and in central France, and in 1777 work began on the Burgundy Canal, which would eventually allow barges to move from the English Channel to the Mediterranean. The improvement of France's main highways, with labor provided by peasants, was even more impressive. Around midcentury the government founded the School of Bridges and Roads, which soon became a model engineering institute.

The collapse of a government-sanctioned investment scheme by John Law in 1720, however, had a regressive effect on French banking and credit. French investors developed a deep suspicion of banks, paper money, and joint-stock companies. Businesspeople tended to rely instead on resources that they or their close relatives could muster and preferred to deal in hard cash rather than commercial paper. On the other hand, stable coinage aided the financing of enterprises. In 1726 the government fixed the value of the principal gold coin and kept it stable thereafter—a notable feat in light of the monarchy's desperate financial needs. On balance, although limited capital and conservative management held back French business enterprises, they dampened but did not suppress the expansion of the economy. France remained a leader in producing wool and linen cloth as well as iron, but it seemed more inclined to produce luxury items or very cheap, low-quality goods. On the other hand, England (with its higher standard of living and strong domestic demand) was more adept at producing standardized products of reasonably good quality.

COTTON: THE BEGINNING OF INDUSTRIALIZATION

The process of early industrialization in England was extremely complex and remains difficult to explain. What seems certain is that a strong demand for cheap goods was growing at home and abroad in the eighteenth century, and important segments of the English community perceived this opportunity and responded to it.

The market for cotton goods was the most propulsive force for change in industrial production. Thanks to slave labor in plantation colonies, the supply of raw cotton was rising dramatically. On the demand side, lightweight cotton goods were durable, washable, versatile, and cheaper than woolen or linen cloth. Cotton therefore had a bright future as an item of mass consumption. But traditional textile manufacturing centers in England (the regions of protoindustrialization such as East Anglia and the Yorkshire districts) could not satisfy the growing demand. The organization and technology of the putting-out system had reached its limits. For one thing, the merchant was limited to the labor supply in his own district; the farther he went to find cottage workers, the longer it took and the more cumbersome it became to pass the materials back and forth. Second, he could not adequately control his workers. Clothiers were bedeviled with embezzlement of raw materials, poor workmanship, and lateness in finishing assigned work. English clothiers were therefore on the lookout for technological or organizational innovations to help them meet a growing demand for textiles.

Machines and Factories Weavers could turn out large amounts of cloth thanks to the invention of the fly shuttle in the 1730s, which permitted the construction of larger and faster handlooms. But traditional methods of spinning the yarn caused a bottleneck in the production process. Responding to this problem, inventors built new kinds of spinning machines that could be grouped in large factories or mills. Richard Arkwright's water frame drew cotton fibers through rollers and twisted them into thread. Not simply an inventor but an entrepreneur (one who combined the various factors of production into a profitable enterprise), Arkwright initially housed his machines in a large factory sited near a river so that his machines could be propelled by waterpower.

At around the same time, James Watt had been perfecting the technology of steam engines—machinery originally used to power suction pumps that would evacuate water from the pits of coal mines. The earliest steam engine had produced a simple up-and-down motion. Watt not only redesigned it to make it far more efficient and powerful but also developed a system of gears to harness the engine's energy into rotary motion that could drive other types of machines. In 1785 Arkwright became one of Watt's first customers when he switched from water power to steam engines as the means of driving the spinning machines in his new cotton factory. With Arkwright (who became a millionaire) and Watt, the modern factory system was launched (*see box*, p. 586).

Spinning factories, however, disrupted the equilibrium between spinning and weaving in the other direction: Yarn was now abundant, but handloom weavers could not keep up with the pace. This created a brief golden age for the weavers, but merchants were eager to break the new bottleneck. In 1784 Edmund Cartwright de-

▸ *Right:* Richard Arkwright not only invented this power-driven machine to spin cotton yarn but proved to be a highly successful entrepreneur with the factory he constructed at Cromford in the Lancashire region.

▸ *Below:* The engineering firm of Bolton & Watt became famous for its steam engines, whose complex mechanisms of cams, gears, and levers could harness the power of steam to a variety of uses in industry and transportation.

Richard Arkwright's Achievement

This celebration of British industrialization, the factory system, and entrepreneurship begins by extolling Richard Arkwright's accomplishments in the 1780s.

"When the first water-frames for spinning cotton were erected at Cromford, about sixty years ago, mankind were little aware of the mighty revolution which the new system of labour was destined by Providence to achieve, not only in the structure of British society, but in the fortunes of the world at large. Arkwright alone had the sagacity to discern, and the boldness to predict in glowing language, how vastly productive human industry would become, when no longer proportioned in its results to muscular effort, which is by its nature fitful and capricious, but when made to consist in the task of guiding the work of mechanical fingers and arms, regularly impelled with great velocity by some indefatigable physical power [such as a steam engine].

"The main difficulty did not lie so much in the invention of a proper self-acting mechanism for drawing out and twisting cotton into a continuous thread, as in the distribution of different members of the apparatus into one co-operative body . . . and above all, in training human beings to renounce their desultory habits of work, and to identify themselves with the unvarying regularity of the complex automaton. To devise and administer a successful code of factory discipline, suited to the necessities of factory diligence, was the Herculean enterprise, the noble achievement of Arkwright. . . . It required, in fact, a man of Napoleonic nerve and ambition to subdue the refractory tempers of work-people accustomed to irregular paroxysms of diligence, and to urge on his multifarious and intricate constructions in the face of prejudice, passion, and envy."

From Andrew Ure, *The Philosophy of Manufactures* (1835).

signed a power-driven loom. Small technical flaws, and the violent opposition of handloom weavers, retarded the widescale adoption of power looms until the early nineteenth century, but then both spinning and weaving were totally transformed. Power-driven machinery boosted the output of yarn and cloth astronomically, while merchants were able to assemble their workers in factories and scrutinize their every move to maximize production. In a factory, one small boy could watch over two mechanized looms whose output was 15 times greater than that of a skilled handloom weaver.

In 1760 Britain imported only 2.5 million pounds of raw cotton; by 1830 it was importing 366 million pounds. Cotton textiles had become the single most important industrial product in terms of output, capital investment, and number of workers. Its production was almost exclusively organized in factories using power-driven machinery at all stages. In the process, the price of cotton yarn fell to about one-twentieth of what it had been in the 1760s. Lancashire, with its abundant waterways and coal deposits to fuel steam engines, became the center of a booming cotton cloth industry, and Manchester, its leading city, became the cotton capital of the world.

III. Innovation and Tradition in Agriculture

In England in 1700, an estimated 80 percent of the population lived directly from agriculture; a century later that portion had fallen to approximately 40 percent. This massive shift of labor and resources from agriculture would have been inconceivable had the countryside not been able to supply a greater abundance of food. English farmers introduced significant improvements in their methods of cultivation, which enabled the countryside to supply the industrial towns with food as well as labor, capital, and markets. On the continent, however, peasant cultivators generally clung tenaciously to traditional ways in agriculture as their only form of security.

CONVERTIBLE HUSBANDRY

A central problem in any agricultural system is the way repeated harvests on the same land eventually rob the soil of its fertility. Since the Early Middle Ages, the usual method of restoring a field's fertility involved letting the land lie fallow for a season (that is, resting it by planting nothing) every second or third year. This allowed bacteria in the soil to take needed nitrogen from the air. A quicker and better method, heavy manuring, could not be used widely because most farmers were unable to support sufficient livestock to produce the manure. Feeding farm animals, particularly with fodder during the winter, was beyond the means of most peasants.

But fallowing was an extremely inefficient and wasteful method of restoring the soil's fertility. One key to improving agricultural productivity therefore lay in eliminating the fallow periods, which in turn required that more animals be raised to provide fertilizer. In a given year, instead of taking it out of cultivation, a field could be planted not with grain but with turnips or with nitrogen-fixing grasses that could supply fodder for livestock. The grazing livestock would in turn deposit abundant quantities of manure on those fields. Thus by the end of that season the soil's fertility would be greater, and next year's grain crop was likely to produce a higher yield than it would have if the field had simply been left fallow the year before.

In the 1730s Charles Townshend (known as "Turnip Townshend") showed the value of planting turnips and other fodder crops in such a rotation system instead of letting the land lie fallow. One of the first British landlords to adopt this approach on a broad scale was Jethro Tull, an agriculturist and inventor. Tull's zeal in conducting his experiments and advocating new farming methods proved infectious. By the late eighteenth century, Norfolk, in the east of England, had achieved particular prominence for such techniques, known as *convertible husbandry.*

With convertible husbandry, innovative or "improving" landlords never let their land lie fallow but always put it to some productive use. They also experimented with techniques designed to enhance the texture of the soil. Where soil was normally too thin to retain water effectively, they added clays or marl to help bind the soil. In those regions where the soil had the opposite problem of clumping too rigidly after rainfalls, farmers lightened the soil by adding chalk and lime to inhibit the clotting.

Eighteenth-century agrarian innovators also experimented with the selective breeding of animals. Some improved the quality of pigs, while others developed new breeds of sheep and dramatically increased the weight of marketed cattle. Soil management and livestock breeding did not depend on any high-tech knowledge or machinery but simply on a willingness to experiment in the management of one's land, and to invest capital to achieve higher yields.

THE ENCLOSURE MOVEMENT IN BRITAIN

To make use of such new methods, farmers had to be free to manage the land as they saw fit. This was all but impossible under the open-field system, which had dominated the countryside in Europe since the Middle Ages. Under the open-field system, even the largest landlords usually held their property in numerous elongated strips that were mixed in with and open to the land of their neighbors. Owners of contiguous strips had to follow the same routines of cultivation. One farmer could not raise grasses to graze cattle when another was raising wheat or leaving the land fallow. The village as a whole determined what routines should be followed and thus effectively managed each holding. The village also decided such matters as how many cattle each member could graze on common meadows and how much wood each could take from the forest. The open-field system froze the technology of cultivation at the levels of the Middle Ages.

Landowners who wished to form compact farms and apply new methods could do so only by enclosing their own properties. Both common law and cost considerations, however, worked against fencing the numerous narrow strips, un-

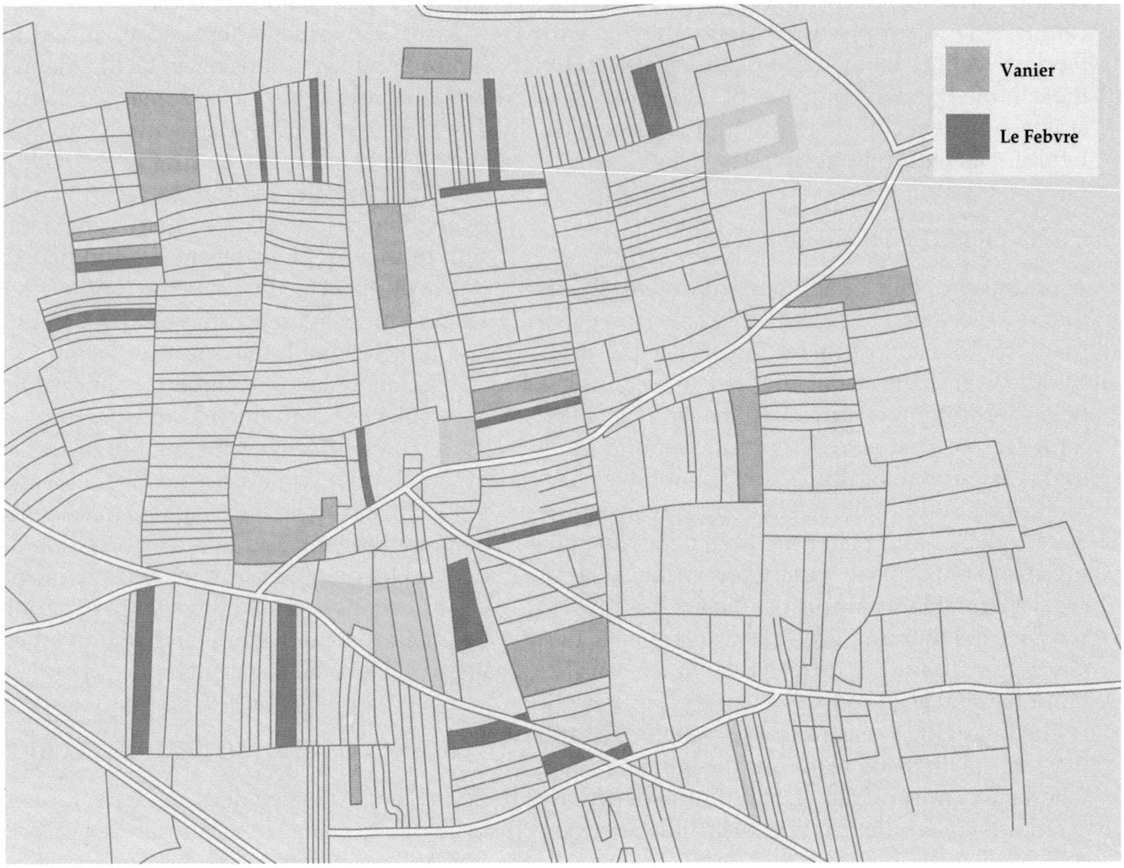

Map 18.1 AN OPEN FIELD VILLAGE IN FRANCE
The land in this Northern French village, originally blocked out in large fields, was subsequently subdivided into small strips owned by individual landowners or peasants. The scattered holdings of two large owners (Vanier and LeFebvre) are indicated by separate colors.

less the property of the entire village could be rearranged, which required the agreement of all the community. Such voluntary "enclosures" were nearly impossible to organize. In England, however, there was an alternative: An act of Parliament, usually passed in response to a petition by large landowners, could order the enclosure of all agrarian property in a village even against the opposition of some of its inhabitants. Then large landowners could fence in their land and manage it at their discretion.

Enclosing properties in a village was difficult and expensive. The lands of the village had to be surveyed and redistributed, in compact blocks, among the members in proportion to their former holdings. But over the course of the eighteenth century, the high rents and returns that could be earned with the new farming methods made enclosures very desirable investments. Numerous acts authorizing enclosure in a village had been passed by Parliament in earlier periods, but a new wave of such acts began to mount around the middle of the eighteenth century. Parliament passed 156 individual acts of enclosure in the decade of the 1750s; from 1800 to 1810 it passed 906 acts. Cumulatively, the enclosure movement all but eradicated the traditional open-field village from the British countryside.

The Impact of Enclosure While enclosure was clearly rational from an economic standpoint, it brought much human misery in its wake. The redistribution of the land deprived the poor of their traditional rights to the village's common land (which was usually divided among the villagers as well) and often left them with tiny, unprofitable plots. Frequently, they were forced to sell their holdings to their richer neighbors and seek employment as laborers or urban workers. However, no massive rural depopulation occurred in the wake of enclosures. For one thing, the actual work of fencing the fields required a good deal of labor, and some of the new husbandry techniques were also labor-intensive. In fact, the new industrial labor force drew as much on small-town artisans and casual laborers as on the dislodged rural poor.

The enclosure movement transformed the English countryside physically and socially, giving it the appearance it retains today of large verdant fields, neatly defined by hedges and fences. Enclosures in Britain led to the domination of rural society by great landlords and their prosperous tenant farmers, who usually held their farms under long leases. Conversely, they resulted in the near disappearance in England of the small peasant-type cultivators still typical of Western Europe. If enclosures did not abruptly push people to the towns, neither did they encourage growth in rural settlements. They were therefore a major factor in the steady shift of population from countryside to city and in the emergence of the first urban, industrial economy.

▸ Livestock and people could range freely over the land in open-field villages after the crops were harvested. The regrouping of scattered parcels and the enclosure of those consolidated properties would put an end to an entire rural way of life.

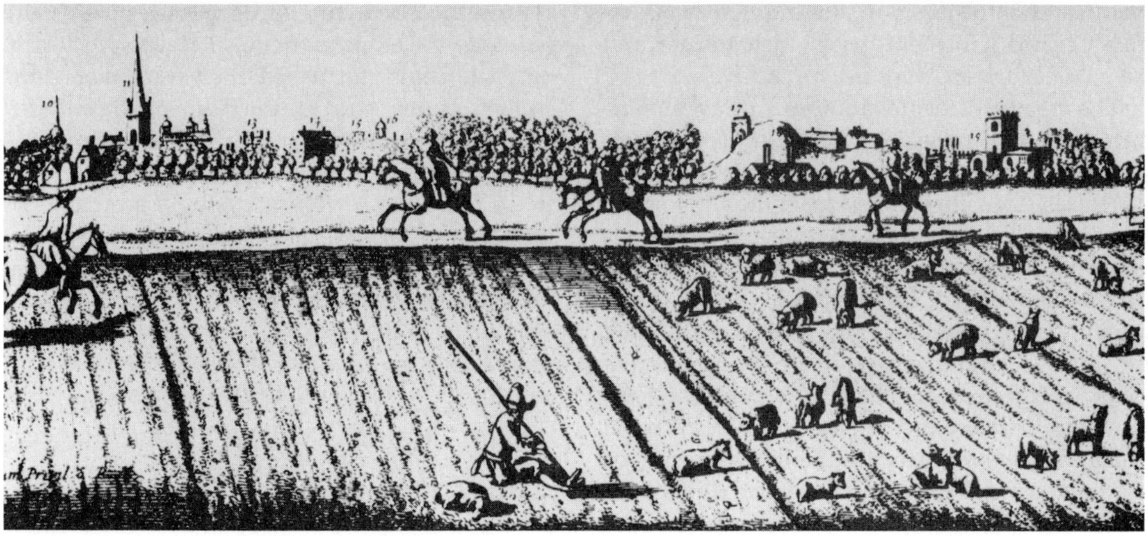

SERFS AND PEASANTS ON THE CONTINENT

On the continent, peasants continued to work their small plots of land—whether owned or rented—in the village of their ancestors. In Eastern Europe, however, the peasants' status was defined by a system of serfdom similar to that which prevailed in Western Europe during the Middle Ages.

Lords and Serfs in Eastern Europe In most of Central and Eastern Europe, nobles retained a near monopoly on the ownership of land and peasants remained serfs, their personal freedom severely limited by the lord's supervision. Serfs could not marry, move away, or enter a trade without their lord's permission. This personal servitude ensured that peasants would be available to provide the labor that the lord required. In return the peasants received access to plots of land (which they did not actually own) and perhaps some rudimentary capital, such as seed for their crops. Much of their time, however, was spent in providing unpaid labor on their lord's domain, the amount of labor service determined by custom rather than law. Labor service often

The Condition of the Serfs in Russia

For publishing this unprecedented critique of the miseries and injustices of serfdom, the author was imprisoned by Catherine II.

"A certain man left the capital, acquired a small village of one or two hundred souls [i.e., serfs], and determined to make his living by agriculture.... To this end he thought it the surest method to make his peasants resemble tools that have neither will nor impulse; and to a certain extent he actually made them like the soldiers of the present time who are commanded in a mass, who move to battle in a mass, and who count for nothing when acting singly. To attain this end he took away from his peasants the small allotment of plough land and the hay meadows which noblemen usually give them for their bare maintenance, as a recompense for all the forced labor which they demand from them. In a word, this nobleman forced all his peasants and their wives and children to work every day of the year for him. Lest they should starve, he doled out to them a definite quantity of bread.... If there was any real meat, it was only in Easter Week.

"These serfs also received clothing befitting their condition.... Naturally these serfs had no cows, horses, ewes, or rams. Their master did not withhold from these serfs the permission, but rather the means to have them. Whoever was a little better off and ate sparingly, kept a few chickens, which the master sometimes took for himself, paying for them as he pleased.

"In a short time he added to his two hundred souls another two hundred as victims of his greed, and proceeding with them just as with the first, he increased his holdings year after year, thus multiplying the number of those groaning in his fields. Now he counts them by the thousands and is praised as a famous agriculturalist.

"Barbarian! What good does it do the country that every year a few thousand more bushels of grain are grown, if those who produce it are valued on a par with the ox whose job it is to break the heavy furrow? Or do we think our citizens happy because our granaries are full and their stomachs empty?"

From Alexander Radischev, *A Journey from St. Petersburg to Moscow* (1790).

took up three days a week, and even more during harvest time. In Russia it was said that the peasants worked half the year for their master and only half for themselves (*see box*, above).

The degree of exploitation in European serfdom naturally varied. In Russia, Poland, Hungary, and certain small German states, the status of the serf scarcely differed from that of a slave. Russian and Polish serfs were in effect chattels who could be sold or traded at their lords' discretion, independent of the land they lived on or their family ties. In Russia the state itself owned many peasants and could assign them to work in the mines and factories of the Ural Mountains. Russian and Polish lords could inflict severe corporal punishment—up to 40 lashes—on their serfs, or six months in prison. Peasants had no right of appeal to the state against such punishments.

Serfdom was not as severe in Prussia or the Habsburg Monarchy, and the state did assure peasants of certain basic legal rights. In theory, peasants could not be expelled from their plots so long as they paid all their dues and rendered all the services they owed, although in practice the lords could usually remove them if they wished to. Since it was increasingly profitable for the lords to farm large domains directly, many felt an incentive to oust peasants from their tenures or to increase peasant labor services beyond customary limits.[1]

[1]In certain regions of Spain and southern Italy this situation had existed for centuries; noble lords monopolized the ownership of land in vast estates, or *latifundia*, on which their nominally free peasants provided the labor.

Lords and Peasants in the West In Western Europe, by contrast, serfdom had waned. Most peasants were personally free and were free to buy land if they could afford it. Peasants were not necessarily secure or prosperous, however. There was not enough land to satisfy the needs of all peasant families, and lack of real independence was the rule. Moreover most French, German, Spanish, and Italian peasants still lived under the authority of a local noble in a system called *seigneurialism.* The peasants owed these lords various dues and obligations on their land, even if the peasants otherwise owned it. Seigneurial fees and charges (for example, a proportion of the harvest, somewhere between 5 and 15 percent) could be a considerable source of income for the lord and an oppressive burden to the already hard-pressed peasant. In addition, the lords administered petty justice in both civil and criminal matters; enjoyed the exclusive privilege of hunting rights across the lands of the village, no matter who owned them; and profited from monopolies on food-processing operations such as flour mills, bread ovens, and wine presses.

Concerned as they were with securing their basic livelihood, few peasants worried about trying to increase productivity with new farming methods. Satisfied with time-tested methods of cultivation, they could not risk the hazards of novel techniques. Along with growing grain for their own consumption, peasant households had to meet several obligations as well: royal taxes, rents, seigneurial dues, the tithe to the local

▸ In Poland and Russia rural lords had direct control over their serfs without intervention by the state. Their powers included the right to inflict corporal punishment.

church, and interest payments on their debts. In short, most peasant households in Western Europe were extremely insecure and relied on custom and tradition as their surest guides.

Peasant Survival Strategies Every peasant household in Western Europe hoped to control enough land to ensure its subsistence and meet its obligations. Ideally, it would own this land. But most peasants did not own as much land as they needed and were obliged to rent additional plots or enter into sharecropping arrangements. Peasants therefore hated to see the consolidation of small plots into large farms, for this meant that the small plots that they might one day afford to buy or lease were becoming scarcer. The lords and the most prosperous peasants, on the other hand, were interested in extending their holdings, just like the "improving landlords" across the English Channel.

When the land that small peasants owned and rented did not meet their needs, they employed other survival strategies. Peasants could hire out as laborers on larger farms or migrate for a few months to other regions to help with grain or wine harvests. They might practice a simple rural handicraft or weave cloth for merchants on the putting-out system. Some engaged in illegal activities such as poaching game on restricted land or smuggling salt in avoidance of royal taxes. When all else failed, a destitute peasant family might be forced to take to the road as beggars.

In their precarious situation, peasants depended on strong family bonds. A peasant holding was a partnership between husband and wife, who usually waited until they had accumulated enough resources, including the bride's dowry, to establish their own household. Men looked for physical vigor and domestic skills in their prospective brides. ("When a girl knows how to knead and bake bread, she is fit to wed," went a French proverb.) In peasant households the wife's domain was inside the cottage, where she cooked, repaired clothing, and perhaps spent her evenings spinning yarn. Wives were also responsible for the small vegetable gardens or the precious hens and chickens that peasants tried to maintain to raise cash to help meet their obligations. The husband's work was outside: gathering fuel, caring for draft animals (if the family owned any), plowing the land, planting the fields, and nurturing the crops. But at harvest time everyone worked in the fields.

Peasants also drew strength from community solidarity. Many villages possessed common lands open to all residents. Poorer peasants could forage there for fuel and building materials, and could inexpensively graze whatever livestock they owned. Since villagers generally planted the same crops at the same times, after the harvest livestock was allowed to roam over the arable fields and graze on the stubble of the open fields, a practice known as vacant pasture. All in all, insecurity and the scarcity of land in continental villages made it risky and improbable that peasants would adopt innovative methods or agree to the division of common land.

The Limits of Agrarian Change on the Continent Change therefore came more slowly to the continental countryside than it did to England. The regions that experienced the most active development were the Netherlands, the Paris basin and the northeast of France, the Rhineland, and the Po valley of Italy—all areas of dense settlement where high food prices encouraged landlords with large farms to invest in agricultural improvements and to adopt innovative English methods.

Like their English counterparts, innovating continental farmers waged a battle for managerial freedom, though the changes they sought were not as sweeping as the English enclosure movement. Most French villages worked the land under an open-field system in which peasants followed the same rhythms and routines of cultivation as their neighbors, with the village also determining the rights of its members on common lands. From the middle of the century on, the governing institutions of several provinces banned obligatory vacant pasture and allowed individual owners to enclose their land; some authorized the division of communal lands as well. But the French monarchy did not adopt enclosure as national policy, and after the 1760s provincial authorities proved reluctant to approve or enforce enclosure ordinances against the vigorous opposition of peasants. Traces of the medieval village thus lasted longer in France and Western Europe than in England.

In contrast to England as well as Russia, the small-holding peasant remained the most typical social type in France. In the peasant "family economy," husband and wife each made vital contributions to the household's productivity.

In France in 1789, on the eve of the Revolution, probably 35 percent of the land was owned by the peasants who worked it. In this regard, the French peasants were more favored than those of most other European countries. But this society of small peasant farms was vulnerable to population pressures and was threatened by sharp movements in prices—two major characteristics of eighteenth-century economic history, as we have seen. The pattern of land distribution in France and the character of rural society, superficially favorable to the peasant, were thus also a source of acute tension in the countryside.

In the regions close to the Mediterranean Sea, such as southern Italy, difficult geographical and climatic conditions—the often rugged terrain, thin soil, and dearth of summer rain—did not readily allow the introduction of new techniques either, although many peasants improved their income by planting market crops like grapes for wine or olives for oil instead of grains for their own consumption. But most peasants continued to work their lands much as they had in the Late Middle Ages and for the same poor reward. Fertile areas near the Baltic Sea, such as east Prussia, benefited from the growing demand for grains in Western countries, but on the whole, Eastern Europe did not experience structural agrarian change until the next century.

IV. Eighteenth-Century Empires

After 1715 a new era began in the saga of European colonial development. The three pioneers in overseas expansion had by now grown passive, content to defend domains already conquered. Portugal, whose dominion over Brazil was recognized at the Peace of Utrecht in 1715, retired from active contention. Likewise, the Dutch could scarcely compete for new footholds overseas and now protected their interests through cautious neutrality. Although Spain continued its efforts to exclude outsiders from trade with its vast empire in the New World, it did not pose much of a threat to others. The stage of active competition was left to the two other Atlantic powers, France and Britain.

MERCANTILE AND NAVAL COMPETITION

The Decline of the Dutch The case of Dutch decline is an instructive counterexample to the rise of French and British fortunes. In the seventeenth century the United Provinces, or Dutch Netherlands, had been Europe's greatest maritime power. But this federated state emerged from the wars of Louis XIV in a much weakened position. The country had survived intact, but it now suffered from demographic and political stagnation. The population of 2.5 million failed to rise during the eighteenth century, thus setting the Dutch apart from their French and British rivals. As a federation of loosely joined provinces, whose seven provincial oligarchies rarely acted in concert, the Netherlands could barely ensure the common defense of the realm.

The Dutch economy suffered when French and English merchants sought to eliminate them as the middlemen of maritime commerce, and when their industry failed to compete effectively. Heavy indirect taxes on manufactured goods and the high wages demanded by Dutch artisans forced up the price of Dutch products. What kept the nation from slipping completely out of Europe's economic life was its financial institutions. Dutch merchants shifted their activity away from actual trading ventures into the safer, lucrative areas of credit and finance. Their country was the first to perfect the uses of paper currency, a stock market, and a central bank. Amsterdam's merchant-bankers loaned large amounts of money to private borrowers and foreign governments, as the Dutch became financial instead of trading brokers.

The British and French Commercial Empires Great Britain, a nation that had barely been able to hold its own against the Dutch in the seventeenth century, now began its rise to domination of the seas. Its one serious competitor was France, the only state in Europe to maintain both a large army and a large navy. Their rivalry played itself out in four regions. The West Indies, where both France and Britain had colonized several sugar-producing islands, constituted the fulcrum of both empires. The West Indian plantation economy, in turn, depended on slave-producing West Africa. The third area of colonial expansion was the North American continent, where Britain's 13 colonies became centers of settlement, whereas New France remained primarily a trading area. Finally, both nations sponsored powerful companies for trade with India and other Asian lands. These companies were supposed to compete for markets without establishing colonies.

The two colonial systems had obvious differences and important similarities. French absolutism fostered a centralized structure of control for its colonies, with intendants and military governors ruling across the seas as they did in the provinces at home. Britain's North American colonies, by contrast, remained independent from each other and to a degree escaped direct control from the home government, although crown and Parliament both claimed jurisdiction over them. British colonies each had a royal governor but also a local legislature of sorts, and most developed traditions of self-government. Nonetheless, the French and British faced similar problems and achieved generally similar results. Both applied mercantilist principles to the regulation of colonial trade, and both strengthened their navies to protect it.

Mercantilism Mercantilist doctrine supported the regulation of trade by the state in order to increase the state's power against its neighbors (see Chapter 15). Mercantilism was not limited to the Atlantic colonial powers. Prussia was guided by mercantilism as much as were Britain and France, for all regarded the economic activities of their subjects as subordinate to the interests of the state.

Mercantilist theory advocated a favorable balance of trade as signified by a net inflow of gold and silver, and it assumed that a state's share of bullion could increase only at its neighbor's expense. Colonies could promote a favorable balance of trade by producing valuable raw materials or staple crops for the parent country, and by providing protected markets for the parent country's manufactured goods. Foreign states were to be excluded from these benefits as much as possible. By tariffs, elaborate regulations, bounties, or prohibitions, each government sought to channel trade between its colonies and itself. Spain, for example, restricted trade with its New World colonies exclusively to Spanish merchant vessels, although smugglers and pirates made a mockery of this policy.

Europe's governments sought to exploit overseas colonies for the benefit of the parent country and not simply for the profit of those who invested or settled abroad. But most of the parties

Commerce increased dramatically in the Atlantic ports of England and France as ships embarked for Africa, the Caribbean, North America, and Spanish America, as well as other parts of Europe. Businesses that supplied those ships or that processed colonial products brought back to Europe grew apace. Shown here, the port of Bristol in England.

to this commerce prospered. The large West Indian planters made fortunes, as did the most successful merchants, manufacturers, and shipowners at home who were involved in colonial trade. Illicit trade also brought rewards to colonial merchants; John Hancock took the risk of smuggling food supplies from Boston to French West Indian planters in exchange for handsome profits.

Empire generally meant "trade," but this seaborne commerce depended on naval power: merchant ships had to be protected, trading rivals excluded, and regulations enforced. This reciprocal relationship between the expansion of trade and the deployment of naval forces added to the competitive nature of colonial expansion. Naval vessels needed stopping places for reprovisioning and refitting. This meant that ports had to be secured in strategic locations—such as Africa, India, and the Caribbean—and denied to rivals whenever possible.

THE GROWTH OF ENGLAND'S FOREIGN TRADE IN THE EIGHTEENTH CENTURY Three-year averages of combined imports and exports.

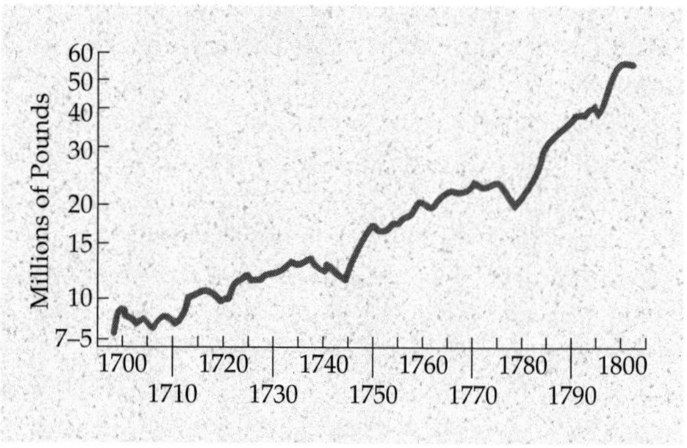

(Adapted from Dean, Phyllis, and Cole, W. A., *British Economic Growth, 1688–1959*, 1964, p. 49.)

THE PROFITS OF EMPIRE

The call of colonial markets invigorated European economic life. Colonial commerce provided new products, like sugar, and stimulated new consumer demand, which in turn created an impetus for manufacturing at home. It is estimated that the value of French commerce quadrupled during the eighteenth century. By the 1770s commerce with their colonies accounted for almost one-third of the total volume of both British and French foreign trade. The West Indies trade (mainly in sugar) bulked the largest, and its expansion was truly spectacular. The value of French imports from the West Indies increased more than tenfold between 1716 and 1788, from 16 million to 185 million livres.

The West Indies seemed to be ideal colonies. By virtue of their tropical climate and isolation from European society, which made slavery possible, the islands produced valuable crops difficult to raise elsewhere: tobacco, cotton, indigo, and especially sugar—a luxury that popular European taste soon turned into a necessity. Moreover, the islands could produce little else and therefore depended on exports from Europe. They could not raise an adequate supply of food animals or grain to feed the vast slave population, they could not cut enough lumber for building, and they certainly could not manufacture the luxury goods demanded by the planter class.

Numerous variations of "triangular trade" (between the home country and two colonial areas) revolved around the West Indies. One pattern began with a ship departing from a British port with a cargo of manufactured products—paper, knives, pots, blankets, and the like—destined for the shopkeepers of North America. Landing at Marblehead, Massachusetts, or Philadelphia, the ship might exchange its goods for New England fish oil, fish, beef, and timber. These would then be transported to Jamaica or Barbados to be traded for sugar that would be turned over to British refineries many months later. Another variation might see a ship set out from Newport, Rhode Island (the chief slaving port in North America), with a cargo of New England rum. Landing in West Africa, it would acquire slaves in exchange for the rum and then sail to the Indies to sell the slaves—for bills of exchange or for molasses, from which more rum could be distilled. French and British manufacturers in the port cities made fortunes by refining or finishing colonial products such as sugar, indigo, tobacco, and furs and reexporting them to other European markets. For colonial commerce was superimposed on a complex pattern of European trade in which the Atlantic states carried off the lion's share of the profits.

SLAVERY, THE FOUNDATION OF EMPIRE

Much of this dynamic global trade rested on slavery. Only endless, backbreaking labor could transform a favorable climate and the investment of speculators into harvested plantation crops (*see box*, below). As a publication of the chamber of commerce of Nantes, France's chief slaving port, publicly argued, without slavery there would be no French colonial commerce at all. At the height of the Atlantic slave traffic, about 88,000 blacks were removed from Africa annually—half in British ships, a quarter in French, and the rest in Dutch, Portuguese, Danish, and American ships (see table on slavery). Over 600,000 slaves were imported into the island of Jamaica in the eighteenth century. The population of Saint-Domingue around 1790 comprised about half a million slaves compared with 35,000 whites of all nationalities and 28,000 mulattoes and free blacks.

MAGNITUDE OF THE SLAVE TRADE

The following figures represent the best current estimate of the number of persons removed from Africa and transported as slaves to the New World during the entire period of the Atlantic slave trade.

British Caribbean	1,665,000
British North America (to 1786)	275,000
United States (after 1786)	124,000
French Caribbean	1,600,000
Dutch Caribbean	500,000
Brazil	3,646,000
Spanish America	1,552,000

Source: Philip D. Curtin, *The Atlantic Slave Trade: A Census*, 1969.

A British Defense of Slavery and the Plantation Economy

"The most approved judges of the commercial interests of these Kingdoms have ever been of the opinion that our West-Indies and African Trades are the most nationally beneficial of any we carry on. It is also allowed on all hands that the Trade to Africa is the branch which renders our American Colonies and Plantations so advantageous to Great Britain; that traffic only affording our plantations a constant supply of Negroe-servants [slaves] for the culture of their lands in the produce of *sugars, tobacco, rice, rum, cotton, pimento,* and all others our plantations produce. So that the extensive employment of our shipping in, to, and from America, the great brood of seamen consequent thereupon, and the daily bread of the most considerable part of our British Manufacturers, are owing primarily to the labor of Negroes; who, as they were the first happy instrument of raising our Plantations, so their labor only can support and preserve them, and render them still more and more profitable to their Mother-Kingdom.

"The Negroe-Trade therefore, and the natural consequences resulting from it, may be justly esteemed an inexhaustible fund of Wealth and Naval Power to this Nation. And by the overplus of Negroes above what have served our own Plantations, we have drawn likewise no inconsiderable quantities of treasure from the Spaniards. . . . What renders the Negroe-Trade still more estimable and important is that near nine-tenths of those Negroes are paid for in Africa with British produce and manufactures only. We send no specie of bullion to pay for the products of Africa. . . . And it may be worth consideration, that while our Plantations depend only on planting by Negroes, they will neither depopulate our own Country, become independent of her Dominion, or any way interfere [i.e., compete] with the interests of the British Manufacturer, Merchant, or Landed Gentleman."

From Malachy Postlethwayt, *The National and Private Advantages of the African Trade Considered* (London, 1746).

A European commercial settlement on the Guinea coast of Africa in the early 18th century. The four compounds belong to Portugal (left), France (centre), England (right) and Holland (right foreground). In the left foreground the French director (numbered 14) returns with his train of servants. (4)

▶ **An early eighteenth-century European commercial settlement on the west coast of Africa consisted of four national compounds: Portuguese, French, English, and Dutch.**

Trafficking in slaves was competitive and risky but highly profitable. The demand for slaves in the West Indies, Brazil, Venezuela, and the southern colonies of North America kept rising, pushing up prices. In both Britain and France, chartered companies holding exclusive rights from the crown originally monopolized the slave trade. They did not actually colonize or conquer African territory but instead established forts, or "factories," on the West African coast for the coordination and defense of their slaving expeditions. Gradually, the monopolies were challenged by other merchants and investors who combined to launch their own ships on slaving voyages. The West Indian planters, who needed more slaves, welcomed all additional sources. The independent traders clustered in port cities like Bristol and Liverpool in England, and by the 1730s they had broken the monopoly on the slave trade.

The Ordeal of Enslavement Europeans alone did not condemn black Africans to slavery. In this period, Europeans scarcely penetrated the interior of the continent; the forbidding topography and the resistance of the natives confined them to coastal areas. The actual enslavement took place in the interior at the hands of aggressive local groups whose chiefs became the intermediaries of this commerce. The competition among European traders for the slaves tended to drive up the prices that African middlemen could command in hardware, cloth, liquor, or guns. In response, some traders ventured into new areas where the blacks might be more eager to come to terms. Increasing demand, rising prices, and competitiveness spread the slave trade and further marred the future of West African society.

Many blacks failed to survive the process of enslavement at all. Some perished on the forced marches from the interior to the coast or on the nightmarish "middle passage" across the Atlantic, which has been compared to the transit in freight cars of Jewish prisoners to Nazi extermination camps in World War II. Since the risks of slaving ventures were high and the time lag between investment and return somewhere from one to two years, the traders sought to maximize their profits by jamming as many captives as possible onto the ships. Medium-sized ships carried as many as 500 slaves on a voyage, all packed below deck in only enough space for each person to lie at full length pressed against neighboring bodies, and with only enough headroom to crawl, not to stand. Food and provisions were held to a minimum. The mortality rate that resulted from these conditions was a staggering 10 percent or more on average, and in extreme cases exceeded 50 percent.

Agitation against slavery by reformers in Britain and France focused initially on the practices of the slave trade rather than on slavery itself. After the 1780s participation in the Atlantic slave trade tapered off, and the supply of slaves was replenished mainly from children born to slaves already in the New World. A dismal chapter in Europe's relations with the outside world dwindled to an end, although the final suppression of slaving voyages did not come for several more decades.

MOUNTING COLONIAL CONFLICTS

In the New World, the population of Britain's North American colonies reached about 1.5 million by midcentury. Some colonists pushed the frontier westward, while others clustered around the original settlements, a few of which—like Boston, New York, and Philadelphia—could now be called cities. The westward extension of the frontier and the growth of towns gave a vitality to the British colonial world that New France appeared to lack. Since there was little enthusiasm among the French for emigration to the Louisiana Territory or Canada, the French remained thinly spread in their vast dominions. Yet France's colonies were well organized and profitable. French West Indian planters underpriced the sugar of their British competitors, while the French trading company in India seemed more effective than its British rival in expanding its operations.

As French fishermen and fur traders prospered in Canada, French soldiers established a series of strongholds to support them, including the bastion of Fort Louisbourg at the entrance to the Gulf of St. Lawrence and a string of forts near the Great Lakes (see Map 18.2), which served as bridgeheads for French fur traders and as a security buffer for Quebec province. In Louisiana, at the other end of the continent, New Orleans guarded the terminus of the Mississippi River. On their side, the British established their first large military base in North America at Halifax, Nova Scotia, contesting French penetration of the fishing grounds and waterways of the St. Lawrence Gulf.

The unsettled Ohio valley was a second focus of colonial rivalry in North America. Pushing south from their Great Lakes trading forts and north from their posts on the Mississippi, the French began to assume control over that wil-

This diagram of "tight packing" below deck conveys the horror of the trans-Atlantic slaving voyages, known as the "middle passage." The drawing was circulated by British antislavery reformers.

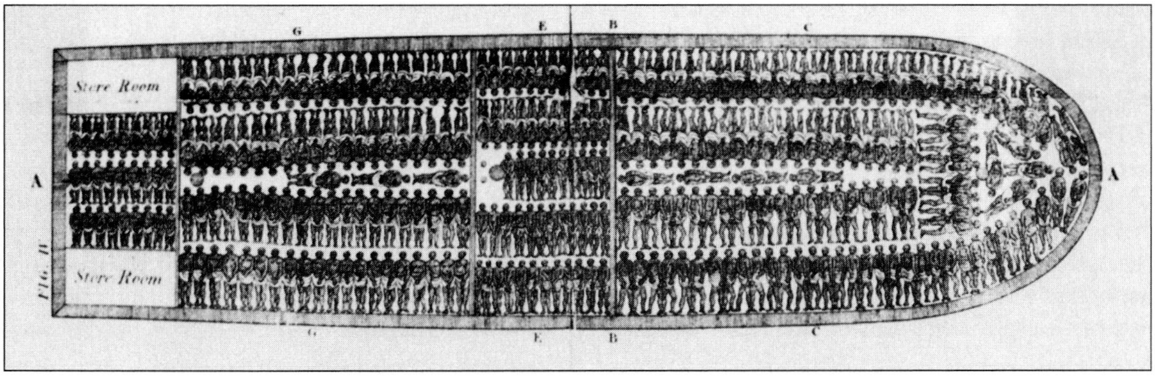

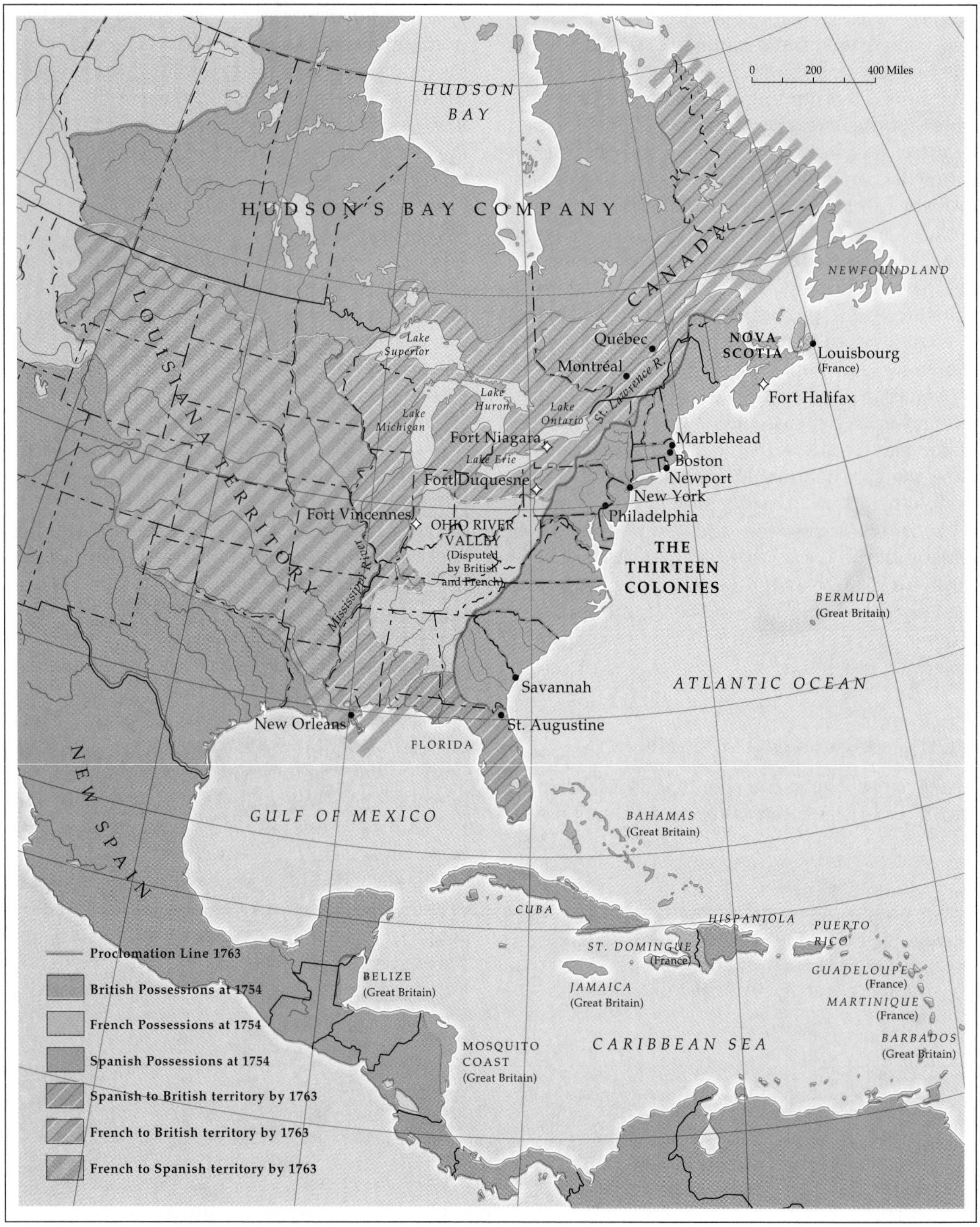

Map 18.2 **ANGLO-FRENCH RIVALRY IN NORTH AMERICA AND THE CARIBBEAN AS OF 1756**

derness. A new string of forts formed pivots for potential French domination of the whole area between the Appalachian Mountains and the Mississippi—territory claimed and coveted by British subjects in the 13 colonies. The threat grew that the French might completely cut off the westward expansion of these colonies. On their side, the French feared that British penetration of the Ohio valley would lead to encroachments on their Canadian territory.

In jockeying for position, both sides sought the allegiance of the American Indians, and in this respect the French gradually gained the upper hand. Because they were traders only, not settlers, the French did not force the Native Americans from their traditional hunting grounds as the British had done repeatedly. Hence the American Indians were willing to cooperate with the French in sealing off the Ohio valley. A large land investment company, the Ohio Company of Virginia, faced ruin with that prospect, and in 1745 it attempted to break the French and Indian hold on the Ohio valley by sending an expedition against Fort Duquesne. Led by a young militiaman named George Washington, the raid failed.

Contrary to a British tradition of letting settled colonies pay for themselves, the home government eventually shouldered the burden of colonial defense. An expedition of British army regulars was sent to do the job that the colonial militia could not accomplish. Limited skirmishes were about to give way to a full-scale war, as each side began to reinforce its garrisons and naval squadrons. In May 1756, after several years of unofficial hostilities, Britain and France formally declared war.

THE GREAT WAR FOR EMPIRE

The pressures created by the competition of states, dynasties, and colonial empires in the eighteenth century exploded in midcentury in Europe's last large-scale war before the French Revolution. Its continental phase, known as the Seven Years' War, centered on the bitter rivalry between Austria and Prussia, but enmeshed Russia, France, and Britain as well. As we saw in Chapter 17, this protracted war ended in 1763 with a peace treaty that essentially restored the status quo. The other phase of this midcentury conflagration revolved around Anglo-French competition for empire in North America, the West Indies, and India. Historians call it the Great War for Empire, and its North American sector was known as the French and Indian War. It was this great global confrontation that produced the most striking changes when the smoke cleared.

The Great War for Empire was one of Britain's high moments in history, the stuff of patriotic legends. The conflict started, however, in quite another fashion. Jumping to the initiative on several fronts, the better-coordinated French struck the first blows. Calcutta in India, the Mediterranean island of Minorca, and several key British forts on the Great Lakes all fell to the French. At the same time, Britain's expeditionary force to the continent, fighting in alliance with Prussia, suffered humiliating defeats. Yet the French had disadvantages that would show in the long run. Spread so thinly in North America, they would be hard put to follow their early success in the French and Indian War. More important, France depended on naval support to reinforce, supply, and move its troops; unfortunately for France, a fairly even naval matchup in the 1740s had turned into clear British naval superiority by the 1750s. British ships of the line outnumbered French ships almost two to one.

Pitt's Strategy When William Pitt became Britain's prime minister in 1758, the tide was about to turn in the Great War for Empire. Pitt, later the Earl of Chatham, was the grandson of a man who had made a fortune in India. Eloquent, supremely self-confident, infused with a vision of Britain's imperial destiny, Pitt had begun his career in Parliament in 1738 by denouncing the timid policies of the government and demanding that France be driven from the seas. Now he had his chance to lead Britain in the battle against its arch rival. Pitt brought single-mindedness and vigor to his task. Although he honored Britain's commitment to Prussia, he attached highest priority to defeating France in the colonial world. His strategy involved an immediate series of offensives and an imaginative use of the British navy. He assigned the largest segment of the British fleet to cover the French home fleet, and he waited.

The French hoped to invade the British Isles

as the surest method of bringing the enemy to the peace table, and the French fleet was ordered to prepare the way. In 1759 major battles were joined between French squadrons from Brest and Toulon and the British ships assigned to cover them. The British decimated the French fleet in these naval battles and thus decided the fate of colonial empires. Henceforth the British had an almost free hand at sea and could prevent France from deploying its superior military forces in the colonial world. Unable to transport men and supplies to its colonies, France could no longer reinforce its garrisons or repel amphibious landings by the British. In every theater of the war, French colonial possessions fell to the British, thanks to Britain's naval supremacy.

In the French and Indian War, for example, Britain's General Wolfe defeated France's General Montcalm in the battle of Quebec in September 1759. Had the French been able to reinforce Montreal, which they still held, they could have launched a counterattack against Wolfe's overextended lines. But Pitt's successful naval strategy had made it impossible for the French to reinforce their overseas garrisons. By September 1760 this last outpost of French power in North America capitulated to the British, who had already ousted the French from the Ohio valley and the Great Lakes area. The same pattern unfolded in India, where soldiers in the employ of the British East India Company enlisted native allies and roundly defeated the French garrison and its allies. Finally, in the West Indies the long duel between the two powers turned into a rout. One by one Britain seized the French islands.

The Peace of Paris In the peace negotiations that followed (concluded by the Treaty of Paris in 1763) Britain did not insist on retaining all its conquests. A war-weary British government was

▶ **British naval power is shown here laying siege to the French stronghold of Louisbourg in July 1758.**

▸ **This painting depicts a British District Officer in 1799 in Madras, one of the regions of the Indian subcontinent where the British began to exercise control after they ousted the French and defeated native forces that challenged them. The official's main function was to supervise the collection of taxes, which he did with the cooperation of local Indian princes and merchants.**

prepared to return certain colonies to France in exchange for an end to the fighting. Since British West Indian planters feared the added competition from the inclusion of the French islands in the British trading system, the British government returned several of them. But France did surrender Canada, which Britain chose to retain, perhaps unwisely; the British occupation of Canada removed the threat of French power, which had actually been an important factor in keeping the restive British colonists loyal to Britain. (On that front, France would soon have its revenge, when it came to the aid of the rebellious colonies in the War for American Independence.)

In the long run, India proved to be Britain's most important colonial domain. Its domination of India began with the Treaty of Paris, which excluded French troops from the subcontinent and left only British influence to have any force. Within a few decades the British moved from organizing profitable commerce in India to occupying and governing much of its territory.

French and English merchants capitalized aggressively on the commercial opportunities afforded by overseas colonies, plantation economies, and slavery, but these traders required backing by their states in the form of naval power. The growth of the British and French empires thus reflected the dynamics of the competitive state system. Those empires also propelled the growth of a global maritime economy and thus became a major factor in the economic dynamism of the eighteenth century. It is well to remember, however, that two totally disenfranchised groups supported the entire structure of state power and mercantile profit: the slaves in the colonies and the serfs, peasants, or agricultural laborers in Europe. Their toil produced the food supplies, staple commodities, and revenues that sustained the merchants, landowners, rulers, armies, and navies of the great powers. The economic future, however, lay not with slavery, serfdom, or seigneurialism but with innovations in agriculture and industrial production that would yield sustained economic growth and whose roots in England we have sketched. Along with the intellectual and cultural transformations to be discussed in the next chapter, these agricultural and industrial innovations heralded the dawn of the modern era.

Recommended Reading

Sources

*Young, Arthur. *Travels in France during the Years 1787, 1788, 1789.* 1972. A critical view of French agriculture by an English expert.

Radischev, Alexander. *A Journey from St. Petersburg to Moscow* [1790]. 1958. The first major exposé of the miseries of Russian serfdom.

*Smith, Adam. *An Inquiry into the Nature and Causes of the Wealth of Nations* [1776]. 1961.

Studies

*Ashton, T. S. *The Industrial Revolution, 1760–1830.* 1962. A brief, classic account of early industrialization in Britain.

*Berg, Maxine. *The Age of Manufactures: Industry, Innovation and Work in Britain, 1700–1820.* 1986. An important revisionist view, emphasizing the persistence of domestic and workshop manufacturing alongside the new factory system.

*Blum, Jerome. *The End of the Old Order in Rural Europe.* 1976. A valuable trove of information on rural conditions, particularly in the regions of serfdom.

Chambers, J. D., and G. E. Mingay. *The Agricultural Revolution, 1750–1880.* 1966. A reliable overview and interpretation.

Coleman, D. C. (ed.). *Revisions in Mercantilism.* 1969. An anthology of views about the nature of mercantilism in early modern Europe.

Crafts, N. F. R. *British Economic Growth during the Industrial Revolution.* 1985. A revisionist statistical study, emphasizing the gradual pace of industrialization.

Craton, Michael. *Sinews of Empire: A Short History of British Slavery.* 1974. An excellent synthesis.

*Davis, David B. *The Problem of Slavery in Western Culture.* 1966. And *The Problem of Slavery in the Age of Revolutions.* 1975. A comparative history of Western attitudes toward slavery, from ancient times to the nineteenth century.

Davis, Ralph. *The Rise of the Atlantic Economies.* 1973.

*De Vries, Jan. *The Economy of Europe in an Age of Crisis, 1600–1750.* 1976. A reliable survey of the European economy before the industrial revolution.

———. *European Urbanization, 1500–1800.* 1984. The development of major cities across Europe.

*Flandrin, Jean-Louis. *Families in Former Times: Kinship, Household and Sexuality.* 1979. From demographic history to the history of marriage and the family.

*Flinn, M. W. *The European Demographic System, 1500–1820.* 1981. A concise overview of the historical demography of early modern Europe.

Forster, Robert. *The House of Saulx-Tavanes: Versailles and Burgundy, 1700–1830.* 1971. A brilliant portrait of an aristocratic family and the peasant communities that supported its life style.

*Available in paperback.

Glass, D. V., and D. Eversley (eds.). *Population in History*. 1964. A collection of pioneering articles in historical demography.

*Gutmann, Myron. *Toward the Modern Economy: Early Industry in Europe*. 1988. Another fine synthesis illustrating the complexity of the European economy.

Hohenberg, Paul M., and Lynn Holen Lees. *The Making of Urban Europe, 1000–1950*. 1985. The impact of protoindustrialization and industrialization on cities.

Hufton, Olwen. *The Poor of Eighteenth-Century France*. 1974. A luminous study of the survival strategies of the indigent who could not sustain themselves on the land, and of the institutions which aided or confined them.

*Landes, David S. *The Unbound Prometheus: Technological Change and Industrial Development in Western Europe from 1750 to the Present*. 1969. A broad and engaging synthesis, emphasizing technological change.

Link, Edith M. *The Emancipation of the Austrian Peasantry, 1740–1789*. 1949. Traces the efforts and frustration of Habsburg agrarian reformers.

*Mantoux, Paul. *The Industrial Revolution in the Eighteenth Century*. 1962. A classic account, emphasizing the early inventions and factories.

*Mathias, Peter. *The First Industrial Nation: An Economic History of Britain, 1700–1914* (2d ed.). 1983. A reliable survey of quantitative and descriptive analysis.

North, Douglass C. *Structure and Change in Economic History*. 1981. Stresses the importance of supportive legal institutions in the coming of industrialism.

*Parry, J. H. *Trade and Dominion: The European Overseas Empires in the Eighteenth Century*. 1971. A panoramic overview.

Price, Roger. *The Economic Modernization of France, 1730–1870*. 1975. A good survey of economic trends and institutions in France.

Ringrose, David. *Transportation and Economic Stagnation in Spain, 1750–1850*. 1970. The factors that impeded economic growth in Spain—a counterexample to British economic growth.

Wilson, Charles. *England's Apprenticeship, 1603–1767*. 1965. An economic history of England before the agricultural and industrial revolutions began.

Wright, William E. *Serf, Seigneur and Sovereign: Agrarian Reform in Eighteenth-Century Bohemia*. Minneapolis, 1966. On the agrarian problem in the Czech domains of the Habsburg Empire.

*Wrigley, E. A. *Population and History*. 1969. A fascinating introduction to the field of historical demography.

Wrigley, E. A., and R. S. Schofield. *The Population History of England, 1541–1871: Studies in Social and Demographic History*. 1981. A reconstruction of population movements.

Joseph II's private orchestra performing after a royal banquet in Vienna, 1760.

CHAPTER NINETEEN

THE AGE OF ENLIGHTENMENT

ALTHOUGH sharp breaks in the intellectual and cultural history of Europe have been rare, the seventeenth, eighteenth, and nineteenth centuries represent three relatively distinct phases of Western cultural development. The seventeenth century, as we have seen, was an age of genius in European thought, a period of great scientific and philosophical innovation. It was also an elitist age in that the audience for cultural activity remained small, while artists and writers generally depended on aristocratic patronage. If we jump ahead to the nineteenth century, we find a thriving middle-class cultural life in Europe's cities and the beginnings of mass literacy. Obviously, then, the eighteenth century was transitional.

During the eighteenth century the impact of scientific knowledge and the growth of religious skepticism matured into a naturalistic world view divorced from religion. There were now important thinkers who no longer believed in Christianity and wished to reduce its influence in society. They argued that there was no reality beyond human society, no afterlife to divert humanity from worldly concerns. Intellectuals developed a strong, sometimes arrogant, sense of their own power to guide society and point it toward change.

Although they were critics of their society, most eighteenth-century intellectuals lived comfortably amid Europe's high culture. They utilized its organized institutions, benefited from a dramatic expansion of publishing, and enjoyed its new literary and musical genres. They had little interest in or understanding of popular culture, however. Their growing sense of "public opinion" referred only to the educated elites of the aristocracy and the middle classes.

I. The Enlightenment

Building on seventeenth-century science, on skepticism in matters of religion, and on a heightened appreciation of the culture of Classical antiquity, eighteenth-century intellectuals approached their role in a new spirit. They believed that human behavior and institutions could be studied rationally, like Newton's universe, and that their faults could be corrected. They saw themselves as participants in a movement—which they called the Enlightenment—that could make educated men and women more understanding, tolerant, and virtuous.

THE BROADENING REVERBERATIONS OF SCIENCE

It is hard to think of two men less revolutionary in temperament than the seventeenth century's René Descartes and Isaac Newton. Both were conservative on matters outside the confines of science, had relatively little concern for social institutions, remained practicing Christians, and wrote only for small learned audiences. Yet their legacy of insight into the world of nature produced in succeeding generations what has been described as "a permanent intellectual insurrection," which unfolded in a spirit undreamed of by either man.

The Popularization of Science While eighteenth-century scientists pondered the cosmologies of Descartes and Newton, nonscientists in England and on the continent applied the methodologies of Descartes, Newton, and the philosopher John Locke to other realms of human thought. They fused the notion of methodical doubt and naturalistic explanations of phenomena into a scientific or mathematical spirit, which at bottom simply meant confidence in reason and a skeptical attitude toward accepted dogmas. They attempted to popularize scientific method, with the aim of transforming the values of Western civilization. Writers translated the discoveries of scientists into clear and even amusing general reading. The literary talents of these enthusiasts helped make household words of Newton and Descartes among educated Europeans.

A more calculating and ambitious propagandist of the scientific spirit was François-Marie Arouet, who wrote under the pen name of Voltaire and was the Frenchman who is virtually synonymous with the Enlightenment. While his chief talents lay in literature and criticism, Voltaire also spent some time studying Newton's work. In 1738 he published a widely read popularization called *Elements of the Philosophy of Newton.* However dry the study of physics, Voltaire argued, it frees the mind from dogma, and its experimental methods provide a model for the liberation of human thought. Moreover, Voltaire related Newton's achievement to the environment of a liberal England that also produced Francis Bacon and Locke, the three of whom Voltaire adopted as his personal Trinity. In his *Philosophical Letters on the English* (1734)—a celebration of English toleration and an indirect attack on religious bigotry, censorship, and social snobbery in France—Voltaire had already noted the respect enjoyed in England by its writers and scientists. He saw this recognition of talent as a crucial component of a free society and as a condition for the achievements of a man like Newton.

Popularizations of scientific method stimulated public interest in science, as mathematicians, cartographers, and astronomers made notable advances in their fields. But further scientific progress was far from automatic. In chemistry, for example, the traditions of alchemy persisted, and phenomena such as fire long escaped objective analysis. At the end of the century, however, a major breakthrough occurred when the Englishman Joseph Priestley isolated oxygen and the Frenchman Antoine Lavoisier analyzed the components of air and water and came close to explaining the process of combustion.

The vogue for science also had a dubious side, apparent, for example, in the great popularity of mesmerism. This pseudoscience of magnetic fields purported to offer its wealthy devotees relief from a variety of ailments by the use of special "electrical" baths and treatments. Although repeatedly condemned by the Academy of Sciences in Paris, mesmerism continued to attract educated followers.

Natural History The most widely followed scientific enterprise in the eighteenth century was

▶ **French chemist Lavoisier conducts an experiment in his laboratory to study the composition of air during the process of respiration.**

natural history, the science of the earth's development—a combination of geology, zoology, and botany. This field of study was easy for the nonscientist to appreciate. Its foremost practitioner was G. L. Buffon, keeper of the French Botanical Gardens—a patronage position that allowed him to produce a multivolume *Natural History of the Earth* between 1749 and 1778. Drawing on a vast knowledge of phenomena such as fossils, Buffon went beyond previous attempts to classify the data of nature and provided both a description and a theory of the earth's development.

Although he was a nonbeliever, Buffon did not explicitly attack religious versions of such events as the Creation; he simply ignored them, an omission of obvious significance to his readers. Similarly, while he did not specifically contend that human beings have evolved from beasts, he implied it. "It is possible," he wrote, "to descend by almost insensible degrees from the most perfect creature to the most formless matter." Buffon's earth did not derive from a singular act of divine creation that would explain the origins of human beings. The readers of his *Natural History* or its numerous popularizations in several languages

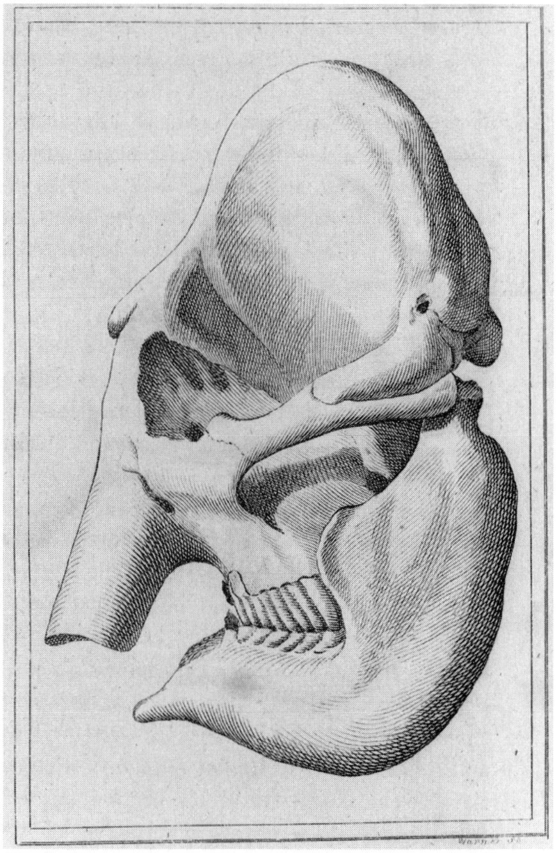

▶ **A plate from the section on fossil remains in Buffon's *Natural History* illustrating the skull of an elephant from India.**

thus encountered a universe that had developed through evolution.

BEYOND CHRISTIANITY

The erosion of biblical revelation as a source of authority is one hallmark of the Enlightenment. This shift derived some of its impetus from seventeenth-century scientists and liberal theologians who were themselves believing Christians but who opposed religious superstition or "enthusiasm," as they called it. They had hoped to accommodate religion to new philosophical standards and scientific formulations by eliminating the superstitious imagery that could make religion seem ridiculous, and by treating the world of nature as a form of revelation in which God's majesty could be seen. The devil, for example, could be considered as a category of moral evil rather than as a specific horned creature with a pitchfork. They hoped to bolster the Christian religion by deemphasizing miracles and focusing on reverence for the Creator and on the moral teachings of the Bible. Their approach did indeed help educated people adhere to Christianity during the eighteenth century. In the final analysis, however, this kind of thinking diminished the authority of religion in society.

Toleration One current of thought that encouraged a more secular outlook was the idea of toleration, as propounded by the respected French critic Pierre Bayle. Consciously applying methodical doubt to subjects that Descartes had excluded from such treatment, Bayle's *Critical and Historical Dictionary* (1697) put the claims of religion to the test of critical reason. Certain Christian traditions emerged from this scrutiny as the equivalent of myth and fairy tale, and the history of Christianity appeared as a record of fanaticism and persecution. Bayle's chief target was Christianity's attempts to impose orthodoxy at any cost (for example, the Spanish Inquisition and Louis XIV's revocation of the Edict of Nantes and persecution of French Protestants). Though a devout Calvinist himself, Bayle advocated complete toleration,

▸ **In 1745, the Habsburg Monarchy expelled an estimated 70,000 Jews from Prague to appease anti-Semitic sentiment.**

Joseph II on Religious Toleration

Between 1765 and 1781 Joseph II was joint ruler of the Habsburg Empire with his pious mother, Empress Maria Theresa. Joseph advocated a utilitarian approach to religious toleration (Document I) but made little headway against Maria Theresa's traditional insistence that the state must actively combat religious dissent. Soon after Maria Theresa's death Joseph promulgated a series of decrees on religion, including a landmark Toleration Edict for Protestants (Document II) and even a special, if somewhat less sweeping, edict of toleration for the Jews of his domains.

(I) LETTER TO MARIA THERESA, JULY 1777

"The word *toleration* has caused misunderstanding. . . . God preserve me from thinking it a matter of indifference whether the citizens turn Protestant or remain Catholics. . . . I would give all I possess if all the Protestants of your States would go over to Catholicism. The word *toleration* as I understand it, means only that I would employ any persons, without distinction of religion, in purely temporal matters, allow them to own property, practice trades, be citizens if they were qualified and if this would be of advantage to the State and its industry. . . . The undisturbed practice of their religion makes them far better subjects and causes them to avoid irreligion, which is a far greater danger to our Catholics. . . ."

(II) TOLERATION EDICT OF OCTOBER 1781

"We have found Ourselves moved to grant to the adherents of the Lutheran and Calvinist religions, and also to the non-Uniat Greek religion, everywhere, the appropriate private practice of their faith. . . . The Catholic religion alone shall continue to enjoy the prerogative of the public practice of its faith. . . . Non-Catholics are in future admitted under dispensation to buy houses and real property, to acquire municipal domicile and practice as master craftsmen, to take up academic appointments and posts in the public service, and are not to be required to take the oath in any form contrary to their religious tenets. . . . In all choices or appointments to official posts . . . difference of religion is to be disregarded."

From C. A. Macartney (ed.), *The Habsburg and Hohenzollern Dynasties* (Harper Torchbook, 1970), pp. 151 and 155–157.

which would allow any person to practice any religion or none at all. An individual's moral behavior rather than his or her creed is what mattered, according to Bayle. Ethics, he argued, do not depend on the Bible; a Muslim, a Confucian, a Jew, even an atheist can be moral.

The most striking success of the eighteenth-century campaign for toleration came with the Edict of Toleration issued by the Habsburg emperor Joseph II on his ascendancy to the throne in 1781. For the first time a Catholic Habsburg ruler recognized the right of Protestants and Jews in his realm to worship freely and to hold property and public office (*see box, above*). Joseph also tried to reduce the influence of the Catholic Church by ordering the dissolution of numerous monasteries on the grounds that they were useless and corrupt. Part of their confiscated wealth was used to support the medical school at the University of Vienna.

Deism Voltaire became the Enlightenment's most vigorous antireligious polemicist. This prolific writer was one of the century's most brilliant literary stylists, historians, and poets. Those talents alone would have assured his fame. But Voltaire was also a dedicated antagonist of Christianity. For tactical reasons, much of his attack against *l'infame* ("the infamous thing"), as he called Christianity, targeted such practices as monasticism or the behavior of priests. His ultimate target, though, was Christianity itself, which, he declared, "every sensible man, every honorable man must hold in horror."

Voltaire's masterpiece, a best-seller called *The Philosophical Dictionary* (1764), had to be published anonymously and was burned by the authorities in Switzerland, France, and the Netherlands. Modeled after Bayle's dictionary, it was far blunter. Of theology, he wrote, "We find man's insanity in all its plenitude." Organized religion is not simply false but pernicious, he argued. Voltaire believed that religious superstition inevitably bred fanaticism and predictably resulted in bloody episodes like the Saint Bartholomew's Day Massacre.

Voltaire hoped that educated Europeans would abandon Christianity in favor of deism, a belief that recognized God as the Creator but held that the world, once created, functions according to natural laws without interference by God. Humanity thus lives essentially on its own in an ordered universe, without hope or fear of divine intervention and without the threat of damnation or the hope of eternal salvation. For deists, religion should be a matter of private contemplation rather than public worship and mythic creeds. Although certain figures in the Enlightenment went beyond deism to a philosophical atheism, which rejected any concept of God as unprovable, Voltaire's mild deism remained a characteristic view of eighteenth-century writers. At bottom, however, this form of spirituality was essentially secular. Broad-minded clergy could accept many of the arguments of eighteenth-century science and philosophy, but they could not accept deism.

THE PHILOSOPHES

Science and secularism became the rallying points of a group of French intellectuals known as the *philosophes*. Their traditionalist opponents employed this term to mock the group's pretensions, but the philosophes themselves used that label with pride. For they saw themselves as a vanguard, the men who raised the Enlightenment to the status of a self-conscious movement.

The leaders of this influential coterie of writers were Voltaire and Denis Diderot. Its ranks included mathematicians Jean d'Alembert and the marquis de Condorcet, the magistrate baron de Montesquieu, the government official Jacques Turgot, and the atheist philosopher baron d'Holbach. Thus, the French philosophes came from both the aristocracy and the middle class. Outside of France their kinship extended to a group of brilliant Scottish philosophers, including David Hume and Adam Smith; to the German playwright Gotthold Lessing and the philosopher Immanuel Kant; to the Italian economist and penal reformer the marquis of Beccaria; and to such founders of the American Philosophical Society as Benjamin Franklin and Thomas Jefferson.

Intellectual Freedom The philosophes shared above all else a critical spirit, the desire to reexamine the assumptions and institutions of their societies and expose them to the tests of reason, experience, and utility. Today this might sound banal, but it was not so at a time when almost everywhere religion permeated society. Asserting the primacy of reason meant turning away from faith, the essence of religion. It meant a decisive break with the Christian worldview, which placed religious doctrine at the center of society's values. The philosophes invoked the paganism of ancient Greece and Rome, where the spirit of rational inquiry prevailed among educated people. They ridiculed the Middle Ages as the "Dark Ages" and contrasted the religious spirit of that era to their own sense of liberation and modernity. In *The Decline and Fall of the Roman Empire* (1776–1788), the historian Edward Gibbon declared that Christianity had eclipsed a Roman civilization that had sought to live according to reason rather than myths.

The inspiration of antiquity was matched by the stimulus of modern science and philosophy. The philosophes laid claim to Newton, who made the universe intelligible without the aid of revelation, and Locke, who uncovered the workings of the human mind. From Locke they went on to argue that human personality is malleable: its nature is not fixed, let alone corrupted by original sin. People are therefore ultimately responsible to themselves for what they do with their lives. Existing arrangements are no more nor less sacred than experience has proved them to be. As the humanists had several centuries before, the philosophes placed human beings at the center of thought. Unlike most humanists, however, they placed thought in the service of change and launched a noisy public movement.

They appeared clamorous to their contemporaries because they had to battle entrenched authority. Religious traditionalists and the apparatus of censorship in almost all countries threatened the intellectual freedom they demanded. The philosophes often had to publish their works clandestinely and anonymously. Sometimes they were pressured into withholding manuscripts from publication altogether or into making humiliating public apologies for controversial books. Even with such caution, almost all philosophes saw some of their publications confiscated and burned. A few were forced into exile or sent to jail: Voltaire spent several decades across the French border in Switzerland, and Voltaire and Diderot both spent time in prison. Although the notoriety produced by these persecutions stimulated the sale of their works, the anxiety took its toll.

By the 1770s, however, the philosophes had survived their running war with the authorities. Some of them lived to see their ideas widely accepted and their works acclaimed. Thus, even if they had contributed little else to the Western experience, their struggle for freedom of expression would merit them a significant place in its history.

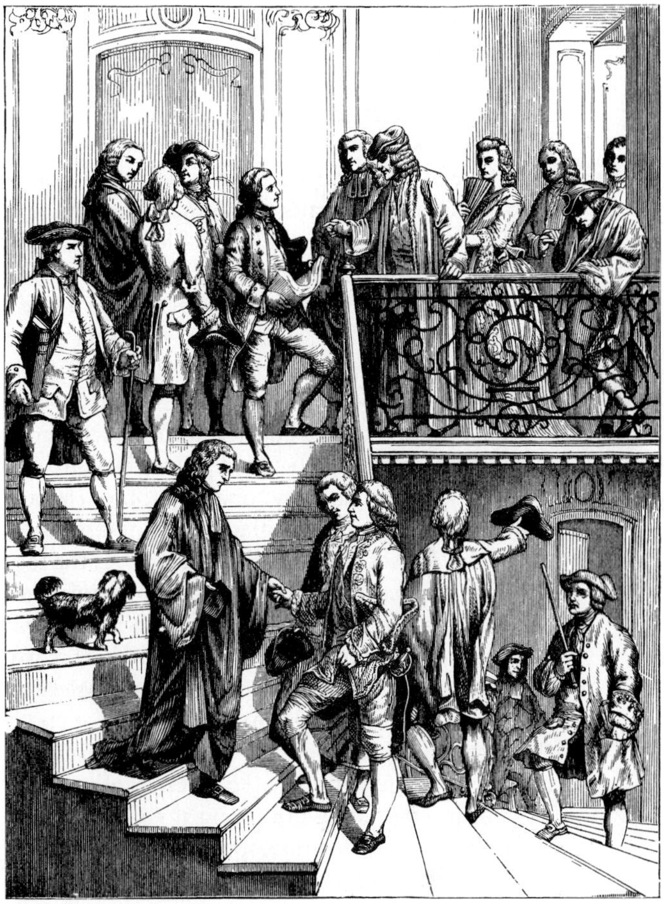

▶ An English engraving entitled "Voltaire's Staircase" suggests how the great writer stood at the center of Europe's literary and intellectual life. The fifth figure from the right at the top, Voltaire is bidding good-bye to d'Alembert.

Social Science But the philosophes achieved far more. In their scholarly and polemical writings, they investigated a wide range of subjects and pioneered in several new disciplines. Some philosophes—Voltaire, for example—were pathbreaking historians. Moving beyond traditional chronicles of battles and rulers' biographies, they studied culture, social institutions, and government structures in an effort to understand past societies as well as describe major events. Practically inventing the notion of social science, they investigated the theoretical foundations of social organization (sociology) and the workings of the human mind (psychology). On a more practical level, they proposed fundamental reforms in such areas as the penal system and education.

The philosophes embedded their study of social science in questions of morality and the study of ethics. Enlightenment ethics were generally utilitarian. Such philosophers as David Hume tried to define good and evil in pragmatic terms; they argued that social utility should become the standard for public morality. This approach to moral philosophy in turn raised the question of whether any human values were absolute and eternal. Among the philosophers who grappled with this challenge, Kant tried to harmonize the notion of absolute moral values with practical reason.

Political Liberty The most influential work of social science produced by the Enlightenment was probably *The Spirit of the Laws* (1748) by the French magistrate Montesquieu. The book offered a comparative study of governments and societies. On the one hand, Montesquieu introduced the perspective of relativism: He tried to analyze the institutions of government in relation to the special customs, climate, religion, and commerce of various countries. He thus argued that no single, ideal model of government existed. On the other hand, he deeply admired his own idealized version of the British system of government; he thereby implied that all societies could learn from the British about liberty.

Montesquieu's sections on liberty won a wide readership in Europe and in America, where the book was influential among the drafters of the United States Constitution. Political liberty, said Montesquieu, requires checks on those who hold power in a state, whether that power is exercised by a king, an aristocracy, or the people. Liberty can thrive only with a balance of powers, preferably by the separation of the executive, the legislative, and the judicial branches of government. Montesquieu ascribed a central role to aristocracies as checks on royal despotism. Indeed, many eighteenth-century writers on politics considered strong privileged groups, independent from both the crown and the people, as the only effective bulwarks against tyranny. To put it another way, Montesquieu's followers thought that the price for a society free from despotism was privilege for some of its members.

Liberal Economics French and British thinkers of the Enlightenment transformed economic theory with attacks against mercantilism and government regulation. We have earlier noted in Chapter 18 Adam Smith's critique of artificial restraints on individual economic initiative. In France, the *physiocrats* similarly argued that economic progress depended on freeing agriculture and trade from restrictions. Since in their view land was the only real source of wealth, they also called for reforms in the tax structure with a uniform and equitable land tax. In opposition to a traditional popular insistence on government intervention to maintain supplies of grain and flour at fair prices, the physiocrats advocated freedom for the grain trade to operate according to the dictates of supply and demand. The incentive of higher prices would encourage growers to expand productivity, they believed, and in this way the grain shortages that plagued Europe could eventually be eliminated, although at the cost of temporary hardship for most consumers.

DIDEROT AND THE ENCYCLOPEDIA

The Enlightenment thus produced not only a new intellectual spirit but also a wide range of critical writings on various subjects. In addition, the French philosophes collectively generated a single work that exemplified their notion of how knowledge could be useful: Diderot's *Encyclopédie* (*Encyclopedia*).

Denis Diderot never achieved the celebrity of his friend Voltaire, but his career proved equally central to the Enlightenment. The son of a provincial knife maker, Diderot was educated in Jesuit schools, but at the first opportunity he headed for Paris. Continuing to educate himself while living a bohemian existence, Diderot developed an unshakable sense of purpose: to make himself into an independent and influential intellectual.

Within a few years, he had published a remarkable succession of writings—novels and plays, mathematical treatises, an attack on inept medical practices, and several works on religion and moral philosophy. His most original writings examined the role of passion in human personality and in any system of values derived from an understanding of human nature. Specifically, Diderot affirmed the role of sexuality, arguing against artificial taboos and repression. As an advocate of what was sometimes called "the natural man," Diderot belies the charge leveled against the philosophes that they overemphasized reason to the neglect of feeling. The thread of religious criticism in these works was also notable. Starting from a position of mild skepticism, Diderot soon passed to deism and ended up in the atheist camp.

Diderot's unusual boldness in getting his works published brought him a considerable reputation but also some real trouble. Two of his books were condemned by the authorities as contrary to religion, the state, and morals. In 1749 he spent 100 days in prison and was released only after making a humiliating apology. At about that time, Diderot was approached by a publisher to translate a British encyclopedic reference work into French. After a number of false starts, he persuaded the publisher to sponsor instead an entirely new and more comprehensive work that would reflect the interests of the philosophes.

The Encyclopedia The *Encyclopedia, or Classified Dictionary of the Sciences, Arts, and Occupations,* an inventory of all fields of knowledge from the most theoretical to the most mundane, constituted an arsenal of critical concepts. As the preface stated: "Our Encyclopedia is a work that could only be carried out in a philosophic century. . . . All things must be examined without sparing anyone's sensibilities. . . . The arts and sciences must regain their freedom." The ultimate purpose of the Encyclopedia, wrote its editors, was "to change the general way of thinking." Written in this spirit by an array of talented collaborators, the expensive 28-volume *Encyclopedia* (1752–1772) fulfilled the fondest hopes of its editors and 4000 initial subscribers.

In such a work, religion could scarcely be ignored, but neither could it be openly attacked. Instead, the editors treated religion with artful satire or else relegated it to a philosophical or historical plane. Demystified and subordinated, religion was probed and questioned like any other subject, much to the discomfort of learned but orthodox critics.

Science stood at the core of the *Encyclopedia,* but the editors emphasized the technological or practical side of science with numerous articles and plates illustrating machines, tools, and manufacturing processes. They praised the roles of mechanics, engineers, and artisans in society and stressed the benefits of efficient production in the advance of civilization. Such emphasis implied that technology and artisanal skills constituted valuable realms of knowledge comparable to theoretical sciences such as physics and mathematics.

On economic topics the encyclopedists tended to echo the physiocratic crusade against restrictions on trade and agriculture. But the opinions and aspirations expressed were those of the elites, whose prerogatives, especially in matters of property, were not being threatened. Articles that might reflect the concerns of the popular masses on such issues as wages or affordable food prices were notably absent. Nor did the *Encyclopedia* take a novel line on questions of government. The authors generally endorsed abso-

Diderot's *Encyclopedia* focused much of its attention on technology. Illustrations of mechanical processes, such as the one shown here for making plate glass, filled 11 folio volumes.

lute monarchy, provided it was reasonably efficient and just. The major political concerns of the editors were civil rights, freedom of expression, and the rule of law.

In retrospect, after the French Revolution, the *Encyclopedia* does not seem very revolutionary. Yet in the context of the times, it assuredly was. The revolution that Diderot sought was intellectual. As he wrote in a letter to a friend, the encyclopedists were promoting "a revolution in the minds of men to free them from prejudice." Judging by the reaction of religious and government authorities, they were eminently successful. "Up till now," commented one French bishop, "hell has vomited its venom drop by drop." Now, he concluded, it could be found assembled between the *Encyclopedia*'s covers.

After allowing the first three volumes to appear, the government banned the *Encyclopedia* in 1759 and revoked the bookseller's license to issue the remaining volumes. As the attorney general of France put it: "There is a project formed, a society organized to propagate materialism, to destroy religion, to inspire a spirit of independence, and to nourish the corruption of morals." Most of the *Encyclopedia*'s contributors prudently withdrew from the project, but Diderot went underground and continued the herculean task until the subscribers received every promised volume, including 11 magnificent folios of illustrations. By the time these appeared, the persecutions had receded. Indeed, the *Encyclopedia* was reprinted in cheaper editions (both legal and pirated) that sold out rapidly, earning fortunes for their publishers. This turn of events ensured the status of Diderot's project as the landmark of its age.

JEAN-JACQUES ROUSSEAU

Arguably the most original and influential eighteenth-century thinker, Jean-Jacques Rousseau stood close to but self-consciously outside the coterie of the philosophes. For Rousseau provided in his life and writing a critique not only of the status quo but of the Enlightenment itself. Obsessed with the issue of moral freedom, Rousseau found society far more oppressive than most philosophes would admit, and he considered the philosophes themselves to be part of the problem.

Young Rousseau won instant fame when he submitted a prize-winning essay in a contest sponsored by a provincial academy on the topic, "Has the restoration of the arts and sciences had a purifying effect upon morals?" Unlike most respondents, Rousseau answered that it had not. He argued that the lustrous cultural and scientific achievements of recent decades were producing pretension, conformity, and useless luxury. Most scientific pursuits, he wrote, "are the effect of idleness which generate idleness in their turn." The system of rewards in the arts produces "a servile and deceptive conformity . . . the dissolution of morals . . . and the corruption of taste." Against the decadence of high culture, he advocated a return "to the simplicity which prevailed in earliest times"—manly physical pastimes, self-reliance, independent citizens instead of fawning courtiers.

Rousseau had no wish to return to a state of nature, a condition of anarchy where force ruled and people were slaves of appetite. But the basis of morality, he argued, was conscience, not reason. "Virtue, sublime science of simple minds: are not your principles graven on every heart?" This became one of his basic themes in two popular works of fiction, *Julie, or the New Heloise* (1761), and *Emile, or Treatise on Education* (1762).

In the first novel Julie is educated in virtue by her tutor St. Preux but allows herself to fall in love with and be seduced by him. In the second half of the novel, Julie breaks away from St. Preux and marries Monsieur de Wolmar, her father's wealthy friend. She maintains a distant friendship with her old lover and rears her children in exemplary fashion, overseeing their education. In the end she overcomes her past moral lapse and sacrifices her own life to save one of her children. Wolmar then brings in the chastened St. Preux to continue the children's education. This tale of love, virtue, and motherhood won an adoring audience of male and female readers who identified with the characters, shed tears over their moral dilemmas, and applauded Rousseau for this superb lesson in the new sensibility.

Emile recounts the story of a young boy raised to be a moral adult by a tutor who emphasized experience over book learning and who considered education a matter of individual self-development. This new kind of man of course required a comparably sensitive wife, attuned to practical matters and without vain aristocratic pretenses. Sophie, the girl in question, received a very different type of education, however, one concerned with virtue but far more limited in its scope. Rousseau depicted men and women liberating themselves from stultifying traditional values, yet in the new relationships he portrayed in these novels, women held a decidedly subordinate position. Their virtues were to be exclusively domestic in character, while the men would be prepared for public roles—a distinction that deeply troubled feminist thinkers in the future (*see box, below*).

Rousseau himself was by no means a saint. His personal weaknesses—including the illegitimate child that he fathered and abandoned—doubtless contributed to his preoccupation with morality and conscience. Nonetheless, his rebellious life as well as his writings greatly impressed the generation of readers and writers coming of age in the 1770s and 1780s. Not only did he quarrel with the repressive authorities of Church and

Mary Wollstonecraft on the Education of Women

***The sharpest challenge to Rousseau's widely shared attitude toward women came only in 1792, with the publication of Mary Wollstonecraft's* A Vindication of the Rights of Woman. *Inspired by the French Revolution's doctrine of natural rights, this spirited writer deplored the fact that society kept women (in her words) frivolous, artificial, weak, and in a perpetual state of childhood. While men praised women for their beauty and grace, they hypocritically condemned them for a concern with vanity, fashion, and trivial matters, yet refused to treat them as rational human beings who could contribute to society as much as men. Her book emphasized the need for educational reform that would allow women to develop agile bodies and strong minds. Along the way Wollstonecraft took particular aim at Rousseau's* Emile.**

"The conduct and manners of women, in fact, evidently prove that their minds are not in a healthy state; for, like the flowers which are planted in too rich a soil, strength and usefulness are sacrificed to beauty. . . . One cause of this barren blooming I attribute to a false system of education, gathered from the books written on this subject by men who, considering females rather as women than human creatures, have been more anxious to make them alluring mistresses than affectionate wives and rational mothers. The understanding of the sex has been so bubbled by this specious homage, that the civilized women of the present century, with a few exceptions, are only anxious to inspire love, when they ought to cherish a nobler ambition, and by their abilities and virtues exact respect.

"[T]he most perfect education, in my opinion, is such an exercise of the understanding as is best calculated to strengthen the body and form the heart. Or, in other words, to enable the individual to attain such habits of virtue as will render it independent. In fact, it is a farce to call any being virtuous whose virtues do not result from the exercise of its own reason. This was Rousseau's opinion respecting men: I extend it to women, and confidently assert that they have been drawn out of their sphere by false refinement, and not by an endeavour to acquire masculine qualities. Still the regal homage which they receive is so intoxicating, that till the manners of the times are changed, and formed on more reasonable principles, it may be impossible to convince them that the illegitimate power, which they obtain by degrading themselves, is a curse, and that they must return to nature and equality. . . ."

From Sandra M. Gilbert and Susan Gubar (eds.), *The Norton Anthology of Literature by Women: The Tradition in English* (W. W. Norton, 1985).

▸ **The French revolutionaries acclaimed both Voltaire and Rousseau and transferred their remains to a new Pantheon. But Rousseau was the man considered by many French people to be the Revolution's spiritual father, as suggested by his position in this allegorical painting of 1793, filled with the new symbolism of liberty and equality.**

state—who repeatedly banned his books—but he also attacked the pretensions of his fellow philosophes, whom he considered arrogant, cynical, and lacking in spirituality. By the 1770s the commanding figures of the Enlightenment, such as Voltaire and Diderot, had won their battles and had become masters of the most prestigious academies and channels of patronage. In a sense, they had themselves become the establishment. For younger writers frustrated by the existing distribution of influence and patronage, Rousseau became the inspiration.

Rousseau's Concept of Freedom What proved to be Rousseau's most enduring work, *The Social Contract*, published in 1762, became famous only after the French Revolution dramatized the issues that the book had raised. (The Revolution, it could be said, did more for the book than Rousseau did for the Revolution, which he neither prophesied nor advocated.) *The Social Contract* was not meant as a blueprint for revolution but rather as an ideal standard against which readers might measure their own society. Rousseau did not expect that this standard could be achieved in practice, since existing states were too large and complex to allow the kind of participation that he considered essential.

For Rousseau, a government distinct from the individuals over whom it claims to exercise authority has no validity. Rousseau denied the almost universal idea that some people are meant to govern and others to obey. In the ideal polity, Rousseau said, individuals have a role in making the law to which they submit. By obeying it, they are thus obeying themselves as well as their fellow citizens. For this reason, they are free from arbitrary power. To found such an ideal society, each citizen would have to take part in creating a social contract laying out the society's ground rules. By doing so, these citizens would establish themselves as "the sovereign." This sovereign—the people—then creates a government that will carry on the day-to-day business of applying the laws.

Rousseau was not advocating simple majority rule but rather a quest for consensus as to the best interests of all citizens. Even if it *appears* contrary to the welfare of some or even many citizens, he believed, the best interest of the community must be every individual's best interest as well, since that individual is a member of the community. Rousseau called this difficult concept "the general will." Deferring to the general will means that an individual ultimately must do what one *ought*, not simply what one *wants*. This commitment derives from conscience, which must do battle within the individual against passion, appetite, and mere self-interest. Under the social contract, to use Rousseau's most striking phrase, the individual "will be forced to be free" (*see box*, p. 619). Thus for Rousseau, individual freedom depends on a political framework involving consent and participation as well as subordination of individual self-interest to the commonweal. More than any of the philosophes, Rousseau argued that individual freedom depends on the arrangements governing the collectivity.

II. Eighteenth-Century Elite Culture

The Enlightenment was merely one dimension of Europe's cultural life. Europe's economic expansion and relative prosperity, discussed in the previous chapter, were matched by a marked increase in publishing activity that served diverse audiences and by the creation of new cultural forms and institutions. Although the aristocracy still dominated society, men and women of lesser social status participated prominently in cultural life. Eighteenth-century elite culture was cosmopolitan, spilling across national borders as well as certain social class lines.

COSMOPOLITAN HIGH CULTURE

As the expansive, cosmopolitan aspects of European high culture are described here, it must be remembered that the mass of Europe's peasants and workers remained virtually untouched by these developments, insulated within their local environments and traditions. But the educated and wealthy, the numerically small and influential elites, enjoyed a sense of belonging to a common European civilization. French was the international language of this culture; even King Frederick II of Prussia favored French over German. Whatever the effects of Frederick's attitude might have been—the German dramatist Lessing, for one, considered it a deplorable cultural prejudice—the widespread knowledge of French meant that ideas and literature could circulate easily past language barriers.

Travel Europeans sharpened their sense of common identity through travel literature and by their appetite for visiting foreign places. Although transportation was slow and uncomfortable, many embarked on a "grand tour," whose

Rousseau's Concept of the General Will

"The essence of the social compact reduces itself to the following terms: Each of us puts his person and all his power in common under the supreme direction of the general will, and, in our collective capacity, we receive each member as an indivisible part of the whole. . . .

"In fact, each individual, as a man, may have a particular will contrary or dissimilar to the general will which he has as a citizen. His particular interest may speak to him quite differently from the common interest: his absolute and naturally independent existence may make him look upon what he owes to the common cause as a gratuitous contribution, the loss of which will do less harm to others than the payment of it is burdensome to himself. . . . He may wish to enjoy the rights of citizenship without being ready to fulfill the duties of a subject. The continuance of such an injustice could not but prove the undoing of the body politic.

"In order then that the social compact may not be an empty formula, it tacitly includes the undertaking, which alone can give force to the rest, that whoever refuses to obey the general will shall be compelled to do so by the whole body. This means nothing less than that he will be forced to be free; for this is the condition which, by giving each citizen to his country, secures him against all personal dependence. In this lies the key to the working of the political machine. . . ."

From *The Social Contract*, Book I, chs. 6–7.

highlights included visits to Europe's large cities (such as London, Paris, Rome, and Vienna) and to the ruins of antiquity—to the glories of the modern and the ancient worlds.

Kings, princes, and municipal authorities were embellishing their towns with plazas, public gardens, theaters, and opera houses. Toward the end of the century, amenities such as street lighting and public transportation began to appear in a few cities, with London leading the way. From the private sector came two notable additions to the urban scene: the coffeehouse and the storefront window display. Coffeehouses, where customers could chat or read, and enticing shop windows, which added to the pleasures of city walking (and stimulated consumer demand), enhanced the rhythms of urban life for tourists and residents alike. When a man is tired of London, Samuel Johnson remarked, he is tired of life.

Travelers on tour invariably passed from the attractions of bustling city life to the silent monuments of antiquity. As the philosophes recalled the virtues of pagan philosophers like Cicero, interest grew in surviving examples of Greek and Roman architecture and sculpture. Many would have agreed with the German art historian Johann Winckelmann that Greek sculpture was the most worthy standard of aesthetic beauty in all the world.

The Republic of Letters Among writers, intellectuals, and scientists, the sense of a cosmopolitan European culture devolved into the concept of a "republic of letters." The phrase, introduced by sixteenth-century French humanists, was popularized by Pierre Bayle (noted earlier as a pro-

This painting of Mme. Geoffrin's Salon in 1755, which dates from 1814, reflects the artist Lemonnier's imagination rather than historical reality. His canvas depicts an assemblage of all the major philosophes and their patrons that never actually took place. Yet it does accurately convey the social atmosphere and serious purpose of the Parisian salons. At the center is a bust of Voltaire, who lived in exile at the time.

ponent of religious toleration), who published a critical journal that he called *News of the Republic of Letters*. The title implied that the realm of culture and ideas stretched across Europe's political borders. In one sense it was an exclusive republic, limited to the educated; but it was also an open society to which people of talent could belong regardless of their social origins. For this reason, European intellectuals felt that their "republic of letters" was a model for a "public sphere" in which political and social issues could be debated freely as well.

Aside from the medium of the printed word, the republic of letters was organized around the salons and the academies. Both institutions encouraged social interchange by bringing together socially prominent men and women with talented writers. The philosophes themselves exemplified this social mixture, for their "family" was composed in almost equal measures of nobles (Montesquieu, Holbach, Condorcet) and commoners (Voltaire, Diderot, d'Alembert). Voltaire, while insisting that he was as good as any aristocrat, had no desire to topple the aristocracy from its position; rather he sought amalgamation. As d'Alembert put it, talent on the one hand and birth and eminence on the other both deserve recognition.

The salons, usually organized and led by women of wealthy bourgeois or noble families, sought to bring together important writers with the influential persons they needed for favors and patronage. The salon of Madame Tencin, for example, helped launch Montesquieu's *Spirit of the Laws* in the 1740s, while the salon of Madame du Deffand in the 1760s became a forum where the philosophes could test their ideas (see figure, p. 620). The salons also helped to enlarge the audience and contacts of the philosophes by introducing them to a flow of foreign visitors, ranging from German princes to Benjamin Franklin. Private newsletters kept interested foreigners and provincials abreast of activities in the Parisian salons when they could not attend personally, but salons also operated in Vienna, London, and Berlin.

The salons placed a premium on elegant conversation and wit. The women who ran them insisted that intellectuals make their ideas lucid and comprehensible to laypeople, which increased the likelihood that their thought and writings would have some impact. The salons were also a forum where men learned to take women seriously, and they constituted a unique cultural space for women between the domestic and public spheres. But the salons' emphasis on style over substance led Rousseau to denounce them as artificial rituals that prevented the display of genuine feeling and sincerity.

Throughout Europe, freemasonry was another important form of cultural sociability that often crossed the lines of class and (less commonly) of gender. Operating in an aura of secretiveness and symbolism, the masonic lodges fostered a curious mixture of spirituality and rationalism. Originating as clubs or fraternities dedicated to humane values, they attracted a wide range of educated nobles, commoners, and liberal clergy, while a few lodges accepted women as well. But toward the end of the century, freemasonry was torn by sectarian controversies and its influence seemed to be diminishing.

The Learned Academies As important for the dissemination of ideas in the eighteenth century as the salons were the learned academies. These ranged from the Lunar Society in Birmingham, a forum for innovative British industrialists and engineers, to state-sponsored academies in almost every capital of Southern and Central Europe, which served as conduits for advanced scientific and philosophical ideas coming from Western Europe. In France, moreover, academies were established in more than 30 provincial cities, most of which became strongholds of advanced thinking outside the capital.

These provincial academies were founded after the death of Louis XIV in 1715, as if in testimony to the liberating effect of his demise. Most began as literary institutes, concerned with upholding traditional values such as purity of literary style. A few academies adhered to such goals well into midcentury, but most gradually shifted their interests from literary matters to scientific and practical questions in such areas as commerce, agriculture, and local administration. They became offshoots, so to speak, of the *Encyclopedia*'s spirit. Indeed, when a Jesuit launched an attack against the *Encyclopedia* in the Lyons

Academy, many members threatened to resign unless he retracted his remarks. By the 1770s the essay contests sponsored by the provincial academies and the papers published by their members had turned to such topics as population growth, capital punishment and penology, education, poverty and welfare, the grain trade, the guilds, and the origins of sovereignty.

A parallel shift in membership occurred. The local academies began as privileged corporations, dominated by the nobility of the region. Associate membership was extended to commoners from the ranks of civil servants, doctors, and professionals. Gradually, the distinction between regular and associate participants crumbled. The academies admitted more commoners to full membership, and a fragile social fusion took place.

▶ **The title page of Samuel Johnson's pioneering *Dictionary of the English Language* (1755 edition), one of the masterpieces of eighteenth-century literature.**

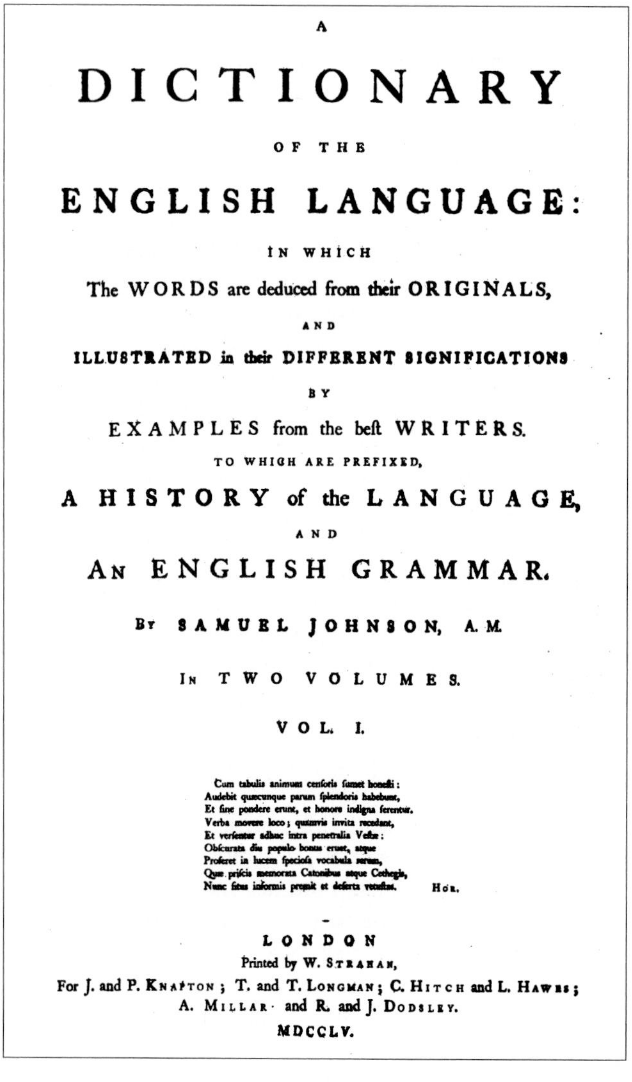
A
DICTIONARY
OF THE
ENGLISH LANGUAGE:
IN WHICH
The WORDS are deduced from their ORIGINALS,
AND
ILLUSTRATED in their DIFFERENT SIGNIFICATIONS
BY
EXAMPLES from the beſt WRITERS.
TO WHICH ARE PREFIXED,
A HISTORY of the LANGUAGE,
AND
AN ENGLISH GRAMMAR.
BY SAMUEL JOHNSON, A.M.
IN TWO VOLUMES.
VOL. I.

Cum tabulis animum cenſoris ſumet honeſti:
Audebit quæcunque parum ſplendoris habebunt,
Et ſine pondere erunt, et honore indigna ferentur.
Verba movere loco; quamvis invita recedant,
Et verſentur adhuc intra penetralia Veſtæ:
Obſcurata diu populo bonus eruet, atque
Proferet in lucem ſpecioſa vocabula rerum,
Quæ priſcis memorata Catonibus atque Cethegis,
Nunc ſitus informis premit et deſerta vetuſtas. HOR.

LONDON
Printed by W. STRAHAN,
For J. and P. KNAPTON; T. and T. LONGMAN; C. HITCH and L. HAWES;
A. MILLAR and R. and J. DODSLEY.
MDCCLV.

PUBLISHING AND READING

The eighteenth century saw a notable rise in publishing that was geared to several kinds of readers. Traveling circulating libraries originated in England around 1740 and opened untapped markets for reading material; by the end of the century almost 1000 traveling libraries had been established. "Booksellers," or publishers—the intermediary between author and reader—combined the functions of a modern editor, printer, salesperson, and (if need be) smuggler. Their judgment and marketing techniques helped create as well as fill the demand for books, since they conceived and financed a variety of works. The *Encyclopedia* originated as a bookseller's project; so, too, did such enduring masterpieces as Samuel Johnson's *Dictionary*, a monumental lexicon that helped purify and standardize the English language. Booksellers commissioned talented stylists to write popular versions of serious scientific, historical, and philosophical works. Recognizing a specialized demand among women readers, they increased the output of fictional romances and fashion magazines, and also began to publish more fiction and poetry by women. In general, the entertainment and instruction of a diverse but educated audience became the focus of most publishers.

Journals and Newspapers Eighteenth-century publishing was notable for the proliferation of periodicals. In England, which pioneered in this domain, the number of periodicals increased from 25 to 158 between 1700 and 1780. In one successful model, Addison and Steele's *Spectator* (1711), each issue consisted of a single essay that sought in elegant but clear prose to raise the reader's standards of morality and taste. Their goal was "to enliven Morality with Wit, and to temper

Wit with Morality. . . . To bring Philosophy . . . to dwell in clubs and assemblies, at tea-tables and coffeehouses." Eliza Haywood adapted this format in her journal, *The Female Spectator* (1744–1756), where she avocated improvement in the treatment of women and greater "opportunities of enlarging our minds." (A comparable periodical in France, the *Journal des Dames*, which appeared in 1759, propagated the writings of the Enlightenment but also raised the question of women's place in society.) Another type of journal published extracts and summaries of books and covered current events and entertainment; one such journal, the *Gentleman's Magazine*, reached the impressive circulation of 15,000 in 1740. More learned periodicals specialized in book reviews and serious articles on science and philosophy.

Most important for the future of reading habits in Europe was the daily newspaper, which originated in England. Papers like the *London Chronicle* at first provided family entertainment and then took on classified advertisements (thereby spurring consumerism and the notion of fashion). English newspapers of course published news of current events, but only after strenuous battles for permission from a reluctant government did they win the right to report directly on parliamentary debates. In France, a handful of major Parisian newspapers enjoyed privileged monopolies in exchange for full compliance with government censorship. This severely restricted their ability to discuss government and politics, although other periodicals published outside France's borders helped satisfy the demand for such coverage in France. With the Revolution of 1789, however, a politically aroused French citizenry provided unimagined opportunities for the growth of political journalism.

"Bad Books" The demand for books and the dynamism of the publishing industry created new employment opportunities for men and women. Although the number of would-be writers swelled, relatively few could develop their talents without constraint or achieve financial independence without patronage. Many remained poverty-stricken and frustrated.

Publishers thus could hire legions of otherwise unemployed writers to turn out the kinds of books for which they sensed a great demand: potboilers, romances, salacious pamphlets, and gossip sheets, which pandered to low tastes. Paid for quantity and speed rather than quality, these hack writers led a precarious, humiliating existence. Booksellers and desperate writers saw money to be made in sensational pamphlets assailing the character of notorious aristocrats, in partisan pamphlets attacking a particular faction in court politics, and in pornography. Sometimes they combined character assassination and pornography in pamphlets dwelling on the alleged perversions of rulers or courtiers. For all its wild exaggeration, such material helped "desacralize" monarchy and created a vivid image of a decadent aristocracy.

To satisfy the public's demand for gossip, character assassination, and pornography in violation of laws regulating the book trade in France, publishers located just across the French border marketed such books and pamphlets clandestinely. They smuggled this material into France—along with banned books by writers like Voltaire and Rousseau—using networks of couriers and distributors. In their sales lists of what they called Philosophic Books, the clandestine publishers lumped together banned books by serious writers along with such illicit publications as *The Scandalous Chronicles, The Private Life of Louis XV,* and *Venus in the Cloister* (a pornographic account of the alleged perversions of the clergy). The police made the same judgment. In attempting to stop the flow of "bad books," they scarcely distinguished between a banned work by Voltaire assaulting religious bigotry and a libelous pamphlet depicting the queen as a corrupt pervert.

LITERATURE, MUSIC, AND ART

Unlike the artistic style of the seventeenth century, generally classified as Baroque, that of the eighteenth century cannot be given a single stylistic label. The nature of the audience and the sources of support for writers and composers also varied considerably. But several artistic trends proved to be of lasting importance: the rise of the novel in England, the birth of romantic po-

▸ **One of the leading French portrait painters, and the most successful female artist of the era anywhere, was Élisabeth Vigée-Lebrun, who enjoyed the patronage of Queen Marie Antoinette. Shown here is one of several portraits that she painted of the French queen.**

etry, the development of the symphony in Austria, and the changing social context of French painting late in the century.

The Rise of the Novel The modern novel had its strongest development in England, where writers and booksellers cultivated a growing middle-class reading public. The acknowledged pioneer of this new genre was Samuel Richardson, a bookseller as well as a writer. With a series of letters telling the story, Richardson's *Pamela, or Virtue Rewarded* (1740) recounted the trials and tribulations of an honest if somewhat hypocritical servant girl. Pamela's sexual virtue is repeatedly challenged but never conquered by her wealthy employer, Mr. B., who finally agrees to marry her. An instant success, this melodrama broke from the standard forms and heroic subjects of most narrative fiction. Richardson dealt with recognizable types of people.

Pamela's apparent hypocrisy, however, prompted a playwright and lawyer named Henry Fielding to pen a short satire called *Shamela*, which he followed with his own novel *Joseph Andrews*. Here comedy and adventure replaced melodrama; Fielding prefaced *Joseph Andrews* with a manifesto claiming that the novel was to be "a comic epic in prose." Fielding realized the full potential of his bold experimentation with literary forms in *Tom Jones* (1749), a colorful, robust, comic panorama of English society featuring a gallery of brilliantly developed characters and vivid depictions of varied social environments.

The novel was thus emerging as a form of fiction that told its story and treated the development of personality in a realistic social context. It seemed to mirror its times better than other forms of fiction, and like the dramas that filled the stage in the second half of the century, most novels focused on family life and everyday problems of love, marriage, and social relations. Novelists could use broad comedy, or they could be totally serious; they could experiment endlessly with forms and techniques and could deal with a wide range of social settings.

In *Evelina or A Young Lady's Entrance into the World* (1778), the writer Fanny Burney used the flexibility of the novel to give a woman's perspective on eighteenth-century English social life. In the form of letters, like *Pamela* and *Julie*, *Evelina* traces a provincial girl's adventures in London as she discovers her true father and finds a suitable husband. While falling back on conventional melodrama, in which marriage is the only happy ending for a young woman, Burney also uses social satire to suggest how society restricts, and even endangers, an independent woman's life. If Burney was ambivalent about the possibilities for female independence in the social world, her own writing, together with other women writers of the period, demonstrated the opportunities for female artistic achievement.

Meanwhile, writers with more didactic objectives perfected a satiric genre called the philosophical tale, as exemplified by the great Irish satirist Jonathan Swift in his *Gulliver's Travels* (1726). The French philosophes favored this form of satire because it allowed them to criticize their society covertly and avoid open clashes with the censors. Thus Montesquieu created a range of mythical foreign settings and travelers from the Levant to ridicule contemporary European morality in *The Persian Letters* (1721). Voltaire similarly achieved great success in his tale *Candide* (1759), a critique of the notion that this was the best of all possible worlds. His exotic characters and incidents disguised an Enlightenment tract against the idiocy and cruelty that he saw in European society.

The Birth of Romantic Poetry During most of this century of innovation in prose fiction, poetry retained its traditional qualities. Still the most prized form of literary expression, poetry followed unchanging rules on what made good literature. Each poetic form had its particular essence and rules; but in all types of poems diction was supposed to be elegant and the sentiments refined. Poets were expected to transform the raw materials of emotion into delicate language and references that only the highly educated could appreciate. In this Neoclassical tradition, art was seen to echo eternal standards of truth and beauty. The poet was not permitted to unburden his soul or hold forth on his own experience. The audience for poetry was the narrowest segment of the reading public—"the wealthy few," in the phrase of William Wordsworth, who criticized eighteenth-century poets for pandering exclusively to that group.

By the end of the century, however, the restraints of Neoclassicism finally provoked rebellion in the ranks of English and German poets. Men like Friedrich von Schiller and Wordsworth defiantly raised the celebration of individual feeling and inner passion to the level of a creed, which came to be known as Romanticism. These young poets generally prized Rousseau's writings, seeing the Genevan rebel as someone who had forged a personal idiom of expression and who valued inner feeling, moral passion, and the wonders of nature. Hoping to appeal to a much broader audience, these poets decisively changed the nature of poetic composition and made this literary form, like the novel, a flexible and more accessible vehicle of artistic expression.

Goethe The writer who came to embody the new ambitions of poets, novelists, and dramatists was Johann von Goethe, whose long life (1749–1832) spanned the beginnings and the high point of the Romantic movement. A friend of Schiller and many of the German writers and philosophers of the day, he soon came to tower over all of them. Goethe first inspired a literary movement known as *Sturm und Drang* (Storm and Stress), which emphasized strong artistic emotions and gave early intimations of the Romantic temperament. The best-known work of *Sturm und Drang* was young Goethe's *The Sorrows of Young Werther* (1774), a novel about a young man driven to despair and suicide by an impossible love.

Courted by many of the princes and monarchs of Germany, Goethe soon joined the circle of the duke who ruled the small city-state of Weimar, where he remained for the rest of his life. There flowed from his pen an astonishing stream of works—lyrical love poetry, powerful dramas, art and literary criticism, translations, philosophic reflections, an account of his travels in Italy, and studies of optics, botany, anatomy, and mathematics. Even though he held official posts in the duke's court, Goethe's literary output never flagged. His masterpiece, *Faust*, occupied him for nearly 50 years and revealed the progress of his art. The first part (published in 1808) imbued with romantic longing the somewhat autobiographical story of a man who yearns to master all of knowledge and who makes a pact with the devil to achieve his goal. But the second part (1831) emphasized the renunciation and determination that came to be Goethe's credo. The final lines are:

> He only earns his freedom and existence
> Who daily conquers them anew.

What had begun in the youthful exuberance and energy of Romanticism ended in an almost classical mood of discipline. No wonder that Goethe seemed to his contemporaries the last "universal man," the embodiment of conflicting cultural values and Western civilization's struggle to resolve them.

The Symphony For Europe's elites, music offered the supreme form of entertainment, and the development of the symphony in music paralleled the rise of the novel in literature. It must be noted at once, however, that a great deal of eighteenth-century music was routine and undistinguished. For much of the century, composers still served under royal, ecclesiastical, or aristocratic patronage. They were bound by rigid formulas of composition and by prevailing tastes tyrannically insistent on conventions. Most listeners wanted little more than pleasant melodies in familiar forms; instrumental music was often commissioned as background fare for balls or other social occasions.

The heartland of Europe's music tradition shifted during the eighteenth century from Italy and France to Austria. Here a trio of geniuses transformed the routines of eighteenth-century composition into original and enduring masterpieces. True, the early symphonies of Franz Joseph Haydn and young Wolfgang Amadeus Mozart were conventional exercises. As light and tuneful as its audience could wish, their early music had little emotional impact. By the end of their careers, however, these two composers had altered the symphonic form from three to four movements, had achieved extraordinary harmonic virtuosity, and had brought a deep if restrained emotionalism to their music. Haydn and Mozart had changed the symphony radically from the elegant trifles of earlier years.

Ludwig van Beethoven consummated this development and assured that the symphony, like the novel and romantic poetry, would be an adaptable vehicle for the expression of creative genius. In each of his nine symphonies, as well as in his five piano concertos, Beethoven progressively modified the standard formulas, enlarged the orchestra, and wrote movements of increasing intricacy. His last symphony burst the bonds of the form altogether. Beethoven introduced a large chorus singing one of Schiller's odes to conclude his Ninth Symphony (1824), making it a celebration in music of freedom and brotherhood. Laden with passion, the music is nevertheless recognizable as an advanced form of the classical symphony. Thus it provides a bridge between the music of two periods: eighteenth-century Classicism and nineteenth-century Romanticism.

Aristocratic and court patronage remained the surest foundation for a career in music during the eighteenth century. Haydn, for example, worked with mutual satisfaction as the court composer for one prince from 1761 to 1790. At the end of his long life, however, Haydn moved out on his own, having won enough international recognition to sign a lucrative contract with a London music publisher who underwrote performances of his last 12 symphonies. In contrast, Mozart had an unhappy experience trying to earn his living by composing. After a few miserable years as court composer for the Archbishop of Salzburg, Mozart escaped to Vienna but could not find a permanent employer. He was obliged to eke out an inadequate living by teaching, filling private commissions, and giving public concerts. Beethoven did much better at freeing himself from dependence on a single patron through individual commissions and public concerts.

The Social Context of Art Unlike the situation in literature and music, there were no notable innovations in the field of painting during most of the eighteenth century. With the exception of the Frenchman Jacques-Louis David, eighteenth-century painters were overshadowed by their predecessors. Neoclassicism remained a popular style in the late eighteenth century, with its themes inspired by antiquity and its timeless conceptions of form and beauty, comparable to the rules of Neoclassical poetry.

The social context of painting, however, was changing. Most commissions and patronage still depended on aristocrats and princes, but the public was beginning to claim a role as the judge of talent in the visual arts. Public opinion found its voice in a new breed of art critics, unaffiliated with official sources of patronage, who reached their new audience through the press in the second half of the century. The Royal Academy of Art in France created the opening for this new

▶ **The kind of art held in high esteem in eighteenth-century France included the sensuous and ornate scenes of aristocratic life in the so-called Rococo style painted by J.-H. Fragonard, such as *Blind Man's Bluff*, shown here (detail).**

voice by sponsoring an annual public exhibition, or "salon," starting in 1737. People could view the canvases chosen by the Academy for these exhibitions and could reach their own judgments about the painters. In this way a "public sphere" of cultural discourse came into being, where once the official word of the Academy had determined the matter of taste and reputation in painting.

David, a brilliant painter in the Neoclassical style, won the greatest renown in this arena of public opinion during the 1780s. He skillfully celebrated the values of the ancient world in such historical paintings as *The Oath of the Horatii* (see figure, bottom of p. 628), *The Death of Socrates*, and *Brutus*. Discarding many of the standard conventions for history painting (and thereby drawing criticism from the Academy), David overwhelmed the public with his vivid imagery and the emotional force of his compositions. His paintings of the 1780s unmistakably conveyed a yearning for civic virtue and patriotism that had yet to find its political outlet in France. Not surprisingly, David became the most engaged and triumphant painter of the French Revolution.

In an entirely different vein, a few eighteenth-century artists chose more mundane and "realistic" subjects or themes for their canvases, parallel in some respects to what novelists and playwrights were doing. Jean-Baptiste Greuze, for example, made a hit in the Parisian exhibitions of the 1770s with his sentimentalized paintings of ordinary people in family settings caught in a dramatic situation, such as the death of a father or the banishment of a disobedient son. William Hogarth, a superb London engraver who worked through the medium of prints and book illustrations, went further down the social pyramid with his remarkable scenes of life among the working classes and the poor.

Instead of the aristocrats or classical figures that most artists chose for their subjects, Jean-Baptiste Greuze painted ordinary French people. His portraits and dramatic scenes (such as *The Father's Curse*) seemed to echo Rousseau's call for honest, "natural" feeling.

The greatest innovation in French painting came in reaction to the artificiality of Baroque and Rococo styles and subject matter, with a return to favor of "noble simplicity and calm grandeur." This Neoclassical style found its supreme expression in the work of Jacques-Louis David. Such history paintings as *The Oath of the Horatii* evoked the ideal of civic virtue in ancient Greek and Roman civilization.

III. Popular Culture

While the cultural world of aristocratic and middle-class elites has been extensively studied, the cultures of artisans, peasants, and the urban poor remain more dimly illuminated. In those sectors of society, culture primarily meant recreation and was essentially public and collective. Popular culture had its written forms, but they were relatively unimportant compared to the oral tradition of songs, folktales, and sayings, which have left fewer firsthand traces in the historical record. Nonetheless, it is possible to suggest the rich variety of cultural and recreational practice among working people.

POPULAR LITERATURE

Far removed from the markets for Voltaire and the *Gentleman's Magazine*, there existed a distinct world of popular literature—the reading matter consumed by journeymen and peasants, the poor and the almost poor, those who could barely read and those who could not read at all. From the seventeenth through the early nineteenth century, but particularly in the eighteenth century, publishers produced for this audience small booklets written anonymously, printed on cheap paper, and costing only a few pennies. These brochures were sold by itinerant peddlers who knew the tastes of their customers; presumably the booklets were often read aloud by those who could read to those who could not.

This popular literature took three major forms. Religious material included devotional tracts, saints' lives, catechisms, manuals of penitence, and Bible stories, all written simply and generously laced with miracles. Readers who were preoccupied with fears of death and damnation sought reassurance in these works that a virtuous life would end in salvation. Almanacs constituted a second type of popular literature, which appealed to the readers' concern for getting along in this life. Almanacs and how-to-live-successfully pamphlets discussed things like the kinds of potions to take for illnesses and featured astrology—how to read the stars and other signs for clues about the future. The third type of pop-

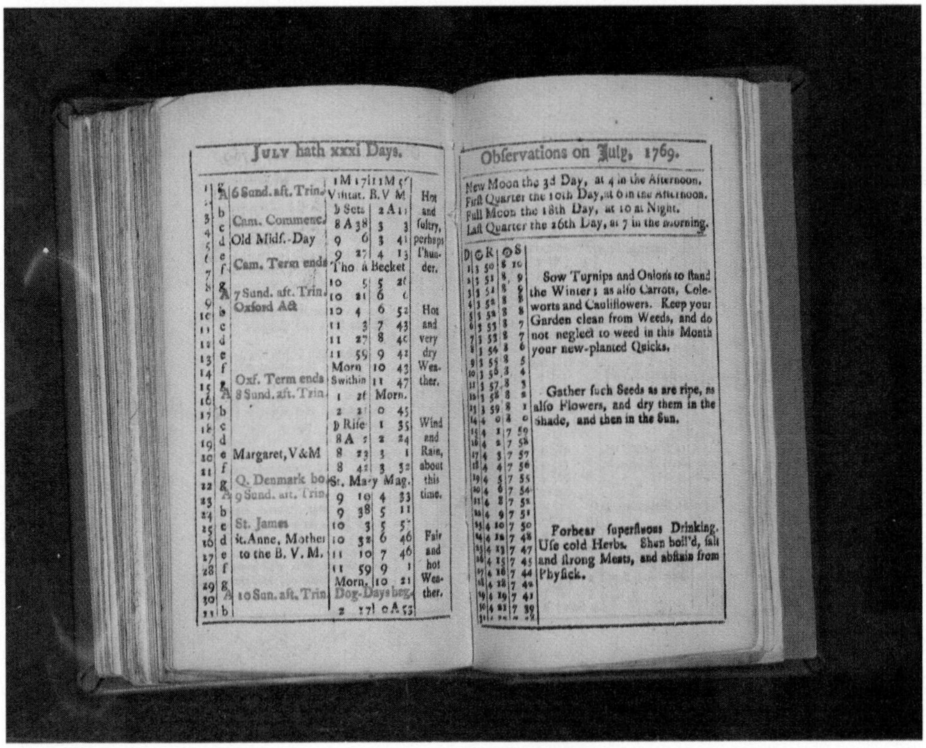

▸ **A page from an English almanac of 1769 on the month of July includes saints' days, information about likely weather patterns, and advice about agricultural matters and health care.**

ular literature provided entertainment: tales and fables, burlesques and crude satires, mixtures of fiction and history in which miraculous events frequently helped bring the story to a satisfactory conclusion.

Although useful information may have trickled down through these booklets, most of them were escapist. The religiosity and supernatural events of popular literature separate it from the growing rationalism and secularism of elite culture. Moreover, it could be argued that by ignoring such problems as food shortages, high taxes, and material insecurity, popular writings fostered submissiveness, a fatalistic acceptance of a dismal status quo. Glimpsing the content of this popular literature helps us understand why Voltaire had no hope of extending his ideas on religion to the masses.

Oral Tradition Almanacs and pamphlets for working people were produced by outsiders, printers and writers who were themselves well educated. Oral tradition encompassed more authentic forms of popular culture: folktales told at

Map 19.1 ESTIMATED REGIONAL VARIATIONS IN FRENCH LITERACY (1780s)

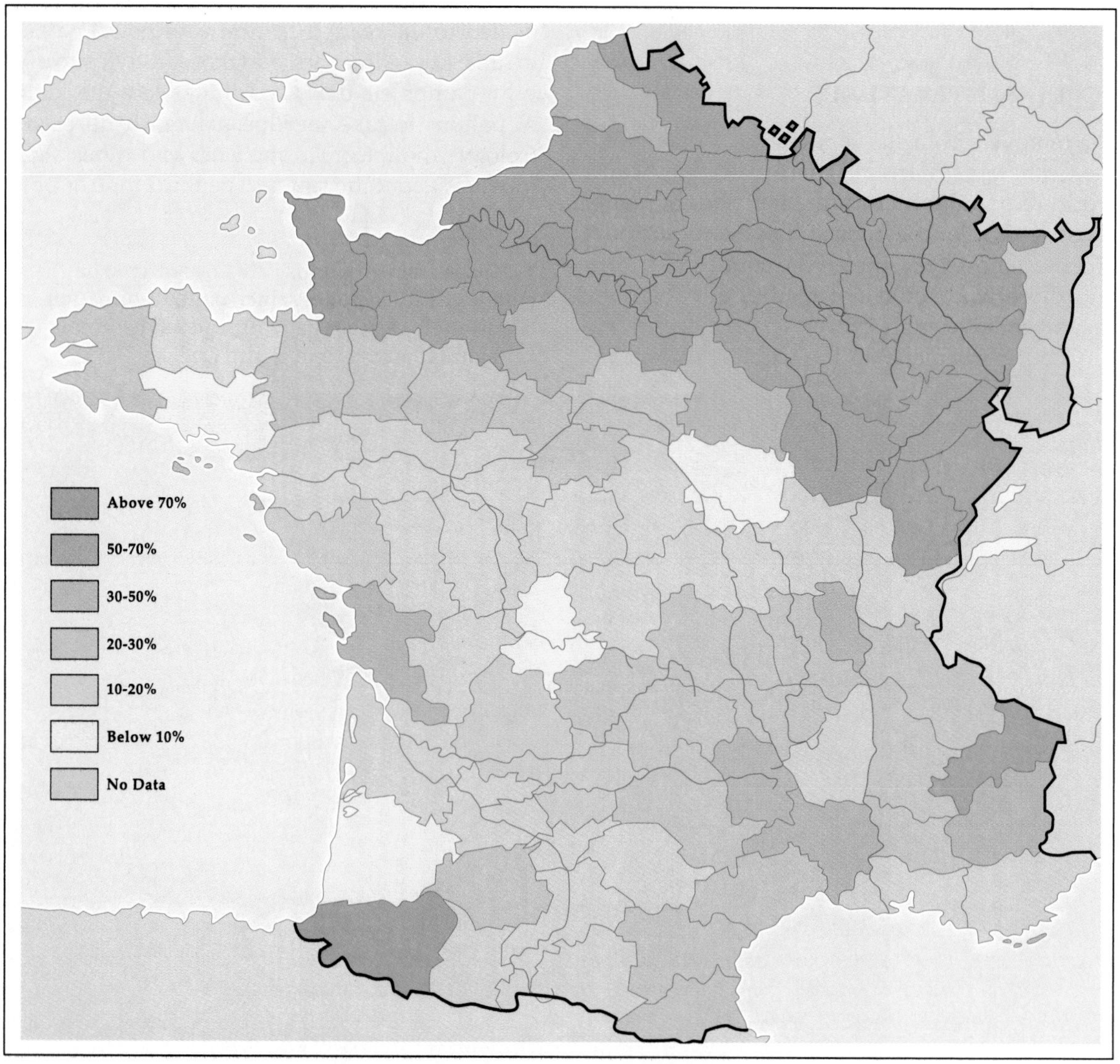

the fireside on long winter nights, songs passed on from generation to generation, sayings that embodied the conventional wisdom of the people.

Themes touching on hunger, sex, or oppression were more likely to turn up in songs or oral tales than in booklets. Songs and tales expressed the joyful bawdiness of ordinary men and women but also the ever-present hardships and dangers of daily life: the endless drudgery of work in the fields, the gnawing ache of an empty stomach, the cruelty of parental neglect or mean stepparents, the desperation of beggars on the road. The most fantastic tales evoked a threatening world where strangers might turn out to be princes or good fairies but might just as well turn into wolves or witches. Oral tradition also celebrated the shrewdness and cunning of ordinary people struggling for survival, in the spirit of the saying: "Better a knave than a fool." Often rendered in local dialects, these tales or songs would have been incomprehensible to an educated Parisian, Londoner, or Viennese.

LITERACY AND PRIMARY SCHOOLING

The Wars of Religion had spurred the spread of literacy and elementary schooling in Europe. Protestantism explicitly promoted literacy so that Christians could read their Bibles directly; strongly Protestant societies such as Scotland, Switzerland, and Sweden had unusually high rates of literacy by the eighteenth century. The Catholic Church, as well, believed that the spread of literacy would serve its cause in the battle against heresy. While teaching reading, Catholic schoolmasters could provide religious instruction and could socialize children into the beliefs and behavior of a Catholic way of life.

A unique study of literacy in France carried out in the late nineteenth century, based on signatures versus X's on parish marriage registers all across the country, indicates a national literacy rate (meaning the ability to read) in 1686 of about 21 percent, which reached 37 percent a century later. These national averages, however, conceal striking regional and social disparities. The south of France had much lower rates than the north/northeast (see Map 19.1), and rural literacy rates lagged significantly behind those of the towns. While agricultural laborers rarely could read, urban artisans were generally literate. The widest gap of all, however, separated men from women, the rates in 1786 being 47 and 27 percent, respectively. Similarly, estimates for England suggest a male literacy rate of slightly under 60 percent and a female rate of about 40 percent.

Primary Education Schooling was not intended to transform society or lift the mass of people out of the situations into which they were born. On the contrary, it was supposed to maintain the social order and reinforce the family in promoting piety and decent behavior among the young. Many among the elites (including Voltaire) were skeptical about the value of education for peasants and laborers. Might it not confuse them, or make it more difficult for them to accept the drudgery to which they seemed destined? Peasant or laboring parents might well have shared such skepticism about educating their young. Education could seem a waste of time when their children could be contributing to the family's livelihood; they might especially begrudge spending the money on tuition that most elementary schooling required.

A village usually hired a schoolmaster in consultation with the pastor or priest; schools usually straddled community and church, since the schoolmaster often served as the pastor's aide. Except in towns that had charitable endowments to support schooling, the parents, the village, or some combination of the two paid the schoolmaster, and for that reason numerous villages did without any schooling. Even a modest tuition could deter impoverished parents from hiring a master, enrolling their children, or keeping them in school for a sufficient time. Since schoolmasters taught reading first and writing separately and later, many pupils, especially girls, were not kept in school long enough to learn how to write anything but their names. Schooling, in other words, was largely demand-driven, the product of a community's level of wealth and interest. When a region achieved a critical mass of literacy, however, interest in schooling generally became more widespread and gradually reached lower down the social scale.

While England and France left primary schooling entirely to the chance of local initiative, the Habsburg Monarchy seriously promoted pri-

▶ **Most eighteenth-century elementary school teachers used the extremely inefficient individual method of instruction, where pupils read to the teacher from whatever book they happened to bring from home, while the other pupils occupied themselves as best they could.**

mary education and thereby became the first Catholic realm to do so. The Habsburg General School Ordinance of 1774 authorized state subsidies, in combination with local funds, for the support of a school in almost every parish. Attendance was supposed to be compulsory, though the state had no way to enforce this. The state also intended to train future teachers at institutions called normal schools. A similar two-pronged strategy was adopted in Prussia under Frederick II at about the same time, although little was done to implement it.

In Prussia, as in most of Europe, schoolmasters remained barely competent and poorly paid. Frederick II indeed had a limiting vision of popular education: "It is enough for the country people to learn only a little reading and writing. . . . Instruction must be planned so that they receive only what is most essential for them but which is designed to keep them in the villages and not influence them to leave." As elsewhere in Europe, the goals of elementary schooling were to inculcate religion and morality, propagate the virtues of hard work, and promote sobriety and deference to one's superiors.

SOCIABILITY AND RECREATION

If the educated elites had their salons, masonic lodges, and learned academies, the common people also formed organized cultural groups. Many journeyman artisans, for example, belonged to secret societies that combined fraternal and trade-union functions. Young unmarried artisans frequently traveled the country, stopping periodically to work with comrades in other towns in order to hone their skills. Artisans also relied on their associations for camaraderie and ritual celebrations. Rivalries among federations of artisan associations occasionally led to pitched battles, however—a far cry from the nineteenth-century ideal of labor solidarity. Married artisans often joined religious confraternities, which honored a patron saint and assured a dignified funeral when they died, or mutual aid societies to which they contributed small monthly dues to pay for assistance if illness or accident should strike.

Corresponding to the coffeehouses of the urban middle classes were the taverns in working-class neighborhoods. These noisy, crowded places catered to a poor clientele, especially on Sunday and on Monday, which working people often took as a day off, honoring (as they put it) "Saint Monday." The urban common people were first beginning to consume wine in the eighteenth century, still something of a luxury except in its cheapest watered form. In England gin was the poor person's drink, cheap and plentiful until the government levied a hefty excise tax after realizing that too many people were drinking themselves into disability and death—a concern depicted in Hogarth's etchings.

More commonly, drinking was not done in that morbid fashion but as part of a healthy and vibrant outdoor life. In England, before the spread of industrialization changed the cultural as well as physical landscape, popular pastimes followed a calendar of holidays that provided occasions for group merrymaking, eating, drinking, dressing-up, contests, and games. Local festivals were particularly comfortable settings for single young men and women to meet each other. The highlight of a country year usually came in early autumn after the summer harvest was in, when most villages held a public feast that lasted several days. In Catholic countries similar festivities

► In his "Gin Lane" etching of 1750, Hogarth depicted the results of excessive gin drinking by the English common people as death, apathy, and moral decay. A cheerful companion piece called "Beer Street," however, suggested that drinking in moderation was an acceptable practice.

were often linked with church rituals. Popular observances included the commemoration of local patron saints, pilgrimages to holy places, and the period of Carnival before Lent.

Sports A growing "commercialization of leisure" in the eighteenth century supported new spectator sports, such as horseracing and boxing matches. Blood sports, constituted a more prevalent popular recreation. Bullbaiting, for example, involved setting loose a pack of dogs on a tethered steer. These events were usually collaborations between a butcher (who provided the steer, its meat to be sold later) and an innkeeper (whose yard served as the arena and who sold refreshments to the spectators). Cockfighting, similar in its gory results, attracted gentlemen and commoners alike, who enjoyed wagering on the outcome.

In early modern Europe, gentlefolk and commoners had been accustomed to mixing in recreational and religious settings: fairs and markets, sporting events, village or town festivals, Carnival in Catholic countries. But in the eighteenth century, as aristocrats and bourgeois alike became more concerned with good manners and refinement, these elite groups began to distance themselves from the bawdy and vulgar behavior of ordinary people. With growing intolerance they censured popular recreational culture in the hope of "reforming" the people into a more sober and orderly life style. Social status was based on birth or wealth, but cultural taste was becoming its behavioral marker.

The philosophes, celebrated members of Europe's cultural establishment by the 1770s, hoped that their society would gradually reform itself under their inspiration. Although these writers criticized their society, they were not its subverters. Distrustful of the uneducated masses—and afraid of popular emotion, superstition, and disorder—they were anything but democrats. Nonetheless, the Enlightenment challenged basic traditional values of European society: from Voltaire's polemics against Christianity through the sober social science of Diderot's *Encyclopedia* to the impassioned writings of Rousseau. Along with a flood of "bad books"—the pornography and scandal sheets of the clandestine publishers—booksellers, writers, and journalists disseminated critical ideas among Europe's educated men and women. The philosophes challenged the automatic respect for convention and authority, promoted the habit of independent reflection, and implanted the conviction that the reform of institutions was both necessary and possible. They promoted a climate in which the status quo was gradually put on the defensive and in which revolution—when provoked under particular circumstances—would not be unthinkable.

Recommended Reading

Sources

Crocker, Lester (ed.). *The Age of Enlightenment.* 1969.

Gendzier, Stephen (ed.). *Denis Diderot: The Encyclopedia: Selections.* 1967.

Mohl, Mary R., and Helene Koon (eds.). *The Female Spectator: English Women Writers Before 1800.* 1977.

*Rousseau, Jean-Jacques. *The Social Contract and Discourses.* 1950.

*Voltaire. *The Portable Voltaire.* 1949, 1977.

Studies

*Baker, Keith. *Condorcet, from Natural Philosophy to Social Mathematics.* 1975. A study of a philosophe who lived to participate in the French Revolution.

Bernard, Paul. *Jesuits and Jacobins: Enlightenment and*

*Available in paperback.

Enlightened Despotism in Austria. 1971. Liberalization and conflict in the Habsburg domain.

Bruford, W. H. *Germany in the Eighteenth Century: The Social Background of the Literary Revival.* 1952.

Capp, Bernard. *English Almanacs, 1500–1800: Astrology and the Popular Press.* 1979. A probing study of the most important genre of popular literature.

*Cassirer, Ernst. *The Question of Jean-Jacques Rousseau.* 1963. Brief and reliable.

*Chartier, Roger. *The Cultural Origins of the French Revolution.* 1991. A synthesis of recent research on publishing, the "public sphere," and the emergence of a new political culture.

*Cragg, G. R. *The Church and the Age of Reason, 1648–1789.* 1966.

Cranston, Maurice. *Jean-Jacques* (2 vols.). 1983, 1991. The most recent study of Rousseau's life and work.

*Crow, Thomas. *Painters and Public Life in Eighteenth-Century Paris.* 1985. A pioneering work on the development of a "public sphere" of critical discourse about art.

Darnton, Robert. *The Business of Enlightenment: A Publishing History of the Encyclopedia.* 1979. The "biography of a book" and of the century's most influential publishing venture.

*———. *The Great Cat Massacre and Other Essays in French Cultural History.* 1984. A notable collection of essays on "the social history of ideas" and on the "mentalities" of peasants and workers.

*———. *The Literary Underground of the Old Regime.* 1982. A pathbreaking book on the clandestine world of hack writers, publishers, and smugglers of illegal books.

Furet, François, and Jacques Ozouf. *Reading and Writing: Literacy in France from Calvin to Jules Ferry.* 1982. An overview of literacy and primary schooling based on quantitative sources.

*Gay, Peter. *The Enlightenment: An Interpretation* (2 vols.). 1966–1969. A masterly, full-bodied exposition of Enlightenment thought.

*———. *Voltaire's Politics: The Poet as Realist.* 1959. A lively and sympathetic portrait.

*Hahn, Roger. *The Anatomy of a Scientific Institution: The Paris Academy of Sciences, 1666–1803.* 1971. The rise and problems of a scientific "establishment."

*Hampson, Norman. *A Cultural History of the Enlightenment.* 1969. A good general introduction.

Herr, Richard. *The Eighteenth-Century Revolution in Spain.* 1958. The reverberations of the Enlightenment in Spain—a case study not discussed in the present text.

*Isherwood, Robert. *Farce and Fantasy: Popular Entertainment in Eighteenth-Century Paris.* 1986. A cultural and institutional history of fairs and popular theater.

Joeres, Ruth-Ellen, and Mary Jo Maynes (eds.). *German Women in the Eighteenth and Nineteenth Centuries.* 1986. Essays on women's writings and women's roles.

Kors, Alan. *D'Holbach's Coterie: An Enlightenment in Paris.* 1976. Focuses on the circle of a leading French atheist.

Korshin, P. J. (ed.). *The Widening Circle: Essays on the Circulation of Literature in Eighteenth-Century Europe.* 1976.

Malcolmson, R. W. *Popular Recreations in English Society, 1700–1850.* 1973. A good survey of a neglected subject.

Melton, James Van Horn. *Absolutism and the Eighteenth-Century Origins of Compulsory Schooling in Prussia and Austria.* 1988. An excellent comparative study.

Palmer, Robert R. *Catholics and Unbelievers in Eighteenth-Century France.* 1939. The response of Catholic intellectuals to the century's philosophic thought.

*Paulson, Ronald. *Hogarth: His Life, Art, and Times* (abridged ed.). 1974.

Payne, Harry. *The Philosophes and the People.* 1976. An analysis of the Enlightenment's liberal elitism.

*Roche, Daniel. *The People of Paris: An Essay on Popular Culture in the Eighteenth Century.* 1987. On the material culture and aspirations of ordinary Parisians.

Schackleton, Robert. *Montesquieu.* 1961. A biography of the French thinker with influence on both sides of the Atlantic.

*Spencer, Samia (ed.). *French Women and the Age of Enlightenment.* 1984. A pioneering collection of essays on a variety of literary and historical themes.

Venturi, Franco. *Italy and the Enlightenment.* 1972. Essays on important Italian philosophes by a leading historian.

*Watt, Ian. *The Rise of the Novel: Studies of Defoe, Richardson, and Fielding.* 1957. The view from England.

Wilson, Arthur. *Diderot.* 1972. An exhaustive, reliable biography of the consummate French philosophe.

The storming of the Bastille.

CHAPTER TWENTY

THE FRENCH REVOLUTION

MOST eighteenth-century monarchs and princes still claimed to hold their authority directly from God and presided over realms composed of distinct orders of citizens, or *estates*, each with its own rights, privileges, and obligations. But forces for change had been building during the century. In France Enlightenment writers, who rarely questioned the basic forms of government, had nonetheless helped to create a "public sphere" of political discourse outside the framework of official monarchical institutions. In contrast, self-confident monarchs in Austria, Prussia, and Russia cultivated a new style of ruling as they imposed reforms from above. Royal innovations there and elsewhere, however, usually met with resistance from aristocracies or local oligarchies who resented encroachments on their privileges. Conflicts over political exclusion and empowerment also erupted in Britain, and in Britain's American colonies local resentments exploded into outright rebellion.

Without question, however, the pivotal event of European history in the eighteenth century was the French Revolution. From its outbreak in 1789, the Revolution transformed the social values and political system of France and resonated across the borders of other European states. When war broke out in 1792, French armies carried revolutionary ideology into neighboring states. Both at home and abroad the new regime faced formidable opposition, and its struggle for survival propelled it in unanticipated directions. The French Revolution's ideals defined the basic aspirations of modern liberal society, but its bloody events dramatized the brutal dilemma of ends versus means.

I. Reform and Political Crisis

"ENLIGHTENED ABSOLUTISM" IN CENTRAL AND EASTERN EUROPE

During the late nineteenth century, German historians invented the concept of "enlightened absolutism" to describe the Prussian and Habsburg monarchies of the eighteenth century. Critical of the ineptitude and weakness of French monarchs in that period, these historians argued that the strength of an enlightened ruler had been the surest basis for progress in early modern Europe. A king who ruled in his subjects' interest, they implied, avoided violent conflicts like those of the French Revolution. Earlier strong monarchs such as Philip II of Spain and France's Louis XIV (who had once declared: "I am the state") had been irresponsible; in contrast, these German historians argued, Frederick II of Prussia symbolized the "enlightened" phase of absolutism with his comment that the ruler is merely the "first servant of the state."

Earlier chapters, however, have demonstrated that monarchs dealt with the same fundamental issues during all stages of absolutism. They always strove to assert their authority over their subjects and to maximize the power of their state in relation to other realms, principally by means of territorial expansion. Any notion that Enlightenment thinking caused monarchs to desist from these efforts is misleading. Still, several eighteenth-century monarchs did initiate reforms from above and did modify their styles of ruling in order to appear more modern or enlightened. Frederick II of Prussia and Catherine II of Russia, for example, lavished praise on Voltaire and Denis Diderot, and those philosophes returned the compliment. For these rulers it may have been simply a question of public relations. Yet the fact that they found it desirable to seem supportive of such controversial writers suggests that absolutism had indeed adopted a new image.

Catherine the Great (who reigned from 1762 to 1796) played this game to its limit. In 1767 she announced a new experiment in the direction of representative government—a policy hailed as a landmark by her philosophe admirers, who were too remote from St. Petersburg to see its insincerity. Catherine convened a Legislative Commission, a body of delegates from various strata of Russian society who were invited to present grievances, propose reforms, and then debate the proposals. In the end, however, she sent the delegates home under the pretext of having to turn her attention to a war with Turkey. Little came of the Legislative Commission except some good publicity for Catherine. In fact, she later promulgated a Charter of the Nobility, which, instead of limiting the nobility's privileges, strengthened their corporate status and increased their control over their serfs in exchange for their loyalty to the throne.

Conceptions of Enlightened Rule in Germany In justification of absolute monarchy, eighteenth-century German writers depicted the state as a machine and the ruler as its mainspring. Progress came from sound administration, through an enlightened monarch and well-trained officials. In keeping with this notion, German universities began to train government bureaucrats, and professors offered courses in the science of public finance and administration called *cameralism.* Before long the governments of Prussia and Austria introduced the rudiments of a civil service system.

The orders for the bureaucracy came from the monarchs, who were expected to dedicate themselves to the welfare of their subjects in return for their subjects' obedience. The framework for this command-obedience chain was to be a coherent body of public law, fairly administered by state officials. According to its advocates, this system would produce the rule of law, a *Rechtsstaat,* without the need for a written constitution or a representative parliament. The ruler and his or her officials, following their sense of public responsibility and rational analysis, would ensure the citizen's rights and well-being.

JOSEPH II AND THE LIMITS OF ABSOLUTISM

Joseph II—coruler of the Habsburg Empire with his mother, Maria Theresa, from 1765 and sole ruler in the 1780s—vigorously promoted reform from above. Unlike Frederick or Catherine, he did not openly identify with the philosophes, and he maintained his own Catholic faith. But Joseph proved to be the most innovative of the century's major rulers, as well as one of its most autocratic personalities. It was a problematic combination.

Sound rule for Emperor Joseph involved far more than the customary administrative and financial modernization necessary for survival in the competitive state system. With startling boldness he implemented several reforms long advocated by Enlightenment thinkers: freedom of expression, religious toleration, greater state control over the Catholic Church, and legal reform. A new criminal code, for example, reduced the use of the death penalty, ended judicial torture, and allowed for no class differences in the application of the laws. By greatly reducing royal censorship, Joseph made it possible for Vienna to become a major center of literary activity. And we have already noted Joseph's remarkable Edicts of Religious Toleration for Protestants and for Jews. But Joseph's religious policies did not stop there. To make the Catholic Church serve its parishioners better, Joseph forced the clergy to modernize its rituals and services. Most of his Catholic subjects, however, preferred their traditional ways to Joseph's streamlined brand of Catholicism. These "reforms" proved extremely unpopular.

Agrarian Reform Joseph's most ambitious policies aimed to transform the economic and social position of the peasants. In this respect the Habsburg emperor acted far more boldly than any other eighteenth-century sovereign. Agrarian reform was generally the weak side of "enlightened absolutism," since Frederick II and Catherine II did little to improve the lot of the peasants or serfs in their realms. Joseph, however, set out to eradicate serfdom and to convert Habsburg peasants into free individuals in command of their persons and of the land they cultivated.

By royal decree Joseph abolished personal servitude and gave peasants the right to move, marry, and enter any trade they wished. He then promulgated laws to secure peasants' control over the land they worked. Finally and most remarkably, he sought to limit the financial obligations of peasant tenants to their lords and to the state. All land was to be surveyed and subject to a uniform tax. Twelve percent of the land's annual yield would go to the state and a maxi-

▶ Joseph II, shown here visiting a peasant's field, actually promulgated his momentous agrarian reform edicts without any significant consultation with the peasants before or after the fact.

mum of 18 percent would go to the lord, in place of previous seigneurial obligations in which peasants owed service to their lord that could consume more than 100 days' labor a year.

Joseph ordered these reforms in an authoritarian fashion, with little consultation and no consent from any quarter. Predictably, they provoked fierce opposition among the landowning nobles. But they also perplexed most peasants, who already distrusted the government because of its arbitrary religious policies. Joseph made no effort to build support among the peasants by carefully explaining the reforms, let alone by modifying their details after getting feedback from the grass roots. As a sympathetic chronicler of Joseph's reign observed, "He brought in his beneficial measures in an arbitrary manner."

His arbitrary manner, however, was not incidental. Joseph acknowledged no other way of doing things, no limitation on his own sovereignty. In reaction to the opposition that his reforms aroused he moved to suppress dissent in the firmest possible way. Not only did he restore censorship in his last years, but he elevated the police department to the status of an imperial ministry and gave it unprecedented powers. By the time he died, in 1790, Joseph was a disillusioned man. His realm resembled less a *Rechtsstaat* than a police state, and his successors quickly restored serfdom.

CONSTITUTIONAL CRISES IN THE WEST

While "enlightened absolutists" reigned in Austria, Prussia, and Russia, political tension and spirited debate over the institutions of government erupted in several Western European countries. To understand these crises we must recall the role of *estates* in European history. The term is both a social and a political signifier. Socially, every person belonged to one legally distinct order or another. The clergy usually constituted the First Estate of the realm, the nobles formed the Second Estate, and both maintained a common aristocratic viewpoint. The remainder of the population constituted the Third Estate. In the past the estates had sent representatives to national and provincial assemblies or diets, which shared in making government decisions. But absolutism had drastically curtailed the political role of the estates, as we have seen in previous chapters. It was the Third Estate's new bid for prominence and power in several countries at the expense of the dominant aristocratic orders that made the late eighteenth century, as one historian calls it, "the age of the democratic revolution."

Monarchs and Aristocrats On one level monarchs and the privileged orders were perennial and natural rivals. The rights and privileges of various groups, especially but not solely the aristocratic orders, reduced the fiscal resources of kings and princes and hampered their ability to pursue internal reform. The privileges and monopolies enjoyed by provinces, towns, and guilds restrained trade, hampered economic growth, and militated against the common welfare. Eighteenth-century struggles over political power often began when rulers initiated changes in traditional political or economic arrangements. While monarchs might wish to allocate a smaller place to nobles in the business of government, nobles would not willingly cede the privileges they held and might demand an even larger share in the exercise of power.

Aristocracies all over Europe thus sought to advance their fortunes and consolidate their roles in their country's traditional or unwritten constitutions. Armed perhaps with the ideas of the French philosophe Montesquieu, who held that privilege is the bulwark of liberty, nobles claimed that they had the exclusive right to serve as ministers of the king as well as the obligation to lead the community in the conduct of its important affairs. In the last decades of the century, the nobility continued to enjoy a near monopoly over high offices in the state, the army, and the Church. In 1781, for example, officers' commissions in the French army were limited almost exclusively to those who could prove descent from four generations of nobility. Aristocrats in several countries demanded that local assemblies of estates, which they expected to dominate, be granted a larger share of political power.

Upheavals over such issues erupted in the Austrian Netherlands (Belgium) and in the Dutch Netherlands, where provincial oligarchies rebelled against the centralizing reforms of their princes: Joseph II in Belgium and the Prince of Orange in the Dutch Netherlands. In each case a more democratic element of unprivileged commoners, including urban artisans, turned these conflicts into triangular struggles, as they took up arms to oppose both princely tyranny and oligarchic privilege. To a certain extent, these Dutch and Belgian "patriots," as they called themselves, provided a foretaste of the French Revolution. Their suppression, in turn, suggested that "counterrevolution" was a force to be reckoned with.

UPHEAVALS IN THE BRITISH EMPIRE

An aggressive monarch, George III, helped ignite political unrest in Great Britain. Unlike his Hanoverian predecessors George I and George II, this king had been born in England and knew its language and its political system well. He was intent on advancing royal authority, but rather than bypass Parliament altogether he simply tried, as Whig ministers had before him, to control its members through patronage and influence. The Whig aristocrats saw this operation as a threat to their own traditional power. Not only did they oppose the king and his ministers in Parliament, but they enlisted the support of citizens' groups outside of Parliament as well. These organizations were calling for political reform, including representation in Parliament proportionate to population, stricter laws against political corruption, and greater freedom of the press.

"Wilkes and Liberty" John Wilkes, a member of Parliament and a journalist, became the center of this rising storm. Wilkes viciously attacked the king's prime minister, and by implication the king himself, over the terms of the Treaty of Paris, which ended the Seven Years' War in 1763. The government arrested him for seditious libel on a general warrant. When the courts quashed the indictment, the government then accused Wilkes of having authored a libelous pornographic poem, and this time he fled to France to avoid prison. He stayed there for four years; but in 1768, still under indictment, he returned to stand once more for Parliament. Three times he was reelected, and three times the House of Commons refused to seat him. With the ardent support of radicals and to the acclaim of crowds in London, who marched to the chant of "Wilkes and Liberty," Wilkes finally took his seat in 1774.

Agitation for parliamentary reform drew support primarily from "solid citizens": shopkeepers, artisans, and property owners who had the franchise in a few districts but were denied it in most others. Thus even without a right to vote, English citizens could engage in politics and mobilize the power of public opinion, in this case by rallying to Wilkes. Most radicals called only for political reform, not for the overthrow of the British political system. They retained a measure of respect for the nation's political traditions, which ideally guaranteed the rights of "freeborn Englishmen."

Rebellion in America Great Britain did face revolutionary action in her 13 North American colonies. George III and his prime minister, Lord North, attempted to force the colonies to pay the costs, past and present, of their own defense. The policy would have meant an increase in taxes and a centralization of authority in the governance of the British empire. Colonial landowners, merchants, and artisans of the eastern seaboard organized petitions and boycotts in opposition to the proposed fiscal and constitutional changes.

The resistance in North America differed fundamentally from comparable movements in Europe. American political leaders did not appeal to a body of privileges that the actions of the monarchy were allegedly violating. Instead they appealed to traditional rights supposedly enjoyed by all British subjects, regardless of status, and to theories of popular sovereignty and natural rights advanced by John Locke and other English libertarian writers. When conciliation and compromise with the British government failed, the American Declaration of Independence in 1776 gave eloquent expression to those concepts. The lack of a rigid system of estates and hereditary privileges in American society, the fluid boundaries that separated the social strata, and the traditions of local government in the colonies—from town meetings in New England to the elected legislatures that had advised colonial governors—blunted the kinds of conflicts between aristocrats and commoners that derailed incipient revolutionary movements in Ireland, Belgium, and the Dutch Netherlands.

These differences help to explain the unique character of the American rebellion, which was

▶ **The committee that drafted the American Declaration of Independence included John Adams, Thomas Jefferson, and Benjamin Franklin, all shown here standing at the desk.**

simultaneously a war for independence and a political revolution. The theories that supported the rebellion, and the continuing alliance between social strata, made it the most democratic revolution of the eighteenth century before 1789. The American Revolution created the first state governments, and ultimately a national government, in which the exercise of power was grounded not on royal sovereignty or traditional privilege but on the participation and consent of the citizens (apart from the numerous black slaves, whose status did not change). Even more important as an historical precedent, perhaps, it was the first successful rebellion by overseas colonies against their European masters.

II. 1789: The French Revolution

Although the rebellion in America stirred sympathy and interest across the Atlantic, it seemed remote from the realities of Europe. The French Revolution of 1789 proved to be the turning point in European history. Its sheer radicalism, creativity, and claims of universalism made it unique. Its ultimate slogan—"Liberty, Equality, Fraternity"—expressed social and civic ideals that became the foundations of modern Western civilization. In the name of individual liberty, French revolutionaries swept away the institutionalized constraints of the old regime: seigneurial charges upon the land, vestiges of feudalism, tax privileges, guild monopolies on commerce, and even (in 1794) black slavery overseas. The revolutionaries held that legitimate governments required written constitutions, elections, and powerful legislatures. They demanded equality before the law for all persons and uniformity of institutions for all regions of the country, denying the claims to special treatment of privileged groups, provinces, towns, or religions. The term *fraternity* expressed a different kind of revolutionary goal. Rousseauist in inspiration, it meant that all citizens regardless of social class or region shared a common fate in society and that the nation's well-being could override the interests of individual citizens.

ORIGINS OF THE REVOLUTION

Those who made the Revolution believed they were rising against despotic government, in which citizens had no voice, and against inequality and privilege. Yet the government of France at that time was no more tyrannical or unjust than it had been in the past. On the contrary, a process of reform had been under way for several decades. What, then, set off the revolutionary upheaval? What had failed in France's long-standing political system?

An easy answer would be to point to the incompetence of King Louis XVI (who reigned from 1774 to 1792) and his queen, Marie Antoinette. Louis was good-natured but weak and indecisive, a man of limited intelligence who lacked self-confidence and who preferred hunting deer to supervising the business of government. By no stretch of the imagination was he an "enlightened absolutist." Worse yet, his young queen, a Habsburg princess, was frivolous, meddlesome, and tactless. But even the most capable ruler could not have escaped challenge and unrest in the 1780s. It is the roots of the political crisis, not its mismanagement, that claim the historian's attention.

The Cultural Climate In eighteenth-century France, as we have seen, intellectual ferment preceded political revolt. For decades the philosophes had questioned accepted political and religious beliefs. They undermined the old confidence that traditional ways were the best ways. But the philosophes harbored deep-seated fears of the uneducated masses and did not question the notion that educated and propertied elites should rule society; they wished only that the elites should be more enlightened and more open to new ideas. Indeed, the Enlightenment had become respectable by the 1770s, a kind of intellectual establishment. Rousseau damned that establishment and wrote of the need for simplicity, sincerity, and virtue, but the word *revolution* never flowed from his pen either.

More subversive perhaps than the writings of Enlightenment intellectuals were the "bad books," the clandestine flow of gossip sheets, libels, and pornography that indirectly, at least, portrayed the French aristocracy as decadent and the monarchy as a ridiculous despotism. Royal officials and philosophes alike regarded the authors of this material as "the excrement of literature," as Voltaire put it. And writers forced to earn their living by turning out such stuff must have been embittered by their plight. Their resentment at being stuck on the bottom rung in the world of letters would explode once the Revolution began in 1789, and many became radical journalists either for or against the new regime. In itself, however, this "literary underground" of the old regime did not cause the Revolution.

Class Conflict? Did the structure of French society, then, provoke the Revolution? Karl Marx, and the many historians inspired by him, certainly believed so. Marx saw the French Revolution as the necessary break marking the transition from the aristocratic feudalism of the Middle Ages to the era of middle-class capitalism. In the words of historian Georges Lefebvre, "The clergy and nobility preserved the highest rank in the legal structure of the country, but in reality economic power, personal abilities and confidence in the future had passed largely to the bourgeoisie. Such a discrepancy never lasts forever. The Revolution of 1789 restored the harmony between fact and law." In this view, the French bourgeoisie, or middle classes, had been gaining in wealth during the eighteenth century and resented the privileges of the nobility, which placed obstacles in the path of their ambition. Though they framed their ideology in universal terms in 1789, the middle classes led the Revolution in order to change the political and social systems in their own interests.

Three decades of research have rendered this

theory of the Revolution's origins untenable. Whether a sizable and coherent capitalist middle class actually existed in eighteenth-century France is questionable. In any case, the leaders of the Revolution in 1789 were lawyers, administrators, and liberal nobles, and rarely merchants or industrialists. Moreover, the barrier between the nobility of the Second Estate and the wealthy and educated members of the Third Estate was porous, the lines of social division frequently (though not always) blurred. Many members of the middle class identified themselves on official documents as "living nobly"—as substantial property owners who did not work for a living. Conversely, wealthy nobles often invested in mining, overseas trade, and finance—activities usually associated with the middle classes. Even more important, the gap between the nobility and the middle classes was as nothing compared with the gulf that separated both from the working people of town and country. In this revisionist historiography, the bourgeoisie did not make the Revolution, so much as the Revolution made the bourgeoisie.

Yet numerous disruptive pressures were at work in French society. A growing population left large numbers of young people in the countryside and the towns struggling to attain a stable place in society. New images and attitudes rippled through the media of the day, despite the state's efforts to censor material it deemed subversive. The nobility, long-since banished by Louis XIV from an independent role in monarchical government, chafed at its exclusion, while the prosperous middle classes too aspired to a more active role. The monarchy struggled to contain these forces within the established social and political systems. Until the 1780s it succeeded, but then its troubles began in earnest.

FISCAL CRISIS AND POLITICAL IMPASSE

When he took the throne in 1774, Louis XVI tried to conciliate elite opinion by recalling the Parlements, or sovereign law courts, that his grandfather had banished in 1770 for their opposition to his policies. This concession to France's traditional "unwritten constitution" did not suffice to smooth the new sovereign's road. Louis' new controller-general of finances, Jacques Turgot, encountered a storm of opposition from privileged groups to the modest reforms he proposed.

Turgot, an ally of the philosophes and an experienced administrator, hoped to encourage economic growth by a policy of nonintervention, or laissez-faire, that would give free play to economic markets and allow individuals maximum freedom to pursue their own economic interests. He proposed to remove all restrictions on commerce in grain and to abolish the guilds. In addition, he tried to cut down on expenses at court and to replace the obligation of peasants to work on the royal roads (the *corvée*) with a small new tax on all landholders. Privately, he also considered establishing elected advisory assemblies of landowners to assist in local administration. Vested interests, however, viewed Turgot as a dangerous innovator. When agitation against him mounted in the king's court at Versailles and in the Paris Parlement, Louis took the easy way out and dismissed his contentious minister. With Turgot went perhaps the last hope for significant reform in France under royal leadership.

Deficit Financing The king then turned to Jacques Necker, a banker from Geneva who had a reputation for financial wizardry. Necker had a shrewd sense of public relations. To finance the heavy costs of France's aid to the rebellious British colonies in North America, Necker avoided new taxes, which gained him wide popularity, and instead floated a series of large loans at exorbitant interest rates as high as 10 percent. (England, through sound management of its public finances and public confidence in the government, financed its war effort with loans at only 3 or 4 percent interest.)

By the 1780s royal finances hovered in a state of permanent crisis. Direct taxes on land, borne mainly by the peasants, were extremely high but were levied inequitably. The great variations in taxation from province to province and the numerous exemptions for privileged groups were regarded by those who benefited from them as traditional liberties. Any attempt to revoke these privileges therefore appeared to be tyrannical. Meanwhile indirect taxes on commercial activity (customs duties, excise or sales taxes, and royal monopolies on salt and tobacco) hit regressively at consumers, especially in the towns. Any tax increases or new taxes imposed by the monarchy at this point would be bitterly resented. At the same time, the cycle of borrowing—the alternative to increased taxes—had reached its limits. New loans would only raise the huge interest payments already being paid out. By the 1780s those payments accounted for about half of the royal budget and created additional budget deficits of perhaps 150,000,000 livres each year!

Calonne and the Assembly of Notables When the king's new controller-general, Charles Calonne, pieced all this information together in 1787, he warned that, contrary to Necker's rosy projections, the monarchy was facing outright bankruptcy. Though no way had yet been found to win public confidence and forge a consensus for fiscal reform, the monarchy had to act and could no longer rely on old expedients. Bold innovations were essential. Calonne accordingly proposed to establish a new tax, called the *territorial subvention,* to be levied on the yield of all landed property without exemptions. At the same time, he proposed to convene *provincial assemblies* elected by large landowners to advise royal officials on the collection and allocation of revenues.

Certain that the Parlements would reject this scheme, Calonne convinced the king to convene an Assembly of Notables, comprising about 150 influential men, mainly but not exclusively from the aristocracy, who might more easily be persuaded to support the reforms. To Calonne's shock, the Assembly of Notables refused to endorse the proposed decrees. Instead, they denounced the lavish spending of the court and insisted on auditing the monarchy's financial accounts. To save the day, Louis dismissed Calonne and appointed one of the notables, Archbishop Brienne, in his place. Brienne now submitted Calonne's proposals to the Parlement, which not only rejected them but also demanded that Louis convene the Estates General, a body representing the clergy, nobility, and Third Estate, which had not met since 1614. Louis responded by sending the members of the Parlements into exile. But a huge outcry in Paris and in the provinces against this arbitrary act forced the king to back down: After all, the whole purpose of Calonne's proposals had been to build public confidence in the government.

Facing bankruptcy and unable to float new loans in this atmosphere, the King recalled the Parlements, reappointed Necker, and agreed to convene the Estates General in May 1789. In the opinion of the English writer Arthur Young, who was visiting France, the kingdom was "on the verge of a revolution, but one likely to add to the scale of the nobility and clergy." The aristocracy's determined opposition was putting an end to absolutism in France. But it was not clear what would take its place.

FROM THE ESTATES GENERAL TO THE NATIONAL ASSEMBLY

The calling of the Estates General in 1789 created extraordinary excitement across the land. The king invited his subjects to express their opinions about this great event, and thousands did so in pamphlet form. Here the "patriot," or liberal, ideology first took shape. Self-styled patriots came from the ranks of the nobility and clergy as well as from the middle classes; they opposed traditionalists, whom they labeled as "aristocrats." Their top priority was the method of voting to be used in the Estates General. While the king accorded the Third Estate twice as many delegates as the two higher orders, he refused to promise that the deputies would all vote together (by head) rather than separately in three chambers (by order). Voting by order would mean that the two upper chambers would outweigh the Third Estate no matter how many deputies it had. Patriots had hoped that the lines dividing the nobility from the middle class would crumble in a common effort by France's elites at reform. Instead, it appeared as if the Estates General might sharpen the lines of separation between the orders.

The Critique of Privilege It did not matter that the nobility had led the fight against absolutism. Even if they endorsed new constitutional checks on absolutism and accepted equality in the allocation of taxes, nobles would still hold vastly disproportionate powers if the Estates General voted by order. In the most influential pamphlet about the Estates General, Emmanuel Sieyès posed the question "What is the Third Estate?"

Thousands of pamphlets were published to discuss the calling of the Estates General in 1789, but the grievances and claims of the Third Estate translated most readily into vivid imagery and caricature; this print was titled "The Awakening of the Third Estate."

and answered flatly "Everything." "And what has it been until now in the political order?" he asked. Answer: "Nothing." The nobility, he claimed, monopolized all the lucrative positions in society while doing little of its productive work. In the manifestos of Sieyès and other patriots, the enemy was no longer simply absolutism but privilege as well.

Unlike reformers in England, or the Belgian rebels against Joseph II, or even the American revolutionaries of 1776, the French patriots did not simply claim that the king had violated historic traditions of liberty. Rather, they contemplated a complete break with a discredited past. As a basis for reform, they would substitute reason for tradition. It is this frame of mind that made the French Revolution so radical.

Cahiers and Elections For the moment, however, the patriot spokesmen stood far in advance of opinion at the grass roots. The king had invited all citizens to meet in their local parishes to elect delegates to district electoral assemblies and to draft grievance petitions (*cahiers*) setting forth their views. The great majority of rural *cahiers* were highly traditional in tone and complained only of particular local ills or high taxes, expressing confidence that the king would redress them. Only a few *cahiers* from cities like Paris invoked concepts of natural rights and popular sovereignty, or demanded that France must have a written constitution, that sovereignty belonged to the nation, or that feudalism and regional privileges should be abolished. It is impossible, in other words, to read in the *cahiers* the future course of the Revolution. Still, these gatherings of citizens promoted reflection on France's problems and encouraged expectations for change. They thereby helped raise the nation's political consciousness.

So too did the local elections, whose royal ground rules were remarkably democratic. Virtually every adult male taxpayer was eligible to vote for electors, who, in turn, met in district assemblies to choose representatives of the Third Estate to the Estates General. The electoral assemblies were a kind of political seminar, where articulate local leaders emerged to be sent by their fellow citizens as deputies to Versailles. Most of these deputies were lawyers or officials, without a single peasant or artisan among them. In the elections for the First Estate, meanwhile, parish priests rather than Church notables formed a majority of the deputies. And in the elections for the Second Estate, about one-third of the deputies could be described as liberal nobles or patriots, the rest traditionalists.

Deadlock and Revolution Popular expectation that the monarchy would provide leadership in reform proved to be ill-founded. When the deputies to the Estates General met on May 5, Necker and Louis XVI spoke to them only in generalities and left unsettled whether the estates would vote by order or by head. The upper two estates proceeded to organize their own chambers, but the deputies of the Third Estate balked. Vainly inviting the others to join them, the Third Estate took a decisive revolutionary step on June 17 by proclaiming that it formed a "National Assembly." A few days later over a third of the deputies from the clergy joined them. The king, on the other hand, decided to cast his lot with the nobility and locked the Third Estate out of its meeting hall until he could present his own program. But the deputies moved to an indoor tennis court and swore that they would not separate until they had given France a constitution.

The king ignored this act of defiance and addressed the delegates of all three orders on June 23. He promised equality in taxation, civil liber-

▸ When the king opened the meeting of the Estates General, the deputies for each estate were directed to sit in three separate sections of the hall.

▸ **Jacques-Louis David's depiction of the Tennis Court Oath, one of the great historical paintings, captures the deputies' sense of idealism and purpose.**

ties, and regular meetings of the Estates General at which, however, voting would be by order. France would be provided with a constitution, he pledged, "but the ancient distinction of the three orders will be conserved in its entirety." He then ordered the three estates to retire to their individual meeting halls, but the Third Estate refused to move. "The assembled nation cannot receive orders," declared its spokesman. Startled by the determination of the patriots, the king backed down. For the time being, he recognized the National Assembly and ordered deputies from all three estates to join it.

Thus the French Revolution began as a nonviolent, "legal" revolution. By their own will, delegates elected by France's three estates to represent their own districts to the king became instead the representatives of the entire nation. As such, they claimed to be the sovereign power in France—a claim that the king now seemed powerless to contest. In fact, however, he was merely biding his time until he could deploy his army to subdue the capital and overwhelm the deputies at Versailles. Twenty thousand royal troops were ordered into the Paris region, due to arrive sometime in July.

THE CONVERGENCE OF REVOLUTIONS

The political struggle at Versailles was not occurring in isolation. The mass of French citizens, politically aroused by elections to the Estates General, was also mobilizing over subsistence issues. The winter and spring of 1788–89 had brought severe economic difficulties, as crop failures and grain shortages almost doubled the price of flour and bread on which the population depended for subsistence. Unemployed vagrants filled the roads, angry consumers stormed grain convoys and marketplaces, and relations between town and country grew tense. Economic anxieties merged with rage over the obstructive behavior of aristocrats in Versailles. Parisians believed that food shortages and royal troops would be used to intimidate the people into submission. They feared an "aristocratic plot" against the National Assembly and the patriot cause.

The Fall of the Bastille When the King dismissed the popular Necker on July 11, Parisians correctly assumed that a counterrevolution was about to begin. They prepared to resist, and most of the king's military units pulled back. On July 14 Parisian crowds searching for weapons and ammunition laid siege to the Bastille, an old fortress that had served as a royal prison, where gunpowder was stored. The small garrison resisted, and a fierce firefight erupted. Although the troops soon capitulated, dozens of citizens were hit, providing the first martyrs of the Revolution, and the infuriated crowd massacred several soldiers as they left the fortress. Meanwhile, patriot electors ousted royal officials of the Paris city government, replaced them with a revolutionary municipality, and organized a citizens' militia to patrol the city. Similar municipal revolutions occurred in 26 of the 30 largest French cities, thus ensuring that the defiance in the capital would not be an isolated act.

The Parisian insurrection of July 14 not only saved the National Assembly but altered the Revolution's course by giving it a far more popular dimension. Again the king capitulated. He traveled to Paris on July 17 and, to please the

The fall of the Bastille was understood at the time to be a great turning point in history, and July 14 eventually became the French national holiday. Numerous prints and paintings evoke the daunting qualities of the fortress, the determination of the besieging crowd, and the heroism of individuals in that crowd.

people, donned a ribbon bearing three colors: white for the monarchy and blue and red for the capital. This *tricolor* would become the emblem of the new regime.

Rural Revolt and the August 4 Decree These events did not pacify the anxious and hungry people of the countryside. Peasants had numerous and long-standing grievances. Population growth and the parceling of holdings reduced the margin of subsistence for many families, while the purchase of land by rich townspeople further shrank their opportunities for economic advancement. Seigneurial dues and church tithes weighed heavily on many peasants. Now, in addition, suspicions were rampant that nobles were hoarding grain in order to stymie the patriotic cause. In July peasants in several regions sacked the castles of the nobles and burned the documents that recorded their feudal obligations.

This peasant insurgency blended into a vast movement known to historians as "the Great Fear." Rumors abounded that the vagrants who swarmed through the countryside were actually "brigands" in the pay of nobles, who were marching on villages to destroy the new harvest and cow the peasants into submission. The fear was baseless, but it stirred up the peasants' hatred and suspicion of the nobles, prompted armed mobilizations in hundreds of villages, and set off new attacks on manor houses.

Peasant insurgency worried the deputies of the National Assembly, but they decided to appease the peasants rather than simply denounce their violence. On the night of August 4, therefore, certain deputies of the nobility and clergy dramatically renounced their ancient privileges. This set the stage for the Assembly to decree "the abolition of feudalism" as well as the end of the church tithe, the sale of royal offices, regional tax privileges, and social privilege of all kinds. Later, it is true, the Assembly clarified the August 4 decree to ensure that property rights were maintained. While personal servitudes such as hunting rights, manorial justice, and labor services were suppressed outright, the Assembly decreed that most seigneurial dues would end only after the peasants had paid compensation to their lords. Peasants resented this onerous requirement, and most simply refused to pay the dues; pressure built until all seigneurial dues were finally abolished without compensation by a more radical government in 1793.

The Declaration of the Rights of Man By sweeping away the old web of privileges, the August 4 decree permitted the Assembly to construct a new regime. Since it would take months to draft a constitution, the Assembly drew up a Declaration of the Rights of Man and Citizen to indicate its intentions (*see box*, p. 651). The Declaration was the death certificate of the old regime and a rallying point for the future. It affirmed individual liberties but also set forth the basic obligation of citizenship: obedience to legitimate law. The Declaration enumerated natural rights such as freedom of expression and freedom of religious conscience but stipulated that even these rights could be circumscribed by law. It proclaimed the sovereignty of the nation and sketched the basic criteria for a legitimate government, which the constitution would eventually amplify, such as representation and the separation of powers. The Declaration's concept of natural rights meant that the new regime would be based on the principles of reason rather than history or tradition.

In his *Reflections on the Revolution in France*, published in 1790, the Anglo-Irish statesman Edmund Burke condemned this attitude, as well as the violence of 1789. In this influential counterrevolutionary tract, Burke argued that France had passed from despotism to anarchy in the name of misguided, abstract principles. Burke distrusted the simplicity of reason that the Assembly celebrated. In his view the complexity of traditional institutions served the public interest. Burke attacked the belief in natural rights that guided the revolutionaries; something was natural, he believed, only if it resulted from long historical development and habit. Trying to wipe the slate of history clean was a grievous error, he wrote, since society "is a contract between the dead, the living, and the unborn." Society's main right, in Burke's view, was the right to be well-governed by its rulers. Naturally this argument did not go unchallenged, even in England. Mary Wollstonecraft countered with *A Vindication of the Rights of Man*, while Thomas Paine's *The Rights of Man*, published in 1792 to refute Burke, won a larger readership than Burke's tract.

Two Views of the Rights of Man

The radical theoretical and practical implications of French revolutionary ideology are suggested in a comparison of two essentially contemporaneous documents. The Prussian General Code, a codification initiated by Frederick the Great and issued in its final form in 1791 after his death, reinforced the traditional prerogatives of the nobility under an umbrella of public law. The National Assembly's Declaration of the Rights of Man and Citizen (1789) established the principle of civil equality, alongside the doctrines of national sovereignty, representation, and the rule of law. While the Prussian General Code exemplifies the old order against which French revolutionary ideology took aim, the Declaration became a foundational document of the liberal tradition.

EXCERPTS FROM "THE PRUSSIAN GENERAL CODE," 1791

- This general code contains the provisions by which the rights and obligations of inhabitants of the state, so far as they are not determined by particular laws, are to be judged.
- The rights of a man arise from his birth, from his estate, and from actions and arrangements with which the laws have associated a certain determinate effect.
- The general rights of man are grounded on the natural liberty to seek and further his own welfare, without injury to the rights of another.
- Persons to whom, by their birth, destination or principal occupation, equal rights are ascribed in civil society, make up together an *estate* of the state.
- The nobility, as the first estate in the state, most especially bears the obligation, by its distinctive destination, to maintain the defense of the state. . . .
- The nobleman has an especial right to places of honor in the state for which he has made himself fit.
- Only the nobleman has the right to possess noble property.
- Persons of the burgher [middle-class] estate cannot own noble property except by permission of the sovereign.
- Noblemen shall normally engage in no burgher livelihood or occupation.

EXCERPTS FROM THE FRENCH "DECLARATION OF THE RIGHTS OF MAN AND CITIZEN," 1789

1. Men are born and remain free and equal in rights. Social distinctions may be based only on common utility.

3. The principle of all sovereignty rests essentially in the nation. No body and no individual may exercise authority which does not emanate expressly from the nation.

4. Liberty consists in the ability to do whatever does not harm another; hence the exercise of the natural rights of each man has no limits except those which assure to other members of society the enjoyment of the same rights. These limits can only be determined by law.

6. Law is the expression of the general will. All citizens have the right to take part, in person or by their representatives, in its formation. It must be the same for all whether it protects or penalizes. All citizens being equal in its eyes are equally admissible to all public dignities, offices and employments, according to their capacity, and with no other distinction than that of their virtues and talents.

13. For maintenance of public forces and for expenses of administration common taxation is necessary. It should be apportioned equally among all citizens according to their capacity to pay.

14. All citizens have the right, by themselves or through their representatives, to have demonstrated to them the necessity of public taxes, to consent to them freely, to follow the use made of the proceeds, and to determine the shares to be paid, the means of assessment and collection and the duration.

III. The Reconstruction of France

THE NEW CONSTITUTION

From 1789 to 1791, the National Assembly acted as a Constituent Assembly to produce a constitution for France. While recognizing the civil rights of all French citizens, it effectively transferred political power from the monarchy and the privileged estates to the body of propertied citizens; in 1790 nobles lost their titles and became indistinguishable from other citizens. The new constitution created a limited monarchy with a clear separation of powers. Sovereignty effectively resided in the representatives of the people, a single-house legislature to be elected by a system of indirect voting. The king was to name and dismiss his ministers, but he was given only a suspensive or delaying veto over legislation; if a bill passed the Assembly in three successive years, it would become law even without royal approval.

The Assembly limited the franchise to "active" citizens, defined as those who paid a minimal sum in taxes; the property qualification was higher for election to public office. Under this system about two-thirds of adult males had the right to vote for the electors who would then choose deputies to the legislature and local officials. Although it favored the propertied, the system was vastly more democratic than the political structure in Britain.

Gender and Race Under the old regime women from prominent families had exercised considerable political influence behind the scenes. Now that the Assembly had established a public sphere of political action with clear ground rules based on elections, would women be admitted to this arena? In petitions to the Assembly and in pamphlets such as Olympe de Gouges' *Declaration of the Rights of Women* (1791), women's rights activists demanded suffrage for women without success. Sieyè spoke for most deputies when he claimed that women's emotional natures made them prone to being easily misled in public affairs. This weakness of character, Sieyès said, made it imperative that women be kept out of public life and devote themselves to their nurturing and maternal roles.

The formal exclusion of women from politics did not mean that they remained passive spectators, however. Women actively engaged in local conflicts over the Assembly's religious policy (discussed below). In the towns they agitated over food prices, and in October 1789 Parisian women led a mass demonstration to Versailles that pressured the king into moving permanently to Paris. Women formed female auxiliaries to local political clubs and organized a handful of independent women's clubs; they participated in civic festivals and helped with relief for the poor. Nor was revolutionary policy indifferent to women's rights. A remarkably egalitarian inheritance law stipulated that all children regardless of gender were entitled to an equal share of a family's estate. And in 1794, an unprecedented system of free primary schools for girls as well as boys was enacted in which the state would pay the teachers' salaries.

As the Assembly excluded women from "active" citizenship without much debate, other groups posed challenges on how to apply "the rights of man" to French society. In eastern France, where most of France's 40,000 Jews resided, public opinion scorned them as an alien race not entitled to citizenship. Eventually, however, the Assembly rejected that argument and extended civil and political equality to Jews. A similar debate raged over the status of the free Negroes and mulattoes in France's Caribbean colonies. White planters, in alliance with the merchants who traded with the islands, were intent on preserving slavery and demanded local control over the islands' racial policy. The planters argued that they could not maintain slavery, which was manifestly based on race, unless free people of color were disenfranchised. When the Assembly accepted this view, the mulattoes rebelled. But their abortive uprising had the unintended consequence of helping to ignite a slave rebellion. Led by Toussaint-L'Ouverture, the blacks turned on their white masters and proclaimed the independence of the colony, which became known as Haiti. In 1794 the French revolutionary government belatedly abolished slavery in all French colonies.

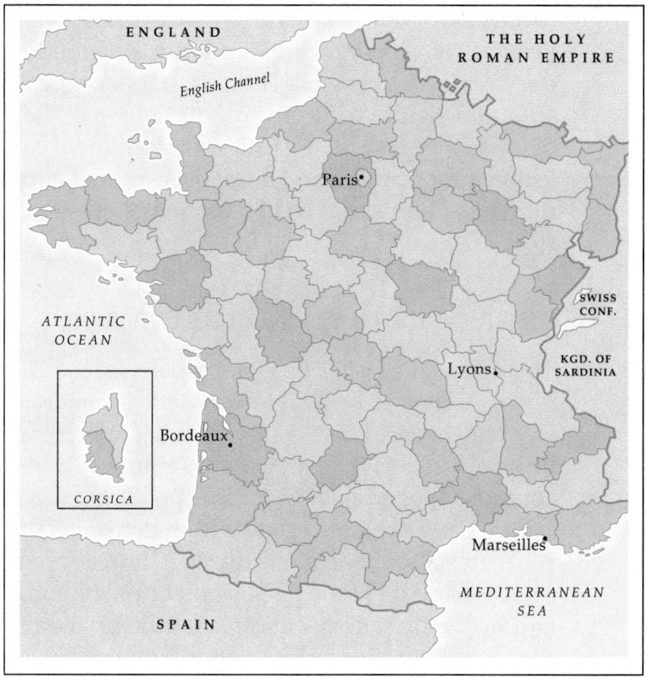

Map 20.1 **REDIVIDING THE NATION'S TERRITORY IN 1789: FROM HISTORIC PROVINCES (*left*) TO REVOLUTIONARY DEPARTMENTS (*right*)**

Redividing the Nation's Territory Within France the Assembly obliterated the political identities of the country's historic provinces and instead divided the nation's territory into 83 departments of roughly equal size (see Map 20.1). Unlike the old provinces, each new department was to have exactly the same institutions. The departments were, in turn, subdivided into districts, cantons, and communes (the common designation for a village or town). On the one hand, this administrative transformation promoted local autonomy: The citizens of each department, district, and commune elected their own local officials, and in that sense political power was decentralized. On the other hand, these local governments were subordinated to the national legislature in Paris and became instruments for promoting national integration and uniformity.

The new administrative map also created the boundaries for a new judicial system. Sweeping away the parlements and law courts of the old regime, the revolutionaries established a justice of the peace in each canton, a civil court in each district, and a criminal court in each department. The judges on all tribunals were to be elected. The Assembly rejected the use of juries in civil cases but decreed that felonies would be tried by juries; also, criminal defendants for the first time gained the right to counsel. In civil law, the Assembly encouraged arbitration and mediation to avoid the time-consuming and expensive processes of formal litigation. In general, the revolutionaries hoped to make the administration of justice faster and more accessible.

The Assembly's clearing operations extended to economic institutions as well. Guided by the dogmas of laissez-faire theory, and by its uncompromising hostility to privileged corporations, the Assembly sought to open up economic life to individual initiative, much as Turgot had attempted in the 1770s. Besides dismantling internal tariffs and chartered trading monopolies, it abolished merchants' and artisans' guilds and proclaimed the right of every citizen to enter any trade and conduct it freely. The government would no longer concern itself with regulating wages or the quality of goods. The Assembly also insisted that workers bargain in the economic marketplace as individuals, and it therefore banned workers' associations and strikes. The precepts of economic individualism extended to the countryside as well. At least in theory, peasants and landlords were free to cultivate their fields as they saw fit, regardless of traditional collective practices. In fact, those deep-rooted communal restraints proved to be extremely resistant to change.

THE REVOLUTION AND THE CHURCH

To address the state's financial problems, the National Assembly acted in a way that the monarchy had never dared contemplate. Under revolutionary ideology, the French Catholic Church could no longer exist as an independent corporation—as a separate estate within the state. The Assembly therefore nationalized Church property, placing it "at the disposition of the nation," and made the state responsible for the upkeep of the Church. It then issued paper notes called *assignats*, which were backed by the value of these "national lands." The property was to be sold by auction at the district capitals to the highest bidders. This plan favored the bourgeois and rich peasants with ready capital and made it difficult for needy peasants to acquire the land, though some pooled their resources to do so.

The sale of Church lands and the issuance of *assignats* had several consequences. In the short run, they eliminated the need for new borrowing. Second, the hundreds of thousands of purchasers gained a strong vested interest in the Revolution, since a successful counterrevolution was likely to reclaim their properties for the Church. Finally, after war broke out with an Austrian–Prussian coalition in 1792, the government made the *assignats* a national currency and printed a volume of *assignats* way beyond their underlying value in land, thereby touching off severe inflation and new political turmoil.

Religious Schism The issue of church reform produced the Revolution's first and most fateful crisis. The Assembly intended to rid the Church of inequities that enriched the aristocratic prelates of the old regime. Many Catholics looked forward to such healthy changes that might bring the clergy closer to the people. In the Civil Constitution of the Clergy (1790), the Assembly reduced the number of bishops from 130 to 83 and reshaped diocesan boundaries to conform exactly with those of the new departments. Bishops and parish priests were to be chosen by the electoral assemblies in the departments and districts, and were to be paid according to a uniform salary scale that favored those currently at the lower end. Like all other public officials, the clergy was to take an oath of loyalty to the constitution.

The clergy generally opposed the Civil Constitution because it had been dictated to them by the National Assembly; they argued that such questions as the selection of bishops and priests should be negotiated either with the Pope or with a National Church Council. But the Assembly asserted that it had the sovereign power to order such reforms, since they affected temporal rather than spiritual matters. In November 1790 the Assembly demanded that all clergy take the loyalty oath forthwith; those who refused would lose their positions and be pensioned off. In all of France only seven bishops and about 54 percent of the parish clergy swore the oath; but in the west of France only 15 percent of the priests complied. A schism tore through French Catholicism, since the laity had to take a position as well: Should parishioners remain loyal to their priests who had refused to take the oath (the nonjuring, or refractory, clergy) and thus be at odds with the state? Or should they accept the unfamiliar "constitutional clergy" designated by the districts to replace their own priests?

The Assembly's effort to impose reform in defiance of religious sensibilities and Church autonomy was a grave tactical error. The oath crisis polarized the nation. It seemed to link the Revolution with impiety and the Church with counterrevolution. In local communities, refractory clergy began to preach against the entire Revolution. Local officials fought back by arresting them and demanding repressive laws. Civil strife rocked thousands of communities.

COUNTERREVOLUTION, RADICALISM, AND WAR

Opposition to the Revolution had actually begun much earlier. After July 14 some of the king's relatives had left the country in disgust, thus becoming the first *émigrés*, or political exiles, of the Revolution. During the next three years thousands of nobles, including two-thirds of the royal army's officer corps, joined the emigration. Across the Rhine River in Coblenz, émigrés formed an army that threatened to overthrow the new regime at the first opportunity. The king himself publicly submitted to the Revolution, but privately he smoldered in resentment. Finally, in June 1791, Louis and his family fled in secret from Paris, hoping to cross the Belgian frontier and enlist the aid of Austria. But Louis was stopped at the French village of Varennes and was forcibly returned to Paris.

Moderates hoped that this aborted escape would finally end the king's opposition to the Revolution. The Assembly, after all, needed his cooperation to make its constitutional monarchy viable. It did not wish to open the door to a republic or to further unrest. Radicals such as the journalist Jean-Paul Marat, on the other hand, had long thundered against the treachery of the king and the émigrés, and against the Assembly itself for not acting vigorously against aristocrats and counterrevolutionaries. But the Assembly was determined to maintain the status quo and adopted the fiction that the king had been kidnapped. The Assembly reaffirmed the king's place in the new regime, but Louis' treasonous flight to Varennes ensured that radical agitation would continue.

The Outbreak of War When the newly elected Legislative Assembly convened on October 1, 1791, the questions of counterrevolution at home and the prospect of war abroad dominated its stormy sessions. Both the right and the left saw advantages to be gained in a war between France and Austria. The king and his court hoped that a military defeat would discredit the new regime and restore full power to the monarchy. Most members of the Jacobin Club—the leading radical political club in Paris—wanted war to strike down the foreign supporters of the émigrés and domestic counterrevolutionaries.

When Francis II ascended the throne of the Habsburg Monarchy in March 1792, the stage was set for war. Unlike his father, Leopold, who had rejected intervention in France's affairs, Francis fell under the influence of émigrés and bellicose advisers. He was determined to assist the French queen, his aunt, and he also expected to make territorial gains. With both sides thus eager for battle, France went to war in April 1792 against a coalition of Austria, Prussia, and the émigrés.

Each camp expected rapid victory, but both were deceived. The French offensive quickly faltered, and invading armies soon crossed France's borders. The Legislative Assembly ordered the arrest of refractory clergy and called for a special corps of 20,000 national guardsmen to protect Paris. Louis vetoed both measures and held to his decisions in spite of demonstrations against them in the capital. For all practical purposes, these were his last acts as king. The legislature also called for 100,000 volunteers to bolster the French army and defend the homeland.

The Fall of the Monarchy As Prussian forces began a drive toward Paris, their commander, the Duke of Brunswick, rashly threatened to level the city if it resisted or if it harmed the royal family. When Louis XVI published this Brunswick Manifesto, it seemed proof that he was in league with the enemy. Far from intimidating the revolutionaries, the threat drove them forward. Since a divided Legislative Assembly refused to act decisively in the face of royal obstructionism, Parisian militants, spurred on by the Jacobin Club, organized an insurrection.

On August 10, 1792, a crowd of armed Parisians stormed the royal palace at the Tuileries, literally driving the king from the throne. The Assembly then had no choice but to declare Louis XVI suspended. That night more than half the Assembly's members themselves fled Paris, making it clear that the Assembly too had lost its legitimacy. The deputies who remained ordered elections for a National Convention to decide the king's fate, to draft a republican constitution, and to govern France during the current emergency. What the events of 1789 in Versailles and Paris had begun, the insurrection of August 10, 1792 completed. The old regime in France had truly been destroyed.

IV. The Second Revolution

By 1792—just three years after the fall of the Bastille—the Revolution had profoundly altered the foundations of government and society in France.

▶ **Like July 14, the assault on the Tuileries of August 10, 1792 led to a brief battle with numerous casualties among the besiegers and infuriated reprisals against the garrison after it surrendered. The event brought the end of the constitutional monarchy and led directly to the founding of the first French Republic.**

The National Assembly swept away absolutism and introduced constitutional government, legislative representation, and local self-government. It repudiated aristocratic and corporate privilege and established civil equality and uniform institutions across the country. Peasants were freed from the seigneurial system, religious minorities from persecution. Yet the Revolution was far from over, and in the short view, one might say that it was only beginning. True, these changes ultimately proved to be the most significant. But they had been won at the price of great opposition, and the old order was far from vanquished. European monarchs and aristocrats encouraged refractory priests, émigrés, and royalists in France to resist, while many ordinary French citizens turned against the revolutionaries for a variety of reasons.

The patriots, threatened in 1792 by military defeat and counterrevolution, were themselves divided. Some became radicalized, while others grew alienated from the Revolution's increasingly radical course and joined its opponents. Each spasm of change produced new opponents at home and abroad, but each increment of opposition stiffened the resolve of the Revolution's partisans. Building on the momentum of August 1792, the Jacobins forged a coalition with urban militants known as the *sans-culottes* (literally, men who wore trousers rather than fashionable knee breeches). The sans-culottes sought to revolutionize the Revolution, to create a democratic republic based on a broadening definition of equality. But the government's responses to the crisis distorted this second revolution. To establish liberty, the Jacobins argued, coercion was required. The ideals of equality became confused with problems of national defense and with the impulse to repress opposition.

THE NATIONAL CONVENTION

The insurrection of August 10, 1792 created a vacuum of authority until the election of a National Convention was completed. A revolutionary Paris Commune, or city government, became one power center, but that bastion of radicalism could not control events even within its own domain. As thousands of volunteers left for the battlefront, Parisians nervously eyed the capital's jails, which overflowed with political prisoners and common criminals. Radical journalists like Jean-Paul Marat saw these prisoners as a counterrevolutionary striking force and feared a plot to open the prisons. A growing sense of alarm finally exploded early in September. For three days groups of Parisians invaded the prisons, set up "popular tribunals," and slaughtered more than 2000 prisoners. No official dared intervene to stop the carnage, known since as the September massacres.

The sense of panic eased, however, with the success of the French armies. Bolstered by units of volunteers, the army finally halted the invaders at the Battle of Valmy on September 20. Two months later it defeated the allies at Jemappes in the Austrian Netherlands, which the French now occupied. Meanwhile, the Convention convened and promptly declared France a republic.

Settling Louis XVI's fate proved to be extremely contentious. While the deputies unanimously found the ex-king guilty of treason, they divided sharply over the question of his punishment. Some argued for clemency, while others insisted that his execution was a necessary symbolic gesture as well as a fitting punishment for his betrayal. Finally, by a vote of 387 to 334, the Convention sentenced Louis to death and voted down efforts to reprieve this sentence or delay it for a popular referendum. On January 21, 1793, Louis was guillotined, put to death like an ordinary citizen. The deputies to the Convention had become regicides (king killers) and would make no compromise with the counterrevolution.

▸ Beset by invasion jitters, and fearing a plot to force open the capital's overcrowded jails, mobs of Parisians invaded the prisons and over the course of three days in September 1792 slaughtered over 2000 prisoners.

▸ **After the National Convention concluded its trial of ex-King Louis XVI and voted to impose the death penalty without reprieve, "Louis Capet" was guillotined and the leaders of the Republic became regicides, king killers.**

Factional Conflict From the Convention's opening day, two bitterly hostile groups of deputies vied for leadership and almost immobilized it with their rancorous conflict. One group became known as the *Girondins*, since several of its spokesmen were elected as deputies from the Gironde department. The Girondins were fiery orators and ambitious politicians who advocated provincial liberty and laissez-faire economics. They reacted hostilely to the growing radicalism of Paris and broke with or were expelled by the Jacobin Club, to which some had originally belonged. Meanwhile Parisian electors chose as their deputies leading members of the Jacobin Club such as Danton, Robespierre, and Marat. The Parisian deputation to the Convention became the nucleus of a group known as the *Mountain*, so-called because it occupied the upper benches of the Convention's hall. The Mountain attracted the more militant provincial deputies and attacked the Girondins as treacherous compromisers unwilling to adopt bold measures in the face of crisis. The Girondins, in turn, denounced the Mountain as would-be tyrants and captives of Parisian radicalism, and held them responsible for the September prison massacres.

Several hundred deputies stood between these two factions. These centrists (known as the *Plain*) were committed to the Revolution but were uncertain which path to follow. The Plain detested popular agitation, but they were reluctant to turn against the sans-culottes, who so fervently supported the Revolution. In the end they would support men or policies that promised to consolidate the Revolution.

THE REVOLUTIONARY CRISIS

By the spring of 1793 the National Convention faced a perilous convergence of invasion, civil war, and economic crises that demanded imaginative responses. Austria and Prussia had mounted a new offensive in 1793, their alliance strengthened by the addition of Spain, Piedmont, and Britain. Between March and September military reversals occurred on every front. The Convention reacted by introducing a military draft, but this, in turn, touched off a rebellion in western France by peasants and rural weavers, who had long resented the patriot middle class in the towns for monopolizing local political power and for persecuting their priests. In the isolated towns of the Vendée region, south of the Loire River, they attacked the Republic's supporters. Priests and nobles offered leadership to the rebels, who first organized into guerrilla bands and finally into a "Catholic and Royalist Army." The Vendée rebels briefly occupied several towns, massacred local patriots, and even threatened the port of Nantes, where British troops could have landed.

Meanwhile, economic troubles were provoking the Parisian sans-culottes. By early 1793 the Revolution's paper money, the *assignats,* had declined to 50 percent of its face value. Inflation was compounded by a poor harvest, food shortages, hoarding, and profiteering. Municipal authorities fixed the price of bread but could not always secure adequate supplies. Under these conditions the government could not even supply its armies.

Spokesmen for the sans-culottes declared that even the Convention and the Paris Commune were insufficiently responsive to popular opinion. They demanded that the Convention purge the Girondins and adopt a program of "public safety," including price controls for basic commodities, execution of hoarders and speculators, and forced requisitions of grain. Behind these demands lay the threat of armed insurrection. This

▶ Bitter fighting in the Vendée between counterrevolutionaries and republicans caused a profound split in the loyalities of Western France, which endured for at least the next hundred years. Each side cultivated its own memories of the event and honored its own martyrs.

pressure from the sans-culottes aided the Mountain in their struggle against the Girondins, but it could easily have degenerated into anarchy. In a sense, all elements of the revolutionary crisis hinged on one problem: the lack of an effective government that would not simply respond to popular pressures but would organize and master them. When the sans-culottes mounted a massive armed demonstration for a purge of the Girondins on June 2, centrist deputies reluctantly agreed to go along. The Convention expelled 23 Girondin deputies, who were subsequently tried and executed for treason.

Factionalism in the Convention reflected conflict in the provinces. Moderate republicans in several cities struggled with local Jacobin radicals and sympathized with the Girondin deputies in their campaign against the Parisian sans-culottes. In the south, local Jacobins lost control of Marseilles, Bordeaux, and Lyons to their rivals, who then repudiated the Convention. As in the Vendée revolt, royalists soon took over the resistance in Lyons, France's second largest city. This was an intolerable challenge to the Convention. Labeling the anti-Jacobin rebels in Lyons and elsewhere as "federalists," the Convention dispatched armed forces to suppress them. In the eyes of the Jacobins, to defy the Convention's authority was to betray France itself.

Map 20.2 CONFLICTS IN REVOLUTIONARY FRANCE

THE JACOBIN DICTATORSHIP

Popular radicalism in Paris had helped bring the Mountain to power in the Convention. The question now was: Which side of this coalition between the Mountain and the sans-culottes would dominate the other? The sans-culottes seemed to believe that the sovereign people could dictate their will to the Convention. Popular agitation peaked on September 5, when a mass demonstration in Paris demanded new policies to ensure food supplies. To give force to the law, urged the sans-culottes, "Let terror be placed on the order of the day." The Convention responded with the Law of the Maximum, which imposed general price controls, and with the Law of Suspects, which empowered local revolutionary committees to imprison citizens whose loyalty they suspected.

Revolutionary Government In June the triumphant Mountain had drafted a new democratic constitution for the French Republic and had submitted it to an unprecedented referendum, in which almost 2 million citizens had overwhelmingly voted yes. But the Convention formally laid the constitution aside and proclaimed the government "revolutionary until the peace." Elections, local self-government, and guarantees of individual liberty were to be suspended until the Republic had defeated its enemies within and without. The Convention placed responsibility for military, economic, and political policy, as well as control over local officials, in the hands of a 12-man Committee of Public Safety. Spontaneous popular action was about to give way to revolutionary centralization.

Maximilien Robespierre emerged as the Committee's leading personality and tactician. An austere bachelor in his mid-thirties, Robespierre had been a provincial lawyer before the Revolu-

The Paris Jacobin Club began as a caucus for a group of liberal deputies to the National Assembly. During the Convention it became a bastion of democratic deputies and middle-class Parisian radicals, while continuing to serve as a "mother club" for affiliated clubs in the provinces.

tion. As a deputy to the National Assembly he had ardently advocated greater democracy. His main political forum was the Paris Jacobin Club, which by 1793 he more or less dominated. In the Convention, Robespierre was inflexible and self-righteous in his dedication to the Revolution. He sought to appease the sans-culottes but also to control them, for he placed the Revolution's survival above any one viewpoint (*see box*, p. 662).

Local political clubs (numbering over 5000 by 1794) formed crucial links in the chain of revolutionary government. The clubs nominated citizens for posts on local revolutionary institutions, exercised surveillance over those officials, and served as "arsenals of public opinion." The clubs fostered the egalitarian ideals of the second revolution and supported the war effort. They also saw it as their civic duty to denounce fellow citizens for unpatriotic behavior, and thereby sowed fear and recrimination across the land.

For the Jacobins tolerated no serious dissent. The government's demand for unity during the emergency nullified the right to freedom of expression. Among those to fall were a group of ultrarevolutionaries led by Jacques-René Hébert, a leading radical journalist and Paris official. They were accused of a plot against the Republic and were guillotined. In reality, Hébert had questioned what he deemed the Convention's leniency toward "enemies of the people." Next came the so-called indulgents. Headed by Georges-Jacques Danton, a leading member of the Jacobin Club, they publicly argued for a relaxation of rigorous measures. For this dissent they were indicted on trumped-up charges of treason and were sentenced to death by the revolutionary tribunal. This succession of purges, which started with the Girondins and later ended with Robespierre himself, suggested, as one contemporary put it, that "revolutions devour their own children."

Robespierre's Justification of the Terror

"If the spring of popular government in time of peace is virtue, the springs of popular government in revolution are at once *virtue and terror*: virtue, without which terror is fatal; terror, without which virtue is powerless. Terror is nothing other than justice, prompt, severe, inflexible; it is therefore an emanation of virtue. . . . It is a consequence of the general principle of democracy applied to our country's most urgent needs.

"It has been said that terror is the principle of despotic government. Does your government therefore resemble despotism? Yes, as the sword that gleams in the hands of the heroes of liberty resembles that with which the henchman of tyranny are armed. Let the despot govern his brutalized subjects by terror; he is right, as a despot. Subdue by terror the enemies of liberty, and you will be right, as founders of the Republic. The government of the revolution is liberty's despotism against tyranny. Is force made only to protect crime?

"Society owes protection only to peaceable citizens; the only citizens in the Republic are the republicans. For it, the royalists, the conspirators are only strangers or, rather, enemies. This terrible war waged by liberty against tyranny—is it not indivisible? Are the enemies within not the allies of the enemies without? The assassins who tear our country apart, the intriguers who buy the consciences that hold the people's mandate; the traitors who sell them; the mercenary pamphleteers hired to dishonor the people's cause, to kill public virtue, to stir up the fire of civil discord, and to prepare political counter-revolution—are all those men less guilty or less dangerous than the tyrants [abroad] whom they serve?

"We try to control revolutions with the quibbles of the courtroom; we treat conspiracies against the Republic like lawsuits between individuals. Tyranny kills, and liberty argues. . . ."

From Robespierre's speech to the Convention on "The Moral and Political Principles of Domestic Policy," December 1793.

The Reign of Terror Most of those devoured by the French Revolution, however, were not its own children but an assortment of armed rebels, counterrevolutionaries, and unfortunate citizens who were swept into the vortex of war and internal strife. As an official policy, the Reign of Terror sought to organize repression so as to avoid anarchic violence like the September massacres. It reflected a state of mind that saw threats and plots everywhere (some real, some imagined). The laws of the Terror struck most directly at the people perceived to be enemies of the Revolution: Refractory priests and émigrés, for instance, were banned from the Republic upon threat of death. But the Law of Suspects also led to the incarceration of as many as 300,000 ordinary citizens for their opinions, past behavior, or social status.

The Terror produced its own atrocities: the brutal drowning of imprisoned priests at Nantes; the execution of thousands of noncombatants during the military campaigns of the Vendée; and the summary executions of about 2000 citizens of Lyons, more than two-thirds of them from the wealthy classes. ("Lyons has made war against liberty," declared the Convention, "thus Lyons no longer exists.") But except in the two zones of intense civil war—western France and the area of "federalist" rebellion in the south (see Map 20.2)—the Terror impressed by examples, not by the execution of entire social groups.

THE SANS-CULOTTES AND REVOLUTION FROM BELOW

The Parisian sans-culottes formed the crowds and demonstrations that produced the Revolution's dramatic turning points (see chart on p.

Air: Ou Courez vous Mr. l'Abbé.
Ne redoutez plus les Brocards.
Gentes Nonettes beaux frocards
De la Metamorphose
He bien
l'Amour rit et pour cause
Et vous mentendez bien.
On me Raze ce Matin, Je me Marie ce Soir.

▸ **At the height of the "dechristianization" movement (which lasted for about eight months in the period 1793–1794), over 18,000 priests renounced their vocations. About a third were also pressured into marrying as a way of proving the sincerity of their resignations. ("They shave me in the morning and have me married by evening.")**

664), but they also threw themselves into a daily routine of political activism during the second revolution of 1792–1794. The sans-culottes were mainly artisans, shopkeepers, and workers—building contractors, carpenters, shoemakers, wine sellers, clerks, tailors, cafe keepers. Many owned their own businesses; others were wage earners. But they shared a strong sense of local community in the capital's varied neighborhoods.

Popular Attitudes The sans-culottes were obsessed with the availability and price of bread. As consumers, they faced inflation and scarcities with fear, distress, and rage, and demanded forceful government intervention to ensure the basic necessities of life. Sans-culotte militants believed in property rights, but they insisted that people did not have the right to misuse property by hoarding food or speculating. As one petition put it, "What is the meaning of freedom, when one class of men can starve another? What is the meaning of equality, when the rich, by their monopolies, can exercise the right of life and death over their equals?" The sans-culotte call for price controls clashed dramatically with the dogma of laissez-faire. By 1793, however, the Jacobins had acknowledged "the right to subsistence" in their new constitution and had instituted price controls under the Law of the Maximum to regulate the economy during the emergency.

Bitterly antiaristocratic, the sans-culottes displayed their social attitudes in everyday behavior. They advocated simplicity in dress and manners, and attacked opulence and pretension wherever they found or imagined them to be. Under their disapproving eye, high society and fancy dress generally disappeared from view. Vices like prostitution and gambling were attributed to aristocrats and were denounced in the virtuous society of the Revolution; drinking, the common people's vice, was tolerated. The revolutionaries symbolized their break with the past

TURNING POINTS IN THE FRENCH REVOLUTION

June 17, 1789	Third Estate declares itself a "National Assembly."
July 14, 1789	Storming of the Bastille and triumph of the patriots.
August 10, 1792	Storming of the Tuileries and the end of the monarchy (followed by the September prison massacres).
January 21, 1793	Execution of Louis XVI.
March 1793	Vendée rebellion begins.
June 2, 1793	Sans-culottes intimidate the Convention into purging the Girondin deputies. "Federalist" rebellion begins in Lyons.
September 5, 1793	Sans-culottes demonstrate for the enactment of economic controls and Terror.
October 1793	The Jacobin dictatorship and the Terror begin: The Convention declares that "the government is revolutionary until the peace."
9 Thermidor year II (July 27, 1794)	Fall of Robespierre.
1–2 Prairial year III (May 20–21, 1795)	Failed insurrection by Parisian sans-culottes for "Bread and the Constitution of 1793."
18 Brumaire year VIII (November 9, 1799)	Coup d'état by General Bonaparte and the "revisionists."

by changing the names of streets and public places to eliminate signs of royalism, religion, or aristocracy. The Palais Royal thus became the Palais d'Égalité ("Equality Palace"). Some citizens exchanged their Christian names for the names of secular heroes from antiquity, like Brutus. And all citizens were expected to drop honorifics like *monsieur* and *madame* in favor of the simple, uniform designation of *citizen*. Even the measurement of time was altered when the Convention decreed a new republican calendar in which the months were renamed, the seven-day week replaced by a ten-day *décadi*, and the year I dated from the establishment of the Republic in 1792.

Popular Politics The Convention believed in representative democracy, with an active political life at the grass roots, but during the emergency it enacted a centralized revolutionary dictatorship. The sans-culottes preferred a more decentralized style of participatory democracy. They believed that the local assembly of citizens was the ultimate sovereign body. At the beginning of the year II (1793–1794), the 48 sections of

▶ The radical activists of the Paris sections—the *sans-culottes* and their female counterparts—made a point of their plebeian forms of dress, their freedom to bear arms, and their egalitarian insignias, such as the red liberty cap.

A Portrait of the Parisian Sans-Culotte

"A Sans-Culotte is a man who goes everywhere on his own two feet, who has none of the millions you're all after, no mansions, no lackeys to wait on him, and who lives quite simply with his wife and children, if he has any, on the fourth or fifth floor. He is useful, because he knows how to plough a field, handle a forge, a saw, or a file, how to cover a roof or how to make shoes and to shed his blood to the last drop to save the Republic. And since he is a working man, you will never find him in the Cafe de Chartres where they plot and gamble. . . . In the evening, he is at his Section, not powdered and perfumed and all dolled up to catch the eyes of the *citoyennes* in the galleries, but to support sound resolutions with all his power and to pulverize the vile faction [of moderates]. For the rest, a Sans-Culotte always keeps his sword with a sharp edge, to clip the ears of the malevolent. Sometimes he carries his pike and at the first roll of the drum, off he goes to the Vendée, to the Army of the Alps or the Army of the North."

From a pamphlet attributed to the sectional militant Vingternier: "A Reply to the Impertinent Question: But What Is a Sans-Culotte?" (1794).

Paris functioned almost as autonomous republics in which local activists ran their own affairs. Political life in Paris and elsewhere had a naive, breathless quality and made thousands of ordinary citizens feel that they held real political power (*see box*, above).

To Robespierre, this ideal of direct democracy appeared unworkable and akin to anarchy. The Convention watched the sans-culottes uneasily, supportive of democratic egalitarianism but fearful of the unpredictability, disorder, and inefficiency of this popular movement. The Mountain attempted to steer between encouraging civic participation and controlling it. From the 48 sections of Paris, however, came an endless stream of petitions, denunciations, and veiled threats to the government. In the spring of 1794 the Convention decided to curb the power of the sections with a series of decrees drastically restricting their rights and activities. By forcibly cooling down the ardor of the sans-culottes, however, the revolutionary government necessarily weakened its own base of support.

THE REVOLUTIONARY WARS

Ultimately, the Revolution's fate rested in the hands of its armies, although no one had thought in such terms in 1789. France's revolutionary ideology had initially posed no direct threat to the European state system. Indeed, the orators of the National Assembly had argued that the best foreign policy for a free society was peace, neutrality, and isolation from the diplomatic intrigues of monarchs. But peaceful intentions did not imply pacifism. When counterrevolution at home coalesced with threats from abroad, the revolutionaries were eager to fight against both. As in most major wars, however, the initial objectives were soon forgotten. As the war expanded, it brought revolution to other states.

The revolutionary wars involved timeless considerations of international relations as well as new and explosive purposes. On the one hand, France pursued the traditional aim of extending and rounding off its frontiers. On the other hand, France now espoused revolutionary principles such as the right of a people to self-determination. As early as September 1791, the National Assembly had declared that "the rights of peoples are not determined by the treaties of princes."

Foreign Revolutionaries and French Armies Even before 1789 "patriots" in Geneva, the Dutch Netherlands, and the Austrian Netherlands (Belgium) had unsuccessfully challenged the traditional arrangements that governed their societies,

Amidst elaborate arrays of symbolism, revolutionary iconography generally used the figure of a woman to represent its ideals. Briefly in the period 1793–1794, however, the Jacobins introduced the more aggressive masculine figure of Hercules to represent the Republic.

and the French Revolution rekindled those rebellious sentiments. Foreign revolutionaries were eager to challenge their governments again, and they looked to revolutionary France for assistance. Refugees from these struggles had fled to France and now formed pressure groups to lobby French leaders for help in liberating their own countries during France's war against Austria and Prussia. Some revolutionaries from areas contiguous to France (Belgium, Savoy, and the Rhineland) hoped that the French Republic might simply annex those territories. Elsewhere—in the Dutch Netherlands, Lombardy, Ireland, and the Swiss Confederation—insurgents hoped that France would help establish independent republics by overthrowing the ruling princes or oligarchies.

Few French leaders were interested in leading a European crusade for liberty, but practical considerations led them to intervention. As the war spilled over into Belgium and the Rhineland, the French sought to establish support abroad by incorporating the principles of the Revolution into their foreign policy. Thus in December 1792 the Convention decided that feudal practices and hereditary privileges would be abolished wherever French armies prevailed. The people thus liberated, however, would have to pay for their liberation with special taxes and requisitions of supplies for French troops. By 1794 France had a permanent foothold in Belgium and soon annexed that territory to the Republic. Yet Robespierre was dubious about foreign entanglements; he believed that liberty had to be secured in France before it could be exported abroad. The Committee of Public Safety thus declined to support a distant Polish revolutionary movement, refused to invade Holland, and attempted to avoid any involvements in Italy.

The Armies of the Republic The fighting men who defended France and carried its revolution abroad were a far different body from the old royal army. The National Assembly of 1789 retained the notion of a professional army but opened officers' careers to ordinary soldiers, especially after most of the royal officer corps emigrated or resigned. At the same time, the concept of the citizen-soldier was introduced in the newly organized national guard, which had elected officers. When the war against the coalition began in 1792 the government enrolled over 100,000 volunteers for short-term service at the front. But when the coalition launched its second offensive in 1793, the inadequacy of the French army demanded drastic innovations.

The Convention responded with the mass levy of August 1793 (*levée en masse*). All able-bodied unmarried men between the ages of 18 and 25 were drafted for military service, without the option of buying themselves a replacement. About 300,000 new recruits poured into the armies, while perhaps 200,000 draftees fled to avoid service. By the end of 1794 the French had almost 750,000 men under arms. With elected officers at their head, the citizen-soldiers marched off to the front under banners that read "The French people risen against the tyrants." The Convention merged these recruits with the regulars of line army into units called demibrigades, so that the professionals could impart their military skills to the new troops.

Military tactics in the field reflected a combination of revolutionary spirit and pragmatism. The new demibrigades did not have the training to be deployed in the well-drilled line formations of old-regime armies. Commanders instead favored mass columns that could move quickly without much drilling. Mass and mobility characterized the armies of the French Revolution. The Committee of Public Safety advised its commanders, "Act offensively and in masses. Use the bayonet at every opportunity. Fight great battles and pursue the enemy until he is destroyed."

The revolutionary government fostered new attitudes toward military life. The military was under civilian control. Discipline applied equally to officers and men, and wounded soldiers received generous veterans benefits. The Convention insisted that generals show not only military talent but the will to win. Many young officers rose quickly to command positions, but some generals fared badly. The commander of the defeated Rhine army in early 1793, for example, was branded a traitor, tried, and guillotined. Mean-

To bolster the professional troops of the line army in 1791 and again in 1792 after the war began, the government called for volunteers, one of whom is shown in this sentimental and patriotic portrait bidding farewell to his family. By 1793, the National Convention had to go further and draft all able-bodied young men.

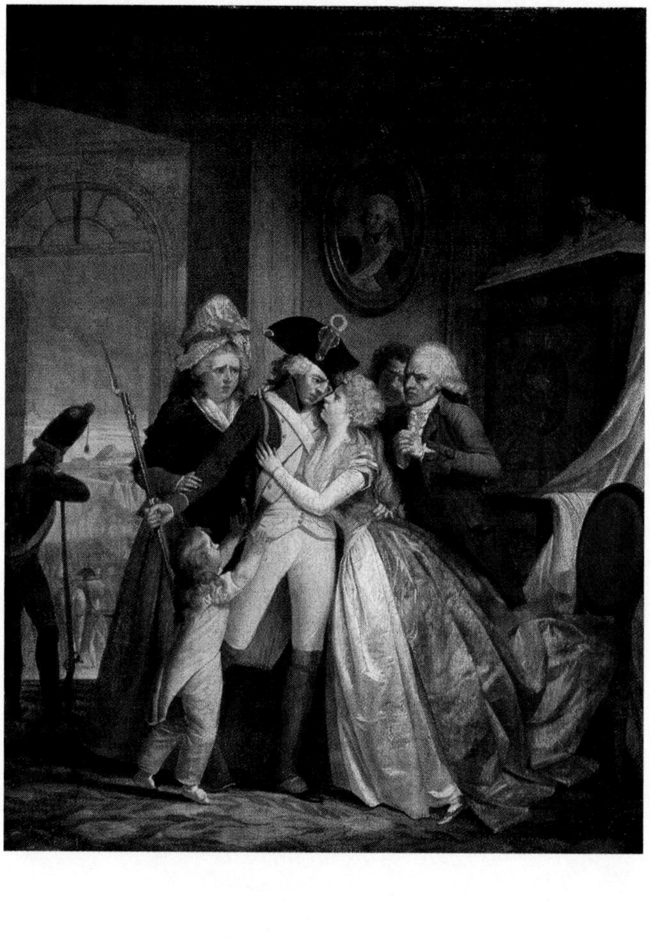

while, economic mobilization at home produced the weapons, ammunition, clothing, and food necessary to support this mass army.

In late 1793–early 1794 the armies of the Republic won a string of victories, culminating in the Battle of Fleurus in June 1794, which liberated Belgium for the second time. French armies also triumphed at the Pyrénées and the Rhine, and forced their enemies one by one to the peace table—first Spain and Prussia, then Piedmont. An army crippled at the outset by treason and desertion, defeat, lack of training and discipline, and collapsing morale had been forged into a potent force in less than two years. Militarily, at least, the revolutionary government had succeeded brilliantly.

To its most dedicated supporters, the revolutionary government had two major purposes: first, to surmount a crisis and steer the Republic to victory; and second, to democratize France's political and social fabric. Only the first objective, however, won widespread adherence. The National Convention held a polarized nation together, consolidated the Republic, and defeated its foreign enemies, but only at enormous and questionable costs. Moderates and ultrarevolutionaries alike resented the stifling political conformity imposed by the revolutionary government. Wealthy peasants and businesspeople chafed under the economic regimentation, and Catholics bitterly resented local "dechristianization" campaigns. The Jacobins increasingly isolated themselves, making enemies on every side. It is not surprising, then, that the security provided by the military victories of 1793–1794 would permit the Convention to end the Jacobin dictatorship and abandon its rhetoric of radical egalitarianism. But the question remained: What would take their place?

Recommended Reading

Sources

*Beik, Paul H. (ed.). *The French Revolution.* 1971.

*Burke, Edmund. *Reflections on the Revolution in France.* 1969. The most influential antirevolutionary book.

Kirchberger, Joe H. (ed.). *The French Revolution and Napoleon: An Eyewitness History.* 1989. Includes key documents and contemporary accounts of the principal events.

*Levy, Darlene, H. Applewhite, and M. Johnson (eds.). *Women in Revolutionary Paris, 1789–1795.* 1979. A documentary history of women activists.

Roland, Manon Jeanne. *The Private Memoirs of Madame Roland* (2d ed.). E. G. Johnson (ed.). 1976. By a woman deeply involved in revolutionary politics, guillotined in 1793 with the Girondins.

Stewart, J. H. *A Documentary Survey of the French Revolution.* 1951.

*Young, Arthur. *Travels in France during the Years 1787, 1788, 1789.* 1972. Invaluable eyewitness testimony by a keen British observer.

*Available in paperback.

Studies

*Bailyn, Bernard. *The Ideological Origins of the American Revolution.* 1967. A classic account of the impact of British libertarian thought on the American colonies.

Bertaud, Jean-Paul. *The Army of the French Revolution.* 1988. A pioneering political and social study of the soldiers and officers of the Republic's armies.

Blanning, T. C. W. *Joseph II and Enlightened Despotism.* 1970. A convenient synthesis on a fundamental subject.

*Chartier, Roger. *The Cultural Origins of the French Revolution.* 1990. On the emergence of a "public sphere" of political discourse in the old regime.

*Christie, Ian. *Great Britain and the American Colonies, 1754–1783.* 1966. A synthesis written from the British viewpoint.

*———. *Wars and Revolutions: Britain, 1760–1815.* 1982. Focuses on British government policy in the age of revolutions.

*Cobb, R. C. *The People's Armies.* 1987. On the paramilitary battalions of sans-culottes, an "instrument of the terror" in 1793–1794.

———. *The Police and the People: French Popular Protest.*

1970. A study of peasants and sans-culottes that should be compared to Soboul's work.

*De Tocqueville, Alexis. *The Old Regime and the French Revolution.* Stuart Gilbert (tr.). 1955. A classic interpretation of the Revolution's genesis first published in the 1850s.

*Doyle, William. *Origins of the French Revolution.* 1980. A reliable synthesis of revisionist historiography; should be compared to Lefebvre's treatment.

*———. *The Oxford History of the French Revolution.* 1989. A readable, detailed narrative.

Egret, Jean. *The French Pre-Revolution, 1787–88.* 1978. A masterly account of the unraveling of the old regime.

Forrest, Alan. *The French Revolution and the Poor.* 1982. A history of good intentions and disappointing results.

*———. *Soldiers of the French Revolution.* 1990. A deft synthesis of recent research.

Furet, François, and Mona Ozouf (eds.). *A Critical Dictionary of the French Revolution.* 1989. A collection of essays, some brilliant and some idiosyncratic, on selected events, actors, institutions, ideas, and historians of the French Revolution.

Gershoy, Leo. *Bertrand Barère, a Reluctant Terrorist.* 1962. Perhaps the best available biography of a revolutionary figure.

Greer, Donald. *The Incidence of the Terror during the French Revolution.* 1935. A statistical study of the geography and social composition of death sentences during the Terror.

*Hampson, Norman. *A Social History of the French Revolution.* 1963. A clear, concise history of the Revolution through 1795.

*Hunt, Lynn. *Politics, Culture, and Class in the French Revolution.* 1984. A pioneering analysis of the imagery and sociology of revolutionary politics.

*Jones, Peter. *The Peasantry in the French Revolution.* 1988. A comprehensive study of the impact of the Revolution on rural society.

*Kennedy, Emmet. *A Cultural History of the French Revolution.* 1989. The Revolution's impact on cultural institutions and artistic activity.

Kennedy, Michael. *The Jacobin Club of Marseilles.* 1973. On the second most important center of Jacobinism.

*Landes, Joan. *Women and the Public Sphere in the Age of the French Revolution.* 1988. A discussion of eighteenth-century thought on women, and of the "gendered republic" of the 1790s.

*Lefebvre, Georges. *The Coming of the French Revolution.* 1967. A classic interpretation dating from 1939 by a major French historian; should be compared to Doyle's treatment.

McManners, John. *The French Revolution and the Church.* 1970. A superb synthesis on a major issue.

*Palmer, Robert R. *The Age of the Democratic Revolution: A Political History of Europe and America, 1760–1800* (2 vols.). 1959–1962. Examines the origins of revolutionary movements in the eighteenth-century comparatively, from America to Poland.

———. *The Improvement of Humanity: Education and the French Revolution.* 1985. A history of good intentions and mixed results.

*———. *Twelve Who Ruled: The Year of the Terror in the French Revolution.* 1941. A modern classic, by far the best book on the subject.

*Popkin, Jeremy. *Revolutionary News: The Press in France 1789–1799.* 1990. An excellent analysis of journalism and the impact of journalists in the revolutionary decade.

*Rudé, George. *The Crowd in the French Revolution.* 1959. Description and analysis of popular participation in the Revolution's crucial turning points.

———. *Robespierre: Portrait of a Revolutionary Democrat.* 1975. An extremely admiring portrait.

———. *Wilkes and Liberty.* 1962. On popular movements for parliamentary reform in England.

Schama, Simon. *Patriots and Liberators: Revolution in the Netherlands 1780–1813.* 1977. An exhaustive but lively account.

Scott, H. M. (ed.). *Enlightened Absolutism: Reforms and Reformers in Later Eighteenth-Century Europe.* 1990. The latest and most comprehensive assessment.

*Soboul, Albert. *The Parisian Sans-Culottes and the French Revolution.* 1964. An abridgment of a landmark French thesis; should be compared to Cobb's treatment.

*Sutherland, Donald. *France 1789–1815: Revolution and Counter-revolution.* 1986. The best general history of the period.

Tackett, Timothy. *Religion, Revolution and Regional Culture in Eighteenth-Century France: The Ecclesiastical Oath of 1791.* 1986. An exhaustive study of the Revolution's first and most fateful crisis.

Venturi, Franco. *The End of the Old Regime in Europe, 1768–1776: The First Crisis.* 1989. Like Palmer's treatment, a comparative European perspective on the period.

*Vovelle, Michel. *The Fall of the French Monarchy, 1787–1792.* 1984. A good synthesis of recent research.

Woloch, Isser. *The New Regime: Transformations of the French Civic Order, 1789–1820s.* 1994. A thematic study of new civic institutions and how they fared, from the beginning of the Revolution to the Restoration of the Bourbons.

General Bonaparte, in an uncompleted portrait by Jacques-Louis David.

CHAPTER TWENTY-ONE

THE AGE OF NAPOLEON

THE second phase of the French Revolution (1792–1794) remains a study in contradictions. On the one hand, the National Convention moved for the first time since ancient Athens to institute a democratic republic: a government without kings, based on universal male suffrage, where popular rights—for example, the right to subsistence and to education for all—were inscribed in the constitution. On the other hand, the Convention responded to the crisis of foreign military threats, internal rebellion, and intense factionalism by establishing a revolutionary dictatorship. Individual liberties disappeared, and terror against "enemies of the people" became the order of the day. With the crisis finally surmounted by repression and military victories in 1794, most members of the Convention wearied of those harsh policies and wished to terminate the Revolution as quickly as possible. They hoped to end the Terror, yet preserve the Revolution's positive gains.

But it proved extremely difficult to jettison the Terror without unraveling the revolutionary changes that had preceded or accompanied it. By 1794 too much blood had been spilled, too many people nursed deep wounds, frustrated aspirations, and social hatreds. The new regime could not easily be steered toward the safe harbor of republican liberty in such a polarized atmosphere. In the end the Revolution was terminated by a dictatorship, which the men of 1789 (schooled in the history of the Roman Republic) had feared from the start. But since the struggle for and against revolution had long since spilled across France's borders, this development held profound consequences throughout Europe as well. After the French Republic succumbed to the Napoleonic dictatorship, the public life of both France and Europe hinged to an unparalleled degree on the will of a single man. How would Napoleon Bonaparte use that power at home and abroad?

I. From Robespierre to Bonaparte

Relatively secure after the military victories of the year II (1793–1794), the National Convention repudiated the Terror and turned against the leading Jacobin terrorists. Jacobinism, however, was now a permanent part of the French political experience, along with antirevolutionary royalism. The political spectrum of modern European history had been created. The surviving revolutionaries attempted to command a centrist or moderate position within this range of opinions, but they proved inadequate to the task. During the four unsteady years of the Directory regime (1795–1799), however, French armies helped bring revolution to other parts of Western Europe, only to provoke a second anti-French coalition. This new challenge brought the weaknesses of the Republic to a head and opened the way to the seizure of power by an ambitious general.

▶ **With its field of guillotines, this Thermidorian caricature ("Robespierre Guillotining the Executioner") portrays Robespierre as a murderous tyrant who had depopulated France.**

THE THERMIDORIAN REACTION (1794–1795)

When the military victories of the year II over the coalition and the Vendée rebels eased the need for patriotic unity, long-standing clashes over personalities and policies exploded in the Convention. Robespierre prepared to denounce yet another group of unspecified intriguers, presumably to send them to the guillotine as he had Hébert and Danton. But his enemies made a preemptive strike and denounced Robespierre to the Convention as a tyrant. The Convention no longer needed Robespierre's uncompromising style of leadership. Moderate deputies now repudiated him along with his policies of terror. The Parisian sans-culottes might have intervened to keep Robespierre in power, but the Jacobins had alienated their one-time allies when they curbed the sans-culottes' political autonomy several months earlier. On July 27, 1794 (9 Thermidor year II in the revolutionary calendar), the Convention declared Robespierre an outlaw and he was guillotined the following day, along with several loyal associates.

Anti-Jacobinism Robespierre's fall broke the Revolution's momentum. As the Convention dismantled the apparatus of the Terror, suspects were released from jail, the revolutionary committees that had spearheaded the Terror were abolished, and some of their former members were arrested in turn. The Convention closed the Paris Jacobin Club, once the main forum for Robespierre's influence, while the political clubs in the provinces gradually withered away. The Convention also extended an amnesty to the surviving Girondins and arrested a few leading deputies of the Mountain. Those who had taken responsibility for the Terror in the year II now found themselves under attack. The anti-Jacobin thirst for retribution eventually produced a "white terror" against the Jacobins and the sans-culottes that resulted in arrests, assassinations, and, in the south of France, wholesale massacres.

Thermidor also released France from the social austerity of the year II. The Jacobins' insistence on public virtue gave way to the toleration of luxury, fancy dress, and self-indulgence among the wealthy. The titles *monsieur* and *madame* reappeared, replacing the republican designation of *citizen*. In keeping with laissez-faire ideology, the Thermidorians rescinded economic controls. With the marketplace again ruled by supply and demand, skyrocketing inflation reignited. Worse yet, the harvest of 1795 proved mediocre, and many consumers suffered worse privations than those they had dreaded during the shortages of 1793. In near-famine conditions, mortality rates rose markedly; police reports spoke of little but popular misery.

The Last Revolutionary Uprising Former militants attempted to spark a political reversal and halt the Thermidorian reaction. In the spring of 1795 sans-culottes began to demonstrate in Paris with the slogan "Bread and the Constitution of 1793." The Thermidorians, however, were moving in the opposite direction. They viewed the Jacobin Constitution of 1793 as far too democratic and looked for an excuse to scrap it altogether. In May sans-culottes launched a poorly organized insurrection (the revolt of Prairial year III). In a grim and desperate gamble they invaded the

▸ The Parisian sans-culottes launched a futile rebellion in the spring of 1795 for "Bread and the Constitution of 1793" in response to hyperinflation and severe food shortages.

Convention's hall, where they won the sympathy of only a handful of deputies. Their hours were numbered. In two days of street fighting, government forces overwhelmed the insurgents. Afterward, 36 sans-culottes were executed, and 1200 more were imprisoned for their activism during the Terror. This proved to be the last mobilization of the Parisian revolutionary crowd and the final eclipse of the egalitarian movement.

THE DIRECTORY (1795–1799)

By the end of 1795, the remaining members of the Convention considered the Revolution over. The extremes had been vanquished, and the time for the "peaceable enjoyment of liberty" seemed at hand. The Thermidorians drafted a new constitution—the constitution of the year III (1795)—proclaimed a general amnesty, and hoped to turn a new page. The revolutionary government, which had replaced the fallen constitutional monarchy in 1793, gave way to a constitutional republic, known as the Directory after its five-man executive.

The Directory's proponents declared that the Republic should "be governed by the best citizens, who are found among the property-owning class." The new constitution said little about the popular rights proclaimed by the Constitution of 1793, like the right to subsistence, public assistance, or free education. The constitution also abandoned the universal male suffrage promised in 1793 and restored the propertied franchise of 1791 and the system of indirect elections. The regime's two-house legislature was designed to moderate the political process, while its five-man executive was meant to prevent the rise of a dictator. The Directory also feared a royalist resurgence. Since genuinely free elections at this point might be carried by the antirepublicans of the right, the outgoing Convention decided to coopt two-thirds of its members into the new legislature, thereby ensuring a substantial degree of political continuity. A royalist revolt against this power grab was easily crushed by government troops.

The Directory wished to command the center of the political spectrum, which one historian has aptly called "the mirage of the moderates." To maintain themselves in power, however, the directorials violated the liberties pledged in their own constitution. They repeatedly purged elected officials, and periodically suppressed political clubs and newspapers on the left and right. In general they refused to acknowledge the legitimacy of organized opposition of any kind. This explains the succession of coups and purges that marked the Directory's four years. Although the repressive measures were mild compared with those of the Terror—deportation usually being the harshest punishment meted out—they ultimately undermined the regime's viability. In the end many moderate republicans walked away from their own creation.

The Political Spectrum For all its repressive qualities, however, the Directory regime was democratic enough to allow most shades of the political spectrum some visibility. The full range of opinions in France, obscured previously by the Terror, was evident during the years of the Directory and would persist with some modifications into the twentieth century. The most important legacy of all, no doubt, was the apathy born of exhaustion or cynicism. Most citizens, especially peasants, had wearied of politics and distrusted all officials whatever government they served. Participation in the Directory regime's annual elections was extremely low.

Within this context of massive apathy, politically conscious minorities showed fierce partisanship. On the right, ultraroyalists (including émigrés, refractory priests, and armed rebels in western France) hoped to overthrow the Republic altogether. Some worked with the exiled Bourbon princes and with British secret agents. More moderate royalists hoped to win control of the Republic's political institutions lawfully, and then bring back the émigrés and refractory priests while stamping out the last vestiges of Jacobinism. (Since Napoleon later effected such changes on his own terms, they would form a major base of his support.)

On the left of the spectrum stood the Neo-Jacobins—democrats in their own eyes, anarchists to their opponents. The Neo-Jacobins adhered to the moderate Republic of 1795 but identified positively with the experience of 1793. They did not advocate a return to the Terror or the use of force to regain power. Instead, the Neo-

Jacobins promoted grass-roots activism through local political clubs, petition drives, newspapers, and electoral campaigns to keep alive the egalitarian ideals of the year II, such as free public education and progressive taxation.

At the far end of the spectrum stood a tiny group of radicals whose significance would loom larger in the next century than it did in 1796. Their leader was François-Noël Babeuf, who had changed his name to Gracchus Babeuf in 1793. The Babeuvists viewed the revolutionary government of the year II as a promising stage that had to be followed by a final revolution in the name of the masses. The Babeuvists advocated a vaguely defined material equality, or communism, for all citizens—a "community of goods," as they called it. They also assigned a key role to a small revolutionary vanguard in carrying out this final revolution. Regarding the present Republic as simply a new form of oppression by the elites, they conspired to overthrow it.

▶ **"The Directory Falls between Two Stools" is a caricature depicting the political dilemma of the Directory, which vainly sought a centrist position between the left and right.**

The Elusive Center The Directory's adherents stood somewhere in the center of this broad spectrum, hostile to royalists and Neo-Jacobins alike and ready to shift their ground with any change in the political balance. Thus, although the Neo-Jacobins had spurned Babeuf's calls for insurrection, after Babeuf's plot was exposed the Directory joined forces with the right. But when the first regular elections in the year V (1797) produced a royalist victory, the Directory reversed field. Backed by influential generals, the government purged newly elected royalist deputies, suppressed royalist newspapers, and allowed the Neo-Jacobins to open new clubs.

After a few months, however, the Directory grew fearful of the revived left. During the elections of the year VI (1798), Neo-Jacobins and Directorial moderates vied for influence in what almost amounted to party rivalry. But in the end the Directory would not risk the results of free elections. Again it intervened: closed down clubs and newspapers, manipulated electoral assemblies, and purged those neo-Jacobins who were elected anyway. Interestingly, at almost the same moment that France's government was quashing its political rivals, leaders of the American republic were reluctantly coming to accept opposition parties as legitimate. In France, however, the Directory would not tolerate organized opposition, and that rigidity contributed to the Republic's demise.

THE RISE OF BONAPARTE

Meanwhile, the Directory years provided unexpected impetus for revolutionary expansion in Europe, which brought into being a half dozen "sister republics" (see Map 21.1), including the Batavian Republic in the Netherlands and the Helvetic Republic in the Swiss Confederation. Revolutionary change also spread through the entire Italian peninsula, as French commanders

Map 21.1 **FRANCE AND ITS SISTER REPUBLICS, 1798**

in the field began to make their own diplomacy. Among them was a young brigadier general named Napoleon Bonaparte.

Bonaparte personifies the world-historic individual—the rare person whose life decisively dominates the course of historical events. Born in 1769 of an impoverished but well-connected family on the French-controlled island of Corsica, Napoleon scarcely seemed destined to play such a historic role. His youthful ambitions and fantasies involved little more than leading Corsica to independence from France. Sent to French military academies, he proved a diligent student, adept at mathematics. Aloof from his aristocratic classmates, whose pretensions he resented, self-reliant and energetic, he became an expert on artillery.

After 1789 the young officer returned to Corsica, but his ambitions ran up against more conservative forces on the island. Eventually, local factional conflict drove him and his family off Corsica altogether. Bonaparte then moved onto a much larger stage. He rose steadily and rapidly through the military ranks, based in part on the luck of opportunities but equally on his ability to act decisively and effectively. While on leave in Paris in 1795, Bonaparte was assigned to the planning bureau of the war ministry. There he advocated a new strategy—the opening of a front in Italy to strike at Austrian forces and push into Germany from the south, while French armies on the Rhine pushed as usual from the west. The strategy was approved, and Bonaparte gained command of the Army of Italy in 1796.

The Making of a Hero Austria's forces outnumbered the French in Italy, but Bonaparte moved his troops rapidly to achieve surprise and numerical superiority in specific encounters. The end result was a major victory that brought the French into the Habsburg domain of Lombardy and its capital, Milan. Bonaparte's overall plan almost miscarried, since the Army of the Rhine did not advance as planned. But this made his own triumphs all the more important to the Directory. And Bonaparte ensured his popularity with the government by making his campaign self-supporting through organized levies on the Italians.

Bonaparte brought a great sense of excitement and drama to the French occupation of Lombardy. His personal magnetism and his talent in manipulating people attracted many Italians. The general encouraged the Italians to organize their own revolutionary movement; the liberation of northern Italy, he believed, would solidify support for his army and enhance his own reputation. This policy distressed the Directory, since it had intended to trade back conquests in Italy in exchange for security on the Rhine frontier. But in the end the Directory endorsed the Treaty of Campo Formio, in which Bonaparte personally negotiated a peace settlement with Austria in October 1797. Austria recognized a new, independent state in northern Italy, the Cisalpine Republic, and left the Rhine question to future negotiations. The Directory regime had found the hero it so desperately needed.

The French now focused their patriotic aspirations on defeating the last member of the first coalition: the hated British enemy. Bonaparte naturally yearned for the glory of accomplishing this feat, and he was authorized to prepare an invasion force. Previous seaborne landings directed at Ireland had failed, however, and Bonaparte too finally had to abandon the scheme because of France's insufficient naval force.

Instead, in the spring of 1798 Bonaparte launched an expedition to Egypt intended to strike at Britain's colonial interests, including the approaches to India. But British naval superiority, in the form of Admiral Horatio Nelson's fleet, turned the expedition into a debacle. The British destroyed the French fleet at the Battle of the Nile, thereby marooning a French army in North Africa. Worse yet, the French were beaten back in several engagements with Turkish forces. Only cynical news management prevented the full story of this defeat from reaching France; instead, the expedition's exotic details and scientific explorations held the attention of the French public. Bonaparte extricated himself from this mess by slipping off through the British blockade, in effect abandoning his army as he returned to France.

THE BRUMAIRE COUP

While Bonaparte floundered in Egypt, the Directory was faltering under political pressures at home. Charges of tyranny and ineptitude accumulated against the directors. Further French expansion into Italy, which produced new sister republics centered in Rome and Naples, precipitated a new coalition against France, consisting of Britain, Russia, and Austria. In June 1799 ill-supplied French forces were driven out of most of Italy and Switzerland.

Widespread discontent with the Directory led to the defeat of many government-sponsored candidates in the spring elections of 1799. The legislature then ousted four of the five directors and named Sieyès, a respected leader of the patriots in 1789, among the replacements. Sieyès and his supporters secretly wished to alter the constitution itself, for they had lost confidence in the regime's institutions, especially its annual elections. These "revisionists" wanted to redesign the Republic along more oligarchic lines, as against the Neo-Jacobins who wished to democratize the Republic. The centrist position had virtually disappeared. The revisionists blocked emergency measures proposed by the Neo-Jacobins in reaction to the new war crisis, and breathed a sigh of relief as French armies rallied and repulsed Anglo-Russian forces in the Batavian Republic and Switzerland. Most of Italy was lost for the time being, but the threat to France itself had passed. Sieyès and the revisionists moved against the Neo-Jacobins by closing their clubs and newspapers, and prepared for a coup.

A General Comes to Power Although no dire military threat remained to propel the country into the arms of a general, the revisionists wished to establish a more centralized, oligarchic republic, and they needed a general's support. Generals were the only national heroes in France, and only a general could organize the force necessary to ensure the coup's success. Bonaparte's return to France from Egypt thus seemed most timely. Bonaparte was not the revisionists' first choice, but he proved to be the best available one. On his trip up from the Mediterranean, people had cheered him warmly, since they knew little of the Egyptian fiasco and saw him in his role as victor of the Italian campaign.

Contrary to the intentions of Sieyès and his fellow conspirators, Bonaparte proved to be the tail that wagged the dog. Once the coup began, he proved to be far more ambitious and energetic than the other conspirators and thrust himself into the most prominent position. Bonaparte addressed the legislature to denounce a mythical Jacobin plot and to demand emergency powers for a new provisional government. Along with two former directors, he was empowered to draft a new constitution; a cooperative rump of the legislature subsequently approved the new arrangements. Thus unfolded the coup of 18 Brumaire year VIII (November 9, 1799).

The Brumaire coup had not been intended to install a dictatorship, but that was its eventual result. In the maneuvering among the revisionists, Bonaparte's ideas and personality prevailed. The plotters agreed to eliminate meaningful elections, which they saw as promoting political instability. They agreed also to enshrine the social ideals of 1789, such as civil equality, and to bury those of the year II, such as popular democracy. The vague notion of popular sovereignty gave way to concentrated authority. The general came out of the coup as the regime's strongman, and Sieyès' elaborate plans for a republican oligarchy ended in the wastebasket. On one other point, the plotters were particularly deceived. With General Bonaparte's assistance they hoped to achieve durable peace through military victory. Instead, the Napoleonic regime promoted unbounded expansion and endless warfare.

II. The Napoleonic Settlement in France

Bonaparte's prime asset in his rapid takeover of France was the resignation of its citizens. Most French people were so weary politically that they saw in Bonaparte what they wished to see.[1] The Committee of Public Safety had won grudging submission through its terroristic policies; Bonaparte achieved that result almost by default. As an effective propagandist for himself and a man of great personal appeal, he soothed a divided France. Ultraroyalists and dedicated Jacobins never warmed to his regime, but most citizens fell between those positions and could find comfort in the prospect of a return to order and stability.

THE NAPOLEONIC STYLE

Napoleon Bonaparte was not a royalist or a Jacobin, not a conservative or a liberal, though his attitudes were flavored by a touch of each view-

[1] It is customary to refer to "Bonaparte" until 1804, when the general crowned himself Emperor Napoleon I.

point. Authority, not ideology, was his great concern, and he justified his actions by their results. The revolutionaries of 1789 could consider Napoleon one of theirs because of his hostility toward the unjust and ineffective institutions of the old regime. He had little use for seigneurialism, the cumbersome institutions of Bourbon absolutism, or the congealed structures of aristocratic privilege, which the Revolution had destroyed. Napoleon valued the Revolution's commitment to equality of opportunity and continued to espouse that liberal premise. Other rights and liberties of 1789 he curtailed or disdained.

Ten years of upheaval had produced a grim paradox: The French Revolution had proceeded in the name of liberty, yet successive forms of repression had been mounted to defend it. Napoleon fit comfortably into this history; unlike the Directory, he made no pretense about it. The social gains of the Revolution would be preserved through political centralization and authoritarian control. Napoleon's field of action was in fact far greater than that of the most powerful eighteenth-century monarch, for no entrenched aristocracy existed to resist him. Thanks to the clearing operations of the Revolution, he could reconstruct at will.

Tragically, however, Napoleon drifted away from his own rational ideals. Increasingly absorbed in his personal power, he began to force domestic and foreign policies on France that were geared to his imperial ambitions. Increasingly he concentrated his government on raising men and money for his armies, and turned his back on revolutionary liberties.

POLITICAL AND RELIGIOUS SETTLEMENTS

Bonaparte gave France a constitution, approved in a plebiscite, that placed almost unchecked authority in the hands of a First Consul (himself) for 10 years. Two later constitutional revisions, also approved overwhelmingly in plebiscites, increased executive power and diminished the legislative branch until it became simply a rubber stamp. The first revision, in 1802, converted the consulship into a lifetime post; the second, in 1804, proclaimed Napoleon hereditary emperor. The task of proposing new laws passed from elected representatives to appointed experts in the Council of State. This new body advised the ruler, drafted legislation under his direction, and monitored public officials. Such government by experts stood as an alternative to meaningful parliamentary democracy for the next century.

The system of local government established by Bonaparte in 1800 came ironically close to the kind of royal centralization that public opinion had roundly condemned in 1789. Bonaparte eliminated the local elections that the Revolution had emphasized. Instead, each department was now administered by a *prefect* appointed by the ruler. The 400-odd subprefects on the district level as well as the 40,000 mayors of France's communes were likewise appointed. With minor changes the

► **Napoleon Bonaparte as First Consul, at the height of his popularity, painted by his admirer J.-B. Gros.**

unquestionably efficient prefectorial system survived in France for 150 years, severely limiting local autonomy and self-government.

Police-state methods finished what constitutional change began: the suppression of independent political activity. From the legislature to the grass roots, France was depoliticized. The government permitted no organized opposition, reduced the number of newspapers drastically, and censored the remaining ones. The free journalism born in 1789 gave way to government press releases and news management. In 1811 only four newspapers remained in Paris, all hewing to the official line. Political clubs were prohibited, outspoken dissidents deported, and others placed under police surveillance. All this silenced liberal intellectuals as well as former political activists.

The Concordat Napoleon's religious policies promoted tranquillity at home and a good image abroad. Before Brumaire the Republic tolerated Catholic worship in theory but severely restricted it in practice. Continued proscription of the refractory clergy; insistence on the republican calendar, with its 10-day weeks that made Sunday a workday; and a drive to keep religious instruction out of elementary schools curtailed the free and familiar exercise of Catholicism. These policies provoked wide resentment among the mass of citizens whose commitment to Catholicism remained intact throughout the Revolution.

Though not a believer himself, Napoleon judged that major concessions to Catholic sentiment were in order, provided that the Church remained under the control of the state. In 1801 he negotiated a Concordat, or agreement, with Pope Pius VII. It stipulated that Catholicism was the "preferred" religion of France but protected religious freedom for non-Catholics. The Church was again free to operate in full public view and to restore the refractory priests. Primary education would espouse Catholic values and use Catholic texts, as it had before the Revolution, and clerical salaries would be paid by the state. Though nominated by the ruler, bishops would again be consecrated by the pope. But as a major concession to the Revolution, the Concordat stipulated that land confiscated from the Church and sold during the Revolution would be retained by its purchasers. On the other hand, the government dropped the 10-day week and restored the Gregorian calendar.

The balance of church-state relations tilted firmly in the state's favor, for Napoleon intended to use the clergy as a major prop of his regime. The pulpit and the primary school became instruments of social control, to be used, as a new catechism stated, "to bind the religious conscience of the people to the august person of the Emperor." As Napoleon put it, the clergy would be his "moral prefects." Devout Catholics came to resent this subordination of the Church. Eventually Pope Pius renounced the Concordat, to which Napoleon responded by removing the pontiff to France and placing him under house arrest.

THE ERA OF THE NOTABLES

With civil equality established and feudalism abolished, Napoleon believed that the Revolution was complete. It remained to encourage an orderly hierarchical society to counteract what he regarded as the excessive individualism of revolutionary social policy. Napoleon intended to reassert the authority of the state, the elites, and, in family life, the father.

In the absence of electoral politics, Napoleon used the state's appointive powers to confer status on prominent local individuals, or *notables*, thus associating them with his regime. These local dignitaries were usually chosen from among the largest taxpayers: prosperous landowners, former nobles, businessmen, and professionals. Those who served the regime with distinction were honored by induction into the Legion of Honor, nine-tenths of whose members were military men. "It is with trinkets that mankind is governed," Napoleon once said. Legion of Honor awards and appointments to prestigious but powerless local bodies were precisely such trinkets, and they endured long after their creator was gone.

Napoleon offered more tangible rewards to the country's leading bankers when he chartered a national bank that enjoyed the credit power derived from official ties to the state. In education, Napoleon created elite secondary schools, or *lycées*, to train future government officials, engineers, and officers. The *lycées* embodied the concept of careers open to talent and became part of a highly centralized French academic system called the *University*, which survived into the twentieth century.

The Civil Code Napoleon's most important legacy was a Civil Code regulating social relations and property rights. Baptized the Napoleonic Code in 1807, it was in some measure a revolutionary law code that progressives throughout Europe embraced. Wherever it was implemented, the Civil Code swept away feudal property relations and gave legal sanction to modern contractual notions of property. The code established the right to choose one's occupation, to receive equal treatment under the law, and to enjoy religious freedom. At the same time, it allowed employers to dominate their workers by prohibiting strikes and trade unions. Nor did the code match property rights with popular rights like the right to subsistence.

Revolutionary legislation had emancipated women and children by establishing their civil rights. Napoleon undid most of this by restoring the father's absolute authority in the family. "A wife owes obedience to her husband," said the code, which proceeded to deprive wives of property and juridical rights established during the 1790s and to curtail the right to divorce, while establishing a kind of double standard in the dissolution of a marriage (*see box*, below). The code also expanded the husband's options in disposing of his estate, although each child was still guaranteed a portion.

The prefectorial system of local government, the Civil Code, the Concordat, the University, the Legion of Honor, and the local bodies of *notables* all proved to be durable institutions. They fulfilled Napoleon's desire to create a series of "granite masses" on which to reconstruct French society. His admirers emphasized that these institutions contributed to social stability amid France's chronic political unrest. One can argue

Family and Gender Roles under the Napoleonic Civil Code

"Art. 148. The son who has not attained the full age of 25 years, the daughter who has not attained the full age of 21 years, cannot contract marriage without the consent of their father and mother; in case of disagreement, the consent of the father is sufficient.

"Art. 212. Married persons owe to each other fidelity, succor, assistance.

"Art. 213. The husband owes protection to his wife, the wife obedience to her husband.

"Art. 214. The wife is obliged to live with her husband, and to follow him to every place where he may judge it convenient to reside: the husband is obliged to receive her, and to furnish her with everything necessary for the wants of life, according to his means and station.

"Art. 215. The wife cannot plead [in court] in her own name, without the authority of her husband, even though she should be a public trader . . . or separate in property.

"Art. 217. A wife . . . cannot give, alienate, pledge, or acquire by free or chargeable title, without the concurrence of her husband in the act, or his consent in writing.

"Art. 219. If the husband refuses to authorize his wife to pass an act, the wife may cause her husband to be cited directly before the court of first instance . . . which may give or refuse its authority, after the husband shall have been heard, or duly summoned.

"Art. 229. The husband may demand a divorce on the ground of his wife's adultery.

"Art. 230. The wife may demand divorce on the ground of adultery in her husband, when he shall have brought his concubine into their common residence.

"Art. 231. The married parties may reciprocally demand divorce for outrageous conduct, ill-usage, or grievous injuries, exercised by one of them towards the other."

that they were skillful compromises between revolutionary liberalism and an older belief in hierarchy and central authority. Detractors point out that they were class-oriented and excessively patriarchal. Moreover they fostered overcentralized, rigid structures that might have sapped the vitality of French institutions in succeeding generations. Whatever their merits or defects, these institutions took root, unlike Napoleon's attempt to dominate all of Europe.

III. Napoleonic Hegemony in Europe

After giving France a new government, Bonaparte's first task was to defeat the second anti-French coalition on the battlefield, especially in northern Italy. The outcome of this campaign against Austria would reinforce or destroy the settlement he had imposed on France after Brumaire. Napoleon's dictatorial tendencies became obvious enough within France, but it was in the arena of international relations that his ambitions lost all semblance of restraint. There he evolved from a general of the Revolution to an imperial conqueror. Napoleon's conquest of Italy, Germany, Spain, and other lands set contradictory responses of collaboration and resistance in motion. French expansion sparked nationalism abroad, but also liberalism and reaction.

MILITARY SUPREMACY AND THE REORGANIZATION OF EUROPE

Bonaparte's strategy in 1800 called for a repeat of the 1797 campaign: He would strike through Italy while the Army of the Rhine pushed eastward against Vienna. Following French victories at Marengo in Lombardy and Hohenlinden in Germany, Austria sued for peace. The Treaty of Lunéville (February 1801) essentially restored France to the position it had held after Bonaparte's triumphs in Italy in 1797.

▶ Deputies from the Cisalpine Republic of Italy proclaim Napoleon Bonaparte their president in 1802.

▶ **Admiral Nelson's heavily armed three-decker ship of the line, which inflicted such devastation on the French fleet at Trafalgar.**

In Britain a war-weary government now stood alone against France and decided to negotiate. The Treaty of Amiens (March 1801) ended hostilities and reshuffled territorial holdings outside Europe, such as the Cape Colony in South Africa, which passed from the Dutch to the British. But this truce proved precarious since it did not settle the future of French influence in Europe or of commercial relations between the two great powers. Napoleon abided by the letter of the treaty but soon violated its spirit. Britain and Austria alike were dismayed by further expansion of French influence in Italy, Switzerland, and North America. Most important, perhaps, France seemed determined to exclude British trade rather than restore normal commercial relations. Historians agree that the Treaty of Amiens failed to keep the peace because neither side was ready to abandon its century-long struggle for predominance.

The Third Coalition A third anti-French coalition soon took shape, a replay of its predecessors. France ostensibly fought to preserve the new regime at home and its sister republics abroad. The coalition's objectives included the restoration of the Netherlands and Italy to "independence," the limitation of French influence elsewhere, and, if possible, a reduction of France to its prerevolutionary borders. Like most such alliances, the coalition would be dismembered piecemeal.

French hopes of settling the issue directly by invading Britain proved impossible once again. At the Battle of Trafalgar (October 1805), Admiral Nelson's fleet crushed an outnumbered and outmanned French navy. Nelson was an innovative tactician who broke rule-book procedures on the high seas just as French generals did on land, and he ensured the security of the British Isles for the remainder of the Napoleonic era.

Napoleon then turned against the Austro-Russian forces. Moving 200,000 French soldiers with unprecedented speed across the continent, he took his enemies by surprise and won a dazzling succession of victories. After occupying Vienna he proceeded against the coalition's main army in December. Feigning weakness and retreat at the moment of battle, he drew his numerically superior opponents into an exposed position, crushed the center of their lines, and inflicted a decisive defeat. This Battle of Austerlitz was Napoleon's most brilliant tactical achievement, and it forced the Habsburgs to the peace table. The resulting Treaty of Pressburg (December 1805), extremely harsh and humiliating for

Austria, imposed a large indemnity and required the Habsburgs to cede their Venetian provinces.

France and Germany By now the French sphere of influence had increased dramatically to include most of southern Germany, which Napoleon reorganized into the Confederation of the Rhine, a client realm of France (see Map 21.2). France had kept Prussia neutral during the war with Austria by skillful diplomacy. Only after Austria made peace did Prussia recognize its error in failing to join with Austria to halt Napoleon. Belatedly, Prussia mobilized its famous but antiquated army; it was rewarded with stinging defeats by France in a number of encounters culminating in the Battle of Jena (October 1806). With the collapse of Prussian military power, the conquerors settled in Berlin and watched the prestige of the Prussian ruling class crumble. Napoleon was now master of northern Germany as well as the south. For a while it appeared that he might obliterate Prussia entirely, but he restored its sovereignty—after amputating part of its territory and imposing a crushing indemnity.

Napoleon was free to reorganize Central Europe as he pleased. After formally proclaiming the end of the Holy Roman Empire in 1806, he liquidated numerous small German states and merged them into two new ones: the Kingdom of Westphalia, with brother Jérôme on the throne, and the Grand Duchy of Berg, to be ruled by his brother-in-law Joachim Murat. His ally Saxony became a full-scale kingdom, while a new duchy of Warsaw was carved out of Prussian Poland. This "restoration" of Poland had propaganda value; it made the emperor appear as a champion of Polish aspirations, compared to the rulers of Prussia, Russia, and Austria, who had dismembered Poland in a series of partitions between 1772 and 1795. Moreover, Napoleon could now enlist a Polish army and use Polish territory as a base of operations against his remaining continental foe, Russia.

France and Russia In February 1807 Napoleon confronted the colossus of the East in the Battle of Eylau; the resulting carnage was horrifying but

Napoleon amidst the carnage on the battlefield of Eylau, the bloodiest engagement to date of the revolutionary-Napoleonic era, where the French and Russians fought each other to a stalemate in 1807.

inconclusive. When spring came, only a dramatic victory could preserve his conquests in Central Europe and vindicate the extraordinary commitments of the past two years. Fortunately for the emperor, the Battle of Friedland in June was a French victory that demoralized Russia's Tsar Alexander I and persuaded him to negotiate.

Meeting at Tilsit, the two rulers buried their differences and agreed in effect to partition Europe into Eastern and Western spheres of influence. Each would support the other's conquests and mediate in behalf of the other's interests. The Treaty of Tilsit (July 1807) sanctioned new annexations of territory directly into France and the reorganization of other conquered countries. The creation of new satellite kingdoms became the vehicle for Napoleon's domination of Europe. Like the French Republic, the sister republics became kingdoms between 1805 and 1807. And it happened that Napoleon had a large family of brothers ready to wear those new royal crowns.

The distorted shape of Napoleonic Europe is apparent on maps dating from 1808 to 1810 (see Map 21.2). His chief satellites included the King-

Map 21.2 **EUROPE AROUND 1810**

dom of Holland, with brother Louis on the throne; the Kingdom of Italy, with Napoleon himself as king and his stepson Eugène de Beauharnais as viceroy; the Confederation of the Rhine, including brother Jérôme's Kingdom of Westphalia; the Kingdom of Naples, covering southern Italy, with brother Joseph the ruler until Napoleon transferred him to Spain and installed his brother-in-law Murat; and the Duchy of Warsaw. Belgium, the Rhineland, Tuscany, Piedmont, Genoa, and the Illyrian provinces had been annexed to France. Switzerland did not become a kingdom, but the Helvetic Republic (as it was now called) received a new constitution dictated by France. In 1810, after yet another war with Austria, a marriage was arranged between the house of Bonaparte and the house of Habsburg. Having divorced Joséphine de Beauharnais, Napoleon married princess Marie Louise, daughter of Francis II, who bore him a male heir the following year.

▸ Emperor Napoleon I on his imperial throne in 1806, by the great portrait painter Ingres. Note the dramatic contrast in appearance with the young, intense military hero of the Republic in David's portrait, which opens the chapter.

NAVAL WAR WITH BRITAIN

For a time it seemed that Britain alone stood between Napoleon and his dream of hegemony over Europe. Since Britain was invulnerable to invasion, Napoleon hoped to destroy its influence by means of economic warfare. Unable to blockade British ports directly, he could try to close off the continent: keep Britain from its markets, stop its exports, and thus ruin its trade and credit. Napoleon reasoned that if Britain had nowhere to sell its manufactured goods, no gold would come into the country and bankruptcy would eventually ensue. Meanwhile overproduction would cause unemployment and labor unrest, which would turn the British people against their government and force the latter to make peace with France. At the same time, French advantages in continental markets would increase with the elimination of British competition.

The Continental System Napoleon therefore launched his "Continental System" to prohibit British trade with all French allies. Even neutral ships were banned from European ports if they carried goods coming from the British Isles. Britain responded in 1807 with the Orders in Council, which in effect reversed the blockade: It *required* all neutral ships to stop at British ports to procure trading licenses and pay tariffs. In other words, the British insisted on regulating all trade between neutral states and European ports. Ships that failed to obey would be stopped on the high seas and captured. In an angry response, Napoleon, in turn, threatened to seize any neutral ship that obeyed the Orders in Council by stopping at British ports.

Thus a total naval war between France and Britain enveloped all neutral nations. Indeed, neutral immunity virtually disappeared, since every ship was obliged to violate one system or the other and thus run afoul of naval patrols or privateers. While the British captured only about 40 French ships a year after 1807 (for few were left afloat), they seized almost 3000 neutral vessels a year, including many from the United States.

The Continental System did hurt British trade. British gold reserves dwindled, and 1811 saw widespread unemployment and rioting. France was affected, in turn, by Britain's counterblockade, which cut it off from certain raw materials necessary for industrial production. But the satellite states, as economic vassals of France, suffered the most. In Amsterdam, for example, shipping volume declined from 1350 ships entering the port in 1806 to 310 in 1809, and commercial revenues dropped calamitously. Out of loyalty to the people whom he ruled, Holland's King Louis Bonaparte tolerated smuggling. But this so infuriated Napoleon that he ousted his brother from the throne and annexed the Kingdom of Holland directly to France. Smuggling was in fact the weak link in the system, for it created holes in Napoleon's wall of economic sanctions that constantly needed plugging. This problem drove the emperor to ever more drastic actions.

THE NAPOLEONIC CONSCRIPTION MACHINE

One key to Napoleon's unrestrained ambitions in Europe was the creation of an efficient administrative state in France and its annexed territories. State penetration of the countryside under Napoleon achieved its most dramatic impact by creating a veritable conscription machine, which continuously replenished the ranks of the imperial army.

The National Convention's mass levy of August 1793 had drafted all able-bodied unmarried men between the ages of 18 and 25. But this unprecedented mobilization had been meant as a one-time-only emergency measure, a temporary "requisition." There was no implication that subsequent cohorts of young men would face conscription into the army as part of their civic obligations. When the war resumed in 1798, however, the Directory passed a conscription law that made successive "classes" of young men (that is, those born in a particular year) subject to a military draft should the need arise. The Directory immediately implemented this law and called up three classes, but local officials reported massive draft evasion in most of the departments. Many French youths found the prospect of military service repugnant. From this shaky foundation, however, the Napoleonic regime developed a successful conscription system.

After much trial and error with the details, timetables, and mechanisms, the system began to operate efficiently within a few years. The government assigned an annual quota of conscripts for each department. Using parish birth registers, the mayor of every community compiled a list of men reaching the age of 19 that year. These youths were then led by their mayor to the cantonal seat on a specified day for a draft lottery. Panels of doctors at the departmental capitals later verified or rejected claims for medical exemptions. In all, about a third of French youths legally avoided military service because they were physically unfit—too short, lame, deformed, or suffering from poor eyesight, chronic diseases, or other infirmities.

In the draft lottery, youths picked numbers out of a box; marriage could no longer be used as an exemption, for obvious reasons. Those with high numbers were spared (for the time being), while those who drew low numbers filled the local induction quota. Two means of avoiding service remained: The wealthy could purchase a replacement, and the poor could flee. True, the regime had a bad conscience about allowing draftees to hire replacements, because the practice made its rhetoric about the duties of citizenship sound hollow. But to placate wealthy notables and peasants with large holdings (who were sometimes desperate to keep their sons on the farm), the government permitted the hiring of a replacement under strict guidelines that made it difficult and expensive but not impossible. The proportion of replacements was somewhere between 5 and 10 percent of all draftees.

Draft Evasion For Napoleon's prefects, conscription levies were always the top priority

The departure of a group of conscripts from the "class" of 1807 in Paris.

among their duties, and draft evasion was the number one problem. Dogged persistence, bureaucratic routine, and various forms of coercion gradually overcame this chronic resistance. From time to time, columns of troops swept through areas where evasion and desertion were most common and arrested culprits by the hundreds. But draft evaders usually hid out in remote places—mountains, forests, marshes—so coercion had to be directed against their families as well. Heavy fines assessed against the parents did little good since most were too poor to pay anything. A better tactic was to billet troops in the draft evaders' homes; if their families could not afford to feed the troops, then the community's wealthy taxpayers were required to do so. All this created pressure on the youths to turn themselves in. By 1811 the regime had broken the habit of draft evasion, and conscription was generally becoming accepted as a disagreeable civic obligation, much like taxes. In fact, just as draft calls were beginning to rise sharply, draft evasion fell dramatically. In 1812 prefects all over France reported that the year's levies were more successful than ever before.

Napoleon had begun by drafting 60,000 Frenchmen annually, but by 1810 the annual quotas had risen steadily to 120,000, and they continued to climb. Moreover, in 1810 the emperor ordered the first of many "supplementary levies," calling up men from earlier classes who had drawn high lottery numbers. In January 1813, to look ahead, Napoleon replenished his armies by calling up the class of 1814 a year early and by making repeated supplementary calls on earlier classes.

IV. *Opposition to Napoleon*

In 1808, with every major European power except Britain vanquished on the battlefield, Napoleon felt that nothing stood in his way. Since Spain and Russia seemed unable or unwilling to stop smuggling from Britain, the emperor decided to deal with each by force of arms, assuming that his design against Britain could then be pursued to its conclusion. On all counts he was mistaken.

Napoleon's confrontations with Spain and Russia proved that his reach had exceeded his grasp.

THE "SPANISH ULCER"

Spain and France shared a common interest in weakening British power in Europe and the colonial world. But the alliance they formed after making peace with each other in 1795 brought only troubles for Spain, including the loss of its Louisiana Territory in America and (at the Battle of Trafalgar) most of its naval fleet. The Spanish royal household, meanwhile, was mired in scandal. Prime Minister Manuel de Godoy, once a lover of the queen, was a corrupt opportunist and extremely unpopular with the people. Crown Prince Ferdinand despised Godoy and Godoy's protectors, the king and queen, while Ferdinand's parents actively returned their son's hostility.

Napoleon looked on at this farce with irritation. At the zenith of his power, he concluded that he must reorganize Spain himself to bring it solidly into the Continental System. As a pretext for military intervention, he set in motion a plan to invade Portugal, supposedly to partition it with Spain. Once the French army was well inside Spain, however, Napoleon intended to impose his own political solution to Spain's instability.

Napoleon brought the squabbling king and prince to France, where he threatened and bribed one and then the other into abdicating. The emperor then gathered a group of handpicked Spanish notables who followed Napoleon's scenario by petitioning him to provide a new sovereign, preferably his brother Joseph. Joseph was duly proclaimed king of Spain. With 100,000 French troops already positioned around Madrid, he prepared to assume his new throne, eager to rule under a liberal constitution and to believe his brother's statement that "all the better Spanish people are on your side." As he took up the crown, however, an unanticipated drama erupted.

▶ **Tricked and cajoled out of the Spanish throne by Napoleon, Ferdinand VII sits unhappily as a virtual prisoner in Bayonne, across the French border.**

Popular Resistance Faced with military occupation, the disappearance of their royal family, and the crowning of a Frenchman, the Spanish people rose in rebellion. It began on May 2, 1808, when an angry crowd in Madrid rioted against French troops, who responded with firing squads and brutal reprisals. This bloody incident, known as the Dos de Mayo and captured in Goya's famous paintings, has remained a source of Spanish national pride, for it touched off a sustained uprising against the French. Local notables created committees, or *juntas,* to organize resistance, mainly by peasants and monks, and to coordinate campaigns by regular Spanish troops. These troops were generally ineffective against the French, but they did produce one early victory: A half-starved French army was cut off and forced to surrender at Bailén in July 1808. This defeat broke the aura of Napoleonic invincibility.

The British saw a great opportunity to attack Napoleon in concert with the rebellious Spanish people. Landing an army in Portugal, the British actually bore the brunt of anti-French military operations in Spain, in what they called the Peninsular War. In a grueling war of attrition, their forces drove the French out of Portugal, and after five years of fighting and many reversals they pushed the French back across the Pyrénées in November 1813. The British commander, the Duke of Wellington, had grasped the French predicament when he said: "The more ground the French hold down in Spain, the weaker they will be at any given point."

▸ The great Spanish artist Francisco Goya memorably captured the brutality of French reprisals against the citizens of Madrid who dared to rebel against the Napoleonic occupation on May 2, 1808.

▸ **In a relentlessly bleak series of drawings collectively entitled "The Horrors of War," Goya went on to record the savagery and atrocities committed by both sides of the struggle in Spain.**

About 30,000 Spanish guerilla fighters helped wear down the French and forced the occupiers to struggle for survival in hostile country. The guerillas drew French forces from the main battlefields, inflicted casualties, denied the French access to food, and punished Spanish collaborators. In short, the Spanish fighters established the model for modern guerilla warfare. Their harassment kept the invaders in a constant state of anxiety, which led the French to adopt harsh measures in reprisal. But these "pacification" tactics only escalated the war's brutality and further enraged the Spanish people.

Together, the juntas, the Spanish regulars, the guerillas, and the British expeditionary force kept a massive French army of up to 300,000 men pinned down in Spain. Napoleon referred to the

Spanish Liberals Draft a Constitution, 1812

"The general and extraordinary Cortes of the Spanish nation, duly organized . . . in order duly to discharge the lofty objective of furthering the glory, prosperity and welfare of the Nation as a whole, decrees the following political Constitution to assure the well-being and upright administration of the State.

"Art. 1: The Spanish Nation is the union of all Spaniards from both hemispheres.

"Art. 3: Sovereignty resides primarily in the Nation and because of this the right to establish the fundamental laws belongs to it exclusively.

"Art. 4: The Nation is obligated to preserve and protect with wise and just laws civil liberty, property and the other legitimate rights of all the individuals belonging to it.

"Art. 12: The religion of the Spanish Nation is and always will be the Catholic, Apostolic, Roman and only true faith. The Nation protects it with wise and just laws and prohibits the exercise of any other.

"Art. 14: The Government of the Spanish Nation is an hereditary limited Monarchy.

"Art. 15: The power to make laws resides in the Cortes with the King.

"Art. 16: The power to enforce laws resides in the King.

"Art. 27: The Cortes is the union of all the deputies that represent the Nation, named by the citizens.

"Art. 34: To elect deputies to the Cortes, electoral meetings will be held in the parish, the district, and the province.

"Art. 59: The electoral meetings on the district level will be made up of the electors chosen at the parish level who will convene at the seat of every district in order to name the electors who will then converge on the provincial capital to elect the deputies to the Cortes.

"Art. 338: The Cortes will annually establish or confirm all taxes, be they direct or indirect, general, provincial or municipal. . . .

"Art. 339: Taxes will be apportioned among all Spaniards in proportion to their abilities [to pay], without exception to any privilege."

From the Political Constitution of the Spanish Monarchy proclaimed in Cádiz March 19, 1812 (translated by James Tueller).

war as his "Spanish ulcer," an open sore that would not heal. Though he held the rebel fighters in contempt, other Europeans were inspired by their example of armed resistance to France.

The Spanish Liberals The war, however, proved a disaster for Spanish liberals. Torn between loyalty to Joseph, who would have liked to be a liberal ruler, and nationalist rebels, liberals faced a difficult dilemma. Those who collaborated with Joseph hoped to spare the people from a brutal war and to institute reform from above in the tradition of Spanish enlightened absolutism. But they found that Joseph could not rule independently; Napoleon gave the orders in Spain and relied on his generals to implement them. The liberals who joined the rebellion organized a provisional government by reviving the ancient Spanish parliament, or *Cortes*, in the southern town of Cádiz. Like the French National Assembly of 1789, the Cortes of Cádiz drafted a liberal constitution in 1812 (*see box*, above), which pleased the British and was therefore tolerated for the time being by the juntas.

In reality, most nationalist rebels despised the liberals. Most rebels were royalists who were fighting for the Catholic Church, the Spanish monarchy, and the old way of life. When in 1814 Wellington finally drove the French out of Spain and former crown prince Ferdinand VII took the throne, the joy of the Cádiz liberals quickly evaporated. As a royalist mob sacked the Cortes building, Ferdinand tore up the constitution of 1812, reinstated absolutism, restored the monasteries and the Inquisition, revived censorship, and arrested the leading liberals. Nationalist reactionaries emerged as the victors of the Spanish rebellion and the Peninsular War.

Independence in Spanish America The Creoles, descendants of Spanish settlers who were born in the New World, also profited from the upheaval in Spain. Spain had been cut off from its vast empire of American colonies in 1805, when the British navy won control of the Atlantic after the Battle of Trafalgar. In 1807 a British force attacked Buenos Aires in Spain's vice-royalty of the Río de la Plata (now Argentina). The Argentines—who raised excellent cattle on the *pampas*, or grassy plains—were eager to trade their beef and hides for British goods, but Spain's rigid mercantilism had always prevented such beneficial commerce. The Argentines welcomed the prospect of free trade, but not the prospect of British conquest. With Spain unable to defend them, the Creoles organized their own militia and drove off the invaders. Gaining confidence from this victory, they pushed aside the Spanish viceroy and his bureaucrats and took power into their own hands, though they still swore allegiance to the Spanish crown. The subsequent upheaval in Spain, however, led the Argentines to declare their independence. After Ferdinand regained the Spanish throne in 1814, he sent an army to reclaim the colony but the Argentines, under General José de San Martín, drove it off, and Argentina made good on its claim to full independence.

Rebellion spread throughout Spanish America, led above all by Simón Bolívar, revered in the hemisphere as "The Liberator." After Napoleon removed the king of Spain in 1808, the Creoles in Spain's vice-royalty of New Granada (encompassing modern-day Venezuela, Colombia, and Ecuador) elected a congress, which declared independence from Spain. An arduous, protracted war with the Spanish garrisons followed, and by 1816 Spain had regained control of the region. But Bolívar resumed the struggle and gradually wore down the Spanish forces; in one campaign his army marched 600 miles from the torrid Venezuelan lowlands over the snow-capped Andes Mountains to Colombia. Finally in 1819 the Spanish conceded defeat. Bolívar's dream of one unified, conservative republic of Gran Colombia soon disintegrated, under regional pressures, into several independent states, but not before Bolívar launched one final military campaign and liberated Peru, Spain's remaining colony in South America (see Maps 21.3a and b on pages 694 and 695).

THE RUSSIAN DEBACLE

Napoleon did not yet realize in 1811 that his entanglement in Spain would drain French military power and encourage resistance in Central Europe. On the contrary, never were the emperor's schemes more grandiose. Surveying the crumbling state system of Europe, he imagined that it could be replaced with a vast empire, ruled from Paris and based on the Napoleonic Code. He mistakenly believed that the era of the balance of power among Europe's nations was over and that nationalist sentiments need not constrain his actions.

Russia now loomed as the main obstacle to Napoleon's imperial reorganization and domination of Europe. Russia, a restive ally with ambitions of its own in Eastern Europe, resented the restrictions on its trade under the Continental System. British diplomats, anti-Napoleonic exiles such as Baron Stein of Prussia, and nationalist reactionaries at court all pressured the tsar to resist Napoleon. Russian court liberals, more concerned with domestic reforms, hoped on the contrary that Alexander would maintain peace with France, but by 1812 their influence on the tsar had waned. For his part, Napoleon wanted to enforce the Continental System and humble Russia. As he bluntly put it: "Let Alexander defeat the Persians, but don't let him meddle in the affairs of Europe." Once again two major powers faced each other with diminishing interest in maintaining peace.

Napoleon prepared for his most momentous military campaign. His objective was to annihilate Russia's army or, at the least, to conquer Moscow and chase the army to the point of disarray. To this end he marshaled a "Grand Army" of almost 600,000 men (half of them French, the

Map 21.3a SPANISH AMERICA BEFORE INDEPENDENCE

LOUISIANA
French 1800–1803; sold to U.S. 1803
UNITED STATES
(from 1783)
TEXAS
ATLANTIC OCEAN
New Orleans
FLORIDA
Spanish 1783–1819; sold to U.S. 1819
REPUBLIC OF MEXICO
1821 / 1821
Gulf of Mexico
Bahama Islands
Havana
Mexico City
Yucatan
Cuba
REPUBLIC OF HAITI
1804
BELIZE
Jamaica
Hispaniola
Puerto Rico
Guadeloupe
Martinique
Barbados
Guatemala
Caribbean Sea
MOSKITO COAST
UNITED PROVINCES OF CENTRAL AMERICA
1821 / 1823
Cartagena
Trinidad
BRITISH GUYANA
Caracas
DUTCH GUIANA
Panama
VENEZUELA
1830
FRENCH GUIANA
REPUBLIC OF NEW GRENADA
1830
Santa Fe de Bogotá
REPUBLIC OF GREATER COLOMBIA
1811
Quito
Galapagos Islands
ECUADOR
1830
EMPIRE OF BRAZIL
1822
Lima
PERU
1821 / 1821
La Paz
Bahia (Salvador)
PACIFIC OCEAN
BOLIVIA
1825
PARAGUAY
1811
Rio de Janeiro
REMAINING COLONIAL POSSESSIONS
Spanish Possessions
British Possessions
French Possessions
Dutch Possessions
URUGUAY
1814 / 1828
Montevideo
Buenos Aires
Santiago
ARGENTINE CONFEDERATION
1810
CHILE
1810 / 1818
PATAGONIA
Date of independence from colonial power
Date of separation from other states
1821 / 1823
Islas Malvinas/ Falkland Islands
British 1765–1770; Spanish 1770–1820

Map 21.3b SPANISH AMERICA AFTER INDEPENDENCE

remainder from his satellite states and allies) and moved them steadily by forced marches across Central Europe into Russia. The Russians responded by retreating in orderly fashion and avoiding a fight. Many Russian nobles abandoned their estates and burned their crops to the ground, leaving the Grand Army to operate far from its supply bases in territory stripped of food. At Borodino the Russians finally made a stand and sustained a frightful 45,000 casualties, but the remaining Russian troops managed to withdraw in order (see Map 21.4). Napoleon lost 35,000 men in that battle; but far more men and horses were dying from hunger, thirst, fatigue, and disease in the march across Russia's unending, barren territory (see plate on p. 697). The greatly depleted ranks of the Grand Army staggered into Moscow on September 14, 1812, but the Russian army was still intact and far from demoralized.

The Destruction of the Grand Army In fact, the condition of Moscow demoralized the French. They found the city deserted and bereft of badly needed supplies. The next night Moscow was mysteriously set ablaze, causing such extensive damage as to make it unfit to be the Grand Army's winter quarters. Realistic advisers warned the emperor that his situation was dangerous, while others told him what he wished to hear—that Russian resistance was crumbling. For weeks Napoleon hesitated. Logistically it was imperative that the French begin to retreat immediately, but that would constitute a political defeat. Only on October 19 did Napoleon finally order a retreat, but the order came too late.

The delay forced an utterly unrealistic pace on the bedraggled army as it headed west. Supplies were gone, medical care for the thousands of wounded nonexistent, horses lacking. French officers were poorly prepared for the march, and the soldiers grew insubordinate. Food shortages compelled foraging parties to sweep far from the main body of troops, and these men fell prey to Russian guerillas. And there was the weather—a normal Russian winter in which no commander would wish to find himself facing a march of several hundred miles, laden with wounded and loot but without food, fuel, horses, or proper clothing. Napoleon's poor planning, the harsh weather, and the operation of Russian guerilla

Map 21.4 THE RUSSIAN CAMPAIGN OF 1812

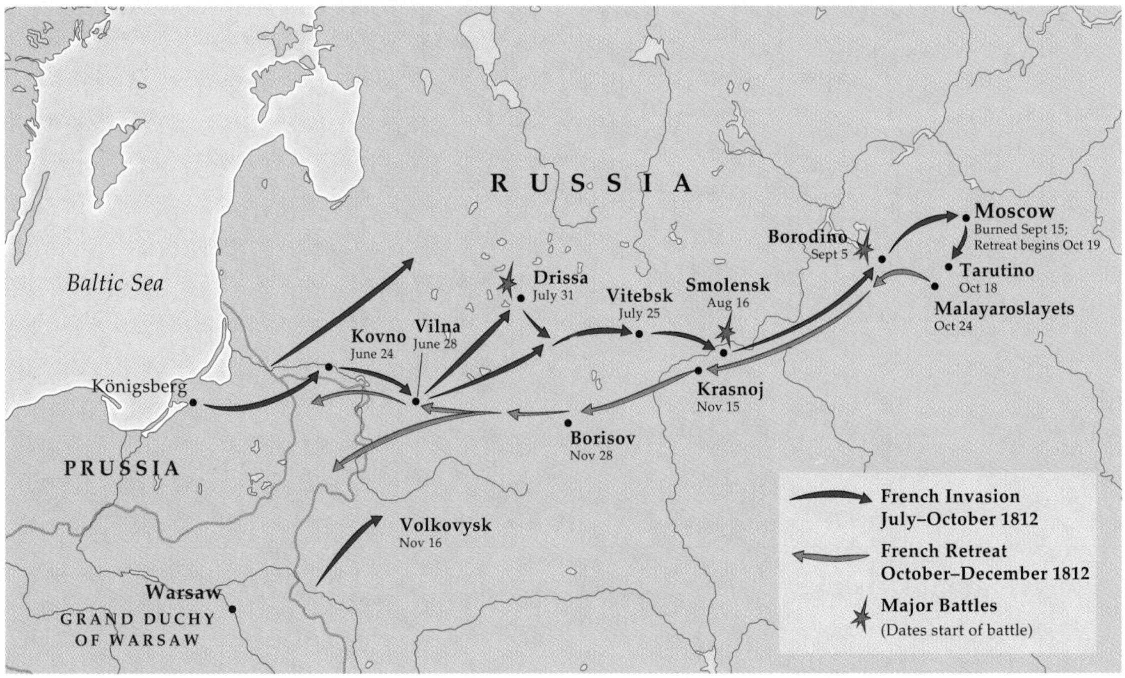

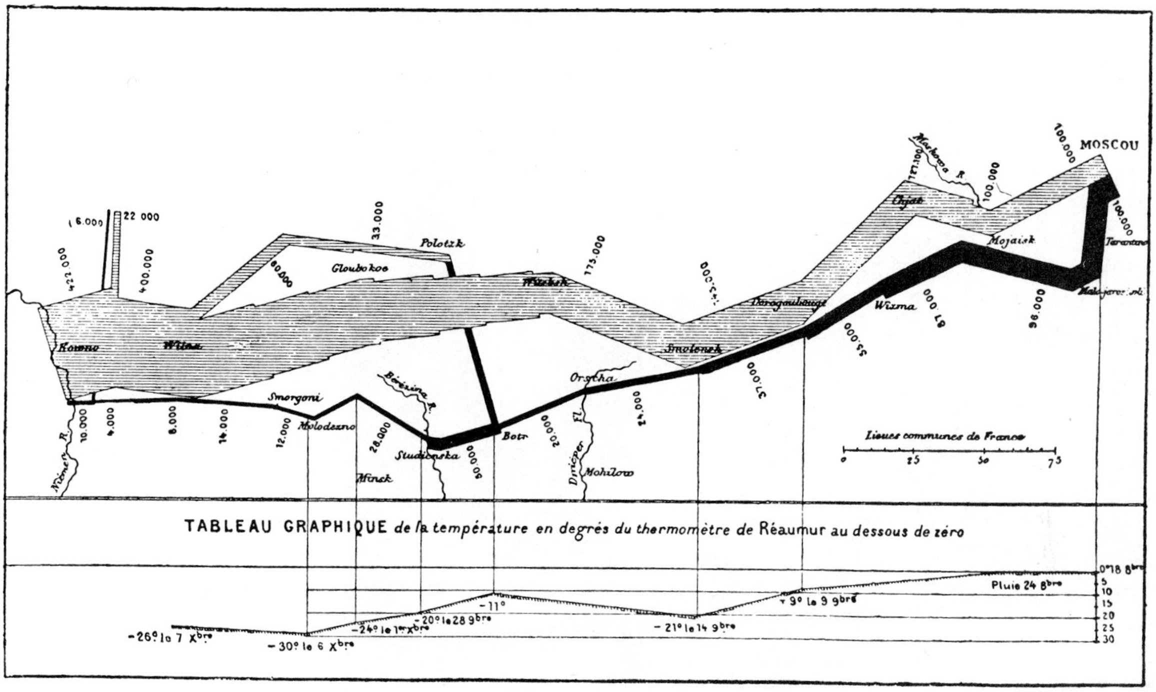

Xbre = December 9bre = November 8bre = October

▸ **This ingenious image, which dates from 1861, demonstrates graphically the attrition in the ranks of Napoleon's Grand Army on its way into and then out of Russia in 1812.**

bands made the long retreat a nightmare of suffering for the Grand Army (see picture on page 698). No more than 100,000 troops survived the ordeal. Worse yet, the Prussian contingent took the occasion to desert Napoleon, opening the possibility of mass defections and the formation of a new anti-Napoleonic coalition.

GERMAN RESISTANCE AND THE LAST COALITION

Napoleon was evidently impervious to the horror around him. On the sleigh ride out of Russia he was already planning how to raise new armies and set things aright. Other European statesmen, however, were ready to capitalize on Napoleon's defeat in Russia and demolish his empire once and for all. Provocative calls for a national uprising in the various German states to throw off the tyrant's yoke reinforced the efforts of diplomats like Prussia's Baron Stein and Austria's Klemens von Metternich to revive the anti-Napoleonic coalition.

Reform from Above in Prussia In Prussia, after the defeat of 1806, the government had introduced reforms intended to improve the quality of the bureaucracy by offering non-nobles more access to high positions and by reducing some of the nobility's privileges. The monarchy hoped thereby to salvage the position of the nobility and the authority of the state. Prussian military reformers adopted new methods of recruitment to build up a trained reserve force that could be rapidly mobilized, along with a corps of reserve officers to take command of these units. Prussia, in other words, hoped to achieve French-style efficiency and military mobilization without resorting to new concepts of citizenship, constitutions, legislatures, or the abolition of seigneurialism. On the level of propaganda and the symbolic gesture, writers in Prussia and other German states called for a popular war of liberation under the slogan "With God for King and Fatherland."

Against this background of Prussian military preparation and growing nationalist sentiment, the diplomats maneuvered and waited. Finally,

▸ **Just as Goya's drawings captured the unique ferocity of the Spanish campaign, this picture evokes the particular agonies of climate and logistics in the Russian debacle.**

in March 1813, King Frederick William III of Prussia signed a treaty with Russia to form an offensive coalition against Napoleon. A great struggle for Germany ensued between the Russo-Prussian forces and Napoleon and his allies. Austria continued to claim neutrality and offered to mediate the dispute, but at a meeting in Prague, Napoleon rejected an offer of peace in exchange for restoring all French conquests since 1802.

In August, as Napoleon learned of new defeats in Spain, Habsburg Emperor Francis finally declared war on his son-in-law. Napoleon called up underage and overage conscripts and was able to field one last army, but his major southern German ally, Bavaria, finally changed sides. A great battle raged around Leipzig for three days in October, and when the smoke cleared, Napoleon was in full retreat. As far as Germany was concerned, the war of liberation had been won. German states were free from Napoleon's domination, but Prussia's rulers were also free from the need to concede further reforms in the political and social order.

The Fall of Napoleon In the belief that he could rely on his conscription machine, Napoleon had rebuffed offers by the allies to negotiate peace in 1813. In fact, however, he reached the end of the line in November 1813 with a desperate call for 300,000 more men to defend France against the allies. Difficulties were inevitable, wrote one prefect, "when the number of men required exceeds the number available." Another reported: "There is scarcely a family that is not oppressed by conscription." Alongside sizable contingents of Italians, Germans, and other foreigners from the annexed territories and satellite states, nearly 2.5 million Frenchmen had been drafted by Napoleon. At least 1 million of those conscripts never returned.

With Napoleon driven back into France, British troops reinforced the coalition to ensure that it would not disintegrate once Central Europe had been liberated. The coalition offered final terms to the emperor: He could retain his throne, but France would be reduced to her "normal frontiers." (The precise meaning of this was left purposely vague.) Napoleon, still hoping for a dramatic reversal, chose to fight, and with some reluctance the allies invaded France. Napoleon led the remnants of his army skillfully but to no avail. The French had lost confidence in him, conscription has reached its limits, and no popular spirit of resistance to invasion developed as it had in 1792. Paris fell in March 1814. The price of this defeat was unconditional surrender and the emperor's abdication. Napoleon was transported to the island of Elba, between Corsica and Italy, over which he was granted sovereignty. After 22 years of exile, the Bourbon dynasty returned to France.

THE NAPOLEONIC LEGEND

For Napoleon, imperial authority—originating with him in France and radiating throughout Europe—represented the principle of rational progress. In his view, the old notion of balance of power among European states merely served as an excuse for the British to pursue their selfish interests. While paying lip service to the notion of Italian, Spanish, and Polish nationhood, he generally scorned patriotic opposition to his domination as an outmoded, reactionary sentiment—exemplified by the "barbaric" guerillas in Spain fighting for king and religion. Modern-minded Europeans, he believed, would see beyond historic, parochial traditions to the prospect of a new European order. Indeed, Napoleon's credibility with some reformers in Europe was considerable. The Bavarian prime minister, for instance, justified his collaboration with France in 1810 in these words: "The spirit of the new age is one of mobility, destruction, creativity. . . . The wars against France offer the [unfortunate] possibility of bringing back old constitutions, privileges, and property relations."

During his final exile, however, Napoleon came to recognize that nationalism was not necessarily reactionary—as one could plainly see in the nationalistic but liberal Cortes of Cádiz of 1812. Progressive thinking and nationalist aspirations could coexist. From exile Napoleon rewrote his life story to portray his career as a series of defensive wars against selfish adversaries (especially Britain) and as a battle in behalf of the

Napoleon Justifies Himself in 1815

"I have cleansed the Revolution, ennobled the common people, and restored the authority of kings. I have stirred all men to competition, I have rewarded merit wherever I found it, I have pushed back the boundaries of greatness. Is there any point on which I could be attacked and on which a historian could not take up my defense? My despotism? He can prove that dictatorship was absolutely necessary. Will it be said that I restricted freedom? He will be able to prove that license, anarchy, and general disorder were still on our doorstep. Shall I be accused of having loved war too much? He will show that I was always on the defensive. That I wanted to set up a universal monarchy? He will explain that it was merely the fortuitous result of circumstances and that I was led to it step by step by our very enemies. My ambition? Ah, no doubt he will find that I had ambition, a great deal of it—but the grandest and noblest perhaps, that ever was: the ambition of establishing and consecrating at last the kingdom of reason and the full exercise, the complete enjoyment, of all human capabilities!"

From B. Las Cases, ed., *Mémorial de Sainte-Hélène.*

nations of Europe against reactionary dynasties. In this way Napoleon brilliantly (if falsely) put himself on the side of the future.

These memoirs and recollections from exile formed the basis of the Napoleonic legend, as potent a force historically, perhaps, as the reality of the Napoleonic experience. The image they projected emphasized how General Bonaparte had consolidated what was best about the French Revolution while pacifying a bitterly divided nation and saving it from chaos. They cast the imperial experience in a deceptively positive light, glossed over the tyranny and unending military slaughter, and aligned Napoleon with pragmatism, efficiency, and modernity (*see box*, p. 699).

The Napoleonic legend also evoked a sense of grandeur and glory that moved ordinary people in years to come. Napoleon's dynamism and energy became his ultimate inspirational legacy to succeeding generations. In this way the Napoleonic legend fed on the romantic movement in literature and the arts. Many young romantics (including the poet William Wordsworth and the composer Ludwig van Beethoven) saw in the French Revolution a release of creativity and a liberation of the individual spirit. Napoleon's tyranny eventually alienated most such creative people. But the Napoleonic legend, by emphasizing the bold creativity of his career, meshed nicely with the emotional exaltation and sense of individual possibility that the romantics cultivated. Napoleon's retrospective justifications of his reign may not be convincing, but one can only marvel at the irrepressible audacity of the man!

In the confrontations between Napoleon and his European adversaries, France still embodied the specter of revolution. Even if the revolutionary legacy in France amounted by that time to little more than Napoleon's contempt for the inefficiency and outmoded institutions of the old regime, France after Brumaire remained a powerful challenge to the status quo. Napoleon intended to abolish feudalism, institute centralized administrations, and implant the French Civil Code in all of France's satellite states. But by 1808 his extravagant international ambitions relied on increasingly tyrannical and militaristic measures. These in turn provoked a range of responses, including nationalist rebellions. Britain and Russia, then Prussia and Austria, joined forces once more to bring the Napoleonic Empire down, to restore the balance of power in Europe, and to reinstall the Bourbons in France. But the clock could not really be set back from Europe's experience of revolution and Napoleonic transformation. The era of modern political and social conflicts had begun.

Recommended Reading (See Also Chapter 20)

Sources

De Caulaincourt, Armand. *With Napoleon in Russia.* 1935. A remarkable account of the diplomacy and warfare of the 1812 debacle by a man at Napoleon's side.

Herold, J. C. (ed.). *The Mind of Napoleon.* 1961.

Thompson, J. M. (ed.). *Napoleon Self-Revealed.* 1934.

*Walter, Jakob. *The Diary of a Napoleonic Foot Soldier.* 1991. A vivid and appalling account of the Russian campaign.

Studies

Alexander, Don. *Rod of Iron: French Counterinsurgency Policy in Aragon during the Peninsular War.* 1985. A case study of French responses to Spanish guerilla warfare.

Anderson, Eugene. *Nationalism and the Cultural Crisis in Prussia, 1806–1815.* 1939. The intellectual roots of German resistance to Napoleon.

*Bergeron, Louis. *France under Napoleon.* 1981. A fresh and insightful evaluation of the Napoleonic settlement in France.

*Carr, Raymond. *Spain 1808–1975.* 1982. An authoritative general history with fine chapters on this period.

*Available in paperback.

Chandler, David. *Napoleon's Marshals.* 1986. By a leading expert on Napoleonic military history.

Cobb, Richard. *Reactions to the French Revolution.* 1972. On the violent aftermath of the second revolution in the provinces.

*Connelley, Owen. *Blundering to Glory: Napoleon's Military Campaigns.* 1988. An irreverent but incisive account of Napoleon's military leadership.

———. *Napoleon's Satellite Kingdoms.* 1965. A study of the states conquered by France and ruled by the Bonaparte family.

Ellis, Geoffrey. *Napoleon's Continental Blockade: The Case of Alsace.* 1981. A case study of the period's economic warfare.

Forrest, Alan. *Conscripts and Deserters: The Army and French Society during the Revolution and Empire.* 1988. A study of popular resistance to revolutionary and Napoleonic conscription.

Gates, David. *The Spanish Ulcer: A History of the Peninsular War.* 1986. On the Spanish rebellion, the French response, and Wellington's expeditionary force.

Geyl, Pieter. *Napoleon, For and Against.* 1949. Napoleon and the historians, as reviewed by a Dutch scholar with no illusions.

*Herold, J. Christopher. *The Age of Napoleon.* 1963. A brilliant popular history of the era.

*Lefebvre, Georges. *Napoleon* (2 vols.). 1959. A general history of the period by a master historian.

———. *The Thermidorians.* 1964. A detailed narrative of 1794–1795.

Lucas, C., and G. Lewis (eds.). *Beyond the Terror: Essays in French Regional and Social History, 1794–1815.* 1983. Local studies by students of Richard Cobb.

*Lynch, John. *The Spanish American Revolutions, 1808–1826.* 1973. A comprehensive account of the independence movements in Spanish America and their aftermath.

Lyons, Martyn. *France under the Directory.* 1975. A brief topical survey of the Revolution's later, unheroic phase.

Marcus, G. J. *A Naval History of England, II: The Age of Nelson.* 1971. The standard history of British naval supremacy.

*Markham, Felix. *Napoleon.* 1966. Perhaps the best biography in English.

Mitchell, Harvey. *The Underground War against Revolutionary France: The Missions of William Wickham 1794–1800.* 1965. On British attempts to subvert the French Republic.

*Palmer, Robert R. *The World of the French Revolution.* 1971. Emphasizes the interplay of French power and indigenous revolutionary movements outside of France.

Rosenberg, Hans. *Bureaucracy, Aristocracy, and Autocracy: The Prussian Experience, 1660–1815.* 1958. On reform from above in Prussia that helped preserve the status quo.

Rothenberg, Gunther. *The Art of Warfare in the Age of Napoleon.* 1978. A good analysis of strategy and tactics.

*Sutherland, D. M. G. *France, 1789–1815: Revolution and Counterrevolution.* 1985. The best general history of France in this period.

Tulard, Jean. *Napoleon: The Myth of the Savior.* 1984. A synthesis by the leading French expert on Napoleon.

Woloch, Isser. *Jacobin Legacy: The Democratic Movement under the Directory.* 1970. On the ideas and practice of democratic activism after the Terror.

Woolf, Stuart. *A History of Italy, 1700–1860.* 1979. An authoritative general history, with fine chapters on this period.

*Woronoff, Denis. *The Thermidorian Regime and the Directory.* 1984. A relatively recent synthesis on France between Robespierre and Bonaparte.

The contrast of new and old: The train from Vienna to Baden frightened the horses in this watercolor done in 1847 by Leander Russ.

CHAPTER TWENTY-TWO

FOUNDATIONS OF THE NINETEENTH CENTURY: POLITICS AND SOCIAL CHANGE

PEACE was a dramatic change for a world accustomed to war. After a generation of fighting, the victorious alliance had established once more that no one state should dominate the continent. They were determined to preserve that balance. The wars against France, however, had been about more than territory or the balance of power; they were also a fight for monarchy and against revolutionary ideas. To the victors, peace and security required that revolution as well as French aggression be prevented in the future. Painfully aware that political order was fragile and that rulers could be toppled from within, the allies sought to restore the social as well as the international equilibrium of prerevolutionary Europe.

They began by redrawing the map, shifting boundaries to create an interlocking patchwork of states that could resist aggression and making sure that those who ruled them were safely conservative. Ironically, the restoration of effective monarchies necessitated fundamental change. Even where the old order had not been swept away, it had been seriously challenged. To reestablish conservative institutions required measures as formal and disruptive as the rejected policies of Napoleon; and these measures, like Napoleon's, would be imposed by force, relying on political authority to ensure stability. Eventually, this focus on politics would prove characteristic of the nineteenth century and itself a source of change. For the next century, while conservatives and progressives battled over how to use politics to reshape society, European society was being independently transformed by industrialization and economic change. The Europe restructured in 1815 to preserve the status quo entered a new era of passionate and volatile politics, of pervasive and rapid change.

I. The Politics of Order

In setting the terms of peace, allied leaders sought stability above all else and expected to achieve it through domestic political arrangements supported by international agreements. Conservative monarchies were to keep order in their own lands, to cooperate in stamping out the threat of revolution anywhere in Europe, and to sustain an intricate balance of power as the guarantee of peace.

THE CONGRESS OF VIENNA

To forge these arrangements, the great international conference known as the Congress of Vienna met in September 1814, an occasion for serious deliberations and elaborate pomp centering on the crowned heads of Austria, Prussia, Russia, and dozens of lesser states. Officials, expert advisers, princesses and countesses, dancers and artists, and the ambitious of every rank flocked to the Austrian capital. Their contrived gaiety and bewigged elegance made the Congress a symbol of aristocratic restoration.

▸ In the tradition of aristocratic portraits, Prince Metternich is conveyed as a polished courtier; the medals, symbolic of his position and power, are also a reminder of the purpose of his policies.

Its business remained the responsibility of the four great powers—Austria, Great Britain, Russia, and Prussia—an inner circle to which France was soon admitted. Prince Klemens von Metternich, who had led the Austrian Empire to this triumph, conducted the affairs of the Congress with such skill that its provisions can be seen as largely his work. Handsome, elegant, and arrogant, Metternich was the epitome of an aristocrat, fluent in all the major European languages, a dandy who dabbled in science and shone in the ballroom. More consistently than any other single figure, he had understood the extent of Napoleon's ambitions and had welded the international alliance that defeated the French emperor. Metternich was named foreign minister of Austria in 1809 and would hold that position for nearly 40 years, tying his vision of European order to Austria's interests. Metternich was generally supported by Lord Castlereagh, England's able foreign minister, but Russia's tsar Alexander I, who acted as his own chief diplomat, was more unpredictable. Educated in the ideas of enlightened despotism, Alexander was now more given to mysticism and conservative fear and was attracted to grandiose programs upsetting to the careful calculations of self-interest by which the Congress reached agreement.

The most pressing issue these statesmen faced was the future of France. Most of the allies favored restoring some sort of monarchy; and the Treaty of Paris, signed in May 1814, had recognized Louis XVIII, a brother of the executed Bourbon, Louis XVI, as king. The treaty also granted France its expanded frontiers gained by 1792. A settlement covering all the territory affected by the Napoleonic wars would take longer. Warily watching one another, the allies soon included Prince Talleyrand, the French representative, in their deliberations. A former bishop who had served the First Republic and then the Directory, he had helped Napoleon to power and been his foreign minister for eight years. Talleyrand was now the indispensable servant of Louis XVIII, using all his famous shrewdness to regain for France its former influence.

▶ **The Congress of Vienna is portrayed here as a kind of elegant salon in which the very clothes these statesmen wore mix the styles of the old regime and the new century.**

The concerns of these men focused on continental Europe, for only Great Britain among the victors had extensive interests overseas, and British designs on South Africa, Ceylon, and Malta were modest enough to be accepted by the other European states. Europe was considered the sphere of the great powers; each closely weighed the claims of the others, and all especially watched Russia, with her mammoth armies, undefined ambitions, and quixotic tsar.

Conflicting interests kept Austria, Prussia, and Russia from dividing up Poland as they had in the eighteenth century, but neither did they want to risk creating an independent state. So Russia received most of Poland to be ruled as a separate kingdom, and Prussia took about half of Saxony—a triumph of Old Regime diplomacy in which each got something (see Map 22.1). Prussia was also given greatly enlarged territories in the Rhineland, ensuring that formidable Prussian armies would stand along the French border. The Austrian Netherlands were absorbed in a new, independent Kingdom of the Netherlands, which created another strong buffer against France and met the British desire that no major power control the Low Countries' important river ports. Austria, in return for ceding the southern Netherlands, acquired Venetia and recovered Lombardy, which greatly strengthened its dominance of northern Italy. The other duchies of northern Italy went to dukes with close Austrian ties (in a touch of chivalry, Marie Louise, Napoleon's now throneless Austrian wife, was given Parma to rule).

The terms agreed upon at Vienna constituted the most extensive European peace settlement since the treaty of Westphalia in 1648.[1] Each of the victors had gained territory, and France was

[1]The Kingdom of Sardinia would have liked Lombardy but got Genoa, the last of the ancient Italian republics to fall. Russia took Finland from Sweden, which in turn got Norway from Denmark.

Map 22.1 EUROPE, 1815

surrounded by states capable of resisting any future French aggression. The final act was signed in June 1815 by the five great powers and by Sweden, Spain, and Portugal, a gracious recognition of their past importance.

The Hundred Days The deliberations of the Congress were interrupted in March 1815 by the terrifying news of Napoleon's escape from exile. He had tried to make the best of ruling the island of Elba and had even showed something of his old flair as he designed uniforms, held receptions, and inquired into the local economy. But the island principality was far too small to contain an emperor's ambition. Landing in the south of France, he was joined by units of the French army as he moved toward Paris. Louis XVIII waited for signs of resistance that did not develop, and then climbed into his carriage and once again headed for the eastern border. Napoleon became the ruler of France without firing a shot. He then tried to negotiate with the allies, but they declared him an outlaw and quickly assembled their troops. After several minor battles, Napoleon was defeated for the last time at Waterloo on June 18 and surrendered to the British. They dispatched him to the more distant island of St. Helena, in the South Atlantic.

Napoleon's dashing venture lasted only a hundred days, but its effects were felt far longer. The terms of peace were altered, and the possibility of restoring a stable monarchy was called into question. Allied armies had quickly defeated Napoleon, and France was required to pay an indemnity and its boundaries reduced to those of 1789 (which entailed the loss of much of the Saar region to Prussia). The Bourbons again returned to the French throne, haunted by the specter of renewed revolution and permanently embarrassed by the ease with which Napoleon had retaken power. Napoleon had used his Hundred Days to soften the memory of his despotism with a series of liberal measures (he even banned slave traffic in the French colonies) and the promise of a constitution. Sent to the more distant island of St. Helena, he continued to propagandize for Bonapartism, redefining it as a means for achieving both national strength and social change. Allied statesmen, with power on their side, remained less concerned with playing to popular opinion.

International Order The restorations of 1815 acknowledged many of the changes of the past 25 years. The Bourbons were restored in France but now governed with a constitution. In Germany, the Holy Roman Empire and hundreds of minor German principalities, all abolished by Napoleon, were not restored but consolidated into 39 states, including Prussia and Austria, and joined in a loose confederation. The statesmen at Vienna were also innovative in their use of experts as advisers on technical matters of history and law. The Congress established the principle that navigation on international riverways should be open to all and set down rules of diplomatic conduct useful to this day. For the next 100 years Europe would be free of European-wide war, and some of the credit for that should go to the complicated arrangements negotiated at Vienna.

The Congress was less impressive in the realm of ideas. Recognizing the need to invoke some general principle to justify such far-reaching arrangements, Talleyrand suggested they were only restoring governments made legitimate by tradition and public support; but that principle gave more weight to public opinion than his colleagues could accept. Aiming for something more stirring, Tsar Alexander proposed a Holy Alliance, an agreement that all states would conduct their affairs according to Christian teachings. That seemed vague enough; and though some were publicly skeptical, nearly all European governments signed. Three refused: The Ottoman sultan cared too little for Christian teachings, the pope cared too much, and Britain rejected any permanent commitments on the continent. Historians, too, have tended to dismiss the Holy Alliance as a meaningless expression of Alexander's mysticism. Yet there was something modern, and maybe wise, in the tsar's desire to give the new order moral appeal.

Proponents of change—Europe's liberals, reformers, and nationalists—would later recall the Congress of Vienna as the occasion when aristocrats danced while foisting reactionary regimes on the people of Europe. They cited not its realistic compromises but the brutal shuffling of territory without regard to the claims of nationality or constitutions. In fact, the new order was not so solid as it seemed. In 1820 and 1821 uprisings occurred in both Italy and Spain, led by young army officers who were influenced by memories of Napoleonic reforms and convinced that individual advancement and efficient government required a constitution. Metternich was quick to call on a "concert of Europe" to use force to snuff the flames of revolution (*see box*, p. 708), but unanimity among the former allies was breaking down. Great Britain disapproved sending Austrian troops into Naples to put down a constitutional government and did not attend the conference that approved French intervention against the revolution in Spain. French troops met little resistance in Spain, and their royal parade was welcomed by conservatives throughout Europe as evidence of the French monarchy's revived prestige. Subsequent talk of reestablishing European authority in Latin America, however, brought stern warnings from Britain and the proud declaration of the Monroe Doctrine from the United States, declaring the Americas outside

Metternich Analyzes the Threat to Tranquillity

On December 15, 1820, Metternich wrote the Habsburg emperor from the international conference he had called to deal with the threat of revolution. Metternich argued that all monarchs must act together against the common threat, which he blamed on the middle class.

"Europe presents itself to the impartial observer under an aspect at the same time deplorable and peculiar. We find everywhere the people praying for the maintenance of peace and tranquility, faithful to God and their Princes. . . . The governments, having lost their balance, are frightened, intimidated, and thrown into confusion by the cries of the intermediary class of society, which, placed between the Kings and their subjects, breaks the sceptre of the monarch, and usurps the cry of the people—that class so often disowned by the people, and nevertheless too much listened to. . . .

"We see this intermediary class abandon itself with a blind fury and animosity . . . to all the means which seem proper to assuage its thirst for power, applying itself to the task of persuading Kings that their rights are confined to sitting upon a throne, while those of the people are to govern, and to attack all that centuries have bequeathed as holy and worthy of man's respect—denying, in fact, the value of the past, and declaring themselves the masters of the future.

". . . The evil is plain; the means used by the faction which causes these disorders are so blameable in principle, so criminal in their application, and expose the faction itself to so many dangers, that . . . we are convinced that society can no longer be saved without strong and vigorous resolutions on the part of the Governments. . . .

"By this course the monarchs will fulfill the duties imposed upon them by Him who, by entrusting them with power, has charged them to watch the maintenance of justice, and the rights of all, to avoid the paths of error . . . and to show themselves as they are, fathers invested with the authority belonging by right to the heads of families, to prove that, in days of mourning, they know how to be just, wise, and therefore strong. . . .

"The Governments, in establishing the principle of stability, will in no wise exclude the development of what is good, for stability is not immobility. But it is for those who are burdened with the heavy task of government to augment the well-being of their people! It is for Governments to regulate it according to necessity and to suit the times. It is not by concessions, which the factious strive to force from legitimate power, . . . that wise reforms can be carried out. That all the good possible should be done is our most ardent wish; but . . . even real good should be done only by those who unite to the right of authority the means of enforcing it."

From *Memoirs of Prince Metternich, 1815–1829*, III, Prince Richard Metternich (ed.), Mrs. Alexander Napier (tr.). First published in English by Charles Scribner's Sons, 1881. From the reprint by Howard Fertig, New York, 1970.

the sphere of European power politics. Metternich's concept of a European concert to maintain order was being circumscribed.

The Concert of Europe was hardly invoked at all when the Greeks revolted against Ottoman Turk rule in 1821. The cries for freedom from the ancient home of democracy excited liberals throughout Europe, an early demonstration that would be repeated throughout the century of the power of nationalist movements. Metternich restrained Russia from rushing to war against the Ottomans as it had in the past; but he could not keep the British and French fleets from intervening in 1827, when the sultan seemed at last about to subdue the Greeks, and Russia declared war a few months later. Greece was granted independence in 1829 on terms arranged by the European powers, stipulating that it must have a king but

▸ **The Greek revolution captured the imagination of many Europeans, and Delacroix's *Greece Expiring* has all the elements of that fascination. Greece is symbolized by an ordinary peasant girl who is also a classical figure of liberty, come alive. The Turk in the background, a colorful and exotic figure of oppression, evokes centuries of conflict. Romanticism, nationalism, and political liberty come together on the stones of Greek culture and the arm of a martyred freedom fighter.**

one who was not a member of the ruling family of a major power. The leading European states altered the status quo after all, partly in response to the public opinion, but they then made sure that the Greek rising would be held in check. Their acute sense of self-interest, their use of force, and their willingness to carve up the Ottoman Empire foreshadowed imperialist policies later in the century.

THE PILLARS OF THE RESTORATION: RUSSIA, AUSTRIA, PRUSSIA

To maintain social order in the nineteenth century, the state would need to be more effective than before in order to maintain large armies and collect more taxes, support a better-trained bureaucracy, dispense justice more evenly, and provide more services. Because they would thus affect the lives of their subjects more directly, governments would have to be more concerned with popular sentiment. Even the most reactionary rulers accepted some of the changes (and the potential for increased power) brought by revolution, war, and Napoleonic occupation. The organization of the state became an issue even in conservative Russia, Austria, and Prussia, the guardians of the European restoration.

The Russian Empire By 1820 Tsar Alexander had abandoned his earlier enthusiasm for new ideas. As Metternich's staunchest ally, he imposed harsh censorship, increased restrictions on universities, and made sure that the constitution granted to the newly organized Kingdom of Poland was largely ignored. On Alexander's death in 1825, a group of young army officers, the Decembrists, attempted a coup and called for a constitution in Russia. Like the leaders of the revolts in Naples and Spain a few years earlier, they saw that as an essential step toward a more efficient and progressive administration. Their poorly planned and isolated conspiracy was easily defeated; but it would be remembered, by conservatives as an ever-present danger and by revolutionaries as part of Russia's radical tradition. Alexander's younger brother, who succeeded him as Nicholas I, was convinced that only a loyal army and his own decisiveness had prevented revolution. He made Russia Europe's strongest pillar of reaction by example at home and willingness to use force abroad. He was a diligent administrator who gave his closest attention to the army and the police and who established a more effective bureaucracy by making it more directly responsible to the state and less attached to the nobility.

All the same, petty corruption, the arrogance of local officials, and fear of change continued to undermine the government's capacity to manage a vast land of varied peoples where communications were poor and few had the voice, the means, or the will to effect reform. Most thoughtful people, including the state's highest officials, agreed that serfdom had become a hindrance to Russia's development. The commissions ordered to study the matter gathered data and noted that hundreds of peasant uprisings had had to be suppressed by force, but they proposed no solution. Despite fears that education bred discontent, the government built schools; and among the literate minority, discussion of Russia's destiny became a compelling theme. The government attempted to establish a kind of official philosophy based on the teachings of the Russian Orthodox Church. Intellectuals who expected Russia to develop along familiar European lines were known as Westernizers. Those who stressed the uniqueness of Russia were called Slavophiles, and they argued that Russia's religion, peasant communes, and traditional culture gave it a unique destiny. Despite this urgent questioning about Russia's place in a changing world and despite loquacious exiles, bitter Poles, angry peasants, and its own immobility, the authority of the Russian state remained. Nicholas would watch with pride in 1848 as his empire escaped the revolutions that swept over most of the thrones of Europe.

The Habsburg Empire Habsburg rule over German, Italian, and Eastern European lands relied on a well-organized bureaucracy. Forged by Maria Theresa and Joseph II, that system of government had enabled Austria to survive the Napoleonic wars without dramatic reform despite repeated defeat. Metternich and others recognized the need for domestic reform, but their projects for better fiscal planning, stronger local government, and recognition of the empire's diverse nationalities came to nothing. Habsburg rule remained locked in stalemate between an increasingly cautious central bureaucracy and a selfish local aristocracy.

Hungary proved particularly troublesome for the Habsburg empire, for though they were a minority, the dominant Magyar aristocracy had a strong sense of their historical identity and a good deal of power. Emperor Francis I grudgingly acknowledged many of their claims, and by the 1840s Magyar had replaced German as the official language of administration and schooling in Hungary. More demands followed. The campaign for a more representative parliament and related reforms was led by Lajos Kossuth, who became Hungary's leading statesman. Through newspapers and public meetings Kossuth was able to reach much of the nation. This widespread agitation, stimulated by the example of nationalist ferment in Italy, encouraged other groups subject to Habsburg rule to claim national rights of their own. Much of Polish Galicia rose in revolt in 1846; but weakened by the bitter antagonism between Polish peasants and their masters, the uprising was soon suppressed. In Croatia and Bohemia, too, angry peasants and nationalists often had different aims. The different national groups opposed to Habsburg rule, often hostile to each other, were also internally divided by class, religion, and language. Although, growing nationalist movements sought to overcome these social divisions, giving broader appeal to the demands of merchants and lawyers for governmental reforms, the fact that the goals of these movements conflicted helped in practice to sustain the empire. At the center, despite much good advice and many promising plans, inaction remained the safest compromise.

Prussia and the German Confederation Germans called the battles against Napoleon from 1813 to 1814 the Wars of Liberation; and after that common national experience, talk of "Germany" meant more than it had before. The Congress of Vienna acknowledged this with the creation of the German Confederation, a cautious compromise that, in calling for some coordination among Germany's many states, tacitly acknowledged the changes the experience of French dominance had wrought. Any stronger union was prevented by the rivalry of Austria and Prussia, distaste for reform among restoration regimes, and the conflicting ambitions of German princes. The Confederation's diet, more a council of ambassadors from member states than a representative assembly, was permitted to legislate only on certain matters—characteristically, restriction of the press was one of them.

In practice, the German Confederation was important in German politics largely when Metternich wished to make it so. He used it, for ex-

▶ **German authorities worried greatly that university students would be a center of political agitation, and this print from a series on student life in the 1820s suggests why. Privileged, educated, and idle young men meeting to drink and smoke were all too likely to talk about politics, spread radical ideas, and maybe even hatch plots.**

ample, to suppress agitation led by nationalist and reformist student groups in the universities. In 1817 some of these groups organized a celebration of the tercentenary of Luther's theses with a rally, the Wartburg Festival. Several hundred young people gathered to drink, listen to speeches full of mystical nationalist rhetoric, sing songs, and cheer as a corporal's cane and a Prussian military manual were tossed into a bonfire. Even symbolic challenges to military authority alarmed governments in both Berlin and Vienna. When a well-known reactionary writer was assassinated, the Confederation was pressed into issuing the Carlsbad Decrees of 1819, which intensified censorship, proscribed dangerous professors and students, outlawed fraternities and political clubs, and required each state to guarantee that its universities would be kept safely conservative (*see box*, p. 712).

Despite these fears, there was less agitation within the German Confederation than in most of the rest of Europe. In fact, the cultural life of these largely rural lands thrived in complacent university and market towns that seemed to eschew politics on a larger scale. Meanwhile, Prussian influence increased. Its national educational system was capped by the new but prestigious University of Berlin, and the state's efficiency extended to measures to stimulate economic growth. The lower tariff duties imposed in 1818 on Prussian territories east and west allowed raw materials free entry, with results impressive enough that within a decade the Prussian tariff was adopted by many of the smaller states Prussia nearly surrounded. By 1833 most German governments except Austria had joined Prussia's

Policing Universities—The Carlsbad Decrees

The Carlsbad Decrees, drafted by Metternich, were adopted by the Diet of the German Confederation in 1819 to be applied in all its member states.

"1. There shall be appointed for each university a special representative of the ruler of each state, the said representatives to have appropriate instructions and extended powers, and they shall have their place of residence where the university is located. . . .

"This representative shall enforce strictly the existing laws and disciplinary regulations; he shall observe with care the attitude shown by the university instructors in their public lectures and registered courses; and he shall, without directly interfering in scientific matters or in teaching methods, give a beneficial direction to the teaching, keeping in view the future attitude of the students. Finally, he shall give unceasing attention to everything that may promote morality . . . among the students. . . .

"2. The confederated governments mutually pledge themselves to eliminate from the universities or any other public educational institutions all instructors who shall have obviously proved their unfitness for the important work entrusted to them by openly deviating from their duties, or by going beyond the boundaries of their functions, or by abusing their legitimate influence over young minds, or by presenting harmful ideas hostile to public order or subverting existing governmental instructions. . . .

"Any instructor who has been removed in this manner becomes ineligible for a position in any other public institution of learning in another state of the Confederation.

"3. The laws that for some time have been directed against secret and unauthorized societies in the universities shall be strictly enforced. . . . The special representatives of the government are enjoined to exert great care in watching these organizations.

"The governments mutually agree that all individuals who shall be shown to have maintained their membership in secret or unauthorized associations, or shall have taken membership in such associations, shall not be eligible for any public office.

"4. No student who shall have been expelled from any university by virtue of a decision of the university senate ratified or initiated by the special representative of the government, shall be admitted by any other university. . . .

"As long as this edict remains in force, no publication which appears daily, or as a serial not exceeding twenty sheets of printed matter, shall be printed in any state of the Confederation without the prior knowledge and approval of the state officials. . . ."

From Louis L. Snyder (ed.), *Documents of German History*, New Brunswick, 1958, pp. 158–159.

customs union, the *Zollverein*, which proved a remarkable spur to commerce. One of the most important steps toward German unification under Prussia had been taken without nationalist intent. Prussia was finding ways to win the benefits of liberal institutions without liberal politics.

THE TEST OF RESTORATION: SPAIN, ITALY, AND FRANCE

The durability of the conservative order that the Congress of Vienna sought to impose would depend less on the autocracies in Russia, Austria, and Prussia than on the new regimes imposed in Spain, Italy, and France. There, revolution and Bonapartism were woven into the fabric of public life. Intensely divided over questions of government, its form, powers, and policies, conservatives and liberals agreed in considering politics as central to everything else.

Spain and Italy In Spain the Bourbon king Ferdinand VII regained his throne in 1814 when Napoleon's army was expelled. Strong enough to denounce the constitution he had promised, Ferdinand was too weak to do much more. He benefited from patriotic resentment against French rule, but his government found no solution for its own inefficiency or the nation's poverty. In Spain's American colonies the revolts led by José de San Martín and Simón Bolívar gained strength, and in 1820 the army that was assembled in Spain to reconquer the colonies mutinied and marched instead on Madrid. The king was then forced to grant a constitution after all, and for three years the constitutional regime struggled to cope with Spain's enormous problems, weakened by its own dissension and its uncooperative monarch. The regime's restrictions on religious orders raised powerful opposition from the Church, freedom of the press produced more devastating criticism, and a constitution in Spain was no help in reconquering the rebellious colonies. When a French army once again crossed into Spain in 1823, this time with the blessing of the Concert of Europe and in the name of order, the Spaniards who had fought French invasion so heroically just 10 years earlier were strangely acquiescent. The constitution disappeared again, but the threat of revolution did not.

In Italy, restoration meant the return to power of the aristocracies the French had ousted and the reestablishment of separate Italian states.[2] Yet the years of Napoleonic rule had established institutions (and hopes) that the new regimes could not ignore, and they promised constitutions, enlightened administration, peace, and lower taxes even though their insecure rulers were hardly prepared to take such initiatives. Cautious, moderately repressive, and conveniently corrupt, they provided the sleepy stability Metternich thought appropriate for Italians. Such an atmosphere bred some conspiracy and rumors of far more. Secret groups began to meet across Italy. Known collectively as the *Carbonari* (charcoal burners), they varied in membership and program. Some talked of tyrannicide, some equality and justice, and some of mild reform; they had in common the excitement of secret meetings, terrifying oaths, and ornate rituals.

By 1820 news of revolution in Spain was enough to prompt revolts in Italy. Young army officers led the demand for a constitution in Naples but then put down a rising in Sicily against Neapolitan rule; and an Austrian army was dispatched to Naples to remove their constitutional regime as well. A similar revolt erupted in Piedmont, and the king abdicated in favor of his son; while awaiting his arrival, the prince regent, Charles Albert, hastily granted a constitution. But when the new monarch arrived, the Austrian army was with him. Piedmont's constitution lasted two weeks. These revolutions, which left Italy's reactionary governments more rigid and Austrian influence more naked, demonstrated the inadequacy of romantic conspiracies but affirmed an Italian radical and patriotic tradition that would continue to grow.

France More than anything else, Europe's conservative order was meant to prevent France from again becoming the center of military aggression or revolutionary ideas, and the restoration there was an especially complex compromise. France was permitted a constitution called the Charter, presented as a gift from Louis XVIII and not as a right. It granted the legislature more authority than Napoleon had allowed but left the government largely in the hands of the king. The old estates were wisely forgotten, replaced by a Chamber of Peers, with hereditary members, and a Chamber of Deputies, chosen by an electorate limited to prosperous landowners. Napoleon's centralized administration and effective system of taxation were willingly kept intact.

The regime's supporters, shaken by Napoleon's easy return during the Hundred Days, were determined to crush their enemies. A violent "white terror" broke out in parts of the countryside as those tainted with a revolutionary past were ousted from local office or even killed. Yet Louis XVIII resisted as best he could the more extreme demands of the reactionary ultraroyalists; land confiscated from the Church and the

[2]Italy was divided into three monarchies, four duchies, and a republic. The Kingdom of Sardinia (Sardinia and Piedmont), the Papal States, and the Kingdom of the Two Sicilies were the monarchies. The Grand Duchy of Tuscany and the duchies of Lucca, Modena, and Parma were all tied to the Habsburgs, who annexed Lombardy and Venetia. The disappearance of the republics of Genoa (part of Piedmont) and Venice left tiny San Marino, safe on its mountain top, the oldest republic in the world.

▸ **This official portrait of Charles X by François Gerard, in the up-to-date romantic style, echoes the portraits of Louis XIV and suggests the way a regime that looked to the past wanted to be seen.**

émigré aristocracy during the Revolution was not returned to them, and most of those who had gained office or wealth since 1789 were allowed quietly to live out their lives. The king and his ministers, moderate and able men, pursued a course of administrative efficiency and political restraint. From 1816 to 1820 they governed well in a relatively peaceful and prosperous country, and Paris became again Europe's most brilliant center of science and the arts.

The Catholic Church, weakened in the intervening years by the loss of property and a decline in the number of new priests, revived remarkably. Missions of preachers toured the countryside calling for a return to the faith, praising the monarchy, and ceremonially planting crosses of repentance for the sins of revolution. The nobles, traditionally rather skeptical in matters of religion, were now more pious; and so, too, for the first time in more than a century, were France's leading writers. To the surprise of many Catholics, however, the Concordat of 1801 remained in effect, another of Napoleon's institutional arrangements to prove remarkably lasting.

Despite its achievements, the regime remained insecure and uncertain, satisfying neither all Catholics nor anticlericals, neither ultraroyalists nor liberals. The assassination of the duke of Berry in 1820 reminded everyone of how fragile the monarchy was. The duke was the son of Louis' younger brother and the last Bourbon likely to produce an heir. The royal line seemed doomed until the widowed duchess gave birth to a son eight months later. Louis XVIII reacted to the assassination by naming more conservative ministers, increasing restrictions on the press, and dismissing some leading professors. The air of reaction grew heavier in 1824 when his brother succeeded to the throne as Charles X. A leader of the ultraroyalists, Charles had himself crowned at Reims in medieval splendor, in a ceremony redolent with symbols of the divine right of kings and the alliance of throne and altar.

The new government gave the Church fuller control of education, declared sacrilege a capital crime, and granted a cash indemnity to those who had lost land in the Revolution. In fact, the law against sacrilege was never enforced; and the indemnity, which helped end one of the most dangerous issues left from the Revolution, was a limited one. France remained freer than most European countries, but Charles's subjects worried about the intentions of an ultraroyalist regime that disliked the compromises on which it rested. Public criticism increased, leading politicians joined the parliamentary opposition, and radical secret societies blossomed. Disturbed by liberal gains in the elections of 1827, Charles X dutifully tried a slightly more moderate ministry, but he could not conceal his distaste for it. By 1829 the king could stand no more. While political disputes grew more inflamed, he appointed a cabinet of ultraroyalists only to have the Chamber of Deputies reject them. He called new elections, but instead of regaining seats, the ultraroyalists lost still more. Determined to show greater firmness than his predecessor, Charles X in 1830 suddenly issued a set of secretly drafted decrees, the July Ordinances, which dissolved the new Chamber of Deputies even before it met, further restricted suffrage, and muzzled the press. Having shown his fiber, the king went hunting.

A shocked Paris slowly responded. Crowds began to mill about, some barricades went up, and stones were thrown at the house of the prime minister. Newspapers disregarded the ordinances and denounced the violation of the constitution, and the government responded with troops enough to raise tempers but too few to enforce order. Charles began to back down; but people were being killed (nearly 700 died in the three days of Paris fighting), some of the soldiers were mingling with the crowds, and liberal leaders were planning for a new regime. Once again, Paris was the scene of a popular uprising and Charles X, victim of what he most detested, abdicated on August 2. For 15 years, and for the only time in its history, France had been administered by its aristocracy, which had performed with probity and seriousness. The nation had prospered at home and enjoyed some success in foreign affairs; but the monarchy had been meant above all to provide political stability, and that the Bourbon regime, the restoration's most important experiment, had failed to do.

II. The Progress of Industrialization

At the same time, politics had begun to show the effects of a larger process of economic and social change. Economic growth stimulated further growth as inventions, the demand for more capital, factory organization, more efficient transportation, and increased consumption reinforced one another. All of society would feel the effects as land ceased to be the primary and surest source of wealth and the poor crowded into cities to seek the wages on which survival depended.

THE TECHNOLOGY TO SUPPORT MACHINES

Industrialization required the efficient use of raw materials, beginning with cheap metals such as iron, which could be formed into machines, and cheap fuel such as coal. The increased importance of iron and coal gave England an important advantage, for it was well supplied with deposits of coal that lay conveniently close to its iron ore.

Fuel, Iron, and Steam The English had increasingly turned to the use of coal as the once-great forests were cut down, and miners had begun taking coal from deeper veins, often beneath the water table. The need for powerful pumps to remove the water stimulated experiments to harness steam. Coal was not useful in smelting iron, however, because its impurities combined with the iron, resulting in an inferior product. For high-quality wrought iron, ironmasters therefore traditionally used charcoal, which was expensive. That stimulated experiments by eighteenth-century engineers in smelting with coke prepared from coal, producing pig iron, which could be cast but not worked or machined. As demand for iron and steel increased, the search for new techniques continued, resulting in the 1780s in the puddling process, the first commercially feasible effort to purify iron using coke alone. It was a breakthrough that convinced ironmasters like John Wilkinson that iron would be the building material of a new age. His improved techniques for boring cylinders made it possible to make better cannons and steam engines; and he built the world's first iron bridge over the Severn River in 1779, experimented with iron rails, launched an iron boat, and at his death was buried in an iron coffin.

Harnessing Steam The development of steam power also had a long history. In the third century, Hero of Alexandria had employed a jet of steam to spin a small wheel, and the account of his experiments, translated into English in 1575, suggested one means by which heat could be converted into motion. The first modern steam engines were based on another principle, however. In the seventeenth century several scientists proved that the atmosphere has weight, and Otto von Guericke in Germany used atmospheric

▸ **The crucial resource of industrialization was coal, and coal mining was one of the earliest industrial activities, employing steam engines to pump water and creating large, polluting enterprises in which hundreds of workers labored as drones, as at this English mine in Northumberland.**

pressure to push a piston through a cylinder, overcoming the efforts of 20 men to restrain it. Such sensational experiments encouraged construction of an "atmospheric engine," which used a partial vacuum; and before the end of the seventeenth century, atmospheric machines in which the condensation of steam created the needed vacuum were being designed both in England and on the continent.

The first commercially successful atmospheric engine was invented in England by Thomas Savery, who described it in a book published in 1702 and significantly entitled *The Miner's Friend*. Used as a pump, Savery's engine was woefully inefficient; but a decade later another Englishman, Thomas Newcomen, returned to the piston and cylinder design, which completely separated the engine from the pump and proved a third more efficient. Newcomen engines were soon being used not only in Great Britain but in France, Denmark, Austria, and Hungary.

The most fundamental step in the development of steam was the work of James Watt, a young mechanic and instrument maker working at the University of Glasgow. In the 1760s he made important improvements on the Newcomen engine, while still relying on atmospheric pressure; but he also recognized the enormous potential in making expanding steam push against a piston. His work took years, for it required new levels of precision in machining cylinders and pistons, new designs for valves, and new knowledge of lubricants and the properties of steam itself. Patented in 1782, Watt's first practical model was nearly three times more efficient than the Newcomen engine. Once he added a system of gears for converting the piston's reciprocating motion to the rotary motion needed to drive most machines, the steam engine had become much more than a pump.

Getting these inventions into use required the business talents of Watt's partner, the Birmingham industrialist Matthew Boulton. He recognized that the demand for cheap power had become more critical with the new inventions in the textile industry (including Arkwright's water frame, Crompton's spinning mule, and Cartwright's power loom). From the 1780s on, the steam engine was being used in factories; and some 500 were built before 1800. Even these early machines represented a remarkable improvement over traditional sources of power. They produced between 6 and 20 horsepower,[3] comparable to the largest windmills and water mills, and did so more reliably and wherever they were needed. An economy traditionally starved for sources of power had overcome that obstacle.

---

[3]The average man working hard can muster about one-tenth horsepower, or about 75 watts; the horse itself works continuously at a power output of only one-half horsepower. James Watt first defined the unit of horsepower as 33,000 foot-pounds per minute, but this could be achieved only by the strongest horses and only for short periods. The largest windmills in the eighteenth century could develop probably as much as 50 horsepower, but perhaps two-thirds of this was lost in friction. The best water mills seem to have produced 10 horsepower, but most of them rarely surpassed 5.

THE ECONOMIC EFFECTS OF REVOLUTION AND WAR

Great Britain's lead over continental countries in goods produced, capital invested, and machinery employed had widened steadily from 1789 to 1815. Nonetheless, there had been economic growth on the continent, too, where the exploitation of resources became more systematic, population increased, transportation generally improved, the means of mobilizing capital for investment expanded, and more and more political and business leaders were concerned with speeding industrial growth. In important respects, the French Revolution and the Napoleonic era had cleared the way for future industrialization. In France, western Germany, northern Italy, and the Low Countries, land tenure was no longer the most pressing economic and social issue. Less constrained by custom and legal restrictions, landowners, including peasant proprietors, could more easily shift their production to meet the demands of a national market. The abolition of guilds and old commercial restrictions had eliminated some obstacles to the free movement of workers and the establishment of new enterprises. The Napoleonic Code and French commercial law not only favored free contracts and an open marketplace but also introduced the advantages of uniform and clear commerical regulations. The French government had exported a common and sensible standard of weights and measures, encouraged the establishment of technical schools (the Polytechnic School in Paris long remained the world's best), and honored inventors and inventions of every sort, from improved gunpowder to new techniques for raising sugar beets. Under Napoleon, Europe had benefited from improved highways and bridges and a large zone of free trade; and the Bank of France, as restructured in 1800, had become the European model of a bank of issue providing a reliable currency.

In the short run, however, the years of war had slowed and disrupted Europe's economic growth. Vast resources in material and men were destroyed or wastefully used up. When peace came, governments were burdened with heavy debts, and returning soldiers had to find ways to support themselves in a changed economy. The Continental System, which had initially swung production and trade in France's favor, had collapsed with Napoleon's fall, bringing down many of the enterprises that it had artificially sustained. Both the instability of political change and renewed British competition discouraged daring capital investment. Great Britain had found compensation in American markets for its exclusion from continental ones and had avoided the shock of military invasion; but it, too, suffered a severe slump in the postwar years when the anticipated continental demand for British goods failed to materialize and the transition to a peacetime economy proved difficult to achieve.

PATTERNS OF INDUSTRIALIZATION

By the mid-1820s, however, British trade was reviving, and by 1830 its economy was being transformed. Although no single industry was yet fully mechanized, the pattern of industrialization was clear. Later, that pattern would be repeated in much of the world, but contemporaries attributed England's leadership to unique advantages. Cotton had become the most important industry; its spinning was mechanized, and its weaving was becoming so as the result not just of mechanization but of a large consumer market. Growth in one economic sector stimulated growth in others. Increased textile production, for example, accelerated the use of chemical dyes; greater iron production required more coal. A few factories in one place encouraged others in the same region, where they could take advantage of the available work force and capital; this concentration of production in turn increased the demand for roads, canals, and, later, railways. All this required more capital, and on the cycle went. In continuity, range of industries affected, national scope, and rate of increase, Great Britain's industrial growth in the first half of the nineteenth century was the greatest humankind had yet experienced.

New inventions became whole industries and were integrated into the economy with dazzling speed. The steam engine's application to rail travel is a classic case. The first successful steam railway line was built in England in 1825; a few years later an improved engine impressed spectators by outracing a horse, and in 1830 the first

Gladstone Argues for Regulating Railroad Fares

Sir Robert Peel supported his young colleague, William Gladstone, in trying to push a bill for the regulation of railroads through the English Parliament. Conflicting interests eventually forced Gladstone's plan to be watered down (there was great fear that the government would seek to purchase private railroad companies and considerable opposition to its regulating them very heavily); but Gladstone won his point, set forth in his speech on July 8, 1844, that Parliament should have a voice in setting rates as a matter of social policy.

"... Of the forty Clauses of the Bill, twenty-four related to the provisions respecting purchase; those from the twenty-fifth to the twenty-eighth related to third-class passengers. He must say that he felt strongly that the case of the third-class passengers by those trains was becoming a national question of great importance, and though averse to any general interference by Government with the management of these Companies, he did think it was wise to make a provision while it could be done without any breach of public faith, whereby those persons—being, as they were frequently, the least able to bear exposure to the cold, and obliged to remove frequently in search of bread, from one part of the country to the other—might be able to transfer themselves at the charge of 1*d*. a mile, without such exposure to the severity of the weather as amounted in many cases to severe personal suffering. It was on that ground they had introduced Clauses which certainly, so far as they went, were of the nature of interference. There were other Clauses regarding the public service, access of the public to the station and yards, conduct of inspectors, the prosecution of Railway Companies who exceeded the powers for which they were incorporated, contracts with Government, loan notes, and other matters so trivial that he need not mention them. . . .

"... With railways the Legislature were dealing with a new system producing new results, and likely to produce unforeseen effects. Was it not wise, then, to make provision for the future? Was it wise to trust themselves to all changes which the next ten or fifteen years might produce with regard to public communication by railway, without a thought for providing for the difficulties that might arise. Was it wise to place themselves in a position in which, whatever might be the exigency, they would be debarred from any interference. . . ."

From *Hansard's Parliamentary Debates*: Third Series, Volume LXXVI, 1844.

passenger line took its riders the 32 miles from Liverpool to Manchester in an hour and a quarter. Just over a decade later, there were 2000 miles of such rail lines in Great Britain; by 1851, there were 7000 (*see box*, above).

Railroads constituted a new industry that stimulated further industrialization. They bought huge quantities of iron and coal, carried food and raw materials to cities, and transported building

▶ **Stephenson's North Star engine of 1837 was meant to be an object of beauty, combining technology and craftsmanship.**

▶ **By 1830 it was possible to conceive of life transformed by technology as in this imagined view of what London's important White Chapel road might soon become, with traffic jams and smog but on an unpaved road with room for dogs.**

materials and fertilizers to the countryside and manufactured products to consumers. And they made it easier for the men and women who crowded into dirt-stained railway cars to travel in search of work. Similarly, the telegraph, developed by a generation of scientists working in many countries and quickly adopted as an adjunct of railroading, expanded to other uses, becoming a military necessity and a conveyor of news to the general public. The most impressive of the early long telegraph lines was Samuel F. B. Morse's from Philadelphia to Washington, opened in 1843. Less than a decade later, Britain laid 4000 miles of telegraph lines, and a cable to the continent was in operation.

Yet the leap from new invention to industrialization was not necessarily direct or predictable. Often dozens of subsidiary inventions or improvements were necessary to make a new machine competitive. Everywhere, but more often on the continent than in Britain, small-scale manufacturing and crafts persisted alongside the new. Machines themselves were usually made of wood and were frequently still driven by wind, waterpower, or horses. But the water-driven mills, charcoal-fired smelters, and hand-powered looms that dotted the countryside would be gradually but relentlessly displaced, as would hundreds of thousands of skilled artisans and rural families working in their homes to make products in the old ways—a transformation that accounted for much of the human suffering occasioned by industrialization.

PRODUCTION IN BELGIUM, FRANCE, AND THE UNITED KINGDOM

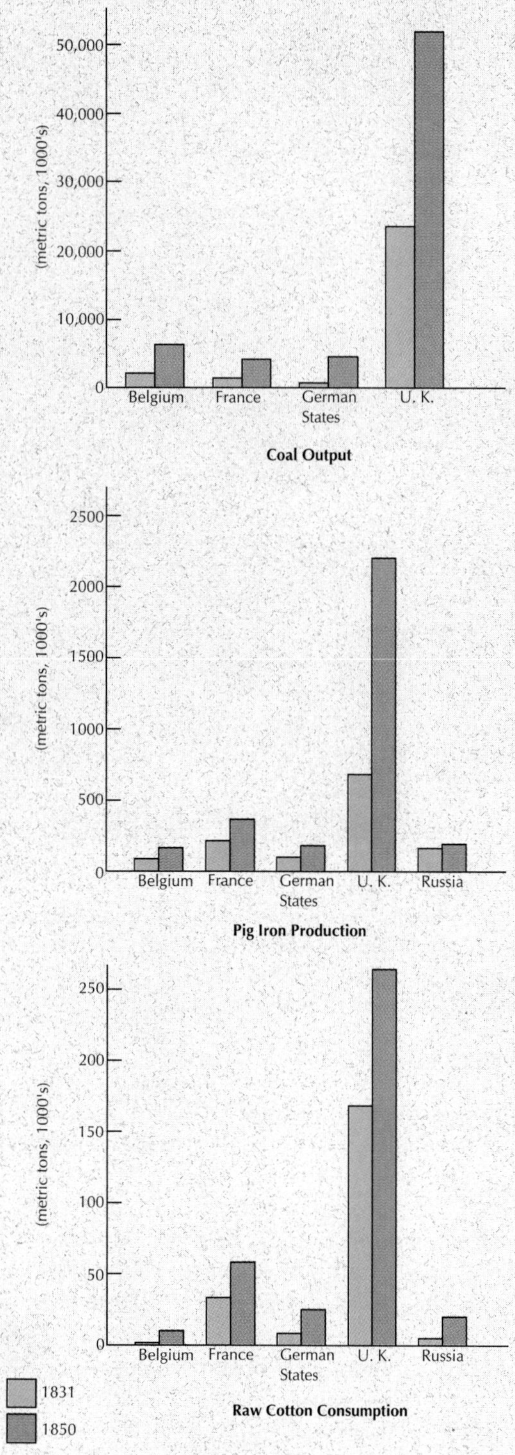

(Source: Mitchell, B.R. *European Historical Statistics, 1750–1970*, 1975, pp. 360–361, 428–429.)

National Differences In 1815 many regions of the continent, including such traditional commercial centers as Barcelona and Naples, had seemed ready to follow the British example of industrial growth, but by the 1850s the zone of industrialization had narrowed to include only northeastern France, Belgium and the Netherlands, western Germany, and northern Italy. Industrial change in this zone was uneven but more extensive than outside it. Countries poorly endowed in coal and iron, such as Italy, faced formidable obstacles. Although Saxony in eastern Germany was an early industrial center, most of Germany remained an area of quiet villages in which commerce relied on peddlers and trade fairs, even though by midcentury the German states were crisscrossed by the continent's largest railway network. Except for pockets of industrial development, Eastern Europe remained a world of agricultural estates. The centuries-old Atlantic triangular trade declined in importance as did the European ports that had depended on commerce in sugar and raw materials, now overshadowed by the export of manufactured goods and the entrepreneurial activity of merchants on both sides of the ocean.

Belgium, which had prospered from its former connections with Holland, built on its tradition of technological skill, its geographical advantages that made it an international trade center, and its access to coal to become the continent's first industrialized nation. Belgium extracted more coal than France or Germany and was the first country to complete a railway network. The French railway system, on the other hand, was not finished until after Germany's, for it was slowed by political conflict despite early and ambitious plans. France's canals, considered good in 1815, had trebled by 1848; and its production of iron, coal, and textiles increased severalfold in the same period. This would have been impressive growth a generation earlier, but Britain's expansion in each of these sectors was several times greater. In iron production, for example, the two countries were about equal in 1800, but by 1850 Britain's output was six or seven times greater. Britain outstripped France still more in textiles and coal, producing by midcentury half the world's total of these as well as iron.

Everywhere increased production led to more commerce and closer international ties as capital, techniques, workers, and managers moved from Britain across the Channel and spread from Belgium and France into the rest of Europe. Finance became so internationally linked that the Bank of France granted an emergency loan to the Bank of England in 1825, only a decade after Waterloo; and the domestic banking policies of the United States, in response to a financial panic in 1837, led to a wave of crises in the financial centers of Europe.

The Role of Government Although many argued that the new prosperity followed from natural economic laws that worked best unimpeded by government, by midcentury the state was centrally involved in the process of economic growth. Railroads required franchises and the power of eminent domain before a spike was pounded. Inevitably, routes, rates, and even the gauge of the track became political matters to be settled by parliaments or special commissions. In Belgium and in most of Germany, railroads were owned as well as planned by the state.

Tariffs, the dominant issue in British politics in the 1840s, became a critical question in every country. In 1846 Britain abolished the tariff on grain, known as the Corn Laws, after a wrenching public campaign. In doing so, the nation expressed confidence in its position as the world's greatest center of manufacture and sided with those who favored trade and a lower price for bread rather than with the landowners, who benefited from higher grain prices. Equally important to economic development was the role of government in banking and currency. Just before the middle of the century, Parliament granted the Bank of England a monopoly on issuing money and, as a guarantee to investors, required companies to register with the government and publish annual budgets. Similar steps were taken across Europe. Before industries could effectively tap private wealth, investors needed assurance that they risked only the money they invested, without being liable (as in a partnership) for all a firm's debts. That assurance required new legislation establishing limited liability and encouraging the formation of corporations, and every major country passed such measures.

The growth of cities and the benefits of new technology created additional social demands involving government. By the 1840s most cities had a public omnibus, some sidewalks, and gas lighting in certain areas. Such services, usually provided by private companies, had to be subsidized, regulated, and given legal protection by government. As their cost and importance increased, so did the state's participation in them, often extending to full ownership. The growing role of government was exemplified by the postal service, which most states had provided since the seventeenth and eighteenth centuries. These postal systems, with few exceptions graft-ridden and unreliable, were inadequate for an industrial era. In Britain demands for improvement led a little-known inventor and radical to propose a solution that captured the thinking of the new age. Using arguments like those of the new economists, he called for standard envelopes and payment in advance by means of an adhesive stamp. Not only would that eliminate graft and reduce costs, but the service would pay for itself because lower rates would increase volume. His reforms, denounced as dangerous and impractical, passed nevertheless in 1840; and within 20 years the volume of mail in Britain increased sixfold. By then, money orders, savings accounts, and the telegraph had been added to postal services. In France mail delivery was extended to rural areas, and by the 1850s every major government was adopting the new system, including the postage stamp, which quickly became the object of a fashionable middle-class hobby.

Effective government, in short, was now expected to further economic development—by subsidizing ports, transportation, and new inventions; by registering patents and sponsoring education; by encouraging investment and enforcing contracts; and by maintaining order and preventing strikes. In the 1840s the leaders of Britain, France, and Belgium busily did these things—in Great Britain the number of government employees increased about fourfold in the first half of the century—and the desire for other states to make governments elsewhere match this performance was an important element in the revolutions of 1848 and the nationalist movements of the period that followed.

The Crystal Palace The British celebrated their position as the masters of industrialization in 1851 with the first international industrial exhibition. Prominent people from the aristocracy,

▶ **A glass cathedral enclosing trees, statues, and fountains, the Crystal Palace organized national exhibits as a kind of encyclopedia of world industry, with subcategories for different products, as in the Indian exhibit at the left.**

▶ **British products dominated the machinery section of the Crystal Palace Exhibition. Here men and women marveled at Joseph Whitworth's lathe for forming railway wheels, a machine for making machines.**

business, and government joined in the planning; and a specially designed pavilion was built in London, a sort of giant greenhouse called the Crystal Palace, which proved to be an architectural milestone. Many governments feared that Britain risked revolution by attracting huge mobs to London, but the admiring crowds proved well-behaved.

The exhibition provided a significant comparison of the relative economic development of the participating countries. Russia displayed primarily raw materials; Austria showed mainly luxury handicrafts. So did the German Zollverein and the Italian states, whose appearance as single economic units foretold the advantages of national unification. Although unable to fill all the space it had demanded, the United States impressed viewers with collections of fossils, cheap manufactured products for use in the home, mountains of dentifrice and soap, and a series of new inventions, including Colt revolvers, a sewing machine, McCormick's reaper, and a vacuum coffin. French machines, which ranged from a much-admired device for folding envelopes to a submarine, were generally considered the most elegant. But British machines surpassed everyone's in quantity, size, and variety. It is, explained London's *Morning Chronicle,* "to our wonderful industrial discipline—our consummately arranged organization of toil, and our habit of division of labour—that we owe all the triumph." By 1850, Great Britain was the wealthiest nation in history,[4] and it would increase its lead over others in goods produced for the next 20 years.

III. The Social Effects

Economic growth on such a scale was accompanied by far-reaching social change. Even in its early stages, industrialization impinged on all of society, from the state to the family, affecting what governments did, the nature of work, women's roles, and childhood. Child labor, tyrannical foremen, teeming slums, and unemployment brought new social problems and required new social policies as the growing prosperity and security of the middle class contrasted all the more sharply with the destitution of the urban poor.

THE DIVISION OF LABOR

The Factory The factory quickly became the symbol of the age. Well before industrialization there had been workplaces where hundreds of people labored under one roof, and conversely even in industrialized societies, most wage earners did not work in factories. But the factory symbolized a different kind of power—the power of steam and of technology, the power of capital to assemble machinery and work force, the power of competition to drive down prices and wages, the power of markets to absorb ever more production and determine what would be produced. Above all, the factory symbolized the capacity of this whole system to change the landscape, to erect or transform cities, and to reshape the lives of masses of men, women, and children.

The factory model was most clearly triumphant in the production of textiles. Spinning and weaving had always been domestic tasks; even in Europe's most important textile centers, where merchants collected the output from hundreds of looms, the actual work was done primarily in the home and involved all the family. The most successful weavers often employed others, so that on average there had been about a half-dozen weavers in a domestic establishment. Pay and working conditions varied from place to place, with the season, and with the ability of middlemen to control the prices of the thread they supplied and the cloth they purchased. Textile factories, on the other hand, required and investment in buildings, machinery, and raw materials far beyond the reach of most weavers; in return, production per worker increased more than a thousandfold with the factory's efficient organization and power-driven machinery. By the 1830s cotton factories in Manchester, larger than most, averaged nearly 300 employees.

This Nasmyth steam hammer looms above the men who endure heat and noise to feed it—in every way the symbol of a new era.

[4]Although all estimates for this period are uncertain, it seems likely that by 1860 the per capita wealth of the French was about two-thirds and of the Germans about two-fifths that of the British.

Under the foreman's close supervision, women kept the textile looms running.

Slowly, these factories drove the older forms of textile production out of business, although their flexibility (and the weavers' hatred of factories) long kept domestic production alive in some regions and for special products. Those who came to work in a factory might be former weavers, but they were likely to be less skilled laborers (often migrants) driven by poverty. Most were women and children, hired to tend power looms, splice thread, or sweep the floor. Children were paid less than women and women less than men, who did the heaviest work and served as carpenters and mechanics. At first, children usually worked with their parents, even in the factories; but increased specialization meant that, like their mothers and fathers, children came to be employed and supervised without regard to family ties.

The workday usually began at 5:30 or 6:00 in the morning and lasted for 12 hours of work plus whatever time was allotted for meals and for recesses (when belts were replaced and machinery fixed). The workroom was usually kept moist, so that the taut thread would break less readily, hot in summer and cold in winter. To the employer, who was concerned to keep the expensive machinery running, the employees were too often lethargic and sullen, prone to drunkenness and indifference. In order to maintain the discipline efficient production demanded, foremen used whips and curses but most of all fines (fines for lateness, for slacking off, for flawed work, for talking, and sometimes even for singing or whistling).

The best employers, like the middle-class reformers and the inspectors subsequently appointed as the result of factory legislation, were shocked by all this and by the workers themselves in whom they discovered foul language, filthiness, poor health, ignorance, and promiscuity. Employers could see no solution beyond more discipline, and nearly all of them opposed such measures as the law finally passed in England in 1847 that limited the workday to 10 hours. Many workers, especially those with established skills—hatters, masons, tanners, typesetters, bakers, and, eventually, steam-engine makers—looked to different solutions. They took the lead in forming labor organizations and agitating for political redress. Although skilled laborers tended to look down on those who worked in factories, the latter were, in income at least, better off than about half of all laborers; and their lot improved a bit as legislation hesitantly restricted hours and set some standards of hygiene and safety.

Differentiation The increased division of labor was not limited to the allocation of work within factories, and sociologists use the term *differentiation* to describe the spread of specialization among groups and institutions that was a characteristic of the nineteenth century. Just as factories separated work from family life, so money exchange and legal contracts differentiated economic from personal or social relationships. Business affairs and governmental functions became more specialized, matters determined by calculation or regulation rather than status or social connection. Maintaining the peace, collecting taxes, inspecting factories and schools, and administering welfare measures fell to separate agencies. In addition, social tasks (such as the registration of births and deaths and provisions for education and charity), that had once been performed more informally and largely by the clergy, were now increasingly absorbed by the state—another reason for the importance of politics in this period. Just as each trade and each locality followed its own course of social change, so each nation differed in the pace and manner of institutional differentiation. Britain, more than continental states, left many public matters to local government and private groups; in France the role of the national government increased, and the German states tended to combine centralizing bureaucracies with considerable local autonomy. Whatever the pattern, the growth of differentiation brought increased professionalization and exposed tensions between government and established interests, national policy and local custom.

The Family To a great many nineteenth-century observers, social change threatened to undermine the family, and moralists of every sort warned that the very institution most central to civilization was in danger. Recent research has suggested a different view. The heightened concern for the family was a response to real stress, but it was also an expression of a growing belief in the importance of the family, which would prove to be an extraordinarily adaptable institution.

Family life in Europe had always been related to social status. For the aristocracy, family encompassed a wide network of relatives, privilege, and power. Women played a critical but subordinate role as carriers of the dowries that joined estates, as managers of large domestic staffs, and as centers of the social circles in which aristocrats met. Among peasants, the family unit might include grandparents or, where plots were large enough, even in-laws, cousins, and nephews. Particularly in the Mediterranean regions, such extended families often shared housing in the village but worked in different nearby fields. When they could, however, a young couple generally set up a household of their own. Where peasants owned land, they had difficulty keeping it intact while giving something to all their children. Bitter disputes were frequent, for the elderly feared dispossession and the children were concerned that they would not get their share in time, whether law and custom required equal division of inheritance as in France, primogeniture (inher-

The bourgeois family at breakfast: perfect domestic harmony, father looks up from the morning newspaper to enjoy the scene of an angelic child and adoring wife, a servant tends to them in front of the Chinese screen that sets off the eating space.

itance by the eldest son) as in England, or other more complicated arrangements.

The family was the basic economic unit, pooling income from various sources and dividing labor in customary ways. Women usually handled household chores and the smaller animals, the men were responsible for the heavier work, and everyone worked together in critical periods of planting and harvest. Often the women had more access than the men to additional sources of income—piecework from a nearby mill or domestic service for the well-to-do—and they played a central role in marketing. Men, on the other hand, were more likely to travel considerable distances, especially in difficult times, in order to pick up a bit of work on roads or docks or at some great landlord's harvest. As population increased, the children were more often pushed out to seek employment in the nearest mills and towns.

For artisans, too, the family was often the unit of production, although the division of tasks by sex was usually more explicit and even small workshops had long tended to exclude women, at least from the better-paid tasks. Working-class women and children were accustomed to long hours of labor; the strain on the family in the industrial age came rather from the lack of housing and the conditions of work. Not only did women and children have to supplement the father's income, but they were less and less likely to work side by side; if taught a trade, children were less likely to learn it from their parents. Sometimes the father, with his preindustrial skills, remained unemployed and did housework while his wife and children earned wages, which the socialist Friedrich Engels believed was another source of "the righteous indignation of the workers at being virtually turned into eunuchs."

Adolescents in factory towns, hardened at an early age, were probably more likely to leave home when their pay allowed, and urban conditions made it more difficult for the family to support the aged and the sick. Such factors did weaken family ties, as did—at least in the eyes of the upper classes—the common practice for working men and women to live together without the trouble or expense of formal marriage rites. Yet among workers, too, the family survived and the home remained a special place expected to provide protection for small children, a haven for wage earners, and temporary shelter for relatives seeking a job.

Women's Roles The fact that women worked for pay may also have slowly lessened their domestic subordination, even if it did not lead very directly to the new and superior stage of family life that Karl Marx thought it might. In the lower-middle class, especially in France, women were as important as, and frequently more visible than, men in operating small shops. The life of the middle-class woman, however, contrasted greatly with that of her poorer sisters, and the role allotted wife and mother became one of the most apparent and important indicators of social status. Women continued to be the organizers, patrons, critics, and ornaments of many of Europe's most cultivated circles; but the middle class isolated women from the harsh competition of business and politics. As the contemporary French historian Jules Michelet complained, "By a singular set of circumstances—social, economic, religious—man lives separated from woman." In Victorian England, gentlemen met in their clubs or withdrew from the ladies after dinner for their cigars and weighty talk.

Victorian discourse often made the ideal of femininity appear to be an idle and pallid creature, encased in corset or bustle, whose tendency to faint was a sign of delicacy. In reality women's roles were far more significant and varied, but the image may well have reflected values widely shared. Allowing a wife to be idle even if her husband worked hard was of course a kind of conspicuous consumption, a partial imitation of aristocratic elegance. There were signs, too, of an unconscious effort to sustain a sort of counterculture. If men must be competitive, hard, and practical, women should be tender, innocent, and gracious—the weak but pure upholders of morality and aesthetic sensibility. The middle-class woman with no estate to manage and few servants to direct was almost literally placed on a pedestal. Neither her needlework nor her piano playing was viewed as serious, but her role in maintaining the protective calm of the home and as exemplar of the moral virtues was.

Unless they had (female) servants, wives of every class—no matter what their other burdens—were expected to prepare and serve the food, wash and mend clothes, and clean the home. Middle-class concern with the family also emphasized, however, the special role of women within the home, which became a private citadel largely closed to the outside world. The liberal dream of combining individualism and social order found its model in the family, where the patriarchal father, devoted mother, and carefully trained children were meant to live in disciplined harmony. Childhood itself lasted longer in the middle class, for manners, education, and character required elaborate preparation. The mother was the core of this home; and books, newspapers, magazines, and sermons filled with accounts of the talents her role required. Motherhood had become an honored occupation, fondly depicted in novels and the new women's magazines founded, like the Parisian *Journal des Femmes* of 1832, to make women "skilled in their duties as companions and mothers."

Clearly, these attitudes were related to the famous prudery of the age and the distrust of sexual passion. In 1818 Thomas Bowdler produced his *Family Shakespeare*, a "bowdlerized" version "in which . . . those words and phrases are omitted which cannot with propriety be read in a family," a strange sensitivity after 200 years of admiration for Shakespeare's dramas. And "the anti-English pollution of the waltz . . . the most degenerating that the last or present century can see" was denounced in *The Ladies' Pocket Book of Etiquette* of 1840. The middle classes sought to maintain an orderly world through convention. At a time when prostitution and drunkenness were believed to have reached new heights, this was more than repression; it was an effort to bend society to the self-discipline on which morality, a thriving commerce, the advancement of knowledge, and personal fulfillment were thought to rest.

THE STANDARD OF LIVING

There is more agreement among historians about the general pattern of social change in the first half of the nineteenth century than about its effects on the standard of living, particularly of the working class. For this period, England is the critical case; and scholars agree that between 1790 and 1840 national wealth about doubled but that the upper classes were the principal beneficiaries. Did workers gain, too? Certainly they were poor, but poverty, even of the bleakest sort, was not new (and the growing protest against such destitution was in itself one of the important changes of the period). The poorest peasants of Sicily who lived in caves, or those of Sweden or Ireland who lived in holes dug into the ground, may have been victims of the social system; they were hardly victims of industrialization.

What *was* new was the terrible crowding in industrial areas and the workers' helpless dependence on their employers. The conditions in which workers lived made poverty more miserable, more obvious to all, and more threatening to the general welfare. The crowding was partly the result of increased population, but it followed directly from the rapid growth of factory towns. There, hastily built housing may often have been drier and cleaner than peasant hovels that had served for centuries; but squeezing whole families into a single room and cramming hundreds and thousands of people into slums with little light, with a single source of insalubrious water, and with no means for disposing of sewage created problems so different in scale as to be different in kind (*see box*, p. 728). Industrialization also added the special hazards of lead and phosphorous poisoning; and the assault on the lungs of coal mining, cotton spinning, and machine grinding helped make tuberculosis ubiquitous. Everywhere in Europe members of the working class were recognized generally to be thinner, shorter, and paler than other people.

The work available had always changed with the seasons and laborers in many regions and trades were accustomed to migrating to follow harvests and other temporary opportunities for work, but industrialization brought an often demoralizing dependence. Most new factories employed between 150 and 300 men, women, and children, whose well-being was largely tied to a single employer. A high proportion of these people were new to the area in which they lived, starkly dependent upon cash to pay their rent, purchase rough cotton for clothes, provide the bread that was the staple of their diet, and buy some candles and coal. For millions, employment was never steady; for millions of others, unem-

Reports on the Housing Crisis in France and Germany

The housing crisis was not limited to cities with a lot of new industry, as these two descriptions, expressing the shock of middle-class reformers, show. The first is from André Guépin,* Nantes au XIXe siécle *(Nantes, 1835); the second, giving Dr. Bluemner's impression of Breslau, is from Alexander Schneer,* Über die Zuständer der arbeitenden Klassen in Breslau *(Berlin, 1845).

". . . If you want to know how he [the poorer worker] lives, go—for example—to the Rue des Fumiers which is almost entirely inhabited by this class of worker. Pass through one of the drain-like openings, below street-level, that lead to these filthy dwellings, but remember to stoop as you enter. One must have gone down into these alleys where the atmosphere is as damp and cold as a cellar; one must have known what it is like to feel one's foot slip on the polluted ground and to fear a stumble into the filth: to realise the painful impression that one receives on entering the homes of these unfortunate workers. Below street-level on each side of the passage there is a large gloomy cold room. Foul water oozes out of the walls. Air reaches the room through a sort of semi-circular window which is two feet high at its greatest elevation. Go in—if the fetid smell that assails you does not make you recoil. Take care, for the floor is uneven, unpaved and untiled—or if there are tiles, they are covered with so much dirt that they cannot be seen. And then you will see two or three rickety beds fitted to one side because the cords that bind them to the worm-eaten legs have themselves decayed. Look at the contents of the bed—a mattress; a tattered blanket of rags (seldom washed since there is only one); sheets sometimes; and a pillow sometimes. No wardrobes are needed in these homes. Often a weaver's loom and a spinning wheel complete the furniture. There is no fire in the winter. No sunlight penetrates [by day], while at night a tallow candle is lit. Here men work for fourteen hours [a day]. . . .

"*Question*: What is the condition of the living quarters of the class of factory workers, day labourers and journeymen?

Reply of the City Poor Doctor, Dr. Bluemner: It is in the highest degree miserable. Many rooms are more like pigsties than quarters for human beings. The apartments in the city are, if possible, even worse than those in the suburbs. The former are, of course, always in the yard, if places in which you can hardly turn round can be called apartments. The so-called staircase is generally completely in the dark. It is also so decrepit that the whole building shakes with every firm footstep; the rooms themselves are small and so low that it is hardly possible to stand upright, the floor is on a slope, since usually part of the house has to be supported by struts. The windows close badly, the stoves are so bad that they hardly give any heat but plenty of smoke in the room. Water runs down the doors and walls. The ground-floor dwellings are usually half underground. . . ."

Reprinted in Sidney Pollard and Colin Holmes (eds.), *Documents of European Economic History*, vol. I, New York, St. Martin's Press, 1968, pp. 494–495, 497–498.

ployment was the norm. It was common for a third of the adult males of a town to be without work, especially in the winter, and pauperism was acknowledged to be the social disease of the century, a condition that included some 10 percent of the population in Britain and only slightly less in France. Workers, of course, suffered most in the periodic economic depressions that baffled even the most optimistic observers. The depression of 1846 was nearly universal, and that of 1857 extended from North America to Eastern Europe. Layoffs in the Lancashire cotton industry ran so high in the 1860s as a result of the American Civil War that at one time more than 250,000

▸ **Hopelessness dominates J. Leonard's painting of the poor coming to the charitable doctor in an endless stream.**

workers, better than half the total, lived by what they could get on relief. The recipes for watery soup handed out by the charitable agencies of every city define the thinness of survival.[5]

Although most workers everywhere suffered from the changing conditions of employment, in some trades and places, they were distinctly better off. Overall, real wages—measured, that is, in terms of what they could buy—may have begun to increase somewhat even before the general rise in wages in the mid-1840s and notably again in the 1850s, though these gains meant less in new factory towns, where workers could be forced to buy shoddy goods at high prices in company stores. Alcoholism was so extensive that in many a factory town paydays were staggered in order to reduce the dangerous number of drunks, a sign of alienation that may also have reflected an increase in available money. Technology brought benefits as well. The spread of the use of soap and cotton underwear were an enormous boon to health, and brick construction and iron pipes had improved housing even for many of the relatively poor by midcentury. Luxuries such as sugar, tea, and meat were becoming available to the lower-middle class and the more prosperous artisans.

The vigorous debate among historians over whether industrialization raised or lowered workers' standard of living in the first half of the century has become in large measure a judgment about the effects of capitalism. But historians generally agree that whatever improvements occurred reached the masses slowly and often could not compensate for the added burdens of

[5]The French chef of the Reform Club of London was much admired for his "good and nourishing" recipe: ¼ lb. leg of beef, 2 oz. of drippings, 2 onions and other vegetables, ½ lb. flour, ½ lb. barley, 3 oz. salt, ½ oz. brown sugar—and 2 gallons of water! It was by no means the cheapest soup. Cited in Cecil Woodham-Smith, *The Great Hunger*, 1964, p. 173.

industrial employment or the growing chasm between the destitute and the regularly employed. In industrial Europe the urban poor remained a subject of baffled concern. The more fortunate workers and the middle classes were unquestionably more prosperous than they had been in the recent past, which made the contrast with the poverty of those beneath them even more striking. A luxury restaurant in Paris (there were over 3000 restaurants of every type there by 1830 in contrast to only 50 or so before the Revolution) might charge 25 or 30 times an average worker's daily wage for a single meal; even modest restaurants charged twice a worker's daily wage—to a clientele that ate three or four times a day, in contrast to the two meals of many workers. From the top to the bottom of society, the gradations in status and wealth were subtle; the differences between the comfortable and the poor were palpable in every aspect of daily life.

In 1815 the reorganization of Europe following the Napoleonic wars had concentrated on politics as the key to social order, but the very meaning of order continued to be challenged by the complex heritage of the French Revolution and the painful drama of industrialization. For the rest of the century, Europeans would strive to understand accelerating social change and the problems that accompanied it. Arguments about how to describe it, what caused it, and how it might be controlled would stimulate great literature, important philosophies, and development of the social sciences, while the more pressing question of what to do about it challenged every political system.

Recommended Reading

Sources

Memoirs of Prince Metternich (5 vols.). Published in the United States in the 1890s, this edition was reissued in 1970. The published memoirs and correspondence of diplomats are a wonderful source, and larger libraries will have editions of the *The Memoirs and Correspondence of Viscount Castlereagh* (12 vols.) and the *Memoirs of the Prince of Talleyrand* (5 vols.). All of these give a lively picture of the Congress of Vienna.

For the subsequent years, *France and the European Alliance, 1816–1821: The Private Correspondence between Metternich and Richelieu*, 1948, is particularly useful.

Wilson, Charles, and Geoffrey Parker. *An Introduction to the Sources of European Economic History, 1500–1800.* 1977.

Studies

*Briggs, Asa. *The Making of Modern England, 1784–1867.* 1967. A wide-ranging and readable survey of English society and politics.

*Carr, Raymond. *Spain, 1808–1975.* 1982. The most balanced and comprehensive account in any language.

*Cipolla, Carlo M. (ed.). *The Industrial Revolution, 1700–1914.* 1973. The essays collected here give a good sense of the range of factors and interpretations important for understanding industrialization.

Davies, Norman. *God's Playground: A History of Poland* (Vol. II). *From 1789 to the Present.* 1981. Effectively studies the development of a nation without a national government.

*Gash, Norman. *Aristocracy and People: Britain, 1815–1865.* 1979. An incisive and balanced account of how British politics adapted to social and economic change.

Goodman, J., and K. Honeyman. *Gainful Pursuits: The Making of Industrial Europe, 1600–1914.* 1988. Attentive to the variety of interests that made industrialization a continuing process.

*Gideon, Siegfried. *Mechanization Takes Command.* 1948. This provocative analysis of the social and aesthetic implications of the machine age has become a classic.

Hamerow, Theodore S. *The Birth of a New Europe: State and Society in the Nineteenth Century.* 1983. A systematic, informative consideration of the major social changes of the nineteenth century, noting their connection to industrialization and the role of the state.

*Henderson, W. O. *The Industrialization of Europe: 1780–1914.* 1969. A general study contrasting developments in England and on the continent.

*Available in paperback.

*Hobsbawm, E. J. *The Age of Revolution, Europe 1789* to *1848*. 1970. A sparkling, influential Marxist assessment of the period.

Kissinger, Henry A. *A World Restored: Metternich, Castlereagh, and the Problems of Peace, 1812–22*. 1957. The author's subsequent fame adds to the interest of this account, which is very sympathetic to Metternich.

Kossman, Ernst H. *The Low Countries, 1780–1940*. 1978. Valuable and balanced treatment of a region that was an important participant in all the trends of modern European history.

*Landes, David S. *The Unbound Prometheus: Technological Change and Development in Western Europe from 1750 to the Present Day*. 1969. Emphasizes the role of technology.

*Macartney, C. A. *The Habsburg Empire, 1790–1918*. 1968. Detailed and authoritative.

Magraw, Roger. *France, 1815–1914: The Bourgeois Century*. 1986. A clear general account attentive to social change.

*Nicolson, Harold. *The Congress of Vienna. A Study in Allied Unity: 1812–1822*. 1970. A lively and balanced account of the process of peacemaking.

O'Brien, Patrick, and Caglar Keyder. *Economic Growth in Britain and France, 1780–1914*. 1978. A thorough examination of statistical methods and data for the period, focusing in particular on wages and productivity.

*Pollard, Sidney. *Peaceful Conquest. The Industrialization of Europe 1760–1970*. 1981. A provocative new study that focuses on the importance of geographical regions and not political units.

Price, Roger. *An Economic History of Modern France, 1730–1914*. 1981. Underlines the importance of modes of communication and transportation in the development of the marketplace.

*Rich, Norman. *Great Power Diplomacy, 1814–1914*. 1992. A classic kind of diplomatic history, in which the century is seen in terms of international relations; includes a very useful bibliography.

Seton-Watson, Hugh. *The Russian Empire, 1801–1917*. 1967. A solid, largely political survey.

*Smith, Bonnie G. *Changing Lives: Women in European History Since 1700*. 1989. Discussion of the major trends affecting all classes, with excellent bibliographies.

*Tilly, Louise, and Joan Scott. *Women, Work and Family*. 1978. Discusses the impact of industrialization on women and on the family economy.

*Trebilcock, Clive. *The Industrialization of the Continental Powers, 1780–1914*. 1981. A synthesis that uses recent research to emphasize the political implications of industrialization.

*Wandycz, Piotr S. *The Lands of Partitioned Poland, 1795–1918*. 1974.

Delacroix's painting presents the revolution of 1830 as the heroic rising of the people, poor and middle class together, being led by liberty into a new era.

CHAPTER TWENTY-THREE

LEARNING TO LIVE WITH CHANGE

EUROPEANS had to learn to cope, in the first half of the nineteenth century, with a world that would not stand still. Intellectual life was dominated by the effort to understand change and by arguments about how to deal with it. In daily life, too, people had to accommodate to new ways of earning a living, to the challenges of city life, and to shifting relations within the family and between social groups. Politics, in turn, was forced to focus not merely on new procedures and new programs but on change itself as something to be welcomed, contained, or resisted. Although more intensely experienced in cities than in the countryside, and in western Europe than in southern or eastern Europe, change—intellectual, social, and political—was becoming a preoccupation everywhere; for it was increasingly understood not just as the result of single events but as a continuing process likely to affect all aspects of society.

I. Theories of Change

Political ideas, social theories, and new movements in the arts were all closely interconnected in the early nineteenth century. New movements reshaped every field of thought, altering the way pictures were painted, poetry was written, statistics were collected, society was analyzed, biology was studied, and history was understood. Several elements served to connect all this creative diversity and increase its impact. The professors, writers, scientists and artists whose works were most influential increasingly saw themselves as having a special place in society because of their unique talents and special knowledge. Primarily male and largely from the middle class, they depended less on patronage than on their connections to established institutions such as academies, universities, publishing houses, magazines, and newspapers. They sought—through exhibitions, public lectures, and publications—to reach others like themselves and beyond them to a broader audience. A central theme in all this intellectual activity was the need to comprehend the French Revolution, and competing interpretations of it were in fact debates about the nature of society.

▶ A convert to Catholicism and a leading student of Gothic architecture, Augustus Pugin was one of the architects of the Houses of Parliament. These illustrations, part of a book of *Contrasts* comparing Catholic and Protestant society, sum up the romantic and conservative critique of modern society for replacing church spires with smokestacks, cottages and craftsmanship with massive tenements and factories, and charities with prisons. (The new prison in the foreground is Jeremy Bentham's Panopticon, designed so that a single guard can see down all the cellblocks.)

CONSERVATIVE THOUGHT

Conservatism grew from opposition to the French Revolution to become what today would be called an ideology—a coherent view of human nature, social organization, political power, and the sources of change that generally justified the status quo. Not that conservatives always agreed. But in arguing for social order, they tended to emphasize the limitations of human understanding, the wisdom of established customs, the value of hierarchy, and the social importance of religion. Conservatives thus mounted a powerful critique not just of radical programs but of modern society itself as perilously inclined toward antisocial individualism and immorality. As a broad school of thought, conservatism would contribute importantly to European intellectual life and political discourse throughout the nineteenth century.

The powerful English prose of Edmund Burke provided from the late eighteenth century on perhaps the most influential formulation of the conservative position. Society, he argued, exists through continuity. By granting special privileges to certain groups, it fulfills social needs in a way conducive to order, achieving a delicate arrangement in which rank is related to social role and in which differences of status, having evolved through time, are therefore acceptable to all. This "natural" historical order was far wiser than the "artificial" plans of radicals, however well-intentioned. The Burkean view thus allowed for gradual change, at least in theory; but in practice, such arguments could be used against any plan for general reform. This tendency was strengthened by a distrust of reason that rejected

De Maistre's Opposition to Reform

Over the course of the past 20 years, most European governments had adopted constitutions, when Joseph de Maistre, writing from exile in Russia, set forth his objections to them in his **Essay on the Generative Principle of Political Constitutions.** ***First published in Russia in 1810 and in Paris in 1814, the essay was reprinted many times.***

"Every thing brings us back to the general rule—*man cannot create a constitution; and no legitimate constitution can be written.* The collection of fundamental laws, which must essentially constitute a civil or religious society, never has been written, and never will be, *a priori.* It is only when society finds itself already constituted, without being able to say how, that it is possible to make known, or explain, in writing, certain special articles; but in almost every case these declarations or explanations are the effect of very great evils, and always cost the people more than they are worth.

" . . . Not only does it not belong to man to create institutions, but it does not appear that his power, *unassisted,* extends even to change for the better institutions already established. . . . *Nothing* [says the philosopher, Origen] . . . *can be changed for the better among men, without God.* All men have a consciousness of this truth, without being in a state to explain it to themselves. Hence that instinctive aversion, in every good mind, to innovations. The word *reform,* in itself, and previous to all examination, will be always suspected by wisdom, and the experience of every age justifies this sort of instinct.

" . . . To apply these maxims to a particular case . . . the great question of parliamentary reform, which has agitated minds in England so powerfully, and for so long a time, I still find myself constrained to believe, that this idea is pernicious, and that if the English yield themselves too readily to it, they will have occasion to repent."

From Scholars' Facsimiles & Reprints, Delmar, New York, 1977, reprinting of the edition of Joseph de Maistre, *Essay on the Generative Principle of Political Constitutions* published by Little and Brown, Boston, 1847.

the ideas of the Enlightenment as dangerously abstract. Society could not be reconstituted by social schemes or formal constitutions because it was a great interconnecting web, and slogans about rights or equality concealed selfish interests and encouraged false hopes.

Conservatives found in history the record of how painfully civilization had developed and how fragile it remained, and many saw evidence in events since the French Revolution not only of human error but of divine will. Christianity was the source of Europe's strength and Christian fear a necessary restraint on humanity's selfish and prideful nature. Without it, society dissolved into revolution and anarchy. Political battles were part of a far larger millennial conflict.

Such views gave conservative thought both militancy and depth. For Europeans used to receiving radical ideas from France, two of the most pungent exponents of conservatism were men who wrote in French, Joseph de Maistre and Louis de Bonald. Society's first task, they argued, is self-preservation. Authority alone can check the selfish wills of individuals, and authority requires undivided sovereignty, social hierarchy, close links between church and state, and the vigilant suppression of dangerous ideas. They thus connected religion to politics and tied the Church to aristocracy and monarchy. Revolution, de Maistre explained, is divine retribution for false ideas (*see box,* above). Conservatism in this form contained little that was human or tolerant. With its praise of hangmen and censors, it spoke only to those who already shared its fears. Terrified of weakening the dikes that held back revolution, it left little room for compromise, divided while calling for unity, and relied on power while speaking of the social good.

LIBERALISM

Liberalism, like conservatism, was not so much a compact doctrine as a set of attitudes; but whereas conservatism emphasized tradition and hierarchy, liberalism was associated with ideas of social progress, belief in economic development, and values associated with the middle class. Confident that their ideas would triumph, liberals generally welcomed change and looked forward to the future.

Liberal Political Ideas Liberal political thought was rooted in the writings of John Locke and of the philosophes; and liberals in the nineteenth century believed that their programs would benefit individuals and society as a whole. A leading French liberal, Benjamin Constant, put the case succinctly: "The liberty of the individual is the object of all human association; on it rest public and private morality; on it are based the calculations of industry and commerce, and without it there is neither peace, dignity, nor happiness for men." By this creed, freedom would lead to morality, prosperity, and progress. The freedom liberals sought was primarily political and legal, and they generally favored a constitution and representative institutions, freedom of the press and of assembly, an extension of the jury system, separation of church and state, public education, and administrative reform. Most liberals were not democrats—political wisdom, they thought, required the advantages of education and leisure—but nearly all believed that giving ideas a free hearing and propertied voters a free voice would result in policies beneficial to all.

▸ Known for his biting satire, Honoré Daumier began the 1830s expecting liberty to bring social and political progress that would light up the sky like fireworks.

Economic Liberalism Although liberal politics and liberal economic theory were closely related, they were nevertheless separable. The advocates of one were not always committed to the other. Still, it was England's example of economic growth as well as political liberty that made it the model of nineteenth-century liberalism. Adam Smith's argument that government intervention in the free play of the market restricted economic forces, which if left to themselves would increase productivity and prosperity, became liberal dogma. As systematically expounded by Englishman David Ricardo in his *Principles of Political Economy and Taxation* (1817), liberal theory became the keystone of modern economics. Ricardo, a financier who became wealthy during the Napoleonic wars and then retired from business, became an important public figure; but his great influence lay in his precise, flat prose that presented economics as a science.

The wealth of the community, Ricardo declared, comes from land, capital, and labor; and these three "classes" are compensated by rent, profit, and wages. A product's value results from the labor required to make it: This was the labor theory of value, which socialists would later use for very different purposes. For Ricardo, this theory led to principles of property similar to those of Locke and to an emphasis on labor saving as the source of profit, which had been foreshadowed by Adam Smith. The value of land or of work was determined not by individual decisions but by economic laws. The poorest land in cultivation simply sustains those who work it; but the most fertile land produces more for the same labor, and that increment constitutes profit, paid to the landlord as rent. As population pressures bring more (and poorer) land into cultivation, rents rise because the difference between the best and worst land increases. Similarly, wages subtract from profit, but the rate of pay is set by an "iron law of wages" (Ricardo's phrase is characteristic). It decrees that when labor is plentiful, the workers tend to be paid at the subsistence level. Short-term fluctuations in prices are the natural regulator within this system, pushing people to activities for which demand is high. Ricardan economics thus extended the sphere of inexorable economic laws to social relations.

For Ricardo, both land and labor are commodities, their value quite unaffected by any sentimental talk about the virtues of rural life or craftsmanship, and society is a congeries of competing interests. Legislation cannot raise wages or prevent the marketplace from working in its natural way; but if people acknowledge economic laws and act in their own best interest, a natural harmony and progress follow.

Ricardo called his subject *political economy*, and a powerful reform movement developed from it. Landed interests, liberals argued, had misused political power for their own benefit while harming the rest of society. Throughout Europe liberal economic theory thus added important weight to demands that special privilege be eliminated (as the French Revolution had done), that governments be responsive to their citizens (who best know their own interests), and above all that the state not try to regulate production and trade. As economic growth became more impressive, it was natural for liberals to add that politicians should adopt some of the openness, efficiency, and energy of the men of action who were transforming the economy.

Utilitarianism The call for political and social reform could also lead to renewed emphasis on the role of the state, as it did in the utilitarianism of another Englishman, Jeremy Bentham. Like the philosophes, Bentham believed he could rationally deduce practical programs from universal principles, and he was ready to write a constitution for Russia or codify the laws of Latin American republics. Bentham began his reform campaign by criticizing the legal system, and he remained all his life an opponent of the precedent-bound courts of England. Some of his most important writings before 1789 appeared first in French (the revolutionaries gave him French citizenship).

In contrast to most philosophes, he rejected the doctrine of natural rights as a meaningless abstraction. In his system utility replaced natural rights as the basis of public policy, and utility was measured by determining the greatest good for the greatest number. In the Enlightenment tradition, he combined plans of detailed reform with a theory of psychology. The good is that which avoids pain and gives pleasure—a calculation all people make for themselves anyway and that better education would enable them to make more wisely.[1] Thus just as self-interest built great industry, so it could create a just and happy society. In contrast to Burke's emphasis on tradition and many liberals' preference for limited government, Bentham gave the state a central role. It should assign penalties for undesirable actions and awards for desirable ones, distributing pain and pleasure to induce socially beneficial behavior.

Bentham's followers, sober intellectuals who called themselves *philosophic radicals*, did not necessarily adopt all his doctrines, but they applied his principles in every sphere. By his death in 1832, they were among the most important reformers of Parliament, law, prisons, education, and welfare. A special group within a larger liberal movement, they shared and contributed to the tendency of liberals everywhere to press for humane reforms on grounds of common sense and natural harmony.

John Stuart Mill Liberals appraised society primarily in terms of opportunities for individual growth and freedom of individual choice, an emphasis that gave some ethical dignity to the pain of industrialization and lent promise to the process of social change. They believed their

[1]Bentham called this the "felicific calculus," but his verbal pomposity was famous: After-dinner walks were "postprandial perambulations."

principles were universally valid; yet, to the perpetual surprise of its adherents, liberalism proved a creed of limited appeal, forever subject to attack and internal division. Enthusiasm for limited constitutional reform was harder to sustain as disagreements arose over how limited it should be. In practice it was not easy to reconcile liberty with order or equal rights with private property. Liberals themselves divided on such issues. Some reduced liberalism to little more than the narrow justification of individual success. Others expanded it until the demand for social justice overshadowed its founding principles of competition and individualism. In each country the temper of liberalism was different, shaped by a national history liberals never wholly dominated.

Its very malleability, however, enabled liberalism to endure as a doctrine and a political force; and its broader meaning is best exemplified in John Stuart Mill, the most important liberal spokesman of the nineteenth century. Mill's father was a leading Benthamite, and he raised his son in the strictest utilitarianism; but the younger Mill gradually came with searching candor to modify received doctrine. Mill was extraordinarily learned—a philosopher, economist, and publicist—and he wrote some of the most influential classics of modern thought. Fearful of the intolerance and oppression of which any social class or political majority was capable, he made freedom of thought a first principle, and he advocated universal suffrage as a necessary check on the elite and proportional representation as a means of protecting minorities. Influenced by Auguste Comte, the French social theorist who was one of the founders of sociology, he acknowledged the critical role of institutions in social organization, and he admitted that the institutions, even liberal ones, suited to one stage of historical development might not be appropriate for another.

▸ This photograph of John Stuart Mill shows a sensitive intellectual who is also distinctly middle class; compare the Ingres portrait on p. 750.

To counterbalance the influence of the established elites, he favored a more open administration, organized interest groups, and workers' cooperatives. Moved by the problems of the industrial poor, he tried to distinguish between production (to which liberal economics could still apply) and distribution (in which the state might intervene in behalf of justice), and he came to see that collective action by the workers could enhance freedom rather than restrict it. He sought a place for aesthetic values within the colder utilitarian doctrine he inherited, and in later years Mill courageously advocated causes, such as the emancipation of women and the confiscation of excess profit, that seemed fearfully radical to most contemporaries (*see box*, p. 739). His liberalism, thus modified and extended, remained firm; and his essay, *On Liberty*, published in 1859, stands as one of the important works of European political theory, a careful but heartfelt, balanced but unyielding declaration that society can have no higher interest than the freedom of each of its members.

THE EARLY SOCIALISTS

Socialist thought offered a radical alternative to conservative and liberal ideologies, varied as each of those were. Among scores of socialist

Mill Opposes the Subjection of Women

John Stuart Mill published his essay,* The Subjection of Women, *in 1869. His arguments were based on familiar ideas about individualism and modern progress, but their extension to women's rights and in such absolute terms went much farther than most contemporary discussion.

"The object of this Essay is to explain, as clearly as I am able, the grounds of an opinion which I have held from the very earliest period when I had formed any opinions at all on social or political matters, and which, instead of being weakened or modified, has been constantly growing stronger by the progress of reflection and the experience of life: That the principle which regulates the existing social relations between the two sexes—the legal subordination of one sex to the other—is wrong in itself, and now one of the chief hindrances to human improvement; and that it ought to be replaced by a principle of perfect equality, admitting no power or privilege on the one side, nor disability on the other.

"... The masters of all other slaves rely, for maintaining obedience, on fear; either fear of themselves, or religious fears. The masters of women wanted more than simple obedience, and they turned the whole force of education to effect their purpose. All women are brought up from the very earliest years in the belief that their ideal of character is the very opposite to that of men; not self-will, and government by self-control, but submission, and yielding to the control of others. All the moralities tell them that it is the duty of women, and all the current sentimentalities that it is their nature, to live for others; to make complete abnegation of themselves, and to have no life but in their affections.

"... So far as the whole course of human improvement up to this time, the whole stream of modern tendencies, warrants any inference on the subject, it is, that this relic of the past is discordant with the future, and must necessarily disappear.

"For what is the peculiar character of the modern world—the difference which chiefly distinguishes modern institutions, modern social ideas, modern life itself, from those of times long past? It is, that human beings are no longer born to their place in life, and chained down by an inexorable bond to the place they are born to, but are free to employ their faculties, and such favourable chances as offer, to achieve the lot which may appear to them most desirable.

"If this general principle of social and economical sciences is ... true, we ought to act as if we believed it, and not to ordain that to be born a girl instead of a boy, any more than to be born black instead of white, or a commoner instead of a nobleman, shall decide the person's position through all life ....

"At present, in the more improved countries, the disabilities of women are the only case, save one, in which laws and institutions take persons at their birth, and ordain that they shall never in all their lives be allowed to compete for certain things. The one exception is that of royalty.

"... The social subordination of women thus stands out an isolated fact in modern social institutions; a solitary breach of what has become their fundamental law; a single relic of an old world of thought and practice exploded in everything else, but retained in the one thing of most universal interest ...."

From "The Subjection of Women" in John Stuart Mill, *Three Essays,* Oxford University Press, Oxford, 1975.

schemes, those of Saint-Simon, Fourier, and Owen were notable for the attention they won among intellectuals and political leaders. All three men had lived through the French Revolution and had personal experience of burgeoning capitalism in the early stages of industrialization, and each of them founded a movement that disseminated telling criticisms of capitalism.

Competition, they argued, is wasteful and cruel, induces hard-hearted indifference to suffering, misuses wealth, and leads to frequent economic crises. They offered instead scores of suggestions for organizing production differently and creating a harmonious, orderly, and truly free society.

As a young French officer, Claude Henri de Rouvroy, Comte de Saint-Simon, fought alongside George Washington at Yorktown. During the French Revolution he abandoned his title, made and lost a fortune speculating in land, and then devoted himself to the difficult career of a seer. Injustice, social divisions, and inefficiency could be overcome, he believed, in a society directed by experts standing above the conflict: scientists, men of affairs (*industriels*), and artists. These specialists, chosen for their ability, would design plans to increase productivity and prosperity for the benefit of all. The integrated, organic quality of Greek city-states and of the Middle Ages could be recaptured in the industrial age with scientists and managers (who would have the authority once granted priests and soldiers), leading humanity to self-fulfillment and love.

Saint-Simon's theories won a significant following especially among the bright engineers at France's École Polytechnique, and an extraordinary number of France's leading engineers and entrepreneurs in the next generation fondly recalled the Saint-Simonian enthusiasms of their youth. In their penchant for planning, their grand economic projects, and their schemes for social reform, they carried elements of his teaching into the world of affairs and respectable politics. There were important Saint-Simonian movements in every country, and later socialists would long sustain his respect for industrialization and the power of planning.

François Marie Charles Fourier had been a traveling salesman before dedicating himself, at the same time as Saint-Simon, to a theory that he firmly believed would rank among the greatest discoveries ever made. His cantankerous yet shrewd writings on contemporary society were so copious that his manuscripts have still not all been printed, despite the devotion of generations of admirers. Largely self-taught, he committed to paper his fantasies of the strange beasts and incredible inventions that would abound in the future. His central concept, however, was an ideal community, the phalanstery (from "phalanx"). Once even one was created, the happiness and well-being of its members would inspire the establishment of others until all of society was converted. A phalanstery should contain some 1600 men and women, representatives of all the types of personality identified in Fourier's elaborate psychology. He listed a dozen passions that move human beings and proposed to organize the phalanstery in such a way that individuals would accomplish the tasks society required simply by doing what they wanted. Each member would perform a variety of tasks, engaging in no one for too long; pleasure and work would flow together. Largely self-sufficient, a phalanstery would produce some goods for export and pay its members according to the capital, labor, and talent that each contributed. Although no phalanstery was ever established exactly as Fourier planned (he even offered designs for the architecture), communities were founded on Fourierist principles from the United States to Romania; and if few of them survived for long, the vision did of a society in which cooperation replaced compulsion and joy transformed drudgery.

Robert Owen was one of the success stories of industrial capitalism: A self-made man, he rose from selling cloth to be the manager and part owner of a large textile mill in New Lanark, Scotland. Owen ran the mill in a way that transformed the whole town, and by the end of the Napoleonic wars, distinguished visitors were traveling from all over Europe to see the miracle he had wrought in New Lanark. The workday was shortened from 17 to 10 hours. New housing eventually allowed an employee's family several rooms; inspection committees maintained cleanliness; gardens were planted and sewers installed. In nursery schools with airy, pleasant rooms, children were given exercise, encouraged to sing and dance, taught without corporal punishment, and trained in the useful arts. Most promising of all, the subjects of this paternalistic kingdom developed a pride in their community, productivity rose, and profits increased.

Owen had, he felt, disproved Ricardo's dismal economic laws and set about establishing ideal

communities elsewhere. Like Fourier's, they would be placed in a rural setting and would supply most of their own needs. Members would take meals and enjoy entertainment in common, and children would be raised communally. The young would be educated to the age of 8 and then engage in productive labor until they were 26; after five years in distributive or managerial jobs, adults would assume the tasks of government, cultivating the sciences and the arts in their increasing leisure time. The controlled environment would assure good character among community members, and the division of tasks would provide them with varied and interesting lives. Standardized production would offer more goods at lower cost (the snobbery that made luxuries attractive would disappear), and higher wages would increase sales (*see box*, p. 742).

A saintly father figure, Fourier instructs his disciplines from a hill overlooking an idyllic setting and an imagined phalanstery, Fourier's orderly community for 400 families.

Even after losing most of his wealth when the community of New Harmony, which he founded in Indiana, failed, Owen remained the single most important figure in the labor movement and in the workers' cooperatives that he helped spread through England in the 1830s and 1840s. But by the time of his death, in 1858, Owen, who had converted to spiritualism, was largely ignored by the world he had sought to remake.

Although there was much in these socialist movements that was easily ridiculed, the values they stressed echoed those of growing workers' movements everywhere. These early socialists

Owen Tells Congress About the Science of Socialism

Robert Owen made a number of trips to the United States in connection with the Owenite community on the Wabash River at New Harmony, Indiana. His international fame was such that on one of these trips he was invited to give two addresses to the United States Congress. In the first he called on Congress to adopt his principles; and in the second—delivered on March 7, 1825—he set out in some detail his plan for a community of up to 5000 people on 1000 or 2000 acres, with a square of large buildings at the center (each 1000 feet long). These buildings would house the "school, academy, and university" as well as washrooms, kitchens, dining halls, dormitories for children over the age of two, and apartments. Owen described the arrangements for central heating and cooling, gardens, manufacturing, and farms, and discussed how the community would be governed by an elected committee. But before entering into such specific matters, he presented the general principles of his program:

"Then it should be ever remembered, that the first principle of the science is derived from the knowledge of the facts, *that external circumstances may be so formed as to have an overwhelming and irresistible influence over every infant that comes into existence, either for good or evil . . . and thus, at pleasure, make any portion, or the whole, of the human race, poor, ignorant, vicious, and wretched; or affluent, intelligent, virtuous, and happy.*

"And thus, also, form man to understand and to practice pure and genuine religion, which never did nor ever will consist in unmeaning phrases, forms, and ceremonies; but in the daily, undeviating practice . . . of charity, benevolence, and kindness . . . [this] is the *universal religion* of human nature.

". . . Having then discovered, as I believe I have, the science of the influence of circumstances, and a rational, and therefore, a pure and genuine religion, the next important consideration is, to ascertain in what manner the new science and the new religion can be applied to produce the promised practical results. I have been frequently urged to apply these principles to the present state of society, and not attempt to disturb it, but endeavor to make them unite harmoniously together. . . . The inventor of the Steam Engine might as well have been required to unite his new machinery with the inefficient and clumsy horse engine. . . . The fact is . . . the system which I propose now for the formation and government of society, is founded on principles, not only altogether different, but directly opposed to the system of society which has hitherto been taught and practised at all times, in all nations.

". . . My conviction is, that, from necessity and inclination, the individual or old system of society, would break up, and soon terminate; from necessity, because the new societies would undersell all individual producers, both of agricultural productions, and manufactured commodities. And from inclination, because it is scarcely to be supposed that anyone would continue to live under the miserable, anxious, individual system of opposition and counteraction, when they could with ease form themselves into, or become members of, one of these associations of union, intelligence, and kind feeling."

From Oakley C. Johnson (ed.), *Robert Owen in the United States*, Humanities Press, New York, 1970.

sought to combine an older sense of community with the possibilities of a new era. They imagined a society enriched by new inventions and new means of production, in which new forms of social organization would foster cooperation and love. Their indictment of capitalism, their insights into the nature of productivity and exchange, and their attention to social planning and education had an impact far beyond their relatively small circles of believers. The dream of brotherhood and of work that was fulfilling echoed through later socialist and anarchist movements; yet nearly everyone ultimately rejected their ideas as impractical and too radical. Bucolic isolation and artisanal production became increasingly unrealistic in the face of industrialization, and these theories were incredibly vague about problems of politics and power.

The nature of their radicalism, however, deserves a closer look. The criticisms of liberal society mounted by Saint-Simon, Fourier, and Owen were not so different overall from the conservative attack. With some restrictions (Saint-Simon, for example, insisted on the abolition of inheritance), they even allowed private property, and none of them was thoroughly democratic. What most shocked contemporaries were their views on the status of women, sexual mores, and Christianity. All rejected the place allotted women in bourgeois society, and Owen not only specified that women should share in governing but believed that their emancipation required lessening their family responsibilities. All wrote of sensual pleasure as good and of its repression as a characteristic European error. The Saint-Simonians publicly advocated free love, and Fourier carefully provided that neither young nor old should be deprived of the pleasures of the flesh. Owen was only slightly less outspoken in his contempt for Christian marriage. At the same time, all three stressed religion as the source of community feeling, brotherhood, and ethics. Their efforts to replace what they had eliminated therefore led to imitations of Christian ritual and foggy mysticism that provided an easy target for their opponents. By the end of the nineteenth century they would be remembered as "utopian socialists"; for by then, socialist thought would center on the more hard-headed and systematic theories of Karl Marx (see Chapter 26).

II. The Structure of Society

SOCIAL CLASSES

Theories of change intermixed with everyday experience to form nineteenth-century perceptions of society. In the old regime, discussion of the "orders" or "ranks" in society had referred to an imaginary social pyramid rising from the lowliest peasant to the ruler. In this idealized picture, each person had an assigned place in that pyramid and social relations were governed by elaborate networks of reciprocal responsibilities. By the beginning of the nineteenth century, increased reference to the "middle" or "middling classes" conveyed a different conception of society. In this view, society consisted of broad strata, called classes, and social relations were matters of free contract between individuals, undetermined by rank or custom. A person's class reflected the status of his or her or her husband's occupation as well as something of the values held, the style of life led, and, later, the political and social interests likely to be favored. Descriptive of an expanding, fluid, unequal, national society, the concept of class gained urgency with the sharpening contrast between the middle class and the urban poor.

The Aristocracy The class most easily identified was the aristocracy. It included all nobles and their immediate relatives, whether they held noble titles or not; members of the upper gentry, who were large landholders and lived like nobles; and (in the ancient commercial cities of the Netherlands, northern Germany, and northern Italy) the established and wealthy patrician families, who dominated the cities though they might not bear titles.

The aristocracy had been a principal target of the French Revolution, and its privileges and influence were further threatened in the nineteenth century by new industrial wealth (which overshadowed the fortunes of large landholders), wider participation in politics, the growth of the state, and cultural change. The aristocracy's relative decline was so clear, in fact, that its continued importance is easily overlooked.

In most countries aristocrats continued to control most of the wealth, were closely allied to an established church, and dominated the upper levels of administration and the military. By training and tone the most international of social classes, aristocrats would remain the preeminent diplomats even where government was dominated by the middle class. They also stimulated some of the most influential critiques of nineteenth-century society, denouncing the middle class for selfishness and materialism, proclaiming urban life morally inferior to rural, and lamenting the loss of gentlemanly honor. The efforts of the aristocracy to defend its position, the means used, and the success achieved provide an important measure of social and political development in each country.

In much of Europe, especially the south and east, the aristocracy held on to local power and tremendous wealth, a social pattern exemplified by the Kingdom of Naples and by Russia. In both states the nobility, constituting only about 1 percent of the population, in effect ruled over most of the peasant masses. Three-fifths of the people in southern Italy lived on baronial estates, and after the defeat of Napoleon the aristocracy there worked with king and church to reestablish its authority. In Russia a fraction of the nobility held one-third of the land, and most of the rest, although owned by the state, was administered by nobles. Tyrants on their estates and dominant over local administration, Russia's aristocracy was a pillar of tsarist rule.

In countries where the nobles made up a higher proportion of the population, the pattern was somewhat different. In Poland, Hungary, and Spain, many of the nobility were extremely poor, and they tended to alternate between desperate allegiance to an empty title and sympathy for radical change, thus becoming another important source of political instability. In some countries, however, aristocrats sought to strengthen their influence through representative government and decentralization, thereby cooperating with political and economic reformers. The confident Magyars took this position in Hungary, and so, even more open-mindedly, did the aristocrats of northern Italy, Belgium, and Great Britain. They were thus prominent during the revolutions of 1848 in Hungary and northern Italy and in the subsequent nationalist movements in those countries. The Belgian aristocracy cooperated with liberals in the revolution of 1830 and afterward, accepting an endless string of concessions and reforms. In England, above all, the aristocracy proved willing to accept liberal programs in exchange for keeping their political prominence. Of the 100 men who served as cabinet ministers in Britain between the reform bills of 1832 and 1867, 64 were sons of nobles; and perhaps four-fifths of the members of Parliament were landholders or their representatives, closely tied to the aristocracy. On the other hand, younger sons and lesser aristocrats in England were more closely associated with the upper-middle class, which lessened the sharpness of social division.

In Prussia, the most influential aristocrats were the Junkers of east Prussia, owners of large estates, some of which included sizable villages. They maintained their traditional position even when the state became the instrument of dramatic and rapid change. Considered crude and ignorant by most of the aristocracies of Europe—which set great store by polished manners, elegant taste, and excellent French—the Junkers had a proud tradition of service to the state and loyalty to their king. In local government, in the bureaucracy, in the army, and at the court, their manners and their values—from rectitude to fondness for dueling, from arrogance to loyalty—set the tone of Prussian public life.

France is thus the European exception, for there the old aristocracy was reduced to a more minor role in national politics after the revolution of 1830. Its members retained major influence in the Church, army, and foreign service, but those institutions were also on the defensive. Yet even in France, aristocrats maintained a strong voice in local affairs and were a major influence on manners and the arts. Everywhere, however, aristocrats were in danger of being isolated from important sources of political and economic power. Lineage was once of such importance that tracing family lines had been a matter of state; now even pride of family was becoming a private matter.

Peasants The overwhelming majority of all Europeans were peasants, a social class as firmly tied to the land and to tradition as the aristocracy. They also felt the effects of change as agriculture became more commercial, its production increasingly intended for market rather than for mere subsistence or local consumption. Profits increased with the cultivation of one or two cash crops and with the use of improved fertilizers and machinery, but these changes were easier for those with more capital and bigger holdings than most peasants enjoyed. Because larger farms were more likely to be profitable, landed nobles, bourgeois investors, and richer peasants sought to expand and consolidate their holdings, a trend encouraged by legislation in much of northern Europe.

The emancipation of peasants from obligations denounced as "feudal"—a change effected by the French Revolution and carried to much of Western Europe by Napoleon, decreed in Prussia as part of the reforms of 1806, and spread to most of Eastern Europe with the revolutions of 1848—encouraged their entry into the commercial market; but these changes also deprived them of such traditional protections against hard times as the use of a common pasture, the right to glean what was left after the first harvest, and the practice of foraging for firewood in the forest. Similarly, the decline of the putting-out system and of local industries took away critical income, especially during the winter months. Gradually and with considerable local variation, peasants were becoming more dependent on the little piece of land to which they had some legal claim or the wages that could be earned from labor. Although additional land was put under cultivation to meet rising demand, especially in the West, it was usually of poor quality and divided into small plots, thus not greatly improving the peasant economy. As governments became more efficient, they reached more deeply into peasant society for taxes and conscripts, while population growth and competition from more distant markets added other pressures.

Peasants, however, were not just passive victims of outside forces. They tenaciously maintained old loyalties to their region, their priests, and their habitual ways; and they were the despair of reformers, who were often defeated by peasant suspicion of outsiders, ignorance, and opposition to change. But peasants also used elaborate ties of family and patronage to build effective social networks, and they were frequently shrewd judges of their interests, cooperating with measures that promised immediate benefits while resisting all others with the skepticism of experience.

Their hunger for land, resentment of taxes and military service, and sense of grievance against those above them could also become a major political force. Peasant involvement made a crucial difference in the early days of the French Revolution, in the Spanish Resistance to Napoleon, in the wars of German liberation, and in the strength of nationalism in Germany and Italy. Rulers were kept on edge by eruptions of peasant violence in southern England in the 1820s; Ireland in the 1830s and 1840s; Wales, Silesia, and Galicia in the 1840s; and on a smaller scale in most other countries. The outbreaks of 1848 would topple the system of feudal service in the Austrian Empire and eastern Prussia, though rural indifference to constitutional claims and workers' demands undermined the urban revolutions there.

► **This idealized picture of prosperous peasants and bustling farmyard is a German lithograph of 1850.**

The peasantry was deeply divided between those who owned land and those who were forced to sell their labor. Some of the former, especially in the West, grew relatively prosperous and joined the influential notables of their region. More of them survived on small plots by being as little dependent on cash as possible, vulnerable to the slightest change in weather or market and supplementing their income by whatever odd jobs family members could find. In most of Europe peasants received only a part of the crops they raised, with the rest going to their landlords. Such arrangements could provide significant security, but they also tended to be inflexible, discouraging adaptation to changes in prices, markets, and technology. Rural laborers were the poorest and most insecure of all, the tinder of violence and the recruits for factory work.

A central problem for nineteenth-century European society was how to integrate the agricultural economy and the masses dependent on it into the developing commercial and industrial economy. By the 1850s the process had gone farthest in France and Great Britain but by opposite means. In Britain the peasantry was largely eliminated as the continuing enclosures of great estates reduced the rural poor to laborers, shifting from place to place and hiring out for the season or by the day. The concentration of landholding in Great Britain was one of the highest in Europe: Some 500 aristocratic families controlled half the land; and some 1300 others, most of the rest. In France, on the other hand, peasants owned approximately one-third of the arable land and were gradually gaining more. They made the most of their situation by favoring crops that required intense cultivation, such as grapes and sugar beets, and by maintaining small-scale craft industries.

Patterns elsewhere lay between these two extremes. Small landholding persisted in western Germany, northern Italy, Switzerland, the Netherlands, Belgium, and Scandinavia, alongside a trend toward the consolidation of larger farms that reduced millions to becoming day laborers. In Germany emancipation from personal obligations to the lord usually required peasants to pay for their freedom with part (often the best part) of the land they had previously cultivated. New historical research has also established that the situation of peasants varied greatly with local conditions—the quality of the soil, the favored crop, government policy, and legal custom.

The clear distinction remained, however, between these Western and Central regions and Eastern Europe, where peasants were more directly subject to the power of the lord, most of all under Russian serfdom. In the West, developments that increased agricultural productivity often made the life of peasants more precarious. In the East, the landowners' authority over their peasants included claims to their unpaid labor, which in Russia ranged from a month or so of work each year to several days a week. The disadvantages of such a system were many, and the eventual emancipation of Russian serfs in the 1860s proved necessary for economic growth and minimal military and administrative efficiency. As urbanization and industrialization advanced, many writers waxed nostalgic for the bucolic purity and sturdy independence of peasant life, but the social and economic problems of the peasantry were, in fact, some of the gravest and most intractable of European society.

Workers Industrial workers attracted far more attention than the peasantry; yet even in Britain industrial workers were a minority among paid laborers (there were more domestic servants than factory hands). Industrial workers, however, were taken to be indicative of the new age be-

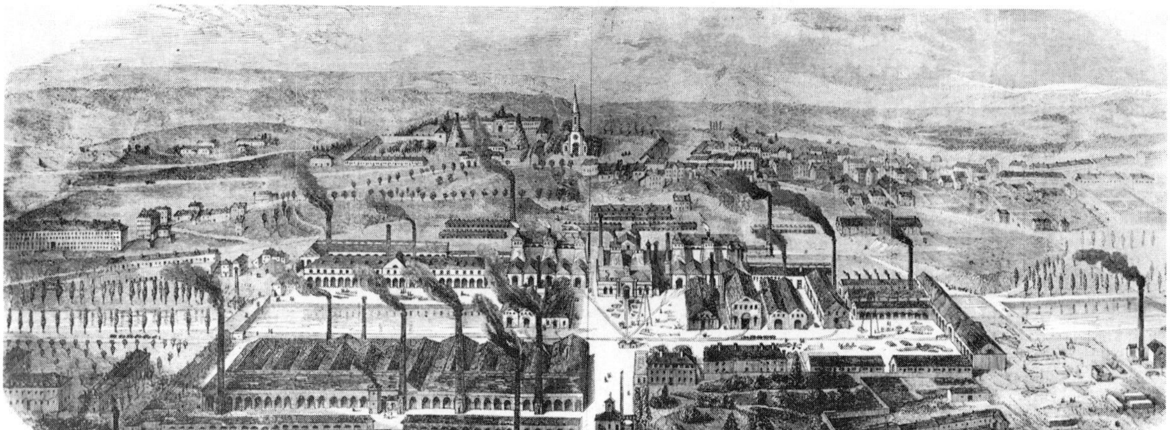

▶ **Le Creusot was a carefully planned and controlled company town that provided housing for the workers in its foundries.**

▶ **An etching of Dean Mills in 1851 shows cotton spinning as contemporaries liked to think of it: women working together with nimble industriousness under the watchful but gentle eye of a sturdy foreman, all in the iron grandeur of an immaculate, orderly, huge new factory.**

cause of the environment in which they lived and worked and because of their absolute dependence on wages set by employers, who could fire them at will and who determined the tasks performed as well as the conditions of work and the length of the workday. To many, such workers seemed a social threat, and in the 1830s and 1840s, serious French analysts wrote of the "dangerous classes" crowding into Paris.

Most factory workers earned too little to sustain a family even when work was steady, and the employment of women and children became as necessary to their survival as it was advantageous to employers, who appreciated their greater dexterity and the lower wages they would accept. The largest factories were cotton mills, where commonly half the laborers were women and a quarter, children. In coal mines, where women and children were hired to push carts and work in the narrower shafts, they made up a smaller proportion of the work force. A class of men, women, and children was thereby formed of people dependent on cash for their subsistence and subject to the rigid discipline of their employers. Awakened before dawn by the factory bell, they tramped to work, where the pace of production was relentless and the dangers from machinery and irate foremen were great. Any lapse of attention during a workday of 14 hours or more, even stopping to help a neighbor, brought a fine and a harsh reprimand. Children were frequently beaten, as men had been before fines proved more effective, and workers were spurred by the hated system of payment for tasks completed. Life was still more precarious for the millions without regular employment, who simply did such tasks as they could find, hauling or digging for a few pence.

Industrial workers were thus set apart by the conditions of their labor, the slums where they lived, and special restrictions such as the *livret*, or passport, that all French workers were required to present when applying for a job and on which previous employers recorded comments on the worker's conduct and performance. Understandably, the powerful worried about the social volcano on which they lived, and the sensitive feared the effect of the immorality and degradation that accompanied industrial life.

The most independent workers were the artisans, who had been stripped of their tight guilds and formal apprenticeships by the French Revolution, by a series of laws passed in Britain in the years before the 1830s, and by a similar process in Germany that was completed by the revolutions of 1848. Nevertheless, artisans continued to ply their crafts in a hierarchy of masters, journeymen, and apprentices, working in small shops where conditions varied as much according to the temper of the master as to the pressures of the market. Skilled workers, from carpenters and shoemakers to mechanics, moved in a less organized labor market but were distinctly better paid than the masses of the unskilled. Although they were vulnerable to competition from machines and new products and, above all, to unemployment during the frequent economic slumps, in general these skilled workers were among the beneficiaries of industrialization. Their real wages tended slowly to increase, and they could expect to earn enough to support their families in one or two bare rooms on a simple diet.

Ignorant and exhausted industrial workers, often strangers to one another, for the most part lacked the means necessary for effective concerted action to improve their lot. Their frequent outbursts of resentment and intermittent strikes usually ended in some bloodshed and sullen defeat. Sometimes riots, demonstrations, and strikes became local revolutions, spreading across the north of England in 1811 and 1812, breaking out in Lyons in 1831 and 1834, Bristol in 1831, Lancashire in 1841, and Silesia in 1844. Significantly, most of these outbursts were led by artisans, who felt most keenly the threat of economic change and held clearer visions of their rights and dignity. Although the authorities usually blamed such disturbances on the sinister plots of a few agitators, they were for the most part expressions of resentment and of a growing sense of a common interest.

Trade unions were banned everywhere except in England after 1824, and even there the laws against conspiracy restricted their activity; but various local organizations had developed since the eighteenth century to take the place of the declining or outlawed guilds. By midcentury more than 1.5 million British workers may have belonged to such groups, called friendly societies in England, which tended to form around a few of the more skilled workers and to meet in secret, often of necessity but also as a sign of brotherhood and trust. Although their members were fond of elaborate rituals and terrifying oaths, these societies served specific purposes that were tellingly modest, such as providing burial costs for members or assistance in times of illness. There were also movements that aimed to increase the workers' control over their lives. Consumers' cooperatives were numerous by the 1830s in England, as were artisan's production cooperatives, often established with church support, in France and Italy. Such programs sometimes became associated with radical politics, a specter likely to rouse crushing opposition even from liberal governments. For the most part, however, these expressions of workers' insistence on their rights and dignity remained small in scale and local in influence.

The hundreds of strikes that occurred throughout Western Europe in the first half of the century suggested what unions might accomplish; but without funds, organizational experience, or effective means of communication, these labor movements usually petered out after a few years or sometimes a few months. Not even the Workingman's Association for Benefiting Politically, Socially, and Morally the Useful Classes, launched with some fanfare in England in 1836, managed to survive for long or bring off the general strike its more radical members dreamed of. Yet these organizations did influence Parliament to favor factory legislation. The meetings, torchlight parades, and special workers' newspapers and tracts all contributed to the growing sense of belonging to a distinctive class. So, above all, did the repression by police and courts that usually followed. By midcentury millions of workers in Britain, somewhat fewer perhaps in France, and smaller numbers elsewhere shared heroes and rituals, believed they faced a common enemy,

THE WORK FORCE IN INDUSTRIAL NATIONS, MID-1850S

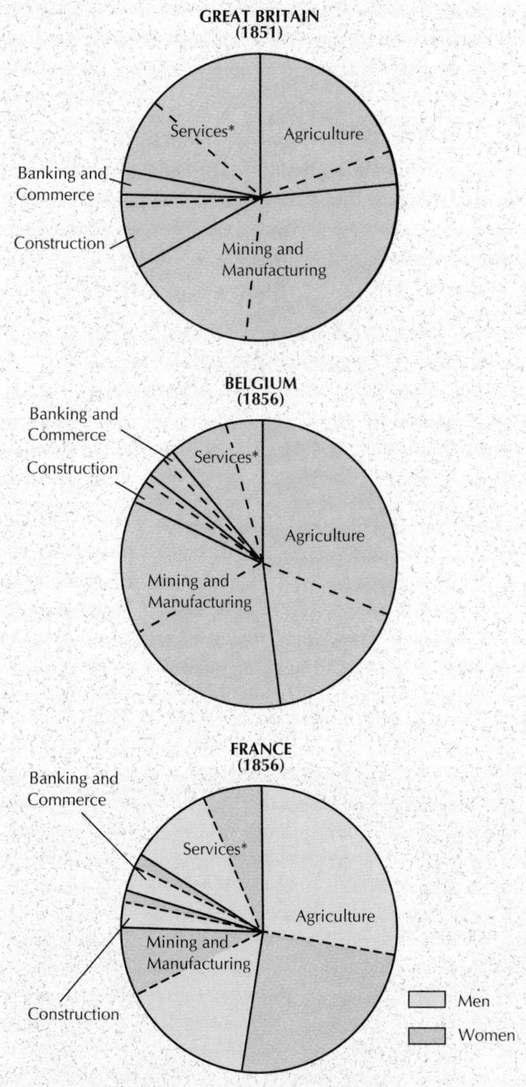

* Including transport and communication, domestic servants, and armed forces.

(Source: Bairoch, P., et al. *The Working Population and its Structure,* Brussels, 1968.)

and adopted organization as the prime means of defending themselves in a hostile world. In Britain the national trades unions of skilled workers formed in the 1830s and 1840s (with only some 100,000 members then) steadily increased their size and influence, reaching more than a million members a generation later.

The vast majority of the working class, however, remained essentially defenseless, possessing meager skills, dependent on unstable employment, and living in the isolation of poverty. Ideas of *fraternité* and *égalité,* of the rights of freeborn English people, and of simple patriotism, often expressed in Biblical prose, communicated a common sense of hope and outrage to the millions of men and women who attended rallies, met in dingy cafés, and read the working-class press (or listened as it was read to them). Newspapers and pamphlets intended for workers were numerous in England after 1815, less widespread in France in the 1830s and 1840s, and present everywhere in 1848. The common themes were people's natural rights, pride of work, and the claims of justice.

The Middle Classes Of all the social classes, the most confident and assertive was the middle class. At the top stood the great bankers, who in London and Paris were often closely connected to the liberal aristocracy and whose political influence after 1830 was considerable. The great industrialists and the wealthiest merchants were more separate from and a little contemptuous of the traditional elites, while at the bottom were the small shopkeepers, office clerks, and schoolteachers, often distinguishable from artisans only by their pretensions. This *petite bourgeoisie* constituted most of the middle class numerically, but the class was epitomized by those between these two groups: most merchants, managers, and upper bureaucrats and nearly all lawyers, doctors, engineers, and professors. The view that such disparate groups made up a social class resulted as much from ideas shared as common interests. Opposed to aristocratic privilege, they saw themselves as the beneficiaries of social changes that allowed talented people to gain security and influence.

They were primarily an urban class and intimately connected with the commerce and politics of city life. In Paris they constituted nearly all of that part of the population (between one-fourth and one-fifth) that was prosperous enough to pay some taxes, have at least one maid, and leave an estate sufficient to cover the costs of private bur-

▸ **Fashion magazines like *La Mode Illustré* kept middle-class women informed of the latest styles and elegant touches to which they might aspire.**

ial.[2] In other cities their proportion was probably somewhat smaller. Among nations, they were most numerous in Great Britain, a sizable fraction in France and Belgium, and a smaller minority elsewhere. The middle class was the only social class that it was possible to fall out of, and people established their membership in it by economic self-sufficiency, literacy, and respectability. Their manner, their dress, and their homes were thus symbols of their status and were meant to express values of probity, hard work, fortitude, prudence, and self-reliance. No matter how favored by birth or fortune, they tended to think of themselves as self-made.

While industrial centers were notoriously drab, the middle-class home became more ornate, packed with furnishings that boasted of elaborate craftsmanship. Women's fashions similarly featured ornamental frills, and shops translated Parisian elegance into forms available to more modest purses. Masculine garb, by contrast, grew plainer, a point of some pride in a practical age; and clerk and banker tended to dress alike. Those who forged great industries out of daring, foresight, and luck; those who invented or built; and those who taught or tended shop or wrote for newspapers came to share a certain pride in one another's achievements as proof that personal drive and social benefit were in harmony and as a harbinger of progress yet to come.

More than any other, the middle class was associated with an ideology; and the triumph of the middle class in this period—so heralded then and by historians since—related as much to constitutionalism and legal equality, individual rights, and economic opportunity as it did to any explicit transfer of power. The conquests of the

▸ **Dominque Ingres portrayed the entrepreneur, Louis Bertrand, as the very epitome of the self-reliant, aggressive man of the industrial middle class.**

[2]Perhaps the most detailed study yet made of the middle class in this period is Adeline Daumard's *La Bourgeoisie parisienne de 1815 à 1848* (1963).

middle class were measured not just by its rise in importance but also by a more general adoption of values associated with it. Even being in the middle, between the extremes of luxury and power and of poverty and ignorance, was seen as an advantage, a kind of inherent moderation. Most of Europe's writers, scientists, doctors, lawyers, and businesspeople would have felt no need to blush on finding themselves called by a London paper in 1807 "those persons . . . always counted the most valuable, because the least corrupted, members of society," or on hearing John Stuart Mill speak a generation later of "the class which is universally described as the most wise and the most virtuous part of the community, the middle rank." Society was understood in terms of social class at a time when the hallmarks of the era—flourishing commerce, science, and technology; great works of art and institutions of culture; triumphant movements of liberalism and nationalism—were seen as achievements of the middle class.

THE CHANGING POPULATION

While Europeans grappled with political, economic, and social changes, they also faced the fact that there were more and more people—more people to feed, more seeking work, and more living in cities.

Demographic Growth The effects of population growth were particularly visible where industrialization was under way, and historians used to think that it had stimulated a rising birthrate with new opportunities for employment, particularly of children. But demographic research has challenged that view, and current explanations emphasize a decline in disease-carrying germs, an increase in the food supply, a lowering of the age at which people married, and, after 1870, some improvement in public sanitation.

Admittedly spotty data suggest that the world experienced a decline in some common diseases beginning in the eighteenth century. Microbes have cycles (like those of locusts but less regular), and remissions had undoubtedly occurred many times before. Now, however, better supplies of food allowed the larger number of babies surviving the perilous years of infancy to reach adulthood and form families of their own.

The food supply rose because of better transportation, more effective agricultural techniques, and the potato. Agricultural associations, usually led by enlightened aristocrats, campaigned for more scientific farming; and the humble potato, not common on the continent before 1750, was a staple of the peasant's diet in most of Europe by 1830.[3] Potatoes are easy to cultivate in a small space and can yield more calories per acre than any other crop. While infant mortality remained enormously high by modern standards, even a slight decline in death rates could make a great difference in the total number of people, so close to subsistence did most Europeans live.

The reasons for the trend toward earlier marriage are less clear, but peasants freed from servile obligations apparently tended to marry and form new households at a younger age. Early marriage was facilitated by the spread of cottage industry, which preceded the new factories and enabled families to add to their income by spinning or weaving at home. The increased number of people in a single generation—only a slight rise in a single decade or province—multiplied in the next generation and led to an enormous increase in the aggregate. As population grew, the proportion who were young and in the childbearing years grew still faster, which increased the ratio of births to the total population. The net result was that the 180 to 190 million Europeans of 1800 had become 266 million by 1850 and 295 million by 1870.

The effects of a larger population were far-reaching. More people consumed more food, and this necessitated more intensive cultivation and the use of land previously left fallow. More people meant a larger potential work force readier to leave the countryside for industrial jobs, and that movement of population became a social change of immeasurable importance. To a lesser extent, an increasing population meant an expanding market for goods other than food, an element of growth that would have stronger impact later in the century. That a greater proportion of the pop-

[3]William L. Langer made an effective case for the potato's importance in "Europe's Initial Population Explosion," *American Historical Review*, 1963, pp. 1–17.

ulation was youthful may have made for increased restiveness and a larger pool of potential radical leaders.[4] There was also a distinction in birthrates by social class, which demographers call *differential fertility.* On the whole, the higher a man stood on the social scale, the fewer the children in his family, which led some to interpret the lower classes' fertility as a lack of foresight and moral restraint and to worry that they would eventually overwhelm society.

The most influential analysis of population was Thomas R. Malthus' *An Essay on the Principle of Population as It Affects the Future Improvement of Society,* first published in 1798 and reissued in many revisions. Observing the Britain of his time, Malthus argued that human population, unless checked by death (through war, famine, or pestilence) or deliberate sexual continence, increases faster than the supply of food. A clergyman, he advocated continence; but he remained pessimistic that human beings were capable of such restraint. An economist as well, Malthus presented demography as a science closely attached to liberal economic theory, with the convenient corollary that the misery of the poor resulted from their own improvidence.

Urbanization At the turn of the century, greater London reached 1 million in population. No European city since imperial Rome had ever approached this size. Paris, with about half that number, would reach 1 million a generation later. The third largest European city in 1800, Naples, had some 350,000 inhabitants; and in all Europe there were then only 22 cities with populations over 100,000. By midcentury there were 47. Great Britain was the leader, with 6 cities over the 100,000 mark; London's population had surpassed 2.5 million by 1856, Liverpool had grown from 80,000 to almost 400,000, and Manchester and Glasgow each had more than 300,000 people. By the 1850s, half of Britain's population lived in towns or cities, making it the most urbanized society since the classical era.

On the continent most old cities increased by at least 50 percent in the first half of the century, and many a town became a city. The major capitals burgeoned. Paris reached a population of nearly 1.5 million by 1850; Berlin almost trebled, to 500,000; and a similar growth rate pushed Brussels to 250,000. St. Petersburg, Vienna, and Budapest all had populations between 400,000 and 500,000.

By the 1860s the English countryside was actually losing people, as were some sections of France. The tide of urbanization was overwhelming, and nearly all the subsequent increase in European population would end up in cities swelling with immigrants, as rural folk moved to nearby villages, villagers to towns, and town dwellers to cities. Clearly, the tide of urbanization was strongest where industry was great, but the growth of ports and national capitals demonstrated the importance of great commercial, financial, and political centers as well.

Society had neither the experience nor the means to cope very well with such an expansion. Urban conditions for all but the reasonably prosperous were unspeakable. Narrow alleys were littered with garbage and ordure that gave off an overpowering stench. The water supply in Paris, better than in most large cities, offered access to safe water only at fountains that dotted the city (the affluent paid carriers by the bucket), and in London the private companies that provided water allowed it to flow only a few hours a day. In most cities the water supply came from dangerously polluted rivers. Sewage was an even more serious problem. A third of Manchester's houses used privies in the 1830s, and a decade later the ratio of inside toilets to population was 1 to 212. In London cesspools menaced health only slightly less than still more public means of disposal.

The most dramatic inadequacy, however, was in housing. A third of Liverpool's citizens lived crowded into dark, cold cellars, and conditions in Lille were similar. In every city the poor of both sexes crowded into filthy, stuffy, unheated rooms; and over the cities, especially manufacturing and mining towns, chemical smog and

---

[4]In 1789 perhaps 40 percent of France's population was between 20 and 40 years old and another 36 percent under 20, the highest proportion of the young that France has ever known. The nationalist organization Young Italy limited membership to those under 40, and probably most of the leaders of the revolutions of 1848 would have met that standard. The relation of youth to revolution is interestingly discussed in Herbert Moller, "Youth as a Force in the Modern World," *Comparative Studies in Society and History,* April 1968.

coal smoke darkened the sky. It is hardly surprising that crime was rampant, that often more than a third of the births were illegitimate, and that the number of prostitutes soared (reaching perhaps 80,000 in London, where 9000 were officially registered; 3600 were registered in Paris).

Maintaining public order became a new kind of problem. Governments had used the police primarily as secret agents whose job was to ferret out real or potential enemies. But the protection of lives and property in great cities, the effective handling of crowds, and the enforcement of local ordinances required something other than spies or the military. London's police force was established by Sir Robert Peel in 1829,[5] and the Paris Municipal Guard was created under Guizot a few years later.

[5]The role played by Sir Robert Peel led to the nickname "Bobbies," by which the police are still called.

▶ **In this famous engraving of London by Gustave Doré, the rhythmic sameness and cramped efficiency of new housing suggest a machine for living appropriate to the age of the railroad.**

For all their misery, cities continued to grow; and through the century the worst conditions were slowly alleviated by housing codes, public sewers, and reliable water supplies. These improvements were made possible in part by industrialization, which gradually provided iron pipes, water closets, gas lighting, better heating, and sounder buildings. Urban life developed a style of its own, increasingly distinct from life in the countryside. Towns clustered around factories and railway stations, and cities teeming with the poor and indigent were also the thriving centers of communication, commerce, politics, and culture.

SOCIAL WELFARE

Social questions were debated in hundreds of speeches and pamphlets, and newspaper articles that worried about pauperism, public health and morals, and class division. These discussions were filled with the appalling facts uncovered through parliamentary and private inquiries in Britain and scholarly investigations in France. Using the rational techniques that seemed to work brilliantly when applied to issues of profits and politics, these humanitarian attempts to improve the lot of the lower class had discouragingly modest results, although individual employers, especially in Britain and Alsace, had some effect by building special housing for their workers, drab barracks that nonetheless seemed marvels of cleanliness and decency.

Middle-class radicals supported efforts like those of the Society for the Diffusion of Useful Knowledge, founded in 1826 to carry enlightenment to the lower classes. They contributed to and gave lectures at night schools for the workingman, many of which were run by the Mechanics' Institutes (of which there were more than 700 in Great Britain by 1850) and by the Polytechnic Association of France (which had more than 100,000 participants on the eve of the revolution of 1848). Thousands of middle-class people personally carried the lamp of truth to the poor in the form of Bibles, pious essays, moral stories, and informative descriptions of how machines worked. Ambitious members of the lower-middle class were, however, more likely than workers to take advantage of these opportunities.

▸ The visitation of the poor by charitable members of the middle class was expected to bring a good example as well as food and clothes.

For the truly poverty-stricken, charities were established at an astounding rate; more than 450 relief organizations were listed in London alone in 1853, and whole encyclopedias cataloging these undertakings were published in France. A revival of Christian zeal provided powerful impetus to such groups in Britain, and on the continent new Catholic religious orders, most with specific social missions, were founded by the hundreds. They sponsored lectures, organized wholesome recreation to compete with the temptations of the tavern, set up trade apprenticeships, provided expectant mothers with a clean sheet and a pamphlet on child care, opened savings banks that accepted even the tiniest deposit, campaigned for hygiene and temperance, gave away soup and bread, supported homes for abandoned children and fallen women, and ran nurseries, schools, and hostels. These good works were preeminently the province of women. Catholic nuns and Protestant matrons in the middle class were expected to uplift the poor by example as well as charity. The Society of St. Vincent de Paul believed that pious men could have a similar effect. Organized in Paris in 1835, it soon spread to all of Catholic Europe, requiring thousands of educated and well-to-do men to visit the poor regularly so that they might teach thrift and give hope by their very presence. Although these heroic efforts were important for some lucky individuals and were a significant means of informing the comfortable about the plight of the poor, they were never adequate to the social challenge. Most of Europe's urban masses remained largely untouched by charity or religion.

In matters of public health, standards of housing, working conditions, and education, governments were forced to take a more active role. By modern standards the official measures were timid and hesitant, and the motives behind them were as mixed as they were in factory legislation, which was favored not only by humanitarians but by landed interests happy to restrict industrialists. Vaccination, enforced by progressive governments, made smallpox less threatening; but beyond that, advances in medicine contributed little to public health. The great work of immunization would come later in the century. The most important medical gain of the 1840s was probably the use of anesthesia in surgery, dentistry, and childbirth.

Serious epidemics broke out in every decade. Typhus, carried by lice, was a constant threat, accounting for one death in nine in Ireland between 1816 and 1819, and infected water spread typhoid fever in city after city. A cholera epidemic, which apparently began along the Ganges River in 1826, spread through East Asia, reaching Moscow and St. Petersburg by 1830; 100,000 people died of cholera in Russia in two years. From Russia it spread south and west, to Egypt and North Africa, to Poland, Austria, and into Germany, where it was reported in Hamburg in 1831. Despite efforts to put ports in quarantine (a move opposed by shipping interests), the disease reached northern England and then France in that same year and continued slowly to the south, taking a ninth of Palermo's population in the period from 1836 to 1837.

Reaction to the cholera epidemic in Britain, France, and Germany revealed much about social change. An official day of fasting, prayer, and humiliation in England and warnings of the archbishop of Paris that the cholera was Divine Retribution expressed the strength of traditional faith and revealed widespread distrust of an era of materialism and its claims to progress.

But governments were expected to act. Torn between two inaccurate theories of how the disease spread,[6] governments mobilized inspectors to enforce such sanitary regulations as existed (not infrequently they faced riots by a populace fearful of medical body snatchers eager to dissect corpses). In Paris and Lille tenements were whitewashed by the tens of thousands, foods inspected, streets and sewers cleaned by official order; and similar steps were taken in the German states and in Britain, where the demonstrated inadequacy of local government prompted establishment of a national Public Health Commission with extraordinary powers over towns and individuals. Carefully collected statistics led to a new understanding of how disease spread and of the importance of social factors for public health. Over the years, doctors and inspectors reported with troubled consciences on the terrible conditions they had found among lower-class neighbors whose quarters they had never visited before. Another cholera epidemic followed in the 1840s and lesser ones thereafter, but the shock and uncertainty of what to do was never again so great. Gradually, hospitals, too, came under more direct state supervision as the cost and complexity of medical treatment increased. By midcentury housing and sanitary codes regulated most of urban construction throughout the West, and inspectors were empowered to enforce these rules.

Liberalism showed its other face in England's handling of the terrible potato famine in Ireland. As the potato blight struck late in 1845, disaster for a population so dependent on a single crop was not hard to predict. For the next several years some of England's ablest officials struggled with bureaucratic earnestness to collect information, organize relief, and maintain order in a corpse-strewn land; yet they did so in a manner so inhibited by respect for the rules of liberal economics and the rights of property that, in practice, only meager relief was offered while millions starved.

In the 1830s and 1840s governments also began reluctantly to regulate child labor, banning employment of those under 9 in textile mills in Britain and factories in Prussia, under 8 in factories in France, and under 10 in mines in Britain. By the end of the 1840s, similar measures had been adopted in Bavaria, Baden, Piedmont, and Russia. Generally, the laws held the workday to 8 or 9 hours for children under 12 or 13, and to 12 hours for those under 16 or 18. In Britain and France there were additional requirements that the very young be provided with a couple of hours of schooling each day. To be effective, such regulations required teams of inspectors, provided for only in Britain, where earnest disciples of Jeremy Bentham applied the laws diligently. This expansion of government authority had been vigorously opposed by industrialists and many liberals; but mounting evidence of the harmful effects of industrial work made the need

[6] The cholera bacillus was finally identified by Robert Koch in 1883.

apparent, and the ability to gather such evidence became one of government's most important functions.

The most bitterly controversial welfare measure of the period was Britain's Poor Law of 1834. The old system of relief required each county to supplement local wages up to a level of subsistence determined by the price of bread. The system, expensive and inadequate to changing needs, was attacked by liberal economists, who charged that it cost too much and discouraged workers from migrating to new jobs. An extensive campaign for reform led to the Poor Law of 1834, based on the Benthamite notion that unemployment had to be made unattractive. Those receiving relief were required to live in workhouses, where discipline was harsh, conditions were kept suitably mean, and the sexes were separated. The new law was resented as a cruel act of class conflict, and it proved unenforceable in much of the nation, though recent studies suggest that it was somewhat less harsh in either practice or intent than its critics charged. On the continent welfare measures kept more traditional forms while gradually shifting the responsibility for them from local and religious auspices to the state.

Public education also became a matter of national policy. Prussia had declared local schooling compulsory in 1716, and efforts to enforce and regulate that requirement culminated in 1807 with the creation of a bureau of education. In the following decades the government, with the cooperation of the Lutheran clergy, established an efficient system of universal primary instruction with facilities to train the teachers now needed and to guarantee that the subject matter taught would remain rudimentary and politically safe. The network of secondary schools was also enlarged but kept quite separate, generally not admitting graduates of the ordinary primary schools. Most of the German states had similar arrangements, establishing nearly universal elementary education. In France the French Revolution had provided the framework for a national system of public schools meant as a substitute for the extensive but more informal and largely religious schools of the old regime. Slowly that vision of a national system of public schools took effect. By 1833 every commune was required to support a public school, and schooling steadily expanded while the quality of teachers improved and the power of inspectors over tightfisted local authorities increased. By the revolution of 1848, three-fourths of France's school-age children were receiving some formal instruction. In Britain conflict between the Church of England and other Protestant churches prevented creation of a state-controlled system of elementary schools, a lack welcomed by those conservatives who opposed educating the masses. Nevertheless, Parliament voted in 1833 to underwrite the construction of private schools, and subsidies for education gradually increased in amount and scope each year thereafter. From Spain to Russia elementary schools were favored by every government and passionately demanded by liberals. The public schools of Europe, inadequate and impoverished, offered little chance of social advancement to those forced to attend them, but few doubted that they could be a major instrument for improving society as well as a force for social peace.

III. The Spread of Liberal Government

These social programs were part of the great age of liberalism that began in 1830, with England as its model, and spread to the continent with revolution in France and the revolt that created Belgium. Europe's conservative powers failed to prevent the establishment of these liberal governments, and the differences between the representative monarchies of the West and the autocratic governments of Central and Eastern Europe now stood in sharp contrast.

GREAT BRITAIN

Britain's withdrawal in the 1820s from Metternich's Concert of Europe represented more than insular habit. The world's leading example of liberalism, Britain was coming to favor liberal programs in other countries, too. But the triumph of liberalism at home had not come without serious conflict.

The turmoil of the postwar years was heightened by the economic crisis that resulted from demobilization and the collapse of wartime markets, and popular meetings echoed with cries of class resentment. The issues were both social and political. The government's economic policies—removal of the wartime income tax and a higher tariff on grains, which made bread more expensive—favored the rich. To change them required reform of the political system; and the agitation for that reform which swept the country was heated and sometimes violent.

The government had responded with repression. Habeas corpus was suspended for the first time in English history in 1817. A mass meeting for reform at St. Peter's Field, Manchester, in 1819 so terrified the local magistrates that they called out troops. In the ensuing charge, hundreds of demonstrators, including women and children, were wounded, and several were killed. With bitter mockery people called it the Peterloo Massacre. Parliament responded by passing the Six Acts of 1819, which restricted public meetings, facilitated the prosecution of radicals, and imposed a stamp tax intended to cripple the radical press. In 1820 the discovery of a clumsy plot to blow up the cabinet at dinner added to the atmosphere of political danger. Support for the established order continued to ebb, and the scandal of George IV's personal life earned public contempt. Old restrictions on Protestant dissenters and Roman Catholics (they could not hold public office, for example) now brought attacks even on the privileges of the Church of England.

Even an unreformed Parliament could be sensitive to public opinion, however, and it began to support temperate compromises on some critical issues. Under the leadership of George Canning, the government gave a voice to people like William Huskisson, a businessman well known for his belief in the new economics. It reduced some tariffs and repealed the Combination Acts that had banned unions, although an amendment effectively outlawing strikes was soon added. As the minister in charge of the Home Office, Sir Robert Peel ceased the prosecution of newspapers and the use of political spies, halved the list of capital crimes, and by creating a police force put civil order in the hands of civil authority. The Tories, who opposed such measures, looked to the conservative duke of Wellington, the prestigious victor over Napoleon at Waterloo, to resist further change; yet as prime minister even he saw the need to push through Parliament a measure he himself disliked, allowing Catholics and religious dissenters to vote and to hold public office. All of these issues—religious freedom, the legitimacy of labor unions, tariffs, restrictions on the press—led to agitation that from London to Ireland increasingly focused on the need to reform Parliament itself. Elections in 1830, required by the death of King George IV and the accession of William IV, only raised the political temperature. In the countryside, laborers set haystacks afire by night; by day, stern magistrates ordered laborers accused of seditious activity transported to Australia.

The Reform Bill of 1832 As public turmoil rose (and British leaders watched with concern the revolution of 1830 in France), a new cabinet presented a bill to reform the electoral system. The measure, initially passed, was approved in the House only after a new election and was then rejected in the Lords until the king reluctantly threatened to create enough new peers to get it through. Each defeat made the public mood uglier, and the king's intervention came amid demonstrations, the burning of the town hall and the bishop's palace in Bristol, and much dark talk about the French example.

The bill itself offered much less than the more outspoken radicals had wanted, but it marked a fundamental change in Britain's electoral system. Suffrage was increased, allowing some 800,000 well-to-do men to vote, based on the property they owned or the rents they paid.[7] More important than the increased suffrage was the elimination of local variation in favor of a uniform national standard which, as many Tories warned, could easily be broadened in the future. Before

[7] This was a considerably broader electorate than that established in either France or Belgium in 1830, though Belgium, the only country to give elected representatives a salary, had in many respects Europe's most liberal constitution. About 1 Frenchman in 160 could vote in 1830; 1 Briton in 32, after the Reform Bill of 1832. About 1 Belgian in 95 could vote by 1840; and 1 in 20, by 1848. Universal male suffrage permits approximately one-fifth of the total population to go to the polls.

the Reform Bill was passed, many boroughs that sent representatives to Parliament were barely villages (the most notorious, Old Sarum, was uninhabited), and the bustling cities of Birmingham and Manchester had had no representatives at all. Perhaps a third of the members of Parliament owed their seats to the influence of some lord. Now representation was at least crudely related to population, and the voices of commerce and manufacturing were both more numerous and louder.

Although restricted suffrage and social tradition (and the open ballot) guaranteed the continued dominance of the upper classes, Parliament was ready after 1832 to turn to other reforms. Slavery was abolished in Britain's colonies in 1833, a victory for Protestant reformers and humanitarian radicals. The Factory Act, limiting the hours children worked,[8] soon followed as well as the Poor Law of 1834. A law granting all resident taxpayers the right to vote in municipal elections challenged aristocratic influence even more directly than the Reform Bill of 1832. When the young Victoria ascended the throne in 1837, representative government was stronger than ever. Her reign of more than six decades would rival that of Queen Elizabeth I as a period of British glory and power, but she would remain subordinate (often against her wishes) to an increasingly flexible political system.

▸ The British House of Commons sat in a new building of gothic splendor that made parliamentary liberty seem ancient and the two-party system inevitable.

Chartism and the Corn Laws Two great popular movements helped define the limits of that political system. Chartism was a huge, amorphous workers' movement, the central aim of which was political democracy, spelled out in what was called the People's Charter.[9] With articulate leaders and a working-class base, Chartists propagandized widely; held huge demonstrations in 1839, 1840, and 1848; and were accused of causing riots that ended with scores of deaths. Although treated by the state as dangerous revolutionaries, their principal tactic was to present Parliament with petitions containing thousands of signatures (*see box,* p. 759). These petitions were summarily rejected, however, and by 1842 the movement was weakening. It failed, despite its size, to find a program that could for long mobilize the masses struggling for survival; and it failed, despite its emphasis on political rather than more threatening economic goals, to stir the consciences of those in power. Angry or desperate workers could riot here or there, but in England they were too isolated from one another and from other classes to gain even their political goals.

The other great popular movement, against the grain tariff, was victorious. The Anti-Corn Law League grew out of urban resentment over the high cost of bread resulting from grain tar-

[8]The work week was limited to 48 hours for children between the ages of 6 and 13, and to 69 hours for those between 14 and 18.

[9]The six points of the People's Charter were universal manhood suffrage, a written ballot, abolition of property qualifications for members of Parliament, payment of the members, constituencies of equal population, and annual elections. All but the last of these were adopted by 1918.

The Great Charter

The Chartist movement reached its peak in 1842 with the presentation to the House of Commons of the Great Charter. There were more than 3 million signatures on this petition calling for universal male suffrage, annual parliaments, lower taxes, and greater attention to the needs of the poor.

TO THE HONOURABLE THE COMMONS OF GREAT BRITAIN AND IRELAND, IN PARLIAMENT ASSEMBLED.

"The petition of the undersigned people of the United Kingdom,

"Sheweth—That Government originated from, was designed to protect the freedom and promote the happiness of, and ought to be responsible to, the whole people.

"That the only authority on which any body of men can make laws and govern society, is delegation from the people.

"That as Government was designed for the benefit and protection of, and must be obeyed and supported by all, therefore all should be equally represented.

"That any form of Government which fails to effect the purposes for which it was designed, and does not fully and completely represent the whole people, who are compelled to pay taxes to its support and obey the laws resolved upon by it, is unconstitutional, tyrannical, and ought to be amended or resisted.

"That your honourable House, as at present constituted, has not been elected by, and acts irresponsibly of, the people; and hitherto has only represented parties, and benefitted the few, regardless of the miseries, grievances, and petitions of the many. Your honourable House has enacted laws contrary to the expressed wishes of the people, and by unconstitutional means enforced obedience to them, thereby creating an unbearable depotism on the one hand, and degrading slavery on the other. . . .

"That the existing state of representation is not only extremely limited and unjust, but unequally divided, and gives preponderating influence to the landed, and monied interests, to the utter ruin of the small-trading and labouring classes.

"That bribery, intimidation, corruption, perjury, and riot, prevail at all parliamentary elections, to an extent best understood by the Members of your honourable House.

"That your petitioners complain that they are enormously taxed to pay the interest of what is termed the national debt, a debt amounting at present to £800,000,000, being only a portion of the enormous amount expended in cruel and expensive wars for the suppression of all liberty, by men not authorised by the people, and who, consequently, had no right to tax posterity for the outrages committed by them upon mankind. . . .

"That your petitioners would direct the attention of your honourable House to the great disparity existing between the wages of the producing millions, and the salaries of those whose comparative usefulness ought to be questioned, where riches and luxury prevail amongst the rulers, and poverty and starvation amongst the ruled.

"That your petitioners, with all due respect and loyalty, would compare the daily income of the Sovereign Majesty with that of thousands of the working men of this nation; and whilst your petitioners have learned that her Majesty receives daily for her private use the sum of £164 17*s.* 10*d.*, they have also ascertained that many thousands of the families of the labourers are only in the receipt of 3 3/4*d.* per head per day. . . .

"That your petitioners believe all men have a right to worship God as may appear best to their consciences, and that no legislative enactments should interfere between man and his Creator.

"That your petitioners maintain that it is the inherent, indubitable, and constitutional right, founded upon the ancient practice of the realm of England, and supported by well approved statutes, of every male inhabitant of the United Kingdom, he being of age and of sound mind, nonconvict of crime, and not confined under any judicial process, to exercise the elective franchise in the choice of Members to serve in the Commons House of Parliament. . . ."

▸ **Mass meetings had been one of the Chartists' most effective devices, and this one held on Kensington Common in London, April 10, 1848, was one of the most publicized. With revolution on the continent and famine in Ireland, radical hopes were as high as conservative fears. The 20,000 who attended this meeting had passed armed soldiers, policemen, and special constables. The expectation of violence explains the small number of women and children in this photograph. What might have been the beginning of a revolution in England was instead the Chartists' last national demonstration.**

iffs—the corn laws—that benefited the land-owning classes. From Manchester the movement spread throughout the country, becoming a kind of crusade, an attack on the privileges of aristocracy in the name of the "productive orders" of society, the middle and working classes. The league's propaganda used the new techniques of popular politics: parades and rallies, songs and speeches, pamphlets and cartoons. Its slogans were printed on trinkets for children, ribbons for women, drinking cups for men. Two manufacturers, Richard Cobden and John Bright, proved effective spokesmen who became influential figures in public life, spreading the gospel of free trade across the land. To the upper classes, such activity seemed in terrible taste; and conservatives argued that the nation's greatness was rooted in its landed estates.

In the face of this sort of coalition of the middle and working classes, however, British politics was more responsive. Twice Sir Robert Peel's government lowered duties on a wide range of items, including grain, but the league demanded more. Finally, in 1845, Peel announced his support for outright repeal of the Corn Laws. The threat of famine in Ireland had decided the issue for him. Almost simultaneously, the Whig leader, Lord John Russell, affirmed his conversion to the principles of free trade. Yet neither man was eager to carry the fight through the houses of Parliament. Ultimately, Peel undertook the task, and in 1846 he shepherded the measure through both the Commons and the Lords. The grain tariff was reduced to almost nothing, and nearly all duties were abolished or greatly lowered. As in 1832, the political system had bent when demands for reform gained widespread support among the middle class, but Peel's courage split his party and ended his ministry. He was jeered by angry

Tories as a young backbencher, Benjamin Disraeli, rose to decry Peel's treachery to the aristocracy. The growing weight of public opinion and the liberal creed had triumphed and thereby expanded the sphere of political attention to include vexing social issues.

THE REVOLUTIONS OF 1830

Reform in Britain had benefited from events on the continent. In France, a provisional government had taken charge upon Charles X's abdication. Organized largely in newspaper offices, it had a faintly republican coloration but soon settled for a liberal monarchy. Most of France was ready to accept that compromise when the Marquis de Lafayette, still a republican and a popular hero, stepped out on the balcony of the Hôtel de Ville to present Louis Philippe as the candidate for the throne. The revolution, brief and largely limited to Paris, was a revolution nevertheless, and any uprising in France was a European event. Minor revolts stimulated by the French example occurred in central Italy, Spain, Portugal, and some of the German principalities, and revolution broke out in Poland. But Austria once again extinguished revolt in Italy, and the Russian army crushed Poland's rebels. Closer to France, the Swiss cantons were forced to liberalize their constitutions, and in the southern Netherlands, Catholics and liberals took the occasion to rise against Dutch rule. This revolt was a direct challenge to the provisions of the Congress of Vienna. Britain, however, opposed any intervention by the great powers, once assured that France had no territorial designs on the Netherlands; and Britain led in arranging international guarantees for the independence of the southern Netherlands, which became Belgium. The British and French then pressured the Dutch to acquiesce.

Belgium The Belgian monarchy established in 1830 was one of the triumphs of liberal constitutionalism; and the new state, which owed its existence both to French restraint and British protection, took as its king Leopold I, who had lived long in England (he was an uncle of Queen Victoria) and who soon married the daughter of Louis Philippe. The constitution went further than France's in guaranteeing civil rights and the primacy of the Chamber of Deputies; and politics continued to revolve around a coalition—rare in Europe—of Catholics and liberals, aristocrats and members of the upper-middle class.

Rapidly becoming the most industrialized nation on the continent, Belgium was prosperous; and if its lower classes were more miserable and more largely illiterate than those of France, that very fact permitted the social isolation of its leaders. Self-confident and satisfied with the new order of things, they built on the administrative traditions left from Austrian and French rule prior to the Dutch and proved themselves remarkably adept at planning railroads, reforming taxes and schools, and making timely political concessions.

Switzerland Liberal institutions spread to Switzerland, too, as part of the international trend, spurred by the revolutions of 1830. Beginning in 1828, some cantons adopted such liberal measures as representative government and freedom of the press, and 10 cantons formed a league in 1832 to agitate for religious freedom and for a stronger, secular central government within the Swiss confederation. These policies were resisted by seven largely Catholic cantons, which were dominated by their aristocracies and soon formed an alliance, the Sonderbund. By 1847 the two leagues were at war. The Sonderbund looked for support from conservative and Catholic states, but none came (the papacy, Austria, and Piedmont had their hands full with revolts in Italy), and the liberal sympathies of Britain and France once again proved decisive. With the Sonderbund's defeat, Switzerland became a federal state with a new constitution, influenced by the example of the United States, that provided for universal male suffrage.

THE JULY MONARCHY IN FRANCE

The symbols of revolution and moderation were neatly combined in France's new monarchy under the House of Orléans, the liberal branch of the royal line headed by Louis Philippe (his father had voted with the Jacobins for the death of Louis XVI). Louis Philippe's posters proclaimed him citizen-king, and the Revolution's tricolor re-

Jeanron del   Ch. Colin sc

▶ **Jeanron's depiction of a Parisian barricade in 1830 (later used to illustrate Louis Blanc's socialist history of the period) presents a more realistic scene of the fighting than Delacroix's more famous version but a very similar heroic vision of workers and middle class together.**

placed the Bourbon flag. Known as the July Monarchy, the new regime began with a constitution presented as a contract the king swore to keep, not as a gift he granted. Similar to the one it replaced, it offered stronger guarantees of political freedom, lowered property requirements for voters (nearly doubling their number to some 170,000, safely restricted to men of means), and replaced the hereditary upper house with lifetime peers. Because most of the old aristocracy resigned their offices, never to return to public life, there was an important change in government personnel. Those who replaced them, professional people and bearers of newer (often Napoleonic) titles, differed from their predecessors more in outlook than in social origin. In his appeal to the people of Paris, Louis Philippe sounded more radical than he was, and the new government hastened to assure Europe's other monarchs that this French revolution would send no militants to sponsor or support revolution elsewhere.

The overriding political question of the 1830s in France was the July Monarchy itself, which was attacked from left and right. Louis Philippe presented himself as a good bourgeois, while the regime's opponents sought broader support. With strong Catholic support, legitimists (those in favor of the Bourbons) campaigned in the countryside and the newspapers. A mass held in Paris on the anniversary of the death of Charles X's son and heir, who had been assassinated in 1820, became a demonstration that in turn prompted an anticlerical crowd to sack and loot the archbishop's palace and a nearby church. In 1832 the duchess of Berry, whose infant son was now the legitimist claimant to the throne, tried to stage an uprising. Republicans were active, too, often in secret groups that had provocative names like the Society of the Rights of Man. When the silk workers of Lyons went on strike, it was viewed as a republican revolt and was suppressed with the bitterness of class hatred by the bourgeois National Guard. That political climate encouraged another contender, the Bonapartist heir, Louis Napoleon, to attempt to stir an uprising in 1836 and again in 1840.

Yet all these attempts failed; and the July Monarchy presented itself as a center of stability and patriotism, even laying claim to the cult of Napoleon I by bringing the emperor's body back from St. Helena and placing it with nationalist pomp in the marble crypt of the Invalides. The government built on the administrative system that had been developed under the Revolution and Napoleon to promote public education, limited social services, and industrialization. With time (and restriction of the press) opposition quieted, and many of the middle-class notables of France rallied to a government of cautious moderation that talked of progress.

A regime largely isolated from workers, peasants, and the old aristocracy had found in nationalism its most effective means of reaching a larger public. Yet it remained divided between those who wanted further reform and wider suffrage and those, like the king himself, who believed the proper balance between liberty and order had been achieved. The former were led by Adolphe Thiers; the latter, by François Guizot. Both were journalists and historians of great talent; but their skillful verbal duels, often models of parliamentarism, failed to mobilize opinion in France as agitation over the Corn Laws had done in England. From 1840 to 1848 the government was dominated by Guizot. A Protestant in a Catholic country, an intellectual in politics, a man who held broad principles rigidly, Guizot had in excess failings common to many liberals of the nineteenth century. He spoke of liberty, progress, and law in eloquent terms that made his cautious practices seem hypocritical. In 1848 the whole regime fell as easily as incumbents losing an election.

The two freest and most prosperous of Europe's great nations had developed similarly since 1830. In both, liberal governments led by able men sought through reasonable compromise, the rule of law, and parliamentary politics to unify their nations and to make "progress" compatible with stability. Discontent and workers' misery, though frightening, were understood in the councils of government primarily as a threat to order. In England reform had to be wrung from a powerful aristocracy that was, in the end, secure enough to cede under pressure. In France the aristocracy counted for little after 1830; but the government, fearful of the more radical hopes for democracy and social justice that it excluded, remained uncertain of its popular support.

SPAIN

The victories of French and British liberalism seemed part of a general trend. In Spain the monarchy itself wooed liberals. When King Ferdinand VII died in 1833, he had carefully arranged for his three-year-old daughter, Isabella, to succeed him. But the king's brother, Don Carlos, denounced the arrangement as illegal[10] and began an uprising that lasted until 1839. The Carlists, who favored autocracy and the traditional claims of Spanish Catholicism, found their greatest support in rural areas and regions of the north resentful of rule from Madrid. Despite eventual defeat, Don Carlos won a place in Spanish legend as a dashing and chivalric hero, protector of old Spanish virtues; and Carlism would remain a conservative rallying cry in every subsequent Spanish revolution.

To win liberal support, the regency ruling in Isabella's name granted a constitution in 1834. Cautiously modeled on the French constitution of 1814, with narrow suffrage and protection of royal power, it established representative institutions as a lasting feature of Spanish politics. Even so modest a step placed Spain in the liberal camp, and Isabella's government relied on extensive support from Britain and France against threats from abroad, an alliance joined by Por-

[10]He cited the Salic law, dating from Merovingian times, which prohibited women from acceding to royal thrones. Generally followed on the continent, it had meant that in 1837 England's Queen Victoria could not also assume rule over Hanover as her father had. In Spain Ferdinand VII had abolished the Salic law in 1830 by what was known as a pragmatic sanction.

tugal after similar concessions there. Internal war brought generals into politics and conflict between moderates (who supported the constitution of 1834 and admired Guizot's France) and the anticlerical progressives (who demanded a democratic constitution and the election of local officials). Only after a couple of military coups did moderates establish a regime in the 1840s strong enough to hold power for a decade. Everywhere, the changes and the aspirations that brought constitutions, limited suffrage, and circumscribed freedoms proved difficult to contain.

From 1815 on, a variety of political experiments, each claiming to be permanent, had been tried in Europe. The problem for conservative regimes was to increase their political effectiveness while preserving as much of the old social order as possible. Liberal regimes experienced the benefits of uniform justice, legal equality, individual rights, and broader political participation but raised the issue of how far such principles could be taken without creating instability. In setting the rules of political life, constitutions and the right to vote were statements about the nature of society, controversial in themselves and subject to change.

Recommended Reading

Sources

Engels, Friedrich. *The Condition of the Working Class in England.* Written in 1844 and available in many modern editions, this influential work by Karl Marx's friend and coauthor paints a dark picture of the working-class slum and conveys the moral outrage radicals felt.

Ure, Andrew. *The Philosophy of Manufactures.* 1835. An early and classic justification of liberal economics, emphasizing its promised benefits for all.

Novels are important sources for understanding nineteenth-century society. Elizabeth Gaskell (*Mary Barton* and *North and South*) and Charles Dickens (*Hard Times* and *Oliver Twist*) provided contemporaries with an influential picture of social conditions in England; Honoré de Balzac's *Père Goriot* set the tone for criticisms of the selfishness of the middle class.

Studies

Berdahl, Robert M. *The Politics of the Prussian Nobility: The Development of a Conservative Ideology.* 1988. Shows how political interests and social structure led to the formation of a conservatism that dominated much of German history.

Bridenthal, Renate, Claudia Koonz, and Susan Stuard (eds.). *Becoming Visible: Women in European History.* 1987. Essays offering a good introduction to the range of topics that recent work in women's history has led historians to understand in a new way.

*Briggs, Asa. *Victorian Cities.* 1970. Colorful studies of the urban politics and social life of individual cities.

Brock, Michael. *The Great Reform Act.* 1974. Analyzes the significance of the Reform Bill of 1832 through a close examination of the political and social forces that brought it about.

*Chevalier, Louis. *Laboring Classes and Dangerous Classes in Paris during the First Half of the Nineteenth Century.* Frank Jellinek (tr.). 1981. This detailed study of the Parisian poor also says much about French society in general during the early years of industrialization.

Church, Clive H. *Europe in 1830: Revolution and Political Change.* 1983. A study that emphasizes the significance of the revolutions of 1830 by noting their transnational connections and impact.

*Davidoff, Leonore, and Catherine Hall. *Family Fortunes: Men and Women of the English Middle Class, 1780–1850.* 1985. A wonderfully rich and concrete picture of the aspirations and concerns of middle-class life.

Dennis, Richard. *English Industrial Cities of the Nineteenth Century.* 1984. A comprehensive study of the special nature and problems of this new kind of city.

Franklin, S. H. *The European Peasantry: The Final Phase.* 1969. Taken together, these essays on different countries reveal not only the striking differences in peasants' lives but the importance of the peasantry for understanding the general history of European nations.

*Hamerow, Theodore S. *Restoration, Revolution, and Reaction: Economics and Politics in Germany, 1815–1871.* 1958. A complex analysis of the relationship of social

*Available in paperback.

classes and the state to economic change in this revolutionary period.

Harrison, J. F. C. *The Early Victorians, 1832–1851.* 1971. A lively account of the personalities and issues that marked the beginning of a new era.

*Heilbroner, Robert L. *The Worldly Philosophers.* 1972. A good introduction to the ideas of the economic liberals.

Himmelfarb, Gertrude. *On Liberty and Liberalism: The Case of John Stuart Mill.* 1974. Penetrating and controversial analysis of the still-controversial philosopher of liberalism.

Holmes, Stephen. *Benjamin Constant and the Making of Modern Liberalism.* 1984. The biographical focus offers a valuable insight into the evolution of liberalism on the continent.

Johnson, Douglas. *Guizot: Aspects of French History.* 1963. Insightful essays focusing on the dominant figure of the July Monarchy and revealing the tensions between aspirations for a liberal society and conservative fear for order.

Katznelson, Ira, and Artistide R. Zolberg (eds.). *Working-Class Formation: Nineteenth-Century Patterns in Western Europe and the United States.* 1986. Significant interpretative essays by some leading scholars that take a fresh look at how working-class awareness was formed and at the values and attitudes associated with it.

*Lichtheim, George. *A Short History of Socialism.* 1975. Well-constructed treatment of the evolution of socialist ideas in their historical context.

*Lindemann, Albert S. *A History of European Socialism.* 1984. Establishes the line of continuity from the early socialists through labor movements and the eventual dominance of Marxism.

*Lukács, Georg. *The Historical Novel.* Hannah and Stanley Mitchell (trs.). 1962. Insightful and learned study of the social significance of the nineteenth-century novel by one of Europe's leading Marxist scholars.

*Manuel, Frank. *The Prophets of Paris.* 1965. An excellent discussion of French utopian thinkers.

Perkin, Harold. *The Origins of Modern English Society, 1780–1860.* 1969. Provides a clear picture of the diverse sectors of English society and how they adapted to the changes of the period.

Price, Roger. *A Social History of Nineteenth-Century France.* 1987. A clear synthesis of recent research that provides an excellent introduction.

*Rudé, George. *The Crowd in History, 1730–1884.* 1964. Argues that there was a fundamental change in the social composition and demands of crowds, and therefore of their significance, after industrialization.

De Ruggiero, Guido. *The History of European Liberalism.* R. G. Collingswood (tr.). 1977. A classic comparison of the different concepts of liberalism that were dominant in each of the major European nations.

Segalen, Martine. *Love and Power in the Peasant Family: Rural France in the Nineteenth Century.* J. C. Whitehouse and Sarah Mathews (trs.). 1983. Shows the active role of peasant society in the process of social change.

*Sewell, William H., Jr. *Work and Revolution in France. The Language of Labor from the Old Regime to 1848.* 1980. An important study that shows the radical potential and continuing strength of a preindustrial working-class culture in the industrial area.

*Shanin, Teodor (ed.). *Peasants and Peasant Society.* 1987. Essays treating the varied aspects of peasant society, reflecting important recent scholarship, especially useful on Eastern Europe.

Snell, K. D. M. *Annals of the Laboring Poor: Social Change and Agrarian England, 1660–1900.* 1985. A pioneering look at the position of the rural underclass in Britain and the transformation of their world in the nineteenth century.

*Stromberg, Roland N. *European Intellectual History since 1789.* 1975. A graceful and thorough presentation of the major trends.

*Thompson, Dorothy. *The Chartists: Popular Politics in the Industrial Revolution.* 1984. A lively and sympathetic account that relates working-class action to the larger social context.

*Thompson, Edward P. *The Making of the English Working Class.* 1964. A remarkable work of sympathetic insight and exhaustive research that continues to influence studies of the working class in all societies.

Walker, Mack. *German Home Towns: Community, State, and General Estate, 1648–1871.* 1971. Sensitive and original treatment of the response of small-town life to political and social change, showing the historical significance of the ambivalence felt toward the state, liberalism, and nationalism.

*Weiss, John. *Conservatism in Europe, 1770–1945: Traditionalism, Reaction and Counter-Revolution.* 1977. Provides a valuable survey of the rich variety and social insight in conservative thought and of the political importance of conservative movements.

Victory and the birth of a new Germany: The Halls of Versailles ring as Prussian officers hail the proclamation of Prussia's King Wilhelm as German Kaiser.

CHAPTER TWENTY-FOUR

NATIONAL STATES AND NATIONAL CULTURES

IN the spring of 1848 revolution swept across Europe from France to Hungary, and within a few weeks governments old and new were forced to give way. These revolts had in common the pressures of economic distress and their emphasis on political freedoms. Their spontaneity in capital after capital demonstrated the widespread belief that liberty and representative institutions could make all the difference. Their internal divisions and eventual defeat taught other lessons. Nationalist appeals could be as powerful as calls for liberty, and a stable state had to develop social programs and an effective bureaucracy to administer them. Over the next 30 years, which saw the unification of Italy and of Germany, much of Europe adopted this model of the modern national state as one that watched closely over the economy and social life, fostered measures for popular education and public health, and gained enhanced prestige from its close association with the institutions of high culture.

I. The Revolutions of 1848

Two years of poor harvests and industrial recession in most of Europe preceded the outbreak of revolution, but economic crisis alone does not make a revolution. In Ireland more than a million people died from starvation during the famine years from 1846 to 1849; yet that tragedy did little more to shake British rule than the Chartist movement. Revolutions occurred where the fear and resentment fed by rising food prices and unemployment found focus in specific political demands.

THE OPENING PHASE

In France an unpopular government's refusal to widen the suffrage led the parliamentary opposition to launch a protest movement that staged large banquets across the country. When a nervous government banned the one scheduled for Paris in late February 1848, some members of the Chamber of Deputies announced they would attend anyway. Crowds gathered in the streets, and workers who could never have afforded banquet tickets started to build barricades. The rituals of revolution had begun, and the king held a review of his citizen militia, the National Guard. When they sullenly refused to cheer him, Louis Philippe, ever sensitive to middle-class opinion, abdicated in favor of his grandson and left for England, much as Charles X had done just 18 years before. This time, too, royal suggestions for succession were ignored, and a provisional government of figures chosen by two rival newspapers appeared at the Hôtel de Ville and declared France a republic. The Paris crowds cheered, and political clubs organized. The new cabinet—led by Alphonse de Lamartine, a handsome and much-admired poet—was dominated by moderates who at first cooperated with more radical members (including a socialist, Louis Blanc). They agreed that the republic should adopt universal male suffrage, a degree of democracy allowed in no other large nation, and that the citizen's right to work was a principle of government, establishing a commission to hold public hearings on problems of labor. Noting that each French revolution "owed it to the world to establish yet one more philosophic truth," the republic abolished the death penalty.

At the same time, the new regime was careful to demonstrate its restraint. It rejected intervention in behalf of revolutions elsewhere, rejected proposals for adopting a red flag as the symbol of revolution in favor of the familiar tricolor with a red cockade, and levied new taxes to balance the budget. Relations with the Catholic Church were the best in a generation, and April elections for a Constituent Assembly took place in good order. Nearly 85 percent of the eligible electorate voted, giving moderate republicans an overwhelming majority. The Second Republic seemed solidly established.

Revolution Spreads As news of the events in France sped across Europe, a conservative nightmare became a reality. Nearly every capital had citizens who found exciting promise in words like "constitution," "rights," "liberty," and "free press." In Hungary the Diet cheered the Magyar leader, Louis Kossuth, as he called, on March 3, for representative government; and in the same week demonstrations with similar demands erupted in the cities of the Rhineland. Revolution broke in the Rhineland and later in Vienna (March 12), Berlin (March 15), Milan (March 18), and Venice (March 22). Each of these revolutions followed a similar pattern. The news from France would attract excited crowds; groups of men—especially journalists, lawyers, and students—would meet in cafés to discuss rumors and newspaper reports; governments would call out troops to maintain order; and with a kind of inevitability, some incident would occur—a shot fired by a soldier insulted once too often or by someone in the crowd with an unfamiliar gun.

Then barricades would rise in the style that came from Paris, constructed of paving stones, a passing coach ceremoniously overturned, nearby trees, and furniture. Barricades became the people's voice, threatening but vague, as workers and professional people, men, women, and children labored together. When blood was shed, the crowd had its martyrs. In Paris corpses were carried around on a cart as a spur to revolutionary determination; in Berlin the king, supporting his fainting queen, acceded to the crowd's demands and paid his respects, bareheaded, to the subjects

▶ **Lamartine persuades the crowd to reject the red flag and let the new French republic keep the tricolor.**

his troops had killed. When new concessions were won, the atmosphere would grow festive. New flags would fly, often a tricolor, an echo of the French Revolution but with colors symbolizing national union. In the almost universal dedication to politics, newspapers and pamphlets appeared in floods (100 new newspapers in Vienna, nearly 500 in Paris). Radicals would seek ever after to recapture the unanimity and joy of a day of revolution. Others, and not just conservatives, would never forget fearsome mobs, fanatical faces, and ugly threats.

Central Europe In the Austrian Empire, the Hungarian Diet had by mid-March established a free press and a national guard, abolished feudal obligations (with compensation to the lords), and required nobles to pay taxes. Everyone noticed the parallel to 1789. Reluctantly Vienna agreed that Hungary could levy its own taxes and direct its own army. The Hungarian example encouraged students in Vienna to demand representative government for Austria as well, and crowds soon clashed with the troops and formed specific demands. In rapid order Metternich resigned, censorship was abolished, a constitution was promised, and firearms were passed out to the students. When students rejected the proposal that everyone but factory workers and servants be allowed to vote, universal male suffrage was conceded. Hungarian autonomy then brought similar demands from Czechs in Bohemia, Croatians in Croatia, and Romanians in Transylvania (these last two domains under Hungarian rule). The old Austrian Empire had all but collapsed.

When Frederick William IV of Prussia learned the incredible news of an uprising in Vienna and the fall of Metternich, he granted the concessions on which he had stalled for months, relaxing censorship and calling a meeting of the Landtag. Fighting broke out anyway, and Frederick William then agreed to remove his hated troops from Berlin, used the evocative word *Germany* in proclamations to "my dear Berliners," and wore the German national colors: black, gold, and red. A constituent assembly was elected in May by universal but indirect suffrage, and when it met in Berlin, where a civic guard now kept order, revolution seemed to have triumphed in Prussia, too. Events in the rest of Germany confirmed that victory. In May, 830 delegates elected by universal male suffrage convened at Frankfurt to write a constitution for all of Germany. They were mostly from the smaller states of the more liberal

▶ **In one of the early triumphs of the 1848 revolutions, the citizens of Milan forced the Austrian Army to leave the city. Everyone now knew how to build barricades, and the whole family helped, using whatever was available.**

west, and more than half of them were lawyers and professors. But there were also businessmen, members of the liberal gentry, and even nobles, suddenly awkward in such society. The great majority favored a monarchical German state with an almost democratic constitution, and the brilliant, difficult, and noisy assembly set about to write a constitution for a united Germany.

The arrangements contrived in 1815 at the Congress of Vienna were under siege in Italy as well, where the kingdoms of Piedmont in the north and Naples (including Sicily) in the south had barely weathered previous revolts, which had also threatened the smaller duchies in between. A well-organized rising in Palermo against rule from Naples was actually the first of the revolutions in 1848; but it was news of the revolution in Paris that made it possible to demand constitutions in Naples, Tuscany, and Piedmont. Even the Papal States got a constitution, though it awkwardly preserved a veto for the pope and the College of Cardinals. Lombardy and Venetia had been ruled as part of the Habsburg empire since 1815, but shortly after the revolution in Vienna, a revolt broke in Milan against the Austrian forces there. They were soon forced to retreat, and the "Five Glorious Days of Milan" were added to the heroic legends of March. Then Venice rose up to reestablish the Venetian republic of old, and the possibility that the Italian peninsula might be freed from foreign rule stimulated a nationalist fervor that forced Piedmont to join the war against Austria.

THE FATAL DISSENSIONS

Everywhere, however, the new freedom exposed divisions among those who had fought for it. In France these divisions were primarily social—between Paris and the countryside, between the middle class and workers. Finding conditions little improved under a republic, workers agitated for a social program and pinned their hopes on the national workshops that had been established as an echo of ideas popularized by the socialist Louis Blanc. Unemployed men from Paris and the countryside enrolled by the tens of thousands, although in practice the workshops were reduced to a mere relief program. To moderate

▶ **A silent street in Paris, its rubble, bodies, and blood—the emblems of revolution defeated in this painting by Ernest Meissonier.**

▶ **An engraving of the violence in Frankfurt in September 1848 contrasts the fighting styles of troops and people.**

republicans they represented a dangerous principle and outrageous waste; and the government ordered them disbanded in June. Workers, who considered the workshops an explicit promise and the beginning of a new era, responded by building barricades in the working-class sections of Paris. For three days the poor fought with the ferocity of hopelessness before the republic's troops systematically crushed the threat to order.

More than a thousand people died; thousands more would be sent to prison or into exile. The June Days remained the very symbol of class conflict for socialists, and after them radicals never quite recaptured their faith that democracy would lead to social justice. Given almost dictatorial powers, Cavaignac took steps to restrict the press, suppress radical societies, and discipline workers. Yet Cavaignac remained a convinced republican; and the assembly continued to write a constitution, which kept universal suffrage and provided for a president elected by popular vote. But after June there was something a little hollow about the Second Republic.

In Germany and Austria, also, revolution uncovered latent conflicts between workers and the middle class and among artisans, peasants, and nobles. But the outcome there was determined more by competing nationalism and the fact that kings still had their armies. The Frankfurt parliament had little sympathy for uprisings by other nationalities against German rule. Instead of protesting the repression of revolution, it congratulated the Austrian field marshal who bombarded Prague, where Czechs had staged a pan-Slav conference, on his German victory; and it applauded the Austrian forces that regrouped in northern

Italy and fought their way back into Milan. It called on the Prussian army to put down a Polish uprising in Posen and to fight against Denmark in Schleswig and Holstein. In September when riots broke out in Frankfurt itself, the assembly invited Austrian and Prussian troops to restore order. Conflicts among multiple nationalities were also strengthening the Habsburgs at home, where the emperor mobilized Croatians, who had been demanding autonomy from Hungary much as Hungary had from Austria.

The armies that soon moved on Frankfurt and Vienna confronted a rising that, like the June Days in Paris, revealed an even greater popular fury and more radical demands than the risings of February and March. That was true in Rome as well, where the pope had proved not to be an Italian nationalist; economic conditions worsened, and a government that had promised much accomplished little. When his prime minister was assassinated, Pius IX slipped across the border into the Kingdom of Naples, and the eternal city assumed the ancient title of the Roman Republic. Venice and France were also republics, and assemblies were still busy drafting constitutions in Vienna, Berlin, and Frankfurt, but there could be no doubt that conservative forces were gaining ground.

THE FINAL PHASE

In December, France elected a president, and the candidates who had been prominent in the new republic finished far behind Louis Napoleon Bonaparte, who won 70 percent of the votes. The ambitious nephew of Emperor Napoleon, he had campaigned as a republican. He had written more about social questions and workers' needs than any other candidate; and he was supported by the Catholic Church and the monarchists, for want of anyone else, as a man of order. Above all, he had his name.[1] Austria, too, found a strong new leader in Prince Felix von Schwarzenberg, who filled the place Metternich left vacant; and in December he persuaded the emperor to abdicate in favor of his 18-year-old son, Francis Joseph I, who could promise a fresh start. In Prussia the king felt confident enough to dissolve the Landtag and promulgate a constitution of his own, one very similar to Piedmont's and Belgium's. Ten months of turmoil had led back to the arrangements of February.

One by one, the remaining revolutionary regimes were subdued. The Frankfurt Assembly, having completed its constitution for a unified Germany, in March 1849 elected the Prussian king as German emperor, only to have him reject a crown from the "gutter," declaring that the ones he recognized came by grace of God. The Frankfurt constitution—with its touching list of old abuses to be abolished, its universal male suffrage and promises of civil rights and education—would never be tested (*see box*, p. 773). New revolutions broke out in the Rhineland, Saxony, and Bavaria, but all of them were quashed in June and July with the aid of Prussian troops. The Habsburgs' multinational armies bombarded the revolutionaries of Vienna into submission and soon turned on Hungary, where a republic had been declared because Schwarzenberg refused to permit Hungary to have a constitution. The Hungarians battled for months against the armies of Austria and against Croatians, several groups of Slavs, and Romanians until Russia intervened in June to seal the fate of the Hungarian republic.

In Italy, too, military force was decisive. Austria defeated Piedmont one more time, leaving it nothing to show for its support of Italian independence except an enormous debt, an unpopular government, a new ruler, a cautious constitution, and the red, white, and green flag of Italian nationalism. Ten years later the constitution and the flag would seem quite a lot; for the time being, Austrian power once again dominated the Italian peninsula. There was soon a further foreign presence in the center of Italy, for Louis Napoleon sent French armies to restore the pope and defeat the Roman Republic, which fought with heroic tenacity for three months before being overrun. The Kingdom of Naples did not reconquer Sicily until May 1849 and only

---

[1] On trial for his attempted coup in 1840, Louis Napoleon had concluded his defense with these words: "I represent before you a principle, a cause, and a defeat: the principle is sovereignty of the people; the cause, that of the Empire; the defeat, Waterloo. The principle you have recognized; the cause you have served; the defeat you want to avenge."

The Frankfurt Constitution

The Frankfurt Parliament completed its work on a constitution for Germany in 1849. It was a long and detailed document, carefully proscribing the repressive acts that had been most common in the preceding years. Its proud assertions of German freedom remain significantly vague, however, about the enforcement of its provisions and what the boundaries of the German nation will be.

THE FUNDAMENTAL RIGHTS OF THE GERMAN PEOPLE

"ARTICLE 1

¶ 131. The German people consists of the citizens of the states which make up the Reich.

¶ 132. Every German has the right of German Reich's citizenship. He can exercise this right in every German land. Reich's franchise legislation shall provide for the right of the individual to vote for members of the national assembly.

¶ 133. Every German has the right to live or reside in any part of the Reich's territory, to acquire and dispose of property of all kinds, to pursue his livelihood, and to win the right of communal citizenship.

The terms for living and residence shall be established by a law of settlement; trade regulations shall be established by regulations affecting trade and industry; both to be set by the Reich's administration for all of Germany.

¶ 134. No German state is permitted to make a distinction between its citizens and other Germans in civil, criminal, and litigation rights which relegates the latter to the position of foreigners.

¶ 135. Capital punishment for civil offenses shall not take place, and, in those cases where condemnation has already been made, shall not be carried out, in order not to infringe upon the hereby acquired civil law.

¶ 136. Freedom of emigration shall not be limited by any state; emigration levies shall not be established.

All matters of emigration remain under the protection and care of the Reich.

"ARTICLE 2

¶ 137. There are no class differences before the law. The rank of nobility is abolished.

All special class privileges are abolished.

All Germans are equal before the law.

All titles, insofar as they are not bound with an office, are abolished and never again shall be introduced.

No citizen shall accept a decoration from a foreign state.

Public office shall be open to all men on the basis of ability.

All citizens are subject equally to military service; there shall be no draft substitutions.

"ARTICLE 3

¶ 141. The confiscation of letters and papers, except at an arrest or house search, can take place with a legally executed warrant, which must be served on the arrested person at once or within the next twenty-four hours.

¶ 142. The secrecy of letters is inviolable.

Necessary exceptions in cases of criminal investigation and in the event of war shall be established by legislation.

"ARTICLE 4

¶ 143. Every German shall have the right freely to express his opinion through speech, writing, publication, and illustration.

The freedom of the press shall be suspended under no circumstances through preventive measures, namely, censorship, concessions, security orders, imposts, limitation of publication or bookselling, postal bans, or other restraints. . . ."

Excerpt from the Frankfurt Constitution, in Louis L. Snyder (ed.), *The Documents of German History*, New Brunswick: Rutgers University Press, 1958.

after a bombardment of Messina that made Ferdinand II known throughout Europe as King Bomba. The last of the revolutionary regimes to fall was the Venetian republic, defeated in August 1849 more by starvation and cholera than by the Austrian artillery that accomplished the unprecedented feat of lobbing shells three miles from the mainland into the island city.

A famous liberal historian has called 1848 "the turning-point at which modern history failed to turn,"[2] and his epigram captures the sense of destiny thwarted that still colors the liberal view of 1848. Current historical analysis of the failures of 1848 generally makes five broad points. First, liberal constitutions, new economic policies, and increased civil rights failed to pull strong and lasting support from artisans, peasants, and workers, whose more immediate needs were neither met nor understood. Second, the revolutions of February and March were made primarily by the middle classes, strengthened by popular discontent; but when radicals sought more than representative government and legal equality, the middle classes worried about order and private property. Isolated from the masses, they were too weak to retain power except in France; and there order came after repression of the urban poor and soon included the erosion of constitutional liberties. Third, the leaders of the revolutions, inexperienced in practical politics, often mistook parliaments for power and left intact the established authorities that would soon turn on them. Fourth, nationalism divided revolutionaries and prevented the cooperation that was essential for durable success. Fifth, no major nation was ready to intervene in behalf of change. Britain was sympathetic, France encouraging, and the United States (its consulates centers of republicanism), enthusiastic; but none of that matched the military assistance Russia gave the Austrian emperor or the formidable armies of Austria and Prussia.

The events of 1848 had significant effects nonetheless. Revolution so widespread measured the failures of restoration, displayed again the power of political ideas, and uncovered the effects of a generation of social change. Many of the gains won in that year endured: The peasants of eastern Prussia and the Austrian Empire were emancipated in 1848 and remained free of servile obligations; Piedmont and Prussia kept their new, limited constitutions. The monarchs triumphant in 1849 punished revolutionaries with execution, flogging, prison, and exile, but they paid more attention to winning some popular support. Liberals would never again depend so optimistically on the spontaneous power of the people, and advocates of social reform would be more skeptical of political liberalism. International power clearly constrained domestic policy, but political leaders of every hue now also recognized the potential force of nationalism.

[2]George Macaulay Trevelyan, *British History in the Nineteenth Century and After*, 1937, p. 292.

II. The Politics of Nationalism

Why nationalism assumed such importance in the nineteenth century and has retained it to the present day remains one of the important questions of modern history. As an ideology, it presents itself as a natural, age-old sentiment arising spontaneously; yet nationalism is essentially a modern phenomenon and often seems to require generations of propaganda. Associated with liberalism in the first part of the nineteenth century, nationalism came to be embraced and used by both the left and the right.

THE ELEMENTS OF NATIONALISM

Nationalism's deepest roots lie in a shared sense of regional and cultural identity, especially as those roots are expressed in custom, language, and religion. These had been greatly affected, even shaped, by the development of the state, whose power and importance had increased since the state building of the seventeenth century. But it was the experience of the French Revolution that established nationalism as a political force capable of mobilizing popular enthusiasm, of reforming society, of creating seemingly irresistible political movements, and thus of greatly adding to the power of the state. Napoleon had sought to appeal to national feeling in much of Europe, most notably Poland and Italy, and on the other side the Allies had used that sentiment somewhat more timidly to recruit opposition to the French in Germany, Spain, and (less successfully) Italy.

Nationalism was also a movement for self-conscious modernization, embraced by people who believed their societies might equal the industrial wealth of England and acquire political systems as responsive and efficient as those of Britain and France. In the course of the nineteenth century, increased communication, literacy, and mobility further stimulated the sense of belonging to a larger but definable community. Nationalism was thus a response to social and economic change, one that promised to bring middle classes and masses together in support of common goals. Nationalists, like conservatives and socialists, stressed the values of community; like liberals, they tended to believe that change could bring progress. As an intellectual movement, nationalism was an international phenomenon, everywhere emphasizing the importance of culture; yet it was informed by cultural Romanticism, with its rejection of the universalism of the Enlightenment. Thus German intellectuals such as Johann Gottfried von Herder and Johann Gottlieb Fichte were characteristic in urging their countrymen to put aside values imported from France in favor of a uniquely German culture.

The exploration of ethnic origins took many forms. A group of German scholars made philology a science, and by the 1830s and 1840s an extraordinary revival of national languages had occurred across Europe. Gaelic was hailed as the national tongue of Ireland; in Finland the first public lecture in Finnish marked a break from the dominant Swedish culture; intellectuals in Bohemia began abandoning their customary German to write in Czech. More remarkable still was the number of languages consciously contrived out of local dialects and invented vocabularies. Norwegian became distinct from Danish, Serbian from other Slavic languages, and Slovak from Czech—all literary languages by the 1840s, each the work of a handful of scholars whose task of establishing a national language was made easier by widespread illiteracy.

This fascination with folk culture and a national past was reinforced by an emphasis on history as popular genre but also a special, scholarly form of knowledge that revealed each nation's historic mission. Germans wrote of a special sense of freedom embodied in Germanic tribes, expanded in the Reformation, and now extended to the state. French historians wrote eloquently of France's call to carry reason and liberty across Europe, and Italian writers proclaimed that Italy was destined to lead Europe once again as it had as the home of Roman civilization and the center of Christianity. The poet Adam Mickiewicz, lecturing in Paris, inspired nationalists with his descriptions of how Poland's history paralleled the life of Christ and had yet to achieve Resurrection. Francis Palacky pioneered in stressing the role of the Czechs as leaders of the Slavs. Such visions were repeated in poetry and drama, which now blossomed in the native tongue and justified resistance to alien rule. Cultural nationalism thus served as a weapon of middle-class self-assertion whereby people who felt cramped by social hierarchy, an unsympathetic bureaucracy, and a stagnant economy could win broader support for their own dreams of progress.

In places subject to foreign rule, such as Hungary or much of Italy, campaigns for agricultural improvement, promoted by the liberal aristocracy, became nationalist programs; and a national tariff, which would enlarge the area of free trade internally and protect native industry, became a nationalist battle cry. Friedrich List, a leading liberal economist, argued from the American example that only behind tariff barriers could a united Germany develop the industry and the vigorous middle class necessary for competitive strength and independence. Everywhere nationalist groups generally demanded public education, more political freedom, and efficient government. Strengthened by its promises of economic growth and its respect for native traditions, nationalism generated political movements of broad appeal, capable of mobilizing popular enthusiasm. Daniel O'Connell's inflammatory speeches won thousands to his Young Ireland organization and its demands for the end of union with Great Britain; by the 1830s he commanded the largest movement of political protest Europe had yet seen.

▸ **Hausmann's rebuilding of Paris began with the demolition of buildings that had stood for centuries.**

A NEW REGIME: THE SECOND EMPIRE IN FRANCE

In France elections had left the Second Republic ruled by a president, Louis Napoleon, who would eventually subvert it, and monarchists, who had not wanted a republic at all but won a majority in the Chamber of Deputies. Often at odds with the deputies, Napoleon continued to play to public opinion; and when, in the third year of his four-year term, the Chamber rejected a constitutional amendment that would have allowed him a second term, he struck. His coup d'état came on the eve of December 2, 1851—the anniversary of the first Napoleon's coronation as emperor in 1804 and of his victory at Austerlitz in 1805. Potential opponents, including 200 deputies, were quickly taken into custody; troops occupied the streets and overran hastily built barricades. At the same time, Napoleon restored universal manhood suffrage, which the conservative Chamber had restricted.[3] Resistance was serious in many parts of France—hundreds were killed and more than 20,000 people arrested—but brief. Three weeks later Napoleon's actions were ratified by more than 90 percent of the voters in a national plebiscite. Exactly one year after this first coup, Napoleon had the Second Republic transformed into the Second Empire and became Emperor Napoleon III, a change even more overwhelmingly supported in another plebiscite. Citizens could do no more than vote yes or no, to accept changes already effected or risk unknown perils.

The Second Empire claimed a democratic mandate but held authoritarian power. It was supported by most businessmen and the Catholic Church, accepted by most monarchists, local no-

[3] They did so by using a residence requirement that excluded "unstable" workers, that is, those who had recently moved.

tables, and peasants. It sponsored programs for social welfare as well as economic growth and promised both peace and national glory. Napoleon III was influenced by Saint-Simonian socialism, attracted by liberal nationalism, and obsessed by belief in his own destiny—Napoleon the Little to his opponents, the Emperor to most of the French.

The economy boomed in the 1850s; and the government fostered economic growth more systematically than any other in Europe, using tax incentives to stimulate investment, making it easier to form companies with limited liability, and adding its own special investment funds (of which the Crédit Mobilier for industry was the most famous). Among its many programs of public works, the rebuilding of Paris was one of the most elaborate. A pioneering venture in city planning, the project typified the imperial style. Plans were reviewed by Napoleon III himself, who favored ostentatious structures of even height, and directed by his extraordinarily able prefect Georges Haussmann. New parks were created and slums cleared, often with painful dislocation for their residents; wide boulevards, planned for their vistas and as an aid to traffic, incidentally made it hard to build barricades. Facades often received more attention than the buildings behind them, but these were now served by a vast new sewer and water system. Such massive projects stimulated land speculation and profiteering; yet the result was a city healthier and more convenient, envied and imitated throughout the world. The court of Napoleon and Empress Eugénie was brilliant, and French prestige in the arts and sciences (enhanced by the fame of Louis Pasteur's discoveries in biology) was never higher. The emperor presented himself as the patron of educational and social reform and, in the Napoleonic tradition, rewarded talent with honors and promotions. He took credit for all this—more, in fact, than was his due.

The Liberal Empire By the 1860s, however, the empire's fortunes were changing, its policies at home and abroad subject to rising criticism. The coalition of interests that had supported Napoleon was breaking up. Foreign ventures intended to extend French influence and satisfy national pride had their political costs. Support of Italian unification antagonized French Catholics, and the attempt to gain imperial glory by intervention in Mexico ended in disaster. Steps toward free trade, including a major tariff agreement with Great Britain in 1860, appealed to liberal economists but upset many producers. At the same time, workers wanted more from the government than public works projects and support for mutual-aid societies. Restrictions of political freedom were increasingly resented, and opponents' criticisms more intense.

Napoleon's response was a gradual liberalization that in 1860 enlarged the role of the legislature and by 1868 included freedom of the press and of assembly; a full-fledged parliamentary system was in place two years later. The government also encouraged worker's organizations and acknowledged the right to strike. Like the establishment of public secondary schools, which the Church opposed, these new measures alienated some old supporters without, however, mollifying an opposition that gained in each election. Republicans held nearly half the lower house in 1869, and a republican was prime minister the following year, which turned out to be the Second Empire's last.

► The ladies and gentlemen of the court and diplomatic corps assembled in 1860 to watch Napoleon III take the imperial prince in a rowboat. The photograph is a reminder of the common touch that was important for an emperor elected by plebescite.

NATIONALISM AND INTERNATIONAL RELATIONS

The conflicts of 1848 and 1849 had suggested the political potential of nationalism, a lesson that Prussia, Austria, Britain, Piedmont, and France would all seek to apply. In 1849 Prussia still hoped to lead a confederation of North German states, finding the nationalist dreams of the Frankfurt assembly more attractive once the assembly itself had no voice. Eager to reassert Habsburg influence in Germany after revolution in Hungary had been quelled, Schwarzenberg shrewdly reconvoked the diet of the old German Confederation, putting the German states in the dangerous position of having to choose between Austrian and Prussian leadership. Austria, with the clear support of Russia, then threatened Prussia with war; before so grave a challenge, Prussia backed down, abandoning its scheme for a German union. Habsburg hegemony over Germany seemed assured.

The British foreign secretary also exploited the nationalist appeal of an assertive policy. Henry John Temple, Viscount Palmerston, was a flamboyant aristocrat, frequently at odds with his cabinet colleagues, often indifferent to procedural niceties, but shrewdly alert to public opinion. Thus he made the claims of one Don Pacifico against the Greek government into an issue of British national honor. An Athenian mob had burned Pacifico's house because he was a Portuguese Jew; but he had been born in Gibraltar and held British citizenship. Palmerston vigorously supported Pacifico's demands for compensation from the Greek government, sending notes, threats, and finally the British fleet to Greece until an indemnity was paid. Palmerston defended his stand in the House of Commons. Dramatically, he recalled the pride of ancient Romans, who could say "*Civis Romanus sum*" ("I am a Roman citizen") and know themselves secure throughout their empire. A British subject, Palmerston declared, "in whatever land he may be, shall feel confident that the watchful eye and strong arm of England will protect him against injustice and wrong." To the public at least, Palmerston was vindicated.

The Crimean War The restless search for international prestige led France and Great Britain to war against Russia in 1854 over competing claims to Jerusalem's holy places by Roman Catholic and Greek Orthodox monks. France, citing traditions ranging from the time of the Crusades to the policies of Cardinal Richelieu, supported the Latin monks and pressed the Ottoman sultan, whose empire included Jerusalem, to grant them specific privileges. Russia, as defender of the Orthodox faith, demanded a protectorate over Orthodox churches within the Ottoman Empire and showed its determination by occupying Wallachia and Moldavia, Danubian lands under Ottoman suzerainty. Britain (inclined to see a threat to its own empire in any expansion of Russian influence in the direction of Persia or Afghanistan) encouraged the sultan to resist Russia's demands.

Negotiations repeatedly broke down; Britain and France sent their fleets into the Aegean Sea, and in October 1853 the sultan exuberantly declared war on Russia. Russian forces destroyed an Ottoman fleet, however, and Britain and France decided to fight Russia to preserve the balance of power in the Middle East. That announcement in March 1854 was greeted with patriotic enthusiasm in London and Paris. Six months after war was declared, British and French forces landed in the Crimea for want of a more convenient battlefield and fought a war conducted with remarkable incompetence on both sides. Russia was unable to mobilize or effectively deploy the large armies that made it so feared, and Britain's supply system proved inadequate for hostilities at such a distance. In 1855 the allies welcomed the aid of little Piedmont and, a full year after invading the Crimea, finally took Sevastopol. Russia sued for peace and agreed to accept terms to be defined at a European congress in Paris.

The Congress signified an important shift in the European balance. It met in Paris rather than Vienna and was preoccupied with issues of nationalism. In 1856 Russia counted for less than it had in 1815, and the conservative alliance of Austria, Prussia, and Russia that had dominated the continent for a generation had broken up over competing ambitions in the Balkans and Germany. The Congress required Russia to cede some territory at the mouth of the Danube River, to surrender its claims to any protectorate over

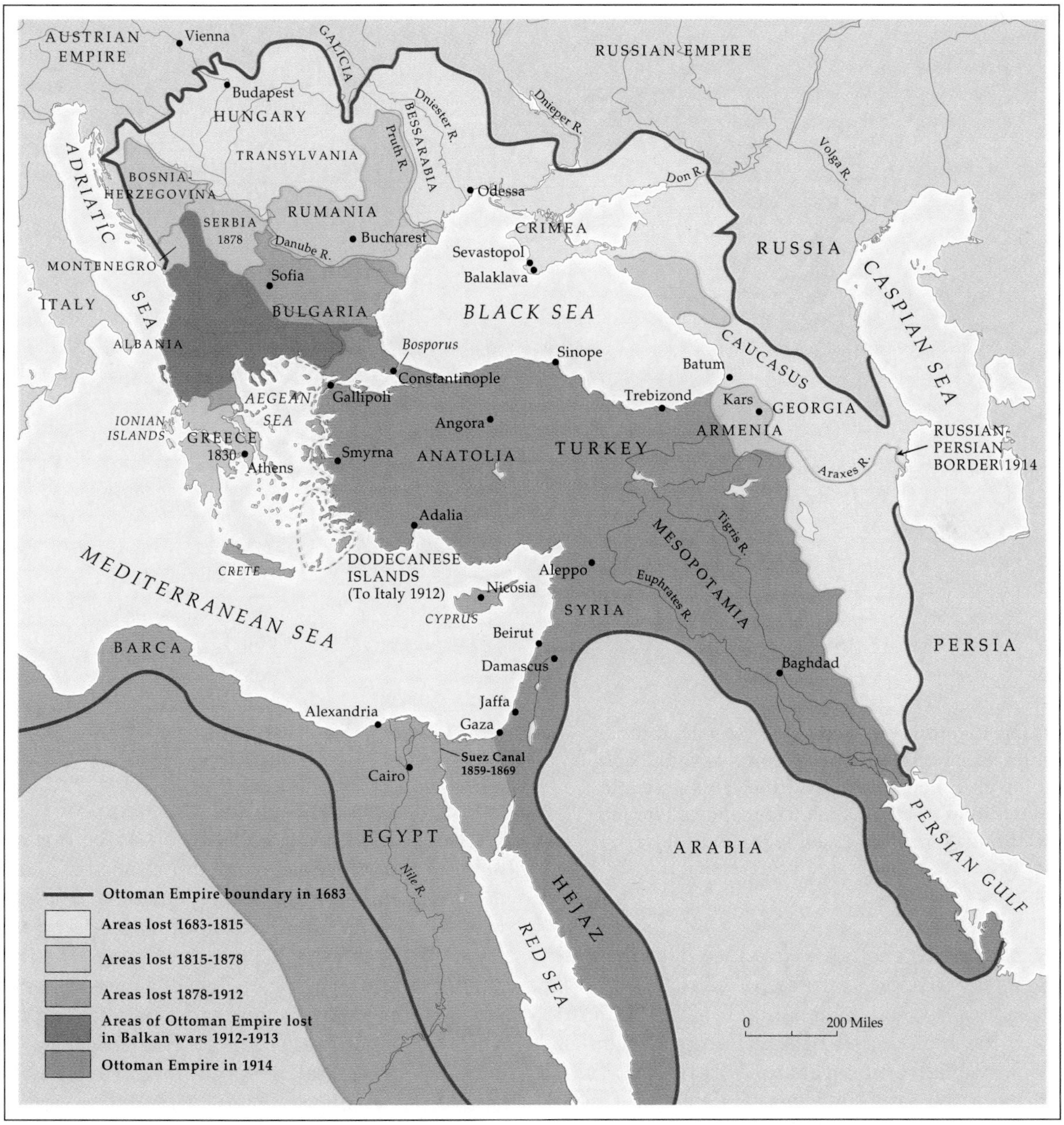

Map 24.1 The Decline of the Ottoman Empire, 1683–1914

Christians in the Ottoman Empire, and to accept a ban on warships in the Black Sea. Only this last point really rankled.

The more troublesome issues all had to do with national claims. Britain and France did not want to give the Danubian principalities to either Russia or Austria. The issue was postponed because the obvious resolution—uniting the two territories and allowing them autonomy, a procedure which began a few years later—would create the basis for a Romanian national state, and Austria was learning to fear nationalism as a threat to the Habsburg empire. Such fears prevented Napoleon III from putting the question of Polish independence on the agenda as he wanted to; but the Congress did discuss the rising discontent in Italy, the only concession Piedmont won for having helped the victors in the Crimea.

The Crimean War generated considerable enthusiasm in Britain and France, with the help of colorful accounts from the front. This dramatic illustration from a British paper shows Florence Nightingale rushing to aid wounded soldiers, a service that made her and professional nurses famous.

Even that was enough to produce patriotic outbursts in Italy and to frighten Austria.

Almost 500,000 soldiers died in the Crimean War, the highest toll of any European conflict from the Napoleonic wars to World War I. Two-thirds of the casualties were Russian, and two-thirds of all losses resulted from sickness and bad care. Yet the outbreak of war produced a surge of enthusiasm no government could ignore. The public diplomacy that led to the war, the parades of magnificently uniformed soldiers, and the heroic stories reported by an aggressive journalism underscored its political importance. Under Western pressure, the Ottoman Empire began to adopt the modernizing institutions of the West; and Russia, sobered by defeat, launched an era of fundamental reform unequaled since the days of Peter the Great. In Italy and Germany the way was opening for still more drastic changes.

A NEW NATION: THE UNIFICATION OF ITALY

Across the peninsula, all the revolutions of 1848 had declared an independent Italy to be one of their primary goals; and in doing so they employed the ideas of Giuseppe Mazzini, one of Europe's most important revolutionaries (*see box*, p. 782). For 15 years, Mazzini had lived in exile, mainly in London, organizing conspiracies and writing thousands of letters and passionate propaganda. His nationalist movement, Young Italy, had stimulated similar efforts in Ireland, Switzerland, and Hungary. Until 1848, the conspiracies he fostered had resulted in tragic failures; yet like the clandestine committees, secret meetings, and smuggled newspapers that surrounded them, these plots, though unsuccessful, had disseminated the belief that once corrupt regimes were toppled, the people would rise in common cause. Revolutionary and democratic, Mazzini was also a moralist who criticized the French Revolution for stressing rights over moral duty and who rejected socialism as materialistic. In nationalism he saw the expression of natural communities, the basis for popular democracy and international brotherhood.

Italy renewed would lead the way. A man of letters steeped in Romanticism, Mazzini nonetheless wrote tellingly about the specific grievances of peasants, artists, professionals, and intellectuals. His influence was especially strong in northern Italy, where in the 1830s and 1840s young lawyers, liberal landowners, and some members of the aristocracy began to find national implications in nearly all they did. Annual congresses of Italian scientists became quiet demonstrations of patriotic aspirations; disputes over where railroad lines should be built became means of expressing discontent with Austrian rule. Literary journals and societies for agricultural improvement took up the nationalist theme.

For Mazzinians, 1848 was the great chance (Mazzini himself was one of the leaders of the Roman Republic), and the defeats that followed were an even greater blow to Mazzinianism than to Italian nationalism. As Austria regained dominance of the peninsula, Mazzini had returned to exile and Italian nationalists began to look elsewhere for leadership. The papacy, restored by French arms, was no longer sympathetic to Italian unity; Austria ruled Lombardy and Venetia repressively, and all the other Italian regimes except Piedmont were Austrian dependencies.

► **In his portraits and in his personal life Mazzini seemed as much a romantic poet as a revolutionary agitator.**

The Role of Piedmont Although a small state, Piedmont held some promise for patriots. It had fought Austria, and its young king, Victor Emmanuel II, though no liberal, ruled with a parliament. The kingdom had a tradition of military strength and bureaucratic rectitude. More recently, its government had encouraged commerce and industry, and its efforts to win trade away from Austria by commercial treaties excited Italians elsewhere. These policies acquired firmer purpose in 1852, when Count Camillo Cavour became prime minister. Cavour was a gentleman-farmer who had traveled in France and England. He believed in economic and scientific progress, representative government with limited suffrage, the rule of law, and religious tolerance. Nationalism he understood primarily as an avenue to modernization, and he found in free trade, sound finances, and railroads a power that could remake Piedmont.

Cavour pursued his liberal goals with tactical brilliance, skillfully using newspapers and parliamentary debate to mold public opinion. He created a centrist parliamentary coalition with which he dominated both king and parliament from 1852 until his death in 1861. In that brief time he established himself as one of the outstanding statesmen of the century. Piedmont's internal strength was Cavour's first concern, but he also sought to make his state the center of Italy's resurgence, the Risorgimento.[4] He welcomed exiles from other parts of the peninsula, encouraged the nationalist press, and sought every opportunity for symbolic gestures of patriotism. He was aided in this by the Italian National Society, one of whose founders was the president of the Venetian republic in 1848. The National Society propagandized for Italian unity under Pied-

[4]*Risorgimento,* now the historian's label for the whole period of Italian unification, was a term meaning "resurgence," often used by nationalists and made the title of a liberal newspaper that Cavour helped to found and edit.

Mazzini's Nationalism

"On the Duties of Man" is one of Giuseppe Mazzini's most famous essays. It was first written in 1844 for Italian workers living in England, and the excerpts here are from the fifth chapter, which was added for a new edition in 1858. Despite the events of the intervening years, Mazzini's romantic faith had changed little. The essay's title was meant to contrast with the French Revolution's Declaration of the Rights of Man, which Mazzini criticized for encouraging selfishness and materialism.

"Your first duties—first as regards importance—are, as I have already told you, towards Humanity. . . . If you do not embrace the whole human family in your affection, . . . if, wheresoever a fellow-creature suffers, or the dignity of human nature is violated by falsehood or tyranny—you are not ready, if able, to aid the unhappy, and do not feel called upon to combat, if able, for the redemption of the betrayed or oppressed—you violate your law of life, you comprehend not that Religion which will be the guide and blessing of the future.

"But what can each of you, singly, *do* for the moral improvement and progress of Humanity? . . . The watchword of the faith of the future is *Association*, and . . . [the] means was provided for you by God when he gave you a country; when, even as a wise overseer of labour distributes the various branches of employment according to the different capacities of the workmen, he divided Humanity into distinct groups or nuclei upon the face of the earth, thus creating the germ of Nationalities. Evil governments have disfigured the divine design. Nevertheless you may still trace it, distinctly marked out—it least as far as Europe is concerned—by the course of the great rivers, the direction of the higher mountains, and other geographical conditions. They have disfigured it by their conquests, their greed, and their jealousy even of the righteous power of others. . . .

"These governments did not, and do not, recognise any country save their own families or dynasty, the egotism of caste. But the Divine design will infallibly be realized. Natural divisions, and the spontaneous, innate tendencies of the peoples, will take the place of the arbitrary divisions sanctioned by evil governments. The map of Europe will be redrawn. The countries of the Peoples, defined by the vote of free men, will arise upon the ruins of the countries of kings and privileged castes. . . .

"O my brothers, love your Country! Our country is our Home, the house that God has given us, placing therein a numerous family that loves us, and whom we love. . . . Our country is our common workshop, whence the products of our activity are sent forth for the benefit of the whole world. . . . In labouring for our own country on the right principle, we labour for Humanity."

From Giuseppe Mazzini, *On the Duties of Man.*

mont's king and established secret committees in most of the cities of Italy. Its members were predominantly liberal aristocrats, local lawyers, and professors; and in calling for Italian unity, it combined Mazzinian rhetoric with hardheaded insistence on the need for international alliances and military force. Economic liberalism largely replaced more generous and vaguer social theories.

Most of all, Cavour depended on astute foreign policy. He had pushed for Piedmont's participation in the Crimean War and was rewarded with the discussion of the Italian question at the Congress of Paris. Using his state's enhanced international position, he argued that Italy repressed would remain a danger to European order. He appealed for liberal sympathy throughout Western Europe, and he courted Napoleon III. At last, in July 1858, Cavour and Napoleon III met secretly. Austria's resentment of Piedmont's growing prominence made it easy to argue that war was inevitable. If France would support Piedmont against Austria, Cavour promised to accept a complicated set of arrangements designed to benefit France and limit Piedmont's expansion. The plan, too delicately balanced to be practical, sought cautious ends through cynical daring.

Austria, watching young Lombards and Venetians escape conscription by streaming to Piedmont as volunteers, determined to end the nationalist threat once and for all. It sent Piedmont an ultimatum so strong that Cavour needed only to reply with cautious dignity in order to have his war. On April 29, 1859, Austria invaded Piedmont, and France went to the rescue of a small state attacked by her giant neighbor.

The rapid movement of large French armies was impressive, but thereafter the war was fought with little tactical brilliance on either side. The Austrians suffered a serious defeat in June, but a larger battle three weeks later was as indecisive as it was bloody. As the Austrians retreated to the fortresses controlling the Lombard plain, Napoleon suddenly lost his taste for war and unilaterally agreed to a truce. The emperors of France and Austria agreed that Piedmont should have Lombardy but not Venetia and that the other Italian states should remain as before.

Formation of the Italian Kingdom Those other Italian states, however, had not survived the excitement of a national war. Gentle revolutions accompanied the march of Piedmontese troops throughout northern Italy. When local patriots gathered in the streets, the dukes of Modena, Parma, and Tuscany simply fled, to be replaced by provisional governments led by members of the National Society. These governments quickly adopted Piedmontese laws and held elections to representative assemblies. The terms of the truce arranged by France and Austria could not be carried out; and after a few months, the provisional governments held plebiscites—a device Napoleon could hardly reject—on the question of annexation to Piedmont. Italians trooped to the polls with bands playing and flags waving, peasants behind their lord and workers with their guilds. The result was as one-sided as in the plebiscites in France. Piedmont's King Victor Emmanuel ruled from the Alps to Rimini on the Adriatic. The province of Savoy and the city of Nice were turned over to France.

Moderate liberals had united half of Italy. Sputtering revolts in Sicily gave more democratic nationalists a chance to lead a different sort of Risorgimento. Former Mazzinians, eager to promote a Sicilian uprising, gathered guns in Genoa and planned an expedition that Cavour dared neither support nor oppose. Its leader would be Giuseppe Garibaldi, Italy's most popular hero. Exiled for his Mazzinian activity in the 1830s, Garibaldi had spent 10 years fighting for democratic causes in South America, returning to Italy in time to take part in the wars of 1848. He had directed the heroic defense of the Roman Republic in 1849 and led the most effective corps of volunteers in 1859. He set sail for Sicily one night in May 1860, with a thousand men, mainly middle-class youths from Lombardy, Venetia, and the Romagna.

No event in the nineteenth century so captured the popular imagination as that daring venture. The Expedition of the Thousand was like some ancient epic come to life in an industrial age: untrained men, wearing the red shirts Garibaldi had adopted in South America, fought with bravery and discipline, enthusiastically supported in the Sicilian countryside. Garibaldi's tactics confused and defeated the Neapolitan gen-

► The handshake of Victor Emmanuel and Garibaldi, which sealed the unification of Italy as their armies met in 1860, became a favorite subject for illustrations of the Risorgimento. This engraving is English.

Map 24.2 THE UNIFICATION OF ITALY, 1859–1920

▶ **A demonstration in Florence's historic piazza della Signoria in 1866 for the annexation of Venetia to the new Kingdom of Italy.**

erals, despite their far larger and better-equipped forces. In two weeks the Red Shirts occupied Palermo and within two months almost all of Sicily. Volunteers flocked to join Garibaldi from all over Italy, and money was raised in his behalf in all the towns of northern Italy and from New York to Stockholm.

The epic continued when, against all odds, Garibaldi sailed across the strait and landed on the Italian mainland. He declared his goal to be Rome itself and not just Naples. That worried Cavour, who considered Garibaldi irresponsible and believed that an attack on Rome might lead Austria and France to intervene on behalf of the pope. So Cavour encouraged uprisings in the Papal States and then sent Piedmontese troops to preserve order. Carefully skirting the area around Rome, they moved south to meet Garibaldi. On September 18, between lines of suspicious men, Giuseppe Garibaldi and Victor Emmanuel rode out to shake hands and unite Italy. Garibaldi added to his legend by thus giving way in the interests of union, and the Piedmontese took over. Plebiscites confirmed the union, and in March 1861 the Kingdom of Italy was proclaimed.

United Italy It included almost all of Italy except for Rome and Venetia. Catholics throughout the world opposed the annexation of Rome which Napoleon III was pledged to protect; and Austrian troops were massed in Venetia. Italy acquired Venetia in 1866 as a by-product of the war between Austria and Prussia. Austria offered it in return for neutrality; Prussia promised that Italy should have it if allied to a victorious Prussia. Italy kept a prior pledge to Prussia and went to war. It fought poorly but got Venetia anyway following Prussia's rapid victory. Rome was annexed when French troops withdrew during the Franco-Prussian War of 1870; the new nation finally had its ancient capital.

More lasting problems remained. To many Italians, especially in the south, unification felt like a foreign occupation, and Italy's leaders were appalled at the poverty and corruption they could not overcome. Pius IX forbade Catholics to take part in national elections and rejected the indemnity and guarantees of protection the government offered. United Italy was poor and overwhelmingly agricultural. It had no coal or iron, and three-quarters of the population was illiterate. With liberal conviction the Italian government assumed the debts of all the former governments and struggled to balance the annual budget. Despite taxes that were among the highest in Europe, Italy continued to lag in schools, railways, and roads. The sale of Church lands failed to benefit peasants as much as hoped, and the lower Piedmontese tariffs brought instant distress to hundreds of small producers. For millions of artisans and peasants, few tangible benefits followed from replacing reactionary dukes with a liberal national state.

A NEW NATION: THE UNIFICATION OF GERMANY

German cultural identity had grown throughout the first half of the nineteenth century, from the battles against Napoleon to the statements of the Frankfurt parliament. It was strengthened by achievements in philosophy, science, literature, and music that were seen as German accomplishments no matter what kingdom, principality, or free city they occurred in. What the political expression of that identity should be was far from resolved, however. The German Confederation was ineffectual; none of the schemes for unification in 1848 had been adopted, and Austria had blocked Prussian plans for leadership in 1850. Yet it was Prussia that created modern Germany.

The Dominance of Prussia Several factors account for Prussia's eventual dominance. One was economic. The Zollverein, the tariff union Prussia led, continued to prosper with industrialization in the Rhineland and Prussia, and by 1853 every German state except Austria had joined it. Another factor was Austria's multiple and multinational preoccupations, and the unification of Italy highlighted the weakening of the Austrian empire. Most important of all was the dynamism of Prussia itself. It was the largest German state, with a powerful army and an efficient administration, and Prussian politics began a new era in 1858 with the rule of William I.[5]

After a long period of reaction in which the press and public discussion were severely repressed, politics had become more open and livelier. Liberal nationalists, particularly in the Rhineland, campaigned for a more representative government; William sought to strengthen the army, and a constitutional crisis resulted. The Prussian constitution of 1850 allowed universal male suffrage but avoided democracy by dividing voters into three classes according to the taxes they paid. Each of three classes elected an equal number of representatives, assuring that those chosen by the two wealthier classes would be a majority. In addition, the king could veto any legislation and appoint the ministers of his choice.

Although designed to ensure conservative dominance, the three-class system had the unexpected effect of magnifying the voice of new industrial wealth, and the majority of the Landtag was now prepared to challenge the monarch. The military budget became their battleground. With William's support, General Albrecht von Roon, minister of war, and Helmuth von Moltke, his chief of staff, proposed to double the army and add to its equipment. Although the proposal was defeated, the government went ahead with its plan. Liberals, who distrusted Prussian militarism and an army dominated by the Junkers, insisted the government must be responsible to the legislature; and the opposition gained in the elections of 1862. Convinced that royal authority was at stake, William called on God and conscience, threatened abdication, and named Otto von Bismarck his chief minister.

[5]William I became regent in 1858—when his brother, Frederick William, was judged insane—and king on his brother's death in 1861.

Bismarck's Leadership Bismarck was a member of the Junker class, better educated than many, whose pride of caste and reactionary views were resented by liberals and whom most conservatives considered to be as erratic and dangerous as Napoleon III. An experienced diplomat familiar with Europe's major capitals, he stood out by reason of his cosmopolitan outlook as much as his enormous self-confidence. For 30 years all of them would have to live with his stinging sarcasm, bruising contempt, and brilliance. Bismarck surprised conservatives with his appeal to nationalism, shrewdly used power wherever he found it, and made success in foreign policy his justification. He lectured the deputies: If Germans looked to Prussia, it was because of its powerful army, not because of any liberal institutions; and he added, in the most famous statement he ever uttered, that "the great questions of the day will not be settled by speeches and majority decisions—that was the mistake of 1848 and 1849—but by blood and iron."

Bismarck dissolved the parliament and used heavy government pressure in the subsequent elections but with little effect. So Bismarck ignored parliament whenever he could and encouraged divisions within the legislature whenever possible. He closed opposition newspapers and manipulated the rest. Promotions in the civil service and judiciary went to those unquestionably loyal; and, once confident of his position, Bismarck spent funds and collected taxes without parliamentary authorization.

In return he offered a remarkable string of foreign triumphs. While blocking Austria's efforts to lead the German Confederation, he courted Russian friendship. When in 1863 Russia repressed a Polish uprising with such severity that Austria, France, and Britain joined in protest, Prussia supported the tsar. Bismarck used conflict over Schleswig and Holstein to assert leadership in German affairs. German nationalists were outraged at attempts by the king of Denmark to annex Schleswig and to extend his authority over Holstein, but Prussia thwarted the German Diet by persuading Austria to join in war against Denmark in January 1864. Bismarck then foiled international negotiations until the Danes were defeated. Schleswig was placed under Prussian administration and Holstein, surrounded by Prussian troops, under Austrian, in an awkward arrangement sure to breed contention between Austria and Prussia.

The Austro-Prussian War, 1866 Friction with the Habsburg empire increased almost daily, and Bismarck prepared for war while ensuring Austria's diplomatic isolation. He dangled visions of territory along the Rhine before Napoleon III, won Italy's support by promising it Venetia, and gained Russia's assurance of neutrality. Both Austria and Prussia were already mobilizing when Prussian troops found an excuse to march into Holstein in June 1866. Initially, Austria had the support of most of the German Confederation, but Hanover surrendered to Prussia within two weeks. Three Prussian armies swept into Bohemia, and at the Battle of Sadowa, Austria suffered overwhelming defeat. The Austro-Prussian War lasted just seven weeks. Experts had predicted a long flight, but Prussia, well-equipped and ready, applied the lessons of the American Civil War, using railroads and telegraph to move with a speed for which Austria was unprepared.

Many Prussian conservatives had been shocked at Bismarck's disrespectful and belligerent treatment of Austria, but now they were eager to demonstrate the end of Austria's dominance and looked forward to significant territorial gains. Instead, Bismarck insisted on leniency, against the wishes of his king and generals. Austria surrendered no territory, but Prussia's gains elsewhere changed the face of Europe; it annexed several states that had sided with Austria,[6] established a confederation of North German states under Prussian leadership, and got the South German states to accept a military alliance with Prussia.

The North German Confederation The North German Confederation was a Bismarckian structure that seemed to protect local interests and to point toward democracy yet assured the dominance of Prussia. It left member states free to regulate their local affairs but joined them through

[6]They were Hanover, Nassau, Electoral Hesse, and Frankfurt.

Crowds cheer as Prussian troops parade through the Brandenburg Gate in Berlin in 1866, celebrating Prussia's victory over Austria and the formation of the North German Confederation.

a common army under Prussian officers and a bicameral federal parliament. The upper house, the Bundesrat, was composed of 43 delegates sent in varying numbers from the separate states; Prussia's 17 gave it more than the one-third necessary for a veto. The lower house, the Reichstag, was elected by universal male suffrage; but the king of Prussia appointed the chancellor, who was responsible to no one else.

After Prussia's victories, the Prussian parliament retroactively legalized the taxes and expenditures Bismarck had imposed. No German nationalist believed Bismarck's federation a satisfactory or permanent solution. Germany's unification, like Italy's, would be achieved in stages and through war and diplomacy. North Germany, Protestant and more industrial than the south, offered a sound foundation for the kind of Germany Bismarck envisioned, as different from the largely agricultural and Catholic south as northern Italy was from Naples. With their own cultural traditions and ancient dynasties, Germany's southern states still looked to Vienna as their traditional center, admired Paris, and remained suspicious of Berlin.

The Franco-Prussian War More than elections and trade were necessary if Germany was to be quickly united, and war with France filled the need. Historians once hotly disputed who was to blame for that war and whether it was "necessary." New research and changing perspectives have lessened the controversy. The war was wanted by Bismarck but first declared by France, the result more of nationalism on both sides than of long-range calculation. It was provoked by competition over influence in Spain. Queen Isabella II had been forced to abdicate in 1868, and the provisional government there, seeking a replacement, picked a Hohenzollern prince. He declined, under heavy French pressure; but a shaky French government, eager to curry popular favor at home, continued to press its case. In a famous interview at the western German spa of Ems, where William I was taking the baths, the French ambassador demanded a public guarantee that the Hohenzollern candidacy would not be put forward again. The king refused and telegraphed a report to Bismarck, who edited the Ems dispatch to make French demands seem more imperious and the king's refusal more abrupt and then released it to the press. Bismarck, Roon, and Moltke correctly assumed that war would follow. The French government responded to the patriotic fury it had helped ignite and declared war on Prussia in July 1870.

France hoped for support from Italy and Austria but had failed to establish formal agreements, and these states remained neutral. The French army, more formidable than Austria's had been, possessed modern equipment in some respects superior to that of the Germans, but the Germans were better prepared and far more decisively led. In rapid movements German armies pushed through Alsace and encircled the French army at Metz. After heavy losses on both sides, another

Map 24.3 **THE UNIFICATION OF GERMANY**

French force, attempting to relieve Metz, was defeated at Sedan in September. There Napoleon III surrendered and was taken prisoner. Major fighting was over, but French resistance continued. Paris, quickly surrounded by German troops, held out under a long siege, and a provisional French government kept an army in the field. An armistice came only at the end of January 1871, when Paris capitulated.

The brief war had profound effects. A German national state was created. In France the Second Empire fell to be succeeded by the Third Republic after bitter internal conflict. France was required to pay an indemnity of 5 billion francs and to cede Alsace and Lorraine, harsh terms that established enmity between France and Germany as a central fact of European affairs.

The German Reich The decision to annex Alsace-Lorraine was primarily a military one, intended to provide Germany with strong fortifications in case of future conflict with France. But it was also a response to the demands of German nationalists, whose support Bismarck still needed, for there were many Germans who did not welcome unification under Prussia. Well before the final French surrender, Bismarck began difficult negotiations with each of the South German states. They had joined in fighting France with a mixture of enthusiasm and fear, but it took concessions, secret funds, and threats to arrive at terms for a permanent union of North Germany. William I was then crowned German kaiser (emperor) in the Hall of Mirrors at Versailles on January 18, 1871, the anniversary of the founding of the Prussian monarchy.

With modifications, the constitution of the North German Confederation was extended to all the new nation, with many domestic affairs reserved to the 25 states that made up the Reich. There was no doubt, however, that the great new nation would be dominated by Prussia. The Second Reich[7] was from its inception a powerful nation. Germany in 1871 was already more populous than France, and its rate of demographic growth was the fastest Europe had ever known. Germany's industrial production increased at an astounding rate. Because it had developed later than Great Britain and France, its industrial equipment was more modern, and the French indemnity added to the available capital. The German government made heavy investments in railroads and spurred industrialization with tax privileges, tariffs, and policies encouraging the formation of large combines, the famous German cartels. German universities led all others in the application of scientific methods to every discipline.

Such rapid growth fed tensions among powerful conservative circles, a growing but insecure middle class, and workers increasingly aware of their distinct interests. Nowhere were materialistic and urban values more intensely attacked than in industrial Germany. Bismarck, worried about internal threats to the new nation, chose to demonstrate the supremacy of the state by moving against two potential opponents: first the Catholic Church and then the socialist party.

Rather grandiosely named the *Kulturkampf* ("Struggle for Civilization"), the conflict with the Catholic Church centered on the state's right to approve appointments, restrict religious orders, and supervise seminaries. Many of these measures were common in much of Europe, but there was a harshness in the new state's execution of them and in the rhetoric surrounding them. Intended to assure the "Germanization" of Alsace and the Polish parts of Prussia (both largely Catholic), they accentuated regional and ideological differences. Yet the *Kulturkampf* was not a success. It made martyrs of many a priest and nun, and Catholics rallied to their Church as a majority of bishops went into exile. The Catholic Center party steadily gained votes, and when the more flexible Leo XIII became pope in 1878, Bismarck sought an understanding with the Vatican. That battle of civilization subsided as Bismarck turned his sights on another growing movement.

Socialism did not offend Bismarck either in its criticism of laissez-faire economics or in its call for the state to be socially active, and he had gotten on well with the leading German socialist of the 1860s, Ferdinand Lassalle. But as socialists sought a mass following and in 1875 established the Social Democratic party, their attacks on autocracy, the military, and nationalism seemed

[7]The old Holy Roman Empire was patriotically honored as having been the first Reich.

Bismarck's Social Program

Between 1883 and 1887 the German parliament passed three laws that created a new model for the role of the state in social legislation. Bismarck introduced the first of these (providing for sickness insurance) in April 1881 in a speech to parliament that reflects the power of his personality as well as the clarity of his reasoning and of his prejudices.

"... For the past fifty years we have been talking about the social question. Since the Socialist Law was passed, I have been repeatedly reminded, in high quarters as well as low, of the promise I then gave that something positive should be done to remove the causes of Socialism.... I do not believe that our sons, or even our grandsons, will be able finally to solve the question. Indeed, no political questions can ever be mathematically settled, as books are balanced in business; they crop up, have their time, and give way to other questions propounded by history. Organic development wills that it shall be so. I consider it my duty to take up these questions without party feeling or excitement, because I know not who is to do so, if not the imperial government.

"Deputy Richter has pointed out the responsibility of the state for what it is now doing. Well, Gentlemen, I feel that the state should also be responsible for what it leaves undone. I am not of the opinion that *laissez faire, laissez aller,* 'pure Manchester policy,' 'everybody takes care of himself,' 'the weakest must go the wall,' 'to him who hath shall be given, from him who hath not shall be taken even that which he hath,' can be practiced in a monarchically, patriarchically governed state....

"An appropriate title for our enterprise would be 'practical Christianity,' but we do not want to feed poor people with figures of speech, but with something solid. Death costs nothing; but unless you will put your hands in your pockets and into the state Exchequer, you will not do much good. To saddle our industry with the whole affair—well, I don't know that it could bear the burden."

From Louis L. Snyder, *The Documents of German History,* New Brunswick: Rutgers University Press, 1958.

dangerous. Using as justification two attempts in 1878 to assassinate the kaiser (neither by a socialist), Bismarck demanded laws repressing socialism. The Reichstag refused, and the election of 1878 in which conservatives and the Center party made some gains was fought largely on that issue. Most socialist publications were banned and socialist meetings prohibited unless supervised by the police. The Social Democrats were, in effect, forced underground, although they were free to speak in the Reichstag, and their party gained support with every election.

The campaigns against Catholics and socialists were abandoned by the 1880s as no longer needed or effective, but they were part of a larger political realignment. The conservatives and Catholics who had resisted the new Germany came to accept it, while liberals, torn between Bismarck's accomplishments and their old principles, grew weaker. A more durable coalition was formed around the tariff of 1879. Its higher duties, a response to the economic problems caused by rapid growth and to a European agricultural depression, protected manufactured and agricultural goods, drawing together the most powerful interest groups in German society. Supported by Junker landlords, industrialists, and nationalists, it gave the conservative state and its powerful leaders their political base. In the 1880s Bismarck also established a system of national insurance to aid workers in times of illness and unemployment and to help provide for pensions upon retirement. Paid for by contributions from employers and workers, these measures became an influential model of modern social policy (*see box, above*).

RESHAPING THE OLDER EMPIRES

In a Europe of industrial growth and national states, war more than ever stood as the ultimate test of the state's efficiency. The wars that made Italy and Germany were understood to require drastic political changes in the nations that lost—Russia in 1856, Austria in 1859 and 1866, and France in 1870.

The Russian Empire Of the 74 million people in Russia, some 47 million were serfs. Their emancipation began in 1861 by the tsar's decree. Intellectuals had argued against serfdom for generations, and peasants spoke through frequent uprisings. Serfdom was constricting economic development, and any major political reforms required its abolition. Defeat in the Crimean War added urgency; and Tsar Alexander II, who had assumed the throne in 1855, announced his commitment to modernization. Quietly he pressed the nobles to lead the way; but while secret committees drafted proposals for ending serfdom, most nobles dragged their feet.

▸ In this 1861 photograph a Russian official is reading to peasants on a Moscow estate the "Regulations Concerning the Peasantry," the decree that abolished serfdom.

Emancipation was thus imposed by edict, a daring step cautiously framed. More than 22 million serfs gained legal rights and were promised title to the land they worked or its equivalent. If they accepted one-quarter of that, they would owe no payments; otherwise they contracted a long-term debt to the state, which compensated the lord. In practice, the lord usually kept the best land for himself and often got an inflated price for the land he lost. Former serfs on the whole found themselves with less land than they needed to support families and make their payments. Although they were required to fulfill other obligations for only two more years, they often remained dependent on their former masters for pasture and water rights and for the wage labor that had become a necessity. A few years later the government liberated all state peasants—nearly 25 million—on somewhat more favorable terms; but Russia's peasants remained a caste distinguishable in dress, speech, and customs, with special laws and punishments, including flogging, applicable only to them.

The law of 1861 also gave the *mir*, or village commune, new importance. It elected its own officials, and they assigned plots of land, decided what would be planted, and assessed the taxes owed the state. The former serfs could not leave the commune or sell their land without permission. The *mir*, which came to be considered a characteristic Slavic institution, thus sustained traditional ways and served as agent of the state while allowing some popular participation. Other reforms followed. In 1864 district councils (*zemstvos*, elected through a three-class system like Prussia's) were made responsible for local primary schools, roads, and welfare. These steps were part of a process that—along with increased schooling, relaxed censorship, and reduced military service[8]—made Russia more like other Eur-

[8]The old system, which required selected serfs to serve 25 years, was changed in 1874 to one of universal service, with generous exemptions and only six years of active duty. Those who completed primary school were liable for only four years of duty; those who finished secondary school, for two years; and those with university education, for just six months.

opean nations. Each reform, however, uncovered more that needed to be done, and leaders remained fearful. Concessions in Poland were followed by revolution in 1863. It was harshly quelled, and Poland's separate status ended. Repression increased in Russia, too, as censorship and police surveillance tightened. While pan-Slavists stressed Russia's special destiny and disdained liberal parliamentarianism as alien, an isolated intelligentsia was drawn to more radical ideas, and conspirators plotted more drastic remedies. Yet when a bomb killed Alexander II in 1881, his son smoothly succeeded him as Alexander III; tsarist Russia could survive an assassination.

The Austro-Hungarian Empire Following the revolutions of 1848, the Habsburg monarchy under the young Franz Joseph I had sought to create a modern, unitary state. For the first time in its history, the empire was subjected to uniform laws and taxes. But military defeat in Italy and then at the hands of Prussia and mounting debts proved that more changes were needed. In 1860 Franz Joseph announced a new federal constitution, giving considerable authority to regional diets. Intended to reduce resentment against high-handed government, it was a failure from the start, opposed by liberals and bureaucrats alike while provoking dangerous arguments among the empire's diverse nationalities. So the emperor reversed himself the next year and established a bicameral parliament for the entire empire. Having stirred visions of local self-government and autonomous nationalities, he now wanted to subordinate local governments to rule from Vienna and parliament, which had a lower house elected by a four-class system that ensured the dominance of the German-speaking middle class.

Hungary in particular objected, led by the liberal nationalist Ferencz Deák, who had campaigned for Hungary's constitution of 1848. Neither side was strong enough to have its way, and the war with Prussia finally brought a compromise. In 1867 Hungary became an autonomous state, joined to Austria only through the emperor, for Franz Joseph became king of Hungary, and through common policies for defense and diplomacy. The emperor had kept his authority in foreign policy, which was what he cared about most, by conceding to one nationality what he denied to others. Within Hungary, domestic politics centered on conflict between the dominant Magyars and the non-Magyar majority and between the diverging interests of Austrian industry and Hungary's great landholders.

Within the Austrian parliament, the emperor turned first to the German liberals, who offended him by their anticlericalism, and then to the Czechs and Poles, who disturbed him with their nationalist demands. More fundamental reform proved difficult; and although ministers were now responsible to parliament, policy rested more on a conservative bureaucracy dominated by Germans. An awkward compromise, the Dual Monarchy gave power to wealthy landlords and merchants; and it rested on the dominance of Magyars (over Romanians, Croatians, and Serbs) and of Germans in cooperation with Czechs and Poles (over Slovenes, Slovaks, and Ruthenians). It lasted for 50 years as one of Europe's great powers, an empire of diversified peoples and cultures, threatened by nationalism, changing even while resisting change, with more freedom in practice than in principle, and sustained at its center by the graceful civilization of Vienna.

III. Nineteenth-Century Culture

Europe's cultural life was as dynamic as its economy and politics. In the nineteenth century the arts were understood to be national and urban rather than centered in courts, salons, or villages (*provincial* had become a pejorative term); and they were remarkable for quantity as well as quality. There were more writers, artists, musicians, and scholars than ever before; and they reached larger audiences through expanding cultural institutions and markets.

CULTURAL INSTITUTIONS

Before the nineteenth century, most paintings and musical compositions were commissioned for a particular place or occasion. Now music moved from palaces, churches, and private salons to public concert halls; artists sold their paintings to any purchaser and, by midcentury, in galleries created for that purpose; and writers found themselves engaged in commercial activity.

Theaters ranged from the new music halls to the great stages and opera houses built (usually by the state) to rank with parliament buildings as monuments of national or civic pride. Most major cities supported choirs, bands, and symphony orchestras, which grew larger and technically more proficient. Conservatories and museums became national public institutions, maintaining official taste and considerably increasing Europe's stock of highly trained artists, musicians, and scholars. Some of the greatest of these institutions—the British Museum in London, the Bibliothèque Nationale in Paris, the Hermitage in St. Petersburg, the Alte Pinakothek in Munich—opened to the public in the 1840s, most in imposing new structures. Lending libraries, charging a few pence per volume, were common even in smaller cities. In Paris the Louvre became the model museum of art that gave access to everyone and expressed the era's understanding of culture by putting works of art in chronological order by country.

Cultural life—associated with the state, tied to a market economy, and promulgating shared values and taste—helped to create national identity and to establish social status. The public it addressed was, for the most part, the same public active in politics, the professions, and business—or rather, such people and their wives. They bought tickets for concerts just as they frequented restaurants with famous chefs, enjoying in both cases pleasures once part of private society and now open to all who had the inclination and money. Participation in this exciting culture also set boundaries of decorum that distinguished the middle class from those below them and defined the distinctive roles thought appropriate to men and women. High culture was expected to sustain those values, although individual artists and intellectuals often criticized them and attacked a system that left creativity dependent on administrators and what would sell to the public—a tension that became the hallmark of modern culture.

This public culture encompassed a wide range of activities. Those who sought self-improvement flocked to public lectures on the sober implications of political economy or the wonders of science or new marvels like photography, which was being enthusiastically applied to the needs of science and exploration, widely used for portraits, and recognized as the newest of the arts.[9] No cultural institution was more important than the press, and the newspaper became a major instrument of culture and politics. By 1830 there were more than 2000 European newspapers, and liberals everywhere fought the censorship, special taxes, and police measures with which governments sought to constrain so awesome a social force. *The Times* of London had a circulation of 5000 in 1815 and of 50,000 by midcentury; two of the most popular French papers, the *Presse* and *Siècle*, reached 70,000.

As newspapers came to rely more on advertising than subscriptions for their revenue, they got larger, published articles on a wider range of topics (including items on fashion and domestic concerns aimed at women), and attracted readers by serializing novels by writers as famous as Honoré de Balzac, the elder Alexandre Dumas, and Charles Dickens. Technology aided these changes. Press services such as the Agence Havas and Reuters quickly adopted the telegraph; and the *London Illustrated News*, which created the picture magazine in 1842, was immediately copied in every large country. Satirical magazines (*Punch* was founded in London in 1840, a few years after the *Caricature* and *Chiarivari* in Paris) made the cartoon a powerful political weapon, raised to art by Honoré Daumier's biting pictures of fat bankers and complacent bourgeois. Technology contributed a flood of technical improvements.

The Cultural Professions Professionalization affected the arts as well. The violinist Niccolò Paganini, who transformed violin technique, commanded huge fees and enormous crowds wherever he played; the soprano Jenny Lind,

[9]Daguerre announced his photographic process to the French Academy in 1839, which persuaded the government to purchase his rights and give the new technique to the world, unencumbered by royalties.

"the Swedish Nightingale," was the rage of Europe as was Franz Liszt, piano virtuoso and composer. Many a young man announced that he was a painter and proudly starved, in Paris if possible, out of loyalty to his career (there were 354 registered artists in Paris in 1789 but 2159 in 1838). A few, among them England's great landscape painter J. M. W. Turner, became wealthy.

The most popular writers—Balzac, Sir Walter Scott, Victor Hugo, Dickens—were able to live by their pen alone, among the most honored figures of their age. There were also many women novelists. Expected to write light romances, they generally were not taken very seriously; and to escape that prejudice a number of women writers adopted masculine pen names. Still, the rising prestige of the professional writer enabled some extraordinary women, like George Eliot (Mary Evans Cross) and Elizabeth Gaskell in England and George Sand in France, to be recognized as influential thinkers. For a new public faced with so much new work to choose from, critics became important; like professors, they were professional intellectuals who guided taste much as the popular books on etiquette and gastronomy taught manners to people of new means and prepared the bourgeois palate for *haute cuisine.*

Cultural Forms Artistic works were valued for a moral seriousness and formality that distinguished them from popular culture. In painting, great historical scenes were the most admired, ranked considerably above genre painting or portraits. Musical forms such as the symphony, concerto, quartet, and sonata were carefully defined and composers then evaluated on their capacity to exploit the possibilities of these forms within the established rules. Ludwig van Beethoven's music was taken as a model of personal expression within formal structure, and it was treated as a kind of profound essay to be studied and savored for itself rather than as part of some larger occasion. The novel's great popularity was related to the social panorama it presented. Balzac attempted in his novels to encompass all the "human comedy" (the phrase contrasted with Dante's divine concerns), showing the wealthy, the ambitious, and the poor in their roles as husbands and wives, soldiers, bankers, politicians, and writers. Novelists used social types to analyze society and challenge the public conscience, and no reformer was more influential than Dickens. Scott's swashbuckling stories of romance and chivalry in an earlier age probed the connection between personal character and social tension in a way that influenced writers throughout Europe. Hugo, Alexander Pushkin, and Alessandro Manzoni promulgated patriotism by connecting high ideals to the national past, painting in words (much as the most admired paintings put on canvas) monumental interpretations of historical events. The novel's most common theme, the conflict between personal feeling (especially romantic love) and social convention, explored critical contemporary issues of individualism and social change.

Conceptions of culture were also strongly gendered. Women were held to have qualities—including a natural sense of beauty and openness to emotion—that made them especially responsive to art. Women were thought to be the principal readers of novels, and novels presented women's lives in ways that underscored the inequities of their social subordination and ultimately enlarged the perception of women's abilities (as in Gustave Flaubert's *Madame Bovary* and Thomas Hardy's *Tess of the d'Urbervilles*). Women were especially associated with the intimate side of middle-class culture, the popularity of poetry, lithographs, watercolor paintings, and piano music[10]—all to be savored in the parlor with the woman of the house at the center.

STYLES AND MOVEMENTS

Romanticism Romanticism, a protean movement that affected all of intellectual life and not just the arts, cannot be captured in any simple definition. Its roots lay in the eighteenth-century reaction against the Enlightenment and the Classical forms and crisp rationality associated with it. Romantic painters emphasized vibrant color and swirling lines more than perfect proportion and control; Romantic novelists favored vivid, personal description and singular settings over balanced sentences and lucid prose; Romantic

[10]Industrial techniques had made the piano, with its iron frame, economical enough to be a common sight in middle-class homes.

▸ **The evocation of nature and time, favorite Romantic themes, made the ruins of Tintern Abbey the subject of a poem by Wordsworth and of this watercolor by J. M. W. Turner.**

musicians broke conventional rules of form and harmony. Thus certain themes emerge as characteristically Romantic: an emphasis on feeling, emotion, and direct experience more than on universality and logic; a fascination with nature understood as raw and unpredictable; interest in the momentary and the unique in human affairs and in history; a search for the organic relatedness of life that goes beyond the analysis of cause and effect; and a belief in the capacity of the individual genius to experience more and feel more deeply than ordinary mortals (*see box*, p. 798).

These themes were important in philosophy, conservative and radical thought, and all the arts; and they were central to ideas of nationalism. Romantic thinkers tended to see rural life, folk culture, and language as natural expressions of the nation. Romanticism was at the heart of the great burst of cultural creativity in Germany at the turn of the century, marked by the works of Georg Friedrich Hegel and Friedrich Schlegel in philosophy and F. W. J. Schelling in literature, and by an outpouring of compositions that made German music the most admired in Europe. Associated with a pride in things German and with a rejection of French universalism, this German Romanticism was taken up in France by figures like Madame de Staël, whose writings introduced many of these German thinkers to French audiences, and René de Chateaubriand, who evoked the moving beauty and social necessity of religion, and in England by Samuel Coleridge, whose writing combined mysticism and sober concern for social order. Romanticism could thus be politically conservative, but it could also—in writers like Percy Bysshe Shelley in England and Victor Hugo in France—present the artist as liberator, leading society into a new age of freedom.

Toward Other Styles Romanticism's concern with the individual hero or genius—found in the paintings of Delacroix, the plays of Hugo, the poetry of John Keats and Shelley—had stressed the artist's personal vision and the capture for eternity of a momentary feeling within a work of art. That emphasis would soon lead some to the cry of art for art's sake, to the claim that the merit of a work lay in its purity, independent of any other purpose. For others, the goal of the artist should be to capture the essence of "modernity," extracting "from fashion whatever element it may contain of poetry within history," in the words of Charles Baudelaire.[11] By midcentury, "Realism" was replacing Romanticism as the dominant style, as writers and painters reemphasized close observation in a socially concerned effort to portray, with sometimes shocking directness, the lives of ordinary people.

There was a wish as well to integrate the arts, which gave lyric opera special resonance in nineteenth-century culture. Opera was first of all theater, combining popular appeal with aristocratic elegance, and performances were impor-

[11]From his essay on the painter, Constantin Guys, in Charles Baudelaire, *The Painter of Modern Life and Other Essays*, Jonathan Mayne (tr. and ed.), 1965, p. 12.

tant civic events. Elaborate plots, often in historical settings, and flowery poetic texts were closely followed along with the varied, tuneful, and complex music, the whole further enriched by ballet, colorful sets, and special effects. The two leading operatic composers were Giuseppe Verdi and his exact contemporary Richard Wagner. Verdi was an Italian national hero, whose compelling and often patriotic music explored human emotion and character in diverse social and political contexts. Wagner carried the search for an artistic synthesis still further. He wrote his own texts, often building with nationalist intent on Germanic myths, and identified his major ideas and characters with specific musical themes to create a whole in which voices, instruments, words, and visual experience were inseparable.

Thus the frequent shifting of styles became in itself a modern characteristic. Innovation was often taken for a sign of genius, and the belief that artists must be in an avant-garde, ahead of their duller public, became a cliché. The arts were never more honored than in the nineteenth century, nor artists more critical of their society.

Courbet, a leader in the shift toward social realism in painting, presents the artist in his studio in touch with all classes of men and women. Many of those portrayed here were well known artists and radicals.

Religion There was comparable ambivalence with regard to religion. In some respects this was a very religious age, for thoughtful people cared greatly about religion. Protestant and Catholic missions campaigned with an intensity not seen since the seventeenth century, and the pious became more militant and turned to social action, preaching temperance, teaching reading, and establishing charities. This focus on the problems of modern life was connected, however, to the fear that religion was losing its social importance. Some intellectuals became bitter anticlericals, seeing in the church the barrier to progress. More typically, especially in England, stern morality and propriety were substituted for theology. Theological works nevertheless accounted for a high proportion of the titles publishers produced. It made headlines when the Abbé Lamennais, once a powerful spokesman of Catholic renewal, broke with the Church in the 1830s because it would not accept the connection he made between Christianity and democracy. The Protes-

Wordsworth on the Role of the Poet

Wordsworth was one of England's most popular poets, and the success of his **Lyrical Ballads** *may have encouraged him to write a preface to the second edition, explaining what he was up to. He points out that his poems differ from Classical poetry with its greater formality and lofty themes, and he justifies his use of ordinary speech. In making his case, he touches on many of the themes characteristic of the Romantic movement.*

"The principle object of these Poems was to choose incidents and situations from common life, and to relate or describe them, throughout, as far as was possible in a selection of language really used by men, and, at the same time, to throw over them a certain colouring of imagination, whereby ordinary things could be presented to the mind in an unusual aspect. . . . Humble and rustic life was generally chosen because, in that condition, the essential passions of the heart find a better soil in which they can attain their maturity, are less under restraint, and speak a plainer and more emphatic language; because in that condition of life our elementary feelings co-exist in a state of greater simplicity, and, consequently, may be more accurately contemplated and more forcibly communicated; because the manners of rural life germinate from those elementary feelings . . . ; and, lastly, because in that condition the passions of men are incorporated with the beautiful and permanent forms of nature. . . .

". . . For all good poetry is the spontaneous overflow of powerful feelings: and though this be true, Poems to which any value can be attached were never produced on any variety of subjects but by a man who, being possessed of more than usual organic sensibility, had also thought long and deeply. . . .

"The Man of science seeks truth as a remote and unknown benefactor; he cherishes and loves it in his solitude; the Poet, singing a song in which all human beings join with him, rejoices in the presence of truth as our visible friend and hourly companion. Poetry is the breath and finer spirit of all knowledge; it is the impassioned expression which is the countenance of all Science. Emphatically may it be said of the Poet, as Shakespeare hath said of man, 'that he looks before and after.' He is the rock of defence for human nature; an upholder and preserver, carrying everywhere with him relationship and love . . . ; the Poet binds together by passion and knowledge the vast empire of human society, as it is spread over the whole earth, and over all time."

From William Wordsworth, "Preface to the Second Edition of *Lyrical Ballads*" as printed in Jack Stillinger (ed.), *William Wordsworth: Selected Poems and Prefaces*, Boston: Houghton Mifflin Company, 1965.

tant David Strauss created a sensation across Europe with his *Life of Jesus*, which appeared in 1835, for it cast erudite doubt on the accuracy of the Gospel, frightening many with the apparent need to choose between historical scholarship and Christ. In Denmark the writings of Søren Kierkegaard starkly explored ethical dilemmas in a passionate search for faith; and his intense, semiautobiographical essays that interweave biblical stories and personal symbols have continued to fascinate twentieth-century thinkers.

The Sense of History A romantic respect for the past, the nationalists' desire to rest their claims on the historical record, and a modern need to understand change reinforced an interest in history. Its systematic study became an admired profession. In England, France, and Germany, national projects were launched for publishing historical documents and for training scholars to interpret them. Some historians were as widely read as novelists, among them Michelet, for whom French history was a dramatic story of the people's fight for freedom, and Thomas B. Macaulay, for whom the history of England was a record of progressive change through moderation and compromise. In each country certain events and themes—in England, the Glorious Revolution of 1688; in France, the Revolution; in Germany, the rise of Prussia—were favored as part of an intense search for national roots, heroes, and patterns of development significant for the present. Many a political leader first gained fame as a historian.

This preoccupation with history, which affected all intellectual life, received its most powerful philosophic expression in the writings of Georg Wilhelm Friedrich Hegel, a German Rhinelander who watched with fascination the unfolding of the French Revolution and the spread of Napoleon's influence. Thoroughly trained in philosophy and Lutheran theology, Hegel set out to establish a philosophy as comprehensive as that of Thomas Aquinas or Aristotle. He was determined to reconcile contradictions between science and faith, Christianity and the state, the ideal and the real, the eternal and the temporal. The key, he believed, lay in the meaning of history and the nature of the historical process.

According to Hegel, that process is dialectical. Society in any era constitutes a thesis, an implicit statement about life and values expressed through social structures and actions. That thesis, however, is never adequate to every need, and its incompleteness generates contrary views, institutions, and practices—the antithesis. Thus every society gives rise to conflict between thesis and antithesis until from that dialectic a new synthesis is molded. This synthesis becomes in turn another thesis that generates a new antithesis. History moves by this dialectic in a steady unfolding of what Hegel called the World Spirit, and it always moves toward greater human freedom and self-awareness. In the ancient East, Hegel said, only one man was free; in Greece and Rome, some were free; in the Germanic Christian kingdoms after the Reformation, all were free. Since the French Revolution, people have consciously acted on history, knowing what they want and fulfilling the World Spirit at the same time. Thus cosmic order and human reason ultimately work together; history has a religious meaning.

Hegel's important philosophy was—as he would have said it had to be—an important expression of his age. Like most nineteenth-century thinkers, he was determined to find eternal meaning in historical change and was convinced that his own nation was the highest articulation of that meaning. After Hegel, philosophy and literary criticism both tended to become increasingly historical, and historians sought more systematically for relationships among all aspects of a culture. Within a generation of his death in 1813, just after another wave of the revolutions he abhorred, some of his followers claimed to find in the Prussian state at war humanity's highest ethical expression, while others—led by Karl Marx, the most famous of the Hegelians—predicted the state's withering away. By then it was a European habit to approach any question of society, culture, or politics in terms of historical change.

In 1848 revolutions had swept across Europe, only to be defeated. But many of the regimes that defeated them absorbed part of the revolutionaries' programs and of their techniques for reaching a broader public. In the period that followed, political reorganization remarkably strengthened the state in many European countries, a tendency underscored by the unification of Italy and of Germany. Nationalism enabled astute political leaders to mobilize diverse support and opened the way for new experiments mediating between the premise of democracy and the guarantee of social order.

Recommended Reading

Sources

Marx, Karl. *The Class Struggles in France, 1848–1850; The Eighteenth Brumaire of Louis Napoleon.* Early and brilliant applications of Marx's ideas to contemporary political events, these essays on the revolution of 1848 in France and on Napoleon's coup d'état also show Marx's power as a polemicist.

Trollope, Frances Milton. *Travels and Travellers.* (2 vols.) 1846. A novelist well known for travel essays, Mrs. Trollope's chatty descriptions contain insightful comments on European society and the position of women on the eve of revolution.

Treitschke, Heinrick. *History of Germany in the Nineteenth Century.* Written shortly after German unification, this vast work exemplifies the importance of history as nationalist propaganda.

Studies

*Agulhon, Maurice. *The Republican Experiment, 1848–1852.* Janel Lloyd (tr.). 1983. An authoritative study of politics and society during the Second French Republic, sensitive to popular attitudes and concerns.

*Alter, Peter. *Nationalism.* 1989. A valuable introduction to the history of European nationalism organized around a very interesting classification of the different kinds of nationalism.

*Anderson, Benedict. *Imagined Communities: Reflections on the Origin and Spread of Nationalism.* 1983. An important and provocative analysis of modern nationalism around the world, stressing its origins in European culture and capitalism.

*Barzun, Jacques. *Classic, Romantic, and Modern.* 1961. A famous and provocative defense of Romanticism by a cultural historian.

*Beales, Derek. *The Risorgimento and the Unification of Italy.* 1982. Concise, skeptical introduction to the history of Italian unification.

Branca, Patricia. *Women in Europe since 1750.* 1978. A helpful survey, emphasizing England and addressing many of the important issues of modern social history.

*Chadwick, Owen. *The Secularization of the European Mind.* 1975. Perceptive, careful introduction to changing patterns of thought affecting attitudes toward religion.

*Gellner, Ernest. *Nations and Nationalism.* 1983. An effort to build a theory by analyzing the relation of industrialization to nationalism.

*Greenfeld, Liah. *Nationalism: Five Roads to Modernity.* 1992. An ambitious comparison of nationalism and state making in England, France, Russia, Germany, and the United States.

Greenfield, Kent R. *Economics and Liberalism in the Risorgimento: A Study of Nationalism in Lombardy, 1814–1848.* 1978. A classic study of the connection between economic change and nationalism.

*Hamerow, Theodore S. *The Social and Economic Foundations of German Unification, 1858–1871* (2 vols.). 1969–1972. The politics and ideas of unification placed in the context of a developing economy.

Hemmings, F. W. J. *Culture and Society in France, 1789–1848.* 1987; and *Culture and Society in France, 1848–1898.* 1971. A literary scholar's provocative and comprehensive analysis of the relationship between cultural styles and social context.

*Howard, Michael. *The Franco-Prussian War.* 1969. Exemplary study of how war reflects (and tests) an entire society.

*Jelavich, Barbara. *History of the Balkans* (2 vols.). 1983. An impressively thorough survey of both society and politics, from the eighteenth century to the present.

*Mack Smith, Denis. *Cavour.* 1985. An expert and well-written assessment of the personalities and policies that created an Italian nation.

*McLeod, Hugh. *Religion and the People of Western Europe, 1789–1970.* 1981. A well-conceived interpretive survey of the impact of social change on religious practice.

*Mosse, George L. *The Nationalization of the Masses: Political Symbolism and Mass Movements in Germany from the Napoleonic Wars through the Third Reich.* 1975. One of the most recent and complete efforts to find the roots of Nazism in popular nationalism.

Pflanze, Otto. *Bismarck and the Development of Germany: The Period of Unification, 1815–1871.* 1963. A balanced

*Available in paperback.

assessment that places each of Bismarck's actions in its larger context.

*Pinkney, David. *Napoleon III and the Rebuilding of Paris.* 1958. Studies the political background to one of the most extensive, influential, and successful examples of urban policy.

*Plessis, Alain. *The Rise and Fall of the Second Empire, 1852–1871.* Jonathan Mandelbaum (tr.). 1985. A balanced assessment of this important political experiment making good use of current scholarship.

Porter, Roy and Mikulá Teich (eds.). *Romanticism in National Context.* 1988. Particularly useful for the student because this volume of interpretive essays includes many on smaller European nations.

*Read, Donald. *England 1868–1914. The Age of Urban Democracy.* 1979. Political change presented in terms of economic and social conditions.

Reardon, B. M. G. *Religion in the Age in Romanicism: Studies in Early Nineteenth-Century Thought.* 1985. An excellent introduction to the formation of one of the most important intellectual traditions of the century.

Riasanovsky, Nicholas V. *Nicholas I and Official Nationality in Russia.* 1959. An important study of how a conservative regime sought to use nationalism to strengthen the state.

Rich, Norman. *Why the Crimean War? A Cautionary Tale.* 1985. A concise synthesis and engaging interpretation of the political and diplomatic problems involving the major powers.

Salvemini, Gaetano. *Mazzini.* 1957. Still the best introduction to Mazzini's thought and its relationship to his revolutionary activities.

Saville, John. *1848: The British State and the Chartist Movement.* 1987. A careful study of why Chartism failed to win its aims at the moment revolution succeeded elsewhere.

*Sperber, Jonathan. *Rhineland Radicals: The Democratic Movement and the Revolution of 1848–1849.* 1993. A significant discussion, very clearly presented, of popular attitudes demonstrating the widespread support for the German revolutions of 1848.

*Stearns, Peter N. *1848: The Revolutionary Tide in Europe.* 1974. Pays attention to conflicting interpretations in bringing together accounts of these diverse revolutions.

Szporluk, Roman. *Communism and Nationalism: Karl Marx versus Friedrich List.* 1988. By drawing attention to the ideas of List, one of the most influential figures of his day, this study suggests that in Central and Eastern Europe nationalism and Marxism were from the first competing programs for modernization and economic development.

Wandycz, Piotyr S. *The Lands of Partitioned Poland, 1795–1918.* 1974. An excellent overview of the history of divided Poland.

*Williams, Roger L. *The French Revolution of 1870–1871.* 1969. An introduction to the long-standing controversies about the Paris Commune.

*Zeldin, T. *France: 1848–1945* (2 vols.). 1973–1977. Reissued in five paperback volumes, 1979–1981. Lively essays on an unusual array of topics that add up to an important look at French society and culture.

The Reverend John Williams was an English missionary who had extraordinary success converting native populations on the islands of the South Seas. He wrote codes of law for them and taught them European construction techniques before moving on to win more converts elsewhere. This painting depicts his arrival in November 1839 on an island in the New Hebrides, where on the following day the natives killed him.

CHAPTER TWENTY-FIVE

EUROPEAN DYNAMISM AND THE NINETEENTH-CENTURY WORLD

ECONOMIC changes were as dramatic as political ones in the second half of the nineteenth century. New technologies, large-scale industry, better communication, and greater capital investment resulted in unprecedented productivity that affected all of society. Intellectual life kept pace, with important scientific discoveries and theories about social systems. These achievements spurred the increased trade, investment, migration, missionary activity, and cultural curiosity that spread European influence to all parts of the globe. With it came the expressions of national power and ultimately the competitive tensions characteristic of European states.

I. The Economics of Growth

The dynamism of Europe's economy in the second half of the nineteenth century was also unprecedented. As economic growth accelerated, it reached into sectors previously little affected and spread beyond Europe's industrial heartlands into most of the continent. While Europe's population grew more rapidly than ever before, the value of manufacturing went up three times as fast. For the first time in history, economic growth became an expectation, and most of society would experience some of its benefits. The model factory, especially the producers of steel and chemicals, coupled large-scale production with new technologies, like those connected to electricity. The impact of these developments was so great that historians often speak of this as the second industrial revolution. Distribution and marketing operated on a larger scale, too, and department stores used new techniques of merchandising to entice a wider public to higher levels of consumption.

THE SECOND INDUSTRIAL REVOLUTION

Industrial growth in this period was closely tied to new technology. By 1890 Europe was producing even more steel than iron. The Bessemer converter developed in the 1860s permitted far higher temperatures in smelter furnaces, and subsequent discoveries made it profitable to use

▶ The Bessemer process of removing impurities from molten iron, which revolutionized the industry, was based on English and American patents; but the Krupp steelworks installed these massive converters in 1862 and continued to lead in steel production in both size and efficiency when this photograph was taken in 1880.

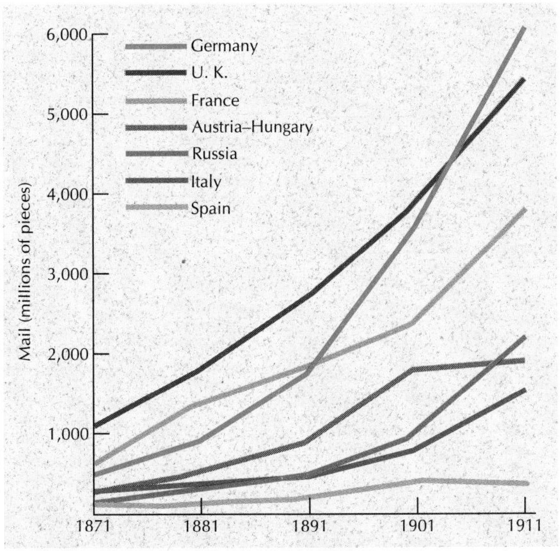

MAIL (MILLIONS OF PIECES) The volume of mail has been used by some scholars as an indicator of modernization, reflecting increased literacy, internal communication, and commercial activity. In these terms, then, the relative position of the several nations on this chart is suggestive of more than gross population, as are the points at which Germany surpasses first France and then the United Kingdom, or at which Russia surpasses Italy and Austria-Hungary.

lower-grade ores. British, German, and French maritime shipping, which doubled between 1870 and 1914, depended on faster and larger steamships. New chemical processes and synthetics led to improved products ranging from dyes, textiles, and paints to fertilizers and explosives. A whole new industry developed to produce and supply electricity, and the demand for large generating stations to distribute power over a wide area increased with the invention of the incandescent lamp. By 1900 the manufacture of generators, cables, and motors, an important new industry in itself, allowed greater and cheaper production in scores of other fields.

Equally striking was the speed with which the new technology was adapted to commercial uses. The telephone, invented in 1879, became a business necessity and an established private convenience within a few decades. The steam turbine, shown in the 1880s to be more efficient than the reciprocating engine, was soon widely employed in ships and factories, fueled by oil as well as coal. Home sewing machines and bicycles were created directly for the consumer market—an indication of the growing purchasing power of the masses. Inventions were now expected to change people's lives. The automobile in the 1890s, the airplane in the 1900s, and the radio a decade later were all greeted with enthusiasm even before their commercial possibilities were established.

National Differences The expansion of the German economy following unification was spectacular. Already rich in natural resources, Germany acquired more raw materials as well as factories with the annexation of Alsace-Lorraine. Its system of railroads provided excellent communications; the famous educational system produced ample numbers of the administrators and engineers the commercial sector now required. The government, which had played an active role in every facet of industrialization, continued to cooperate with business interests. Military needs stimulated basic industry, and a growing population provided an eager domestic market. German factories, being newer than those of Britain or France, employed the latest and most efficient equipment, obtaining the necessary capital through a modern banking structure. By 1900 those plants were far bigger than anyone else's, and firms engaged in the various stages of production often combined in huge cartels that dominated an entire sector of industry, as Germany became preeminent in new fields such as chemicals and electricity (*see box,* p. 806). German salespeople appeared all over the world with catalogs in local languages and products suited to local conditions, selling with a drive and optimism British merchants resented as bad manners.

The older industrial economies of Great Britain, Belgium, and France continued to grow but more slowly; yet by 1900 France's industrial production, despite the loss of important textile and iron centers in Alsace, about equaled Great Britain's a generation earlier, when Britain had led the world. French iron production more than doubled in the first 25 years of the Third Republic, and new processes made the nation's ore output second only to that of the United States. In value of production per capita, a figure that sug-

Making the Deals that Created a Cartel

Cartels, strongest in Germany, existed in other countries, too. Here the general manager of an iron rolling mill that made rails describes how in 1878 a cartel of rail producers came to be formed in Austria.

"In 1878 there were in Austria-Hungary nine rail rolling mills with an annual capacity of about 120,000 tons. A large part of these mills had been set up in the years 1869–73, that is to say in a period in which railway building flourished in Austria-Hungary as never before.... The picture changed in the course of 1873. The lines that had been started were being finished, but no new ones were being built....

"I was then the general manager of one of these rail rolling mills.... If our works did not get an annual minimum quantity of orders of 10,000 tons, it would be faced with the impossibility of employing its work force. We should have had to close and face bankruptcy.... My task was therefore a simple one; to get orders at all costs.

"In 1878.... on the day when contracts were awarded [by the Kaiser Franz-Joseph Railway], the manager ... told me: 'Yours was the lowest; but since two other works are also prepared to come down to our price, I shall divide the order into three parts.... ' I tried to make representations; in vain, the decision stood. After I had left the office of the managing director, I met the managers of the other two works which had come down to my price. Because of the years of bitter competition, our personal relations had also suffered, but this time we shook hands, and the rail cartel, the first cartel in Austria, the model for other later cartels, also in Germany, was born. At the moment when it became clear that no works could succeed in getting sufficient orders to stay fully employed, each reached the conviction that there was nothing left but at last to attempt to get higher prices. The course of the tendering negotiations with the Franz-Joseph Railway had shown the way. We reached agreement to distribute the total demand according to certain ratios among all the works, and sought then to get the highest prices possible in the light of foreign competition, and the rates of freight and of customs duty."

Karl Wittgensteing, "Kartelle in Österreich" in Gustav Schmoller (ed), *Über wirtschaftliche Kartelle in Deutschland und im Auslande,* Leipzig, 1894, as quoted in Carroll and Embree, *Readings in European History since 1814,* 1930.

gests something of a nation's standard of living, France remained ahead of Germany, though behind the British Isles.

By the turn of the century, Great Britain, whose industrial superiority had seemed a fact of nature, was clearly being surpassed in some of the critical indexes of production by the United States and Germany. Although the economy did continue to expand, its state of health became a serious issue in English public life, and economic historians remain fascinated by the question of why an economy once so dynamic grew sluggish. Several factors stand out. British plants and equipment were old, and owners hesitated to undertake the cost of modernizing or replacing them. Well-established firms often made it hard for new companies to get a start. Without technical secondary schools like those of Germany and France, English schooling remained weak in technical subjects and provided less opportunity for social mobility than on the continent. Indeed, social attitudes, always difficult to analyze precisely, may explain more than strictly economic factors. British industrialists, slow to appreciate the mere specialist and resistant to new ways, became less venturesome and perhaps a little complacent. Even so, London remained the financial capital of the world—a world in which industrialization was rapidly spreading to Sweden and Italy, Russia and Japan.

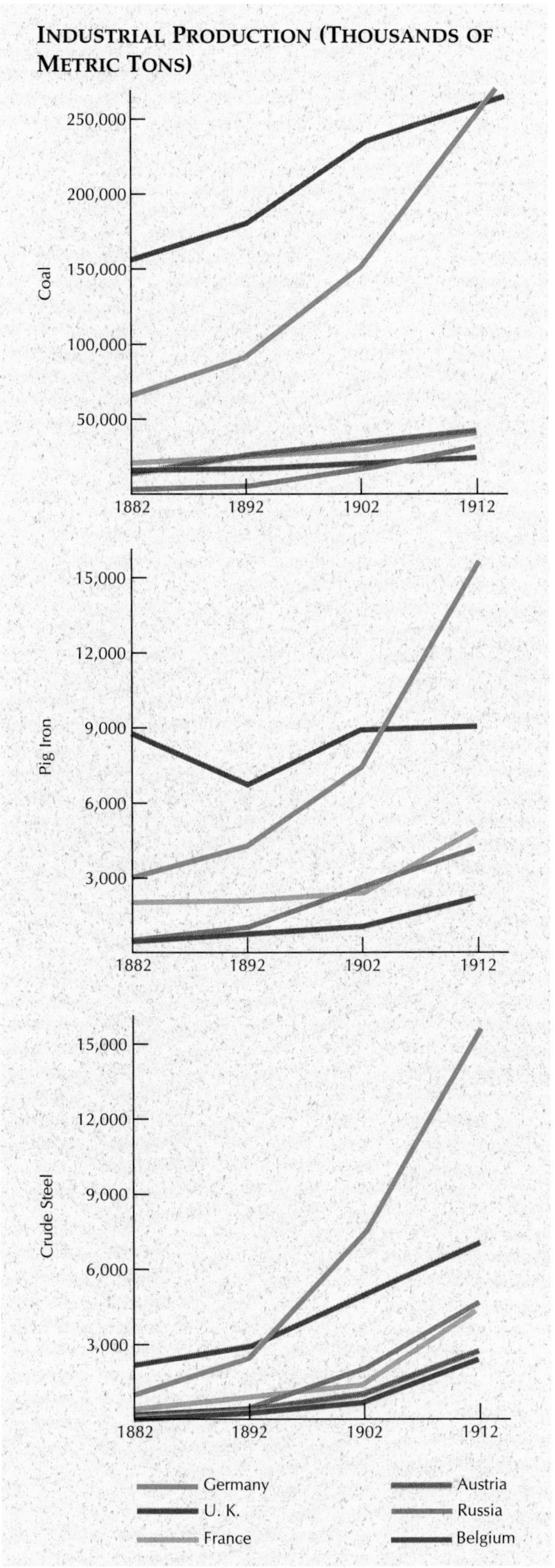

That important change was tied to others. Industrialization no longer depended so directly on the possession of critical natural resources like coal and iron ore but could be accomplished with foreign investment and imported technology. Newly industrializing countries, reluctant to leave their fate to market forces and the interests of foreigners, expected the government and investment banks to play a large part in encouraging economic growth.

Agriculture and the Long Depression Although greater prosperity and growing populations increased the demand for food, the percentage of the population that made its living in agriculture continued to decline, down to only 8 percent in Britain, 22 percent in Belgium, and 35 percent in Germany toward the end of the century. In France, which maintained a more balanced economy (as did the Netherlands and Sweden), 43 percent of the population lived off the land. But everywhere the wider use of machinery and chemical fertilizers increased the capital investment required for farming, and improved transportation intensified international competition. These factors encouraged much greater specialization. The most famous example is Denmark, where agriculture began to center on a highly capitalized and profitable dairy industry. But in France, too, wheat and sheep production declined in favor of wine grapes and sugar beets, which farmers could raise more profitably. Britain now imported almost all its grain, and Germany, a great deal.

Global connections were increasingly important. Civil war in the United States, which cut off Europe's supply of cotton from the southern states, caused unemployment in England's mills and created a boom for Egyptian cotton. After 1865, cheaper grain from the Americas and Eastern Europe, especially Russia, poured into Europe on larger ships and improved railroads, pushing prices down at a time when farmers needed cash for the improvements required to make farming profitable. More young men abandoned the countryside, and landed interests pressed their governments for help in the face of recurrent agricultural crises. The most common response was protective tariffs, and these were raised in France, Germany, Austria, Russia, Italy,

Economically Active Population, ca. 1900

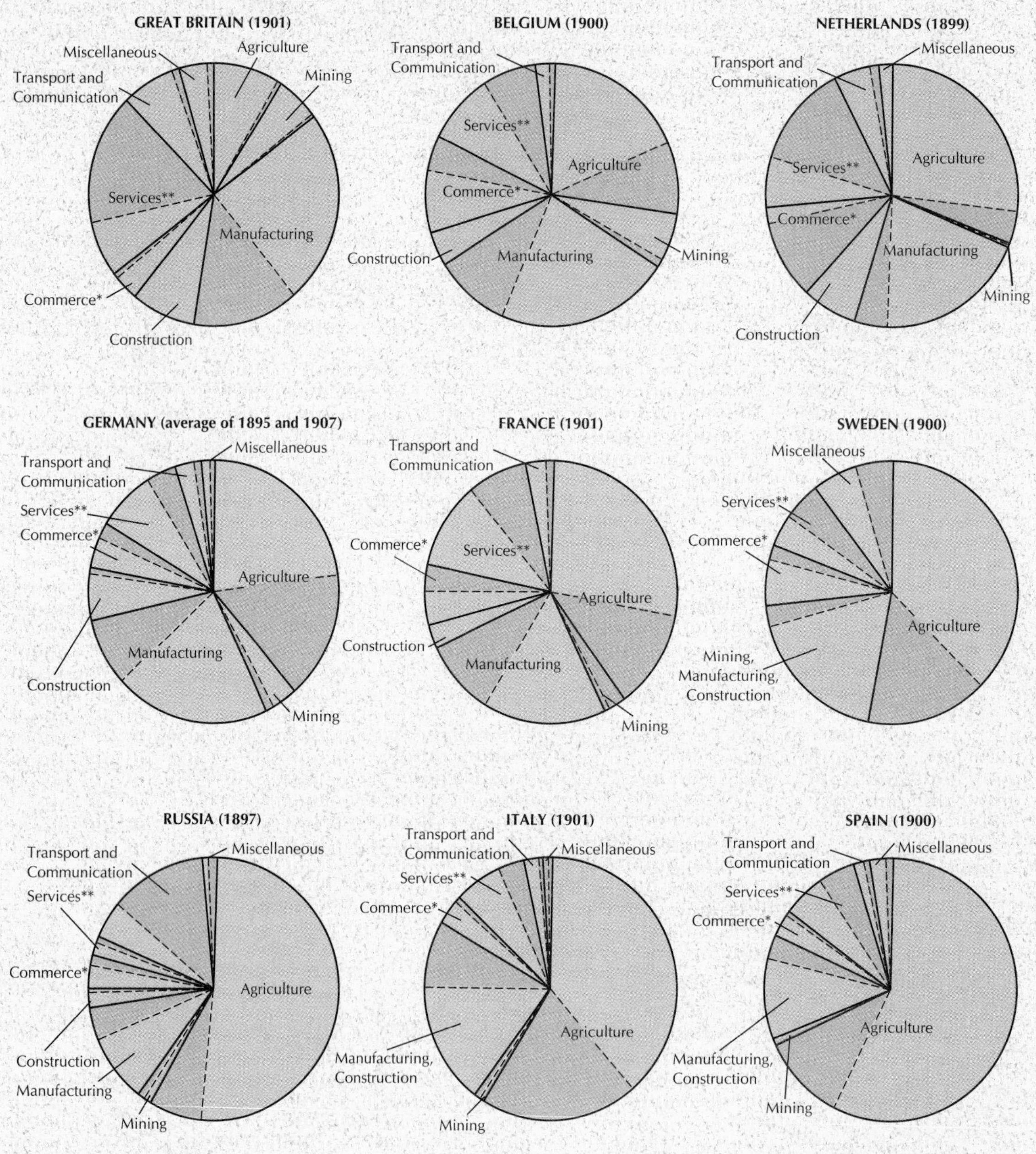

*Commerce includes banking, utilities, real estate, and insurance.
**Services includes armed forces and domestics.

(Source: Bairoch, P., *The Working Population and Its Structure*, 1968, p. 119) and Spain. Initially applied primarily to agriculture, the new tariffs were soon extended to manufactured goods as well, reversing the trend from the 1830s to the 1870s toward liberal policies favoring free trade.

But the trade barriers did not stop the general decline in prices. Strangely, the second industrial revolution occurred in one of the longest and most severe periods of deflation in European history. From the 1870s to 1896, prices, interest rates, and profits fell, with far-reaching effects. This dynamism in which one part of the economy soared while another declined was socially disruptive. Handicraft industries, which had survived side by side with mechanized manufacturing throughout Europe, were forced out of business. So were numerous smaller and less efficient industrial firms. As competition sharpened, many industrialists welcomed the support governments could give through tariffs, state spending, and colonial policies. The great boom in railroad building ended, and governments had to save socially or politically important lines deserted by bankrupt companies. Economic demands became a central theme of politics as more and more of economic life centered on great factories owned by large corporations (and closely tied to banks and government) that employed hundreds or even thousands of workers who, in turn, increasingly organized into industrial labor unions.

The Demographic Transition Europe's population continued to grow even more rapidly than before during the second industrial revolution—from 295 million in 1870 to nearly 450 million by 1914—but the age distribution or demographic profile was different from that of any previous period. Europe's population increased despite the fact that in most of Europe birthrates had begun to decline, and it did so because mortality rates were falling still more steeply. This pattern of a declining birthrate accompanied by a more rapidly falling mortality rate, which is called the *demographic transition,* continues in our own time and has become one of the marks of modernity that spread from Europe to the rest of the world.

Death rates initially declined because of lower infant mortality rates, a result of improved sanitation, better diet, and the virtual elimination of diseases such as cholera and typhus. By the turn of the century, improvements in medical care lowered mortality rates among adults as well. This brought an increase in population growth despite the declining birthrate. The lowering of mortality rates thus reflected the benefits of industrial prosperity, but the declining birthrates marked a subtler change.[1] The number of children in a family was becoming more a matter of choice, aided by the spread of contraception; and where bourgeois values took root and child labor declined, workers followed the upper classes in the trend toward later marriage, fewer births, and smaller families.

Although the issues are complicated and the statistics uncertain, the estimates of crude birthrates in about 1910 suggest the social significance of this changing pattern: Birthrates were highest in Romania, Bulgaria, Portugal, Hungary, Italy, and Spain; they were lowest in Switzerland, Belgium, and France. Parents who were confident their children would live, who wanted them to inherit property and receive some education, chose to have fewer of them. Before 1850 population growth had been higher in Western than in Central and Eastern Europe. That pattern was now reversed, and the enormous increases in populations to their east gave the French added reason to fear Germany's larger and younger population and the Germans cause to worry in turn about the Russian giant. Another outcome of population growth was a new mobility as countless numbers of people moved from countryside to town and from town to city. Mainly the young and the poor, they were responding to new ambitions as well as perennial misery. In doing so, they added to the sense of restless change within Europe. In most cities a majority of residents had been born elsewhere.

These economic, demographic, and social changes reached into the peasant hut and the urban slum. Meat and white bread became regular, although not daily, parts of the diet for most people in the industrialized countries. Commerce of-

[1] *Birthrate* is used here as the more familiar term, but *fertility rate*—the ratio of the number of children born to the number of women of childbearing age—is the more precise term preferred by demographers.

fered cheap products at fixed prices, and jobs in sales and distribution provided new opportunities to rise into the lower-middle class. Women, particularly those between the ages of 15 and 25, still constituted about one-third the work force, concentrated in poorly paying jobs. Most working-class women continued to supplement the family income by such tasks as taking in washing, sewing, or making artificial flowers or matchboxes, usually with the aid of their small children. If domestic service remained the primary occupation for young girls, those with some education could increasingly consider teaching, nursing, or clerical work. As they became better paid, male industrial workers were pleased to see their wives give up their factory jobs, and unions argued for a "family wage" to make that possible. Ordinary people thus shared in and contributed to society's growing population and productivity, its new ideas and stronger institutions, and Europe's dynamism, which was being felt around the world.

II. Europe's Knowledge of the Larger World

Knowledge was expanding, too. Scientific discoveries underlay technological innovation, and science itself was becoming ever more organized into distinctive specialities pursued by professional researchers. Their theories could be understood, however imprecisely, by the educated public; and their success in establishing laws of nature rekindled the hope that laws of social development might similarly be discovered and beneficially applied. This quest for knowledge, fame, and wealth through the study of nature and society stretched around the globe.

THE CONQUESTS OF SCIENCE

The clearest intellectual triumphs were in the natural sciences. Hailed as contributions to general philosophy, new findings were expected to affect learning in every sphere and to have practical effects on the economy and ordinary life.

Physics *Thermodynamics*, the study of the relationship between heat and mechanical energy, became the core of nineteenth-century physics. Building on theorems stated by Nicolas Sadi Carnot early in the century, it developed in many directions at once, addressing both practical problems of steam engines and fundamental properties of matter. By midcentury the combined work of scientists in many countries established that laws predicting the behavior of gases could be applied to the field of mechanics. This culminated in the mathematical formulation of the two fundamental laws of thermodynamics. One states the principle of the conservation of energy: Energy can be transformed into heat or work, and heat or work can be transformed into energy, but energy can be neither created nor destroyed. The other law declares that any closed physical system tends toward equilibrium, where heat becomes uniformly distributed, a state in which the system cannot be used to produce work.[2] In practical terms, this means that heat can be made to do work only when connected through an engine to a cooler body. Philosophically, it invites speculation about the universe as a giant machine in which the level of energy must inexorably decline.

The study of magnetism advanced in a similar way from the work of Michael Faraday. He had shown in the 1830s and 1840s that lines of magnetic force are analogous to gravity and that electricity can induce magnetism (and vice versa—the principle of the dynamo). In 1873 James Clerk Maxwell published equations that described the behavior of electricity, magnetism, and light in terms of a single, universal system. Thus gravity, magnetism, electricity, and light were all related. By the end of the century, physics had established mathematical laws of theoretical beauty and practical power extending from the universe to the atom, which was then conceived of as a miniature solar system. Thermodynamics led to the development of more efficient sources of power. The investigations of electricity led to the telegraph by midcentury and

[2] The measure or amount of energy unavailable for work is called *entropy*, a term coined by the physicist Rudolf Clausius in 1865.

▶ **Michael Faraday at work in his laboratory at the Royal Institution.**

to electric lights and motors for hundreds of uses a generation later.

Chemistry The fundamental generalizations of chemistry are contained in the periodic law and periodic table published by Dmitri Mendeleev in 1869. Compounds and elements had been clearly distinguished for only half a century, and the difference between molecules and atoms came to be generally accepted only in 1860. Yet Mendeleev's table established a marvelous symmetry, so precise that the elements could all be charted by atomic weight, with similar elements occurring at regular intervals. This regularity even allowed for the prediction of unknown elements that would, when discovered, fill the gaps in the table.

The recognition of germs and the realization that they were not spontaneously generated had more immediate results, for in the 1860s the discoveries of Louis Pasteur in France led to the techniques for destroying germs called *pasteurization*, which were of crucial importance to the wine, dairy, and silk industries. As a result of his work in immunology, Pasteur also developed a preventive vaccine against rabies. In England Joseph Lister discovered that germs could be killed by carbolic acid, and the application of that knowledge made surgery a reasonable remedy rather than a desperate gamble. A decade later Robert Koch in Germany showed that different diseases were caused by distinct microbes, discovered the microorganism responsible for tuberculosis, and opened the way to new techniques in bacteriology and in the battle against communicable diseases. Advances such as these not only improved agriculture and medicine but also stimulated the drive to make sanitation and public health into systematic sciences.

Such achievements resulted from the efforts of hundreds of scientists, freely exchanging ideas across national boundaries, working with precise methods and the logic of mathematics. Experiments admired in the 1820s seemed crude by the 1870s, and science became the province of carefully trained professionals rather than inspired amateurs. Research demanded even more systematic organization and larger and more expensive laboratories. The success of science stimulated a general expansion of education, and most of the disciplines that constitute the modern university achieved their separate identity, establishing professional organizations and scholarly journals, in the late nineteenth century. Tangible evidence of practical benefits, as well as intellectual pride, sustained the optimistic view that science progressed at an unprecedented pace for the benefit of all humankind.

SOCIAL SCIENCE AND IDEAS OF PROGRESS

Auguste Comte The philosophy of Auguste Comte (1798–1857), enormously influential from midcentury on, was characteristic of much nineteenth-century thought. Clearly rooted in the ideas of the Enlightenment, it gave greater attention to the process of historical change. Like Hegel a few years earlier, Comte sought to erect a comprehensive philosophical system that would encompass all human knowledge, and like him, Comte believed that his own era had opened the final stage of historical development. Comte was especially impressed, as were most contemporary intellectuals, by the social role of religion, the conquests of natural science, and the possibilities of human progress. For many years private secretary to Saint-Simon, Comte retained a confidence characteristic of the early socialists that society would soon be reorganized on rational principles.

He systematically elaborated his philosophy, which he called *positivism*, in 10 volumes published between 1830 and 1845; and these, with his other writings, established positivism as an international movement even before his death in 1857.[3] The key to civilization, he argued, is humanity's understanding of the world, which has developed through three historical stages. In the first, the theological stage, humankind interpreted everything in terms of gods who lived in nature. In the second, or metaphysical stage, people learned through Christianity to think in more abstract terms. In the third, or positive stage now dawning, human understanding was becoming scientific through objective and precise observation followed by generalization in the form of scientific laws. Every science, he argued, has already passed through the first two stages and into the third—astronomy first, then physics, chemistry, and biology. Now a new science, *sociology* (Comte coined the term), must crown the progression.

While thus honoring the role of established religion, Comte announced its demise, substituting a "religion of humanity" of his own invention. Some devoted followers accepted his complex scheme whole. But Comte's importance rests rather in the wider acceptance of the view that civilization progresses with the increased knowledge discovered through scientific method and that the great need now was for the scientific study of society and of humankind itself. This creed inspired and shaped much of the rapid development of the social sciences—economics, political science, anthropology, sociology, and psychology—achieved later in the century.

Marxism No theory about society and history has proved more influential than the work of Karl Marx. Marx was born in 1818 into a middle-class Rhineland Jewish family that had prospered with the lifting of civil disabilities that accompanied the revolutionary armies from France. He was an able student and received an excellent education at the leading German universities. Too radical

[3]Later, the term *positivism* came to refer not so much to Comte's specific theories as to a method: the construction of logical theories based on facts established through empirical research.

to be permitted an academic career, he turned to journalism and became editor of a famous liberal newspaper, the *Rheinische Zeitung*. But his attacks on censorship and his views on economics led the Prussian government to demand his removal, and in 1843 Marx left for Paris. There he met other exiles and leading French radicals, men to whom he would later give the dismissive and enduring label of "utopian" socialists, and established a friendship with Friedrich Engels that would become a lifetime's collaboration.

Trained in German philosophy, abreast of contemporary economics, and in touch with the currents of radical thought, Marx began in Paris the systematic development of his own ideas. He outlined his theory of history in a powerful, apocalyptic tone in the *Communist Manifesto*, written jointly with Engels, which was published just before the revolutions of 1848. Little noticed at first, it proved to be one of the great pieces of propaganda of all time, a specific program and a general call to action combined with a philosophy of history. Marx devoted the rest of his life—from 1849 to 1883, which he spent in poverty-stricken exile in London—to the painstaking elaboration of his ideas in essays, letters, and the comprehensive treatise *Das Kapital*, the first volume of which was published in 1867. Engels, who shared Marx's exile in Britain, edited the second and third volumes, which appeared in 1885 and 1894.

Marx wrote with verve on contemporary affairs—his essays on the revolutions of 1848 and Louis Napoleon's coup d'état are classics—but fundamentally he wanted, like so many thinkers of his time, to build a comprehensive philosophical system. Later in the century his followers would compare him with Darwin as the "discoverer" of the "law" of history: dialectical materialism. The dialectic came from Hegel, who had said that history evolved through the struggle between thesis and antithesis leading to a synthesis, the next stage of history. Marx kept the idea of a dialectic but rejected Hegel's idealism—the view that the dialectic works through ideas that constitute the spirit of the age—and insisted instead that any society rests fundamentally on the organization of its economy, on its mode of production.

Political systems, Marx said, grow from these material underpinnings, and in each system, the dominant social class expresses the needs, values, and interests associated with a particular mode of production. The agricultural economy of the Middle Ages required the feudal system with its particular social values and laws, upheld by the landowning aristocracy. That system produced its antithesis in the middle class. But the industrial society of capitalism, dominated by the middle class, was now producing a new antithesis embodied in the rising working class. Class conflict is the mechanism of historical progress, and the triumph of the proletariat will bring a new synthesis, a classless society. By its own inevitable laws, history would thus lead to a new era, one similar to the future envisioned by other so-

Something of the power of his personality shows through in this photograph of Karl Marx, bourgeois and scholar (with reading glass).

cialists. In the classless society, people would no longer be forced into the inequality capitalist production required. At present, the primary purpose of the state was to protect property and enforce inequality, but in the new era the state would wither away, unneeded.

Revolutions, in this analysis, mark the arrival to power of a new class. They are, however, more than mere transfers of power. A new class brought changes in law, religion, and customs, which it then maintained in its own interest. The middle class, in Marxist terms, has represented a great, progressive force. But capitalism, despite all the ideologies and social institutions designed to shore it up, will fail through its own internal contradictions.

Marx's detailed analysis of capitalism took much from the classical economists (at a time when they were beginning to be outmoded). The value of a product, he insisted somewhat obscurely, comes from the value of all the labor required to produce it—to transform raw materials into manufactured goods. The capitalist makes a profit by keeping part of the value added by the labor of others, that is, by exploiting the working class. But capitalists must compete with each other, and to do so, they are forced to lower prices, which, in turn, reduces profits. This has two effects. First, the capitalist must exploit labor more harshly, cutting wages to the minimum required for subsistence. Second, the smaller producers will fail, which will lead to increased concentrations of capital and force more and more members of the middle class into the proletariat, the class of people who have nothing but their labor to sell. Thus a shrinking capitalist class suffering from declining profits will face a growing proletariat. Capitalism therefore lays the basis for socialism by depriving all but a few of property. The contradictions will be resolved when the whole system fails.

Many of Marx's specific predictions now seem wrong. Although some of the rich have grown richer, the poor are not poorer as Marx predicted. Marx simply did not see much that is central to the modern economy—ever-expanding technology, the spread of ownership through public sale of stocks, and mass consumption. He did not anticipate the social effects of literacy, popular democracy, and mass communication. Marxist psychology is inadequate, with little acknowledgment of the loyalties and the irrationality so important in human personality. He sought to combine in one system Hegel's most difficult ideas, the economic theories of liberalism, the "scientific" method of positivism, and the moral vision of socialism—a combination awkward at best. Such critical terms as *class* and *state* remained ambiguous, and the concept of class struggle, applied elastically to a single event and to centuries of history, lost its analytic force. The goal of history, according to Karl Marx, is the classless society; yet he sketched that condition only vaguely and left unanswered fundamental questions about it and about the means of obtaining it.

The Appeal of Marxism Despite such weaknesses, and the theory's every flaw has been widely broadcast, Marxism has deeply affected all modern thought, shaped the policies of all sorts of governments, and provided a core for some of the most powerful political movements of the last hundred years. Such impact requires explanation, and perhaps four points can capture something of the answer.

First, Marxism not only sees society as a whole and explains historical change but demands systematic and detailed analyses of the interrelationship of social values, institutions, politics, and economic conditions. It also suggests methods for conducting such analyses. These qualities and the impressive body of important Marxist studies that have resulted account for its continuing importance in all the social sciences.

Second, Marxism accepts and indeed hails industrialization as inevitable and beneficial even while accepting most criticism of industrial society. Many reformers dreamed of green gardens and simpler days; but Marx believed that the machine can free human beings from brute labor and that it can, through greater productivity, provide well-being for all. Industrialization could be made to provide solutions to the very problems it created. Thus Marxism has had special appeal for societies eager to modernize.

Third, the theory is rich in moral judgments without having to defend any ethical system. Although social values are considered relative, and those of his opponents are denounced as hypocritical, Marx's own rage at injustice rings out in a compelling call to generous sentiments that rejects sentimentality.

Finally, Marxism not only claims the prestige of science but offers the security of determinism. Knowing where destiny leads, Marxists can accept the uneven flow of change, confident that any defeats are temporary. Opponents are to be recognized and fought less for what they say or do than for what they represent—for their "objective" role in the structure of capitalism. Their concessions do not alter their destiny, and the Marxist is free to adopt whatever tactics will further the inevitable movement of history toward the victory of the proletariat. Just as Marx believed that small (quantitative) changes may lead to sudden qualitative ones, so Marxists can favor short-term reforms as well as revolution. The variety inherent in Marx's system has been a source of bitter division as well as strength among socialists, but it has helped keep Marxism more vigorous and coherent than any other of the grand theories spawned in the nineteenth century.

Charles Darwin and Darwinism A more concrete and more shocking theory of human progress emerged from Charles Darwin's *On the Origin of Species*, a milestone in the history of science published in 1859.[4] With sober caution, Darwin had worked much as Comte said a scientist should. Born into a well-known family of clergy and doctors with ties to many of England's leading intellectuals, Darwin had difficulty in finding a suitable career. But his respect for facts led him to collect evidence about natural history from every available source—his own observations from travel in the South Seas, the work of others, the lore of farmers. He first formulated his concept of natural selection in 1838, but not until Alfred R. Wallace independently developed a very similar theory could Darwin be persuaded to publish his findings. Although Darwin's presentation was the more fully and carefully developed, the parallel theories of the two men suggest how much both owed to ideas already current.

▶ **With self-conscious art, the photographer of an elderly Charles Darwin suggested some timeless mystery.**

Biologists had shown the relationship between biological form and function in impressive detail; geologists had begun to analyze the earth in terms of natural forces, without recourse to sudden cataclysms or divine intervention; classical economists, especially Malthus, had stressed the importance of the cruel conflict for food, which Darwin made the essential key to natural selection.

Darwin established that the variety of species is potentially infinite—rejecting the Classical and Christian ideas of immutable forms in nature—and argued that there is an almost constant modification of species, each tested in the universal struggle for existence. He not only presented detailed evidence for evolution but described its mechanism: Only those well adapted to their environment survived to reproduce, as their progeny would. Over millions of years, through the

[4]The full original title of Darwin's work suggests its broad and provocative implications: *On the Origin of Species by Natural Selection, or the Preservation of Favoured Races in the Struggle for Life.* The first edition sold out on the day of publication.

process of natural selection, more complex or "higher" forms of life emerged, each expanding as the environment permitted and competition for food and survival dictated.

This scientific theory, expressed with caution and supported by massive evidence, almost instantly became the center of controversies that raged throughout Europe for a generation. Evolution, mutable species, survival determined by brute conflict rather than divine will—each of these challenged established assumptions in science and theology. Nor did Darwin hide his belief that the same laws apply to the development of human beings and beasts. This seemed to many a scandalous disregard of divine providence and Christian teaching. Nowadays, most theologians and scientists generally agree that there is no necessary conflict between the concept of evolving species and Christian doctrine, but such tolerance required a distinction between the study of natural laws and religious tradition that few in the nineteenth century were willing to make.

Those eager to apply science to society quickly extended these principles to more current concerns, a tendency that came to be called *social Darwinism.* Few of the claims of social Darwinism were logically necessary extensions of Darwin's views; but reference to his grand theories added universal meaning, scientific prestige, and a new vocabulary to contemporary debate. Social Darwinists tended to ignore the unimaginably long time span in which Darwinian theory operated and to extend the formal concept of species by loose analogy to groups, classes, nations, or civilizations. An invitingly tough-minded way to argue, social Darwinism was used to support reform (better education and social welfare constitute a higher stage of evolution, and this improved environment will produce a superior species). Thomas Huxley, the greatest intellectual propagandist for Darwin's theories, battled clergymen who rejected human evolution as contrary to the Bible, but his conception of social Darwinism held it to be consonant with the teachings of Indian philosophy, Buddhism, ancient Greece, and Christianity (*see box*, p. 817). But Darwinism was commonly used to justify competition in the marketplace or between nations (as the mechanism of evolution in which the fittest triumph). It could also be cited to explain the domination of men over women or Europeans over other races as the natural result of evolution. At its most extreme, social Darwinism presented the law of the jungle as realistic, scientific, and beneficial. Usually not so unmodulated, the assumptions of social Darwinism nevertheless infiltrated many aspects of late nineteenth-century social thought. Combined with (often fallacious) theories of genetics, they reappeared in ideas of genetic determinism that took many forms. These included loose talk about national characteristics and theories that ranked races as superior or inferior, the codification of traditional views defining innate differences in men and women, elaborate systems for identifying criminal types by physiology, a science of eugenics that looked for ways to discourage the unfit from breeding, and the emergence of inherited characteristics as a literary theme in novels and drama.

Herbert Spencer One of the grandest statements of the laws of progress was the *Synthetic Philosophy* of Herbert Spencer, published in a series of studies that first appeared in 1860 and continued to 1896. Spencer's ideas were closely tied to those of Comte and Darwin, and his contemporaries ranked him among the major philosophers of all time. Spencer's central principle, which made progress "not an accident, but a necessity," was the evolution of all things from simplicity to complexity, from homogeneity to diversity. With heavy erudition, he traced this process in physics and biology, sociology and psychology, economics and ethics. Such comprehensiveness was part of his appeal, and he applied his theses to physical matter, to human understanding, and to social institutions. He was admired for his claim to be hardheaded and practical; but while he refused to worry about the metaphysical abstractions of traditional philosophy, he maintained the assumptions of a narrow and rigid liberalism.

Spencer argued that the marketplace is the true test of the fittest, and that it must be uninhibited by state intervention even in behalf of welfare or public education. When he died in 1903, much of his work was already outmoded. Strict laissez-faire had been abandoned even by most liberals, his sort of rationalism had come under heavy attack, and the disciplines of the so-

Huxley's Social Darwinism

"Evolution and Ethics," a much reprinted lecture that T. H. Huxley gave at Oxford in 1893, was perhaps the most famous statement of what can be called the gentle interpretation of the social implication of Darwin's theories.

"Man, the animal, in fact, has worked his way to the headship of the sentient world, and has become the superb animal which he is, in virtue of his success in the struggle for existence. The conditions having been of a certain order, man's organization has adjusted itself to them better than that of his competitors in the cosmic strife. In the case of mankind, the self-assertion, the unscrupulous seizing upon all that can be grasped, the tenacious holding of all that can be kept, which constitute the essence of the struggle for existence, have answered. For his successful progress, throughout the savage state, man has been largely indebted to those qualities which he shares with the ape and the tiger; his exceptional physical organization; his cunning, his sociability, his curiosity, and his imitativeness; his ruthless and ferocious destructiveness when his anger is roused by opposition.

"But, in proportion as men have passed from anarchy to social organization, and in proportion as civilization has grown in worth, these deeply ingrained serviceable qualities have become defects.... In fact, civilized man brands all these ape and tiger promptings with the name of sins, he punishes many of the acts which flow from them as crimes; and, in extreme cases, he does his best to put an end to the survival of the fittest of former days by axe and rope.

"... The history of civilization details the steps by which men have succeeded in building up an artificial world within the cosmos. Fragile reed as he may be, man, as Pascal says, is a thinking reed: there lies within him a fund of energy operating intelligently and so far akin to that which pervades the universe, that it is competent to influence and modify the cosmic process.

"... Moreover, the cosmic nature born with us and, to a large extent, necessary for our maintenance, is the outcome of millions of years of severe training, and it would be folly to imagine that a few centuries will suffice to subdue its masterfulness to purely ethical ends. Ethical nature may count upon having to reckon with a tenacious and powerful enemy as long as the world lasts. But, on the other hand, I see no limit to the extent to which intelligence and will, guided by sound principles of investigation, and organized in common effort, may modify the conditions of existence, for a period longer than that now covered by history. And much may be done to change the nature of man himself."

From Thomas H. Huxley, *Evolution and Ethics and Other Essays*, New York: D. Appleton and Company, 1916.

cial sciences had moved toward subtler theories. His confidence that universal laws of development enshrined the values of middle-class English Protestants would soon seem quaint.

The Study of Other Societies Interest in other societies was a significant current in European thought, always engaged with its Classical roots and shaped by centuries of conflict with Islam. Curiosity about other ways of life had increased in the age of exploration, stimulated by the reports of missionaries and the experience of trade, conquest, and rule. Subsequently, enlightenment thinkers had made the systematic observation of other societies a way to study the effects of diverse environments, customs, and political forms. Admiration for the Chinese or Persians was a device for criticizing European societies while searching for universal patterns in human behavior. This effort to establish a science of society continued in the nineteenth century. An important part of liberal economic theory and utilitarianism, the effort expanded with the experience of industrial change, to be furthered by ideas of historical evolution and increased contact with other lands.

Much as Darwinian ideas were influenced by economic theory and discoveries in geology, so anthropology, which now became a distinctive field of study, bore the imprint of the new work in sociology and history and of increased contact with the Americas and Asia. Many of the great scholars of ancient law and of linguistics developed their methods through the study of Indian civilization. And many of the leading advocates of reform in England formed their views from the experience of governing in India. Confident of their own place on the evolutionary scale, Europeans tended to see other societies as recapitulating their own historic past, a view that encouraged both affectionate interest and disdain for cultures stuck in a distant past. At the same time, Europeans learned from non-European civilizations. That was obviously true of the social sciences, but it occurred in many other fields as well. Asian and later African art influenced the arts in Europe, and European medical practice adopted herbs and drugs used elsewhere. On the whole, however, these growing global connections strengthened the sense that Europe's was a distinctive civilization and the one that led the world.

▸ Increased familiarity with Chinese and Japanese art strongly influenced Western artists interested in new styles, including the impressionists or their friend, James McNeill Whistler, who painted this portrait of *The Princess of the Land of Porcelain* in 1864.

THE EUROPEAN PRESENCE AROUND THE GLOBE

From the French Revolution to the last third of the nineteenth century, European influence on other continents was not primarily a matter of conquest but came rather from cultural, economic, and political connections. The energy of Europe and its example nevertheless spilled across the world in multiple ways: humanitarian opposition to slavery, denunciations of the treatment of Native Americans, Christian missions, political advice, trade, exploitation, and military conflict. Whatever the intent or the mixture of motives, the result was disruptive; for the European presence brought with it irrepressible power.

The Apparent Decline of Colonial Empires Most liberals truly believed that the age of empire, which they associated with an outmoded mercantilism, had passed; and the example of Latin America seemed to prove the point. In the 20 years from 1804 to 1824, France lost control of Haiti, Portugal of Brazil, and Spain of all the rest of Latin America save Cuba and Puerto Rico. Deeply affected by the examples of the French and American revolutions, the independence movements of Latin America were in turn models of the kind of nationalism and state making that would soon sweep Europe. Although subsequent conflicts among the new states of Latin America created plenty of opportunities for British and French involvement, empire was not at issue. Garibaldi had been hailed as the hero of two worlds when he returned to Italy from Latin America in 1848, because it was believed he fought on both continents for the same principles of freedom and national independence. Creoles, the descendants of Europeans who now ruled Latin America, maintained and strengthened their cultural ties to Spain and France. They followed the latest continental trends in music and literature, fashion and science; shared an intellectual life close to Europe's (positivism was especially strong in Latin America); adapted constitutions modeled on that of the United States; and purchased the goods brought by English merchants.

Independence from European rule did not eliminate European influence or the reasons for opposing it. Local efforts to throw off foreign domination could also increase the European presence, which happened as the power of the Ottoman Empire declined. Intervention from Britain and France had ensured the independence of Greece; and they fought the Crimean War, which increased their influence in the region, to restrict Russia's claims against the Ottoman Empire. In Egypt the Ottoman governor in the first half of the century, Mohammed Ali, set out on an independent course that included not only alliance with France but the adoption of institutions like those of the Napoleonic state. That led Egypt to war with Turkey (1832–1833, 1839–1841) and conquest of the Sudan, but it also established French as the language of administration in Egypt and opened the country to other European influences. As early as 1833, Saint-Simonian engineers arrived with plans for building a Suez Canal, a project that eventually led to European dominance in Egypt. During the same period, Russian pressure on Afghanistan and Persia brought British counterpressure. The pattern was significant. To resist one European state, local leaders turned to another European state for help. Demands for special concessions and offers of military alliances would result in the sending of military and political advisers. The process begun with efforts to strengthen Egyptian autonomy had increased European interests there.

▸ After elaborate ceremonies, the opening of the Suez Canal in 1869 was marked by a parade of ships, including new steamships and a sailboat with the lateen sail characteristic of the Mediterranean. Both the empress Eugénie of France and the emperor Franz-Josepf of Austria attended the ceremonies for which the Khedive of Egypt commissioned Verdi to write an opera, *Aida*, first performed two years later.

Explorers and Missionaries Exploration could have practical and scientific importance (as in the continued search for a northwest passage across northern Canada, which incidentally benefited whaling) but was no longer expected to reveal previously unknown civilizations. Europeans, and the European presence was usually not accompanied by claims of sovereignty. David Livingston made his way across central Africa in the 1850s, opposing the slave trade while stimulating interest in that vast continent. Campaigns against the slave trade led to the French creation of Libreville in the Congo in 1847 as a haven for freed slaves and to British intervention in parts of East Africa. The British and French governments followed their missionaries in competing for influence in Madagascar, and the Ethiopian emperor turned to the English for support against his local enemies. The possibility of more radical changes was beginning to be noticed. Liberia, where the first colonists of American blacks arrived in 1822, became an independent state in 1847.

Christian missionaries were important in Asia, too, where they had been active for centuries; but traders and European governments began to show greater interest in protecting their nationals. The English reformers who objected to slavery also opposed the opium trade between India and China, long a source of profit for English merchants. Yet Chinese efforts to restrict that trade resulted in a conflict with Britain that was settled by the cession of Hong Kong (1841) and the granting of special rights to foreigners. The impact of missionaries contributed to the Taiping Rebellion (1850–1864), in which a Chinese-led millenarian movement incorporating elements of Christian religion and social discontent produced revolts that threatened the Chinese empire. Battling for survival, the Chinese government was forced to grant new concessions to Britain, the United States, France, and Russia for trade, the protection of missionaries, and extraterritorial rights. In 1860 British and French forces occupied Peking and burned the summer palace in retaliation for the seizure of their envoys, and Russia took Vladivostock—a step recognized by China's Department of Foreign Affairs, a ministry not needed before.

Concern to protect India, which stirred British interest in Afghanistan, also led to wars in Burma and the opening of Siam to European trade in 1855. The persecution of Christians in Cochin China led to hostilities against French and Spanish forces, which occupied Saigon in 1858, the beginning of a relationship that led in 20 years to the transformation of the eastern provinces of Cochin China into French Indochina. A revolt in Java against the Dutch (1825–1830) resulted in their tightening their rule over the entire Dutch East Indies. The mistreatment of American castaways in Japan prompted the arrival of an American fleet with demands that went beyond that issue to include trade. The result was a treaty with the United States signed in 1854 and quickly followed by similar ones between Japan and the major European nations, ending Japan's centuries-old policy of isolation. In all these instances what began as local issues had resulted in the exercise of European military and political power. The privileges Europeans demanded usually did not include outright control, but the increased European presence, upsetting to local institutions and customs, accelerated the process that led to greater European domination.

Direct Rule in Algeria and India Algeria, however, exemplified another kind of empire. Invaded by France's Bourbon monarchy in 1830 just prior to its fall, Algeria was slowly conquered by succeeding French regimes. Significantly, each new government found itself extending the efforts of its predecessors, expanding the area directly controlled and adopting an ever more centralized and French administration until Algeria was made part of metropolitan France after 1848.

Similarly, British engagement in India also moved toward direct rule. For much of the century, the East India Company, under charter from the British government, exercised authority through local princes. But empire building was in fact under way during the governor-generalship of Lord William Bentinck (1828–1835). Efforts to maintain order led to border skirmishes that increased the territory under British command and to campaigns against the bands of *thags* (the source of the English word *thugs*) that broadened British policing. In London reformers denounced corruption within the East India Company and demanded humanitarian measures, which had the effect of extending British interests and responsibilities. The custom of *sati* (in which a widow placed herself on her husband's funeral pyre) was banned, the production of tea and coffee encouraged, and trade opened to merchants not connected to the company. Administrative reforms were followed by the commissioning of Thomas Macaulay, historian and reformer, to design a law code. India's first railroad was built in 1853, and a school system was established the following year. This increased British involvement in Indian life, which often ran counter to traditional practices and religious beliefs, provoked resistance and then the shock of rebellion in 1857. It began with the revolt of the native troops the British employed in northern India and spread to popular risings that were eventually put down after terrible atrocities on both sides. In Britain, public opinion was outraged, against ungrateful Indians but also at the brutality of their own officials. The upshot was more reforms of British administration, further annexations of Indian territories to guarantee more acceptable politics, and the promotion of the governor-general to viceroy. The British crown had established direct sovereignty over India.

The Impact of Money and Migration These worldwide arrangements and interventions stemmed from more than the superiority of European arms and technology. European insistence on the universal applicability of European laws and standards of conduct accompanied the thousands of resolute missionaries and avid traders who poured across the globe. In the Middle East, Africa, and Asia local rulers recognized that self-protection and their own ambitions required that they try to deal with those traders, seek alliances with these powerful foreign nations, and adopt some of their techniques and institutions. All that required money, which Europeans were ready to lend. As debts mounted, payments often fell into arrears, which became a justification for more forceful European intervention. Efforts at modernization in Egypt, which resulted in the completion of a railway from Alexandria to Cairo and concession of the right to construct the Suez Canal to Ferdinand de Lesseps, also included Egypt's first foreign loan in 1854. A serious burden by 1863, the debt grew to be 30 times larger in the following decade. The Bey of Tunis was so badly in debt by 1869 that he accepted international (meaning European) control of Tunisian finances. And Mexico's suspension of debt payments in 1861 had led to the joint intervention by Britain, Spain, and France which blossomed into Louis Napoleon's disastrous efforts to establish a lasting influence there. He arranged to have Archduke Maximilian of Austria made Mexican emperor, but the new regime was soon toppled and Maximilian executed in 1867. It was not so much official plans that injected the promising and threatening influence of Europe as burgeoning commerce and capital, the power of technology and arms, and the ambitions of emissaries, army officers, and merchants.

Migration Ordinary people also carried European languages and cultures around the world in

EMIGRATION FROM EUROPE

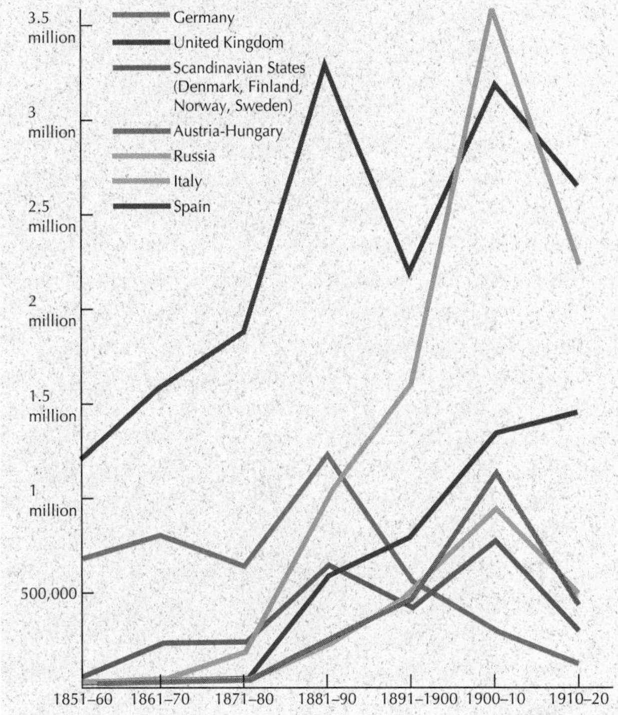

(Source: Mitchell, B. R., *Europe Historical Statistics, 1750–1970*, p. 135. Copyright © 1970 by Columbia University Press. Reprinted with permission of the publisher.)

the greatest voluntary movement of peoples in human history. This wave of migration continued a century-old trend but on an unprecedented scale. The growth of population, an established pattern of migration from rural areas to cities, unemployment in Europe and opportunities in the New World, larger boats and cheaper fares, and visions of a better life all pushed Europe's lower classes to crowd into the steerage of ship after ship.

Between 1875 and 1914 some 26 million Europeans emigrated overseas, more than half of them to the United States, with Latin America the next most common destination. More people left the United Kingdom than any other country, going to Australia, Canada, and South Africa as well as to the United States; in proportion to population the greatest exodus was from Ireland. Before 1890 the United Kingdom, the Scandinavian countries, and Germany sent migrants in the

▸ **C.J. Staniland's picture of *The Emigrant Ship* shows English men (mainly young) and some women crowding on board ship to start a new life overseas. By this time, toward the end of the century when emigration from Europe was at its height, the ships were larger and the voyage shorter and less dangerous than it had been a generation earlier.**

highest proportion to their population. After 1890 the leaders were the United Kingdom, Italy, Spain, and Portugal. But every nation except France (Europe's major receiver of immigrants) contributed significant numbers to the movement. Perhaps a third of those who left their native land to go overseas eventually returned home, where they added to the number of Europeans concretely informed of the larger world.

III. Modern Imperialism

THE MEANINGS OF IMPERIALISM

Throughout European history, the great example of empire was ancient Rome, which was evoked by the tsars of Russia, the Habsburg monarchs, and both Napoleons when they called themselves *emperors*. In the late nineteenth century, however, imperialism came to mean European rule overseas, and nowadays the term commonly includes economic and cultural domination that may or may not involve direct political control. Thus current studies of imperialism include the spread of a world market, from the trade in luxuries and slaves of the seventeenth century to the multinational corporations of today.

European imperialism, understood in this sense, increased enormously throughout the nineteenth century but especially from the 1860s on. Trade expanded both in value and in geographical range. Wherever commerce took them, Europeans built docks and warehouses, established companies, and made new investments. Whether directed from Europe, by European settlers, or by local merchants, these commercial enterprises adopted European techniques of management, accounting, and technology. Businesses expanded by attracting European capital, and much of the profit they generated was returned to European banks and investors. Thus tied to foreign markets, such enterprises, in turn, transformed local economies through their labor policies and their purchases of local goods and services. This complex process was further stimulated by improved communication. Steamships required better ports, more reliable and expensive provisions, and larger cargoes. Telegraph lines connected India to Europe in 1865, and a cable ran from Vladivostok to Shanghai, Hong Kong, and Singapore by 1871. By the 1880s rail lines operated on every continent; and more were being built, all requiring European equipment, engineers, and investment. By the turn of the century the automobile began to generate a demand not only for highways and bridges but also for a steady flow of petroleum, the basis for new international corporations.

In the same period universities on the European model were established from Constantinople to India; and students from China, Japan, India, and the Middle East became familiar figures in European and American centers of learning. All these developments had fundamental social and political implications for daily life and for traditional elites in Latin America, Asia, and Africa. It is the cumulative effect of this process—which increases Western wealth and prestige while disrupting and transforming non-Western societies and which corrodes non-European traditions and cultures while feeding Western interests and power—that the term *imperialism* evokes today.

Bordeaux had been a major Atlantic port for centuries, but in the 1860s Eduoard Manet could still portray the harbor as a colorful clutter of fishing boats and vessels for coastal shipping.

When contemporaries spoke of imperialism then (and they spoke and wrote about it a great deal), they generally meant a European state's intervention in and continuing domination over non-European territory. This emphasis reflected a striking new reality. In the single generation preceding World War I, European states spread their political dominion over vast territories with breathtaking speed. Dramatic evidence of

By the end of the century shipping was associated with power and empire as in this painting by Frederick Scarborough, which shows lighters ready to tend to the needs of the great steamships in the habor of London, the world's greatest port.

Europe's dynamism, imperialism was justified as progress—carrying higher civilization and Christianity to backward lands—as well as national interest. Most of the newly acquired lands had few European settlers (the primary means of exploiting local wealth in the past), and most of them lay in tropical zones Europeans had heretofore found unappealing and unhealthy. This imperialism was a turning point in other ways. Not only was imperialism now central to international relations and a reason to abandon free trade, but this imperialism infected public discourse with ideas of superiority (based on ethnicity, class, or gender) and national political campaigns with a competitive nationalism.

EXPLANATIONS OF IMPERIALISM

Such rapid and far-reaching developments demand explanation, and by the turn of the century, the opponents of imperialism in particular had an explanation for the pervasive imperial fever. In 1902 J. A. Hobson, a British economist, published *Imperialism: A Study*, a critical tract that has been heavily attacked by subsequent scholars yet remains the starting point of modern analysis (*see box*, p. 825). Writing during the Boer War (discussed below), Hobson was eager to show that imperialism offered little to restless Europeans or to commerce. Emigrants, he noted, preferred to go to the Americas, and Britain's trade with the European continent and the Americas was far greater and growing faster than its trade with its colonies.

Hobson found the economic explanation of imperialism to lie in the influence of speculators and financiers, a small number of people who controlled great wealth and looked for quick profits by investing outside Europe. Such people used their social and political connections to have their government protect their investments in undeveloped lands, and they exploited the missionaries, soldiers, and patriotic dreamers who glorified empire. Imperialism thus stemmed from the manipulation of public opinion in the interest of certain capitalists.

Hobson's analysis inspired the still more influential theory of V. I. Lenin. The leader of Russia's Marxist revolutionaries, Lenin provided a Marxist interpretation of a subject on which Marx had written little. In *Imperialism: The Last Stage of Capitalism* (1916), Lenin agreed that the stimulus behind empire building was basically economic and that the essence of colonialism was exploitation. Imperialist ventures, Lenin argued, grew not just from the policies of a few but from the very dynamics of capitalism itself. Competition both lowered profits and resulted in monopolies, forcing surplus capital to seek investments overseas. The alternative, to enlarge the domestic market by raising wages, would be uncompetitive and thus further reduce profit. Imperialism was therefore the last "stage" of capitalism, the product of its internal contradictions. Lenin would add during World War I that imperial rivalries, involving whole nations, led to wars that further hastened the end of capitalism. *Imperialist* became an epithet for a system considered decadent as well as immoral.

Current Views Although influenced by these views, most historians have remained uncomfortable with them. Economic explanations contribute little to an understanding of the actual process of imperial conquest, in which capitalists were often reluctant participants. They do not explain why imperialists called for political control beyond treaty rights or for the swift spread of European power into areas that offered small financial return; indeed, European investment and trade remained much greater with developed noncolonial countries than with colonies. Nor do economic arguments tell us much about the role of the popular press, explorers, earnest missionaries, and ambitious soldiers in pressing hesitant politicians to imperial conquest.

Many factors help explain the sudden increase in the pace and importance of European imperialism in the late nineteenth century, although all analysts today would agree that economic interests, at least in the long run, were certainly important. Even early in the century the European economy had been closely tied to imports of raw materials such as cotton, tea, and timber, and policies that guaranteed those supplies had been welcomed. A general increase in trade and the growing demand for rubber, oil, and rare metals spurred the search for natural resources. Stiffening competition in international commerce and

The Interpretation of Imperialism

Debate on the interpretation of imperialism has not ceased since the publication of J. A. Hobson's* Imperialism: A Study *in 1902. The work went through many editions and remains worth reading today. Hobson was a highly respected British economist and social scientist, and his study is filled with statistics and careful argument. His conclusions capture some of the essence, and polemic tone, of the case he made.

"If Imperialism may no longer be regarded as a blind inevitable destiny, is it certain that imperial expansion as a deliberately chosen line of public policy can be stopped?

"We have seen that it is motivated, not by the interests of the nation as a whole, but by those of certain classes, who impose the policy upon the nation for their own advantage. . . . The essentially illicit nature of this use of the public resources of the nation to safeguard and improve private investments should be clearly recognized.

". . . Analysis of Imperialism, with its natural supports, militarism, oligarchy, bureaucracy, protection, concentration of capital and violent trade fluctuations, has marked it out as the supreme danger of modern national States. The power of the imperialist forces within the nation to use the national resources for their private gain, by operating the instrument of the State, can only be overthrown by the establishment of a genuine democracy. . . ."

Joseph A. Schumpeter, who was born in Austria, achieved international fame with the publication of* The Theory of Economic Development *in 1912, when he was 29 years old. The famous essay titled "The Sociology of Imperialism," written a few years later, was an extension of his interest in economic growth under capitalism and was in part a rebuttal of economic explanations of imperialism, particularly those of Hobson and of Marxists from Lenin on. Imperialism, Schumpeter argued, was not a natural outgrowth of capitalism but rather a leftover from the precapitalist era centered in the policies of the aristocracy.

"Here we find that we have penetrated to the historical as well as the sociological sources of modern imperialism. It does not *coincide* with nationalism and militarism, though it *fuses* with them by supporting them as it is supported by them. It too is—not only historically, but also sociologically—a heritage of the autocratic state, of its structural elements, organizational forms, interest alignments, and human attitudes, the outcome of precapitalist forces which the autocratic state has reorganized, in part by the methods of early capitalism. It would never have evolved by the 'inner logic' of capitalism itself. This is true even of mere export monopolism. It too has its sources in absolutist policy and the action habits of an essentially precapitalist environment. . . . But export monopolism, to go a step further, is not yet imperialism. And even if it had been able to arise without protective tariffs, it would never have developed into imperialism in the hands of an unwarlike bourgeoisie. If this did happen, it was only because the heritage included the war machine, together with its socio-psychological aura and aggressive bent, but because a class oriented toward war maintained itself in a ruling position. This class clung to its domestic interest in war, and the pro-military interests among the bourgeoisie were able to ally themselves with it. This alliance kept alive war instincts and ideas of overlordship, male supremacy, and triumphant glory—ideas that would have otherwise long since died. It led to social conditions that, while they ultimately stem from the conditions of production, cannot be explained from capitalist production methods alone. And it often impresses its mark on present-day politics, threatening Europe with the constant danger of war.

"This diagnosis also bears the prognosis of imperialism. The precapitalist elements in our social life may still have great vitality; special circumstances in national life may revive them from time to time; but in the end the climate of the modern world must destroy them."

(Continued)

Wolfgang Mommsen, a distinguished member of a family of famous historians, for years served as director of the German Historical Institute in London and as professor of history at the University of Düsseldorf. His **Theories of Imperialism** *began as a series of lectures given at the University of Amsterdam in 1970, and it reflects the complexity and ambiguities of current interpretations.*

"Despite the changes in our attitude towards the imperialist age now that the classic type of formal imperialism has become a thing of the past, a remarkable degree of continuity can be seen in both bourgeois and Marxist studies of the subject. The broad lines of a possible interpretation of imperialism were already laid down by such classic theorists as Hobson, Hilferding, Schumpeter and Lenin; later writers have endeavoured, on the basis of these studies, to produce more differentiated models taking into account recent research and developments in the world situation. An important new light is cast by recent British research, which on the one hand has developed the idea of 'informal imperialism' and thus widened the scope of the enquiry in general, and on the other has drawn attention to the independent role of the 'periphery,' especially the indigenous ruling classes, which have often had much to do with the character, timing and direction of imperial expansion.

"It must be said that the older theories of imperialism have lost much of their usefulness because they are too Eurocentric and also tend to reduce the whole phenomenon to a single cause. A modern theory which gives due weight to the periphery, while recognizing that its so-called crises were themselves the result of informal European penetration, is better able to comprehend the phenomenon of third-world underdevelopment without necessarily subscribing to the tautologies of neo-Marxist theory. The 'objectivist' argument that imperialist processes were generally stimulated by the marginal groups in European society, in conjunction with 'men on the spot,' gives sufficient reason to review the 'endogenous type of theory' according to which imperialism is a necessary outcome of the policies or economic structures of the industrial states. Finally, it seems as though the long discredited political theories of imperialism are to some extent enjoying a 'comeback,' chiefly in combination with sociological and socio-economic explanations. The 'official mind' is certainly not nowadays conceived as brashly imperialist, as was formerly the case. The picture is rather one of statesmen who were powerless to control the self-propelled course of imperial expansion, which began with more or less informal methods and then called for the use of formal power in one case after another, often against the wishes of the politicians concerned.

"Classic economic theories of imperialism, whether Marxist or bourgeois, have lost much of their attraction. . . . In the present state of research into the subject it appears to us that a new form of theory is required which would not simply repeat the traditional formulae. . . . On the other hand, a new theory should not, as is frequent in the Western world, content itself with regarding imperialism as a thing of the past: it must take account of the after-effects of imperialism in the world as we know it, not least the disturbing fact that the gap between rich and poor nations is growing steadily wider. Many may even develop nostalgia for the days of formal colonial rule, when the European powers were, at least in principle, responsible for developments at the periphery, whereas today they are formally relieved of the burden. But the question remains of how far these developments are rooted in the era of formal imperialism, and whether the forms of economic, cultural and political dependence which have survived the end of colonialism are not partly to blame for the 'development of underdevelopment' in many parts of the third world. Any modern theory of imperialism must face the question of how far the international capitalist system contains latent or manifest imperialist tendencies, or even whether it *is* manifestly imperialist. . . ."

From J. A. Hobson, *Imperialism: A Study*, London: George Allen & Unwin, Ltd., 1961 (sixth impression of the third revised edition of 1938, first published in 1902). Excerpts from pp. 356, 358, 360; From *Two Essays by Joseph Schumpeter: Social Classes, Imperialism,* Heinz Norden (tr.), New York: Meridian Books, 1951, pp. 97–98; Wolfgang J. Mommsen, *Theories of Imperialism,* P. S. Falla (tr.), Chicago: The University of Chicago Press, 1980.

rising tariffs taught businessmen to seek the backing of their governments. By the late nineteenth century a society familiar with self-made men was readier to believe that new lands offered the chance to make a quick fortune. Technology, too, played a part. Not only was regular trade with distant places made easier, but dynamite lessened the difficulty of building roads, while modern medicine reduced the dangers of the tropics. Coaling stations that enabled navies to remain far from home and telegraph posts acquired strategic as well as commercial importance, a fact that argued for military and political protection.

IMPERIALISM'S DOMESTIC CONNECTIONS

The Organization of Society Beyond such rational calculations, imperialism flourished because of values Europeans held and the institutions of their own society. There had been an enormous increase throughout Europe in religious missions. Many of the hundreds of new religious orders and missionary societies initially created in response to the social problems of industrialization also sent increasing numbers overseas to convert the heathen. For churches often at odds with the culture of their day and in conflict with the state, here was a dramatic outlet and a welcome reassurance of their importance in modern life. British, Swiss, and German missionaries were competing for souls on the Nigerian coast well before the area had been targeted by any foreign office.

Imperial activities had particular importance for members of the aristocracy, especially in Britain and France. The younger sons of aristocratic families in Britain had a long tradition of government and military service, and now their best chances for the experience of governing and of military command were in the empire. In France, where the Republic turned anticlerical after 1875, Catholic and monarchist nobles who were largely excluded from public positions at home could find them in the colonies. Aristocrats, after all, expected to feel distant from the people they ruled, and the language of subordination was applicable to both European and colonial societies. Descriptions of ignorant, lazy, uncooperative natives were much like those used by the upper classes to complain about workers and peasants at home. While conservatives were often tempted to use empire to argue for the necessity of inequality, labor leaders and radicals were equally quick to note the parallels, to compare the treatment of strikers and radicals to the brutality of imperial armies, and to protest that the poor workers and peasants (in Wales, Scotland, southern Italy, or southern Germany) were treated like colonial subjects.

State Policy and Public Opinion Even the campaigns for reform at home proved remarkably relevant to imperial rule. Governments were increasingly engaged in collecting statistics, providing for public health, building schools, and establishing welfare programs, and they found it natural to undertake similar measures in their colonies. Officials with colonial experience proved particularly useful back home. Organizing hospitals in the tropics taught doctors and nurses about health care in the slums; and the courts, police, and prisons being built across Europe and in the United States (which had pioneered in creating them to rehabilitate criminals) were equally useful for maintaining order in the colonies. Even the work colonies and model farms sponsored by religious communities and utopian socialists had coercive imperial imitations. Britain's best-known organization in the campaign for public education was called the British and Foreign Schools Society. Indeed the arguments for such measures, from schooling to railroads, were similar at home and abroad: Overcoming isolation and ignorance in the colonies was much like making good citizens in the nation. In both cases governments saw themselves combating local dialects, provincial outlooks, corruption, and lack of civic spirit.

The glorification of empire, which appealed effectively to nationalism, contained other ideological messages as well. Descriptions of encounters with native peoples were rich in images of Europeans mistaken for gods, of a superiority in knowledge and technology that made dominance inevitable and usually beneficial, and they were often written in gendered language that equated European qualities with masculine virtues (rationality, decisiveness, dominance) and those

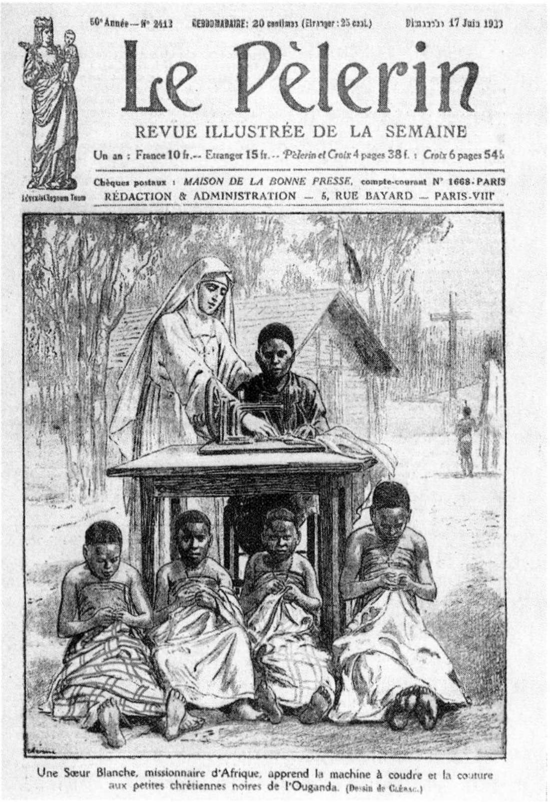

▸ **This illustrated French Catholic weekly presented the popular European view of imperial influence: a saintly (and beautiful) member of the White Sisters teaches a well-behaved group of newly converted Ugandan girls to use a sewing machine. Faith, order, civilization, and technology went together. At home, too, Catholic orders emphasized the importance of teaching poor girls a useful trade.**

of other societies with feminine ones (intuitive sensitivity, passivity, subordination). Mass-circulation newspapers gloried in imperialism, writing of adventure and wealth and of Christianity and progress in the virile language of force.

To the people of the late nineteenth century, exploration and conquest were high and noble adventure. Geographical societies became prominent in every European country, proudly acclaiming yet another association of new knowledge with increased power. Press reports made popular heroes of daring men like Henry M. Stanley, who followed the rivers of South Africa and penetrated the interior of the Congo, and Pierre de Brazza, who traveled up the Congo River, overcoming hardship and danger after dismantling a steamship so it could be carried around the rapids. Exploration seemed, in itself, an expression of progress, the brave adventurer the personification of individual initiative. If the explorer also gained wealth, that completed the parable. The missionaries who risked their lives to build a chapel in the jungle and convert the heathen made for appealing stories of humane concern and heroic sacrifice, while social Darwinists could hardheadedly note the inevitable conflict of race with race and the resultant spread of civilization, by which they meant, of course, their own.

Where class tensions were high and domestic conflict serious, colonial expansion offered all citizens a share in national glory and gain. Rudyard Kipling's poems of imperial derring-do in exotic lands hail the simple cockney soldier; whatever his lot at home, he was a ruler abroad. Thus in politics, imperialism, like nationalism, cut across social divisions. It was an important part, especially in Great Britain and Germany, of the political resurgence of the right, allowing conservative groups strong in the army, the Church, and the aristocracy to ally themselves with commercial interests in a program of popular appeal. Employment as well as glory was promised as the fruit of a policy of strength. Significantly, imperialism never achieved comparable political effect in France, the nation with the second largest of the European empires, though this empire, too, was built principally by soldiers and priests. The right fumbled its effort at mass appeal in the Dreyfus affair; patriots were preoccupied with avenging the loss of Alsace and Lorraine to Germany, and French nationalism retained ideas associated with the Revolution that often conflicted with those of imperialism. Still, imperial triumphs were welcomed when they came. Everywhere empire offered the appeal of individual daring and direct action in a society becoming more bureaucratized, gave openings to groups often disparaged at home, and illustrated popular ideologies with concrete tales of risk, gain, glory, and conquest.

Imperialism in Britain Imperialism became an increasingly important issue in Britain's domestic politics and one of the important points of difference between the parties. Liberals had generally joined the call for the reform of British rule in

India following the great uprisings of 1857, and that precedent made it easier in 1867 to pass the important act that gave Canada the self-governing autonomy of dominion status. The Liberal commitment to imperial reform included criticism of many of the techniques of imperial expansion from ambiguous treaties to armed attack; and the Liberal leader, William Gladstone, won the election of 1880 after campaigning against the immoral and un-Christian imperialist policies of the Conservatives. Yet it was the Liberals who occupied Egypt just over a year later, for Gladstone could not withstand the public outcry once incidents occurred that were deemed a threat to British interests and a challenge to British honor.

The Conservatives, led by Benjamin Disraeli, embraced empire in principle as well as in practice. When the debt-ridden Khedive of Egypt (who ruled as monarch representing the nominal sovereignty of the Ottomans) had to sell a large bloc of Suez Canal shares, Disraeli had snatched the chance to get them for Britain and thus gain a voice in Egyptian affairs. As prime minister, he had Queen Victoria declared Empress of India in 1876, a flamboyant title that caught the popular imagination, and imperialism proved politically popular even as it began to draw the British into armed conflicts around the world.

The most costly of these conflicts—in blood, money, and prestige—was the Boer War (1889–1901) in South Africa. Ultimately a conflict between the Dutch-speaking white farmers called *Boers* and the British government, its origins were far more complex. The Boers, who had lived in South Africa for centuries, resented Britain's organization of the Cape Colony and in the Great Trek of 1835–1837 had literally moved away, across the Orange River, where they established two (frankly racist) republics and were almost

▸ This engraving of 1897 typically shows Cecil Rhodes as popular hero. Leaving the Cape Town railway station, his carriage is drawn by a private army (called the Matabili boys after the Zulu warriors) through a crowd meant to depict the romance and color of empire.

constantly at war with neighboring African peoples. From the Cape Colony British forces, too, were often at war, most significantly with the powerful Zulus. The situation became more explosive in the 1870s and 1880s with the discovery of diamonds and gold in the Boer republics. The rush was on. Prospectors poured in, mining companies amassed enormous wealth, railroads were hurried to completion, and African blacks were forced to work for meager wages or be driven away.

Ambitious Englishmen on the scene urged the expansion of the territory under British rule, and the most notable among them was Cecil Rhodes, who had gained a near monopoly of the world's diamond production before he was 30. He became prime minister of the Cape Colony and used his position to scheme and propagandize for a South African federation dominated by the British. By 1890, the Boer republics were swarming with British citizens and surrounded by British colonies. Conflicts between the two groups grew more heated, and in 1899 the Boers declared war. British forces rapidly occupied the major cities of the Boer republics, but it took two years to subdue the Boers' skillful guerrilla resistance. The rest of Europe watched that slow progress with surprise and then shock as farmhouses were destroyed and homeless Boers herded together in guarded areas called *concentration camps*. In Great Britain, however, the Boer War produced patriotic fervor.

PATTERNS OF IMPERIALISM

Despite the general popularity of imperialist ideas, few wholehearted imperialists held high political office even in Great Britain. The history of colonial conquest in this period was less one of long-range schemes than of a series of decisions that appear almost accidental when viewed singly. Frequently, individual explorers, traders, or officers—acting independently of their home governments—established claims in a given region through treaties with native leaders whose agreement was won by fear, the lure of profit, the promise of investment, or the hope of help against some nearby enemy. Once so involved, European interests proved difficult to dislodge. In the process of enforcing contracts and maintaining order, Europeans on the scene often exceeded their instructions and then sought the backing of their governments after the fact. Anxious not to appear weak in the eyes of voters or of other powers, the governments acquiesced in their initiatives; trading concessions and protectorates became colonies. This pattern of expansion required little premeditation. Applying their own laws and practices to other cultures, Europeans were surprised when natives failed to honor Western rules, and they responded with increased force.

Even those Europeans attracted by non-Western cultures or devoted to helping local populations, in the name of Western religion and medicine, undermined their host societies—introducing alien ideas, institutions, and technology and overwhelming them by sheer wealth and power. There is, in fact, a whole other history of imperialism now being written from the perspective of the indigenous peoples that shows how native political, economic, and religious organization was disrupted by the arrival of outsiders. To the confident people of empire, such unstable conditions left no alternative but further European control.

Africa Despite the growing pressures of traders, missionaries, and officers, despite the vigorous exploration of the Congo sponsored by King Leopold II of Belgium and the increasing conflicts between the British and the Boers, European involvement in Africa had produced only limited territorial claims prior to 1875. Twenty years later, seven European states had partitioned almost the entire continent.

The Suez Canal was completed in 1869, and after 1875 France and Britain were the largest shareholders. Determined to protect their investments, they established joint control over Egyptian finances. In 1882, however, a nationalist revolt by the Egyptian army against both the khedive and foreign influence threatened this arrangement. The British government decided to mount a show of strength (the French parliament refused to allow France to take part), and the Royal Navy bombarded Alexandria to teach Egyptians that contracts must be met. In the resulting chaos, the British attempted to restore order, and that quickly led to their occupying

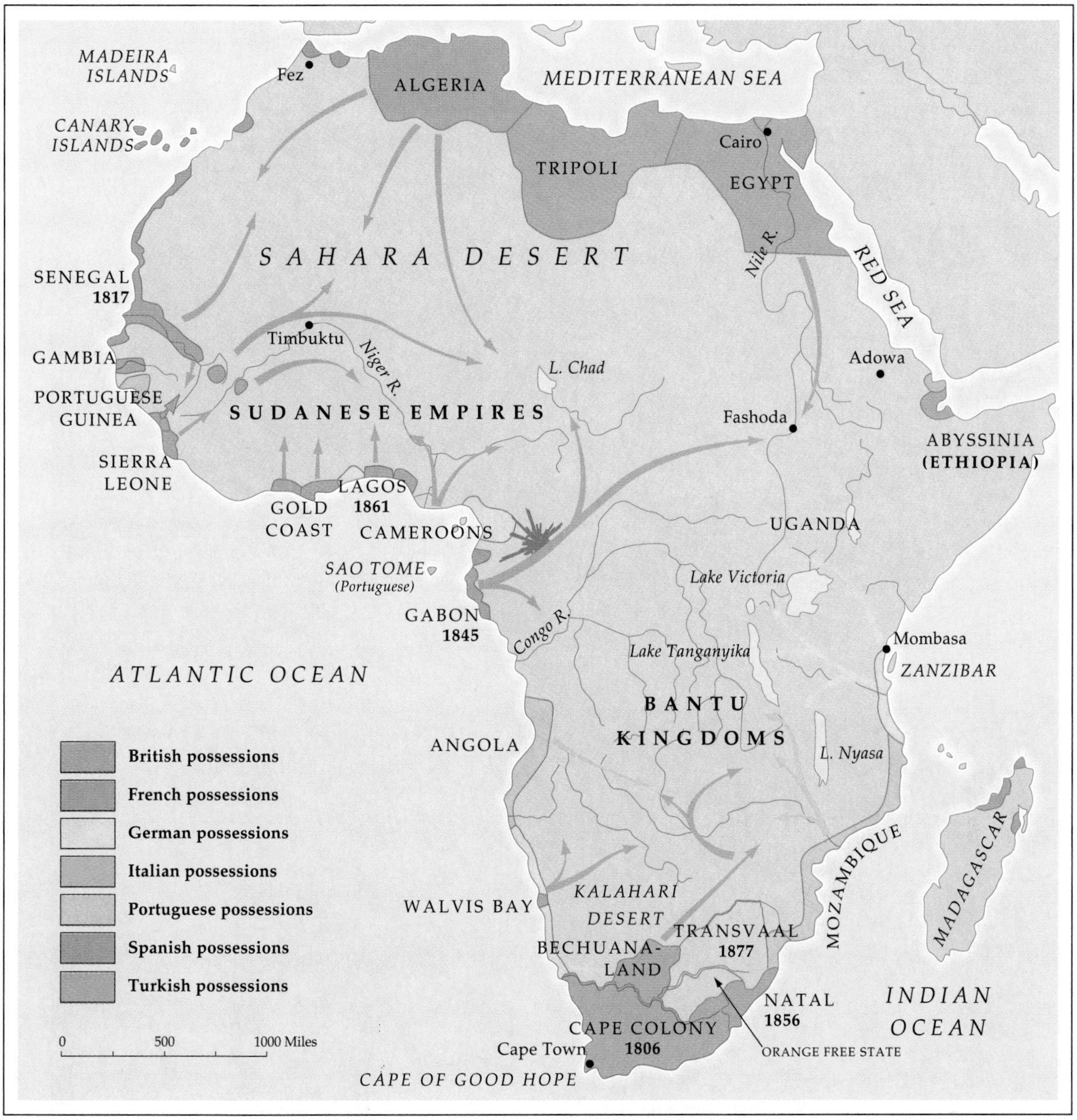

Map 25.1 **AFRICA, 1885**

Egypt, which remained under their rule until after World War II. In Tunisia a similar pattern of increased foreign investments followed by a financial crisis and intricate diplomatic maneuverings brought about French occupation in 1881. Both events accelerated the European competition for African empire.

In sub-Saharan Africa, European nations found themselves drawn piecemeal into scores of treaties that prescribed arrangements for societies they little understood and fixed boundaries in areas whose geography was barely known. European governments, although reluctant to accept responsibility for all that their ambitious citizens did, were afraid to disown any local advantage because Africa had become a site of competition among European states. The International Association for the Exploration and Civilization of Central Africa, founded in Brussels in

▸ **A latecomer to African empire, Germany shared the general sense that Europeans were bringing civilization to a primitive world, the results of which were lampooned in this German cartoon on the effects of Teutonic order in Africa.**

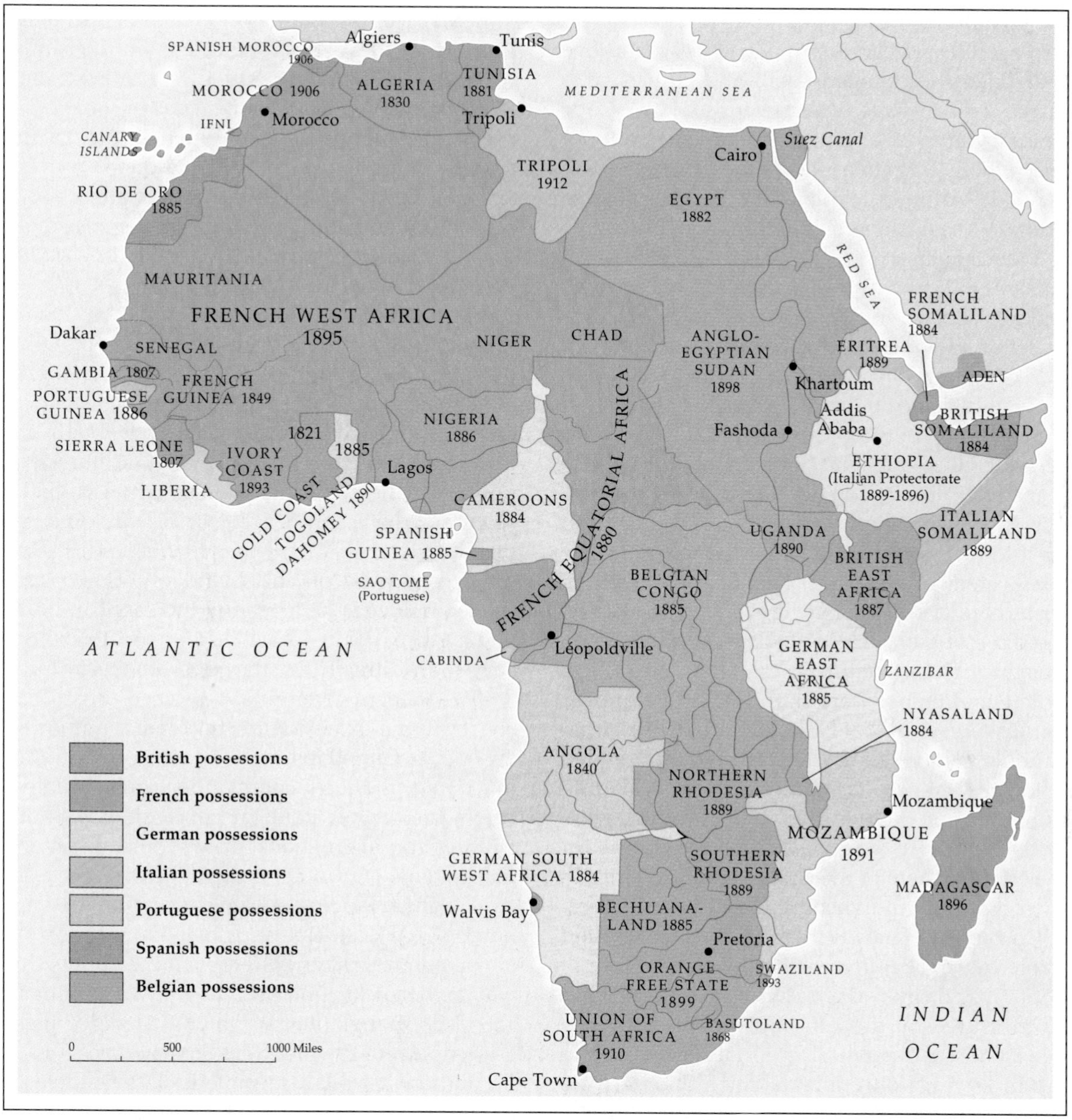

Map 25.2 **Africa, 1914**

1876, quickly became a private operation of Leopold II. The association paid less attention to its lofty aims of furthering science and ending slavery than to the vast territorial claims it might make by sponsoring Stanley's explorations. From their outposts along the west coasts, the French, English, Spaniards, and Portuguese hurried to push into the hinterlands of what are now Senegal and Nigeria.

As the European states were drawn into the scramble for Africa, they sought through diplomacy to lessen the clear danger that clashes there would lead to war in Europe. At Berlin in 1885 the powers established rules for one another. The most important was that coastal settlement by a European nation would give it claim to the hinterlands beyond. Straight lines drawn from haphazard coastal conquests cut across the little-known indigenous cultures, but they restrained the anarchy of European ambition. The powers also agreed at Berlin to prohibit slavery; and five years later they banned liquor and limited arms in the zone between the Sahara and the Cape Colony. Humanitarian considerations had not been wholly forgotten, and by the turn of the century, the ruthless exploitation of the Belgian Congo was considered an international scandal.

French gains in West Africa were the most extensive of all, and in 1898 a group of soldiers who had pushed two-thirds of the way across the continent at its widest point arrived at Fashoda, on the Nile, a few days before the British, who were moving into the Sudan. Both nations considered the encounter of their troops at Fashoda a matter of national honor, and imperialists plotted on maps how dominance over Africa was at stake. The French imagined holdings stretching from west to east across the continent, controlling the headwaters of the Nile. The British talked in terms of territory and maybe even a railway from the Cape of Good Hope to Cairo, a north-south axis through the continent. Thus for weeks Great Britain and France were on the brink of war over the obscure outpost at Fashoda, sought by neither nation's general staff. The confrontation ended when the French, facing serious political divisions at home, chose to give way. In South Africa, British victory in the Boer War paved the way for the establishment of the Union of South Africa in 1910, a partial fulfillment of Rhodes's ambitions.

Those who bravely planted their flags and wrote out treaties for chieftains to sign did not doubt that theirs was a beneficial achievement to be measured by mission hospitals and schools, new roads and political order, as well as their profit. By 1912 only Liberia and Ethiopia were formally free of European domination. The social, cultural, religious, and political life of Africans was everywhere submerged under an imposed European order based on raw power and used for prestige and profit, whatever its other intentions.

Southeast Asia India remained the jewel of the British Empire, the envy of all imperial powers. As a trading partner, India stood on a par with France (only the United States ranked higher in British commerce). India's wealth and the prestige of its culture made it the very symbol of empire. Many of the leading figures of British political life made their reputations in the India service, and their techniques of administration through local lords and British courts were often proclaimed as models of enlightened rule. Yet the growth of trade and industry did not prevent devastating famines in the 1890s, and concessions to local government only stimulated increasingly organized and nationwide demands for a native voice in political life.

East of India and south of China, only Siam (Thailand) preserved its independence of European control through its willingness to modernize—that is, to adopt European forms of political and economic organization—and through the countervailing pressures of the three European powers in neighboring realms, who, in effect, constrained one another. The British annexed upper Burma in 1886 and part of Malaya in 1896; the Dutch were on the island of Borneo; and French influence had steadily increased in Cambodia and Cochin China during the 1860s, despite the indifference of the governments in Paris.

The French government seemed unable to constrain the extension of its colonial authority. Whenever Christians were attacked or a trader murdered, the local commander pressed native rulers for further political concessions without waiting for instructions from home. Even the modest goal of providing their enclave with a secure frontier—a European conception that ignored social realities—usually led to war and expansion into another ancient realm. France in this way eventually found itself at war with China in 1883; and though the parliament voted down the government of Premier Jules Ferry, France's leading imperialist, the war nevertheless resulted in an enlarged French protectorate, reorganized in 1887 as French Indochina. By the 1890s France had begun the kind of full-scale program to build roads and schools and headquarters that marked a well-run colony.

China and Japan The weakness of China and the strengthening of Japan were the central realities of Asian history in the second half of the nineteenth century. Both proud nations had sought to keep intruding Europeans at a distance, and both failed, but with contrasting results. For the huge Chinese Empire, with its administrative

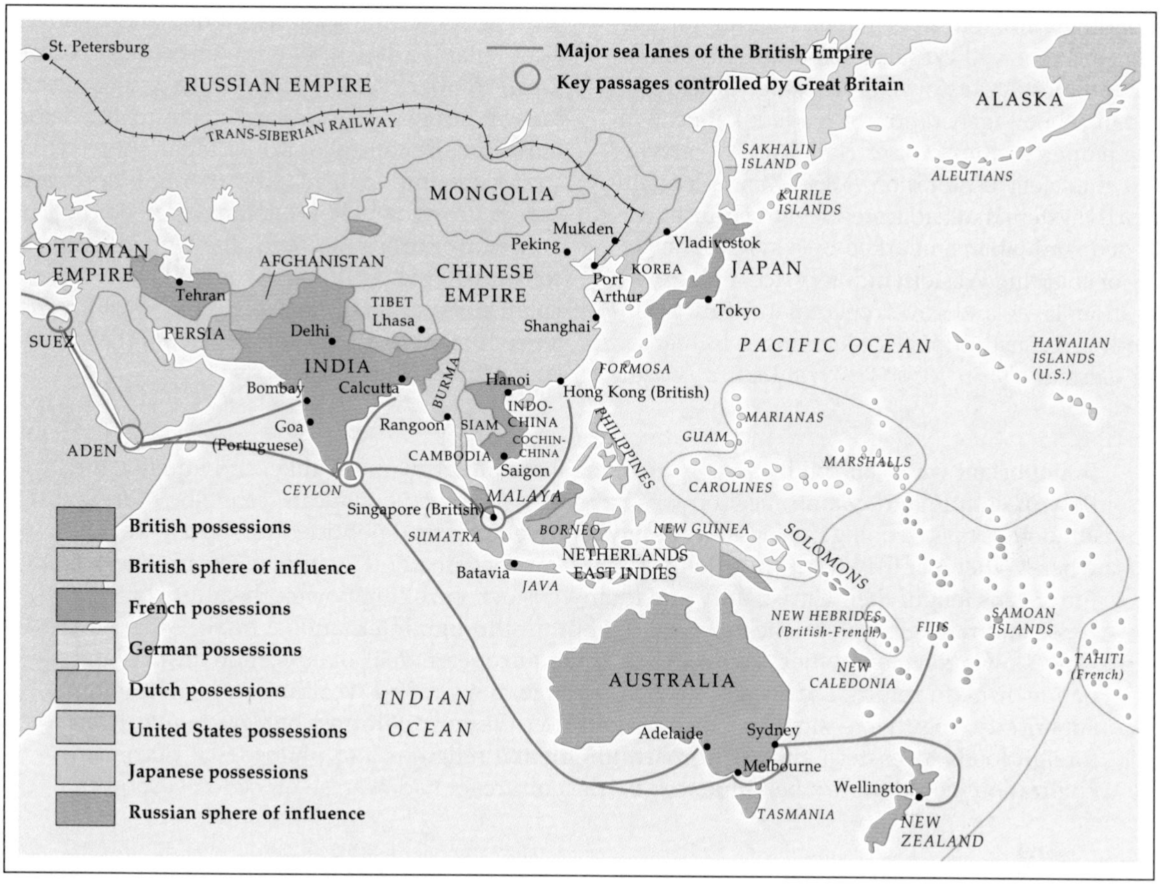

Map 25.3 IMPERIALISM IN ASIA

system threatened by inefficiency and provincial warlords, Western missionaries and traders were especially disruptive. Thus the French gains in Indochina, the extension of Russian interests in Manchuria, the arrival of more and more missionaries, and further trading concessions were all part of a continuing process. Again and again, a local riot, a missionary murdered, or a contract broken would lead to renewed demands and military intervention from Western powers.

And European governments now competed with each other in the systematic exploitation of new opportunities. In 1898 China's inland waters were opened to foreign shipping (mainly British), and the Germans laid claim to Kiaochow Bay, as Germany and Japan joined the competition for claims on China. Chinese efforts to raise revenues, reform administration, and stimulate railroads required, in turn, further loans from and concessions to Western nations. The Boxer Rebellion (1900–1901)—a complicated response by local militias outraged at foreigners and the weakness of their own government—brought another round of violence. Scores of Western missionaries, agents, and some diplomats were killed, prompting heavy military intervention, especially by Russia and Germany. When order was restored, China agreed to a large indemnity. Ironically, the only defense against European imperialism even in a great and ancient nation like China appeared to be a westernization that deepened European influence. That accelerated changes that resulted in the revolution of 1911, led by Sun Yat-sen, and the establishment of the Chinese Republic.

Japan, which for centuries had preserved its isolation, had been successfully pressed to permit trade with the West and protect foreigners; and there followed the familiar pattern of misunderstandings, broken agreements, antiforeign feeling, and renewed Western demands. But domestic political transformation came quickly in Japan. A new generation of leaders joined with the emperor, after a brief civil war, in carrying out the Meiji Restoration (1868). An essentially feudal system that had lasted seven centuries was ended, and Japan embarked on a systematic policy of adapting Western industry, technology, education, laws, and governmental institutions, including a constitutional system (much influenced by Germany's) in 1889. The resultant economic growth, efficient administration, and modern army enabled Japan, like the imperialists of the West, to attack China and win easy victories in the war of 1894–1895. Japan's gains included Formosa and the control of Korea. Japan showed that successful imperialism, like the ambitions and power from which it stemmed, need not be limited to Europeans. With the United States in control of the Philippines, an outcome of the Spanish-American War (1898), the Western system of power relations dominated Southeast Asia and encircled the globe.

In important ways, all civilizations were being forced to grow more alike, and initially, the flow of culture and communication was primarily one-way: European technology, dress, etiquette, ways of doing business, wage payment, religion, and political ideas spread everywhere. Wherever they went and whether they came for gain or out of humanitarian concern, Europeans taught their Christianity and their ways of controlling power, the utility of their roads and railways and medicine, the lure of profit through international trade. Other cultures slowly developed their own ways of using European ideas of education, justice, and nationalism. In return, Europeans enjoyed prestige, power, and wealth. Confident in their superiority, they were slow to borrow from non-Western cultures; but gradually, from foreign foods to Eastern and African art, to Oriental religions and philosophy, European civilization would in turn be influenced by the cultures it had been so quick to overpower.

Recommended Reading

Sources

Darwin, Charles. A number of volumes provide good selections from Darwin's writings, which demonstrate his gifts for observation and his reflectiveness. Some eight volumes of his *Correspondence* have appeared in the new edition edited by F. Burckhardt and Sydney Smith, which began in 1985. It shows him to have been a well-connected and self-aware intellectual.

Lugard, Frederick J. D. *The Rise of Our East Africa Empire* (2 vols.). 1893. This colorful account provides a superb example of the mixture of qualities in a dynamic English imperialist: curious and arrogant, well-intentioned and domineering.

Studies

*Avineri, Shlomo. *The Social and Political Thought of Karl Marx.* 1971. There are dozens of excellent introductions to Marx's thought; this one stands out for the clarity and freshness of its treatment.

*Barzun, Jacques. *Darwin, Marx, and Wagner.* 1958. This famous essay finds a good deal to connect three of the most famous thinkers of midcentury.

Bowler, P. *Evolution: The History of an Idea.* 1989. Combining recent work in the history of science with more general intellectual history, this book traces the various conceptions of evolution in different fields.

Burrow, J. W. *Evolution and Society: A Study in Victorian Social Thought.* 1968. A distinguished essay on the origins of anthropology and the scientific study of society in Britain.

*Available in paperback.

Cameron, Rondo. *France and the Economic Development of Europe, 1800–1914.* 1961. Demonstrates the importance of capital and engineers for the economic growth of Europe and the important role played by France in the development of Central and Eastern Europe.

Clark, Ronald W. *The Survival of Charles Darwin.* 1984. A detailed biography, which also discusses the impact of Darwin's work.

*Fieldhouse, D. K. *The Colonial Empires: A Comparative Study from the Eighteenth Century,* 1982. A valuable introduction to this complicated subject that combines older and newer approaches in looking at imperialism around the world.

Headrick, Daniel R. *The Tools of Empire: Technology and European Imperialism in the Nineteenth Century.* 1981. The author discusses an array of fascinating examples in arguing convincingly for the importance of technology in European domination.

*Himmelfarb, Gertrude. *Darwin and the Darwinian Revolution.* 1968. Relates Darwinian ideas to the intellectual currents of the age, not just in geology and other sciences but in liberal thought as well.

Hobsbawm, Eric. *The Age of Empire, 1875–1914.* 1987. An interesting interpretive essay emphasizing England that argues for the importance of imperialism in domestic life.

Kennedy, Paul. *The Rise of the Anglo-German Antagonism, 1860–1914.* 1980. This massive study of international relations includes economic and political factors as well as imperialism in accounting for the rising tension between the two nations.

Kiernan, V. G. *European Empires from Conquest to Collapse, 1815–1960.* 1981. A good survey of European imperial activity around the globe.

Kindelberger, Charles. *Economic Growth in France and Britain, 1851–1950.* 1964. Comparing the two economies reveals a good deal about the role of the state and social structure in the economic history of each.

*McLellan, David. *Karl Marx. His Life and Thought.* 1977. Considers the more youthful writings as well as *Das Kapital,* bringing out their essential unity.

Milward, Alan S., and S. B. Saul. *The Development of the Economies of Continental Europe, 1850–1914.* 1977. Excellent study of the second great wave of industrialization, which shows the significant difference between this later continental experience and the earlier English one.

*Mommsen, Wolfgang J. *Theories of Imperialism.* P. S. Falla (tr.). 1977. A careful assessment of the dominant approaches, which argues the need for a new theory without producing it.

Reddy, William M. *Money and Liberty in Modern Europe: A Critique of Historical Understanding.* 1987 A critical look at the social impact of the expansion of capitalism in England, France, and Germany, probing the nature of the inequality that resulted.

*Robinson, Ronald, John Gallegher, and Alice Denny. *Africa and the Victorians: The Climax of Imperialism.* 1961. An influential study that has affected all subsequent writing through its emphasis on the importance of the domestic history of the societies subject to imperialist pressure and its argument for the continuity in European imperialism.

Rotberg, Robert I. *Africa and Its Explorers: Motives, Methods, and Impact.* 1970. A lively account that incorporates modern scholarship on European imperialism.

———. *The Founder: Cecil Rhodes and the Pursuit of Power.* 1988. A biography that uses psychology and the astounding events of Rhodes's life to explain the dynamic of imperialism in Africa.

*Owen, Roger, and Bob Sutcliffe (eds.). *Studies in the Theory of Imperialism.* 1972. Telling essays evaluate current and older theories, while case studies treat particular historical examples; a heterogeneous collection, both Marxist and non-Marxist.

*Thornton, A. P. *The Imperial Idea and Its Enemies: A Study in British Power.* 1959. A well-written account of the appeal of imperialism in Britain and of the movement against it.

Wiener, Martin. *English Culture and the Decline of the Industrial Spirit, 1850–1980.* 1981. Argues that English society and culture never really held the values or accepted the social practices necessary to sustain economic growth.

The Metropolitan Museum of Art

This early and famous painting by Claude Monet, which partakes of the impressionists' delight in scenes of outdoor leisure and in seascapes, also conveys the calm satisfactions of middle-class life against a background of the commerce plying the English Channel that made such a life style possible.

CHAPTER TWENTY-SIX

The Age of Progress

IN the last decades of the nineteenth century, European society was becoming distinctively more urban, more productive, and more organized. Expanding trade and production lifted the general standard of living, and more people had more choices about schooling, where to live, life style, and leisure than ever before. After 1870, most governments acknowledged some civil rights and, having adopted representative forms, depended more on public opinion. All of this justified widespread optimism that Europe and North America had entered a new era of progress.

The dynamic societies that created these opportunities also generated sharp tensions among interest groups and social classes and strident arguments over systems of values. These conflicts tended increasingly to be expressed through large-scale organizations—businesses, labor unions, state bureaucracies, churches, and political parties—and this institutional element may ultimately have encouraged accommodation and compromise, but for decades these clashes seem grave threats to social peace. This period of an expansive and innovative culture was also marked by extraordinarily powerful criticisms of modern society and by political battles within each nation over the kind of society to construct for the future.

I. The Belle Époque

With a touch of nostalgia, the period has come to be called the *belle époque,* a phrase evocative of the Paris of the 1890s, the city of lights where the Eiffel Tower was new, the grand boulevards were crowded with cafés, and great department stores propagandized for consumerism. It was the era in which millions of Europeans came to share an urban life of public ceremonies, strolls through parks, relaxation and light entertainment. Regular leisure for the masses was part of an essentially new way of life that offered something for every taste and pocketbook.

▸ **Department stores, like this one in Paris—a combination of theater and commercial display—were the seductive symbols of consumerism and prosperity.**

POPULAR CULTURE

Traditional festivals and games, once tied to the local region, had gradually become less important than other amusements. With each change to a new popular medium, from operetta to music hall to vaudeville and—after the turn of the century—silent films, a larger part of the population shared in public entertainment. Popular culture thus tended to become more uniform within each nation and across Europe. It also became more formal (the Marquis of Queensberry rules for boxing, for instance, date from 1867) and increasingly commercial, in the music hall and on the athletic field, in the circus and at amusement parks. Leading actors and actresses became stars whose offstage lives were part of their fascination. Entertainment was an important business, whose clientele included families from the lower-middle and working classes (*see box,* p. 842). Soccer, once the sport of elite English secondary schools, became professional (most of the famous teams of Europe were formed around the turn of the century), attracting huge, noisy Sunday crowds. While workers shared these urban entertainments, the middle classes began to crowd summer resorts and to play games like golf and tennis, which had recently adopted new sets of rules. This profitable popular culture helped bridge the social gap between workers and the middle class, between town and city, and in doing so assumed and helped create an audience with common tastes. Newspapers had similar effects as publishers learned to increase their circulation (several now approached daily sales of a million copies) through sensational articles and colorful features written in a direct and less literary style. Like the millions of popular novels (now more specialized into romances, adventure stories especially for children, and penny thrillers), such writing abandoned any pretense to cultivated taste, further separating formal from popular culture.

Education These changes were related to another of immeasurable importance: For the first time in Western history, in the major nations at least, a majority of the adult population could read and write. By the 1880s governments almost everywhere, recognizing the importance of literacy to politics and industry, had made education universal and compulsory and had reduced or eliminated school fees. In 1850 Prussia was the only major nation in which a majority of the adult population could read and write; by 1900 more than 90 percent of the adult population of Germany, France, and Great Britain was literate, and the proportion elsewhere was climbing rapidly. Mass schooling was usually limited to a few years of the most elementary subjects, and aside from special supplementary instructions in workers' classes, night schools, and special vocational institutes, few of the poor had any opportunity for further training. The amount and kind of education received was one of the clearest distinctions between the middle class and those below it. Nevertheless, the schooling available to everybody would be steadily extended and access to secondary school, technical school, and university gradually increased.

THE ROLE OF ORGANIZATIONS

National systems of schooling were characteristic of the era in their reliance on large, formal, hierarchical institutions. As governments took on increased responsibilities for public health, social welfare, transportation, the post, and the telegraph, the civil service expanded, carrying its orderly procedures and hierarchical system deep into society. Businesses, too, tended to become bigger and more bureaucratic, with a few large companies dominating many national industries from steel and shipping to retail sales. Smaller firms thus tended to organize in associations that could represent their interests with government and in the marketplace. Labor, too, was increas-

▶ **The street life and vaudeville of Paris provided an international model, and all Europe's great cities delighted in an urban life that provided attractions for every class.**

G. B. Shaw Explains the Appeal of Popular Theater

The famous playwright George Bernard Shaw was even better known as a drama critic. In this review published in the April 9, 1898, issue of* The Saturday Review, *a prestigious general magazine, he contrasts the high culture of the theaters in London's West End, where internationally admired artists such as Sarah Bernhardt performed, with the more vaudeville-like popular theater.

". . . The Britannia Theatre is in Hoxton, not far from Shoreditch Church, a neighbourhood in which the *Saturday Review* is comparatively little read. The manager, a lady, is the most famous of all London managers. . . . Over 4000 people pay nightly at her doors; and the spectacle of these thousands, serried in the vast pit and empyrean gallery, is so fascinating that the stranger who first beholds it can hardly turn away to look at the stage. Forty years ago Mrs. Sara Lane built this theatre; and she has managed it ever since. It may be no such great matter to handle a single playhouse. . . ; but Mrs. Lane is said to own the whole ward in which her theatre stands. Madam Sarah Bernhardt's diamonds fill a jewel-box: Mrs. Lane's are reputed to fill sacks.

". . . The enthusiasm of the pit last night, with no stalls to cut it off from the performers, was frantic. There was a great throwing of flowers and confectionery on the stage; and it would happen occasionally that an artist would overlook one of these tributes, and walk off, leaving it unnoticed on the boards. Then a shriek of tearing anxiety would arise, as if the performer were wandering blindfold into a furnace or over a precipice. Every factory girl in the house would lacerate the air with a mad scream of 'Pick it up, Topsy!' 'Pick it up, Voylit!' followed by a gasp of relief, several thousand strong, when Miss Topsy Sinden or Miss Violet Durkin would return and annex the offering. I was agreeably astonished by Miss Topsy Sinden's dancing. Thitherto it had been my miserable fate to see her come on, late in the second act of some unspeakably dreary inanity at the West End. . . . At the Brittania Miss Sinden really danced, acted, and turned out quite a charming person. I was not surprised; for the atmosphere was altogether more bracing than at the other end of the town. These poor playgoers, to whom the expenditure of half a guinea for a front seat at a theater is as outrageously and extravagantly impossible as the purchase of a deer forest in Mars is to a millionaire, have at least one excellent quality in the theatre. They are jealous *for* the dignity of the artist, not derisively covetous of his (or her) degradation. . . . Altogether, I seriously recommend those of my readers who find a pantomime once a year good for them, to go next year to the Britannia, and leave the West End to its boredoms and all the otherdoms that make it so expensively dreary."

From George Bernard Shaw, "The Drama in Hoxton," in *The Saturday Review*, April 9, 1899, reprinted in George Rowell (ed.), *Victorian Dramatic Criticism* (London: Methuen & Co., 1971).

ingly organized in national trade unions for particular industries, and they in turned grouped together (especially in Germany and Britain) to increase their political influence and economic weight. In every industrial country from the 1880s on there were great strikes in which these behemoths battled whole industries while competing with them for political protection and public support. Political parties, too, tended to adopt some form of national organization and a permanent staff, especially where universal male suffrage had been adopted. With its Marxist program, national organization, and thousands of local centers for recreation and instruction, the German Social Democratic party was the most impressive example of all.

Associational life had come to dominate other activities, too. Physicians, lawyers, engineers, and teachers all had their professional associations that set standards, lobbied governments, and conferred prestige. This institutionalization of society was in many respects a source of stability, establishing norms for and giving order to rapidly expanding activities, as well as providing internal discipline and the means for negotiating conflicting interests in the larger society. Like political parties, associations offered a means whereby scattered groups and new interests could make their presence felt in public life.

"The Woman Question" Everywhere, from the 1860s on, women had begun to organize movements of their own. Often divided over goals and tactics, these movements tended to fall into three types. The first and largest were led by middle-class women. Usually cautious in outlook, they could effectively demonstrate the contradictions between cultural ideals of female purity and motherhood and a social reality that subjected millions of women to desperate poverty and sometimes brutal conditions. The meeting of the International Congress of the Rights of Women, which brought together representatives from 12 countries on the occasion of the Paris exposition of 1878, can be taken as a signal that women's issues were becoming a regular part of the public agenda. By the 1880s and 1890s, this growing awareness of women's issues brought more explicitly feminist and radical organizations to the fore, particularly in Germany, England, and France. Aware that their demands required fundamental social change, these organizations were often drawn toward the Labour and Social Democratic parties, but met a mixed response from male workers worried about competition from women and from many feminists worried that laws regulating women's work would also tend to preserve paternalistic attitudes and close off new opportunities.

A third response centered in the growing women's trade union movement, which was concerned primarily with the immediate problems of pay and working conditions. Employers' resistance, the nature of women's work, and low pay made unionization difficult, however, as did the resentment of men who saw women as a threat to their jobs and higher wages. When a British trade union leader declared it men's "duty as men and husbands . . . to bring about a condition of things where wives should be in their proper sphere at home," he spoke for most of his sex of every class (and quite possibly for a majority of women). The fact remained that in the late nineteenth century most women in industrial nations worked for wages from their early teens until they married and increasingly continued working after marriage as an often essential contribution to family income.

The increase in the number of women workers was especially noticeable where industrialization was more recent, in Germany, Italy, and the Scandinavian countries. The proportion of women who worked for pay was highest in France—about 40 percent. (The proportion of married women who worked was twice as high there as in England.) Jobs remained tightly tied to gender. More women in England and Germany were employed as domestic servants than in any other field. Next came work as a laundress, seamstress, chambermaid, or waitress. Only about one-fifth of working women were employed in factories, where they were usually assigned tasks associated with domestic skills. In the textile industries the proportion of women workers steadily rose to become the majority everywhere. Paid less than men in any case (from one-half to two-thirds as much for comparable work), women were less numerous in the burgeoning industries of the sec-

▸ New developments like the small electric motor created new jobs for women as in this German metal-working plant.

▸ **Middle-class women were the leaders in feminist movements, and efforts to organize women workers concentrated on industrial work; but far more women earned money in menial drudgery like these women in a French laundry.**

ond industrial revolution than in more stagnant ones where pay was lower; and far more women than men did piecework, making buttons or cardboard boxes in shops or at home. The garrets of every city were filled with women living in tiny rooms where they worked late into the night making hats, artificial flowers, and lace. There were also many new jobs in the service sector—washing, ironing, and mending clothes—the classic employment for the young woman newly arrived in the city.

But there were some significant changes in women's employment, and these were helpful to the women's movement generally. With the spread of elementary schooling, women slowly took over as bookkeepers, office clerks, and secretaries, occupations in which prestige, opportunities for advancement, and pay declined as they came to be women's work. Some professions also opened to women, especially nursing (primarily provided by nuns in Catholic countries) and teaching in elementary school. By the end of the century three-quarters of the elementary school teachers in England were women, as were more than half the teachers in Sweden and France and one-fifth of those in Germany. The expanding field of social work began to pay the sort of middle-class women who as charitable workers had pioneered in its creation. Small shops, and, more slowly, the great department stores also hired women as clerks, preferably women from the lower-middle class who were trained to speak and dress in the ways considered proper by a bourgeois clientele. A few of the famous stores provided dormitories for their women employees, although the city life of single women who supported themselves and lived alone continued to worry moralists and titillate readers of the sensational press.

The resistance to these women's movements was formidable, and feminists found themselves combating customary attitudes in every social class, as well as the prejudices of doctors who insisted on women's physical weakness and psychological instability and of social Darwinists who declared that civilization required women to concentrate on their biological function. Nevertheless, dominant attitudes did begin to change. Women's colleges were established at Oxford

▸ **This advertisement in a German magazine was typical in selling not just an inexpensive means of transport but the joys of youth, style, and a new freedom for women.**

▶ **Renoir's festive scene of the outdoor Sunday dance at *Le Moulin de la Galette*, an outdoor cafe in Paris, which catered to the working class and the lower-middle class as well as artists, is characteristic of the impressionists' interest in urban life.**

and Cambridge in the 1870s; and in Italy, where universities had never been closed to women, Marie Montessori's lectures at the end of the century on "the new woman" were widely hailed. Outstanding achievements by individual women (and their number was growing) in science, medicine, education, literature, art, economics, and social reform challenged stereotypes; and it was far less unusual now for women to attend school, ride bicycles, and speak at public meetings and demonstrations. As women lived longer and bore fewer children, legal and cultural constraints that assumed their lives would be circumscribed by marriage and motherhood became harder to defend. By 1910, most European nations had passed laws protecting women workers; increasing women's rights to dispose of property, share in decisions affecting their children, and take part in civic life (the ban forbidding women to attend public political meetings in Germany was lifted in 1908); allowing wives independent control of the money they earned (1884 and 1910 in France); and even establishing a minimum rate for piecework (England, 1910). Wherever suffrage was universal for men, demands that women be allowed to vote were rising.

THE ARTS

The creative arts continued to flourish, benefiting from high prestige and ever larger and more sophisticated audiences. Yet the forms and styles employed grew so diverse that the arts hardly seemed to speak for a single civilization. One reason for the change (and the one most welcomed) was the trend toward national styles. The use of folk elements and distinct traditions gave an instantly recognizable national identity to English or Russian novels and French, German, or Russian music. Another reason for the variety of artistic styles was the tendency of artists to act as social critics, thereby bringing into the realm of aesthetics issues of politics and values that troubled society. Thus the tension between the individual and society, between the artist's personal perceptions and the unstable conventions of a world undergoing rapid change, remained a central theme of nineteenth-century art. These concerns and then the reaction against them in favor of a "purer" art led to a bewildering variety of competing movements. "Naturalism," the "Pre-Raphaelites," "Impressionism," the "Decadents," "Symbolism"—such self-conscious labels for new artistic movements were frequently proclaimed with angry manifestoes against previous art and present culture.

Much influenced by the impressionists, Vincent van Gogh was one of the important artists to move away from their emphasis on cohesion and control in favor of vigorous strokes that made a dazzling, and often fervently mystical, personal statement. By 1890, when he painted this picture of a village church, impressionism was being superseded.

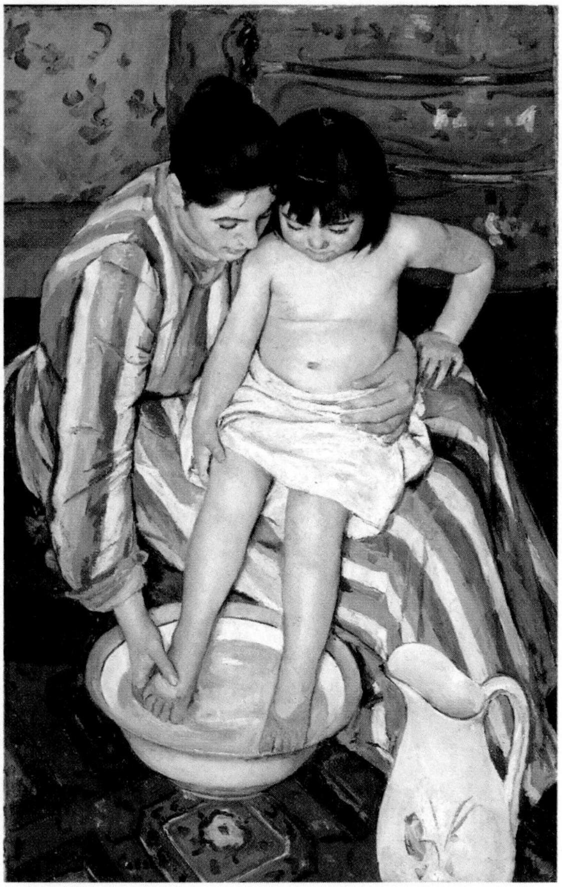

The American, Mary Cassatt, was the first woman painter to achieve recognition as a member of the impressionists. The unusual composition, which emphasizes the relationship between mother and daughter, is characteristic of the experimentation found in many impressionist works (with composition, the effects of thick paint on the surface, and strong patches of color) that pointed in directions that would be explored by the next generation of painters.

Naturalists claimed that the artist, like a scientist, should present life in objective detail after careful research. This aim was particularly suited to the novel; and Emile Zola, with his precise descriptions of industrial and Parisian life, was a master of the school. Determinism, the view that behavior was determined by blood inheritance or social class, was a favorite theme in this Darwinian age. It proved especially effective on the stage where the protagonist's destiny inexorably unfolded before the new audience gradually won over to realistic drama.

For the realistic painters of midcentury and for England's Pre-Raphaelites (who took their name from the pious and simpler art of the early Renaissance), much of a painting's importance had lain in its subject matter and message. A new generation of painters broke with this tradition to concentrate on capturing the effects of light and color almost as if the artist's brilliance in analyzing and recreating such effects was in itself the purpose of painting. In 1867 some of the artists denied exhibition space at the annual Paris Salon established the Salon des Refusés, proudly contesting the validity of official taste. These are the painters we remember, for they included some of the leaders of Impressionism, whose golden age was the 1870s and 1880s, among them Auguste Renoir and Claude Monet. They and the Post-Impressionist Paul Cézanne were recognized in their own lifetimes as ranking among the great artists of Western history, but painters only slightly younger, like Paul Gauguin and Vincent van Gogh, turned to still newer and more personal styles.

Thus each of the arts tended to develop on its own terms. Architecture, the most immediately social of all the arts, was the least innovative. Perhaps the tension between individual and society that was fruitful elsewhere was stultifying to so public and functional an art. Even when they achieved real beauty, the great buildings of the nineteenth century were eclectically dressed in the styles of other periods. Churches evoked the spiritual coherence of the High Middle Ages; banks and public buildings expressed in stone the civic virtues of Greece and Rome. Even apartment houses usually imitated some earlier epoch, as if to make new wealth feel more secure. Only at the very end of the century were the structural and aesthetic possibilities hidden in railroad sheds, bridges, and exhibit halls developed into a new architectural style that included the skyscraper.

The international style known as art nouveau turned its back on the practical and efficient industrial world of the turn of the century and delighted in applying ornamental arabesques to everything from wrought iron to poster lettering and printed cloth. Poetry, like painting, became an increasingly private expression, often obscure, indifferent to conventional morality, and constructed according to complex aesthetic doctrines. The fashionable fascination with death, languid despair, and perfumed aestheticism was called *decadent* by its critics, a label the artists willingly accepted until that term gave way to Symbolism. A movement of French poets that spread throughout Europe, Symbolism interpreted the things one sees and describes as signs of a deeper and more spiritual reality. Art, like life itself, was to be complexly understood on several levels of meaning at once, and individual style became a personal conquest, a private bridge between the artist's identity and external society. In the decade preceding World War I still more radical

The Metropolitan Museum of Art

▶ With playful elegance, art nouveau was even more influential in the design of household objects than in architecture. Graceful curvilinear suggestions of natural objects were echoed in the shape of vases, gates, and furniture in porcelain, metal, and wood. Georges de Feure, who made this vase, had a whole room of porcelain on display at the Paris Exposition of 1900.

▸ **In Norway Edvard Munch's use of symbolism pointed the way to German expressionism, using color and line to convey the anxiety underlying ordinary life as in this bitter comment on the tragedy of the *Dance of Life*.**

changes (changes that would shape the art of the twentieth century) further separated the artist from the broader public. That separation, and the low quality of popular entertainment and mass journalism, seemed to some an ominous new threat to Western culture. For most contemporaries, however, European culture at the end of the century was characterized primarily by an extraordinary commitment to education and to the dissemination of knowledge, encouraging evidence (along with political liberty and industrial prosperity) of progress.

II. Attacks on Liberal Civilization

This dynamic, prosperous Europe with its constitutional liberties could be seen as fulfilling much of liberalism's promise; yet liberalism came under a heavy critique as many intellectuals joined with artists in expressing contempt for middle-class society, radicals sought the end of the capitalist system, and conservatives and Christians mounted new attacks on liberal values. These attacks had their intellectual foundations in well-developed systems of thought, but they had their greatest impact in organized movements that clamored for public attention and fought for political power.

THE FIRST INTERNATIONAL

Marx may have done most of his work in the library of the British Museum, but he and Engels intended to lead an effective social movement. When in 1864 a group of English labor leaders called a small international conference in London, Marx readily agreed to come as a representative of German workers. The International Working Men's Association, usually called the First International, was founded at that meeting, and Marx dominated it from the start. He did his best to replace traditional radical rhetoric about truth and justice with the hard language of Marxism. During the eight years of the First International, he gradually succeeded in expelling those who disagreed with him.

The French members were generally followers of Louis-Auguste Blanqui and Pierre Joseph Proudhon, socialists for whom Marx had little use. He dismissed the Blanquists, with their fondness for violence and dreams of conspiracy, as romantic revolutionaries; and his earliest socialist writing had criticized Proudhon's plans for workers' cooperatives and his sympathy for anarchy. Marx also antagonized the English members of the International who did not accept his emphasis on revolution or his claim that the Paris Commune of 1871 (discussed below) was "the glorious harbinger of a new society."

Marx's most important conflict, however, was with Mikhail Bakunin. A Russian anarchist, Bakunin had established himself in 1848 as one of Europe's more flamboyant revolutionaries (*see box*, p. 849). Later sentenced to exile in Siberia, he escaped in 1861 and eventually joined the International in 1867. Bakunin respected Marx and understood his materialist philosophy, while Marx seems to have felt some of the fascination of Bakunin's personality. But Bakunin supported nationalism and praised the revolutionary spirit of countries like Italy and Spain, whereas Marx insisted that the revolutionary cause was inter-

Bakunin on Why He Opposes the State

A professional revolutionary, Mikhail Bakunin took part in the Polish revolution of 1863 and spent most of the next six years in Italy organizing workers there. In 1870 he took part in an uprising in Lyons aimed at creating a regime like that of the Paris Commune, which he greatly admired. In the spring of 1871 he was in Geneva, where he published three lectures "To the Swiss Members of the International," part of which is given here. Always eager to present his interpretation of European history and his arguments for anarchism, he was an important figure in the International Workingmens Association until his conflicts with Marx led to his expulsion in 1872.

"This ruination and general oppression of the working masses, and partly of the bourgeois class, had for its pretext and as its acknowledged goal the grandeur, power, and magnificence of the monarchical, nobiliary, bureaucratic, and military State, a State which had usurped the place of the Church and proclaimed itself a divine institution. Accordingly, there was a State morality entirely different from, or rather wholly opposed to, the private morality of men. Private morality has an everlasting basis that is more or less recognized, understood, accepted, and achieved in every human society, insofar as it is not vitiated by religious dogmas. This basis is nothing but human respect, respect for human dignity and for the right and freedom of every human individual. To respect [these principles] is a virtue; to violate them, on the contrary, is a crime. State morality is wholly opposed to this human morality. The State presents itself to its subjects as the supreme goal. Virtue consists of serving its power and grandeur, by all means possible and impossible, even contrary to all human laws and to the good of humanity. Since everything which contributes to the power and growth of the State is good, everything contrary to them is bad, be it even the noblest and most virtuous action from the human point of view.

"... The contradiction lies in the very idea of the State. Because the worldwide State has never been realized, every State is a limited entity comprising a limited territory and a somewhat restricted number of subjects.

"... This is why we are passionate opponents both of the State and of every State. For so long as there exist States, there will be no humanity; and so long as there exist States, war and its horrible crimes and inevitable consequences, the destruction and general misery of the peoples, will never cease.

"So long as there are States, the masses of the people will be *de facto* slaves even in the most democratic republics, for they will work not with a view to their own happiness and wealth, but for the power and wealth of the State. And what is the State? People claim that it is the expression and the realization of the common good, universal rights and freedom. Well, whoever so claims is as good a liar as someone who claims that God Almighty is everyone's protector. Ever since the fantasy of a Divine Being took shape in men's imagination, God—all gods, and among them above all the God of the Christians—has always taken the part of the strong and the rich against the ignorant and impoverished masses. Through His priests, He has blessed the most revolting privileges, the basest oppressions and exploitations.

"The State is likewise nothing but the guarantor of all exploitation, to the profit of a small number of prosperous and privileged persons and to the loss of the popular masses. In order to assure the welfare, prosperity, and privileges of some, it uses everyone's collective strength and collective labor, to the detriment of everyone's human rights. In such a set-up the minority plays the role of the hammer and the majority that of the anvil."

From Mikhail Bakunin, "Three Lectures to Swiss Members of the International" given in 1870, translated and reprinted in Robert M. Cutler (ed.), *Mikhail Bakunin: From Out of the Dustbin: Bakunin's Basic Writings, 1869–1871* (Ann Arbor: Ardis Publishers, 1985).

national and most certain to triumph where industrialization was farthest advanced. The Russian's delight in conspiracies and plots seemed childish to the German expatriate; and Bakunin, who distrusted any state, found a dangerous authoritarianism in Marx and Marxism.

The 1872 meeting, at which Bakunin was expelled, was the First International's last, for Marx and Engels then let the association die. Its membership had never been large or even clearly defined. Yet it played a part in building a workers' movement by disseminating Marxism, by teaching others to view each strike or demonstration as part of a larger conflict, by stressing the international ties of workers in a period of nationalism, and by exemplifying the advantages of militant discipline. In these ways and in its intolerance of doctrinal error and its intense polemics, the First International helped set the tone of the growing socialist movement.

SOCIALISM AND ANARCHISM

Between 1875 and World War I, socialist parties became an important part of political life in nearly every European country. Except in Great Britain, most of them were at least formally Marxist. As they began to win elections, socialists disagreed over whether to follow a more moderate policy aimed at electoral success or adhere rigidly to the teachings of Marx. The most common compromise combined moderate policies with flaming rhetoric, and the Second International, formed in 1889 with representatives from parties and unions in every country, sought to maintain doctrinal rigor and socialist unity. The Marxist critique of liberalism and capitalism was spread through books, newspapers, and magazines; in parliamentary debate; and in every election.

Labor organizations outside Germany were not often consistently Marxist, but trade unions were everywhere class-conscious, frequently tempted by anarchism and suspicious of politics. Their membership soared, with millions of workers paying dues in the industrialized countries, and the strike became the common expression of social protest. Skilled artisans, threatened by new modes of production yet strengthened by their own traditions of cooperation, often continued to be the leaders in militant action; but the successful organization of labor in larger factories led to a great wave of strikes that were larger, better organized, and more orderly than any that had come before. Most people did not distinguish very clearly among the various radical movements and associated socialists and labor leaders with the anarchist "propaganda of the deed," violent acts that made headlines. In the 1880s and 1890s, bombs were thrown into parades, cafés, and theaters in cities all over Europe, and individual anarchists assassinated the president of France in 1893, the prime minister of Spain in 1897, the empress of Austria in 1898, the king of Italy in 1900, and the president of the United States in 1901. Such incidents were followed by the arrest of radical suspects, spectacular trials, and denunciations of leftists.

But bomb throwers and assassins were only a tiny part of the broad anarchist movement. Anarchism's intellectual tradition was continuous from the time of the French Revolution. Its most famous figure after Bakunin was Prince Peter Kropotkin, an exiled Russian aristocrat. Kropotkin was a theorist whose gentleness and compassion made him a kind of spiritual leader, but his prescriptions for what he called anarcho-communism did not unify the movement. Some anarchists stressed individualism, some pacifism, and some the abolition of private property. All rejected imposed authority and denounced the state as a repressive machine serving the interests of wealth. They won their largest following among the poor who felt crushed by industrialization: immigrants to the United States, peasants in southern Spain, artisans and some industrial workers in Italy and France. Anarchism was an influential element in the opposition to bureaucratic centralization and to militarism, and it appealed to artists and writers who shared the anarchists' contempt for bourgeois values, while contributing heroes and martyrs to the growing mystique of the radical left.

Socialism, anarchism, and trade unions addressed feelings of brotherhood, justice, and common interest that had developed within working-class life. Expressed in songs and speeches—at meetings, demonstrations, and strikes—they reflected shared values and experiences developed over generations. This common culture was reinforced as the conditions of labor became more similar in different industries and as housing patterns created working-class districts. Radical movements linked the immediate issues of working-class life to broad principles and to national politics in a powerful challenge to the established system. Nevertheless and despite working-class leaders' insistence on the importance of class unity, the left was far from united as conflicts over tactics as well as principles exposed differences between skilled and unskilled workers, between workers in established trades and new industries, between men and women, and between labor unions and political parties.

THE CHRISTIAN CRITIQUE

Attacks on liberalism also came from the pulpits of every Christian denomination. Individualism, the charges ran, is often mere selfishness; religious tolerance masks indifference to moral issues; progress is another name for materialism. Churches tended to reject the growing claims of the state, especially in education and welfare, and many Protestants and Catholics denounced the values and injustices of capitalist society as forcefully as did the socialists.

The Roman Catholic Church was particularly hostile to liberalism. In 1864 Pope Pius IX issued an encyclical, *Quanta Cura,* with a syllabus of "the principal errors of our time" attached. Taken from earlier statements by the pope, its 80 items were written in the unbending tones of theological dispute. The syllabus listed false propositions, for example, that "it is no longer expedient that the Catholic religion should be held as the only religion of the State, to the exclusion of all other forms of worship." Catholics more politic than the pope were quick to point out that to declare that opinion not to be true is not the same as advocating religious intolerance, but such subtleties were easily lost. The syllabus denounced total faith in human reason, the exclusive authority of the state, and attacks on traditional rights of the Church; but its most noted proposition was the last, which declared it false to think that "the Roman Pontiff can, and ought to, reconcile himself, and come to terms with progress, liberalism and modern civilization."

The Vatican Council of 1869–1870, the first council of the Church in 300 years, confirmed the impression of intransigence. It was a splendid demonstration of the Church's continued power, and prelates came from around the world to proclaim the dogma of papal infallibility. It declared that the pope, when speaking *ex cathedra* (that is, formally from the chair of Peter and on matters of faith and morals), is incapable of error. This had long been a traditional belief, and its elevation to dogma confirmed the trend toward increased centralization within the Church and affirmed the solidarity of Catholics in the face of new social and political dangers. Even as the council met, the outbreak of the Franco-Prussian War allowed the Italian government to take the city of Rome from the pope and make it the capital of Italy, but governments throughout Europe wondered if Catholics who followed an infallible pope could be reliable citizens of a secular state.

The expanding role of government, especially in matters of education and welfare, made conflicts between church and state a major theme of European life. Theories of evolution, positivism, and biblical criticism put defenders of traditional belief on the defensive and made them seem opponents of science. Politicians, on the other hand, worried about the influence of the churches in elections, especially as men who had never voted before, particularly in rural areas and among national minorities, were called to the polls. In the United Kingdom, the Church of England had steadily been stripped of its special privileges in moves opposed at every step by the clergy, by most peers, and by many conservatives; but religious differences continued to inflame the Irish question. As chancellor of the new German state, Bismarck launched and then abandoned attacks on the Catholic Church as his government relied more and more on the Catholic Center party. In Russia the Orthodox Church became, in effect, a department of state, used to strengthen the dominance of Russians in the multinational empire, while the Austrian government, in contrast, broke its close ties (and its concordat) with the Roman Catholic Church in an effort to lessen nationalist opposition to rule from Vienna. The conflict between church and state was most open and bitter, however, in Spain, Italy, and France, where it was the central political division of the 1880s and 1890s.

Generally, these conflicts subsided somewhat after the turn of the century. Relatively secure states, having established the breadth of their authority, tended to become more tolerant; and anticlericalism came to seem outmoded as governments faced the rising challenge from the left. The churches, too, became more flexible, in the style of Pope Leo XIII (1878–1903), who established an understanding with Bismarck and encouraged French Catholics to accept the Third Republic.

At the same time, Christianity displayed renewed vigor. There was a general revival of biblical and theological studies, marked in the Roman Catholic Church by emphasis on the theology of St. Thomas Aquinas, whose arguments for the compatibility of faith and reason brought greater clarity and confidence to Catholic positions. Christian political and social movements learned to mobilize enormous support and became more active in social work (the Protestant Salvation Army was founded in 1865). This engagement in charity, religious missions at home and overseas, education, labor unions, and hundreds of special projects not only strengthened Christian social influence but gave concreteness to the outspoken denunciations by religious leaders of immoral and unjust conditions. In his social encyclicals, especially *Rerum Novarum*, issued in 1891, Leo XIII added a powerful voice to the rising cry for social reform. He restated Catholic belief in private property, the sanctity of the family, and the social role of religion, but he went beyond these well-known views to speak to modern industrial conditions. The Catholic Church, he wrote, recognizes the right of workers to their own organizations and to "reasonable and frugal comfort"; but the state, he warned, should not favor any single class, and society must not consider human beings as merely a means to profit. Strongest in rural areas and with more support among women than men, Christian churches knew a lot about those who had not necessarily benefited from modern social change. They now made more effort to reach workers and the middle class, urban groups whose special needs had often been overlooked in the past, and they spoke more readily for the discontented as they came to rely less on close ties to the state. By 1910 Christianity was more respectable among intellectuals, more active in society, and more prominent in politics than it had been since the early nineteenth century. Whether of the political left or right, Protestants and Catholics found in Christian teaching a whole arsenal of complaints against liberalism and industrial capitalism.

BEYOND REASON

Until World War I European political thought remained predominantly liberal, but some of its optimism was fading. Liberals themselves worried more about problems of community and social justice, and others questioned the power of human reason and argued for leadership by a small elite. The Frenchman Georges Sorel shared the growing suspicion that public opinion owed more to prejudice than to reason. Like many intellectuals, he felt contempt for middle-class society, but he argued that its overthrow would not come in the way predicted by Marx. His most important book, *Reflections on Violence* (1908), postulated rather that historic changes like the rise of Christianity and the French Revolution come about when people are inspired by some great myth beyond the test of reason. As a myth for his times, he proposed the general strike, a possibility then much discussed by European unions. Sorel thus contributed to the widespread syndicalist movement, which called on workers' organizations, or *syndicats*, to bring down bourgeois society. And he rejected bourgeois rationalism in favor of violence as an expression of the will that could create powerful political movements. Like many contemporary writers in Italy and Germany, he found the energy for change in humanity's irrationality.[1]

Sorel's countryman, Henri Bergson, the most eloquent and revered philosopher of his day, expounded gentler, more abstract theories; yet he, too, pictured much that is best in human understanding as arising not from reason but intui-

---

[1]Vilfredo Pareto and Sorel, both trained as engineers, are usually grouped together with Robert Michels as leading theorists of the new political "realism."

tively from subjective and unconscious feelings. Bergson was close to contemporary movements in the arts, psychology, and religion; and he believed society needed the new spirit of energy and common endeavor could be achieved through spontaneity, translating feeling into action.

The revolutionary challenge such ideas contained was clearest in the works of Friedrich Nietzsche. He, too, emphasized human will in a philosophy that lashed contemporary civilization on every page. His disdain for ideas of equality and democracy was balanced by his hatred of nationalism and militarism; he rejected his society not only for what it was but also for what it meant to be. The only hope for the future was the work of a few, the supermen who would drop the inhibitions of bourgeois society and the "slave morality" of Christianity. Nietzsche's tone had the violence of a man trying to bring everything crashing down, but he was no mere nihilist. He wrote his passionate aphorisms as a man in terror for himself and his world. A deeply original thinker, he was a child of his times in his approach to culture and history but above all in his anger.

Anti-Semitism and the Right Like Nietzsche's philosophy, anti-Semitism, which he detested, was part of the rising current of opposition to liberal society. Anti-Semitism in the 1890s was more than a continuation of centuries-old prejudices, and it was remarkably widespread. Venomous assertions of Jewish avarice and lack of patriotism were used to discredit the entire republic in France and the opponents of imperial policy in Great Britain. Sixteen deputies from anti-Semitic parties won seats in the German Reichstag in 1893, and Germany's prestigious Conservative party added anti-Semitism to its program (*see box*, p. 854). The lord mayor of Vienna from 1895 to 1910 found anti-Semitism invaluable in his electoral victories, and anti-Semitism was an official policy of the Russian government from the terrible pogroms of 1881 on.

There is no simple explanation for a phenomenon seemingly so contrary to the major trends of the century, but scholars note that Jews were often perceived as a symbol of liberal, capitalist society. They had received their civil rights at the hands of Napoleon and in liberal revolutions, lived primarily in urban environments, and found their opportunities for advancement in the expanding professions and businesses of the nineteenth century. They were prominent leaders in many of the most venturesome enterprises, important scientific discoveries, and striking social theories. Nationalism, especially in Germany, had come to stress folk culture and race; by attacking Jews, conservatives could make the liberal, capitalist world itself seem alien to national traditions. Crude adaptations of Darwinism gave racial theories a pseudo-scientific panache,[2] and indeed quack science generally flourished, for credulity was encouraged by the fact that much of academic science, especially physics, was no longer comprehensible to the layperson. Theories of conspiracy gave concrete and simple explanations for the baffling pace of social change, offering the hope that by circumscribing specific groups—such as the Jews—society could resist change itself.

Neither irrationalism nor anti-Semitism belongs inherently to a single political persuasion, but both were used primarily by the political right in the decades preceding World War I. Rightist movements revived notably in these years, building among those social groups that felt most harmed by the changes of the century: aristocrats, rural people, members of the lower-middle class whose status was threatened, and many Christians. Often incongruously, they defended established constitutions—the House of Lords in Britain, the concordat with the Roman Catholic Church in France, three-class voting and government independent of the Reichstag in Germany, limited suffrage and an intrusive monarchy in Italy, the authority of the tsar in Russia. They added to this conservatism contemporary concerns about the shallowness of middle-class

---

[2]An important example is Houston Stewart Chamberlain's *The Foundation of the Nineteenth Century*, published in Germany in 1899. A Germanophile Englishman, son-in-law and intense admirer of Richard Wagner, who had become more anti-Semitic, Chamberlain traced all that was best in European civilization to its "Aryan" elements. The work was widely admired until the collapse of the Nazi regime.

The Argument of Anti-Semitism

Anti-Semitism became more organized and more vocal in most European countries in the 1880s. Despite important variations of tone and tactic in each nation, certain myths and themes were common to most of these movements. In 1883 a German publication calling itself* The Journal for the Universal Rally for Combatting Jewdom (Zeitschrift für die Allgemeine Vereinigung zur Bekämpfung des Judentums) *repeated many of these themes. The article was presented in the form of a petition to Chancellor Bismarck, calling for a ban on Jews holding important offices and a restriction on their immigration.

"... Wherever Christian and Jew enter into social relations, we see the Jew as master and the native-born Christian population in a servile position. The Jew takes only a vanishingly small part in the hard work of the great mass of our people; in field and workshop, in mines and on scaffolding, in swamps and canals—everywhere it is only the calloused hand of the Christian that is active. But it is above all the Jew who harvests the fruits of this labor. By far the greatest portion of capital produced by national labor is concentrated in Jewish hands. Jewish real estate keeps pace with the growth of mobile capital. Not only the proudest palaces of our cities belong to the Jewish masters (whose fathers or grandfathers crossed the borders of our fatherland as peddlers and hawkers), but the rural estate—this highly significant and conserving basis of our state structure—is falling into Jewish hands with ever greater frequency.

"Truly, in view of these conditions and because of the massive penetration of the Semitic element into all positions affording power and influence, the following question seems justified on an ethical as well as national standpoint: *what future is left our fatherland if the Semitic element is allowed to make a conquest of our home ground for another generation as it has been allowed to do in the last two decades*? If the concept of 'fatherland' is not to be stripped of its ideal content, if the idea that it was our fathers who tore this land from the wilderness and fertilized it with their blood in a thousand battles is not to be lost, if the inward connection between German custom and morality and the Christian outlook and tradition is to be maintained, then an alien tribe may never, ever rise to rule on German soil. This tribe, to whom our humane legislation extended the rights of hospitality and the rights of the native, stands further from us in thought and feeling than any other people in the entire Aryan world.

"The danger to our national way of life must naturally mount not only when the Jews succeed in not only encroaching upon the national and religious consciousness of our people by means of the *press*, but also when they succeed in obtaining state offices, the bearers of which are obliged to guard over the idealistic goods of our nation. We think above all of the professions of *teacher* and *judge*. Both were inaccessible to Jews until very recently, and both must again be closed if the concept of authority, the feeling for legality and fatherland, are not to become confused and doubted by the nation. Even now the Germanic ideals of honor, loyalty, and genuine piety begin to be displaced to make room for a cosmopolitan pseudo-ideal."

From *Schmeitzer's Internationale Monatsschrift: Zeitschrift für die Allgemeine Vereinigung zur Bekämpfung des Judentums*, 1883, reprinted and translated in Richard S. Levy (ed.), *Antisemitism in the Modern World* (Lexington: D.C. Heath and Company, 1991).

culture and the evils of unchecked capitalism. A reinvigorated right tried, frequently with success, to make patriotism and national strength their battle cry, learning to make an effective mass appeal. Denounced by Marxists as defenders of reactionary capitalism, they declared socialism the menace of the hour and the natural consequence of liberal error.

Thus critics from the right and the left gained vigor from attacking the very changes that most people still labeled progress. So many simultaneous assaults created grave political crises in many states. How those were resolved in each country was crucial in reshaping its political system, and by 1910 it looked as if the international trend was for government to accept more responsibility for social justice, politics to become more democratic, and society to grow more tolerant. Overall, Europeans had never been so free to move about as they wished and say what they liked.

III. Domestic Politics

The state—the center at which political parties, economic interests, and ideologies competed—had become the focus of patriotism, a sponsor of culture, an agent of economic growth, and a source of public welfare. Governments learned the importance of winning popular support and discovered new ways of gaining it. In many respects political systems were more similar at the end of the nineteenth century than they had been since before the French Revolution, and everywhere they faced some of the same issues. Yet each nation evolved its own distinctive response, its own way of balancing the pressures for continuity and change, the interests of business and agriculture, the values of old aristocracies and new elites, the claims of workers and factory owners, and the demands for democracy and the preservation of hierarchy.

There were certain issues that every political system had to deal with. One was who should participate in political life. The trend was to increase suffrage until every adult male had the right to vote, and in many countries extending that right to women had become a burning issue by the turn of the century. Each political system also found its own ways of constraining democracy, through royal prerogatives, a conservative second chamber, or limits on what legislatures could do. Another issue had to do with the role of the state, its responsibility for social welfare (including education, housing, and public health) and its economic policies (especially as they affected trade and labor unions). Specific institutions and groups—such as the church, the military, or the aristocracy—sought to enlist the state on their side. Sometimes these competing interests could be balanced (as in tariffs that protected both industry and agriculture) or resolved through compromise (as in reforms that preserved social distinctions but expanded access to public schooling or access to positions in the civil service). Sometimes these conflicts reinforced ideological divisions that threatened to undermine the political system itself.

Nearly every country also struggled with the very definition of national community and whether some groups—ethnic minorities, foreigners, Catholics, Jews, anarchists, or socialists—should be excluded as alien or of uncertain loyalty. These issues, which expressed basic hopes and aroused passionate fears, could become extremely disruptive; and how a society responded to this challenge was an important measure of its political system and restatement of its national tradition. Peaceful resolutions were possible: When Norway voted for separation from Sweden in 1905, the decision was accepted on both sides, and the two nations lived thereafter in harmony, among the most democratic in the world. Not surprisingly, comparative politics became a formal academic subject in this period; the similarities among European political systems made their differences more revealing.

FRANCE: THE THIRD REPUBLIC

In France political conflict revolved around the form of government. Defeat in the Franco-Prussian War of 1870 was fatal to Louis Napoleon's Second Empire. Shortly after his surrender, Parisian crowds cheered the proclamation of a republic; and new leaders sought to mobilize the nation as an earlier republic had done in 1792. German forces quickly surrounded Paris, but Léon Gambetta, the most dynamic of the republicans, made a daring escape, flying off in a balloon to set up headquarters and organize resistance outside the capital. French forces, strengthened by newly recruited peasants, even made some gains until, overmatched, they were pushed back in December. Paris remained under

▸ Onlookers reacted with fury when the Versailles government sent troops into Paris to seize artillery left in the city after the siege. Shouts and stones led to shots and bloodshed, then someone recognized Generals Lecomte and Clément-Thomas. They were lined up and shot, while citizens watched (and someone took a photograph).

German siege. Refusing to surrender, its citizens held out for four months. They cut down the trees of the boulevards for fuel, slaughtered pets, and emptied the zoo as a starving city continued to resist during a winter as severe as any on record. But heroism and patriotic fervor could not defeat a modern army, and at the end of January Paris capitulated. German troops marched into a denuded and quiet city.

France's newly elected assembly met at Versailles and quickly accepted peace on German terms. The assembly, divided between monarchists (elected as proponents of peace) and republicans, could not agree, however, on the form of government. It compromised by naming Adolphe Thiers, a moderate politician who had been prominent in the July Monarchy 30 years earlier, as chief of the "Executive Power," thereby postponing the issue of whether France was to have a king or a president.

The Paris Commune Thiers knew that his government must establish control of Paris, which had been cut off from the rest of France. As a first step, he decided to disarm the city's National Guard. When troops from Versailles tried to remove some cannons, however, they were confronted by an angry crowd. Shots were fired; and by day's end, two generals lay dead. Faced with insurrection, Thiers withdrew his army, determined first to isolate the revolution and then to crush it. The municipal council of Paris, in another echo of the French Revolution of 1789, declared the city a self-governing commune and prepared to fight. While German armies idly watched, the French engaged in civil war.

Many of the well-to-do had left Paris during the armistice, but the poor and the radical remained. Hardened by months of siege, their resentments mounted as the government at Versailles stopped payments to the National Guard, the only income for many Parisians, and suddenly ended the moratorium on personal debts (including rents) that had been in effect while Paris was under siege. The Paris Commune included moderate and radical republicans, some followers of Pierre Joseph Proudhon and Louis-Auguste Blanqui, militant socialists in the tradition of Saint-Simon and Fourier, and a few members of the Marxist First International. Its program, favoring democracy and federalism, was not very specific on other matters; and it had little time to experiment.

The conservative assembly in Versailles sent its armies to assault the Paris Commune, and the hatred between them was exacerbated by the recent anguish of war, siege, and defeat as well as by the long-standing differences, ideological and social, between rural France and the capital. The two sides fought for competing visions of what the nation should become, and they fought with rising fury. On both sides hostages were taken and prisoners shot (the communards executed the archbishop of Paris), and it took almost two months of bloodshed before government troops broke into the city in May. Even then the fighting continued, barricade by barricade, into the working-class quarters, where the group commanded by Louise Michel—the most famous of hundreds of militant *citoyennes* who would later tell her captors, "I belong entirely to the Social Revolution"—was among the last to fall. Solid citizens shuddered at revolutionary excess (and especially at the part played by women), but on the whole, the victors were more brutal. Tens of thousands of Parisians died in the streets, and summary courts-martial ordered execution, imprisonment, or deportation for tens of thousands more.

Throughout Europe, the commune raised the specter of revolution. From the first, Marxists hailed it as a proletarian rising, the dawning of a new era, though Marx was indignant with the communard's lack of revolutionary daring and their respect for property and legality. Former communards became the heroes of socialist gatherings for the next generation, and to this day the cemetery where many of them were executed remains a shrine honored by socialists and communists.[3] Historians have been at great pains to show how little socialism, still less Marxism, there was in the Paris Commune (it respectfully left the Bank of Paris intact); yet myth has its historical importance, too. This indisputably was class conflict, and the rage on both sides was more significant than mere differences of program. After 1871 a proletarian revolution became a credible possibility to radical and conservative alike, and working-class movements pointed to the martyrs of the Commune as evidence of the selfish cruelty of bourgeois rule.

The Founding of the Third Republic Remarkably, a stable republic gradually emerged from this unpromising beginning. The administrative structure of the French state remained, stronger than any political group, and Thiers used it effectively. The loan needed to pay the indemnity to Germany was soon oversubscribed. As elections produced victories for moderate republicans, monarchists feared that their chance was slipping away. They managed to oust Thiers in favor of one of their own while they looked for a chance to restore the monarchy. They never found it. They themselves were divided between the conservative supporters of the grandson of Charles X and those who favored the grandson of Louis Philippe. The two factions differed on issues of democracy, social policy, relations with the Church, and even symbolism (the more conservative claimant refused to accept the tricolor, the flag of French patriotism, because it was the flag of revolution). Meanwhile moderate republicans continued to gain in popularity, and in 1875 the assembly passed a law declaring that "the president of the republic" should be elected by the two legislative houses. The Third Republic was thus quietly established, without ringing phrases, as the government that, as Thiers put it, divided Frenchmen least. There was to be a Chamber of Deputies, elected by direct universal male suffrage, and a Senate indirectly elected by local officials. In elections the following year, republicans captured two-thirds of the seats in the Chamber and almost half those in the Senate. The presidency, which had been so strong under Thiers, was still in monarchist hands; but its authority continued to decline, and that established a further precedent. The Third Republic, a regime of compromise which had earned acceptability by crushing the Commune and accepting a conservative Senate, would have a weak executive. It would last longer than any French regime since 1789. Successive republican governments guaranteed political freedom and deferred to the middle class while France's public institutions preserved the remarkable continuity that had characterized them after 1800. Economic growth, less dramatic than in Great Britain or Germany, was also less disruptive; France had found its own balance between the demands for order and the need for change.

The Trials and Triumph of the Third Republic For 20 years, from 1879 to 1899, the leading politicians were moderate republicans who found in lack of daring the best guarantee of stability and in anticlericalism their most popular plank. Strong defenders of free speech and individualism, they recognized unions but initiated few projects of public works or social welfare. In the 1880s they made elementary education in state schools compulsory and established restrictions on the Catholic Church that were intended to weaken its political influence, policies that carried the parliamentary conflicts between left and right into the villages of France. The republic's cautious leaders did not evoke much popular enthusiasm, however, and political crises were fre-

[3]A century later a Russian sputnik proudly carried to the moon not only a Soviet flag but a red flag from the Commune of 1871.

▶ **Every stage of the Dreyfus affair was the occasion for public demonstrations. *Le Petit Journal*, which had the largest circulation of any Paris newspaper, printed this scene of a crowd of magistrates and ordinary citizens hailing the news in February 1898 that Zola has been convicted of libel.**

quent. In 1889 General Georges Boulanger gained such popularity by speeches expressing concern for workers and patriotic denunciation of Germany that there was danger of a coup d'état. A few years after that danger had passed, scandals threatened the government. Companies planning a canal through Panama went bankrupt, and investigations into them uncovered political graft. There followed a stormy campaign against republican politicians, liberal newspapers, and Jewish financiers. Only when the regime seemed close to toppling did its defenders pull together.

The Third Republic's great trial came with the Dreyfus case. In 1894 a court-martial convicted Captain Alfred Dreyfus, a Jew and a member of the General Staff, of providing the German military attaché with secret French documents. Although the sensational press shouted Jewish treachery, the issue only became the center of public attention three years afterward, when evidence appeared suggesting another officer had been guilty. Generals, refusing to reopen the case, spoke darkly of honor and state secrets, and the right-wing press hailed their patriotism. The controversy escalated with charges and countercharges in parliament and the press, a series of sensational trials, and huge public demonstrations. The nation was divided. The majority of Catholics, monarchists, and conservatives joined in patriotic indignation against Jews and socialists who were allegedly conspiring to sell out France and weaken a loyal army. The left—intellectuals, socialists, and republicans—came to view Dreyfus as the innocent victim of a plot against republican institutions. Figures like the novelist Emile Zola, who was twice convicted of libel for his efforts, led in demanding a new trial. The military courts, however, were reluctant to admit past mistakes. A courts-martial in 1898 acquitted the man who forged the principal evidence against Dreyfus and a year later convicted Dreyfus a second time but "with extenuating circumstances," a confusing ruling that led to a presidential pardon. The defenders of Dreyfus won the battle for public opinion, though barely,[4] and that victory set the tone of subsequent French politics, cementing traditions of republican unity on the left and greatly reducing the political influence of the Church and monarchists. Years of polemics and confrontation, however, left deep scars.

From 1900 until World War I, government was in the hands of firm republicans who, despite their cautious position on social issues, called themselves the Radical party. They set about purging the army of their opponents and launched new attacks on the Church that subsided only with the passage of a law separating church and state in 1905. Yet they administered with restraint. Solicitous of the "little man," of small businessmen and peasant farmers, they solidified support for the republic. Indeed, part of

[4]A few Dreyfusards continued collecting evidence and finally won acquittal in a civil trial in 1906. Dreyfus was then decorated and promoted to the rank of major.

the Third Republic's achievement was its ability to draw radical politicians to moderate policies. A socialist even entered the cabinet in the aftermath of the Dreyfus affair (thereby earning the condemnation of the Second International for cooperating in a bourgeois state). Despite frequent strikes, a labor movement that doubled its membership in this period never produced the more revolutionary general strike so much talked about. The prime minister from 1906 to 1909 was Georges Clemenceau, a man once associated with the radical left who now effectively combined policies of reform and conciliation. On the eve of world war, France, prosperous and stable, appeared to have surmounted its most dangerous divisions.

GERMANY: THE REICH

Until 1890 Bismarck dominated German public life with an authority few modern figures have equaled, establishing a pattern his successors would strain to maintain. The architect of so successful a system was understandably scornful of criticism, and a chancellor so overweening won many enemies; but Bismarck was untouchable until William II ascended the throne in 1888. Twenty-nine years old, bright but ill-prepared, William was infatuated with all things military, anxious to make himself loved, and eager to rule. He disagreed with parts of Bismarck's foreign policy and opposed the antisocialist laws, but theirs was primarily a conflict of wills. In 1890 the emperor, impatient with Bismarck's paternal arrogance, forced his resignation. Succeeding chancellors (there were four between 1890 and 1917) served until the dissatisfaction of some powerful faction led to their replacement.

Post-Bismarckian Tensions Bismarck's policies had allowed for great concentrations of political and economic power in a rapidly expanding society, one in which court, army, bureaucracy, and business were treated as semiautonomous interests. Holding the system together while balancing the demands of parliament and public opinion was the growing challenge Bismarck's successors faced. They sometimes tried to match his dazzling foreign policy, and they followed him in attending to the army. Bismarck won a sizable electoral victory in 1887 on the issue of enlarging the army over parliament's objections, and military appropriations were a source of intense conflicts again in 1893, 1898, and 1911–1913; each time the army grew larger, the government's statements became more nationalist, and society seemed more divided.

Germany's conservatives had also learned from Bismarck the value of appealing to the public, and they did so through the strident propaganda of political leagues—the Landlords', Peasants', Pan-German, Colonial, and Naval Leagues—organized in the 1890s. Well-financed by Prussian Junkers and some industrialists, these leagues campaigned for high tariffs, overseas empire, and the military, with attacks on socialists, Jews, and foreign enemies. As pressure groups, they won significant victories, as with the naval bill of 1898, which proposed to create a fleet that could compete with Britain's. In addition to building railroads, roads, and schools, the government extended the comprehensive social welfare programs begun under Bismarck, and William II was hailed as "the Labor Emperor" for supporting social security, labor arbitration, the regulation of workers' hours, and provisions for their safety.

But Bismarck's assurance that such measures would weaken socialism was not realized. The well-organized Social Democrats continued to

▸ At a mine entrance in the Ruhr in 1912, striking German mine workers read an official proclamation warning that the police are authorized to shoot.

gain in the 1890s, and they became the largest party in the Reichstag in 1912 (and the strongest socialist party in Europe) despite the distortions of the electoral system. Socialists also dominated Germany's vigorous labor unions, which had 2.5 million members by 1912, and an influential subculture with its own newspapers and libraries and recreation centers. In theory, at least, the Social Democrats remained firm revolutionaries, formally rejecting the revisionism of Eduard Bernstein. In his book *Evolutionary Socialism* (1897), he argued that many of Marx's predictions had proved wrong and that socialists should place less emphasis on economic determinism or revolution and seek instead to improve working conditions and strengthen democracy. The subject of international debate, Bernstein's theories implied a less militant socialism willing to cooperate with other democratic parties, and it was an important moment in the history of socialism when Germany's powerful Social Democrats chose instead to make a rigorous Marxism their official policy.

An angry rigidity had developed in Germany's politics. The last peacetime chancellor (and the first of bourgeois origin) Theobald von Bethmann-Hollweg took office in 1909. A cautious bureaucrat who presided over a bureaucracy rife with cabals, he tried to placate parliament and hold in check a royal court where people spoke openly of using the army against radicals. Bethmann-Hollweg's mild programs for reform came to nothing. The continent's most powerful nation remained dominated by Prussia, where voting continued to be by the three-class system, and Germany's chancellor remained responsible to the crown and not to the Reichstag.

ITALY

Italy's liberal monarchy was committed to modernizing the nation while balancing the budget and steadily sponsoring modest reforms, but the political system in which only the well-to-do could vote and where the government kept its parliamentary majority by means of political favors made it hard to win broad popular support. As a hero of Italian unification and former radical, Francesco Crispi, prime minister in the late 1880s and 1890s, tried to change that. His policies—which included anticlericalism, a trade war with France, and imperial adventure—proved divisive instead. Crispi resorted to martial law to put down peasant protests, and in 1894, now frankly relying on the army, he attempted to win over the public by establishing an Italian protectorate in Ethiopia. Instead Crispi had to resign in 1896 when 25,000 Italian troops were nearly wiped out at Aduwa by well-prepared Ethiopian forces four times their number.[5]

Domestic unrest increased, however, both in the poverty-stricken agrarian south and in the rapidly industrializing north, where anarchist bombs, socialist demonstrations, and waves of strikes culminated in riots that reached revolutionary scale in Milan in 1898. Order was restored at the cost of bloodshed, the suppression of scores of newspapers, and a ban on hundreds of socialist, republican, and Catholic organizations. Many argued for still firmer measures; yet the Chamber of Deputies, although frightened, refused further restriction of civil liberties, a stand supported in the elections of 1900. In Italy, as in France at the same time, the political campaign of a revitalized right was defeated by parliament and public opinion.

The political system acquired a broader base of support under Giovanni Giolitti, prime minister from 1903 to 1914. He acknowledged the right to strike, nationalized railroads and life insurance, sponsored public health measures, and in 1911 supported universal male suffrage. Giolitti also encouraged Catholics to enter the national politics they had boycotted since 1870, and he, too, acquiesced in an imperial venture. Italy went to war against the Ottoman sultan in 1912, took Rhodes and the other major Dodecanese Islands, and landed at the port city of Tripoli in Libya, all of which the sultan ceded. The year of war inspired an enthusiasm Italian governments had rarely enjoyed. The economic problems of the south remained grave and the discontent of more and more militant workers largely unappeased, but the Italian economy, less developed than that of the great industrial powers, experienced the fastest growth rate in Europe during

[5]Subsequent governments held on to Eritrea as an Italian colony.

the decade ending in 1914. An often isolated and sometimes corrupt government would prove an easy target for critics from the left and the right, and they were the notable winners in the elections of 1913, the first under the broadened suffrage.

RUSSIA

In Russia the pressures for political change were held in check for a generation by official policies that centered on a program of "Russification," meant to create a united nation. Alexander III had become tsar in 1881 on his father's assassination, an event that he believed resulted from too much talk about further reform following the abolition of serfdom. He sought instead to achieve stability by using the Orthodox Church and the police to extend an official reactionary ideology through public life, and he gave nobles an increased role in regional councils, the *zemstvos*, and rural administration. Local governors were authorized to use martial law, to restrict or ban the religions and languages of non-Russian peoples, and to persecute Jews.[6] These policies were continued with equal conviction but less energy by Tsar Nicholas II, who ascended the throne in 1894. Unrest increased nevertheless in cities and in the countryside, and many in the government searched for other ways of achieving the solidarity repression had failed to create.

War, and the patriotism it evokes, was thus welcomed in 1904, when Japan suddenly attacked the Russians at Port Arthur. Russia had leased Port Arthur from China in 1898 as part of its expansion into East Asia and Manchuria. For years these moves had troubled the Japanese, and Russia had neither kept its promises to withdraw nor acknowledged Japan's proposals for establishing mutually acceptable spheres of influence. The war was a disaster for Russia. Surprise attack was followed by defeats in Manchuria, the fall of Port Arthur, and the annihilation of a large Russian fleet that sailed around the world only to be sunk in Japanese waters. In the treaty, signed at Portsmouth, New Hampshire—the United States, like Japan, wished to demonstrate its status as a world power—Russia ceded most of its recent gains, including Port Arthur and the southern half of Sakhalin Island, and recognized Japanese interest in Korea.

The Revolution of 1905 So dramatic a defeat increased pressure for major reforms just as the Crimean War had 50 years before, but this time the pressure came from deep within Russian society. Peasant agitation had been on the rise since a terrible famine in 1891. Secret organizations were growing among the non-Russian nationalities, and workers drawn to St. Petersburg and Moscow by industrialization had begun to form unions. The Social Revolutionaries, a party combining the traditions of populism and terrorism, grew more active; and the Marxist Social Democrats, hitherto composed of rather disparate groups, now organized in exile and strengthened their ties within Russia. In this atmosphere liberal members of the *zemstvos* held a national congress in 1904, though forbidden to by the government, and insisted on civil liberties. Then in January 1905 striking workers in St. Petersburg, demanding a national constitution as well as the recognition of labor unions, marched on the Winter Palace to petition the tsar. They carried icons and sang "God save the tsar"; when they had assembled, the army opened fire, killing scores and wounding hundreds more.

"Bloody Sunday" led to agitation so widespread that in March the tsar promised to call an assembly of notables and announced immediate reforms: religious toleration, reduced restrictions on Jews and non-Russian nationals, and cancellation of part of the payments peasants owed for their land. Agitation for a constitution only grew stronger, expressed through urban strikes, peasant riots, and mutinies in both the army and navy. In August the tsar conceded more, declaring he would consult a national assembly, the Imperial Duma. Many close to the throne were shocked by so radical a step; the response of a public wanting something more concrete was a wave of strikes. For the last 10 days of October, Russia's economic life came to a halt, the most effective general strike Europe had ever seen. It

[6]One of history's famous forgeries, the *Protocols of the Elders of Zion*, was published (and written) by the Russian police in 1903. The protocols purported to be the secret minutes of a Jewish congress that revealed a conspiracy to control the world.

▸ **On "Bloody Sunday" in January 1905 protesters, led by a priest and carrying a petition to the Tsar, marched to the Winter Palace where they were fired on by Russian soldiers. That bloodshed, following rising demands for a representative assembly, marked the beginning of the Revolution of 1905; thousands of people died that day.**

won from the tsar the October Manifesto, which granted a constitution.

Crowds danced in the streets; but proponents of change were divided. Those willing to work with this constitution, which guaranteed freedom of speech and assembly but was vague on much else, became known as Octobrists. Liberals who insisted on a constituent assembly and broader guarantees formed the Constitutional Democratic party, called Cadets for short. On the left, socialists and revolutionaries rejected compromise, and the St. Petersburg Soviet, a committee of trade union leaders and socialists, called another general strike. It was only partially successful, and an emboldened government arrested the leaders of the Soviet in December and bloodily defeated the Moscow workers who revolted in protest. The Fundamental Laws announced in May 1906 defined the limitations of the tsar's concessions. He would keep the power of veto, the right to name his ministers, and full command of the executive, the judiciary, and the armed forces; the national legislature would have an upper house in addition to the Duma, with half its members appointed by the tsar. Elections under this new system, however, brought the Cadets a large majority, which demanded representative government. Nicholas then disbanded the legislature and held new elections, but they produced an even more radical assembly; and it, too, was disbanded. Only a new electoral law favoring the propertied classes ensured conservative majorities in subsequent legislatures.

The Revolution of 1905 had nevertheless brought important changes. Russia now had parliamentary institutions and organized parties, the power of the aristocracy had been greatly reduced, and the nation was clearly set on a modern course. The prime minister from 1906 to 1911, Peter Stolypin, reformed education and administration and strove to stimulate the economy with programs that abandoned the *mir* system of communal lands in favor of the full private ownership of land and other programs that created land banks and social insurance. With the aid of foreign capital, the pace of industrialization rapidly increased. While discontent among workers and poorer peasants remained serious and radical movements were sternly repressed, the Cadets were finding it possible to work with the new system. Liberals throughout Europe rejoiced that the giant of the East had at last begun to follow the path of Western progress.

AUSTRIA-HUNGARY

The political problems of Austria-Hungary were revealed not so much in crises as in stalemate. Creation of an autonomous regime in Hungary led to conflicts with the rest of the empire that remained critical until the turn of the century, exacerbated by the divergent economic interests of industrializing regions and agrarian Hungary. Further reforms were stymied by the imperial court, the aristocracy, and the bureaucracy. The pillars of the empire, they settled instead on a cautious prime minister, Count Eduard von Taafe, who held office from 1879 to 1893. Taafe's parliamentary support included Czechs and Poles, who wanted concessions Taafe's other supporters would not accept. Inaction was thus the safest course as social change led to further disagreements. The spread of education, for instance, heightened conflict over the language to be used in schools. In response to workers' agitation, Taafe proposed welfare measures while repressing socialists, steps that antagonized both left and right. After his fall, governments came to rely more on decree powers and the support of the crown than on parliamentary support. With universal manhood suffrage, introduced without conviction in 1907, the Christian Socialists and the Social Democrats became the two largest parties. Neither was acceptable to the leaders of the empire, and they were kept out of office while competing for support primarily in the city of Vienna, where the Christian Socialists gained sway by combining social programs with demagogic anti-Semitism.

Within Hungary the Magyars remained dominant over other nationalities by requiring that their language be used in government and schools, by tightly controlling the electoral system, and by subverting the bureaucracy through corruption. Their efforts to win greater independence from the imperial government and to protect the interests of large landowners weakened the empire. When in 1903 they demanded greater autonomy for their own army, they touched one issue about which Emperor Francis Joseph I cared too much to yield. He suspended the Hungarian constitution, ruled without parliament, and frightened the Magyars into submission by threatening to subject them, a minority in their own country, to universal male suffrage. Magyars and the empire needed each other; and Magyar politics, admired in the 1840s as a model of liberal nationalism, had turned by 1906 into the defensive strategy of a threatened aristocracy. For mutual survival the leaders of Austria and Hungary avoided dangerous changes and relied on imperial foreign policy to strengthen from the outside a political system in danger at home.

SPAIN

Spain developed a remarkable tradition of parliamentarism in which governments were careful to keep the support of the army, the Church, big business, and regional interests. By emphasizing the economy, a liberal coalition held power from 1854 to 1863, years in which Spain experienced on a smaller scale the waves of speculation, railroad building, economic growth, and ostentation associated with the Second Empire in France. But growth brought new demands that old alliances, palace intrigue, and electoral manipulation could not check. The government's conservative successors led in 1868 to the flight of the unpopular Queen Isabella II and to revolution.

The leaders of the revolution were political moderates who quickly agreed on a constitutional monarchy with universal manhood suffrage, trial by jury, and freedom of religion and the press. It proved easier to adopt a new constitution, however, than to find a new king. Candidate after candidate declined to become entangled in Spanish politics and the sort of international complications that precipitated the Franco-Prussian War. The king finally found gave up the throne after three years of rising opposition from forces on the left and right. The subsequent republic lasted only two years before the military installed Isabella's son on the throne as Alfonso XII. He began his reign in 1875 with a new constitution closer to the one in effect at midcentury than to the more democratic ones that had succeeded it. In a parliamentary system based on limited suffrage, the Conservative and Liberal parties alternated in power with little change in policy, a system that masked the bitter divisions between regionalists and centralists, Catholics and anticlericals, the poor and the propertied by keeping the state relatively weak. As in Russia and Austria, however, industrialization exacerbated these tensions. Nor could the government establish a consistent program for the colonies, meeting unrest in Cuba with alternating policies of repression and laxity. Cuban resistance became guerrilla war, and in 1898 the United States entered the conflict with an imperialist enthusiasm of its own. Spain was forced to withdraw from Cuba and to cede Puerto Rico, Guam, and the Philippine Islands to the United States.

Those losses led to a great deal of soul searching. A group of Spanish intellectuals known as the generation of 1898 brought new vitality to Spanish public life, but neither caution of conservatives nor the mild reforms of liberals could stem the increasing dissension in which the Church denounced the liberals while growing anarchist and socialist movements attacked the whole establishment. In 1909 these conflicts burst forth in a week of violence in Barcelona during which churches were burned and looted and private citizens were murdered. Yet the authorities soon restored order, and Spanish politics continued its familiar course.

GREAT BRITAIN

From Russia to Spain, European nations had adopted parliamentary systems; and until the end of the century, Britain provided the model of how such a system was supposed to work. Legislation addressed the most pressing social issues, however cautiously; and parliament gradually reduced legal inequalities, opening the civil service to those who passed competitive examinations, removing legal disabilities on Jews, and eliminating special taxes on behalf of the Church of England. At the same time order was maintained through respect for law, toleration, and social deference. There were serious domestic tensions, but they were attenuated by a thriving two-party system.

The Parties of Gladstone and Disraeli The creation of modern political parties led by two brilliant leaders facilitated Britain's adaptation to change. William Gladstone was instrumental in transforming the Whigs into the Liberal party, and Benjamin Disraeli led in making the Tories into the modern Conservative party. Gladstone was a skilled parliamentary tactician sympathetic to liberal reformers and even radicals, for whom political liberalism was a moral cause. Somewhat hesitantly, he made increased suffrage, which had been talked about for a generation, a central plank; but his complicated bill was defeated in Parliament. Instead, Disraeli persuaded his startled party to support a simpler, more generous reform, which passed in 1867. It doubled the electorate by extending the right to vote to all men who paid property taxes directly or indirectly through rent (about one adult male in three). Equally important, even major reforms were now part of the systematic competition for popular favor. The parliamentary clashes of Gladstone and Disraeli became a dramatic part of British public life.

This enlarged electorate gave the Liberals a great victory; and for six years Gladstone's first ministry fundamentally altered the relations between government and society. State aid to elementary schools, both religious and secular, brought Britain closer to universal education. The Liberals also reformed the army (even the purchase of commissions was abolished, despite great resistance from the House of Lords) and disestablished the Anglican Church of Ireland (so that an overwhelmingly Catholic population no longer paid taxes to support a Protestant church). Recognizing the festering poverty and discontent in Ireland, they passed laws that restricted the abuses of absentee landlords and provided peasants some protection against eviction. The elections of 1874 returned the Conservatives to power, and they were more willing than the Liberals to expand the authority of the state. A public health act established a national code for housing and urban sanitation; and new measures allowed striking workers to picket, making unions more effective. These social concerns, often called Tory democracy, which offered a British parallel to the policies of Bismarck and Napoleon III, became the cornerstone of the revived Conservative party.

Gladstone in turn adopted the principle of universal male suffrage, which became law with the Third Reform Bill in 1885. Men with an independent place of residence could now vote, and it says much about the life of the poor that this one requirement—which excluded domestic servants, sons living with parents, and those with no permanent address—was enough to exclude roughly one-third of all adult males. Gladstone's perpetual compromises, however, were losing their appeal; and imperial issues were his undoing. His renewed efforts in behalf of Irish peasants failed to satisfy Irish nationalists who wanted an independent Irish parliament. When Gladstone acquiesced to home rule, in 1886, his party split; and an important group of Liberals allied with the Conservatives. They were led by Joseph Chamberlain, a radical in social matters, who had adopted the popular cause of imperialism. Conservative governments would hold office for 16 of the next 19 years between 1886 and 1905.

► London's dock workers had gained national sympathy with their orderly demonstrations in the great strike of 1899 and had won some of their demands, but the agitation and unrest continued. Here, during a subsequent strike, police guard a convoy of food trucks making their way to city markets.

Rising Social Tensions While projecting British power around the world, Conservative governments were active at home. In 1888 and again in 1894 they restructured local government, a traditional source of the aristocracy's political power, making country councils elective and thus more democratic. They extended the reforms of the civil service, and in an act of 1902 established a national education system that for the first time included secondary schooling. Yet these important changes did not address the needs of the working class, whose rising dissatisfaction was marked by the dramatic strikes of London match girls in 1888 and dock workers the next year. The strikes, which won public sympathy, were part of a "new unionism" that included unskilled workers in a more militant labor movement. Social conflict became public in Britain as never before; and the Labour party, formed in 1900, which brought together many union representatives and some prominent intellectuals who favored democratic socialism, added to it.

Conservatives resisted the social programs demanded by the Labour and Liberal parties and hoped that the popular appeal of empire would keep them in power. Instead, in 1906 the Liberals won the most one-sided electoral victory since 1832. They immediately established systems of workers' compensation, old-age pensions, and urban planning. These measures—and the expanding arms race—required new revenues, and in 1909 David Lloyd George, the chancellor of the Exchequer, proposed a "people's budget." A skilled orator who delighted in the rhetoric of class conflict, he promised to place the burden of social welfare costs squarely on the rich. An aroused House of Lords rejected his budget, an unprecedented act that forced a constitutional crisis and new elections. The king's threat to appoint hundreds of additional peers finally forced the upper house to accept not only the hated budget but also a major change in the constitution. New legislation established that the Lords could no longer veto money bills or any measure

Emmeline Pankhurst on Women's Rights

Emmeline Pankhurst founded the Women's Social and Political Union in 1903. As the militant leader of the British suffragettes, she won headlines and eventually significant support for her cause with her disruptive tactics and powerful speeches. Her fame was international by the time she went on a speaking tour in Canada in 1912, where on January 14 she gave a long speech from which this passage is taken. Delighting her audience with stories of the resistance she had met, she focused on the right to vote but made clear that her vision of women's roles was much broader.

"There has been a great deal of talk lately of new legislation for those who are about to enter into marriage. Women should have a say as one of the contracting parties. There are the questions of divorce and of the training of children. Who knows better of these matters than do women? There are also the trades and professions which are at the present time open to women. It is only right that we should have some say in the legislation concerning us. We have heard much of the English divorce law. It is a disgrace to any civilized country. The only redeeming feature of the matter is that the bulk of men are better than the law allows. But there is the minority, and the law should be severe for them. They are as bad as the law allows them to be. If woman only had weight in politics this would be rectified soon. She will serve to call more attention to such questions of national welfare. If we are to have any divorce law at all, and that is a much-debated question, it should be a law that is equal both for man and woman. Unless women get the vote we have no guarantee that it will be so.

". . . Men are responsible if they allow the present condition of things to continue. Women have the power to work out their own salvation. But as it is, if a woman is ruined, if a child is injured, man is responsible for it all. It is a responsibility I would not care to have, and, as things are, I would not be a man for all the world. If women fail as men have failed, then they will bear the burden with them. But since men cannot protect and shield us, let us share the duty with them, let us use our power so that woman may be a participant, not to tyrannize over man but to take a share in the responsibilities of ruling, without which there is no real representative government. What we really are interested in in this fight is the uplifting of the sex and better conditions of humanity than men can secure. In the legal home there is but the man. What we want is the combined intelligence of man and woman working for the salvation of the children of the race. This will make for the world a better time than ever before in its history. It will raise mankind to heights of which now it has little conception. We must only make this last fight for human freedom that as the class distinction disappeared so that sex distinction may pass, and then you will get better things than men can by themselves secure."

From Emmeline Pankhurst, "The Last Fight for Human Freedom," speech given in Canada in 1912, in Brian MacArthur, *Twentieth-Century Speeches* (New York: Viking, 1992).

that passed the Commons in three successive sessions.

The peers' intemperate outburst, which cost them so much, was part of a general rise in social tension. From 1910 to 1914 strikes increased in frequency, size, and violence; a general strike became a real and much-talked-of threat. Women campaigning for the right to vote interrupted public meetings, invaded Parliament itself, smashed windows, and planted bombs. Arrested, they went on hunger strikes until baffled statesmen ordered their release. Such behavior from ladies was shocking in itself; but as the movement gained strength, recruiting women (and some men) from every social class, its outraged attack on smug male assumptions reinforced the rising challenge to a whole social order (*see box*, p. 866). Nor was the threat of violence limited to the left. In 1914 the Commons for the third time passed a bill granting Irish home rule, which made it immune to a veto in the House of Lords. The Protestants of northern Ireland, with support from many in England, openly threatened civil war. Squads began drilling, and the British officer corps seemed ready to mutiny rather than fight to impose home rule on Protestant loyalists.

The outbreak of world war generated the national unity that neither imperialism nor social reform had been able to achieve. But if the death of Queen Victoria in 1901 had symbolized the end of an age of British expansion, the ascent of George V to the throne (1910–1936) marked the opening of new and terrible conflicts. Edward VII's brief reign (1901–1910) would soon be remembered a little sadly as the Edwardian era, a happy time of relaxed confidence in prosperity, progress, and peace.

In a short period every European nation had faced major political crises; yet as political systems worked to balance class conflict and clashing interests, the trend toward greater democracy and large-scale organization seemed irresistible. For good or ill, there had been no revolutions for a generation, save in backward Russia, and no European war, facts contemporaries often cited as proof of progress. In most countries there was greater freedom of expression, more political participation, more leisure, increased literacy and education, and better health care than in the past. In general, productivity and prosperity, already at levels never achieved before, continued to rise. Science and technology promised still greater wonders. Even in retrospect, the level of creativity in the arts and scholarship and the growth of knowledge and professional standards in every field remain impressive. Yet the civilization that achieved all this was bitterly denounced not only for its manifest injustices, which by contrast with its achievements seemed all the more blatant, but more fundamentally for its lack of coherent values, for its materialism, for the ugliness of industrial society, and for the privileged position of a middle class portrayed as self-serving and philistine. Perhaps European society was evolving toward solutions of these deficiencies, as many believed. We cannot know, because suddenly in 1914 the very compromises that had held society together and kept the peace exploded—not in revolution, but in total war.

Recommended Reading

Sources

MacDougall, H. A. (ed.). *Lord Acton on Papal Power.* 1973. A leading figure in Britain's intellectual life and thoughtful historian, Lord Acton was a committed Catholic who was also an outspoken opponent of the doctrine of papal infallibility proclaimed at the Vatican Council in 1871. This collection of his public writings and private correspondence with important contemporaries provides a touching glimpse of Acton's anguish as well as the widespread attention these issues received.

Snyder, Louis L. *The Dreyfus Case: A Documentary History.* 1973. These well-edited documents convey the passions this famous affair evoked and the broad implications all sides saw in it.

Weintraub, Stanley. *The Yellow Book: Quintessence of the Nineties.* 1964. The stories and articles in this collection are all taken from the most daring literary quarterly of the day; nearly every piece is an exercise in the rejection of Victorian proprieties, and in that respect characteristic of the new movements in the arts.

Studies

Berghahn, Voker R. *Germany, 1871–1914: Economy, Society, Culture, and Politics.* 1993. A thematic survey unusual in its breadth, particularly attentive to public culture and social structure.

Berlanstein, Lenard R. *The Working People of Paris, 1871–1914.* 1984. Looks at the important changes in the lives of wage earners, in the nature of work, and in the workplace, as well as their impact on working-class movements.

Boxer, Marilyn, and Jean Quataert. *Socialist Women: Socialist Feminism in the Nineteenth and Twentieth Century.* 1978. Looking at the important figures, the book explores the tortured ambivalence among socialists toward feminism in all the major countries.

*Craig, Gordon. *Germany: 1866–1945.* 1978. A well-written and capable analysis that stresses the failure of liberalism to overcome preindustrial forces as a key to public life.

*Dangerfield, George. *The Strange Death of Liberal England.* 1935. A skillfully and argumentatively written description of a society in crisis that has influenced subsequent interpretations of the period.

*Derfler, Leslie. *Socialism since Marx: A Century of the European Left.* 1973. Thoughtful discussion of the movements that stemmed from Marx, showing their variety, creativity, and contradictions.

*Evans, Richard J. *The Feminist Movement in Germany, 1894–1933.* 1976. Establishes the importance of these movements and their connection to German politics and parties more generally.

*———. *The Feminists: Women's Emancipation in Europe, America, and Australia.* 1979. The similarities and differences in feminist campaigns reveal a good deal about the dominant ideologies, social structure, and politics of their respective societies.

*Gay, Peter. *The Education of the Senses.* 1984. A sensitive treatment of sexuality during the Victorian Age, and the first part of a major study of the values of the bourgeoisie, written from a Freudian perspective.

Gillis, John R. *Youth and History: Tradition and Change in European Age Relations, 1770 to the Present.* 1981. An original study of youth transformed by social change that highlights the late nineteenth-century as a pivotal period.

*Hughes, H. Stuart. *Consciousness and Society: The Reorientation of European Social Thought, 1890–1930.* 1958. A gracefully written and indispensable analysis of the currents of modern thought in this time of transition from midcentury certitudes.

Johnson, Douglas. *France and the Dreyfus Affair.* 1966. A standard account of the affair that explains its extraordinary impact.

*Joll, James. *The Anarchists.* 1964. Provides a particularly clear discussion of the ideas and motives of very disparate groups, all claiming to be anarchist.

*———. *The Second International, 1889–1914.* 1966. A general history of the socialist movement in this period, with striking portraits of the major figures.

Kern, Stephen. *The Culture of Time and Space 1880–1918.* 1983. An imaginative study of ideas and experiences related to technological and cultural change reflected in art, literature, politics, and social life.

Lidtke, Vernon. *The Alternative Culture: Socialist Labor in Imperial Germany.* 1985. A significant analysis of how German socialists created Europe's most organized working-class subculture.

*Löwith, Karl. *From Hegel to Nietzsche: The Revolution in Nineteenth-Century Thought.* 1964. A sober essay on the pessimistic and irrationalist transformations in modern thought and the powerful insights that resulted.

*Available in paperback.

Lyons, Francis S. *Ireland since the Famine.* 1971. A broad social history of a society in crisis.

*Mayeur, Jean-Marie, and Madeleine Rebérioux. *The Third Republic from Its Origins to the Great War, 1871–1914.* J. R. Foster (tr.). 1984. A balanced synthesis of recent scholarship on the establishment of a stable republic amidst social conflict.

Miller, Michael. *The Bon Marché: Bourgeois Culture and the Development of the Department Store.* 1981. A fascinating study that explores the department store as a significant cultural institution.

Moses, Claire. *French Feminism in the Nineteenth Century.* 1984. Reveals the vigor of a feminist movement quite different from its British and German counterparts.

*Mosse, George L. *The Crisis of German Ideology.* 1964. Looks for the currents of Nazi ideology in the views of nation and race embodied in the popular ideas and movements of the late nineteenth century.

Pugh, Martin. *The Tories and the People, 1880–1935.* 1985. A study of the basis for and limitations of the Conservatives' mass appeal.

*Pulzer, Peter G. *The Rise of Political Anti-Semitism in Germany and Austria.* 1964. A clear and balanced survey of a difficult topic that shows the remarkable scope of anti-Semitism.

Ralston, David B. *The Army of the Republic, 1871–1914.* 1967. Treats a question of central importance to the establishment of democracy: the problem of the military in France both before and after the Dreyfus affair.

Rearick, Charles. *Pleasures of the Belle Époque.* 1985. Captures the cultural and social vitality of the period, emphasizing popular culture and the uses of leisure.

*Robertson, Priscilla. *An Experience of Women: Pattern and Change in Nineteenth-Century Europe.* 1982. A social and intellectual history of middle- and upper-class women in Western Europe, useful for the breadth of its coverage.

*Romero, Patricia W. *E. Sylvia Pankhurst: Portrait of a Radical.* 1987. This biography of Britain's feminist leader gives a good sense of the development of the movement overall.

*Schorske, Carl E. *Fin-de-Siècle Vienna: Politics and Culture.* 1980. Unusually sensitive and imaginative assessment of one of the important moments in European cultural history.

Seton-Watson, Christopher. *Italy from Liberalism to Fascism.* 1967. A thorough general, political account of Italy in its first period of rapid industrialization.

*Shattuck, Roger. *The Banquet Years.* 1968. A brilliant study of the role of artists in late-nineteenth-century Paris, showing the connections among social attitudes, institutions, and the birth of modernism in the arts.

Sheehan, James J. *German Liberalism in the Nineteenth Century.* 1978. An important assessment of a much disputed and critical issue, the place of liberalism in German intellectual and political life.

Stone, Norman. *Europe Transformed, 1878–1919.* 1984. An insightful and fresh new survey of the period, outlining the weaknesses of the liberals.

Tannenbaum, Edward R. *1900: The Generation before the Great War.* 1976. Interesting essays on the major facets of society.

*Wagar, Warren W. *Good Tidings: The Belief in Progress from Darwin to Marcuse.* 1972. A wide-ranging account of the period's principal yet beleaguered concepts.

*Weber, Eugen. *Peasants into Frenchmen: The Modernization of Rural France, 1880–1914.* 1976. A provocative treatment stressing the resistance of rural France to the pressures for change and the lateness of their arrival.

Wehler, Hans-Ulrich. *The German Empire 1871–1918.* Kim Traynor (tr.). 1985. A comprehensive structural analysis that synthesizes the most recent empirical research.

*Wohl, Robert. *The Generation of 1914.* 1979. Theories of generations in conflict are related to the intellectual and political discontent preceding World War I in this important book.

A British surgeon and painter, Henry Tonks, was sent to the front in 1917 to paint this scene of a dressing station at the Somme, where officers classify the wounded while the artillery barrages go on.

CHAPTER TWENTY-SEVEN

WORLD WAR AND DEMOCRACY

IN 1914 Germany, Russia, Austria-Hungary, France, and England suddenly went to war—a war different from any that had gone before, one that permanently altered society and politics, and a war that even in retrospect stands as the dividing point between two eras. Interpreting its origins is thus crucial to any understanding of modern history and still the subject of controversy. The war itself strained the belligerents' every resource, and ultimately its outcome transformed the political map. As it ended and well-established states crumbled, there were dramatic opportunities for change, often accompanied by revolution, and the complicated settlement that followed tried to make democracy universal and to ensure that there would not be another world war.

I. The Coming of World War

Explanations for the outbreak of war begin with international relations. The unification of Italy and Germany and the defeat of France in 1870 had fundamentally altered the balance of power in Europe, and international relations were further complicated by imperialism, expanding trade, and nationalism. The foreign ministries of Europe worked assiduously to keep all this under control through diplomacy that was conducted by gentlemen, largely in secret, and according to elaborate rules.

THE DEPENDENCE ON ALLIANCES

Bismarck, whose skillful diplomacy had created the Second Reich, continued using that skill to make the new German nation secure from any foreign threat. For 20 years he dominated international relations, and his policies led to an extraordinary system of alliances that eventually hardened into a threatening arms race.

▶ Bismarck dominated the Congress of Berlin in 1878 much as he dominates this portrait which shows him being congratulated by the Russian delegate, with Count Andrassy of Austria-Hungary on his left.

The Bismarckian System Bismarck showed his dominance at the Berlin Conference of 1878, which met to deal with a crisis in the Balkans. The immediate issue was a sudden expansion of Russian influence there. In 1879 Russia had renounced the ban on sending its navy into the Black Sea (imposed after Russia's defeat in the Crimean War), and in 1876 Russian armies fought the Ottomans, effectively enough to force the sultan to accept a treaty that ceded to Russia territory across the Caucasus Mountains, enlarged Montenegro and Serbia, and granted full independence to a large and autonomous Bulgaria, which everyone believed would be a Russian puppet. This was more than the other great powers were willing to allow, and they pressured Russia to accept an international conference to set the final terms of peace. Bismarck directed that conference to a settlement that recognized the independence of Serbia, Romania, and Montenegro; lessened the gains of the other victors; and granted autonomy to a greatly reduced Bulgaria. Austria-Hungary, which considered these gains for national states in the Balkans to be threatening to its interests, was authorized to occupy Bosnia and Herzegovina (which nevertheless remained under Ottoman rule). In addition Britain's occupation of Cyprus was confirmed and Tunis in effect promised to France.[1] The balance achieved extended Russian, Austrian, and British interests at the expense of a weakening Ottoman Empire and acknowledged, but did not really address, the nationalist ambitions and demands for reform that ran across the Balkans. It was a pattern for preserving peace characteristic of imperialism.

Bismarck also used the Berlin Conference in Germany's interest. He persuaded Austria-Hungary, worried by Russian ambitions in the Balkans, to sign a mutual defense pact a year later that would be the foundation of German foreign policy. It promised that each nation would come

[1]The southern part of Bulgaria, Rumelia, remained under Turkish rule as a separate province. The Romanian provinces of Wallachia and Moldavia had been joined in 1862 and received their own prince two years later. A Hohenzollern, he became King Carol in 1881. The tsar's nephew was elected to the Bulgarian throne.

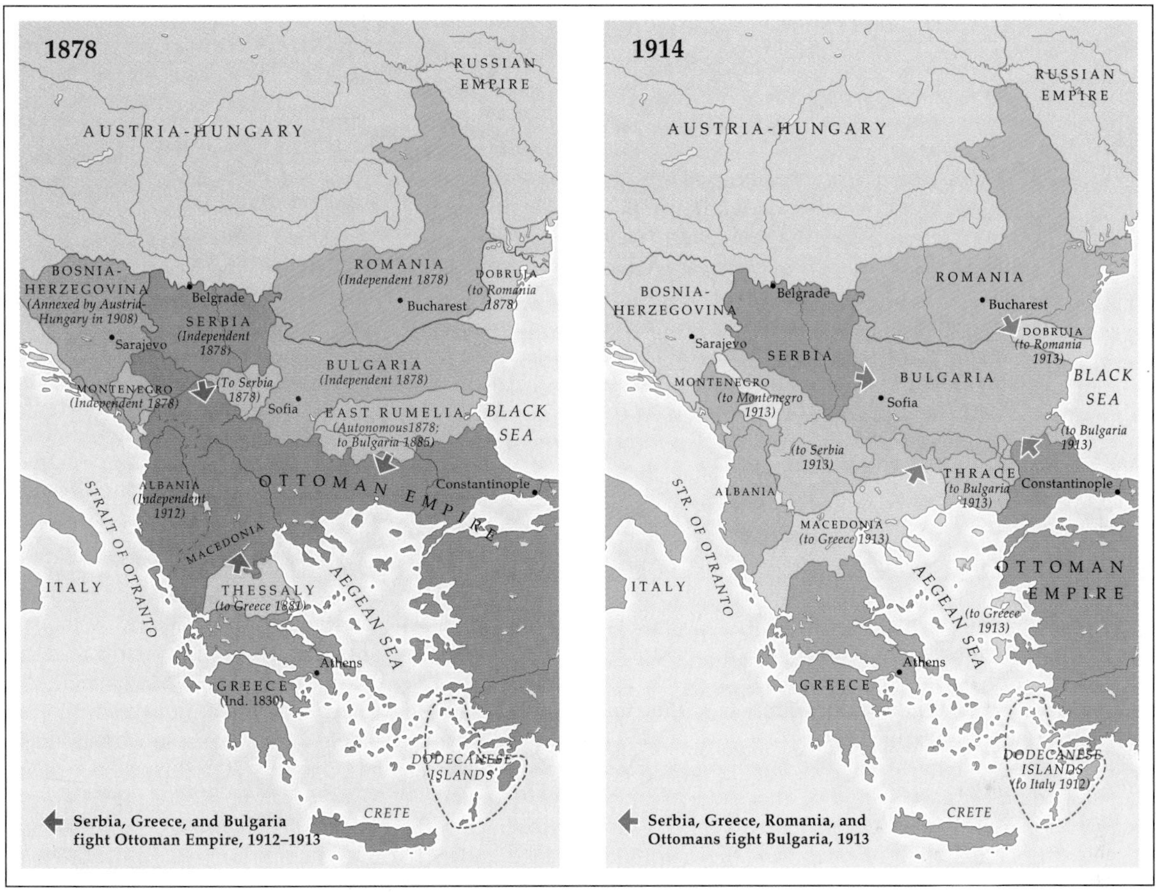

Map 27.1 The Balkans, 1878–1914

to the defense of the other if either was attacked by Russia. Russia might be a threat, but the Berlin Conference had also shown Russia's diplomatic isolation, so in 1881 Bismarck audaciously persuaded Russia to join Germany and Austria-Hungary in promising to remain neutral in the event of war between any of them and a fourth power. To these understandings, Bismarck added a third—the Triple Alliance of Italy, Germany, and Austria-Hungary—a renewable five-year pact first signed in 1882. Made possible by Italy's resentment of France's occupation of Tunis the year before, the triple alliance in effect achieved the diplomatic isolation of France, whose resentment over the loss of Alsace-Lorraine Bismarck continued to fear (*see box*, p. 874).

Formally, these treaties were defensive, although the secrecy surrounding them fostered a sense of insecurity. They gave Germany an international influence rare in peacetime, but holding them together took great skill. Italy and Russia had more reasons for conflict with Austria-Hungary than with anyone else. Disagreements in the Balkans led Russia and Austria-Hungary to let their alliance lapse in 1887, and Bismarck could only partially repair the damage by signing a separate Reinsurance Treaty with Russia, promising the neutrality of one if the other was at war. To persuade Italy to renew the Triple Alliance in 1887, Bismarck had to recognize Italian ambitions in the Balkans, Africa, and elsewhere.

The Shifting Balance After Bismarck's dismissal in 1890 German diplomacy was erratic and often abrasive. His successors recognized the importance of the alliance, but it was easy from Berlin to overlook a new factor that could draw others together—common fear of Germany. When Germany let the Reinsurance treaty with Russia ex-

The Terms of the Triple Alliance

These articles are from the treaty of 1912 in which Austria-Hungary, Germany, and Italy renewed the Triple Alliance for the fifth time since 1882. This version essentially continued earlier ones, except for articles VI through XI, not printed here, which dealt rather vaguely with the Balkans, Ottoman territories, Egypt, and North Africa. With respect to those regions, the signatories reassured each other that they preferred to maintain the status quo but promised mutual understanding and even support if Austria-Hungary or Italy found it necessary temporarily to occupy territory in the Balkans or if Italy had to take measures against French expansion in North Africa. The promises of support to Italy indicated the higher price now required to keep Italy in the Alliance.

"ARTICLE I. The High Contracting Parties mutually promise peace and friendship, and will enter into no alliance or engagement directed against any one of their States.

"They engage to proceed to an exchange of ideas on political and economic questions of a general nature which may arise, and they further promise one another mutual support within the limits of their own interests.

"ARTICLE II. In case Italy, without direct provocation on her part, should be attacked by France for any reason whatsoever, the two other Contracting Parties shall be bound to lend help and assistance with all their forces to the Party attacked.

"This same obligation shall devolve upon Italy in case of any aggression without direct provocation by France against Germany.

"ARTICLE III. If one, or two, of the High Contracting Parties, without direct provocation on their part, should chance to be attacked and to be engaged in a war with two or more Great Powers nonsignatory to the present Treaty, the *casus foederis* will arise simultaneously for all the High Contracting Parties.

"ARTICLE IV. In case a Great Power nonsignatory to the present Treaty should threaten the security of the states of one of the High Contracting Parties, and the threatened Party should find itself forced on that account to make war against it, the two others bind themselves to observe towards their Ally a benevolent neutrality. Each of them reserves to itself, in this case, the right to take part in the war, if it should see fit, to make common cause with its Ally.

"ARTICLE V. If the peace of one of the High Contracting Parties should chance to be threatened under the circumstances foreseen by the preceding Articles, the High Contracting Parties shall take counsel together in ample time as to the military measures to be taken with a view to eventual cooperation.

"They engage, henceforth, in all cases of common participation in a war, to conclude neither armistice, nor peace, nor treaty, except by common agreement among themselves.

"ARTICLE XII. The High Contracting Parties mutually promise secrecy as to the contents of the present Treaty."

From Sidney Bradshaw Fay, *The Origins of the World War* (New York: The Macmillan Company, 1930).

pire, France pressed the Russian government for an understanding that became a full alliance by 1894. France and Russia would each support the other in case of an attack from Germany or another member of the Triple Alliance aided by Germany. An accord between the Russian autocracy and the French republic had seemed politically impossible, although Russia had already turned to France for loans and arms purchases. Now the tsar greeted French delegates while a band played the "Marseillaise," previously outlawed in Russia as a song of revolution.

In response, German diplomats sought to assert Germany's importance in world affairs while renewing their efforts to reach some understanding with Great Britain. Those aims conflicted. In 1896, for example, William II sent a telegram congratulating the president of the South African Republic after the Boers had defeated a small private army organized by Englishmen. Intended to show the British how much they needed German friendship, the gesture was merely resented. The kaiser's talk of the "yellow peril" during a period of turmoil in China, when he instructed his soldiers to behave like the barbaric Huns of old, did nothing to enhance his reputation for stability. Neither did the talk of a "natural" alliance between the Teutonic and Anglo-Saxon races while Germany simultaneously explored a continental coalition against Great Britain. The concrete issue in contention was the expanding German navy, and some negotiated limit seemed possible until the Germans demanded a formal alliance first. The British concluded that the German fleet was aimed at them.

At the same time the colonial competition between Great Britain and France, which had seemed to risk war, was giving way to mutually defined spheres of influence. Following the confrontation at Fashoda in 1898, the French set about turning humiliation into good relations. They accepted British domination in Egypt in return for Britain's recognition of French interests in North Africa, particularly Morocco; and in the Anglo-French Entente Cordiale of 1904 France and Great Britain eliminated the major issues of imperial conflict between them from Siam to Newfoundland and from the Niger River to North Africa. Formally a mere understanding, the Entente implied much more, as the exchange of public visits between Edward VII and the president of France was meant to demonstrate.

THE HARDENING OF ALLIANCES

Germany's diplomatic position remained strong; and German leaders reasoned that an assertive foreign policy would demonstrate that strength. But the tenor of international relations was changing. As armaments increased and treaties proliferated, each power became more obsessed with its own security, and public opinion grew more sensitive to questions of national honor. Within seven years, three diplomatic crises—each of which initially seemed a German victory—in fact brought Germany's opponents closer together.

The first of these crises arose over Morocco. France, its designs there well known, had carefully won acquiescence from the other powers except for Germany; and the German chancellor, Bernhard von Bülow, demanded an international conference to settle Morocco's future. He expected the conference to expose France's isolation, and indeed the architect of French policy, the foreign minister Théophile Delcassé, was forced from office before the conference met at Algeciras in 1906. The agreement they reached recognized Morocco's international status but also the primacy of French interests. But the crisis was a disaster for German diplomacy. Only Austria-Hungary loyally voted with its ally. Italy, Russia, Great Britain, and the United States (now a regular participant in such international agreements) supported France; and Germany's threatening tactics led French and British officials to begin talks about their mutual military interests.

The second crisis arose over the Balkans. Serbia, led by a new king and a radical nationalist government, had become Austria-Hungary's primary Balkan antagonist; and Ottoman influence there seemed likely to grow following the revolution of 1908 (led by the Young Turks, who were determined to modernize their nation). Austria-Hungary decided it was time to annex Bosnia and Herzegovina; and this time Russia, where Slavophiles were outraged, demanded an international conference. Britain and France supported that demand; and Germany, though angered by the suddenness of the annexation, supported Austria-Hungary's move. Diplomatic crises were becoming tests of alliances (and, significantly, Italy expressed resentment at not being consulted by Austria-Hungary rather than loyalty to the Triple Alliance). When France had recognized Italian ambitions in Libya in 1902, the two nations pledged neutrality if either was attacked by a third power. Although the Triple Alliance was renewed in the same year, Italy now sat on the fence between the Franco-Russian and the Austro-German alliances.

The third major crisis once again involved Morocco, which France now wanted to annex. It had consulted all the European powers, and talks with Germany seemed to be going well when suddenly in 1911 the Germans sent the gunboat *Panther* to the Moroccan port of Agadir—as a show of power, a classic imperialist gesture—and asked for all of the French Congo as the price for accepting French annexation of Morocco. Both the demands and the method seemed excessive, and in Great Britain David Lloyd George publicly denounced them. Once again, eventual compromise (France would cede parts of its Congo lands and bits of its other African territories adjacent to German colonies) counted for less than the rising tension and growing international distrust of the Germans.

The dangers of a European arms race, especially Anglo-German naval competition, were thus very apparent; and two great conferences on disarmament and compulsory arbitration were held at The Hague in 1899 and again in 1907. No power was willing to sacrifice any of its strength, but Germany's delegates bluntly rejected any limitation on their sovereign right to make war. And at that moment Kaiser William complained to the British press that England should be grateful for German neutrality in the Boer War. The public recriminations by British statesmen and journalists that these events provoked were part of an important shift in policy. In 1902 Britain ended its long tradition of refusing peacetime alliances by signing a treaty with Japan. An accord between France and Russia and Japan in 1907, defining areas of interest and agreeing to preserve the integrity of China, opened the way for a more important entente between Great Britain and Russia resolving points of contention from the Black Sea straits to Persia, Afghanistan, and Tibet. Thus the Triple Entente was formed, an informal coalition of France, Russia, and Britain that now balanced the Triple Alliance. Its implications became clear when Britain decided in 1912 to withdraw its battleships from the Mediterranean, where the French navy would take their place, and concentrate its fleet in the North Sea to face Germany.

The Balkan Challenge The two coalitions glared menacingly at each other, and for each of them turmoil in the Balkans became a test of strength. The ferment of nationalism, modernization, militarism, and shaky parliamentarism there echoed European-wide trends but was complicated by centuries of oppression, by disputed boundaries (most of recent invention), and by social, ethnic, and religious rivalries. These conflicts were quickly enmeshed in the competition between Russia and Austria-Hungary and, beyond that, in the ambitions of Germany (with railway and economic interests in the peninsula) and Italy (whose defeat of Turkey in 1912 triggered the first Balkan War).

In the fall of 1912 Bulgaria, Serbia, and Greece declared war on Turkey and in a few months drove the Ottomans from all their remaining European holdings except Constantinople. After a partial truce and months of border skirmishes, the great powers hammered out the terms of peace at the end of May 1913. One month later Serbia and Greece, quickly joined by Romania and Turkey, again went to war, this time against Bulgaria, the big winner in the previous war. This war ended in a few weeks, but local anger and international concern did not. The great powers pressured the belligerents to accept peace, but their primary attention was directed toward each other.

In this context the antagonism between Austria-Hungary and Serbia became potentially explosive as Austria-Hungary used threats to force Serbia to abandon some of its nationalist claims and conspiratorial groups of Serbian nationalists continued to agitate on behalf of fellow Slavs living under Austrian rule in Bosnia and Herzegovina. Against this background Archduke Francis Ferdinand, the heir to the Austrian and Hungarian thrones, chose to parade in Sarajevo, the capital of Bosnia, on June 28, 1914. If the archduke wished to demonstrate the solidity of Habsburg rule, there were others eager to demonstrate their opposition to it. As his car moved down the street, a bomb just missed him, and then other conspirators who lost their courage failed to fire as his car passed by. At that point his driver made a wrong turn and started to back up, and yet another young Bosnian revolutionary fired point-blank, killing both the archduke and his wife.

For the leaders of Austria-Hungary, convinced the Serbian government was involved in the assassination, a strong response was imperative. They dispatched a special emissary to Berlin, where he was promised Germany's full support, and on July 23 they sent an ultimatum to Serbia. Meant to be unacceptable, it gave Serbia 48 hours in which to apologize, ban all anti-Austrian propaganda, and accept Austria-Hungary's participation in investigations of the plot against Francis Ferdinand. Serbia replied with great tact, accepting all terms except those that diminished its sovereignty, and offered to submit even these to arbitration. Great Britain proposed an international conference, to which France and Russia reluctantly agreed, and Germany hinted that Serbia and Austria-Hungary alone should settle the matter. Another crisis seemed about to pass when, on July 28, Austria-Hungary declared war on Serbia.

The system of international relations built over the last 40 years was breaking down. Austria-Hungary was, in fact, not yet ready to fight. Germany and Great Britain still hoped the Austrians would limit themselves to occupying Belgrade and then agree to an international conference. But Russia could not let Austria-Hungary unilaterally extend its sway in the Balkans or seem to abandon its role as protector of the Slavs. On July 29 Russia ordered partial mobilization, making clear that it was aimed only at Austria-Hungary. The following day the Russians discovered they lacked the organization for a partial call-up and announced a general mobilization instead. On July 31 Germany proclaimed a state of readiness, sent Russia an ultimatum demanding demobilization within 12 hours, and requested France to declare what it would do in case of a Russo-German war. France answered that it would act in its own interests and then mobilized but held its troops 10 kilometers (about 6 miles) from the German frontier to prevent any incidents. The Germans, who had planned next to demand that France guarantee its neutrality by surrendering its border fortresses, were unsatisfied. On August 1 Germany mobilized and declared war on Russia. Convinced this meant war on the Western front as well, Germany invaded Luxemburg and sent an ultimatum to the Belgians demanding unobstructed passage for its troops. On August 3 Germany declared war on France and invaded Belgium. The following day Great Britain declared war on Germany. Within 48 hours each nation had 2 million soldiers under orders. World War I had begun.

The assassination of Archduke Francis Ferdinand and his wife in Sarajevo, painted as a dramatic moment when a single act affected the course of history.

The Origins of World War The question of what caused the Great War—or, more simply, who was to blame—would become an important issue in European politics. The eventual victors in that war blamed Germany so insistently that they would write its guilt into the peace treaty four years later. Most historians have considered that assessment one-sided, at the very least. German scholars rejected it with special force, which explains the furor some 40 years later (and after another world war) that greeted the research of the German historian Fritz Fischer. He found evidence that Germany's leaders had, in fact,

▸ **By 1912 this Krupp factory at Essen was devoted to the arms race that was consuming an increasing proportion of Europe's energy and wealth.**

looked forward to war and nurtured almost boundless ambitions for military dominance. But the question remains without a final answer, for the causes adduced depend very much on how long-range a view one takes.

The immediate cause, the assassination of the archduke, almost did not happen. The tensions that made it so significant had a long history in the Balkan governments' struggles to establish themselves, in Austria-Hungary's declining power, and in each nation's fears for its safety. Human judgment was also involved, and individual statesmen and governments can be blamed for Austria-Hungary's untoward haste in attacking Serbia, Germany's irresponsible support of Austria-Hungary, Russia's clumsy and confused diplomacy, and France's eagerness to prove loyalty to the Russians. British leaders were at fault as well. Not wanting to admit that they were already attached to one side, they failed to warn the Germans that an attack on France meant war with Britain.

Such an analysis, however, may make statesmen seem to have been more autonomous and therefore more to blame than they were. The system of alliances that was intended to achieve security had been hardened by habit, military imperatives, and domestic politics. The fear that cemented these commitments was related to Britain's conviction that empire required supremacy at sea; France's eagerness to revenge the defeat of 1870 and regain Alsace-Lorraine; Russia's 150 years of territorial expansion; Italy's need to show itself a great power; Austria's dependence, since Metternich, on foreign policy to sustain a shaky regime; and Germany's fear of encirclement and use of prestige abroad to reduce conflict at home.

The arms race itself contributed to the outbreak of war. In 1889 Great Britain had adopted the principle that its navy must equal in size the two next-largest fleets combined, and in 1906 it had launched the *Dreadnought*, the first battleship armed entirely with big guns. By 1914 Britain had 29 ships of this class afloat and 13 under construction. The German navy had 18, with 9 being built. The standing armies of France and Germany doubled between 1870 and 1914, and all able-bodied men had some military responsibilities from the age of 20 to their late fifties. Strategy was a factor, too. Germany's victory over France in 1870 had been understood to prove the superiority of the Prussian system of universal conscription, large reserves, and detailed military planning. Furthermore, it was believed that technology gave an attacker overwhelming advantages. But it took immense organization and many days to locate millions of reservists, get them to their proper units, equip them, and then effectively deploy them. Mobilization—in the eyes of some diplomats, a cumbersome but effective show of seriousness—was considered by military men in each country to be an essential act of self-defense. By 1914 it had become tantamount to war. Even slight disadvantages in numbers, weapons, speed, or tactics might prove fatal. Thus each increase in manpower and weapons was quickly matched, often with enormous effort; France, for example, had only 60 percent of Germany's potential manpower and yet equaled its rival through more burdensome conscription. The arms race, justified by the fear that it was meant to allay, fed on itself.

Such expenditures of money and resources had to be justified to parliaments. Thus, ultimately, these enormous forces, like foreign policy, rested on domestic politics. In every country political parties competing for broader support found an effective appeal in nationalist programs that promised to overcome domestic conflicts. Special interests associated with the military and empire joined all who feared a rising tide of socialism in dramatizing issues of national honor. This was especially the case in Germany, where economic growth and social change threatened the political system that preserved the dominance of Prussia and of the Junker class.

Few Europeans really wanted war; yet its outbreak was hailed with joy everywhere. The strain of economic, demographic, and imperial com-

▸ Summer hats in the air, an August crowd in London's Trafalgar Square cheers the declaration of war on Austria, as it had a week earlier the announcement of war with Germany. Similar scenes occurred throughout that week of 1914 in France and Germany.

petition prepared many to welcome with relief the confrontation of armed conflict; and its excitement provided a unity and common purpose otherwise missing. In immediate terms, world war could have been avoided; in a larger sense, it was a product of the social structures it nearly annihilated.

▸ **In Berlin during August 1914, German volunteers march down the street hailing their good fortune; they will soon fight for their country.**

II. The Course of the War

THE SURPRISES OF THE FIRST TWO YEARS

For decades European military staffs had prepared detailed plans for the situation they now faced. The French intended to drive into Alsace and Lorraine in coordinated dashes that reflected their almost mystic belief in the spirit of a patriotic offensive. German strategy began from the desire to avoid fighting on two fronts simultaneously: A plan adopted years earlier assigned minimal forces to hold the Russians in the East and to slow the expected French attack in Alsace while Germany's main armies were to wheel through Belgium down through Paris and knock France out of the war before Russia could bring its massive armies into play or British aid could make a difference. That strategy, which envisioned the German army as a coiled spring to be released the moment war began, required the invasion of neutral Belgium, further labeled Germany as the aggressor, and determined Britain's entry into the war.

Map 27.2 **THE WESTERN FRONT**

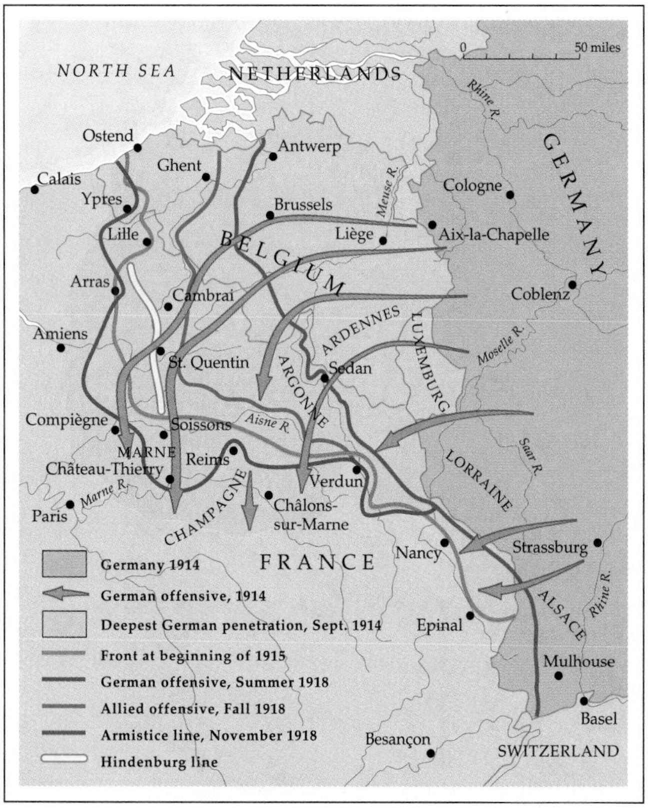

All the belligerents in 1914 assumed that modern warfare would make for brief wars of rapid movement, but in a few months it began to be clear that the war being fought was not the one planned, though commanders were slow to admit it. Increased fire power gave defensive forces unexpected strength, cavalry was ineffectual, and the common soldier proved able to absorb more punishment than anyone had thought possible. After making some slight gains, the French offensive in Alsace was stopped, with heavy losses on both sides. The Germans were more nearly successful. The French command had underestimated by half the forces they would face at the outbreak of war, and in the first weeks the Germans drove to within 30 miles of Paris. But the German army was as battered as the defenders, its casualties as high, and its lines of communi-

cation and supply were dangerously stretched.

These factors, added to unanticipated Belgian resistance, infuriated and worried German commanders. The arrival of a small British force sooner than expected and unanticipated Russian advances led the indecisive German chief of staff, Helmuth von Moltke (nephew of the field marshal who had led Germany to victory in 1866 and 1870), to modify the army's well-established plan. He ordered troops intended for the Western front to the East and sent extra forces to Alsace in hope of a breakthrough there. The German army cut east of Paris, instead of running beyond it as planned. After each bloody encounter, the Allies had retreated but were not routed, and German officers were surprised they took so few prisoners.

On the other side, the French commander in chief, Joseph Joffre, remained imperturbably confident of the ultimate success of a great French drive. In September the French launched a counteroffensive along the Marne River that saved Paris and hurled the Germans back to the natural defenses of the Aisne River. There, despite repeated Allied attacks, the Germans held. In the next few months the armies tried to outflank each other but succeeded only in extending the front northward to the sea. With changes of only a few miles, the battle lines that were established at the end of 1914 would remain those of the Western front for the next four years. France had not been knocked out of the war, but Germany held a tenth of its territory and nearly all of Belgium.

▸ Newly mobilized French recruits pose in front of the flower-decked train that will carry them off to military duty.

▸ **Massive German forces cross the Schara river, the opening of the drive into Galicia in May 1915 that would carry the Central Powers into Russia.**

On the Eastern front, Russian armies scored important gains in early August, taking eastern Galicia from Austria-Hungary and beginning an invasion of eastern Prussia in the north. Moltke talked in panic of a general retreat until the battle of Tannenberg late in August. There generals Paul von Hindenburg and Erich Ludendorff, who soon became Germany's greatest war heroes, surrounded and destroyed a Russian army and then pushed on almost to Warsaw before being stopped. In the south, Austria-Hungary halted the Russian advance with German aid and took Belgrade despite the strong resistance of the Serbian army. By the end of 1914, Germany and Austria-Hungary had made impressive gains at every hand, and the entry of the Ottoman Empire on their side threatened Britain and France through the eastern Mediterranean all the way to Suez.

War of Attrition On the Western front especially, the great armies found themselves bogged down in a terrifying kind of siege warfare. Artillery became increasingly important, and shells were fired at rates unimaginable a few months before, devastating the pockmarked land and making any movement difficult. Dug into trenches and clinging to pillboxes, neither side could be uprooted. Military units worked out complex systems of communication by laying cables, building bridges, and maintaining roads and railways. For the first time, poison gas was used, but the German troops could not follow up the momentary gains their new weapon permitted.

Again and again, the Allied armies attempted to mount a great offensive, only to be stopped after gaining two or three miles and losing hundreds of thousands of men. Battles were now numbered—the Second Battle of Ypres (April–May 1915), the Second Battle of Artois (May–June), the Second Battle of Champagne (September–November), the Third Battle of Artois (September–October); and after a year's bloodshed, the Western front remained essentially the same. Nothing broke the stalemate, neither desperate new offensives nor Italy's entry into the war. Italy had announced its neutrality when war broke out, declaring the attack on Serbia an offensive action outside the terms of the Triple Alliance. Both sides then negotiated with Italy, and Britain and France could offer much more. In April 1915 Italy signed a secret agreement, the Treaty of London, and committed itself to the Allies, as the opponents of Germany and Austria-Hungary had come to be called. In return Italy was promised considerable territory along its border with Austria-Hungary, important Dalmatian islands, and expansion of its colonial holdings. Italy declared war in May and soon ad-

▸ **Desolation surrounded weary Allied soldiers as they made their way across the mud on the battlefield at Ypres.**

Map 27.3 WORLD WAR I

vanced to a line along the Isonzo River. Eleven battles would be fought along that line in the next two years.

Early in 1916 the Germans launched another all-out offensive to knock France out of the war. They stormed the fortifications at Verdun. Knowing the French would be determined to hold, their aim was more to bleed the enemy than to take territory. For days shells poured down, and then the Germans attacked in overwhelming numbers. From February to July 1916 the fighting continued at full pitch. German forces captured two outlying forts, but the French managed a brief counterattack. Verdun held; and though the French losses, more than 300,000 men, weakened the subsequent Allied offensive, Germany casualties were only slightly less. The Allied attack in the Battle of the Somme, from July to November, brought still heavier casualties and a maximum advance of seven miles. The doctrine of the offensive, like general morale, was sinking in gore. If tactics could not guarantee victory, then attrition, systematically exhausting men and resources, was the alternative.

There was more movement on the Eastern front but no decisive result. The Central Powers

▸ **The ruins of Verdun stood like a broken tombstone after the siege that bled both armies.**

(Germany, Austria-Hungary, and the countries on their side) launched an offensive through Galicia in May 1915, drove forward a hundred miles, and followed that with a general offensive in July. By late September—while their new ally, Bulgaria, pushed into Serbia—the Central Powers were massed on a line from Riga in the north to the easternmost part of Hungary. Russia lost Poland and Lithuania. The following year, however, in one of the few really well-conducted Russian campaigns, General Alexis Brusilov regained a large part of those losses. The effort cost Russia a million men, and it lacked the capacity to do more. Although the Russian offensive brought Romania into the war on the Allied side, Austria-Hungary took Bucharest at the end of the year.

Naval strength, so significant to the arms race, proved more important in terms of supply lines than combat. The single large-scale attack by sea, the dramatic landing of Allied forces on the Gallipoli peninsula in April 1915, was a failure. The Allies were grateful to withdraw in December without having either opened the Dardanelles as a pipeline to Russia or forced the Ottomans out of the war. Britain's naval blockade of Germany was more effective. As it began to hurt, Germany countered in 1915 by announcing a submarine blockade of Britain; but the angry reaction of neutrals, led by the United States, forced them to abandon the tactic. The sinking of passenger ships—most sensationally the *Lusitania*, killing more than a thousand civilians—gave way in 1916 to attacks on armed merchant ships and then, in the face of American warnings, to the renunciation of "unlimited" submarine warfare. The one great naval battle of the war, at Jutland in May 1916, was indecisive. British and German fleets lost the same number of ships, though the tonnage of British losses was twice as great. Thereafter the feared German fleet stayed in its harbors.

ADJUSTMENT TO TOTAL WAR

By every measure, this was war on an unprecedented scale, and adjustment to its demands strained the very fabric of society. The first response was national unity. The German parliament unanimously voted the funds for war, the public convinced that theirs was a just and defensive war. The French hailed their "sacred union," and a leading socialist joined the cabinet. In Great Britain the Liberal government soon gave way to a coalition that included Conservatives, and in Russia the government seemed almost popular.

Domestic Mobilization There was also immediate dislocation. At first, factories closed and unemployment rose despite conscription; a labor shortage followed as war production became crucial. Everywhere agricultural output dropped, contributing to the food shortages of subsequent years. Prices rose rapidly and consumer hoarding further strained faltering systems of distribution. Just as the rules of warfare were bent or shattered by unlimited submarine warfare, poison gas, and a blockade that included consumer goods, so governments extended their powers to move workers, censor the press, control railroads and shipping, and direct the economy. Unprepared for the ever greater amounts of ammunition and supplies the war required, governments quickly learned to use paper money, rationing, and central planning.

In Great Britain the government requisitioned supplies and forced industry to new efficiency. Despite voluntary enlistments that raised the largest army in British history, it had to adopt conscription in 1916, a step Winston Churchill would call "the greatest revolution in our system since the institution of feudalism under William the Conqueror." Rebellion in Ireland that Easter was quickly put down; yet it was a serious diversion for British troops and a disturbing reminder of how cruelly war tested every weakness in the social structure.

Germany, deprived of critical raw materials, developed the most fully controlled economy of any of the combatants, under the brilliant direction of Walther Rathenau. Private firms were organized into sectors of production so that the most important could be favored, inefficient firms closed, and national planning enforced. The chemical industry developed ways of making rubber substitutes, manufactured fertilizers from nitrates in the air and textiles from wood pulp, and culled aluminum from local clays. Substitutes, which made *ersatz* an international word, included chestnut flour and clover meal used in the "war bread" that, like meatless days and conscription, soon made civilians feel the burden of all-out war.

In the first weeks of the fighting, France lost half of its iron ore and coal fields and more than half its heavy industry; yet as commissions established quotas and allocated supplies, production steadily increased. Although Joffre exercised virtually dictatorial powers and censorship was severe, the tradition of political dispute was in large part preserved. In France, as in Great Britain, civilian authority had begun to reassert itself in 1915.

Great Britain, France, and Germany were the states that adjusted most effectively to the new challenge of fielding vast armies while increasing industrial production and maintaining intricate logistical networks. These were feats that the Austro-Hungarian and Russian empires could not match. Their industries were less well developed; supplies and trained manpower were often lacking. Equally important, neither government knew how or dared try to squeeze from the economy the quantities of food, ammunition, and clothing that war required. Russian armies increasingly showed the effects of fighting ill-fed and ill-shod, with inadequate weapons and ammunition, and without good communication. (Orders to Russian troops were broadcast uncoded, and the German ability to intercept them contributed to Ludendorff's reputation as a great tactician.) In adversity, Austria-Hungary could not rely on the continued loyalty of subject peoples, and soldiers were carefully dispatched to zones far from their native lands so as not to be fighting against people who spoke their own language.

The Social Effects By the winter of 1916–1917, the strains were visible to all. Everywhere on the bloodied continent, Europeans were thinner and more shabbily dressed, overworked, and grieved

Meet the "Khaki Girls"

The two women who wrote this brief article, published in June 1917 in* The Englishwoman*, a lady's magazine, present it as an upbeat account of the dedication of women workers, but it is also a document about class distinctions.

"We got out of the tram and walked up the short, muddy path, past the sentry, who with fixed bayonet guards the entrance to A_3, the 'shop' in which we work. It was twenty minutes past two—ten minutes before the hour for the shift to begin—so there were plenty of our fellow-workers passing through the door. Among the three hundred girls employed on this shift there are not more than four of five lady-workers, so the crowd was made up of 'khaki girls', the colloquial name given to the industrial hands, originating from the fact that when women were admitted last July to the munition shops they wore khaki overalls, which since have been replaced for economical reasons by those made of black material.

"We had grown accustomed to the sight of the endless procession of girls pouring into the factory . . . all of the same type, rather wild, yet in their quieter moods giving an impression of sullen defiance, ready to answer you back if you should happen to tread on their very tender corns. So long, though, as you keep off those corns, and do not let these wayward creatures feel you are intruding nor provide yourself with anything which they have not, even though it be merely a newspaper to sit upon in preference to a dusty board, they will show their good nature to you—and they have plenty. Then there is their good humour and their gay spirits. No matter how strenuous the work, nor how wearing the hardships, they will always give out from this wonderful gaiety of spirits, and keep the ball rolling with their sense of humour—obvious and childlike—running as it does mostly to nicknaming, pelting the mechanics with orange peel, or skipping with a rope of steel shavings cut from the shell on the lathe.

"Every one of them carries a brown or green despatch-case. Most of them are flashily dressed: a cherry-coloured coat, a black-and-white check skirt, a satin blouse trimmed with swansdown, a hat, small in shape but too large to fit, so it drops over one eye, and down-trodden boots, is typical of what they wear. Some of them are exceedingly pretty; they are all heavily powdered, and in some cases rouged. Their hair is dressed with great care, and even if it does fall about their eyes it is not untidiness, but an effect purposely arranged by the aid of the small mirror—often a beautiful thing to look upon, either encrusted with shells or mounted on scarlet plush—carried in that despatch-case which is the essential part of a khaki girl's equipment, since it contains the food with which she is obliged to provide herself.

"We stood in the doorway a moment looking at the sun shining down upon the river. 'Do you think the Zeppelins will come tonight?' one of us said to the other. 'It will be a good night for them.' 'There's no moon.' 'Nor wind—and they were at Paris last night.'

"Then we went to our work, and the absorption of screwing plugs into shells, turning them on the lathe, taking them out and gauging them, working to exceed the standard number, swallowed up every other thought."

From Brenda Girvin and Monica Coxens, "Meet the 'Khaki girls' " in *The Englishwoman,* June 1917, reprinted in E. Royston Pike, *Human Documents of the Lloyd George Era* (London: George Allen & Unwin, 1972).

by the endless losses of husbands, sons, and homes. Poor crops and overloaded transportation systems further reduced the diet; this was Germany's "turnip winter," when the best organized of the domestic war economies could barely keep its people healthy.

Society itself was subtly altered from the first month, when Belgian refugees poured into France, until years after the war. The strains of war were changing society. As the queue became a kind of public rite and rationing a way of life, distinctions of social class blurred. Each government awkwardly tried to restrict the consumption of alcohol and worried about rising rates of illegitimacy. At first, the outbreak of war had seemed to overcome conflict between genders as well as classes. Women would sustain the home front (and most feminists turned into active supporters of their nation's war effort) while their men fought. Propaganda, too, reinforced traditional gender roles, emphasizing the enemy's brutality toward women and the maternal care that nurses provided the wounded. Soon, however, governments were eager for women in general to go to work. British women were asked in 1915 to take any jobs they could, and by 1917 the government denied contracts to employers unwilling to hire women (*see box*, p. 886). The French government forbade hiring men for certain jobs that women could do; and the Krupp works, which had no women employees in 1914, counted 12,000 by 1917. In munitions industries in particular, the number of women workers steadily rose to become one-third or more of the total. Women also tilled the soil and served as bus conductors, firefighters, and office workers in addition to doing more direct war work. Inevitably, questions arose about unequal pay and whether men might be permanently displaced. Patriotic commitment to the common cause masked issues of women's work on which labor leaders remained as ambivalent as ever.

Although general labor agitation remained below prewar levels, signs of growing discontent among workers had to be taken seriously. Trade unions were treated with new respect, and officials began to talk of the benefits to be granted after the war to those making such heavy sacrifices now. Even the kaiser spoke of ending the three-class voting system in Prussia and hinted at a government that would be responsible to parliament, while the House of Commons, in a notable reversal, declared its support in principle for women's suffrage. Meanwhile, month upon month of bloodshed in muddy, disease-filled trenches took a psychological as well as physical toll. Morale was sinking.

Changes in Leadership Having gained the initiative on the Eastern front, the Central Powers indicated their willingness to discuss a settlement in December 1916; but the Allies' terms were wholly unacceptable. The war would continue, and the belligerents looked to new leaders. In France Joffre's intolerance of civilian leaders brought his downfall in December 1916; and he was replaced by the tactful and dashing General

► **In March 1917 women demonstrated in Petrograd, demanding that the rations of soldiers' families be increased.**

Robert Georges Nivelle, who planned a massive new offensive. This one, he promised, would break through German defenses. In Germany two heroes of the Eastern front had been promoted. Hindenburg received overall command and with Ludendorff took charge of campaigns in the West in the fall of 1916. To destroy the shipping on which Britain depended, Germany returned to unlimited submarine warfare in January 1917. Aware that this might bring the United States into the war, the Germans calculated that Britain would have to sue for peace before American power could make a difference.

The political changes were more revealing. Lloyd George, made minister of war in June 1916, became prime minister in December. Eloquent and energetic, once a radical orator who had terrified the upper classes, he now seemed the kind of popular and decisive leader who could galvanize the British war effort. After morale hit a dangerous low, the French turned to the fiery Clemenceau as premier again in November 1917. Change had come to Russia too—through revolution. In March 1917 the tsar had been forced to abdicate, and a new provisional government proclaimed sweeping democratic reforms while promising to continue the war. Both sides knew that Russia was now more vulnerable than ever but that its immense resources had yet to be effectively tapped. For the Allies these changes in Russia gave the war itself new meaning. Now democracies were fighting together against authoritarian governments. A war that involved the people more fully than any before took on an ideological meaning. The Allies' sense of democratic purpose was strengthened in April when the United States—resentful that Germany was sinking its ships and making overtures to Mexico that included promises of the return to Mexico of lands now part of the United States—declared war on Germany.

THE GREAT TRIALS OF 1917–1918

In the fighting itself, neither new leaders nor shared ideals seemed to make much difference (*see box*, p. 889). On the Western front, Nivelle launched his great offensive in April and May 1917 despite multiple handicaps. The Germans had strengthened their defenses; disagreements arose between the British and French commands; and some French troops, dispirited by two years of endless death on the same desolate terrain, mutinied, refusing to fight. The Second Battle of the Aisne and the Third Battle of Champagne took a toll as great as their predecessors and made even slighter gains. Nivelle was replaced by General Henri Philippe Pétain, the hero of Verdun, who began a concerted effort to raise morale, but it would be months before France dared another offensive. The British went ahead with plans for an attack in the north, spurred by the desperate need to knock out at least some of the submarine bases from which German U-boats were sinking such enormous tonnages that the Admiralty openly wondered how many months Great Britain could last. The noise of battle could be heard in England, and hundreds of thousands of men fell, but the British fared no better in the Third Battle of Ypres (July–November) than had the French in their spring offensive. British morale, too, was shaken; yet stalemate continued. Germany's submarine warfare had come close to its goal, but Allied losses dropped to a tolerable level in mid-1917 with the development of the convoy in which fleets of armed ships accompanied merchant vessels across the ocean. With America's entry into the war, the tonnage those convoys delivered increased.

Elsewhere the picture was different. On the Eastern front, Russian advances in July soon turned into almost constant retreat, and in November the communists gained control of the government. They invited all nations to join in peace without annexations or indemnities, then entered into independent negotiations with the Central Powers. The most populous of the Allies had been defeated. Able now to engage more troops on the Italian front, Germany and Austro-Hungary launched a concentrated attack there in October, scoring an overwhelming victory at the Battle of Caporetto. Italy's armies collapsed as tens of thousands died, surrendered, or deserted. But the Italians regrouped along the Piave River; Britain and France rushed in reinforcements, and the Austro-German onslaught was slowed and then stopped.

Wilfred Owen Describes Trench Warfare

Wilfred Owen's moving poems about World War I were published after he was killed in action in 1918, and they continue to be widely read. His first tour of duty had ended when he was sent home suffering from "shell shock." Some months later, he was back in France; and on January 4, 1917, he wrote his mother that "on all the officers' faces there is a harassed look that I have never seen before," adding, "I censored hundreds of letters yesterday, and the hope of peace was in every one of them." He was back in the fighting a few days later, when he wrote her this letter.

Tuesday, 16 January 1917
[2nd Manchester Regt, B.E.F.]

"My own sweet Mother,

"... I can see no excuse for deceiving you about these last 4 days. I have suffered seventh hell.

"I have not been at the front.

"I have been in front of it.

"I held an advanced post, that is, a 'dug-out' in the middle of No Man's Land.

"We had a march of 3 miles over shelled road then nearly 3 along a flooded trench. After that we came to where the trenches had been blown flat out and had to go over the top. It was of course dark, too dark, and the ground was not mud, not sloppy mud, but an octopus of sucking clay, 3, 4, and 5 feet deep, relieved only by craters full of water. Men have been known to drown in them. Many stuck in the mud & only got on by leaving their waders, equipment, and in some cases their clothes.

"High explosives were dropping all around us, and machine-guns spluttered every few minutes. But it was so dark that even the German flares did not reveal us.

"Three quarters dead, I mean each of us ¾ dead, we reached the dug-out, and relieved the wretches therein. I then had to go forth and find another dug-out for a still more advanced post where I left 18 bombers. I was responsible for other posts on the left but there was a junior officer in charge.

"My dug-out held 25 men tight packed. Water filled it to a depth of 1 or 2 feet, leaving say 4 feet of air.

"One entrance had been blown in & blocked.

"So far, the other remained.

"The Germans knew we were staying there and decided we shouldn't.

"Those fifty hours were the agony of my happy life.

"Every ten minutes on Sunday afternoon seemed an hour.

"I nearly broke down and let myself drown in the water that was now slowly rising over my knees.

"Towards 6 o'clock, when, I suppose, you would be going to church, the shelling grew less intense and less accurate: so that I was mercifully helped to do my duty and crawl, wade, climb and flounder over No Man's Land to visit my other post. It took me half an hour to move about 150 yards.

"I was chiefly annoyed by our own machine-guns from behind. The seeng-seeng-seeng of the bullets reminded me of Mary's canary. On the whole I can support the canary better.

"In the Platoon on my left the sentries over the dug-out were blown to nothing. One of these poor fellows was my first servant whom I rejected. If I had kept him he would have lived, for servants don't do Sentry Duty."

Reprinted from *Wilfred Owen: Collected Letters,* in Jon Clover and Jon Silkin, *The Penguin Book of First World War Prose* (New York: Viking, 1989).

The Last Year Although the Russians stopped fighting in February 1918, the Central Powers did not. Their eastward march ended only with the Treaty of Brest Litovsk, signed in March. Russia surrendered Russian Poland, the Baltic provinces, the Ukraine, and Transcaucasia. Germany had acquired invaluable wheat and oil and a respite on one front when it needed them most. But merely patrolling such immense gains required great numbers of badly needed troops, and the incredibly harsh terms of the treaty stiffened resistance elsewhere. Both Lloyd George and President Wilson now stated formal war aims that expressed their confidence in victory and put revolutionary emphasis on the right to self-government.

On the Western front, the Germans, their reserves of manpower and resources nearing exhaustion, opened a great offensive. Attacking sector after sector from March through June, they made the greatest advances seen there in four years. It was a triumph of careful strategy, improved tactics, heavy artillery, and gas. To correct the weakness of divided command, the Allies named General Ferdinand Foch supreme commander of all their forces; and they retained their reserves while the Germans exhausted theirs. Enemy guns once more bombarded Paris before the Allied counteroffensive began in July. Slowly, then faster, the Germans were driven back over the familiar and devastated landscape. By the end of August, German armies had retreated to the Hindenburg line. The Allies continued their push in battles of the Argonne and Ypres in September and October, gaining less rapidly than hoped or expected but now inexorably nevertheless.

Elsewhere the Central Powers collapsed more dramatically. In the Middle East Turkish and German troops were defeated by British and Arab forces led by T. E. Lawrence, whose exploits became part of the romantic lore in which this war was poorer than most. In October the sultan was deposed, and a new government sued for peace. Combined Serbian, French, British, and Greek forces under French leadership drove up the Balkan Peninsula. Bulgaria surrendered at the end of September, and the Allies moved toward Romania. Czech, Yugoslav, Romanian, and (Austrian) Polish movements for independence, encouraged by the Allies, gained strength throughout 1918. The Austro-Hungarian Empire was disintegrating. Austria-Hungary attacked once more on the Italian front but withdrew after heavy losses. Its armies, defeated at Vittorio Veneto at the end of October, began simply to dissolve as the various nationalities left for home and revolution. Czechoslovakia and the kingdom later called Yugoslavia both declared their independence. In November Austria-Hungary surrendered unconditionally to the Italians.

Ludendorff had demanded that Germany seek an armistice at the end of September, but that required political changes as well. Twice in 1917 Kaiser William II had promised to make his cabinet subject to a majority in the Reichstag; and in October 1918, he appointed Prince Max of Baden chancellor to begin this transformation from above. Ludendorff resigned his command at the end of October, and Germany asked for peace on the terms of President Wilson's Fourteen Points. But Wilson now insisted on a democratic German government with which to negotiate and the evacuation of occupied territories. While German leaders hesitated, they faced the threat of revolution at home. A liberal believer in parliamentary government, Prince Max represented a compromise that might have worked earlier but now could not, in the face of uprisings in the name of peace, democracy, and socialism. Germany threatened to break apart. Prince Max pleaded with William to abdicate and, when revolt spread to Berlin, announced that he had done so without waiting for the kaiser. Kaiser William II abdicated on November 9 after a mutiny in the German fleet and revolution in Munich. The German Republic was proclaimed, the government handed over to Friedrich Ebert, the leader of the Social Democrats; and a German armistice commission sent to meet with Foch. It agreed to terms on November 11. By then Allied troops were approaching the German borders in the West and had crossed the Danube in the East, taken Trieste on the Adriatic, and sailed through the Dardanelles. In the meantime, revolution was sweeping Central Europe.

The Effects of World War I The war itself had some of the effects of revolution. Even among the Allies, it had forced such changes that no one could be sure what postwar society would be like. Having shown the capacity to mobilize society for war, governments would now be held more responsible than in the past for society's needs in peacetime, as evidenced in a spate of postwar legislation on housing, education, and pensions. Clemenceau, Lloyd George, and Wilson, the spokesmen of victory, had all been vigorous reformers; but now they watched with apprehension the revival of the radical left. From Germany east, new regimes and sometimes whole new nations replaced the defeated states. In Germany itself, radical groups staged a number of local revolts, and the air of instability was sustained by *Freikorps* ("free corps"), mercenary squads made up of ex-soldiers available to any movement that could pay them for street fighting and marauding. Throughout Central Europe political conflict adopted the techniques of force.

Life in wartime had affected social classes differently. Even where there was no open revolution, the aristocracy and other traditional elites had been weakened by the general democratization of political life and by the decline in purchasing power that resulted from inflation, reduction in the value of land, and increased taxes (especially in England). A middle class confident in 1914 found itself after the war exposed and vulnerable, its savings threatened, its possibilities limited, its values challenged. Those on salary or fixed income suffered relatively more from inflation than those on workers' wages; middle-class life became less lavish, and there were fewer servants (some 400,000 English women left domestic service in the course of the war). Workers, particularly the skilled, were on the whole relatively well off. Although rates of pay usually lagged behind inflation, the years of full employment and more jobs for women had increased family income; and trade unions used their greater influence to maintain shorter hours and higher pay. Peasants, though declining in number, were also often better off, helped by the demand for food and by inflation, which made it easier to pay off their debts.

Even ordinary manners and dress were different. Gentlemen had abandoned their top hats when forced to use public transportation; women's clothes grew simpler and their skirts shorter. Women of the working class took to wearing cosmetics and high-heeled shoes and smoking and drinking in public, as did their middle-class sisters. Such changes in customs, even more than the increase in violent crime and juvenile delinquency, shocked moralists who associated them with casual encounters between the sexes, increased illegitimacy, and the popularity of dance halls. The way people looked and acted thus joined the disruptions of wartime and postwar political rhetoric in suggesting a more mobile and fluid society in which old customs and patterns of proper behavior had been so altered that they might never be recaptured. Millions of refugees represented a deeper displacement, but millions more (especially peasants and women) would choose not to return to their old way of life.

The psychological impact of war is harder to prove; but throughout society, there was a tendency following the war to expect instability. Intellectuals suffered what one historian has called "minds scorched by war"; and among the populace, a cynical distrust of leaders and institutions seems to have spread after years of wartime promises. There was a cleavage, too, between those who had fought and those who stayed home, those whose lives were transformed and those who had more nearly maintained business as usual. Bitterness about the inequalities of sacrifice surfaced in denunciations of war profiteers. At the same time, few forgot and some would yearn for the thrill of combat, the sense of common purpose, and the vision of national unity that war had brought.

There were economic gains—new technologies, such as automobiles and airplanes, radio, and some chemicals, were stimulated by their wartime use—but the losses were more tangible. World trade had been disrupted and Europe's place in it transformed. In 1914 Europe was the world's greatest lender of money; in 1918 its nations were debtors. The physical destruction of property, aside from the billions lost in war material, was greatest in Belgium and France. In France alone, thousands of bridges and factories as well as a million buildings were destroyed. Total European production in the 1920s would fall below the level of 1913.

All this required enormous adjustments from individuals, institutions, and society as a whole. So did the war's simplest accomplishment: the

▸ **It would take years to recover from the damage to roads and bridges and private housing in Belgium and northeastern France. The French village of Craonne, where Napoleon once won a battle and which was the scene of fighting in 1917 and 1918, looked like this in 1919.**

killing of from 10 to 13 million people, perhaps one-third of them civilians. Moreover, for every soldier who died, two or three were wounded; millions were maimed for life. The casualty figures tell much about the history of the first third of the twentieth century (see accompanying table). Among the armed forces, casualties ran about 50 percent for the major combatants except France, whose losses were higher. Able to mobilize some 7 percent of its population, Russia could only estimate fatalities. Germany mobilized some 16 percent and France, 19 percent. In each country whole classes from the elite schools were virtually wiped out. For France, with its older population and low birthrate, the war was a demographic catastrophe in which a large part of an entire generation disappeared on the Western front. And throughout Europe, the one-armed, and one-legged, and the blind would live on, supported by pensions and performing menial tasks, in silent testimony to the cost of total war.

MILITARY FATALITIES IN WORLD WAR I (MAJOR POWERS)

Germany	1,900,000
Russia	1,700,000
France	1,400,000
Austria-Hungary	1,200,000
British Empire	900,000
Ottoman Empire	700,000
Italy	600,000
United States	100,000

With all this before them, the leaders of exhausted nations sat down to make a lasting peace. The gigantic effort victory required had been fueled by the vision of a better world in which governments would use their increased powers to ensure greater justice and fuller democracy. With Wilson as its moralistic voice, democracy—meaning popular participation in public life and opportunity for all—seemed a guarantee of peace. There must be an end, Wilson urged, to the old secret diplomacy that juggled spheres of influence and national interests without regard for public opinion.

III. The Peace

The Revolutionary Situation . Russia's was the most important revolution that resulted from World War I, but there were many others. Among the defeated nations, only Bulgaria's government survived. By default as well as victory, the Allies seemed free to construct the Europe of peaceful democracies foreshadowed in so many of their wartime statements of principle. Instead, the diplomats assembled at the Paris Peace Conference found their task complicated by the very extent of victory and beset by more interests than they could satisfy. So grand an undertaking fed the extremes of hope and disillusionment, while far from Paris, more direct means were being used to shape the postwar world.

From Ireland to Asia Minor, nationalist movements sought to capture power. The peoples suddenly released from Habsburg and Russian rule fought to define the boundaries of their new nations. In the Baltic lands, Lithuanian, Estonian, and Latvian republics marked their independence by war with Russia, but Lithuania was also at odds with the new republic of Poland. Poland, in fact, faced conflict on all its other borders as well—against Russians, Ukranians, Czechs, and Germans. The creation of Czechoslovakia and the new kingdom of Yugoslavia led to renewed warfare as Czechoslovakia was attacked by Hungary, and in the Balkans the kind of hostility that had preceded World War I broke out again as Romania attacked both Hungary and Yugoslavia.

Russia's communists had good reason then to hope that revolution would sweep from East to West, and Marxists throughout Europe looked to the miraculous events in Russia as the beginning of the socialist future they had so long imagined. In March 1919 delegates from a score of countries met in Moscow to establish the Third International. Communists were active in the Baltic states, and Lenin's friend Béla Kun led a communist government in Hungary in 1919 until Romanian armies ended his brief reign. There was communist agitation in Vienna, where the provisional government of truncated Austria looked forward to union with the new German republic.

Marxists had long seen special revolutionary promise in highly industrialized Germany with its class tensions and strong socialist movement. In Germany's defeat and new government they saw the fulfillment of old portents. In January 1919 a communist revolt broke out in Berlin, and in the following spring another managed for a few weeks to make Bavaria a Soviet republic. Both uprisings were quickly defeated by remnants of the German army, and Russia remained the center of the communist world.

THE PEACE TREATIES

President Wilson's Fourteen Points had won acceptance as a basis for defining a new European order. They dealt mainly with territorial adjustments but made the ideal of self-determination of peoples a matter of policy. Wilson's call for free trade and open seas had long been part of the liberal canon. His attention to the dangers of colonial warfare, the need for disarmament, and the benefits of open diplomacy was more radical, but it echoed the common belief that such steps would have averted war. Wilson's final point, and the one closest to his heart, called for a League of Nations to guarantee the safety of all. The American president's talk of "impartial justice," "peace that will be permanent," and covenants "sacredly observed" caught the imagination of the world.

At the Paris Peace Conference, which opened in January 1919, all parties agreed not to repeat the mistakes of the Congress of Vienna a century earlier. No defeated nations would take part in the early discussions; no German Talleyrand would divide the Allies. The atmosphere was one of sober business, organized around commissions of expert advisers. Thirty nations had joined the Allies, at least formally,[2] but the major decisions would be taken by the five big powers—France, the United Kingdom, Italy, Japan, and the United States. In practice, since most questions did not directly concern Japan, primary authority resided in four men: Clemenceau,

[2]The newly created nations of Yugoslavia, Czechoslovakia, and Poland were treated as Allies; the new republics of Austria, Hungary, and Germany as the defeated Central Powers.

▶ **When Woodrow Wilson paraded through the streets, Parisians cheered the representative of a new democratic era as well as an ally in victory.**

Lloyd George, Premier Vittorio Orlando, and Wilson. Disagreements among the Big Four soon became the center around which the negotiations turned. All were elected leaders, sensitive to public opinion, faced with grave domestic problems, worried by the turmoil in Central and Eastern Europe. Experienced politicians, they knew they had to hurry.

The Treaty with Germany To settle by May the complicated terms for peace with Germany was a remarkable achievement. Haste itself probably made the treaty more severe than it might otherwise have been. Commissions, assuming their proposals would be subject to later bargaining, tended to begin with maximum terms, but these were often simply written into the treaty itself.

The territorial provisions were not extremely harsh. Germany lost territory and colonies but remained a great state. Except for Alsace-Lorraine, however, the new boundaries were a source of continuing difficulties. France did not get the left bank of the Rhine. Instead, the Allies were to occupy the Rhineland for 15 years; and the coal-producing regions along the Saar River, while remaining under German sovereignty, would be supervised by France unless a later plebiscite by universal suffrage determined differently. Plebiscites would also decide whether Germany would surrender part of Schleswig to Denmark or part of upper Silesia to Poland.

The Polish provinces of eastern Prussia, where Germans formed about 40 percent of the population, were immediately ceded to Poland, creating the controversial Polish corridor to the sea. That corridor awkwardly separated eastern Prussia from the rest of Germany; and although a majority of the population within it was Polish, its

Map 27.4 TERRITORIAL SETTLEMENTS, 1919–1926

outlet was the German port city of Danzig, restored to its ancient status as a free city. Poland would always feel insecure with an arrangement the Germans never accepted.

Germany was to have no large artillery, submarines, or military air force, and no more than 100,000 men under arms—requirements that would have looked different if they had led to the general disarmament the treaty implied. The lists of matériel Germany had to deliver to the

Allies were more punitive: horses and railway carriages, quantities of coal, most of its present ships, and some new vessels to be specially built. The required reparations were more burdensome still. Despite fine talk of not requiring an indemnity, the Allies declared that Germany should pay for civilian damages. The claims of Belgium, a neutral attacked without warning, were easily justified; and Clemenceau could argue that the most destructive fighting had occurred in Belgium and France. But Lloyd George had campaigned on a platform of making Germany pay. He insisted, over American objections, on including Allied military pensions as civilian costs. Pandora's box was opened. Germany was made liable for sums unspecified and without foreseeable end and forced to accept "responsibility" for losses from a war "imposed . . . by the aggression of Germany and her allies." The "war guilt clause" became a subject of controversy in every country and a source of bitter resentment, official and private, in every part of Germany.

Finally, in German eyes, the treaty was an intolerable *Diktat*, which German delegates had no chance to discuss until it was already drafted, when only minor objections were accepted. Faced with these terms, the German government resigned, and the parliament at first rejected the treaty's stipulation of German guilt. But when the Allies held firm, parliament angrily acquiesced. The treaty was signed on June 28, 1919, the fifth anniversary of the assassination at Sarajevo, in the Hall of Mirrors at Versailles, where Bismarck and William I had announced the German Empire 48 years before. The symbolism was complete.

▸ The Treaty of Versailles was signed by elected political leaders in the Hall of Mirrors at Versailles and presented as a great public event, in self-conscious contrast to the Congress of Vienna a century earlier.

The Other Treaties For the Big Four, Italy's aims were especially difficult, and Italian insistence upon them particularly irksome. The Treaty of London of 1915 had promised Italy much of the Slavic-speaking lands of the Dalmation coast, and the Italian delegates expected to get them. Wilson was determined to prevent further violations of the principle of nationality beyond allowing Italy, for strategic reasons, to have the Tyrol south of the Alpine Brenner Pass, a German-speaking area formerly held by Austria. Using a press interview, Wilson in effect asked the Italian people to reject the position of their representatives at the conference, and the Italian delegation withdrew in protest, to a great outpouring of nationalist feeling at home. Eventually, Italy was given the Istrian Peninsula and some islands but not Dalmatia. For years to come, Italian resentment would be a disruptive issue in Italian domestic politics.

With the signing of the Treaty of Versailles, the Big Four dispersed, leaving the details of the remaining settlements to their foreign offices. The treaty with Austria in September was closely modeled on the treaty with Germany, but reparations and demilitarization, including naval restrictions, hardly seemed appropriate for the shaky little landlocked Austrian republic. Boundaries for the other new states were settled on the basis of nationality in some cases and strategic needs in others. Treaties with Bulgaria in

November and with Hungary in June 1920 gave Bohemia to Czechoslovakia on historical grounds, but Hungarian claims to a larger historical kingdom were largely ignored. Like Austria, Hungary lost almost three-quarters of its former lands. Although Bulgaria surrendered relatively little territory, its resentment over its borders equaled that of the others. Every state of Eastern Europe could cite some injustice it had suffered, usually with exaggerated statistics and with tales, too often true, of inhumane treatment. Railways, economic ties, "natural" boundaries, historical claims, and nationality simply did not coincide. It would fall to the new League of Nations to make these arrangements work.

There would be much to negotiate. The fate of many territories was determined later, some by plebiscite. The promise of just treatment for minorities, an expression of the Allies' decent intent, would confront the sensitivity of new states about protecting their sovereignty. Much just did not work. The reparations required from Austria, for example, were divided among the new states carved out of the former Habsburg empire, which left some of them paying reparations to others, a perpetual source of dissension.

The final treaty, with Turkey, was not signed until August 1920, and much of it never went into effect. The Allies' aims had been contradictory all along, and the postwar situation spawned indigenous movements in the former Ottoman Empire as complex and uncontrollable as those in Eastern Europe. During the war, the Allies had encouraged Arab nationalism, but their sympathy faded afterward. The Russian and Habsburg empires no longer competed for influence there, and the Soviet government's release of earlier secret Allied plans for partitioning the Ottoman Empire reinforced suspicions that in Britain and France an old imperialism overshadowed commitment to any new arrangements. Turkey's territorial integrity was assured by the political effectiveness it gained under Mustafa Kemal; and although the independence of Arabia was recognized, internal conflict made its real status uncertain.

The more pressing need was to create a political order for the eastern shores of the Mediterranean, and the solution reached was defined as temporary. France was to have a supervisory authority in Syria; and a vaguely defined area—carved into Palestine, Trans-Jordan, and Iraq—would be subject to British authority, as would Egypt, despite its claims to independence. Aside from recognizing the presence of Britain and France in the Middle East, the treaty settled little, and lasting boundaries would be determined only through the conflicts and diplomacy of the next few years. British intentions in separating Palestine from Trans-Jordan were especially confusing. In 1917 the British foreign secretary, Arthur Balfour, had promised that a "national home" for Jews would be created in Palestine; but the Balfour Declaration, exemplifying the nationalistic propaganda and humanitarian concern of that difficult year, had also guaranteed the rights of the Muslims there. The future of Palestine was uncertain, and subsequent British statements provided little clarification.

In their effort to codify French and British interests, these arrangements did lead to an important innovation. Colonial territories were declared "mandates" of the League of Nations and assigned to classes. The parts of the Ottoman Empire newly placed under British or French rule were Class A mandates, states considered on the verge of self-government. Most of the reassigned African territories (primarily former German colonies) were Class B mandates, ones in which European rules were to guarantee freedom of religion, prohibit trade in liquor and arms, refrain from subjecting natives to military training, and encourage commerce. Class C mandates were primarily Pacific islands, to be ruled essentially as colonies. In every case, the mandate power had to submit annual reports to the League of Nations for review. Like much else in the treaties, the system of mandates can be seen both as an expression of conscience toward the rest of the world and as a device for absorbing former German colonies while legitimating continued European dominance.

The Mixed Outcome Not since 1848 had liberal conceptions so thoroughly dominated European politics. There was much to hope for in the call for self-determination and plebiscites, the League of Nations, the system of colonial mandates, and the establishment of representative regimes throughout Central Europe. By 1920, however, the limitations of what had been accomplished at Paris were all too apparent. Much done there reflected a cold assertion of national interest and a realistic appraisal of power, but the Allies had propagandized standards of high principle and injected ideology into international affairs. Living in a time of revolutionary changes they largely welcomed, the statesmen who forged the peace were not revolutionaries. They never managed to find a place for Russia at the conference. They took little account of the social and economic complexities of Eastern Europe. Believers in democracy, they were baffled by the turmoil it created. They stimulated nationalist movements but recognized the dangers of nationalism. Slogans that sounded radical in November 1918 gave way to frightened insistence on order a few months later. None of the leaders of democracy yet fully understood how much had changed.

Disillusionment came quickly. In March 1920 the Senate of the United States rejected the treaties for the final time. Having claimed moral leadership, America would in the end not enter the League of Nations. In the process, it added France to the list of aggrieved states, for France had abandoned demands for further weakening Germany in return for a joint guarantee against German aggression from the United States and Great Britain, which it did not get. China refused to sign the treaties because of terms that gave Japan, in addition to other gains, extensive rights in China. Japan was offended by the conference's refusal to formally declare all races equal.

The reparations were denounced in a brilliant and influential pamphlet, in which the English economist John Maynard Keynes castigated the Carthaginian peace the victors had exacted.[3] He argued that the Allies owned one another more money than Germany could pay and that reparations would merely slow the recovery of Europe's economy. His analysis helped undermine confidence in the terms of peace, but his prescriptions—cancellation of international war debts and recognition that the international economic system was essentially artificial—were as utopian in their way as any of Woodrow Wilson's points. His criticisms, like those that for decades would ring from party platforms in every country, tended to exaggerate how much of the postwar world could be shaped by worried statesmen quarreling in Paris.

[3]John Maynard Keynes, *The Economic Consequences of the Peace*, 1920; and the famous rebuttal, Etienne Mantoux, *The Carthaginian Peace: or the Economic Consequences of Mr. Keynes*, 1946. The reference is to the harsh peace terms that Roman senators demanded upon the defeat of Carthage in the Third Punic War, 149–146 B.C.E.

IV. The Era of Democracy

THE NEW REGIMES

From Finland to the Balkans, most of the states of Eastern Europe were new, and most of them had democratic constitutions. The disappearance of the Russian, Austrian, and Ottoman empires opened the way for systematic modernization using the administrative institutions and practices they left behind. Schools were built by the thousands and functioned fairly effectively despite issues of language and nationality. Stability was threatened, however, by economic, social, and ethnic conflict. New tariff barriers interrupted the flow of trade within the former empires, compounding the dislocations of war and the burden of reparations. Extensive help from the new League of Nations soon proved essential to creating stable economies. Growing populations, widespread illiteracy, and lack of capital plagued economic development.

Only Austria and Czechoslovakia had advanced industries that could compete in European markets; elsewhere, land remained the central economic issue. Independence brought the eviction of "foreign" landlords and the breakup of large estates in the Baltic countries and land reform in Bulgaria, Romania, and Czechoslovakia. Less effective than expected, such measures fed accusations of special treatment for favored nationalities and regions. In Poland and still more in Hungary (where 40 percent of the peasants were landless and 90 percent held less than 3 hectares, or 7.4 acres), the great estate owners of the aristocracy succeeded in protecting their interests.

Peasant parties, dominant in Eastern Europe, often combined agrarian radicalism with distrust of urban values, modernizing changes, or parliaments. These social conflicts intersected with ethnic and religious differences. The German minorities in Poland, Czechoslovakia, Hungary, and Bulgaria were generally among the resented well-to-do. Town-country antagonism also often set rural Slovaks at odds with the Czechs of industrialized western Czechoslovakia. Anti-Semitism was especially virulent in Poland and Romania, where it was partly an expression of rural hostility toward village money lenders and urban values. In Yugoslavia the claims of Greek Orthodox Serbians to be the "national" people angered the Roman Catholic Croatians and Slovenes. Macedonians—divided among Yugoslavia, Greece, and Bulgaria—agitated in all three countries and produced chaotic insurrection in Bulgaria from 1923 to 1925.

Such circumstances encouraged military intervention in politics, as in the new Greek republic and in the authoritarian rule in Hungary of Admiral Miklós Horthy, regent for an empty throne, who abolished the secret ballot in rural areas. But most of the governments of Eastern Europe worked more or less within their constitutions; and Czechoslovakia, under President Tomáš Masaryk and Foreign Minister Eduard Beneš, became a model of the order, freedom, and prosperity democracy was supposed to bring.

The Weimar Republic of Germany The provisional government had been established just in time to sign the armistice. It talked proudly of the German "revolution" and promulgated decrees promising democracy, freedom of speech, a return to the eight-hour workday, and improvements in social security. Frightened of a communist revolution, the government quickly reached an accommodation with the army, which was already encouraging the legend that it had not lost the war but had been stabbed in the back by politicians and radicals at home. General Wilhelm Groener, who replaced Ludendorff as Hindenburg's principal aide, promised to assist the government provided it would not meddle in the army's affairs. President Ebert accepted those terms; and when an uprising of left-wing Marxists, the Spartacists, gained control of most of Berlin in January 1919, the army crushed the revolt and shot its leaders. Lenin's best hope for a communist revolution in Germany died with them. One of those murdered was Rosa Luxemburg, who had drafted the Spartacist platform, which called for a proletarian revolution. An effective leader and impressive intellectual, she had urged the Spartacists to avoid useless violence and had recognized that most workers remained loyal to Ebert's social democratic government. But she would not abandon her party when hotter heads chose armed conflict. Her death was a lasting blow to the radical left, and the government's reliance on the army a blow to Germany's new democracy.

▸ Friedrich Eberts took the oath of office as provisional president of Germany in February 1919; note the absence of men in uniform.

Committed democrats, nevertheless, Germany's new leaders held elections in January 1919 for a constituent assembly. It met in Weimar, with nearly three-quarters of the delegates intent on installing a republic. They wrote a thoroughly democratic constitution that joined proportional representation to universal suffrage. The president, directly elected for a seven-year term, would nominate the chancellor, or prime minister, who would have to be approved by the Reichstag. The Reichsrat, the upper house, would still represent the single states but with reduced powers. In the new Germany, government would be responsible to parliament, minorities would be fairly represented, the aristocracy would hold

▸ **By November 1923 German children could play with their nation's worthless paper money.**

no political privilege, and civil rights and private property would be guaranteed. With women voting, the Social Democrats in power, and a broad spectrum of parties, German politics was launched on a new course.

The gravest problem of these years was inflation. Early in 1923 French and Belgian forces occupied the Ruhr district following Germany's failure to make the coal deliveries required as reparations. The local populace responded with passive resistance, a kind of general strike that made the occupation fruitless. The resulting dislocation and scarcity drastically accelerated the already serious inflation. The German government, which from 1920 on found it easier to print more money than to raise taxes, continued that practice in 1923 as its expenses rose (it provided payments to the striking workers of the Ruhr) and its revenues declined. The German mark, valued at 4 to 1 U.S. dollar in 1914 and 9 to 1 in 1919, was exchanged at 500 to 1 by 1922. Its subsequent fall was cataclysmic. One dollar was worth 18,000 marks in January 1923; 350,000 marks in July; nearly 5,000,000 in August; and inflation accelerated after that. New money was run off the presses at top speed, and old notes with additional zeros printed on them were rushed to the banks before they, too, became valueless. Prices changed within hours, always upward. By November a newspaper could sell for nearly 100 billion marks (*see box*, p. 901).

By the end of the year a restructuring was begun. The government imposed stringent new financial measures, aided by foreign loans, a moratorium on reparations, and subsequently a new schedule of payments. Some fortunes had been made, especially by speculators and financiers during the inflation; many large industries and property owners had fared quite well. Small businesses were more often hurt, as were nearly all wage earners. Savings held in cash had been wiped out, but a slow recovery began.

At the height of the Ruhr crisis, a little-known man named Adolf Hitler led a nationalist *Putsch*, or coup, in Munich. More notable for Ludendorff's participation, it was quickly defeated, and the plotters' punishment was ludicrously light. Ludendorff was acquitted, and Hitler was given a five-year sentence in comfortable prison quarters, where he composed *Mein Kampf* ("My Struggle") during the 13 months he actually served. It was reasonable to believe in 1924 that Germany was on the road to stability, and a period of notable prosperity followed.

But the divisions in German society were sharpening. The leading statesman was Gustav Stresemann, who sat in every cabinet, usually as foreign minister, from 1923 to his death in 1929. A nationalist of the center-right, he acquiesced in the army's violations of the disarmament clauses, but the right denounced him for his conciliatory tone toward former enemies and for bringing Germany into the League of Nations. German workers felt little was being done for them. The middle class could not forgive the inflation. Prosperity and moderate policies were a relief from the assassinations and revolts of the earlier years, but they produced no significant group with primary loyalty to the existing regime. The political extremes were growing at the expense of the center. When President Ebert died in 1925, a rightist coalition elected General von Hindenburg as his successor, defeating the candidate supported by

German Inflation

The German statistical office published this description of the effects of inflation in 1923. Obviously concerned that foreigners did not understand how bad the effects of inflation were, the account also expresses the rising insecurity of the middle class.

"The greater part of the population has been forced down far below their old standard of living, even with regard to the most important necessities of life.

"Consequently the foreigner, for example, who has visited Germany since the war, would do well to ask himself whether, in the overcrowded first-class railway carriages, he has found many Germans, or whether in the best seats at the theatre Germans are in the majority. He would do well to inquire whether in fashionable places of entertainment the German or the foreign public predominates, and if he does see Germans present spending their money for light entertainment, let him consider whether these are the majority of the German people. He must not forget either that many people today are influenced by the psychological fact that saving is no longer of any use: 100 marks today will perhaps be only 50 marks tomorrow. He who before the war, for example, had saved 5,500 marks could purchase for that amount furniture for a middle-class flat of three rooms as well as clothing, for a married couple with two children. In the middle of February 1923 (with an average dollar rate of 27,819 for February) the same person, for the same articles, would have had to spend 26.3 million marks in paper money. The man who did not spend the 5,500 marks, but preferred to save it together with the interest thereon might have over 7,000 marks today, with which, however, he cannot even buy a shirt! Who would care to 'save' under such conditions? Does the stranger realize, moreover, that such violent changes in the valuation of German money have meant for many thousands of German savers the annihilation of their savings? Does the stranger see the formerly well-to-do men and women of the middle class who today with a heavy heart carry their old family jewellery to the dealer, in order to prolong their physical existence a little longer? He who before the war could spend the interest on 1 million marks was a rich man, even up to 1919 he could still live upon it with reasonable comfort; today he is poor, for with his 50,000 marks interest he can today barely provide his own person with the necessities of life for a week! Does the stranger see the women and girls from the higher circles, even up to the highest, who are compelled to take up some occupation or who help to eke out the family income by working in their homes for a miserable wage? Does the stranger see the 1½ millions of war cripples, who are struggling desperately to earn their living, because the pensions that the State can afford to pay them are utterly inadequate? . . ."

From Statistisches Reichsamp, *Germany's Economic and Financial Situation, An Exhibit of After-Effects of the World War*, 1923, in Sidney Pollard and Colin Holmes (eds.), *Documents of European Economic History*, Vol. 3: *The End of Old Europe, 1914–1939* (New York: St. Martin's Press, 1972).

both the Center and the Social Democratic parties; significantly, the 2 million votes given the Communist nominee would have made the difference.

INTERNATIONAL RELATIONS

From 1924 to 1930 the conduct of international affairs really did reflect some of the idealism of the Paris Peace Conference. The League of Nations, formally established in 1920, successfully resolved a number of disputes, despite the absence of the United States, Britain's greater concern for its empire, and France's tendency to use the League for its own security. Its special commissions helped restructure the disjointed economies of new states, aided refugees, and set international standards for public health and working conditions. In the late 1920s, at least, the decisions of the Permanent Court of International Justice were treated with great respect as steps toward the rule of law.

Crises over debt payments were dealt with more directly by the major powers. As Germany fell behind in its payments, the Allies took the position that they, in turn, could not pay their war debts to the United States. Some compromise was essential, and in 1924 the nations involved accepted the proposals of an international commission of financial experts, headed by the American banker Charles G. Dawes. The Dawes Plan fixed Germany's reparations payments on a regular scale, established an orderly mode of collection, and provided loans to Germany equal to 80 percent of the reparations payment due the first year of the plan. The plan did not admit any connection between Allied debts to the United States and German reparations to the European victors, but it did end the worst of the chaos. For the next six years, Germany, fed by loans largely from the United States, made its reparations payments on schedule. The issue seemed forever resolved with the adoption of the Young Plan in 1929, which finally set a limit to Germany's obligations (59 years), reduced annual payments, and ended foreign occupation of the Rhineland. Under the leadership of American bankers, the interests of international capital had come to shape policy in the name of economic necessity.

The Locarno Era International efforts to outlaw war foundered on definitions of aggression, but they led to a series of treaties known as the Locarno Pact in 1925. The major agreement—entered into by Germany, Belgium, France, Great Britain, and Italy—secured Germany's western frontier as defined by the Versailles treaty; all parties promised to arbitrate their disputes. In addition, France pursued a more traditional diplomacy, signing a mutual-defense alliance with Poland and Czechoslovakia. A continental war caused by German aggression now seemed impossible.

The optimism of the Locarno era was capped by the Kellogg-Briand pact of 1928. The French had suggested that the American entry into World War I be commemorated by a friendship pact, and the Americans proposed to include others as well. More than a score of nations signed the pact, which contained no troubling provisions for enforcement and renounced war "as an instrument of national policy."

From 1921 on, some League commission was always studying the problem of disarmament. Given the enormous cost of capital ships (Britain no longer aspired to maintain a fleet twice the size of any other), naval disarmament seemed especially promising. At the Washington Conference of 1921–1922, called by President Warren G. Harding, the United States, Great Britain, Japan, France, and Italy agreed after some difficulty to fix their relative strength in capital ships at current levels,[4] not to expand their naval bases, and even to scrap some of their larger vessels. About smaller ships there had been less agreement, but the Washington Conference produced tangible results. Never again did disarmament discussions prove so fruitful. At Geneva in 1927 and London in 1930, Italy (citing the special needs of its geography) and France (arguing that all forms of disarmament should be discussed together) refused to accept a treaty. By 1935 Japan would reject even the Washington accord.

Attempts to limit land and air arms were even less successful. League commissions could not agree on which were offensive weapons, whether a professional army was comparable to a reserve force, and whether limitations should be expressed in terms of budgets, weapons, or men. German and Russian proposals that their military weakness be made a standard for other nations to reach by disarming only aroused suspicion. When the conference on general disarmament that these League commissions prepared was finally called in 1932, the dream of arms restrictions was more remote than ever. Discussions continued at length, but before agreements were reached, Hitler had come to power in Germany, and a new arms race ensued.

THE ESTABLISHED DEMOCRACIES

Except for Italy, where Fascism came to power, democracy at first fared rather well. Belgium, despite the war's destruction and conflicts over language and religion, recaptured its place among

[4]This was defined as parity between the United States and Great Britain at 525,000 tons apiece in capital ships; 315,000 tons for Japan; and 175,000 tons each for France and Italy.

Europe's most prosperous and freest countries. Although the Netherlands faced nationalist unrest in its colonies, especially the East Indies, such problems hardly threatened democratic institutions at home. The Scandinavian countries, while often at odds among themselves, sustained effective democracies. Women's suffrage there (Norway, 1907; Denmark, 1914; Sweden, 1919) and in Weimar Germany and Great Britain had neither destroyed the family nor cleansed politics, but it proved to be a natural expansion of democracy.

Society had not been radically reformed, although in every country the most militant Marxists felt strengthened by the presence of the Soviet Union as an international homeland for the proletariat. But the founding of Communist parties and allegiance to the Soviet Union split and weakened the left in domestic affairs. Economic recovery, though slower than expected, brought a general prosperity by the mid-1920s that contributed to the electoral victories of moderate and conservative parties. Constitutional democracy was the European norm, and many were convinced that even the Soviet Union and Italy would in time become more like their neighbors.

The real social changes of this period were usually not the result of deliberate policy. Employment in services such as sales and office work increased more rapidly than in industry, and the number of domestic servants declined. In most countries more women were gainfully employed than before the war (at those jobs thought suitable for women), despite a sharp decline from the wartime peak and despite the strong tendency for women to leave work upon marriage. The number of (middle-class) youths enrolled in universities increased sharply, and the automobile, especially in Britain and France, began to alter middle-class life. Generally, the central government now spent a higher proportion of national wealth; and although most of that went to the military, to interest on the national debt, and to pensions—all costs left from the war—some of it was used to lay the basis for broader measures of social security for all. Politically, both business interests and labor unions exercised a more direct influence, essentially supporting the effort to recapture economic stability. Yet despite periods of prosperity and a genuine boom in certain industries, the 1920s did not provide the steady growth of the prewar decade. Economic uncertainty, increased by inflation and unemployment, tended, like the disillusionment over reparations or the specter of Bolshevism, to favor caution.

France Life in France quickly returned to prewar patterns. The nation had become *par excellence* the land of the middle class, the artisan, and the peasant proprietor fiercely attached to a tiny plot of land. Though the cornucopia of reparations they had expected never materialized, ordinary people accomplished miracles of reconstruction, carefully making their new buildings look as much as possible like those destroyed. The Chamber of Deputies elected in 1919 at the height of patriotic pride in victory was the most conservative since the founding of the Third Republic; and politics, too, focused on restoration.

Depreciation of the franc, for a century one of the world's stablest currencies, became the focus of President Raymond Poincaré's conservative program. Inadequate taxation during the war (it took great political courage to raise taxes in France) lay at the root of the problem, and budgetary contraction was the preferred solution. Economic security and protection from aggression were pursued with a rigidity that showed the psychological as well as the economic and demographic costs of war. In the subsequent prosperity, competent leaders presided over governments content with policies that permitted domestic stagnation and encouraged rigidity in foreign affairs. Poincaré's concern for national honor and a stable currency appealed to a cautious middle class much as the complicated maneuvers of Aristide Briand, the leading figure of the 1930s, did to parliamentarians, but neither encouraged the French to face more difficult long-term issues of working conditions, social inequality, or mass culture.

The United Kingdom In the United Kingdom also, the 1919 elections—the first in which women (those over 30) were allowed to vote—produced an overwhelming victory for the leaders who promised to extract enough from Germany to make winning the war worthwhile. Lloyd George remained prime minister, but his government was essentially conservative. The breakup of the wartime coalition exposed the Liberal party's decline; and in 1924 new elections

▸ **Demonstrations and parades were banned in Dublin and Belfast, where an armored car stands ready to put down any trouble; violence had become an expected part of political struggle in Ireland.**

brought the Labour party briefly to power. Except for recognizing the Soviet Union, Labour did little to recall its leftist origins. For most of that decade, Britain was led with dull caution by the Conservatives and Stanley Baldwin, who inherited problems of unemployment, Irish nationalism, and a changing empire.

A crisis in the coal industry led to a 10-day general strike in 1926. Frightened by the bitter class conflict, many of the well-to-do volunteered in maintaining essential services, thus helping to break the strike. That and the antilabor legislation which followed did much to deepen the resentment of the British workers. The Irish question was equally explosive. The promise of home rule had been suspended during the war, and the Easter Rebellion of 1916 had been firmly suppressed. In 1919, however, the most militant Irish nationalists, led by the Sinn Fein (meaning "We Ourselves") party, refused to take their seats in the House of Commons and met instead at Dublin in a parliament of their own, the Dail Eireann, where they declared Ireland independent. To this defiance the London government responded slowly and ineptly, finally choosing to suppress the Sinn Fein party and with it Irish independence. To support that policy, the government sent reinforcements to the Royal Irish Constabulary in numbers sufficient to spread the fighting without ending it, and these soldiers soon became the most hated symbol of British repression. Violent civilian resisters called themselves the Irish Republican Army; and against civilian terrorists, the British could look only foolish or brutal. By the 1920s the two sides were fighting a bloody war.

With pressure mounting at home and abroad for some settlement, the British government in 1920 passed an Ireland act, creating two Irish parliaments, one in the predominantly Catholic areas of the south and west, and the other in the predominantly Protestant counties of the northeast. Sinn Fein combated this division of the island in almost two more years of fighting. In December 1922 the Irish parliament at Dublin in the Catholic south proclaimed, with British acquiescence, the existence of the Irish Free State, which included all Ireland except the six northern counties of Ulster. As Northern Ireland, these counties maintained the traditional union with Great Britain, an uneasy peace that preserved the basis for further tension and conflict.

Only in imperial affairs were habits of flexible compromise more productive. Canadian complaints led the Imperial Conference of 1926 to a significant new definition of all dominions as "autonomous communities . . . equal in status . . . united by a common allegiance to the crown and freely associated as members of the British Commonwealth of Nations." Autonomous in all domestic and foreign affairs, dominions accepted ties to the British crown as the expression of common traditions and loyalties. Given legal sanction by the Statute of Westminster in 1931, this conception of empire proved a skillful adaptation to new conditions crowned by the stability, prosperity, and loyalty of dominions such as Canada, New Zealand, and Australia.

The nations of Europe had stumbled into the most destructive war in their history, forcing them to harness the political systems, organizational skills, and technology that had made them powerful. The war had probed every social weakness; eliminated the German, Austro-

Hungarian, and Russian empires; and left the victors only marginally better off than the losers. In the course of the war and as part of its justification, the winning alliance had promulgated universal values of democracy; and though these values were tainted in the practical decisions of the peace, they were to some extent embraced across the continent. Gradually, stability and prosperity did return to much of Europe. If broader hopes lost their luster, the institutions that expressed them remained in place. Only the next round of challenges would reveal whether that was enough to compensate for opportunities missed.

Recommended Reading

Sources

Chapman, Guy. *A Passionate Prodigality.* 1966. No war stimulated a richer literature, and this searing account of the personal experiences of an English soldier, first published in 1933, is among the best of these works.

*Nicholson, Harold G. *Peacemaking, 1919.* 1965. The retrospective analysis of an experienced diplomat who was a disillusioned participant at the Versailles Conference.

Studies

Becker, Jean-Jacques. *The Great War and the French People.* 1985. Shows the multiple ways in which the war was a turning point in French life.

Cannadine, David. *The Decline and Fall of the British Aristocracy.* 1990. Traces the extraordinary erosion of the position of a dominant class from the Lloyd George budget of 1906 through World War I and the changes that have followed.

Carsten, F. L. *Revolution in Central Europe, 1918–1919.* 1972. An important treatment of these significant outbreaks following the war.

Falls, Cyril B. *The Great War.* 1961. A skillful account of the war by a noted military historian.

Feldman, Gerald D. *Army, Industry and Labor in Germany, 1914–1918.* 1966. A fundamental analysis of the war's effects on institutions and power in Germany.

*Ferro, Marc. *The Great War, 1914–1918.* 1973. This stimulating, outspoken essay emphasizes the economic and social impact of the war.

*Fischer, Fritz. *Germany's Aims in the First World War.* 1967. The reassessment that became a center of controversy among Germany historians.

Fridenson, Patrick (ed.). *The French Home Front, 1914–1918.* Bruce Little (tr). 1992. A valuable collection of essays by social historians on the effects of wartime on the lives of industrial workers.

*Fussell, Paul. *The Great War and Modern Memory.* 1975. A lively study of the cultural impact of the war denouncing modern warfare in all its aspects.

*Joll, James. *The Origins of the First World War.* 1984. Draws upon the vast literature dealing with a question that was once extremely controversial to establish a balanced perspective.

Kennedy, Paul (ed.). *The War Plans of the Great Powers, 1880–1914.* 1979. Places the arms race in the context of imperialist and political pressures that underlay the process of planning leading up to the war.

Kocka, Jürgen. *Facing Total War: German Society 1914–1918.* Barbara Weinberger (tr.). 1984. A leading social historian's assessment of the domestic impact of the war on Germany.

Marwick, Arthur. *War and Social Change in the Twentieth Century: A Comparative Study of Britain, France, Germany, Russia and the United States.* 1975. Develops the case for the revolutionary effects of World Wars I and II on the domestic economy of modern society.

*Mayer, Arno J. *Politics and Diplomacy of Peacemaking: Containment and Counterrevolution at Versailles, 1918–1919.* 1967. Argues that fear of Bolshevism shaped the terms of peace more than publicized principles.

Miller, S. (ed.). *Military Strategy and the Origins of the First World War.* 1985. These essays assess the role of the military in the decisions that led to war.

Williams, John. *The Home Fronts: Britain, France, and Germany, 1914–1918.* 1972. Pulls together a variety of evidence of the war's domestic impact.

Williamson, S. R., Jr. *The Politics of Grand Strategy: Britain and France Prepare for War, 1904–1914.* 1969.

Winter, J. M. *The Great War and the British People.* 1986. A balanced assessment of the effects of the war on British society.

*Available in paperback.

This idealized image of Lenin addressing the people conveys the power of Lenin's oratory skills and the sense that his leadership began a new era. The portrait of impassioned workers, soldiers and sailors, men and women—all inspired by their leader and the careful placement of Stalin just behind Lenin—reveal the painting as the subsequent official view of the Soviet government. One of the marks of the new era in Europe was, in fact, the effective propaganda of single-party states.

CHAPTER TWENTY-EIGHT

The Great Twentieth-century Crisis

TWO important exceptions stood against the liberal political trend following World War I. While most European nations embraced a standard form of representative government, Communists consolidated their hold on Russia and Fascists seized power in Italy. At first, these new regimes remained relatively isolated and seemed to have only limited impact on Europe generally. Soon, however, their examples affected politics in every nation. Almost everywhere, parties on the left split between socialists and a more militantly revolutionary Communist party with close ties to Russia, and new movements on the right sprung up in imitation of the nationalist tone and military style of Italian Fascism.

The disruptive political conflicts that ensued were enlarged by the broader cultural and economic crises. In the physical and social sciences provocative new theories not only challenged old assumptions but invited skepticism about absolute truths and traditional values. A flourishing popular culture, flippant and commercial, resonated less with nineteenth-century confidence than with the experience of World War I and the promise of some revolutionary transformation of society that was central to both communism and fascism. By 1930 the disaster of economic depression exposed the weaknesses of parliamentary democracy for all to see and cast further doubt on the future of liberalism. Nearly everywhere, communists gained support among workers and intellectuals, and fascist regimes gained power in nation after nation.

I. The New Revolutions

RUSSIAN COMMUNISM

The February Revolution When world war broke out in 1914, Russia's parliament (the Duma) and local councils (or *zemstvos*) had helped coordinate the war effort. But when the Cadet party maintained its insistence on further liberal reforms, the Duma was suspended. Resentful that political aims should be pursued in wartime—they still did not see that a more representative government could strengthen the war effort—the tsar and his officials grew more isolated from the country. More skilled as a military strategist than as a head of state, Tsar Nicholas II grandly departed to command his army, leaving Tsarina Alexandra and those closest to her to oppose any program for reform. Her chief confidant was Grigori Rasputin, an ignorant and corrupt mystic whose influence symbolized the decadence of this regime.

Throughout 1916 signs of Russia's failures accumulated. Production and transportation were undependable, war refugees filled the roads, inflation soared, and food shortages became critical. The resulting discontent reached into the highest circles, where there was even talk of deposing the tsar. In November in the reconvened Duma, Pavel Milyukov, the Cadets' leader, courageously delivered a bitter attack on the government. In December a group of nobles murdered Rasputin. Strikes spread; and in March 1917, when strikers filled the streets of Petrograd,[1] their economic demands quickly broadened to include political issues; and the army could not be relied on to oppose them. Once again, much as in 1905, the Soviet of Workers' and Soldiers' Deputies became the voice of revolution, and they joined with a Duma committee in seeking a provisional government. They prepared to resist any tsarist force that might be sent against them. None came; the tsar had nowhere to turn. The military situation was desperate, the government in disarray, and the tsar unpopular. Nicholas II abdicated, and the February Revolution[2] was hailed with joy and relief throughout the country.

The provisional government's central figure was Milyukov; its only socialist was Aleksandr Kerensky, a member of the Social Revolutionary party and vice-chairman of the Petrograd soviet. The new government quickly established broad civil liberties, an amnesty for political prisoners, and the end of religious persecution. It also proposed granting a constitution to Finland, which Russia ruled, and independence to Russian Poland. Declaring its support for an eight-hour day for workers and the abolition of class privileges, it left most other social issues to a constituent assembly, which it promised to call soon.

In fact, the parties of revolution sharply disagreed on these issues. The Cadets, who dominated the provisional government, came to accept the idea of a republic, political democracy, and distribution of land with compensation to former owners. To their left, the Social Revolutionary party and the Menshevik wing of the Social Democratic party, which was especially strong in the soviets forming across the nation, demanded more drastic reforms. Some of them were willing to postpone these further reforms until after the war, which, like the Cadets, they still meant to win. The more radical of them stressed an early end to the war, without yet advocating an immediate armistice. For the time being, the soviets, watching from the outside and ever ready to criticize, allowed the provisional government its chance. To the left of all these factions stood a small group known as the Bolsheviks.

The Bolsheviks In 1898 Russian Marxists had secretly formed the Social Democratic party, which functioned mainly in the conspiratorial

[1]St. Petersburg was a German name, and in 1914 Nicholas had changed it to the Russian *Petrograd.* The capital until 1918, the city would become Leningrad in 1924 and St. Petersburg again in 1991.

[2]These events occurred on March 8–12 according to the Gregorian calendar used throughout the West. Russia, however, had never abandoned the older Julian calendar (which continues to be the calendar of the Orthodox Church). The revolutions of March 8–12 and November 7, 1917, according to the Gregorian system were dated 13 days earlier according to the Julian, and they continue to be called the February and October revolutions.

world of exile. At the party's second congress, held in Brussels and London in 1903, it had split into two groups, called the Bolsheviks (majority) and Mensheviks (minority); in fact, the Bolsheviks rarely had a majority, but these nicknames stuck. Their differences were theoretical, organizational, and personal. The theoretical issues, which engaged Marxists everywhere, were fought with the special intensity of revolutionaries far from home and power. On the whole, the Mensheviks placed greater emphasis on popular support and parliamentary institutions, which implied cooperation with other parties. The Bolsheviks stressed instead the need for a disciplined revolutionary party to instruct and lead the masses, who were otherwise likely to settle for immediate gains rather than the European revolution that would bring about socialism. Led by Georgi Plekhanov and V. I. Lenin, the Bolsheviks denounced as enemies all who did not join them. Only later would these party battles waged in foreign cities prove significant for Russian history.

Neither Mensheviks nor Bolsheviks had played a central part in the Revolution of 1905. The ideas of socialism that spread in Russia after 1905 were not so much those of the Bolsheviks as those of the Mensheviks and Social Revolutionaries, who were less consistently Marxists and closer to the peasants. Although Plekhanov tried on his own to heal the breach in the Social Democratic party, Lenin's conception of iron discipline allowed little room for compromise; and Plekhanov, too, was soon consigned to the Mensheviks. Removed from events in Russia, Lenin continued from Switzerland to organize selected followers, denounce the heresies of others, and develop his theoretical view of the special role a militant party should play in a country that, like Russia, was just achieving modern capitalism. The party could achieve its aims, he argued, only by recognizing the revolutionary potential in the peasants' hunger for land (most Marxists considered the peasantry a socially backward class and land ownership opposed to socialism). Thus the Bolsheviks, although they lacked a large following in Russia, had a theory of how to make a revolution.

Lenin also considered World War I a civil war among capitalists, and in a sense that theoretical stand gave Lenin his chance, for it suggested to the Germans that his presence in Russia as an agitator might be useful in undermining the Russian war effort. In April 1917 the Germans arranged to send Lenin by sealed train through Germany and Scandinavia to Russia. Lenin, however, had something grander than mere agitation in mind; and once again it began from a practical solution to a doctrinal problem. Marxists were ambivalent in their attitude toward the February Revolution, which they welcomed as progressive but tended to disdain as a bourgeois revolution and not the victory of a proletariat. Lenin offered another interpretation: Revolution in Russia was part of a larger revolution about to sweep all of Europe. Socialists had no interest in the capitalistic war, which Russia's provisional government continued to support, but the Bolsheviks could take advantage of the situation to push the revolution beyond its bourgeois phase to a "second stage" that would make Russia capable of joining in the international revolution destined to take place soon. In this second stage of Russia's revolution, Lenin reasoned, the soviets would be the true representatives of the proletariat. That in turn dictated the tactics the Bolsheviks should follow; they must gain the leadership of the soviets. Historians have emphasized Lenin's tactical flexibility, but in April his views seemed impossibly dogmatic even to radicals. It was the force of his personality, his political skill, and his oratory that kept him leader of the Bolsheviks.

Summer Crisis While the soviets meanwhile were building a national organization that claimed authority over railroads, telegraph lines, and troops, the provisional government was falling apart. Its members disagreed over war policy and land reform; its police and officials were abandoning their posts. Workers continued to strike, and nationalist movements erupted in Latvia, Georgia, and the Ukraine. Army morale was sinking when in March the Petrograd soviet issued its famous Order Number I: Officers would be chosen by their men and the army run by elected committees. The order was adopted in most military units, and a good part of the army simply melted away. A radical change in political leadership was imperative. Milyukov resigned, four more socialists joined the cabinet, and Kerensky, an energetic leader and effective orator, became the cabinet's leading figure.

The Bolsheviks were feeling some frustration, too, for the revolution seemed to be proceeding without them. At the first all-Russian Congress of Soviets in June, the Bolsheviks could weaken support for Kerensky, but they gained only a little over 100 of the more than 800 delegates. In July they attempted a coup in Petrograd, which was decisively defeated. Many of its leaders were arrested, and Lenin fled to Finland. Kerensky saw his chance to establish a more effective and stable government. That, he believed, required one successful military offensive, which had been prepared as carefully as possible, and an escape from the disruptions created by the soviets. The offensive failed, and the national congress of all interests called to show that the soviets were isolated instead revealed how deeply divided the whole nation was over war aims and social policy. Cities were torn by strikes and demonstrations as the situation at the front grew more perilous. In the countryside, manor houses were burned and landlords murdered as peasants rioted for land.

The army's commander in chief, General Lavr Kornilov, convinced that a strong military hand was what the nation needed, led an attack on Petrograd in September. Kerensky asked the soviets (and thus the Bolsheviks as well) to defend the government. Most of Kornilov's men had refused to follow his orders, and the threat passed quickly. Bolshevik leaders had been released from prison, however, and Bolshevist propaganda was gaining ground with simple slogans promising peace, land, and bread—issues at the heart of daily life, for which the provisional government had no clear solutions. The Bolsheviks won control of the soviets in Moscow and Petrograd, electing Leon Trotsky chairman of the latter. Trotsky, who had worked with Lenin in exile, had until recently stood somewhat aloof from party conflicts. Now firmly in Lenin's camp, he proceeded to organize the armed forces in Petrograd. With the Social Revolutionaries supporting

▶ **The armed civilians in the foreground are Red Guards, demonstrating their might and protecting the Bolshevik leaders addressing a large crowd of workers.**

peasant expropriation of land, the provisional government was left politically alone in a city it could not control trying to rule a nation in chaos and still at war.

The October Revolution Lenin boldly decided to seize power, to the dismay of many in his party. When the second all-Russian Congress of Soviets met on November 7, he would confront it with a new government. Kerensky began countermeasures a few days before that date, but it was too late. On November 6, Red Guards (squads of armed workers), sailors, and soldiers captured the Winter Palace and strategic points throughout the city. A simultaneous movement in Moscow won control of the city in a week. Lenin announced to the Congress that the Bolsheviks held power and sent out a young officer to take command of the armies. At each stop along his route, the troops enthusiastically cheered his announcement of the Bolshevik coup, and their commanders could only acquiesce. Kerensky, who had escaped from the capital, tried to muster support; but the one group of Cossacks who moved on Petrograd was soundly defeated. The world's first Communist government had taken office (*see box*, p. 912).

"All power to the Soviets!" had been one of the Bolsheviks' most effective slogans, and the Congress readily approved the one-party cabinet Lenin presented it. The rudiments of a new form of government emerged: The Congress of Soviets replaced parliament and elected a Central Executive committee to advise the Council of People's Commissars, or cabinet. From the very first Bolshevik rule did not depend on any elected body. Elections for the promised constituent assembly, held at the end of November, would be the last open competition among parties for more than 70 years. The Bolsheviks won a quarter of the seats, other socialist parties more than 60 percent, conservatives and liberals the rest. As the assembly met on its second day, the military guards told it to adjourn.

Lenin provided a basis for such ruthlessness in his pamphlet "The State and Revolution," written in Finland in the summer of 1917. It used the Marxist conception of the state as the coercive organ of the ruling class to argue that once the Bolsheviks held power, the proletariat would be that ruling class; dictatorship, Lenin reasoned, was the only way to lead backward Russia through so advanced a revolution. Lenin justified dictatorship as the transition to that higher historical stage Marxists envisioned in which the state would no longer be necessary. Nationalization of land and factories would achieve socialism. Communism would follow once everyone learned to work for the good of society and production met the needs of all. In the interim, the single party, the "vanguard of the proletariat," would be model and guide. The party, as Lenin envisioned it, would sustain its enthusiasm by sincere discussion in which differences would be reconciled and criticisms would keep officials on their toes. By his combination of theory, attention to such immediate issues as bread and land, and ruthless but flexible tactics, Lenin placed himself beside Marx as a founder of modern communism.

Toward a Communist Society Millions of workers, soldiers, and peasants had joined in pulling down the old system, and the Bolshevik leaders were determined to snatch their historical moment. The day after taking the Winter Palace, the new government decreed that land, livestock, and farm equipment belonged to the state but was to be held "temporarily" by peasant committees, thereby legitimizing the rural revolution that was taking place anyway. No peasant was to work for hire, and committees of the poor would supervise the allocation of land and produce. Workers' committees would share in factory management, and everyone would be paid according to the work done (the state's new leaders assigned themselves laborers' salaries). All social titles and military ranks were abolished. "People's tribunals" and workers' militias replaced tsarist courts and police. Church and state were separated; the equality of the sexes was decreed and followed by regulations allowing divorce by mutual consent. Even the alphabet was reformed and the Gregorian calendar adopted. In the next few months, railroads, banks, and shipping concerns were nationalized; foreign trade became a state monopoly, and Russia's debts were repudiated. The various nationalities of Russia were declared equal and granted the right of secession; Finland separated from Russia in

Two Accounts of Revolution in Russia

The culmination of the Russian Revolution came on November 7, 1917, when the Communists captured the Winter Palace, which was then the seat of the Kerensky government. Eyewitnesses saw the event very differently. The first account is by Pitirim Sorokin, a young member of the Social Revolutionary party, who would soon go into exile, where he would have a distinguished career as a professor of sociology at Harvard. In his memoir,* Leaves from a Russian Diary, *he recalled that day. The second description is from* Ten Days That Shook the World, *the famous book by John Reed, an American journalist who admired the Bolsheviks.

◆ "Lying ill all day on my bed, I listened to the steady booming of the cannon and the spatter of machine-guns and crack of rifles. Over the telephone I learned that the Bolsheviki had brought up from Kronstadt the warship *Aurora* and had opened fire on the Winter Palace, demanding the surrender of members of the Provisional Government, still barricaded there. At seven in the evening I went to the Municipal Duma. With many matters before us, the immediate horror that faced us was this situation at the Winter Palace. There was a regiment of women and the military cadets were bravely resisting an overwhelming force of Bolshevist troops, and over the telephone Minister Konovalov was appealing for aid. Poor women, poor lads, their situation was desperate, for we knew that the wild sailors, after taking the Palace, would probably tear them to pieces. What could we do? After breathless council it was decided that all of us, the Soviets, Municipalities, Committees of Socialist Parties, members of the Council of the Republic, should go in procession to the Winter Palace and do our utmost to rescue the Ministers, the women soldiers, and the cadets. Even as we prepared to go, over the telephone came the despairing shout: 'The gates of the Palace have been forced. The massacre has begun. . . . Hurry! The mob has reached the first floor. All is over. Goodbye. . . . They break in. They are. . . .' The last word . . . from the Winter Palace was a broken cry. . . .

◆ "Carried along by the eager wave of men we were swept into the right-hand entrance, opening into a great bare vaulted room, the cellar of the east wind, from which issued a maze of corridors and staircases. A number of huge packing cases stood about, and upon these the Red Guards and soldiers fell furiously, battering them open with the butts of their rifles, and pulling out carpets, curtains, linen, porcelain plates, glassware. . . . One man went strutting around with a bronze clock perched on his shoulder; another found a plume of ostrich feathers, which he stuck in his hat. The looting was just beginning when somebody cried, 'Comrades! Don't touch anything! Don't take anything! This is the property of the People!' Immediately twenty voices were crying, 'Stop! Put everything back! Don't take anything! Property of the People!' Many hands dragged the spoilers down. Damask and tapestry were snatched from the arms of those who had them; two men took away the bronze clock. Roughly and hastily the things were crammed back in their cases, and self-appointed sentinels stood guard. It was all utterly spontaneous. Through corridors and up staircases the cry could be heard growing fainter and fainter in the distance, 'Revolutionary discipline! Property of the People. . . .' "

From Roger Pethybridge (ed.), *Witnesses to the Russian Revolution* (Secaucus, N.J.: Citadel Press, 1964).

December 1917, though the Bolsheviks struggled to prevent the Ukraine and the ethnic groups of the Baltic regions from following suit.

Revolutionary measures also made way for a regime of terror. A new secret police, the Cheka, differed from the old in determination more than method. The citizens who sat on the new committees and tribunals often combined revolutionary enthusiasm with personal vengeance, and tens of thousands lost their property, their rights, and their lives for "mistaken" alliances, "false" ideas, or "suspect" gestures. Such practices, which helped the regime solidify support, also threatened to undermine the regular procedures of government.

The most pressing issue was to find a way out of the war. The Bolsheviks had asked all nations to accept peace without annexations. When rebuffed, they shocked the world by publishing secret Allied agreements. Then in February 1918 a delegation headed by Trotsky, having failed to arrange terms of peace with Germany, proposed a policy of no peace, no war: Russia would just stop fighting. The Germans advanced to within 100 miles of Petrograd. In March the Russians accepted the Treaty of Brest Litovsk. Russia surrendered more than 1 million square miles of territory to Germany, including a third of its arable land, a third of its factories, and three-quarters of its deposits of iron and coal. It granted the independence of Finland, Georgia, and the Ukraine; left to Germany the disposition of Russian Poland, Lithuania, Latvia, and Estonia; and ceded parts of Transcaucasia to the Ottoman Empire. The communists paid this high price for peace, confident that revolution in Germany would soon nullify the kaiser's gains.

The peace treaty, like the course of the revolution itself, had also demonstrated the discontent among non-Russian nationalities, and in July a new constitution tried to meet that problem by declaring Russia a federation—the Russian Soviet Federated Socialist Republic (R.S.F.S.R.). Great Russia, extending through Siberia, was the largest member. Ostensibly, political power rested with the local soviets, organized by occupation and elected by the votes of all men and women, excluding members of the clergy, former high officials, and bourgeois "nontoilers." These soviets elected delegates to the congress of soviets of their canton, the smallest administrative unit, and each of these congresses in turn sent delegates to a congress at the next administrative level. The system, which continued by steps up to the all-Russia Congress, allowed considerable control from the top. The constitution did not mention the Russian Communist party, as it was now named, which became the real center of political authority. Its Central Committee elected the smaller Politburo, which shared ruling power with the governing Council of People's Commissars, and Lenin was the dominant figure in both.

Civil War The Bolsheviks remained surrounded by enemies. In March Allied troops in small numbers had landed in Murmansk, Archangel, and Vladivostok to prevent the supplies shipped to Russia from falling into German hands, but those detachments might also be used to support a change of regime. In addition, the government had reluctantly permitted a Czech brigade of some 30,000 men to go by rail from the Eastern front to Vladivostok in order to sail around the world to the Western front. On the long train journey, the Czechs clashed with some Hungarian prisoners of war; the fighting spread, and the Czechs, aided by Russian anti-Bolsheviks, captured one train station after another. Allied leaders decided to take the opportunity and ordered the Czechs to move back along the railway toward the center of Russia. At the same time, a number of tsarist generals, among them the army's former commander-in-chief, Kornilov, were preparing to lead a small but excellent army of Cossacks against the Bolsheviks. It was the beginning of a civil war that would last for two terrible years.

While Trotsky undertook to organize the new regime's army, its opponents formed fighting units in many regions; anti-Bolsheviks of every stripe, including the Social Revolutionaries, organized in hundreds of villages and towns. Across Russia, food riots, battles over land, skirmishes between workers and bourgeois, and ethnic hatred added to the violence. With the economy near collapse, the Bolsheviks adopted "War Communism," a program to extract from a country in chaos just enough men and supplies to fight a war through requisitioning, terror, police repression, and propaganda. With the firm leadership of Lenin, the military talent of Trotsky, and above all the mistakes of their enemies, they won.

By mid-1919 armies under former tsarists were the principal threat. One pushed from the Urals toward Moscow but was stopped before another took Kiev in August and reached within 300 miles of Moscow by October, while a third stood only 30 miles from Petrograd. Thereafter the tide turned. The antigovernment armies, weakened by their conflicting ambitions, did little to win popular support; and areas under their control experienced a terror less efficient but at least as brutal as under the revolutionaries. With each defeat, more of their troops melted away until they were hardly more than marauding bands. By the end of 1919, they were in general retreat. Their most important group withdrew to the Crimea early in 1920 and stubbornly fought on before finally heeding Allied advice and evacuating the men remaining in November 1920.

The Communists had to fight against Poland as well. In conjunction with the Versailles treaty, an Allied commission had set the Russo-Polish border along a line that assigned to Poland most areas in which Poles were a clear majority. Poland wanted more and, citing cultural and historical arguments, insisted on its boundary of 1772, well to the east. Rejecting Russian offers of compromise, Poland sent an army into the Ukraine in March 1920. Within a month it took Kiev, but the Ukranian nationalists who had fought the Russians were unwilling to fight for the Poles. In August the Red army, by now a relatively efficient military machine, launched an assault that soon threatened Warsaw. An effective Polish counterattack led in 1921 to compromise after all. With Russia's western border now fixed, it was possible to settle boundary with Turkey as well. Ignoring local independence movements, the two states assigned Armenia and Georgia to the Soviet federation, and Kars and Ardahan to Turkey. Fighting continued in Asia until 1922 when Japan withdrew from eastern Siberia. The Soviet Union was firmly in Communist hands.

The New Economic Policy Under War Communism, regimentation and bloodshed were the means of survival, and by using them, the Communist party had become increasingly powerful; yet most of the countryside was still subject to the whims of local party officials and roving bands of armed men. Cities were partially empty, a million Russians had gone into exile, tens of millions more had died, manufacturing produced less in 1920 than in 1913, foreign trade had almost ceased, and poor harvests raised the specter of famine. Requisitions spurred resistance, and black markets flourished. Thus the mutiny of sailors at the Kronstadt naval base in March 1921 was an ominous sign.[3] These were the sort of men who had made the October Revolution possible; and though they were soon quelled and their demands for political liberty rejected, Lenin recognized the need for change.

He announced the New Economic Policy (NEP), a major turning point in the development of Communist Russia. To many, the NEP seemed a departure from Marxism, but Lenin saw Russia's problems as the result not of flaws in Marxist theory but of having stormed the "citadel of capitalism" too fast. Russia suffered from old habits hard to uproot and from a lack of the technical experts and managers a modern economy required. With noteworthy pragmatism, Lenin proposed a moderate course the Bolsheviks would earlier have opposed.

Under the NEP, peasants were no longer subject to requisitions but rather to a tax in kind. Businesses employing fewer than 20 workers could be run as private enterprises, and nationalized industries could be leased to foreigners as a way of training Russians in efficient methods. Fiscal reforms guaranteed a stable currency, helping Russia's external trade to emerge from the pattern of barter into which it had fallen. Recovery was slow. Millions died in the famine of 1920–1921 despite the extensive aid of the American Relief Administration, and not for another six years would production reach prewar levels. Abandoning the hope of creating Communism all at once, the NEP was nevertheless the reaffirmation of Communist determination. Every social institution was recruited to help create a stable new society. Cooperatives and trade unions, newspapers and public meetings taught efficiency and pride in class and nation, as did the school system, which was improved and extended. The curriculum stressed official doc-

[3]Denounced as part of an international counterrevolutionary conspiracy, the members of the Kronstadt base who were captured after the mutiny was crushed were subject to executions and deportations, and for 70 years the event was cited in Soviet histories as an example of the kinds of forces arrayed against the revolution. In 1994 Boris Yeltsin announced the rehabilitation of these rebels, and the event was used as evidence that the brutality of Communist rule had begun with Lenin's ruthlessness.

▶ **Uncomfortable with the pomp of conventional armies, the Bolsheviks were nevertheless proud of the forces that had won the civil war. Here Trotsky reviews the Moscow Brigade of the Red Army.**

trines. Workers' children were favored for admission, and teachers were urged to abandon old-fashioned rote learning. The problems of ruling over multiple nationalities had eased somewhat with the cession of so much territory in the Treaty of Brest Litovsk, and three-quarters of the remaining population could be called Russian. Non-Russian nationalities were encouraged as never before, and a certain relaxation permitted the Orthodox Church to function in a restricted fashion.

In practice, the Communist party, which remained a restricted elite, was the most important instrument of rule. Organized in a hierarchy that paralleled the bureaucracy, it reached into every aspect of public life—factories, hundreds of new centers for adult education, and youth associations, propagandizing, encouraging, and explaining. In 1922 cultural activities were placed directly under the Ministry of Education, and the Western artistic movements recently welcomed were discouraged in favor of books and art that met the current definition of communist aesthetics: realistic in style, popular in appeal, and useful to the new order. Issues of practical policy were thrashed out within the government and the party, but to be on the losing side could be politically and sometimes personally fatal. In foreign policy, the Communist government gave signs of seeking normal relations; and by 1924, the year of Lenin's death, every major power except the United States had recognized the new regime. Still an object of fear to liberals and conservatives, the new Communist state became a source of inspiration and hope for the far left throughout Europe.

ITALIAN FASCISM

Postwar Europe witnessed another experiment in a new form of government in Italy, economically, the least developed of the major Western powers. Italy had just barely met the demands of total war; the end of war brought inflation, unemployment, and talk of revolution. In many places peasants simply confiscated the land they had long been promised; and when in 1920 industrialists met a series of strikes with lockouts, workers answered by occupying factories. Social issues largely ignored for 20 years challenged the established system. The peace treaty, too, was disillusioning. Although granted considerable territory, Italy got less than expected, and its treatment by the other Allies was often humiliating. Disposition of the Dalmation port of Fiume was still being argued in 1919 when a private expedition led by Gabriele d'Annunzio dramatically captured it for Italy. The nation's most famous living poet, d'Annunzio ruled Fiume for more than a year at the head of an "army" of the unemployed, whose nationalist frenzy and vulgar slogans were for many a welcome contrast to the wordy frustration of diplomacy. Eventually, the Italian government evicted him, but he had shown the effectiveness of direct action in a nationalist cause.

The Victory of Fascism The Fascist movement was born amid these crises. The term *fascio*, meaning "bundle," comes from an ancient Roman symbol of authority—a bundle of sticks, individually weak but strong in unity. Echoes of imperial Rome were part of the Fascist mystique. The movement centered around Benito Mussolini, whose polemical skills won him promotion to the editorship of the Socialist party newspaper until he was expelled in 1915 for favoring Italy's entry into the war. Mussolini, who established another paper, became one of Italy's noisiest nationalists, using the rhetoric of the left to denounce liberalism and parliamentary indecision, and the slogans of nationalism to castigate Marxists. Fascism grew from this heritage; both a movement and a party, it employed propaganda, symbols, and activism in new ways, making party militants in their black shirts seem another kind of army.

At first the Fascists had little electoral success, but the changing nature of Italian politics offered them multiple opportunities. The elections of 1921 were the first in Italy with universal male suffrage, and two newer, well-organized mass parties overshadowed the traditional leaders and groups. The Catholic Popular party demanded major reforms, but much of its real strength came from rural and conservative groups. The Socialists, for all their increased strength, were weakened by the split with their left wing, which formed a Communist party, inspired by the Bolsheviks' success in Russia. The aging Giolitti, who had been a dominating prime minister in the prewar era, tried to patch together a personal coalition that included the Fascists in a "national bloc" of candidates. The Fascists, who had won no seats in 1919, gained 35 in the new Chamber; and instead of being domesticated to parliamentary ways as Giolitti expected, they used the campaign to demonstrate their style. Fascist squads in black shirts planted bombs, beat up opponents, and disrupted meetings, enjoying violence and intimidation while denouncing Marxists as a threat to order.

When left-wing unions called a general strike in 1922, raising fears of revolution, Mussolini's Black Shirts grew more threatening and started taking over town councils by force. While politicians struggled to find a parliamentary majority, the Fascists staged a march on Rome in October. Motley squads of party militants moved on the capital in a grand gesture of revolt while Mussolini cautiously waited in Milan. Belatedly, parliamentary leaders called for martial law, but King Victor Emmanuel III refused: The gesture of revolt had been enough to capture power. Mussolini dashed to Rome, where the king invited him to form a cabinet, claiming the office both as a matter of perfect legality and by right of conquest. Mussolini at 39 became prime minister of a coalition government, and in the elections of 1924, Fascists won a massive victory. Intimidation and fraud contributed to this success, but most Italians were willing to give the new party a chance.

In the following year, it became clearer what a Fascist regime would mean. Giacomo Matteotti, a Socialist who bravely stood before the entire Chamber to enumerate Fascist crimes, was subsequently murdered in gangland style. As public condemnation mounted, Mussolini's government seemed about to topple, but the opponents of Fascism were no more able to unite now than when they had been stronger. The Fascists gradually isolated first the Socialist and then the Popular party, which was weakened by the Vatican's distaste for its program of social reform. By 1925 all the opponents of Fascism had been expelled from the legislature, and newspapers either printed what they were told or risked suppression. The Fascist period had begun.

To many in and out of Italy, it seemed merely that the nation at last had a strong, antisocialist leader. Some distinguished Italians were associated with the regime in various ways, men such as the poet Gabriele d'Annunzio, the sociologist Vilfredo Pareto, the composer Giacomo Puccini, the playwright Luigi Pirandello, and some of the avant-garde artists called Futurists. Even moderates found it hard to believe that a party whose program contained so many contradictions—Fascists praised revolution and promised a strong state, defended property and called for social change, advocated order and used violence—could be dangerous for long.

Fascist Rule Mussolini moved slowly to institutionalize his power. A series of special laws passed by 1926 declared the Duce (leader) of Fascism the head of state with the right to set the Chamber's agenda and to govern by decree. For 20 years, nearly all the laws of Italy would be issued in that way. Opposition parties were outlawed, scores of potential opponents arrested, and the civil service and judiciary purged of anyone thought too independent. Italy's newspapers were filled with pictures of Mussolini overawing

Mussolini and his bodyguard of Black-Shirted party members in paramilitary uniforms give the Fascist salute. The propaganda and rituals developed by Italian Fascists would be imitated across Europe.

visitors, captivating vast throngs, leaping hurdles on horseback, flying airplanes, harvesting grains. No story was too silly: The Duce recited the cantos of Dante from memory, he worked all night (the light in his office was carefully left on), he inspired philosophers and instructed economists, American razor blades were inadequate to the toughness of his beard, and his speed in race cars frightened experts. Slogans such as "the Duce is always right" and "Believe, Obey, Fight" soon covered walls throughout Italy. The victory of an Italian athlete or the birth of a child to a prolific mother became an occasion for hailing the new order as Mussolini's propaganda pumped pride and confidence into a troubled nation. Despite considerable skepticism, the good news and sense of energy were welcome. Mussolini's sensitivity to the masses brought to Italian government a popular touch that it had lacked. By 1931 when the government demanded that all professors sign a loyalty oath, only 11 refused. With most people frightened into silence and organized resistance shattered, the regime had little to fear from some secret Communist groups and an underground centered in France.

The authoritarian single party, completely subordinate to the Duce, reached into every city and town with its own militia, secret police, and tribunals. Recruited in its early years mainly from among the unemployed and alienated, the Fascist party soon won hundreds of thousands of new members eager for the advantages it offered until by the 1930s the party decided to accept members more selectively in an effort to increase discipline. There were associations for Fascist teachers, workers, and university students. In youth organizations for every age group over four years old, the next generation wore black shirts, marched, and recited official slogans. Citizens were to replace the handshake with the extended right arm of the Fascist salute,[4] and regulations established the Fascist names to give one's children and the form of address to use with one's friends.

Fascist doctrine, never wholly consistent, denounced the principles of the French Revolution and of majority rule but hailed "the people." The much advertised principle of authority was reduced to simple obedience to the Duce. Authority itself was deemed purer when arbitrary. There was said to be a Fascist style in art and philosophy, sport and war. A candid irrationalism suspicious of intellectuals and traditional culture stressed the virtues of intuitive "thinking with

▸ These ten-year-old boys were not, official propaganda declared, just playing at being soldiers but were ready with half-size rifles and lunch kits to defend their country. Millions of Italian children were enrolled in five organizations: one for boys and girls 6 and 7 years old, two separate ones for boys and girls 8 to 13, and two more for those 14 to 17. For the four years after that, they could belong to the Young Fascists.

[4]The salute was a stylized form of the greeting used in ancient Rome and portrayed in the statue of Marcus Aurelius that since the Renaissance had stood on the Capitoline Hill in Rome, where Michelangelo designed a piazza to frame it. The salute quickly became an international symbol.

Fascist Doctrine

The most carefully constructed single statement of Fascist doctrine was the article "Fascism: Doctrine and Institutions," written in 1932 for the **Enciclopedia Italiana,** ***one of the most impressive intellectual works accomplished under the Fascist regime. Although the article was officially listed as by Mussolini himself, most of it was written by Giovanni Gentile, a noted philosopher who was an early supporter of Fascism.***

"It [Fascism] is opposed to classical liberalism which arose as a reaction to absolutism and exhausted its historical function when the State became the expression of the conscience and will of the people. Liberalism denied the State in the name of the individual; Fascism reasserts the rights of the State as expressing the real essence of the individual. . . . The Fascist conception of the State is all-embracing; outside of it no human or spiritual values can exist, much less have value. Thus understood, Fascism is totalitarian, and the Fascist State—a synthesis and a unit inclusive of all values—interprets, develops, and potentiates the whole life of a people.

". . . First of all, as regards the future development of mankind—and quite apart from present political considerations—Fascism does not, generally speaking, believe in the possibility or utility of perpetual peace. It therefore discards pacificism as a cloak for cowardly supine renunciation in contra-distinction to self-sacrifice. War alone keys up all human energies to their maximum tension and sets the seal of nobility on those peoples who have the courage to face it. . . .

"Fascism denies the materialistic conception of happiness. . . . This means that Fascism denies the equation: well-being = happiness, which sees in men mere animals, content when they can feed and fatten, thus reducing them to a vegetative existence pure and simple.

"After socialism, Fascism trains its guns on the whole block of democratic ideologies, and rejects both their premises and their practical applications and implements. Fascism denies that numbers, as such, can be the determining factor in human society; it denies the right of numbers to govern by means of periodic consultations; it asserts the irremediable and fertile and beneficent inequality of men who cannot be levelled by any such mechanical and extrinsic device as universal suffrage.

". . . The State, as conceived and realized by Fascism, is a spiritual and ethical entity for securing the political, juridical, and economic organization of the nation, an organization which in its origin and growth is a manifestation of the spirit. The State guarantees the internal and external safety of the country, but it also safeguards and transmits the spirit of the people, elaborated down the ages in its language, its customs, its faith. The State is not only the present, it is also the past and above all the future. Transcending the individual's brief spell of life, the State stands for the immanent conscience of the nation."

Taken from the version of the article, "Fascism: Doctrine and Institutions," in the *Enciclopedia Italiana,* reprinted in S. William Halperin (ed.), *Mussolini and Italian Fascism* (Princeton: D. Van Nostrand Company, Inc., 1964), an Anvil Book under the general editorship of Louis L. Snyder. I have Americanized the spelling.

the blood" and the joy in war. As the antithesis of the decadent materialism of the democracies, Italy would influence the world and reclaim the heritage of imperial Rome (*see box,* above).

The Corporate State The most discussed element of Fascism, the corporate state, was partly facade, partly an institutional expression of ideology. The idea was to organize each sector of production into a huge confederation, or corporation. Each corporation encompassed a syndicate of employers and one of workers, each headed by party members appointed by the government. Corporations were to establish industrywide policies and wage scales, and by 1926 the system was sufficiently in place to outlaw strikes, lockouts, and independent unions. In 1934 the number of corporations was set at 22,[5] the Duce, as president of each corporation, appointed its council of delegates, and they sat in the National Council of Corporations. These institutions, which never attained real autonomy, were further undercut by the strength of established interests and by Mussolini's habit of legislating by decree; but they were presented as the Fascist alternative to liberal forms of representation, replacing conflict with coordination.

The new order in its 20 years did not remake Italy, which never became as orderly, efficient, or docile as Fascists wished. A quiet and safely intellectual opposition, exemplified by Benedetto Croce, was tolerated; and the twentieth century would witness greater tyranny and worse brutality. But freedom was crushed, the jails filled, hundreds of prominent figures exiled to dreary southern towns or desolate islands. The measure of the regime lies as much in the control it sought and the quality of its goals as in its failure to achieve them.

Domestic Policies Fascist economic policy sought autarky, or national economic self-sufficiency, and emphasized industrialization and technology. Initial distrust of big business soon attenuated, but the government remained active in economic affairs and often favored nationalization. For reasons of prestige, the value of the lira was set to equal the French franc, which hurt Italian exports and required restrictions that led to a painful deflation. In the interest of self-sufficiency, the government launched its famous battle of grain in 1926, which succeeded (with enormous hoopla) in doubling grain production at great cost in efficiency. Output per capita declined in the Fascist era. Generally, the industrial giants in steel, automobiles, rubber, and chemicals found it easy to deal with (and often to manipulate) Fascist bureaucracy. At the same time, subsidies to weak industries, financed through the Institute for Industrial Reconstruction established in 1933, led to a significant extension of government ownership. By 1940 real wages were down in both industry and agriculture.

Efforts to keep peasants on the land and to increase the birthrate at most merely slowed the contrary trends. But the regime did score some notable achievements, which it vigorously advertised. The criminal activities of the mafia were suppressed, the malaria-infested marshes near Rome were drained, new railroads were built, and some superhighways were launched. Enormous building projects contributed to employment. Workers benefited from the creation of centers with recreation halls, meeting rooms, and libraries in most towns and programs for vacations at seaside or mountain resorts. Family bonuses gave the poor an increased sense of security, and educational reforms put more people in school for longer periods.

Fascism's most publicized accomplishment was its accommodation with the Vatican. Although Mussolini and most of his early followers were thoroughly anticlerical, the Fascist government adopted many measures the Church would welcome, putting crucifixes in classrooms and raising the budget for clerical salaries and church repairs. The Lateran treaties of 1929 ended 60 years of conflict between Italy and the Church. The treaties recognized the tiny area of Vatican City as an independent state, and related agreements established religious teaching in public schools, guaranteed that marriage laws would conform to Catholic doctrine, promised to restrict Protestant activities, and set the indemnity to be paid the Church for its losses during Italian unification.

A dispute that had seared the consciences of millions of Italians was at last resolved. Abroad, the agreement suggested that Fascism had won special favor from the papacy, an impression little dimmed by an encyclical of 1931 that warned against the worship of the state or by subsequent conflicts between Fascists and Church officials. Although these conflicts were bitter, Catholics

---

[5]A corporation covered an entire sphere of production, from raw materials to manufacture and distribution; and the corporations were divided into three groups: I—grains, fruits and vegetables, wines, edible oils, beets and sugar, livestock, forestry and lumber, and textiles; II—metals, chemicals, clothing, paper and printing, construction, utilities, mining, and glass and pottery; III—insurance and banking, fine arts and liberal professions, sea and air transportation, land transportation, public entertainment, and public lodging.

▸ The techniques of modern art combined with evocations of ancient Rome in Fascist posters like this one for an exhibition in 1933 on the eleventh anniversary of the Fascist revolution.

were on the whole more generous toward Mussolini's regime than they had been toward its liberal predecessors.

Within the country, potential opponents were baffled by Mussolini's apparent successes and, surrounded by propaganda, felt isolated and uncertain of what to believe. Indeed, most Italians probably shared some pride in their nation's heightened prestige. Outside Italy, important groups in all European and many South American nations sang the praises of Fascism's "bold experiment" that ended petty squabbling, ran the trains on time, kept order, and eliminated the threat of communism.

II. The Distinctive Culture of the Twentieth Century

Russian Communists and Italian Fascists boasted that they represented new ideas based on new principles, and these movements found much they could use and much that contributed to their popularity in current thought. Psychology, literature, and art explored the irrational and surreal. The sciences uncovered complexities in nature that made uncertainty a theoretical principle, and theories of society adopted a tough-minded "realism" that spoke of power and interest more than values. Norms of behavior that had been considered the essence of civilization just a generation earlier were now called into question. The cultural achievements of the twenties, exciting and creative in many realms, were also disquieting.

FREUDIAN PSYCHOLOGY

No one disturbed accepted views more deeply than Sigmund Freud, a Viennese physician whose clinical studies had taken him gradually from an interest in neurology to the study of psychiatry. Freud followed the method—close and detailed observation—of medical science, and his writings were as careful in their logic as in their literary elegance. Freud had done his most important work before 1914, and in many ways he was old-fashioned. For the most part, he accepted as socially necessary the norms of behavior of the nineteenth-century middle class. He was deeply influenced by ideas of evolution, and his metaphors and assumptions betray the liberal economist's conception of human nature. His interest in the phenomenon of hysteria and his use of hypnosis built on the work of others to create a startling view of the human mind which he insisted could be universally applied.

In treating neurotics, Freud found that they often experienced relief of their symptoms by recalling forgotten events under hypnosis. He concluded that the recollection itself was crucial, not for its accuracy but as an expression of the psychic reality with which the patient had been unconsciously struggling. Within the unconscious,

Although Freud believed his theories had universal, scientific validity, his consultation room in Vienna unmistakably reflected the cultivated taste of a Central European of the upper-middle class in the late nineteenth century, from its tiled stove and afghans to its pictures and ancient sculptures.

conflicting urges contended in what Freud labeled the *id*. Here universal basic desires (similar to instincts) seek satisfaction, and Freud found the most troublesome and psychologically significant desires to be sexual. The *ego* tries to channel and control these desires, directed to do so by the *superego*, which (rather like the conscience in more traditional conceptions) imposes a socially conditioned sense of what is acceptable behavior. Thus mental life is marked by perpetual tension between the id and the superego.

Most of this conflict, uncomfortably mediated by the ego, is unconscious; for one of the mind's responses is to repress from consciousness the id's desires. Most people remain unaware of their own deepest motivations. Repression, however, causes an enormous mental strain that often finds an outlet in neurotic behavior. As the patient comes to face and understand what is being repressed, neurosis is relieved. From this conception of the human psyche, Freud developed an elaborate, subtle, and shocking theory which ascribed sexual lusts to every person at every age. The idea of infant sexuality was especially offensive to contemporaries, but so was the notion of the Oedipus or Electra complex, through which the boy's angry competition with his father (or the daughter's with her mother) could produce an unconscious guilt-ridden wish for one parent's death so that the child could possess the other parent. Few in Freud's time could tolerate this ascription of base desires to decent people. Freudian theory proclaimed such decent people were merely the most repressed. It also considered religion the satisfaction of infantile and obsessive needs and even the greatest human achievements to be the result of sublimation, diversion of the id's demands to other and higher purposes.

Psychoanalysis, the name Freud gave his body of theory and his therapeutic technique, calls on the analyst not to pass judgments but rather to help the patient discover aspects of self that proper society held to be quite simply unmentionable. By implication, these ideas and therapeutic techniques called for a shift in aesthetic and intellectual standards. Freud valued hypnosis and later free association as modes of expression in which hidden connections emerged without the intervention of narrative or logic. He considered whatever seemed real to the psyche to be important; dreams and slips of the tongue were serious expressions of psychic conflict. He pioneered ways of comprehending life and literature on several levels at once and provided the model for doing so.

In the 1920s the broad implications of Freud's discoveries gained wider public recognition despite continued hostility. If repression leads to neuroses, one extrapolation went, then greater sexual freedom and, above all, greater candor will produce healthier people. This remains perhaps the most widespread popular notion drawn from Freudian teaching, though it was not a view he held. Related to this is the belief that guilt is evil, a kind of Christian perversion of human nature. Freudian insights encouraged literary and personal introspection and supported the view that childhood is the most important phase of life. Although his theories stimulated new visions of a freer and happier life, Freud's dark conclusion was that "the price of progress in civilization is paid in forfeiting happiness." For civilization is based on the repression of primitive and still very powerful drives, which may burst forth at any moment. Freud, who feared the revolt he foresaw, died in 1939, driven into exile by the anti-Semitism of the Nazis.

Freudians strove to maintain this doctrine whole as science and therapy, treating deviations as heresies. The best known of these was the work of the Swiss psychologist Carl G. Jung, who broke with Freud and developed the theory of the collective unconscious, our common psychic inheritance expressed especially in the symbols and rituals of religion. Jung's somewhat looser and more mystical perspectives have fascinated religious thinkers, attracted theorists of nation and race, and influenced philosophers and artists. The concepts and vocabulary of psychoanalysis soon penetrated a whole culture.

THE HUMANITIES

Art and Literature Some artists in the postwar period—the Surrealists, with their dreamlike canvases, are an example—applied Freudian ideas directly, and in his manifesto of Surrealism (1924), the writer André Breton proclaimed the liberation of the subconscious. Quite independent of Freud, explorations of the irrational fairly exploded in prose and poetry. The novels of Marcel Proust, Franz Kafka, and James Joyce most clearly mark the change in style and content. Marcel Proust died in 1922, soon to be hailed as one of the great stylists of the French language. His long novel, *Remembrance of Things Past*, built an introverted and delicately detailed picture of upper-class Parisian life into a monumental and sensitive study of one man's quiet suffering, which became a model of interior monologue, of the novel in which the subject is not action seen from the outside but feelings observed from within. Franz Kafka, who wrote in German though born in Prague, died in 1924, leaving instructions for his manuscripts to be burned. They were not, and they came to be accepted as quintessentially modern, with their realistic and reasonable descriptions of fantasies that convey the torture of anxiety. In *The Trial* the narrator tells of his arrest, conviction, and execution on charges he can never discover, an exploration of the psychology of guilt that foreshadows the totalitarian state. James Joyce's international fame came with the publication of his novel *Ulysses* (1922), the presentation on a mythic scale of a single day in the life of a modest Dubliner, written in an exuberant, endlessly inventive game of words in which puns, cliché, parody, and poetry swirl in a dizzying stream of consciousness. Virginia Woolf, who used related devices in her novels, was especially important as a leader in British intellectual circles. Active in progressive political causes, Woolf was also a feminist, and the subtlety of her reflections on women's concerns would be more noticed and become even more influential toward the end of the century than in her own time.

Not all of the most important writers turned

▶ **Like many German expressionists, Otto Dix challenged the public with a series of paintings that simultaneously lampooned and celebrated the decadence of life in Berlin in the Weimar era.**

away from objective, chronologically precise narrative. But even those who made use of more familiar techniques tended—like Thomas Mann in Germany, André Gide in France, and D. H. Lawrence in England—to explore topics and attitudes offensive to convention. In all the arts, shock became one of the points of creative expression. Dada, a movement that originated during World War I, put on displays, part theater and part art exhibition, of noisy nonsense and absurd juxtapositions that were intended to infuriate the Parisian bourgeoisie. Italian Futurists, poets and playwrights as well as artists, promised to build a new art for a technological age—"The world has been enriched by a new beauty: the beauty of speed"—and in their manifesto of 1909 issued a call to "burn the libraries . . . demolish the venerated cities" (*see box*, p. 925). The Fauves in France and the Expressionists in Germany and Scandinavia gloried in their reputation for wildness in the style and content of their paintings as well as in their conduct. Where more sober traditions prevailed—as in the carefully con-structured, cerebral poetry of William Butler Yeats and of the younger Ezra Pound and T. S. Eliot—foreboding and obscurity intertwined. Works of art became more difficult to comprehend. Cubist and Expressionist painters, like composers using the 12-tone scale and dissonance, deliberately eschewed the merely decorative or pleasant and seemed eager to incorporate violence and amorality. Today the richness and profundity of the greatest of these works are readily apparent; but to contemporaries, they were more threatening than attractive, dangerously widening the chasm between "serious" art and the popular culture most intellectuals disdained.

Philosophy The philosopher most widely read in the 1920s was Oswald Spengler, whose *Decline of the West* appeared in 1918. Spengler treated whole civilizations as biological organisms, each with a life cycle of its own, but his fame rested

The Futurist Manifesto

The Futurist movement was announced in typically provocative language in the "Manifesto of Futurism," written by Filippo Marinetti and published in the Paris newspaper* Le Figaro *in 1909.

MANIFESTO OF FUTURISM

"1. We intend to sing the love of danger, the habit of energy and fearlessness.

"2. Courage, audacity, and revolt will be essential elements of our poetry.

"3. Up to now literature has exalted a pensive immobility, ecstasy, and sleep. We intend to exalt aggressive action, a feverish insomnia, the racer's stride, the mortal leap, the punch and the slap.

"4. We say that the world's magnificence has been enriched by a new beauty; the beauty of speed. A racing car whose hood is adorned with great pipes, like serpents of explosive breath—a roaring car that seems to ride on grapeshot—is more beautiful than the *Victory of Samothrace*.

"5. We want to hymn the man at the wheel, who hurls the lance of his spirit across the Earth, along the circle of its orbit.

"6. The poet must spend himself with ardor, splendor, and generosity, to swell the enthusiastic fervor of the primordial elements.

"7. Except in struggle, there is no more beauty. No work without an aggressive character can be a masterpiece. Poetry must be conceived as a violent attack on unknown forces, to reduce and prostrate them before man.

"8. We stand on the last promontory of the centuries! . . . Why should we look back, when what we want is to break down the mysterious doors of the Impossible? Time and Space died yesterday. We already live in the absolute, because we have created eternal, omnipresent speed.

"9. We will glorify war—the world's only hygiene—militarism, patriotism, the destructive gesture of freedom-bringers, beautiful ideas worth dying for, and scorn for woman.

"10. We will destroy the museums, libraries, academies of every kind, will fight moralism, feminism, every opportunistic or utilitarian cowardice.

"11. We will sing of great crowds excited by work, by pleasure, and by riot; we will sing of the multicolored, polyphonic tides of revolution in the modern capitals; we will sing of the vibrant mighty fervor of arsenals and shipyards blazing with violent electric moons; greedy railway stations that devour smoke-plumed serpents; factories hung on clouds by the crooked lines of their smoke; bridges that stride the rivers like giant gymnasts, flashing in the sun with a glitter of knives; adventerous steamers that sniff the horizon; deep-chested locomotives whose wheels paw the tracks like the hooves of enormous steel horses bridled by tubing; and the sleek flight of planes whose propellers chatter in the wind like banners and seem to cheer like an enthusiastic crowd."

From R. W. Flint (ed.), *Marinetti: Selected Writings*, R. W. Flint and Arthur A. Coppotelli (trs.) (New York: Farrar, Straus and Giroux, 1971).

Spengler's View of History

Oswald Spengler was an obscure German teacher before the publication of* The Decline of the West *in 1918. A philosophy of history in two substantial volumes, it presents an original and systematic analysis of world history. The erudition is remarkable, and Spengler elaborately categorizes the societies of Asia and Europe while discussing all sorts of topics, beginning with the meaning of numbers and ideas of destiny. The study's central device, however, is to analyze the arts as the symbolic expression of entire civilizations. The passage quoted here is from the last two paragraphs in the book. The final chapter—which follows chapters on the state, politics, and money—is entitled "The Form-World of Economic Life (B): The Machine." Although conceived and largely written before the outbreak of World War I, the work was inevitably read as a commentary on the postwar world and prediction of the future.

". . . The *private* powers of the economy want free paths for their acquisition of great resources. No legislation must stand in their way. They want to make the laws themselves, in their interests, and to that end they make use of the tool they have made for themselves, democracy, the subsidized party. Law needs, in order to resist this onslaught, a high tradition and an ambition of strong families that finds its satisfaction not in the heaping-up of riches, but in the tasks of true rulership, above and beyond all money-advantage. *A power can be overthrown only by another power,* not by a principle, and no power that can confront money is left but this one. Money is overthrown and abolished only by blood. *Life* is alpha and omega, the cosmic onflow in microcosmic form. It is *the* fact of facts within the world-as-history. Before the irresistible rhythm of the generation-sequence, everything built up by the waking-consciousness in its intellectual world vanishes at the last. Ever in History it is life and life only—race-quality, the triumph of the will-to-power—and not the victory of truths, discoveries, or money that signifies. *World-history is the world court,* and it has ever decided in favour of the stronger, fuller, and more self-assured life—decreed to it, namely, the right to exist, regardless of whether its right would hold before a tribunal of waking-consciousness. Always it has sacrificed truth and justice to might and race, and passed doom of death upon men and peoples in whom truth was more than deeds, and justice than power. And so the drama of a high Culture—that wondrous world of deities, arts, thoughts, battles, cities—closes with the return of the pristine facts of the blood eternal that is one and the same as the ever-circling cosmic flow. The bright imaginative Waking-Being submerges itself into the silent service of Being, as the Chinese and Roman empires tell us. Time triumphs over Space, and it is Time whose inexorable movement embeds the ephemeral incident of the Culture, on this planet, in the incident of Man—a form wherein the incident life flows on for a time, while behind it all the streaming horizons of geological and stellar histories pile up in the light-world of our eyes.

"For us, however, whom a Destiny has placed in this Culture and at this moment of its development—the moment when money is celebrating its last victories, and the Cæsarism that is to succeed approaches with quiet, firm step—our direction, willed and obligatory at once, is set for us within narrow limits, and on any other terms life is not worth the living. We have not the freedom to reach to this or to that, but the freedom to do the necessary or to do nothing. And a task that historic necessity has set *will* be accomplished with the individual or against him."

"Ducunt Fata volentem, nolentem trahunt."

From Oswald Spengler, *The Decline of the West,* Charles Frances Atkinson (tr.) (New York: Alfred A. Knopf, 1970).

on the dire prediction of his title: World War I had begun the final act of Western civilization (*see box*, p. 926). José Ortega y Gasset's *The Revolt of the Masses*, published in 1930, was hardly more optimistic. The masses, he warned, were destined to use their rising power to destroy civilization's highest achievements. Scores of other writers joined in scorn for modern culture as vapid and directionless.

The most striking innovation in philosophy came, however, from another tradition entirely and was monumentally set forth in *Principia Mathematica* (1910) by Bertrand Russell and Alfred North Whitehead, which became the cornerstone of analytic philosophy. On the continent a group known as the Vienna Circle developed a related system, Logical Positivism; and the work of Ludwig Wittgenstein, especially his *Tractatus Logico-Philosophicus* (1921), influenced both schools of thought. Wittgenstein attempted in a series of numbered propositions "to set a limit to thought." Analytic philosophy holds that philosophers should concern themselves only with what is precise and empirically demonstrable. By insisting on such rigor and seeking through symbolic logic to attain the precision of mathematical reasoning, analytic philosophers tended to exclude most of the general questions of public concern. The issues theologians and moral philosophers had argued about for centuries were too imprecise to merit debate. Like the earlier positivists, analytic philosophers consciously emulated the natural sciences, but their stress on the lean language of mathematics led away from positivist confidence in knowledge. The philosopher's task is to analyze every statement, stripping away connotations and values that do not convey precise meaning, however, appealing. "My propositions," Wittgenstein concludes in the *Tractatus*, "serve as elucidations in the following way: anyone who understands me eventually recognizes them as nonsensical. . . ." Philosophy, too, generated doubt and turned to its own specialized challenges.

THE SCIENCES

Science had also, since the turn of the century, moved beyond the layperson's comprehension. Even when the achievements of science were apparent to everyone, they often rested on theoretical advances that overturned established certainties. And the fields in which scientists worked became ever more highly specialized.

The Nature of Matter One line of scientific investigation stemmed from an experiment by two Americans, Albert A. Michelson and Edward W. Morley, in 1887. By demonstrating that the speed of light leaving earth was the same whether the light traveled in the direction of the earth's movement or against it, they challenged the established theory that the universe was filled with a motionless substance called "ether," which was thought necessary because waves could not function in empty space. The implications were fundamental, and exploring them led Albert Einstein to his theory of relativity, which he set forth in two brief papers published in 1905 and 1915. They were of the highest philosophical as well as scientific interest: Space and time are not absolute, he said, but must be measured in relation to the observer and on the most fundamental levels are aspects of a single continuum.

As Einstein developed his theory of relativity, physicists were also achieving a new understanding of matter. Wilhelm Roentgen's discovery of x-rays in 1895 had given the first important insight into the world of subatomic particles. Within two years the English physicist J. J. Thomson showed the existence of the electron, the subatomic particle that carries a negative electrical charge. The atom was thus not the basic unit of matter. By the turn of the century Pierre and Marie Curie, among others, had found radium and other materials to be radioactive; that is, they emitted both subatomic particles and a form of electromagnetic radiation. Soon, largely through the work of the English physicist Ernest Rutherford, radioactivity was identified with the breakdown of heavy and unstable atoms. These discoveries made it possible to link the structure of atoms with Dmitri Mendeleev's periodic table of elements. Elements with similar chemical properties were also similar in their atomic structures. A simpler and clear understanding of matter seemed in the offing.

But continuing research soon revealed phenomena Newtonian physics could not explain. In 1902 the German physicist Max Planck challenged Newtonian assumptions by announcing that energy in the subatomic world was released or absorbed not in a continuous stream but in discrete, measurable, and apparently irreducible units, which Planck called quanta. Energy, in effect, possessed many of the properties of matter. This finding implied that matter and energy might be interchangeable, and Einstein incorporated the insight into his theory of relativity in the famous equation $E = mc^2$. Energy (E) is equivalent to mass (m) times the square of the speed of light, a constant (c), which means that at least in theory, small quantities of matter could be turned into enormous amounts of energy. In this respect Newtonian physics was wrong; matter could be transformed after all. In 1919 Rutherford produced changes in the structure of the nitrogen atom by bombarding it with subatomic particles, and other atomic changes were soon produced in the laboratory.

▸ Einstein's face remains one of the best known icons of the twentieth century, a symbol of humanity, universal genius, and Jewish exile.

By the mid 1920s, however, physicists had to face troubling anomalies. Planck's quantum theory, though verified in numerous experiments, considered particles to behave in probabilistic rather than absolutely regular patterns—a concept Einstein himself could never wholly accept. Furthermore, electromagnetic radiation, including visible light, seemed to behave like a flow of particles in some circumstances and as a wave (a regular disturbance of particles in which the particles themselves do not advance) in others. No fixed model of any element's atoms was possible, the German physicist Werner Heisenberg argued, for at that level measurement interfered with the variables measured, and scientists could only describe an atom's probable structure. In a few years conceptions of matter had been transformed. At the subatomic level, matter consisted mostly of empty space and did not behave with absolute regularity. Moreover, the energy and mass of a subatomic particle could not be measured simultaneously, because the measurement of one altered the apparent values of the other—a disturbing effect that Heisenberg appropriately named "the uncertainty principle." In the subatomic world and in the stellar universe, the position and purpose of the observer fundamentally affected what was observed.

The new theories proved powerful tools, but physicists who chose to philosophize about such matters now spoke in humbler and more tentative tones. Physics became one of the most prestigious, highly organized, and expensive of human activities, recognized rather than understood by the public through its applications: x-ray technology, the electron microscope, and eventually the controlled fission of atomic energy. Newtonian principles, physicists insisted, still obtained in most cases, as solid and predictable as ever. But there was a loss as well. The Western world had long looked to the sciences for confirmation of its philosophy and even its theology. In the twentieth century no popularizer would build a general outlook on society from the latest scientific discoveries as Voltaire had once done from the ideas of Newton.

The Biological and Social Sciences Although the new work in other fields of science was less revolutionary, it often had immediate impact.

Knowledge of the mechanisms of heredity furthered scientific breeding of animals and the creation of plant hybrids that would greatly increase the productivity of agriculture. The isolation of viruses, first achieved in the 1890s, gave medicine a new armory and led the way to invaluable drugs, most notably penicillin, discovered in England by Sir Alexander Fleming and Sir Howard Florey in 1928.

The understanding of society was deeply affected by two giants of modern sociology, the Frenchman Emile Durkheim and the German Max Weber, whose work is central to modern social science. Durkheim's use of statistical tools and Weber's use of the "ideal type" to analyze how societies function remain influential as does their concern with the customs and beliefs that hold society together. Both, for example, emphasized the importance of religion yet were concerned not with its metaphysical truth but its contribution to the development of the state and of capitalism. Both stressed the threat to society when group norms broke down and saw that danger in modern trends. Through this emphasis on the function of communal values rather than their validity, and on the role of myth and ritual in all societies including our own, anthropology, sociology, and history have tended to share psychology's insistent relativism.

▸ **A school of handcrafts, art, and architecture, the Bauhaus defined a modernist aesthetic; and buildings like this one designed by Walter Gropius in 1925 pioneered the functional, International style that would dominate the most admired architecture of the next fifty years. Part of the explosive creativity of the Weimar years, the school broke up with the advent of Hitler when many of its members left Germany, most for the United States.**

PUBLIC CULTURE

To the public at large, developments in science and the arts were associated with the prosperity and brash excitement of the twenties. Science meant the spread of automobiles, radios, and airplanes; new trends were known through colorful stylish advertising, risqué literature, and vibrant theater. The surprising crisp architecture and applied design of Walter Gropius' Bauhaus school in Germany, with its emphasis on relating form to function, began to win a following, and there was curiosity about the still more daring endeavors in France of Le Corbusier to envision a wholly modern city as a machine for living.

In motion pictures the distortions of time and perspective through flashbacks and close-ups were less disturbing than when conveyed through words or on canvas. Even the frothiest romance or adventure story of the silent screen could contain subliminal themes of social or national concern, reflecting the experiences of World War I in themes of abandonment in France and of betrayal in Germany.[6] Motion pictures became more popular and more profitable than any form of entertainment had ever been. Movie theaters were built on the most elegant streets of Paris, London, and Berlin, gaudily combining the exoticism of a world's fair with reassuring luxury. Egyptian and Greek motifs, marble columns, fountains, mirrors, and statues reinforced the fantasies on the screen. The Gaumont Palace built in Paris in 1919 became an international model, with its 5000 plush seats and an orchestra pit for 80 musicians. Berlin's 300 cinemas included the Sportspalast, redone for motion pictures in 1920, which boasted of being the largest movie theater in the world. By the mid-twenties, Britain, France, Germany, and Italy each counted their movie theaters in the thousands.

Crowds of people from every stratum attended the same movies; and women came, even without male escorts. Influenced by the movies, middle-class and working-class families in the 1920s were more likely to be talking about the same things, and women especially could more easily imagine a different and better life. Reviews and movie magazines helped to provide the publicity essential to success in a business that relied on stars and vast distribution networks. American companies did all this very effectively, filling screens around the world. The United States made more films than any other country. Japan was second and Germany third, with Europe's largest film company. The rapid transition to talking pictures between 1929 and 1930 underscored national differences, and every country had some ministry empowered to monitor the presentation on the screen of sex and violence. In 1919 an English Watch committee condemned a film of the Johnson-Jeffries fight, fearing it could "demoralize and brutalize the minds of young persons." Sunday showings were an issue for years. Politics was present, too. Many countries restricted or banned German films in the 1920s; France, generally the most tolerant, in effect pro-

▶ **Gaudy movie palaces like this Parisian theater, one of the first, became prominent monuments in every city, offering the masses an exotic luxury previously associated with the great opera houses.**

[6]Paul Monaco develops this interpretation in *Cinema & Society: France and Germany during the Twenties,* 1976.

scribed films made in the Soviet Union where, with Lenin's encouragement, the director Sergei Eisenstein brilliantly showed how well suited the medium was to depicting official views of the revolutionary power of the masses.

While moralists worried about the cynicism of mass entertainment and the amoral excess of nightlife in cabarets and theaters, millions joined a kind of dizzying celebration. Middle-class families bought their first car; millions from every class, their first radio. Sophistication was a kind of shibboleth, used to justify lipstick, short skirts, alcohol, and one brash fad after another but also to underscore the cosmopolitanism that valued American jazz, openly learned from African art, and welcomed the new. For perhaps the only time, Berlin rivaled Paris as a European artistic center, more famous as the home of acid satire in art and theater than for its thriving cultural institutions of a more traditional sort. Modernism turned its back on gentility.

III. Totalitarianism

THE RETREAT FROM DEMOCRACY

Democracy was in retreat across Europe within less than a decade after the Paris Peace Conference. By 1929 authoritarian regimes had violated or eliminated the liberal constitutions of Hungary, Spain, Albania, Portugal, Lithuania, Poland, and Yugoslavia as well as Italy. By 1936 political liberty had been suppressed in Romania, Austria, Bulgaria, Estonia, Latvia, and Greece as well as Germany. Most of these countries were among the poorest in Europe, but their political difficulties illustrate the broader trend. Divided over issues of social reform, nationality, and religion—differences amplified by new and angry socialist and peasant parties—they suffered increased disruption with each economic crisis and foreign threat.

Authoritarianism in Eastern Europe Authoritarian leaders often flirted with fascism on the Italian model only to find it dangerously uncontrollable. Hungary was among the first to turn to authoritarian rule. Behind a constitutional facade, the Magyar aristocracy relied on a rigged electoral system to maintain its political dominance, protect its privileges, and stifle land reform. Under Admiral Horthy, who became head of state in 1920, the regime made sure that any threats of democracy were kept in check. Hungary was drawn to Italy both as another opponent of the peace treaties and as a model of order. In the 1930s fascist trappings increased, and successive governments became more anti-Semitic; yet Hungary never became a full-fledged modern dictatorship, and the government dissolved the most threatening fascist parties in 1939. Romania's liberal government began to give way even before Carol II was called to the throne in 1930.

▸ The men of Romania's fascist Iron Guard movement marched in green shirts, its women's corps in green skirts.

King Carol admired Mussolini and secretly subsidized the Iron Guard, a fascist organization whose political violence and anti-Semitism imitated the worst of fascism in other countries. The government stripped most Jews of land and citizenship, tightened censorship, and imposed martial law, but the disruptions that followed and pressure from Britain and France brought a shift in policy. By 1938 the king led the way in suppressing fascist activities.

In Yugoslavia, King Alexander I assumed dictatorial powers in 1929 in an effort to tame the divisive forces of Croatian, Slovenian, and Serbian nationalism. But as these conflicts continued, he tried a restricted parliamentarianism. The regent, who directed affairs after his death in 1934, pursued a similar course, drawn at first to the example of Germany and Italy, and then deciding by 1939 that Yugoslavia's international position and internal stability would best be served by a federal and democratic system. In Bulgaria a military coup ended parliament, parties, and free speech in 1934, and the regime moved closer to fascism as it sought both urban and rural support. But by 1936 the king was restricting the military, banning some fascist groups, and talking of constitutions. Fear of Germany and the need for French support was one reason these regimes turned away from fascism, but there was another. Authoritarians, attracted to fascism because of its ability to mobilize a mass following in the name of order, were soon threatened by ambitious fascists and by public resentment of fascist tactics.

The Republics of Poland, Greece, and Austria Although republican regimes were necessarily in touch with public opinion, their political systems were easily disrupted and as threatened as any other by international pressures. Poland, especially, suffered from having powerful neighbors, and Poles disagreed on whether their national interest lay with Germany, Russia, or France. Socialists and Catholics, conservative landowners and radical peasants, looked in different directions for outside support as they battled each other, and the resulting instability brought Marshal Jozef Pilsudski to the fore. A former socialist, he took power in 1926 in a military revolt; and even after he resigned in 1930, once his supporters had gained a majority in parliament, Poland continued to be ruled by men from the military. Unable to quell the noisy conflicts of fascists and socialists and without a popular base, they persisted in trying to strengthen a nation badly hurt by the worldwide economic depression of the 1930s.

The Greek republic, founded in 1924, lasted little more than a decade. Its liberals gradually lost ground to the monarchists, and a republican attempt at a coup could not prevent a plebescite in 1935, manipulated by monarchists, from leading to the return to the throne of King George II. When liberals made gains in the 1936 elections, General Joannes Metaxas proclaimed himself dictator and clung to power in fascist style by balancing severe censorship and the abolition of political parties with extensive social welfare, public works, and armament.

In Austria the republic was undermined by the sharp division between a Catholic German countryside and a cosmopolitan imperial Vienna that no longer had an empire to administer. The Socialists, out of power since 1926, had little strength beyond the city, while the Christian Socialists—whose nineteenth-century programs of welfare, nationalism, and anti-Semitism had influenced the young Hitler—moved steadily toward fascism. In the 1920s each party had established its own paramilitary organization, and their violent clashes became a regular part of Austrian politics. Chancellor Engelbert Dollfuss drew Austria closer to Italy and ruled by decree, suspending parliament, outlawing Communists, and, by 1934, banning all parties except his own Fatherland Front. The Socialists responded with a general strike, and the government replied by bombarding Karl Marx Hof, the public housing that Viennese socialists had been so proud of, an act that symbolized the end of Austrian democracy. A new constitution, elaborately corporative and claiming inspiration from papal encyclicals, was announced in 1934 but never really put into operation. Events in Germany, where Hitler and the Nazis had come to power, now overshadowed everything else in Austrian politics. In July a group of Austria's Nazis assassinated the Austrian chancellor. Although the Anschluss, or union with Germany, that they thought would follow did not come immediately, Austria's authoritarian government, having repressed the left, had little basis from which to resist growing Nazi pressure.

Dictatorship and Civil War in Spain Spain—with its overstaffed army, discontented workers, militant anarchists, and socialists—was already a strife-torn nation in 1921 when its army in Spanish Morocco was routed by Berber tribesmen. The resulting turmoil at home temporarily ended in 1923 when General Miguel Primo de Rivera issued a *pronunciamento* in time-honored style and assumed office as de facto dictator. Without a clear program, he used the themes of modern antiliberalism and Mussolinian techniques, dividing the left with extensive welfare programs and establishing a political party of his own. Experiments with corporatism followed, but by 1926 intellectuals, businessmen, the Church, and the army were restive. As economic depression hit, the government faltered, King Alfonso lost his taste for Primo de Rivera's attempt at a fascist constitution, and the dictator went into exile. The king, who now presented himself as the protector of liberty, tried another military government, which experimented in turn with both martial law and the promise of constitutionalism, but all the old problems remained. When republicans and socialists triumphed in the municipal elections of 1931, Alfonso also chose exile.

The second Spanish republic briefly held its divergent supporters together with progressive labor legislation and welfare programs ill-adapted to Spain's economy. It granted autonomy to Catalonia but left unresolved other regional conflicts and the critical problem of effective land reform. Its policies separating church and state and secularizing education infuriated half of Spain without satisfying the anticlericals. A conservative government and then one based on a coalition of the parties of the left could not keep opposition from growing more radical, both on the far left and on the right, where a movement called the Falange (in direct imitation of Italian Fascism), founded by José Antonio Primo de Rivera, the dictator's son, grew stronger. Systematic street violence was commonplace by 1936, when a group of generals announced their revolt. The Spanish Civil War that followed was seen from the first as part of the European battle between the fascist right and the Marxist left. The insurgent officers counted on support from Italy, Germany, and Portugal, where Antonio de Oliveira Salazar had already established his dominance over a single-party, corporative, conservative, and Catholic state.

International Fascism Whether they won power or not, Europe's fascist movements had much in common. Generally influenced by Italian Fascism, they looked and sounded similar. They liked uniforms, starting with a shirt of one color. Cheap to buy and easy to adopt, it made a group of supporters (however few or poor) look like a movement, a historical force. They used paramilitary organization that promised decisive action to remake society through discipline and force. They created drama in the streets—noise, marches, colorful demonstrations, symbolic acts, and real violence—that undermined convention while advertising fascism as something new and powerful. They borrowed heavily from working-class movements and used all the devices of democratic politics, while seeming to stand outside the corrupting process of compromise and responsibility. Populist tactics were thus attached to the promise of order. Fascists nostalgically evoked the enthusiastic patriotism of World War I to offer simple solutions to real problems. The disruption and inequity of capitalism, class conflict, a faltering economy, and aimless governments were the fault of enemies—liberal politicians, Marxist revolutionaries, Jews, and foreigners. Although they were ridiculed and denounced in fascist propaganda and rallies, those enemies were credited with hidden powers. Fascist force was needed to overcome them and make the nation a single, orderly, prosperous community.

There was more to these movements than their simple myths, camaraderie, and sinister attraction to violence. Fascists addressed real fears. They spoke to a rural society that felt threatened by urbanization, to small-business people threatened by the competition of large corporations and to all businesspeople threatened by workers' demands and government intervention, to a middle class threatened by socialism, to the privileged threatened by democracy, to the unemployed threatened by continuing economic depression, to the religious threatened by a secular society. Everywhere, they played on fear of a communist revolution.

They could do all this by borrowing freely from ideas current throughout Europe. They used socialist criticisms of liberalism and capitalism, conservative values of hierarchy and order, and intellectual denunciations of modern culture. They amplified a widespread contempt for parliamentary ineffectiveness, used doctrines of race made familiar by war and imperialism, and laid claim to the nationalism that every government liked to invoke. At the same time, as admirers of technology and organization, fascists promised to create more modern societies. And they laid claim to corporatism, which Mussolini's Italy proclaimed the wave of the future. Corporatist thought had a long history, and its current form emphasized organizing society, and parliament, by occupational groups instead of interests or parties. This, it was argued, would preserve natural hierarchies while avoiding the divisiveness of class conflict or conventional politics. The idea of an integrated society sharing a common purpose gained attractiveness during the international depression and prestige with Pope Pius XI's encyclical *Quadragesimo Anno* ("In the Fortieth Year") issued in 1931 on the anniversary of Leo XIII's *Rerum Novarum.* The new encyclical went further in rejecting the injustices of capitalism and the solutions of Marxism, and it called instead for a harmony based on religion and cooperation through corporative organization. Many anxious people found in that papal pronouncement a sympathy for fascism that seemed to justify overlooking its deeply antireligious quality.

The appeal of fascism was not limited to poor nations. Its ambiguities made it applicable everywhere. In Britain, Sir Oswald Mosley, once considered a likely Labour prime minister, founded the British Union of Fascists. In Belgium, fascism benefited from the antagonism between Catholics and anticlericals and between French-speaking Walloons and Dutch-speaking Flemings, who were increasingly sympathetic to fascism and the Nazis. In the Netherlands a National Socialist movement rose to prominence in the 1930s, and there were a number of fascist and protofascist movements in France, including the *Action Française,* which had become prominent in the furor of the Dreyfus case. Led by Charles Maurras, its denunciations of the bourgeois republic were echoed by fascist parties everywhere; but the *Action Française* lacked the mass appeal of full-fledged fascism and was overshadowed in the 1930s by other movements of uniformed young militants eager to take to the streets.

The Great Depression Above all, fascist and Marxist movements benefited from a worldwide economic depression that seemed to many the death knell of capitalism and undermined social and political stability. On October 24, 1929, the price of stocks on the New York Exchange began to plummet. Suspecting that speculation had pushed stock prices too high, nervous investors sold their shares. Day after day tens of millions of dollars in paper assets disappeared. Such panics were not new, and they had spread from New York to Europe in the previous century. Now, however, the United States was the world's wealthiest nation, and this panic quickly settled into full-scale depression as banks failed, businesses cut back, consumption declined, factories closed, and unemployment rose. Although its banks and exchanges were shaken, the European economy was hurt more by the decline in world trade and the gradual withdrawal of American investments and loans. Financial panic hit Europe in May 1931 when Austria's largest bank nearly went under. That started a run on Austrian and German banks and then spread as it had in the United States to other sectors of the economy and to other nations.

The late twenties had been years of boom in the United States and of general prosperity in Europe, but the Depression exposed deep-seated problems. Europe, which lost huge amounts of foreign investments during the war, had not regained its prewar percentage of world trade (about half), and American investments in Europe increased dramatically throughout the twenties. Too much of the international economy rested on the unproductive passing of paper from the United States to Germany as loans, from Germany to the Allies as reparations, and from the Allies to the United States as payment of war debts; and the United States raised tariffs in 1922 and again in 1930 to levels that made it nearly impossible for Europeans to earn dollars by sell-

▸ **Unemployed workers from Glasgow set out for London on a "famine march" in 1934.**

ing to Americans. Not all industries recovered after the war. Coal and textile industries had long been sliding toward chronic depression. Former trade patterns had not revived, especially among the underdeveloped new countries of Eastern Europe, and economic difficulties were increased by Germany's inflation and Russia's withdrawal from commerce. Much of the prosperity of the 1920s rested on new processes and on new products such as automobiles and synthetic fabrics. These proved vulnerable to the withdrawal of American investment and the decline in consumer confidence, for the Great Depression also revealed that for millions of Europeans 10 years had not been long enough to overcome the effects of World War I.

By 1932 the world's industrial production was two-thirds of what it had been in 1929. Unemployment climbed to more than 13 million in the United States, 6 million in Germany, and nearly 3 million in Great Britain. Among leading industrial nations, only France, with its balanced economy and lower fertility rate, escaped a crisis of unemployment. Since the war, and especially in democracies, governments were expected to deal with economic problems. They looked first for international help. The reparations system broke down amid the world economic crisis, and European nations declared that they therefore could not make debt payments to the United States, which refused to acknowledge the connection between reparations and international debt. Instead, President Hoover proposed that all intergovernment debt payments be suspended; his proposal, quickly accepted in 1932, was supposed to be temporary but in fact marked the end of both kinds of payments.

Other crises loomed. Austria's banking system had been saved from bankruptcy with British loans; but the deepening depression and other financial burdens forced Great Britain to abandon the gold standard, which meant it no longer guaranteed the value of the pound sterling. The important bloc of countries that traded in sterling followed suit. Tantamount to devaluation, this threatened chaos for international monetary exchanges and trade; and so the League of Nations sponsored a World Economic Conference that met in London in 1933. Begun with visions of high statesmanship, it ended in failure. When the United States also went off the gold standard, the structure of credit and exchange that had been one of the signal achievements of liberal finance fell apart. For a century nations, like so many bankers, had supported international financial stability by honoring these rules of liberal economics, and that historic era had ended.[7]

National Responses In this crisis democracies responded first to domestic pressures. Austria and Germany sought a customs union, which was opposed by France and rejected by the World Court. Nearly everyone raised tariffs and import quotas, further reducing trade, while domestic programs protected interests that were political. Liberals were at a loss as to what else to do, and socialists were no better prepared to solve the problems of declining commerce, insufficient capital, and—most pressing of all—unemployment. Socialists could find some vindication in the evident weakness of capitalism, but their favorite nostrum, the nationalization of industry, was barely relevant. In practice, they adopted rather orthodox measures of budget reduction while supporting whatever palliatives for unemployment could be suggested, though the dole, the most common one, strained the budgets they wanted to balance. Growing Communist parties let no one forget that while a whole international system had been collapsing, Soviet production advanced at a steady pace.

Gradually, economic conditions did improve; and by 1937, production in Germany, Britain, and Sweden was well above the 1929 level, though below that mark in the United States, Italy, Belgium, and France. Government intervention, which changed economic and political life, was often as socially divisive as the Depression itself. The democracies that had dominated Europe faced the double threat of communism and fascism with a heavy burden of failure.

THE RISE OF TOTALITARIANISM

Dictatorship has been recognized since ancient times as a particular political form, one way to maintain political order. The most important dictatorships of this century were different enough, however, to merit a separate term. Their use of a single political party, devotion to a leader, mass communications, economic controls, and force in the name of an imposed, official ideology with the declared purpose of transforming society is what is meant by *totalitarianism.* The term emphasizes a system of rule more than the specific policies that usually accompanied it: oppression, terror, forced agreement beyond mere acquiescence, and the effort through party and state to shape every aspect of life and crush "enemies" who were defined by race, occupation, region, or religion.

Useful as the concept of totalitarianism is, it has also come under heavy criticism for a number of reasons. In practice, none of the totalitarian regimes achieved total control. Authorities often bent to customs and institutions they could not afford to offend and negotiated with entrenched interests. Inefficiency and duplication were characteristic. Officials and party members often bickered among themselves. No totalitarian ideology was entirely coherent or unanimously embraced, and there were important differences among totalitarian systems. The values promulgated in Soviet Russia and Nazi Germany were not at all the same. Italy's claim to be totalitarian was largely propaganda, and most fascistic regimes did not maintain the pretense. Even so, totalitarianism is a useful term for underscoring the newness of the political systems based on boundless intrusion,

[7]Karl Polanyi elaborated on the significance of the abandonment of the gold standard in a famous essay, *The Great Transformation: The Political and Economic Origins of Our Time.*

thought control, secret police, vast armies, and official brutality that distinguished the twentieth century.

HITLER'S GERMANY

The Nazi regime won power in a democracy with an advanced economy and a strong administrative tradition. It took advantage of selected elements of German history, from militarism and nationalism to the weakness of the Weimar Republic, much as it played upon the social shocks Germany had recently suffered, including defeat in war, failed revolutions, clashing ideologies, and a depression that brought the most extensive unemployment in Europe.

The Rise of Nazism As a young man, Adolf Hitler was undistinguished, his ambition to be an artist thwarted when the Academy in Vienna rejected his application. Service in World War I had been a kind of salvation, providing comradeship and some accomplishment: He was promoted in the field. In Munich after the war, he found brief employment spying on the small German Worker's party, which the army considered dangerous, and took to addressing political rallies in the beer halls, where he learned the potential of a movement that combined the personal loyalty of a paramilitary core with mass appeal and where he molded the speaking style that would make him Führer. His speeches combined crude accusations, a messianic tone, and simple themes repeated in a spiraling frenzy. Race and universal struggle were the core of his message. Germans were victims of vast conspiracies mounted by foreign powers, capitalists, Marxists, Freemasons, and (above all) Jews—the gutter anti-Semitism Hitler had absorbed in Vienna. Jews were behind war profits, reparations, inflation, and depression; but Marxism was also Jewish, and Communists were agents of the Jewish conspiracy. Internationalism and pacifism were Jewish ideas intended to destroy Germany as the bastion of Western (Aryan) civilization. Life was a desperate struggle won by the ruthless, and Germany's destiny was victory over these enemies, who attacked the nation with the Versailles treaty, economic disasters, Communists, Jews, moral decay, and abstract art. These diverse attacks had a common target, the German *Volk*, the German people whose primitive virtues must be welded into an irresistible force.

Hitler had named his party the National Socialist German Workers' party, and the Nazis were one of many such nationalist movements when in 1923 Hitler had led them in the Munich *Putsch*. After its failure and Hitler was sent to prison, the book he wrote there, *Mein Kampf*, won little notice, for it was a turbulent, repetitious outpouring of his political views interlarded with demoniac statements about how human beings are manipulated by fear, big lies, and simplistic explanations. In prison and after his release in 1925, Hitler worked to reorganize and strengthen the party. To the SA, his street army of brownshirted storm troopers, he added the SS, an elite corps in black uniforms who served as his bodyguards and special police. The party picked up some ideas and useful phrases from Moeller van den Bruck, a literary figure respected in conservative circles, whose book *The Third Reich* advocated a corporative and nationalist regime. And the party established its own newspaper, edited by Alfred Rosenberg, who expanded Hitler's racist ideas in *The Myth of the Twentieth Century*, published in 1930, which was significant as part of the effort to establish an official ideology if not for its turgid contents.

Even with an ideology and with organizations in place, the Nazis had limited success. The party's membership of 60,000 in 1928 was not enough to have much weight in German politics. It had some notable assets, however. General von Ludendorff had joined Hitler in the 1923 *Putsch*, and other officers might cooperate. Some circles of Bavarian conservatives and Rhineland industrialists showed interest in the movement, and in 1929 the Nazis gained national prominence with a petition against the Young Plan. Its aim was to put a final limit on reparations, but the Nazis opposed all reparations and declared it high treason not to renounce the war-guilt clause of the Versailles treaty. Four million Germans signed. If Hitler's intensity and bad manners offended many, others felt the fascination of a personality that radiated power; and he soon gathered a group of absolutely loyal men: Hermann Göring, an air ace; Joseph Goebbels, journalist and party propagandist; and Heinrich Himmler. They worked ceaselessly to enlarge the party, orchestrate the impressive rallies, and terrorize their opponents. The Nazis were gaining attention and support. In 1930 they became the second-largest party in the Reichstag, and the following year a group of Rhineland industrialists promised the Nazis financial support.

By the 1930s, the party was broadly based, and the question of what groups were first drawn to the Nazis had been the subject of historical controversy, because different interpretations of Nazism rest on the answer. Workers were probably the biggest single group of members, but most workers continued to favor socialists and communists. Disproportionately large numbers of Nazi supporters were small-business people and tradespeople, civil service employees, and (to a lesser extent) farmers—all groups fearful of losing status. In the Depression, promises of recovery, higher agricultural prices, and more employment (tens of thousands found jobs in the SA and SS) combined with a call to rebuild the army and save society from socialism had ideological appeal for many. In 1931 an array of right-wing nationalists joined the Nazis in a manifesto denouncing the "cultural Bolshevism" of the Weimar Republic, which hinted that, once they seized power, the Nazis would protect only those who had joined them now. The Nazis spoke simultaneously like a government in office and like an underworld gang, and they demonstrated their seriousness by beating up Jews and socialists.

Collapse of the Weimar Republic The Social Democrats led the government that faced the Great Depression and did the best they could with a shaky parliamentary majority and an uncooperative president. In 1930 the government resigned, to be replaced by the Center party and Heinrich Brüning, a cautious man with little popular appeal. President von Hindenburg allowed this government to enact measures by decree, something he had denied the Social Democrats. But a nation in crisis was in political stalemate, with an unalert, reactionary president and a Reichstag incapable of producing a stable majority; like the country, it was divided among multiple parties, each with its own agenda of outrage. Hindenburg's sporadic interventions only made this worse; repeated elections raised the heat but brought no resolution.

The elections of 1930 gave Nazis over a hundred new seats from which they contemptuously disrupted parliamentary proceedings. His confidence growing, Hitler became a candidate for president in 1932, when Hindenburg's term expired. Worried politicians persuaded the nearly senile field marshal to run for reelection. Ludicrously cast as the defender of the constitution, the 84-year-old Hindenburg won handily; but Hitler got over 13 million votes. When Brüning proposed a financial reform that included expropriation of some East Prussian estates, Hindenburg dismissed him and turned to Franz von Papen, a friend of important army officers and Junkers. Hoping to create a right-wing coalition, von Papen lifted Brüning's ban on the SA and SS, named four barons and a count to his cabinet, and declared martial law in Prussia, to unseat the socialist government there. The outcry led Hindenburg to call another election. It resulted in a Nazi landslide. With 40 percent of the Reichstag's seats, it was by far its largest party. Hindenburg avoided naming Hitler chancellor by refusing to grant him the full decree powers he insisted on. The nation was sent to the polls again, and this time the Nazis lost a little but remained the largest party.

Hindenburg then named another chancellor, General Kurt von Schleicher, a conventional army man who made an easy target for the Nazis, Communists, and the disgruntled von Papen, who thought he saw his chance. Confident he could use Hitler but contain him, von Papen persuaded the men around Hindenburg to appoint Hitler the head of a coalition government. Of the 12 men in Hitler's cabinet, only two others were Nazis; but Hitler, the leader of an unsuccessful *Putsch* 10 years before, took office late in January 1933. The political system lost its flexibility as the anti-Weimar parties of left and right gained ground. While the number of votes for Marxist parties remained nearly constant, the Communist share of them grew; and the Nazis increasingly garnered the votes of the right.

Hitler almost immediately called another election. Previous campaigns had been ugly, but this was one of systematic terror, especially in Prussia, where Hermann Göring was now minister-president and the police were electoral agents. The climax came with the burning of the Reichstag, a fire that the Nazis loudly blamed on the Communists. Hindenburg agreed to issue special laws—Ordinances for the Protection of the German State and Nation—that ended most civil liberties, including freedom of the press and assembly. The voters gave the Nazis 44 percent of the seats, enough, with the Nazis' nationalist allies, for a bare majority. Hitler pressed on. Communists were expelled from the Reichstag, conservatives wooed with calls to nationalism, and the Center party enticed with promises to respect the privileges of the Catholic Church. By March Hitler dared demand a special enabling act that gave him, as chancellor, the right to enact all laws and treaties independent of constitutional restraints for four years. Of the 566 deputies left in the Reichstag, only 94 Social Democrats (out of 121) voted no. Blandishment and terror had done their work, but the tragedy went deeper: German politics offered no clear alternative to Hitler.

▸ **Nazi party troops march out of the rally on Nuremberg Party Day, 1933, carrying victory banners proclaiming "Germany Awake."**

Consolidating Nazi Rule Hitler's regime moved quickly to destroy the potential for opposition. It established concentration camps, first on private estates and then in larger and more permanent institutions. By July all parties except the National Socialist had been outlawed, and soon all competing political organizations disappeared. In the elections of November 1933, the Nazis won more than 90 percent of the vote. They restructured government, purged the civil service and judiciary, outlawed strikes, and clamped stricter controls on the press. In a few months Hitler had achieved fuller power than Mussolini had managed in years.

Hitler's most serious potential rivals were within his own party, and his solution was barbarically simple. On a long weekend in June 1934, leaders of the Nazi left wing were shot or stabbed. So, among hundreds of others, were General von Schleicher and his wife, some Catholic leaders, some socialists, and some taken by mistake. Hitler admitted to 74 deaths; subsequent estimates raise the figure to as many as a thousand. The Night of the Long Knives proved that any horror was possible; and the purge, like the noisy accusations of homosexuality that accom-

panied it, established the tone of Germany's new order. When Hindenburg died in August, Germans voted overwhelmingly to unite presidency and chancellorship in the person of Adolf Hitler, who took the official title of *Führer* ("Leader").

▶ Under Hitler, labor battalions also marched. By 1938 this "shovel brigade" could parade through the streets of Eger, a German town near the Czech border, on its way to extend the road from the newly annexed Sudetenland.

Administrative and Economic Policies The federal states lost their autonomy through a policy of *Gleichschaltung* or coordination; and a law of March 1933, which had expelled Jews from public service and universities, made all government employees appointees of the Führer. New people's courts heard secret trials for treason, now very broadly defined, and rewritten statutes allowed prosecution for intent as well as for overt acts. Arrest and detention without charge or trial became a regular practice. At the same time, the Nazi party was restructured to parallel the state, with administrative *Gaue* ("regions") headed by a party Gauleiter, its own office of foreign affairs, and its own secret police, the Gestapo, which infiltrated both the bureaucracy and the army.

Economic policies scored impressive successes. Unemployment dropped steadily thanks to great public works projects—government offices, highways, public housing, reclamation and reforestation. Many of these projects used special labor battalions, in which one year's service was soon compulsory. Later the burgeoning armaments industry and growing armed forces eliminated the problem of joblessness entirely. By spending money when more traditional governments thought it essential to balance their budgets, the Nazis reduced unemployment more effectively than any other Western nation.

Such programs were expensive, and they were paid for in several ways. A currency scheme largely designed by Hjalmar Schacht, a brilliant economist, required that payments for foreign trade be made with special marks whose value was altered according to the goods and the nations involved. Goods Germany bought were paid for in marks redeemable only through purchases in Germany. Tantamount to barter, this system increased Germany's self-sufficiency and influence in countries dependent on its markets. Additional revenues came from property confiscated from Jews, high taxes, forced loans, and carefully staged campaigns urging patriotic Germans to contribute their personal jewelry to the state. Ultimately, costs would be covered by printing paper currency, with effects long hidden by a war economy and the exploitation of conquered lands. By 1945 the mark had fallen to about 1 percent of its 1933 value.

Labor policies met related goals. Strikes were

outlawed and the mobility of workers regulated. The National Labor Front, which represented all workers and management, froze wages and directed personnel in the interests of business and government, while propaganda advertised new benefits, including the summer camps and special cruises that were part of the Nazi program of Strength Through Joy, and the special role of Aryan women as breeders of the race. The military had reasons for gratitude, too. Disregarding the disarmament clauses of the Treaty of Versailles (which Germany formally repudiated in 1935), Hitler pushed rearmament from the first. With the return of universal compulsory service in 1935 and the creation of an air force, Germany was soon spending several times as much on arms as Britain and France combined. If regular officers resented Nazi paramilitary organizations and looked down on the Nazis as their social inferiors, they nevertheless accepted the oath of personal loyalty Hitler required. Strengthened by his diplomatic successes, Hitler asserted control more directly in 1938, removing the minister of war, the chief of staff, and more than a dozen generals amid public tales of private vice. At the same time the foreign minister, an old-style nationalist who had served since 1933, was replaced by Joachim von Ribbentrop, a good Nazi and no aristocrat at all. The army and foreign service, strongholds of traditional conservatives, were under the Nazi thumb.

Religious and Racial Policies The churches presented a different challenge. A concordat with the Vatican in 1933 gave the state some voice in the appointment of bishops while assuring the Church authority over Catholic orders and schools. Protestant denominations agreed to form a new body, the Evangelical Church, under a national bishop whom Hitler named; but when the bishop declared a need to "Aryanize" the church, dissidents formed the separate Confessional Church. The minister for Church Affairs was authorized to confiscate ecclesiastical property, withhold funds, and have pastors arrested; but in practice the state kept religion in line more

► **The six-pointed star and the word *Jude* scrawled on this Berlin department store in 1938 were a warning to good Aryans not to shop there.**

Goebbels' Populist View of German Culture

As minister of propaganda in the German government, Joseph Goebbels was also president of the Reich Chamber of Culture, an organization divided into separate sections for the various arts and for film, radio, and the press. Artists had to belong in order to exhibit, perform, or be published. The speech quoted here was an address given by Goebbels to the annual Congress of the Chamber and the Strength Through Joy organization held in Berlin in November 1937. Goebbels' efforts were at their peak, and he reported proudly on the campaign against decadent art (which included much of the modern art today most admired), on the abolition of art criticism, and on the new recreation homes for veterans and the elderly, saying, "Nothing similar has even been tried ever or anywhere else in the world."

"My Führer! Your excellencies!
My racial comrades!

"Organization plays a decisive role in the lives of peoples. . . . For every organization must demand that its members surrender certain individual private rights for the benefit of a greater and more comprehensive law of life. . . .

"The purging of the cultural field has been accomplished with the least amount of legislation. The social estate of creative artists took this cleansing into its own hands. Nowhere did any serious obstructions emerge. Today we can assert with joy and satisfaction that the great development is once again set in motion. Everywhere people are painting, building, writing poetry, singing, and acting. The German artist has his feet on the ground. Art, taken out of its narrow and isolated circle, again stands in the midst of the people and from there exerts its strong influences on the whole nation.

". . . . True culture is not bound up with wealth. On the contrary, wealth often makes one bored and decadent. It is frequently the cause of uncertainty in matters of the mind and of taste. Only in this way can we explain the terrible devastations of the degeneration of German art in the past. Had the representatives of decadence and decline turned their attention to the masses of the people, they would have come up against icy contempt and cold mockery. For the people have no fear of being scorned as out of step with the times and as reactionary by enraged Jewish literati. Only the wealthy classes have this fear. . . . These defects are familiar to us under the label "snobbism." The snob is an empty and hollow culture lackey. . . . He goes in black tie and tails to the theater in order to breathe the fragrance of poor people. He must see suffering, which he shudderingly and shiveringly enjoys. This is the final degeneration of the rabble-like amusement industry. . . . The Volk visits the theater, concerts, museums, and galleries for other reasons. It wants to see and enjoy the beautiful and the lofty. That which life so often and stubbornly withholds from the people . . . here ought to unfold before their eyes gleaming with astonishment. The people approach the illusions of art with a naïve and unbroken joyousness and imagine themselves to be in an enchanted world of the Ideal. . . . The people seek joy. They have a right to it.

". . . 'Hence bread and circuses!' croak the wiseacres. No: 'Strength Through Joy!' we reply to them.

"This is why we have thus named the movement for the organization of optimism. It has led all strata of the people by the million to the beauties of our country, to the treasures of our culture, our art, and our life. . . . The German artist of today feels himself freer and more untrammeled than ever before. With joy he serves the people and the state. . . . National Socialism has wholly won over German creative artists. They belong to us and we to them.

". . . In this hour, we all look reverently upon you, my Führer, you who do not regard art as a ceremonial duty but as a sacred mission and a lofty task, the ultimate and mightiest documentation of human life."

Speech of Goebbels reprinted in George L. Mosse, *Nazi Culture: Intellectual, Cultural and Social Life in the Third Reich,* Salvator Attanasio and others (trs.) (New York: Grosset & Dunlap, 1966).

through the local harassment of individual clergymen. Some priests and ministers cooperated with the regime—enthusiastically supporting war, race, and Reich. Most resisted at least the more outrageous demands made of them, and some individuals spoke out courageously. In 1937 Martin Niemoeller, the leader of the Confessional Church, was arrested for his opposition to Nazism; and Pope Pius XI condemned both the deification of the state and Nazi racial doctrine. In the following years some Catholic churches were burned, and members of religious orders were frequently tried on morals charges.

Nazism had always made much of its anti-Semitism, and the Nuremberg laws of 1935 not only removed Jews from the public service (anyone with one or more Jewish grandparents was considered a Jew) but declared Jews mere subjects who were no longer citizens and prohibited marriage or sexual intercourse between Jews and Aryans. Subsequently, Jews were expelled from one activity after another, required to register with the state, and ordered to give their children identifiably Jewish names. In 1938 the murder of a German diplomat by a young Jewish boy touched off a new round of terror. Many Jews were arrested, and the SS led an orgy of violence (named *Kristallnacht* from the "night of broken glass") in which Jews were beaten and murdered, their homes and businesses smashed, and synagogues burned. A fine of 1 billion marks was levied on the Jews of Germany, and they were barred from the theater and concerts, forbidden to buy jewelry, forced to sell their businesses or property, denied access to certain streets, and made to wear a yellow star. Worse would come.

For most Germans, life went on much as before but a little better, and there was a new excitement in the air. From the beginning, the Nazis' publicity had been flamboyant, their posters striking, and their rallies well staged; after the movement came to power, propaganda became a way of life. Torchlight parades, chorused shouts of *Sieg Heil!* ("Hail to victory!"), book burnings, the evocation of Norse gods, schoolyard calisthenics, the return to Gothic script—a thousand occasions offered Germans a feeling of participating, of being swept up, and implicated, in some great historical transformation. At the Reich Chamber of Culture, Joseph Goebbels saw to it that cinema, theater, literature, art, and music all promoted Nazism (*see box*, p. 942). Things primitive and brutal were praised as Aryan; any who opposed or even doubted the Führer ceased to be German. Warfare was for this new regime its natural condition.

STALIN'S SOVIET UNION

Fascists insisted that they were the only effective enemies of communism, but Mussolini took much from the Soviet example of a revolutionary movement with dictatorial powers. For Communists, on the other hand, dictatorship was incidental and supposedly temporary. No one knew who Lenin's successors would be when he died in January 1924 or even how the succession would be determined. For more than a year, Lenin had been ill and nearly incapacitated, but his prestige had precluded any public scramble for power, and many expected a more relaxed government by committee to follow. In a famous letter, Lenin had assessed two likely successors: Trotsky, whom he called overconfident but the best man in the Politburo, and Stalin, whom Lenin found "too rude" though an able organizer.

Over the next three years, Russia's leaders publicly debated the complex issues of Communist theory and practical policy. Trotsky led those who clung to the traditional vision of revolution spreading across Europe and favored an uncompromising radical program at home and abroad. Stalin declared that the Soviet Revolution must survive alone, a "revolution in one country." No theoretician, and little informed about the world outside Russia, Stalin was not wholly at ease in these debates with more intellectual and experienced opponents. But they, in turn, underestimated his single-minded determination. The Politburo formally adopted his position in December 1925. His victory rested on more than ideas.

As general secretary of the party's Central Committee, Stalin was the link between the Politburo and the party organization below it, and he could count on the loyalty of party officials, many of whom he had appointed. He played effectively on personal antagonisms and on resentment of Trotsky's tactless arrogance. When the Politburo elected three new members at that December meeting, all were Stalin's associates. He then effectively eliminated his opponents. When leading figures publicly sided with Trotsky, Stalin labeled the break in party solidarity a threat to Communism. Trotsky and Grigori Zinoviev—the head of the Comintern, the Third International, whose prominence made him dangerous—were expelled from the Politburo in 1926 and from the party in 1927. The left was broken, and Zinoviev recanted his "mistake" the following year. So did Nikolai Bukharin, perhaps the party's subtlest theoretician and a leader of the right. Trotsky, who refused to change his mind, was exiled and then deported, continuing from abroad his criticism of Stalin's growing dictatorship. None of these veterans of the October Revolution had attempted to oust Stalin; even Trotsky, who built the Red Army, never tried to use it against him. Old Bolsheviks fervently accepted the need for party loyalty, and Stalin made sure that the open debates of those early years would not recur.

The First Five-Year Plan: Agriculture In aims and enforcement, the First Five-Year Plan reflected some of the qualities that had brought Stalin to the top. It shamelessly incorporated ideas Stalin had denounced just months before, but it was thoroughly his in the bold assumption that Russia could be transformed into an industrial power by mobilizing every resource. By 1928, when the plan was launched, Russian production had regained prewar levels in most sectors; but Lenin's New Economic Policy had depended heavily on private entrepreneurs in commerce and peasant owners in agriculture. The task now was to create a socialist economy, and the first step was to collectivize agriculture.

With the improved techniques and the mechanization that peasants had on the whole resisted, Soviet agriculture would produce enough to feed industrial workers and to export grain to pay for the imported machinery industrialization required. Russian peasants, however, continued to withhold their goods from market when agricultural prices fell. Some 4 or 5 percent of them had the means to hire labor and lend money within their villages, which gave them a hold over the local economy. Calling them *kulaks*—the old, pejorative term for grasping merchants and

▶ **Farmers, women as well as men, drive imported tractors out of one of the Soviet Union's Machine Tractor Stations to work fields where such mechanization had been rare.**

▸ **Villagers watch with anticipation for the first light bulb in Bryansk Province to be switched on, an achievement of the First Five-Year Plan.**

usurers—the government mounted a sweeping campaign of propaganda and police action against them as famine threatened. It seized their grain (informers were given a quarter of any hoard uncovered), killed hundreds of thousands of people, and deported untold numbers of them to till the unbroken soil of Siberia. Peasants destroyed crops and animals rather than let the government have them.

The explosive antagonisms of rural society were out of control, and Stalin had to intervene in 1930 to halt a virtual civil war. By then, more than half the peasants were in collective farms, but the conflict badly hurt production, contributing to serious famine in 1932–1933. A kind of compromise followed. Even on collective farms peasants were permitted individual plots and privately owned tools. Larger machinery was concentrated at Machine Tractor Stations, which became the rural base for agricultural agents and party officials. By 1933 output was sufficiently reliable to permit the state to concentrate on the most massive and rapid industrialization in history.

The First Five-Year Plan: Industry According to the five-year forecast, industrial production was to double in less than five years, and in some critical areas, such as electrical power, to increase sixfold. More than 1500 new factories were to be put into operation, including large automobile and tractor plants, and there were projects on a still grander scale, among them a Dnieper River power station and a great coal and iron complex in a whole new city, Magnitogorsk. These goals were indeed met somewhat ahead of schedule, and there was only slight exaggeration in the government's proud claim to have made Russia an industrial nation almost overnight.

To pay for that achievement, indirect taxes were levied, wages increased only slightly, planned improvements postponed, peasants displaced, and their land collectivized. Food and most consumer items were rationed, with allotments varying according to one's contribution to the plan. Success required much more than money. Unskilled or poorly trained, laborers were unaccustomed to the pace now required: Turnover was high; output and quality, low. The state resorted to a continuous work week and moved special "shock brigades" of abler workers from plant to plant. Women and young people were urged into industrial jobs. "Socialist competition" pitted groups of workers and whole factories against each other for bonuses and prizes; piecework payment, once a hated symbol of capitalism, became increasingly common. Violators of shop rules were fined; malingering, pilfering, and sabotage (often loosely defined) became crimes against the state. "Corrective" labor camps, initially a mode of prison reform, became another way to get more work done. Special courses in factories and enlarged technical schools trained new managers and engineers to replace the foreigners who were still essential to efficient industrial production.

In effect, an entire nation was mobilized, and the need for social discipline replaced an ear-

▶ **This Soviet poster of 1930 hails the International Day of Women Workers, part of the government's extended campaign to encourage women to work in factories.**

lier emphasis on revolutionary enthusiasm. In schools, the formal examinations, homework, and academic degrees, recently abolished, began to return; and classroom democracy gave way to greater authority for the teacher. The state praised the virtues of marriage, discouraged divorce and abortion, and rewarded prolific families. Associations of writers, musicians, and artists worked on propaganda for the plan. Mass organizations of youth and workers met for indoctrination, and within the party, criticism or even skepticism was akin to treason. Hundreds of thousands of party members were expelled, and new recruits were carefully screened. "Overfulfillment" was triumphantly announced in 1932; the miracle of industrialization came with creation of a Russian totalitarianism.

Growth in the Decade before World War II The Second (1933–1937) and Third (1938–1942) Five-Year plans continued the push for industrialization at somewhat lower pressure. Consumer goods were more available, and rationing was eliminated by 1936. Standards of quality rose, and dramatic improvement in transportation, especially domestic aviation, made previously remote territories accessible. By 1939 Soviet Russia ranked third among the world's industrial producers behind only the United States and Germany, producing 24 times more electrical power and 5 times more coal and steel than in 1913. Literacy among those over school age rose from below 50 percent in 1926 to more than 80 percent in 1939. As millions moved to cities, the number of higher schools, libraries, and hospitals doubled or tripled. In these years one-seventh of the population moved to the cities, where a higher proportion lived than ever before, and over 90 percent of peasant households were on collective farms serviced by the Machine Tractor Stations.

Announcing that the stage of socialism had been reached, the Soviet Union adopted a new constitution in 1936. The changes it made were mainly formal. Direct voting by secret ballot replaced the cumbersome indirect elections for the Soviet of the Union. The other house, the Soviet of the Nationalities, represented the republics, which on paper had considerable autonomy. The two houses together elected the Council of Ministers (the term *Commissars* thus passed away) and the Presidium, which legislated and whose chairman was head of state. The constitution recognized the Communist party as "the vanguard of the working people" and provided social and political guarantees that Communists hailed as the most democratic in the world. Ninety-six percent of the population voted in the next elections, 98 percent of them for the list the party presented.

Stalinism A more confident government showed signs of relaxing its campaigns against potential enemies. Some political prisoners were amnestied in 1935, and a more controlled political police, the NKVD, replaced the sinister secret police. The campaign against religion abated. Opportunities for advancement in this expanding economy were great. White-collar classes got more respect, the military had officers again, and foremen were reinstalled in factories. The expression of opinion, however, remained tightly controlled. Writers, Stalin commented ominously, were "engineers of human souls." Although harassed less than during the First Five-Year Plan, intellectuals had long since learned the necessity of caution. The Russian Academy of Science's grants of money and prestige were never far from politics.

At the center of Soviet society stood Stalin, adulated as leader in every activity. Works of art were dedicated to him, factories named after him. His picture was everywhere. Patriotism overshadowed the socialist internationalism of an earlier generation, and Stalin was taking his place with Ivan the Terrible and Peter the Great among the molders of Russia. With no official position other than party secretary, he demonstrated his awful power in the great purges of the late 1930s. Directed against engineers, Ukrainian separatists, former Mensheviks, and party members accused of being counterrevolutionaries, the purges were touched off by the assassination in 1934 of Sergei Kirov, a member of the Politburo who had been a close associate of Stalin's (although Stalin himself was probably behind the assassination).

Party and state combined to root out a great conspiracy. Zinoviev and members of the "left opposition" were twice tried for treason and were executed in 1937. Other public trials followed: party leaders and army officers in 1937; and members of the "right opposition," Nikolai Bukharin and other old Bolsheviks, in 1939. To the outside world, the indictments seemed vague and the evidence unconvincing. Yet the accused consistently confessed—the effect of torture perhaps, or the wish to protect their families, or maybe the final act of faith by men who had always believed in the inevitable course of history and believed that anyone resisting it was "objectively" a traitor. A reign of terror swept the country, feeding local vendettas until Stalin called a halt in 1939. The dead were countless; jails and labor camps were bursting with prisoners, perhaps 10 million. More than twice that many had gone into exile. Soviet totalitarianism had grown to be ominously like that of Germany and Italy, except for the values it professed.

Throughout Europe, the democracy, recovery, and prosperity of the postwar period had crumbled. The provocative and brilliant culture of the twenties apparently fostered either skepticism or violence. Ideological divisions were deeper than ever. Hesitant and ineffectual democracies seemed especially weak in contrast to the confident vigor of fascism, Nazism, and communism, inventors of a new kind of political system with an unprecedented ability to mobilize entire societies and a boundless capacity for brutality. Rather helplessly, reasonable observers could only speculate whether the rising tensions were bound to dissipate or destined to explode.

Recommended Reading

Sources

Ciano, Count Galiazzo. *Diary, 1937–1938.* 1952; *Diary, 1939–1943.* 1947. The diaries of Mussolini's son-in-law and, eventually, foreign minister are often self-serving; but they give a vivid picture of the intrigue and confusion at the center of the Fascist regime.

Ortega y Gasset, José. *The Revolt of the Masses.* 1957. First published in 1932, this essay by one of Spain's leading philosophers and historians, an important work in its own right, is also a significant document of the disquiet intellectual elites felt over the effects that increased specialization and mass society were having on the traditional culture of the West.

Reed, John. *Ten Days That Shook the World.* Available in many editions, this classic account of the Russian revolution was first published in 1922. John Reed went to Russia as a journalist and radical. His enthusiastic and perceptive report on the revolution captures both the excitement of the moment and the communist revolution's dramatic and international appeal.

Studies

*Allen, William S. *The Nazi Seizure of Power: The Experience of a Single German Town, 1930–1935.* 1965. A much-used microcosmic study.

*Arendt, Hannah. *The Origins of Totalitarianism.* 1958. This important study begins with a profoundly pessimistic application of hindsight to the imperialism and anti-Semitism of the late nineteenth century to make the case for Nazi totalitarianism as a phenomenon rooted in Western history.

Bessel, Richard. *Life in the Third Reich.* 1987. Essays by leading historians using the latest research to provide fresh interpretations of various aspects of Nazi rule.

*Bracher, Karl D. *The German Dictatorship.* Jean Steinberg (tr.). 1970. A major synthesis of work on the origins, structure, and impact of the Nazi movement.

Broszat, Martin. *The Hitler State: The Foundation and Internal Structure of the Third Reich.* 1981. Uses the methods of current social history to show the complexity and confusion of Nazi rule, emphasizing its operation in daily life.

*Bullock, Alan. *Hitler: A Study in Tyranny.* 1971. The best biography of Hitler and one that gives an effective picture of Nazi society.

*Carr, E. G. *The Bolshevik Revolution 1917–1923* (3 vols). 1985. The most comprehensive single study.

Carsten, F. L. *The Rise of Fascism.* 1967. The careful synthesis of a distinguished scholar that looks at the varieties of fascist regimes.

*De Felice, Renzo. *Interpretations of Fascism.* Brenda Huff Evertt (tr.). 1977. A very thoughtful review of the interpretations of Italian Fascism.

Fitzpatrick, Sheila. *The Russian Revolution, 1917–1932.* 1982. A valuable, fresh overview that emphasizes social conditions.

*——— (ed.). *The Cultural Revolution in Russia.* 1978. Essays treating varied aspects of the effort to create a new culture.

*Available in paperback.

Gay, Peter. *Weimar Culture: The Outsider as Insider.* 1968. A wide-ranging essay arguing that the vigorous cultural life of Weimar Germany was shaped by those viewed as marginal to Germany's traditional culture.

Kater, Michael H. *The Nazi Party. A Social Profile of Members and Leaders, 1919–1945.* 1984. An impressive analysis of the relevant statistical data on the social origins of Nazi party members.

Kershaw, Ian. *The Nazi Dictatorship: Problems and Perspectives of Interpretation.* 1985. A significant assessment that provides an excellent introduction to and interpretation of a vast literature.

Kindleberger, Charles P. *The World in Depression, 1929–1939.* 1973. A study of the origins of the Depression and of responses to it in different countries.

*Kolb, Eberhard. *The Weimar Republic.* P. S. Falla (tr.). 1988. A comprehensive account of the difficulties and failures of Germany's experiment with democracy.

Koonz, Claudia. *Mothers in the Fatherland: Women, the Family, and Nazi Politics.* 1987. Shows the importance of gender policies to Nazi ideology and rule.

Lebovics, Herman. *Social Conservatism and the Middle Classes in Germany, 1914–1933.* 1969. Looks at individual figures to explore the development of an ideology of conservatism that prepared many members of the middle class to be sympathetic to the Nazi movement.

Lee, Stephen J. *The European Dictatorships: 1918–1945.* 1987. A comprehensive and systematic comparison of Communist Russia, Fascist Italy, and Nazi Germany.

Lewin, Mosche. *The Making of the Soviet System: Essays in the Social History of Interwar Russia.* 1985. Explores the complex roots and real limitations of the regime in a period of revolutionary change.

Mack Smith, Denis. *Mussolini.* 1981. An informed, skeptical account by the leading English scholar of modern Italy.

*Nettl, J. P. *The Soviet Achievement.* 1967. Effectively tackles the difficult task of assessing both the economic development of the U.S.S.R. and its social cost.

*Nolte, Ernst. *Three Faces of Fascism.* Leila Vennewitz (tr.). A learned effort to place the intellectual history of fascism in France, Germany, and Italy in the mainstream of European thought.

*Nove, Alec. *An Economic History of the USSR.* 1982. A compact survey through the Brezhnev years, which concentrates on the formation of economic policies.

Peukert, Detlev J. K. *Inside Nazi Germany: Conformity, Opposition, and Racism in Everyday Life.* 1987. Makes use of a great deal of recent research to explore the effects of Nazi tyranny on ordinary life and the difficulties of opposition to it.

*Pipes, Richard. *The Formation of the Soviet Union.* 1964. A clear, comprehensive, and very critical treatment of Soviet rule.

*Schoenbaum, David. *Hitler's Social Revolution: Class and Status in Nazi Germany. 1933–1939.* 1966. A topical discussion contrasting theory and practice in the social policies of the Third Reich.

Tannenbaum, Edward R. *The Fascist Experience: Italian Society and Culture, 1922–1945.* 1972. A wide-ranging effort to recapture the meaning in practice of Fascist rule.

Thompson, John M. *Revolutionary Russia, 1917.* 1989. A good overview of what the revolution meant for ordinary life throughout the country.

*Tucker, Robert C. *Stalin as Revolutionary, 1879–1929: A Study in History and Personality.* 1973. Sensitively explores the shaping of Stalin's character as a key to his use of power.

*Ulam, Adam B. *Lenin and the Bolsheviks.* 1969. Combines the study of ideas and of policy to explain Lenin's triumph.

Weinberg, Gerhard L. *The Foreign Policy of Hitler's Germany.* 1970. A major study by a leading American diplomatic historian that helps explain Hitler's early successes.

*Woolf, S. J. (ed.). *Fascism in Europe.* 1981. Essays on the countries that offer major examples of fascist movements.

A women's unit pulls in one of the barrage balloons used for defense in the Battle of Britain. The weighted cables dangling beneath the balloons prevented low-level flights by German bombers.

CHAPTER TWENTY-NINE

The Nightmare: World War II

WORLD War II was the centerpiece of a long trial of European civilization. The war itself represented more than a conflict of nations, and the terrors of the battlefield were exceeded by the deliberate, systematic horrors of genocide, torture, and concentration camps. The war followed from a breakdown in international relations, which in turn had economic, social, and cultural causes. For more than a decade Europe had experienced a kind of ideological civil war that undermined established institutions and exposed every weakness in the social fabric. When war broke out, it rewarded organization, technology, and ruthlessness; and horrors committed against civilians rivaled those of the battlefield. After the war, a devastated continent filled with millions who had lost homes, family, health, and hope struggled just to make society function. The achievement of stability and prosperity by the 1950s really was the European miracle.

I. Democracy on the Defensive: The Path to War

Liberal democracy, and the restructuring of European states which made that the nearly universal European model by 1920, was everywhere on the defensive in the 1930s. Confident regimes—Communist, Fascist, and Nazi—moved dramatically to meet the challenge of the Depression and to create social unity, in the process tightening their hold on power; while Europe's democracies responded uncertainly, forever compromising in order to sustain unstable majorities that reflected the social and ideological dissension that politics could not overcome.

SOCIETIES DIVIDED

Economic recovery by the mid-1930s did not lessen these divisions, even though standards of living were rising again. Agriculture became more productive by becoming more mechanized and scientific, changes that required increased capital (thus favoring larger holdings) and employed fewer laborers. Workers benefited from better transportation, mechanical refrigeration, cheaper clothes, and more leisure; but it took organized conflict for them to pry better wages from employers. Many employees now enjoyed a shorter work week, but work itself was more subject to "American" efficiency on speeded-up assembly lines. The middle classes recouped much that inflation and depression had undermined, but not their former confidence. Small business and craft industry suffered much more than larger corporations, which were the first to benefit from the economic upturn; both remained fearful of unions and socialism.

Cultural life, too, continued to be unsettling. Where not restricted by the state, the sciences, social sciences, and the arts became more international. Easier communication, increased mobility, and exile brought the achievements of Russian ballet, Bauhaus architecture, and Russian, German, and Italian scientists and scholars to Paris, London, and, most of all, the United States. New cultural movements seemed all the more foreign, politicized, and ideological. In Paris, the Spanish painter Pablo Picasso became the dominant figure of twentieth-century art, restlessly experimenting with one new style after another. His most political work, *Guernica*, was a searing comment on war prepared for the Spanish pavilion at the Paris World's Fair of 1937. Social scientists, poets, and novelists probed the theme of alienation in a faceless mass society and participated in political conflicts. Some artists defended the "experiments" of Hitler and Mussolini; far more joined Marxist groups, convinced that socialism could achieve equality and preserve culture, which to many intellectuals seemed threatened as never before by the frothy commercialism of talking motion pictures and radio.

Enthusiastically taken up by the general public, and skillfully used in the propaganda at which the totalitarian regimes excelled, the new media did much to bridge the chasm between rural and urban life. Not given to thoughtful discourse and moral uplift, mass entertainment sharpened the distinction between high and popular culture. The transformation of Soviet society and the energy of the propaganda that advertised new, better-lit factories and vacation resorts in Germany and Italy offered a striking contrast between the ideologically coherent, purposeful, orderly societies of a single party and the aimless dislocation and dissension to be found in the democracies.

Ideological Conflict All of Europe seemed divided in a great ideological battle. Intellectual arguments and newspaper articles alike took on apocalyptic tones that made the bland decencies of bourgeois democracy seem barely relevant to the modern world. While the strident claims of radicals and fascists dominated the debate, four major groups expressed a revived commitment to freedom. The most prominent was Marxist. The Russian Revolution had enthralled millions of Europeans with visions of economic progress in a backward nation and of social equality and high culture in a mass society. This appeal grew as capitalist economies staggered and reached a peak with the Soviet constitution of 1936. At the same time, socialists and even Communists insisted on the importance of justice, equality, and liberty, asserting that dictatorship in the Soviet Union was a special case.

NUMBER OF MOTOR VEHICLES

The number of automobiles in a society reflects its general wealth, adaptation to a consumer economy, and changing patterns of communication. (Note that the United Kingdom, France, and Italy each had about 40 million people; Germany had 65 million.) This graph gives evidence of impressive prosperity and change; by 1935 France and the United Kingdom had one vehicle for every 20 people.

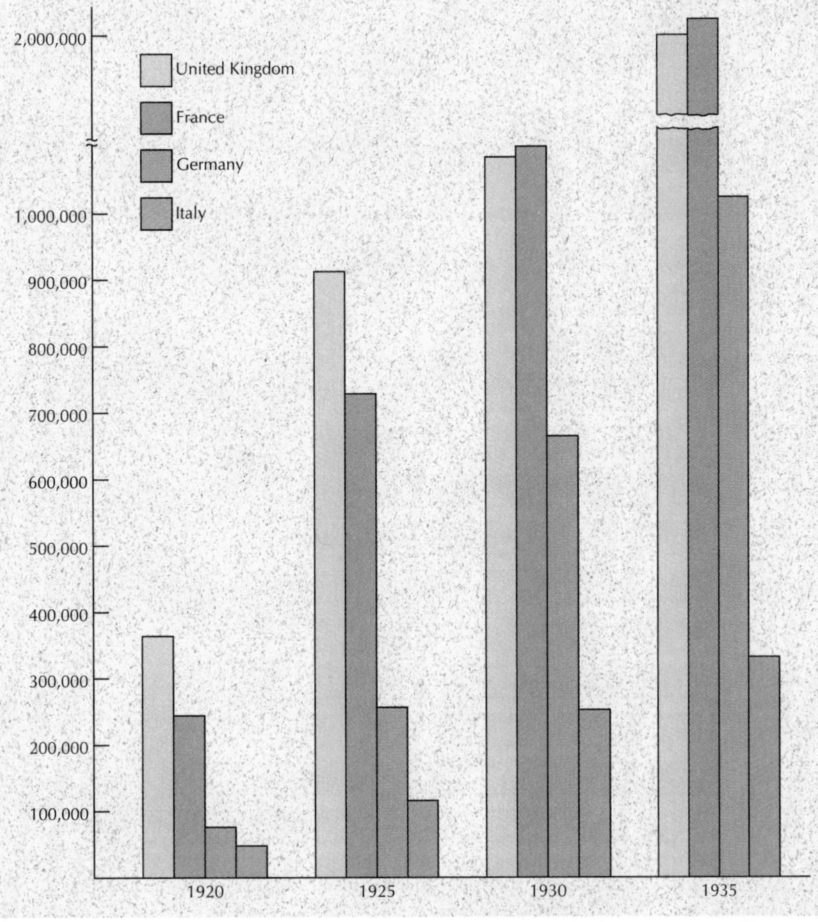

APPROXIMATE NUMBER OF RADIOS LICENSED FOR EVERY 100 PEOPLE IN 20 SELECTED COUNTRIES (1938)

Radio was an important new instrument of communication and propaganda. These statistics suggest that most families in the United Kingdom had a radio, that nearly everyone could sometimes listen to the radio in Finland and Austria, and that from Italy to Portugal, millions of people heard the radio only on special occasions when speakers blared in public places.

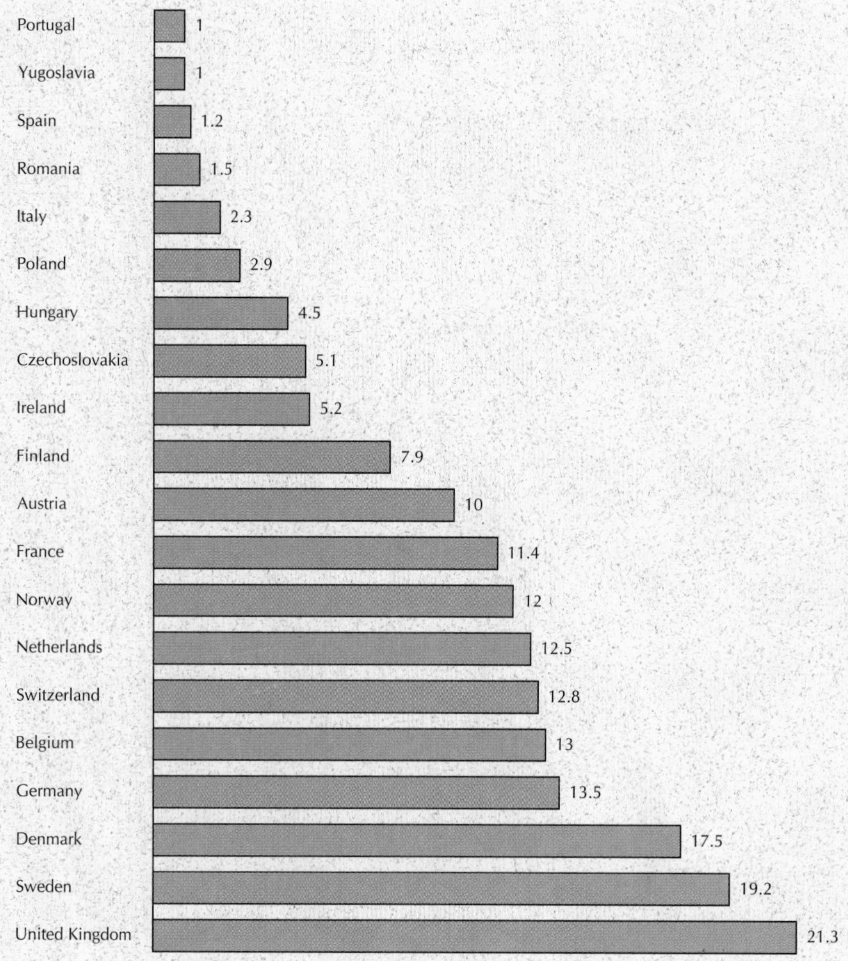

In Christian thought, traditional arguments against the idolatry of the state gained new meaning. The Protestant Karl Barth and the Catholic Jacques Maritain built on firm theological orthodoxy to stress the importance of individual freedom and social justice. Similar concerns emerged in the influential work of the Russian Orthodox Nikolai Berdyaev and the Jewish scholar Martin Buber. From a more secular perspective, noted poets and novelists such as W. H. Auden, Thomas Mann, and André Malraux wrote powerfully in behalf of human dignity and social justice, warning of the dangers of power and the evils of war. Nor were liberals silent. Most vigorous in the politics and universities of Britain and France, they were also heard even in Fascist Italy. In his important *History of European Liberalism,* Guido de Ruggiero argued that liberal values, modified yet again, offered a practical path to stability and progress; and Benedetto Croce made liberty the central theme of his historical and philosophical writings.

Economic theory also contributed to the argument for political freedom through the work of John Maynard Keynes, whose book *The General Theory of Employment, Interest and Money* appeared in 1936. Keynes rejected classical views of economic man and the self-regulating economy. Few people, he argued, consistently act in their own financial interest, for no one is free of ideas, values, and tastes that shape actions. Nor do iron economic laws inexorably dictate a pattern of booms and busts. To Keynes, massive unemployment was not only intolerable but proof that capitalism must not be left to its own devices. At the same time, he dismissed Marxism as outmoded. Instead he offered a sophisticated theory that called on governments to smooth out the economic cycle. When the economy lagged, the government should lower interest rates to encourage production and finance public works and social welfare to stimulate consumption. As the economy expanded, the opposite policies should check inflation and excessive speculation. Keynes advocated granting government a more active role while preserving free markets. In effect he gave a theoretical foundation for practices already partially adopted under Swedish socialism, the French Popular Front (see below), and the American New Deal, President Franklin D. Roosevelt's program of social and economic reform inaugurated in 1933.

An advocate of capitalism, Keynes defended it by denying that its social evils were inevitable; most capitalists denounced him as a socialist. Few thinkers were neutral. With socialist anger, Auden, the British poet who chose to live in America, warned capitalists that "the game is up for you and for the others. . . ."[1] T. S. Eliot, the American poet who chose to live in Britain, proposed still tougher choices in a voice of Christian outrage: "The term 'democracy' . . . does not contain enough positive content to stand alone. . . . If you will not have God (and He is a jealous God) you should pay your respects to Hitler or Stalin."[2]

Political Uncertainty The economic crisis of the Great Depression was followed from the mid-1930s on by rising international dangers, and both sets of problems weakened parliamentary politics. Conservative parties pursued balanced budgets with results that embittered the unemployed; liberals compromised their traditional principles by supporting tariffs and subsidies that had few positive results; and socialists, weakened by competition from communists, antagonized workers by accepting weak welfare measures in the interest of better-balanced budgets. Issues of foreign policy added further complications as traditional positions shifted. Conservatives, historically supporters of military strength, were now inclined to downplay the dangers rising from Italy and Germany. The left tended to abandon its antimilitary rhetoric and stress the need to resist the fascist states. Not many democracies remained in Europe as Finland and Czechoslovakia, whose economic growth and political freedom had made them models of the new postwar nations, felt the pressure of their stronger neighbors. Increasingly, the cause of democracy depended primarily on Britain and France.

---

[1] W. H. Auden, "Consider This and In Our Time," in *A Little Treasury of Great Poetry,* Oscar Williams (ed.), Charles Scribner's Sons, 1947, p. 689.

[2] T. S. Eliot, *The Idea of a Christian Society,* Harcourt Brace, 1960.

Great Britain In Britain a Labour victory in 1929 had made Ramsay MacDonald prime minister once again. His economic policies followed the standard advice of experts in making drastic cuts in welfare and unemployment payments, measures that divided his own party and led to his forming a national government with members from all three parties, in effect a conservative government in disguise. The Labour party expelled MacDonald amid bitter recriminations, but the government survived to adopt controls on foreign exchange and to increase tariffs, policies that split the Liberals. When MacDonald resigned in 1935, tired and unloved, his coalition government had overseen a slow recovery of the British economy, redefined imperial relations, and initiated some cautious steps toward government planning. It had done so by pursuing conservative policies, and in the process MacDonald had struck a devastating blow to the proletarian movement to which he had devoted his life.

Conservative Stanley Baldwin then returned for his third time as prime minister, after campaigning as a strong supporter of the League of Nations, in which he actually had little interest. With a complacency that masked indecision, he helped Britain avoid political extremes. The parliament elected with him, which would continue to sit through 1945 as the longest-lived in modern history, would later reveal a wealth of talent that was testimony to the continued vitality of British political life. Even the crisis of 1936 could be seen in retrospect as a comforting assertion of tradition. King Edward VIII acceded to the throne, only to insist upon marrying an American divorcee. He was forced to abdicate; and the transition to George VI went smoothly, quelling talk of the end of the monarchy. At the time, however, British institutions appeared weak. As international affairs grew more ominous, the uncertainty of British policy further weakened the capacity of continental states to resist the expansionist policies of Germany and Italy; and doubts about Britain's role increased in 1937 when Baldwin turned the prime ministership over to his earnest chancellor of the Exchequer, Neville Chamberlain, who was convinced that through caution and compromise he must avoid the danger of another war.

France France experienced the Depression later and less severely than other highly industrialized countries; but when the decline came, it lasted. The left, which had won the legislative elections of 1932 as the French began to feel the economic slump, found it difficult to construct a reliable majority (Socialists refused to participate in bourgeois governments), leading to unstable administrations that were committed to reducing expenditures and protecting established interests. Outside parliament, rightist factions, including the fascist Croix de Feu (Cross of Fire), grew increasingly noisy. Their uniformed militants led demonstrations against parliament on February 6, 1934, that resulted in more bloodshed than Paris had seen since the Commune of 1870; and many believe that the Third Republic nearly died that day. France seemed more bitterly divided than at any time since the Dreyfus affair at the turn of the century. The exposure of a gigantic investment swindle perpetrated by one Serge Stavisky, who had benefited from important political connections, became the basis for a campaign in which protofascist groups used the now familiar devices of uniforms, anti-Semitism, propaganda, and demonstrations. To meet the emergency, Gaston Doumergue, a former president of the republic, was recalled from retirement to take the premiership, empowered to govern by decree. The sober old man, supported by every party except the royalists and the Marxists, held office for nine calming months before giving way to a parliament that insisted on its prerogatives but little else.

The elections of 1936 brought a dramatic change. Moderate republicans, Socialists, and Communists formed an anti-fascist Popular Front (a cooperation made possible by the decision of the Comintern, the international association of Communist parties directed from the Soviet Union, permitting Communists to ally with other parties). The three parties agreed not to run against each other on the second, or runoff, ballot; and such rare solidarity brought the left a resounding victory and France its first Socialist premier: Léon Blum, a learned, humane intellectual and a Jew—attributes that made his enemies all the more distrustful. Even as the new government took office, it faced a wave of strikes by workers determined to collect the fruits of their victory. They occupied factories, which many conservatives mistook for the revolution they dreaded. Eventually the strikes ended as the government pushed through legislation that provided for a general 12 percent increase in wages, two-week paid vacations, a 40-hour work week, and compulsory arbitration. Other reforms were soon added. Public works were launched, the Bank of France (long distrusted by the left) was restructured, the arms industry was nationalized, veterans were given increased pensions, and small businesses were offered subsidies. But each of these measures, like the devaluation of the franc, which in 1937 could no longer be avoided, frightened the business classes. New programs proved hard to finance, the economy more accessible to regulation than to stimulation. Blum's government—one of the Third Republic's most admired and most hated—had hardly begun the tax reforms its plans required when, after a year in office, it was defeated in the conservative senate. The Popular Front itself soon broke up. Subsequent governments were less ambitious amidst political feuds and public slander. Meanwhile, France's carefully constructed international position was collapsing.

THE FAILURES OF DIPLOMACY

The internationalism of the twenties was failing. The question of reparations had been abandoned rather than resolved; and the sense of unreality in European diplomacy was underscored by the absence of the Soviet Union, which was effectively ostracized, and the limited participation of the United States, which was absorbed in domestic affairs. The League of Nations had little independent authority. China protested to the League when Japanese troops occupied the major cities of southern Manchuria in 1931. After two years of deliberations a League committee recommended that Japan be ordered to withdraw. Japan withdrew from the League instead and in 1933 renounced the limitations on its naval strength that were part of the international agreements that had seemed so promising a decade earlier. Then Germany withdrew from the London conference on disarmament and from the League of Nations as well.

Governments did make some effort to counterbalance the threat of Germany's rapid rearmament. The Little Entente—an alliance of Czechoslovakia, Yugoslavia, and Romania, each also allied to France—drew closer together, and Greece and Turkey joined this French sphere in 1934. But Hungary and Bulgaria remained outside it, authoritarian states attracted to Italy and impressed by Germany's resurgence. For a while, Italy seemed the key to the balance of power in Europe. Austrian Nazis abandoned their attempt in 1934 to force the unification of Austria and Germany through a coup d'état when Italian troops were rushed to the border, and Mussolini used his heightened prestige to form the so-called Stresa Front with France and Great Britain in 1935 after Germany publicly renounced the disarmament clauses of the Versailles treaty. But in fact the great powers quickly went their separate ways. France signed a mutual assistance pact with the Soviet Union, which was loudly opposed by many at home, worried Britain, and frightened Poland. Britain and Germany negotiated an agreement that the German navy, excluding submarines, should not exceed 35 percent of the British fleet—dealings that outraged France. Italy and Germany meanwhile prepared to take advantage of these international differences.

The First Moves of Italy and Germany In October 1935 Italy began an invasion of Ethiopia, seemingly an old-fashioned imperialistic venture preceded by carefully arranged understandings with Britain and France. But the enthusiastic bombings of defenseless populations and the racist propaganda that accompanied the attack signaled something new. Europeans were shocked, and the League of Nations, declaring Italy an aggressor, promptly banned the sale of essential war materials to Italy. Most of Europe seemed united in this crucial test of the League's peacekeeping powers; but the embargo, though it angered Italy and caused some hardship, did not stop the war, partly because the most important commodity of all, oil, was not included. And there were those in France and Britain who considered Italy's friendship more important than the League. They included the two foreign ministers: Pierre Laval, a slippery politician who had drifted steadily to the right, and Sir Samuel Hoare, an experienced conservative diplomat. Secretly, they arranged a settlement that would, in effect, give Italy most of Ethiopia. When the plan was leaked to the press, public outrage forced both men to resign; but their plan delayed efforts to add oil to the list of sanctions and undermined confidence in the two democracies. By May 1936, Ethiopia had capitulated, and Italy soon celebrated the formal lifting of the embargo. The ineffectiveness of the League of Nations had been exposed for all to see.

Germany then began to exploit its opportunities. The world knew that Germany, like everyone else, was rebuilding its fighting forces; and when in 1936 German troops marched into the Rhineland, which had been demilitarized by the Versailles treaty, there was no compelling international response. Italy this time did nothing. France, unwilling to act alone as it had in 1923, consulted the British, who urged France to acquiesce. The German troops were cheered by their countrymen in the Rhineland just as they had been the year before when France returned the Saar to German control following a plebiscite that had been overwhelmingly in favor of German rule. The initiative belonged to the fascist powers in their search for radical changes in the international balance. Britain and France were internally divided; the Eastern European nations were stalemated by fear of the Soviet Union as well as of Germany, and Hitler played skillfully on the bad conscience the Versailles treaty had created, using shrill propaganda and shifting demands for which Western diplomats were ill-prepared.

The Spanish Civil War Civil war in Spain drove home the sense that all of Europe was divided into two camps destined for a life and death struggle. In 1936 the army's best units, stationed in Spanish Morocco, rose up against the Spanish republic; and General Francisco Franco soon emerged as their leader. Little interested in doctrines or ideologies, he recognized the utility of a modern mass appeal and a disciplined movement. Known as the Nationalists, the movement remained dominated by the army, which held somewhat aloof from the monarchists yet appealed to them in addition to the fascistic Falangists, most of the clergy, and all others who saw in these different groups salvation from anarchy and communism. Italy and Germany quickly proffered their support and formed the Rome-Berlin Axis to guarantee their cooperation; and Germany and Japan signed an Anti-Comintern Pact declaring their mutual sympathy and op-

▸ A French gendarme leads members of the International Brigade who, with the fall of the Spanish republic, made their way across the French border to safety.

position to communism. The Nationalist cause had become ideological and international.

Spain's government had the support of republicans, socialists, communists, anarchists, labor groups, and Catalan and Basque nationalists, a loose and badly split coalition of Loyalists. Seeing themselves as the defenders of democracy against fascist aggression and of social justice against reactionary forces at home, they looked to the democracies for support but received little except from the thousands of idealistic young men who went to Spain to fight as volunteers in national units like the Lincoln Brigade and the Garibaldi Brigade (which had its greatest moment when it defeated troops of the regular Italian army sent by Mussolini).

Most of the Spanish navy remained loyal to the republic, and one of the insurgents' first problems was to get their armies from Spanish Morocco to the mainland, where many garrisons had risen in support of the Nationalists. By July, Italian and German planes were providing the needed transport. The help of the fascist powers—in the form of military advisers, planes, tanks, and ammunition as well as significant numbers of Italian troops—remained essential. Mussolini welcomed the chance to enhance Italian prestige, and Hitler used the opportunity to test new German military technology.

Only the Soviet Union gave reliable if limited aid to the Loyalists—until 1938, when Stalin decided to cut his losses. Blum's government in

▸ Pablo Picasso used the still unfamiliar techniques he had mastered to protest the bombing of the Spanish town of Guernica by German planes in 1937. The huge, dark canvas, a political act in opposition to Franco and the Spanish nationalists, foreshadowed modern warfare's brutal impact on civilian life. Kept in the United States for nearly fifty years, the painting can now be exhibited in a democratic Spain.

France favored the Loyalists but feared the domestic and international consequences of openly aiding them; Britain's Conservative government shared France's caution, but with a deeper distaste for the radicals of Madrid and a greater hope for good relations with Italy. The democracies thus chose neutrality; and under pressure, Germany and Italy pretended to agree. An international commission to prevent foreign intervention sustained the legalisms that starved the republic, honoring international law while undermining it. As aid to the Nationalists flowed in from the fascist powers, Britain and France looked the other way.

Foreign aid, trained troops, better military organization, and modern weapons made the victory of Franco's forces almost inevitable. They nearly won Madrid and the war itself in the summer of 1936, but the Loyalists held on and in a last-minute counterattack broke the Nationalists' assault. For more than two years, despite poor equipment and internal conflict, the republicans fought on, heartened by occasional victories. As the war progressed, the Loyalists became increasingly dependent on the Soviet Union for supplies, and that plus the Communists' organizational skills made the Communists increasingly influential among the Loyalists. To the disgust of his Axis supporters, Franco conducted a war of attrition. Not until the spring of 1939, when Soviet supplies had ceased to come and Britain had signed special treaties of friendship with Italy, did the Spanish republic finally fall. Thousands of refugees wearily crossed into France while Franco filled Spain's capacious prisons with potential enemies, undid the republic's social measures, and restored the power of the Church over education. Franco then joined the Anti-Comintern Pact and took Spain out of the League of Nations. The civil war had cost more than a million Spaniards their lives, many of them at the hands of firing squads and mobs. The bombing of the town of Guernica by German aircraft in 1937 made people shudder before the vision of what war now meant for civilians, and the tales of atrocities on both sides fed the angry arguments between left and right throughout Europe and the United States. The one clear lesson was that democracies, fearful and divided, had accepted defeat while the Axis acted.

The Anschluss For 18 months Hitler orchestrated a series of escalating crises that culminated in the outbreak of World War II in September 1939. In February 1938, with the outcome of civil war in Spain still uncertain, Hitler began to pressure Austria. He summoned the Austrian chancellor, Kurt von Schuschnigg, to the Führer's fortified mountain retreat at Berchtesgaden and subjected him to a humiliating harangue that won a promise to include Austrian Nazis in Schuschnigg's cabinet. On returning home, Schuschnigg felt braver and decided to hold a plebiscite in the hope that public opinion would rally to save Austria's independence. Hitler, furious, massed his army on the Austrian border, and Schuschnigg realized his position was hopeless. He had earlier disbanded the Socialist party, the strongest opponent of union with Germany, and Italy warned it would not oppose the German moves. The friendless Austrian chancellor was replaced by Artur von Seyss-Inquart, a Nazi, who invited German troops to restore order. They did so on March 13, and within a month Austria's annexation to Germany was almost unanimously approved in a plebiscite run by the Nazis. The dream of union with Germany, *Anschluss*, had been fulfilled; Hitler's popularity at home rose still higher, and German influence spread more deeply into the Balkans. Britain and France merely protested.

Czechoslovakia and the Munich Pact Two weeks after the Austrian plebiscite, Hitler demanded autonomy for the Sudetenland, an overwhelmingly German-speaking section of Czechoslovakia. Although this challenge to the Czech republic was far more daring—Czechoslovakia was a prosperous industrial state protected by a respectable army, well-fortified frontiers, and mutual-aid treaties with both France and Russia—the parallel with Austria was lost on no one. Supported by its allies, Czechoslovakia mobilized, and Hitler ordered the Sudeten Nazis to quiet down. But Czechoslovakia was vulnerable. The republic, dominated by the more prosperous Czech region, was barely able to maintain the loyalty of the Slovaks; and it met the additional threat of a pro-Nazi party (which had won more votes than any other in the elections held in 1935) only by restricting political parties. The great powers remained divided. Chamberlain wanted to parlay directly with Germany, believing that no nonnegotiable British interest was at stake in the Sudetenland, and he rejected suggestions from the United States and the Soviet Union for a meeting to consider means of restraining the Nazi dictator. Many in France and England, deeply alarmed at how close to war they were, doubted that fighting for Czechoslovakian sovereignty over a German population was worth the risk.

Throughout the summer, Sudeten Nazi leaders negotiated with the Czech state in an atmosphere heated by demonstrations there and in Germany. In August, Chamberlain, with French concurrence, sent his own emissary to mediate while German troops held maneuvers on the Czech border and Hitler pointedly toured Germany's fortifications in the west. Hitler's speeches became more bellicose, and Chamberlain decided, once again with French support, to visit the Führer at Berchtesgaden. When they met on September 15, Hitler raised the stakes, demanding annexation of the Sudetenland. Britain and France advised Czechoslovakia to submit. Desperately, the Czechs sought some escape, but only the Soviet Union was ready to support resistance. In a week Chamberlain flew back to Germany with the good news that Czechoslovakia had agreed to Hitler's terms, only to find them changed again: German troops must occupy the ceded territory immediately. The Czechs would have no time to move factories and military supplies or provide for citizens who wished to evacuate. A shocked Chamberlain said no, and for five days the world listened for war.

Then, persuaded by Mussolini, Hitler agreed to a meeting with the duce and the prime ministers of Britain and France. They met on September 29, 1938, in Munich, where just 15 years earlier Hitler had failed to capture the town hall. Now he dealt with nations. During an afternoon and evening of discussions, Hitler was granted all he asked. Neither the Soviet Union nor Czechoslovakia was consulted. The next day Czechoslovakia submitted to Hitler's terms and ac-

Map 29.1 EUROPE, 1935–1939

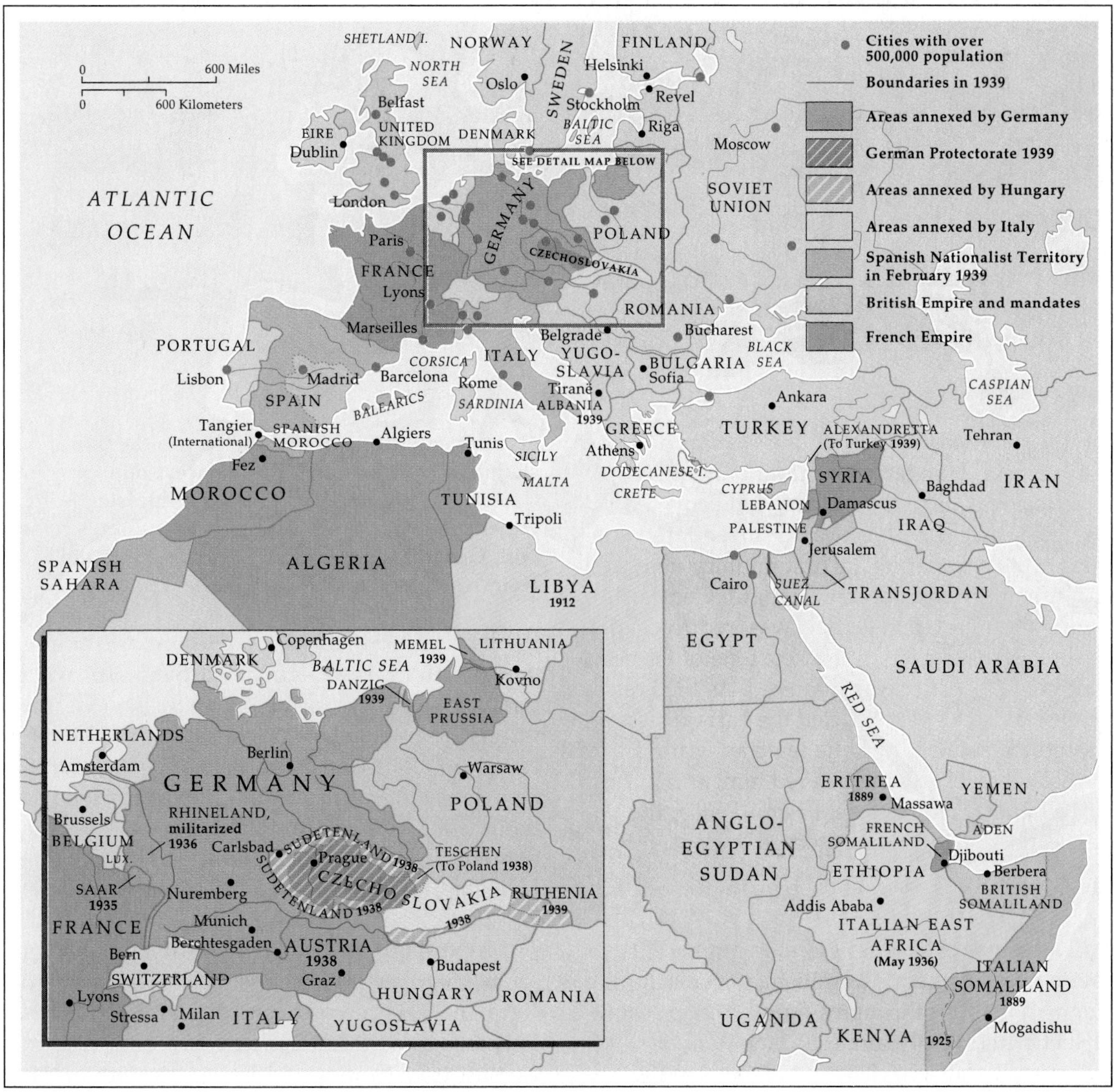

▶ **Hitler and Mussolini on the way to the train station after the Munich conference. Count Galeazzo Ciano, the Italian foreign minister, is on Hitler's left; Hermann Göring on Mussolini's right with General William Keitel, Rudolf Hess, and Heinrich Himmler among those behind them.**

cepted demands added at the last minute by Poland and Hungary for additional pieces of Czechoslovak territory they had long coveted. At a single stroke, Czechoslovakia surrendered one-third of its population, its best military defenses, and much of its economic strength. Central Europe's strongest democracy was reduced to a German dependency, and a keystone of France's continental security was shattered. As the French prime minister's plane circled the Paris airport on his return from Munich, he watched with dread the crowd below. But it cheered him, and in Britain, Chamberlain became a hero. Peace, the papers echoed, had been preserved.

Poland and World War German might, Hitler's speeches, virulent anti-Semitism, goose-stepping troops marching through Central Europe, news of life in the newly annexed lands and in Germany itself—all gave Jews, ethnic groups the Nazis labeled non-Aryans and therefore inferior, peoples along the German borders, and whole nations reason for terror. Early in 1939 German troops occupied all of Czechoslovakia (except for an additional piece taken by Hungary) and annexed the seaport of Memel from a terrified Lithuania. The pretext of absorbing only German peoples had now been abandoned. Chamberlain, believing that not even Nazis could want world war, led those who hoped concessions could appease Hitler; but in fact most of England and France had become resigned to the need to stop Germany with force. Inspired by Hitler's success, Italy began a noisy campaign to get Nice and Corsica from France and in the summer of 1939 invaded and annexed Albania. The Rome-Berlin Axis was formally tightened into the "Pact of Steel." Germany kept European chancelleries quaking with demands for nonaggression pacts, and late in August the leader of the Nazi party in Danzig, which had been established as a free city carved from Polish territory as a result of the Versailles treaties, declared that his city must be returned to the fatherland. Denunciations of the Versailles boundaries and claims that Germans living within the Polish corridor were being persecuted clearly indicated that Poland was next. As they had all summer, Britain and France renewed their pledges to protect Poland.

The summer's most important contest, however, was for the allegiance of the Soviet Union, and Hitler won that, too, with the sudden announcement of a Russo-German nonaggression pact. Russia had made overtures to Britain and France for a guarantee of the territorial integrity of all the states between the Baltic and Black seas. But the Western powers, reluctant to grant a Communist nation such extensive influence, had responded weakly. In May 1939, Stalin replaced his foreign minister, Maxim Litvinov, the eloquent spokesman for a pro-Western policy, with Vyacheslav Molotov, a tougher and less cosmopolitan old ally. Since 1935 the Soviet Union had advocated disarmament, supported the League of Nations, supplied Loyalist Spain, and offered support to Czechoslovakia; but Stalin feared that the democracies would welcome a war between Germany and Russia. Hitler, on the other hand, offered the Soviet Union a free hand in Finland, Estonia, Latvia, eastern Poland, and part of Romania, in the event that Germany sought any changes in its own eastern border. The Russo-German agreement, a masterpiece of cynicism arranged between the sponsors of antifascist fronts and the authors of the Anti-Comintern Pact, shocked a world that was still unaccustomed to totalitarian flexibility.

The last days of August resounded with formal warnings and clarifications between the Western powers and Germany. On September 1, Germany invaded Poland. Britain and France mobilized, sent Germany an ultimatum, and declared war on September 3, 1939. One year after surrendering democratic Czechoslovakia, they would fight for authoritarian Poland.

II. European and Global War

One argument for the policy of appeasement was that it enabled Britain and France to buy time. They had been vigorously strengthening their armed forces, and the domestic consensus that war required was slowly taking shape. But much remained to be done; Germany had gained, too, in territory and power, and now there was no time left.

AXIS TRIUMPHS, 1939–1941

Blitzkrieg and Phony War For two years the Axis scored one victory after another. Having carefully prepared the invasion, Germany attacked Poland with overwhelming force in the first blitzkrieg, or "lightning war." Poland fell in less than a month, and Hitler suggested that the war could now end. Few were tempted by his hints of peace. Concerned to strengthen its frontiers against Germany, the Soviet Union attacked Finland in November and met such fierce resistance that it did not gain all its demands until the following spring. Having regained boundaries close to those of the last tsars, Russia could afford to wait. The Western powers had been waiting, too. Hitler refrained from attacking along the French border, and the Allied commanders resolved not to risk precious planes too soon or to repeat the pointless assaults of World War I.

This was the so-called phony war, during which arms production and mobilization speeded up, the world waited, and little happened. The strain was bad for morale. With the Soviet Union standing aside from the conflict, French Communists now said the war was a mistake; their party was suppressed. Paul Reynaud, energetic and determined, replaced Daladier as premier as the Allies prepared to defend Norway, an obvious German target. On April 9, Germany attacked Denmark, taking it in a day, and captured Norway's most important strategic points in short order, which gave Germany bases for numerous assaults on British ships and cities. After a wide-ranging and often angry parliamentary debate, Chamberlain resigned in May, and

▸ **Warsaw, October 5, 1939: German tanks, fresh from their lightning destruction of the Polish army, pass in review before Adolf Hitler.**

Winston Churchill became prime minister of an all-party government. A Conservative who believed in empire and an opponent of appeasement, Churchill was a political maverick given his chance by disaster. His decisiveness and eloquence made him one of England's greatest leaders.

The Fall of France On May 10, and without warning, German troops flooded the Netherlands and Belgium. The Dutch, who had expected to escape war as they had since Napoleon I, surrendered in five days. The better-prepared and larger Belgian army held out for eighteen days. On May 14 a skillfully executed German offensive broke through the Ardennes forest, thought to be impervious to tanks, reached Sedan, and drove to the Channel, trapping the Belgian and British forces fighting there and much of the French army. The German air force, the Luftwaffe, controlled the skies, and the Allies' proudest achievement in the battle for France was the evacuation from the port town of Dunkirk of 340,000 troops pinned against the sea. They left for Britain in a motley flotilla of naval vessels, commercial ferries, and private sailboats, a symbol of heroism and inferior preparation.

The Allied defense of France was broken. German forces renewed the attack on June 5 and took Paris in a week. Anxious lest he miss the war entirely, Mussolini attacked France on the tenth; France surrendered on June 16, 1940. The armistice was signed in the railway car used for Germany's surrender in 1918. More ironic still, the man who chose to sign for France was the World War I hero of Verdun, Marshal Henri Philippe Pétain.

Hitler seemed invincible and the blitzkrieg some terrible new Teutonic force, a totalitarian achievement other societies could not hope to equal. In fact, however, many of the tactical ideas on which it rested were first put forward by British and French experts, including a French officer, Charles de Gaulle. The blitzkrieg was the result not so much of new technology but of new strategy. It combined air attacks with rapid movements of motorized columns to overcome the advantages defensive positions had previously enjoyed. Tanks roared through and behind enemy lines, a maneuver requiring speed and precision that were nearly forbidden in older theories. In the flat terrain of Poland, Germany's panzer tank divisions quickly encircled the enemy; in France, they often assaulted troops so far in the rear that they had not yet prepared for battle. The aim was less to capture ground than to break up communications, using air power to disorient and terrify the retreating army. Even the machine-gunning of French roads clogged with civilian refugees and the bombing of Rotterdam had their place in the campaign to demoralize.

French strategy had relied too much on the defensive strength of the Maginot Line, a system of fortifications extending from the Belgian border to Switzerland, and on the assumption that Germany would respect the neutrality of Belgium and the Netherlands. The French had powerful tanks of their own but had been slow to deploy them; their air force was momentarily weakened as they changed models. Memories of the last war weakened morale during the phony war, and policy was undermined by politics rife with suspicion of the British, of the army, of the politicians, of the left. Pétain, who believed France must now make its way in Hitler's Europe, blamed the Third Republic, and for a moment the nation turned to the octogenarian marshal with stunned unanimity. He accepted terms of surrender that put three-fifths of the country under Nazi occupation and allowed French prisoners of war to be kept in Germany.

▶ **French refugees with all the possessions they can carry clog the roads, expecting to be able to escape the German armies in 1940 as their parents had 30 years before.**

The unoccupied southeastern part of France was to have its own government, established at Vichy, where a reconvened parliament maneuvered by Pierre Laval named Pétain chief of state. The new regime, known as Vichy France, was a confused coalition of militant fascists and the traditional right, and it would never be really independent of Germany. After adopting bits of corporatism and some fascist trappings, it settled into a lethargy of its own, an often willing collaborator in Hitler's new order, ruling a truncated state as rife with intrigue, personal ambition, and shifting alliances as the Third Republic it so heartily denounced.

The Battle of Britain Great Britain now stood alone. Unprepared for such enormous victories so soon, German officers planned their invasion

▸ **In the hopfields of Kent in southeastern England, the pickers and their families took refuge in trenches during the air raids.**

of Britain while, beginning in June 1940, their bombers roared over England in sustained attacks that many believed would be enough to force surrender. Instead, in September the projected invasion was postponed, while the air attacks continued. The German navy had suffered enough damage in encounters with the British to favor caution, and by the spring even the air raids were letting up. The waves of German planes flying across the Channel sustained losses far greater than those of Britain's Royal Air Force. British fighter planes, particularly the newer designs, proved at least the equal of the German; and they were aided by new techniques of antiaircraft defense, including radar, an English development that was the most critical addition to military technology in these years. At first the air raids concentrated on ports and shipping, then on airfields, and finally on cities, leaving great burning holes in London and completely destroying the industrial city of Coventry. But the diversity of targets dissipated the economic and military effects of the bombing, and the terror from the skies seemed to raise morale in a nation ever better organized and more fiercely determined to carry on. Merely to survive from June 1940 to June 1941 was a kind of victory, in what Churchill memorably called Britain's "finest hour."

The Balkans and Eastern Europe With all the continent from Norway to Sicily to the Atlantic in their own hands or in the friendly ones of dictators in Spain and Portugal, the Axis powers looked eastward. In October 1940, Italian forces moved from Albania into Greece only to be pushed back, and Hitler had to bail out Mussolini, further squeezing the Balkan States, which were rapidly losing their independence. In June 1940, the Soviet Union had stretched its pact with Germany to take Bessarabia from Romania. After Hungary and Bulgaria also took some of Romania for themselves, Hitler announced that he would protect the rest of the country. In fact all three Eastern European nations were already implicated in Hitler's mapmaking and were closely tied to Germany. It was no great step for them to join the Axis, welcome German troops in March 1941, and cooperate with Germany in attacking Yugoslavia, which had hesitated too long over whether to join the Axis, and Greece, which had fought Mussolini too well.

The attack was launched in April 1941 and swept through both countries within the month. Some Greek and British forces pulled back to Crete, only to be forced out almost immediately by attacks from German gliders and paratroops, history's first. The Allies retreated to Egypt, where British forces had held off an Italian attack launched from Italy's neighboring colony of Libya. The Axis now threatened to dominate the Mediterranean, too.

Then on June 22 German forces attacked the Soviet Union. The Russians had long feared such a move; yet the Soviets appeared genuinely surprised, at least by the timing and the size of the German invasion (*see box*, p. 967–968). The assault, in three broad sectors, was the largest concentration of military power that had ever been assembled, and once more the blitzkrieg worked its magic. Germany's armored divisions ripped through Russian lines and encircled astonishing numbers of troops, crossing the vast lands Russia had acquired since 1939, taking Riga and Smolensk in July, reaching the Dnieper in August, claiming Kiev and the whole Ukraine in September. Then the pace slowed; but while one German force lay siege to Leningrad in the north, a second hit Sevastopol in the south and moved into the Crimea, and by December still another had penetrated to the suburbs of Moscow. There the German advance stopped temporarily, halted by an early and severe winter, by strained supply lines, and (at last) by sharp Russian counterattacks. The territory now held by Germany had accounted for nearly two-thirds of Russia's production of coal, iron, steel, and aluminum, as well as 40 percent of its grain and hogs.

Stalin Appeals to Patriotism

Stalin, apparently in a state of shock, was silent for the first week after German forces invaded the Soviet Union. Finally, on July 3, 1941, he spoke by radio to the Soviet people. His address acknowledged initial defeats, invoked the example of Russian victories over invaders in the past, and emphasized that the Allies were fighting together against Nazi tyranny. But he also called in striking detail for ordinary citizens to continue the fight by destroying anything that might be helpful to the invader (which became known as the "scorched earth" policy) and by constant sabotage.

"Comrades! Citizens! Brothers and Sisters! Men of our Army and Navy!

"I am addressing you, my friends!

"The perfidious military attack on our fatherland, begun on 22 June by Hitler's Germany is continuing.

"In spite of heroic resistance of the Red Army, and although the enemy's finest divisions and finest air-force units have already been smashed and have met their doom on the field of battle, the enemy continues to push forward, hurling fresh forces into the attack.

"Hitler's troops have succeeded in capturing Lithuania, a considerable part of Latvia, the western part of White Russia, and a part of the western Ukraine.

". . . A grave danger hangs over our country.

"How could it have happened that our glorious Red Army surrendered a number of cities and districts to the Fascist armies?

"Is it really true that German Fascist troops are invincible, as is ceaselessly trumpeted by boastful Fascist propagandists? Of course not!

"History shows that there are no invincible armies, and never have been. Napoleon's army was considered invincible, but it was beaten successively by Russian, English, and German armies. Kaiser Wilhelm's German army in the period of the first imperialist war was also considered invincible, but it was beaten several times by Russian and Anglo-French forces.

"The same must be said of Hitler's German Fascist army today. This army has not yet met with serious resistance on the Continent of Europe. Only on our territory has it met serious resistance, and if as a result of this resistance the

(Continued)

finest divisions of Hitler's German Fascist army have been defeated by our Red Army, it means that this army, too, can be smashed and will be smashed as were the armies of Napoleon and Wilhelm.

"There can be no doubt that this short-lived military gain for Germany is only an episode . . . , while the tremendous political gain of the USSR is a serious and lasting factor that is bound to form the basis for development of decisive military successes. . . .

"In case of a forced retreat of Red Army units, all rolling stock must be evacuated, to the enemy must not be left a single engine, a single railway car, nor a single pound of grain or a gallon of fuel.

"Collective farmers must drive off all their cattle and turn over their grain to the safekeeping of state authorities for transportation to the rear. All valuable property including nonferrous metals, grain, and fuel which cannot be withdrawn must without fail be destroyed.

"In areas occupied by the enemy, guerrilla units, mounted and foot, must be formed, diversionist groups must be organized to combat enemy troops, to foment guerrilla warfare everywhere, to blow up bridges, roads, damage telephone and telegraph lines, and to set fire to forests, stores, and transports.

"In occupied regions conditions must be hounded and annihilated at every step and all their measures frustrated.

"This war with Fascist Germany cannot be considered an ordinary war. It is not only a war between two armies, it is also a great war of the entire Soviet people against the German Fascist forces.

"The aim of this national war in defense of our country against the Fascist oppressors is . . . aid to all European peoples groaning under the yoke of German Fascism.

"In this war of liberation we shall not be alone.

"In this great war we shall have loyal allies in the peoples of Europe and America, including German people who are enslaved by Hitlerite despots.

"Our war for the freedom of our country will merge with the struggle of the peoples of Europe and America for their independence, democratic liberties. It will be a united front of peoples standing for freedom and against enslavement."

Speech of Joseph Stalin on July 3, 1941, quoted in Brian MacArthur (ed.), *The Penguin Book of Twentieth-Century Speeches* (New York: Viking, 1992).

As the war engulfed all of Europe,[3] German power at the end of 1941 was at its height, encompassing between 7 and 10 million soldiers, a superb air force, and a navy that included more than 150 submarines which would sink nearly 400 Allied ships in the summer of 1942. Italy added sizable forces that were especially important in Africa. And yet Axis dominance was short-lived.

TURNING POINTS

From the 1930s on, the fascist powers had held the initiative in politics, international relations, and war. Japan's attack on the United States in 1941 continued that pattern, but it also marked the beginning of a significant change. War in the Pacific made this a truly global war—involving Asia, the Middle East, and North Africa—and the addition of American power helped tip the balance toward the Allies. Axis propaganda was losing effect in the face of reality and the Allied claim to the humane traditions of Western civilization; and they now began to take the initiative as Russia, the Americas, and the British Empire set out to reconquer Europe.

The United States Enters the War Despite its deep partisanship for France and Britain, the United States had remained technically at peace, even as the American government sold weapons to private firms for transfer to Great Britain and traded 50 old American destroyers for the lease of British bases in the western Atlantic. The

[3]Only Sweden, Spain, Portugal, Switzerland, and Eire remained even technically neutral by grace of geography.

United States, which Roosevelt called "the arsenal of democracy," extended loans, first to Britain and then the Soviet Union; and in August, Churchill and Roosevelt met at sea to draft the Atlantic Charter, which envisioned a world "after the destruction of the Nazi tyranny" that included collective security and self-determination for all nations in which "all the men of all the lands may live out their lives in freedom from fear and want." Ideological commitment, however, did not bring the United States into the war.

Japan did that. Its attack on Manchuria in 1931 had been followed by a series of aggressive actions, from war with China starting in 1937 to the conquest of French Indochina in 1941. Tension between the United States and Japan increased with each new act of Japanese aggression, and America replied to the assault on Indochina with sanctions. Anticipating more, Japan gambled that the United States could be rendered nearly harmless in one blow, an attack on the American Pacific fleet at Pearl Harbor. The raid, on December 7, was devastating, and the United States declared it an act of war. All sides immediately recognized that the wars in Asia, Europe, and North Africa were one. Germany and Italy declared war

Map 29.2 THE HEIGHT OF AXIS POWER, 1942

▸ **American servicemen survey the ruins on an airfield at Pearl Harbor; the United States had entered the war.**

on the United States three days later. Unless the Allies were driven from the seas, the industrial and military power of the United States might make a decisive difference in a war fought around the world.

Stalingrad Winter snows raised the specter of a continuing two-front war, which Hitler had sworn to avoid. For all its losses, Russia's Red Army was intact; and its scorched-earth policy in retreat left the Germans little to live on. To secure its massive victories, Germany had to knock Russia out of the war. But the siege of Leningrad, the attacks on Moscow, and even a drive into southern Russia in the summer of 1942 that took Sevastopol (and desperately needed grain) did not accomplish that. The crucial battle of the Eastern front took place at Stalingrad (now Volgograd) from August to October 1942. A breakthrough for the Germans at that strategic center would open the way to the oilfields of southern Russia.

By September the Germans had penetrated the city and fighting continued from building to building. The heroic defense gave Russia time to amass more troops than the Germans thought were available, and in the meantime Germany's own supplies dwindled. A Russian counterattack encircled the German army, which Hitler frantically ordered to stand its ground. When it finally surrendered, in February 1943, less than one-third of its 300,000 men were left. The giant Russian pincers had cost the Germans more than half a million casualties. Stalingrad was the turning point of the war on the Eastern front.

Air Power and the Invasion of North Africa The Axis position in the West was eroding, too. The losses German submarines inflicted were less crippling after 1942, and Allied air supremacy extended to the continent, where thousands of tons of explosives were dropped on Germany each month in 1942, a rate that would increase fivefold in 1943. The Americans bombed strategic targets during the day; the British preferred nighttime area bombing, with a city itself as the target. The inferno created by the firebombing of Hamburg in 1943 was a horror to be exceeded two years later in a yet more massive raid that leveled Dresden, a cultural center without important industry. The Germans were unaware, of course, that in London the secret codes they believed unbreakable had been cracked as early as 1940, giving the Allies an advantage that would be more important as the war progressed.[4]

The Allies also regained control of the Mediterranean. The battle lines in North Africa had ebbed and flowed, as General Erwin Rommel, the German "desert fox," and Britain's General Bernard Montgomery parried each other's thrusts in the deserts between Libya and Egypt. In October 1942 the German *Afrikakorps* drove to El Alamein in Egypt but were defeated there. Then in November British and American forces conducted the largest amphibious action yet attempted, landing in Morocco and Algeria to attack the *Afrikakorps* from the west. The campaign was an important test of green American troops and of Allied coordination, under an American commander, General Dwight D. Eisenhower. It succeeded, and by May 1943 and after heavy losses, the Axis powers had been pushed out of Africa.

Shortly after the Japanese attack on Pearl Harbor, Roosevelt and Churchill had agreed to give priority to the war in Europe. The decision acknowledged the bonds of Western culture, the importance of European industrial power, and the fear that Russia might not long survive without massive help. After costly stands at Bataan and Corregidor, the United States lost the Philippine Islands early in 1942. Japan had the upper hand, but the situation in the Pacific began to stabilize in the course of 1942. A naval engagement in the Coral Sea in May brought no clear-cut victory to either side but reduced the immediate threat of further Japanese gains, and a Japanese attempt to invade Midway Island in June was driven off.

COMPETING POLITICAL SYSTEMS

War on this scale required the coordination of entire economies and cooperation from every sector of society. After their slow start, Britain and the United States achieved that with impressive effect. The Soviet Union proved far stronger than expected, and Germany, the state in theory most devoted to militarism, managed in practice less well than its enemies.

The Allies As bombs rained down on Britain, support there for the war effort was more nearly unanimous than in any other country in the world. Civilians accepted sacrifice and welcomed the end of unemployment, and the government commanded national resources as effectively as any in the world. The United States also mobilized its full economic resources, by the end of 1942 producing more war matériel than all its enemies combined. Ships, planes, arms, and munitions from American factories and food from American farms flowed across the oceans to Britain and the Soviet Union.

Even before 1939 Stalin had adopted the policy of industrializing the more backward regions east of the Urals, a safe distance from Russia's western border, and in the months preceding Hitler's attack in 1941 hundreds of factories were moved there piece by piece. Despite its enormous losses of productive capacity, the Soviet Union was able throughout the war to produce most of the military supplies it needed. Central planning, rationing, military discipline, and the employment of women were not such a dramatic change in this communist regime, but the acceptance of rationing, increased hours of labor, the destruction of homes, the death of loved ones, and the loss of men and territory required patriotism of a rather old-fashioned and bourgeois sort. Patri-

[4]The code was cracked in a project named Ultra, using devices that foreshadowed the computer. The secret of Ultra was not revealed until long after the war, and historians are still assessing its impact. The information the Allies gained through Ultra appears to have been especially important in the Battle of Britain, the protection of Atlantic shipping, later in the war in Egypt, and (above all) in the Normandy landing.

otism became the dominant theme of Soviet public life.

Nazi Rule Until 1943 German civilians did not experience hardships comparable to the sacrifices of the Soviets or the lowered standard of living of the British. Nor was German output much greater than at the war's outset. The illusion, fed by military success and propaganda, that the war would soon be over encouraged interim measures. Competing elements of the Nazi party and the government often worked at cross purposes, and distrust made it difficult for the Nazis to cooperate effectively with science and industry. Only when Albert Speer was given increased powers over the economy did coordination improve. In mid-July 1943 German production was twice what it had been in 1939, despite Allied bombing. A year later it was three times the prewar level.

Germany certainly benefited from its vast gains of territory rich in resources, industry, and manpower; but the system that took so naturally to ruthless conquest was less well adapted to ordinary life. The Nazis alienated those they conquered with their labor conscription, racial policies, and oppressive brutality. A high percentage of Ukrainians, for example, had welcomed liberation from Russian rule, but brief acquaintance with Nazis treatment of the "racially inferior" Slavs discouraged their cooperation. Nazi rule was most severe and most destructive in Eastern Europe, and less harsh among the "Aryan" populations of the Nordic lands. In France food rations provided only about half the minimum that decent health requires. Germany's most crucial need was for workers, and slave labor was an answer in accord with Nazi racial theory. About 1 million French workers, and eventually some 5 million Slavs, were shipped like cattle to labor in Germany. By 1944 the 8 million foreign workers in Germany constituted one-fifth of the work force.

Genocide The hysteria of racial hatred dominated rational planning. Brutalized and starving workers could hardly be efficient. Transporting and guarding slave laborers became an enormous, corrupting, and expensive enterprise. Hounding Jews and Gypsies and cramming Jews into ghettos, however, was less an extension of the war effort or of the brutality of war itself (the massacre of prisoners taken on the Eastern front may have been a precedent) than the implementation of Nazi racial theory. In 1942 a secret meeting of the regime's high officials escalated the terror of years into a formal systematic policy, "the final solution of the Jewish question"—extermination (*see box*, p. 973). By 1945, nearly 6 million Jews and probably as many others (Poles, Gypsies, and Magyars especially) had died in concentration camps like Auschwitz, Buchenwald, and Dachau. These camps were also supposed to be centers of production: A Krupp arms factory, an I. G. Farben chemical plant, and a coal mine were part of the Auschwitz complex. But the chief product of Auschwitz was corpses, at a rate that reached 12,000 a day.

The extermination camps remain the ultimate nightmare of modern history. Beating and torturing prisoners of war was not new, though rarely so common as under the Nazis, but the industrial organization of death in Nazi camps raises terrifying questions about modern civilization. Hundreds of thousands of people were involved in operating those camps and in rounding up men, women, and children to be shipped to them. At first, the victims were primarily Slavs and Jews from the conquered lands of Eastern Europe; then Jews from Western Europe were hunted down and added to the flow. They came by trainload, huddled in boxcars, hungry, thirsty, frightened, and confused. Upon arrival at the camps, the weakest and least "useful" were sent to showers that proved to be gas chambers. The others were given uniforms, often with patches that distinguished into neat categories the common criminals, political prisoners, homosexuals, Communists, Jehovah's Witnesses, Slavs, and Jews. Many were literally worked to death or were killed when they could work no longer. The prisoners themselves, reduced to blind survival, were caught up in this dehumanized world of beatings, limited rations, constant abuse, and contempt, in which gestures of cooperation or shrewd selfishness might gain another day of life. German clerks and bureaucrats kept elaborate records of names, stolen possessions, and corpses, which were efficiently stripped of gold fillings and useful hair before being turned to

A Crematorium

At a meeting of high Nazi officials on January 20, 1942, Reinard Heydrich, Plenipotentiary for the Preparation of the Final Solution of the European Jewish Question, spoke proudly of the liquidation of the Jews already accomplished and of the concentration camps already established but called for a further step. "We have the means, the methods, the organization, experience, and people. And we have the will. This is a historic moment in the struggle against Jewry. The Führer has declared his determination . . . [and sees destruction of the Jews] as exterminating fatal bacteria to save the organism. . . . We will work effectively but silently."

Nazi extermination camps indeed followed strikingly similar procedures, and the following description of the Birkenau camp is typical of hundreds of survivors' testimonies. It was written by a French doctor, André Lettich, who was a member of the "special commando" squad, whose job it was to empty the crematoria of corpses and make them ready for the next round.

"Until the end of January 1943, there were no crematoria in Birkenau. In the middle of a small birch forest, about two kilometres from the camp, was a peaceful looking house, where a Polish family had once lived before it had been either murdered or expelled. This cottage had been equipped as a gas chamber for a long time.

"More than five hundred metres further on were two barracks: the men stood on one side, the women on the other. They were addressed in a very polite and friendly way: 'You have been on a journey. You are dirty. You will take a bath. Get undressed quickly.' Towels and soap were handed out, and then suddenly the brutes woke up and showed their true faces: this horde of people, these men and women were driven outside with hard blows and forced both summer and winter to go the few hundred metres to the 'Shower Room'. Above the entry door was the word 'Shower'. One could even see shower heads on the ceiling which were cemented in but never had water flowing through them.

"These poor innocents were crammed together, pressed against each other. Then panic broke out, for at last they realised the fate in store for them. But blows with rifle butts and revolver shots soon restored order and finally they all entered the death chamber. The doors were shut and, ten minutes later, the temperature was high enough to facilitate the condensation of the hydrogen cyanide, for the condemned were gassed with hydrogen cyanide. This was the so-called 'Zyklon B', gravel pellets saturated with twenty per cent of hydrogen cyanide which was used by the German barbarians.

"Then, *SS Unterscharführer* Moll threw the gas in through a little vent. One could hear fearful screams, but a few moments later there was complete silence. Twenty to twenty-five minutes later, the doors and windows were opened to ventilate the rooms and the corpses were thrown at once into pits to be burnt. But, beforehand the dentists had searched every mouth to pull out the gold teeth. The women were also searched to see if they had not hidden jewelry in the intimate parts of their bodies, and their hair was cut off and methodically placed in sacks for industrial purposes."

From J. Noakes and G. Pridham (eds.), *Nazism, 1919–1945: A History in Documents and Eyewitness Accounts*, vol. II (New York: Schocken Books, 1988).

ashes that could be used as fertilizer. Doctors invented new tortures under the guise of medical experiments to benefit the Aryan race. Yet even the SS guards—like the camp commandants, the people who arranged for trains, and the businessmen who bid for contracts to build gas ovens—employed euphemisms rather than acknowledge what was really happening. The

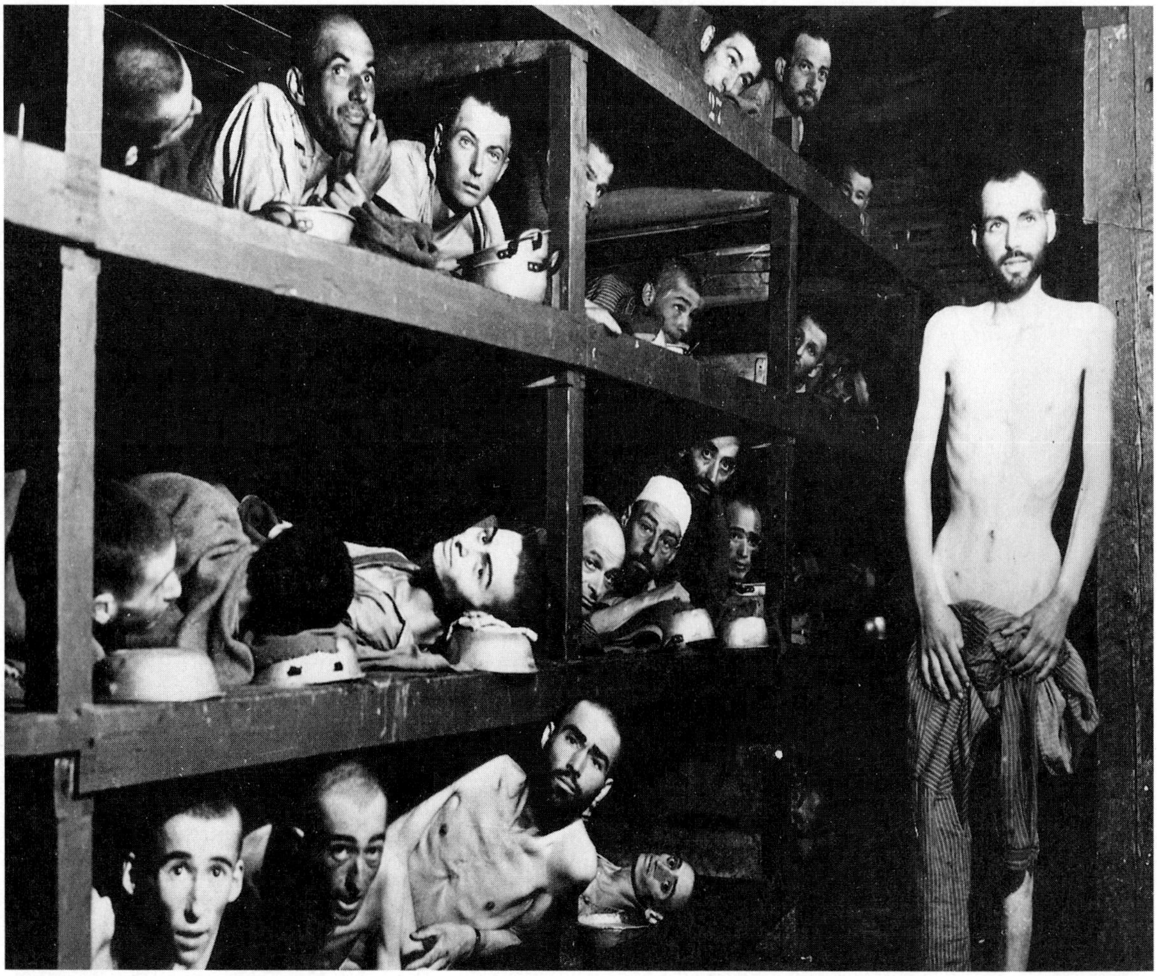

▸ **The laborers' barracks at Buchenwald at the end of the war.**

residents of nearby towns rarely discussed what was carried in the trains rumbling by or asked about the odor that settled over the countryside from crematoria smokestacks. Nor did the Allies quite believe or choose to act on the stories that filtered out of Germany about atrocities on a scale too terrible to comprehend.

Resistance Movements Millions of Europeans came to rely on the British Broadcasting Corporation for news and for encouragement in occupied lands, where every act of opposition took on symbolic significance. Gradually, against great odds, organized resistance movements formed. Some developed around neighborhood groups; many were connected to prewar political parties. Always composed of a small minority, these partisan movements achieved particular strength in Denmark and Norway, the Netherlands, France, and Yugoslavia. Many of them received material aid and guidance from governments-in-exile operating from London, the most notable being the Free French, headed by General de Gaulle.

Nazis reprisals for acts of resistance were meant to be horrible. When Czechs assassinated the new Reich Protector of Bohemia and Moravia in June 1942, the Germans retaliated by wiping out the village of Lidice, which they suspected of hiding the murderers: Every man was killed; every woman and child deported. On a single day in 1943, the Germans put 1400 men to death in a Greek village. Hundreds of towns across occupied Europe had their memorials, a burned-out building or a ditch where clusters of civilians had been massacred.

Yet the underground movements continued to grow, and their actions became a barometer of the course of the war. In France, partisan activities expanded from single exploits—smuggling Allied airmen out of the country, dynamiting a bridge, or attacking individual German officers—to large-scale operations closely coordinated from London. Norway's resistance helped force the Germans to keep 300,000 troops there and away from more active fronts. In Yugoslavia, two groups of partisans maintained an active guerrilla war, although the British decision to support the group led by Tito all but ensured his control of the country at the end of the war. After the Allied invasion of Italy, partisan groups there maintained an unnerving harassment of Fascist and Nazi forces. Even in Germany itself some members of the army and the old aristocracy began to plot against Hitler, and in July 1944 a group of conspirators planted a bomb under the table as the Führer conducted a conference with his staff. Hitler escaped serious injury, but the sense that he was doomed had spread to the heart of Germany.

ALLIED STRATEGY

By 1943 the Axis was on the defensive but had the advantage of holding contiguous territory with direct lines of supply. The Allies continued to disagree as to how they should attack Hitler's "fortress Europe." Russia had repeatedly urged opening a second front on the continent, and most of the American military command favored an immediate invasion. The British warned against the high cost of such an invasion, and with Roosevelt's support, Churchill prevailed. Instead, the Allies successfully invaded North Africa, ending the threat to Egypt. When that was not followed by landings on the continent, the Russians suspected that they and the Germans were being left to annihilate each other. The Americans, too, now favored an attack on the mainland, but the British argued for tightening the blockade of Germany and for making more limited assaults in the eastern Mediterranean and on what Churchill called the "soft underbelly" of southern Europe.

More than military strategy was at stake. The Allies, who said less about their long-range goals than they had during World War I, were divided. Stalin looked forward to regaining the Polish territory lost in 1939 (Poland could be compensated with territory taken from a defeated Germany). The British correctly warned that that would be unacceptable to the Americans and hoped to place Anglo-American troops where they could

▸ **The scene that greeted the Allies on entering Lansberg concentration camp. American forces required several hundred German civilians in the area to come look at it as well.**

have a voice after the war in the disposition of Eastern Europe, for they recalled the earlier communist aim of revolution across the continent (and the aim of imperial Russia before that for expansion into Eastern Europe). In London the exiled leaders of the Eastern European countries agitated for their own nationalist goals, alarmed by Stalin's references to the need for "friendly" governments along Russia's borders.

The Casablanca Conference and the Fall of Italy With such issues before them, Roosevelt and Churchill met at Casablanca in January 1943. There they decided (to the Russians' disgust) to invade Sicily and agreed to demand the unconditional surrender of Italy and Germany, an expression of moral outrage against fascism that was meant as well to prevent the Soviet Union and the Western Allies from making any separate deals with the enemy. Welcomed by public opinion among the Allies, the refusal to negotiate with the Axis was subsequently criticized for strengthening their desperate defense after defeat was inevitable.

In July a mammoth amphibious assault carried Anglo-American forces into Sicily. A victim of his own propaganda, Mussolini had consistently overestimated Italian strength. As the invaders advanced, the Fascist Grand Council in a secret session voted Mussolini out of office. The duce was arrested, and Marshal Pietro Badoglio was named prime minister. A coalition of monarchists and moderate Fascists then sought an armistice. But Committees of National Liberation had sprung up throughout Italy; composed of anti-Fascists from liberals to Communists, these Committees wanted nothing to do with Badoglio, a Fascist hero who had led the campaign in Ethiopia, or with the king, who had bowed to Mussolini for 20 years. Again the Allies were divided. Britain favored the monarchy and feared leftist influence in the Committees. The Americans leaned toward the Committees but agreed that the Russians should be excluded from the Allied military government that would be installed in Italy. Stalin accepted that decision, knowing that arguments about spheres of influence would be useful to Russia elsewhere; and he encouraged Italy's Communists to be flexible in cooperating with the arrangements the Anglo-Americans preferred.

In September Allied forces landed in southern Italy, where they were well entrenched by the end of the month. The German army, however, had snatched control of the rest of the peninsula. Although the Allies captured Naples in October, their campaign in Italy soon bogged down in difficult terrain and in the face of fierce German resistance. In a daring rescue, German paratroops snatched Mussolini from prison and took him to northern Italy, where he proclaimed a Fascist republic that was blatantly a German puppet. As Italy's anti-Fascist partisans became effective, Italians, their country a battleground for foreign armies, were caught in civil war.

The Teheran Conference Italy was not the first place in which the Allies indicated they might compromise with tainted regimes. At the time of the North African invasion, Admiral Jean François Darlan, a former vice premier of Vichy France and commander of its armed forces, had happened to be in Algiers. Eisenhower's staff had quickly agreed to make him governor-general of French Africa provided his forces would not resist the Allied invasion. De Gaulle had been outraged. He had claimed to represent a free France since his first call for continued resistance in 1940 and his organization, from London, of French forces that fought with the Allies. His hauteur, his insistence on a voice in Allied policy, and his success in winning support in the French colonies had made his relations with Britain and the United States difficult at best. The assassination of Darlan in December 1942 eased the situation some, but the British and Americans had continued to deal with the Vichy regime even after the Germans, in response to the North African invasion, occupied all of France. Now, watching events in Italy, Europe's governments-in-exile shared Stalin's concerns about Allied policy.

Finally, in December 1943, Roosevelt, Churchill, and Stalin met for the first time, at Teheran. The conversations were not easy. Previously, the British had mediated between the United States and the Soviet Union, but now the Americans took a middle position. They reached a tentative understanding that Russia would accept a

Stalin, Roosevelt, and Churchill, meeting for the first time at Teheran, reached an understanding that laid the groundwork for Allied cooperation in pursuing the war.

boundary with Poland similar to the one proposed in 1919, and they left open the question of what kind of government a liberated Poland might have. Their unity thus preserved by postponing the most difficult issues, the Allies could plan vigorous prosecution of the war. Stalin promised to declare war on Japan as soon as Germany surrendered, and Churchill's proposal for an invasion of the Dardanelles was rejected. The British and Americans agreed instead to land in France in the following year.

THE ROAD TO VICTORY

The Allies progressed slowly in Italy, taking five months to fight their way past a costly new beachhead at Anzio. In December 1943, King Victor Emmanuel III announced he would abdicate in favor of his son, and Badoglio gave way to a cabinet drawn from members of the Committees of National Liberation. Italy then officially joined the Allies; and the slow push northward, while the main Allied forces were held for the invasion of France, was aided by partisan risings against Nazi occupation. On one mountain ridge after another the Germans held the advantage of entrenched positions. Only in May 1944 did Allied armies finally seize the old Benedictine abbey of Monte Cassino, north of Naples, after a destructive bombardment. Rome, the first European capital to be liberated, fell in June. German resistance converged on the so-called Gothic Line, running from Pisa to Rimini. Not until it was pierced in September 1944, after months of bloody fighting, could further drives lead to the capture of Ravenna (in December) and Bologna, Verona, and Genoa (in April 1945). By then German resistance had ceased.

The Russian Front Russia's successes were more spectacular. In the spring of 1943, the Ger-

Map 29.3 **THE ALLIED VICTORY IN WORLD WAR II**

mans could still launch an offensive of their own, but it slowed within weeks. In July the Russian army began a relentless advance that continued, with few setbacks, for almost two years. With armies now superior in numbers and matériel, Soviet forces reached the Dnieper and Kiev by November. In February 1944 they were at the Polish border. They retook the Crimea in the spring, Romania surrendered in August, and Finland and Bulgaria fell a few weeks later.

The Western Front For months Germany was subjected to constant pounding from the air, and the Germans knew an invasion across the English Channel was imminent. They believed it would come in the area around Calais, the shore closest to England, as a series of calculated feints seemed to indicate. Instead, on June 6, 1944, the Allies landed in Normandy. The largest amphibious landing in history, it put 150,000 men ashore within two days, supported by 5000 ships and 1500 tanks. In a complex series of landings made possible by overwhelming control of the air and aided by a poorly coordinated German defense, but effected only with heavy loses, Eisenhower's Allied force poured onto the French beaches. More than a million men disembarked within a few months. In July they broke through the German defense and began a series of rapid drives through France. A second amphibious attack, in southern France in mid-August, led to swift advances inland that were greatly aided by well-organized French resistance groups. On August 24 the Parisian underground rose against the Germans, and French forces under Charles de Gaulle quickly entered the cheering city. Brussels fell a week later, and 10 days after that, American troops crossed the German frontier.

Germany had launched a "miracle" weapon in June, the relatively ineffective V-1 pilotless plane, and it was followed in September by the far more dangerous V-2 rocket. Had the Nazis recognized its potential earlier, the effects might have been devastating. The V-2 flew faster than the speed of sound and was almost impossible to intercept; but these rockets were hard to aim, and were too few and too late to be decisive. More threatening was a counterstroke through the Ardennes in December that rocked the Allied line back. The Battle of the Bulge, the last offensive the Germans would mount, cost about 70,000 men on each side before the Allies regained the initiative in January 1945.

The Yalta Conference When Allied leaders held their last wartime meeting, at Yalta in February 1945, Russian troops occupied part of Czechoslovakia and stood on the German frontier of Poland. The decisions of the Big Three at Yalta, which were widely hailed at the time, later became the most controversial of World War II. The hurried meeting dealt with four broad issues, each a measure of the Allies' mutual distrust.

They agreed to the creation of a United Nations Organization. The Soviet Union asked for 16 votes, one for each of its republics, to counterbalance the votes of the British Commonwealth and of Latin America, which the United States was expected to dominate. That request was reduced to 3, and the veto demanded by the Soviet Union was restricted slightly. Russia

Charles de Gaulle, the epitome of French resistance, greeted by Parisians on the day of the city's liberation in August 1944.

promised to declare war against Japan within 90 days of Germany's defeat in return for the territories it had surrendered to Japan in 1905 and a sphere of influence in Manchuria. A more contentious issue was the treatment of Germany. Each of the Big Three was assigned a zone of occupation, and Russia reluctantly agreed to a zone for France as well. Russia's demands for huge reparations and "labor services" were so troubling that specific terms had to be postponed. The creation of new governments for the liberated nations, the most difficult issue of all, could not be postponed much longer; yet every proposal exposed fundamental differences between the Soviet Union and the Western powers. The form of Italy's government was in fact now largely set, as was de Gaulle's ascendance in an independent France. The main issue was Soviet dominance in Eastern Europe.

In most of the countries they occupied, the Russians were tolerating broad coalitions that included all the old antifascist parties, but the Soviets would not allow a role for the Western powers, even restricting Allied observers. When Churchill had visited Moscow four months earlier, he had proposed a division of interests: The Soviet Union would have predominance in Romania and the largest influence in Bulgaria, Britain would have a free hand in Greece, and the two powers would recognize their equal interests in Yugoslavia and Hungary. Such crude understandings, however, offered few guarantees, though Stalin remained silent when Britain inter-

▶ In February 1944 an American sergeant who spoke German, believing he faced six or seven Germans, called on them to surrender—56 came forward.

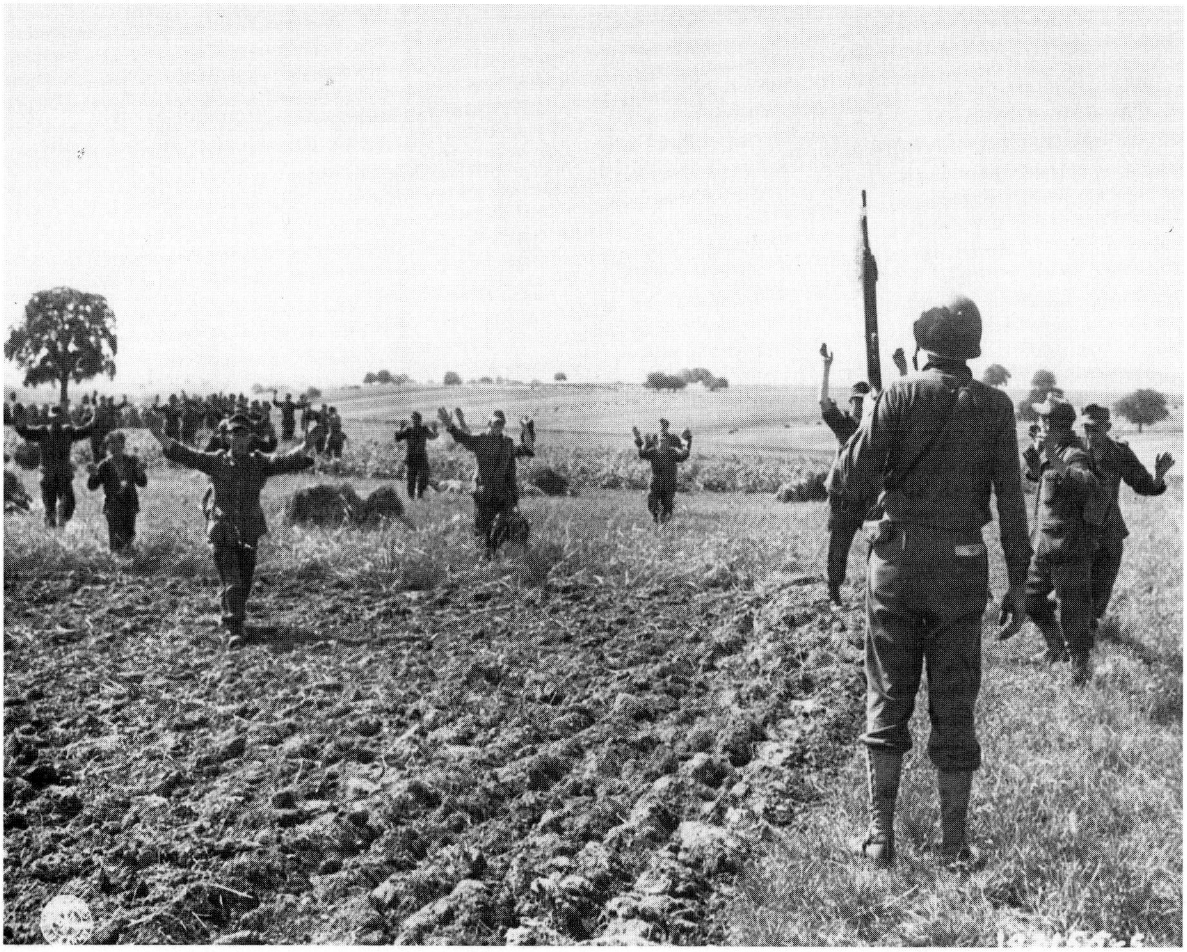

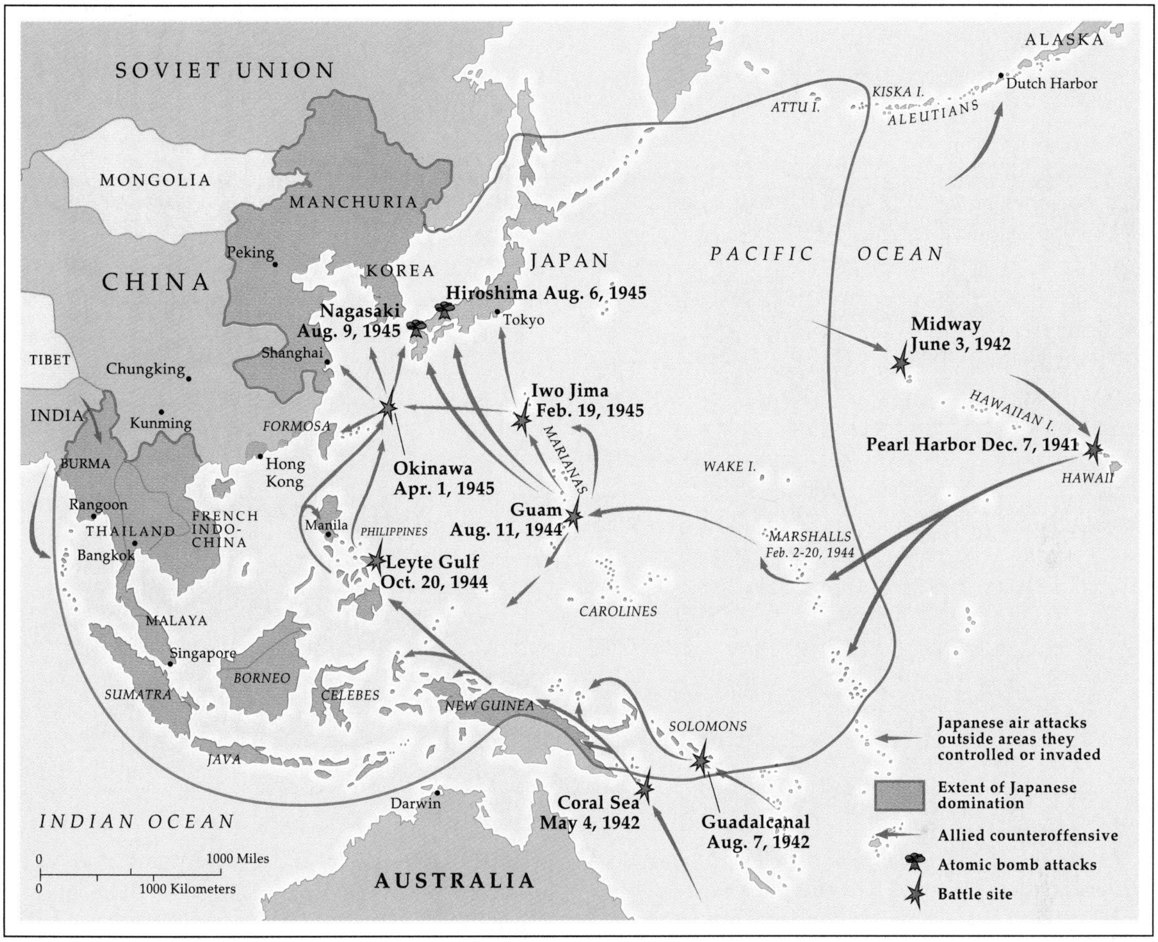

Map 29.4 **World War II in the Pacific**

vened in the civil war raging in Greece to rout the leftists. Stalin had exercised his own free hand in Poland after the Polish underground arose against the Germans in August 1944. As Soviet troops approached Warsaw, the Russians simply halted their advance until the Germans had wiped out the resistance fighters, who were closely tied to the anti-Communist Polish government in London. Cynically drawn spheres of influence were in fact not adopted at the Yalta Conference, but the conference's formulas, with their references to democratic governments and free elections, would in the end be interpreted by those with guns.

The Final Months As the Allies pushed into Germany from all sides, it became clear that Berlin would be the final battleground. Fearing that Hitler planned a last desperate stand at his mountain retreat at Berchtesgaden, in the south German mountains, Eisenhower halted the eastward advance of American and British armies at the Elbe River. The Russians took Berlin, where Hitler had ordered a defense to the death, thus ensuring the maximum destruction of the capital. The Führer committed suicide on April 30, 1945; his aides burned his body, which has never been found. Four days later a group of German officers signed the final unconditional surrender. The war in Europe was over.

World conflict would continue in Asia for four months more. It was expected to last much longer, even with the Russian help that had seemed so necessary at Yalta. Despite massive bombing and repeated naval victories, Allied progress toward Japan through the islands and

▸ **Hiroshima, the victim of one of science's great achievements. The world had entered a new era of warfare, and for a generation the Japanese would suffer from the environmental destruction and the effects of radiation.**

jungles of the Pacific had been laborious and bloody. During the three months following Germany's surrender, air raids obliterated Japan's navy, industrial plants, and large parts of its cities: Nearly 200,000 people were killed in Tokyo in just one week. But still the Japanese would not surrender.

On August 6 the new president of the United States, Harry Truman (Roosevelt had died in April), authorized the use of a new weapon that had been developed after years of secret research, the atomic bomb. In one blow, half of the city of Hiroshima disappeared from the face of the earth, and a quarter of its 320,000 inhabitants were killed. On August 9 the Americans dropped an even more powerful atomic bomb on the city of Nagasaki. The Soviet Union declared war on Japan on August 8; and on September 2, 1945, Japan surrendered unconditionally. The atomic bomb, an extraordinary achievement of science and technology made possible by great wealth and scores of European scientists driven to sanctuary in the United States, permitted a great democracy to end World War II by unleashing a new order of terror upon humanity. Later, many would question the morality of using so terrible a weapon; and even in the jubilation of victory, leaders reordering a shattered world now knew that another war might bring the end of civilization.

III. The Reconstruction of Europe

For years Europeans would have to deal with the effects of death, destruction, and the displacement of millions of people. Overcoming such fundamental problems on so vast a scale was the central achievement of the next decade and the sober preoccupation of individuals, institutions, and governments. Even among the victors and newly liberated, euphoria was brief as people set about their daily tasks in an uncertain world of economic hardship, social dislocation, and political division.

IMMEDIATE PROBLEMS

The Devastation In contrast to World War I, a majority of the fatalities in World War II were civilian. For every soldier killed, two were either wounded or taken captive. But civilian losses are harder to categorize than those of soldiers, and often there was no one to do the counting. The Germans murdered more than 12 million people in concentration camps, half of them Jews; and across Europe millions more civilians died just for being where armies chose to bomb or shell or shoot. In all, the European casualties in World War II were five or six times greater than in World War I (only for Britain and France were they lower). The Soviet Union lost about 20 million people; Poland, about 6 million (including 3 million Jews); Germany, nearly 5 million. So the total European casualties of World War II—dead, wounded, or crippled by inhumane treatment—remain an estimate, a number hard to comprehend in its gruesome total or ghostly imprecision: some 45 to 55 million people.

Europe's industrial capability in 1945 was perhaps half what it had been in 1939; and only parts of such major cities as Frankfurt, Dresden, Brest, and Toulon were still standing. The continent's most important ports, bridges, and rail lines had been all but destroyed. Agriculture was also hard hit. Large areas of farmland in France, Italy, and Germany could not be cultivated; the number of cattle in France had been reduced by half. In the winter of 1945–1946, starvation was a threat in many places, and in some, such as Vienna, thousands died of famine. Disease was an ever-present danger, too, although penicillin helped limit the epidemics that erupted. The rationing of food and clothes (and black markets selling illegally) continued in many countries into the 1950s, and Europeans looked to the United States and the Soviet Union for relief as Allied troops occupied the continent.

In addition to the millions without jobs or housing, there were more refugees in Europe than ever before in history. Some 8 million slave laborers in the Third Reich and millions in concentration camps were put on trains headed back to where their homes had been. There were German prisoners of war and Allied prisoners in Germany. More than 7 million Soviet citizens in Germany, included defectors, had no place to go. Some 2 million Poles and Czechs returning from prison in the Soviet Union joined millions of Ukrainians and Poles who moved west to stay on the other side of the shifting border with Russia. Romanians drove out Hungarians; Czechs expelled Hungarians and Germans. Millions of Germans whom the Nazis had transplanted to Poland in the interests of Germanization were forced to leave, and many of the 1.5 million Poles the Nazis had evicted wanted to go back home. The question of where national boundaries should be drawn, which had so troubled the peacemakers of Versailles, was settled now by first drawing the lines and then pushing inconvenient nationalities across them.

Most of those who carried their few belongings along unfamiliar roads were civilians, perhaps 60 million in all, a majority of them women and children, who had lost their homes and livelihood. Separated from kin and possessions, they struggled to survive in strange lands that were impoverished by war. We will never know how many died or were abused or robbed. Governments tried to make nice distinctions between the homeless (those in or near their own country) and displaced persons (who were mostly stateless—some 12 million were so registered in 1945), and they tried to separate criminals from others. Abandoned factories and warehouses, even former concentration camps, were used to house refugees. When facilities were specially built, they were usually crude barracks without plumbing or electricity and were meant to be temporary. Bit by bit the fortunate were assigned a destination, but "unaccompanied children," the disabled, and the aged were harder to place. In 1960, 15 years after the war had ended, there were still

32,000 refugees in 107 camps in Europe, sharing tiny quarters and communal toilets.

THE POLITICAL FRAMEWORK

There was no great peace conference after World War II. When the leaders of the Soviet Union, Great Britain, and the United States met at Potsdam for two weeks in July 1945, they hardly knew each other. President Harry Truman had been in office only three months following the death of Roosevelt, and in the midst of the meeting Clement Attlee replaced Churchill, who had been defeated in the British elections.

The Peace Terms The Potsdam meeting outlined the future of Germany but left details for the future. The Allies readily agreed that all Nazi institutions must be abolished, German arms production prohibited, and German industry controlled. Democracy and free speech were to be restored. In the meantime Germany was divided into four zones of occupation, and so was Berlin, isolated in the Soviet zone. Germany's eastern border was moved westward to the Oder and Neisse rivers, enlarging Poland. During the next year, the foreign ministers of the four principal Allies (now including France) drafted treaties for the other defeated states, but their meetings soon became a forum for quarrels between the Russians and the other three. Italy, Romania, Hungary, Bulgaria, and Finland each ceded minor territories to its neighbors. Austria, like Germany, remained divided into four occupied zones and without a formal treaty. The Potsdam conference had also laid down the terms for peace with Japan. The Soviet Union would get some territory, and the European nations would regain their Asian colonies. But the prime beneficiaries were China and, above all, the United States, whose troops were to occupy Japan and which already held most of the strategic islands in the Pacific.

Within Europe, the first concern was to root out fascism. In countries the Nazis had occupied, there were summary executions of collaborators and some public prosecutions, notably in France, where Pierre Laval and Marshal Pétain were tried. In Germany itself, however, the numbers involved made de-Nazification difficult. Millions of forms were filled out and hundreds of trials held, but the drive against former Nazis soon waned. Determined to establish some lasting standard, the Allies created an international tribunal to try Hitler's closest associates for crimes against humanity. The trials, held in Nuremberg in 1945 and 1946, were also intended to inform the German people of the full horror of Nazi rule. The appalling revelations of those solemn hearings were followed by restrained judgments—only 12 of the 22 prime defendants were condemned to death, and 3 were acquitted.

International Agencies The belief in international law that underlay the Nuremberg trials and the United Nations Organization was tempered by a determination to learn from the past. This peace would not be punitive; and devastated nations, defeated enemies as well as those liberated from German rule, must be helped. Even before the UN had its charter; its first agency, the United Nations Relief and Rehabilitation Administration, had been created late in 1943. UNRRA played a major role in the reconstruction of postwar Europe, organizing relief of food and medical supplies and coordinating international loans. To avoid the dangerous inflation that had followed World War I, a conference at Bretton Woods, New Hampshire, in 1944 created the International Monetary Fund and an International Bank for Reconstruction and Development. Those institutions, with nearly $20 billion in assets, furthered reconstruction and capital investment by supporting stable currencies.

But the main instrument of peace was to be the United Nations, and a few months after the Yalta meeting, 51 countries had approved the United Nations Charter at a special conference held in San Francisco. The charter established a General Assembly of all members to determine policy; a decision-making Security Council of 11 nations to supervise "the maintenance of international peace"; and various economic, social, and legal agencies. Permanent Security Council seats were reserved for the United States, the Soviet Union, China, Great Britain, and France, each with a right to veto any Council action; the remaining six seats were filled by election from among the other member states.

▸ Göring, Hess, and von Ribbentrop (the first three on the left in the prison's dock) listen to the proceedings at the beginning of the Nuremberg trial for war crimes.

The presence of the United States and the Soviet Union in the UN was a promising contrast to the League of Nations, but their conflicts soon dominated international relations. Germany was in effect divided in two, with the eastern part under Soviet occupation; and within the UN, Russia and the United States competed for the support of the nations of Asia, Africa, and Latin America that were not yet formally tied to one of the two major blocs. Although Britain and France were on the Security Council and Scandinavians served as the UN's general secretaries until 1961, the United Nations reflected a redistribution of international power in which Europe was no longer dominant.

THE DIVISION BETWEEN EAST AND WEST

Everywhere liberation opened a battle for domestic power. Communists had played a leading part in resistance movements, and their prestige was high. Initially they joined in the general demand for democracy and social justice. On one issue after another, however, communists and socialists soon found themselves in bitter conflict with the center and the right. As each side fought for power, the lines between them hardened and their conflicts became part of the larger competition between the Soviet Union and the United States.

Eastern Europe: Puppet Regimes Soviet troops occupied Eastern Europe from the Adriatic to the Baltic. Three formerly independent states—Estonia, Latvia, and Lithuania—became Soviet re-

Churchill Sees an Iron Curtain

On March 5, 1946, Winston Churchill gave a speech at Westminster College in Fulton, Missouri, that immediately received worldwide attention. After years of official emphasis on the cooperation among the wartime Allies, its directness was shocking. In effect, it announced the Cold War.

"A shadow has fallen upon the scenes so lately lighted by the Allied victory. Nobody knows what Soviet Russia and its Communist international organization intends to do in the immediate future, or what are the limits, if any, to their expansive and proselytizing tendencies. I have a strong admiration and regard for the valiant Russian people and for my wartime comrade, Marshal Stalin. There is deep sympathy and goodwill in Britain—and I doubt not here also—towards the peoples of all the Russias and a resolve to persevere through many differences and rebuffs in establishing lasting friendships. We understand the Russian need to be secure on her western frontiers by the removal of all possibility of German aggression. We welcome Russia to her rightful place among the leading nations of the world. We welcome her flag upon the seas. Above all, we welcome constant, frequent and growing contacts between the Russian people and our own people on both sides of the Atlantic. It is my duty, however, for I am sure you would wish me to state the facts as I see them to you, to place before you certain facts about the present position in Europe.

"From Stettin in the Baltic to Trieste in the Adriatic, an iron curtain has descended across the Continent. Behind that line lie all the capitals of the ancient states of Central and Eastern Europe. Warsaw, Berlin, Prague, Vienna, Budapest, Belgrade, Bucharest and Sofia, all these famous cities and the populations around them lie in what I must call the Soviet sphere, and all are subject in one form or another, not only to Soviet influence but to a very high and, in many cases, increasing measure of control from Moscow.

". . . An attempt is being made by the Russians in Berlin to build up a quasi-Communist party in their zone of Occupied Germany by showing special favours to groups of left-wing German leaders. At the end of the fighting last June, the American and British Armies withdrew westwards, in accordance with an earlier agreement, to a depth at some points of one hundred and fifty miles upon a front of nearly four hundred miles, in order to allow our Russian allies to occupy this vast expanse of territory which the Western Democracies had conquered.

"If now the Soviet Government tries, by separate action, to build up a pro-Communist Germany in their areas, this will cause new serious difficulties in the British and American zones, and will give the defeated Germans the power of putting themselves up to auction between the Soviets and the Western Democracies. Whatever conclusions may be drawn from these facts—and facts they are—this is certainly not the Liberated Europe we fought to build up. Nor is it one which contains the essentials of permanent peace."

Reprinted in Brian MacArthur, *The Penguin Book of Twentieth-Century Speeches* (New York: Viking, 1992) and available in many other places.

publics; and Russia annexed territory from East Prussia, Poland, Hungary, and Romania. In the ostensibly autonomous states of Eastern Europe, the Soviets discouraged independent revolutions like those that followed World War I but skillfully used social issues and crude coercion to establish friendly governments. Then leading anti-Communists would be excluded from the governing coalition; and later a campaign of propaganda, pressure, and sudden arrests would eliminate the non-Communist parties from power until a single-party dictatorship on the Soviet model had consolidated its position with purge trials and secret police (*see box* above).

With Soviet production at less than two-thirds of its prewar level, the Five-Year Plan announced in 1946 openly depended on the ransacking of East Germany and the other occupied areas for materials. In the eastern zone of Germany, the Soviet Union followed the same procedures effective in the states of Eastern Europe. Early in 1946 the Russians forced a merger of East Germany's Social Democratic party with the smaller Communist party, and Soviet control was soon complete. After expropriating much of German industry and restricting trade with the West, the Russians gradually allowed the eastern zone to increase its industrial activity and granted it independent status in 1949 as the German Democratic Republic.

In Romania the Communists forced King Michael into exile late in 1947. Poland, where the Communists were weakest, had been promised free elections. When these were held in 1947, repressive measures against the minority Peasant party left the Independent Socialists with an overwhelming majority. In a few months the Peasant party was purged, the Catholic Church persecuted, the Independent Socialist party subordinated to the communist Workers' party, and a Russian placed in command of the army.

Czechoslovakia had a notable democratic tradition, and the president and the foreign minister, Eduard Beneš and Jan Masaryk, were its heirs. But in 1948, the Communists, the largest party, threatened to take over the country with Russian support. Beneš gave way, and Masaryk died in a mysterious fall from a window. Hungary's coalition government had an anti-Communist majority until a dubious election in 1949 gave the Communists control. In each case Britain and the United States protested, with little effect, and the new regimes established close links with the Soviet Union. Albania and Bulgaria became solid members of the Communist bloc by 1950.

Only Yugoslavia followed a different course. Marshal Tito easily won the 1945 national election, and the Communists dominated the government; but Tito resisted Soviet efforts to influence his foreign and domestic policies. After having joined the Cominform, which had replaced the Comintern and was similarly designed to coordinate international Communist activity, Yugoslavia broke with its neighbors in 1948, using ties with the West to resist economic and political pressure from the East—an example to others of how small states could use the tense balance between the superpowers.

Western Europe: The Politics of the Past Despite their altered circumstances, most Western countries returned to prewar patterns of parliamentary life, although Spain and Portugal remained defiant dictatorships. The governments of the Low Countries and Scandinavia established much-admired social programs. Women now voted nearly everywhere and contributed their voice to heightened concern with social issues. Generally, reconstruction took precedence over reform. West Germany's federal structure and two dominant parties, the Christian Democrats and the Social Democrats, recalled the pre-Nazi Weimar Republic. Ironically, at war's end Germany's industry was in better shape than that of any other nation, and the Allies soon relaxed restrictions on its economic activity. Early in 1949 they acknowledged the ad hoc division of Germany and recognized its western sections as the Federal Republic of Germany. For the next 14 years, West Germany's chancellor was Konrad Adenauer, the head of the Christian Democrats. Mayor of Cologne from 1917 to 1933, he was 73 years old in 1949, a firm and conservative leader closely allied with the United States, who promoted an atmosphere of efficient calm.

In France, the new Fourth Republic looked much like the Third. Political life was shaped by three large parties—the Communists, the Socialists, and a new Catholic party of the left, the MRP (Popular Republican Movement). They wrote a constitution that kept the executive subordinate to the legislature as it had been before and soon pushed the domineering de Gaulle from office as provisional president. The nation was in fact effectively engaged in the enormous effort of reconstruction; but unstable governments, Communist intransigence, and labor agitation won more popular attention and spurred a revival of de Gaulle's popularity and disillusionment with the Fourth Republic.

Italy, too, became a republic, when more than 54 percent of the electorate voted to replace the monarchy in 1946. Governments were dominated by the Christian Democrats, a party that was in itself a coalition held together primarily by opposition to the Communists. Alcide De Gasperi, the party's leader from 1945 to 1953, was prime minister during most of that period. A wily politician, he ostracized the Communists—the largest Communist party in the West—and took advantage of a split among Socialists to bring Italy into close alliance with the United States. The Christian Democrats won the crucial elections of 1948, aided by extensive American pressure, and launched a program of moderate reform, including efforts to revitalize the economy of southern Italy and stimulate industry in the north. Italian politics had returned to the unheroic tradition of parliamentary deals that the Fascists had overturned, and De Gasperi's skillful maneuvering

Map 29.5 THE COLD WAR OF THE 1950S

among diverse interests set a pattern that would last for nearly 50 years.

In many respects, postwar politics brought greater change to Great Britain than to the new regimes on the continent. Churchill's defeat in the elections of 1945 was a turning away from wartime unity and sacrifice. With an enormous majority, the Labour party under Clement Attlee launched a massive program of nationalization, taking over the Bank of England and a wide range of major industries, including coal, transportation, electricity, and iron and steel. It also instituted extensive welfare programs and established public housing, national insurance, and free medical care for all. True to its principles, the Labour government also began the withdrawal from the empire to which men like Churchill had been so attached, granting India independence in 1947.

Cold War In 1947 distrust between the Soviet Union and the United States hardened into a worldwide military, political, and ideological conflict quickly dubbed the Cold War. As Russia tightened its grip on Eastern Europe, the American president announced the Truman Doctrine, promising military and economic aid to nations in danger of communist takeover. His immediate concern was civil war in Greece and Turkey, where local communists were aided by neighboring Yugoslavia. Britain, which up to that point had provided the countervailing force against the communists, declared it could no longer sustain its military power and influence in the eastern Mediterranean, and the United States was taking over. Money and supplies poured into Greece, and this American response, combined with Yugoslavia's break with Russia, enabled the Greek government to crush the opposition by 1949. Turkey, slowly moving toward democracy, received similar assistance. Opposition to communism and Soviet influence, understood to operate as an international conspiracy, had become the focus of American policy.

A few months after the announcement of the Truman Doctrine, Secretary of State George Marshall unveiled an imaginative plan to stimulate European recovery—and overcome the European economic crisis in which communism seemed likely to prosper. The United States would offer massive economic aid to all nations still recovering from the war. Russia forbade the Eastern European states from participating in the American program and established its own Council of Mutual Economic Assistance (Comecon) instead. Communist parties throughout the West opposed the Marshall Plan despite its obvious benefits to recovering nations, and the United States encouraged the isolation of the Communists, who were excluded from coalition governments in France and Italy in 1947 and from all government positions in Switzerland in 1950. West Germany banned the party itself in 1956. The two halves of Europe followed the lead of their powerful patrons.

Fear of the growing German economy and America's support for anticommunist movements everywhere stimulated Russia's tightening hold over the satellite states in Eastern Europe. Believing that Berlin was becoming a dangerous outpost of Western power, the Soviet Union suddenly closed off overland access to the former German capital. War seemed imminent. The United States responded with an extraordinary airlift: For nearly a year a steady stream of flights ferried in all West Berlin's supplies. By the time the Soviets backed down, Germany had officially become two separate states, one on each side of the Cold War.

When the Soviet Union tested its own atomic bomb in 1949, the United States saw it as a direct challenge. Truman announced that work was under way on the even more devastating hydrogen bomb. But the loss of a monopoly on atomic weapons made ground forces seem essential to deter Soviet aggression without resorting to atomic war. Consequently, in 1949 the North Atlantic Treaty Organization (NATO) was created to coordinate the military planning of the United States, Canada, and 10 Western European states,[5] which now received U.S. military aid. The Russians replied with the Warsaw Pact of Communist states in 1955.

At first, the Cold War had been primarily a conflict over Europe, waged as a competition for

[5]Great Britain, France, Belgium, the Netherlands, Luxemburg, Italy, Portugal, Denmark, Norway, and Iceland were the European members. Greece and Turkey would be added in 1952; West Germany, in 1955.

▶ **The world was as impressed as the children of Berlin by the airlift that carried supplies to the city and completed 277,264 flights in a year.**

public opinion as well as international power. Even domestic issues formed along pro-American or pro-Soviet positions. But with Eastern Europe isolated behind what Churchill called the "iron curtain" and Communists excluded from political power in the West, the focus of the Cold War shifted. When the Communist North Koreans invaded South Korea in 1950, the United States at once asked the United Nations to intervene, and the UN (Russia happened to be temporarily absent) called for an international army to stop the North Koreans. The Cold War was now worldwide. Having marked the lessened autonomy of the European nations, the conflict spread to colonial issues and events in the Middle East and Asia (*see box*, p. 991–992).

The Loss of Empire Part of a larger process of worldwide change, the contraction of European empires was a prominent sign of the decline in European power; European states lacked the finances and military might (or confidence in their colonial mission) that empire required. At the end of the war, Britain and France briefly renewed some of their old rivalries in the Middle East but withdrew in 1946 from the new states of Lebanon and Syria. Trans-Jordan became independent, foreign troops left Iraq and Iran, and negotiations began for British forces to depart from Egypt and the Sudan. In Asia, Japan had taken Indonesia from the Dutch, Indochina from France, and much of Malaysia from Britain; and restoring empire was different from sustaining it. Nearly everywhere nationalist movements demanded independence, strengthened by the displacement of European and Japanese rule, experience in combat, anti-imperialist propaganda, and the disruption of capitalist ties. The United

States was traditionally unsympathetic to European empires, and the Soviet Union encouraged local communist movements in nationalist opposition to imperialism. In Europe itself, parties on the left generally favored independence movements and insisted that promised concessions be granted.

India, where the spiritual message and personal qualities of Mohandas K. Gandhi won worldwide admiration and built a powerful movement, was granted independence from Britain in 1947. Simultaneously, violent conflict between Hindus and Muslims led to recognition of an independent Pakistan. Sri Lanka (Ceylon) and Burma gained their independence from Great Britain in the following year. France had recognized Vietnam as a free state in 1945, but fighting over the rest of Indochina would continue for years. The Dutch, too, tried to reimpose their rule over Indonesia, which won its freedom in 1949 only after years of combat.

Pulling out of empire was not easy. Despite Arab hostility, Great Britain undertook the creation of separate Jewish and Muslim states in Palestine. Mounting terror campaigns from both sides notwithstanding, the British decided to remove all their troops in May 1948, and the United Nations, eager to give Jews a refuge following Hitler's persecutions, endorsed the creation of the state of Israel. The Arabs invaded the day the British left but were driven back despite numerical superiority, and UN mediators were able to bring about a shaky truce that confirmed Israel's existence.

The Soviet Union Denounces the United States While Calling for Arms Reduction

Andrei Vishinsky, the Russian delegate to the United Nations, spoke to the General Assembly on November 1, 1948, proposing steps toward arms reduction and control of atomic weapons. The address was testimony, however, to the global range of the Cold War. Most of it consisted of a lengthy denunciation of the policies of the United States, which was accused of undermining the United Nations; of intervening against democracy and peace in Korea, Greece, Indonesia, and Palestine; and of harming Europe's economy with the Marshall Plan while forming a military alliance with the nations of Western Europe aimed at the "freedom-loving" states of Eastern Europe.

"The policy of the USSR is a consistent and constant policy of expanding and strengthening international cooperation. This follows from the very nature of the Soviet State. A socialist State of workers and peasants deeply interested—a State, I repeat, which is deeply interested in the establishment of the most favorable conditions for peaceful creative work in the building of a socialist society. The foreign policy of the Soviet Union pursues the course of co-operation among all countries prepared for peaceful cooperation. The USSR consistently fights against any plan and measures and designs intended to create a gap, a cleavage, among peoples. It fights for the realization and implementation of democratic principles which were born out of the war.

"Such is not the case with the present foreign policy of the United States. After the termination of the recent world war, the Government of the United States has changed its foreign policy: from a policy of fighting against aggressive forces, the United States has passed over to a policy of expansion. It is now attempting to realize plans for world domination. It is in open support in various countries of the most reactionary and monarcho-fascist regimes and groups and rendering to them systematic aid with money and armaments for the suppression of democratic national liberation movements in these countries; organization of military alliances or blocs, the construction of new military air and naval bases as well as the expansion and reconstruction in accordance with the

(Continued)

newest military technical requirements of old bases established during the war with Germany, Japan, and Italy; furthermore, unchecked propaganda of a new war against the Soviet Union and the new democracies of Eastern Europe; a wild race of armaments; a true worship of the cult of the atomic bomb and allegedly a means of escape from all the dangers and misfortunes threatening the capitalistic world: these are the principal aspects, the characteristic features, of the foreign policy of the United States of America at present.

"Such a policy is inciting the psychosis of war, sowing restlessness and fear among the broad masses which strive for peace and peaceful creative labor. Such a policy has nothing in common whatsoever with a policy of peace.

"[A] . . . map by the ESSO Company of New York is of the same insolently arrogant and war-inciting nature. This map is published by the Standard Oil Company of New Jersey. It is called, quite provocatively, 'The Map of the Third World War.' That is what they are publishing in the United States—the Map of the Third World War! They are handing them out to motorists. This map, with provocatively militant appeals, carries the heading: 'Pacific Theatre of Military Operations.' The map is an example of the malicious war propaganda against the Soviet Union and the new democracies of East Europe.

". . . The reactionary circles of the United States and the United Kingdom as well as of countries such as France, Belgium, and others, do not confine themselves to slander and abuse alone. This campaign is now being headed not only by amateurs from the family of retired politicians, statesmen, Senators and Members of Parliament, but also by persons now holding high official posts in the Governments of the United States, the United Kingdom, France and some other countries.

". . . On the instructions of the Soviet Union Government the delegation of the USSR proposes to the General Assembly, for the purpose of strengthening the cause of peace and removing the menace of a new war which is being fomented by expansionists and other reactionary elements, the adoption of the following resolution:

". . . as the first step in the reduction of armaments and armed forces to reduce by one-third during one year all present land, naval, and air forces. . . .

". . . to prohibit atomic weapons as weapons intended for aims of aggression and not for those of defense;

". . . to establish within the framework of the Security Council an international control body for the purpose of the supervision and control of the implementation of . . . [these] measures. . . ."

Speech by Andrei Y. Vishinsky to the United Nations, November 1, 1948, from *Vital Speeches of the Day*, Vol. XV, No. 2, New York.

Internal conflicts in the new nations in fact tended to draw European states back into the political life of their former colonies. The leaders of the new states often made calls for legal procedures and appeals to old interests that resonated in Britain and France with conservatives and the military, while the presence of communist movements triggered Cold War concerns. Pakistan committed itself to the West, India tried to steer a middle course, and a major communist revolt broke out in Burma immediately after independence. In Vietnam the French were encouraged by the United States to resist the French-educated Communist leader Ho Chi Minh, who organized a brilliant guerrilla campaign to unify the nation. He was strongly supported by Russia and by the most formidable of the newly Communist states, China, where, after long civil conflict, the Communists under Mao Zedong consolidated power in 1949. That costly war in Indochina ended only with the capture of a major French base at Dien Bien Phu in 1954 and French withdrawal from Vietnam. As a counterweight to communist gains in Asia, the United States promoted the economic revival of a now democratic Japan and gave strong economic and military support to Taiwan (a large island off China still held by the Chinese nationalists). The Americans also promoted a Pacific equivalent to NATO in the Southeast Asia Treaty Organization (SEATO), in which Britain,

Pakistan, Australia, New Zealand, and various Asian states were to join the United States in common defense.

European domination had left a heritage of ties to international capitalism, of bureaucracy and parties organized on Western models, and of nationalist and socialist ideas increasingly tempered by local traditions and indigenous forms of organization; but the resolution of these struggles was outside European control. Cold War competition, however, increased great power support for one side or the other in local conflicts, as in Iran, where Soviet influence rapidly waned as American economic aid rose. This competition in some respects benefited independence movements in Africa, which could play the superpowers against each other in seeking outside support. Still, Great Britain sustained the Commonwealth of Nations, binding former colonies in a sometimes influential international club, although it could not resolve conflicts between its members. The fiercely anti-British republic of Eire rejected the Commonwealth when its independence was formally recognized in 1949. France's *Union Française* gave French-speaking former colonies a voice in France's own political affairs and sustained valuable connections with the elites of the new nations, but hardly functioned as an empire.

IV. European Recovery

Europe's economy as well as its political life depended heavily on the Soviet Union and the United States; yet from 1947 to 1957 economic growth was great. With rising prosperity, governments developed social policies that set new standards for equity and well-being. Even so, European states could not successfully challenge the hegemony of the superpowers.

ECONOMIC REVIVAL

For all the shortages of capital and supplies, the homeland of the Industrial Revolution had important resources in its skilled population and infrastructure. The need to rebuild factories and transportation networks offered the chance to adopt the most efficient machinery and methods, and the millions of displaced people added to a skilled labor force as rates of employment slowly increased. European nations also had access to a backlog of unexploited technology; and as these new techniques became more important, European societies were well placed to take advantage of atomic power, the jet engine, the rocket engine, television, computers, antibiotics, and frozen foods. This remarkable resilience was reflected in demography. In contrast to World War I, birthrates actually increased in nonbelligerent nations as well as in England and France during World War II, and in Germany they declined by less than they had during the previous war. This European "baby boom," though not so large as in the United States, lasted until 1963, helping to replace some of the losses of war and to expand domestic markets.

The Role of the Soviet Union and the United States The recovery of Eastern Europe depended heavily on the Soviet Union, which through strenuous efforts had, by 1953, exceeded prewar industrial output, and leaders such as Nikita Khrushchev confidently predicted that the U.S.S.R. would surpass America. As the economy expanded, however, the costs of administration increased disproportionately, and the inefficiencies of centralized management became more pronounced. Without a free market, planners had difficulty judging costs and performance; agriculture was a major disappointment. The cereal harvest in 1953 was only slightly larger than in 1913.

The Soviet Union nevertheless provided an important market and economic stimulus for the countries of the Communist bloc, which organized their economies along the Russian model. All but Poland collectivized farmlands, and all instituted five-year plans to achieve rapid industrialization. In varying degrees, these governments adopted elements of a mixed economic system—"goulash socialism," as Hungary's compromise has been called: The state retained ownership of most means of production, but managers operated within the structure of a largely free market. The formula first proved most successful in the already advanced economies of Czechoslovakia and East Germany. Eastern Europe, though dramatically less prosperous than the West, had the highest rate of economic growth in its history by the 1950s.

The Western European nations looked to the United States for help, and in 1946 it extended $4.4 billion in long-term credit to Great Britain and, subsequently, $1.2 billion to France. Only with the Marshall Plan in 1947 did the United States acknowledge the scale of Europe's economic problems as depleted currency reserves and inflation threatened to undermine recovery. Over the next four years, more than $15 billion was channeled into Europe under the direction of the Organization for European Economic Cooperation (OEEC), which 18 Western states established for this purpose. Subsequently, the European Payments Union (1950–1958) was created to regulate currency exchanges. The imports from the United States that the Marshall Plan made possible benefited the American economy and helped, through the planning required as well as the goods made available, to lay the foundations for rapid recovery. In the three years from 1948 to 1950, the combined gross national product of the OEEC participants increased at an annual rate of 25 percent. By 1952 it was approximately half again larger than it had been in 1938, and per capita income was a third higher. Western Europe had never been wealthier.

The Role of Government Throughout Western Europe the economic importance of the public sector increased greatly. In part this was an extension of wartime measures and a result of immediate postwar social needs. In part it was a new attitude toward public policy. Immediately after the war, Britain and France had nationalized much of their heavy industry and banking system, and in Italy the Fascist regime had bequeathed to the state huge publicly owned conglomerates that directed hundreds of firms in some of the critical sections of industry and energy. West Germany alone made no effort to expand the number of state-owned industries, but there, too, the government had an important role (as it had during the war) in coordinating economic growth. State ownership gave no assurance of efficient management, good labor relations, or a high return on capital; but it encouraged governments to develop economic policies to guide both public and private enterprises in the interests of overall growth. With the Monnet Plan (1946–1950), France set the model of loose but effective control (building on policies developed under the Vichy regime) and of relying on refined methods of national accounting and highly trained "technocrats." Comparable plans were devised from Britain to Israel, especially in Scandinavian and Mediterranean countries. In West Germany the largest banks and a private trade association with close government ties played a similar role.

The policies of European governments were closely comparable in their programs to protect workers and their families against sickness, impoverished old age, and unemployment. Great Britain provided the earliest and (Sweden excepted) probably the most complete example of what has come to be called the welfare state. Its cornerstone was the National Health Service, inaugurated in 1948, which assumed nearly the total cost of medical, dental, and hospital care for all residents of the United Kingdom. Although they structured it differently, continental governments also provided universal health care, family allowances with payments for minor children, housing programs, and a growing array of social services. By reducing insecurity, these measures also stimulated consumption. To meet their cost, states raised taxes and became more efficient in collecting them, in the process accumulating large reserves that they used for investment according to their economic plans.

POLITICAL LIMITS

By the early 1950s, European society had taken on a new look of health and stability. Not surprisingly, the political balance shifted toward the center and center right, although that meant something different in each country, while Cold War fears weakened the left.

Western Europe Only in Scandinavia did socialists continue in office. In Britain the Conservatives regained power in 1951 and held it for the next 13 years, ending rationing and lowering taxes but not undoing most of the Labour program. The coronation of Queen Elizabeth II in 1953 was celebrated as the symbol of a new era of prosperity. Italy's Christian Democrats turned more to the right, while keeping the Communists isolated, and West Germany under Adenauer became a model of stable prosperity and even won diplomatic recognition from the U.S.S.R. despite joining NATO in 1955. A notable easing of international tension permitted the Allies to agree on a peace treaty for Austria and the withdrawal of their occupation forces in the same year.

Similar trends in France, however, brought down the Fourth Republic. The government had in many respects performed very well, though just how well would become clearer in the prosperity of the 1960s. But coalition governments and party conflicts recalled the weaknesses of the Third Republic. In 1954 an able prime minister of the center-left, Pierre Mendès-France, seemed about to make the system work. His promising vision included finishing negotiations to extricate France from Indochina and a dynamic program of political reform and social modernization. He accomplished the first, but the rest of his program stalled in party bickering as the political center was weakened from right and left. Supporters of Charles de Gaulle and an angry movement of small shopkeepers and farmers, the people bypassed by the benefits of modernization, gained in the elections of 1956 as did the Communists, which made the other parties on the left more hesitant to support the government.

In that situation external crises were too much. The question of forming a common European military command was troublesome enough, but the question of Algeria proved fatal. There, a revolt against French rule was growing, and from 1954 to 1958 the Algerian question brought down more French governments than any other issue. A French colony since 1830, Algeria had a sizable French population that had lived there for generations, and many in France reacted with horror to tales of atrocities against their compatriots by Algerian nationalists, demanding that they not be abandoned. In the spirit of the Cold War, army officers who had been fighting colonial uprisings in Africa and Asia since 1945 saw themselves holding the line alone against communist conspiracy around the world. They redoubled their repression and demanded that their sacrifices not be scuttled by treacherous "politicians" ready to concede autonomy or independence to Algeria. At the same time, leftists and intellectuals expressed outrage at the atrocities committed by the French army and at the kind of democracy that would wage war against Algerians seeking to govern themselves.

As these tensions reached a peak in 1958, a group of French army officers seized political control in Algeria and threatened to move against the government of France. Faced with that challenge, a majority of the National Assembly turned to de Gaulle to unify the country and pacify the military insurgents. Upon his announcement that he would once again serve the nation, they invested him with extraordinary powers for six years. He led France for the next ten. Although de Gaulle had been shrewdly ambiguous in his pronouncements on Algeria, the army, the center, and the right all found him acceptable. He used that strength to win support for a new constitution that was overwhelmingly approved by popular referendum in September 1958. It established the Fifth Republic as a presidential regime with a chief executive indirectly elected for a seven-year term. De Gaulle was chosen president two months later, and Gaullists became by far the largest party in parliament, where the Communists were reduced to a handful.

The president moved cautiously on the Algerian question, quietly weakening and dispersing the leaders of the military revolt. Only gradually did it become clear that de Gaulle would accept Algerian self-determination, a proposal approved by three-quarters of the voters in a referendum held in January 1961. Effectively isolated, the most intransigent of the officers formed a secret army and for 18 months indulged in terrorism in France and Algeria. But the French president, having arranged peace with the Algerian rebels, declared war on the army rebels. By the end of 1962, they had disbanded, Algeria was independent, and France's presidential regime could turn to other questions.

The Soviet Union After 30 years of dictatorship, Joseph Stalin died of a stroke in 1953. The shock and sense of loss in the Soviet Union was compounded by the problem of succession, something its Communist government had faced only once before. It went surprisingly smoothly, and a form of collective leadership emerged. Only in 1956–1957 did it become clear that Nikita Khrushchev was the dominant figure. The competition for leadership involved two principal issues. Stalin's last years had brought heavy repression (with terror), ugly anti-Semitism, and a party line enforced on everything from socialist realism in the arts to the fallacious genetic theories of Trofim Lysenko. Many wanted that to change. The second issue was the standard of living sacrificed to the demanding goals of the latest five-year plan, but even Stalin had hinted that it might be time to increase consumption as well as industry. Khrushchev had seemed conservative on the need for change, and his triumph showed again that control of the Communist party remained the key to power. Still, the infighting that brought him to the top, which included sudden dismissals and even executions, was followed not by purges but by the reassignment of his opponents to less prominent positions.

With a speech to the Twentieth Party Congress in 1956, Khrushchev established his new direction. He attacked the "cult of personality" under Stalin, naming many of Stalin's excesses, his paranoid distrust, his interference in the conduct of war, and his responsibility for the purge trials of the 1930s. Nothing like it had occurred before. Myths central to the nation's enormous sacrifices for a generation were suddenly unmasked. The charges circulated widely in secret and then more openly, with unsettling effects in the Soviet Union, Eastern Europe, and Communist movements everywhere. Streets and squares were renamed; statues and pictures disappeared. With the thaw[6] following Stalin's death, a freer and more open society appeared in prospect. Although Khrushchev quickly clamped down on criticism amid rising complaints about domestic problems and rumblings from within the Soviet bloc, restraints were never again so rigid or arbitrary as they had been under Stalin. When the Soviet Union celebrated the fortieth anniversary of the Russian Revolution in 1957 by launching the world's first space satellite, Sputnik, Russia's status as a state both powerful and stable seemed to be dramatically confirmed.

FORAYS AT INDEPENDENCE

The Nations of the Soviet Sphere The Communist governments of Eastern Europe closely mimicked Soviet rule in the idolization of Stalin and the ruthless use of secret police and internment camps as well as in general policy. But resentments at the Soviet Union's open exploitation of its neighbors emerged publicly after Stalin's death. Within three months, the workers of East Berlin were in the streets proclaiming a general strike to protest increased production quotas that they blamed on the Soviet Union. Russian tanks rushed in to put down the revolt, but it had long-lasting effects. Walter Ulbricht became the new leader of East Germany and offered a program of higher wages and better living conditions even while strengthening dictatorship. Still tightly tied to the Soviet Union and limited in its autonomy, East Germany expanded its trade with West Germany and developed a voice of its own in the councils of Communist countries.

A workers' protest in Poland in 1956 even won support from within the Communist party among nationalists who were critical of Russian policies. Again Soviet forces intervened. They were jeered, and the Polish party elected Wladyslaw Gomulka its party secretary over the pro-Russian candidate. Gomulka, a firm Communist, dominated the government until 1970 by convincing the Russians of his loyalty to the Soviet alliance while nevertheless arguing that socialist states needed to follow national paths that were different from Russia's. Poland demanded and got a share of the war reparations that Germany paid, negotiated economic aid from the United States, and mitigated its repression of the Catholic Church and Polish intellectuals.

The risings in Hungary ended more tragically. Riots in October 1956 were fiercely anti-Russian; and the Russian troops at first withdrew from Budapest, seemingly disposed to accept Hungary's increased autonomy. Then Imre Nagy, who had been arrested for "right-wing deviationism" the year before, became premier. Bowing to popular

[6] The metaphor of the thaw, which has come to be generally applied to these changes in domestic and foreign policy, is derived from a novel of that title by the noted Russian fiction writer and journalist Ilya Ehrenburg.

pressure, he agreed to replace the alliance with Russia with a policy of neutrality. The Soviet leaders pressured, threatened, and finally sent their army to attack in force, crushing the revolution in 10 days of bitter fighting. Rebel radio stations pleaded for the Western aid many Hungarians expected, but none came. Washington denounced Russian imperialism but remained preoccupied with the crisis in its own alliance over Suez (see below). Russia had made it clear that satellite regimes could not break with Soviet policy, and the Western nations in effect acknowledged a Russian sphere of influence. Hungary suffered a heavy-handed Soviet occupation and harsh repression, and a new wave of refugees left the country. Nagy himself was eventually executed by the Russians; yet his successor, Janos Kadar, slowly led the country on a more national course.

No other Communist nation was able to follow the example of independent Yugoslavia, where reconciliations with Khrushchev in 1954 and 1957 did not affect Yugoslavia's trade with the West or its experiments at decentralization. Albania, the most backward country on the continent and isolated from the Soviet sphere by geography, formed closer ties to mainland China in diplomatic and dogmatic opposition to Russia; and Romania, like Bulgaria among the most Stalinist of the satellite regimes, distanced itself slightly by seeking better relations with the West. Little more was possible.

Western Europe Britain and France, too, were restive at their subordination to a stronger ally; and the United States wanted to strengthen European defenses by rearming Germany, a measure the French could hardly welcome and one that Russia was determined to prevent. As a safeguard, in 1952 the French had proposed the creation of a European Defense Community (EDC), in effect a European army that would benefit from German strength without facing the risks of a separate German military force. Although accepted by most of the European members of NATO and pushed by the United States, its im-

Soviet tanks occupy the streets of Budapest; the uprising of October 1956 has been crushed.

plication of permanent continental engagement was distasteful to the British and growing doubts in France, increased by resentment of extraordinary American pressure, led the French parliament to reject the EDC in 1954. European governments were asserting their independence.

The British asserted themselves again when there was a crisis in relations with Egypt, a former colony where they continued to have special knowledge and ties. Gamal Abdel Nasser's government was distrusted in the West for its nationalism, its radical domestic program, and its willingness to accept aid from nations in the Communist bloc. When the Western powers, following the United States, refused aid for the construction of a high dam across the Nile at Aswan, Nasser nationalized the Suez Canal, which was still owned by a British-controlled company. Britain led in demanding a strong response and, after international efforts at compromise broke down, conspired with Israel and France to take military action. Israel attacked Egypt in October 1956, and that attack was immediately followed by an Anglo-French bombardment and occupation of the canal banks. Because both the Soviet Union and the United States opposed the entire venture, the United Nations was able to force a ceasefire within a week and the withdrawal of foreign troops shortly afterward. Nothing had been gained by this return to old tactics that aroused anti-imperialist sentiment everywhere while at the same time demonstrating England and France's continuing dependence on American approval, a subordination that remained even though Britain soon became the third nation to possess a hydrogen bomb and France would later be the fourth.

The European Economic Community In several respects 1956–1957 marked a turning point in European affairs. The period of postwar recovery was over, and the launching of Sputnik implied a new equilibrium in the competition between the two superpowers, each with its established spheres of dominance and network of alliances. Khrushchev's policies and the reactions to them in Eastern Europe indicated that communist regimes might in time become less rigidly authoritarian, but had established firm limits as to the changes that would be allowed. Crises over Algeria and Egypt, in many respects a last gasp of old imperial dreams, brought changes in personnel and policy in Britain and a new constitution in France. In retrospect, however, the most important turning point in 1957 was the treaty of Rome signed by Belgium, the Netherlands, Luxemburg, France, Germany, and Italy. It created the European Economic Community to go into effect January 1, 1958.

From 1948 on, governments participating in the OEEC had recognized that the free movement of capital and labor as well as of finished products was beneficial to economic growth. But efforts to create a tariff union had failed except for agreements among Belgium, the Netherlands, and Luxemburg (the Benelux countries). There had also been talk about the advantages of political integration; and a meeting at The Hague in 1948, chaired by Winston Churchill, discussed the formation of a Council of Europe and established a Council of Ministers and a Consultative Assembly, with headquarters at Strasbourg. The powers of the Council of Europe were very limited, however; and it became clear that few governments, least of all Great Britain's, were willing to surrender any sovereignty or significant decision-making power to a supranational authority. Two leading French supporters of European integration, the economist Jean Monnet and the foreign minister Robert Schuman, then decided to proceed one step at a time. They tackled the economically disadvantageous separation of French iron ore from German coal, which had plagued relations between the two nations for nearly a century. Their efforts led to an imaginative solution, the creation of the French-German Coal and Steel Authority in 1950, which in effect guaranteed equal access to these resources. Two years later, propelled by the euphoria of recovery, Italy and the three Benelux countries joined to establish the European Coal and Steel Community (ECSC), the real kernel of a common market. Each member appointed a representative to the ECSC's executive body, which would coordinate the production and distribution of the coal and steel critical to industrial growth. As this union proved its economic value, its authority increased and stimulated renewed visions that it could lead to an economic and political federation.

The treaty of Rome was a limited agreement. It established, as an addition to the ECSC, an agency to coordinate the development of atomic energy, and it declared that the six nations should eliminate tariffs among themselves through a series of gradual steps and establish a common tariff toward all others. The treaty's larger significance would depend upon what sense of community evolved in practice, and that was uncertain. Britain refused to participate; and France, which in the Fourth Republic had been a major proponent of such measures, would soon adopt the Fifth Republic, which sounded much less internationalist. Nevertheless, six states that had often been at war at least declared that they were now "determined to establish the foundations of an ever closer union among the European peoples."

These democracies were determined to prevent the kind of policies that had led to war 20 years before, when democracy itself was widely challenged and totalitarianism was newly invented. Europe's war, like its ideological divisions, had spread around the world; and it had taken a worldwide mobilization to defeat the Axis. The exhausting triumph over fascism and Nazism was a victory for European civilization; and afterward, European nations recovered with astonishing speed. On the whole they adjusted realistically to the loss of empire and international preeminence, while accepting the ideological and geographical division of the Cold War. Neither communists nor democratic capitalism managed in victory to create the societies they promised, and neither prosperity nor carefully contrived political stability necessarily resolved old conflicts. If Europe seemed to be beginning a new era, Europe's economic, social, and cultural place in the modern world remained unclear.

Recommended Reading

Sources

*Churchill, Sir Winston S. *The Second World War* (6 vols.). 1948–1954. Each volume of Churchill's detailed account can be read singly, and all are rich in documents and his masterly prose (he was awarded the Nobel prize for literature in 1953), which recapture the drama and meaning of the century's greatest war.

**Hitler's Table-Talk.* Hugh Trevor-Roper (ed.). 1988. Isolated in his headquarters, Hitler liked at mealtime to discourse on all sorts of topics with his closest aides. From 1941 to 1944 he allowed notes to be taken on these discussions, and this is a translation of the transcript, edited by his secretary, Martin Bormann. Hitler's opinionated ramblings and reminiscences have a chilling fascination.

Monnet, Jean. *Memoires.* 1978. The chief architect of the European Community here reveals the intellectual roots of his vision and the personal style that made him so effective.

*Available in paperback.

Studies

Allsop, Kenneth. *The Angry Decade: A Survey of the Cultural Revolt of the 1950s.* 1969. Captures very well the postwar disillusionment that undermined political and social consensus.

*Aron, Raymond. *The Imperial Republic: The United States and the World, 1945–1973.* 1974. A leading French thinker of the time analyzes the period of American dominance.

Branson, N., and M. Heinemann. *Britain in the 1930s.* 1971. Ably demonstrates the interrelationship between the social and economic stress of the period and political stagnation.

Brown, Colin, and Peter J. Mooney. *Cold War to Détente, 1945–1980.* 1981. A largely narrative account of relations between the superpowers.

Calvocaressi, Peter. *The British Experience 1945–1975.* 1978. A comprehensive study of British life in a period of imperial decline and economic difficulty.

Carr, Raymond. *The Civil War in Spain.* 1986. A comprehensive and unusually balanced study that effectively uses recent research to put the events of the war in the context of Spanish history and international relations.

Colton, Joel C. *Léon Blum: Humanist in Politics.* 1966. The biography of this appealing figure is particularly useful for the period of the Popular Front.

*Crossman, Richard H. (ed.). *The God That Failed.* 1950. The moving testimony of former Marxists about their lost faith during the era of Stalin and in itself a document of the Cold War.

*Crouzet, Maurice. *The European Renaissance since 1945.* 1971. An optimistic essay on the politics, society, and culture of postwar Europe that reflects the hopes that underlay the years of prosperity and the growth of the European Community.

*Dahrendorf, Ralf. *Society and Democracy in Germany.* 1969. A German sociologist assesses the special qualities of German society and its implications for the postwar West German republic.

Dawidowicz, Lucy S. *The War against the Jews, 1933–1945.* 1976. An extensive and thoughtful consideration of the twentieth century's greatest horror.

*DePorte, A. W. *Europe between the Superpowers.* 1979. A stimulating assessment of Europe's place in the postwar bipolar system.

Feis, Hebert. *From Trust to Terror: The Onset of the Cold War, 1945–1970.* 1970. Written before Western policies had come under heavy criticism in the West by an expert in international relations and the world economy, this work holds up well.

Fejto, François. *A History of the People's Democracies: Eastern Europe since Stalin.* 1971. A careful study of the conflicts and variety among Eastern European states under Soviet dominance.

Gilbert, Martin. *The Second World War: A Complete History.* 1989. Pulls together the latest research to cover the war and the home fronts of the major participants.

Grosser, Alfred. *The Western Alliance: European-American Relations since 1945.* 1983. A clear-headed account of how international relations have worked in practice.

*Hoffman, Stanley, et al. *In Search of France.* 1965. A group of distinguished scholars attempt to define the unique patterns of French political and social life and to explain the significance of the Fifth Republic.

Knox, MacGregor. *Mussolini Unleashed, 1939–41: Politics and Strategy in Fascist Italy's Last War.* 1982. A thorough and insightful analysis of Fascist foreign policy and strategic aims as well as of the regime's many weaknesses in pursuing them.

*Laqueur, Walter. *Europe since Hitler.* 1982. One of the ablest of the surveys of contemporary Europe that sees Europe as a whole.

La Feber, Walter. *America, Russia, and the Cold War.* 1967. Consistently argues for the responsibility of the United States in creating the Cold War.

*Liddell-Hart, Basil H. *History of the Second World War.* 1980. The crowning work of this renowned strategist and military historian.

*Maier, Charles S. *In Search of Stability: Explorations in Historical Political Economy.* 1987. Essays relating economic interests to the ambitions, limitations, and bitter divisions of European politics between the wars.

*——— (ed.). *The Origins of the Cold War and Contemporary Europe.* 1978. Essays by leading scholars seeking not so much to lay blame for the Cold War but to study its connection to domestic societies.

Michel, Henri. *The Shadow War: The European Resistance, 1939–1945.* 1972. Combines recent scholarship in a solid study of the most attractive (and romanticized) aspect of world war.

Middlemas, Keith. *Power, Competition and State.* Vol. I: *Britain in Search of Balance, 1940–1961.* 1986. A clear assessment of the pressures that shaped British society and politics.

Milward, Alan S. *The Reconstruction of Western Europe, 1945–1951.* 1984. Concludes that the economic boom of the fifties and sixties began as early as 1945, through the role of government policy in establishing international economic interdependence.

*———. *War, Economy and Society 1939–1945.* 1977. Examines the interdependence of economic planning and military strategy and its implications for the postwar period.

*Neff, Donal. *Warriors at Suez.* 1981. Well-researched and comprehensive, this dramatic account by a journalist focuses on the political leaders of the nations involved in the highly significant crisis of 1956.

*Paxton, Robert. *Vichy France: Old Guard and New Order, 1940–1944.* 1972. Stresses the continuity and lasting significance for French society and institutions of this twilight period.

*Payne, Stanley G. *The Franco Regime, 1936–1975.* 1987. A fair-minded account that sees the bases of Spain's subsequent transformation in Franco's later years.

Postan, Michael M. *An Economic History of Western Europe, 1945–1964.* 1967. A noted economic historian analyzes the roots of European recovery.

Rioux, Jean-Pierre. *The Fourth Republic, 1945–1958.* 1987. A close look at and a critical assessment of the politics of the period.

Sherwin, M. J. A. *A World Destroyed: The Atomic Bomb and the Grand Alliance.* 1975. A scholarly and balanced account of this controversial and complicated subject.

*Ulam, Adam B. *Expansion and Coexistence: The History of Soviet Foreign Policy, 1917–1973.* 1974. An expert appraisal of the consistent patterns and political pressures underlying Soviet policy.

Wilkinson, James D. *The Intellectual Resistance in Europe.* 1981. A wide-ranging and sensitive assessment of the content and legacy of the resistance and its place in contemporary thought.

In November 1989 the East German government suddenly granted free access to West Berlin; the spontaneous celebrations that followed became the symbol of one of history's great turning points. The breach of the Berlin wall seemed a victory as great as any commemorated by the Brandenburg gate in the background.

CHAPTER THIRTY

CONTEMPORARY EUROPE

IN the 1950s it had been possible to imagine that the industrial societies of Eastern and Western Europe would become more alike, but a decade later it was clear that they were moving in different directions. Western Europe was developing a new kind of economic base that emphasized services and information, and social relations were changing as women gained greater independence, a larger part of the population had access to advanced education, and immigrants from rural areas and other lands changed the urban landscape. With its prosperity and measures of social welfare, Western European societies offered a model that undermined neighboring dictatorships and internal movements of opposition. The European Community developed institutions and patterns of cooperation that pointed to European Union. These changes in turn fostered new, and often disquieting, intellectual movements that altered the ways of understanding society itself. Eastern European societies, with their entrenched one-party systems and directed economies, found it increasingly difficult to match this process of change and then unexpectedly collapsed.

I. Postindustrial Society

For 30 years, from the 1950s on, Europe's economic growth continued. Every nation became richer than it had ever been before; and as standards of living rose, life styles changed along with the ways of creating wealth. Industrial production no longer dominated the economy, for the service sector employed more and more people in office work, sales, and personal services. Societies structured in this way have come to be called, a little misleadingly, *postindustrial*, to indicate the fundamental transformation. North America and Western Europe were its pioneers. There the changes postindustrial society implies were exuberantly embraced, while in Eastern Europe they occurred more slowly and with greater difficulty.

EUROPE'S ADVANTAGE

Historically, much of Europe outside the Soviet Union had been economically handicapped by limited natural resources and sources of energy. The coal fields of Britain, West Germany, and Eastern Europe and the iron ore fields of France and Sweden were critical to industrialization in the nineteenth century and for industrial production in the first two-thirds of the twentieth century. These assets have been supplemented in the last generation by the exploitation of other sources of energy, especially the oilfields in the North Sea but also of natural gas in Italy. More important, however, is the fact that such resources have become less crucial; for economies today create wealth primarily through the efficient transformation of raw materials, which can be imported, and through services. And Europe excels in the attributes that now matter more for economic expansion: great amounts of capital and institutions to facilitate its rapid investment, advanced technology, experienced managers, skilled and willing workers, efficient marketing, rapid communication, high levels of education, adaptable societies, and high consumption.

Infrastructure During the 1960s every nation launched new road-building projects, and by 1980 the most important of these had been completed in France, the Benelux countries, and Germany and were nearing completion in Great Britain and on the Iberian peninsula. Superhighways now run from Stockholm to south of Valencia and from Naples to Hamburg. Railroads, valued for passenger travel as well as for transport (and usually considered a service to be provided by the state more than a source of profit), have been extensively modernized. In 1981 French trains, which hold world speed records, began to carry passengers from Paris to Lyons at 165 miles per hour. A tunnel under the English Channel, a project considered for centuries, opened in 1994 to provide direct automobile and rail links between Britain and the continent. Water transport along coasts, rivers, and canals is relatively inexpensive; and air travel, dense in all of Europe, is especially important across the expanses of Russia. Western European nations have also been technological leaders in electronic communication. Radio and television reach into nearly every home with programming that crosses national boundaries, and Europe has been a leader in innovative applications of computer technology.

Steadily increasing productivity requires high rates of investment in new technologies, and in Western Europe governments, banks, insurance companies, and stock markets have been eager to support the employment of robots, microchips, and satellite communication. Since the 1980s,

▸ High-speed electric trains poised for their dash from Paris to Lyons.

there has been a strong trend toward privatization, placing in the hands of profit-making firms much of the economic activity previously directed by governments; but until then, economic growth was often greatest in mixed economies, a characteristic European mixture of private enterprise and state planning. From infrastructure to personal consumption, European society readily adapted to the frequent changes in organization, production, and marketing of modern economies, which reduce costs while adding new products and activities.

These changes have been accompanied by increased agricultural productivity in the West, although the number of people who work the land has continued to decline (in Ireland, one of the West's least developed nations, 60 percent of the work force was employed in agriculture in 1960 but only 20 percent in 1980). By the 1980s, nearly one-half the tractors in the world were used in Europe. With only about 3 percent of the world's farmland, Western Europe produced nearly one-third of the world's dairy products and 15 percent of the world's eggs, potatoes, and wheat (of which France alone was the fifth largest producer and the former Soviet Union was the largest, followed by the United States, China, and India).

Education Modern society also requires that a large proportion of the population be much more highly educated than in the past. In Europe that required major changes in the educational system, reforms that in the late 1960s and early 1970s were a source of controversy and even of demonstrations and riots. Traditionally, secondary education has been the great dividing point. Before the reforms, a small fraction of students were admitted to secondary schools that were noted for their demanding and, usually, classical curriculums and that served as the gateway for entrance to a university. Many more students went to secondary schools where training was more vocational, and half or more of all students beyond the ages of 12 or 14 went directly to work. Despite efforts to make this segregation a matter of academic performance, in practice social class made a critical difference. Reforms aimed at making the system more democratic. In the West the increased enrollment in the more prestigious forms of secondary education was accompanied by a move toward "comprehensive" schools, more like the American high school, which less sharply segregate the college-bound. Broadening access to universities in turn required them also to change dramatically.

▶ The skyscrapers of Frankfurt, one of Europe's greatest commercial centers, loom over the statue of Schiller, Germany's great eighteenth-century playwright.

Despite the creation of hundreds of new institutions, often with American-style campuses, enrollments in many places have swollen beyond their capacity. National patterns still reflect differing traditions, but the tendency has been for educational systems to become more similar across Western Europe and for enrollments everywhere to increase. The European nations with the highest proportion (roughly one-fifth to one-third) of people 20 to 24 years old enrolled in universities are the Netherlands, Sweden, Denmark, France, Italy, and Norway. Those with the lowest proportion (less than 10 percent)—Yugoslavia, Spain, and Portugal—are the poorest nations; and nearly all the rest of Europe falls in between. The Communist regimes of Eastern Europe gave preference to the children of workers and party members but enlarged total enrollments more slowly than in the West, where this expansion slowed in the 1980s; and cutbacks in government spending (especially severe in Great Britain) reopened unresolved issues of fair access, quality, general culture, and prospects for employment.

This emphasis on education is related to other changes in the economy and in society. While employment on farms and in factories declined, it increased in occupations that demand further training. This more extensive education required that society have the increased wealth to fund schools and support children for a longer period before they begin to work. As social mobility became a more universal goal, the advantages enjoyed by middle-class children were challenged, although never overcome despite serious efforts to create educational equality.

Changes in the opportunities for women were more dramatic. By the 1980s, the proportion of women in higher education was approaching that of men in much of Western Europe; and they constituted one-third of the students even in the Netherlands, the lowest proportion in Western Europe. Women everywhere have become more prominent in all the professions and in politics. In Britain, France, and Germany, women make up some 40 percent of the work force; and as their number increased, labor unions came to pay more attention to their needs, in Italy, for example, winning released time for paid educational leave in special courses for working women. Child care is widely provided by European governments and employers, so that women are in effect encouraged to think in terms of careers. On the average, however, women workers continue to earn less than men (between two-thirds as much in Britain and four-fifths as much in France), but social attitudes and gender relations are clearly changing, as the steady stream of articles and television programs on these topics indicates.

Urban Life Postindustrial society is essentially urban, and Europe had long experience in making that adjustment. Its well-organized cities were relatively well-prepared to assume new functions. At the same time, people with more wealth and leisure often wanted more space and privacy than cities offered. While the inner core of older cities lost population, the urban agglomeration expanded across the surrounding suburbs. One-fifth of the population of France lives within an hour's drive of Paris, and nearly that proportion of Britain's population is similarly close to London. Volgograd stretches for 45 miles along the river after which it was named, and some 14 cities of the former Soviet Union have a population of over a million. In general, the new highways, extended subways, and bus lines that push the cities outward rarely keep pace with the congestion of traffic at their core. As similar-looking skyscrapers rise in the city centers and in new business centers around what had been the periphery, similar residential districts sprawl across the outskirts.

In the 1950s new housing tended, East and West, to look like dreary concrete barracks and often provided few of the services necessary to create a sense of community. In nearly every country, whole new cities, often bleak and artificial, surround the metropolis: Five towns of 24,000 people each were placed around Paris; twenty-four such towns now surround Moscow. Since the 1970s the trend has shifted to new urban hubs on a smaller scale, carefully planned to have shopping, recreational, and cultural centers of their own as well as some light industry so that much of the working population need not commute. Many of these ventures—those in Scandinavia were among the first (Tapiola, outside Helsinki, being one of the most successful)—have proved to be attractive models, widely imitated, mixing large and small modern buildings, pleasant streets, and restful green spaces. From the 1960s on, European governments invested in expensive projects of urban renewal, refurbishing urban centers across much of Western Europe, often with stunning effects; Europe has some of the world's most interesting experiments in urban planning. Cities like Rome and Vienna found that banning traffic from the narrow, medieval streets of their old centers made them more attractive (and expensive) for shops and housing. Although loud laments accompanied the closing of Les Halles in Paris, the great sheds built in the Second Empire for the provisioning of the capital, the efficiency and improved traffic that resulted were (like the controversial but exciting new cultural center and apartments that replaced Les Halles in the 1970s) undeniable benefits. In London, the produce sellers of Covent Garden gave way to a cultural center; and Billingsgate, the fishmarket that gave the language a word for verbal abuse, closed in 1981. Although the effects in terms of social cohesion and convenience are disputed, far more Europeans are comfortably housed with more living space and better hygiene than ever before.

Social Welfare By every measure, the standard of living of the working classes has risen impressively, but the gap between wage earners and the very rich has narrowed only slightly in the West (income distribution is least uneven in Sweden and the Netherlands). In Communist Europe professional people and officials lived at a much higher standard and with far greater freedom of choice than workers or peasants, an important element in the unpopularity and ultimate downfall of those governments.

Throughout Europe, the full impact of these inequalities has been softened by complex provisions for social security, free education (in most of Europe even universities do not charge tuition), universal medical care, and a wide variety

▸ **The glass structures that replaced Paris's central market evoke the iron and glass pavillions built a century earlier but now contain shops, museums, and a media center. New apartment buildings stand in the background. Leveling the crowded old mercantile buildings surrounding the market also provided a view of the gothic church of St. Eustache that had not been seen for centuries.**

of family benefits and services. Not surprisingly, in the nations of Western Europe rates of infant mortality have declined and rates of longevity have improved to become among the highest in the world. In Communist Europe good housing remained scarce, and there were long waiting lists for cramped apartments; but housing and transport were kept relatively cheap. In the West, too, governments extensively subsidized low-income housing (in the 1980s about one-third of new housing in Germany was government sponsored, one-half in Great Britain, two-thirds in Sweden and France). Elaborate programs provide for the elderly, whose proportion of the population has increased as people live longer and families have fewer children (birthrates in Europe are now generally the lowest in the world, lowest of all in Italy, where the average per family is but 1.3 children).

Social differences are more acceptable in periods of rapid economic growth. As growth slowed in the 1980s, the cost of social programs began to weigh more heavily. Taxes in Western Europe have been relatively high, absorbing between 21 and 24 percent of the gross national product (GNP). In theory they should fall most heavily on the rich, although in practice they often do not. As early as the 1970s unemployment had begun to rise, depressing whole regions that had never enjoyed industrial prosperity (such as Ireland, large parts of Spain and Portugal, and southern Italy), as well as areas dependent on declining industries. On the whole, programs of special subsidies and tax incentives meant to ease conditions in these areas have had disappointing results; and by the 1990s endemic unemployment had become one of Europe's most pressing social problems, with young people and foreign immigrants hardest hit.

New Issues: Foreign Workers and the Environment Unemployment had virtually disappeared in the industrial zones during the 1960s, and large numbers of people from the less developed periphery began moving to more prosperous regions. Southern Italians went to northern Italy, Switzerland, and Germany; Spaniards, Portuguese, and North Africans to France; Yugoslavs and Turks to Germany; African and Caribbean blacks, Indians, and Pakistanis from former colonies to England. Although most often employed as domestic servants, street sweepers, and the least skilled industrial workers, they also contributed to Europe's economic miracle. By the 1970s

▸ **Many German cities have districts, like this one in Cologne, that almost look as if they were in Turkey.**

these immigrants made up 17 percent of the work force in Switzerland, some 8 percent in Germany, and only slightly less than that in France. Often different in physical appearance, language, and culture from the majority of those around them, they were drawn together and forced by poverty to live in slums that quickly became ghetto subcultures, resistant to and misunderstood by the larger society. Without the full protection of citizenship, resented by native workers competing for jobs and higher pay, despised as sources of crime and heavy welfare costs, these migrants recreated some of the gravest social problems of the early nineteenth century, now exacerbated by prejudices of race and color. Nevertheless, many of these immigrants gradually came to see themselves as permanent residents. Many acquired citizenship, as their children automatically did (except in Germany). This second generation went to local schools and for the most part adopted local ways, and government programs lessened the housing crisis. Immigrant families, however, were the first to feel the effects of any economic downturn. Their problems, and the prejudice against them, were problems for which most European societies were ill prepared (*see box*, p. 1010).

Everywhere economic growth brought pollution that contaminated the air, waterways, and countryside as it poured from factories and automobiles and littered the landscape. Monuments and scenic places revered for centuries came to be seriously threatened; yet Western Europe was slow to respond, and in Eastern Europe the problem was ruthlessly ignored. The Rhine became one of the most polluted of international waterways, and high concentrations of mercury have been recorded in Geneva's Lac Leman. It is now dangerous to bathe in or eat fish from much of the Baltic and Mediterranean seas. Escaped industrial gases have caused illness and death in the outskirts of Milan, and the magnificent palaces of Venice were discovered to be slowly sinking, apparently because the earth beneath their pilings gives way as underground water is pumped up on the mainland for industrial use. The remaining monuments of ancient Greece and Rome and the ornate facades of Gothic churches in city after city crumble and crack from the vibrations and fumes of modern traffic.

Governments intent upon stimulating growth were reluctant to impose the restrictions and undertake the expense required to protect the environment until strong ecology movements in Germany, Britain, the Low Countries, and France forced their hand. Huge demonstrations against nuclear power and environmental parties, known everywhere as the green parties, became politically important; and several international agencies now enforce European standards against pollution. Although more remains to be done, the gains have been impressive. Stern regulations eliminated the smog that had plagued London since the sixteenth century, killing thousands of people as recently as 1952. The Thames has become a clean river for the first time in centuries. Nearly every building in Paris was cleaned in the 1960s and 1970s, stripping away the somber, dark patina of soot accumulated through 150 years of industrialization. By the 1980s, citizens' movements, well-organized programs for recycling, and strict regulations were changing the landscape across Europe; and European states had become leaders in international measures to protect the environment. Green parties complicated old political alignments, but at least parts of their programs have been embraced by larger parties, and their political importance continues; the effects have been socially and economically beneficial.

European Cooperation Western Europeans have increasingly come to see themselves as belonging to a region of shared values and culture, an awareness in part imposed by political experience from World War II and the Marshall Plan to the Cold War and NATO.[1] But idealism, facilitated by prosperity and a half century of peace,

---

[1]Geographers list 19 nations as belonging to Western Europe: Austria, Belgium, Denmark, Finland, France, Greece, Iceland, Ireland, Italy, Lichtenstein, Luxemburg, the Netherlands, Norway, Portugal, Spain, Sweden, Switzerland, the United Kingdom, and West Germany. All of these save Finland now belong to the Council of Europe, which also includes Cyprus, Malta, and Turkey.

Belgium, Denmark, Iceland, West Germany, Italy, Luxemburg, Netherlands, Norway, Portugal, Turkey, the United Kingdom, Canada, and the United States belong to NATO, as do France and Greece, although their armed forces no longer are under NATO command.

A Turkish Girl Arrives in Germany

Aynur, a young Turkish girl, published in a Turkish newspaper a very personal and frank account of her life in Germany. She had gone to Germany with her mother to live with her father, who had worked there several years. Leaving her village elementary school behind, she went to a Turkish school in Germany and lived there into her teens. As she adopted new ways, she became alienated from her family, found German friends only among groups of homosexuals and drug addicts, and eventually made several visits to Turkey in search of old ties to her extended family and native culture. She ends her account with the comment, "On my birth certificate it is written that I am a 'Turk.' But in the full sense, more correctly, with my thinking, I am not completely a Turk. I do not want to be a German either." In the passage quoted here, she describes her first days in Germany.

"A bustle of activity commenced as soon as the plane landed in Berlin. Everyone wanted to disembark. I looked for the sun as soon as we went out, but it wasn't to be seen. I thought I was before a gray wall. The weather was cloudy and rainy. Later on I started looking for blond people. I always thought that all Germans were blond.

"We took a taxi. I was watching out of the window. I was trying to see the white houses which I had dreamed about. All around were large brick buildings. There were no people in sight on the wide boulevards. I was constantly asking my father, 'Which one looks like our house?'

"Finally we got out of the taxi. I was looking around to find the house that they lived in. My father, pointing to a somewhat larger door, said, 'You enter here.' An old door, all the edges of which were broken, and a somewhat large building from which the plaster was falling. After we entered through the large door and went through the small concrete courtyard, we started climbing the stairs. The holding-on places were broken.

"Suddenly all of my illusions were shattered. Pessimism and dejection overcame me. We climbed until the fourth floor. My father opened the door. A small hallway, a living room, and a kitchen. That was all there was to the home. The toilet was outside, they said.

"I asked myself, 'Is this our house?' I withdrew to a corner and started to investigate the living room. In the middle a faded rug was laid. Around it stood a few old armchairs. The only new thing was a fairly large television that stood in the corner. Forgetting everything, we started playing with the television. At each press of a button, a different film appeared.

"Six of us started to live together in the one-room house. This situation did not strike me as odd. In our village, too, we used to live all together. Since I had not had any different living experience, this did not seem unusual.

"My older sister and I did not get out of the room for a period of three months. We were afraid, and moreover, our father was not giving us permission. Our only tie to the outside was a window facing the courtyard. Children were playing in the courtyard. My only wish was to play with them. From time to time I was able to talk through the kitchen window with our neighbor's daughter, who was a year older than I. I was impatiently waiting for her return from school. My first friend in Germany was this girl.

"Her hair was cut very short. She looked like a very modern girl. We went down together to the courtyard entrance to play. I gained a little courage. After that I started going to their home.

"We used to wear skirts over pajamas in our village. My father had bought slacks for us in Istanbul. From then on we wore slacks under our skirts instead of pajamas. Slowly I began to imitate my friend. When no one was at home, I would take off my skirt and walk around in my slacks. At other times, I would take off my slacks and walk around in just my skirt. My older sister was not able to dare to do this. She would sit at the window as my look-out.

"For a long time when we went outside, we wore slacks under our skirts."

Story by Aynur, Akural (tr.), published in Ilhan Basgöz and Norman Furniss (eds.), *Turkish Workers in Europe* (Bloomington, Indiana: Turkish Studies, 1985).

contributed, too. One expression of that idealism is the Council of Europe, founded in 1949. A forum with no binding powers, its member states must uphold individual freedom and the rule of law—which meant that Spain, Portugal, and Greece were excluded when ruled by dictators and so, too, initially were all the nations of Eastern Europe. The Council now has 27 members, and its committees and assembly meet in Strasbourg where they establish general policies on common political and social issues and adjudicate complaints against any member state for violations of the Council's statutes. The aspirations it represents (the Council's anthem is Beethoven's "Ode to Joy") have made its flag a popular symbol on buildings and private automobiles across the continent.

The greatest force for European cooperation has been the European Community (EC), which grew from the creation in 1958 of a limited economic community or common market by France, Germany, Italy, and the three Benelux countries. At the time, Great Britain refused to join. Reluctant to accept permanent political ties to the continent or to loosen its Commonwealth connections, Britain led instead in creating the European Free Trade Association (EFTA). A looser association joined by Sweden, Norway, Denmark, Austria, Switzerland, and Portugal, it set more limited goals (free trade among its members, for example, but not a common tariff). The ensuing competition between the two groups was closely watched. Sweden, with the most socialist economic system, and Switzerland, with the most thoroughly free market system, had achieved the highest per capita income in the industrial world. In rate of growth, however, the United Kingdom remained last among major European countries, and the states of the European Community enjoyed the highest increase in per capita productivity at an amazing rate of over 4 percent a year.

The European Community By 1968 (sooner than its organizers had expected) all tariffs between members of the Community had been abolished; and in 1973, after extended negotiations, Great Britain, Ireland, and Denmark joined the European Community.[2] Twice before Britain had asked for membership with special concessions (to protect it from the Community's agricultural policies and to preserve its Commonwealth interests) only to be blocked by De Gaulle's opposition and by a general concern that separate arrangements could undermine the Community's coherence. Together the nine members of the European Community now surpassed the United States in the production of automobiles and steel, and by 1979 they surpassed the United States in total GNP as well. Steps toward fuller economic integration among the nine were more difficult, however, especially with regard to agricultural policy. The Community's subsidies of agricultural products resulted in costly stockpiles as each nation sought benefits for its own farmers. Britain, which imports most of its food and has fewer farmers, was required to contribute far more toward the cost of these subsidies than the EC spent in Britain; and its vigorous protests forced adjustments that led to some reform of agricultural policies in 1981. That continuing issue was complicated, however, by the further enlargement of the Community to include Greece in 1981 and Spain and Portugal in 1986, all countries with strong and competing agricultural interests.

The process of integrating the economies and societies of the Community's 12 states continued nevertheless, and that increasingly involved broader social and political issues. In 1972 the heads of government of the EC countries began meeting regularly several times a year, an important step toward more coordinated policies. Every six months another government serves as chair, often making it a point of pride to push for some new acccomplishment. Ordinary affairs are handled by the Community's permanent Council, with a representative from each member state, and by a large bureaucracy with headquarters in Brussels, directed by an appointed Commission. On many complicated economic and legal matters EC officials were acting as an independent executive. In 1979 a mechanism was created for regulating exchange rates, and the citizens of each member nation began voting directly for delegates to the Community's parliament, where the representatives sit according to party rather

[2]In a surprising referendum, Norwegians voted not to join the European Community, one of many signs of resistance to the Community's centralizing tendencies and to its domination by France and Germany—concerns that have been strongest in the Scandinavian countries and in Britain.

▶ **Flags of the member states fly outside the Brussels headquarters of the European Union.**

than nationality.[3] The establishment of an elected parliament, one official declared, "marks the birth of the European citizen." The parliament's powers remained very limited, but in the 1980s the Council was empowered to make some decisions without unanimous agreement from all member states; the Community's institutional autonomy was growing. The decisions of the Community's Court of Justice led to increasingly uniform regulations (on standards of product quality, insurance, and environmental issues, for instance) and to common legal rights for migrant workers. Special grants to poorer regions—including the northwestern part of the British Isles, southern Italy, and the poorer members generally (Ireland, Portugal, Spain, and Greece)—brought those regions closer to the Community's general level of prosperity; and the Community gained a voice in matters long considered the exclusive concern of national governments.

Steps toward European Unity Remarkable as it has been, the Community's growth has not been a steady progress nor gone unopposed. The Preamble to the 1957 treaty establishing the EC expressed the desire "to lay the foundations of ever-closer union among the peoples of Europe . . . and to ensure economic and social progress by common action. . . ." Over the next 30 years that lofty rhetoric was frequently ignored by politicians and ridiculed by journalists, as often acrimonious conflict over issues both minute and grand stifled new initiatives. There was thus some surprise when Jacques Delors, the unusu-

[3]The complexities of representation are exemplified by the fact that France, Great Britain, Italy, and West Germany were given 81 representatives each (a large enough number to ensure Scotland and Wales more representatives than Denmark or Ireland). The Netherlands and Belgium were each allotted 25, but Belgium preferred 24 (so that the Flemings and Walloons would have equal representation), which meant a gift of 1 representative to Denmark, which has 16. Ireland has 15 representatives; Luxemburg, 6; Greece, 24; Portugal, 24; and Spain, 60.

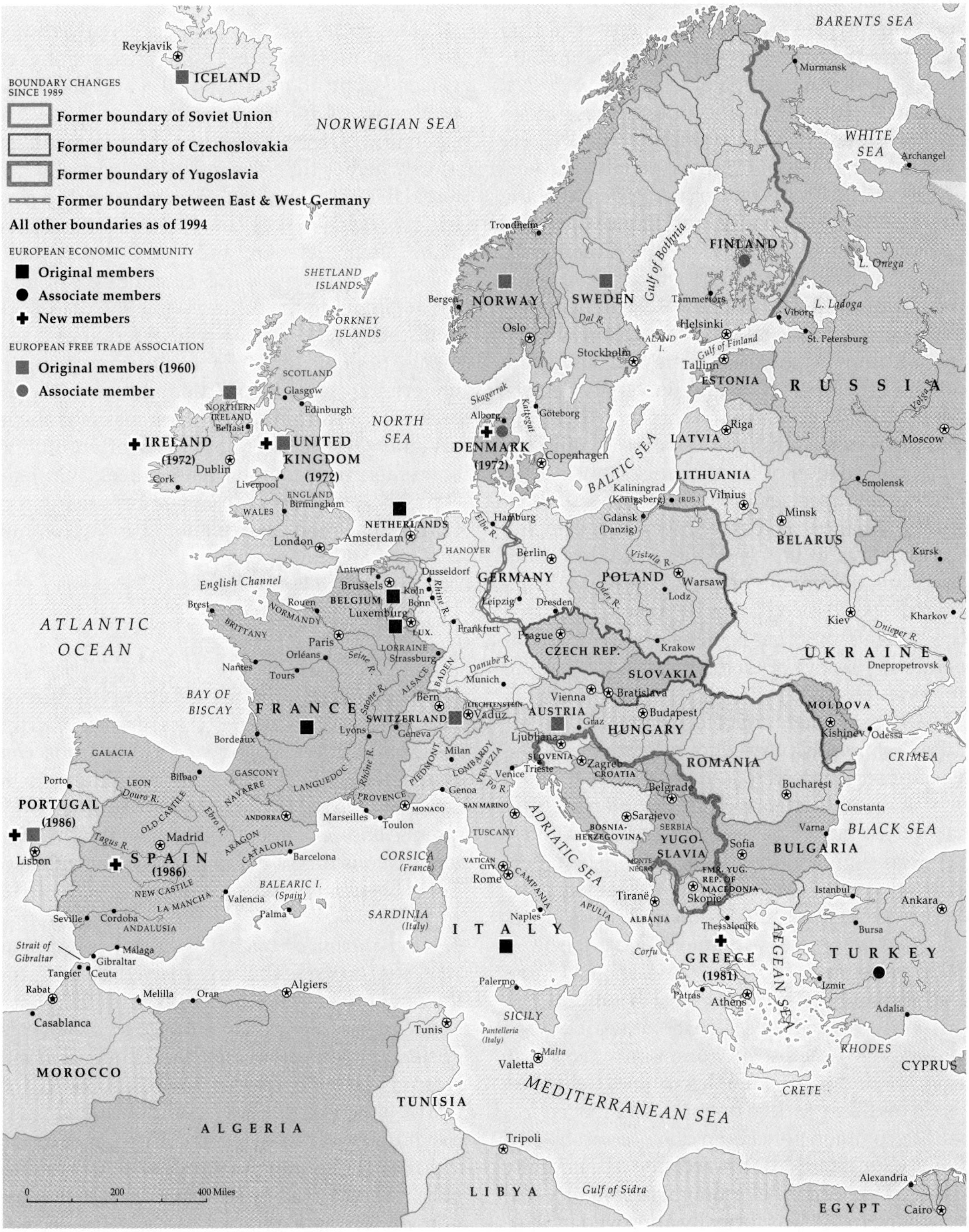

Map 30.1 EUROPE SINCE WORLD WAR II

ally effective president of the Community's executive body, the Commission, succeeded in winning support in 1986 for the Single European Act. In addition to Community programs in education (hundreds of thousands of students now regularly study in another European country), research, and environmental protection, the Act declared that by the end of 1992 there would no longer be any restrictions within the Community on the movement of goods, services, workers, or capital. With minor exceptions, these terms were met; and that has brought some striking changes in the lives of ordinary people. The border checkpoints between Germany, Belgium, the Netherlands, Luxembourg, and France have disappeared, and all citizens of the Community carry a community passport and cross national boundaries without restriction. Any of them may open a bank account, take out a mortgage, receive medical care, or practice a profession anywhere in the EC, for the licenses and university degrees of one are recognized in all the others. Vast arrays of national regulations had to be made uniform; and in anticipation of these changes, businesses, government agencies, and schools set about forming alliances across borders and bringing their practices in line with those of other countries. Thus the impact of the Community in individual societies continues to go beyond formal requirements as organizations and individuals begin to think and operate in terms of the Community as a whole.

With this momentum before them, the leaders of the Community pressed for more changes, and the 12 nations agreed to a treaty signed at Maastricht in the Netherlands in the beginning of 1992 that was so far-reaching it had to be separately approved within each member nation, by plebiscite or vote of the national parliament. The Maastricht treaty granted some increased power to the Community's parliament, gave the EC a major voice in a common social policy (from which Britain won exemption partly on principle and partly because the Conservatives opposed the generous benefits the Community required), began plans for a common currency (allowing Britain and Denmark to opt out), and looked forward to common policies on defense and foreign affairs. But attitudes toward the Community changed as domestic economies faltered. Although the treaty was formally approved in 1993, in nation after nation the votes were so close and the treaty passed with so many conditions that its larger significance was undermined. Rising resentments of the Community's bureaucratic regulations and the complexity of the treaty made it an easy target for opponents of its government sponsors. In each country there was strong, organized opposition as national coalitions formed combining all the interests that feared they had something to lose. There was disagreement, too, as to whether the EC should focus on closer internal ties or on broadening its membership. Austria, Sweden, Norway, and Finland applied to become members soon; and the Czech republic, Poland, and Hungary had all indicated an interest in joining in the future. While the roadblocks to further political union remain serious, governments hesitant, and the future uncertain, the underlying movement continues nonetheless, pushed, for the moment at least, more by the individual decisions of hundreds of institutions and enterprises than by governments. On January 1, 1994, the European Community became the European Union, and planning for a common currency and foreign policy was slowly and cautiously revived.

THE SEARCH FOR ALTERNATIVES

Social democratic principles greatly influenced Western Europe's domestic programs, but capitalism and liberal confidence in free trade were cornerstones of the European Community. In the 1960s and 1970s a number of quite different economic and political programs had fought for alternative visions of the future, less dependent on established elites and consumerism.

The Revolution of 1968 For a few weeks in May 1968 the students of Paris seemed to recapture the revolutionary spirit of 1848, with their barricades of paving stones and trees, imaginative posters, and mocking slogans. Students briefly acted as an independent political force in Germany, Italy, Great Britain, and the United States, too, in 1968 and 1969. Inspired by the movements of national liberation in Africa and Asia and appalled by the war in Vietnam, they denounced imperialism as a product of capitalist societies that used consumer goods to mask inequality and injustice and excoriated the rigidities of the educational system to which they were subject. As revolutions, these movements failed. Labor unions and the traditional left were suspicious of privileged college students; liberals and conservatives were offended by bad manners and violence. In elections following these upheavals, the majority of voters turned to parties that emphasized order. These protest movements nevertheless stimulated important reforms, especially of education; and their style of protest, their challenges to middle-class values, and their questioning of authority have remained important elements in public discourse.

In Czechoslovakia the optimism of 1968, when Alexander Dubček came to power, was even shorter lived. As Communist party secretary, he was able to adopt a program of liberalization calling for greater autonomy for Slovakia and for freedom of speech, assembly, and religion. Students there, too, were enthusiastic for this "communism with a human face"; but Moscow saw it as an intolerable danger to the stability of Eastern Europe. In the largest military operation in Europe since World War II, troops from the Soviet Union, East Germany, Hungary, and Poland invaded Czechoslovakia in August. Dubček was soon ousted; and of his springtime program, only Slovakian autonomy was allowed to stand.

▶ **After weeks of student demonstrations in Paris, police use buses to cordon off the Sorbonne shortly before storming the university and evicting the students in June 1968.**

The End of Dictatorship in Greece, Portugal, and Spain Despite the power concentrated in the modern state, revolutions were possible. In Greece they came primarily as military coups. In 1967, army officers overthrew the unstable parliamentary system and eventually the monarchy itself, but then in 1973, the military dictatorship was forced to give way to civilian leaders who restored democracy. The failure of the military was part of a larger lesson. To strengthen a fragile but modernizing economy, Greece's repressive military rulers had needed to draw closer to Western Europe, where there was little inclination to deal with dictators. As the military regime, weakened by conflict with Turkey over control of Cyprus, gradually felt compelled to restore freedoms, its own unpopularity was exposed. Political tensions remained high under the socialist government that won victory in 1981 as it stridently asserted its independence of America's Cold War policies; but the course of Greek development toward democracy and economic growth was well under way—marked by admission to the European Community—by the time charges of corruption cost the Socialists their support in 1989.

Portugal and Spain had been ruled by dictators since the 1930s, and their end was even more remarkable. In Portugal the Salazar regime, which had paralleled Franco's long period of rule in Spain, continued in milder form even after Salazar became incapacitated in 1968. While opposition remained stymied at home, it grew stronger in Portuguese Guinea, Angola, and Mozambique, where Portugal relied on brute force to hold on to its empire. Condemned in the United Nations, by African states, and by most European nations, the overtaxed government was suddenly seized in April 1974 by a group of army officers promising full freedom and civil rights as well as self-determination for the colonies. The response was overwhelming. Crowds danced in the streets and cheered smiling soldiers whose rifles were decorated with flowers.

The euphoria could not last. A poor and backward country, Portugal faced raging inflation and declining production. While peasants claimed the land they had long coveted, socialist and communist unions competed for support among the workers, business groups struggled to defend their interests, and many prominent businessmen left the country. The army leaders themselves were ideologically divided, and for two years cabinets were formed and fell after only a few months in the face of revolts from left and right. Nevertheless, the nationalization of banks and industry was followed by free elections in 1975 and 1976 and by the election of the moderate General António Ramalho Eanes as president. Reasonable stability followed as the Socialists overshadowed the Communists to become the largest political party and centrist coalitions brought Portugal closer to the other governments of Western Europe. The elections of 1985–1986 that accompanied Portugal's joining the European Community made Mario Soares, a Socialist and former prime minister, Portugal's first democratically elected civilian president in 60 years.

The political transformation in Spain was more gradual. Franco retired in 1973 but skillfully kept his influence until his death two years later. In 1969 Franco had called for Juan Carlos, the grandson of Spain's last king, to take the empty throne as in effect his heir; and the new king proved both more committed to democracy and more adept than expected. Many feared a recurrence of civil war, and with freedom old animosities reappeared in the open but then subsided as the voters approved a new constitution in 1978. Greater regional autonomy reduced agitation from separatists (although Basque terrorist movements remained), a split in the Communist party reduced pressure from the left, and the failure of a military coup in 1981 cleared the way for a stable democracy. Long dormant, Spanish society was changing. Only in 1950 had the gross national product regained the level of 1935, but growth increased more rapidly in each succeeding decade, exploding in the 1970s and 1980s. Under the premiership of the extremely popular Socialist Felipe Gonzales, the Spanish economy radically restructured. Gonzales supported the decision to join NATO even when it seemed unpopular and led Spain into the European Community in 1986, ending Spain's long isolation.

Terrorism Elsewhere in Europe some radical groups, rather than abandon their fading hope for revolution, turned to terrorism. In the semisecret world of international crime, espionage, and arms deals that prospered in the Cold War, the skills and equipment necessary for a terrorist campaign were not hard to come by. Although terrorists were few in number, the complexity and urban anonymity of modern society made it vulnerable. Small groups could not expect to gain power directly, but they could hope to provoke the authorities into repressive responses that in turn would alienate the larger public. German terrorists made business leaders as well as politicians their targets until they were defeated by severely efficient police. Basque terrorists shook several Spanish governments with bombs and murders but accomplished little more, although some Spaniards, especially in the army, demanded military action. In Italy, Marxist and neo-Fascist underground bands competed in kidnappings and bombings accompanied by revolutionary proclamations. In 1978 the Red Brigades followed a series of dramatic actions by kidnapping Aldo Moro, a Christian Democrat who was sympathetic to the left. As the nation held its breath, the police searched for him in vain until his bullet-riddled body was found in a car abandoned in Rome near the headquarters of the major political parties. From Communists to conservatives, the public responded with firm outrage, and the state neither collapsed nor turned to repression. Clearly counterproductive, terrorism was on the wane when the Red Brigades captured an American NATO commander in 1982; and the police, armed with information garnered from years of trials and investigations, were able to capture a number of terrorists and free their hostage, dealing a serious blow to their movement. Such incidents, like the shooting of Pope John Paul II by a Turkish terrorist in 1981, provoked outcries about the alienation and violence of modern society but changed it very little.

Terrorism was most effective when it fed regional or religious hatreds that provided a popular base. In Northern Ireland, where Catholics believed they should be part of the Irish Republic and Protestants insisted on keeping British rule, terrorism rose to the level of continuous war. The Irish Republican Army, an underground organization repudiated by the Irish Republic, and extremist Protestant groups killed hundreds of innocent people. As the number of martyrs mounted, the British government had to postpone its program for local rule. Despite a growing desire on all sides for some workable solution, issues of nationality, discrimination, and repression allowed violence to prevent a resolution. There were also incidents of terrorism in Europe that were associated with the conflicts of the Middle East. Supporters of the Palestine Liberation Organization, seeking a Palestinian state, killed Israeli athletes at the Munich Olympic Games in 1972, and in the 1970s other Muslim terrorists placed bombs in Paris stores or aimed them at American tourists. In response, security measures and heavily armed police became more prominent on European streets, but society was not seriously disrupted. Terrorism had become more a means of demonstration than a path to revolution.

Communism and Eurocommunism In contrast, Communist parties in Western Europe were seeking by the 1980s to broaden their appeal. Italy's party, the largest Communist party outside the Soviet bloc, was especially innovative. It sponsored dozens of publications aimed at women, students, and intellectuals as well as workers and held great public celebrations that had elements of an industrial exhibit and a rock concert with lectures and seminars on the side. The spectacle and the content were impressive, even if there was less sense of revolutionary community than in the years right after the war. The party's tone had become less doctrinaire, and it was less inclined to hold up the Soviet Union as the model of the future than it had been 20 years before. The members of the Italian party elected to the European Parliament chose to sit with the Socialists from other countries rather than the Communists. By the end of the decade they voted to change their name, dropping the term *Communist* altogether and removing the hammer and sickle from their flag.

Everywhere Communists concentrated less on revolution than they used to. In the West, years of electoral and union activity had established party positions on scores of immediate, practical issues. Arguing for social justice and political freedom invited commitment to pluralism and democracy; criticizing Soviet policies in Eastern Europe, as many Communist now did, opened prospects for alternative programs. This came to be known as Eurocommunism; and Italy's Communist party was its model and major proponent.[4] In this new tack the party made use of the ideas of Antonio Gramsci, a Communist hero who had died in prison under Fascism. Gramsci was one of the ablest of modern Marxist theoreticians, and in the 1970s his writings, most of which had only recently been published, would gain an extraordinary influence among intellectuals and social scientists throughout Western Europe and the United States. Gramsci's Marxism emphasized the role of culture in shaping social behavior and maintaining the dominance of elites. At a practical level, that justified flexible respect for the liberal and even religious values generally admired in the West (and touted in Cold War rhetoric as the antithesis of Communism). Under the leadership of Enrico Berlinguer, a suave and attractive politician, the Italian party formally declared its support of civil rights, mul-

[4]Communist parties had traditionally attracted nearly one-third of the electorate in Italy, one-fifth in France and Finland, one-eighth in Spain, and much less elsewhere: about 5 percent in Sweden, 4 percent in Denmark, 3 percent in Belgium, 2 percent in Greece and the Netherlands, and less than 1 percent in West Germany and Great Britain. The parties in Portugal, briefly powerful after the revolution there, and in Finland were the two least inclined to Eurocommunism.

tiple parties, and free elections. The electoral successes and increased esteem that followed broadened the Italian Communist party's influence at home and abroad and eventually led the French Communist party, traditionally among Europe's most Stalinist, toward a similar stance. Even before that, both parties had denounced the Soviet invasion of Czechoslovakia in 1968; and Italian Communists even accepted NATO. With the liberalization in Spain, the Spanish Communist party also adopted a Eurocommunist stance.

The Soviet Union exerted heavy pressure on these Western Communist parties to conform to its leadership and restore the unity of European Communism, but by the sixtieth anniversary of the Russian Revolution in 1977, Eurocommunism marked a new schism in the Communist ranks. Even non-Communist Marxists remained skeptical, however, noting that Communist parties remained highly centralized, intolerant, suspicious of the European Community, and on foreign policy closely tied to Soviet and anti-American positions. With the prosperity of the 1980s, it was the socialist parties of Italy, France, Spain, Portugal, and Greece that gained power; and the appeal of Eurocommunism began to fade. The decline of radical alternatives on the left and right, which left the societies of Western Europe seeming more alike, also made it easier to build toward a European Union.

II. Understanding the Present

CONTEMPORARY CULTURE

Liberation from war and repression had stimulated a burst of creativity in the 1940s and 1950s, which in form and content clearly continued prewar culture. In the period that followed, radically new perspectives led to efforts, in every field, to rethink culture itself. Collectively known as *postmodernism*, these challenges to older conceptions of culture have been a principle source of the ideas, vocabulary, and creative expression most characteristic of contemporary intellectual life.

Postwar Creativity In much of Europe the end of fascism and world war unleashed ideas and artistic styles long banned. Sudden exposure to work previously produced in secret and in the United States, much of it the work of European émigrés, was an exciting stimulus. Artists already famous in the 1930s, like the painter Pablo Picasso and the poet T. S. Eliot, could simultaneously be honored as grand old figures and savored with a freshness usually reserved for the young. This continuity in the arts was tempered by somber reflections on the intervening experience of dictatorship, war, and postwar dislocation.

Neorealism flourished, especially in Italy, where the novels of Ignazio Silone and Alberto Moravia gave incisive, detailed accounts of the daily lives of little people buffeted by movements and events beyond their control, and where the films of Roberto Rossellini and Vittorio de Sica combined the harsh eye of the candid camera with sympathy for the minor characters who are society's victims and its strength. In Germany the plays of Bertolt Brecht, who moved to East Berlin in 1949, pursued similar themes but with a firm Marxist purpose; and the savagely satirical novels of Heinrich Böll extended the once-shocking surrealism of Franz Kafka to interpret Central Europe's experience of the twentieth century.

The New Wave The arts had never been more international, but their humane concerns were expressed in very individual terms. The novels of Alain Robbe-Grillet and the films of Jean François Truffaut, Ingmar Bergman, and Federico Fellini were personal essays, held together by the sensitivity and imagination of a single creator and by images simultaneously surreal and real. Identified in France as the *nouvelle vague* of the 1960s, this style had its counterpart in all the arts; and the focus on personal perception encouraged experimentation. In painting, abstract expressionism gave way to a great variety of styles often deliberately disturbing and garish—Pop Art, Op Art, and the satirically representational. The most admired sculptor was the English artist Henry Moore, whose huge reclining figures—with their combination of clean lines, solid masses, and empty spaces—were directly influenced by African art. Younger artists, however, experimented with ways to make the familiar new by using common objects, materials of every sort, and strange forms, and by creating gigantic "environmental" sculptures composed of lines traced across deserts or plastic wrapping stretched around whole buildings. Composers, too, shifted from the modernist formalism of the 12-tone scale and dissonance to the new sounds of *musique concrète* (everyday noises and musical sounds carefully arranged on spliced tapes) and of electronic music in the manner of the American John Cage and the German Karlheinz Stockhausen.

Although artists sought ways to stimulate the senses and open the minds of a public bombarded by images and sensations, few artistic conventions remained to be breached. One device was to absorb and distort technology for aesthetic purposes, playing on the ambiguity of flashing lights, random noise, plastics, and mechanical motion. Another was to break the barriers between "serious" and commercial art. As a result, advertising and movies have become more sophisticated and the music of popular entertainers, like the Beatles and many folk singers, became artistically more serious and complex.

ADAPTING VALUES

Developments in the arts paralleled those in other realms of thought. The horrors of genocide, totalitarianism, and war challenged traditional beliefs and reopened questions about values and the nature of knowledge, which were often seen as resting not on absolute or objective truth but on the needs and circumstances of the moment.

Existentialism One of the most influential movements of the postwar period, existentialism, offered a radical solution to the problem of ethics. Life may be absurd and meaningless, the French philosopher Jean-Paul Sartre argued, but to take any action is to make a decision, and that is to make a personal moral choice. Building on the prewar work of Karl Jaspers and Martin Heidegger in Germany, Sartre constructed a radical individualism that centered on moral responsibility. In the worst of circumstances, human beings were nevertheless free to make some choices; and in a world without ultimate meaning, the sum of the choices made gave each life its moral meaning. The soldier could refuse to torture; the civilian could choose to resist custom or authority. Underneath its relentless pessimism, Sartre's existentialism held out the hope that a life of quiet heroism remained a possibility; and Sartre's version of existentialism—set forth in essays, dramas, and criticism—became enormously influential in the postwar period.

Expressed with great power in the novels of Albert Camus, these ideas not only fit a mood and met a need but offered many points of connection with other doctrines of human liberation. There were Christian existentialists and existentialist Marxists; positivists, liberals, and Freudians adopted much of existentialism's vocabulary and incorporated many of its insights. Like neorealism, existentialism found value in blind experience, but it spoke more clearly to moments of crisis than to the search for some larger meaning.

Christianity In the public anguish over values that has marked the postwar period, Christian voices, individually strong, have collectively had a rather uncertain effect. Leading theologians—also mainly men of an older generation, like Jaspers, Karl Barth, and Jacques Maritain—were studied with renewed interest. The Protestant Paul Tillich and the Catholic Pierre Teilhard de Chardin achieved a large following with their systematic claims for the relevance of Christianity to every facet of modern life.

Reflected in the postwar vigor of Christian political parties, this confidence in the relevance of Christianity illumined the papacy (1958–1963) of Pope John XXIII. He was extraordinarily popular, admired by Protestants as well as Catholics and by peasants and workers as well as intellectuals. Determined to recast the Church's position in modern life, he called the Vatican Council, which opened in 1962 and was dedicated to *aggiornamento*, a renewal to bring the Catholic Church up to date not just organizationally but in social policy as well. The Council made the leadership of the Church far more international, directed attention to the concerns of developing nations, made

▶ **Prelates from around the world stand as Pope Paul VI is carried on his throne into St. Peter's during the Vatican Council. Amid Renaissance splendor the leaders of the Catholic Church set about the task of *aggiornamento*.**

respect for Jews a formal policy, and expressed belief in religious liberty. Putting the individual believer's comprehension above institutional uniformity, it ordered that Masses be conducted in the vernacular instead of Latin. These changes encountered resistance, and with Pope John's death before the Council was completed, the Church turned to more cautious consolidation of doctrine and structure. Calls for more radical measures, such as more autonomy for national Church councils or ending the requirement that priests be celibate, have been firmly resisted. Confronting the dangers of the Cold War and the practices of modern life, the major Christian Churches tended to become more outspoken about moral behavior than social reform. While some Christian groups battled for radical programs of social justice and disarmament, established churches attacked rising divorce rates and pornography. The rise in church attendance in the 1950s was followed by a decline that included a steady drop in the number of clergy.

CONCEPTIONS OF SOCIETY

In the late twentieth century, competing social theories have been important to intellectual life and public policies. Theories of modernization optimistically envisioned economic and political development for all, and tried to determine how to achieve it. Marxist theoretical work, more critical of modern society, strengthened Western social sciences, and newer trends challenged both the methods of social science and the assumptions of Western superiority they encouraged.

Modernization and Marxism Social and political thought in the 1950s combined efforts to explain the recent past with prescriptions for dealing with the present. Theories of modernization traced a line of progressive development from absolute monarchy to liberal democracy; and in doing so, they sought to explain where nations that—like Germany, Italy, and Spain—did not sustain democracy had gone wrong. Answers to these historical questions could then guide policies toward developing nations around the world, helping them to achieve democratic stability. Such theories, especially pervasive in the United States, influenced the social sciences throughout the West. Scholars demonstrated how intricately social changes were interrelated; increased political freedom and economic growth required changes in law, education, and values. The integrated view of society and how it changes stimulated interdisciplinary research that was methodologically sophisticated, and it led Western scholars to give increased attention to the non-Western world. Much of it remains important for its findings and as methodological models of social scientific research. Its foundation has been heavily attacked, however, for assuming some universal pattern of development, for making an idealized description of the United States a goal required of all, for stressing consensus and compromise while ignoring social and political conflict, and for serving as a Cold War ideology in competition with Soviet Marxism.

Indeed, Marxist thought, also attached to ideas of progress, was the principal source of alternative conceptions. Varieties of Marxism, extending far beyond the rigid doctrines of communism, were influential throughout European intellectual life, especially in England and Italy, in the late 1960s and 1970s. In their flexibility and subtle insights, these neo-Marxist analyses made lasting contributions to the understanding of society and culture. Much of this new thinking emerged from the writings of the Frankfurt school. Founded in Weimar Germany, its leaders were forced into exile by Hitler (most of them went to the United States) and gained a wide readership in the postwar period. As social theorists, they incorporated modern sociology and psychology (especially Freudian ideas) with their profound distaste for mass culture and contemporary society. One of their members, Herbert Marcuse, who wrote learned essays that systematically criticized the commercialism and illusory freedoms of contemporary society, became a hero to leaders of the student revolts of 1968. The pervasiveness of Marxist thinking also owed a great deal to the work of Antonio Gramsci, whose writings gained almost universal admiration. Like the more doctrinaire Hungarian Georg Lukacs, Gramsci was a communist intellectual who took culture seriously, not simply as a reflection of society's material structure but in its own right. Pondering why the proletariat often shared bourgeois values and how elites maintained their authority, Gramsci developed the concept of cultural hegemony as the process through which the values and styles promulgated by an elite become, through custom and education, a part of the social fabric, accepted across social classes to shape thought and action within an entire nation. Ideas and works of art hailed as universal could be made instruments of domination.

Postmodernism A related challenge to the dominant culture occurred in many fields of creativity. The arts tended to become less austere and less concerned with the principles that academies taught and critics adhered to, a change particularly clear in architecture. For some 30 years, modern architecture, exemplified by the Bauhaus school, had developed an international style that favored the pure and simple forms of cube and rectangle and the simplicity of unadorned walls of glass. The newer styles rejected that aesthetic and deliberately featured unexpected shapes, echoes of older styles, pitched roofs with gables, and whimsical ornamentation; and because they rejected the international style of modernism, they were called *postmodern*. By extension, postmodern is also used to describe current directions in literature and scholarship that similarly turn away from rules of logical exposition and explicit evidence to search for the underlying meanings that convey suppressed needs and feelings. In the social sciences postmodernists expose the codes of domination in established theories and cultural practices, and by doing so, they can enthusiastically incorporate ethnic and folk cultures, playfully ignoring formal rules to better convey multiple and often contradictory perspectives.

Michel Foucault This attention to how people perceive themselves acquired more radical implications in the work of Michel Foucault, perhaps the most influential thinker of the 1980s, particularly in the United States and England. Foucault was trained as a philosopher, and his work achieved an international resonance much as Sartre's had a generation earlier. He consistently acknowledged his debt to Nietzsche and made use of Marx (although the extent of his Marxism is disputed). He was close to the French historians of the *Annales* school, whose emphasis on social history has affected historical study everywhere, and he absorbed much from the French anthropologist Claude Lévi-Strauss, who believed that every aspect of a supposedly primitive society—its kinship systems, customs, rituals, and myths—can be analyzed as the extension of unstated, complex, and integrated structures of thought. These hidden structures, Lévi-Strauss declared, reflect the nature of the human mind, a view that led him to an admiration of premodern societies comparable to that of many modern artists.

All these currents are present in Foucault, but most of all he built on the rising science of semiotics, the study of the signs by which human beings communicate. In Foucault's hands, semiotics provided the means for reinterpreting modern history and civilization. His periodization was conventional: Modernity emerged in the late eighteenth century and was heralded by the French Revolution. But he up-ended the conventional interpretations of what modernity meant. Medicine, psychology, and prison reform were instruments of a new social discipline, more mental than physical even when it was directed at the body. Thus the scientific observation of other people, however neutral or objective it claims to be, is also a means of controlling behavior through shared *discourse*—a crucial Foucauldian term. Discourse establishes the framework of understanding, categorically excluding some possibilities and urging others. It is a form of power, and power is one of Foucault's central concerns. Discourse functions within society to make power diffuse and pervasive, independent of public intent. Thus the very institutions and reforms of the nineteenth century that historians usually described as humane and progressive were an exercise of social power, constraining individuals while seeking their concurrence. Foucault's ideas (like his witty, perceptive, and involuted style) provided a new and effective way to challenge not just the acknowledged evils of modern society but the laws, institutions, practices, and conception of knowledge on which it rests. Without offering a solution, they are an arsenal of weapons with which to unmask intellectual claims to authority or objectivity (*see box*, p. 1023).

Poststructuralism and Gender Studies A further powerful attack on the apparent neutrality of logical reasoning and of philosophical and scientific categories is heavily indebted to Jacques Derrida. Like Foucault, a French cultural critic who uses the tools of semiotics and philosophy, Derrida, too, has more followers in the United States than in Europe. He studies literature by concentrating on the text and subjecting it to a technique he named *deconstruction*. The linguistic signs of which a text is composed are not straightforward—not *transparent*, to use a deconstructionist term—but carry multiple associations attached to the contexts from which they emerged. These signs contained in the text are then (mis)translated in the mind of the reader. Thus no text has one stable meaning but communicates on many levels at once and differently to different people. Deconstruction, the exploration of

Foucault on Sexual Discourse

One of Michel Foucault's last major works was* The History of Sexuality, *which explored the topic from ancient Greece to the present. In the selection here he touches on several of his major themes.

"But there may be another reason that makes it so gratifying for us to define the relationship between sex and power in terms of repression: something that one might call the speaker's benefit. If sex is repressed, that is, condemned to prohibition, nonexistence, and silence, then the mere fact that one is speaking about it has the appearance of a deliberate transgression. A person who holds forth in such language places himself to a certain extent outside the reach of power; he upsets established law; he somehow anticipates the coming freedom. This explains the solemnity with which one speaks of sex nowadays. When they had to allude to it, the first demographers and psychiatrists of the nineteenth century thought it advisable to excuse themselves for asking their readers to dwell on matters so trivial and base. But for decades now, we have found it difficult to speak on the subject without striking a different pose: we are conscious of defying established power, our tone of voice shows that we know we are being subversive, and we ardently conjure away the present and appeal to the future, whose day will be hastened by the contribution we believe we are making. Something that smacks of revolt, of promised freedom, of the coming age of a different law, slips easily into this discourse on sexual oppression. Some of the ancient functions of prophecy are reactivated therein. Tomorrow sex will be good again. Because this repression is affirmed, one can discreetly bring into coexistence concepts which the fear of ridicule or the bitterness of history prevents most of us from putting side by side: revolution and happiness; or revolution and a different body, one that is newer and more beautiful; or indeed, revolution and pleasure. What sustains our eagerness to speak of sex in terms of repression is doubtless this opportunity to speak out against the powers that be, to utter truths and promise bliss, to link together enlightenment, liberation, and manifold pleasures; to pronounce a discourse that combines the fervor of knowledge, the determination to change the laws, and the longing for the garden of earthly delights. This is perhaps what also explains the market value attributed not only to what is said about sexual repression, but also to the mere fact of lending an ear to those who would eliminate the effects of repression. Ours is, after all, the only civilization in which officials are paid to listen to all and sundry impart the secrets of their sex: as if the urge to talk about it, and the interest one hopes to arouse by doing so, have far surpassed the possibilities of being heard, so that some individuals have even offered their ears for hire.

"But it appears to me that the essential thing is not this economic factor, but rather the existence in our era of a discourse in which sex, the revelation of truth, the overturning of global laws, the proclamation of a new day to come, and the promise of a certain felicity are linked together. Today it is sex that serves as a support for the ancient form—so familiar and important in the West—of preaching. A great sexual sermon—which has had its subtle theologians and its popular voices—has swept through our societies over the last decades; it has chastised the old order, denounced hypocrisy, and praised the rights of the immediate and the real; it has made people dream of a New City. The Franciscans are called to mind. And we might wonder how it is possible that the lyricism and religiosity that long accompanied the revolutionary project have, in Western industrial societies, been largely carried over to sex."

From Michel Foucault, *The History of Sexuality*, Vol. I: *An Introduction*, Robert Hurley (tr.) (New York: Vintage Books, 1990).

multiple and hidden signification, thereby directly denies the existence of absolutes and rejects any pretense to objectivity.

Together, these currents of contemporary thought have come to be called *poststructuralism,* which describes itself as having moved beyond scientific models with their concern for logical structures, empirical evidence, and fixed categories. Poststructuralism is political in its drive to expose the asumptions hidden under general statements, assumptions that are attached to interests and power. Under the influence of poststructuralism, techniques of literary analysis have become central to contemporary theories of society. This new understanding of social custom, from forms of courtesy and dress to organizations and law, as constructing a culture of dominance has radically affected much modern scholarship. It has stimulated a large body of theory and transformed research on imperialism and women.

The need to take a new look at how imperialism functioned obviously reflected current events, decolonization, the relative decline in European power, the importance of the non-Western world, and the often difficult efforts to

A French View of the Feminist Movement

A prominent French intellectual, novelist, philosopher, and critic, Julia Kristeva is a leading feminist who brings the techniques of deconstruction to her writings on women, as this comment in an interview published in 1974 makes clear.

"Feminism can be but one of capitalism's more advanced needs to rationalize: Giscard d'Estaing, wishing to liquidate certain gaullist archaisms, invented the Secretary for the Status of Women. It's better than nothing, but it's not exactly right either. In the twentieth century, after suffering through fascism and revisionism, we should have learned that there can be no socio-political transformation without a transformation of subjects: in other words, in our relationship to social constraints, to pleasure, and more deeply, to language. What is politically 'new' today can be seen and felt in modern music, cartoons, communes of young people provided they do not isolate themselves on the fringes of society but participate in the contradiction inherent in political classes. The women's movement, if it has a raison d'être, seems to be part of this trend; it is, perhaps, one of its most radical components. In every political apparatus, whether on the Right, or the Left, the movement, by its negativity, indicates what is otherwise repressed: that 'class consciousness' for example, is not unrelated to the unconscious of the sexed speaker. The trap that is set for this demystifying force, a force that the women's movement can be, is that we will identify with the power principle that we think we are fighting: the hysterical saint plays her pleasure against social order, but in the name of God. The question is: 'Who plays God in present-day feminism?' Man? Or Woman—his substitute? As long as any libertarian movement, feminism included, does not analyze its own relationship to power and does not renounce belief in its own identity, it remains capable of being coopted both by power and an overtly religious or lay spiritualism. Besides, it is spiritualism's last great hope. The solution is infinite, since what is at stake is to move from a patriarchal society, of class and of religion, in other words from pre-history, toward—Who knows? In any event, this process involves going through what is repressed in discourse, in reproductive and productive relationships. Call it 'woman' or 'the oppressed social class': it's the same struggle, and you never have one without the other. It seems to me that the movement's most urgent task is to make the ideological and political machines understand this complicity. But this implies that we change our style, that we get out a bit from 'among women,' from among ourselves, that each one of us in our respective fields fights against social and cultural archaisms."

From an interview with Julia Kristeva published in Elaine Marks and Isabelle de Courtivron, *New French Feminisms: An Anthology* (Amherst: The University of Massachusetts Press, 1980).

shake off Western cultural and economic domination. Similarly, the rising interest in women's studies stems in large part from the social changes that have given women greater access to education and independent careers and public life. The interest in social history and the lives of ordinary people has contributed, too; but much of the excitement and influence of this research, which extends beyond particular topics, comes from the methods and theories it embodies. Thus women's studies, more strongly in the United States but also in Europe, too, are concerned not just with what women do but with gender. In current usage the term *gender* refers not just to biology but to a whole social construction, fabricated from custom, from views about the nature of women and men, and above all from seemingly neutral distinctions such as strength/weakness, rationality/irrationality, and public/private. In this light a great deal of history, anthropology, and sociology have been rethought and rewritten. The results, which have brought new interpretations of society and culture, past and present, have also given new strength within Europe to campaigns in behalf of groups previously marginalized and to feminist movements (*see box*, p. 1024).

III. The Politics of Prosperity

Even without the exuberant consumerism that filled the shops of Western cities, Eastern Europe discovered that economic growth and political stability could generate new challenges to the established order. Not only did the contrast between East and West grow more striking, and in agricultural as well as industrial production, but earlier achievements in heavy industry came to count for less economically than new technologies and services.

COMMUNIST COUNTRIES: THE PROBLEM OF RIGIDITY

The U.S.S.R. The Soviet Union's most impressive achievement, admired throughout the world, had been its industrial growth. By the 1960s the Soviet economy was second in overall production and wealth only to that of the United States. In 1961 it sent the first man into orbit around the earth; and as the world's largest producer of steel, iron, and more recently oil, the U.S.S.R. was apparently gaining on the West. Brash and outspoken, Khrushchev suggested that the Soviet government had no desire to risk these achievements in international confrontation and that it would give more attention to consumer products and adequate housing.

Like de-Stalinization, such policies opened the possibility of a new evolution in Soviet rule, but it proved difficult to accomplish. Khrushchev's plans to increase agricultural production failed, and the question of whether to invest in consumer goods or heavy industry revived longstanding conflicts within the highest circles. Many Kremlin leaders worried, as well, about growing restiveness in Eastern Europe and the rift with China, which since 1956 had begun denouncing the Soviet Union's international policies as a betrayal of communism. When, in the process of solidifying his authority, Khrushchev antagonized the military, they and his opponents in the Politburo and the Central Committee felt strong enough to speak against him. He was voted out of office in 1964 and sent into quiet retirement.

The orderly transition was promising in itself, but Khrushchev's successors were tough party technicians. Leonid Brezhnev emerged as the dominant figure, with a firm grip on power and no fresh solutions to the problems that had defeated Khrushchev. The cold-blooded invasion of Czechoslovakia, continuing agricultural crisis (which required the purchase of American grain in 1972 and 1975 and improved relations between the superpowers), and the need to import industrial technology, particularly from Italy and France, were all signs of a system failing to adapt to change.

Questions of civil rights also tarnished the international image of the Soviet Union. Boris Pasternak's novel *Doctor Zhivago*, like Khrushchev's denunciation of Stalin, had exposed the repressive and seamy aspects of Soviet life. Awarded the Nobel prize for literature in 1958, Pasternak was not permitted to go to Stockholm to receive it. The case of Alexander Solzhenitsyn caused still greater international furor. His *Gulag Archipelago*

▶ **Soviet science and industry gained enormous prestige with the first successful orbit of a space vehicle in 1957; and later, the atmosphere of détente made it possible to hold exhibits like this one in Los Angeles in 1977.**

was a haunting account of the terrors of the Soviet concentration camps, and he, too, was prevented from receiving the Nobel prize in 1970. Four years later he was arrested and then deported, joining a chorus of Russian writers and scientists whose criticisms, widely published outside the U.S.S.R., became increasingly known in their own country. There was increasing criticism, too, over the plight of Soviet Jews, subject to discrimination and attack, and then intermittently permitted to emigrate.

Gorbachev's Gamble When Brezhnev died, he was succeeded by Yuri Andropov (1982–1984) and Konstantin Chernenko (1984–1985), elderly and ailing party figures who exemplified the bureaucratic grayness of Soviet rule. Thus the appointment in 1985 of Mikhail Gorbachev to be general secretary of the Communist party—at 54 the youngest man to lead the Soviet Union since Stalin—marked a new era, even if it began with the familiar problems of stifling inefficiencies and alienation (absenteeism and alcoholism among the work force had become serious problems) in an economy sapped by heavy military expenditures.

Gorbachev gradually revealed a personality and daring that led him in startling new directions. He recognized that without radical reform the Soviet system could not meet the growing demand for consumer goods and a higher standard of living and could not sustain the arms race with the United States. Already a vast drain on the economies of both countries, the cost and danger of that competition greatly increased as President Reagan expanded armaments and announced his strategic defense initiative, which envisioned a high-tech shield of satellites and missiles to make America invulnerable to attack.

Gorbachev's goals of a more flexible and productive economy revealed the need for fundamental restructuring of Soviet society. He wanted to decentralize decision making, but that required more open communication, greater authority for local managers, and reducing the role of the Communist party. To accomplish all this, he had to increase his power, overcome entrenched resistance, and reduce international pressures.

His efforts made *perestroika* (political and economic restructuring) and *glasnost* (greater openness) international words and won him admirers around the world, but the benefits of his program came slowly. Achievements in foreign policy came more readily and made him internationally the most popular figure in Soviet history. He campaigned against the threat of nuclear war; and at a summit meeting with Reagan in 1986 Gorbachev suddenly proposed breath-taking reductions in nuclear arms that nearly won Reagan's acquiescence before aides hurriedly dissuaded him. Gorbachev also determined that he must stop the dangerous drain on Soviet lives, wealth, and morale caused by the war in Afghanistan. Soviet troops had been sent there in 1979 to support a Communist government entangled in a bloody guerrilla war, a war waged by rebels heavily supported by the United States. In 1987 Gorbachev began a staged withdrawal.

More surprising, he took an approach to Eastern Europe parallel to his own policy of glasnost, allowing the governments of Eastern Europe to make similar changes. That new tolerance was necessary to protect his reforms at home and to justify ending the Soviet Union's costly barter arrangements with the Comecon nations, by which they received Soviet oil at prices below the world market and Russia was saddled in return with

▸ For years Gorbachev was mobbed by enthusiastic well-wishers whenever he visited Western Europe and the United States; his trip to West Germany in 1990, where he was accompanied by Chancellor Kohl, was one of his last triumphal tours.

products it did not need from Eastern Europe. But once launched, glasnost was hard to contain. When some of the East European nations began to request the departure of Soviet troops and to replace their Communist regimes, Gorbachev accepted that, too. Required by his larger goals, such concessions troubled already hostile hardliners at home, where each step for reform revealed the need for more, and each gesture toward glasnost increased public expectations and criticisms.

Ethnic Conflict A still greater danger to Soviet stability arose from the explosion of nationalist unrest that in 1988 produced demonstrations and violent clashes all along the Soviet Union's eastern frontier—in Georgia, Moldavia, and the Ukraine—while the Baltic republics of Latvia, Lithuania, and Estonia built upon more recent memories of independence. Fervent but carefully controlled demonstrations encouraged the Baltic States to write new laws and constitutions as if they were already autonomous. Gorbachev dangled promises, argued for the benefits of membership in the U.S.S.R., restrained his own army, and delayed any final decision. At the same time, in the Soviet Union's southern republics, Azerbaijanis and Armenians engaged in open war, inflamed by conflicts that were ethnic (Azeri and Armenians had fought for centuries), religious (Shi'a Muslims and Armenian Orthodox Christians), social (the Armenians had generally been wealthier and better educated), political (involv-

▸ **Lithuanian crowds hold up a banner that says, "Ivan Go Home" and cheer as a Soviet soldier is burned in effigy. This demonstration in April 1990 followed two years of similar agitation.**

ing territory and relations with Moscow), and economic (the oil industry of Azerbaijan was in a slow decline). Eventually Soviet troops attempted to separate the combatants but without trying to exercise the full authority the Soviet state had previously held.

Throughout most of the multinational U.S.S.R., Russians had long enjoyed privileged status, and many resented losing it. As members of the Soviet Union's largest republic, Russian nationalists, too, mobilized in the name of culture (with appeals to the Orthodox Church), order (attractive to the military and some party members), and race (including virulent anti-Semitism). Nationalism was as grave a challenge to Gorbachev as bloated bureaucracy and stores with empty shelves. The bonds of ideology, institutions, and custom that had held a great state together were beginning to look weak.

Eastern Europe The Soviet presence remained the central fact of politics in Eastern Europe; yet differences that had been submerged became increasingly important. Yugoslavia, the maverick among Communist states, cautiously established better relations with its Communist neighbors but firmly maintained its independence in foreign policy. Domestically, too, it combined a limited market economy and decentralized factory management with state ownership and single-party elections that permitted competing candidates. Despite crackdowns, some significant dissent was permitted, and Yugoslavia's federal structure was strong enough to survive Tito's death in 1980. But it could not provide the restructuring necessary to pull the country out of an economic downturn nor prevent a rise in crippling ethnic and political tensions.

▸ Lech Walesa addressing workers outside a factory in Zyrardow, not far from Warsaw in October 1981. The scene, reminiscent of the long history of labor movements except for the television cameras, marks the rising power of the Solidarity movement.

The "Brezhnev doctrine" had declared that a "threat to socialism" in one country was a threat to all; and the invasion of Czechoslovakia had been followed by efforts to strengthen the economic ties that bound the nations of Comecon, but the countries of Eastern Europe were looking westward for increased trade and badly needed loans. Not content with its allotted role as a Soviet granary, Romania launched its own course of industrialization and an independent foreign policy. That made the Romanian leader, Nicolae Ceausescu, welcomed in the West even as he became an increasingly brutal and repressive tyrant at home. East Germany, the second industrial power among Communist states (and the seventh in Europe), oscillated between friendly overtures toward and suspicious rejection of West Germany much as it alternated concessions with repression at home in an effort to meet the discontent that exploded in riots in the early 1970s.

The winds of change were stronger still in Poland and Hungary. There and in Czechoslovakia cultural ties to the rest of Europe remained strong and the influential Catholic Church now became more outspoken. Protests against the police expressed a growing restiveness in Hungary, which had one of the strongest and most consumer-oriented of the Eastern European economies. In Poland riots in 1976 forced postponement of a rise in food prices, and strikes in 1980–1981 led to the recognition of Solidarity, an organization of independent trade unions led by Lech Walesa, who became a national hero. That movement, which received strong support from the Catholic Church, was even strong enough to prompt a change of government, but the new party head, General Wojciech Jaruzelski, soon resorted to martial law and clamped down on Solidarity. Amidst rising public resentment at the economic and political cost of the Soviet connection, the Polish government relied on force as much as ever.

CAPITALIST COUNTRIES: THE CHALLENGE OF RECESSION

Western democracies had grown accustomed to economic growth, which promised gains for all segments of society. When it slowed, political conflict sharpened and new issues came to the fore. Ecological movements gained at the polls, and regional movements acquired new strength. The traditional programs of left and right were losing relevance, and weakened governments grappled with problems deeply embedded in their social and economic systems.

The Energy Crisis and Inflation European economies were instantly vulnerable when in October 1973 the oil-exporting nations (mainly in the Middle East) banded together in a cartel to raise international prices. Europe imported nearly two-thirds of its energy in the form of petroleum, and only the Soviet Union could meet its own energy needs through domestic production. In response to higher prices, Western nations redoubled efforts to develop domestic sources of energy. Over the next decade the exploitation of North Sea oilfields made Norway self-sufficient and Britain nearly so, and the Netherlands developed Europe's largest fields of natural gas. But Europe's energy consumption continued to rise, and increased self-sufficiency depended heavily on nuclear energy. By 1976 over half of the world's nuclear power plants operating or under construction were in Europe, where France became the world leader.

These measures and the collapse of oil prices in 1986 eased the immediate economic crisis, but its effects remained important. A growing environmental movement, especially strong in Germany, protested reliance on nuclear power; and opposition increased with the meltdown of a nuclear reactor at Chernobyl in the Soviet Union in 1986, which sent radioactive clouds over much of Central Europe, briefly disrupting agriculture and renewing concern for safety everywhere, although the full extent of the deaths and injuries from radiation within the Soviet Union only came to be known some years later.

In addition, the high cost of energy added to inflationary pressures. Nuclear energy proved more expensive than anticipated, and European governments taxed petroleum heavily, in the long term an environmentally wise inducement to energy efficiency. Inflation became a pressing problem. Among major capitalist nations, only West Germany consistently managed to hold the rate of inflation below 5 percent. It rose to an annual rate of increase in 1975–1976 of over 20 percent in Britain and Italy (30 percent in Portugal) and undermined planning, savings, and trade, while squeezing salaried employees and many workers. This widespread inflation resulted from more than the price of energy, and it called into question policies on which prosperity had rested: deficit financing by governments, the rising cost of increased imports, the willingness of businesses to maintain profits by raising prices, and the general anticipation that prices would continue to rise. Changing these policies threatened the political equilibrium, initiating debates about social programs and wages that reopened ideological and class conflicts—a political struggle that became especially bitter in Britain and Italy.

Economists worried about *stagflation,* the paradoxical combination of economic stagnation and rising prices, and then about a more familiar condition, recession. Everywhere unemployment was rising. In Britain classic tight-money policies insisted upon by Britain's Prime Minister Margaret Thatcher slowed inflation—although it remained surprisingly high—at the price of jobs. By 1982, 12 percent of Britain's work force was unemployed. Elsewhere, slightly less draconian measures succeeded in slowing inflation; but in France and Italy, too, unemployment rose to about 8 percent, levels not experienced since World War II. In Germany, the rate climbed to 6 percent. Foreign immigrants were hardest hit, which meant that the recession was soon felt in poorer countries, and the next group hardest hit was the young, a fact of frightening political and social implications.

Europe was undergoing a major and painful economic transition as its now-aging industries faced increased competition from the Japanese and from new plants in other parts of the world (often ones built with European capital). And the capacity of governments to respond was limited, inhibited by a rising public campaign against high taxation as well as disagreement about what national policies could accomplish. A great deal of economic activity relied on payments in cash or barter, an "underground economy" that avoided taxes and regulation and was believed to account for nearly 10 percent of GNP in most of Europe (only in Italy was the proportion

► **France invested more heavily in nuclear energy than any other country. Well run and efficient the French plants provoked little public opposition, but not even a mural of a child at the beach could make the giant stacks seem to belong in their bucolic surroundings.**

thought to approach its importance in the United States, where estimates placed it between 7 and 25 percent of GNP). The economic pressures that mattered most were international; domestically, they reinforced an unexpected rise in regionalism, which complicated national politics in every European country. Outspoken regional movements, which appealed to local pride in a distinctive local culture, denounced long-accepted national policies on the grounds that their region was being economically and politically disadvantaged; and as these movements generated support, they became an effective rallying point for opposition to the programs and social changes that a few years before had been accepted as concomitants of modern growth.

Opening to the Left: Italy In 1983 Bettino Craxi became Italy's first Socialist prime minister. A wily politician, he had personally rebuilt the Socialist party; his arrival in power was the result of a long-term political trend. The Italian Republic had been dominated by the Christian Democrats since its founding. Dependent upon alliances with smaller parties to stay in power, they excluded the Socialists and Communists from government while parceling out patronage directly and through the vast array of government-owned enterprises. While the economy boomed—Italy had enjoyed the longest period of economic growth of any nation—politics often sank into immobility in a labyrinthine process of semisecret negotiations and deals. The public grew increasingly restive; and from 1958 on there had been growing talk of an "opening to the left," which might woo Socialists away from their Communist allies and permit a left-center coalition. Italy's rapid modernization, the need for administrative reform, and the change in Catholic attitudes associated with Pope John XXIII finally made a coalition including Socialists possible in 1963; it lasted until 1972.

The process of compromise, however, remained infinitely complex. Few ministries survived a whole year as unprestigious governments succeeded each other and a sprawling, inefficient bureaucracy administered the state. In a tension-filled nation undergoing rapid social change, the maintenance of reasonable stability was an impressive achievement. The governing parties were held together primarily by opposition to the Communists, in many respects Italy's most dynamic party. Well-organized and skillfully led, they made steady gains and won the chance to try out some of their practical proposals in many of the regional governments finally established in the 1970s (although called for in the constitution). The Communists won local offices in much of the north and most of Italy's largest cities, where they instituted popular programs and enhanced their reputation for probity and efficiency. The time had come, they argued, for a "historic compromise," a coalition of Communists and Christian Democrats to rule in the name of reform. For several years such an arrangement seemed all but inevitable, until Craxi set the Socialists on the opposite course, gaining at the polls and making his party indispensable to a governing coalition. In office Craxi brought a new decisiveness to government, but hoped-for reform of the political system, which the turn to the left had been expected to produce, had to be subordinated to more immediate economic issues.

Opening to the Left: France The growth of the left in France was somewhat surprising after the years of Gaullist supremacy. By 1962, with a firm majority in the Chamber of Deputies, Charles De Gaulle guaranteed the stability and even the popularity of the Fifth Republic. Both foreign and domestic policy centered on him. While relying on able, even brilliant, technocrats to administer the state, he kept parliament docile and used plebiscites and public relations to ensure public support independent of parties. Despite France's prosperity, De Gaulle had won the presidential election of 1965 (the first by direct popular vote since 1848) only on the second ballot. The opposition, led by François Mitterrand, benefited from resentment of an often arbitrary bureaucracy and of De Gaulle's paternalism, from discontent among workers convinced they were not receiving their share of France's increasing wealth, and from a broader dissatisfaction with many of the effects of growth itself, including inadequate urban housing and neglect of underdeveloped regions.

Such attitudes fired the student revolt in May 1968, which nearly toppled the regime. Millions of workers went on strike as students occupied buildings and battled with police. The storm was weathered with firmness and promises of reform; but the Fifth Republic was never the same, although Gaullists gained impressively in elections held that June, for the student radicals frightened much of French society. Extensive reforms followed. The educational system was drastically overhauled, increasing options and access and giving both students and parents a larger voice at every level. Social programs were broadened and a complex set of changes made the civil service more responsive. De Gaulle's new program culminated in plans, both far-reaching and vague, for greater decentralization of government. This step was to be approved in a referendum that left the details to the president; but the voters refused their support, and in April 1969 De Gaulle resigned.

His immediate successor, Georges Pompidou, was a firm Gaullist, but the new government was more open and more willing to reconsider established policies. And that change in tone was accentuated with the presidential election of 1974. Valéry Giscard d'Estaing won with a campaign that struck many as American in its techniques and popular appeal. A member of the government's majority but not of the Gaullist party, Giscard d'Estaing promised a more accessible and democratic government reaching from reform-minded Gaullists to the Socialists. The Socialists, however, remained allied to the Communists; and their program combined a fresh emphasis on improving the quality of life through attention to culture, leisure, and urban problems with more traditional demands for the nationalization of many industries and more equitable distribution of income. Although most voters appeared closest to the center, French politics remained divided between a more or less Marxist left and a technocratic right.

▶ The bicentennial of the French Revolution, which had once divided all of Europe, was the occasion in 1989 for patriotic celebrations and as a triumph for human rights.

The left got its chance with the alliance of Socialists and Communists that Mitterrand negotiated and with which he won the presidential election of 1981. Their followers danced in the streets, and the new government began with dramatic measures that nationalized many heavy industries and most banks, raised wages and benefits, and increased social expenditures. Much of this was clearly popular, but the daring gamble failed to stimulate an economy hurt by distrust within the business community, the fall of the franc, and an unfavorable international economy that suffered from slowed growth and high interest rates. The Communists, whom Mitterrand had effectively isolated from major policy decisions, withdrew their support in 1984, and the president turned to policies of austerity, deflation, and investment in high technology more like those of his predecessors than his own platform. The Socialists lost their parliamentary majority in 1986, and the Fifth Republic had to experiment with a split government in which president and prime minister were from different parties. To the surprise of many, that arrangement worked quite well, winning Mitterrand reelection and the Socialists a renewed majority in 1988 with a program that now focused on economic modernization, military strength, and support of the European Community.

Where socialists held office in the mid-1980s, the programs to which they were most attached—increased social services, better education, more vacation time, and a larger voice in the workplace for employees—appeared unaffordable. Like their opponents, they abandoned industries that were no longer competitive and favored investment in new technologies. The new social problems—large pockets of endemic unemployment that remained even after a general economic upturn, drug addiction, and racial conflict—were ones for which the traditional programs of left or right had few solutions.

A Shift to the Right: Germany In West Germany political issues tended to be overshadowed by the satisfying fact of prosperity as the Federal Republic surpassed the United States in world trade. Even the significant change in 1969 to a government led by the Social Democrats did not lessen the commitment to encouraging investment, expanding trade, and preventing inflation. Often surprisingly conservative in their economic policies, the Social Democrats pursued democratization in other ways, carrying through educational reforms and expanding social services. Their most venturesome measure required all firms with more than 2000 employees to have a central board of directors, half of whose members are elected representatives of labor. Yet even as Germany won a more central place in European affairs, dissension was growing within both major parties; and the discovery that one of prime minister Willy Brandt's aides was a Soviet spy forced Brandt's resignation in 1974, in favor of the firmly centrist Social Democrat Helmut Schmidt. In 1982 the Christian Democrats regained office under Helmut Kohl, responding to the unfavorable economic climate by cutting back on social services. Still, the changes were slight, and the new government was almost as eager as its predecessors to maintain good relations with the East.

In the face of such continuity, the new concerns in German politics were associated with the Greens, a group whose environmentalist and antimilitary program recalled the student movement of the 1960s, and a small but worrisone nationalist movement. These groups were not a political threat to Kohl's conservative leadership, nor were the Social Democrats, who were weakened by their internal divisions. Germany, like France, turned more and more to the European Community to provide a program for the future and to shape its international role.

A Shift to the Right: Great Britain Until Margaret Thatcher became prime minister, continuity also marked British policy as the two dominant parties alternated in power. Conservatives (in office from 1951 to 1964, 1970 to 1974) placed greater emphasis on the role of the private sector but largely accepted the extensive welfare programs and mixed economy they inherited. Conversely, Labour governments, constrained by the plight of the British economy, pressured their trade-union constituents to accept wage limits and reduced public expenditures. They accepted the need to balance the budget, to halt the fall in the value of the pound, and to reassure creditors, including the International Monetary Fund, which imposed further restraints. These were not the measures Labour's constituents had voted for, but Labour governments did work to improve public services, especially transportation, and to make education more democratic, favoring comprehensive high schools and an impressive expansion of higher education. On newer issues—the policies of the European Community, discrimination against black immigrants, and demands for regional assemblies in Scotland and Wales—each of the two parties was internally divided. Britain's overwhelming problem, however, remained economic; and neither North Sea oil nor membership in the European Community solved it. Plants were not modernized nor productivity improved at the pace of other leading industrial nations, and inflation further depressed the rate of investment.

Analysts found it easier to lay the blame—on the enormous cost to Britain of World War II, unimaginative and weak business managers, an inadequate educational system, the selfish conservatism of labor unions, the high costs of welfare and defense—than to prescribe remedies. In office during the peak of the recession of the 1970s, the Labour party bore the brunt of the public reaction, and that brought the Conservatives to power in 1979 under the firm leadership of Margaret Thatcher. She remained in office until 1990, longer than any prime minister in this century. A doctrinaire advocate of free enterprise, Thatcher reversed the course of British domestic policy, and both major parties became more ideological. Out of power, Labour was dominated by its left wing, leaving space for a third-party coalition of Liberals and right-wing Labourites, which did well at the polls but could not gain power. That divided opposition helped the Conservatives to stay in office.

The results of Conservative policies were mixed. The British economy was restructured, and a rise in productivity in the late 1980s increased prosperity. At the same time, high unemployment and reductions in social services, including education, exacerbated some of the fundamental problems of British society. And the political system as a whole found it difficult to confront the issues of a global economy, European union, unemployment, and racial division. Admired for her decisiveness, Thatcher was also widely disliked; and she greatly strengthened her political position with her appeal to nationalist fervor in 1983. Argentina had suddenly attacked the Falkland Islands (which Britain had held and Argentina claimed for more than a century), and Thatcher took much of the credit for Britain's victory after initial setbacks. That dedication to national interest made for abrasive relations with the European Community, which ultimately contributed to the opposition within her own party that forced her to resign.

EUROPE'S PLACE IN THE WORLD

For some 30 years Europe's position in world affairs was largely shaped by the effects of decolonization, the Cold War, and Western Europe's great wealth in a global economy. Decolonization, which seemed to follow from defeat and weakness, became a source of strength. The Cold War, while measuring the limitations of European power, encouraged a broad movement for increased cooperation among European nations; and Western Europe's wealth pushed it toward a larger role in international relations.

Decolonization After having given up their protectorates in the Middle East and been driven out of their colonies in Asia, the imperial powers still held most of Africa. Europeans on the scene—officials, businesspeople, and residents—did what they could to prolong European rule with grants of autonomy and promises of aid. By now they knew, however, that the age of empire was over, and most African states won their independence in the 1960s. Seen from Africa, the struggle was often bitter. In Europe the loss of empire no longer carried the kind of trauma that had marked the "fall" of India, Indonesia, Indochina, and Algeria.

Negotiated settlements made it easier to preserve other relationships, not just in the formal connections of the British Commonwealth and its French counterpart, the French Community, but through cultural ties important in education, legal systems, and administrative institutions. Economic interests also sustained a European presence, and some factions in Africa's internal conflicts turned for support to Britain, France, the Soviet Union, and the United States. These links could lead to more direct interventions as in 1979, when Britain supported white-ruled Rhodesia's transformation into black-ruled Zimbabwe and when France intervened during civil strife in Chad and the Central African Republic in the 1980s. Around the world, nations wanting not to be too closely aligned with the Soviet Union or the United States often preferred to work with familiar European states no longer running empires.

Bipolar Stability The limits of European autonomy in foreign affairs had been demonstrated in the Suez crisis and the Soviet invasion of Hungary. Militarily, the Warsaw Pact and the NATO alliance institutionalized dependence on the superpowers, and for a while the lines of opposition hardened. In 1961 East-West tension seemed lit-

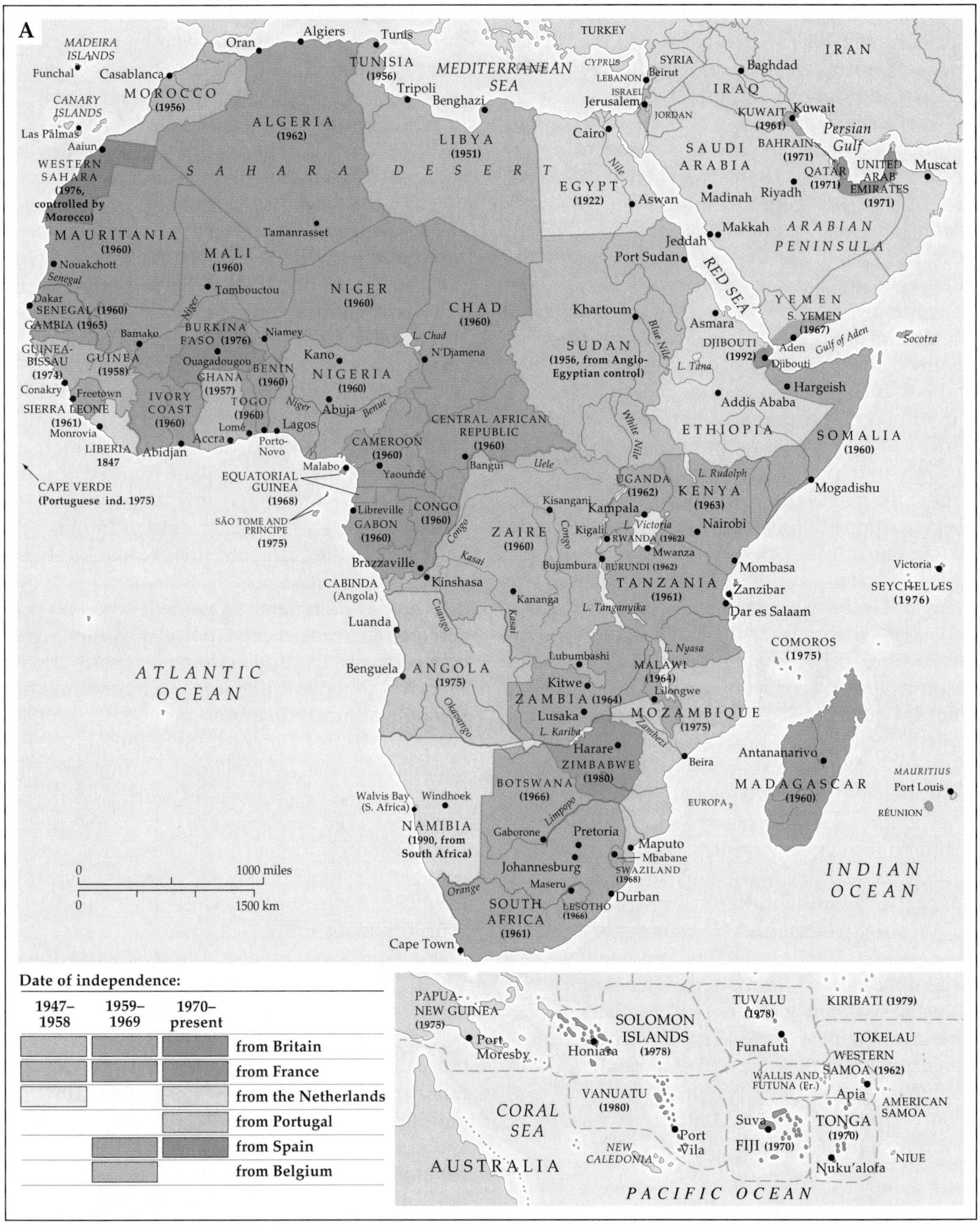

Map 30.2a THE INDEPENDENCE OF EUROPE'S FORMER COLONIES

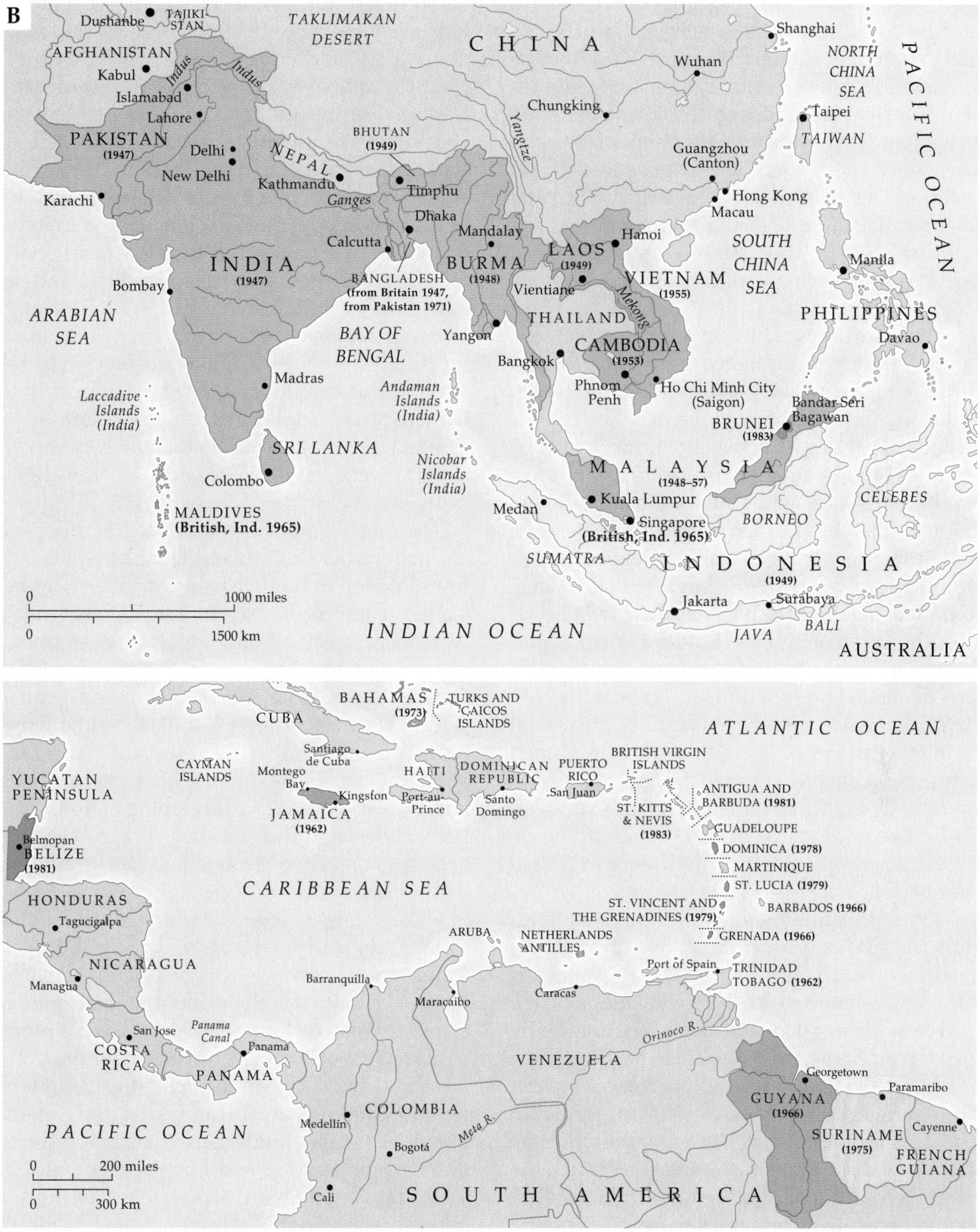

Map 30.2b THE INDEPENDENCE OF EUROPE'S FORMER COLONIES *(Continued)*

erally cast in stone when East Germany built a long gray wall across the center of Berlin, eventually extending it along its entire western border. East Germany's determination to keep its citizens from leaving made the division of Germany permanent. There was another ominous crisis in 1961, when the United States sponsored an invasion of Cuba aimed at the overthrow of Fidel Castro. It failed, and in the following year the Russians began to base missiles on Cuba. For a moment, war seemed imminent, until as the Americans massed their fleet, the Soviets withdrew their missiles. These crises underscored a mutual interest in not disturbing the balance of power, and the growing rift between the Soviet Union and China reinforced the need for regular diplomatic exchanges between the superpowers.

Only Albania among European Communist governments sided with China against the Soviet Union. Generally, European governments used their influence to favor East-West negotiations at summit conferences and on specific issues. They promoted agreements on space exploration in 1967, the beginning of the Strategic Arms Limitation Talks in 1969, and the extension of such agreements to issues of human rights at the Helsinki Conference in 1975, attended by nearly all the European states in addition to the United States and Canada. Through trades, loans, and technical agreements, the governments of Western Europe encouraged those of Eastern Europe toward whatever autonomy they were willing to attempt.

As European international relations stabilized, Germany gradually asserted some of the political weight its wealth implied. The Social Democrats were less committed to the inevitability of the Cold War than Adenauer had been, and Willy Brandt used his negotiating skill in making a new opening to the East. The resulting treaty between West Germany and the Soviet Union, signed in 1970, was a milestone, which earned Brandt the Nobel peace prize. While the treaty left open the possibility of a peaceful reunification of Germany, it accepted Germany's eastern boundary, pointed to a normalization of the status of Berlin, still divided between Soviet and Western occupation, and paved the way for extensive relations between West Germany and the governments of Eastern Europe. In time, increased trade culminated in the agreements of 1981–1982 for a natural gas pipeline to be built from Russia to Germany, Italy, and France.

These steps encouraged the governments of Eastern Europe to more independent policies, and in the West many, especially on the left, demanded greater independence of the United States. Demands that Europe become a zone free of the nuclear weapons of either side culminated in 1981 in demonstrations that saw nearly half a million young people marching in Bonn and perhaps another million in other capitals. Each of the Western nations reassumed some of its traditional policies. Great Britain benefited from reliance on close ties to the United States, and in the United Nations the Scandinavian countries positioned themselves as mediators between the superpowers and as friends of nonaligned countries.

The most flamboyant search for an independent policy was De Gaulle's. France had been the fourth nation to become a nuclear power, and De Gaulle continued that buildup. Resentful of American policy toward France, he set upon a course that by 1966 led to the withdrawal of French forces from NATO command (and of NATO forces from French soil), although France remained a member of the alliance. France strengthened its relations with Eastern Europe and increased its aid to developing nations. After De Gaulle left office in 1969, France's policies grew less assertive but retained their traditional autonomy.

Close relations with Germany enabled France to take the lead in strengthening the European Community, toward which Britain remained more hesitant. As their international role increased, Western European nations were prominent in the worldwide competition for the sale of arms and were central to such effective international economic organizations as the International Monetary Fund, the Organization for Economic Cooperation and Development, and the Trilateral Commission, a privately based group of business and political leaders from Europe, the United States, and Japan. For all their problems, the stable and prosperous societies of the West had reason to look confidently to the future, as an unprecedented revolution swept across Eastern Europe.

IV. The End of an Era

THE MIRACLES OF 1989

The contradictions of Communist rule were clear, but no one expected its total collapse. For years, the pattern had been for Eastern European governments to recognize that greater efficiency and popular feeling required that they loosen controls and lessen repression. Then those steps would expose further institutional blockage and deeper dissent, and the government would clamp down.

Poland That happened in Poland, where economic crisis and the growth of the Solidarity movement led to martial law. Solidarity continued its propaganda with wit and daring from the underground, and the visit of the Polish pope, with its appeal to patriotic and religious feeling, occasioned more demonstrations. This time the government's response was different, for it did not want or no longer dared to rely solely on repression, and Moscow seemed to favor further reform. In 1988 Gorbachev had announced before the United Nations that the Soviet Union would allow its allies to go their own way, and that policy would now be tested.

General Jaruzelski relaxed martial law and released some political prisoners as anger and frustration increased and the Polish economy worsened. In February 1989 the government was prepared once again to recognize the legitimacy of Solidarity, but it now demanded free elections. When the government hesitated, Gorbachev signaled that Poland was on its own. Thus in April a pact was signed recognizing Solidarity and promising free elections. When they took place, Solidarity won almost all the seats. Communist party members, stunned and frightened, did not know what to do. After various formulas for compromise failed, Solidarity took over the cabinet in August, the first non-Communist government in what for 40 years had been called the Soviet bloc.

Hungary and East Germany Hungarians were well aware of events in Poland, for political discussion and economic activity were generally more open there than in other Communist countries. By April 1989 even some Hungarian party officials talked of the need for free speech, civil rights, and the protections of private property. In the annual May Day celebrations, the official demonstration was dwarfed by another, sponsored by the opposition, and in June a huge demonstration honored the uprising of 1956. Even some members of the government chose to attend. In October the Hungarian Communist party flexibly changed its name to the Socialist party, and parliament promised free elections for the following year.

The power of people aroused suddenly seemed irresistible. Many old-line Communist leaders remained convinced that a show of strength would be enough to keep their hold on power; but the efforts of Erich Honecker, East Germany's party leader and prime minister, showed that that might not work. In October soldiers beat and arrested demonstrators in East Berlin; Honecker resigned a week later. Gorbachev announced his disapproval of the use of force; censorship was ineffectual because anyone in East Germany could watch West German television, and the East German republic seemed simply to be emigrating. Every day hundreds of people, especially the young and those with marketable skills, abandoned their country. They went to Hungary, where they mobbed the West German embassy seeking visas and the embarrassed Hungarian and West German governments arranged for special trains to carry them west. Honecker's successor, Egon Kranz, stunned everyone on November 9, 1989, by announcing that East Germany's borders would be opened that very day. The guards could not at first believe their orders. Then late at night they shrugged and stepped aside as hoards of people pushed through the gates of the Berlin wall. Hundreds cheered and waved from atop that symbol of oppression before strolling past the well-stocked shops of West Berlin. The celebrations continued in front of the television cameras for days, even after work crews began dismantling the wall. The flow of people did not stop; thousands came each day, some just looking, others wanting a different life in West Germany. In a few weeks meetings once held in secret took place throughout East Germany in churches and public squares as the police watched and then withdrew. The government's promises for reform and official pleas for order were drowned in revelations of past corruption, talk of uniting the two Germanies, and the public's accumulated frustrations.

The Final Round in Eastern Europe For a while the harsher East European governments—Czechoslovakia, Bulgaria, and Romania—remained unscathed by these changes around them. But there had already been a number of demonstrations in Prague when in October 40,000 people protested in Wenceslas Square. After riot police beat up on demonstrating students, 200,000 people filled Wenceslas Square; and a few days later 300,000 came to shout and sing and jingle keys as a good-humored suggestion that it was time for the Communists to leave. In

Havel's Inaugural Address

Vaclav Havel is perhaps the most widely admired of the new leaders of Eastern Europe, and his literary skill and philosophic bent made him a particularly effective spokesperson. In his inaugural address on January 1, 1990, as president of the Czech Republic, he commented on the historical meaning of the dramatic changes that brought him to office.

"My dear fellow citizens, for forty years you heard from my predecessors on this day different variations of the same theme: how our country flourished, how many million tons of steel we produced, how happy we all were, how we trusted our government, and what bright perspectives were unfolding in front of us.

"I assume you did not propose me for this office so that I, too, would lie to you.

"Our country is not flourishing. The enormous creative and spiritual potential of our nation is not being used sensibly. Entire branches of industry are producing goods which are of no interest to anyone, while we are lacking the things we need. A state which calls itself a workers' state humiliates and exploits workers. Our obsolete economy is wasting the little energy we have available. A country that once could be proud of the educational level of its citizens spends so little on education that it ranks today as seventy-second in the world. We have polluted our soil, our rivers and forests, bequeathed to us by our ancestors, and we have today the most contaminated environment in Europe. Adult people in our country die earlier than in most other European countries. . . .

"But all this is still not the main problem. The worst thing is that we live in a contaminated moral environment. We fell morally ill because we became used to saying something different from what we thought. We learned not to believe in anything, to ignore each other, to care only about ourselves. Concepts such as love, friendship, compassion, humility, or forgiveness lost their depth and dimensions, and for many of us they represented only psychological peculiarities, or they resembled gone-astray greetings from ancient times, a little ridiculous in the era of computers and spaceships. Only a few of us were able to cry out loud that the powers that be should not be all-powerful, and that special farms, which produce ecologically pure and top-quality food just for them, should send their produce to schools, children's homes, and hospitals if our agriculture was unable to offer them to all. The previous regime—armed with its arrogant and intolerant ideology—reduced man to a force of production and nature to a tool of production. In this it attacked both their very substance and their mutual relationship. It reduced gifted and autonomous people, skillfully working in their own country, to nuts and bolts of some monstrously huge, noisy, and stinking machine, whose real meaning is not clear to anyone. It cannot do more than slowly but inexorably wear down itself and all its nuts and bolts."

From Brian MacArthur (ed.), *The Penguin Book of Twentieth-Century Speeches* (New York: Viking, 1992).

▸ **May 1990: Having pulled a statue of Lenin to the ground, Romanian workers remove the cable from his neck.**

now familiar rites, slogans were written everywhere, posters appeared, and new political groups formed. By December the best organized of these, Civic Forum, had won power and elected its leader, Vaclav Havel, the popular playwright whose plays had long been banned, president of Czechoslovakia (*see box,* p. 1040).

Even Bulgaria and Romania, with less-developed economies and weaker traditions of political participation, could not escape the historic pressure for change. They met it very differently. Bulgaria's Communist party, which still took its cues from the Soviet Union, responded with shrewd promptness. In November, Todor Zhivkov, party secretary for 35 years and head of state for 27, was forced from office and then jailed amid plans for free elections. Romania suffered weeks of bloodshed. When crowds gathered in December, the government did not hesitate to shoot. Still the crowds formed; and with rising violence in the streets, Ceausescu, Romania's dictator, tried to make his escape. He was caught and executed by firing squad on Christmas day, but it took a week to end the fighting between the remaining special police loyal to Ceausescu and the army, which supported the new leaders. Everywhere Romanian flags waved, a conspicuous hole in their center where the Communist insignia had been. The last Communist government west of the Soviet Union (except for Albania) had fallen.

As stunning as the sudden end of Communism was the ease with which it came. Economic failure and resentment of Soviet dominance explained a good deal, but more than specific policies was being challenged. Workers and Catholics in Poland, party members and entrepreneurs in Hungary, and students and intellectuals in Czechoslovakia had joined with ordinary citizens in angry alienation. Rarely does politics produce failure on such a scale. Everywhere massive demonstrations showed the impact of television in their effect and in their very style, which was much like the protest movements of the West. Inspired by the events around them, the people spoke out to express a universal hunger for freedom and a shocking cynicism about the regimes under which they had lived for more than 40 years. Massive contempt washed away the pomp of officialdom and the power of party ideology and arbitrary police.

Within months, the meaningful elections and unaccustomed freedoms that promised a new era had also resurrected old divisions—ethnic, social, and ideological. Freedom illumined not only the appalling failures and corruption of the fallen regimes but also the problems still to be faced. All at once, the Eastern Europe of 1990 looked much like that of the 1920s. Moderate conservatives gained the lead among the multiple parties of Hungary and expressed nationalist resentment of the treatment accorded the Hungarian population in Romania. Czechoslovakia, with the internationally admired Havel elected president of the republic, found itself debating yet again the relations of Czechs and Slovaks. As Poland risked the drastic medicine of sudden conversion to a market economy, rifts appeared within Solidarity. In Bulgaria, Communist party members won most of the seats in free elections, and in Romania leaders who claimed no longer to be Communists showed little willingness to allow real democracy. East Germans voted for those who promised the most rapid assimilation into the German Federal Republic.

The Disintegration of the U.S.S.R. Gorbachev, who favored gradual reform, had hardly expected change in Eastern Europe to move so fast or be so sweeping. A hero in Western Europe and the United States, he was never so popular at home, where problems were mounting. Efforts to make the economy more responsive to markets threatened jobs, and attempts to make one sector more efficient ran afoul of related sectors still operating in the old ways. The new price structure increased inflation, uncertainty, and hoarding. By 1990, the transformation of the economy had bogged down. Many in the party and the army resented the erosion of their authority and watched with horror the weakening of the Soviet Union's international position. To overcome their resistance, Gorbachev needed a strong political base. He called for a huge Congress of People's Deputies as a step toward greater democracy. It met in 1989, elected Gorbachev president of the Soviet Union, and made way for competing parties by rejecting the constitution's claim that the Communist party must be preeminent. Open discussion went further, with attacks on old abuses, denunciations of the KGB, and a rising chorus of competing ethnic demands. Estonia and then Lithuania had already declared their sovereignty, and fighting raged between Armenia and Azerbaijan. While Gorbachev proposed greater autonomy for the Union's republics, Russian nationalists launched frankly racist campaigns, and figures like Solzhenitsyn warned against allowing Western decadence to infiltrate Russian society.

Caught between left and right, Gorbachev in 1990 and 1991 clamped down on the media and allowed the army to threaten that it would restore order in the Baltic republics. Among the opponents of this authoritarian turn, Boris Yeltsin, the head of the Communist party in Moscow, stood out. An outspoken populist, he reached ordinary people as Gorbachev never had; and in 1991 he was elected President of the Russian republic. Other enemies of Gorbachev were active, too. When he took his August vacation in the Crimea, hard-liners in Gorbachev's own government, the military, and the KGB staged a coup. Tanks filled the streets as the coup's leaders announced that Gorbachev had been replaced. Beyond that, they seemed to have no plan. Yeltsin held firm against the coup, crowds pleaded with the soldiers not to act, miners in Siberia went on a strike that threatened to spread, demonstrators marched in city after city, and some of the army turned to Yeltsin. Within two days, Gorbachev was back and the leaders of the coup in prison. Across the nation, Communist party offices were closed and sometimes looted as people pulled down the symbols of Communism.

Gorbachev, now overshadowed by Yeltsin, to whom in effect he owed his return to office, could rely on neither left nor right as he tried to maintain continuity and the Soviet state itself. Only eight of the fifteen Soviet republics responded to his call for a meeting; and in October 1991 Russia, Ukraine, Belarus, and Kazakhstan declared that the Soviet Union had ceased to exist. No significant group fought to save it as the looser Confederation of Independent States was formed to replace it; and Gorbachev resigned, a victim of the revolution he had unleashed.

EUROPE WITHOUT COLD WAR

The fall of communism meant the end of the Cold War, and the policies and assumptions with which hard-headed policy makers in East and West had lived for 50 years had to be rethought. No one could know the implications of such fundamental changes in international relations and domestic politics. New leaders scrambled to establish stable support, and those who remained in office struggled not to seem outdated.

German Unification Chancellor Kohl pushed for immediate unification of East and West Germany, moving faster than many Germans thought wise, outmaneuvering the opposition parties, and capturing popular enthusiasm. By the end of 1989, he had gained the support of the United States and then of France, in effect forcing a reluctant Britain to join in negotiations with the Soviet Union about German unification. Many were frightened at the prospect. Kohl reassured the West with the promise that an enlarged Germany would be fully integrated into the European Community. The Soviet Union resisted the increase in NATO's strength that was likely to follow, but such concerns were rooted in an era quickly passing. By May 1990 the victors of World War II—the Soviet Union, the United States, Britain, and France—joined with the two Germanies to write a treaty that was finally signed in August. In return for its promise to respect the border with Poland and to limit the size of its combined army, Germany could unify, free to remain in NATO. Germany had become Europe's second largest and its richest and most powerful state.

For Germans, however, the benefits were not immediate. The East German economy, which had been the most productive in Eastern Europe, revealed enormous weakness. Its outmoded and inefficient industry could not compete in the dynamic economy of the West. Investment flowed more slowly to the East than expected, and East Germans resented their dependence on their Western compatriots who were dismantling their institutions and their economy while unemployment rose. West Germans in turn struggled with a flood of immigrants from the East and the rising cost of aid to the East.

Effects on Western Unity In Western Europe, too, the consequences of German unification were far-reaching. As German expenditures rose, Germany battled inflation by raising interest rates. For the other nations of the Community, whose currencies were officially tied to the mark, Europe's dominant currency, that meant rising interest rates, slowed growth, and increasing unemployment. By 1993, the entire system threatened to break down, and it was preserved in principle only by allowing a much greater fluctuation in exchange rates, which permitted the other nations of the Community to devalue against the mark and lower interest rates.

That loosening of economic bonds was a blow to European unity, and it was accompanied by others. Distrust of Germany, most open in Britain, combined with rising domestic resistance to further steps at European union. Although the prior agreements for uniform policies and the free movement of goods and services within the Community were carried out as promised by the end of 1992 and the Maastricht treaty, with significant national exemptions, was finally ratified, the future of the European Union was uncertain. The promised common foreign policy and single European currency would have to wait. Although the Union's continued importance was not in doubt (economic and cultural ties increased even as politicians hesitated), commitment to its social programs and ambitious plans weakened in the face of tighter budgets and domestic divisions. Even its success reopened old questions. Britain, for example, welcomed applications for membership from Austria, Sweden, Norway, and Finland as a path to a wider, looser Community. Germany and France wanted the strengthening of the Union's institutions to continue, preferring that additional members—Hungary, Poland, and the Czech Republic had indicated their desire to join—first spend a period as associated states.

There were other domestic effects as well. In Italy, the powerful Communist party reorganized as the Party of the Democratic Left; and the fading of a communist threat deprived the dominant Christian Democrats of their central plank. When charges of corruption uncovered a vast network of graft, by which the major parties (especially the Socialists and Christian Democrats) had been funded, the political system itself threatened to collapse. It did not, but a vast and confusing political and economic restructuring had to begin. The public mood of contempt for the old political class and a new electoral system (reducing the importance of proportional representation, which had favored party lists) created opportunities for new political formations but seemed at first to favor extremists. Suddenly, the public life of prosperous Italy looked rather like Eastern Europe's.

Throughout Europe, the weakening of the traditional left, now suspect, and the anti-Communist right altered politics. So did a resentment of foreigners, heightened by unemployment. In Italy a new party, the Northern League, gained ground in the prosperous north by combining in one program the denunciation of African immigrants, of the less-developed south, and of government corruption. In France the xenophobic campaigns of the National Front, aimed especially at Muslims from North Africa, made immigration a national issue; and the coalition that defeated the Socialists in 1993 immediately took steps to restrict the presence of foreigners. Immigrants drawn to the wealthy West and crowded in slums that became centers of crime were an international problem, but the problem was especially acute in Germany, where hundreds of thousands of people made their way from the faltering economies of Eastern Europe. In hundreds of incidents, gangs of skinheads and neo-Nazis burned immigrant housing and beat foreigners, an ominous reminder of Germany's past.

Transition in Eastern Europe The states of Eastern Europe faced the kinds of problems that broke up the Soviet Union. The end of censorship revealed governments more in debt and industries more outmoded and inefficient than even Communism's enemies had suspected. Industrial pollution on an enormous, sometimes life-threatening scale was an especially difficult problem for new governments in a strapped economy. Even when there was a clean sweep at the top, the new leaders had to rely on suspect elites and dubious institutions. Unsure of the loyalty or competence of their own administrations, they attempted drastic and often painful reforms while the new freedom exposed conflicts long hidden. Poland undertook the most radical shift to a market economy, and economic indicators showed dramatic gains. That was often not the experience of ordinary citizens, however, and the leading candidates in the elections of 1993 were the former Communists, who promised to slow the transition while sustaining it. In Russia, Hungary, Poland, and the Czech Republic there were signs of promising if uneven economic growth, but pleas for greater foreign aid and investment were only partially met.

In many areas economic crisis was overshadowed, and heightened, by ethnic and religious conflict. The peaceful division of Czechoslovakia into the Czech Republic and Slovakia was a defeat for Havel that, opinion polls indicated, was not really wanted by majorities in either country. But the relentless drive to capitalism in the more prosperous Czech regions and the ambitions of Slovak political leaders forced the establishment of separate states. Former Communists, in fact, proved particularly adept at stirring ethnic resentments, especially in the former Soviet Union and, most tragically of all, in Yugoslavia. Ethnic differences among and within its six republics had not prevented its effective functioning as a state, even after the death of Tito. Politically and economically, it had moved a long way from the Soviet model. When in the 1980s the Yugoslav republics of Croatia and Slovenia began to criticize the economic and political policies of the Serbian-dominated national government as unfair to them, that was not altogether new nor necessarily fatal to the federation. More general criticism of Communist rule increased throughout the country, however, with the fall of Communist governments elsewhere. The Serbian Communists resisted reform and instead gained support by appealing to Serbian nationalism. In 1990–1991 four of Yugoslavia's republics declared their independence. Slovenia and Macedonia managed to secede relatively unscathed, but the independence of Croatia and Bosnia-Herzegovina was opposed by large Serb populations within their borders. The Serbian government chose to support the armed resistance of these populations; ideological and regional differences became ethnic civil war, in which each side, recalling past injustices, committed new atrocities. Truces were signed and then broken, for uncontrolled local units knew their ethnic brothers in neighboring republics would support them no matter what they did. Slaughter and rape destroyed whole villages. By 1993 the Serb forces had recaptured about one-third of Croatia and nearly two-thirds of Bosnia-Herzegovina, a republic in which Serbs, Croatians, and Muslims had once been proud of peacefully living together.

Yeltsin Holds On Russia faced all these problems, too, plus a crisis over the legitimacy of its government. There were movements for auton-

BOUNDARY CHANGES SINCE 1989
- Former boundary of Soviet Union
- Former boundary of Czechoslovakia
- Former boundary of Yugoslavia
- Former boundary between East & West Germany

All other boundaries as of 1994

* Greece disputes right of former Yugoslav Republic of Macedonia to use of name "Macedonia"

BORDER DISPUTES
1 Croatia-Serbia
2 Hungary-Slovakia

SIGNIFICANT NATIONALIST MOVEMENTS
1 France (Brittany)
2 Great Britain (Scotland)
3 Great Britain (Wales)
4 Italy (Sardinia)
5 Italy (Tyrol)
6 Spain (Basque Region)
7 Spain (Catalonia)

REMOVAL OF HOLDOVER RUSSIAN TROOPS AND WEAPONS
1 Baltic States
2 Bulgaria
3 Czech Republic, Slovakia
4 Germany (former East Germany)
5 Hungary
6 Poland
7 Ukraine

AREAS OF VIOLENT CONFLICT OR OPEN WAR
1 Armenia–Azerbaijan
2 Georgia–Abkhazia
3 Moldova
4 Bosnia-Herzegovina, former Yugoslavia
5 Northern Ireland
6 Persian Gulf War
7 Israeli-Palestinian conflict
8 Kurdish-Turkish-Iraqi conflict

ETHNIC-BASED TERRITORIAL DISPUTES
1 Hungarian populations in Slovakia
2 Hungarian poulations in Romania
3 Russian populations in Crimea (Ukraine)
4 Russian populations in Georgia
5 Russian populations in Azerbaijan
6 Russian populations in Baltic States

Map 30.3 ETHNIC AND TERRITORIAL CONFLICT IN EUROPE SINCE 1989

omy within many of Russia's regions, and relations with the other republics of the former Soviet Union, now joined in the weak Confederation of Independent States, could be sustained only by letting many major issues go unresolved, while negotiating over and over about control of the military, territory, and property. As president of Russia, Yeltsin pushed for drastic economic reform. The effects, though limited, were painful. Unemployment rose as the ruble all but collapsed and production fell to about half what it had been a few years before. Managers did not know how to adjust to a market economy, and efforts in one section were stymied by inefficiency in others. Many officials and former party members resisted change altogether. As repression eased, criminal gangs flourished and ugly groups of nationalists and neo-Nazis as well as angry Communists found numerous supporters.

The chance for a peaceful transition depended on Yeltsin's authority, and he tried to make it constitutional. Free elections in 1991 had produced a Congress of People's Deputies in which Yeltsin's supporters were outnumbered by his opponents—Communists, nationalists, members of the military, and representatives of regional movements—and the president compromised. By appointing moderates to safe positions and ignoring the Congress when he could, Yeltsin avoided direct confrontation. But parliament resisted many of his measures, refused him the fuller powers he sought, and threatened him with a vote of no confidence. As resistance stiffened and his own popularity declined, Yeltsin risked a national presidential election in the spring of 1993 and won. His opponents, however, increasingly dominated parliament, and in September Yeltsin declared the parliament dissolved, calling for new elections in a few months.

Several hundred of the opposition delegates refused to obey. Holed up in their skyscraper, they prepared for a siege, collected arms, and called on the people and the army for support.

▶ **The Soviet army surveys the streets of Moscow in October 1993 after having preserved Yeltsin's hold on power by storming the parliament's White House, where opposition leaders had barricaded themselves.**

Although the army remained silent and the government hesitant, after two weeks some crowds had begun to gather outside the parliament to shout their opposition to Yeltsin. Although they were a very mixed group, they heartened the delegates inside. Amid calls to bring the government down, shots were fired from within the parliament; some armored cars were captured, and an attack was launched on television studios across town. Finally, after a brief bombardment, the army stormed the parliament. Its leaders were captured, and the revolt was put down. A hundred or more people died in Moscow, more bloodshed than the city had seen since 1917. The public seemed either to support Yeltsin or be indifferent, and the army had proved dependable. But the need to rely on the military, like Yeltsin's measures against parliament and indifference to the rulings of the supreme court, was troubling proof that Russia had not achieved a constitutional system or the rule of law.

International Implications Europeans watched the slaughter in Yugoslavia with horror and joined in urging the United Nations to act, and the UN ultimately sent some 14,000 troops on peace missions that were unable to maintain the truces they helped negotiate or even consistently to bring relief supplies to besieged civilians. In fact NATO could not agree on what action to take, and the European Community was divided along lines reminiscent of the period before World War I, as Germany hurriedly recognized Croatian and Slovenian independence. Plans for the future were no easier. The United States, with British support, emphasized the continued importance of NATO, despite the end of the Cold War; Germany and France thought in terms of a more autonomous European force.

The breakup of the Soviet Union brought other international problems. Its nuclear warheads were now in four states: Russia, Ukraine, Belarus, and Kazakhstan. Diplomats struggled to make sure that all but Russia's would be dismantled. Cooperative responses from the republics were accompanied by requests for financial aid, but resources were limited. Germany had all it could handle with the costs of unification, and the United States was struggling with a huge deficit. That deficit had come about in large part from the military buildup under President Reagan, an arms race that was one of the pressures that led Gorbachev to reform. Even with a slow decline in defense expenditures, America's debt and domestic needs left little room for any program like the Marshall Plan a half century earlier, however great the need to encourage stability in Eastern Europe.

Ironically, the end of the Cold War had a clearer impact on international relations outside Europe. Russia supported the American-led attack on Iraq, following its invasion of Kuwait in 1991. Once the superpowers ceased to compete, all sides in the Middle East had to reassess their positions. Without Soviet support, the Muslim states of the Middle East could only lose by diplomatic intransigence and indirect attacks on Israel, which in turn knew it was no longer so important as a Cold War bastion sure of unending American aid. After decades in which one side insisted on an independent Palestinian state and the other refused to negotiate until Muslim states recognized Israel's right to exist, Palestinians and Israelis reached a remarkable agreement in 1993 to negotiate on limited Palestinian autonomy. In Africa and Southeast Asia, the United Nations, no longer hobbled by a permanently divided Security Council, began to play the role envisioned at its founding, pacifying local conflicts and providing humanitarian aid.

If European affairs suddenly appeared more complex without the harsh simplicity of bipolar conflict, that complexity reflected the astounding gains of 50 years of peace. To be sure, capitalism brought dangerous dislocation across the continent; freedom, for all its benefits, allowed ethnic conflict. Dynamic change made politics livelier but more unpredictable, although the changes in people's lives that resulted from the West's extraordinary prosperity hardly seemed to depend on politics. Equality has yet to be achieved, and increased wealth has been accompanied by the signs of alienation revealed in drug abuse and xenophobia. The lack of consensus that may contribute to a vibrant intellectual life does little to assuage anger, frustration, and disillusionment. Nevertheless, however uncertain the future, Eastern Europe is freer than ever before in its history; and Western Europe, whatever the domestic problems, is more united than it has ever been. Just a few generations ago very few people expected that by the end of the twentieth century, in an increasingly global society, Europe would remain a favored continent, enviable in its wealth, liberty, and culture.

Recommended Reading

Sources

Ash, Timothy Garton. *The Magic Lantern: The Revolution of '89 Witnessed in Warsaw, Budapest, Berlin, and Prague.* 1990. An eyewitness account by a particularly keen and informed observer.

de Beauvoir, Simone. *Memoirs of a Dutiful Daughter.* James Kickup (tr.). 1959; *All Said and Done.* Patrick O'Brian (tr.). 1974. An important intellectual and writer with an international following and Sartre's close friend, de Beauvoir's memoirs give a sense of the intellectual life of the times and are important to the history of contemporary feminism.

Gorbachev, Mikhail. *Perestroika: New Thinking for Our Country and the World.* 1989. This presentation of his vision of the future is as revealing for the issues it does not address as for its specific recommendations.

Studies

*Albertini, Rudolf von. *Decolonization. The Administration and Future of the Colonies, 1919–1960.* Francisca Garvie (tr.). 1982. A solid account that focuses on Britain and France and is especially valuable for his historical depth.

*Ardagh, John. *France in the 1980s.* 1987. A fascinating examination of the fabric of daily life, with an eye on the development of the whole period since 1945 and France's position in Europe.

Ash, Timothy Garton. *In Europe's Name: Ostpolitik, Germany, and the European Question.* 1993. An outstandingly perceptive commentator on current European affairs assesses the process of German unification and its implication for the future of Europe.

*———. *The Polish Revolution: Solidarity.* 1984. Rich in insights into the social roots, techniques, ideas, and effectiveness of a moment that captured worldwide attention.

*Beer, Samuel H. *Britain against Herself.* 1982. A subtle and expert analysis of political and social stalemate in Britain.

Berger, Suzanne (ed.). *Organizing Interests in Western Europe: Pluralism, Corporatism, and the Transformation of Politics.* 1981. Important assessments of the political balance of power by some of the leading American social scientists.

Brown, B. E. *Protest in Paris: Anatomy of a Revolt.* 1974. The student revolt in Paris subjected to scholarly study.

*Craig, Gordon. *The Germans.* 1983. A noted historian's insightful, handsomely written, and critical assessment of German society.

*Ellul, Jacques. *The Technological Society.* John Wilkinson (tr.). 1964. One of the most striking and influential of contemporary attacks on the effects of technology.

*Heidenheimer, Arnold, J., Hugh Heclo, and Carolyn Adams. *Comparative Public Policy: The Politics of Social Choice in Europe and America.* 1975. Studies the background and implications of the varied approaches to social policy, written as the limitations of these programs were becoming apparent.

*Heilbroner, Robert G. *An Inquiry into the Human Prospect.* 1980. An analysis based on the literature of modern social science in which a well-known student of European economic history and thought uses that knowledge to look into the future.

*Helias, Pierre-Jakez. *The Horse of Pride: Life in a Breton Village.* June Guicharnaud (tr.). 1980. A compelling account of a preindustrial society about to be transformed.

Hennessy, Peter, and Anthony Seldons. *Ruling Performance: British Governments from Attlee to Thatcher.* 1987. Contrasting perspectives on British politics in radically different governments.

*Available in paperback.

Hoffmann, Stanley, and Paschalis Kitromilides. *Culture and Society in Contemporary Europe.* 1981. An anthology of essays by leading intellectuals attempting to evaluate the condition of Europe.

*Hooper, John. *The Spaniards: A Portrait of the New Spain.* 1987. An engaging look at the European society that went through the greatest transformation in the last 20 years.

Hoskins, Geoffrey. *The Awakening of the Soviet Union.* 1990. An excellent overview of how change came to a society that had resisted it for so long.

*Hughes, H. Stuart. *The Sea Change: The Migration of Social Thought, 1930–1960.* 1977. A major study of the role of European intellectuals in the United States and their contributions to modern social thought.

*———. *Sophisticated Rebels.* 1990. An intellectual historian considers the nature of dissent in the West as well as Eastern Europe in the critical years of 1988 and 1989.

*Hulsberg, Werner. *The German Greens: A Social and Political Profile.* 1988. A systematic treatment of the strongest of the European environmental movements.

*Jay, Martin. *The Dialectical Imagination. A History of the Frankfurt School and the Institute of Social Research, 1923–1950.* 1973. A rewarding study of some of the most influential thinkers of modern social science written with a keen understanding of the intellectual background and prejudices from which they wrote about modern society.

Katzenstein, Mary F., and Carol M. Mueller (eds.). *The Women's Movements of the United States and Western Europe.* 1987. These collected essays make for a book with wide coverage that underscores some striking national differences.

*Kavanagh, Dennis, and Anthony Seldon (eds.). *The Thatcher Effect.* 1989. A variety of critical appraisals of Thatcher's policies.

Kennedy, Paul. *Preparing for the Twenty-First Century.* 1993. A historian's skeptical look at power relations in the near future.

Keylor, William R. *The Twentieth-Century World. An International History.* 1984. A stimulating attempt to break out of the traditional national boundaries.

Lewin, Moshe. *The Gorbachev Phenomenon.* 1988. A brilliant analysis written as the phenomenon was unfolding and that relates current events to the developments in Soviet society over the previous 50 years.

*Mandelbaum, Michael. *The Nuclear Revolution: International Politics before and after Hiroshima.* 1981. A thoughtful study, making good use of parallels from the diplomacy of earlier eras to assess the implications of the nuclear age for international relations.

Marrus, Michael R. *The Emergence of Leisure.* 1974. A historical study that identifies one of the important characteristics of modern life as an important historical trend.

Merkl, Peter H. *The Federal Republic at Forty.* 1989. A distinguished political scientist evaluates the German republic that has lasted far longer than the Weimar Republic.

*Parker, Geoffrey. *The Logic of Unity.* 1975. Usefully analyses the forces for European unity from a geographer's perspective.

Payne, Stanley G. *Politics and Society in Twentieth-Century Spain.* 1976. A historian's recognition that Spain's remarkable modernization had firm foundations in the past.

Poster, Mark. *Existential Marxism in Postwar France.* 1975. An able analysis of an intellectual movement that had a wide impact on its generation.

Riddle, Peter. *The Thatcher Decade: How Britain Has Changed during the 1980s.* 1989. An unusually positive assessment of the long-term effects of the Thatcher period on British society.

Williams, Raymond. *Communications.* 1976. A leading British writer and historian reflects on the role of communication in modern societies.

EPILOGUE

To some extent we all think historically, for the history of the world in the last 200 years has made awareness of change an essential part of our outlook on society. We assess the present by contrasting it with the past; our fears and hopes for the future are largely based on historic trends that seem to forecast conditions to come. Publicists announce "revolutions" in everything from world politics, technology, and social mores to fashions; and politicians confidently predict what "history will say" even about their own decisions. Obviously, our thinking about the present and the future depends in part on the quality of our understanding of the past.

THE PRESENT AND THE PAST

Historical understanding begins with a sense of historical perspective. When the Berlin Wall came down and Europe's Communist regimes collapsed, everyone recognized in those dramas a major historical watershed. These great changes were all the more striking because they were unintended, not the aim of any policy but the effect rather of a surge of popular feeling among millions of Eastern Europeans wanting the freedom and prosperity enjoyed in Western Europe. Such sudden change, facilitated by modern mass communication and peacefully achieved, made it easy to believe, in both East and West, that a wholly new era had begun and that the world had entered an age of disarmament, liberal governments, and capitalist economies.

Historical Perspective That may yet prove to be the case, but assumptions of such total change need to be tempered with historical perspective, which suggests four reasons for caution. The first is simply that great transformations are difficult, and the strains they create can have unexpected results. The history of the Reformation, the expansion of Europe, the French Revolution, industrialization, and the revolutions of 1848 are sufficient reminders of that.

Second, historical perspective tempers assumptions about sweeping change, for there is often surprising continuity in social life. Established patterns matter. Differences persist even today between those parts of Europe that belonged to the Roman Empire and those that did not, between those that experienced the Protestant Reformation and those that did not. If the nations of Eastern Europe were to be ranked today according to the relative strengths and weaknesses of their economies and political systems, they would stand in relation to each other much as they did 70 years ago, following World War I and the collapse of the Habsburg Empire.

Many observers, of course, have noticed this; and facile analogies to the past have become as common as simplistic assumptions that everything is different. Commentators on current events in Eastern Europe point to parallels with Russia in the nineteenth century and the arguments then between Slavophiles and Westerners, to the surge of nationalism in the nineteenth century that led to the unification of Italy and Germany, and to ethnic and religious conflicts in Europe going back to the Middle Ages. Such examples can be invaluable when used analytically to explore how contemporary issues evolved and how societies evoke the loyalties that enable them to function. Historical awareness, which should lessen surprise at the renewed vigor of nationalism in Eastern Europe, may also remind us that in the future communism may be recalled nostalgically by those now suffering from the dislocations its fall has brought about. Such analogies are inherently selective, however, and easily manipulated; historical processes are usually complex and often contradictory.

Finally, historical understanding recognizes that human history is contingent on many factors; identifying trends does not predict outcomes. When Gorbachev came to power, it was part of a process of adaptive reform that seemed likely to strengthen the Soviet Union. Almost no one imagined that it would soon cease to exist. Good historical thinking leaves room for unforeseeable decisions, unexpected results, the play of multiple forces, the sudden intersection of trends and interests that were previously separate, and sheer accident.

Letting the Present Reopen the Past Historical understanding is constantly renewed by new research and by the stimulus of changes in our own times. The social concerns of the twentieth century stimulated new schools of social and demographic history that have fundamentally altered our vision of the European past. From the 1950s through the 1980s the harsh realities of the Cold War caused many to look at the past in terms of power politics, the competition between capitalism and communism, and the rise of superpowers. Such a focus led scholars to emphasize aspects of history they might otherwise have neglected, and this emphasis pointed to the importance of historical trends that in turn supported particular interpretations of the Cold War itself. With the end of the Cold War, the emphasis changes, and we see more clearly the effects it had not just on international relations and military policies but on political parties, social programs, and basic freedoms around the world. That changed perception leads to a rethinking of the past and a reassessment of the present.

These changing views of the past and its relationship to the present show most simply in the choice of periodization. In the 1950s and 1960s, it was common to say that the world had entered the Atomic Age, because the promise of atomic energy and the fear or atomic warfare seemed to shape an era. In the 1990s references to the Atomic Age are rare because both that promise and that fear have faded. Should either become a dominant factor once more, the term and this periodization of history will be used again. Similarly, the promise that World War I would make the world safe for democracy is now remembered primarily as a bitter irony; but should stable democracies in fact become the European norm, the process that accomplished this might well be seen as having been at work since 1918.

Many historians, diplomats, and politicians once identified the decline of Europe as one of history's major trends and thus considered that a new era began in the 1940s, when a continent tragically dominated by the Axis was plunged into a war that destroyed Europe's international power and subjected it to Soviet and American domination. In 1940 France dropped from the ranks of the world's most powerful states, Germany did so five years later, and in the 1950s even victorious Great Britain could no longer sustain an international position comparable to that of the United States and the Soviet Union. The economic crises of the postwar period and the loss of colonial empires thus seemed to confirm a process of relative decline in Western Europe's strength. And in the 1950s Arnold Toynbee's widely admired multivolume *Study of History* echoed the earlier gloom of Oswald Spengler in proclaiming that the millennium of European preeminence in world history had come to an end.

Shifting dates just a few years, however, could produce a periodization that points to a new era in European history beginning in the 1950s and marked by rapid social change, unprecedented prosperity, and the trend toward European union. Neither periodization is wrong; each fits a different set of questions. The questions asked of historical evidence may evolve from prior research, from a body of theory, or from current concerns. The findings that result lead to new understanding and, in turn, new questions. To think about European history in terms of current issues can thus be fruitful both for historical research and for insight into the present. Many of the world's pressing problems, after all, have roots in the history of Europe.

A GLOBAL ERA

Communication, technology, and trade at the end of the twentieth century all seem to be creating a new kind of global society, accelerating a trend that goes back to a restless Europe's expansion through the crusades, the voyages of discovery, the conquest of the New World, the spread of Dutch and British trade in the seventeenth century, the building of empires in North America and India a century later, imperial rule in the age of imperialism, and the extension of Western interests in the competition of the Cold War. This expansion involved knowledge of the world and its peoples, bloodshed, idealism, and greed. There is no reason to think that the process of building a global society will be simpler or have political and cultural effects that are any less mixed.

Europe and the World Despite its great wealth, Europe will not again dominate the world as it once did. Having learned to exercise their diplomatic influence in the interstices of Cold War competition, European nations have become accustomed to a limited role in many international matters, a circumstance like that in which many states of the former Soviet Union now find themselves. Because Europeans have been more consistently interested in other societies—as objects of exploration, study, conversion, and exploitation—than people from any other region, European ideas, institutions, and techniques have spread around the world and are in many places so much a part of local history that they are no longer merely European. These cultural encounters, whatever their motive and however enriching, have also created a long history of misunderstandings, abuse, and resentment that is felt in world politics today. Western influence, brute power, and new technologies have not, however, obliterated local differences. Indeed, within Europe itself the ability of local cultures to adapt to outside pressures while preserving something of their identity has been significant throughout history, for regional differences have survived the laws, the armies, and the roads of ancient Rome; the demands of national states; the intrusion of railroads, newspapers, and universal schooling; and the impact of telephones, television, and computers.

The Modern Economy Economic growth, once primarily a Western preoccupation, is now a universal goal. The power of the Japanese economy and the extraordinary growth of other Asian economies are as significant (and as great a competitive challenge to Europe) as the economic expansion of the United States in the nineteenth century. Many expect this pattern of growth to extend through much of the rest of Asia, including the giant economies of China and India, to accelerate in Mexico and much of South America, and to include parts of the Middle East. Europe would be only a small part of such an economic world, despite the advantages of its developed infrastructure and its historic ties to all parts of the world, ties reinforced in the last generation by Western Europe's role as the principal source of assistance to developing nations.

The economic institutions and markets that developed in Europe from the Middle Ages on produced a capitalism in which comparative economic advantages rarely last. The decline of some of the great commercial centers of the Middle Ages was followed by the relative decline of Renaissance Italy, then Spain, and then the Netherlands. These shifts in relative economic strength speeded up with industrialization. England had the world's most productive economy and was the world's greatest trader for much of the nineteenth century, only to be overtaken by Germany and the United States. These competitive changes are hard to predict, however, and sometimes reversible. As late as 1960 almost no one expected France and then Italy to surpass Britain, nor would anyone have anticipated the recent rapid growth of Spain. Sudden economic transformations remain possible, even though the capacity to adapt can benefit from tradition, capital, technology, infrastructure, and education, as Germany's impressive recovery from defeat in two world wars suggests. Although the resources and technologies that matter most today are far different from those that were important in the past, Europe's wealthiest regions at the end of the twentieth century are much the same ones that were the wealthiest one or two, and even five or six, centuries ago.

The Limits of Growth There is no certainty that economic growth will continue, although, since the industrial revolution, societies expect it to. Because of those expectations, even mild economic downturns can have serious social and political consequences. The revolutions of 1848, the political crises at the end of the nineteenth century, the revolutions in Russia, the rise of fascism, and the fall of communism were all related to economic crises. There is now concern that, even if productivity continues to rise, many may never feel its benefits and that a prosperous economy that leaves out large sectors of the domestic population will challenge the social principles and the political stability of modern Europe at least as seriously as industrialization and the Great Depression. Great benefits may flow from free trade and world peace, but neither is likely to last if today's international economic inequalities should persist or grow greater.

Furthermore, perpetual growth may be doomed by demographic and ecological constraints. Industrial expansion in nineteenth-century Europe benefited from growing populations, but now demographic factors have a negative economic effect. In Europe an aging population requires more services and produces less, and in many parts of the world populations grow faster (thanks in large part to modern medicine) than the economy, thereby reducing the standard of living. Furthermore the environment may not be able to support limitless growth. Thus the rest of the world may not be so lucky as Europe was in the past when, just as the supply of timber or grain or some other resource seemed likely to run short, unexploited sources of energy, new agricultural techniques, and the expansion of trade permitted a timely readjustment. There was nothing automatic about such responses, and many economies were seriously harmed by environmental abuses such as overgrazing and excessive logging. Italy suffered for centuries from the erosion of a mountainous terrain that had been stripped of trees to supply the shipbuilders of ancient Rome and of the medieval maritime republics. Since the Renaissance, cities have tried to regulate pollution, and in the sixteenth and seventeenth centuries states tried to control practices likely to cause flooding or threaten the game nobles liked to hunt. Until the end of the eighteenth century, however, Europeans usually understood environmental disaster in terms of disease and natural catastrophes, such as earthquakes and volcanic eruptions. Now, environmental catastrophes resulting from human actions are a greater preoccupation. Western European societies spend a great deal of money to combat the pollution they create, and the far graver effects of pollution in Eastern Europe, which are just beginning to be measured, will be a burden at least through the next generation. Everywhere, environmental issues produce new challenges to the status quo, favoring policies that run counter to the immediate interests of specific groups and sometimes of whole regions, cutting across traditional political parties, and pushing the state into new areas of activity. Concern for the environment has also spurred new movements that challenge the established political order because they cut across old social divisions and parties, recruiting support from those on the right as well as the left who distrust politics, formal institutions, and established interests.

THE POWER OF THE STATE

Modern economic life has added to the responsibilities of the state, which is expected to provide a stable currency and banking system, and at least some of the investments, the trade arrangements, the education, the detailed information on economic and social matters, and the means of communication that postindustrial societies require.

Economic and Social Planning Such tasks have led the state into extensive long-range planning. In the French system, a planning office with a large staff of experts and a consultative assembly representing business, labor, and governmental agencies both creates long-range programs and drafts legislation for parliamentary action. Most other European countries have comparably comprehensive arrangements, and nearly all have sought to manage their economies (indirectly through tax and fiscal policies and sometimes directly through nationalized industries and subsidies) and to shape their society (through policies on housing, welfare, and education).

In principle, the social system known as the welfare state and established throughout Europe implies the reallocation of wealth from the well-to-do to the less fortunate. In practice, the middle of society probably benefits as much as the poor, and the accompanying tax burden is in fact too great to fall on the rich alone. The cost and many of the policies of the welfare state have come under attack. Nevertheless, most Europeans expect the state to continue to ensure that no citizen need worry about going hungry, facing illness without medical care, or being destitute in old age.

The importance of governmental functions has helped to make governments' bureaucratic mode of organization a pervasive model, adopted throughout society and expected, in principle, to be efficiently organized for well-defined tasks, rational and objective in dealing with specific problems, and operated by people selected for their talent and technical training, who are promoted on merit (as well as seniority). Each nation has its own bureaucratic style reflecting its own history—the independent role of the aristocracy in England, the service tradition of the Junkers in Prussia, the centralization of royal and Napoleonic government in France, which was adopted in many other countries. The institutions with which governments deal—political parties, businesses, unions, education systems, hospitals—tend to manifest a similarly bureaucratic organization.

In practice, of course, no government agency is removed from special interests and political prejudices, and this makes bureaucracy itself a central issue of modern politics. Bureaucratic organization can inhibit social flexibility; and in democracies its procedures tend to be resented and its cost unpopularly tangible in taxation. In the past decade many European politicians have increasingly criticized the prominent role of the modern state. West Germany's economy became Europe's largest while limiting the government's direct role in economic affairs. In England the Conservative party under Margaret Thatcher launched a systematic campaign to limit the government's direction of the economy and to dismantle the welfare state. Governments in France and Italy are selling off government-owned industries; and the nations of Eastern Europe are, to varying degrees and often at great social pain, allowing prices, wages, production, and distribution to be largely determined by the free market.

Reversing the Historic Trend From the Carolingian and Norman monarchies of the Middle Ages and the city-states of Renaissance Italy to the present, the steady growth of the state has shaped European history. The national monarchies of Spain, France, and England made the state an instrument for creating military might, dispensing uniform justice, and supporting a national culture. With the French Revolution and Napoleonic rule the role of the state increased enormously, its intrusive efficiency expanding as it more fully engaged more of the citizenry. The demands of democracy, the needs of two world wars, and the ambitions of fascism and communism added still more to the state's power and the range of its influence. The European form of the national state was adopted around the world and became the basis of international organization.

Arguably, the state's position as the dominant social organization is now being called into question. There were always smaller political units that seemed to work very well, and in much of Europe regional and federal movements seek to recapture the advantages of smallness and homogeneity, a tendency furthered in the breakup of the Soviet Union. At the same time, international corporations operate across national boundaries, making decisions that affect every aspect of economic life from investment to employment. The European Union has shifted many of the traditional functions of the state, and one of the principal objections to the Maastricht treaties, heard throughout the European Community, was that the Community was being transformed into something too much like a state. The state has become an object of suspicion, not so much for being the captive agent of the ruling class (the classic Marxist reason) or as a threat to individual liberty (the traditional liberal fear) but simply as a concentration of power dedicated to its own interests. To some extent a similar criticism is applied to other large organizations—business corporations, political parties, and universities. A distrust of institutions is echoed in the resurgent regionalist movements within most European nations and in movements like environmentalism and feminism, which operate beyond ordinary politics (always focused on the state) and are known collectively as the new social movements.

Even in effective democracies, the political process often seems far removed from the people, a sort of private game based on the manipulation of public opinion. Save for self-interest, the great political parties have largely lost the clarity of purpose with which they emerged from the resistance movements after World War II. The Christian Democrats, who dreamed of a Christian social vision above politics and were among the first to see the promise of European unity, have become just another coalition mediating among established influences, where they have survived at all. The socialists, once sure their hour had come, remain torn between allies on the left and in the center and weakened by the charges of corruption that followed their time in power. No longer confident of their old panaceas, they are neither the incisive critics nor the innovative leaders they once showed promise of being.

If the economic and social roles of the modern state are being challenged, so is its most traditional role as the locus of military power. With the end of the Cold War and with only one superpower, what will be the nature of (and the need for) military preparedness? By restricting warfare to regional conflicts, international cooperation may reduce the importance of a state's military strength. Among the remarkable changes that have made negotiations possible between Palestinians and Israelis, blacks and whites in South Africa, and Catholics and Protestants in Northern Ireland is the combination of effective international pressure on national states and a new willingness among the states themselves to talk about issues that traditional concepts of national sovereignty once ruled out of consideration.

▸ **Burning a poster of the cover of Salman Rushdie's *Satanic Verses*, Kuala Lumpur, March 1989.**

QUESTIONS OF VALUES

International pressure is ideological as well as military and economic, and there are signs that certain values are coming to be more widely accepted as universal human rights applicable everywhere. Individuals, on the other hand, face the fact that greater liberty, knowledge, and prosperity increase the range of the difficult choices before them.

Human Rights Western civilization has characteristically believed that its principles were universal. Greek philosophy searched for truths applicable to everyone, and Roman law was extended wherever Roman civilization could reach. Christian belief always emphasized the need to carry Christian teachings to all peoples, and in the last two centuries Europeans have variously but confidently proposed capitalism, liberalism, Marxism, and democracy as ideals to be universally embraced.

Now many in Western society put great value on cultural diversity and criticize Eurocentrism. The result is an ironic self-consciousness about advocating human rights around the world, because their very conception may be "fundamentally a product of the liberal imagination, reflecting the complacent cultural imperialism of the modern Western world."[1] In 1989 Salman Rushdie, an Indian Muslim educated in England, published *Satanic Verses*, a novel that in its references to Muhammad seemed to the Ayatollah Khomeini to be blasphemous. To Khomeini the book was the latest of many assaults from Western culture on an Islamic way of life; and supported by the other leaders of Iran, he pronounced a death sentence on Rushdie and on all who, knowing the book's contents, participated in its publication. Rushdie was forced into hiding, and Western intellectuals and political leaders expressed outrage and reaffirmed their commitment to freedom of expression. Crowds of militant Muslims demonstrated in the streets of England, India, Pakistan, the Middle East, and North Africa protesting against insults to Islam and the imposition of Western values.

The Problem of Choice But these are not just differences between East and West, for there is conflict within Europe and America between those who give absolute priority to individual rights and those who place social values first, between those who insist on the right of individuals to make moral choices, even wrong ones, and those who insist that society and the state must embody and enforce some absolute truths. The movement to accord to women all the opportunities for education, careers, and independent activity permitted to men can thus be seen as a logical extension of individual rights and also as the dangerous destruction of a tradition that built the family around the distinctive domestic role of women. Such conflicts between social needs and

[1]Stephen Shute and Susan Hurley (eds.), *On Human Rights: The Oxford Amnesty Lectures 1993*, New York, 1993, p. 3.

personal aims were explored in Classical Greek drama, wrestled with by the Church fathers, and recast during the Renaissance and the Reformation. The great intellectual battles of the Enlightenment were often fought on just these issues, and they have remained divisive ever since.

Several factors, however, have made these disputes especially difficult at the end of the twentieth century. Mobility, education, science, and market economies have broadened the range of personal choices. Matters such as diet and dress that were once simply determined by custom have become personal statements, and people are expected to make wise choices about their life style and their occupation, about where they live and how they spend their leisure.

Furthermore, decisions about even such intimate choices as marriage and divorce, contraception, and abortion are surrounded by public discussion and debate—in which religious leaders, moralists, and feminists disagree—and thus become at the same time issues of personal identity and of social ethics. Belief in the importance of the family and the value of individual achievement may be as high as it has ever been, but there is widespread fear that the institution of the family is being undermined by change, that personal accomplishment is not valued as it once was, and that society is losing its moral compass.

There is little reassurance in the fact that alarm over threats to the family has been heard from thousands of pulpits for centuries; that serfdom, slavery, and poverty have also endangered the family; and that the Christian view of human nature and the Freudian view of the human psyche both acknowledge that the constraints of family life are difficult to accept. Still, the family has survived the effects of industrialization, which separated household members for nearly all their waking hours, moved millions of people to new places, and deprived the family of the traditional social support of relatives and village custom. Indeed, the expectations of the family have steadily increased since the eighteenth century. The Victorian conception of the Christian family raised the norms for loyalty and comity, and marriage in the twentieth century is expected to be a mutual choice and a delightful partnership in which child rearing lasts longer and is more intensive than ever before.

Culture Europe's cultural life expresses related tensions and uncertainties without contributing much to their resolution. While Europe's many cultures maintain their distinctiveness, a European cultural identity also appears to be thriving, one that is part of a wider Western culture but also distinct. Popular and commercial culture share music, styles of dress, and films; while Eurovision allows national networks to share Europe-wide transmissions, and the ease of travel adds to this strengthened pan-European sense of similarity and shared interests. American television programs are almost as popular in Europe as American movies were in the 1920s, and American motion pictures dominate European cinema. Nevertheless, at negotiations on the General Agreement on Tariff and Trade in 1994, the countries of the European Union supported France in insisting that their mass media must reserve some support for European productions. What defined popular culture as European was its origins more than its content or function.

Formal or high culture, too, has become more international than it was in the nineteenth century. Exiles from Hitler's Europe and Stalin's Russia made high culture more international and transatlantic. Today, European research in the sciences and humanities often has a distinctly European flavor (frequently using teams of people from different countries or Europeans from one nation teaching in another). In the arts individual performers, orchestras, and works of art move freely across European national borders, and student exchanges with the European Union have become the norm. No previous civilization supported so much scholarship, so many centers of learning, or so many artists. Nevertheless, contemporary commentators are less confident than Enlightenment thinkers tended to be when they compared ancient and modern culture and argued that the moderns had the advantage, combining ancient wisdom with new knowledge. At the end of the twentieth century, few intellectuals find evidence of progress in European culture.

In part this unease reflects an odd separation between popular and formal culture. The great literary works of all ages are taught in schools and universities and are still read with pleasure, and more people than ever before hear classical music and visit museums and art galleries. Yet popular culture as commercial entertainment suggests a quite different set of values, and the tendency to make serious culture academic, a matter of special study by experts, may suggest some decline in its power to attract. The very forms that defined high culture in the nineteenth century—long novels and epic poems, symphonies, operas, impressive museums—have by current standards become terribly demanding of time and money. And they have lost the support lavished on them by the regimes of Eastern Europe, where, ironically, communism affectionately sustained this older bourgeois culture.

If the moral earnestness of that nineteenth-century culture seems out of date, so does the continued search for shocking new effects, which the twentieth-century avant-garde used to attack that established high culture. Modern doubt about human rationality and disdain for elites have made anti-intellectualism respectable, and there has been a remarkable revival of interest in the occult. Computers, after all, can also be used to plot astrological charts. European civilization has tended to take culture as the most significant expression of society, and we identify the eras of European history in terms of their characteristic cultural achievements. That leads to some disquiet about our own era, when the role of culture seems clearer when in opposition than as an expression of commitment. Still, when Czechoslovakia came to life, it picked a playwright as president.

The Nature of Community Conflicts over social justice, moral values, and culture make for great disagreements over what a social contract might contain or whether society rests at all on the kinds of principles that Locke and Rousseau described and on which liberalism was founded. Many now argue that a sense of alienation, which Marx attributed primarily to the faulty organization of production, has become more general, affecting not just craftsmanship but attitudes toward society and work in general, taste in entertainment, and the prevalence in modern Western societies of crime and drug addiction. Or perhaps this behavior is not so different from the alcoholism of Hogarth's London or the centuries of peasant revolts, highway robbery, cockfighting, prostitution, and public hangings of earlier centuries.

Freedom, some argue, has gone too far, and prosperity has proved to be morally dangerous. Highly organized societies leave individuals feeling powerless and manipulated, despite the apparent array of choices before them. Significantly, social control, a central concern in the writings of the Frankfurt school and Michel Foucault, has become a favorite subject for social research, which finds it operating through advertising and education as well as through religion and custom, laws and institutions. The effect, these critics argue, is to keep the disadvantaged docile and to obscure issues of social justice. While the majority of Western Europeans have enjoyed increased freedom and a rising standard of living, a significant minority suffers unemployment, segregation, and discrimination. Suddenly, the question of what kind of social contract should be extended to foreign immigrants or to citizens who merely lack the skills most in demand has become one of the burning issues of modern Europe.

Around the world, nationalism and vibrant religious movements demonstrate the power of community feeling, raising the question of whether Europeans will once again turn to such movements as they have in the past and whether postindustrial societies can satisfy the desire for social solidarity. Although fundamentalist religious movements remain weak in most of Europe, there is a significant Catholic fundamentalist movement in Italy; a Protestant one in Northern Ireland; Muslim ones in Britain, France, and Russia; and Orthodox ones in the former Soviet Union. Religious clashes have been endemic in Europe—part of medieval battles against heretics and Muslims, warfare between Protestants and Catholics, and modern conflicts between church and state.

Religion can mobilize opposition to current social trends, as in the frequent campaigns against immoral ways whether of dress or drugs; to the state, as in the Solidarity movement in Poland; and to other social groups, as in the enduring conflict in Ireland. Under John Paul II, elected pope in 1978 (and the first non-Italian pope in 455 years), the Roman Catholic Church has become more resolutely conservative and outspoken on

The Saint Louis Art Museum, Purchase: Gift of Mr. and Mrs. Joseph Pulitzer, Jr., by exchange.

▶ *Anselm Kiefer*
BURNING RODS

theological, institutional, and moral issues while remaining a vigorous critic of modern materialism and the injustices of capitalism. Conceivably, religious issues could heighten some of the conflicts in contemporary European society as they did in the 1920s and 1930s.

Ethnic conflict, too, has rarely been absent in European history, and Yugoslavia in the 1990s provided frightening proof that it remains possible for political leaders to inflame ethnic hatreds for their own purposes. Such efforts are in fact under way in much of Eastern Europe, and parties opposed to foreigners have gained attention and votes in France, Germany, and Italy. Western societies, which have generated the most powerful ideas and most effective movements opposed to racism, have also spawned virulent racist movements.

The memory of Nazi genocide must affect any assessment of Western civilization and any evaluation of modern history. That such horror could proceed as systematic policy in the heart of Europe means that no country is automatically immune, and evidence has steadily grown of the widespread willingness to cooperate with the Nazis, not just in Germany but in the occupied countries as well. Recent revelations of mass murder under the Soviet regime underscore a fearful sense of what modern society is capable of, and nationalist movements anywhere in Europe are bound to evoke that fear. By making the hatred of Jews a principle, Nazism effectively strengthened the sense of national identity and appealed to the worst in human beings.

For all the evil that has been committed in its name, national sentiment remains strong throughout Europe. As the Falkland war and the union of East and West Germany showed, political leaders can play no stronger card. At the same time, Western Europeans now know each other better and in the last half century have been drawn closer together than ever before. The question is whether the sense of community can be fulfilled by pride in a more integrated Europe and by regional loyalties, encouraging a largely symbolic nationalism.

The Consolation of History Since every era tends narcissistically to believe that its problems are unique, the assumption deserves to be doubted. Europe today faces no threat comparable to the barbarian invasions of ancient Rome or the Black Death. If social change now is rapid, we have learned to expect and even anticipate it; the changes that followed the fifteenth century or those in the hundred years after 1780 may well have been more shocking and harder to absorb. We should not let nostalgia make it seem that earlier ages enjoyed a confidence and comforting unanimity denied to us. Rarely in Western history has a single philosophy or set of values enjoyed undisputed hegemony. The view that other eras were informed by a single spirit is largely the product of distance, which makes outlines clearer and fissures more obscure. The competing claims of throne and alter and the disputes about forms of transubstantiation were once as socially shattering as issues about public and private ownership, ethnic minorities, or abortion and euthanasia are today.

Good causes can be served by ordinary people with all the normal human flaws. The resistance movements that fought fascism and are rightly honored throughout Western Europe were often built around old feuds and resentments. If the future is uncertain, as futures always are, it means that what human beings choose to do can make a difference. In history long-term trends and accident intersect; cultural and economic elements, politics, and personality interact; new ideas, tradition, and memory help form the future. The western tip of the Eurasian peninsula can be expected to continue generating the tensions, dangers, discoveries, institutions, ideas, and dreams that have made the Western experience a fascinating experiment.

Photo and Text Credits

PHOTOS

Chapter 1: Opener: NASA; p. 6: Georg Gerster/Comstock ♦ p. 7: Giraudon/Art Resource ♦ p. 10: Hirmer Fotoarchiv ♦ p. 12: Fred J. Maroon/Photo Researchers ♦ p. 13: Elliot Erwitt/Magnum ♦ p. 14: The British Museum ♦ p. 15: The Metropolitan Museum of Art, Rogers Fund, 1931. (31.3.166) ♦ p. 16: Photo, M. Büsing/Bildarchiv Preussischer Kulturbesitz ♦ p. 17: C. M. Dixon ♦ p. 19: Gianni Tortoli/Photo Researchers ♦ p. 24: Princeton University Press/Art Resource ♦ p. 25: Hirmer Fotoarchiv ♦ p. 27: George Holton/Photo Researchers ♦ p. 28: Photograph by Dr. G. G. Cameron; The University Museum, University of Pennsylvania (Neg # ANEP Plate 462) **Chapter 2:** p. 30: Nimatallah/Art Resource ♦ p. 32: The British Museum ♦ p. 34: Top, Erich Lessing/Art Resource. Bottom, C. M. Dixon ♦ p. 35: C. M. Dixon ♦ p. 36: Top, C. M. Dixon. Bottom, Michael Holford ♦ p. 37: Top, C. M. Dixon. Bottom, Michael Holford ♦ p. 38: C. M. Dixon ♦ p. 47: Nimatallah/Art Resource ♦ p. 50: Michael Holford ♦ p. 51: American School of Classical Studies at Athens ♦ p. 55: American School of Classical Studies at Athens: Agora Excavations ♦ p. 56: Both, Hirmer Fotoarchiv ♦ p. 57: Scala/Art Resource **Chapter 3:** p. 62: Erich Lessing/Art Resource ♦ p. 66: Naples, Archeological Museum. Photo, © Luciano Pedicini/Index ♦ p. 67: Photo, Johannes Laurentius, 1992/Bildarchiv Preussischer Kulturbesitz ♦ p. 69: Scala/Art Resource ♦ p. 70: The British Museum ♦ p. 72: Michael Holford ♦ p. 73: Acropolis Museum, Athens ♦ p. 74: John W. Snyder/The Stock Market ♦ p. 75: Hirmer Fotoarchiv ♦ p. 77: Unknown, perhaps a pupil of Lysippos, "Statue of a Victorious Athlete." Last quarter of 4th century B.C. Bronze, H: 151.5 cm. Collection of the J. Paul Getty Museum, Malibu, California ♦ p. 78: Scala/Art Resource ♦ p. 80: C. M. Dixon ♦ p. 81: Courtesy the Museum of Fine Arts, Boston; p. 83: C. M. Dixon ♦ p. 84: Scala/Art Resource **Chapter 4:** p. 88: Scala/Art Resource ♦ p. 90: Alinari/Art Resource ♦ p. 91: Scala/Art Resource ♦ p. 93: Trëe; p. 93: Alinari/Art Resource ♦ p. 101: Scala/Art Resource ♦ p. 102: Unknown, "Man of the Republic." Graeco-Roman. Contribution, Purchase of E. P. Warren. Courtesy of Museum of Fine Arts, Boston ♦ p. 105: Giraudon/Art Resource ♦ p. 107: Michael Holford ♦ p. 109: Brian Brake/Photo Researchers ♦ p. 112: C. M. Dixon **Chapter 5:** p. 116: Scala/Art Resource ♦ p. 120: Trëe ♦ p. 121: C. M. Dixon ♦ p. 123: Nimatallah/Art Resource ♦ p. 124: C. M. Dixon ♦ p. 126: Trëe ♦ p. 127: H. C. Kinne/Comstock ♦ p. 129: Michael Holford ♦ p. 134: Hirmer Fotoarchiv ♦ p. 136: C. M. Dixon ♦ p. 138: Erich Lessing/Art Resource ♦ p. 141: Both, Scala/Art Resource ♦ p. 143: Alinari/Art Resource ♦ p. 144: Scala/Art Resource ♦ p. 147: Alinari/Art Resource **Chapter 6:** p. 150: Scala/Art Resource ♦ p. 155: The Huntington Library, San Marino, CA ♦ p. 156: The Metropolitan Museum of Art, gift of J. Pierpont Morgan ♦ p. 158: The British Museum ♦ p. 160: Biblioteca Medicea Laurenziana, Florence. Photo, D. Pineider ♦ p. 161: Walters Art Gallery, Baltimore ♦ p. 162: Art Resource ♦ p. 163: Florence, Bibliotheca Seminario Vescovile/Photo, P. Tosi/Index ♦ p. 164: Stiftsbibliothek, St. Gallen. Photo, Carsten Seltrecht ♦ p. 165: Left, The Pierpont Morgan Library, New York. M.429, f. 183. Right, Bibliothèque Nationale, Paris ♦ p. 166: The Board of Trinity College Library Dublin ♦ p. 176: Bibliothèque Nationale, Paris ♦ p. 177: Scala/Art Resource ♦ p. 178: Bibliothèque Nationale, Paris **Chapter 7:** p. 180: 32.62: Leaf from a Qur'an. Egypt, 9th–10th century. 20.5 × 29.1 cm. Courtesy of the Freer Gallery of Art, Smithsonian Institution, Washington, D.C. ♦ p. 182: Scala/Art Resource ♦ p. 183: The Metropolitan Museum of Art, Gift of J. Pierpont Morgan, 1917 ♦ p. 186: Bibliothèque Nationale, Paris ♦ p.; 187: Moscow, Historical Museum; photo, Ecole des Hautes Etudes, Paris ♦ p. 190: Bibliothèque Nationale, Paris ♦ p. 191: Tibor Bognár/The Stock Market ♦ p. 193: Giraudon/Art Resource ♦ p. 196: General Research Division, New York Public Library. Astor, Lenox, Tilden Foundations ♦ p. 199: Courtesy of The Arthur M. Sackler Museum, The Edwin Binney, 3rd Collection of Turkish Art at the Harvard University Art Museums ♦ p. 203: Bibliothèque Nationale, Paris ♦ p. 204: J. Messerschmidt/Leo de Wys ♦ p. 206: The British Museum ♦ p. 207: The Bodleian Library, University of Oxford. Ms. Marsh 144, page 273 ♦ p. 208: Fridmar Damm/Leo de Wys **Chapter 8:** p. 210: By Permission of The British Library ♦ p. 215: Giraudon/Art Resource ♦ p. 221: Giraudon/Art Resource ♦ p. 223: Erich Lessing/Art Resource ♦ p. 227: André Held ♦ p. 229: Giraudon/Art Resource ♦ p. 230: Collection Viollet ♦ p. 232: Erich Lessing/Art Resource ♦ p. 236: Archiv für Kunst und Geschichte ♦ p. 238: University Library of Freiburg-im-Breisgau ♦ p. 239: Victoria and Albert Museum, London/Art Resource ♦ p. 242: Top, Bibliothèque Nationale, Paris. Giraudon/Art Resource ♦ p. 243: Casimir/Leo de Wys ♦ p. 244: Marburg/Art Resource ♦ p. 245: Giraudon/Art Resource **Chapter 9:** p. 248: Vienna, Austrian National Library ♦ p. 251: Collection Viollet ♦ p. 252: Scala/Art Resource ♦ p. 253: Bibliothèque Nationale, Paris ♦ p. 257: Bettmann ♦ p. 259: Master and Fellows of Corpus Christi College, Cambridge ♦ p. 261: New York Public Library ♦ p. 262: Chroniques de France, fol. 333r. Copyright Bibliothèque royale Albert 1er, Bruxelles ♦ p. 263: Apostolic Library, Vatican City ♦ p. 264: The Granger Collection ♦ p. 269: Scala/Art Resource ♦ p. 271: The Pierpont Morgan Library, New York. M. 716.1 ♦ p. 276: Scala/Art Resource ♦ p. 277: Left, Marburg/Art Resource. Right, Lauros-Giraudon/Art Resource ♦ p. 279: The British Museum **Chapter 10:** p. 282: By Permission of The British Library ♦ p. 284: By Permission of The British Library ♦ p. 285: Stadtsbibliothek Nuremberg (Ms.) Amb. 317.2°, f. 10r ♦ p. 287: Both, Bibliothèque Nationale, Paris ♦ p. 288: Bibliothèque Nationale, Paris ♦ p. 290: The British Museum ♦ p. 292: Bibliothèque Nationale, Paris ♦ p. 294: Scala/Art Resource ♦ p. 296: The Bodleian Library, University of Oxford, MS. BODL. 264. fol., 218r ♦ p. 297: The Granger Collection ♦ p. 302: By Permission of The British Library ♦ p. 303: Bibliothèque Nationale, Paris ♦ p. 306: Scala/Art Resource ♦ p. 309: Erich Lessing/Magnum **Chapter 11:** p. 312: By Permission of The British Library ♦ p. 317: Art Resource ♦ p. 318: By Permission of The British Library ♦ p. 321: Giancarlo Costa/Index ♦ p. 322: E. Harold Hugo ♦ p. 323: New York Public Library ♦ p. 324: Bibliothèque Nationale, Paris ♦ p. 325: Giraudon/Art Resource ♦ p. 326: Alinari/Art Resource ♦ p. 328: Scala/Art Resource ♦ p. 333: Bibliothèque Nationale, Paris ♦ p. 335: By Permission of The British Library ♦ p. 337: Scala/Art Resource ♦ p. 338: Giancarlo Costa/Index ♦ p. 339: Erich Lessing/Art Resource **Chapter 12:** p. 346: Reproduced by courtesy of the Trustees, The National Gallery, London ♦ p. 352: Top, Alinari/Art Resource. Bottom, Giancarlo Costa/Index ♦ p. 357: Giraudon/Art Resource ♦ p. 358: Scala/Art Resource ♦ p. 362: Erich Lessing/Art Resource ♦ p. 363: Top, David Ball/The Stock Market. Bottom, Alinari/Art Resource ♦ p. 364: Top, Erich Lessing/Art Resource. Bottom, Giraudon/Art Resource ♦ p. 365: Scala/Art Resource ♦ p. 366: Scala/Art Resource ♦ p. 367: Scala/Art Resource ♦ p. 370: Erich Lessing/Art Resource ♦ p. 373: A. Dürer, "The Riders on the Four Horses From the Apocalypse" c. 1496. Woodcut. The Metropolitan Museum of Art, Gift of Junius S. Morgan, 1919. (19.73.209) ♦ p. 377: Pisa, Museo Nazionale di S. Matteo/Soprintendenza B.A.A.A.S., Pisa **Chapter 13:** p. 382: Archiv für Kunst und Geschichte ♦ p. 385: Erich Lessing/Art Resource ♦ p. 387: Hans Sebald Beham, German, 1500–1550. "Large Peasant Holiday." Woodcut, 1535. 36.2 × 114.2 cm. (Sections 1 and 2). Potter Palmer Collection, 1967.491. Photograph © 1993, The Art Institute of Chicago. All Rights Reserved ♦ p. 388: Erich Lessing/Art Resource ♦ p. 390: Erich Lessing/Art Resource ♦ p. 391: Erich Lessing/Art Resource ♦ p. 392: Victoria and Albert Museum, London/Art Resource ♦ p. 394: Scala/Art Resource ♦ p. 398: Bildarchiv Preussischer Kulturbesitz ♦ p. 399: Scala/Art Resource ♦ p. 402: Germanisches Nationalmuseum Nurnberg ♦ p. 404: Bibliothèque Nationale, Paris ♦ p. 407: Bibliothèque Publique et Universitaire, Geneva ♦ p. 411: Erich Lessing/Art Resource ♦ p. 413: Giraudon/Art Resource ♦ p. 417: Erich Lessing/Art Resource **Chapter 14:** p. 420: Reproduced by courtesy of the Trustees, The National Gallery, London ♦ p. 423: Bettmann ♦ p. 425: Petrus Christus, "St. Eligius." 1449. Oil on Wood. 39 × 33⁷⁄₁₆". The Metropolitan Museum of Art, Robert Lehman Collection, 1975 (1975.1.110) ♦ p. 426: Museum Boymans-van Beuningen, Rotterdam ♦ p. 427: Erich Lessing/Art Resource ♦ p. 430: New York Public Library ♦ p. 433: Giraudon/Art Resource ♦ p. 435: National Maritime Museum, London ♦ p. 439: By Courtesy of The National Portrait Gallery, London ♦ p. 450: Rare Books and Manuscripts Division, New York Public Library, Astor, Lenox, and Tilden Foundations ♦ p. 451: Erich Lessing/Art Resource ♦ p. 452: Kunsthistorisches Museum, Vienna ♦ p. 455: Reproduced by courtesy of the Trustees, The National Gallery, London ♦ p. 457: The Pierpont Morgan Library, New York. PML 52863 **Chapter 15:** p. 460: Musée Cantonal Des Beaux-Arts, Lausanne ♦ p. 462: Reproduced by courtesy of the Trustees, The National Gallery, London ♦ p. 463: National Maritime Museum, Greenwich ♦ p. 464: New York Public Library ♦ p. 465: Erich Lessing/Art Resource ♦ p. 468: Anne S. K. Brown Military Collection ♦ p. 471: Herzog Anton Ulrich-Museum, Braunschweig. Museum photo, B. P. Keiser ♦ p. 472: Reproduced by courtesy of the Trustees, The National Gallery, London ♦ p. 475: Deutsches Historisches Museum, Berlin, Germany ♦ p. 477: Hamburger Kunsthalle ♦ p. 480: By Courtesy of The Marquess of Salisbury. Photo, The Fotomas Index ♦ p. 483: The Granger Collection ♦ p. 486: Giraudon/Art Resource ♦ p. 489: Bibliothèque Nationale, Paris ♦ p. 491: The Granger Collection **Chapter 16:** p. 496: Mauritshuis, The Hague ♦ p. 498: Giraudon/Art Resource ♦ p. 501: New York Public Library ♦ p. 505: Bettmann ♦ p. 509: The British Museum, Department of Prints and Drawings ♦ p. 513: Reproduced by courtesy of the Trustees, The National Gallery, London ♦ p. 514: Scala/Art Resource ♦ p. 515: Oronoz ♦ p. 516: G. Anderson/The Stock Market ♦ p. 517: Scala/Art Resource ♦ p. 519: Scala/Art Resource ♦ p. 520: Scala/Art Resource ♦ p. 523: Scala/Art Resource ♦ p. 526: Bibliothèque Nationale, Paris ♦ p. 528: Photo: Private collection **Chapter 17:** p. 532: The Wallace Collection, London ♦ p. 534: Giraudon/Art Resource ♦ p. 536: The Wallace Collection, London ♦ p. 542: Giraudon/Art Resource ♦ p. 548: Tass/Sovfoto ♦ p. 551: Sir Joshua Reynolds, "Lady Smith (Charlotte

Delaval) and her Children (George Henry, Louisa, and Charlotte)." Oil on canvas. 55⅜ × 44⅛". The Metropolitan Museum of Art, Bequest of Collis P. Huntington, 1900 (25.110.10) ♦ p. 553: By Courtesy of the Trustees of Sir John Soane's Museum, London ♦ p. 554: Samuel Scott, "The Building of Westminster Bridge." Oil on canvas. 24 × 44⅜". The Metropolitan Museum of Art, Purchase, Charles B. Curtis Fund and Joseph Pulitzer Bequest, 1944 (44.56) ♦ p. 561: Staatliche Schlösser und Garten, Schloss Charlottenburg, Potsdam ♦ p. 563: Scala/Art Resource ♦ p. 564: The British Museum ♦ p. 565: Radio times Hulton Picture Library ♦ p. 568: Giraudon/Art Resource **Chapter 18:** p. 574: Joseph Vernet, detail, "Port of Marseilles" 1759. Musée de la Marine. Photo RMN ♦ p. 577: General Research Division, The New York Public Library. Astor, Lenox, and Tilden Foundations ♦ p. 579: Raspal, "Atelier de Couture en Arles." 1760. Photo Bulloz ♦ p. 583: J. Vernet, "Construction of a Road." Giraudon/Art Resource ♦ p. 585: Both, The Science Museum, London ♦ p. 591: Bettmann ♦ p. 593: Nicolas-Bernard Lépicié, "Cour de Ferme." Paris, Musée du Louvre. Photo RMN ♦ p. 595: City of Bristol Museum and Art Gallery/Bridgeman Art Library ♦ p. 598: From "Voyage du Chevalier des Marchais en Guinée" by J. B. Labat, 1730 ♦ p. 599: Courtesy of the New-York Historial Society ♦ p. 602: New Brunswick Museum ♦ p. 603: Thomas Hickey, "Colonel Kirkpatrick with Attendants." Courtesy of the National Gallery of Ireland **Chapter 19:** p. 606: Martin van Meytens, "Banquet for the Wedding of Joseph II and Isabella von Parma in 1760," 1763. Archiv für Kunst und Geschichte ♦ p. 609: Top, Bettmann. Bottom, from "Natural History General and Particular" by George Buffon. Courtesy Brooklyn Public Library ♦ p. 613: Bettmann ♦ p. 618: Nicolas H. Jeurat de Bertry, "Allegory of the Revolution with a Portrait Medallion of J. J. Rousseau." Giraudon/Art Resource ♦ p. 620: Lemonnier, "Salon of Mme. Geoffrin, 1725." Giraudon/Art Resource ♦ p. 622: Mary Evans Picture Library ♦ p. 624: Giraudon/Art Resource ♦ p. 627: Jean-Honoré Fragonard, "Blindman's Buff," detail, c. 1765. Samuel H. Kress Collection. © 1995 National Gallery of Art, Washington ♦ p. 628: Jean-Baptiste Greuze, "The Paternal Curse." Giraudon/Art Resource ♦ p. 628: Jacques Louis David, "The Oath of the Horatii." Scala/Art Resource ♦ p. 629: New York Public Library, General Research Division, Astor, Lenox, and Tilden Foundations ♦ p. 632: Bibliothèque des Art Décoratifs, Paris. Photo Jean-Loup Charmet Tallandier ♦ p. 633: Hogarth's "Gin Lane" & "Beer Lane." The Metropolitan Museum of Art, Harris Brisbane Dick Fund, 1932 **Chapter 20:** p. 636: Musée Carnavalet/Photo Bulloz ♦ p. 639: Austrian Press & Information Service ♦ p. 642: John Trumbull, "The Declaration of Independence, 4 July 1776." Yale University Art Gallery, Trumbull Collection ♦ p. 646: Bibliothèque Nationale/Roger-Viollet ♦ p. 647: Bibliothèque Nationale/Photo Bulloz ♦ p. 648: Jacques Louis David, detail from "Oath of the Tennis Court at Versailles, June 20, 1789." Giraudon/Art Resource ♦ p. 649: Houet, "The Storming of the Bastille." Musée Carnavalet/Photo Bulloz ♦ p. 656: Jean Duplessi Bertaux, "Storming of the Tuileries, August 10, 1792." Giraudon/Art Resource ♦ p. 657: Musée Carnavalet/Photo Bulloz ♦ p. 658: Musée Carnavalet/Photo Bulloz ♦ p. 659: Jules Benoit-Levy, "Battle of Cholet" 1794. Giraudon/Art Resource ♦ p. 661: Masquelier, "A Session of the Jacobin Club." Giraudon/Art Resource ♦ p. 663: Bibliothèque Nationale ♦ p. 664: Photo Bulloz ♦ p. 666: Left, Photo Bulloz. Right, Collection Viollet ♦ p. 667: F. L. J. Watteau, "The Departure of the Volunteers." Musée Carnavalet/Bridgeman Art Library **Chapter 21:** p. 670: Jacques Louis David, "Napoléon Bonaparte" sketch. Giraudon/Art Resource ♦ p. 672: Giraudon/Art Resource ♦ p. 673: LeSeure, lack of bread in Paris 1795. Photothèque des Musées de la Ville de Paris, © Spadem 1995 ♦ p. 675: Musée Carnavalet/Photo Bulloz ♦ p. 679: Musée Légion d'Honneur/Photo Bulloz ♦ p. 682: Nicolas André Monsiau, "The Council of the Cisalpine Republic Proclaims Napoleon President," 1802. Giraudon/Art Resource ♦ p. 683: Nicholas Pocock, "Nelson's Flagships at Anchor." National Maritime Museum, London ♦ p. 684: C. Meynier, "The Day After the Battle of Eylau, February 9, 1807." Giraudon/Art Resource ♦ p. 686: J. A. D. Ingres, "Napoleon I Enthroned." Giraudon/Art Resource ♦ p. 688: Boilly, "The Departure of Conscripts at St. Denis," 1807. Musée Carnavalet/Photo Bulloz ♦ p. 689: Musée Carnavalet/Photo Bulloz ♦ p. 690: Erich Lessing/Art Resource ♦ p. 691: Francisco de Goya y Lucientes, "The Disasters of War: Populacho." Etching. Harris 148. 1st Edition. The Norton Simon Foundation ♦ p. 697: The Russian Campaign, by C. J. Minard ♦ p. 698: Photo Archives, Nationalbibliothek Austria **Chapter 22:** p. 702: Archiv für Kunst und Geschichte ♦ p. 704: The Mansell Collection ♦ p. 705: Archiv für Kunst und Geschichte ♦ p. 709: Giraudon/Art Resource ♦ p. 711: Archiv für Kunst und Geschichte ♦ p. 714: Chateau de Versailles/Giraudon/Bridgeman Art Library ♦ p. 716: Mary Evans Picture Library ♦ p. 718: Science Museum, London/Bridgeman Art Library ♦ p. 719: National Railway Museum, York/Bridgeman Art Library ♦ p. 722: Top, Guildhall Library, London/Bridgeman/Art Resource. Bottom, Guildhall Library, London/Bridgeman Art Library ♦ p. 723: Science Museum, London ♦ p. 725: Tallandier ♦ p. 729: Musée des Beaux-Arts, Valenciennes/Bridgeman Art Library

Chapter 23: p. 732: Louvre, Paris/Bridgeman Art Library ♦ p. 734: New York Public Library ♦ p. 736: Collection Viollet ♦ p. 738: The Granger Collection ♦ p. 741: Archiv für Kunst und Geschichte ♦ p. 745: Archiv für Kunst und Geschichte ♦ p. 746: Collection Viollet ♦ p. 747: The Mansell Collection ♦ p. 750: Top, Photo Bulloz. Bottom, Giraudon/Art Resource ♦ p. 753: New York Public Library ♦ p. 754: Jean-Loup Charmet ♦ p. 758: Houses of Parliament, Westminster, London/Bridgeman Art Library ♦ p. 760: Royal Archives, Windsor Castle ♦ p. 762: Collection Viollet **Chapter 24:** p. 766: Bismarck Museum/Bildarchiv Preussischer Kulturbesitz, Berlin ♦ p. 769: Musée du Petit Palais, Paris/Giraudon/Bridgeman Art Library ♦ p. 770: Top, Milan, Museo del Risorgimento. Photo, G. Costa/Index. Bottom, Giraudon/Art Resource ♦ p. 771: The Granger Collection ♦ p. 776: Lauros-Giraudon/Art Resource ♦ p. 777: Harlinque-Viollet ♦ p. 780: The Granger Collection ♦ p. 781: The Granger Collection ♦ p. 783: Culver ♦ p. 785: Scala/Art Resource ♦ p. 788: Archiv für Kunst und Geschichte ♦ p. 792: Novosti/Sovfoto ♦ p. 796: Victoria and Albert Museum, London/Art Resource ♦ p. 797: Scala/Art Resource **Chapter 25:** p. 802: Maidstone Museum and Art Gallery, Kent/Bridgeman Art Library ♦ p. 804: Ullstein Bilderdienst ♦ p. 811: Courtesy of the Director of the Royal Institution, London ♦ p. 813: The Granger Collection ♦ p. 815: New York Public Library ♦ p. 818: James McNeill Whistler (American, 1834–1903). "Rose and Silver: The Princess from the Land of Porcelain," 1863–1864. Oil color on canvas: 199.9 × 116.1 cm. Courtesy of the Freer Gallery of Art, Smithsonian Institution, Washington, D.C. 03.91 ♦ p. 819: Mary Evans Picture Library ♦ p. 822: Bradford Art Galleries and Museum/Bridgeman Art Library ♦ p. 823: Top, Buhrle Foundation, Zurich/Bridgeman Art Library. Bottom, Rowles Fine Art, Powis/Bridgeman Art Library ♦ p. 828: Mary Evans Picture Library ♦ p. 829: The Granger Collection ♦ p. 832: The Granger Collection **Chapter 26:** p. 838: Claude Monet, "Garden at Sainte-Adresse" Oil on Canvas. 38⅝ × 51⅛". The Metropolitan Museum of Art. Purchased with special contributions and purchase funds given or bequeathed by friends of the Museum 1967. (67.241) ♦ p. 840: Tallandier ♦ p. 841: Christie's, London/Bridgeman Art Library ♦ p. 843: Bettmann ♦ p. 844: Top, Göteborg Konstmuseum/Edimedia. Bottom, Mary Evans Picture Library ♦ p. 845: Erich Lessing/Art Resource ♦ p. 846: Left, Erich Lessing/Art Resource. Right, Mary Cassatt, American, 1844–1926. "The Bath" 1891–92. Oil on canvas. 39½ × 26". Art Institute of Chicago. Robert A. Waller Fund, 1910.2. Photograph © 1994, The Art Institute of Chicago. All Rights Reserved ♦ p. 847: Georges de Feure, porcelain vase. c. 1900. 12½" height. The Metropolitan Museum of Art, Purchase, Edward C. Moore, Jr. Gift, 1926. (22.228.9). Photograph by Schecter Lee ♦ p. 848: Nasjonalgalleriet, Oslo/Bridgeman Art Library ♦ p. 856: Collection Viollet ♦ p. 858: Edimedia ♦ p. 859: Ullstein Bilderdienst ♦ p. 862: Sovfoto ♦ p. 865: Bettmann **Chapter 27:** p. 870: Imperial War Museum ♦ p. 872: Staatliche Museen, Berlin/Archiv für Kunst und Geschichte ♦ p. 877: Bettmann ♦ p. 878: Archiv für Kunst und Geschichte ♦ p. 879: Bettmann ♦ p. 880: Ullstein ♦ p. 881: Tallandier ♦ p. 882: Top, Archiv für Kunst und Geschichte. Bottom, Imperial War Museum ♦ p. 884: AP/Wide World ♦ p. 887: VA/Sovfoto ♦ p. 892: Roger-Viollet ♦ p. 894: The Granger Collection ♦ p. 896: National Portrait Gallery, Smithsonian Institution, Washington/Art Resource ♦ p. 899: Keystone/Ullstein ♦ p. 900: Archiv für Kunst und Geschichte ♦ p. 904: UPI/Bettmann **Chapter 28:** p. 906: Itar-TASS/Sovfoto ♦ p. 910: Sovfoto ♦ p. 915: Ria-Novosti/Sovfoto ♦ p. 917: AP/Wide World ♦ p. 918: UPI/Bettmann ♦ p. 921: Studio Pizzi/Index ♦ p. 922: Edmund Engelman ♦ p. 924: Archiv für Kunst und Geschichte ♦ p. 928: Karsh, Ottawa/Woodfin Camp & Associates ♦ p. 929: Erik Bohr/Archiv für Kunst und Geschichte ♦ p. 930: Tallandier ♦ p. 931: UPI/Bettmann ♦ p. 935: Mary Evans Picture Library ♦ p. 939: Archiv für Kunst und Geschichte ♦ p. 940: UPI/Bettmann ♦ p. 941: UPI/Bettmann ♦ p. 944: Sovfoto ♦ p. 945: Novosti/Sovfoto ♦ p. 946: Edimedia **Chapter 29:** p. 950: Imperial War Museum ♦ p. 958: Robert Capa/Magnum ♦ p. 959: © 1995 ARS, NY/SPADEM, Paris/Art Resource ♦ p. 962: Ullstein ♦ p. 964: AP/Wide World ♦ p. 965: Lapi-Viollet ♦ p. 966: Topham/The Image Works ♦ p. 970: Navy Department/National Archives ♦ p. 974: Bettmann ♦ p. 975: UPI/Bettmann ♦ p. 977: UPI/Bettmann ♦ p. 979: Robert Capa/Magnum ♦ p. 980: UPI/Bettmann ♦ p. 982: AP/Wide World ♦ p. 985: Bettmann ♦ p. 990: Fenno Jacobs/Black Star ♦ p. 997: UPI/Bettmann **Chapter 30:** p. 1002: D. Aubert/Sygma ♦ p. 1004: Peter Beattie/Gamma-Liaison ♦ p. 1005: Luc Novovitch/Gamma-Liaison ♦ p. 1007: Charles Graham/Leo de Wys ♦ p. 1008: Regis Bossu/Sygma ♦ p. 1012: Steve Vidler/Leo de Wys ♦ p. 1015: UPI/Bettmann ♦ p. 1020: AP/Wide World ♦ p. 1026: AP/Wide World ♦ p. 1027: R. Bossu/Sygma ♦ p. 1028: Reuters/Bettmann ♦ p. 1029: Giansanti/Sygma ♦ p. 1031: Philippe Psaila/Gamma-Liaison ♦ p. 1033: D. Aubert/Sygma ♦ p. 1041: Reuters/Bettmann ♦ p. 1046: Anthony Suau/Gamma-Liaison **Epilogue:** p. 1057: Reuters/Bettmann ♦ p. 1060: Anselm Keifer, "Burning Rods." 1984–87. Mixed media on canvas. The St. Louis Art Museum. Purchase: Gift of Mr. and Mrs. Joseph Pulitzer, Jr., by exchange.

TEXT

Chapter 2: p. 39: Bernal, Martin. Abridged excerpt from *Black Athena: The Afroasiatic Roots of Classical Civilization Volume 1,* 1987, pp. 17–23. Copyright © 1987 by Martin Bernal. Reprinted by permission of Rutgers University Press. ♦ p. 39: Lefkowitz, Mary. Excerpt from *The New Republic,* February 10, 1992. Reprinted by permission of Professor Mary Lefkowitz, Wellesley College, MA. ♦ p. 42: Sappho, untitled excerpts. In Guy Davenport, trans. *Archilochos, Sappho, Alkman.* 1984. Reprinted by permission of University of California Press, Berkeley. **Chapter 3:** p. 68: Thucydides. Abridged excerpt from *The Peloponnesian War, Book V,* pp. 89–105. Rex Warner, ed. Copyright © Rex Warner, 1954. Reproduced by permission of Penguin Books Ltd. ♦ p. 71: Plato. Excerpt from *The Last Days of Socrates.* Hugh Tredennick, trans. Copyright © Hugh Tredennick, 1954, 1959, 1969. Reproduced by permission of Penguin Books, Ltd. **Chapter 5:** p. 146: Saint Augustine. *Confessions, VIII.* In Whitney Oates, ed. *Basic Writings of Saint Augustine.* J. Pilkington, trans. Copyright © 1948 by Random House, Inc. Reprinted by permission of Random House, Inc. **Chapter 6:** p. 158: Tacitus, Cornelius. Excerpt from *The Agricola and the Germania.* H. Mattingly, trans. Copyright © the Estate of H. Mattingly, 1948, 1970. Reproduced by permission of Penguin Books Ltd. **Chapter 7:** p. 194: Cross, S. H., ed. Excerpt from *Russian Primary Chronicle,* pp. 62–63. trans. O. P. Sherbowitz-Wetzor. The Medieval Academy of America. Publication No. 60, 1953. Reprinted by permission of the Medieval Academy of America, Cambridge, MA. ♦ p. 200: Muhammad. Excerpt from *The Koran.* Trans. N. J. Dawood. Copyright © N. J. Dawood, 1956, 1959, 1966, 1968, 1974, 1990. Reproduced by permission of Penguin Books Ltd. **Chapter 8:** p. 228: Suger, Abbot of St. Denis. Excerpt from *Vie de Louis VI Le Gros.* Waquet, ed. Trans. David S. Spear. Société d'Edition "Les Belles Lettres," 1964, pp. 172–179. © Les Belles Lettres, Paris. Reprinted by permission. **Chapter 9:** p. 272: Pope Boniface VIII. *Unam Sanctam,* 1302. In Brian Tierney, ed. *The Crisis of Church and State 1050–1300.* Prentice-Hall, 1964, pp. 188–199, 191. © 1964, 1992. Used by permission of the publisher, Prentice-Hall/A Division of Simon & Schuster, Englewood Cliffs, NJ. **Chapter 10:** p. 297 and 300: Knolles, Richard. *A Generall Historie of the Turkes.* In John J. Saunders, ed. *The Muslim World on the Eve of Europe's Expansion.* Adapted by Theodore K. Rabb. Prentice-Hall, 1966, pp. 20–22, 25–26. Used by permission of the publisher, Prentice-Hall/A Division of Simon & Schuster, Englewood Cliffs, NJ. ♦ p. 304: Carroll, Harry J., Jr.; Embree, Ainslee T.; Mellon, Knox, Jr.; Schrier, Arnold; & Taylor, Alastair M.; eds. Excerpt from *The Development of Civilization: A Documentary of Politics, Society and Thought,* Vol. I. Scott, Foresman, 1961, pp. 217, 220. Reprinted by permission of HarperCollins College Publishers. **Chapter 11:** p. 316: Boccaccio, Giovanni. Excerpt from *The Decameron.* In Ferdinand Schevill, ed. *The First Century of Italian Humanism.* New York: Russell & Russell, 1967, pp. 32–34. Reprinted by permission of Simon & Schuster. ♦ p. 334: Excerpt from *The Trial of Jeanne d'Arc,* 1438. In Bernard, Leonard & Hodges, Theodore B.; eds. *Readings in European History,* 1958, pp. 181–182. Copyright © 1958 by Macmillan College Publishing Company. Reprinted with the permission of Macmillan College Publishing Company. **Chapter 12:** p. 369: d'Este, Isabella. Letters, 1502, 1505, 1504. In D. S. Chambers, ed. *Patrons and Artists in the Italian Renaissance.* London: Macmillan, 1970, pp. 123–130 and 147–148. Reprinted by permission of The Macmillan Press Ltd. ♦ p. 379: Hus, Jan. Letter, 1415. In Matthew Spinka, ed. *The Letters of John Hus,* pp. 195–197. 1972 © Columbia University Press, New York. Reprinted with permission of the publisher. **Chapter 13:** p. 389: Table adapted from Febvre, Lucien & Martin, Henri-Jean. *The Coming of the Book: The Impact of Printing 1450–1800.* Trans. David Gerard, 1976, pp. 178–179 and 184–185. Reprinted by permission of Verso/New Left Books, London. ♦ p. 397: Luther, Martin. Preface, 1545. Trans. from the Latin by Theodore K. Rabb from Otto Schell, ed. *Dokumente zu Luther's Entwicklung.* Tubingen: J. C. B. Mohr, 1929, pp. 191–192. Reprinted by permission ♦ p. 415: St. Theresa. Excerpt from her autobiography, begun 1562. In E. Ellison Peers, *The Life of Theresa of Jesus,* pp. 258–260, 273–274. Reprinted by permission of Sheed & Ward, Kansas City, MO. **Chapter 14:** p. 423: Elliott, John H. Table adapted from *Imperial Spain, 1469–1716.* London: Edward Arnold, publisher, 1964, p. 175. Reprinted by permission of Professor Sir John Elliott, Oriel College at Oxford University, England. ♦ p. 431: Morison, S. E. Excerpt from *Admiral of the Ocean Sea: A Life of Christopher Columbus,* 1942, pp. 670–671. Reprinted by permission of Little, Brown & Company. ♦ p. 431: Sale, Kirkpatrick. Excerpt from *The Conquest of Paradise: Christopher Columbus and the Columbian Legacy,* 1990, pp. 209–210 and 362. Reprinted by permission of Alfred A. Knopf, Inc. **Chapter 15:** p. 489: Elliott, John H. Table adapted from *Imperial Spain, 1469–1716.* London: Edward Arnold, publisher, 1964, p. 175. Reprinted by permission of Professor Sir John Elliott, Oriel College at Oxford University, England. **Chapter 16:** p. 502: Galileo Galilei and Kepler, Johannes. Letters dated from 1597. In Giorgio de Santillana, *The Crime of Galileo,* 1955, pp. 11, 14–15. Copyright © 1955. Reprinted by permission of the publisher, University of Chicago Press. ♦ p. 521: de Vries, Jan. Table from *The Economy of Europe in an Age of Crisis, 1600–1750,* 1976, p. 5. Reprinted by permission of Cambridge University Press. **Chapter 17:** p. 537: Louis XIV. Memoirs, c. 1665–1670. In Thompson, J. M., ed. *Lectures on Foreign History, 1494–1789,* 1956, pp. 172–174. Reprinted by permission of Blackwell Publishers, Oxford. ♦ p. 557: Locke, John. Excerpt from *The Second Treatise of Civil Government,* 1690. Thomas P. Peardon, ed. Reprinted with permission of Macmillan College Publishing Company. Copyright © 1952 by Macmillan College Publishing Company, Inc. **Chapter 18:** p. 596: Exhibit adapted from Dean, Phyllis, and Cole, W. A. *British Economic Growth, 1688–1959,* 1964, p. 49. Reprinted by permission of Cambridge University Press. **Chapter 19:** p. 611: Joseph II: Edict, 1781. In Macartney, C. A., ed. Excerpts from *The Habsburg and Hohenzollern Dynasties,* 1970. Copyright © 1970 by C. A. Macartney. Used by permission of HarperCollins Publishers, Inc. ♦ p. 617: Wollstonecraft, Mary. Excerpt from *A Vindication of the Rights of Woman,* 1792. From Sandra M. Gilbert and Susan Gubar, eds. *The Norton Anthology of Literature by Women: The Tradition in English.* Copyright © 1985 by Sandra M. Gilbert and Susan Gubar. Used by permission of W. W. Norton & Comapny, Inc. ♦ p. 619: Rousseau, Jean-Jacques. Excerpt from "Concept of the General Will." In G. D. H. Cole, ed. and trans. *The Social Contract,* Book I, Chapter 6: "The Sovereign." London: Everyman's Library, 1950. © David Campbell Publishers Ltd., London. **Chapter 21:** p. 692: Political Constitution of the Spanish Monarchy, 1812. Excerpt trans. James Tueller. Copyright James B. Tueller 1993. Reprinted by permission. **Chapter 22:** p. 708: Metternich, Prince Richard. Excerpt from *Memoirs of Prince Metternich, 1815–1829,* III. Prince Richard Metternich, ed. Trans. Mrs. Alexander Napier. First published in English by Charles Scribner's Sons, 1881. From the reprint by Howard Fertig, New York, 1970. p. 970. Reprinted by permission of Charles Scribner's Sons, an imprint of Macmillan Publishing Company. ♦ p. 712: Metternich, Prince Richard. Excerpt from The Carlsbad Decrees, 1819. In Louis L. Snyder, ed. *Documents of German History.* New Brunswick: Rutgers University Press, 1958, pp. 158–159. Copyright Louis L. Snyder. ♦ p. 728: Pollard, Sidney & Holmes, Colin; eds. *Documents of European Economic History,* Vol. I, *The Process of Industrialization,* Chapter 15. "The Conditions of the Working Classes in France, 1840": Andre Guépin, *Nantes Au XIXe Siecle,* 1835; and "The Conditions of the Working Classes in Germany, 1845": Alexander Schneer, "Uber die Zustände der arbeitenden Klassen in Breslau," 1845. Copyright © S. Pollard and C. Holmes 1968. Reprinted by permission of St. Martin's Press, Inc. **Chapter 23:** p. 749: Bairoch, P.; Deldycke, T.; Gelders, H.; & Limbor, J. M. Exhibit from *The Working Population and Its Structure,* from the series *International Historical Statistics, Vol. I,* 1968. Reprinted by permission of Editions de l'Université de Bruxelles. **Chapter 24:** p. 773: Frankfurt Parliament. Excerpt from The Frankfurt Constitution, 1849. In Louis L. Snyder, ed., *The Documents of German History.* New Brunswick: Rutgers University Press, 1958. Copyright Louis L. Snyder. ♦ p. 791: von Bismarck, Otto. Excerpt from speech, 1881. In Louis L. Snyder, ed., *The Documents of German History.* New Brunswick, Rutgers University Press, 1958. Copyright Louis L. Snyder. **Chapter 25:** p. 808: Bairoch, P.; Deldycke, T.; Gelders, H.; & Limbor, J. M. Exhibit from *The Working Population and Its Structure,* 1968, from the series *International Historical Statistics, Vol. I,* p. 119. Reprinted by permission of Editions de l'Université de Bruxelles. "Europe Historical Statistics" by B. R. Mitchell. Copyright © 1970 by Columbia University Press. Reprinted with permission of the publisher. ♦ pp. 825–826: Hobson, J. A. Excerpt from *Imperialism: A Study,* 1961, pp. 356, 358, 360. (Sixth impression of the third revised edition of 1938, first published in 1902.) Reprinted by permission of HarperCollins Publishers Ltd., London. ♦ pp. 825–826: Schumpeter, Joseph. Excerpt from *Imperialism and Social Classes,* 1951, pp. 128–130. Trans. Heinz Norden. © Copyright 1951 Augustus M. Kelley, Inc. Reprinted by permission. ♦ pp. 825–826: Mommsen, Wolfgang J. Excerpt from *Theories of Imperialism.* Translated by P. S. Falla, 1980. Reprinted by permission of the publishers, George Weidenfeld & Nicolson Ltd., London. **Chapter 26:** p. 842: Shaw, George Bernard. Excerpt from "The Drama in Hoxton," from *The Saturday Review,* April 9, 1898. In George Rowell, ed. *Victorian Dramatic Criticism.* Reprinted by permission of The Society of Authors, on behalf of the Bernard Shaw Estate. ♦ p. 849: Bakunin, Mikhail. Excerpt from "Three Lectures to Swiss Members of the International," 1870. In Robert M. Cutler, ed. and trans. *The Basic Bakunin,* Prometheus Books, 1993. Reprinted by permission of Professor Robert M. Cutler, Laval University, Quebec. ♦ p. 854: Excerpt from *Schmeitzer's Internationale Monatsschrift: Zeitschrift für die Allgemeine Vereinigung zur Bekampfung des Judentums,* 1883. In Richard S. Levy, ed. and trans. *Antisemitism in the Modern World.* Reprinted by permission of D. C. Heath & Company, Lexington, MA. **Chapter 27:** p. 874: Fay, Sidney Bradshaw. Excerpt from *The Origins of the World War,* Vol. II, 1930, pp. 547, 548, 550. Copyright 1930 by Macmillan Publishing Company. Reprinted with permission of Macmillan Publishing Company. ♦ p. 886: Girvin, B. & Coxens, M. Excerpt from "Meet the 'Khaki Girls'" from *The English Woman,* June, 1917. In E. Royston Pike, *Human Documents of the Lloyd George Era,* 1972, pp. 164–165.

Reprinted by permission of Routledge, London. ♦ p. 889: Owen, Wilfred. Excerpt from *Wilfred Owen: Collected Letters.* In Jon Clover and Jon Silken, *The Penguin Book of First World War Prose.* 1989. Reprinted by permission of Penguin Books Ltd, London. ♦ p. 901: Pollard, Sidney and Holmes, Colin, eds. *Documents of European Economic History,* Vol. 3, *The End of Old Europe, 1914–1939,* Chapter 4, Doc. 4b. Statistisches Reichsamt, "Germany's Economic and Financial Situation, An Exhibit of After-Effects of the World War, 1923." Copyright © Sidney Pollard and Colin Holmes 1972. Reprinted by permission of St. Martin's Press, Inc. **Chapter 28:** p. 912: Sorokin, Pitrim Alexandrovitch. Excerpt from *Leaves from a Russian Diary.* Boston: E. P. Dutton, 1920. Expanded edition Beacon Press, 1950. Copyright © 1950 by Pitrim A. Sorokin. Reprinted by permission of Beacon Press, Boston, and Reed, John. Excerpt from *Ten Days That Shook the World,* 1919. Both in Pethybridge, Roger, ed. *Witnesses to the Russian Revolution.* Copyright © 1964 George Allen and Unwin Ltd. Used by arrangement with Carol Publishing Group. ♦ p. 925: Marinetti, Filippo. "Manifesto of Futurism," *Le Figaro,* 1909. In R. W. Flint, ed. *Marinetti: Selected Writings,* 1971. Trans. R. W. Flint and Arthur A. Coppotelli. Copyright © 1971, 1972 by Farrar, Straus & Giroux, Inc. Reprinted by permission of Farrar, Straus & Giroux, Inc. ♦ p. 926: Spengler, Oswald. Excerpt from *The Decline of the West.* Trans. Charles Frances Atkinson. Copyright © 1926 by Alfred A. Knopf, Inc. Reprinted by permission of the publisher. ♦ p. 942: Goebbels, Joseph. Address, 1937. In George L. Mosse, ed. *Nazi Culture: Intellectual, Cultural and Social Life in the Third Reich.* Trans. Salvator Attanasio et al. Reprinted by permission of Dr. George L. Mosse, University of Wisconsin, Madison. **Chapter 29:** pp. 967–968: Stalin, Joseph. Speech, 1941. In Brian MacArthur, ed. *The Penguin Book of Twentieth Century Speeches.* Copyright © 1992 Brian MacArthur. Reprinted by permission of Viking Penguin. ♦ p. 973: Lettich, Andre. Eyewitness account. In J. Noakes and G. Pridham, eds. *Nazism, 1919–1945: A History in Documents and Eyewitness Accounts,* Vol. II. Copyright © 1988 by Department of History and Archeology, University of Exeter. Published by Pantheon Books, a division of Random House, Inc. Reprinted by permission of Schocken Books. ♦ p. 986: Churchill, Winston. Speech, 1946. In Brian McArthur, ed. *The Penguin Book of Twentieth Century Speeches.* Copyright the Estate of Sir Winston S. Churchill. Reproduced with permission of Curtis Brown Ltd., London on behalf of the Estate of Sir Winston S. Churchill. ♦ pp. 991–992: Vishinsky, Andrei. Speech. 1948. In Daly, Tom, ed. *Vital Speeches of the Day,* Vol. XV, No. 2. Reprinted by permission of City News Publishing Company, Mount Pleasant, South Carolina. **Chapter 30:** p. 1010: Aynur. Personal account. In Ilhan Basgoz and Norman Furniss, eds. *Turkish Workers in Europe.* Trans. Akural. Turkish Studies Program, Indiana University at Bloomington. ♦ p. 1023: Foucault, Michel. Excerpt from *The History of Sexuality,* Vol. I, *An Introduction.* Trans. Robert Hurley, Jr. Copyright © 1976 by Gallimard. Reprinted by permission of Georges Borchardt, Inc. ♦ p. 1024: Kristeva, Julia. Interview, 1974. In Elaine Marks and Isabelle de Courtivron, eds. *New French Feminisms: An Anthology.* Trans. Marilyn A. August. In *Tel Quel* 59, published by Editions du Seuil, Paris. Copyright © 1974 by Julia Kristeva. ♦ p. 1040: Havel, Vaclav. Inaugural address, 1990. In Brian MacArthur, ed. *The Penguin Book of Twentieth Century Speeches.* 1992. Copyright © Brian MacArthur, 1992. Reprinted by permission of Viking Penguin.

INDEX

Index Note: The b after a page number refers to boxed material, the f to a figure, the m to a map, and the n to a note.

CONTEMPORARY EUROPE